The Routledge Handbook of Strategic Communication

The Routledge Handbook of Strategic Communication

Edited by *Derina Holtzhausen*
and Ansgar Zerfass

NEW YORK AND LONDON

First published 2015
by Routledge
711 Third Avenue, New York, NY 10017

and by Routledge
2 Park Square, Milton Park, Abingdon, Oxon, OX14 4RN

Routledge is an imprint of the Taylor & Francis Group, an informa business

Library of Congress Cataloging-in-Publication Data
The Routledge handbook of strategic communication/edited by Derina Holtzhausen, Ansgar
Zerfass.
pages cm
Includes bibliographical references and index.
1. Communication in organizations. 2. Communication in management. 3. Business
communication. I. Holtzhausen, Derina Rhoda. II. Zerfass, Ansgar, 1965-
HD30.3.R684 2015
658.4′5—dc23
2014016226

ISBN: 978-0-415-53001-9 (hbk)
ISBN: 978-0-203-09444-0 (ebk)

Typeset in Bembo Std and ITC Stone Sans
by Swales & Willis Ltd, Exeter, Devon, UK

Printed and bound in the United States of America by Publishers Graphics,
LLC on sustainably sourced paper.

Contents

Contents

Contents

Contributors

Helle Kryger Aggerholm, PhD, is associate professor and director of corporate communication studies at the Department of Business Communication, Business and Social Sciences, Aarhus University, Denmark. Her major research areas are strategic communication, strategy communication within a strategy-as-practice context, organizational communication, change and crisis communication, and language as social interaction. Her most recent research has appeared in international academic journals such as *Journal of Management Inquiry*, *International Journal of Strategic Communication*, *Public Relations Review*, *Business Ethics: A European Review*, and *Corporate Communication*.

Claudia Auer works as a research associate at the Institute of Media and Communication Science of Ilmenau University of Technology, Germany. Her research interests include public diplomacy, crisis communication, organizational communication and political communication 2.0.

William L. Benoit, PhD, is professor of communication studies at Ohio University, Athens, OH. He developed and has applied image repair theory. He has published in a variety of journals, including *Journal of Communication*, *Communication Monographs*, *Human Communication Research*, the *Quarterly Journal of Speech*, and *Public Relations Review*. Bill Benoit is currently revising his book, *Accounts, Excuses, and Apologies: A Theory of Image Restoration Discourse*.

Günter Bentele, Dr., is professor emeritus at Leipzig University, Germany, where he held the first chair for public relations in the German-speaking countries university from 1994 to 2014. Prior to this he worked as an associate professor at Bamberg University, Germany, from 1989 to 1994. His research interests include public relations theory, public relations history and ethics of public communication. He has authored and coauthored more than 40 books, including the *Handbuch der Public Relations* (3rd ed., 2015) and the *Lexikon der Kommunikations- und Medienwissenschaft* (2nd ed., 2013).

Sergio Bulgacov, PhD, is professor at São Paulo Business School, Brazil. He gained his doctorate at Getúlio Vargas Foundation (FGV), Brazil. His research interests are in strategy content and process.

W. Timothy Coombs, PhD, is professor in the Nicholson School of Communication at the University of Central Florida, Orlando, FL. His crisis books include the award-winning *Ongoing*

Crisis Communication, Code Red in the Boardroom, and the co-edited *The Handbook of Crisis Communication* with Sherry Holladay. His other works include two award-winning books with Sherry Holladay, *Public Relations Strategy and Application: Managing Influence* and *It's Not Just PR*. Articles by Tim Coombs have appeared in *Management Communication Quarterly*, *Public Relations Review*, *Journal of Communication Management*, *International Journal of Strategic Communication*, and *Journal of Public Relations Research*.

Alex Curry is a graduate research assistant at Brigham Young University, Provo, UT. Prior to coming to BYU, he worked in California in the office of Governor Arnold Schwarzenegger from 2005 to 2010. During his time in that office, he went from writing personal correspondence for the governor to supervising the office's executive writers unit, which produced personalized letters, proclamations, and other official messages from the governor.

Stephanie Dixon is senior consultant with Deloitte Consulting in Vancouver, Canada, where she specializes in governance, change management and organizational effectiveness to build and sustain capacity for business transformation in both public and private sectors. She is a graduate of the MSc Double Degree Program in Global Media and Communications with the London School of Economics, England and the Annenberg School at the University of Southern California, Los Angeles, CA.

Mats Eriksson, Dr., is associate professor in media and communication studies at Örebro University, Sweden, where he also gained his doctorate. His research mainly concerns strategic communication and public relations in the field of crisis, risk, and emergency communication. His work has appeared in academic journals such as *Journal of Contingencies and Crisis Management*, *Journal of Communication Management* and *International Journal of Strategic Communication*. He has carried out research projects on many crisis situations in Sweden, funded by, for example, the Swedish National Board for Psychological Defense, the Swedish Civil Contingencies Agency and the Swedish emergency dispatch Centre, SOS Alarm. Mats Eriksson's most recent research concerns Internet and mobile communication technology in this crisis communication context.

James L. Everett, PhD, is professor and chair of the Department of Communication, Languages and Cultures at Coastal Carolina University, Conway, SC, and adjunct professor at Queensland University of Technology, Brisbane, Australia. His research interests focus on the social ecology of organizations, and he has published in *Communication Theory*, *Public Relations Review*, *Emerging Perspectives in Organizational Communication*, and the *Handbook of Public Relations Theory and Practice*.

Jesper Falkheimer, PhD, is professor in strategic communication in the Department of Strategic Communication, Lund University, Campus Helsingborg, Sweden. He is also rector for Campus Helsingborg and has combined his research with management positions for several years. His research interests focus on strategic communication in general, often from a social theory approach, and more specifically on crisis communication, place branding and media strategy. Jesper Falkheimer has authored several books and chapters in international anthologies. His work is published in journals such as *International Journal of Strategic Communication*, *Public Relations Review*, *Corporate Communications: An International Journal*, and *Journal of Contingencies and Crisis Communication*.

Finn Frandsen is professor of corporate communication and the director of the Centre for Corporate Communication (CCC) in the Department of Business Communication, at the School of Business and Social Sciences, Aarhus University, Denmark. His research interests include crisis management and crisis communication, environmental and climate communication, and the institutionalization of strategic communication in private and public organizations. His work has appeared in *Management Communication Quarterly, Public Relations Review, International Journal of Strategic Communication, Corporate Communication: An International Journal, Public Relations Inquiry, The Handbook of Crisis Communication, The SAGE Handbook of Public Relations,* and *The Routledge Handbook of Language and Professional Communication.*

Magnus Fredriksson, PhD, is senior lecturer at the Department of Journalism, Media and Communication, University of Gothenburg and visiting scholar at the Department of Media and Informatics, Uppsala University, both in Sweden. His research interests encompass corporate identity, corporate media work and crisis communication and the role of mediatization, institutionalization and other structural conditions for these practices.

Alexander Fritsch is editor of an international in-house magazine at the Bosch Group, a global supplier of technology and services based in Stuttgart, Germany. He graduated from Ilmenau University of Technology, Germany, and has worked as a newspaper journalist. At the United Nations Office of the High Commissioner for Human Rights, he was involved in implementing and evaluating a global communication campaign.

Kirk Hallahan, PhD, is professor of journalism and technical communication at Colorado State University, Fort Collins, CO. His research interests include applications of new technology in strategic communication, communications campaigns, and crisis communications and issues management. He was a co-founder of *International Journal of Strategic Communication.*

Mats Heide, PhD, is professor in strategic communication at the Department of Strategic Communication, Lund University, Campus Helsingborg, Sweden. His research interests focus on strategic communication in general, and more specifically on crisis communication, change communication and organizational learning. Heide has co-authored several textbooks (in Swedish) within his research interests, and his work has been published in *International Journal of Strategic Communication, Corporate Communications: An International Journal* and *Journal of Contingencies and Crisis Communication.*

Sherry J. Holladay, PhD, is a professor at the Nicholson School of Communication at the University of Central Florida in Orlando, FL. Her research interests include corporate social responsibility, reputation management, crisis communication, activism, and stakeholder relations. Her work has appeared in *Journal of Public Relations Research, Public Relations Review, Management Communication Quarterly, Journal of Communication Management, and International Journal of Strategic Communication.* She is co-author of *It's Not Just PR: Public Relations in Society, Public Relations Strategies and Applications: Managing Influence,* and *Managing Corporate Responsibility: A Communication Approach.* Sherry Holladay is also co-editor of *The Handbook of Crisis Communication.*

Derina Holtzhausen, PhD, is professor and director of the School of Media and Strategic Communications at Oklahoma State University, Stillwater, OK. Her research interests include the theoretical development of strategic communication, the potential of communication activism for practice, and the impact of organizational variables on professional communication practice. Since moving from South Africa to the USA in 1997, she has published a book and more than 30 articles and book chapters and presented more than 30 papers at national and international conferences. For seven years she was co-editor of *International Journal of Strategic Communication,* which she co-founded.

Øyvind Ihlen, Dr., is a professor at the Department of Media and Communication, University of Oslo, Norway. He has published over 60 journal articles and book chapters, and written or edited eight books, including *Public Relations and Social Theory: Key Figures and Concepts* (2009) and the award-winning *Handbook of Communication and Corporate Social Responsibility* (2011). His research focuses on strategic communication and journalism, using theories of rhetoric and sociology on issues such as the environment, immigration and corporate social responsibility.

Emanuele Invernizzi is professor emeritus of public relations and corporate communication management at IULM University of Milan, Italy, where he is also director of the executive master program in corporate public relations. His main scientific contributions in the last few years have been ten books, and several articles published in international and national scientific journals, on strategic public relations and organizational and entrepreneurial communication. He was president of EUPRERA (European Public Relations Education and Research Association) from 2010 to 2011.

Rita Järventie-Thesleff, Dr., is a professor of practice and CEMS Academic Director at the Department of Communication in the School of Business, Aalto University, Helsinki, Finland. Her research interests include strategic change, strategy-as-practice, strategic communication, branding and sense-making. Recently, she has focused on media convergence and on the strategic challenges that the digital technology and the emerging participatory media culture bring about for organizations.

Winni Johansen, Dr., is a professor of Corporate Communication and director of the executive masters program in corporate communication, Department of Business Communication, School of Business and Social Sciences, Aarhus University. Her research interests include crisis management and crisis communication, institutionalization of strategic communication, environmental communication, change communication, and public relations. Her work has appeared in *Management Communication Quarterly, Public Relations Review, International Journal of Strategic Communication, Corporate Communication: An International Journal, Public Relations Inquiry, Rhetorica Scandinavica, LSP and Professional Communication, Hermes: Journal of Language and Communication Studies, The Handbook of Crisis Communication, The SAGE Handbook of Public Relations,* and the *Handbook of Pragmatics*.

Kim A. Johnston, PhD, is a senior lecturer in the School of Advertising, Marketing and Public Relations, QUT Business School, Brisbane, Australia. Her research is focused on strategic and internal communication, particularly cultural knowledge and behavior of organizational members. She is a member of a QUT Business School high potential research group and works collaboratively to identify and investigate internal organizational communication for strategic outcomes. She is on the editorial board of *Journal of Public Relations Research*.

Eyun-Jung Ki, PhD, is an associate professor in the Department of Advertising and Public Relations at the University of Alabama, Tuscaloosa, AL. She is a fellow of The Plank Center for Leadership in Public Relations. Her research areas include developing measurement scales; testing models linking crisis, relationship, attitudes, and behaviors; examining new technologies in public relations; and evaluating ethics in the public relations field. She edited and published the second volume of *Public Relations as Relationship Management: Relational Approach to the Study and Practice of Public Relations*.

Kenneth E. Kim, PhD, is assistant professor in strategic communication at the School of Media and Strategic Communications, Oklahoma State University, Stillwater, OK. His research focuses on cognitive effects of a variety of advertising tactics with an emphasis on strategic message use and its impact on persuasiveness. His scholarship has been recognized with the best papers award from the *International Journal of Advertising*, and the *Association for Education in Journalism & Mass Communication*. His scholarly research has appeared in *Health Communication* and *Journal of Medical Marketing*.

Spiro Kiousis, PhD, is professor of public relations, executive associate dean, and the director of distance education at the College of Journalism and Communications at the University of Florida, Gainesville, FL. His current research interests include political public relations, political communication, and new media. Specifically, this interdisciplinary research explores the interplay among political public relations efforts, news media content, and public opinion in traditional and interactive mass-mediated contexts.

Sarabdeep Kochhar is director of research at the Institute of Public Relations (IPR), Washington, DC. Prior to joining the IPR, she worked as a PhD researcher in the Department of Public Relations at the University of Florida, Gainesville, FL, USA. She holds graduate and undergraduate degrees from universities in the USA and India. Sarabdeep has worked with the Government of India as a public relations manager, as a consultant with Burson-Marsteller in Bangalore, India, with the Department of Architecture at the University of Oklahoma, and with the Institute of Research and Training in the USA.

Kirsten Kozolanka, PhD, is an associate professor in the School of Journalism and Communication at Carleton University, Ottawa, Canada. Previously, she worked in political offices and in government communications. She is the editor of *Publicity and the Canadian State: Critical Communication Perspectives*.

Bobbi Kay Lewis, PhD, is an associate professor of strategic communication and the associate director of undergraduate studies at Oklahoma State University, OK. She concentrates her research on social media and strategic communications, social learning and media effects. She has published articles in several journals, including the *Journal of Advertising Education*, *Public Relations Journal*, and *Public Relations Review*. Lewis co-authored a chapter in the book, *Social Media: Usage and Impact*. Professor Lewis worked in advertising for almost 10 years before joining academia.

Martin Löffelholz, Dr., is rector of the Swiss German University in Jakarta, Indonesia, and director of the Ilmenau Centre for Public Diplomacy Research and Training at the Institute of Media and Communication Science, Ilmenau University of Technology, Germany. He specializes in political communication, organizational communication, international communication, and war and crisis communication. Martin Löffelholz has (co-)authored more than 300 academic publications which have appeared in English, German, Arabic and Indonesian. Furthermore, he has written or (co-) edited 16 books, including *The ASEAN Guide. A Journalist's Handbook to Regional Integration in Southeast Asia* (with Danilo A. Arao), *Global Journalism Research. Theories, Methods, Findings, Future* (with David H. Weaver), and *Kriegs- und Krisenberichterstattung. Ein Handbuch* (with Christian F. Trippe and Andrea C. Hoffmann).

Marlene Marchiori, PhD, is post-doctoral fellow in organizational communication at Purdue University, West Lafayette, IN. Her doctorate is from the University of São Paulo (USP), and she also studied at the Theory, Culture and Society Centre at Nottingham Trent University, England. She is a professor at the graduate program of the Management School at State University of Londrina (UEL), Brazil, and lead researcher at the National Council for Scientific and Technological

Development (CNP). Her research interests include organizational communication and public relations and theoretical and practical perspectives in the area of strategy. Marlene Marchiori is the author of *Cultura e Comunicação Organizacional: um Olhar Estratégico sobre a Organização* (2006; 2nd ed.: 2008), and editor of *Comunicação e organização: reflexões, processos e práticas* (2010), and of the collection *Faces da cultura e da comunicação organizacional* (10 volumes). She is a consultant in the areas of culture, communication and strategy as practice.

Tino G.K. Meitz, Dr., is associate professor in the Department for Empirical Media Research, University of Tuebingen, Germany. From 2013 to 2014 he was deputy full professor for Media Reception and Media Effects Research at Augsburg University, Germany. Tino's research focuses on media effects, especially cognitive information processing and memory. Another main research strand focuses on reception and effects of strategic, persuasive communication; in this regard he is interested in advertising as well as health communication. His publications in 2014 have comprised chapters in *Handbuch Werbeforschung*, *Gesundheitskommunikation* (with A. Kalch and M. Groß) and *Handbuch nichtstandardisierte Methoden in der Kommunikationswissenschaft* (with G. Zurstiege and A. Ort) and an article in *Journal of Experimental Psychology: Learning, Memory, and Cognition* (with M. Huff and F. Papenmeier).

Johanna Moisander, Dr., is a professor of organizational communication in the Department of Communication at Aalto University School of Business, Helsinki, Finland. Her research interests currently center on discursive and practice-based approaches to management and organization studies, and consumer culture theory (CCT). She has published in, among others, *Organization Studies*, *Organization*, *European Societies*, *Consumption, Markets & Culture*, and *Scandinavian Journal of Management*.

Juan-Carlos Molleda, PhD, is professor in the Department of Public Relations and director of the MAMC Global Strategic Communication of the College of Journalism and Communications at the University of Florida, Gainesville, FL. He is also an affiliated faculty of the UF Center for Latin American Studies and a Fulbright Senior Specialist. Between 1987 and 1993, he obtained his major work experience from a Venezuelan financial consortium, acting as manager of public relations, corporate communication, advertising, and promotions. He also worked at Blue Cross and Blue Shield of South Carolina and the global public relations firm Burson-Marsteller Latin America.

Priscilla Murphy, PhD, is professor emerita of strategic communication at Temple University, Philadelphia, PA. Her research interests include international communication, complexity and game theories, social and semantic networks, crisis communication, and reputation.

Cynthia Nichols, PhD, is an assistant professor of strategic communications at Oklahoma State University; Stillwater, OK. Her research interests lie in social media and media effects—specifically related to politics, sports, body image and children. Prior to pursuing a PhD at the University of Alabama in 2010, she worked in the marketing departments of two different corporations in the USA.

Howard Nothhaft, PhD, is assistant professor in strategic communication at the Department of Strategic Communication, Lund University, Campus Helsingborg, Sweden. His research interests lie in the area of communication strategy and the implications of strategic communication on democracy. He has published in *International Journal of Strategic Communication*, *Journal of Communication Management* and in various handbooks in English and German.

Allison Noyes is a doctoral candidate studying strategic organizational communication at USC Annenberg School for Communication and Journalism, Los Angeles, CA. Her specific research

Contributors

interests focus on collaboration, culture, and communication-centered organizational change management. Since coming to Annenberg, Allie has worked on research and training projects with a variety of nonprofit organizations, the U.S. Navy, the World Bank, and organizations from the entertainment industry. The focus of her dissertation research is on collaborative capacity in a hospital organization.

Janis Teruggi Page, PhD, is senior professorial lecturer at American University, Washington, DC. Before entering academia, she was a media marketing executive for 20 years. Her current research focuses on visual rhetoric, political communication, and corporate social responsibility. She has published in, among other journals, *Communication, Culture and Critique, Visual Communication Quarterly, Journal of American Folklore*, and in the book series *Assessing Evidence in a Postmodern World*.

Josef Pallas, Dr., is associate professor at the Department of Informatics and Media and the Department of Business Studies, Uppsala University. His research covers areas such as mediatization, corporate communications and corporate governance. His work is published in well-recognized journals and international books. Two of his current research projects focus on mediatization of public sectors—especially universities—and production of business news.

Willem Pieterson, Dr., is the C.O.O. at research and consulting company Syndio Social. He holds a PhD cum laude in communication and specializes in networked forms of organizational communication and multi-channel communication strategies. He has published over 40 scholarly papers in journals such as *Government Information Quarterly* and *International Review of Administrative Sciences* and at conferences such as ICA and HICSS.

Kenneth D. Plowman, PhD., is an associate professor of communication at Brigham Young University, Provo, UT. The focus of his research is on strategic management, conflict resolution and leadership in public relations. He spent 15 years in the field of public relations in Washington, DC, first as a press secretary and then as a legislative director for several different congressmen, and later on in a public relations agency. Plowman's career has followed a dual track, the other one, from which he has now retired, being in the U.S. Army Reserve. He finished his career as chief of public affairs for detainee operations in Iraq, 2007–2008.

Juliana J. C. Raupp, Dr., is a professor of organizational communication at the Institute for Media and Communication Studies, Free University of Berlin, Germany. Her research areas include strategic political communication, the relationship between media and politics, risk and crisis communication in the public sector, and social network analysis. She has published articles in, among others, *Journal of Communication Management, Public Relations Review*, and *SCM Studies in Communication/Media*. She has written books (in German) on *Opinion research. The use of polls in political communication* (2007), and, with Jens Vogelgesang, on *Media evaluation. An introduction into theory and practice* (2009). With Stefan Jarolimek and Friederike Schultz she edited a book (in German) on *CSR. Foundations in communication, disciplinary perspectives, and methodological challenges*.

Patricia Riley, PhD, is a professor based at the Annenberg School, University of Southern California, Los Angeles, CA. She is known for her work on institutional politics, organizational culture change related to communication and information technologies, and strategic argument. She founded and directs the Global Communication MA Program that is jointly taught with the London School of Economics, England. She also directs the USC Annenberg Scenario Lab which

xv

focuses on developing the organizational capacity for foresight and strategic planning through narratives, argument and sensemaking, as well as the World Bank–Annenberg Summer Institute in Communication and Reform where she is working on a strategic communication grant (funded by USAID) on counter-trafficking in Indonesia. Her work has appeared in such books as *Organizational Communication and Change*, *Organizational Culture*, *Advances in Leadership Research* and the *Handbook of Organizational Communication*, and in journals such as *Administrative Science Quarterly*, *Communication Quarterly*, *Journal of Computer Mediated Communication*, *Journal of Management*, *Argument and Advocacy*, and *Communication Reports*.

Stefania Romenti, PhD, is an assistant professor in public relations and corporate communication at IULM University of Milan, Italy, where she teaches public relations, and adjunct professor at IE Business School, Spain, where she teaches the measuring of intangibles and KPIs in communication. She is vice-director of the executive master program in public relations (IULM University). She is also part of the teaching research commission of the PhD program on corporate communication at IULM University. She centers her research on strategic communication, the influence of communication on corporate reputation, stakeholder management and engagement, dialogue, social media, measurement and evaluation. She has written and co-written over 80 international publications in communication management and public relations and published various academic articles in international communication and management journals, such as *International Journal of Strategic Communication*, *Journal of Communication Management*, *Corporate Communication: an International Journal*, *Public Relations Review*, and *MIT Sloan Management Review*. She works as reviewer for *Corporate Communication: an International Journal*, as well as for international conferences such as the European Public Relations Education and Research Association (EUPRERA) annual congress and the Annual Conference on Public Relations History. She is a member of EUPRERA and of the Federazione Relazioni Pubbliche Italiana (Ferpi).

Constanze Rossmann, Dr., is full Professor of Communication at the Department of Media and Communication Science, University of Erfurt, Germany. She worked as a guest professor at the University of Zürich, Switzerland at the Hannover University of Music, Drama and Media and at the Johannes Gutenberg University of Mainz and completed her PhD and habilitation at the Ludwig Maximiliano University, Munich. In 2012 she co-founded the Interest Group on Health Communication within the German Communication Association and is speaker of the group. Her research interests include health communication, media use, and media effects.

Liane Rothenberger, Dr., works as senior researcher and lecturer at the Department of Media Studies at the Institute of Media and Communication Science, Ilmenau University of Technology, Germany. She studied Journalism at the Catholic University of Eichstätt-Ingolstadt, Germany, and graduated in 2005 with a study about the Foreign Correspondents' Association of Germany. In 2008 she received her doctorate degree for a study about the program development of "arte", the French–German TV channel. Her research interests include research on journalism, terrorism as communication, normativity, intercultural and international communication.

Hagen Schölzel, Dr., is an associated researcher in the project "New Media, Modern Democracy" (NEMO) at Lund University, Campus Helsingborg in Sweden. Previously he worked at Leipzig University in Germany, where he obtained a doctorate in political communication.

Andreas Schwarz, Dr., is senior lecturer and executive head of the Department of Media Studies at Ilmenau University of Technology in Germany. Since 2006 he has been managing director of the International Research Group on Crisis Communication. His research has been published in journals like *Public Relations Review, International Journal of Strategic Communication, the Journal of Public Relations Research*, and *Communications Journal*. Besides crisis communication, his research interests include public relations, journalism and cross–cultural communication. He teaches in the areas of public relations, journalism, communication theory and crisis management.

Charles C. Self, PhD, is professor emeritus at the University of Oklahoma. He is the former dean of the Gaylord College of Journalism and Mass Communication and former director of its Institute for Research and Training. He held the Edward L. Gaylord Research Chair. He is also former president of the Association for Education in Journalism and Mass Communication, the Council of Communication Associations, and the Association of Schools of Journalism and Mass Communication.

Cheryll Ruth Soriano (PhD) is an associate professor of communication at De La Salle University in the Philippines. She is interested in the politics and dialectics of new media engagement by cultural minorities and social movement organizations. Her works, which explore the multiple intersections of cultural activism, citizenship, ritual, gender, alternative development, and new media engagement, have been published in *Media, Culture and Society, Telematics and Informatics, Journal of Creative Communications, Mobile Media & Communication, Journal of Communication Management*, and *Electronic Journal of Information Systems in Developing Countries*. She is currently involved in a book project on Asian perspectives in digital culture. She obtained her PhD in Communications and New Media from the National University of Singapore.

Jesper Strömbäck, PhD, is the Lubbe Nordström Professor and Chair in journalism, and professor in political communication, at Mid Sweden University. He is also research director at the Centre for Political Communication Research at Mid Sweden University, Sundsvall, Sweden. His research mainly focuses on political news coverage, political campaigning and marketing, political public relations, the mediatization of politics, and public opinion formation.

Alice Srugies works as a research associate at the Institute of Media and Communication Science of Ilmenau University of Technology, Germany. She is particularly interested in public diplomacy, international and intercultural communication, political communication, journalism and media effects.

Gail Fann Thomas, EdD, is associate professor of Management at the Naval Postgraduate School (NPS) in Monterey, CA. In addition to her teaching in the Graduate School of Business & Public Policy, she is program manager for strategic communication in the Center of Executive Education, NPS. Her research focuses on the role of discourse in institutionalization, the use of social and semantic network analysis to study the longitudinal effects of strategic discourse, and the impact of inter-organizational collaboration on organizational performance. She has been published in *Journal of Business Communication, International Journal for Conflict Management, Journal of Applied Behavioral Science*, and *Journal of Business & Technical Communication*, among others.

Christa Thomsen, PhD, is associate professor and head of the Department of Business Communication, School of Business and Social Sciences, Aarhus University, Denmark. Her major research areas are corporate communication and strategic corporate social responsibility communication. Her focus is corporate social responsibility, strategy communication and implementation, corporate social responsibility communication as corporate change, management communication and conversations, network and cross-sector social partnership communication, and employer branding. Her most recent research has appeared in international academic journals such as *Journal* *of Management Inquiry, International Journal of Strategic Communication, Journal of Communication Management, Business Ethics: A European Review, Journal of Modern Accounting and Auditing,* and *Corporate Communications.*

Simon Møberg Torp, PhD, is dean of the Faculty of Humanities at University of Southern Denmark. Previously he has been head of department of Marketing & Management and director of research in strategic communication and management. He holds a PhD in Business Administration and an MA and BA in Philosophy and Organizational Culture and Communication. Besides his research on the theoretical and philosophical aspects of strategic communication, he has published widely on integrated communication, marketing communications and leadership. Simon Møberg Torp has written numerous journal articles and contributed to handbooks and anthologies published by Routledge, SAGE and Pearson. He has edited and co-authored two textbooks. In 2008 he won a best paper award at one of the world's leading conferences within one of his research fields. He has acted as a consultant in the sphere of communication, management and intercultural understanding in Danish and international companies.

Piet Verhoeven, Dr., is senior lecturer and researcher at the College and Graduate School of Communication and the Amsterdam School of Communication Research (ASCoR) at the Department of Communication Science of the University of Amsterdam, The Netherlands. His research involves corporations in the mass media.

Mikko Villi, Dr., is lecturer in media and communication studies at the Department of Social Research, University of Helsinki, Finland. He acts also as the director of the Communication Research Centre, CRC, at this university. Villi's research interests include new communication technology and forms of communication, in particular in mobile, visual and digital media. Lately, he has focused his attention on social media, the media industry and the media ecosystem, where different media, devices and actors converge.

Robert I. Wakefield, PhD, is an associate professor of communication at Brigham Young University, Provo, UT. He concentrates his research on stakeholder relations and reputation in transnational entities, examining the impacts of globalization, culture, activism, and other factors on these global practices of public relations. Before becoming a full-time scholar, Professor Wakefield practiced and consulted on strategic public relations in 25 nations between 1990 and 2005.

Rebecca Weintraub, PhD, is a clinical professor of communication at the Annenberg School for Communication and Journalism, University of Southern California (USC) in Los Angeles. She is the director of both the on-campus and online Masters of Communication Management. In addition to teaching in those programs, she provides strategic communication consulting and executive education for a variety of corporate, non-profit and government organizations. Prior to coming to USC, she was director of corporate communication for executive and employee communication at Hughes Electronics, and a Senior Consultant at the consulting firm of Towers Perrin (now Towers Watson).

Kelly Page Werder, PhD, is an associate professor and the director of graduate studies in the School of Mass Communications at the University of South Florida, FL. She is co-editor of *International Journal of Strategic Communication.*

Lindsay Young, PhD, is post-doctoral researcher at the University of Chicago with the Chicago Center for HIV Elimination (CHHE). She received her PhD from Northwestern University. Her work focuses on the relationship between information and communication networks and knowledge-building and decision-making processes as well as using network-based interventions for social and behavioral change.

Ansgar Zerfass, Dr., is professor of strategic communication at the University of Leipzig, Germany, and professor in communication and leadership at BI Norwegian Business School, Oslo, Norway. He serves the research community as president of the European Public Relations Education and Research Association, Brussels, and editor of the *International Journal of Strategic Communication*. Ansgar Zerfass holds a university degree and doctorate in business administration and a habilitation in communication science. He has published 30 books and more than 200 journal articles and book chapters on strategic communication, corporate communications, measurement, and online communication.

Guido Zurstiege is professor and chair of the Division of Empirical Media Research at the Department of Media Studies, University of Tübingen. He is chair of the temporary working group on advertising research in the European Communication Research and Education Association (ECREA). He is member of the editorial board of *International Journal of Strategic Communication*.

Introduction

Strategic is a much contested, albeit neglected, concept in communication studies. One of the reasons for this neglect is that strategic communication may be associated with persuasion in its most negative sense. However, others argue that strategic intent is inherent in all communication. From this perspective strategic communication extends well beyond its practical application in various fields of practice. In particular, thinking about communication as situated at the center of society requires reflections on the frameworks of power and interests in which communication is enacted in all kinds of organizations. These include corporations, non-profit organizations, activist groups, political parties or movements, government organizations, and all other kinds of actors who form part of the patchwork of today's culture.

This handbook explores the field of strategic communication from a multi-disciplinary perspective. It provides insights into ongoing discussions that build an emerging body of knowledge. The journey started with the first edition of the *International Journal of Strategic Communication* in 2007, which has since served as a platform for building knowledge with several special issues on topics like institutionalization, the public sphere, consulting, financial communication and so forth. The ongoing debate fueled the first ever interdisciplinary *Pre-Conference on Strategic Communication*, held at the Annual Conference of the International Communication Association in Chicago in 2011, where researchers from 17 countries presented peer-reviewed papers. The conference was so stimulating and influential in shaping thinking about what strategic communication is or can be that it led to this volume, the *Routledge Handbook of Strategic Communication*. Once the project took shape several scholars who did not participate in the conference were invited to submit chapters to fill in important gaps in what the editors perceived as the emerging body of knowledge of strategic communication.

This volume covers four focus areas. Part 1 reviews different metatheoretical approaches to the field. Part II investigates the impact of organizational variables on strategic communication and part III focuses on the communication between strategic communicators and their stakeholders and audiences. Part IV deals comprehensively with different areas of practice.

Chapter 1 by Derina Holtzhausen and Ansgar Zerfass expands on the original definition of the field proposed by Hallahan, Holtzhausen, Van Ruler, Verčič, and Sriramesh (2007) to include an emphasis on the public sphere as an important construct for strategic communication. It follows developments in communication theory and our understanding of how meaning creation emerges from the communication process. Finally, it identifies common interests across areas of practice that are underdeveloped and that require the need for additional research.

Several chapters deconstruct the term *strategy*, albeit from different perspectives. In chapter 2 Howard Nothhaft and Hagen Schölzel do an outstanding review of the original work of the first strategist, Carl von Clausewitz. Their work is an example of how native speakers can help us interpret original, seminal works and make us aware of the origin of words and their interpretations, in this case the concept of *strategy* in the military. They particularly show how guerilla warfare, as originally defined, can help us get to grips with current trends in communication practice. In chapter 3 Simon Møberg Torp reviews the history and role of strategy in communication science from ancient Greece until the present day and comes to the conclusion that the communicative turn has been supplemented by a strategic turn in which most communication is now viewed as having strategic intent.

The next chapters deal with the philosophical foundations of the public sphere in Western society. In chapter 4, Günter Bentele and Howard Nothhaft discuss European perspectives on communication in the public sphere. Charles C. Self responds in chapter 5 with an American approach to the same topic based on the work of American philosopher John Dewey. Both chapters hold that communication in the public sphere is crucial to democracy and that communication already is public action.

Part I concludes with metatheoretical approaches to strategic communication. Lindsay Young and Willem Pieterson provide an application of network theory to a practical communication problem in chapter 6. They argue communication has become so complex as a result of the emergence of information and communication technologies and networked forms of social organization, that traditional communication theories no longer inform strategic communication. In chapter 7 Priscilla Murphy similarly questions the success of strategic communication once it has left the controlled organizational environment and become part of a diffused and challenged public arena. She too proposes social network theory as fundamental to the understanding of strategic communication and argues that communicators need to accept that the outcome of participation in the issues arena is unpredictable. The section concludes with Øyvind Ihlen and Piet Verhoeven's review of the application of social theories to strategic communication in chapter 8. They highlight the importance of legitimacy, reflection, power and language to understanding the ethical and political consequences of strategic communication practice.

As mentioned, part II deals with the impact of institutional and organizational factors on strategic communication. The first three chapters of this section focus on organizational factors that inhibit excellence in strategic communication. Magnus Fredriksson and Josef Pallas apply a neo-institutional analysis in chapter 9 to explain why it is often difficult for organizations to execute strategic communication goals and objectives. They conclude that strategic communication is inhibited by institutional structures, although it also actively participates in constituting those structures.

In chapter 10 Kim Johnston and James Everett show how organizational culture and knowledge influence the interpretation of the organization's environment in the process of strategic communication planning. Helle Kryger Aggerholm and Christa Thomsen use a case study in chapter 11 to show how polyphony in management messages counteracts persuasive intent and creates uncertainty and confusion.

This section also investigates the role of executives and how the process of strategizing contributes to communication in organizations. Marlene Marchiori and Sergio Bulgacov show in chapter 12, at the hand of a case study, how the interaction of strategies and practices are fundamental to the creation of meaning in organizations. This comes about because humans communicatively constitute strategy through interaction and social practices that involve communication and language. In chapter 13 Patricia Riley, Gail Thomas, Rebecca Weintraub, Allison Noyes, and Stephanie Dixon present the findings of a study on the intersection between good governance and communication in networks and organizations to build communication capital.

Emanuele Invernizzi and Stefania Romenti provide a unique perspective on the importance of entrepreneurial theory for strategy formulation in chapter 14. They use four case studies to show

how an entrepreneurial orientation provides a useful conceptual framework for valuing different approaches to strategic communication formulation in organizations. Chapter 15 places the spotlight on the communication competencies of organizational executives. Finn Frandsen and Winni Johansen review research on the impact of executives' roles, competencies, identities and legitimacy on strategy and strategizing. Part II concludes with Kirk Hallahan's clear articulation of the roles of organizational goals and communication outcomes in organizational strategizing. He argues effective goals should mutually benefit the organization and its constituencies and effective communications objectives should lead to behavioral outcomes in audiences.

Part III focuses on the communication and interaction between the strategic communicator and stakeholders and highlights a number of key concepts. In chapter 17 Kelly Page Werder reviews the progress of research on message strategies from the 1980s to the present day. She proposes synthesizing theories from both public relations and advertising into a single theoretical perspective that clarifies the identification, description, and explanation of the message variable in the strategic communication process. Her study shows how the ability of strategic communicators to interact with a wide variety of interactants is the unique domain of strategic communication.

Kenneth E. Kim's review of framing strategies in message design in chapter 18 further elaborates on the importance of understanding the impact of specific messages on specific target audiences. As in the previous chapter the author shows how message strategy is a unique aspect of strategic communication practice in a wide range of persuasion disciplines. He argues that the effects of message frames, especially individual–societal and attribute–goal frames, provide a guideline for developing effective messages. Similarly, William Benoit's discussion of image restoration strategies in chapter 19 reflects the importance of message strategies during crisis situations.

In chapter 20 Janis Teruggi Page makes a unique contribution by focusing on visual messages. This is one of the most neglected areas of research in strategic communication, even though visual messages have never been as prominent as they are at this time. Her semiotic analysis of a communications campaign in Abu Dhabi shows the powerful ability of strategic communication to reinforce cultural values through visual means, which underscores the need for visual literacy in the interpretation of visual stimuli.

The final two chapters in part III argue for participative practices in strategic communication. In chapter 21 Eyun-Jung Ki reviews the dimensions of relationships, both in terms of actions that cultivate relationships and the dimensions that actually measure them. She calls for more research on the impact of new communication technologies, particularly social media platforms, and on the ability of strategic communicators to cultivate relationships. Jesper Falkheimer and Mats Heide answer this call in chapter 22 by arguing that participation is the foundation of new forms of communication. Because participants have so many opportunities to control the communication they receive, the notion among strategic communicators that communication can be controlled needs to be rejected in favor of the acceptance that organizations have little control over their messages.

Part IV deals with areas of strategic communication practice. This section shows just how far strategic communication research has come in a short time and how pervasive the practice is. Each of the 15 chapters in this section deals with a different area of practice and explores the notion of strategic communication as deliberate, planned and executed by a person assigned to that purpose. It also emphasizes that, no matter how much strategizing and planning take place behind the scenes, the ultimate aim is to communicate in the public sphere.

In chapter 23 Robert I. Wakefield, Kenneth D. Plowman, and Alex Curry place strategic communication in the context of public relations and find that the ability to communicate strategically helps public relations practice to become institutionalized. After studying the impact of organizational changes on public relations practice they conclude that public relations practice has to be in a process of continuous re-institutionalization to be effective. On a similar note Tino G.K. Meitz and Guido Zurstiege examine strategizing in advertising in chapter 24. Focusing on advertising agencies, they argue that the concept of strategy has been added to creativity and efficiency as a third organizing idea. However, the use of strategy in advertising is at best murky. They found strategy is used ritualistically as a benchmark to validate creativity and efficiency in order to justify advertising budget allocation and spending. As a result strategy often is used as post-rationalization for advertising campaigns.

The next two chapters deal with political communication but from very different perspectives. In chapter 25 Spiro Kiousis and Jesper Strömbäck do a comparative analysis of political communication from public relations and marketing perspectives respectively. They find that a public relations approach offers the most comprehensive framework for strategic political communication. They offer a conceptual model of stakeholder engagement in the political context that integrates both reputation management and relationship cultivation. In chapter 26 Kirsten Kozolanka also compares the use of a strategic communication approach to a political marketing approach in government communication. She argues that the conservative Canadian government has used the political marketing approach to solidify marketing behavior as a more technologized and advanced version of strategic communication. This approach, and strategic communication in the political environment in general, does not serve the public interest because it focuses on certain elite stakeholder groups to the exclusion of the public interest.

Constanze Rossmann places strategic communication campaigns at the center of health communication in chapter 27. She advocates a campaign approach that is theory-driven and outcomes-focused. Like many other authors in the volume she emphasizes the challenges that lie in the task of changing attitudes and behaviors, which seem even more daunting in the area of health communication. She discusses the unintended consequences of campaigns that counteract the original campaign objectives and argues that it is important for health communicators to declare the persuasive intent of their work.

The next four chapters investigate the role of strategic communication in social change. In a case study of two minority groups in the Philippines, Cheryll Ruth Soriano explains how these groups use technology to navigate complex local and global forces (chapter 28). She shows how they strategically use production and distribution processes to reaffirm their minority identity and challenge the forces that undermine their minority culture and struggle. In chapter 29 Martin Löffelholz, Claudia Auer, and Alice Srugies provide a thorough review of the domain of public diplomacy and highlight its strategic communication dimensions. They describe two broad strategic approaches to public communication: centralized versus diffused and decentralized. In the centralized approach the government is central to public diplomacy efforts. In the decentralized approach there is no centralized agency promoting public diplomacy. In this instance a country's organizations perform that role.

Andreas Schwarz and Alexander Fritsch provide a comprehensive review of the use of strategic communication in non-governmental organizations in chapter 30. They anticipate an increased proficiency in the ability of these organizations to manage their reputation and influence public perceptions, which will expand their global impact. In chapter 31 Liane Rothenberger explores the use of terrorism as communication strategy. She argues terrorist groups should be treated like professional organizations seeking maximum publicity. She argues studying terrorists' communication strategies will allow for the development of counter-strategies that can negate the communication intent of terrorist campaigns.

The following three chapters share the theme of crisis communication. W. Timothy Coombs and Sherry Holladay place crisis communication in the context of strategic communication in terms of the management of meaning during a crisis and the focus on behavioral outcomes (chapter 32). They argue crisis communication has developed as a unique field of strategic communication and that crisis management, reputation management, issues management, and risk management all form part of the knowledge base required of crisis managers. In chapter 33 Mats Eriksson explores crisis communication in the context of social media impact. He questions the ability of crisis managers to execute strategy in the face of social media and proposes improvisation and crafting of real-time messages as an alternative to implementing previously defined strategies. Juliana Raupp further elaborates on the crisis communication theme in these chapters by investigating the strategic context of risk communication in chapter 34. She argues the field is complicated by the fact that risk is a highly contested and contextualized social construction. As a result it is a conflict-laden negotiation process and the practice is always situational.

Rita Järventie-Thesleff, Johanna Moisander and Mikko Villi show in chapter 35 how top-down organizational change processes result in emergent bottom-up change processes. They found that it would be important for management to provide guidance to those emergent processes. Strategic communicators should focus on creating a sense of collective understanding and engagement by supporting active participation in the processes of sense-making rather than focusing on information transmission.

One of the most consistent themes in this volume is the impact of social media on strategic communication. In chapter 36 Bobbi Kay Lewis and Cynthia Nichols survey the theoretical approaches to studying the phenomenon of social media. They situate these theoretical approaches in the domain of strategic communication and conclude with introducing social learning theory as an important driver in the formation of communities of practice.

Part IV concludes with a global perspective. Juan-Carlos Molleda and Sarabdeep Kochhar show how the complexity of global strategic communication increases because of demands from organizations and stakeholders with local and transnational roots (chapter 37). Their case study shows that coordination, control, and standardization are essential to the success of multinational campaigns.

This volume provides the first comprehensive review of research in the strategic communication domain. There are some important omissions, particularly in the area of branding, consumer behavior and marketing. In this volume the major focus of strategic communication is still in the "soft" disciplines where it is much harder to determine and measure outcomes. Nonetheless, the fog is slowly clearing and a comprehensive picture, if not a coherent theoretical approach, is emerging.

The editors thank the contributors to this volume for their perseverance, their unique contributions, and the original thinking that epitomizes all the work in this volume. We appreciate the ongoing support of Melissa Powers (Oklahoma State University), Dawie Bomman (Universities of Leipzig and Pretoria), and Linda Bathgate and Ross Wagenhofer (Routledge). We hope that the debate will continue and new ideas will be stimulated by the thoughts and debates presented here.

Reference

Hallahan, K., Holtzhausen, D. R., Van Ruler, B., Verčič, D., & Sriramesh, K. (2007). Defining strategic communication. *International Journal of Strategic Communication, 1*(1), 3–35.

Part I

Conceptual Foundations of Strategic Communication

1

Strategic Communication

Opportunities and Challenges of the Research Area[1]

Derina Holtzhausen and Ansgar Zerfass

Strategic communication is a term that has become quite popular in communication science education in the second decade of the twenty-first century. Originally only used for a niche, that is, communication programs in the domain of national governments and the military (Farwell, 2012; Paul, 2011), it is now increasingly popular as an umbrella concept embracing various goal-directed communication activities usually covered by public relations, marketing and financial communications, health communications, public diplomacy, campaigning, and so forth. In the United States, many universities have merged formerly distinct public relations and advertising programs into strategic communication curricula. In Europe, strategic communication is often used to signal a managerial approach to the field of integrated communications for all kinds of organizations. In Asia and Australia, strategic communication is a concept used in the professional field, in education and in literature alike (e.g., Mahoney, 2013).

However, strategic communication is not just a term used in substitution for disliked or ill-reputed concepts. It is a distinct approach focusing on the process of communication which offers complementary insights and open up new fields for interdisciplinary research. This chapter will review the original definition (Hallahan, Holtzhausen, Van Ruler, Verčič, & Sriramesh, 2007) and its expansion (Holtzhausen & Zerfass, 2013). Subsequently it will reflect on those perspectives on the field's theoretical foundation that have emerged over the past few years, and consider the factors that contribute to successful strategic communication practice.

Evolution of the Concept

Since the publication of the article "Defining Strategic Communication" (Hallahan et al., 2007, p. 243) in the inaugural issue of the *International Journal of Strategic Communication*, the definition put forward in that article has been used to explore, limit, argue, debate and study strategic communication. By the end of 2013 the article had been cited numerous times in other journal articles and had been downloaded more than 2,000 times. Not much has changed since 2007 in terms of the definition of strategic communication. However, much has been clarified and at this time a better picture emerges of what goes into a strategic communication process, what defines its success, what the impact is on the public sphere and what the commonalities are among different areas of strategic communication practice.

The 2007 article brought about an identity crisis, particularly in the public relations scholarly community, which has long held that strategic communication is its specific domain. This anxiety is unnecessary because the study of strategic communication has never been intended to replace other areas of practice but has merely tried to explore what the different communities of practice can learn from each other and so break down the silos we have erected around ourselves.

Four reasons why the study of strategic communication is necessary and prudent were provided in the 2007 article: problems in differentiating between traditional communication activities; the changes in technology that makes it increasingly difficult to differentiate between different forms of communication; the increase in methods organizations use to communicate directly to stakeholders; and the fact that purposeful communication is "the fundamental goal of communication by organizations" (Hallahan et al., 2007, p. 10).

There is indeed a great deal of overlap between the different domains of practice, as this volume shows, and many of the developments in the field of strategic communication have emerged from public relations scholars. On the other hand, scholars of advertising, political, health and crisis communication, public diplomacy, management communication and marketing have since 2007 made important contributions to researchers' understanding of strategic communication.

Defining the Field

Hallahan et al. (2007) defined strategic communication "in its broadest sense, (as) communicating purposefully to advance (the organization's) mission" (p. 4). They also held that strategic communication "implies that people will be engaged in deliberate communication practice on behalf of organizations, causes, and social movements" (p. 4). The article further elaborated on the concept of *strategy* and argued that being strategic does not necessarily mean being manipulative, because practitioners often decide that being inclusive and collaborative will be more strategic and effective than being propagandistic or manipulative. However, influencing the levels of knowledge, changing or maintaining attitudes and influencing the behaviors towards issues, products or services remain the preferred outcomes for strategic communication.

Yet another property of the first definition was a focus on practice or action and on the role of the practitioner who serves as an agent communicating on behalf of others. Thus, rather than merely concentrating on the strategic communication process it also focused on the factors that enable or prevent communicators to execute a communication plan. Finally, the article pointed to the importance of *communication* in the strategic communication process as opposed to a strategic organizational process that does not necessarily revolve around communication. The strategic communication process typically is a communication process that follows from an organization's strategic plan and focuses on the role of communication in enabling the organization's strategic goals and objectives. Two communication models were discussed. The transmission model followed from Shannon and Weaver (1949) and eventually evolved in discussions of two-way symmetrical and two-way asymmetrical communication in public relations literature (L. A. Grunig, Grunig, & Dozier, 2002). The interactive or ritualistic model of communication, following Carey (1989), has its foundation in symbolic interactionism and organizational communication and focuses on how messages and people themselves are shaped during the communication process.

This foundation remains largely intact at this time, although Holtzhausen and Zerfass (2013) proposed a more comprehensive, single definition incorporating most of the attributes above, with the inclusion of the public sphere. They proposed the following definition: "Strategic communication is the practice of deliberate and purposive communication that a communication agent enacts in the public sphere on behalf of a communicative entity to reach set goals" (p. 74). Following Holtzhausen (2008), communicative entities "cover the full spectrum of economic and social sectors, such as trade and industry, politics, nonprofit and government agencies, activist groups, and even celebrities in the sports and entertainment industries" (p. 4849). While strategic communicators indeed do a great deal of work outside of the public sphere, such as managing communication programs and communicating with internal stakeholders, the ultimate aim is to maintain a healthy reputation for the communicative entity in the public sphere.

Set against this more advanced definition, this chapter will review each of the attributes of the definition with the purpose of assessing previous and new theoretical approaches to the study of the field. First, it will review the philosophical foundations of strategic communication, particularly as they pertain to the public sphere, before moving to the role of practitioners and the organizational environment in which strategic communication is practiced, and finally to an assessment of the actual communication process in its various contexts.

Strategic Communication and the Public Sphere

The notion of control of public dialogue has always been inherent in the debate on the role of strategic communication. Habermas (1979, 2006) in particular has been critical of the ability of those in power to hire powerful agents to communicate on their behalf and so influence and skew public debate. His work was largely influenced by the reality that, at that time, the media were crucial in shaping and instigating public discourse, with the assumption that the media were neutral in this role and thus open to influence by strategic communicators.

Popular understanding of the public sphere has changed, particularly during the past decade, with the increasingly important role of the Internet, which brought a radical expansion of the public sphere and a marginalization of the major public media. While Bentele and Nothhaft (2010) argued the virtual sphere can only exist in a solid and real society that surrounds it, they also contended that

> The dominant characteristic (of the public sphere) is that the communication sphere, to a degree, collapses structural constraints, such as time, distance, technical limitations, and physical handicaps of the person, to mention a few. The public sphere is not a place of gathering as the *Tingstead* any more (sic). Neither is it a force field of media attention constituted by a limited amount of actors. It is a network of points of interest. Something, e.g., a brand, the swine-flu, a politician or any other topic, is in the public sphere because communicators, who are points in the network of communications, communicate about it.
>
> *p. 112*

They argued that the public sphere is now controlled by the truthfulness of the statements issued in the public communication sphere as perceived by the public. If strategic communicators can argue that their communication is in the public interest and contributes to the wellbeing of society, and if their arguments are accepted as such, they will make a contribution to the public sphere, even if they use their own communication platforms to do so.

In an analysis of the contribution of Dewey to the understanding of the public sphere, Self (2010) argued that Dewey believed discourse in the public sphere already was action, which was preserved in the form of shared meaning. Thus, for Dewey, discourse was already action that shaped the public sphere and subsequently society. Similar to Bentele and Nothhaft (2010), Self (2010) argued that the public became activists through participating in the public sphere, which eventually led to solving society's problems. Whereas in the past the consequences of public deliberation, because of mediators, only vaguely reflected the public debate "now the relation between public communication and public action seems to grow more and more ominous" (Bentele & Nothhaft, 2010, p. 114).

What sets the current public sphere apart from that of the 20th century is that it is more participative rather than representative. There still are some major media who contribute to the public sphere but *contribute* here is the key word rather than *mediate*. Whereas the media was the main force in presenting different viewpoints representing society in the 20th century, digital media now allows members of the public to directly participate in public debate without going through these mediated channels. Thus the public sphere has become participative rather than representative. Now everybody matters in what is a communication sphere rather than a public sphere.

Public versus Private

To understand the role of strategic communication in the public sphere it is important to briefly review the difference between the public and the private, which also is called "The good Life" (Kohlberg, Levine, & Hewer, 1984, pp. 229–230). Traditionally the public sphere was viewed as the arena where the wealthy, aristocratic and well-connected were expected to make a contribution. Women, peasants and tradespeople were typically excluded from the public sphere because they were viewed as second-class citizens who did not have the necessary competency, education and background to make decisions for themselves. Thus, the public sphere belonged to a very select group of people; it was a place where equals met, that is, the free and the privileged. This perspective led to the well-known quote that "The Personal is Political" (Hanisch, 1970), also often presented as "The private is political."

Although this scenario has now changed with a public sphere that is more accessible to a variety of voices than ever before, it nonetheless highlights the split between the public and the private, which also frames the role of strategic communication in the public sphere. If strategic communicators are participants in the public sphere and the role of the public sphere is to solve society's problems, they have a responsibility to present debatable issues to the public sphere. If not, their work will be ridiculed. Individuals who wish to manipulate the public sphere to their own benefit without bringing ideas and arguments that contribute to the public debate will be rejected, as is the case in the United States when Donald Trump used his own brand to make unfounded political statements about President Barack Obama's birthplace (Swindell, 2011). Trump has no elected status and has never run for office and the way he used his public profile to insert himself into a political debate was met with ridicule. Since that public humiliation Trump has been quite absent in the public sphere. This is an example of how arguments in the public sphere are rejected when they are not authentic or do not contribute to the improvement of society.

The inclusion of the public sphere in a definition of strategic communication is therefore valuable in debating the role of the practice. In addition to its many other attributes the role of strategic communicators should surely include helping others gain access to the public sphere through good, thoughtful arguments that can advance the interests of the communicative entity while contributing to the improvement of society. That in itself already represents strategic action, as per Dewey (1954). Furthermore, many strategic communicators will attest to the notion that the pervasiveness of the public sphere makes them more thoughtful about what and how they communicate about issues, even when they communicate in the marketing and branding context. As Bentele and Nothhaft (2010) succinctly pointed out, the public sphere has become "a corridor that limits your maneuverable space when trying to make sense out of reality" (p. 114).

While technology facilitates public communication, there also are indicators that it might pose a future danger to that very important contribution through the process of "*datafication*", which means putting phenomena "in a quantified format so it can be tabulated and analyzed" (Mayer-Schönberger & Cukier, 2013, p. 77). Datafication is the process underlying the concept of big data, and which allow people to collect vast quantities of data through the use of algorithms. While it allows for the collection of vast amounts of data, it simultaneously allows for the collection of unique data from individuals, which already is used to target communication with those individuals, particularly on the Internet. Anybody who has shopped online will know how the products and services searched beforehand keep cropping up while one is using the Internet.

What people do not realize is the extent to which they offer up information willingly in the era of big data simply because the nature of this kind of data is so different from what we generally perceive as data. Mayer-Schönberger and Cukier (2013) described datafication as the ability to (take) information about all things under the sun – including ones we never used to think of as information at all, such as a person's location, the vibrations of an engine, or the stress on a bridge – and transform it into a data format to make it quantified.

p. 15

This data is vastly different from statistical data, as the authors explain. Because of the sheer quantity of data available it questions the need for statistical analysis, which is based on random sampling and analysis of subsets of populations. Because big data focuses on real-time data and the collection of multiple data sets on, for instance, one individual, "the danger shifts from privacy to probability: algorithms will predict the likelihood that one . . . will default on a mortgage (and be denied a loan), or commit a crime (and perhaps get arrested in advance)" (p. 16). There is already evidence that gaming companies are collecting evidence on gaming behavior of individuals and translating that into a profile of the individual that determines her or his suitability for certain types of jobs based on how the individual progresses through a game (Wheatley, 2013).

In the same way big data poses a danger to individual privacy it also poses a danger to the public sphere. It will be very tempting to strategic communicators to rather communicate with individuals on issues, products and services based on algorithms that expose attitudes and behaviors than to communicate with them through open and public communication. This issue highlights the tension between the role of the public and private spheres in society. Although it is not apparent, the danger of big data for individual privacy is directly linked to the public sphere. When this kind of data and the ability to communicate with individuals did not exist, the public sphere was the way in which people were informed and educated themselves on social issues. This also ensured that policy and other issues were debated openly and transparently. When the need for communicating publicly on issues of public concern disappears society loses its ability to collectively protect itself from less transparent practices. For instance, hypothetically a pharmaceutical company might develop a controversial product such as a vaccine and only market it to doctors and individuals who, based on big data, have the potential to develop the disease. At present such a product will most likely be advertised and discussed in the media in an effort to promote it. The company might, however, be tempted to keep the information from the public sphere because it is controversial. Because they have the names and profiles of people who might be possible patients they can with ease personalize messages to those individuals and keep all controversy from the public.

Thus, although certain communication can and should sometimes be private, it is crucial that some information be released in the public sphere for debate and discussion. It will be important for strategic communicators to keep the balance between these two interests and not to be tempted to keep private communication that should have been public and transparent.

The Nature of Communication in the Strategic Process

The notion that communication can be controlled and regulated is now largely redundant. In fact, one of the most important emerging perspectives in strategic communication is the rejection of linearity in the communication process. It is indeed tempting to still teach and adhere to Shannon and Weaver's (1949) transmission model, which is simple and easy to grasp. It also still has a use in the sense that it reminds practitioners in particular to think about media used for a particular communication process, message construction, and target audiences (Boromisza-Habashi, 2013). As Bell, Golombisky, and Holtzhausen (2002) argued, the transmission model only investigated "how we get information from here to there" (p. 5). While this remains a valid question, the more important one really is: "What happens to communication in that process and how is meaning shaped and co-created?"

Both symbolic interactionism (Bauer, 1964; Blumer, 1969; Carey, 1989; Thayer, 1968) and postmodernism (through the extensive writings of Michel Foucault and Jean-François Lyotard) have deeply changed perspectives on the role of communication in organizations and society, and they both form the basis of today's communication theories. Collectively known as the constitutive model of communication, these theories represent "a dialogical-dialectical disciplinary matrix" (Craig, 1999, p. 120) that represents seven different theoretical approaches to communication theory and, broadly speaking, focuses on how individual and shared meanings are shaped through the communication process itself. What is particularly important here for the communication strategist is to understand that all meaning is constructed through a communication process that often focuses on opposing arguments, through what Ermarth (2001, p. 211) referred to as the "linguistic in-between." Without communication there cannot be co-construction of meaning. For the strategic communicator this might occasionally be in a face-to-face context but it mostly relates to communication through other channels.

Whereas the transmission model focuses on how to get information from one point to another, constitutive communication focuses on the importance of communication to bring about actual change and action, as Dewey (1954) argued. From this perspective the role of the strategic communicator is not to send information via the most effective channel, although that is an important starting point. More importantly, the role of the practitioner is to send information that can act as the point of departure for meaning creation between a communicative entity and its stakeholders, which can actually lead to social change and social action. Indeed, an organization has to act publicly (Hallahan, 2010). Instead of transmitting information, with the underlying assumptions that one can control communication so transmitted, strategic communication increasingly focuses on the process of communication, which might take place over long periods of time and stretch over time long after a message has been transmitted.

With their focus on action, it is also important for strategic communicators to understand and utilize "*mediatization*," which "*is a concept used to analyze critically the interrelation between changes in media and communication on the one hand, and changes in culture and society on the other*" [italics in original] (Couldry & Hepp, 2013, p. 197). Mediatization goes beyond media effects:

> Put simply, something is going on with media on our lives, and it is deep enough not to be reached simply by accumulating more and more specific studies that analyze this newspaper, describe how that program was produced, or trace how particular audiences make sense of that film on a particular occasion.
>
> *p. 191*

As "social" communicators strategic communication practitioners and audiences use the media on a daily basis, meaning here media in their broadest sense to include all forms of Internet and electronic communication. In the past strategic communication largely focused on mediatization from an institutional perspective. In this perspective media are institutions that have to be understood through "media logic"—understanding how the media operate—and is the reason why politicians and other interest groups who wish to have access to the media hire communication practitioners to do this work for them (p. 196). However, following the constitutive model of communication described above, it is important for communication practitioners to also be aware of how the media are and can be used to shape social and cultural realities.

From a theoretical perspective it is the convergence of these two strong theoretical traditions in communication that sets strategic communication apart from other communication disciplines. It forces academics and practitioners alike to consider both the constitutive nature of all communication and the role of media in the strategic communication process. Thus, instead of only viewing media as channels of communication and audiences as the receivers of messages, strategic communicators needs to consider how meaning is shaped in the interaction process involving stakeholders and the media practitioners use and how stakeholders interpret and recreate media content in the process. Only then will strategic communicators truly understand how their practices impact and shape society and bring about change.

The Concept of Emergence

When one lets go of control of communication and meaning creation, the sheer messiness of the communication process can be overwhelming. However, to have a realistic and pragmatic perspective on communication one has to embrace the messiness, risk taking and chaos of communication practice.

One outflow of this reality is the now-familiar concept of *emergence* (Mintzberg, 1990; Quin, Mintzberg, & James, 1991), which often describes strategizing in organizations, and that follows from the concept of constitutive communication, that is, a ritualistic rather than a linear process. Emergent strategy is dependent on the participation of many people including external stakeholders to provide a true richness to the process. Notions of strategy as control have largely been dispelled, depending on how the strategic planning process is executed.

Nonetheless, there is place for both a functionalist and an emerging strategic process in organizations, which depends on transformational and visionary leadership and broad stakeholder participation (Sloan, 2006). Even in transformational leadership the concept of emergence embedded in leadership communication has taken hold (Mitra, 2013). The dialogic activities of the transformational leader allow for change and transformation and result in the transformation of the leader herself. Mitra argues the processes of "both leadership and transformation are incredibly complex, contingent, and interconnected through communication" (p. 397), which all contribute to the messiness of the organizational communication environment.

Communication therefore remains the foundation for both transformational leadership and stakeholder participation, as Sloan (2006) argued. Hafsi and Howard (2005, p. 243) argued strategy takes place at an intellectual and practical level and consists of five elements, namely, a leader's statement, a community's statement, a guide, building competitive advantage, and a relationship with the environment. Communication underscores all facets of strategizing, albeit functionalist or emergent.

A functionalist approach to communication planning requires a regular review of the strategic plans. While emergent strategy similarly focuses on the continuous shaping of strategy through communication, it also is closely linked to daily strategic thinking and actions of communication practitioners at all levels, focusing on practice and tactics to support the overall strategy. Creativity and innovation is an essential part of strategy execution (Bigler, 2004).

Lastly, emergent strategy emphasizes an important role for strategic communicators, namely, to ensure broad participation of stakeholders, particularly internal stakeholders. This has the potential to be a stumbling block for communicators because they have to convince organizational leaders that internal stakeholders can add value to the process, and have to assuage the fears of middle managers who often feel threatened by communicative processes that might expose their weaknesses. Holtzhausen (2012) argued strategy is "the most inclusive, although conflicting and contradictory, descriptions of the field of communication practice" (p. 158). It is inclusive because it "emphasizes communication as a management practice . . . (and) allows for the study of participatory communication practices, which include stakeholder communication, change management, and complex analyses or organizational environments and their contribution to emergent strategy" (p. 158). It also, as mentioned, requires the application of both the overarching theoretical approaches in communication, namely constitutive communication and mediated communication.

Communalities Across Areas of Practice

Despite many attempts to formulate global theories of communication practice, they all fall apart in the face of situational variables such as culture; economic, political and media systems; organizational variables such as culture, products or services; and many other factors (e.g., Bardhan & Weaver, 2011; Sriramesh & Verčič, 2003). The result is that strategic communication practice is highly situational and that a normative theory of the field is neither practical nor desirable. There are, however, a few practices, approaches or problems that relate to most areas of practice, whether in public diplomacy, politics, government, non-profit or for-profit, and that became evident from the works published in strategic communication specifically since the Hallahan et al. (2007) article and also the chapters in this volume. The most obvious communalities are stakeholders and audiences, media channels, the desire for behavioral outcomes, reputation management, and agency.

Stakeholder–Audience Concepts

In strategic communication stakeholders come in different names and forms, depending on the nature of the communication. For instance, in political communication they might also be called constituents or voters and in non- and for-profits they might come in the form of communities, volunteers, consumers, shareholders, and so forth. Each area of strategic communication practice has several individuals or groups of people with unique features who are affected by the organization or have the ability to affect the organization. So, for the purposes of this discussion, let us call them stakeholders (Phillips & Freeman, 2010).

Depending on the issue at hand, stakeholders can indeed be defined very broadly. For instance, a corporation or industry that benefits greatly from tax breaks needs to view the taxpaying community as a stakeholder group to whom it should be accountable. Although this does not mean that a group of taxpayers should be involved in the strategic planning process, it does mean that transparency and fiscal responsibility should be priorities in the strategic communication process.

One of the biggest problems in strategic communication is the segmentation of stakeholders based on the pre-determined skill sets of the communication practitioners involved, e.g., human resources practitioners communicate with employees, marketing communicators communicate with consumers, public relations practitioners communicate with publics and the media, other practitioners target business-to-business, and so forth. Although these communicators need to work together, this often does not happen because they do not have the knowledge to communicate beyond their expertise or are cautious of exceeding their scope of responsibilities. This leads to unnecessary fragmentation of strategic communication activities in organizations. This is often exacerbated in education when communication practice is taught as public relations, advertising, marketing, political or health communication (Holtzhausen, 2008).

From the onset the strategic communication project focused on finding those commonalities in practice that will alleviate this problem. One way of determining what a strategic communication practitioner should do is to originate the strategic communication process with the stakeholder-centered approach once the strategic plan has determined the different stakeholder groups. This means instead of determining communication activities on the skill set or specific organizational charge of the communicator, strategic communicators should have the ability to communicate equally well with stakeholders who are consumers, activist groups, communities, other businesses, individual power holders, to mention a few, as well as the media. That is what a unified body of strategic communication should mean, and it is the reason why many universities have ceased to teach students in previously defined professional categories in favor of broader professional communication education. This allows graduates with the requisite skill sets and knowledge bases to communicate equally well with all stakeholder groups using all available media channels and so provide a more holistic approach to strategic communication practice.

Channels

New communication technologies now also demand this broader knowledge of strategic communicators. In the past, media channels were much more controlled and acted as true communication intermediaries. Holtzhausen (2008) argues that new media platforms, such as the Internet and social media, allow strategic communicators to overcome these divisions and provide them with much more opportunity to follow a holistic approach that allows for both persuasive and collaborative communication depending on the stakeholders involved. Adopting a stakeholder-centered approach helps strategic communicators to use a wide variety of communication techniques while maintaining consistent messages across communication platforms. These can include purchased media space; owned media such as websites, blogs, and social media; and earned media, which refers to publicity, retweets, Facebook Likes, and comments to online postings.

Furthermore, as discussed earlier in this chapter, new analytics now provides the ability to micro-segment audiences or even to target individuals, providing more opportunities to tailor messages to individual stakeholder needs. New communication technologies support many different networks, which bring many different kinds of people together in multiple networks (Barney, 2004). Stakeholders belong to many different networks simultaneously and each network represents a different stakeholder identity. This further emphasizes the need for a thorough knowledge of different stakeholder groups, an understanding of the different networks they participate in and the communicator's ability to reach them through different media and platforms.

Behavioral Outcomes

A cohesive focus on the behavioral outcomes of stakeholders has consistently been one of the most neglected areas in strategic communication, although this is one metric most expected from practitioners. This also is partly due to the differentiation between areas of practice. Public relations practitioners generally focus their attention on attitudes and communicative action as outcomes of their work, whereas advertising practitioners and marketers focus on Return on Investment (ROI).

However, in the case of advertising ROI is not a realistic measure either. While advertising contributes to marketing outcomes, it is only a small part of the overall marketing effort. Advertisers struggle as much with measuring the direct outcome of advertising initiatives as public relations practitioners do with assessing the outcomes of their efforts. This is evident from two theoretical approaches in advertising and public relations respectively that focus on behavioral communication outcomes, namely the theory of planned behavior in advertising (Fishbein & Ajzen, 2010), which mostly focuses on the purchase behavior of consumers, and the situational theory of publics in public relations (J. E. Grunig, 1989, 1997). Both these theories are predictive in the sense that they predict how communication behavior will lead to actual behavior. The situational theory of publics predicts when members of publics will become activists. The theory of reasoned action argues behavioral intent is a reasonably reliable predictor of purchasing behavior, assuming a person is able to act and his or her goals have not changed. Bringing these two theoretical strands together has been the major focus of Werder and Schweickart (2013), who have made considerable strides in this regard.

Nonetheless, the ability of strategic communicators to link their work directly with desired outcomes remains one of the most allusive endeavors of the field. Christen and Hallahan (2013) similarly focus on the need for behavioral outcomes of strategic communication campaigns and argues that even the desired behavioral outcomes are unclear and contested. Hallahan points out that most of the concepts used to measure behavioral outcomes, such as relationships, reputation, engagement, and so forth, are quite vague and once again cannot be tied directly to the work of strategic communicators alone.

One area that strategic communicators have neglected, and which might provide guidance in determining behavioral outcomes, is consumer behavior, typically the domain of marketers. An area of consumer behavior that relates to both the situational theory of publics and the theory of reasoned action is the Behavioral Sequence Model (BSM) (Rossiter & Percy, 1997), which might further enhance researchers' understanding of behavioral outcomes. Despite the fact that many strategic communicators resolutely ignore the role of visual images in building relationships and reputation, the BSM focuses on the process of decision-making in the purchasing process and is related to a product's brand. Percy and Rosenbaum-Elliot (2012) argued that there is a strong relationship between the purchase of the final product or service and brand awareness and brand attitude. This directly ties media strategy to the decision-making process. Understanding the decision-making process is a key factor. Percy and Rosenbaum-Elliot identify five decision roles in the consumer process: initiator, influencer, decider, purchaser and user. They argue, "An important key to effective marketing communication is to identify the point in the decision process at which a message of some kind might make a positive contribution" (p. 135). What is noteworthy about this approach is the way in which they tie message strategy to desired behavioral outcomes and media selection.

Realistically, the work of strategic communicators might always be viewed as an indirect contribution to organizational goals unless stakeholder behavior can be tied directly to those goals. This might well be possible in the near future when big data and the use of special algorithms can establish the correlation of strategic communication strategies, stakeholder behavior and organizational outcomes.

The Imperative of Reputation

Reputation management has traditionally been the purview of business and management scholars (Carroll, 2013). Lately, the role of communication in establishing and managing corporate reputation has become more prominent in the strategic communication literature but there is no consensus on a definition or the constructs that would measure reputation (Stacks, Dodd, & Men, 2013). It clearly "takes a village" to establish an organization's reputation because its financial performance, corporate citizenship and employee relations, among others, all contribute to reputation.

In a recent study in German corporations top executives and communicators shared the opinion that a communication strategist should mainly foster trust and create positive images (Zerfass, Schwalbach, Bentele, & Sherzada, 2014). These findings illustrate the importance of reputation management. However, although many try to enhance reputation, measuring reputation as a component of strategic communication is at best vague (Liehr, Peters, & Zerfass, 2010). In a summary of key constructs used to measure reputation Stacks et al. (2013) identified visibility, credibility, authenticity, transparency, trust, relationships, and confidence as the drivers of reputation outcomes such as "supportive stakeholder behavior and beneficial business outcomes" (p. 570).

Measuring country reputation has some overlap with corporate reputation measurements but also differs in important ways. Yang, Shin, Lee, & Wrigley (2008) applied the Fombrun-RI Country Reputation Index (CRI) to measure South Korea's reputation and identified emotional appeal; physical appeal; financial appeal; leadership appeal; cultural appeal; political appeal and global appeal as the constructs that should be used to measure country reputation. In a longitudinal study with three waves of data collection over 14 months Fullerton and Holtzhausen (2012) used these constructs and their measures to determine the impact of the 2010 FIFA World Cup on the reputation of the host country, South Africa, among Americans. Their analyses consistently yielded a more parsimonious measurement of country reputation, namely, assessment of the country's leadership, affection for the country, and perceptions of a culture unique to the country. In all three waves these three constructs explained more than 70% of the variance in measuring country reputation. In an attempt to determine the role of country image in determining country reputation the researchers asked respondents to provide five words that came to mind immediately when they thought of South Africa (Holtzhausen & Fullerton, 2013). Although a direct relationship between the quantitative and qualitative data could obviously not be established, an analysis of the 973 different words or short phrases extracted from a total 3,183 mentions did reflect the attitudes of respondents in the reputation scale. This serves to indicate that the images people recall when they think of a country or region are valid units of analysis for determining reputation.

The above review of reputational constructs indicates that researchers have some way to go before reaching agreement on the measurement of reputation and also that measuring reputation might be situational. It also shows that isolating the unique role strategic communicators play in establishing reputation is particularly difficult. Nonetheless, it also is apparent that reputation management is one of the roles strategic communicators have in common, no matter the context.

The Agency of Communication Practitioners

The discussion on reputation management as inherent in all strategic communication work also has bearing on the expectations employers have of strategic communicators. The definition of strategic communication put forward in this chapter includes the concept of strategic communicators as acting on behalf of another or others. *Principal-agency theory* holds that principals (owners, shareholders) appoint agents (managers) to act on their behalf (Pratt & Zeckhauer, 1991). This happens when organizations grow too large for principals to do all the work, or when they become geographically dispersed so that principals cannot physically be present. Principals control agents to act on their behalf through contracts, measuring expected outputs and rewards (Hatch & Cunliffe, 2013).

Although this is not the only theory of organizational control, it is relevant to strategic communication because of the discipline's agency role in organizations. What makes this problematic for strategic communicators is that there are often divergent expectations of the role of the communication professional in organizations (Zerfass et al., 2014). The success of the relationship between principal and agent is based on the clarity of roles and expectations for outputs against which the performance of agents can be measured. Divergence between the principal and agent on expected performance outcomes can lead to disastrous results for this relationship (see Holtzhausen, 2012 for a comprehensive discussion of communication agency). These discrepancies are often further exacerbated in twenty-first century organizations with less clearly-defined organizational structures and hierarchies (Nolan & Wood, 2003). Traditional approaches propose regulative solutions like mechanisms of control and hierarchical planning to solve the inherent challenges of principal-agency relationships. However, agency in modern organizations is a multi-faceted phenomenon that includes networks of delegation and responsibilities as well as governing structures reaching far beyond markets and hierarchies—values and norms as well as common scripts and shared beliefs are guiding behavior (Zerfass et al., 2014). From this point of view, strategic communication requires a basic understanding and support for its key principles by employers and top executives alike. This means that walls within education have to be torn down—not only within communication schools, but also between the latter and business schools, engineering departments and others, who often stick to transmission models of communication and functional modes of aligning action.

Challenges in Strategic Communication Research Methods

Strategic communication research is also related to the previous discussion, particularly research relating to the measurement of campaign outcomes, roles and performance expectations of practitioners. As mentioned already in this chapter, it is difficult to measure directly the contribution of communicators to ROI and other key organizational metrics. The argument that many communication practices, such as the prevention of crises and monitoring debates among stakeholders to guide strategic decisions, cannot be measured in financial terms remains valid.

This might be changing as big data provide other avenues of directly linking practitioner communication actions to the behavioral actions of stakeholders. For instance, with a smart algorithm a practitioner's post on a company website can follow the person clicking on and reading the post to her subsequent actions generated by that post. The algorithm can compile a quite comprehensive profile of that unique visitor, which can provide an indication of the way in which the original post affected the reader. Mayer-Schönberger and Cukier (2013) explain that big data not only refers to data sets with millions of data points but also to comprehensive data of, for instance, the complete DNA profile of a single human being. One can thus argue that through the use of big data one can collect a comprehensive data set of a single person's actions and behaviors that can help communicators to better track individual behavior of stakeholders as they relate to communication activities of the organization. While CEOs are still reluctant to embrace big data because of high costs, lack of knowledge and understanding, and the data's inability to provide specific solutions to business problems, 79% of executives believe they will embrace big data in the next five years because it will reach its full potential in the next two to five years (Loechner, 2014).

Big data is already occupying the thoughts of many researchers on the challenges this development brings to traditional data collection methods, for example traditional quantitative survey methodology and qualitative data collection such as the in-depth interview (Boyd & Crawford, 2013; Savage & Burrows, 2007; Smith, 2013). Describing it as a "coming crisis," Savage and Burrows (2007, p. 885) point out that big data will eventually make survey research redundant. Because survey research works with samples of populations it can never provide the same comprehensive data big data provides, particularly in institutional contexts, such as those strategic communicators occupy. They argued that "where data on whole populations are routinely gathered as a by-product of institutional transactions, the sample survey seems a very poor instrument" (p. 891). One example they mentioned is how telephone records of clients of a telephone company can provide better data on communication networks than traditional network analysis could ever accomplish. Another example is Amazon, which bases its marketing of books not on a survey of demographic and sociographic data of clients but rather on the information it has collected from each individual client to identify which books he might be interested in. Millions of data points are collected on individuals over their lifetime and as a result these organizations "can hence bypass the principles of inference altogether and work directly with the real, complete, data derived from all the transactions in the system" (p. 891). This is exactly the type of proprietary data that strategic communicators can obtain from their organizations, and that is generally inaccessible to academic researchers.

It will be very important for strategic communicators to become familiar with big data, its benefits and its shortcoming. Smith (2013) raised serious concerns over the thoughtless use of data, particularly that which is collected on the Internet, through social media, or using existing administrative databases as mentioned above. Although he yielded that new communication technologies are useful in the study of public opinion, he believes survey research can still provide a more accurate reflection of public opinion. He argued for the hybrid use of big data and survey research to "boost standard surveys of public opinion and other topics with auxiliary data from alternative sources" such as social media and the Internet (p. 226).

The measurement of social and online media indeed provides new methods for measuring strategic communication outcomes. However, strategic communicators still have to come to grips with the real value of these metrics. Baym (2013) argued that although social media metrics and big data are used to determine their economic value, qualitative analysis of social media "may be more appropriate for assessing social and personal values" (p. 1). Unique visitors, site visits and click-throughs might provide data on the number of visitors but they do not provide the rich data that the qualitative analysis of Twitter feeds, retweets and Facebook Likes or comments can provide.

Conclusion

The above discussion does not only reaffirm some of the basic foundations of the field of strategic communication; it also introduces new perspectives and challenges, particularly in terms of how the performance of strategic communicators are measured. The performance expectations of strategic communicators are still ill-defined, which is a direct result of the principal-agent relationship.

Strategic communicators also face a challenge in truly embracing processes of meaning-making beyond the transmission of messages and in bringing about and measuring behavioral outcomes that are aligned with the strategic goals of the communicative entity and the public interest. It will be up to academics, researchers and communication professionals to discuss, debate and investigate these issues. The first decade of the twenty-first century has introduced many new developments that could never even be imagined as little as ten years ago. The chapters in this book are a first attempt to address some of these issues and problems while also providing a map for future research.

Linking research on communication and the public sphere, organizations and stakeholder relationships and strategy and decision-making in multiple agency settings, to the quest to define and evaluate measurable results that drive overall organizational goals, remains a major challenge. Interdisciplinary approaches are needed that deviate from the well-known paths, that is, traditional theories and research methods of single disciplines like public relations, organizational communication, advertising or public diplomacy—to name just a few examples. Combining insights from several fields might, in a first step, result in concepts that could be criticized as being more speculative and less focused than traditional approaches. But the reality of social life and strategic communication is neither segmented in boxes nor dedicated to serving the rules of the academic community.

Strategic communication is a complex and emergent phenomenon that requires appropriate theories and studies. In a review of the articles published in the *International Journal of Strategic Communication* from 2007 to 2013 Holtzhausen and Zerfass (2013) found that the vision set out in Hallahan et al. (2007) to find commonalities in practice across multiple disciplines was well underway. However, strategic communication was still a work in progress and by no means a mature field. The study determined that strategic communication was indeed a process used in many different communication fields but that the process itself might have limited usefulness for many fields. They argued, for instance, that not all health communication is strategic and not all strategic communication is health related. Similarly, the concept of *publics* defines public relations but in strategic communication publics are but one stakeholder group. This also is true for the concept of *consumers* in marketing or *voters* in political communication. Nonetheless, this does point to the most important goal of the strategic communication process: to find commonalities among areas of communication practice that can inform all academics and practitioners and help build a new group of practitioners who have a much broader understanding of what strategic communication truly entails.

Researchers should be courageous and join the journey towards a research agenda that really matters for the practice. Communication science has often be criticized for not being involved in policy-making and not answering key questions of society in the information age—like the distribution of power (Castells, 2009) and privacy (Buchmann, 2013). The field of strategic communication offers multiple opportunities to explore these and other upcoming issues from the point of communicators whose activities shape the field, from their principals who set goals and expect results, from stakeholders who are involved in processes of communication and reality construction, and from the public sphere, which can be served by professional and transparent communication aligned to strategic goals.

Note

1 The authors wish to thank Kirk Hallahan, Colorado State University, for his insightful review of this chapter.

References

Bardhan, N., & Weaver, C. K. (Eds.). (2011). *Public relations in global cultural contexts. Multiparadigmatic perspectives*. New York: Routledge.

Barney, D. (2004). *The network society*. Malden, MA: Polity Press.

Bauer, R. A. (1964). The obstinate audience: The influence process from the point of view of social communication. *American Psychologist, 19*, 319–328.

Baym, N. K. (2013). Data not seen: The uses and shortcomings of social media metrics. *First Monday, 18*(10), 1–16.

Bell, E., Golombisky, K., & Holtzhausen, D. R. (2002). *Communication Rules!* School of Mass Communication. University of South Florida. Tampa, FL.

Bentele, G., & Nothhaft, H. (2010). Strategic communication and the public sphere from a European perspective. *International Journal of Strategic Communication, 4*(2), 93–116.

Bigler, W. R. (2004). *The new science of strategy execution. How established firms become fast, sleek wealth creators.* Westport, CT: Praeger.

Blumer, H. (1969). *Symbolic interactionism: perspectives and method.* Englewood Cliffs, NJ: Prentice-Hall.

Boromisza-Habashi, D. (2013). Which way is forward in communication theorizing? An interview with Robert T. Craig. *Communication Theory, 23*(4), 417–432.

Boyd, D., & Crawford, K. (2013). Critical questions for Big Data. *Information, Communication & Society, 15*(5), 662–679.

Buchmann, J. (Ed.). (2013). *Internet privacy: options for adequate realisation.* Heidelberg, Germany: Springer VS.

Carey, J. W. (1989). *Communication as culture. Essays on media and society.* Boston, MA: Unwin-Hyman.

Carroll, C. E. (2013). Corporate reputation and the multi-disciplinary field of communication. In C. E. Carroll (Ed.), *The handbook of communication and corporate reputation.* (pp. 1–10). Malden, MA: Wiley-Blackwell.

Castells, M. (2009). *Communication power.* Oxford, England: Oxford University Press.

Christen, C. T., & Hallahan, K. (2013). Psychological processing. In R.L. Heath (Ed.), *Encyclopedia of public relations* (2nd ed.) (Vol. 2, pp. 705–709). Thousand Oaks, CA: Sage.

Couldry, N., & Hepp, A. (2013). Conceptualizing mediatization. *Communication Theory, 23*(3), 191–202.

Craig, R. T. (1999). Communication theory as a field. *Communication Theory, 9*, 119–161.

Dewey, J. (1954). *The public and its problems.* Athens, OH: Ohio University Press. (Original work published 1927).

Ermath, E. D. (2001). Agency in the discursive condition. *History and Theory, 40*, 34–48.

Farwell, J. P. (2012). *Persuasion and power: the art of strategic communication.* Washington, DC: Georgetown University Press.

Fishbein, M, & Ajzen, I. (2010). *Predicting and changing behavior: The reasoned action approach.* New York, NY: Psychology Press.

Fullerton, J., & Holtzhausen, D. (2012). Americans' attitudes toward South Africa: A study of country reputation and the 2010 FIFA World Cup. *Place Branding and Public Diplomacy, 8*(3/4), 1–15.

Grunig, J. E. (1989). Sierra Club study shows who become activists. *Public Relations Review, 15*(3), 3–24.

Grunig, J. E. (1997). A situational theory of publics: Conceptual history, recent challenges, and new research. In D. Moss, T. MacManus & D. Verčič (Eds.), *Public relations research: An international perspective* (pp. 3–48). London, England: International Thomson Business Press.

Grunig, L. A., Grunig, J. E., & Dozier, D. M. (2002). *Excellent public relations and effective organizations. A study of communication management in three countries.* Mahwah, NJ: Lawrence Erlbaum Associates.

Habermas, J. (1979). *Communication and the evolution of society.* Boston, MA: Beacon Press.

Habermas, J. (2006). Political communication in media society—Does society still enjoy an epistemic dimension? The impact of normative theory on empirical research. *Communication Theory, 16*(4), 411–426.

Hafsi, T., & Howard, T. (2005). Reflections on the field of strategy. In S. W. Floyd, J. Roos, C. D. Jacobs & F. W. Kellermanns (Eds.), *Innovating strategy process.* (pp. 239–246). Malden, MA: Blackwell.

Hallahan, K. (2010). Being public. Publicity as public relations. In R.L. Heath (Ed.), *Sage handbook of public relations* (pp. 523–545). Thousand Oaks, CA: Sage.

Hallahan, K., Holtzhausen, D. R., Van Ruler, B., Verčič, D., & Sriramesh, K. (2007). Defining strategic communication. *International Journal of Strategic Communication, 1*(1), 3–35.

Hanisch, C. (1970). The personal is political. In S. Firestone & A. Koedt (Eds.), *Notes from the second year: Women's liberation.* New York: Sulamith Firestone and Anne Koedt.

Hatch, M. J., & Cunliffe, A. L. (2013). *Organization theory. Modern, symbolic, and postmodern perspectives* (3rd ed.). Oxford, England: Oxford University Press.

Holtzhausen, D., & Fullerton, J. (2013). The 2010 FIFA World Cup and South Africa: A study of longer term effects and moderators of country reputation. *Journal of Marketing Communications.*

Holtzhausen, D. R. (2008). Strategic communication. In W. Donsbach (Ed.), *The International Encyclopedia of Communication* (Vol. 10, pp. 4848–4855). Malden, MA: Blackwell.

Holtzhausen, D. R. (2012). *Public relations as activism. Postmodern approaches to theory and practice.* New York, NY: Routledge.

Holtzhausen, D. R., & Zerfass, A. (2013). Strategic communication—Pillars and perspectives on an alternate paradigm. In K. Sriramesh, A. Zerfass, & J.-N. Kim (Eds.), *Current Trends and Emerging Topics in Public Relations and Communication Management* (pp. 283–302). New York, NY: Routledge.

Kohlberg, L., Levine, C., & Hewer, A. (1984). Synopses and detailed replies to critics. In L. Kohlberg (Ed.), *Essays on moral development*. (Vol. 2). San Francisco, CA: Harper & Row.

Liehr, K., Peters, P., & Zerfass, A. (2010). Reputation messen und bewerten – Grundlagen und Methoden. In J. Pfannenberg & A. Zerfass (Eds.), *Wertschöpfung durch Kommunikation: Strategisches Kommunikations-Controlling in der Unternehmenspraxis* [Value creation by communication] (pp. 153–164). Frankfurt, Germany: Frankfurter Allgemeine Buch.

Loechner, J. (2014). *Big data pros and cons*. Retrieved January 28, 2014, from http://www.mediapost.com/publications/article/216665/big-data-pros-and-cons.html.

Mahoney, J. (2013). *Strategic Communication - Principles and Practices*. South Melbourne, Australia: Oxford University Press.

Mayer-Schönberger, V., & Cukier, K. (2013). *Big Data. A revolution that will transform how we live, work, and think*. Boston, MA: Houghton Mifflin Harcourt.

Mitra, R. (2013). From transformational leadership to leadership trans-formations. *Communication Theory, 23*(4), 395–416.

Nolan, P., & Wood, S. (2003). Mapping the future of work. *British Journal of Industrial Relations, 41*(2), 165–174.

Paul, C. (2011). *Strategic communication: origins, concepts, and current debates*. Santa Barbara, CA: Praeger.

Percy, L., & Rosenbaum-Elliot, R. (2012). *Strategic Advertising Management* (4th ed.). Oxford, England: Oxford University Press.

Phillips, R. A., & Freeman, R. E. (Eds.). (2010). *Stakeholders*. Cheltenham, England: Edward Elgar.

Pratt, J. W., & Zeckhauer, R. Z. (Eds.). (1991). *Principals and agents: The structure of business* (2nd ed.). Boston, MA: Harvard Business School Press.

Quinn, J. E., Mintzberg, H., & James, R. M. (1991). *The strategy process: Concepts, contexts, and cases*. Englewood Cliffs, NJ: Prentice Hall.

Rossiter, R., & Percy, L. (1997). *Advertising communication and promotion management* (2nd ed.). New York, NY: McGraw-Hill.

Savage, M., & Burrows, R. (2007). The coming crisis of empirical sociology. *Sociology, 41*(5), 885–899.

Self, C. (2010). Hegel, Habermas, and community: The public in the new media era. *International Journal of Strategic Communication, 4*(2), 78–92.

Shannon, C. E., & Weaver, W. (1949). *The mathematical theory of communication*. Urbana, IL: University of Illinois Press.

Sloan, J. (2006). *Learning to think strategically*. Burlington, MA: Elsevier.

Smith, T. (2013). Survey-research paradigms old and new. *International Journal of Public Opinion Research, 25*(2), 218–229.

Sriramesh, K., & Verčič, D. (Eds.). (2003). *The global public relations handbook*. Mahwah, NJ: Lawrence Erlbaum Associates.

Stacks, D. W., Dodd, M. D., & Men, L. R. (2013). Corporate reputation measurement and evaluation. In C. E. Carroll (Ed.), *The handbook of communication and corporate reputation* (pp. 561–573). Malden, MA: Wiley-Blackwell.

Swindell, C. (2011, May 20). GOP needs viable candidates, *Charleston Gazette*.

Thayer, L. (1968). *Communication and communication systems in organization, management and interpersonal relations*. Homewood, IL: Irwin.

Werder, K. P., & Schweickart, T. (2013). *An experimental analysis of message strategy influence on receiver variables: Advancing an integrated model for explaining the communication behavior of publics*. Paper presented at the 16th Annual International Public Relations Research Conference., Miami, FL.

Wheatley, M. (2013). How The Gambling Industry Is Betting On Big Data. siliconANGLE. Retrieved on July 25, 2014 from http://siliconangle.com/blog/2013/08/20/how-the-gambling-industry-is-betting-on-big-data/

Yang, S.-U., Shin, H., Lee, J.-H., & Wrigley, B. (2008). Country reputation in multidimensions: Predictors, effects, and communication channels. *Journal of Public Relations Research, 20*(4), 421–440.

Zerfass, A., Schwalbach, J., Bentele, G., & Sherzada, M. (2014). Corporate communications from the top and from the center: Comparing experiences and expectations of CEOs and communicators. *International Journal of Strategic Communication, 8*(2), 61–78.

2

(Re-)Reading Clausewitz
The Strategy Discourse and its Implications for Strategic Communication

Howard Nothhaft and Hagen Schölzel

In 2003, communication scholar Benita Steyn pointed out that the term 'corporate communication strategy' remained ill-understood, having seldom received proper academic treatment in the scientific community. Steyn wrote that

> [t]he concept 'strategy' is well-known in management theory and practice. The concept of 'corporate communication strategy', however, has received little attention in the public relations (corporate communication) body of knowledge. There is mention of a strategic role for the corporate communication practitioner, but few explanations or descriptions of what corporate communication strategy means in a strategic organizational context.
>
> *Steyn, 2003, p. 168*

Steyn's call for coming to grips with communication strategy came late, it seems. It came at a time when the term was already *en vogue* with practitioners, having been on everybody's lips for at least a decade. In 1997, Tibbie (cited in Steyn, 2003) had remarked that "it is increasingly difficult to pick up any pitch document without finding chapters on 'strategic direction', 'communications strategies', 'strategic' messages and so on" (p. 357). Steyn makes clear, however, that widespread usage and thorough understanding do not necessarily go hand in hand. She agrees with Tibble, who points out that the term *strategic* has been used very sloppily (Tibble, 1997, p. 358) and has been "bandied around like a mantra" (p. 357). She also agrees with Lukaszewski (2001) who referred to strategy-making as one of the mysterious areas of public relations practice—thus again, like Tibble, invoking the vocabulary of the esoteric.

It is curious, however, that Steyn then limits her explorations of strategy to the business administration and management literature. That the word *strategy* ultimately derives from the classical Greek word στρατηγός, denoting a military commander and being in use in the 6th century BC, is well-known. Also known is the fact that the most frequently cited strategy definition goes back to Prussian military theorist Carl von Clausewitz (1780–1831), whose magnum opus *Vom Kriege* [On War] (version 1989 and 1991) probably represents the single most influential treatise on strategy.

Scholars concerned with strategic communication are, of course, aware that the concept of strategy is rooted in military theory. Nevertheless, the scientific community has seldom displayed more than a limited interest in the military classics. That is particularly puzzling when one considers that the literature of strategic management, often idolized, brims over with references, implicit and explicit, to

Sun-Tzu, Machiavelli, Clausewitz, Mao, Guevara and their contemporary heirs. Hinterhuber (1990), to name one example, develops a book on *Wettbewerbsstrategie* (competitive strategy) from Prussian military theory, referring not only to Clausewitz but also to Scharnhorst, Gneisenau and Moltke.

There are reasons for this reluctance. Indeed, one could argue that communication is the very opposite of warfare, war denoting a state of non-communication, that is, unwillingness to understand the other. It is important to note, however, that strategy is ultimately concerned with *conflict*, not necessarily with *force;* although Clausewitz, dealing with armed conflict, warns against artificial attempts to separate the two in warfare (*On War*, I.I.1.3). Strategy is about *winning* or *prevailing*, one could say, not necessarily about violence. If it was otherwise, the concept would not have been easily adopted by management theory and business administration; although we would argue that twenty-first century business cannot be understood without understanding brutality. But then again, the desire to shun the dichotomous, distinctly asymmetric vocabulary of winning versus losing so prevalent in business and management texts might have been another reason to avoid military discourse in *strategic communication literature,* which sometimes seems to confuse the academic treatment of public relations with public relations for public relations.

We believe, conversely, that there is lot to gain from a glimpse at military theory once semantic sensibilities have been overcome. Clausewitz, in particular, is recommended reading for practitioners and theorists of strategic communication for two additional reasons. Clausewitz not only worked in what we would term today "public relations" during the Prussian reform era (Ritter, 1931, p. 46), but also identified, in his early writings (*Principles of War*, III.1, (*version* 1812), the '\"capture of public opinion"' as one of three general principles of strategy (the other two being the destruction of the hostile army and the seizure of its resources and means). It is from this perspective, then, that the authors propose to reread military theory, and Clausewitz's *On War* in particular, with a view to clarifying the concept of *strategic* in strategic communication.

The starting point is a passage in *On War* in which Clausewitz gives a stunningly straightforward answer to a question with which, in the authors' opinion, generations of writers on management and business strategy have struggled, with a greater or smaller degree of success, namely *what to concern yourself with when concerning yourself with strategy*.

> The first, the supreme, the most far-reaching act of judgment that the statesman and commander have to make is to establish (. . .) the kind of war on which they are embarking; neither mistaking it for, nor trying to turn it into, something that is alien to its nature. This is the first of all strategic questions and the most comprehensive.
>
> *On War*, I.1.27 *1989, pp. 88–89*

To address this issue this chapter briefly provides a methodological orientation before touching on three topics. However, we return repeatedly to the concept of *supreme act of judgment*, that is, the question of the nature of the conflict one is embarking on. The three topics are organized under the following headings. First, *Reading Clausewitz: Learning from the classics,* in which we argue that Clausewitz's careful dialectic reasoning about the relation of politics, people and professionals; about the distinction of art, science and craft; and about means, aims and ends paves the way out of fruitless debates in strategic communication literature. Next, *Rereading Clausewitz: Parallel developments in warfare and communication*, in which we adopt the argument that since the invention of *professional* armies, their very regularity has been confronted by people's uprisings as well as by antagonists waging irregular, asymmetrical or guerrilla warfare—guerrilla meaning here *small war*. The early nineteenth century saw not only the refinement of the grisly practice but also the development of substantial theories of people's wars and guerrilla warfare. We want to trace the discourse and its major concepts insofar as they are relevant for strategic communication. Last, in *Re-rereading Clausewitz: deconstruction*, we conclude the article with a counter-point, a *demontage* of our hero, a deconstruction of Clausewitz. Knights and Morgan (1990) have convincingly argued that Clausewitz and his contemporaries, being middle-class, created a (pseudo-)scientific discourse on *the art of warfare* in order to protect their position as experts with an exclusive problem-solving capability. We argue that communication specialists nowadays pursue a similar strategy, and encounter similar problems.

Methodological Orientation

In the inaugural issue of *International Journal of Strategic Communication*, the board of editors dedicated itself to the question of what strategic communication is and, in particular, what the qualification *strategic* implies (Hallahan, Holtzhausen, van Ruler, Verčič, & Sriramesh, 2007). The editors pointed to the fact that, nowadays, in a twenty-first century oscillating between late modernism and post-modernism, the term strategic must be considered a "rich" concept (p. 11). Although it is still associated with a predominantly modernist management approach, as Hallahan et al. point out, a lot of alternative readings of the term co-exist.

The authors of course agree with the editors' decision not to limit the discourse to narrow-minded, exclusive concepts which, by way of definition, mask out exciting alternative perspectives. But then, to deliberately remain on the level of heuristic vagueness is not a satisfactory state of affairs for a professional field or research domain. It is necessary to further our understanding by sharpening and deepening the understanding of the term *strategy*. We do not believe, however, that one needs to strive for an essential definition of strategy; neither do we believe in the popular approach of synthesizing a compromise out of the plethora of strategy definitions, schools and models. The third way, which we wish to pursue here, is to discuss the core ideas of major authors who visibly and invisibly have shaped the field, of whom the first and foremost is Clausewitz. We believe, then, that familiarity with Clausewitz's core ideas furthers our understanding of strategy simply by furthering our understanding of the genealogy of the strategic discourse, and that that, therefore, is valuable *in itself* for strategic communicators. To clarify their points the authors will cite selected passages of Clausewitz's magnum opus, but also other writers, aligned or contraposed, including "practitioners" such as Mao Tse-tung (1936/1938/1966), Ernesto "Che" Guevara (1965, 2003a, 2003b), Harry Summers (1982), Rupert Smith (2006), and "theorists" and historians such as Friedrich Engels and Karl Marx (passim), Basil Liddell Hart (1991/1929/1954), Robert Asprey (1994), Peter Paret (2007), Michael Howard (1993), Carl Schmitt (2007), Herfried Münkler (1990), and Andreas Herberg-Rothe (2008). We do believe that our selection does not do injustice to Clausewitz, but readers should be aware that we are dealing with ideas taken out of the context of a grand edifice of thought. *On War* is a substantial, highly complex and ultimately provisional book, and any attempt to summarize Clausewitz's dialectical, multi-layered thinking within a couple of lines is doomed to distort.

Reading Clausewitz: Learning from the Classics

First, Clausewitz's careful dialectic reasoning in *On War* and other minor and earlier writings paves the way out of some fruitless debates in strategic communication. In order to understand the nature of strategic communication, we argue, professional strategic communicators must develop a mature understanding of the status of the concept of strategy, the viability of the idea of systems of strategy, and the relationship between craft, science and art.

The Status of the Concept of Strategy

Clausewitz's classical rendering defines tactics as teaching "*die Lehre vom Gebrauch der Streitkräfte im Gefecht*" ["the use of armed forces in engagement"] whereas strategy teaches "*die Lehre vom Gebrauch der Gefechte zum Zweck des Krieges*" ["the use of engagements for the object of the war"] (*On*

War, II.1). As has been mentioned, Clausewitz's classic definition of strategy with its inherent sub-ordination of tactics is still taught in business schools and military academies today. It is interesting to note, moreover, that Drucker (1909–2005) made a lasting impression, with a definition for effectiveness and efficiency very similar in structure—a distinction easily and frequently confused with Clausewitz's. For Drucker there is a difference between doing things right (tactics = efficiency?) and doing the right things (strategy = effectiveness?) (Drucker, 1993/1967).

What is often overlooked when dealing with *On War*, however, is that Clausewitz did not claim originality for his definition. Clausewitz conceded, even argued, that he derives his understanding from the general and accepted *usance* of the time:

> This distinction between tactics and strategy is now almost universal, and everyone knows fairly well where each particular factor belongs without clearly understanding why. Whenever such categories are blindly used, there must be a deep-seated reason for it. We have tried to discover the distinction, and have to say that it was just this common usage that led to it. We reject, on the other hand, the artificial definitions of certain writers, since they find no reflection in general usage.
>
> *On War, II.1*

It is striking, we believe, that Clausewitz's early nineteenth century lines may well serve as a description of the state of the professional discourse in the communication management literature about 200 years later. What Clausewitz seems to be saying, in modern terms, is that strategy, in his times, was a *buzzword* but that there is something substantial behind or in the concept, that is, a "deep-seated reason" ("*tiefer Grund*"). Although there has been no lack of buzzwords in the communication management discourse of the late twentieth and early twenty-first century, strategy might have been the most persistent. The concept has been so astonishingly persistent that one wonders whether belittling it as another buzzword does the term justice. The concept, in its richness and complexity, has recently started a remarkable career as a umbrella term and may emerge as the missing link between marketing communications, public relations, organizational communication and other disciplines—a view expounded by Falkheimer and Heide (2007) and Hallahan et al. (2007).

What needs to be learned from Clausewitz is that the concept of strategy may very well be *both* a buzzword *and* a substantial concept. Accepting the duality would at least explain the irritating yet unsurprising state of the professional discourse during the turn of the century. As has been described, scholars such as Steyn (2003) argued it may be time to get to grips with a term that had been, by then, in widespread use for years or even decades. Furthermore, the duality is by no means unnatural or new. It is often the case with professional terms enjoying long-term use that they serve a double need. The term strategy, thus, is *broad* and *vague* enough to come in handy as a catch-all phrase conveying a vague sense of overall importance. It also is *deep* and *complex* enough, with 2,000 years of etymology, to elaborate at length about it. The upshot is that strategy is *there*. It is there as something that modern theorists would call a *discursive practice*, and it is actually from a careful analysis of practice that Clausewitz arrives at his theory.

The Concept of Systems of Strategy

In retrospect, Clausewitz appears as a prototypical writer of the late eighteenth and early nineteenth century. Paret (2007) convincingly traced the influences in Clausewitz's thinking to contemporaries such as philosopher Fichte and educational reformer Pestalozzi and, above all, to Kant—not in substance, but in form and mode of reasoning. It is also true that Clausewitz, as a military man, was a member of a small but influential circle of reformers grouped around the prominent figures of Scharnhorst and Gneisenau, eager to transform the Prussian state. What is less well known is that

Clausewitz by no means represented the mainstream of military thinking of his age. Clausewitz started his career as a military writer by arguing *against* the mainstream, the popular mainstream at least, and at the time of his early death in 1831 at 51 years of age he was still considered an outsider. Clausewitz's writings have stood the test of 200 years of time, however, and what was considered mainstream and the height of theoretical achievement by then, has been relegated to the archives as historical curiosity. Thus, for communication scholars it is interesting to ask what has been discarded over time and what has been regarded as substantial.

We wish to argue that the substantial element of Clausewitz's thinking is his very urge to deal with the *essentials* of his object of study, in his case war. Although *On War* contains a lot of practical advice on eighteenth and nineteenth century military operations, Clausewitz always refused to be drawn into dogmatic debates or to set up systems. Clausewitz's severe criticism of the writings of military theorists Dietrich Heinrich von Bülow (1757–1807) and Antoine Jomini (1779–1869), who were quite *en vogue* at the time, reveals Clausewitz's piercing eye and urge to get to the heart of the matter by *methodical reasoning*. Bülow, for example, although not a distinguished military man himself, was one of the most frequently read military writers of the time (for the following cf. Paret, 1989). His thoughts reflected the age by proposing a military theory along *mechanical* and *geometrical* lines, declaring actual combat and tactical engagements insignificant in comparison with strategy comprehended as a system of lines of support, operational bases and angles of approach. Clausewitz, in contrast, argued that strategy and combat cannot and must never be disconnected. In a simile that delighted Friedrich Engels in particular (Howard, 1989, p. 43), Clausewitz (I.I.2.) argued that for all small and large operations in war, "decision by arms is for all major and minor operations in war what cash payment is in commerce." ["*Die Waffenentscheidung ist für alle großen und kleinen Operationen des Krieges, was die bare Zahlung für den Wechselhandel ist*"]. At the time, Bülow's theories seemed in accordance with the realities of the battlefield, to be sure. Warfare had indeed developed into a game of maneuver and counter-maneuver, with actual battle being very rare during the *fin de siècle*.

Napoleon Bonaparte (1769–1821), however, swept away the artificialities of contemporary military theory, inflicting one crushing defeat after the other on the *anciens régimes* because he was prepared to pay in cash, that is, because he actively sought decision in battle. What needs to be learned from this historic example, thus, is that theorists should take care never to artificially separate the 'bloody' groundwork of the tactical from the high, clinical realm of the strategic level. Just as wars are not decided by strategies but by successful engagements decided in one's own favor *due to superior strategy*, communication strategies do not communicate, do not convince—people, products, services and messages do. Furthermore, the dream of arriving one day, by theory, at a 'scientific system' of communication management or strategic communication is just that: a dream.

Craft, Science and Art

Bülow belonged to the generation of writers whom Clausewitz's writings swept away, just as Bonaparte's armies swept away the armies of Prussia in 1806. Writers like Bülow, as Paret's (1989) account argues, wanted to turn the military art into a science in line with the causal-mechanical world view of the time. Clausewitz, as we will see, re-introduced the human, psychological element: the genius of the respective commanders, the spirit of the soldiers, the friction of details and minutiae, and also violence, hatred, passion, and fear.

With a view to the Napoleonic age, Clausewitz seems vindicated: Napoleon, by psychology, or by what we might label masterful leadership and skillful propaganda today, achieved stunning success out of proportion to the material means available. Contrarily, in a larger historical context, the two world wars of the twentieth century and the military operations of the twenty-first seem to favor a return to the simple and straightforward causal-mechanical view; not in the rather complicated sense of Bülow, but in a simpler sense. With the exception of Vietnam, which is interesting for that very reason, the side commanding overwhelming material and technological superiority prevailed; and the way to material and technological superiority was paved by science and economic prosperity. Clausewitz did see that, however. In a distinction later referred to by Summers (1982, ch. 4) he differentiated two categories of activities characteristic of war, namely *preparation for war* on the one hand, and *war proper* on the other. Clausewitz wrote:

> The knowledge and skills involved in the preparations will be concerned with the creation, training and maintenance of the fighting forces. . . . The theory of war proper, on the other hand, is concerned with the use of these means, once they have been developed, for the purposes of the war.
>
> *On War, II.1*

Preparation for war and war proper, Clausewitz explained earlier, stood in about the same relationship as the craft of the swordsmith to the art of fencing (*On War*, II.2). Expressed in modern terms, thus, Clausewitz clearly saw that certain areas in the conduct of war lend themselves to the scientific method while others do not.

US military writer Summers (1982, 42–51), in his analysis of the US failure in Vietnam, brilliantly transposes Clausewitz's analysis to the 1960s. Summers argued that one reason for US failure was the quantitative-economic paradigm in the US Department of Defense under the aegis of Secretary Robert McNamara. McNamara, one of the "whizz kids" in the Ford Motor Company, brought commercial systems analysis and quantitative statistics to bear not only on defense *budgeting* but also on *operations* in Vietnam (for a thorough critique that is controversial for framing Vietnam predominantly as a guerilla war see Asprey, 1994). Although senior observers such as Henry Kissinger conceded that systems analysis, overall, was more often right than wrong, the quantitative paradigm, which was perfectly applicable to *preparation for war*, eroded the capability to fight the *war proper* (1979). Kissinger (1979, as cited in Summers 1982, p. 48) described the impact McNamara's whizz-kids, Allan C. Enthoven and K. Wayne Smith in particular, had on the military establishment:

> A new breed of military officers emerged: men who had learned the new jargon, who could present the systems analysis arguments so much in vogue, more articulate than the older generation and more skillful in bureaucratic maneuvering. On some levels it eased civilian-military relationships; on a deeper level it deprived the policy process of the simpler, cruder, but perhaps more relevant assessments which in the final analysis are needed when issues are reduced to a test of arms.
>
> *p. 48*

There is a double lesson for communication management in this comment. First, communication managers need to understand that, as in war, there are areas of communication management that lend themselves to the scientific method while others do not. Preparing for communication management can be organized along scientific lines; communication management proper, as it unfolds in real time and space, can only be *supported* by scientific approaches. It is particularly important to emphasize Clausewitz's message at a time when elaborate systems of controlling communication are being developed and balanced scorecards and strategy maps have become accepted tools. The systems help in preparation, to be sure. But they neither do the actual fighting nor the actual communication for you. The other, second issue is of course the well-known organizational fact of life that it is far easier to talk the talk than to walk the walk. There is a tendency in modern management to adopt a clinical, scientific discourse which seems perfectly rational, until it is confronted with the 'irrationality' of reality.

Rereading Clausewitz: Parallel Developments in Warfare and Communication

Clausewitz's *On War* is the result of decades of practical experience and a lifelong attempt to come to grips with its object of interest, that is, *warfare,* which is different from the *theory* of warfare. But *On War* would have been inconceivable had its author not witnessed far-reaching changes sweeping away the established systems with its concurrent theories and practices. Thus, it seems appropriate for us to ask which far-reaching changes we can observe in *communication practice* today. With Clausewitz in mind we also must ask how contemporary developments influence *our* theoretical understanding.

Surprisingly, the strategic communication community can learn a great deal from Clausewitz and from current attempts in military theory to make sense from what is currently happening in strategic communication. We refer, here, to current trends that have changed the rules: trends such as genuine grassroots campaigning, autonomously organized social movements, and diverse forms of "irregular" communication practices like counter-public-activity, guerrilla-marketing, hacking-activities or "irregularities" in political communication, the growing number of filibusters in the U.S. Senate, for example. It is not a coincidence, we believe, that these practices often refer metaphorically to two forms of warfare, namely, *people's wars* and *guerilla wars*. These became important military concepts in Clausewitz's times and were theoretically outlined, at least in a sketchy way, for the first time in Clausewitz's earlier work and later condensed into *On War*. Clausewitz's sketchy approach was subsequently elaborated upon both in practice and in theory by some of his great admirers during the nineteenth and twentieth centuries.

The Relationship of Organizational Set-Ups and Actions in the Field

While delving deeper into the distinction of cabinet wars, people's wars and guerrilla wars, we have to take into account that *On War* was never finished (see Paret 1989). Although the textual corpus exists completely, the larger part of it is provisional. Clausewitz wanted to rework it but died before doing so. What he had planned in the revisions, it seems, was to emphasize two different ideal types of wars with different logics of conflict. The first type is a limited conflict, which in Clausewitz's time was a typical eighteenth century cabinet war, the end of which might be, for example, to settle a quarrel about borderlines between two states. The second ideal type of war, conversely, is a deeply political conflict, the end of which is to shatter, destroy and abolish an adversary in a political sense. The conflict between early revolutionary, later Napoleonic, France on the one side and the ancient European monarchies on the other, in Clausewitz's time, was a conflict of the second type—a contest for the political existence of different conceptions of society.

In Clausewitz's distinction of different types of conflict, sketched but not thoroughly elaborated, we encounter the idea of a deep structural connection between the 'organizational logic' of a system engaging in war, and its concrete military action. In other words, when two systems clash in a battle for survival, the operations by which they engage in the struggle are expressions of their organizational logics. It is in this area that Clausewitz's famous phrase 'war is a continuation of politics by other means' finds an alternative, second meaning. War cannot only be understood as a *tool* of politics, it might be viewed as an *expression* of it. In *On War* Clausewitz was of course employing the German term *Politik*, a very vague notion connoting three different political dimensions of *polity, policy* and *politics,* which are political institutions, political programs or tasks, and the logic of political procedures, that is, ways of doing things. It is precisely because of this ambiguity that one can find two different English translations of Clausewitz's famous dictum: "war is a continuation of *policy* by other means", and "war is a continuation of *politics* by other means". The term one chooses is not *only* a matter of translation, whether one finds the right version or not. Clausewitz seems to be employing the German term in different ways and sometimes in its opaque ambiguity. Mostly he seems to be thinking of policy, and in those passages war appears as a means to realize political programs or to achieve a certain political will. Here war is a *tool*. But one can find also passages where he is obviously thinking about politics, that is, the logic of a political process being *expressed* in the organizational structure of a particular political system.

To understand what Clausewitz was thinking of when he related politics and warfare one has to take into account that Clausewitz's theory of warfare and his strategic thinking developed and matured in a unique historical situation. By the end of the eighteenth and during the beginning of the nineteenth century Europe had been a battlefield for decades. During the Napoleonic Wars French armies conquered nearly the whole continent—from Spain in the south west to the Russian capital Moscow in the far north east of Europe. This great military success was not only due to Napoleon's outstanding abilities, but also the result of the very idea that war is a continuation of an organizational set-up of a social system by a specific form of action. Clausewitz wrote:

> In the last decade of the eighteenth century, when that remarkable change in the art of war took place, when the best armies saw part of their doctrine become ineffective and military victories occurred on a scale that up to then had been inconceivable, it seemed that all mistakes had been military mistakes. It became evident that the art of war . . . had been surprised. . . . But is it true that the real shock was military rather than political? . . . Clearly the tremendous effects of the French Revolution abroad were caused not so much by new military methods and concepts as by radical changes in policies and administration, by the new character of government, altered conditions of the French people, and the like. That other governments did not understand these changes, that they wished to oppose new and overwhelming forces with customary means: all these were political errors.
>
> *On War, VIII.6.B*

The French armies during the Napoleonic Wars seemed not only invincible because of the strategic capabilities of Bonaparte and his marshals, but also due to the *political changes* in all three fields of polity, politics and policy of the French Revolution they were bringing with them. They inspired not only French soldiers, but also many other people all over Europe, with revolutionary new ideas of how to organize society and how to organize military institutions. What is important here for our topic of military strategy and strategic communication, is the fact that warfare, in Clausewitz's thinking, is inextricably linked to the organizational (political) condition of a war-making system. Napoleonic warfare was influenced by French revolutionary political developments and was successful because of it. Napoleon's real strategic achievement can be seen in translating the new revolutionary political conditions into the field of warfare, forging out of a new society the strongest military force of the era (Schmitt, 2007, p. 3).

Once we have grasped the historical development in the realm of military theory and practice, some striking parallels with contemporary developments in the world of strategic communication emerge. Reformulating Clausewitz, we postulate that if communication is a continuation of politics, then that does *not* describe communication as a neutral tool to achieve whatever aim—on the contrary. How and what an organization communicates will and must be intertwined with its organizational form: it must and will be an expression of its purpose. In Clausewitz's words, it is the relationship of a political purpose and an operational objective (*On War*, VIII.2).

Forms of Conflict and Concepts of Communication

As mentioned, Clausewitz distinguished between three different forms of war: cabinet wars, people's wars and guerrilla wars. It is not too far-fetched to claim that classical, professional campaigns bear a strong resemblance to cabinet wars, grassroots campaigns might be understood as people's wars, and guerrilla communications could correspond to guerrilla wars. The important point, however, is that the categories do not only capture different instruments or tools, but different patterns or types of conflict.

Clausewitz's theoretical distinction arises from analyzing developments in the practice of warfare during the Napoleonic Wars. The new revolutionary thinking, being politically relevant since the French Revolution, was opposed to the thinking of the *anciens régimes*, and resulted in a revolution of warfare: the people's war. The relatively small armies of the ancient European monarchies, consisting of mercenaries or gang-pressed soldiers, were confronted with armies consisting of a mass of volunteers or conscript soldiers. To put it simply, French armies mustered a larger number of more motivated soldiers than their opponents, which was one important reason why Napoleon was able to conquer nearly all of Europe in a few years. A paradoxical detail, however, is the fact that although these new revolutionary developments in the political field impacted warfare in the strongest way, on the surface they had nearly no impact on what military action looked like. While the French Revolution changed the political condition in France, and some organizational conditions of French armies, it did not fundamentally change the way the French fought (see Asprey 2000 and 2001 for a military history of Napoleon's campaigns). It is true that the French soldiers marched faster with less baggage, endured longer in the field without food, and attacked with more spirit and depth, but the weapons they carried, the maneuvers they executed, the whole face of war remained familiar. Napoleon did not re-invent regular warfare, he cannot, even, be considered particularly innovative. What he did followed established standards and rules. The military action of a people's war might be understood, thus, as the military action of a cabinet war brought to perfection or taken to extremes.

The greatest lesson lies in the fact that contemporary observers, despite experiencing the differences as shattering defeats, were slow to grasp the roots of Napoleon's dominance. To a lot of contemporaries, Napoleonic armies and the new kind of People's War appeared similar to monarchies' mercenary armies and their cabinet wars. And the reason was that the root causes were deeply buried. The powerbase of revolutionary and early Napoleonic France, which had tapped into the energies of the people *en masse*, was fundamentally different from the powerbases of Prussia or Britain or Russia (see Smith, 2006, for a concise introduction). We argue, therefore, that the distinction of people's wars and cabinet wars bears a striking resemblance to the distinction of grassroots campaigns and classical campaigns. Grassroots campaigns differ from classical, professional campaigns because of the constitution of the powerbase, but on the surface the communication looks very similar. What we contest, here, is the widespread belief that the same tactical and strategic principles apply no matter which organization communicates which issue. The disaffection of the people with politics might have something to do with professional campaign managers and spin doctors who attempt to apply cabinet war principles to what should and must, essentially, be a people's war.

Guerrilla warfare, to turn to the third type, differs from classical cabinet wars not only in the organization of the powerbase, but also in the way fighting occurred. The Spanish guerrilla war against French armies from 1808 to 1814 counts as the second important politico-military development to take place in Clausewitz's times. While Napoleon was defeating several armies of European powers, including Prussia, Russia, Austria, Italy and Spain, and their diverse coalitions, his army was unable to defeat an uprising undertaken autonomously by the Spanish people after the regular Spanish army's defeat. This new Spanish adversary was a relatively small one, estimated to comprise 50,000 militiamen, while Napoleon's army, part of the strongest military force in this time, numbered about 250,000 experienced soldiers (Schmitt, 2007, p. 6). Despite their great advantage, the French proved unable to defeat the Spanish. The reason was that guerrilla warfare differed fundamentally from the regular military actions the French army was prepared for.

The birth of guerrilla warfare is often dated back to the early 1800s in Spain because the actual expression was coined there—*guerrilla* meaning 'small war' in Spanish. But the practice is much older. Asprey (1994), for example, traced guerilla warfare back to Ancient Persia. However, it was at this time that a systematic *theory* of guerrilla warfare took shape in Prussia, and in the very circles Clausewitz moved in (Schmitt, 2007). Some military advisers of the Prussian king Friedrich Wilhelm III (1770–1840) were reflecting systematically about the phenomenon of small wars that they observed in Spain. In 1813, their ideas led to the king's *Verordnung über den Landsturm* [Ordinance on the citizen force], that is, a legal text ordering the Prussian people to resist by all means to public authorities in case of foreign occupation (Friedrich Wilhelm III, 1813). The edict gave a detailed plan on how to disturb public order by means of everyday instruments and weapons, and the king even decreed that some excessive or riotous mobs against law and order were better than a peaceful country leaving the enemy all his troops for military action (Friedrich Wilhelm III, 1813, p. 83). The decree established "a state of legalized anarchy," as Clausewitz called it (*On War*, VI.26). Thus, on the one hand the existence of the Prussian king's *Verordnung* indicates how strong French revolutionary armies were in comparison to the monarchist mercenary armies, and on the other how strong the forces unleashed by a people's war were in comparison to the force of a cabinet war. For Prussian strategists in 1813, there seemed to be no regular military means left to resist Napoleon. On the other hand, guerrilla warfare was a smart weapon with which to fight against the armies of a people's war, namely by activating irregular forces against the regular enemy.

By reflecting on guerrilla warfare, we come to better understand the two dimensions of organizational logics and actual, concrete and specific actions. A people's war means that the full force of a nation-state is unleashed and placed in the service of war—not only, as in the cabinet war, the fractions which the ruler or sovereign trusts to be armed and is able to pay out of his own pocket. The way people's wars are fought, however, is *conventional* mostly for the reason that the conventional form of warfare, in a military *Babbage principle*, is designed to make use of ordinary people who are always available in abundance, whilst heroes are always in short supply.

Guerrilla warfare, in contrast, differs *qualitatively* in both dimensions: organization and action. A guerrilla organization is marked by extremely decentralized structures, sometimes without any central command. Guerrilla war is a series of autonomous actions executed by different more or less independent groups or individuals, which does not necessarily add up to a series at first glance. Guerrilla organization is a form of organization, which was developed to resist in a very inferior position against stronger forces. The weapons of guerrillas, thus, are almost always simple everyday implements (in Friedrich Wilhelm's edict, for example, hayforks and peasant hatchets). The example of Spain shows that a guerrilla organization in its own mountainous terrain can be extraordinarily efficient—a small number of militiamen armed with simple means resisted the strongest military force of its time. Several other examples, especially of anti-colonial wars during the twentieth century, prove the point further. Nevertheless, as several theorists have pointed out, guerrilla wars are ultimately not conflicts to win but conflicts to resist defeat. In order to win, the decentralized guerrilla activity needs to coalesce into a more regular organization, that is, the regular force of a people's war (Mao, 1936, pp. 90–91; Guevara, 2003a, pp. 45).

Translating our observations into the field of strategic communication, we argue that guerrilla communications, that is, a plethora of communication activities denoted as 'guerrilla' forms of communication, almost always characterize an inferior position in conflict and represent 'irregular' ways to communicate (Schölzel, 2012).

The phenomenon of *guerrilla communication* poses the question of whether to win a conflict or whether to change its rules. In one definition, Clausewitz describes war as "an act of force to compel our enemy to do our will" (*On War*, I.1). In contrast Chinese revolutionary Mao Zedong, who was one of the most influential theorists of guerrilla warfare and a great admirer of Clausewitz, defined the ends of war as surviving a struggle and destroying the adversary (Mao, 1938, p. 171). He was not thinking of *physical* survival or destruction, but of *political* survival or destruction, arguing, again, on the level of organizational structures and activities, not only on the level of military action. While Clausewitz's definition referred to his own first ideal type of war, a conflict of equal adversaries, or "countless duels," which "go to make up war," as he wrote (*On War*, I.1), Mao referred to the second ideal type, a struggle between different types of social organizations. Guerrilla wars, understood in Mao's way, are (comparable to revolutionary people's wars) conflicts between different logics of social organizations and their different ways of doing things. Guerrillas usually find themselves in a dramatically inferior position in such a struggle. They are not *external* adversaries of a state, but *internal* contesters of a societal order, which they perceive as illegitimate and want to overthrow. Thus, 'regular' conflicts are conflicts aimed at winning within an existing ruling framework, and 'irregular' conflicts are conflicts breaking existing rules and aiming to change a system's procedures.

The main idea here, which we believe is also relevant for strategic communication, is that strategy in regular conflicts can be understood as finding the best way to apply general rules to win a game. Irregular conflicts, in contrast, are rule-breaking games where conflicting parties, on the one hand, try to implement their own rules, and, on the other hand, try to interrupt the adversary's game. In such conflicts, every strategic move is a double-sided move: breaking rules and establishing a new game. We can find these productive and destructive dimensions of guerrilla conflicts in classical writings, for example Guevara (2003a, p. 37, p. 163), and also in contemporary concepts of guerrilla marketing as 'irregular' business politics and advertisement. In marketing, Levinson (1984) and Ries and Trout (1986) represent the constructive dimension, and Kotler, Keller and Bliemel (2007, pp. 1124–1127) the destructive dimension. Both dimensions may lead to a third effect, which is a transitional process, namely, changing rules at a larger level. Military guerrillas, for example, fought throughout the twentieth century to change political systems in various respects (Münkler, 1990, p. 16). In contemporary military discussions we can find notions like *Networks* or *Swarms* as metaphors describing today's outcomes of recent transition processes in organizing warfare (Arquilla & Ronfeldt, 2000, 2001). The irregulars of the nineteenth and twentieth centuries' guerrilla wars are to be found, today, in postmodern ideas of "guerrilla" network organizations or swarm intelligence as new forms of "regular" warfare.

This is highly relevant for strategic communication today because for several years now we have been observing a rapid development of communication practices, partly due to fast-growing technological developments, partly due to shifting social values and changing relationships. Whoever reflects on strategic communication in the times of the Social Web, should take a close look at guerrilla theory. If we are correct in describing many contemporary organizations as structured along the lines of absolute monarchies, and a dominant conception of strategic communication referring to classical cabinet wars, then obviously there exists a kind of structural conflict with the concept of *network society* (Castells, 1997; Van Dijk, 1999) and its *swarming* phenomena. Strategic communication, therefore, not only has to take into account rules of 'classical' communication but also the 'rules' of 'strategic' rule-breaking games. These general reflections lead back to our initial question: the problem of how to adequately conceptualize strategic communication today.

Strategic Communication by Deploying Utterances

In the contemporary lingo of communication consultants the guerrilla metaphor is used as a catch-all concept to describe a wide variety of creative or innovative forms of communication. Creativity and innovation do not mainly refer here to the organizational set-ups behind concrete communicative action, but apply first and foremost to the activities and the means of communication that appear as irregular.

The type of strategic communication referred to remains conceptualized along the lines of a paradigm of information flow, information transfer, information submission, or the like. This paradigm originates from information theory and the treatment of problems of technical transition of information. Based on this way of thinking, several models of communication have been developed during the last few decades, from simple container and stimulus-response models by way of two-way exchange models towards complex models of feedback-flows of information. But these models are not well suited to understand guerrilla communication because its technical vision does not recognize phenomena of semantics or discursive practices. The relevance of typical guerrilla-like communication, such as word-plays, communicative violation of all kinds of rule (from typography to legal norms), or seemingly mindless utterances, is not to capture information flow. It is interesting to note that art schools, where some years all aspects of creative and innovative communication practices have been developed and taught, have far fewer difficulties in coming to grips with this. They offer approaches of communication that are based on semantics, on linguistic theory or discourse theory. While the seemingly mysterious phenomena of creative communication are not mysterious at all from their point of view—they are simply discursive practices—the approach of art schools does not seem to be very sensitive to problems of strategic communication. But the guerrilla metaphor in communication may serve as a vehicle to develop an understanding of communication that is based on discursive approaches, and is sensitive to strategy and tactics, or, in different words, to the *conflict dimension* of communication. And military theory, especially concepts of guerrilla warfare, may help to trace a way toward such an understanding (Schölzel, 2012, pp. 47–82).

In *On War*, Clausewitz established a close relationship between warfare and communication. The fact that war has communicative dimensions seems a trivial finding. First, the term *lines of communication* (meaning supply lines) was in use before the word "communication" had anything to do with media. Second, one could think about communication in the sense of exchanging information. This kind of communication is certainly necessary to conduct and execute military operations, as captured in the modern military phrase C^3 (command, control, communication). Third, one could also think about influencing public opinion by communicating about a given war, which is relevant to establishing or maintaining a motivational element. These three dimensions can be traced in all military struggles, sometimes as decisive elements. Triumphs and failures in battle are often explained as results of superior communication or, conversely, failures or breakdowns of communication. Any gain or loss of troops, material or territory has always been the object of either intense news coverage or of efforts to cover up the very same. What we have here are communicative activities *in* warfare or *about* warfare. It seems Clausewitz also thought about another relationship, namely, the idea not only that communication is a corollary element of warfare, but that warfare in itself might be understood *as a form of communication*. Clausewitz for example asked rhetorically:

> Do political relations between peoples and between their governments stop when diplomatic notes are no longer exchanged? Is not war just another expression of their thoughts, another form of speech or writing? Its grammar, indeed, may be its own, but not its logic.
>
> *On War, VIII.6.B*

A prominent reflection of warfare as a kind of communication in itself is Guevara's concept of *foco guerrillero*, developed in the Cuban and the Bolivian campaigns during the late 1950s and the early 1960s. He conceived that a single military operation was meant not only to hit an adversary, but also to communicate to the people. Its function was to be a meaningful event in a double sense by integrating a military and a communicative effect. First, in a military sense, an operation planned and conducted according to the concept of *foco guerrillero* was a single, focused operation of a guerrilla campaign. Its military aim was to hit and defeat the opponent by a surprise attack at one specific point of weakness, thus weakening him by this operation in a general sense. Guerrilla war boils down to a great number of individual tactical operations without an overall operational strategy. The second, communicative effect, however, was to create *utterances (Äußerungen)*, which are expressions, speech acts, and communicating to the people that they should join the revolutionary uprising. As a communicative event, the military operation should focus the people's attention on the existence and the relative success of the revolutionary guerrilla movement, and the necessity as well as the possibility to fight against an oppressive regime. Both were represented in the focused military operation (Guevara, 1965, p. 15).

In today's conceptions of networked warfare and military swarming, every maneuver is now regarded as intertwined with communication processes. There are mixed forms of physical and communicative conflicts in a broad spectrum between "nonmilitary modes of conflict" and "information-oriented warfare" (Arquilla, Ronfeldt, Fuller & Fuller, 1998, p. 8) for which "managing . . . information flows" plays a crucial role (Arquilla & Ronfeldt, 2000, p. viii). Netwar and Swarming describe doctrines of warfare, in which the difference between war and communication is blurring because communication itself plays a decisive role in conflicts. Elements of military conflict count themselves as forms of communication. The relevance of communication thus "refers not only to communication media and the messages transmitted, but also to the increasingly material 'information content' of all things" (Arquilla & Ronfeldt, 2000, p. iii).

What Arquilla and Ronfeldt (2000) appear to be thinking of when they speak of "information content of all things," (p. iii) is a kind of utterance or even *performative utterance* of military actions or, more generally, of all entities that are relevant elements in conflict. Strategy appears here not only as a problem of managing information flows but also (or maybe first and foremost) as a problem of managing systematically the relationships of different utterances that are relevant in conflict. The lesson for strategic communication, thus, is that strategic communication is about deploying utterances to form a discursive environment via campaigns or other complex processes of communication management, or deploying single but relevant utterances as a guerrilla action (Schölzel, 2012, pp. 329–339). Those utterances then establish specific relationships with their targets and may support the probability of a certain intended behavior. Further reflections may help to put into perspective current conceptions of strategic communication still implicitly or explicitly relying on the idea of communication as a kind of information flow. These reduced and one-sided concepts, we argue, are in dire need of complementary discursive conceptions.

Re-ReReading Clausewitz: Deconstruction

We conclude by deconstructing Clausewitz and thus, to a degree, our own writing. Clausewitz is often regarded as the high priest of strategy. As modern Germany emerged due to Prussian leadership, he is also regarded as one of the spiritual fathers of German militarism—to a considerable extent responsible, his critics maintain, for the two world wars of the twentieth century. Judged only from the substance of his theory, it is very strange that Lidell-Hart (1991/1929/1954), in particular, elevated Clausewitz to this dubious height. Erich Ludendorff, the generalissimo dominating the German High Command from 1916 onwards, with Hindenburg as his figurehead, proposed a concept totally opposite to Clausewitz and indebted to Moltke (the Elder), who was, as Howard (1989) found, a great admirer but not a great reader of Clausewitz. In Erich Ludendorff's (1865–1937) deluded worldview the military did not serve the state: the state existed only to organize the existential total war of the races (see Asprey 2005 for an account of Ludendorff in perspective).

When dealing with Clausewitz, it is important to realize that the man and his work have become *iconic*, which means what he *really* says is less important and open to interpretation. What counts is the *aura*. One glance is enough to see what aura Carl Philipp Gottlieb von Clausewitz (hereafter Clausewitz) brings to a discourse. Firstly, the man writes in the tradition of German idealist philosophy in a style that is notoriously rigorous, complicated and inaccessible. Clausewitz *is* German, moreover. Second, *On War* is a lengthy book. It adds up to nearly 600 pages in some editions. It was never finished and as a consequence it is badly structured, at times muddled, at other times tedious, which ensures that few will actually read it from cover to cover. Yet, third, Clausewitz, despite his philosophical style, is a writer of the highest order and it is possible to pick and quote passages of piercing clarity. Finally, when actually read and studied, Clausewitz is a thinker of enormous substance. The fact that eminent and serious scholars, such as Princeton professor Peter Paret, have devoted much of their work to the man, without exhausting the subject, may serve as evidence.

Specifically, many people are interested in the iconic character of Clausewitz because, as sociologists Knights and Morgan (1990) have argued, Clausewitz's concept of strategy lies at the very core of a discourse that created the concept of *professionals* and a *professional class*, first in the military, then in business.

> The formation of strategic discourse, the ability to 'see' the correct strategy and implement it was the role of the professional officer class. This class developed out of classical traditions of 'chivalry' and 'honor' but it was not until the early nineteenth century that expertise as opposed to status became a defining characteristic. The access to a professional ideology legitimated the power of the military elite: in this ideology, military strategy and tactics studied at the emerging officer's schools of the day, played a central role along with skills of leadership and scientific understanding of weapons systems.
>
> *p. 477*

Micklethwait and Wooldridge (1996) agreed with Knights and Morgan's claim that business appropriated the logic of the military elite: "If nothing else, managers have always fancied themselves as an officer class. Strategy is what separates them from the sergeants" (p. 160).

It is therefore not an exaggeration to say that Clausewitz and *On War* are keystones in the architecture of a discourse that is highly relevant to today. What is interesting for communication scholars is that there are two intertwined efforts going on at present that very much resemble the establishment of a professional officer class in the eighteenth and nineteenth centuries. First, there is the effort to adapt the discourse and terminology of 'PR-reborn-as-strategic communication' in a way that it emulates the discourse in strategic management. The effort is apparently directed *upwards*, the idea being to gain access to the professional officer class, or even to the general staff—to gain access to the keys that unlock the boardroom, as Bütschi and Steyn put it (2006). Second, there is the effort of universities and other institutions of higher education, it seems, to erect a barrier. The barrier, possibly facilitated by the Bachelor/Master distinction, is erected between candidates who receive training and education for largely technical or operational jobs in communication management on the one hand, and candidates who are initiated into the higher realms of strategy on the other that might or not to be functional. What is interesting, however, is that the former is offered a 'practical' education with hands-on experience, while the other is being brought into touch with 'theory'.

The assumption that theory prepares for real strategic decision-making, as opposed to creating an aura of importance, is highly debatable, however. From the first part of *On War*, the only part authoritatively completed, it is clear that Clausewitz would have contested it. But what is even more important, we argue, is to understand that there is no such thing as a purely and exclusively *communicative* campaign or conflict. Campaigns and conflicts are about something and conducted by someone against or for someone else. So first and foremost the issue or topic needs to be mastered. To socialize students into believing a few principles of communication will go far in any kind of campaign or conflict will go against Clausewitz's admonition: one has to establish the kind of 'war' on which one is embarking; neither mistaking it for, nor trying to turn it into, something that is alien to its nature. This, to echo Clausewitz, is the first of all strategic questions and the most comprehensive.

References

Arquilla, J., & Ronfeldt, D. (2000). *Swarming and the future of conflict*. Santa Monica RAND Corporation. Retrieved from http://www.rand.org/pubs/documented_briefings/DB311.html.

Arquilla, J., & Ronfeldt, D. (2001). *Networks and netwars. The future of terror, crime, and militancy*. Santa Monica: RAND Corporation. Retrieved July 28 2014, from http://www.rand.org/pubs/monograph_reports/MR1382.html.

Arquilla, J., Ronfeldt, D., Fuller, G., & Fuller, M. (1998). *The Zapatista "Social Netwar" in Mexico*. Retrieved June 15, 2014, from http://www.rand.org/pubs/monograph_reports/MR994.html

Asprey, R. (1994). *War in the shadows. Classic history of guerrilla warfare from Ancient Persia to the present* (2nd ed.). London: Little, Brown & Company.

Asprey, R. (2000). *The rise and fall of Napoleon. Volume I: The rise*. London, England: Abacus.

Asprey, R. (2001). *The rise and fall of Napoleon. Volume II: The fall*. London, England: Abacus.

Asprey, R. (2005). *The German High Command at war*. Lincoln, NE: IUniverse.

Bütschi, G., & Steyn, B. (2006). Theory on strategic communication management is the key to unlocking the boardroom. *Journal of Communication Management, 10*(1), 106–109.

Castells, M. (1997). *The rise of the network society. The Information Age: Economy, society and culture* (Vol. 1). Malden. MA: Blackwell.

Drucker, P. (1993). *The effective executive*. New York: Harper Business. (Originally published in 1967).

Falkheimer, J., & Heide, M. (2007). *Strategisk kommunikation: En introduktion* [Strategic communication: An introduction]. Lund, Sweden: Studentlitteratur.

Figes, O. (2010). *The Crimean War*. New York, NY: Metropolitan Books.

Guevara, E. C. (1965). Der Sozialismus und der Mensch in Kuba [Socialism and Man in Cuba]. In E. C. Guevara, (2003b): Ausgewählte Werke in Einzelausgaben. Band 6: Der neue Mensch–Entwürfe für das Leben in der Zukunft [Selected works in separate volumes. Volume 6: The new man-concepts for life in the future] (4th ed.). Bonn: Pahl-Rugenstein, pp. 14–36.

Guevara, E. C. (2003a). Ausgewählte Werke in Einzelausgaben. Band 1: Guerillakampf und Befreiungsbewegung [Selected works in separate volumes. Volume 1: Guerrilla conflict and liberation movement] (4th ed.). Bonn: Pahl-Rugenstein.

Guevara, E. C. (2003b). Ausgewählte Werke in Einzelausgaben. Band 6: Der neue Mensch–Entwürfe für das Leben in der Zukunft [Selected works in separate volumes. Volume 6: The new man-concepts for life in the future] (4th ed.). Bonn: Pahl-Rugenstein.

Hallahan, K., Holtzhausen, D., van Ruler, B., Verčič, D., & Sriramesh, K. (2007). Defining strategic communication. *International Journal of Strategic Communication, 1*(1), 3–35.

Herberg-Rothe, A. (2008). Die wunderliche Dreifaltigkeit. Clausewitz allgemeine Theorie des gewaltsamen Konfliktes [The peculiar trinity. Clausewitz's General Theory of Violent Conflict]. *Österreichische Militärische Zeitschrift, 88*(2), 163–173.

Hinterhuber, H. (1990). Wettbewerbsstrategie.2.2, völlig neu bearbeitete Auflage [Competitive strategy. 2nd, fully revised edition] Berlin, Germany; New York, NY: DeGruyter.

Howard, M. (1989). The Influence of Clausewitz. In C. von Clausewitz, *On War* (M. Howard & P. Paret, Eds. and Trans.), pp. 27–44. New Jersey: Princeton University Press.

Kissinger, H. (1979). *White House years*. Boston, MA: Little, Brown & Company.

Knights, D., & Morgan, G. (1990). The concept of strategy in sociology. A note of dissent. *Sociology, 24*(3), 275–483.

Kotler, P., Keller, K. L., & Bliemel, F. (2007). *Marketing-Management. Strategien für wertschaffendes Handeln* [Marketing management. Strategies for value reation]. (12th rev. ed.) München, Germany: Pearson Studium.

Levinson, J. C. (1984). *Guerrilla marketing: Secrets for making big profits from your small business*. Boston, MA: Houghton Mifflin Company.

Liddell-Hart, B. (1991). *Strategy* (2nd rev. ed.). New York, NY: Meridian. (First and second editions published in 1929 and 1954.)

Lukaszewski, J. E. (2001). How to develop the mind of a strategist. *IABC Communication World, 18*(3), 13.

Mao Tse-tung (1936). Strategie des chinesischen revolutionären Krieges [Strategy of the Chinese revolutionary war]. In Mao Tse-tung (1966), *Theorie des Guerillakrieges oder Strategie der Dritten Welt* [Theory of guerrilla warfare, or strategy of the Third World], pp. 35–102. Reinbek: Rowohlt.

Mao Tse-tung (1938). Über den verlängerten Krieg [On protracted war]. In Mao Tse-tung (1966) *Theorie des Guerillakrieges oder Strategie der Dritten Welt* [Theory of guerrilla warfare, or strategy of the Third World] (pp. 133–204). Reinbek: Rowohlt.

Mao Tse-tung (1966). *Theorie des Guerillakrieges oder Strategie der Dritten Welt* [Theory of guerrilla warfare, or strategy of the Third World]. Reinbek: Rowohlt.

Micklethwait, J., & Wooldridge, A. (1996). *The witch doctors. What the management gurus are saying, why it matters and how to make sense of it*. London: Random House/Mandarin.

Münkler, H. (1990). *Der Partisan. Theorie, Strategie, Gestalt* [The partisan. Theory, strategy, gestalt]. Opladen: Westdeutscher Verlag.

Paret, P (1989). The Genesis of On War. In Clausewitz, C. v.: *On War* (M. Howard & P. Paret, Eds. and Trans.), pp. 3–26. New Jersey: Princeton University Press.

Paret, P. (2007). *Clausewitz and the State*. Princeton, NJ: Princeton University Press.

Ries, A., & Trout, J. (1986). *Marketing Warfare*. Singapore: McGraw-Hill.

Ritter, G. (1931). *Stein. Eine politische Biographie. Zweiter Band: Der Vorkämpfer nationaler Freiheit und Einheit* [Stein. A political biography. Second volume: Activist for national freedom and unity] Stuttgart and Berlin, Germany: Deutsche Verlagsanstalt.

Schmitt, C. (2007). *Theory of the Partisan. Intermediate Commentary on the Concept of the Political*. New York, NY: Telos Press.

Schölzel, H. (2012). *Guerillakommunikation. Genealogie einer politischen Konfliktform* [Guerilla communication. Genealogy of a mode of political conflict]. Bielefeld, Germany: transcript.

Smith, R. (2006). *The Utility of Force. The Art of War in the Modern World*. London, England: Penguin.

Steyn, B. (2003). From strategy to corporate communication strategy: A conceptualisation. *Journal of Communication Management, 8*(2), 168–183.

Summers, H. (1982). *On Strategy*. New York, NY: Presidio.

Tibbie, S. (1997). Developing communications strategy. *Journal of Communication Management, 1*(4): 356–361.

Van Dijk, J. (1999). *The Network Society. Social Aspects of New Media*. London, England: Sage.

von Clausewitz, C. (1989). *On War*. (M. Howard & P. Paret, Eds. and Trans.). New Jersey: Princeton University Press.

von Clausewitz, C. (1991). *Vom Kriege* [On war] (19th ed.). Bonn, Germany: Dümmler.

von Clausewitz, C. (2010). *Principles of War. A supplement to the courses taught to the Crown Prince in person*. CreateSpace: Kindle Edition. (Original work published 1812).

Wilhelm III, Friedrich. (1813). Verordnung über den Landsturm [Ordinance on the citizen force]. In J. Schickel (1970) (Ed.), *Guerilleros, Partisanen. Theorie und Praxis* [Guerillas, partisans. Theory and practice] (pp. 69–87). München: Hanser.

3

The Strategic Turn in Communication Science

On the History and Role of Strategy in Communication Science From Ancient Greece Until the Present Day

Simon Møberg Torp

This chapter presents the idea that the communicative turn has been supplemented with a *strategic turn* in connection with the development of strategic communication as an organizational discipline and practice, which has resulted not only in everything—or almost everything—being regarded as communication, but also in everything—or almost everything—being regarded as strategic communication. The scope of organizational communication has been broadened to include virtually everything an organization says and does, and everyone who is affected by the organization's existence and activities. The historical background for this strategic turn is outlined in the form of a series of theoretical and philosophical points in the history of Western communications theory: the Athenian or Greek understanding of communication as revealed in Plato and Aristotle, the Roman understanding of communication as seen in Cicero and Quintilian, notions about communication associated with St Augustine in the Middle Ages, the Renaissance, the seventeenth century, the Age of Enlightenment, the nineteenth century, modern rhetoric, the communicative turn, and finally the strategic turn. These periods are analyzed on the basis of Stanley Deetz's theory of the dual concern and dual goal of conceptions of communications. From one period to another, perceptions of communication have varied between whether communication is primarily seen as a question of how, through the communicative processes, people acquire an opportunity to contribute to opinion formation and decision-making, or whether communication is primarily perceived as a means to fulfill certain goals and achieve control. The development of the role and status of communication in relation to markets and marketing communication is reviewed briefly in order to show which concern or goal—effectiveness or participation—has dominated in various historical eras. Finally, the chapter discusses whether the difference between effectiveness and participation has been dissolved or challenged in connection with the strategic turn. The question is raised as to whether the broadening of the scope of strategy in communication has led to the colonization of communication or to an increased opportunity for participation in organizational communication, and perhaps even contains an emancipatory potential.

The Dual Nature of Communication

According to Deetz, all communication, regardless of which area of society it derives from, and how it plays out, is—and has always been—suspended between the goals or ideals of participation and effectiveness (Deetz, 1992). The way in which we have considered these qualities has varied histori-cally. In some eras, communication theory and its development has been preoccupied with effec-tiveness, and with the associated instrumental and ends/means-oriented orientation. This approach centered on the effect of our communication and how we can use communication to exercise control, resulting in the consequent marginalization of the participative aspect of communication. In other eras, the ideal of participation in the communicative process has been accorded priority, at the expense of effectiveness.[1] Deetz defined participation and effectiveness as follows:

> *Participation* deals with who in a society or group has a right to contribute to the formation of meaning and the decisions of the group—which individuals have access to the various systems and structures of communication and can they articulate their own needs and desires within them. *Effectiveness* concerns the value of communicative acts as a means to accomplish ends—how meaning is transferred and how control through communication is accomplished.
>
> *Deetz, 1992, p. 94*

Participation and effectiveness are not fixed entities or goals, but normative ideals that enter into and are determinate for every communication process. Both effectiveness and participation are social constructions that arise from the communicative contexts in which people find themselves. Neither effectiveness nor participation ever appear in fully realized forms in the communication. A crucial factor in connection with all communications is the question of which of the two communicative objectives is the predominant normative ideal (p. 164). If we examine the above definition of effectiveness, we find that the concept has a close affinity with the concept of strategy. Strategy may be defined as a plan of action intended to accomplish specific goals (*The American Heritage Dictionary*, 2006, p. 1712).

Key Moments in the History of Communication in Relation to the Strategic Aspects

The following discussion highlights some key moments and theorists in the history of communica-tion, in order to elucidate how the view and discussion of the essence and role of communication, especially in relation to the strategic aspects, has appeared in various historical eras. Here it is inter-esting to observe that reflections on communication's (immanent) strategic potential are as old as communication theory itself. In order to understand the development of communication theory and the nature of communication—or perhaps rather its culture—within Western civilization, we need to return to classical Greece. The story of the birth of communication theory and its "childhood" is also the story of philosophy and rhetoric. This is quite natural, as philosophy, being the mother of all sciences, was at that time a universal science. Reflections and discussions about communication theory took place within philosophy, inter alia under the label of *rhetoric*. Rhetoric is thereby the West's oldest science of communication (Kjeldsen, 2001, p. 18).

Almost from its emergence, rhetoric has been the object of suspicion (Fafner, 2000, p. 7). Eloquence has been viewed as the potential refuge of deception. In classical Greece, Plato stood as the prime exponent of this skeptical attitude toward rhetoric.

Plato

An extremely elegant (re)playing of the theme of the role of communication can be found in several of Plato's dialogues.[2] Below I will briefly attempt to show how Plato, in the youth dialogue *Apology* and the manhood dialogues *Gorgias* and *Phaedrus,* discussed rhetoric or the art of speech,[3] and what we today would label the *strategic aspects* of speech. In *Apology*, rhetoric is presented as a means of manipulation and a technique of enabling falsehoods to appear true. In *Gorgias*, rhetoric is also rejected as pure demagoguery without connection with the truth, while in *Phaedrus*, rhetoric in an ideal form, characterized by being closely interwoven with philosophy in its recognition of the truth, is again brought back into the fold and made acceptable. The ideal rhetoric, like philosophy, seems to communicate the truth, posing demands on the speaker not only to be eloquent, but also to be in possession of insight (Johansen, 1991, p. 492; Plato, *Gorgias* and *Phaedrus*, *version* Plato, 1992b, 1992c).

The Apology

In Socrates's famous speech in his own defense, rhetoric plays an important role. Here Plato allowed Socrates to markedly distance himself from the speech of his accuser, which he said did not contain a grain of truth, but on the contrary was a rhetorically well-formed contribution "duly ornamented with words and phrases" (Plato, *Apology*, *version* Plato (n.d.). Rhetoric, seen here as a means to manipulate and obtain untruths to appear true, is thereby placed in sharp contrast to the truth (Fafner, 2000, p. 8), which does not need to be dressed up in such a sophisticated disguise. *Apology* begins with Socrates asserting that, due to the prosecutor's eloquent presentation, he has nearly forgotten who he really is. It is clear that Plato believed that words, if adequately formulated and well-presented, can give someone a mistaken view of the actual nature and context of things, including who one really is. Socrates complains that his accusers, in order to warn the spectators against letting themselves be deceived by him, have asserted that he is an excellent speaker, which he himself finds to be false, "unless by the force of eloquence they mean the force of truth" (*Apology*).

This implies that truth is an intrinsic part of speaking well. The accusers, as such, are in agreement with Socrates regarding the capacity of eloquence to persuade and convince, but believe that it is Socrates, and not themselves, who masters (and perhaps abuses) this skill. In a passage at the beginning of *Apology*, where truth is contrasted with eloquence, rhetoric is made the object of suspicion:

> Well, as I was saying, they have hardly uttered a word, or not more than a word, of truth; but you shall hear from me the whole truth: not, however, delivered after their manner, in a set oration duly ornamented with words and phrases. No indeed! but I shall use the words and arguments which occur to me at the moment; for I am certain that this is right, and that at my time of life I ought not to be appearing before you, O men of Athens, in the character of a juvenile orator.
>
> *Plato, Apology*

Gorgias

In *Gorgias*, too, rhetoric is rejected as demagogy. Socrates is extremely curious to know what the special object of rhetoric is, because all fields use words. Gymnastics and medicine, for example, utilize words to deal with the body and its state of health (449 B–E). The essential thing is that the words concern something, namely that which is the object of science. The words are thus not in themselves the most important object. They function as the medium through which insight is disseminated. In rhetoric, however, the material and the object of attention are the words, in and of themselves (449 B). Pressured by the eager and persistent interrogator, Gorgias concludes that the object of rhetoric is no less than the greatest good (452 B), and the most important and most valuable thing in life (451 B). The more specific and elaborate explanation for what the field of rhetoric consists of—and hereby also the greatest good—which Plato allowed Gorgias to present, is very interesting in that it very clearly communicates a sense of, not only what the real Gorgias could possibly have believed about these matters, but also to a great extent Plato's view of rhetoric, and the reason why his aversion to it, at the time, was so pronounced.

Gorgias speaks (in 456 A) of the incredible power of rhetoric, and how rhetoric takes "all other forces into its service and makes them submissive" (p. 129). As an example, he says a speaker would be better equipped than a doctor to convince a patient who is hesitant to undergo an unpleasant treatment; and the doctor, if he had to compete in words with the rhetorician in the Assembly for the position of doctor, would fall short, despite his professional skills. Speakers are much more capable than any skilled professionals of speaking persuasively on various topics. Professional knowledge is thus not a requirement for being able to convince people within a given area.

Rhetoric is not the only field that aspires to the goal of persuasion. At several points in the dialogue, it appears teaching something, be it arithmetic or anything else, is for Gorgias also to persuade (453 A–E). Socrates reaches the conclusion—and with the help of his maieutic ingenuity, also involving his conversation partner—that two kinds of persuasion exist: that which imparts insight and knowledge (*episteme*) to the listeners, and that which communicates opinion, but is devoid of knowledge and insight (*doxa*) (454 C). The form of persuasion rhetoric masters is the latter.

Here we also see a possible beginning of the recognition of the extent and diversity of persuasion, which was radicalized later on in Aristotle, but also a clear distinction in relation to the lack of faith in knowledge. According to Gorgias, rhetoric is neutral. It can be used to speak about everything, and for and against everyone (456 A). In other words, there is nothing within rhetoric that is immanent, or that compels or encourages the speaker to do or promote the good. The teachers of the art of rhetoric instruct their pupils in eloquence with the intention that they will use their skills in a righteous way. If this is not the case, one cannot blame the teacher (457 B). Asked whether knowledge of right and wrong, the bad and the good, is a prerequisite or initial condition for being able to learn the art of speech at all, or whether it is possible to learn it through teaching in the métier (459 A), Gorgias states that he believes himself able to teach a pupil who is ignorant of right and wrong these things as a supplement to rhetoric.

This incites Socrates to a series of arguments that reveal self-contradictions and inconsistency in Gorgias's reasoning. He who possesses insight into right and wrong, according to Socrates, is just, and the just man is characterized by acting justly (460 A). Earlier in the dialogue, Gorgias said rhetoric can be used for both good and foul purposes. It is thus very characteristic that for Plato or Socrates, knowledge about and insight into the good, the correct and the just also entails acting in this way. People who act wrongly or commit injustices are thus not truly in possession of insight into the good. In Socrates's opinion, rhetoric is but a contemptible and unpraiseworthy practical skill, the sole purpose of which is to create pleasure and enjoyment. He categorizes rhetoric under the concept of flattery, together with cookery, personal adornment[4] and sophistry. Rhetoric demands no specialized insight or competencies, but rather slyness and a natural ability to win people over (462 C–464 A). It is clear that Gorgias, in Plato's probably slightly caricatured rendition, does not see participation and the creation of mutual understanding as the real purpose of communication. Rather, it is the establishment of asymmetrical relations, power and manipulation, which is viewed as the most essential aspect, and to which rhetoric aspires.

Phaedrus

In *Phaedrus*, the tone towards rhetoric becomes milder. Here it is not a question of completely rejecting rhetoric at any price, but of discovering what a scientific and systematic theory and method of rhetoric would look like. There is a great similarity between medicine and rhetoric; both disciplines concern themselves with the analysis of nature. In the former case, it is the nature of the body, and in the latter, the nature of the soul. While for the doctor the goal is health, the goal for the rhetorician is to give people the desired persuasions and power of action (269 D)—that is, persuasion which the rhetorician desires for the individual. These persuasions are not purely subjective, but, like medicine, dependent on objective scientific expertise which is the result of thorough investigation. In

Phaedrus, a defense plea is made for a kind of target group-determined form of address. Yet again, one is surprised by the contemporary relevance of Plato's works, despite their being written 2,400 years ago. "The task of speech is to lead souls," as he so poetically formulates it, and in order to do this, the speaker must be in possession of knowledge about different forms of souls. Some people permit themselves to be persuaded by one form of speech, others by another (271 C). The rhetorician, in order to persuade his audience, must therefore have an intimate knowledge of the nature of the human soul and the effect on it of the various means of communication. This is strategic communication in its essence. But the strategy is not a means which can be used for anything at all. In order to learn to master communication strategically and in a targeted way, an understanding of the soul is required. Knowledge is a precondition for being able to speak well.

Aristotle

All arts and sciences persuade, according to Aristotle, in each of their areas. Rhetoric and the sciences no longer stand opposed to each other as two incompatible qualities, as they did in Plato's *Gorgias* and in the *Apology*. Rhetoric is defined as the teachings of the various possible means of persuasion. These means of persuasion are quite simply the object of rhetoric, and persuasion is viewed as being an inherent part of the scientific practice itself. Thus, it is not only rhetoric that can persuade.

> Rhetoric may be defined as the faculty of observing in any given case the available means of persuasion. This is not a function of any other art. Every other art can instruct or persuade about its own particular subject-matter; for instance, medicine about what is healthy and unhealthy, geometry about the properties of magnitudes, arithmetic about numbers, and the same is true of the other arts and sciences. But rhetoric we look upon as the power of observing the means of persuasion on almost any subject presented to us; and that is why we say that, in its technical character, it is not concerned with any special or definite class of subjects.
>
> *Aristotle, Rhetoric, 1, 2 (version* Aristotle, n.d.*)*

In the first book of rhetoric, Aristotle distinguished between *ethos*, *pathos* and *logos*. Ethos is the speaker's credibility or character, pathos the human emotions that are aroused in the audience and with which the speaker must be familiar in order to provoke them intentionally, and logos is internal cohesion of speech which is directed at reason (see for example Höffe, 1992). In Aristotle we find an extremely extensive *persuasio* concept which includes all forms of linguistic address, including both informative and referential language use, as well as the conative and directive functions of language, and even effects of a non-linguistic kind. Therefore, the three aforementioned qualities— ethos, pathos and logos—are also considered as different means of persuasion. The human being is basically persuasive: we affect and are affected by others (Fafner, 2000, pp. 32–33, 39). The non-argumentative means and the extra-subjective goals in Aristotle's rhetoric have led some researchers to believe that there is an inconsistency in the theory, due to the opposition and tension between these and the means which build upon the power of argument (Rapp, 2002).

The reception and dissemination of Aristotle's ideas reveal a rather uneven history. It has often been ignored that the Athenian or Greek theory and understanding of communication rests upon a democratic foundation, with the citizens' participation in the public debate playing an essential role. However, it should be added that far from everyone in the Athenian society was found worthy of the title of "citizen". Slaves and women were excluded (Deetz, 1992). As Deetz wrote, for Aristotle the purpose of rhetoric was not primarily a means of providing someone with an advantage over others. Rhetoric and dialectics were two sides of the same coin. Dialectics was viewed as a social and collective process, through which the individual moved forwards, in conjunction with others, towards insight and truth.[5] When Aristotle speaks of effectiveness, the concept should be seen in the light of the Athenian concept of democracy. It is not about the effective presentation of the truth, but about making this truth effective. In other words, effectiveness must be placed at the service of truth, not the reverse.

> The social problem he addressed was not effective presentation of truth but how to make truth effective. The Athenians were concerned with effectiveness as a means of promoting greater equalization of participation so that the optimal conditions for the emergence of truth would be present.
>
> *Deetz, 1992, p. 95*

This decontextualized reading of Aristotle has entailed a unilateral focus on the effectiveness aspect of his theory—a view also present in the Roman/Latin understanding of communication.

The Roman/Latin Understanding of Communication

After the Classical period, the primary center for reflections about communication and the development of communication theory became Rome, where among others, Cicero and, later, Quintilian, who lived in the early centuries of our era, made important contributions. Cicero and Quintilian are often mistakenly put in the same category, and Latin or Roman communication theory is discussed as though it were a practically homogenous entity. However, there is a distinct difference in nuance.

Cicero

In *De Oratore*, Cicero let Crassus express his deep fascination with the enormous power and effectiveness associated with oratory, when he wrote that there is:

> [. . .] no more excellent thing than the power, by means of oratory, to get a hold on assemblies of men, win their good will, direct their inclinations wherever the speaker wishes, or divert them from whatever he wishes.
>
> *De Oratore, I, viii, 30, (Cicero, 1967)*

Originally, speech and knowledge were a unity, and the same teachers taught "both right actions and good speech" (Cicero, 2009, III, 57). The goal was to turn the pupil into a "speaker of words and a doer of deeds" (Cicero, 2009, III, 57–58), but to Cicero's great regret, these two things had become separated. Cicero was concerned with *humanitas* (humanity) and discussed, through the personae appearing in *De Oratore*, whether rhetoric is grounded in culture and humanity, or whether it is merely a technique (Johansen 1991, p. 615). Technical skills can enable you to become an "accomplished speaker" but to be in "possession of eloquence" (Cicero, 1967, I, xxi, 94) requires that one possesses a comprehensive knowledge; that one is cultured (Cicero, 1967, I, xv, 67–xvi 72; Cicero, 1967, II, xvi, 66—68). According to Cicero, it was through speech that *humanitas* was realized. The ideal orator must also be virtuous or moral (Cicero, 1967, I, xv, 67–69; Cicero, 1967, II, xvi, 67–68; Cicero, 2009, III, 55), and the more skilled the rhetorician, the more important it was that this person was also moral.

> [T]he greater the power is, the more necessary it is to join it to integrity and the highest measure of good sense. For if we put the full resources of speech at the disposal of those who lack these virtues, we will certainly not make orators of them, but will put weapons into the hands of madmen.
>
> *Cicero, 2009, III, 55*

The requirements toward the eloquent speaker or the ideal orator were so many that few people—if indeed any—were able to live up to them (Cicero, 1967, I, v, 19; Cicero, 1967, I, xvii, 74 –xxi, 95), but it was an ideal worth striving for. Ideals, however, are one thing; practice is another. In practice, the rhetoric of the late Republic was often compromised in relation to ethics (Williams, 2009, p. 325) and Cicero himself, in his forensic speeches, such as *Pro Milone* (Cicero, 1891), has been accused of abusing rhetoric in the service of effectiveness—to remain in the terminology of this chapter—and of trying to get a murder to appear to be legitimate self-defense. According to Williams, Plato would have regarded this as an expression of the "pervasive lack of ethical concern for truth and justice" inherent in rhetoric (Williams, 2009, p. 326).

Quintilian

In *Institutio oratorio*, Quintilian defined rhetoric as "bene dicendi," speaking well (Quintilian, *version* 1933, II, xvii, 37, p. 342). *Bene*, like the Aristotelian communication concept, contains a duality and should be understood as both achieving what one wants by using speech in an effective way, and at the same time showing the way toward the good in an ethical sense (Fafner, 2000, p. 17). The only difference between Man and "all other living creatures that are subject to death," according to Quintilian, is that God gave Man "the gift of speech" (*Institutio oratorio*, II, xvi, 12–13, p. 323). This ability, or gift, is one that we should appreciate. The fact that oratory can be used, not only for good things, but also for bad, should not cause us to reject rhetoric. After all, even necessary things like food and drink, water and fire, can have both good and harmful effects, and even the sun and moon can do damage, but by its nature, this does not mean that we should stop eating and drinking and reject these things (II, xvi, 5–9, pp. 319–321).

Quintilian made use of a further analogy to illustrate that one should not renounce rhetoric as a bad thing in itself, even though it can be used both for good and for evil or inferior purposes: the sword is good in the soldier's hands, but harmful in the robber's (II, xvi, 10, p. 323). For Quintilian, then, the question of whether rhetoric leads to a good or bad result depended on whether the practitioner is a good man, with good motives and intentions. As a general rule, the orator will use his skills in the service of truth, but there may be instances in which the "public interest demands that he should defend what is untrue" (II, xvii, 36, p. 341).

That Quintilian—and, we might add, Cicero—necessarily focused on *the good person*, is due to the fact that the relationship between truth and expression known from the Greek concept of communication was breached in the Roman understanding (Deetz, 1992). Hence, the individual is burdened with a decisive responsibility. While for Aristotle the truth derived from communication itself—communication is so to speak pregnant with truth—and truth and expression are therefore two sides of the same coin, in the Roman variant the individual was both the precondition and the goal. The individual could possess the truth, and the truth was given as a pre- and extra-communicative quality. Communication was viewed as a medium through which the individual could promote his own views and interests (Deetz, 1992, pp. 96–98). In the Athenian democracy, participation was the underlying precondition for and therefore also a naturally embedded part of the understanding of communication; communication was the site, the locus, from whence the truth emerged. In Rome, participation and truth were viewed as being extrinsic to the act of communication itself. In judging Quintilian, Deetz is possibly a bit too idealistic in his reading of Aristotle. Deetz fails to notice the significance of the personality for Aristotle. For Aristotle, the speaker's credibility, or ethos, also played an important role. If one accepts Deetz's view of the Greek concept of communication, one can say that means and ends were more closely linked in the Greek than in the Roman understanding, in which communication was to a greater extent reduced to the status of a means.

The Middle Ages: Augustine

In the early Middle Ages St. Augustine[6] turned classical rhetoric into a Christian art of speaking and preaching. In *De Doctrina Christiana* (Augustine, *version* 1958), Augustine attempted to show that the rules of eloquence appear in the Bible and that the Bible also follows these rules. The biblical authors were highlighted as models of true eloquence. At the beginning of the fourth book of *De Doctrina Christiana*, which has been called the first great Christian work of rhetoric (Burke, 1969, p. 49) and the first manual of Christian eloquence (Conley, 1994, p. 77), Augustine explained why the art of rhetoric was important for advocates of Christian doctrine. Rhetoric could be used to promote both truth and falsehood, and "who would dare to say that truth should stand in the person of its defenders unarmed against lying?" (*De Doctrina Christiana*, IV. 2, p. 118). By the truth, Augustine—unlike Plato—meant a religious truth, namely, the Christian faith. For Augustine, rhetoric was thus a means—or a weapon—to be used in the fight against heresy and evil and in the struggle to spread Christianity.

> While the faculty of eloquence, which is of great value urging either evil or justice, is in itself indifferent, why should it not be obtained for the uses of the good in the service of truth if the evil usurp it for the winning of perverse and vain causes in defense of iniquity and error?
>
> *De Doctrina Christiana, IV. 2, pp. 118–119*

It has been asserted that Augustine, in connection with his conversion to Christianity in the year 387, broke with his view of rhetoric. Fafner (1995, p. 132), however, argued this could not be the case, as rhetoric is an unavoidable part of human life. Augustine, like Plato earlier, rejected superficial and bad rhetoric. In this way, Augustine broke not only with the Sophists' formal rhetoric, but also with his own view, as it was precisely this kind of rhetoric that he had practiced and popularized prior to his conversion. Augustine was trained at the school of rhetoric in Carthage, which provided the most superior form of training at the time, and prior to his conversion he worked as a teacher of rhetoric in Carthage and Rome. For Augustine, it was the capacity of communication to effectively disseminate the religious truths in the form of the Christian gospel, which lay at the center of his thinking. The purpose was to create a religious *communitas* and achieve charity (Roer, 2011, p. 48).

The Renaissance

It has been said that in the Renaissance the classical period was reborn, and with it the art of rhetoric.[7] Having been bound to Christianity in the previous period, in which the Church fathers believed language should serve the sacred cause, language in the Renaissance, with its general secularization, became "sacred" in itself (Fafner, 1995, p. 174). Man was moved to the center—a state of affairs labeled "humanism"—and the view of language became anthropocentric (p. 172). As language was viewed as possessing an absolutely critical role for human beings, rhetoric once again became, as in antiquity, a central issue. It is essential to the understanding of rhetoric in the Renaissance that rhetoric must be seen not merely as a superficial teaching of speaking, but as something that joined with philosophy, so that wisdom and eloquence—*sapienta* and *eloquentia*—went hand in hand. The poet Francesco Petrarca (Petrarch), by re-discovering or reviving Cicero, can be accorded most of the honor for re-establishing the connection between rhetoric and philosophy. Petrarch's spiritual descendant, Coluccio Salutati, saw the ideal person as a combination of the philosopher, the rhetorician and the poet (p. 177)—someone who could think, feel and act (p. 54). On the basis of this holistic view, which characterizes thinking about communication during this period, the Renaissance has been considered a golden age of rhetoric. Several rhetoricians have even asserted that the revival of rhetoric was not only a result of the Renaissance, but an essential precondition for the Renaissance itself (Lindhardt,1987, p. 39).

The Seventeenth Century

In the seventeenth century the view of rhetoric changed. From being considered a dialectical *controversia*[8] discipline (Conley, 1994, p. 162), which concerned itself with seeing things from different sides, rhetoric was now viewed as a method of affecting the emotions of the listeners. The philosophers Francis Bacon, René Descartes and Thomas Hobbes, all of whom were brilliant rhetoricians, had few kind words to say about rhetoric. They either rejected it outright, or viewed it as inferior to philosophy (Roer, 2011, p. 57; Conley, 1994, p. 163). Like most other disciplines, rhetoric too has had its upswings and downturns, and according to Fafner (1995, p. 464), history has clearly shown there is not necessarily a link between the disciplinary upswings and downturns and the degree of respect for rhetoric as a discipline. In the seventeenth century, the extension and popularity of rhetoric was widespread, and the field enjoyed great respect. But the rhetoric that was cultivated was a partial rhetoric, which reduced the field to a doctrine of style and a vehicle for literary scholars (p. 464). Which is to say, this was another period in which the understanding of communication, and the ideal, emphasized the aspect of effectiveness.

The Enlightenment Understanding of Communication

With the Enlightenment, the understanding of communication changed. While prior to the Reformation it was primarily the King and the Church who were seen as standing in direct communicative relationship to God, it became possible with the Reformation for the individual to read the Bible and to be in direct, personal contact with God (Deetz, 1992, p. 97). This individualization of the relationship with God, whereby religious communication was no longer mediated or disseminated by higher societal powers, enabled the individual to participate in communication in a new way. One could say people who formerly stood *outside* the religious communicative act could now step *inside* communication as central actors. Politically, the changes found expression in the French and American revolutions (p. 17). Here again, the individuals' participation—in this context in the political process—was the cornerstone. Even though the Enlightenment, the Reformation and the French and American revolutions can be said to have inherited or revived elements of the Athenian understanding of communication, there is a major difference: while for the Greeks it was a case of reaching *the* truth and knowledge about the nature of the world through communication (by way of dialectics), in this new era, the dynamic was that of ensuring the individual's rights, and possibility, by using reason, to arrive at a truth (p. 97).

The Nineteenth Century

The nineteenth century is sometimes spoken of as "rhetoric's fight to the death" and "the death of rhetoric'" (Fafner, 1995, p. 448).[9] This is despite the fact that the nineteenth century, due to political developments such as the introduction of popular sovereignty and the entry of ideologies, was in many ways an exciting period in terms of rhetoric (Roer, 2011, p. 62). Nevertheless, rhetorical theory did not enjoy much attention from prominent thinkers in this period, and to the extent that it did so, the view expressed was usually negative (Kock, 2011, p. 63). As in the seventeenth century, the focus was on effectiveness and the more instrumental aspects of communication. Several treatises were published on lecturing and the art of reading aloud. During this period, rhetoric was considered to be largely a matter of how opinions could be imposed upon and emotions aroused among the listeners. An important element here is that the aesthetic aspects of communication were also discussed, as the control of these aspects was viewed as being of critical importance for the possibility of effectively moving the audience (Fafner, 1995, p. 464). As a concept and as a discipline, rhetoric was at a low point (p. 442; Kock, 2011, p. 63). Rhetoric was considered to be nothing but forms and clichés, while in the university milieu, the ideal of good science was taken from the natural sciences (Roer, 2011, p. 62).

Recent Rhetoric and Communication Theory

Persusasio, according to recent rhetoric and communication theory, is not, as in antiquity, a one-way process in which there is a listener or recipient who passively waits to be persuaded or convinced. Today, both parties are considered to be speakers and listeners, and persuasion is a reversible process (Fafner, 2000, p. 43) through which people jointly arrive at the best answer. In going beyond monologically-oriented rhetoric, the concept of *pistis*—or what in Latin is called *fides*—becomes relevant. *Pistis* means inter alia, trust or faith. Trust is both the prerequisite and the goal of persuasion when persuasion is viewed as having a dialogical nature (p. 43). People must have a basic level of faith and trust in each other to be able to talk together—otherwise communication is, so to speak, meaningless. If the persuasive process is to succeed, there must be *pistis*. *Pistis* is the necessary biological, psychological, social and linguistic prerequisite for all rhetorical situations, from informal conversations to negotiations to teaching (p. 43). Burke (1969, p. 55) formulated it as, "You persuade a man only insofar as you can talk his language by speech, gesture, tonality, order, image, attitude, idea, identifying your ways with his."[10] The extent or the degree of *pistis* has the possibility, through dialogue, of evolving. The opposite can also be the case if the required trust is violated. The fact that the communication has an intentional and strategic character does not, therefore, negate the idea that it also builds upon a foundation of trust. Intentionality, the strategic aspect, need not necessarily be conceptualized as in opposition to sincerity and the desire for mutual understanding.

The Communicative Turn: Everything is Communication

During the twentieth century it became more and more popular to view everything—or nearly everything—as communication. The communicative turn, or the linguistic turn, means the role of language and communication is accorded a privileged status. In the more radical versions of this view, language and communication are elevated to the point of containing everything. A linguistic turn has taken place within many different disciplines, such as philosophy, history, cultural studies, and social sciences. It is, however, important to be aware that what is collectively labeled *the* linguistic turn in reality covers a multiplicity of turns and perspectives, such that it would be more correct, even within the individual fields, to speak of the linguistic *turns* (Alvesson & Kärreman, 2000; Bredsdorff, 2003). Within discourse theory, Laclau and Mouffe (1985) have for example formulated a radical theory in which the discursive has priority. A general and systems theoretical perspective that everything is communication can be found in the work of Luhmann (1995) and the theorists inspired by him.[11]

In an organizational context, this means that organizations do not merely consist of communication in a metaphorical sense. Organizations literally *are* communication (Højlund & Knudsen, 2003). Within the branch of organizational research called CCO (Communicative Constitution of Organization) (Putnam and Nicotera, 2009), organizations are considered to be constituted in and through human communication (Cooren, Kuhn, Cornelissen & Clark 2011). From this perspective, communication is not only a variable, on a par with a variety of other variables in or in relation to an organization; communication is "the means by which organizations are established, composed, designed, and sustained" (Cooren et al., p. 1150). The organization is thus not merely a "container" within which or from which one communicates; the organization comes into existence through communication.

The Montreal School is one of the foremost proponents of this line of thinking (Taylor & van Every, 2000; 2011; Cooren, 2000; 2010; Taylor, Cooren, Giroux & Robichaud 1996; Cooren, Taylor & Every, 2006). Under the inspiration of various theoreticians and research fields, such as conversational analysis, systematic functional linguistics, social psychology and ethnomethodology, adherents of the Montreal School speak of organizations emerging from communication. The thesis that everything is communication in one sense or another can be found in many variants and much of the constructionist wave may be said to be indebted to this line of thinking.

The Strategic Turn

In certain respects, what emerges in the strategic turn is a new understanding of communication and organization, with the use of such terms as *corporate communication*, *corporate branding*, and *integrated communication*. The boundary between the organization's external and internal communication disappears and the traditional organizational boundaries are transcended. Both employees and external stakeholders become targets located within the organization's communicative universe (Torp, 2009). The scope of organizational communication broadens to include virtually everything an organization says and does, and everyone who is affected by the organization's existence and activities. In the most ambitious interpretations of this broadened concept of communication, the effort extends from the external integration of visual design to the internal integration of the organization's culture and "soul" (Torp, 2009). One can say a dual movement has taken place: not only is everything viewed as communication, but also as *strategic* communication. In other words, a strategic turn has followed the linguistic turn. The strategic turn is not a substitute for the communicative turn, but an additional perspective that transforms all communication into strategic communication. In terms of communication theory, the strategic turn need not necessarily be synonymous with the conviction that all communication *is* basically strategic. It can also be seen as the expression of the attempt or effort to make all—or much—communication strategic. Strategic communication can be defined as the "purposeful use of communication by an organization to fulfill its mission" (Hallahan, Holtzhausen, Ruler, Verčič & Sriramesh, 2007, p. 3). Strategic communication encompasses several different areas, including public relations, advertising and marketing (p. 16), all of which have in common that they deal with influence and persuasion. It is characteristic of strategic communication that it is intentional, and carried out with a specific objective.

Where managers and communication specialists formerly focused on that communication which took place in formal forums and through formal channels, the strategic turn entails that informal communication within and outside the organization is also included. This sphere, which formerly escaped management's attention, is now considered relevant and important for the organization's strategy. This change nourishes a far stronger connection and identification on the part of the employees with the organization than was previously the case. In the view of the communication scholars Christensen and Morsing (2005, p. 52), the symbolic and behavioral dimensions of corporate branding imply employees must now be involved. The employees, in their everyday work are now expected to comply with and redeem the promises made by the brand. From a critical perspective, these authors pointed out that identification is an important part of corporate branding since members of the organization are often "expected to align their personal values with the identity of the corporate brand" (Christensen, Morsing, & Cheney, 2008, p. 70). Employees must themselves be incorporated into the organization and hence become walking embodiments of the corporate brand. They are expected not merely to communicate about the brand but to live it (Christensen & Morsing, 2005). And not only *on the job* but also *outside the job*. The Danish bank Sparekassen, which in 2007 won an award as *Europe's Best Financial Workplace*, and which was twice selected as Denmark's best workplace[12], has as its slogan: "You are Sparekassen even when you are not at work" (Brønserud, 2004). The firm's strategic focus is thus not limited to the communication which emanates from or takes place within the firm itself.

Strategic communication is also part of the employees' mindset, behavior and communication during their leisure time. Anders Gronstedt, president of an American consulting firm, described the situation whereby strategic communication has become all-encompassing:

> Integrating the work of everyone in the company, not only of communication professionals, is necessary because companies communicate with everything they do. The performance of the products and services, accuracy of the billing, and the treatment of employees, are all communicating powerful messages to the stakeholders.
>
> *Gronstedt, 1996, p. 39f*

Strategic communication has often been depicted as necessarily asymmetrical and top-down (Hallahan et al., 2007, p. 14). However, Hallahan and colleagues argued that this need not be the case. The strategies can also emerge from below. Strategic communication does not focus simply on the managers; there is also a focus on the employees and the communication specialists' intentional activities with regards to the presentation and promotion of organizations (p. 7).

Marketing Communication

Strategic communication, as stated above, also includes public relations, advertising, and marketing (Hallahan et al., 2007, p. 16). An essential factor in the strategic turn within communication regarding organizations and firms is the effect from marketing and marketing communication. The next section will briefly discuss the history of marketing communication in terms of the aforementioned distinction between the fundamental goals of participation and effectiveness. Within the world of marketing, too, there has been a communicative turn.[13] But this turn is a special, often normative, variant. Schultz and Kitchen (2000, p. 55) argued "Communication is becoming the heart and soul of marketing" and in their view it intervenes in the firm's strategies and organizational culture. Schultz, Tannenbaum and Lauterborn (1994) described this form of *integrated marketing communications* (IMC) thus:

> We have turned all forms of marketing into communication and all forms of communication into marketing. We have integrated our messages and our goals. We have built a seamless stream of communication with the customer.
>
> *p. 58*

When Schultz et al. wrote that integrated marketing communication has turned all forms of marketing into communication, it is relatively innocent and in no way especially new in a theoretical sense. Several researchers (e.g., Bouchet, 1991) have asserted that marketing is communication. Jefkins (1990, p. 2) stated "Marketing is in the communication business" and DeLozier (1976) held that all the *P*'s (Product, Price, Place and Promotion) possess a marketing communication aspect. An essential difference regarding the presentation of marketing as a form of communication, however, is that Schultz et al. (1994) did not view marketing as something which is communication per se. Among the latter, marketing, via IMC, has been turned into communication. And when it is postulated that all forms of communication are marketing, far greater and more serious themes suddenly come into play.[14]

Markets Were Once Conversations

This raises the question of whether one can speak of a strategic turn within marketing communication at all, or whether marketing communication is characterized precisely by being instrumental and having effectiveness as its primary goal. According to Searls and Weinberger (2001), this has not always been the case. They argued markets are, or once were, nothing more than conversations.[15] This is what markets *should* be and with the Internet's conversational nature, they can become so again.[16] Prior to the era of industrialization and mass communication, there were whole millennia during which markets were conversations:

> The first markets were markets. Not bulls, bears, or invisible hands. Not battlefields, targets, or arenas. Not demographics, eyeballs, or seats. Most of all, not consumers. The first markets were filled with people, not abstractions or statistical aggregates; they were the places where supply met demand with a firm handshake. Buyers and sellers looked each other in the eye, met, and connected. The first markets were places for exchange, where people came to buy what others had to sell—and to talk. The first markets were filled with talk.
>
> *p. 76*[17]

It was not the sale that was the original purpose of the market, but the conversation. The conversation sometimes led to a sale and a purchase; but buyers and sellers were equal, and a transaction was not something preceded by a manipulative act. The final goal of the conversation was not given in advance. It grew or emerged from the encounter between the parties. The interaction was truly social and built upon a commonality of interests, taking place face-to-face, without mediators such as firms, corporations and media. The role of the participants was to a large extent a dual one.[18] People were often both buyers and sellers at the same time, buying and selling different products. Searls and Weinberger presented a somewhat romantic view of markets, in what French historian Braudel called the market's "elementary form" (1992, p. 29). Braudel described how these markets, which in German are called *Hand-in-hand* and *Auge-in-Auge* (eye-to-eye) and where the exchange is more honest, transparent and direct, have survived throughout history. Braudel explained: "If this elementary market has survived unchanged down the ages, it is surely because in its robust simplicity it is unbeatable" (1992, p. 29). In *The Cluetrain Manifesto,* the authors (Searls & Weinberger, 2001) subscribed to a simple, linear view of historical development. Braudel, by contrast, saw the various market configurations as historically co-existing.

> The market spells liberation, openness, access to another world. It means coming up for air. Men's activities, the surpluses they exchange, gradually pass through this narrow channel to the other world with as much difficulty at first as the camel of the scriptures passing through the eye of a needle. Then the breaches grow wider and more frequent, as society finally becomes a 'generalized market society'. Finally, in this context, refers to the passage of time. These breaches never take place at the same date or in the same way in different regions. So there is no simple linear history of the development of markets. In this area, the traditional, the archaic and the modern or ultra-modern exist side by side, even today.
>
> *p. 26*

The Conversation is Interrupted: Market(ing) Communication in the Era of Industrialization

With industrialization, the raison d'être of the market changed. It was no longer the conversation and the encounter between equal parties that was decisive. The relationship became asymmetrical. It became a question of having power over the process and its outcome. One party in the relationship was reduced to a means. The customer went from being a subject to being an object, from being a participating subject in the conversation at the market to being an object for (or in) the market. Searls and Weinberger (2001, p. 78) wrote "Power swung so decisively to the supply side that the word 'market' became a verb: something you do *to* customers". One could perhaps say that marketing went from being the phenomenon in which you lead your animals and take your produce *to* the market, to becoming something to which someone is subjected. The classical management and production principles are also reflected in this understanding of the market. Just as workers were considered to be replaceable entities, the relation to the consumers also became less personal. The customer was transformed into a passive consumer. Mass production created uniform products, and mass communication created consumers with uniform needs to purchase the goods produced. One could say the conversation and the sale exchanged places. In the conversational market, the conversation was the intrinsic part and the sale extrinsic. Or to soften the argument a bit, one could say the conversation and sale were inseparable processes in the market. In or on the market of industrialization, the sale has become the intrinsic part, while the conversation has been relegated to the extrinsic. The conversation, which contains the participative aspect of communication, was downgraded, and effectiveness was elevated to become the governing and omnipotent principle.

Marketing Communication in the Era of Social Media

With a point of departure in Braudel's (1992) assumption of the coexistence of different market configurations, we can assert that what the Internet and social media have done, if one follows Searls and Weinberger's (2001) view of the Internet's potential and capacity, is not to re-establish the lost conversation but to create the possibility for a transfer and an evolution of the elementary market's conversational mode to re-emerge in new communication platforms. In other words, the conversation has now been broadened and—for some control-fixated organizations, no matter how undesirable—has found its way even into the large firms. Some of these organizations have desperately sought to limit the degree of freedom provided by the Internet by instituting monitoring systems or by reducing their employees' use of Facebook, Twitter and other social media (Stanton & Weiss, 2000).[19] Social media and new forms of marketing, such as viral marketing, have altered the conditions for communication and the relationship between the sender and the receiver. Up until now it has been a widespread view that stakeholders, be they employees or customers, were people whom one communicated *to* or *with*. Now the effort is to communicate *through* the stakeholders and turn the recipients into disseminators of, or perhaps even ambassadors for, one's message. It may well be true that the conversation which Searls and Weinberger celebrate has become a possibility with the Internet and social media, but it is clear the conversation and the ideal about it can be—and has been—used or abused for manipulative and instrumental non-dialogical and non-conversational purposes. Similarly, the ideal of dialogue has been abused within both organizational communication and marketing communication.

Summary and Conclusions

As this chapter shows, reflections about and discussion of the strategic aspects and potential of communication are as old as communication theory itself. Here the point of departure is Deetz's theory that "all conceptions of communication share with the community a dual concern with *participation* and with *effective presentation*" (Deetz, 1992, p. 94). From one historical era to another, communication has primarily been viewed either as a question of how people, through the communicative process, are given an opportunity to contribute to public opinion and decision-making, or as a means of achieving specific goals and acquiring control. Just as one can identify which fundamental communicative goals belong to different eras, and which paradigms have predominated, one can also distinguish at a meta-theoretical level between effectiveness-oriented and participation-oriented communication theorists and practitioners.[20] Participation-oriented communication theorists view the priority placed on effectiveness as a goal in communication as being synonymous with manipulation. They consider this perspective to be inferior, and even illicit and illegitimate. This attitude may be related to the fact that in the periods when the instrumentalist view of effectiveness has predominated, it has neglected or refused to recognize the significance of communication's participative aspect and avoided any concern with integrating the actors into the communicative process. Theorists who support a participative communication approach believe the primary and perhaps only goal of the instrumentalist view has been to exert influence over and control these actors. In other words, there has been a partial and reductionist understanding of communication. The effectiveness-oriented communication theorists and practitioners, for their part, find the idea of participation as the primary goal of communication to be uninteresting. Insofar as the effectiveness-oriented theoreticians and practitioners deal with or incorporate the participatory aspects of communication, this is not as a goal in itself, but as a means of exerting influence and control. In other words, participation is merely a tactic placed in the service of effectiveness.

It is important to maintain the view that communication is not *only* about participation or *only* about effective presentation. Communication has a persistently dual character and a dual focus. It is important to maintain this duality in strategic communication as organizational discipline and practice, to ensure that the understanding does not become reductionist. In connection with strategic communication as an organizational discipline and practice, it now seems to be possible for goals and communication concepts to interact in a way that is different to that of the past. With the strategic turn, effectiveness and participation have been brought together in a new way in relation to organizational communication. One might even say that in certain cases, there is an effort or attempt to dissolve the difference between the fundamental goals of communication; that attempts are made to create a new hybrid in which participation is used to promote effectiveness, while effectiveness is used to promote participation. Certainly it can be debated whether the two fundamental communication goals are in principle incompatible, and cannot therefore be amalgamated into a new common goal, or whether the effort is illusory and simply has the goal, or certainly the consequence—whether intended or not—of ensnaring people in an illusory concept of genuine participation in combination with effectiveness, while in reality this is simply effectiveness in disguise.

Depending on how one views the strategic turn, it can either be seen as a case of colonization (Habermas, 1984) or as pregnant with entirely new possibilities for participation. This is because the informal aspects of the organization's life and the informal means of communication have been placed on the agenda and are enjoying increased attention on the part of management.[21] On the basis of the colonization perspective, it may be asserted that the expanding scope of strategy that has taken place in connection with the development of strategic communication has caused effectiveness and strategy to impose themselves on all aspects of human life and all forms of communication. The actors and the recipients become a part of the communication process, but the real goal of the communication is effectiveness, not participation. Participation is thereby apparently reduced to a means or a tactic. Whereas participation in classical Athens was the precondition for achieving insight and knowledge, via the path of dialectics enacted within a community, participation after the strategic turn has become instrumentalized; the community and truth are no longer the final objectives. Participation is now, as in Athens, an intrinsic part of the very act of communication and the communication process, but the character of the act and the participation in it are very different, just as the goal is also different.

If, on the basis of the participation perspective, strategic communication is perceived, conceptualized and practiced as something that is not necessarily one-sided, asymmetrical, managerial and top-down but rather as a process that can also emerge from below, one could claim the development of strategic communication practically corresponds to the view of communication developed during the Reformation, when ordinary people suddenly received the opportunity to take part in communication with God. From standing outside the communication process itself, and merely being its passive targets, individuals now have the potential to become the central actors in the communication process, due to the possibilities social media accord them and, by extension, *the scope of strategy* to include basically all communication.

Notes

1 According to Deetz, communication theories can be typologized and the historical development periodized on the basis of which the two aforementioned objectives or ideals have predominated (1992, p. 94).

2 The Stephanus references are not very precise in the above-mentioned text, as the Stephanus pagination, which was originally from 1578, and which has since been used in many editions of Plato's works, is not especially detailed in Høeg and Ræder's edition of Plato's collected works (Platon, *version* 1992a, 1992b, 1992c). Nevertheless, in order to preserve the precision, the Stephanus pagination, which is at the top of the page in the Danish edition, has been added.

3 Socrates did not believe that rhetoric could properly be called an art (461 D), and in the dialogue, he accuses one of the dialogue's other actors, Polis, of having elevated rhetoric into an art (Plato, *The Apology of Socrates, version* 1992a).

4 Allen used the terms "pastry-cooking" and "cosmetics" in his translation of Gorgias (Plato, *Dialogues, version* 1984, pp. 248 ff).

5 Deetz quotes from Paolo Valesio's Novantiqua–Rhetorics as a Contemporary Theory (1980), in which Valesio shows how dialectics and rhetoric have been viewed in certain eras as standing in diametrical opposition to each other. In the Renaissance, the opposition was used in the anti-rhetorical incantation, later to be expressed in connection with the modern separation of the concept of truth from rhetoric (Deetz, 1992, p. 95).

6 St. Augustine of Hippo.

7 Some researchers have stated that the Renaissance represents a break with medieval thinking, while others have argued for a continuity of development (Roer, 2011, p. 51).

8 Protagoras believed that a case should always be seen from two sides, which in Latin came to be called controversia.

9 The year 1750 is sometimes cited as the symbolic year of the death of rhetoric, as it was then that the scholastic rhetoric tradition was confronted with a serious challenge from, and in certain respects replaced by, aesthetics, with Alexander Baumgarten as the most renowned exponent at that time (Fafner, 2009). However, it was more the beginning of a slow death, or as formulated above, a fight to the death. As we now know, rhetoric did not die. The twentieth century, from the latter half onward, is considered by some to be a golden age of rhetoric.

10 However, it may be argued that this identification and willingness to 'put oneself in the other's place' that Burke outlines here is false, in the sense that one simply feigns empathy, and that in reality the act is an attempt to manipulate in order to obtain what one wants. This would then be a question of the effectiveness of communication in achieving a given goal.

11 Luhmann is in fact critical of the linguistic turn, and because of his autopoetic perspective, he views the communication concept very differently. In the article "Wie ist Bewusstsein an Kommunikation beteiligt?", in a hidden address to Habermas, Luhmann stated that "In social theory, the primacy of language theory and the concept of intersubjectivity must be abandoned, and in their place enters the concept of the self-referential closed system of social communication" (cited in Harste: Niklas Luhmanns konstruktion af samfundsteori i Autopoiesis) [Niklas Luhmann's construction of social theory in Autopoiesis]. (Jacobsen, 1992; see also Bredsdorff, 2003, p. 20).

12 In 2010, the bank was declared the second-best workplace in Europe for workplaces with up to 500 employees by the Great Place to Work Institute.

13 Unlike some of the aforementioned positions, this idea does not build upon a scientific, theoretical or philosophical basis, but has more the character of a practical viewpoint. It is not asserted that everything is communication.

14 Naturally, there are also many opponents of this trend within the field of marketing. Duncan and Moriarty (1998) do not accept the assumption that all human action is basically governed by communication—or at any rate, as no more than a theoretical idea. They label this assumption "the communication fallacy" (p. 2).

15 "Conversation is a profound act of humanity. So, once, were markets" (Searls & Weinberger, 2001, p. 77).

16 Searls and Weinberger's presentation does not seem to be simply idealistic-historical, but real-historical, i.e., a description of the actual historical process.

17 The phrase "markets were filled with talk" evokes a container metaphor which harmonizes poorly with the other metaphors used to describe this market's original form. Nor does it accord with the idea that markets are conversations. If markets can be said to be filled by or with talk, the market pre-exists prior to this.

18 The choice of the word roles might not please these authors, as they seem to believe that people in the market at that time did not pretend to be other than themselves. Even their names equalled their brands and the products they produced and exchanged (Searls & Weinberger, 2001, p. 77), with, for example, English-language names such as Miller, Baker, Brewer and Hunter.

19 The control is not necessarily derived from the desire to prevent conversations as such, but may be due to the fact that a part of these conversations is not relevant for the work carried out and therefore draws attention away from the work. Investigations of employees' use of time spent on personal e-mail correspondence, Facebook, private web-surfing and the like have shown that some employees spend inordinate amounts of time on such activities during a normal working day (Conner, 2012a; 2012b).

20 For a more detailed and sophisticated classification of the various perspectives within communication, see Craig (1999).

21 One might even argue that the strategic turn contains an emancipatory potential.

References

Alvesson, M. & Kärreman, D. (2000). Taking the Linguistic Turn in Organizational Research. Challenges, Responses, Consequences. *The Journal of Applied Behavioral Science, 36*(2), 136–158.

Aristotle. (n.d.). *Rhetoric.* Retrieved from http://etext.library.adelaide.edu.au/a/aristotle/a8rh/book1.html. (Retrieved January 24, 2013).

Augustine, St. (1958). *On Christian doctrine.* (D. W. Robertson, Trans.). New York, NY: Liberal Arts Press.

Bouchet, D. (1991). Marketing as a specific form for communication. In H. H. Larsen, D. G. Mick, & C. Alsted, (Eds.), *Marketing and Semiotics. Selected Papers from the Copenhagen Symposium,* pp. 31–51. Copenhagen, Denmark: Handelshøjskolens Forlag.

Braudel, F. (1992). *The Wheels of Commerce. Civilization and Capitalism: 15th-18th Century.* Vol. 2. (S. Reynolds, Trans.). Berkeley, CA: University of California Press.

Bredsdorff, N. (2003). *Diskurs og konstruktion. En samfundsvidenskabelig kritik af diskursanalyser og socialkonstruktivismer [Discourse and Construction: a sociological critique of discourse analyses and social constructivisms].* Gylling, Denmark: Forlaget Sociologi.

Brønserud, H. E. (2004). Retrieved from http://www.jak.dk/forening/blad04/z5–04_Etiskregnskab.html. (Accessed January 24, 2013).

Burke, K. (1969). *A Rhetoric of motives.* California, CA: University of California Press.

Christensen, L. T. & Morsing, M. (2005). *Bagom corporate communication* [Behind corporate communication]. Gylling, Denmark: Forlaget Samfundslitteratur.

Christensen, L. T., Morsing, M. & Cheney, G. (2008). *Corporate communications. Convention, complexity and critique.* London, England: Sage.

Cicero, M. T. (1891). *The Orations of Marcus Tullius Cicero.* (C. D. Yonge, Trans.). London, England: George Bell & Sons. Retrieved from http://www.perseus.tufts.edu/hopper/text?doc=Perseus%3Atext%3A1999.02. 0020%3Atext%3DMil.%3Asection%3D1 Cicero (1967). *De Oratore* [On the Ideal orator]. (E. W. Sutton, & H. Rackham, Trans.). Loeb Classical Library. Cambridge, MA: Harvard University Press.

Cicero (2009). De Oratore [On the Ideal orator]. Excerpt. (J. M. May & J. Wisse, Trans.). In J. D. Williams (Ed.), *An introduction to classical rhetoric: Essential readings.*Chichester, England: Wiley-Blackwell.

Conley, T. M. (1994). *Rhetoric in the European Tradition.* Chicago, IL: University of Chicago Press.

Conner, C. (2012a (July 17)). Employees really do waste time at work. *Forbes.* Retrieved from http://www.forbes. com/sites/cherylsnappconner/2012/07/17/employees-really-do-waste-time-at-work/ (Accessed October 8, 2014).

Conner, C. (2012b (November 15). Employees really do waste time at work, II. *Forbes.* Retrieved from http:// www.forbes.com/sites/cherylsnappconner/2012/11/15/employees-really-do-waste-time-at-work-part-ii/ (Accessed October 8, 2014).

Cooren, F. (2000). *The organizing property of communication.* Amsterdam, Holland: John Benjamins.

Cooren, F., Taylor, J. R. & Every, E. J. van. (2006). Communication as organizing: Empirical and theoretical explorations in the dynamic of text and conversation. Mahwah, NJ: Lawrence Erlbaum Associates.

Cooren, F. (2010). *Action and agency in dialogue: Passion, incarnation and ventriloquism.* Amsterdam, Holland: John Benjamins.

Cooren, F., Kuhn, T., Cornelissen, J. P. & Clark, T. (2011). Communication, organizing, and organization: An overview and introduction to the special issue. *Organization Studies, 32*(9), pp. 1149–1170.

Craig, R. T. (1999). Communication theory as a field. *Communication Theory, 9*(2), pp. 119–161.

Deetz, S. A. (1992). *Democracy in an age of corporate colonization. Developments in communication and the politics of everyday life.* New York: State University of New York Press.

DeLozier, M. W. (1976). *The Marketing Communication Process*. New York: McGraw Hill.

Duncan, T. & Moriarty, S. E. (1998). A communication-based marketing model for managing relationships. *Journal of Marketing 62*(2), 1–13.

Fafner, J. (1995). *Tanke og tale* [Thought and Speech]. Copenhagen, Denmark: C.A. Reitzels Forlag.

Fafner, J. (2000). *Retorik. Klassisk & moderne* [Rhetoric. Classical & modern]. Copenhagen, Denmark: Akademisk Forlag.

Fafner, J. (2009). Retorik. In *Den Store Danske—Gyldendals åbne encyklopædi* [Entry on Rhetoric from The Great Danish—Gyldendal's Open Encyclopaedia]. Retrieved from http://www.denstoredanske.dk/Kunst_og_kultur/Litteratur/Stilistik,_retorik_og_metrik/retorik (accessed October 8, 2014).

Gronstedt, A. (1996). Integrated communications in America's leading total quality management corporations. *Public Relations Review 22*(1), 25–42.

Habermas, J. (1984). *The theory of communicative action*. (T. McCarthy, Trans.). Boston, MA: Beacon Press.

Hallahan, K., Holtzhausen, D., van Ruler, B., Verčič, D. & Sriramesh, K. (2007). Defining strategic communication. *International Journal of Strategic Communication, 1*(1), 3–35.

Harste, G. (1992). Niklas Luhmanns konstruktion af samfundsteori [Niklas Luhmann's construction of social theory]. In J. C. Jacobsen (Ed.), *Autopoiesis* (pp. 59–96). Copenhagen, Denmark: Forlaget politisk revy.

Höffe, O. (1992). Aristoteles (384–322 f. Kr.) (K. K. Jensen, Trans.). In O. Höffe (Ed.), *Filosofi. Antikken & Middelalderen fra Førsokratikerne til Cusanus* [Philosophy: antiquity and the middle ages from the Presocratics to Nicholas of Cusa], pp. 59–90. Copenhagen, Denmark: Politikens Forlag.

Højlund, H. & Knudsen, M. (Ed.). (2003). *Organiseret kommunikation—systemteoretiske analyser* [Organized communication—system theory analyses]. Frederiksberg, Denmark: Samfundslitteratur.

Jefkins, F. (1990). *Modern marketing communications*. Glasgow, Scotland: Blackie.

Johansen, K. F. (1991). *Den europæiske filosofis historie (Bind 1)* [History of European philosophy(Vol. 1]. Viborg, Denmark: Nyt Nordisk Forlag Arnold Busck A/S.

Kjeldsen, J. E. (2001). Skandinavisk retorikvidenskab. Mediesamfundets udfordringer til to afgrænsninger af retorikken som videnskab og fag [Scandinavian rhetorical studies: the challenges of the media society in defining rhetoric as a science and subject]. *Rhetorica Scandinavica 20*, 18–31

Kock, C. (2011). Retorikken i nyere tid [Modern rhetoric], In R. Jørgensen & L. Villadsen (Eds.), *Retorik. Teori og praksis* [Rhetoric: Theory and practice], (pp. 63–83). Gylling: Samfundslitteratur.

Laclau, E. & Mouffe, C. (1985). *Hegemony and socialist strategy*. London, England: Verso.

Lindhardt, J. (1987). *Retorik* [Rhetoric]. Copenhagen, Denmark: Munksgaard.

Luhmann, N. (1995). *Social Systems*. (J. Bednarz Jr. & D. Baecker, Trans.) Stanford, CA: Stanford University Press.

Plato (1984). *The dialogues of Plato*. Vol. 1 (R. E. Allen, Trans.). New Haven, CT; London, England: Yale University Press.

Plato. (n.d.). *Apology* (B. Jowett, Trans.). *The Internet classics archive*. Retrieved from http://classics.mit.edu/Plato/apology.html (accessed October 8, 2014).

Plato. *Gorgias*.(B. Jowett, trans). *The Internet Classics Archive*. Retrieved from http://classics.mit.edu/Plato/gorgias.html (accessed October 8, 2014).

Platon (1992a). Sokrates' forsvarstale. In *Platon Skrifter 1* [The Apology of Socrates. Plato: Writings 1]. (C. Høeg & H. Ræder, Trans.) (p. 267–296). Gylling, Denmark: Hans Reitzels Forlag.

Platon (1992b). Gorgias. *Platon Skrifter 2*. (Plato: Writings 2). (C. Høeg & H. Ræder, Trans.). (p. 117–222). Gylling, Denmark: Hans Reitzels Forlag.

Platon (1992c). Faidros. *Platon Skrifter 6*. (Plato: Writings 6). (C. Høeg & H. Ræder, Trans.). (p. 13–92). Gylling, Denmark: Hans Reitzels Forlag.

Putnam, L. & Nicotera, A. (2009) (ed.). Building theories of organization: The constitutive role of communication. New York: Routledge.

Quintilian. (1933). *The Institutio Oratoria*. (H. E. Butler, Trans.). Loeb Classical Library. Cambridge, MA: Harvard University Press.

Rapp, C. (2002) Aristotle's Rhetoric. *The Stanford Encyclopedia of Philosophy (Summer 2002 Edition)*, Edward N. Zalta (Ed.), retrieved from http://plato.stanford.edu/archives/sum2002/entires/aristotle-rhetoric/ (accessed October 8, 2014).

Roer, H. (2011). Den retoriske tradition [The rhetorical tradition]. In R. Jørgensen, R. & L. Villadsen (Eds.), *Retorik. Teori og praksis* [Rhetoric: theory and practice] (pp. 37–62). Gylling, Denmark: Samfundslitteratur.

Schultz, D. E., Tannenbaum, S. I. & Lauterborn, R. F. (1994). *[Integrated Marketing Communications] The New Marketing Paradigm*. Chicago, IL: NTC Business Books.

Schultz, D. E. & Kitchen, P. J. (2000). *Communicating globally. An integrated marketing approach*. London, England: Palgrave.

Searls, D. & Weinberger, D. (2001). Markets are conversations. In R. Levine, C. Locke, D. Searls & D. Weinberger (Eds.), *The Cluetrain Manifesto: The end of business as usual*. New York: Basic Books.

Stanton, J. M. & Weiss, E. M. (2000). Electronic monitoring in their own words: an exploratory study of employees' experiences with new types of surveillance. *Computers in Human Behavior, 16*(4), pp. 423–440.

Taylor, J. R., Cooren F., Giroux, N. & Robichaud, D. (1996). The communicational basis of organization: Between the conversation and the text. *Communication Theory, 6*(1), pp. 1–39.

Taylor, J. R. & Every, E. J. van (2000). *The emergent Organization. Communication as Its Site and Surface*. Mahwah, NJ: Lawrence Erlbaum Associates.

Taylor, J. R. & Every, E. J. van (2011). *The situated organization: Case studies in the pragmatics of communication research*. New York: Routledge.

The American heritage dictionary (4th ed.) (2006). Boston, MA: Houghton Mifflin Company.

Torp, S. (2009). Integrated Communications: From one look to normative consistency. *Corporate Communications: An International Journal, 14*(2), 190–206.

Williams, J. D. (2009). *An introduction to classical rhetoric: Essential readings*. Wiley–Blackwell.

4

Strategic Communication and the Public Sphere From a European Perspective[1]

euro centrism?

Günter Bentele and Howard Nothhaft

Scholars researching strategic communication, public relations, communication management or other related fields, at least in the Western world, have a tendency to treat the *public sphere* as a given. Although sociologists, philosophers and political theorists quarrel about the details, common sense reassures us that by and large the public is aware of what *Öffentlichkeit,* as is called in German, is about. But as soon as one engages in discussion it becomes clear that common sense is, in fact, not commonly understood. The concept is disputed along with others such as *political, society* or *democracy*. Even people from the same country do not always agree on what is public and what is private. And the question of what belongs in the public sphere, what normatively should be the object of public debate while in reality something else is being debated publicly, while others think it should not be debated, seems to be particularly complex. The following chapter traces the influential conceptualization of the public sphere in the works of Jürgen Habermas and Hannah Arendt respectively and builds further theory on this continental or 'European' tradition of thinking about the public sphere.

Historical Aspects

It would be convenient and safe to begin a treatise on the public sphere in the eighteenth century, when the phrase began to mean more or less the same as it does today (cf. Hölscher, 1978). Many authors do this – however, we shall go further back in history because we believe that the existence of the public sphere is not only a product of Enlightenment philosophy or liberal democratic reasoning. The public sphere as we know it today is also the contemporary phenotypical manifestation of *anthropological constants,* that is, characteristics of the human animal, the *zoon politikon,* and the way it lives together with other members of its species. What we refer to as the public sphere in our hypercomplex modern societies is certainly something that only emerges with higher forms of civilization that have risen beyond mere survival. But the public sphere of the late twentieth and early twenty-first century is the functional equivalent of other institutions in simpler, that is, less complex, modes of living. Over centuries, certain characteristics of the human beings' way of living together have been transposed in accordance with the realities of their respective societies, civilizations or cultures. But if one were to postulate that there was no public sphere, or a negligible public sphere, in a particular period of time, for example the Middle Ages, one would need to explain why this was, and what stood in its place.

From 'Primitive' Societies to Classical Antiquity

The idea of a public life, as opposed to *private affairs* on the one side and *affairs of office* on the other, can be dated back to classical European antiquity, that is, Greek (~750—50 BC) and Roman times (~250 BC–500 AD). Whether the concept goes back even further, and whether there was a *proto-public life* in ancient Egyptian, Babylonian, and Sumerian civilizations, is difficult to say with certainty. For our further discussion it is important to bear in mind, however, that these ancient cultures pursued grand projects such as the building of the great pyramids or coping with the great rivers, respectively the Nile, the Euphrates and the Tigris. This suggests some concern for the well-being of the public, admittedly, but first and foremost such projects served to unite the people under their ruler's yoke.

The Public, the Private and the Secret: the Duality of the Public Sphere

German-American philosopher Hannah Arendt (1906–1975) famously argued that participation in the common, shared or public sphere of the *polis*—by listening and engaging in discussion at the public place, the *agora*—was a privilege of the free, that is, those who had risen above caring for daily subsistence and the necessities of the private household, the *oikos* (cf. Arendt, 2010, pp. 38–47; for English see Arendt, 1958). Habermas (1990, pp. 57–58; 1962), one of the world's eminent thinkers about *Öffentlichkeit* (Calhoun, 1992), adds that it was in the public sphere of the polis that equals met as equals (*homoioi*) to determine who was the most noble (*aristoiein*). It was in the public sphere that the truth came to light while the cruel necessities of everyday life were shamefully hidden away in the household. That also meant, conversely, that a harsh and revealing light was shed on individuals vying for acclamation in the public sphere. The affairs of private men who were not interested in politics—so-called *idiōtēs*, the roots of the modern word 'idiot'–, and who therefore did not lead a full life according to the classical *ideal*, were left in the dark. We have here, an important *motif* and a *dominant metaphor*: a duality characterizing the public sphere from its very beginnings to the globalized world of the twenty-first century. Once the necessities of life are taken care of, the *zoon politikon* seems to develop the urge to distinguish itself among equals. The public sphere, be it the blogosphere, the coffee house, the village marketplace or the fire around which the warriors squat, constitutes a place where one can get up and step out into the light. And the metaphor of light and darkness (Imhof, 2003, p. 194) already conveys the duality: The place is bathed in harsh light because it is a place of acclamation as well as a mechanism of control. That is why the *concept of publicness* has two opposites: private on the one hand, secret on the other. The individual is left in darkness as long as she or he lives a private life only, but if she or he wants power and influence, that is, public office, she or he has to be able to cope with the light. What she or he does is no longer private because if someone is in charge of the fate of the tribe or the kingdom or the empire her or his every aspect (health, opinions) is important—therefore they cannot be allowed to be secret.

The Public Sphere is the Sphere that Matters

Habermas (1990, p. 57), among others, pointed out the seemingly inherent normative power in everything classical. Educated Europeans have been brought up in the belief that the world of classical antiquity constituted a high point of civilization: in the case of ancient Greece, a real democracy. It is important to remember, however, that quasi-democratic structures are quite common among so-called primitive or barbaric societies. The *ting,* for example, was both governing assembly and court of law in Germanic tribal societies, and the term is traceable in the denotations of parliaments of Nordic countries, for example, in Denmark (*Folketing*), Norway (*Storting*) or Iceland (*Althing*). It is also the root of the English word *thing* and German word *Ding*. Although the political circumstances surrounding the ting were entirely different, the similarities should not be explained away. As was the case in classical antiquity, only the free gathered in the ting; the ting took place at a special location, the *tingstead;* the ting constituted a peaceful deliberation of equals among equals as the *Thingfriede* guaranteed that reason rather than armed force prevailed.

A modern observer would quickly point out that the democratic ideal was flawed because it did not include the unfree, such as peasants and slaves, children and women. But that is a revealing observation in itself. It reveals the modern assumption that the individual human being is the basic building block of society. It is by no means a necessary assumption because in contrast to animals living alone, a single individual normally has a tough time to fend for itself in nature. Slaves, children and women, an ancient Greek would have argued, do not count in their own right because their fate is bound up with the fate of the household, which constituted the smallest indivisible element. What we have to realize, thus, is that the public sphere as a place for acclamation and a mechanism of control (of equals by equals) was democratic in its very nature. It is, however, not democratic in the modern sense of the word. The public sphere was not the place for everyone to gather, but the sphere for the ones that matter in their respective culture, civilization or society. The idea that everyone matters is very new. In the Athenian polis the free gathered in the agora because the man unburdened by work, the man liberated to lead the good and real life, represented what mattered in the polis. The ting was the heart of a culture described as military democracy and consequently only the warriors assembled; the man holding a spear mattered.

Being and Representing

Members of twenty-first century societies have a tendency to implicitly assume that power and influence derive from positions one holds in organizations, more often than not temporary positions which denote representational power. It is important to realize, however, that the head of the household participating in debates in the agora did not represent his household, but himself—a point we return to later. In the early and primitive democracies, we have governance by assemblies where everyone counts for himself and makes himself count by being physically present. Imhof (2003) has pointed out that the origin of the public sphere, "die Urform der Öffentlichkeit" (p. 204), is the assembly. The oldest form of legitimation thus arises from saying something in the assembly and giving everyone the possibility to speak up against it. What is often overlooked, however, is that assemblies can be very diverse in character. Figure 4.1 illustrates the differences. On the far left side, Figure 4.1a represents a radical democratic type of assembly where everyone present matters and everyone who matters is equal. Note that the public sphere, the arena, is empty. Its boundaries are made up by the individuals who matter but no one actually takes the space in the center. What we

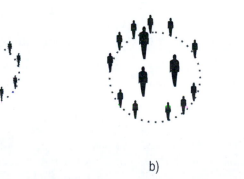

a)　　　　　　　　　　b)　　　　　　　　　　c)

Figure 4.1　Basic Types of Assembly as Public Spheres

have here comes closest, we believe, to Habermas's ideal of discourse as the ideal speech situation (Habermas 1997a, 1997b). The public sphere is not dominated by people, but by arguments thrown in the ring. Figure 4.1b looks similar but has larger-than-life individuals, not arguments, acting in the public sphere. If one speaks up against a proposition, one speaks up against the man. It is important to realize, however, that the individuals are in the arena because they dare to be there, not because they are entitled to be there.

Any individual on the boundary may step into the ring at any time. The difference becomes clear when we look at Figure 4.1c. This figure represents actual actors in the arena and potential actors drawing the boundaries of the arena, but we also have an audience. The audience belongs to the class that matters, otherwise it would not be there. But it does not belong to the class that actually or potentially acts in the arena. No matter what the reason is, there is only a limited pool of individuals who can afford to, are allowed to, or are educated enough to act in the arena. And there is no guarantee that the audience in the outer circle has the same criteria for what should be in the public sphere, for what is interesting, or for what concerns all, as the inner circle of potential or actual actors. In fact, it seems to be one of the recurring problems of every theory of *Öffentlichkeit* that congruence of the inner and outer circle, of audience, potential and actual actors, is very rare. The congruence, be it assumed or factual, is what is later referred to as *public opinion* (cf. Habermas, 1990, pp. 343–359; Noelle-Neumann, 2002), which is not equivalent to statistical representation of each individual member of the audience.

Technical Limits of Co-Presence

It is clear that having a class of actors distinguished from the audience creates a tendency for the actors to limit the access to the actor class by rigidly enforcing the entry criteria they themselves fulfil. It seems safe to assume, however, that apart from any ideological manipulation on behalf of one group, the underlying reason for moving from Figure 4.1a to Figure 4.1c and beyond, namely to *representation,* is the growing complexity of communities and the technical limit to actual physical co-presence of humans. That is particularly true when the humans are supposed to engage in meaningful debate: 50,000 people in a football-stadium are a mass, not an assembly. It is by no means a coincidence that the size of governing assemblies which allow every member to participate in a debate, such as our modern parliaments, is around 500 in maximum size. Data from the Interparliamentary Union shows, for example, that of 260 parliamentary bodies registered worldwide only 15 consist of more than 500 members; amongst them is the Ninth European Parliament, which has 736 members, and which is famous for regular absences (cf. the data collated by the Interparliamentary Union on www.ipu.org). Bodies divided into speakers and voters, such as the Athenian Courts which assembled up to 6,000 people but did not allow questions, only a yes or no vote, could be much larger.

Athenian Democracy versus Roman Republic: Political versus Societal

The term public is not Greek, of course, but Latin. As is commonly known, *republic,* as a political concept, derives from the term *res publica* which, in turn, denotes a public affair, *something concerning everybody.* A republic, as opposed to a monarchy, is defined by the fact that the people (*populi*) are the sovereign. As Cicero (106–43 BC), maybe the most eminent theorist of the Roman Republic, makes clear, *the people* does not simply mean a mass assembly, but a congregation of people who agree on a common law for a common purpose *(utilitatis communione sociatus).* Arendt (2010, p. 38) points out, however, that the word *social,* from which the term *society* derives, does not exist in the Greek language. What emerges with the Roman Republic, although it might have been in existence before, is something that was understood differently during the Athenian democracy.

The very elitist political–private divide was dissolved, it seems, by introducing a third element, namely *society*. Arendt (2010, p. 47) argues that the concept of society evolved as the necessities of daily life, the household affairs hitherto left in the dark as private, entered into the light of the public–political sphere. Figure 4.2 illustrates the difference. The duality of politics versus private had suddenly become a trinity.

1. The arena of the *political* was in itself a trinity: (a) the center of the state, represented by holding *offices of state* and political *power* on the one hand, (b) the *public life* (acclaiming and controlling office-holders) with political *influence* on the other (cf. Habermas, 2006, p. 417, for the differentiation), and (c) the *audience,* again acclaiming and controlling office-holders and candidates.
2. There was private life, in the circle of the family under the *paterfamilias*.
3. Finally, there was an intermediary *societal sphere,* which was neither purely political nor purely private, where one has to live and be seen as living as society demands: a sphere which was private, but not secret. It was here, suddenly, that the private affairs of political office-holders became important. It was here, also, that office-holders needed to discuss the common good, meaning the material, private welfare of everybody or a large number of people. And it was here as well, Arendt (2010, p. 53) argues, that the notion of the *public household,* or alternatively *a national economy* emerges.

The concept of the state constituting a kind of super-household that takes care of the individual households and the individuals is so self-evident to people in the twenty-first century that it is difficult to imagine its absence. But Arendt (2010, p. 38; p. 42) argues also that a public household was alien to the Hellenic mind: To the much simpler and less interrelated life in the polis, the necessities of life, at least in political theory, were considered private and separate, as shown in Figure 4.2. The ancient polis was not a public household and not even a society in today's sense, as the Roman Republic began to be. The change was reflected in the topics deliberated in the public sphere and the arguments that could be successfully employed to gain access and garner public support: what we would call the *public calculus.* One needs to be aware that in the Athenian democracy, every private interest, be it commercial, artistic or otherwise, was banned from political deliberation: a fact that led Max Weber to dub the Athenian democracy a "*pensionopolis*" populated by "consumerist proletariat" (Weber, 1924, p. 147; see also Arendt, 2010, p. 46). If a citizen possessed land outside

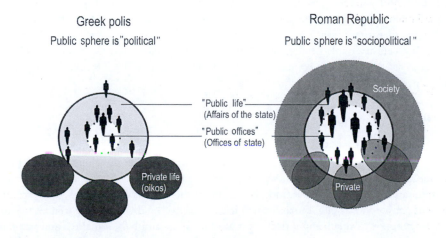

Figure 4.2 The "Invention" of Society

the polis, he was not allowed to vote on whether or not the countryside outside the walls should be scorched in a burned earth policy. In the Roman Republic the separation was no longer absolute. Societal and private interests, the interests of the Patrician houses in particular, began to infringe on the political. Individual actors—the most prominent possibly being Julius Caesar, a PR case *par excellence*— portrayed their personal interests in the public sphere as political, societal, or socio-political, namely, as Rome's interest, as *res publica*. Public office, for example, governorship of a foreign province, was shamelessly regarded as an opportunity to make a private fortune. But at the same time to rise to public office one had to spend a fortune on public projects such as *panem et circenses,* feeding and entertaining the masses, that is, doing good in a way that strongly foreshadowed the mores of modern corporate social responsibility. Conversely, society began to pervade private life to a degree that Romans found it necessary to retire to the country in order to "escape."

From Feudalism to the Enlightenment: From Enforcing Society to Representing It

After the collapse of the Roman Empire, the political order proposed by Cicero was not resurrected. The political order emerging in medieval Europe after the period referred to as *the Dark Ages* was by and large feudal in character. Scholars (e.g., Habermas, 1990, p. 60) generally agree that, although the categories *privatus* and *publicus* still existed due to the traditions of Roman Law, there was no such thing as a public sphere separate from offices of the state on the one hand and private life on the other hand. In the feudal state, private power, towards the *familia* or towards feudal vassals, was not exercised in contrast to the political power of office-holders but as a form of it. Both forms of power derived from one source, the rule of the land; both forms of power upheld, to put it simply, the God-given order of things. Arendt (2010, pp. 38–45) draws attention to two aspects here: the nature of political power on the one hand and the markedly spiritual character of the Middle Ages on the other.

What is Political Power?

The first point is that the feudal view of the *paterfamilias,* the head of the family, was to conceive of him as a little political ruler: a family monarch. Nothing, Arendt (2010, p. 38) argues, could be more contrary to the ancient conception of politics as the affairs of the polis. The head of the oikos was not a political but a *private* ruler—and as such his power was unbounded and unchallengeable. Unbounded and unchallengeable political power, in contrast, was alien to the ancient Athenian democracy. Not only, as Arendt argues, because the power of the tyrant was bounded by the united citizens but because unchecked *political* power constituted a contradiction in itself. Although the Greek polis seems far away, one needs to bear the distinction in mind. After all, the twenty-first century is a century of clashes between private and corporate interests, where the CEO considers himself the *paterfamilias* of his company (the word *company* derives itself from *cum panis,* that is sharing bread, a necessity of life, with each other).

The Worldly and the Spiritual

The second point of importance about feudal Europe is the role of the Christian church (Arendt, 2010, p. 44; pp. 65–70). After the collapse of the Roman Empire, the church provided the one and only public body to identify with. After *the good life* of the polis as a philosophical and the Roman Empire as a military project, the Catholic Church was the grand project of Western Europe. The duality of private versus public transformed itself, thus, to the duality of the *worldly* and the *spiritual*. Interestingly enough the metaphorical contrast of darkness and light remained and was embodied in architecture and art. Private life was a place of darkness and squalor, whereas the spiritual was one of light and glory. St. Augustine, one of the eminent "doctors of the church" (Russell, 2006, p. 314) makes it clear in his text *City of God* by contrasting two cities. In one area the human being is base, weak and selfish, in the other he is lifted to a realm of the sublime, albeit a *post-mortem* one.

The Christian church transposed the human desire to distinguish itself in a grand and noble project, to be part of a grand project that would outlive itself, towards the contra-factual, towards the afterlife. The grand project of feudal Europe was in essence spiritual—and the only secular project that united Europe, the crusades, proves the point. It also becomes clear why the *states,* if the term is appropriate, expanded the realm of private rule until everyone was incorporated into the body politic, until no-one was a free man (free women being inconceivable at that time anyway) except the monarch who, in turn, was responsible to God. The development took centuries, of course, and it also took centuries until it was adequately reflected in theory.

Perhaps the most stringent and disillusioned theoretical conception is to be found in Hobbes's *Leviathan* (1651). The famous title page displays the absolute monarch as consisting of hundreds of citizens bound together by social contract. The very same idea was summed up succinctly, although with a different theoretical foundation, by perhaps the most absolute European monarch, the French King Louis XIV (1638–1715), who insisted he had been appointed by God: *L'état, c'est moi,* he is alleged to have said.

Herrschaftskommunikation and repräsentative Öffentlichkeit

Subsequently, as Habermas also argues, it became increasingly necessary to establish a new basis of legitimacy. To be precise, it became necessary to communicate the old basis in a new way to plug the gap the argument of the God-given order of things used to fill. The basis of the old and new legitimation was *superiority,* in person, in heritage, in blood. In the old way, superiority was demonstrated when and if challenged: a simple peasant was no match for a highly trained professional warrior clad in chain mail or iron and living his life in accordance with a warrior code of courage and honor. In the new way it was represented *before* it was challenged and in order to avoid the challenge. The representation of the superiority of the ruling class *for* the public, not *in* the public, is what Habermas calls "repräsentative Öffentlichkeit" (representative public sphere) (cf. Habermas, 1990, pp. 58–67). A kind of representative public sphere already existed in medieval Europe. One just has to imagine the effects of a Catholic mass, held in mysterious incomprehensible Latin, in a cathedral incomparable to any other edifice, to understand that the church had practiced representation of power [*Herrschaftskommunikation*] *par excellence.*

But with the undermined credibility of the church, and a higher emphasis on the individual as opposed to God, worldly representation became more and more important. Worldly power representation in the *Renaissance* was different in character, with the educated *courtier* as the ideal. But the basic idea was the same: The ruling class demonstrated its superiority by modelling itself, and by being the ideal of the time; by distinguishing itself, in clothing, in habit, in language, and thus by illuminating itself in front of the amazed masses. The message communicated by the pomp and splendor of Renaissance rulers such as England's Queen Elizabeth I (1533–1603) is clear: We are so far apart, peasant, burgher, craftsman, that it is inconceivable that you have the same rights and freedoms as we have.

As the states became more centralized, especially in Britain and France, so did representation (cf. Habermas 1990, 58 – 67). The aristocracy was now assembled at the royal court to add to the glamour and glory of the monarch. The Baroque era transferred the court festivities away from the people to pompous residences but that only added to the overawing effect. Refinements of court etiquette led to even more distinguished clothing and habit, but did not alter the general character of a representative public sphere enacted to dazzle the people: to exclude, not to include. There was no public control of what was going on behind the doors of the Vatican in Rome, the *palazzi* of the Medici in Italy or behind the doors of Versailles in Paris, and the respective power-holders would not have accepted the concept. The papacy in the Middle Ages did not meddle in European affairs on behalf of a mandate by the people, but to represent God's power on earth. Until the end of the *anciens régimes* the possession of a certain territory and the well-being of the people populating it were considered a private affair of the ruling family: politics was not a matter of society, but was secret and arcane.

The Duality of the Public Sphere Revisited—or the Pursuit of Private Affairs

While the citizens of the cities gained power during the late Middle Ages and the Renaissance, one might ask why the following centuries brought absolutism. Arendt (2010, pp. 81–89) argues that the rising merchant and commercial classes did not necessarily press for expansion of the public sphere but for expansion of the private sphere. The merchant and commercial class did not want to be included in the affairs of the state as much as it wanted to be excluded from interference: The citizens wanted a stable framework in order to concentrate on making money. Here, again, we have the basic duality of the public sphere as a place for acclamation on the one hand, and a mechanism of control on the other—but nested in the framework of a much more complex, multilayered and functionally differentiated society (as analyzed by Marx, Durkheim, Tönnies and Weber, for example and as cited in Imhof, 2003, pp. 196–197). Suddenly, society not only offered one playing field to distinguish oneself amongst equals, but many playing fields. One could rise in the world and distinguish oneself, at least in the eyes of one's equals, as an artist, scholar, merchant, soldier, or even bureaucrat. The price, of course, was that one had to concentrate on one's private affairs, or one's private public sphere, so to speak. Note that nowadays, in the twenty-first century, a career in a global corporation is as complex, that is, as political, as a career in public office—a fact which links with the observation of Roman author Pliny the Younger (Arendt, 2010, p. 74) that to the slave the household of the *paterfamilias* is the same as the Republic for the citizen.

From the Enlightenment to Modernity: From Action to Behavior

If one describes the era from the Middle Ages onwards as the era of superiority of the person, the period thereafter can be described as the era of superiority of reason. The core idea of Enlightenment, as it was put forward most stringently and pointedly by German philosopher Immanuel Kant (1724–1804), is that humankind may not rely on tradition or scripture or the guidance of others but on the faculty of its very own reasoning. Kant, of course, needs to be appreciated against the backdrop of the general intellectual climate and amidst other eminent political philosophers such as Jean-Jacques Rousseau (1712–1778), John Locke (1632–1704), Jeremy Bentham (1748–1832), John Stuart Mill (1806–1873) and Alexis de Tocqueville (1805–1859). What the ideals of the Enlightenment meant for the development of the concept of the public sphere in liberal democracies, and later in bourgeois society and social welfare mass democracy, is portrayed and analyzed by Habermas's habilitation thesis covering *Strukturwandel der Öffentlichkeit* [Structural Transformation of the Public Sphere], hereafter *Structural Transformation*) (Habermas 1962, 1989). It is not necessary to repeat the main arguments *en bloc*: Habermas's reasoning is well-known, it is highly complex and detailed, and we refer to it repeatedly in the course of the article, particularly when it comes to Habermas's critique of modern mass democracies. What is important, however, is to emphasize some subtle but important shifts that characterized the Age of Reason.

The Two Eyes of the Public: Society, the Intimate Sphere and its Counterpart Celebrity

We have traced the rise of *society* as a concept interrelated with but ultimately different from the *political* in its original sense in Habermas's and especially Arendt's works. The political, we observed, was concerned with being a member of a state, with the higher functions of the human—whereas the lower functions of existence as a member of the species were hidden away in the private. Society, in contrast, meant that the hitherto private affairs of material welfare—of everything we refer to as social today—became a matter of public interest and public deliberation. The world of the political in the polis was maybe not as harsh as the world of the barbaric warrior, but competitive nevertheless. It was, as we would say in modern parlance, a world for adults. But at least it was well-defined and the individual (i.e., individual male) was permitted to take refuge in his private sphere.

The emerging modern society held together by the state as some kind of super household, in contrast, pervaded each and every aspect of life, from birth to death. The modern welfare society takes care of the individual, but it also keeps it in a state of dependent semi-childhood an ancient Greek presumably would have considered humiliating. One is expected to *behave* in society which is, as Arendt (2010) takes great care to prove, not at all the same as *acting*. French philosopher Rousseau, by rebelling against society's all-pervasiveness, defined the intimate sphere as a kind of sanctum in which original humanity, original in the double sense of the word, was unspoiled by society (cf. Arendt, 2010, pp. 49–50; Habermas, 1990, pp. 238–247). Here, the individual was moved by deep emotions instead of enacting superficial sentiment. Here, the individual was a natural human being (exactly what the Greeks despised), not a conforming member of society.

In our modern understanding the word *intimate* seems to be defined in a similar, but nevertheless different, way. Although the intimate sphere is undoubtedly pervaded by society, it is a sphere that is granted as a refuge and protected from the public eye. For example, when British yellow press newspaper *News of the World,* in 2008, covered the story of Formula One functionary Max Mosley being whipped and tortured by prostitutes dressed in Nazi-like attire, the public's interest was immense, its disgust genuine. But the courts ruled, under so-called "privacy law," that the newspaper had no right to publish the story: Formula One is a private business and Max Mosley's sexual preferences are intimate affairs as long as they do not have a bearing on his ability to represent it.[2] Media observers consequently fear a *Mosley effect,* that is, media coverage of the rich and powerful being silenced.

It is by no means a coincidence, Arendt argues (2010, pp. 48–49), that Rousseau described the intimate sphere in contrast to society, not in contrast to politics. It is the public eye constituted from private people crammed together in society that is interested in Mr. Mosley's sexual aberrations, not the political public eye whose ultimate institutions are court, jail, and police (in other countries that would have been different, of course). What fascinates private people is the fact that an individual dares to misbehave. What irritates and outrages is the fact that the individual, being rich and powerful, misbehaves in secret, whereas the ordinary citizen deems him or herself under constant surveillance by peers, neighbors, and colleagues. Misbehavior, thus, seems to be one of the few forms of acting in an all-pervading society: either misbehavior "enjoyed" by the individual in secret—or breaking the mold and doing what is necessary to get a tough job done (which might not be enjoyable but is *gratifying,* as taking over a job in the public eye lends "importance" to the individual). One only has to look at the typical ingredients of the Hollywood action movie to see that transgressing societal borders in the course of some higher purpose, action instead of behavior, is a basic building block of entertainment and fiction today.

The twentieth and early twenty-first century is marked by another phenomenon related to the intimate: the celebrity. It is clear that there always have been famous people, for example, war heroes, explorers, theater actors. But what is a relatively new phenomenon, probably going back to the star system of Hollywood and the early publicity activities of people such as P. T. Barnum (cf. Grunig & Hunt, 1984, pp. 28–30), is the short-lived fame routinely and professionally manufactured by media and publicity agents working hand in hand to satisfy each other's needs. We define a celebrity as someone who is first and foremost famous *for being famous*. As such, a celebrity is much more, and also much less, than a prominent person. German chancellor Angela Merkel is a prominent person because of high public office, but she is not a celebrity. The interesting thing about celebrities such as Paris Hilton is that in the ultimate stage of celebrity status the duality of the public sphere already encountered in antiquity is fused. The celebrity lives its whole life, it seems, in the glaring light of the public. But with the celebrity it becomes clearer than ever that the public sphere cannot be reduced to the political—it is societal. For what the societal and not political audience really is interested in is not the public performance, but the private, the intimate sphere. People want to know about the celebrity's secrets. It is for the very reason that the celebrity is not really expected to do something that everything the celebrity does has the potential of being action. What the celebrity says or does, even if it is completely irrelevant to society by any other standards, is construed as a statement. That is particularly true for misbehavior, of course, which reinforces the notion that the celebrity—liberated of the pressure to earn a daily living, by the way—leads the true and free life of late modernity.

People as Representatives of Organizations

The celebrity, in a way, is the heir of the free of the polis. Because the celebrity is rich and famous, everything the celebrity does that is dictated by wanting; it is action, not necessary and expected behaviour. It is that very fact that, for instance, makes a testimonial by supermodel Heidi Klum valuable—even though everyone knows she is paid for it. The normal citizen, in contrast, is bound by societal expectations and the need to earn a living, in particular. The office-holder, the person who is in public life because of responsibility, is bound by something else. Chancellor Merkel is not a free agent but bound by the fact that she does not speak for herself but as a representative of her party, her government, and Germany—in short, she represents some kind of organization or institution. It is by no means a coincidence that modern sociology started to question the scope of "real" human action in society, and it seems safe to say that modern currents, such as systems theory in the Luhmann tradition (1987) or neo-institutionalism (DiMaggio & Powell, 1983), portray the human as *behaving* rather than acting. But the "iron cage"[3] hailed and lamented by Max Weber (e.g., 1920, p. 203) as limiting the selfish actions of individuals in the most rational type of government, the bureaucracy, was nested in a grand project, namely the nation-state. Late modern society does not seem to offer a grand project any more. The "war on terror" does not seem to inspire as much enthusiasm as the medieval crusades did.

The Public Sphere and Organizations and Institutions

Figure 4.3 displays the same basic layout as the Roman Republic but with crucial differences. One difference is the existence of organizations, as illustrated by the house-like squares on the border. Another difference is that full-blooded individuals, as illustrated by the figures, are far outnumbered

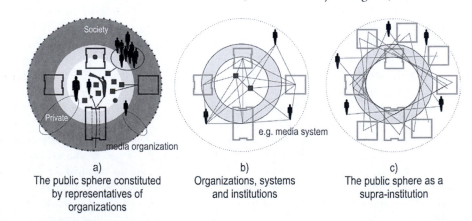

a)
The public sphere constituted by representatives of organizations

b)
Organizations, systems and institutions

c)
The public sphere as a supra-institution

Figure 4.3 The Public Sphere

by representatives, illustrated by squares. Both figures and squares constitute actors. Gerhards (1994) and Gerhards and Neidhardt (1990), for example, differentiate various types of speakers, namely representatives, advocates, experts, intellectuals and journalists as commentators (cf. Bentele, 2005, p. 709; Bentele, Liebert, & Seeling, 1997, pp. 225–226). In Figure 4.3a, representatives are displayed as being bound to and on the payroll of organizations professionally, whereas advocates articulate the more or less aggregated interests of certain groups in society, not always being bound to them. Media professionals, for example journalists, talk show hosts, and television presenters, are privileged because they have a guaranteed speaker role in the public—they are thus equipped with a mega-phone.

In modern societies there are very few individuals who act in public life representing only themselves. The place for the modern individual is in society, but by the aid of modern mass media everyone enjoys a reserved seat in the ranks of the audience of the public sphere. One also enjoys a privileged sphere that is defined as outside society's demands and pressures, the intimate sphere. There are individuals, of course, who really act in the public sphere as full-blooded individuals. One type is the larger-than-life *celebrity* who is not only interested in upholding celebrity status but displays some social agenda, such as George Clooney. Another type is the eminent intellectual, who is "free-floating" (Mannheim, 1929), and who gains access to the public sphere by virtue of fielding outstanding arguments: people like Jürgen Habermas, Peter Sloterdijk, or Gertrud Höhler. The expert is another type similar but not equivalent to the intellectual, as he/she is bound to the system, which gives him/her expert status. A third type, finally, is the individual gaining access by taking the short-cut through a media organization, as portrayed by the sluice in the house at 6 o' clock position in Figure 4.3a. Here we have the 15-minutes-of-fame-people fed to the public by shows such as *Germany's Next Top Model* and *Deutschland sucht den Superstar* or its equivalents around the world. All actors pursue strategies and strategic communication, of course. As Neidhardt (1994, p. 18) points out, however, there are two stages in public rhetoric: The first is the *thematization stage* and the second is the *persuasion stage*. First, actors have to gain access to the public sphere. Only when their topic is debated, they can convince people that their point of view on the topic is right. It is by no means a detail that society and the sphere of potential actors, that is, public life, is not separated by a line as is the case in Figures 4.1 and 4.2. Modern society is open in a way that with enough pressure or good arguments any group may gain access to the outer circle of public life and may even dispatch a person, after a while turning into a representative, to the inner circle. That is the fact Habermas admitted to having underrated in the 1990 foreword to *Structural Transformation* (1990, p. 15; pp. 31–33). It is also worth noting that the inner circle is constituted, as was the case in Figures 4.1 and 4.2, by potential actors on the boundaries. In modern societies the warrior with a spear is not the only type of potential actor. In fact, most of the boundary is constituted by abstract concepts, as represented by the black dots: the accepted routines, customs and traditions of the sociopolitical life—in effect, the rules, resources and modalities Giddens (1986) points to in his *Theory of Structuration*. Some arguments are protected and, if the need arises, even enforced by watch-dog organizations, such as the one represented by the top square.

In the ancient and primitive systems, the routines, customs and traditions rested in the heads of the potential actors. The real difference, again, lies in the fact that modern society is infinitely more complex and much more constituted by organizations and institutions. Figure 4.3a displays organizations on the surface as houses, be it a private company such as BMW, a private media organization such as CNN, a public broadcaster such as the BBC, a non-governmental organization such as Greenpeace, or a public organization such as the courts, the police, or jails. That is the way the normal citizen views everyday life. But if we imagine for a moment that we could draw a map of relevant interactions, relations and connections—relevant with a view to a certain aspect such as finance, legality, welfare—we would see a diagram like Figure 4.3b, although much more complex and confusing. We would see systems in which different houses had different functions, some crucial and irreplaceable, some redundant. We would also see some persons in the private realm connected to almost every aspect of this or that system. Again the system is not visible in itself, unlike the institutions the systems guarantee. The financial system, for example, consists of a lot of banks and a few state-owned or -controlled organizations. Individually, the banks are redundant but if a lot of large banks fail at the same time, the whole system is in danger, as we have experienced lately. The institution the financial system establishes, and which we everyday experience, is money. The media are, in fact, another system. What we experience as manifestation of the media system, and the journalistic sub-system, is news.

The Public Sphere as a Supra-Institution

Figure 4.3c answers the question what the public sphere really is and what it always has been, we believe: a kind of a supra-institution. The supra-institution emerges and is sustained by a lot of individuals, organizations, institutions interacting in a certain way, pursuing certain strategies, with certain arguments. The interactions are depicted as sub-surface because the actors concerned do not necessarily intend to sustain the public sphere but, as *Systems Theory* makes us aware, by pursuing certain strategies with certain arguments they effectually do sustain it. Conversely, other actors who try to uphold the public sphere as a normative ideal actually undermine and weaken the supra-institution.

The public sphere is not simply another institution or sub-system of society on a par with others, because it is concerned with not only a single matter, such as finance, legality, or welfare—it is concerned with all. We link up here with Luhmann's (1990, p. 181; cf. also Marcinkowski, 1993, p. 118; Gerhards, 1994, p. 87; Imhof, 2003, p. 202) representation of the public sphere as a mirror that helps society to observe itself. This comparison has one advantage and one disadvantage, however. The advantage is that the idea of a mirror conveys that the public sphere is not identical to society but offers a reflection of it. What we have described as representatives, thus, are reflections of groups of interest in society. The disadvantage is the implicit assumption that there is a causal congruence between what is going on in the shadows of society and what is going on in the brightly lit public sphere. We believe that a perfect and perfectly clean public sphere, to return to our earlier metaphor, does indeed reflect or illuminate the concerns of the people and groups in society in a kind of isomorphic way. But that is a normative ideal. Neither the cleanliness of the mirror nor the mirror itself is guaranteed by any single institution or establishment.

The Mass Media Beyond Modernity

We have not yet treated the one phenomenon which perhaps is most important: *mass media* (for the concept of *media society* cf. Jarren & Donges, 2006). But we have good reason for postponing the discussion. Although the rise of mass media over the course of centuries has been of fundamental importance for almost every change in society since the invention of the printing press, the concepts of mass media, society and public sphere have in some way gone hand in hand. The public sphere as we have portrayed it was a sphere in the center of one particular society. The framework for the modern mass media, radio and television, moreover, was the nation state: a state whose institutions constituted both the core and the boundary of the society in question.

Since the beginning of the twenty-first century, however, nation states, mass media and the public sphere have seemed to go their separate ways. The European Union, as has been repeatedly emphasized, is a supra-national state with many functions a state has, but there is no corresponding supranational public sphere at its center, no corresponding European society (cf. Brüggemann, Hepp, Kleinen-von Königslöw & Wessler, 2009; Imhof, 2003, p. 206). The majority of European citizens, we dare say, perceive Brussels as an elitist circle populated by a bureaucratic aristocracy. Despite millions and millions spent on communication, politics in the European Union has not much in common with the affairs of the Greek polis deliberated upon in the agora, and much more in common with the behind-closed-doors machinations of the *Ancien Régime* (cf. Sloterdijk, 2009). But that is not only the fault of the Brussels élite, of course: it is at the same time the fault of the people.

The role of the mass media in integrating modern society, and especially in integrating the modern welfare state mass democracies, scarcely needs mentioning. The earlier mass newspapers, and, later, radio and television, once and for all masked the problem we discussed earlier as technical limits of co-presence. Mass media did not solve the participation problem of the audience–candidate divide, to be sure, but watching the news on television certainly gave the feeling of being part of a society with a center, a society in which people acted and things went right or went wrong; or one that pursued a grand project, be it to fight communism, terrorism or global warming. We believe, therefore, that the development of non-national, non-society-oriented mass media, such as satellite television, the internet, and corporate media, goes hand in hand with *individualization,* a sense of decoupling from society at large—and from big politics at the center of that one society, in particular. Individualization, however, does not necessarily mean retreating towards the intimate sphere and the family circle, which is what happened, for example, in Germany in the era of the *Biedermeier* (a period of political withdrawal in Germany, in arts, architecture, and culture, equivalent to the British *Regency* and the French *Empire*). Individualization as it plays out in the early twenty-first century seems to make good use of the technical possibility to connect to, access, and act in spheres all over the world. We shall return to this point later.

A Model of the Mid-Modern and Late-Modern Public Sphere

Our review of the history of Western European civilization as it relates to the concept of the public sphere has revealed that it is interrelated with other concepts and is entangled with ideas that are at the very core of our civilizations, societies or political systems today. What we wish to do now is to integrate the ideas discussed thus far. We present two models of society with their respective public spheres: first, a model of a modern society with a center, and second, a model of a late modern society that is characterized by the fact that it no longer has a center.

The Mid-Modern Public Sphere: A Society of Organizations

Figure 4.4 shows our model of the modern society, which was valid until the turn from the twentieth to the twenty first century. As has been repeatedly emphasized, the dominant feature of this model is that it is characteristic of a society of organizations, that is, organizations, not people, are the principal actors. The power-plays of organizations are central in such a society. Consider that the recent trend in public relations towards personalization revolved around giving a face to the company, and not returning to the human as agent of action in the style of the entrepreneurial personality (cf. Eisenegger & Wehmeier, 2009). Transparency means throwing a light on what is going on behind the fences and walls and in the executive suites of corporations (cf. Szyszka, 2009, for the concept of *functional transparency*).

The Mass Media Arena, Assembly and Encounter
Levels of the Public Sphere

Maybe the most obvious difference from the earlier illustrations lies in the fact that the experience of modern society is mass mediated in many instances; that is, it is constituted by mass media signified by the antennae connecting to private homes. As we said earlier, the technical problem of limited co-presence is brushed aside once and for all. Everyone can be audience without leaving home: The public sphere is *ubiquitous*. It happens somewhere but it can be experienced, as a media surrogate, everywhere. In comparison, society is also drawn in a lighter grey, symbolizing that liberal society

Günter Bentele and Howard Nothhaft

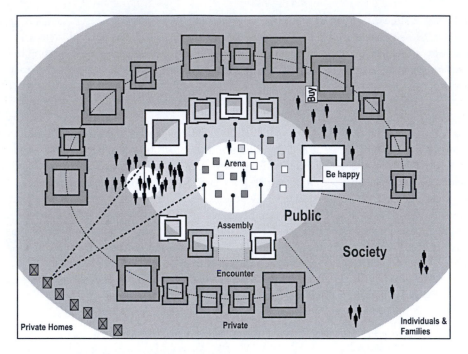

Figure 4.4   The Public Sphere of Modern Societies

is much more tolerant on the one hand, much better illuminated on the other; that is, the light of society illuminates the homes of the individual families. Homosexuality, which was considered a threat to the established order of things in medieval Europe, is accepted as perfectly fine private behavior in a liberal society; a father beating up his children is not a private affair any more, despite the closed doors of the family home. In the late twentieth and early twenty-first century, the two eyes of the public, that is, society's eye demanding *conformity* and the state's political eye demanding *legality,* pierce the closed doors.

As sociologists Gerhards and Neidhardt (Gerhards & Neidhardt, 1990; Gerhards, 1994) have pointed out, the ubiquity of the public sphere leads to three levels of experiencing society: the *encounter level,* the *assembly level* and the *mass media (arena) level.* The experience of modern society, thus, is by no means exclusively mass-mediated. That is a fact too often ignored by theorists prematurely postulating that nothing happens if it does not happen in the media. For instance, if television reports people demonstrating in the streets, the individual may leave her house and go and have a look. The individual then experiences society and its public sphere on the encounter level, as it does when it engages in a conversation about politics *au trottoir* (Luhmann, 1986, p. 75). If the individual decides to take part in the demonstration it experiences society and its public sphere on the *assembly level,* the outer circle: Here we have the sphere covered by the *Situational Theory of Publics* (cf. Grunig & Hunt, 1984, pp. 147–161), and by Hauser's concept of the *rhetorical public sphere* (Hauser, 1998). The individual gains access to the *arena* of society, the inner circle, when it is invited to an established political talk show or when it is singled out to say something on television on the spot of the demonstration. A politician speaking in the parliament, the *Bundestag,* is not automatically public. In the model illustrated in Figure 4.4, the speech takes place in one of the white houses; it becomes public, however, by media attention covering it or, the more frequent case, by the politician making a statement in the public arena.

The arena proper, thus, is no longer only a structure but appears as a kind of force field constituted by media coverage. The capacity of the arena does not constitute a problem in itself any more, as it is mass-mediated: One can receive information about the events in the arena everywhere. The limiting factor is the interest of the people, a condition that has been described as *attention economy* (Franck, 1998). That is particularly the case because information about events in the public sphere is now in competition with other mass media content, namely fiction and entertainment (*Be Happy!*) on the one side, and advertising and marketing (*Buy!*) on the other. Here is the well-known diagnosis of the Frankfurt school's left-wing intellectuals Horkheimer and Adorno that the common people are misled, confused and distracted from proper political participation by the culture industry (cf. Imhof, 2003, pp. 198–199; Müller-Doohm, 2000). Habermas (1990, pp. 225–342, para 16–23) goes even further and complains that the inner circle is taken over by representatives of private interests (represented by dark squares). In 2006, almost 40 years after the first edition of *Structural Transformation*, Habermas's rendering is less categorical, but nevertheless emphasizes inequality and power structures:

> Given the high level of organization and material resources, representatives of functional systems and special interest groups enjoy somewhat privileged access to the media, too. They are in a position to use professional techniques to transform social power into political muscle. Public interest groups and advocates tend likewise to employ corporate communications management methods. It follows that compared with politicians and lobbyists, the actors of civil society are in the weakest position.
>
> *Habermas, 2006, p. 419*

Three Types of Organization

Figure 4.4 depicts three kinds of houses representing organizations, namely, white, light grey and dark grey. The dark grey houses are organizations that are private, not necessarily in ownership, but in interest. The light grey houses are organizations that are public, again not necessarily in owner-ship, but in interest, such as public broadcasters. The white houses are state-governed organizations (*öffentliche Körperschaften),* such as ministries, authorities, regulation boards, and the police. For the purpose of understanding strategic communication, the exact sociological criteria are not of great importance. What is important is the perception. A light grey house is a house that is perceived as pursuing some higher objective although it is not bound to the common good, but to a certain good for a certain group of people. It is by virtue of this perception that houses conquer a position in the inner circle of society, whereas houses pursuing purely private aims, for example profit maximiza-tion for shareholders, are kept out. They are represented nevertheless by certain powers in political parties, and other interests such as trade associations. In post-war Germany, from 1950 to 1990, for example, the inner circle of society was comparatively stable: A couple of corporatist actors, parties, associations and very large companies *did* politics. However, as the empty spot indicates, sometimes houses that do not fulfil the criteria any more are torn down. That is what has happened, to a degree, to the trade unions in Germany. Others may take their place at some point. The Green Party, for example, gained an established position in the inner circle of society during the 1980s in Germany.

The Power Plays of the Houses

The public sphere emerges out of the power plays in the same way as the public sphere of the ting or the polis emerged from people gathering at a special place. The power plays are not visible to the ordinary citizens in everyday life. Nevertheless, it is important not to confuse the power plays of organizations with the systemic relations depicted in Figures 4.3b and 4.3c. Systemic relations can only be grasped on the macro level by a hypothetical outside observer. The antagonism of individual banks, for example, can be *functional* (*eufunctional*) or *dysfunctional* for the financial system regardless of what CEOs of banks, experts or politicians believe or what is said or done. The competitions, antagonisms and coalitions existing in society are played out by organizations acting. Thus, the public sphere is established, maintained and to a degree controlled by organizations; organizations, like people, that first and foremost pursue the aim of surviving themselves, but also organizations, which, unlike people, do not have private lives to retire to. No matter what they do, organizations will not pack up by themselves and say, "Well, we're not needed any more." They will find reasons why they are needed, that is, legitimate themselves, and only if threatened with extinction will they find new areas in which to busy themselves. What they do to survive is public action at first, but the action also affects the structure of society and the public sphere, in particular. Structure and action are two sides of one coin, in the very same way as Giddens's Theory of Structuration (1986) describes it.

The Late Twentieth and Early Twenty-First Century Arena: A Society of Communications

Figure 4.3 still describes, we believe, a variety of public phenomena, but it does not describe the public sphere of late modern society in the twenty-first century as we experience it today, at least not fully and satisfactorily (one has to be aware that when Habermas wrote *Structural Transformation* he had no personal experience of television, cf. 1990, p. 29). The picture painted in Figure 4.3 seems old-fashioned because it is static. The core of the model is that organizations occupied a certain position in twentieth century society, and it was that very position that guaranteed the right to dispatch representatives to the arena. During the last quarter of the twentieth century, we believe, the rather established system, described as corporatist, gradually changed. The change was driven by numerous factors, but apart from a general maturation of society it is impossible to single out reasons. The most important technical step was the spread of the internet.

One social driver of change, we believe, was a clear though one-sided development, namely, the rise of public relations, as Habermas pointed out in 1962 (Habermas, 1990, pp. 289–292). What differentiates Figure 4.4 from Figure 4.3, thus, is the fact that organizations not only started to act in the public sphere to further their interests, for example by press and media work, but also by contributing to their own public spheres by *publishing* themselves. The antennae on organizations in Figure 4.4 illustrate the public activities of organizations. The lighted circles symbolize that organizations, through public relations, illuminate their own activities. What gradually emerged during the last decades of the twentieth and the first decade of the twenty-first century by the intermeshing of organizational public activity is a public sphere of communications that takes place on a shiny, well-lit stratum above society. The metaphors of the polis resurface here. Again we have a sphere of real necessities, which is considered a darker place below the lighted public sphere; and the individual, it seems, still wants to be lifted out of the squalor of everyday life.

The well-lit world constituted by organizations putting themselves in a good light is the sphere constructivist communication theorists such as Merten (2008) refer to when postulating that the twenty-first century citizen lives, at least to a degree, in a fictitious world. Taken at face value, the world the individual experiences is, indeed, fictitious, brave and new. It is a world where insurance companies are *partners,* soap brands are *friends,* and science-fiction series, talk shows and reality TV provide role models for adolescents in para social interaction. But it is entirely misleading to construe the individual as living only in this sphere, as being caught up in an artificial world. The individual is quite used to the brave new world and, contrary to theoretical expectation, by and large acts quite competently in it. One reason for this is, of course, that the normal individual experiences the everyday discrepancies not only between the inside and outside of the organization it works in, as it did in the mid twentieth century, but also the discrepancies between the communication sphere and the social sphere. It is by no means a coincidence that the old twentieth century society *shines through* the fabric of the emergent twenty-first century sphere on the left-hand side of Figure 4.5. No matter

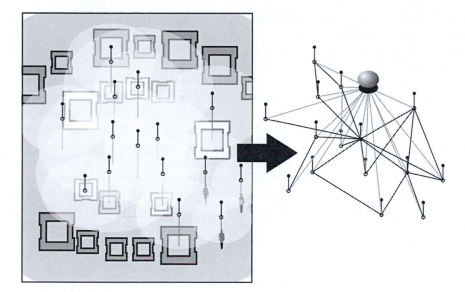

Figure 4.5   The Public Sphere of Late Modern Societies

how much you are involved in the blogosphere, occasionally you go to a pub, your bicycle is stolen, or your neighbors talk behind your back.

The dominant characteristic of the twenty first century public sphere, thus, is not that it is virtual, because with the upper and lower sphere co-existing it is not. The dominant characteristic is that the communication sphere, to a degree, collapses structural constraints, such as time, distance, technical limitations, and physical handicaps of the person, to mention a few. The public sphere is no longer a place of gathering as the *tingstead*. Neither is it a force field of media attention constituted by a limited amount of actors. It is a network of points of interest. Something, for example a brand, the swine-flu, a politician, or any other topic, is in the public sphere because communicators, who are points in the network of communications, communicate about it. The illustration on the right-hand side of Figure 4.5 illustrates that communication involves a dual relation: someone you communicate *with* (black lines), to whom you *push* your communication towards or who *pulls* communication from you; and something you communicate about (grey lines), an *object of reference*. What we see, consequently, is a network of communicators talking about an object of reference with each other. It is here that the perspective expounded by Peters (2007, p. 329; Peters & Wessler, 2006; see also Brüggemann et al., 2009, p. 394) begins to be the only one that makes sense: namely, that public spheres are spheres of communication characterized by a high density of communication and, furthermore, defined by the density within the sphere as being higher than the density towards the outside of the sphere.

Normative and Epistemological Aspects

We have come a long way from Athenian democracy to the globalized, late modern society of today. As we have announced from the very beginning, the models presented have been rather descriptive. In conclusion we want to touch upon *normative aspects* that have a bearing on strategic communication.

A lot of theoretical effort has been spent, it seems, on arguing why and how the court of public opinion is capable of passing judgment, and declaring a matter legitimate or not; or why and when public deliberation can be expected to be rational, fair or good. It appears to us, however, that the theoretical discussion about what constitutes a clean public sphere, and by whose interests the public discourse is muddied (Habermas, 2006, p. 416), undermined, bought, colonized or refeudalized, is not only age-old, but theoretical and practical at the same time. The purely theoretical search for a neat formula by which to decide what belongs to a clean, unspoiled, genuinely democratic public sphere, is futile. Strategic communication in the public sphere always means arguing that your interest is *also* in the interest of the public, of society in general, in some way or another. And it is the number 1 counterstrategy to generously declare your opponents' interest legitimate, yes—but legitimate only *as a private* affair. That is the reason, incidentally, why public relations suffers from such a bad reputation (for this argument see Nothhaft, 2010, pp. 202–204): If the proponent *succeeds* in gaining access to the public arena, it is because the issue at hand is accepted as a genuine political question, worthy of public attention. If the proponent fails, however, his interest is refused as "attention-seeking," as "populism," as "mere public relations." Public relations' bad image, thus, is at least partly due to the fact that successful public relations does not appear to be public relations. What we need to understand, thus, is the dynamic calculus by which selection and deselection of matters as worthy of public deliberation, as worthy of public support, works in reality in the here and now.

Epistemological Assumptions: a Reconstructive Approach

Apart from the normative ideal that the matters deliberated in the public sphere should be worthy of public deliberation, there is another normative ideal, which is, we believe, much simpler and more straightforward; namely, the principle that what is said in the public sphere should be true. We have already alluded to the temptation to employ constructivist theory to construe the twenty-first century public sphere as a purely and exclusively virtual public sphere that has severed every link with societal reality—reality being a questionable concept in the constructivist framework anyway. We believe that that is misleading: The public sphere does not exist without a society around and underneath it. Synchronically, here and now, people believe what they see on television or read in the newspaper because it is in the media. But when one looks at trust in media diachronically, over time, actors and representatives in the public sphere need to connect to what is going on in society, otherwise trust in the media erodes fairly quickly, as was the case in the former GDR where few people believed in the official version of events. Whether connecting means reflecting (causal congruence), reconstructing or constructing is an epistemological question. Our position, expounded by Bentele (2008a, 2008b), quite clearly is that connecting means re-constructing. A true statement reconstructs in the light of the public sphere what is going on in the semi-darkness of society. A politician who says "what the people think" does not necessarily mirror what is out there in society. As it is, the facts out there are, indeed, a questionable concept. The politician offers a version of his own, of course. But it is not a version that she makes up as she wishes but a version that makes sense, and one that does not contradict what the audience factually experiences every day. If you tell everybody that socialism is a blessing when the shelves in the shop are empty, people will not believe it after a while but will begin to believe you are a liar or crazy—in any case, unfit to govern. In other words, there is a corridor that limits your maneuverable space when trying to make sense out of reality (Bentele 2008a, p. 158).

The audience grants that actors in the public may have a different perspective, that they may select other things as important and that they construct a different sense out of the situation, but perspective, selection and construction have limits beyond which the communicator discredits her or himself (Bentele, 2008a, pp. 152–158). That is particularly true, of course, when other communicators appear who deliberately discredit the actor in question by pointing out, for example, errors, contradictions, and discrepancies. Figure 4.5 depicts, thus, that the virtual public sphere is virtual with a twist. The twist is that structural properties, the fact that one actor represents a multinational company and another a small antidiscrimination office, no longer carries any privilege. When an organizational representative claims something, for example, she cannot rely on being the only one who has access to the organization's private and secret interior, that is, the inner courtyard of the house. Another actor, maybe from within the same house, may raise an antenna at any time and claim the opposite, for example, type a critical blog entry. As such, on even ground, strategic communication has indeed returned to equals meeting equals to determine who is best.

We conclude by pointing out one consequence of our two-layered model: As communication becomes increasingly self-referential in fragmented, self-contained publics, it appears necessary to dedicate more and more research towards *transfer processes* between the upper stratum and the lower, that is, answering *how, when and why* public communication leads to public action, to political measures, to societal change. When something was publicly discussed in the early and mid twentieth century, we argue, the debate would lead to consequences vaguely mirroring the deliberation. In the 1970s and 1980s, every Monday the powerful in Germany trembled: What would *Der Spiegel,* the investigative news magazine, uncover? Arguably, that is no longer the case. Trends, media hypes, and scandals come and go from time to time with unpredictable overreactions as consequences, frequently without any "real" consequences at all. The twenty-first century appears to be characterized by a lot of communication but the relation between public communication and public action seems to grow more and more significant. Researchers in public relations and strategic communications are the one group of scholars, it seems, who can come to grips with this phenomenon.

Notes

1 This chapter appeared as an article in *International Journal of Strategic Communication*, *4*(2), 93–116. 2010. It is reprinted with the permission of the publisher.
2 The fulcrum of the court case in Britain, astoundingly, was the question whether the "orgy" was a "Nazi orgy." Daily Mail columnist Stephen Glover recounts the judge's argumentation:

Though German had been spoken during the orgy, and though uniforms had been worn and there had been play-acting which seemed to evoke concentration camps, the judge did not accept that it had been an Nazi affair. He concluded that if it had been he would have found in the newspaper's favour since Mr. Mosley was a public figure and "the people of all races and religions" with whom he had to deal might have been shocked." But as, in his view, it was not a Nazi orgy, he believed that Mr Mosley was entitled to his privacy.

Glover continues, quite reasonably:

Mr. Justice Eady's distinction between Nazi and non-Nazi orgies is obviously crackers. http://www.dailymail.co.uk/debate/article-1238131/STEPHEN-GLOVER Max-Mosley-abhorrent-behaviour-law-protects-rich-powerful.html

3 Weber's original expression is "stahlhartes Gehäuse," literally "shell as hard as steel," but translated by Talcott Parsons as "iron cage." Weber himself refers to the concept in various texts but the one quoted is perhaps the most famous and influential.

References

Arendt, H. (1958). *The human condition*. Chicago, IL: Chicago University Press.
Arendt, H. (2010). *Vita Activa. Vom tätigen Leben* [The human condition]. München, Germany: Piper.
Bentele, G. (2005). Public sphere (Öffentlichkeit). In R. L. Heath (Ed.). *Encyclopedia of public relations* (Vols 1 and 2, pp. 707–710). Thousand Oaks, CA: Sage.
Bentele, G. (2008a). Ein rekonstruktiver Ansatz der Public Relations [A reconstructive approach to public relations]. In G. Bentele, R. Fröhlich & P. Szyszka (Eds.), *Handbuch der Public Relations. Wissenschaftliche Grundlagen und berufliches Handeln* [Handbook of Public Relations. Scientific foundations and professional practice]. *Mit Lexikon. 2., korrigierte und erweiterte Auflage* (pp. 147–160). Wiesbaden: VS.
Bentele, G. (2008b). Public relations theory: the reconstructive approach. In A. Zerfass, B. van Ruler and K. Sriramesh (Eds.), *Public relations research* (pp. 19–31). Wiesbaden: VS.
Bentele, G., Liebert, T. & Seeling, S. (1997). Von der Determination zur Intereffikation. Ein integriertes Modell zum Verhältnis von Public Relations und Journalismus [From determination to intereffication. An integrated

model of the relation between public relations and journalism]. In G. Bentele & M. Haller (1997), *Aktuelle Entstehung von Öffentlichkeit. Akteure–Strukturen–Veränderungen* [The Formation of the Public Sphere: Actors, Structures, Transformations] (pp. 225–250) Konstanz: UVK.

Brüggemann, M., Hepp, A., Kleinen-von Königslöw, K., & Wessler, H. (2009). Transnationale Öffentlichkeit in Europa: Forschungsstand und Perspektiven [The transnational public sphere in Europe: Research status and perspectives]. *Publizistik, 54*(3),391–414.

Calhoun, C. (1992). *Habermas and the public sphere*. Cambridge, MA: MIT Press.

DiMaggio, P. & Powell, W. (1983). The iron cage revisited: Institutional isomorphism and collective rationality in organizational fields. *American Sociological Review, 48*(4), 147–160.

Eisenegger, M. & Wehmeier, S. (2009). *Personalisierung der Organisationskommunikation. Theoretische Zugänge, Empirie und Praxis* [Personalization of organizational communication. Theoretical approaches, research and practice].Wiesbaden: VS.

Franck, G. (1998). *Die Ökonomie der Aufmerksamkeit. Ein Entwurf* [The attention economy. A sketch]. München, Germany: Hanser.

Gerhards, J. (1994). Politische Öffentlichkeit. Ein system- und akteurstheoretischer Bestimmungsversuch [Structures and Functions of the Modern Public Sphere]. In F. Neidhardt (Ed.), *Öffentlichkeit, öffentliche Meinung, soziale Bewegungen. Sonderheft 34 der Kölner Zeitschrift für Soziologie und Sozialpsychologie*. 77–105.

Gerhards, J. & Neidhardt, F. (1990). Strukturen und Funktionen moderner Öffentlichkeit. In Discussion Paper FS III. Berlin: Wissenschaftszentrum Berlin. 90–101.

Giddens, A. (1986). *The constitution of society. Outline of the theory of structuration*. Cambridge, England: Polity Press. (Original work published 1984).

Grunig, J. & Hunt, T. (1984). *Managing public relations*. Fort Worth, TX: Harcourt Brace Jovanovich.

Habermas, J. (1989). *The structural transformation of the public sphere: an inquiry into a category of bourgeois society*. Cambridge, England: Polity Press.

Habermas, J. (1990). *Strukturwandel der Öffentlichkeit* [The structural transformation of the public sphere]. Frankfurt, Germany.: Suhrkamp. (Originally published in 1962).

Habermas, J. (1997a). *Theorie des kommunikativen Handelns. Band 1. Handlungsrationalität und gesellschaftliche Rationalisierung* [Theory of Communicative Action. Vol. 1. Reason and the Rationalization of Society]. Frankfurt, Germany: Suhrkamp.

Habermas, J. (1997b, 1981b). *Theorie des kommunikativen Handelns. Band 2. Zur Kritik der funktionalistischen Vernunft* [Theory of Communicative Action. Vol. 2. Lifeworld and System: A Critique of Functionalist Reason]. Frankfurt, Germany: Suhrkamp.

Habermas, J. (2006). Political communication in media society—does democracy still enjoy an epistemic dimension? The impact of normative theory on empirical research. *Communication Theory*, 16, 411–426. Based on a paper presented at the 56th ICA Annual Convention, Dresden, Germany.

Hauser, G. (1998). Vernacular dialogue and the rhetoricality of public opinion. *Communication Monographs, 65*(2), 83–107.

Hölscher, L. (1978). Öffentlichkeit [Public sphere]. In O. Brunner, W. Conze & R. Kosseleck (Eds.), *Geschichtliche Grundbegriffe* [Basic historical concepts] (Bd. 4, pp. 413–468). Stuttgart, Germany: Klett-Cotta.

Imhof, K. (2003). Öffentlichkeitstheorien [Public sphere theories]. In G. Bentele, H.-B. Brosius & O. Jarren (Eds.), *Öffentliche Kommunikation. Handbuch Kommunikations- und Medienwissenschaft* [Communication in the public sphere. Handbook of communication and media science] (pp. 193–209). Wiesbaden: Westdeutscher Verlag.

Jarren, O., &Donges, P. (2006). *Politische Kommunikation in der Mediengesellschaft* [Political communication in media society]. Wiesbaden: VS.

Luhmann, N. (1986). *Ökologische Kommunikation: Kann die moderne Gesellschaft sich auf Ökologische Gefährdungen einstellen?* [Ecological communication. Can modern society adapt to ecological threats?] Opladen: Westdeutscher Verlag.

Luhmann, N. (1987). *Soziale Systeme. Grundriss einer Allgemeinen Theorie* [Social systems. Outline of a general theory]. Frankfurt, Germany: Suhrkamp.

Luhmann, N. (1990). Gesellschaftliche Komplexität und öffentliche Meinung [Societal complexity and public opinion]. In N. Luhmann, Soziologische Aufklärung 5 [Sociological enlightenment 5] (pp. 170–182). Opladen: Westdeutscher Verlag.

Mannheim, K. (1929, 1995). *Ideologie und Utopie* [Ideology and utopia]. Bonn: Friedrich Cohen.

Marcinkowski, F. (1993). *Publizistik als autopoietisches System* [Journalism as autopoietic system]. Opladen: Westdeutscher Verlag.

Merten, K. (2008). Konstruktivistischer Ansatz [Constructivist approach]. In G. Bentele, R. Fröhlich & P. Szyszka (Eds.), *Handbuch der Public Relations. Wissenschaftliche Grundlagen und berufliches Handeln* [Handbook of Public Relations. Scientific foundations and professional practice]. *Mit Lexikon. 2., korrigierte und erweiterte Auflage* (pp. 136–148). Wiesbaden: VS.

Müller-Doohm, S. (2000). Kritische Medientheorie–die Perspektive der Frankfurter Schule [Critical media theory—the perspective of the Frankfurt School]. In K. Neumann-Braun & S. Müller-Doohm (2000), *Medien- und Kommunikationssoziologie. Eine Einführung in zentrale Begriffe und Theorien* [Media and communication sociology. An introduction to central concepts and theories] (pp. 69–92). Weinheim: Juventa.

Neidhardt, F. (1994). Öffentlichkeit, Öffentliche Meinung, Soziale Bewegungen [The public sphere, public opinion and social movements]. In Neidhardt, F. (Ed.), Öffentlichkeit, öffentliche Meinung, soziale Bewegungen. Sonderheft 34 der Kölner Zeitschrift für Soziologie und Sozialpsychologie. 7–41.

Noelle-Neumann, E. (2002). Öffentliche Meinung [Public opinion]. In E. Noelle-Neumann, W. Schulz & J. Wilke (Eds.), *Fischer Lexikon Publizistik Massenkommunikation* (pp. 392–406). Frankfurt, Germany: Fischer.

Nothhaft, H. (2011*). Kommunikationsmanagement als professionelle Organisationspraxis Theoretische Annäherung auf Grundlage einer teilnehmenden Beobachtungsstudie* [Communication Management as professional organizational practice. Theoretical approach on the basis of a participatory observation]. Wiesbaden, Germany: VS.

Peters, B. (2007). *Der Sinn von Öffentlichkeit. Herausgegeben von Hartmut Wessler, mit einem Vorwort von Jürgen Habermas* [The purpose of the public sphere]. Frankfurt, Germany: Suhrkamp.

Peters, B. & Wessler, H. (2006). Transnationale Öffentlichkeiten–analytische Dimensionen, normative Standards, sozialkulturelle Produktionsstrukturen [Transnational public spheres—analytical dimensions, socio-cultural production structures]. In K. Imhof, H. Bonfadelli & O. Jarren (Eds.), *Demokratie in der Mediengesellschaft* [Democracy in media society] (pp. 125–144). Wiesbaden: VS.

Russell, B. (2006). *History of Western Philosophy*. Abingdon: Routledge.

Sloterdijk, P. (2009, December 20). Das 21. Jahrhundert beginnt mit dem Debakel vom 19. Dezember 2009. Alles, was vorgibt, an der Macht zu sein, erscheint von jetzt an wie ein hohles Ancien Régime: Ein Gespräch mit dem Philosophen Peter Sloterdijk über die Folgen von Kopenhagen. *Süddeutsche Zeitung*.

Szyszka, P. (2009). Organisation und Kommunikation. Integrativer Ansatz einer Theorie zu Public Relations und Public Relations-Management [Organization and Communication. Integrative Approach to a Theory of Public Relations and Public Relations Management]. In U. Röttger (Ed.), *Theorien der Public Relations*. Grundlagen und Perspektiven der PR-Forschung [Theories of public relations. foundations and perspective of PR research]. (pp. 135–150).

Wiesbaden: VS. Weber, M. (1920). Die protestantische Ethik und der Geist des Kapitalismus [The Protestant Ethic and the Spirit of Capitalism]. In M. Weber, Gesammelte Aufsätze zur Religionssoziologie [Collected Essays in the Sociology of Religion]. Bd. 1 (pp. 17–206). Tübingen: J.C.B. Mohr (Paul Siebeck).

Weber, M. (1924). Agrarverhältnisse im Altertum [The Agrarian Sociology of Ancient Civilizations]. In M. Weber, M., *Gesammelte Aufsätze zur Sozial- und Wirtschaftsgeschichte* [Collected Essays in Social and Economic History]. (pp. 1–288). Tübingen: Mohr.

5

Dewey, the Public Sphere, and Strategic Communication

Charles C. Self

Two twentieth-century philosophers and theorists had a profound impact on thinking about discourse in the twentieth century. John Dewey in the United States and Jürgen Habermas in Europe conceptualized publics and discourse in ways that have reshaped the concepts and practices of strategic communication at the opening of the twenty first century.

Among the most persistent concerns for scholars and practitioners has been the role of discourse in the *public sphere*. Grunig (1989) said that early twentieth century one-way, asymmetrical models of discourse focused on selling ideas to publics. "They (have) presupposed that the organization knows best . . . that the public would benefit by cooperating . . . that if dissident publics had 'the big picture' or understood the organization these publics would willingly 'cooperate' with the organization" (p. 32).

Grunig suggested a two-way symmetrical model of discourse with situated publics would better produce excellence (Grunig, 1997). He suggested more effective emphasis on long-term outcomes had begun to replace the older manipulative model of discourse. He argued such a new approach would facilitate understanding and the interdependence of the organization and its publics. He acknowledged John Dewey's influence on the concept of situated publics (Grunig & Hunt, 1984, p. 143; Grunig & White, 1992).

Meanwhile in Germany, Jürgen Habermas developed a formal discursive approach. It emphasized structured face-to-face argumentation within the public sphere reflecting the lifeworld of lived experience. Peters (1993) credited Habermas with reinvigorating the role of publics in public dialog:

> Habermas has done a great service by reconstructing the largely forgotten concept that still lies, officially, at the foundation of constitutional government: the idea of a sovereign, reasonable public, nourished by the critical reporting of the press and engaged in the mutually enlightening clash of arguments.
>
> *p. 544*

More recently, Kent and Taylor (2002) suggested that a broader concept of *dialogue* should be incorporated into public relations practices. They traced the roots of dialogue to multiple philosophical positions and defined the basic tenets of dialogue. They suggested dialogue "predates symmetrical communication by decades" and facilitates a shift in public relations from managing communication toward building and maintaining relationships (p. 23; see also Taylor, 2011, and Kent, 2011). They pointed out that dialogue is not just about achieving consensus, but facilitates debate and advocacy in public policy formation. They outlined five assumptions, tenets, or features that expand the complexity of dialogue beyond two-way symmetry: mutuality (collaboration), propinquity (authentic engagement), empathy, risk, and commitment (Kent & Taylor, 2002, p. 24).

Pearson (1989) traced changing concepts of dialog through competing "sets of epistemological assumptions": objectivism, relativism, and intersubjectivism. Rhetoric from the "objectivist" point of view assumed that managers acted toward publics in socially responsibly ways assuming that corporate actions would produce social goods. "Relativistic approaches" revealed the failure of social responsibility and a collapse of universal moral principles producing a "passive quietude" and "cynical (and self-centered) activism" in managers and publics alike. "Intersubjectivism" thrust discourse back to the center of strategic communication. Pearson said it produced organizational theory that emphasizes "the symbolic dimension of interorganizational relationships . . . dialogic or dialectical . . . that never remain static and in which seeming oppositions or contradictions are transcended in favor of more complex relationships of mutual dependency" (p. 121). Such discourse is grounded on a "genuine class of attitudes, equal control for participants, and risks for all parties to the dialogue" (p. 125).

Some dialogic scholars have adapted the ideas of classical rhetorical thinking to dialogic communication (Marsh, 2001 & 2003; Skerlep, 2001; Ihlen, 2011; Taylor, 2011; Troup, 2009). Others have adapted approaches such as the structural sociological framework of Bourdieu (Benson, 2008; Edwards, 2012), Foucault (Motion, 2005), and political economy (Motion & Weaver, 2005). Some have even denounced the "infatuation with dialogue," calling dissemination and reconciliation "more ethical" than symmetry (Stoker & Berg, 2006, pp. 7 & 17).

Thus, strategic communication as the theory, research and practice of discourse has been grounded in broad sets of assumptions: on the one hand, organizational communication was said to be an appropriately *strategic* and goal-oriented activity that managed discourse to accomplish organizationally defined goals and outcomes; on the other hand, organizational communication was said to be *dialogic,* devoted to building relationships, understanding, and authentic debate through discourse or dialog in the public sphere. The emphasis on dialog stands in contrast to the emphasis on instrumental strategies to manipulate public opinion and modify public behavior by reinforcing strategic messages (Bybee, 1999). The dialogic approaches emphasize equal participation by publics, authenticity in discourse, and shared understanding (Grunig, 1989; Pearson, 1989; Kent and Taylor, 2002). These authors assumed that meaning is built and problems are solved through dialog and discourse with identifiable publics.

The emphasis upon building relationships through dialog has led, at the opening of the twenty first century, under the influence of postmodern thought, to an emphasis on "emergent approaches" to the role of dialog and communication (Ströh, 2007, p 203). These include theorizing dialog as networks (Castells, 2000, 2007), complexity (Stacey, 2003; Stacey & Griffin, 2006), activism (Holtzhausen, 2007, 2012), chaos (McNair, 2006) and even liquid modernity (Bauman, 2000). These authors have argued that communication is dialectic, aimed not at consensus but at accepting, embracing, and even celebrating difference and diversity as the foundation for acting and problem solving.

Differences in understanding the nature of discourse have become more urgent as digital media technologies and social media have restructured options for dialogue with publics (Castells, 2000, 2003, 2005, 2007; McNair, 2006; Jenkins, 2006; Shirky, 2008; Curtis et al., 2009) and growing numbers of organizations have embraced social media.

Roots

The concepts about the nature of communication, publics, and purpose are grounded in philosophical traditions that competed for adoption as the new *science* of communication developed in the late nineteenth century and early twentieth century (Delia, 1987; Self, 2009; Self, 2013; Gerbner, 1983; E. M. Rogers, 1994; Hardt, 1979).

The competing views can be traced to Greek disagreements about rhetoric (Marsh, 2003). However, much of the recent emphasis on discourse has been derived from the work of Dewey and Habermas. Both traced many of their assumptions to the German Idealists, particularly the ideal dialectic of G. W. F. Hegel. They shared symmetrical, dialectical assumptions and perspectives. They diverged, however, in critical ways that have much to say about the current debates over the role of symmetrical, relational, and dialectic discourse in the age of digital media and social networks.

These differences center on the *nature of publics* and the relationships of social institutions to publics, the *nature of discourse* and how it is undertaken, and the *purpose of discourse* and the goals appropriate to its use.

Habermas is perhaps best understood today because he is still writing, but Dewey's work has influenced a great deal of thought about discourse and publics and has been reengaged with in recent years. Both of these philosophers addressed publics and discourse, but they did so in quite different ways.

Both saw publics as complex. Both suggested that the importance of discourse and deliberation begins with Immanuel Kant, G. W. F. Hegel, and the other German Idealists. Both embraced the pragmatic assumptions that emerged from the work of Charles Peirce, William James, George Herbert Mead and other American Pragmatists in the United States. However, Habermas called his "formal," rules-based approach to discourse "universal pragmatics" (Habermas, 1998, pp. 21–103) or "quasi-transcendental," (Aboulafia, 2002, pp. 4 & 5) whereas Dewey clearly embraced an aggressively anti-foundational (Dewey, 1929a, especially pp. 3–25), even atheoretical and experimental, vision of discourse (Dewey, 1925/1929b, pp. 166–207) closer to postmodern, network, and complex theory approaches.

The American Pragmatists embraced Hegel's dialectic, contingent approach to dealing with problem resolution (Shook & Good, 2010; Hegel, 1977). That approach became the foundation for Dewey's naturalized, experimental empiricism and the discourse influence model of conflict resolution. It forms the basis for acts of pragmatic problem solving whose results are constantly measured and reevaluated in terms of their consequences. It is the foundation of Dewey's education theory, his theory of logic and scientific inquiry, and his dynamic conception of democracy (Shook, 2010, pp. 44–55; Good, 2010, pp. 73–89).

The pragmatic vision also shaped Habermas's critical, dialogical answer to Max Weber's instrumental rationality. Habermas has acknowledged defending "a kind of Kantian pragmatism," appropriating "Peirce's pragmatist conception of knowledge" (Habermas, 2002, pp. 223–224; see also Antonio & Kellner, 1992). Furthermore, he has described his perception that the pragmatists share his links to Hegel: "From the outset, I viewed American pragmatism as the third productive reply to Hegel, after Marx and Kierkegaard, as the radical-democratic branch of Young Hegelianism, so to speak," (as quoted in Aboulafia, 2002, p. 2).

This arc of discourse became stronger over the course of the twentieth century with the development of speech act theory (Searle, 1983), structural semiotics (Cobley, 2010), and Richard Rorty's neo-pragmatic emphasis on "language games" (Rorty, 1989/2007, pp. 1–22, esp. 5, 74–75). It can be found more recently in emerging forms of *network semiotics* (Self, 2013) and, arguably, in several forms of postmodernism, including Derrida's textual notions of deconstruction and "democracy-to-come" (Derrida, 2003, p. 9).

This article will examine Habermas's *public sphere* and *communication for understanding* and Dewey's *radical pluralism* and *fallibilistic indeterminacy* as versions of discourse essential to the emerging theories of strategic communication appropriate to the changing digital media systems and network semiotic strategies of the early twenty-first century.

Their differences define the core tension about discourse and strategic communication today. Those differences center on interpretations of the three central assumptions about discourse: the notion of public, the nature of discourse, and the purpose of public discourse.

Jürgen Habermas

Jürgen Habermas is generally acknowledged as one of the most important European philosophers of the second half of the twentieth century. Thomas McCarthy called him "the last great rationalist," whose goal is nothing short of a critique of rationalism (McCarthy, 1984, p. vi). Habermas himself has suggested the three-fold goal of his theory of communicative action is

1. to explore an integrated concept of rationality,
2. to construct a "two-level concept of society to connect the 'lifeworld' of communities with the 'system' paradigms" of mass societies, and
3. to develop a theory of modernity that explains modernity's social pathologies and paradoxes (Habermas, 1981/1984, p. x).

These tasks are founded on a lifetime of critical theory, scholarship, and engagement with a surprisingly eclectic range of philosophers, critical thinkers, and political analysts.

"Habermas moves brilliantly among these discourses to vindicate a 'postmetaphysical' reason, which 'detranscendentalizes' as it retains the 'idealizing force of context-transcending' forms" (Bookman, 2002, p. 65). He drew on Kant, Hegel, Marx, the Frankfurt School, the developmental approaches of Piaget and Kohlberg, the German *linguistic turn,* the speech-act theorists Austin and Searle, and the American Pragmatists, especially Peirce and Mead.

This work produced Habermas's concept of the *public sphere,* now widely embraced in the sociology of media and communication studies (Benson, 2009) though it has been surprisingly under-studied in the professional literature (Jensen, 2001). Discourse lay at the heart of Habermas's project. His work focused on communication, discourse, and argumentation. *The Structural Transformation of the Public Sphere* (Habermas, 1989/1991) was a critical examination of a social space for un-coerced discourse. The two-volume *The Theory of Communicative Action* (Habermas, 1981/1984) detailed the framework for discourse in this public sphere. It expanded his critical theory of modernity and provided the foundation of the *communicative rationality* of the *lifeworld* of everyday experience. Communicative rationality was contrasted with the *strategic rationality* of modern instrumental *systems* destructive to intersubjective understanding and action within the public sphere (Habermas, 1981/1984, Vol. 1, pp. 10 & 168–185; see also Habermas, 1974/2005, particularly pp. 54–55).

Habermas revitalizes intersubjective understanding through discourse in the modern lifeworld. He is anti-foundational. He moves away from transcendental visions of ontology and establishes in their place a *quasi-transcendental ontology* based in rules of discourse.

> While it appears that Habermas has put a greater distance between himself and the transcendental *a priori* over the years—for example by emphasizing the fallibilistic nature of even the presuppositions of argumentation—he cannot yield to what he views as relativism and irrationality (in pragmatism).
>
> *Aboulafia, 2002, p. 5*

As a result, he has developed a formalized account of discourse that clings to structural linguistic rules of argumentation and validity that govern intersubjective understanding and deliberative democracy. This sets him apart from Dewey and from postmodernism.

His critique of modernity is that modernism became burdened with a rationalism that separated and subordinated human psychological processes to communication strategies. Those strategies manipulated human behavior by manipulating communicative interactions. These interactions undermined both intersubjective understanding and social processes. They subjected human beings to manipulative practices of power and domination based on instrumental communication discourses and strategic rationality.

His account of the decline of community discourse and argumentation in the public sphere described the expansion of the instrumental rationalization of communication processes, "manufactured publicity," and "non-public opinion" (Habermas, 1991, pp. 211–222) and the way they undermined the essential elements of discourse.

His approach was more formal, more narrowly focused, than that of Dewey and the American Pragmatists. Although it shared Dewey's anti-foundational and fallibilistic posture, it emphasizes intersubjective understanding and consensus through discourse. In place of Dewey's emphasis on shared experience, transactional discourse, experimentation projects, and assessment of consequences, Habermas constructed an understanding of discourse grounded in *a priori* structures of argumentation derived from Austin and Searle's speech act theory (Habermas, 1970).

Habermas's concept of *public* emerges from his account of the transformation of the public sphere. That account defined public by who is admitted to participate in the realm of the public. He distinguished public from private. Public spaces allow private individuals to assemble for discourse and disputation about their common good (see Habermas, 1991, pp. 1–26). The public sphere is that space where private individuals assemble and make up the public.

Habermas's concept of *discourse* is defined by the nature of the interaction in the public sphere. In the *Structural Transformation,* discourse changes from manipulation by representation in the Middle Ages to deliberation among equals in the Enlightenment and back to manipulation by strategic rationalization in the modern era. In *The Theory of Communicative Action,* he divided discourse into the two types: strategic rationalization and communicative understanding. Strategic rationalization is instrumental, goal oriented, and manipulative, aimed at selling already defined objectives to the public. Communicative understanding is un-coerced argumentative speech that follows the rules of speech acts and validity claims (Habermas, 1981/1984, pp. 24–27) within the "contexts of action" of "a few social arenas or 'fields'" (p 31).

Habermas's concept of *purpose* for discourse is communicative understanding and consensus for further interaction. He wrote:

> What makes communicative reason possible is the linguistic medium through which interactions are woven. This rationality is inscribed in the linguistic telos of mutual understanding. . . . In seeking to reach an understanding, natural-language users must assume, among other things, that the participants pursue their illocutionary goals without reservations, that they tie their agreement to the intersubjective recognition of criticizable validity claims, and that they are ready to take on the obligations resulting from consensus and relevant for further interaction.
>
> *Habermas, 1996, pp. 3–4*

As Haas (2004) put it:

> Habermas argued that a genuinely democratic public sphere comes into being when the interactions are focused on issues of common concern to citizens, equally accessible to all those potentially affected by those issues, based on rational-critical deliberation and subject to normative standards of evaluation.
>
> *p. 180*

Habermas argued mediated forms of communication are crucial for democracy. Burkart (2007) said, "a central effort of Habermas' thinking is to reconstruct universal conditions of understanding within the human communication process" (p. 249).

Habermas's *The Theory of Communicative Action* emphasizes the dual forms of rational discourse, manipulative strategic rationality, aimed at accomplishing strategic objectives, and argumentation aimed at consensus, intersubjective understanding, and common goals. He suggested both are at work in modern societies, but strategic rationality dominates community systems undermining the lifeworld. On the other hand, discourse for understanding feeds the lifeworld. This dual structure of strategic and communicative, system and lifeworld, encapsulates Habermas's attempt to address individual freedom and community norms (for a detailed discussion of this issue see Joas, 1991, Rosenthal, 2002, and Ingram, 2002, particularly pp. 83–86).

Habermas embraced a universal pragmatics of communication grounded in assumptions that human beings use deliberation and argumentation to achieve intersubjective understanding of common needs to enable conjoint action (Habermas, 1998, pp. 21–103).

Thus, Habermas made three crucial assumptions: First, he assumed publics are communities of individuals grouped by their discourse in a lifeworld of stable connections. Second, he assumed discourse consists of structured arguments grounded in rules of argumentation and language. Third, he assumed the appropriate goal of discourse is to achieve communicative understanding and consensus.

John Dewey

John Dewey has been recognized as probably the most important American philosopher of the first half of the twentieth century (Jackson, 2006, p 54; see also McDermott, 1973a & 1973b). He is considered one of "the principle pragmatists" (Margolis, 2006, p. 2) crucial to founding American Pragmatism (Fott, 1991, p. 29). He was one of the most important educational theorists of the twentieth century and has had an impact on scholarship in both psychology and the political sciences.

Margolis argues that the key components of Dewey's account of Pragmatism include:

1) A Darwinian and Hegelian reading of naturalism, 2) A Peircean and Jamesian reading of meaning and truth, and 3) a rejection of final goals or values in moral and community life . . . he features as his principle organizing intuition what he calls 'an indeterminate situation' (LW 12:108–9) . . . (which) yield(s) constructive and provisional forms of realism (without fixity or privilege), and which, rightly grasped, are themselves finally grounded in a pragmatist rendering of reflexive experience suggestively close to the governing conception of Hegel's *Phenomenology* (never explicitly drawn upon, however).

2006, p. 8

Dewey advocated an *anti-elitist* and *anti-foundational* vision of democratic decision-making (Rogers, 2010). That vision was articulated in *The Public and its Problems* (Dewey, 1927/1954) among many other publications (see Westbrook, 1991). The book was Dewey's answer to Walter Lippmann's critique *The Phantom Public* (Lippmann, 1925), which Dewey called "perhaps the most effective indictment of democracy as currently conceived ever penned" (Bybee, 1999; Carey, 1989/1992, pp. 74–82; Self, 2010; Schudson, 2008).

Dewey argued that actions form publics and that the "soul of democracy" is "wider and fuller" than political machinery—"universal suffrage, recurring elections, political accountability, trial by peers and so on." Democratic public action has two parts: "One is normative: the basis in a community's laws, customs, and institutions. A second is epistemic: the collaborative process of *inquiry* with which a democracy can identify, prioritize, and solve problems (through) 'conjoint communicated experience' (MW 9:93)" (Hildebrand, 2011, p. 591; Hildebrand, 2008).

Public

Dewey's *public* emerged from problem solving as acts of discourse, not from essences or membership. He said that individual and group action embodies public. Public emerges, submerges, and reemerges as joint acts create consequences, as they affect people and are affected by others. "The line between private and public is to be drawn on the basis of the extent and scope of the consequences of acts which are so important as to need control, whether by inhibition or by promotion" (Dewey, 1927/1954, p. 15).

> Appeal to a gregarious instinct to account for social arrangements is the outstanding example of the lazy fallacy . . . We must . . . start from acts which are performed, not from hypothetical causes for those acts, and consider their consequences. We must also introduce intelligence, or the observation of consequences *as* consequences, that is, in connection with the acts from which they proceed.
>
> *Dewey, 1927/1954, pp. 10–12*

For Dewey, action was grounded in "three key themes: the relationship between the individual and society, the legitimacy of majoritarianism, and the significance and meaning of political deliberation" (Rogers, 2010, p. 69). The idea of deliberation was central to his thought about the relationships between businesses and publics.

He argued that publics are (networks or) relationships of action assembled to solve problems. Public relationships evaporate as problems are solved, although they sometimes leave behind social structures created to solve the problem and that are sometimes mistaken to define public. Dewey argues that public is "conjoined action," not membership or structure (Dewey, 1939a, p. 10).

Carey (1997) critiqued the sustainability of this idea of public. He suggested the expansion of strategic instrumental interests had overwhelmed the ability of emergent publics to cope:

> Dewey argued that a public interest arises whenever there are indirect consequences of individual private transactions. Therefore, the public and a public interest came into existence whenever externalities were created. But while externalities had steadily expanded, the domain and competence of the public had steadily shrunk. The interdependencies created by industry and commerce were nowhere matched by the interdependencies of public life.
>
> *pp. 71–72*

However, Dewey's vision was that publics emerge, and will always emerge, to the extent that experience with problems demands that publics form and act.

Discourse

Dewey (1929a) saw *discourse* as symbolic action, or what he called *transactions* "of connective relations or 'capacities'" with human beings and non-human experience (Dewey and Bentley, 1949/1960/1975, pp. 270–271; see also Ryan, 1997). "Participation in activities and sharing in results are additive concerns. They demand communication as a prerequisite. Only when there exist *signs* or *symbols* of activities and of their outcome can the flux be viewed" (Dewey, 1927/1954, p. 152). Discourse, he said, allows action to be "preserved as meanings." Those meanings allow conjoint experience to be considered, transmitted and converted into "what, metaphorically, may be termed a general will or social consciousness: desire and choice . . . communicable and shared by all concerned" (p. 153).

He argued transient acts of discourse emerge from experience to solve problems then dissolve back into private concerns. Private individuals experience problems, share their experiences through discourse, join together to plan solutions, advocate experimental approaches to solve problems, and assess the outcomes of those approaches through discourse. This discourse sometimes leaves behind traces in the social structures of political machinery, but that machinery does not comprise democratic action nor ensure discourse. Democratic action and discourse remain perpetually fallible, indeterminate, and contingent. They constantly change. He wrote:

> The constructive office of thought is empirical—that is, experimental. 'Thought' is not a property of something termed intellect or reason apart from nature. It is a mode of directed overt action. . . . Ideas and idealism are in themselves hypotheses not finalities. Being connected with operations to be performed, they are tested by the consequences of these operations, not by what exists prior to them. . . . Action is at the heart of ideas. The experimental practice of knowing . . . discloses that knowing is itself a kind of action, the only one which progressively and securely clothes natural existence with realized meanings.
>
> *pp. 166–167*

Shared experience and *deliberation* about solutions are the heart of Dewey's idea of joint action (Eldridge, 1996). He thought language was the center of democracy as shared ideas in place of democracy as political machinery. Eldridge (1996) explained Dewey's distinction in this regard this way:

> He valued the processes of open, informed communication so much that he thought they should characterize the many ways in which we interact with one another and not be limited to the narrowly and formally 'political' . . . To be a democrat was to commit oneself to participation in the intelligent give and take of our common life.
>
> *p. 11*

For Dewey (1927/1954), *discourse* was the relationships of experience shared in signs and symbols to enable projects (or experiments) to be planned to solve problems:

> To learn to be human is to develop thought, the give-and-take of communication, an effective sense of being an individually distinctive member of a community . . . who contributes to a further conversion of organic powers into human resources and values. But this translation is never finished.
>
> *p. 154*

Public opinion for Dewey is the network of discourse relationships. He wrote:

> Opinions and beliefs . . . presuppose effective and organized inquiry. Unless there are methods for detecting the energies which are at work and tracing them through an intricate network of interactions to their consequences, what passes as public opinion will be 'opinion' in its derogatory sense rather than truly public, no matter how widespread the opinion is. . . . Opinion casually formed and formed under the direction of those who have something at stake . . . can be *public* opinion only in name.
>
> *pp. 177–178*

Purpose

Dewey's (1927/1954) *purpose* of public acts or discourse is problem solving: sharing experience, identifying problems, developing passible solutions to problems, and assessing results of those solutions. Such discourse is always fallible and can only happen within complex and perpetually indeterminate circumstances. Dewey emphasizes that success or failure can only be assessed through continuing discourse about the experiences of their consequences.

Tools can be evolved and perfected only in operation; in application to observing, reporting and organizing actual subject-matter; and this application cannot occur save through free and systematic communication . . . Record and communication are indispensable to knowledge. Knowledge cooped up in a private consciousness is a myth, and knowledge of social phenomena is particularly dependent upon dissemination, for only by distribution can such knowledge be either obtained or tested.

pp. 167, 176–177

Dewey's act of *problem solving* is experience shared, experiment planned and results assessed. He denounced "final causes" and "final solutions" for problems found in causal theories (Dewey 1929a, pp. 3–25; 1925/1929b, pp. 40–77; 1938, pp. 60–80). He held that all solutions were contingent, fallible, and always indeterminate. He rejected fixed essences, whether they were theological, metaphysical, or natural. He believed that problems were defined in the play of relationships of experience shared (inquiry) and projects planned (discovery) through discourse. This play was complex and indeterminate. It was created in connections made through thought and discourse, not in universal essences waiting to be discovered.

There is one common character of all such scientific operations which it is necessary to note: They are such as to disclose relationships

Dewey, 1929a, p. 125

Real things may be as transitory as you please or lasting in time as you please; these are specific differences like that between a flash of lightening and the history of a mountain range. In any use they are for knowledge 'events' not substances. What knowledge is interested in is the correlation among these changes or events

p. 128

It is a declaration that this is the effective way to *think* things; the effective mode in which to frame ideas of them to formulate their meanings

p. 134

The authority of thought depends upon what it leads us to through directing the performance of operations.

p. 137

Dewey argued solutions to problems were built through discourse (discovery). Those solutions had to be evaluated in discourse about the consequences of those solutions in social experience. He suggested that systematic thinking involved inquiry (shared experience) and discovery (constructed solutions) to create experimental judgment about possible consequences, followed by assessment of outcomes that always remained contingent and open to revision (Dewey, 1938; Dewey, 1891).

Dewey's idea of problem solving was what he called the "experimental" method of directed overt action. His idea of empiricism was based in naturalized experience, or the actual lived experience of individuals jointly developing solutions to problems (Dewey, 1927/1954, p. 202; McDermott, 1973a, pp. xxiii–xxix; Dewey, 1906/1973a; Dewey, 1939/1973b).

Dewey believed judgments were always *contingent* and subject to revision. Ideas were instruments for testing solutions in a constantly shifting universe of contingencies. He called this kind of thought "methods of action" as opposed to abstract reflection (Dewey, 1929a, p. 36). And he believed that all publics involve such democratic acts of inquiry and discovery. Anything else was domination in one of its many forms.

> Democracy is belief in the ability of human experience to generate the aims and methods by which further experience will grow in ordered richness. Every other form of moral and social faith rests upon the idea that experience must be subjected at some point or other to some form of external control; to some 'authority' alleged to exist outside the processes of experience. . . . If one asks what is meant by experience in this connection my reply is that it is the free interaction of individual human beings with surrounding conditions, especially the human surroundings, which develops and satisfies need and desire by increasing knowledge of things as they are. Knowledge of conditions as they are is the only solid ground for communication and sharing; all other communication means the subjection of some persons to the personal opinion of other persons. Need and desire—out of which grow purpose and direction of energy—go beyond what exists, and hence beyond knowledge, beyond science. They continually open the way into the unexplored and unattained future.
>
> *Dewey, 1939b, pp. 16–17*

Where Habermas saw members comprising publics, Dewey saw acts of discourse. Where Habermas saw the discourse in rules of argumentation, Dewey saw symbols embodying relationships of experience. Where Habermas saw understanding and consensus, Dewey saw perpetually fallible problem solving that required constant reassessment.

Richard Rorty, Postmodernism, and Semiotic Networks

Margolis (2006) argued Dewey's 1925 account in *The Development of Pragmatism* established "classic pragmatism" (p. 4). It drew together the work of Peirce and James revitalizing pragmatism at a crucial moment of its development (Margolis, 2006; Leary, 2009; Dewey, 1925/1929b). This revitalization laid the foundation for scholars such as Habermas in Europe and Putnam and Rorty in the United States to expand and reinterpret Pragmatism and its relationship with the critical, structural and postmodern accounts of globalized society.

Hickman (2007) opened his book *Pragmatism as Post-postmodernism* this way: "I take as my point of departure the now famous remark by Richard Rorty, that when certain of the postmodernists reach the end of the road they are traveling they will find Dewey there waiting for them" (p. 13). He went on to quote Ermarth on the two key assumptions of postmodernism:

> First, the assumption that there is no common denominator—in 'nature' or 'God' or 'the future'—that guarantees either the one-ness of the world or the possibility of neutral or objective thought. Second, the assumption that all human systems operate like language, being self-reflexive rather than referential systems—systems of deferential function which are powerful but finite, and which construct and maintain meaning and value.
>
> *p. 15, quoting Ermarth, 1998*

These postmodern assumptions undermined what Ermarth called the "one-world hypothesis," a unified view of the world that formed the foundation of modern thought. (Ermarth, 2001, p. 202).

Hickman (2007) argued John Dewey's "classical pragmatism" long ago embraced both of those key assumptions. "For those who are interested in coming to grips with the problems and prospects of our increasingly technological culture, classical Pragmatism appears to offer significant advantages over some currently popular versions of 'neo-pragmatism'" (p. 48).

Morris (1999) suggested Dewey is claimed for postmodernism but is better called postpositivist.

> It is no coincidence that Dewey was reviled as a positivist 'anti-philosopher' in his day and claimed for postmodernism in our own. His thinking does proceed along two distinct axes, naturalist and speculative, the point of the latter being to give expression to precisely those parts of experience which elude naturalist categories.
>
> *p. 608*

Among the most eloquent expressions of neo-pragmatism is Rorty's version. Rorty has re-engaged the American Pragmatic tradition (and particularly Dewey) from a postmodern perspective and has engaged in intense debates with other arguably postmodern thinkers including Derrida (Mouffe, 1996). He has suggested Foucault and Derrida share with Nietzsche "suspicions about the tradition of Western philosophy—suspicions which they share with the American pragmatists" (Rorty, 1996, p. 13). He argues,

> Derrida seems to me as good a humanist as Mill or Dewey. When Derrida talks about deconstruction as prophetic of 'the democracy that is to come,' he seems to me to be expressing the same utopian social hope as was felt by these earlier dreamers.
>
> *p. 14; see, for example, an account of Derrida's perpetually indeterminate*
> *and experimental "democracy-to-come" in Derrida, 2003; see also Reynolds, 2009*

Rorty is called a "neo-pragmatist" (Hickman, 2007, p. 48; see also Mounce, 1997). Like Dewey, he rejected ideas as transcendental truths and replaced them with ideas of consequences. He, too, viewed knowledge as fallible and subject to revision. He, too, emphasized the role of discourse or language games (see, also, Lyotard, 1979/1984, pp. 9–10) in asserting the grounds for human understanding. He, too, argued contingency and the fallibility of knowledge replace metaphysical ontology. He, too, suggested language is the foundation for the intersubjective *solidarity* essential to community. He, too, joined Dewey in arguing "our experience in (and of) the world is an active affair to which we contribute in different ways—we act, depending on the contextual settings, in a specific way. And, what is more, we are bound to the way we construct and use the languages, i.e., the *talk* on what we experience—what *we* experience" (Ljunggren, 2003, p. 364). He argued the "ironist" (Rorty, 1989/2007, p. 73) must embrace contingency precisely because knowledge is grounded in the interplay of contingent language.

Unlike Habermas and Dewey, Rorty (1989/2007) argued the relationship between community obligation and individual freedom divides into private freedom and the public irony (or contingency). He argued unguarded individuals are often immersed in a "final vocabulary" that "they employ to justify their actions, their beliefs, and their lives" (p. 73). However, in public, the "final vocabularies" (p. 73) of different individuals clash—come into conflict—leading to conflicting views of the situation and possible outcomes of action. This conflict produces an "ironic attitude" (p. 74) that recognizes the contingency of their language, their moral deliberation, their conscience, and their community.

Rorty (1989/2007) separated himself (and Dewey) from Habermas. He argued that Habermas's universal pragmatics is still the search for a means of validating a final version of truth.

> Habermas thinks it essential to a democratic society that its self-image embody the universalism, and some form of rationalism, of the Enlightenment. He thinks of his account of 'communicative reason' as a way of updating rationalism. I want not to update either universalism or rationalism but to dissolve both and replace them with something else. I see Habermas's substitution of 'communicative reason' for 'subject centered reason' as just a misleading way of making the

same point I have been urging: a liberal society is one which is content to call 'true' (or 'right' or 'just') whatever the outcome of undistorted communication happens to be, whatever view wins in a free and open encounter.

p. 67

He suggests that contingency, what Dewey has called the indeterminacy of a "precarious and perilous" world (1925/1929b, p. 42), undermines Habermas's project:

> It is precisely this claim of universal validity which what I have called the 'contingency of language' makes implausible, and which the poeticized culture of my liberal utopia would no longer make. Such a culture would instead agree with Dewey that 'imagination is the chief instrument of the good'
>
> *Rorty, 1989/2007, p. 69*

It is this fallibility within the indeterminacy of decision-making in planning and problem solving that the postmodernists celebrate. It is what connects them with Dewey's vision of discourse founded on shifting networks of social, material, and verbal relationships upon which to project experiments of future consequences for action. And it connects them with what Bernstein calls their "primary task":

> Rorty's deepest affinities are with what he calls 'literary culture.' The narrative that he unfolds is one where representatives of literature culture such as Bloom, Foucault, and Derrida replace professional philosophers as the dominant voice in the present conversation of mankind. Dewey is one of Rorty's heroes. . . . Rorty, too, is an apologist for those very democratic virtues that were so central for Dewey and which he sought to make concrete. There is an important difference of emphasis here between Rorty and Habermas—one which also reveals the common ground they share. . . . the practical tasks for achieving what Dewey once delineated as the primary task of democracy—'the creation of a freer and more humane experience in which all share and to which all contribute.'
>
> *Bernstein, 1982, pp. 352–353*

Derrida, too, celebrated the centrality of this "undecidability" and the humane goals of decision-making. He argued:

> The necessity for thinking to traverse interminably the experience of undecidability can, I think be quite coolly demonstrated in an analysis of the ethical or political decision. . . . we would find that undecidability is irreducible within them. If one does not take rigorous account of undecidability, it will not only be the case that one cannot act, decide or assume responsibility, but one will not even be able to *think the concepts of decision and responsibility*.
>
> *Derrida, 1996, p. 86*

An emerging, *network* semiotics (Self, 2013), is powerfully exhibited in digital mediated communication, particularly in online social networks. Network theory sets about representing a "pattern of connections in a given system" (Newman, 2011, p. 20). Social network theory represents "a set of actors or nodes along with a set of ties of a specified type (such as friendship) that link them" (Borgatti & Halgin, 2011, p. 1169; see also Monge and Contractor, 2003; Scott, 2000). Semiotics examines how meaning is generated within the systems of relationships represented in such networks. As Ferdinand de Saussure said, language "is a storehouse filled by the members of a given community through their active use of speaking . . . For language is not complete in any speaker; it exists perfectly only within a collectivity" (Saussure, 1996, p. 43). Semiotics in all its forms examines how connected acts of representation generate meaning (Cobley, 2010, pp. 3–12).

Thus, collections of relationships represented in networks generate meaning. Kull (2010), following Uexküll, suggested that the *Umwelt,* or the self-constructed world of relationships for even non-human organisms, generates meaning (p. 43). Brunor Latour (1991/1993) suggested that collections of human and non-human "hybrids" generate meaning. And Matthew Fuller (2005) referring to a collection of media objects asserted that "materialism also requires that the capacities of activity, thought, sensation, and affect possible to each composition whether organic or not are shaped by what it is, what it connects to, and the dimensions of relationality around it" (p. 174).

Collections of human and nonhuman relationships illustrate patterns of perpetually shifting undecidability, meaning and identity (Castells, 2000, 2003; McNair, 2006; Hassan, 2003). From Foucault (1994) to Lyotard (1979/1984) to Baudrillard (1995) to Derrida (1998), the postmodernists have reminded us that knowledge is no unified grand narrative but a situated narrative grounded in the time and the relationships of human and non-human experience. This is the fallibility and undecidability described as experience, nature and art by Dewey (1925/1929b, pp. 354–393). It is the lived experience of changing environments produced within the complex relationships of "transactions" (Dewey and Bentley, 1949/1960/1975, pp. 67–69). Dewey argued that existence is changeable and rendered stable only when we hold it stable in our verbal constructions of it (Dewey, 1925/1929b, pp. 40–77).

A great deal has been written about the potential of digital technologies to enable powerful, but transient patterns of social action to be built through discourse around events (Shirky, 2008; Jenkins, 2006; Sunstein, 2006). These emerging networks of mediated discourse and unstable relationships have been described as combinations of social and material ecologies (Fuller, 2005). Bauman suggested the connections that emerge are fluid and impermanent but full of economic and social consequences (Bauman, 2000).

Strategic Communication

At the opening of the twenty-first century, the arc of discourse has returned to Dewey (Hickman, Heubert, & Reich, 2009; Perry, 2001). His influence waxed and waned across the twentieth century, influencing thinking about discourse in strategic communication from start to finish. Carey (1989/1992) has discussed his impact on theories of social influence. Grunig has acknowledged his impact on his development of the situational theory of publics and his symmetrical theories (Grunig & Hunt, 1984). Rorty (1996) and Hickman (2007) have suggested Dewey waits at the terminus of postmodern thought. And social network theory has been linked through Kurt Lewin's field theory and typological psychology and Festinger's balance theory (Scott, 2000) with the American Pragmatists and Dewey (Joas, 1993).

Habermas and Dewey described the power of discourse in this postmodern digital age of networks and their insights have been rediscovered in the fluid patterns of dialog that have emerged in the virtual, global public sphere of the twenty-first century digital media (Dahlgren, 2005; Hytten, 2009; Neubert, 2010; Papacharissi, 2002; Downey & Fenton, 2010) and culture of remote connectivity (Papacharissi, 2010).

At the opening of the twenty-first century, strategic communication scholarship and practice is concerned with dialog and with publics. Kent (2011) has suggested that this demands "long-term thinking and planning . . . that requires some friends" (p. 552). Taylor (2011) suggested that competing discourses construct competing images of the world and that public relations can extend organizational discourse into the "wrangle" of public discourse creating social capital and empowering enlightened choice (Taylor, 2011, esp. p. 442).

However, too often publics still are defined by membership instead of acts, and discourse still is defined as information management (Ströh, 2007, pp. 199–203; Holtzhausen, 2007, pp. 359–362).

Ströh (2007) suggested that such approaches have been replaced by a new emphasis on "constant interaction, participation, change and self-organizing growth" (p. 205). She said social institutions are organic systems of actions created by the constantly changing relationships that make up the whole system. They are complex systems of constant change better approached through engagement and facilitation (even of conflict) than management, control, and consensus (p. 215). She emphasized embracing an inherent uncertainty of outcomes always present in social organizations.

Holtzhausen called for communicators to be activists. She suggested that public relations professionals should place less emphasis on idealizing cooperation and harmony and more on conflict and resistance (p. 365). She suggested that public relations professionals should help identify "tensors" or points of conflict within complex systems and serve as "boundary spanners" to promote dialectical exchange around conflict (pp. 367–368; see also Holtzhausen, 2012, esp. pp. 25–35).

Murphy (2007), following Stacey (1996), explained the futility of prediction and control in complex systems. "If a system may be accurately and completely described by reducing it to its component parts, then it is merely complicated; but if a system is truly complex, it is more than the sum of its parts," she writes (p. 129). Stacey and Griffin (2006) pointed out that complex organizations encompass the continuous interplay of self-organizing and emergent interactions among individuals and groups that constantly evolve in predictable and unpredictable ways as those interactions merge and diverge over time. Thus, what an organization becomes as a whole follows no blueprint and often produces surprising outcomes (pp. 7–9).

Peters (1993, pp. 561–562) argued that strategic communication and information management have undermined the public sphere by *representing* or showing off the manipulative decisions taken unilaterally by organizations even if they have consulted the public.

In his 2006 lecture at the 56th Annual International Communication Association Conference, Habermas (2006) described the problems of connecting the lifeworld of everyday experience with the systems paradigms in mass societies. He suggested the goal should be to reintegrate rationality through the rule-governed discourse of argumentation to recreate intersubjective understanding. He described the "indicators of contingent constraints" on "the normative requirements of deliberative politics" (Habermas, 2006, p. 420) and suggested that mediated discourse has to be independent of interference and responsive to citizens' voices about problems and proposed solutions (pp. 420–421).

Overlapping themes emerge from twenty-first century examinations of discourse: the fallibility of knowledge, the complexity and shifting boundaries of institutions as social networks, the indeterminacy of outcomes, the requirement for continuing collaboration with acting publics, the commitment to risk-taking in mutual engagement with constituencies. Holtzhausen (2012) has suggested that the twenty first century communication practitioner operates in a "state of awareness" for the multiple identities manifest in public acts and public discourse (pp. 221–225).

In the early twentieth century, Dewey articulated many of these twenty-first century themes. He suggested sustained discourse about the relationships that make up experience, about problem-solving experiments, and about continuous assessment in complex, indeterminate environments. He suggested viewing organizations as communities of engaged interaction among shifting patterns of relationships rather than as static entities.

> Mobility may in the end supply the means by which the spoils of remote and indirect interaction and interdependence flow back into local life, keeping it flexible, preventing the stagnancy which has attended stability in the past, and furnishing it with the elements of a variegated and many-hued experience. Organization may cease to be taken as an end in itself. . . . Organization as a means to an end would reinforce individuality and enable it to be securely itself by enduing it with resources beyond its unaided reach. (Dewey, 1927/1954, p. 216)

Dewey's vision presented organizations as shifting networks of discourse, engaging acting publics, sharing diverse experiences of social and material life, defining problems individuals encounter, debating conflicting ideas about how to solve those problems, and constantly assessing the success of solutions by sharing the experiences of individuals with those solutions.

Such discourse is not focused on consensus. It is focused on individual experience and individual needs. The constant interplay of the discourse, the dialectic of lived experience, generates, not consensus, but an encompassing and always indeterminate synthesis that is the complex network we call the organization, including its acting publics. Any attempt to freeze those shifting relationships into a fixed essence inevitably creates a false sense of certainty (Dewey, 1929a, pp. 26–48). For Dewey publics are networks of acts. They emerge in discourse. Their purpose is sharing experience, solving problems and assessing the consequences. Communicators who facilitate that ongoing process, linking participants across networks as publics, and promoting their discourse across the organization, also facilitate the continuous inquiry into problems, the discovery of solutions, and the shared assessment of outcomes.

In recent scholarship, public relations practitioners have been urged to play precisely this role within their organizations. Digital media and social networks make it possible for institutions to rebuild sustained flexible discourse partnerships of shared experience among individuals and groups. As problems (and publics) arise, those discourse partnerships make joint inquiry possible. They enable collaborative discovery and problem solving (experiments) to develop conjointly within transient public acts among an organization's networks of constituencies. Discourse partnerships empower continuing joint assessments of consequences. They offer the means for further joint action to produce conjoint solutions and assessments of solutions. As problems are solved, they offer the means that lead back to sustained shared experience of individuals and institutions.

Habermas and Dewey suggested a renewed vision of discourse in communication at the opening of the twenty-first century that would depart from the strategic management of communication that dominated the twentieth century. They offered innovation at the moment new forms of mediated communication demand innovative discourse. These emerging views of classic and neo-pragmatism are echoed in the literature on networks, relationships, complexity, and postmodernism and offer a comprehensive rationale for approaches that hold the promise of sustained public engagement and conjoined problem solving within the fluid virtual communities of the twenty-first century.

References

Aboulafia, M. (2002). Introduction. In M. Aboulafia, M. Bookman, & C. Kemp (Eds.), *Habermas and pragmatism* (pp. 1–13). London and New York: Routledge.

Antonio, R. J., & Kellner, D. (1992). Communication, modernity, and democracy in Habermas and Dewey. *Symbolic Interaction, 15*(3), 277–297.

Baudrillard, J. (1995). *Simulacra and simulation* (S. F. Glaser, Trans.). Ann Arbor, MI: University of Michigan Press.

Bauman, Z. (2000). *Liquid modernity*. Cambridge, England: Polity.

Benson, R. D. (2008, May). *Public relations in the public sphere: Habermas, Bourdieu, and the question of power.* Paper presented at the annual meeting of the International Communication Association, Montreal, Canada.

Benson, R. (2009). Shaping the public sphere: Habermas and beyond. *American Sociology, 40,* 175–197.

Bernstein, R. J. (1982). What is a difference that makes a difference? Gadamer, Habermas, and Rorty. In *Proceedings of the biennial meeting of the Philosophy of Science Association, Vol. 1982, Volume Two: Symposia and Invited Papers*. Chicago, IL: University of Chicago Press on behalf of the Philosophy of Science Association.

Bookman, M. (2002). Forming competence: Habermas on reconstructing worlds and context-transcendent reason. In M. Aboulafia, M. Bookman, & C. Kamp (Eds.), *Habermas and pragmatism* (pp. 65–79). London: Routledge.

Borgatti, S. P., & Halgin D. S. (2011). On network theory. *Organization Science, 22*(5), 1168–1181.

Burkart, R. (2007). On Jürgen Habermas and public relations. *Public Relations Review, 33,* 249–254.

Bybee, C. (1999). Can democracy survive in the post factual age? *Journalism and Communication Monographs, 1*(1), 29–62.

Carey, J. W. (1979). Foreword. In H. Hardt, *Social theories of the press: Early German & American perspectives* (pp. 9–14). Beverly Hills: Sage.

Carey, J. W. (1992). *Communication as culture: Essays on media and society*. New York: Routledge. (Original work published 1989).

Carey, J. W. (1997). Communications and economics. In E. S. Munson & C. A. Warren (Eds.), *James Carey: A critical reader* (pp. 60–75). Minneapolis, MN: University of Minnesota Press.

Castells, M. (2000). *The rise of the network society* (2nd ed.). Oxford, England: Blackwell.

Castells, M. (2003). *The power of identity: Economy, society and culture* (2nd ed.). Oxford, England: Blackwell.

Castells, M. (2005). *End of millennium* (2nd ed.). Oxford, England: Blackwell

Castells, M. (2007). Communication, power and counter-power in the network society. *International Journal of Communication, 1,* 238–266.

Cobley, P. (Ed.). (2010). Introduction. In *The Routledge companion to semiotics* (pp. 3–12). New York: Routledge.

Curtis, L., Edwards, C., Fraser, K. L., Gudelsky, S., Holmquist, J., Thornton, K., & Sweetser, K. D. (2009). Adoption of social media for public relations by nonprofit organizations, *Public Relations Review, 36*(1), 90–92.

Dahlgren, P. (2005). The internet, public spheres, and political communication: Dispersion and deliberation. *Political Communication, 22,* 147–162.

Delia, J. G. (1987). Communication research: A history. In C R. Berger & S. H. Chaffee (Eds.), *Handbook of communication science* (20–98). Newbury Park, CA: Sage.

Derrida, J. (1996). Remarks on deconstruction and pragmatism. In C. Mouffe (Ed.), *Deconstruction and pragmatism* (pp. 77–88). New York: Routledge.

Derrida, J. (1998). *Of grammatology*. Baltimore, MD: The Johns Hopkins University Press.

Derrida, J. (2003). The 'world' of the enlightenment to come (exception, calculation, sovereignty). *Research in Phenomenology, 33,* 9–52.

Dewey, J. (1891). *Outlines of a critical theory of ethics*. Ann Arbor, MI: Register Publishing.

Dewey, J. (1929a). *The quest for certainty: A study of the relation of knowledge and action (Gifford lectures)*. New York: Minton, Balch & Company.

Dewey, J. (1929b). *Experience and nature (Lectures upon the Paul Carus Foundation, First Series)*. Chicago, IL: Open Court Publishing Company. (Original work published 1925).

Dewey, J. (1938). *Logic: The theory of inquiry*. New York: Henry Holt and Company.

Dewey, J. (1939a). The future of liberalism or, the democratic way of change. In *What is democracy? Its conflicts, ends and means* (pp. 3–10). Norman, OK: Cooperative Books.

Dewey, J. (1939b). Creative democracy—The task before us. In L. A. Hickman & T. M. Alexander (Eds.), *The essential Dewey, volume 1: Pragmatism, education, democracy* (pp. 340–343). Bloomington, IN: Indiana University Press.

Dewey, J. (1954). *The public and its problems*. Athens, OH: Ohio University Press. (Original work published 1927).

Dewey, J. (1973a). The experimental theory of knowledge. In J. McDermott (ed.), *The philosophy of John Dewey: Volume I, the structure of experience* (pp. 175–193). New York: G. P. Putnam's Sons. (Original work published 1906).

Dewey, J. (1973b). Having an experience. In J. McDermott (ed.), *The philosophy of John Dewey: Volume II, the lived experience* (pp. 554–573). New York: G. P. Putnam's Sons. (Original work published 1939).

Dewey, J. & Bentley, A. F. (1975). *Knowing and the known*. Westport, CT: Greenwood Press. (Original work published 1949/1960).

Downey, J., & Fenton, N. (2010). New media, counter publicity and the public sphere. *New Media & Society, 5*(2), 185–202.

Edwards, L. (2012). Exploring the role of public relations as a cultural intermediary occupation. *Cultural Sociology, 6*(4), 438–454.

Eldridge, M. (1996). Dewey's faith in democracy as shared experience. *Transactions of the Charles S. Peirce Society, 32*(1), 11–30.

Ermarth, E. D. (1998). Postmodernism. In the *Routledge Encyclopedia of Philosophy*. (7:587–590). Edward Craig (Ed.). London: Routledge.

Ermarth, E. D. (2001). Beyond history. *Rethinking History: The Journal of Theory and Practice, 5*(2), 195–215.

Foucault, M. (1994). *The order of things: An archeology of the human sciences*. New York: Vintage.

Fott, D. (1991). John Dewey and the philosophical foundations of democracy. *The Social Science Journal, 28*(1), 29–44.

Fuller, M. (2005). *Media ecologies: Materialist energies in art and technoculture*. Cambridge, MA: MIT Press.

Gerbner, G. (Ed.). (1983). *Ferment in the field: Journal of Communication (Special Issue), 33*(3), 4–5.

Good, J. A. (2010). Rereading Dewey's permanent Hegelian deposit. In J. R. Shook & J. A. Good (Eds.), *John Dewey's Philosophy of Spirit, with the 1897 Lecture on Hegel* (pp. 56–89). New York: Fordham University Press.

Grunig, J. E. (1989). Symmetrical presuppositions as a framework for public relations theory. In C. Botan & V. Hazelton (Eds.), *Public relations theory* (pp. 17–44). Hillsdale, NJ: Lawrence Erlbaum Associates.

Grunig, J. E. (1997). A situational theory of publics: Conceptual history, recent challenges and new research. In D. Moss, T. MacManus, & D. Verčič (Eds.), Public relations research: An international perspective (pp. 3–48). London: International Thomson Business Press.

Grunig, J.E., & Hunt, T. (1984). *Managing public relations.* New York: Holt, Rinehart and Winston.

Grunig, J. E., & White (1992). The effect of worldviews on public relations theory and practice. In J. E. Grunig (Ed.), *Excellence in public relations and communication management* (31–64). Hillsdale, NJ: Lawrence Erlbaum Associates.

Haas, T. (2004). The public sphere as a sphere of publics: Rethinking Habermas's theory of the public sphere. *Journal of Communication, 54*(1), 178–184.

Habermas, J. (1970). Towards a theory of communicative competence. *Inquiry: An Interdisciplinary Journal of Philosophy, 13*(1–4), 360–375.

Habermas, J. (1984). *The theory of communicative action, Vol. I and II,* (T. McCarthy, Trans.). Boston: Beacon Press. (Original work published 1981).

Habermas, J. (1991). *The structural transformation of the public sphere: An inquiry into a category of bourgeois society.* Cambridge, MA: MIT Press. (Original work published 1989).

Habermas, J. (1996). *Between facts and norms.* (W. Rehg, Trans.). Cambridge, MA: MIT Press. (Original work published 1992).

Habermas (1998). *On the pragmatics of communication* (edited by Maeve Cooke). Cambridge, MA: The MIT Press.

Habermas, J. (2002). Postscript: Some concluding remarks. In M. Aboulafia, M. Bookman, & C. Kemp (Eds.), *Habermas and pragmatism* (pp. 223–233). London and New York: Routledge.

Habermas, J. (2005). The public sphere: An encyclopedia article (1964) (S. Lennox & F. Lennox, Trans.) *New German Critique, 3,* pp. 49–55. (Original work published 1974).

Habermas, J. (2006). Political communication in media society: Does democracy still enjoy and epistemic dimension? The impact of normative theory on empirical research. *Communication Theory, 16*(4), 411–426.

Hardt, H. (1979). *Social theories of the press: Early German and American perspectives.* Beverly Hills, CA: Sage.

Hassan, R. (2003). *The chronoscopic society: Globalization, time and knowledge in the network economy.* New York: Peter Lang Publishing.

Hegel, G. W. F. (1977). *Phenomenology of spirit* (A. V. Miller, Trans.). New York: Oxford University Press.

Hickman, L A. (2007). *Pragmatism as post-postmodernism: Lessons from John Dewey.* New York: Fordham University Press.

Hickman, L. A., Heubert, S., & Reich, K. (Eds). (2009). *John Dewey between pragmatism and constructivism.* New York: Fordham University Press.

Hildebrand, D. L. (2008). *Dewey: A beginner's guide.* Oxford: Oneworld Publications.

Hildebrand, D. L. (2011). Pragmatic democracy: Inquiry, objectivity, and experience. *Metaphilosophy, 42*(5), 589–604.

Holtzhausen, D. R. (2007). Activism. In E. L. Toth (Ed.), *The future of excellence in public relations and communication management: Challenges for the next* generation (pp. 357–379). Mahwah, NJ: Lawrence Erlbaum Associates.

Holtzhausen, D. R. (2012). *Public relations as activism: Postmodern approaches to theory & practice.* New York: Routledge.

Hytten, K. (2009). Deweyan democracy in a globalized world. *Educational Theory, 59*(4), 395–408.

Ihlen, Ø. (2011). On Barnyard scrambles: Toward rhetoric of public relations. *Management Communication Quarterly, 25*(3), 455–473.

Ingram, D. (2002). The sirens of pragmatism versus the priests of proceduralism: Habermas and American legal realism. In M. Aboulafia, M. Bookman, & C. Kemp (Eds.), *Habermas and pragmatism* (pp. 83–112). London: Routledge.

Jackson, P. W. (2006). John Dewey. In J. R. Shook & J. Margolis (Eds.), *A companion to pragmatism* (pp. 54–66). Oxford, England: Blackwell.

Jenkins, H. (2006). *Convergence culture: Where old and new media collide.* New York: New York University Press.

Jensen, I. (2001). Public relations and emerging functions of the public sphere: An analytical framework. *Journal of Communication Management, 6*(2), 133–147.

Joas, H. (1991). The unhappy marriage of hermeneutics and functionalism. In A. Honneth & H. Joas (Eds.), *Communicative action: Essays on Jürgen Habermas's The Theory of Communicative Action* (J. Gaines & D. L. Jones, Trans.) (pp. 97–118). Cambridge: MIT Press.

Joas, H. (1993). *Pragmatism and social theory.* Chicago, IL: University of Chicago Press.

Kent, M. (2011). Public relations rhetoric: Criticism, dialogue, and the long now. *Management Communication Quarterly, 25*(3), 550–559.

Kent, M., & Taylor, M. (2002). Toward a dialogic theory of public relations. *Public Relations Review, 28,* 21–37.

Kull, K. (2010). Umwelt and modeling. In Paul Cobley (ed.), *The Routledge companion to semiotics* (pp. 43–56). New York: Routledge.

Latour, B. (1993). *We Have Never Been Modern.* (Catherine Porter, Trans.). Cambridge, MA: Harvard University Press. (Original work published 1991).

Leary, D. E. (2009). Between Peirce (1878) and James (1898): G. Stanley Hall, the origins of pragmatism, and the history of psychology. *Journal of the History of the Behavioral Sciences, 45*(1), 5–20.

Lippmann, W. (1925). *The phantom public.* New York: Harcourt Brace.

Ljunggren, C. (2003). The public has to define itself: Dewey, Habermas, and Rorty on democracy and individuality. *Studies in Philosophy and Education, 22,* 351–370.

Lyotard, J. F. (1984). *The postmodern condition: A report on knowledge.* (G. Bennington & B. Massumi, Trans.). Minneapolis, MN: University of Minnesota Press. (Original work published 1979).

Margolis, J. (2006). Introduction: Pragmatism, retrospective and prospective. In J. R. Shook & J. Margolis (Eds.), *A companion to pragmatism* (pp. 1–10). Oxford, England: Blackwell.

Marsh, C. W. (2001). Public relations ethics: Contrasting models from the rhetorics of Plato, Aristotle, and Isocrates. *Journal of Mass Media Ethics, 16*(2 & 3), 78–98.

Marsh, C. W. (2003). Antecedents of two-way symmetry in classical Greek rhetoric: The rhetoric of Isocrates. *Public Relations Review, 29*(3), 351–367.

McCarthy, T. (1984). Translator's introduction. In J. Habermas, *The theory of communicative action I* (pp. v–xxxvii). Boston, MA: Beacon Press.

McDermott, J. J. (Ed.). (1973a). *The philosophy of John Dewey: Volume I, the structure of experience.* New York: G. P. Putnam's Sons.

McDermott, J. J. (Ed.). (1973b). *The philosophy of John Dewey: Volume II, the lived experience.* New York: G. P. Putnam's Sons.

McNair, B. (2006). *Cultural chaos: Journalism, news, and power in a globalised world.* London: Routledge.

Monge, P., & Contractor, N. (2003). *Theories of communication networks.* New York: Oxford University Press.

Morris, D. (1999). How shall we read what we call reality? John Dewey's new science of democracy. *American Journal of Political Science, 43*(2), 608–628.

Motion, J. (2005). Participative public relations: power to the people or legitimacy for government discourse? *Public Relations Review, 31,* 505–512.

Motion, J., & Weaver, C. K. (2005). A discourse perspective for critical public relations research: Life sciences network and the battle for truth. *Journal of Public Relations Research, 17*(1), 49–67.

Mouffe, C. (1996). *Deconstruction and pragmatism: Critchley, Derrida, Laclau & Rorty.* London: Routledge.

Mounce, H. (1997). *The two pragmatisms: from Peirce to Rorty.* New York: Routledge.

Murphy, P. (2007). Coping with an uncertain world: The relationship between excellence and complexity theories. In E. L. Toth (Ed.), *The future of excellence in public relations and communication management: Challenges for the next generation* (pp. 119–134). Mahwah, NJ: Lawrence Erlbaum Associates.

Neubert, S. (2010). Democracy and education in the twenty-first century: Deweyan pragmatism and the question of racism. *Educational Theory, 60*(4), 487–502.

Newman, M. (2011). *Networks: An introduction.* Oxford: Oxford University Press.

Papacharissi, Z. (2002). The virtual sphere: The internet as a public sphere. *New Media & Society, 4*(1), 9–27.

Papacharissi, Z. (2010). *A Private Sphere: Democracy in a Digital Age.* Cambridge: Polity Press.

Pearson, R. (1989). Business ethics as communication ethics: Public relations practice and the idea of dialogue. In C. H. Botan & V. Hazleton (Eds.), *Public relations theory* (111–131). Hillsdale, NJ: Lawrence Erlbaum.

Perry, D. K. (2001). *American pragmatism and communication research.* Mahwah, NJ: Lawrence Erlbaum Associates.

Peters, J. D. (1993). Distrust of representation: Habermas on the public sphere. *Media, Culture and Society, 15,* 541–571.

Reynolds, A. (2009). The afterlife of dead metaphors: On Derrida's pragmatism. *Revista de Letras, 49*(2), 181–195.

Rogers, E. M. (1994). *A history of communication study: A biographical approach.* New York: The Free Press.

Rogers, M. L. (2010). Dewey and his vision of democracy. *Contemporary Pragmatism, 7*(1), 69–91.

Rorty, R. (1996). Remarks on deconstruction and pragmatism. In C. Mouffe (Ed.), *Deconstruction and pragmatism* (pp. 13–18). New York: Routledge.

Rorty, R. (2007). *Contingency, irony, and solidarity.* Cambridge: Cambridge University Press. (Original work published 1989).

Rosenthal, S. B. (2002). Habermas, Dewey, and the democratic self. In M. Aboulafia, M. Bookman, & C. Kemp (Eds.), *Habermas and pragmatism* (210–222). London: Routledge.

Ryan, F. X. (1997). The "extreme heresy" of John Dewey and Arthur F. Bentley II: A star crossed collaboration? *Transactions of the Charles S. Peirce Society, 33*(3), 1003–1023.

Saussure, F. de (1996). The object of linguistics. In P. Cobley (Ed.), *The communication theory reader* (pp. 37–47). New York: Routledge.

Schudson, M. (2008). The "Lippmann-Dewey debate" and the invention of Walter Lippmann as an anti-democrat 1986–1996. *International Journal of Communication, 2,* 1031–1042.

Scott, J. P. (2000). *Social network analysis: A handbook* (2nd ed.). Thousand Oaks, CA: Sage

Searle, J. R. (1983). *Intentionality, an essay in the philosophy of mind.* New York: Cambridge University Press.

Self, C. C. (2009). The evolution of mass communication theory in the twentieth century. *The Romanian Review of Journalism and Communication, 6*(3), 29–42.

Self, C. C. (2010). Hegel, Habermas, and community: The public in the new media era. *International Journal of Strategic Communication, 4*(2), 78–92.

Self, C. C. (2013). Who. In P. Cobely & P. Schultz (Eds.), *Theories and models of communication Vol. I* (pp. 351–368). London: Routledge.

Shirky, C. (2008). *Here comes everybody: The power of organizing without organizations.* New York: Penguin Press.

Shook, J. R. (2010). Dewey's naturalized philosophy of spirit and religion. In J. R. Shook & J. A. Good, *John Dewey's philosophy of spirit, with the 1897 lecture on Hegel* (pp. 3–55). New York: Fordham University Press.

Shook, J. R. & Good, J. A. (2010). *John Dewey's philosophy of spirit, with the 1897 lecture on Hegel.* New York: Fordham University Press.

Skerlep, A. (2001). Re-evaluating the role of rhetoric in public relations theory and in strategies of corporate discourse. *Journal of Communication Management, 6*(2), 176–187.

Stacey, R. D. (1996). *Complexity and creativity in organizations.* San Francisco: Berrett Koehler.

Stacey, R. D. (2003). *Strategic management and organizational dynamics: The challenge of complexity.* Harlow, England: Prentice Hall.

Stacey, R. D., & Griffin, D. (Eds.). (2006). *Complexity and the experience of managing in public sector organizations.* New York: Routledge.

Stoker, K. L., & Berg K. T. (2006). Reconsidering public relations' infatuation with dialogue: Why engagement and reconciliation can be more ethical than symmetry and reciprocity. *Journal of Mass Media Ethics, 21*(2–3), 156–176.

Ströh, U. (2007). An alternative postmodern approach to corporate communication strategy. In E. L. Toth (Ed.), *The future of excellence in public relations and communication management: Challenges for the next generation* (199–220). Mahwah, NJ: Lawrence Erlbaum Associates.

Sunstein, C. R. (2006). *Infotopia: How many minds produce knowledge.* Oxford, England: Oxford University Press.

Taylor, M. (2011). Building social capital through rhetoric and public relations. *Management Communication Quarterly, 25*(3), 436–454.

Troup, C. L. (2009). Ordinary people can reason: A rhetorical case for including vernacular voices in ethical public relations practice. *Journal of Business Ethics, 87*(4), 441–453.

Westbrook, R. B. (1991). *John Dewey and American democracy.* Ithaca, NY: Cornell University Press.

6

Strategic Communication in a Networked World

Integrating Network and Communication Theories in the Context of Government to Citizen Communication

Lindsay Young and Willem Pieterson

The relative health of a democracy is in large part a function of the quantity and quality of information that flows between government institutions and citizens. Bimber (2003) argued American society has undergone a series of information revolutions whereby changes in information *costs, flows,* and *distributions* have had profound implications for the balance of power between governments and citizens. Facilitating these shifts are revolutions in communication technology, which have led to information abundance, low-cost accessibility, a more symmetric distribution, and a more networked, nonlinear flow.

Three broader societal changes accompany these changes, which might have broader implications for the management of strategic communication between organizations and their clients. First, there is a change in the structure of society (van Dijk, 2006). Once organized in a pillarized, vertical fashion, whereby governments exercise power over citizens, society now is increasingly organized around a networked logic that emphasizes horizontal relationships and the power of flows (as opposed to flows of power) (Castells, 2009). Second, individualization (Castells, 1996; van Dijk, 2006) makes it more difficult to reach citizens in a ubiquitous, uniform fashion. Finally, the foundation of *trust* between governments and citizens has changed. Previously, trust in government derived from a sense of morality, whereas now trust is more often rooted in direct judgments of governmental performance (Uslaner, 2002). Together these changes have spawned a wealth of scholarship aimed at re-theorizing familiar concepts like the public sphere (Fraser, 1990; Downey & Fenton, 2003), civic engagement (Putnam, 2000), and collective action (Castells, 1996; 2009).

However, we argue that emerging out of these fundamental shifts is a far more practical concern to which communication scholars have paid little attention: *How can governments harness the power of network flows in order to engage in more effective communication with citizens?* Governments and citizens have reason to communicate and interact frequently. In a formal fashion, citizens may contact governmental groups with questions regarding a multitude of topics (e.g., the provision of social services), and governments strategically use information platforms and campaigns to communicate with and influence citizens. Less formally, citizens often desire an opportunity to exercise their rights to participate in the political system and engage in dialogue with its representatives.

Although it has been suggested that traditional mass media campaigns are, in many cases, ineffective in reaching people and in influencing peoples' preferences (Petty, Brinol, & Priester, 2009), especially in light of the societal shifts discussed above, it appears that governments continue to push their information via allocution mechanisms (Weiss & Tschirhart, 2007) through mass media to citizens, leaving little opportunity for citizens to initiate dialogue with the change agents behind governmental campaigns. Furthermore, as Bandura (2001, p. 286) argued: "The absence of individualized guidance limits the power of one-way mass communications," thus challenging the effectiveness of such campaigns.

In light of the communication obstacles laid before them, citizens who have questions or a desire to engage in political discourse are more inclined to inform themselves through their social and media networks (Estabrook, Witt, & Rainie, 2007) rather than rely on institutional sources. This undermines governmental credibility and degrades the image of governmental authority (Bimber, 2003). Even if government groups are willing to integrate new technological platforms into their communication repertoire, Reddick (2005) notes that the increase in available media from which citizens can access information and contribute feedback complicates devising effective strategies for communication outreach. Similarly, marketing studies show the difficulties advertisers have ensuring effective message delivery to consumers, which they attribute to consumers' reliance on social ties for product information and referrals as opposed to information sponsored by producers (Katona & Mueller, 1995).

Taken together, the changes in our society and the technology-driven alterations in communication infrastructure lead to two important related questions for communication theorists and practitioners. First, *to what extent are current communication theories capable of capturing the complexities that our changing society and communication infrastructure caused?* And second, *to what extent are current theories capable of informing the design and implementation of an effective communication campaign between governments and citizens?*

In this chapter we argue traditional theories of communication that presume linear flows, hierarchical authority, and direct effects are too simplistic to capture the (communication) complexities of contemporary society and are too rigid to capture the flexible and context-specific nature of the communicative behaviors of citizens. Relying on the assumptions these models espouse to guide strategic communication decisions exacerbates the communicative ineffectiveness of government organizations and contributes to their overall frayed relationships with citizens. We take an initial step toward correcting the misalignment between the communication realities of citizens and the practices of government communicators by establishing a networked-communication framework suited for strategic communication research and practice. This framework challenges current communication theories and (governmental) practices along four dimensions:

1. the nature of the audience
2. the overall multiplexity of citizens' source and channel repertoires
3. the varied motivations behind individuals' channel selections
4. the embeddedness of information flows within a social context.

To begin, we provide an annotated picture of the shifts in communication theory, particularly regarding how they conceptualize processes of influence, and examine research regarding government–citizen interaction to highlight mechanisms believed to affect this crucial relationship. Next, in light of changes to the communication environment in which governments and citizens are embedded, we explicate an enlightened set of propositions regarding communication flows that take as their starting point our networked reality. We argue that these propositions should serve as the foundation for strategic communication efforts between governments and citizens. To exemplify the grounded insights that a practitioner can glean if she allows the logic of these propositions to guide her approach to campaign design and implementation, we draw on data from a network study the authors conducted in the context of a municipal climate change initiative. We conclude by offering recommendations for practitioners on how to translate theoretical insights into actionable practices in the field.

The Evolution of Communication Theory

Theories of interpersonal influence have evolved from linear transmission models, to two-step models, to multi-stage diffusion models, and most recently to a more holistic networked framework. Traditional thinking about communication flows and social influence emphasizes formal media channels (e.g., newspapers, television, radio, and the Internet) as sources of information and influence. Granting media this status reflects presumptions in early mass communication scholarship, most notably the work of Lasswell (e.g., 1948), that the relationship between media and audience is a direct one. Dubbed the "Hypodermic Needle" Hypothesis, this belief became the dominant paradigm for understanding the flow of information as a direct and linear process. Other models predicated on a similar set of principles followed, such as Shannon and Weaver's (1949) *Mathematical Theory of Communication.*

The limitations of such linear models become apparent in their application to the study of mass communication effects and interpersonal influence. The main problem stems from the epistemological assumptions made in these models regarding the nature of information, how it is transmitted, and what we do with it. Information is treated as if it were a physical entity, like a material object, that can be moved around at will. Moreover, these assumptions lead to the miscalculation, "that the individual mind is an isolated entity, separate from the body, separate from other minds, and separate from the environment in which it exists" (Rogers & Kincaid, 1981, p. 38). Therefore, what goes missing from these linear, one-way models is the role played by one's social/relational environment in the communication process.

The first challenge to direct effect perspectives came in the form of the *"two-step flow"* hypothesis derived by Lazarsfeld and colleagues. Social theorists, such as Tarde and Simmel, viewed social phenomena like public opinion as products of relations between individuals interdependently connected in a network of affiliations (Mattelart & Mattelart, 2004). Lazarsfeld and his colleagues (1944) validated the notion that ideas are relationally constructed, finding that interpersonal interactions with opinion leaders often mediated the relationship message producer and message consumer and, therefore, affected the development of an individual's decisions and opinions.

The "two-step flow" model is aptly credited for refocusing communication research on the mediating role of interpersonal ties in the flow of information between institutions, mass media and various publics. However, it has not escaped familiar critiques of being too linear and oversimplified. For example, in some instances influence may occur in one step, as when media have direct impact on an individual, but in other instances a multistage communication process may occur (Rogers & Kinkaid, 1981).

To advance our understanding of the relational dynamics of information flows, Rogers (2003) posited his well-known *Diffusion of Innovations (DOI) Theory.* Consisting of four main elements, the diffusion of new ideas is thought to involve

1. an *innovation*
2. that is communicated through certain *channels*
3. over *time*
4. among the members of a *social system.*

Like the "two-step flow" model, *DOI Theory* empirically demarcates the roles opinion leaders or "early adopters" play in processes of influence. However, it more clearly delineates information flows as occurring within holistic networks as opposed to simple dyadic relationships between an individual and an opinion leader. For example, opinion leaders exert influence on audience behavior via their personal contact, but additional intermediaries called change agents and gatekeepers are also included in the process of diffusion. Thus, Rogers accounts for different types of people in the social system likely to influence the decision cycle at different stages of its evolution.

Challenges have also been brought to bear on the *DOI* model, primarily for ignoring the context of communication, defining interlocutors as isolated atoms, and painting influence as a process of one-way, linear causality (Mattelart & Mattelart, 2004). Revisiting his thinking, Rogers proposed to replace the diffusion model with an explicit networked model of communication, called the *convergence model* (Rogers & Kincaid, 1981). From a convergence perspective, the goal of communication is not simply to influence or persuade in a top-down manner, but rather to promote mutual understanding and agreement. As such, communication is understood to be a "dynamic, cyclical process over time that is characterized by (1) mutual causation rather than one-way mechanistic causation, and emphasizing (2) the interdependent relationship of the participants, rather than a bias toward either the source or the receiver of messages" (p. 69).

More recently, communication scholars Monge and Contractor (2003) have brought networks to the forefront of communication scholarship. They described communication networks as "the patterns of contact that are created by the flow of messages among communicators through time and space" (p. 3). As such, communication networks are conceptualized as the emergent outcomes of routinized interactions and exchanges that subsequently have important social and behavioral consequences for the individuals embedded within them (Freeman, 2004).

As a process, then, *influence* is one thing that happens within a communication network as information and ideas flow between individual actors in the system. For those who seek to promote attitudinal or behavioral changes within a community or social network, identifying the patterns of information exchange within that network is a crucial step in being able to effectively gain support for those changes. In the context of health communication, simulations that compared traditional allocation models of communication with networked multi-step flows showed that the allocution model missed a key point in the spread of information: "the diffusion of the advisory from its initial audience to others" (Dhanjal, Blanchemanche, Clémençon, Rona-Tas, & Rossi, 2012). Instead, they found that the networked approach to dissemination was more effective in spreading the information throughout the targeted population.

In sum, theory development has progressed, but incrementally, in its shift away from traditional linear models toward networked perspectives on the flow of information. This is a trend that is even more pronounced when we consider the development of specific theories describing the communicative relationships between governments and citizens. We now turn to the current state of research and theory development about this relationship.

Government–Citizen Interaction in a Networked Society

One of the key developments in contemporary society is the arrival of the Internet, a development that has changed the way citizens interact with one another and with governmental agencies (McNeal, Hale & Dotterweich, 2008; Reddick, 2005). Recognizing the salience of the Internet as a communication platform, many governments are moving services online and adopting electronic media to communicate with citizens. This new approach to governance is referred to as e-government, which Gartner defines as: "the continuous optimization of service delivery, constituency participation, and governance by transforming internal and external relationships through technology, the Internet and new media." (Baum & Di Maio, 2000).

Amidst the rise of the Internet in the 1990s emerged utopian visions of how the relationship between governments and citizens would change. The Internet was believed to be an ideal infrastructure to make governments more citizen-centric and to improve communications. As Symonds (2000) prophesized, "Within the next five years the internet (*sic*) will transform not only the way in which most public services are delivered, but also the fundamental relationship between government and citizens" (p.3).

However, several practical realizations have since emerged that challenge the idealism expressed behind these claims. First, although the Internet hosts and facilitates media such as websites, email, chat, and social media (e.g., Twitter, Myspace and Facebook), citizens' preferences for communicating with government agencies are not necessarily following suit. Rather, research shows that when citizens interact with governments they use *more* media—old and new—in parallel with one another (Pieterson & Ebbers, 2008). Citizens do not simply replace their traditional media preferences with newer counterparts.

Second, Web 2.0 tools, such as social media, have enhanced the information capital of an individual's personal network (Resnick & Carroll, 2002). Prior to the emergence of social media, citizens typically received their information about public issues through institutional sources. Now, social media like Facebook and Twitter facilitate information exchanges within peoples' social networks (Boase, Horrigan, Wellman, & Rainie, 2006; Ellison, Steinfield, & Lampe, 2007), making government-sanctioned communication less relevant to their opinion formation. For governments, these changes have made it more difficult to manage the flows of information amongst citizens using only formal communication channels.

A general dearth of knowledge regarding how people actually use and perceive digital channels also exacerbates the information management difficulties government communicators face. Missing from working knowledge is a detailed picture of how people position the Internet as an information source as compared to informal contacts, television, newspapers, libraries, and other sources (Savolainen & Kari, 2004). From research on information search behaviors we know that information exchanges often entail multiple stages of searching, evaluating, and reflecting (Ramirez, Walther, Burgoon, and Sunnafrank, 2002). We also know that exchanges often involve multiple sources. For example, young people often triangulate their search strategy, using multiple sources at the same time (Roberts, 2000). But understanding why people choose certain media over others or in combination is even more complicated to unpack. Studies of media choice behavior show these choices are in many cases habitual, influenced by emotions, and situation-dependent (Pieterson, 2009). For these reasons, it is difficult for governments to predict when and for what purpose a citizen will deploy certain media to get information.

Confounding things further is the role intermediaries play as catalysts between governments and citizens or businesses (Millard, 2006). As a broker between governments and their clients, intermediaries not only supply governmental clients with information about government regulations, but also help them complete—often complex—transactions online (Van den Boer, Van de Wijngaert, Pieterson, & Arendsen, 2012; Jansen, Van de Wijngaert & Pieterson, 2010). While it may be desirable to involve intermediaries in service strategy, identifying these intermediaries and integrating them into a working system of information exchange is yet another challenge facing strategic communication and information management efforts.

In summary, these developments point to the need for a networked perspective regarding the relationship between governments and citizens; however, we have little knowledge about governmental communication in its social context (Kinder, 1998). With its focus on relational dynamics within a larger environmental context, social network analysis is a valuable tool for unpacking some of these questions. However, few studies exist that examine the networked context of government-citizen interaction. Furthermore, although social network analysis has been used extensively to see how information flows through networks of individual actors (Freeman, 2004), less attention has been paid to how individuals and organizations interact, including the role various communication channels play in these interactions.

In light of the inadequacy of more traditional perspectives on communication processes, we explicate a set of theoretically grounded assumptions regarding communication flows that take as their starting point our networked reality. We argue these assumptions should serve as the foundation for strategic communication efforts between governments and citizens and should be brought to bear on data collection procedures in applied strategic communication research settings.

Data Site and Collection Procedures

To exemplify the insights strategic communication practitioners can gain from integrating our networked propositions into audience research, we provide empirical support for each assumption based on an exploratory study we conducted in the context of a climate change initiative in the City of Chicago called *The Chicago Climate Action Plan (CCAP)*. What follows is a brief description of this site and data collection procedures.

Data Site

The *Chicago Climate Action Plan (CCAP)* is a citywide initiative to reduce its carbon footprint and pave a path toward a more sustainable future. Recognizing that community dynamics should influence the nature and direction of strategic outreach, CCAP agents made a concerted effort to learn more about the community-based social contexts in which environmental decisions are made, particularly decisions made by everyday citizens in their daily routines.

South Chicago is one such setting. An ethnically diverse community, South Chicago has an African American population of 62%, a Latino population of 33.4%, and a white population of 5.6%; it is largely working-class and low income, with a median income of $34,279. Born out of the growth of the American steel industry in the nineteenth century and embedded in ecological richness, the cultural identity of South Chicago remains largely entwined in these dualistic realities—industrialization and ecological integrity. Combined, these characteristics made South Chicago an appealing site for further investigation.

Data Collection Procedures

As research partners in the CCAP initiative, we conducted a network survey amongst South Chicago residents in order to map and assess their information environments. Data was collected using a three-part structured questionnaire, each section designed to elicit information about individuals' organizational, media, and peer-based sources of information, respectively. Surveys were administered in person by six trained interviewers who themselves lived in South Chicago and who shared high levels of knowledge and understanding about the social structure of their community. Survey data was collected using *C-IKNOW* (*Cyber-infrastructure for Inquiring Knowledge Networks on the Web*), a web-based software tool designed to collect and analyze survey-based network data.

The Sample

Survey participants were recruited using a snowball sampling technique called *respondent driven sampling* (Heckathorn, 2002). A first wave of respondents, referred to as *seeds*, was selected on the basis of fit to particular demographic profiles constructed to represent key demographic groups in the community. As members of the community, interviewers were assigned one to two profiles and asked to identify individuals within their personal network of family, friends, and acquaintances that fit the profile(s) they were assigned.

After the seeds completed the survey, they each named one to three peers they thought would be willing to take the survey. These referrals became the next wave of respondents, and each subsequent wave of participants was populated using the same referral system. In the case that a chain dissipated because referral(s) could not be reached or refused to participate, interviewers were instructed to start a new chain by targeting a new person who matched the original seed profile to which they were initially assigned.

In total, 285 residents completed the survey. Of these, 54% were male and 46% were female. Nearly 65% had at least "some college" experience, with 19% of those having a bachelor's degree and almost 4% having a graduate degree. About 75% of respondents fell between the ages of 19 and 39 years, of which about 40% were 30–39 years old.

An Integration of Theory and Practice

Based on the analysis of communication theories and the government-citizen setting, we now present four propositions that offer starting points for the development of a new perspective on government-citizen communication that have both theoretical and practical implications.

Network Assumption #1: Audiences Will Display Multidimensionality in their Communicative Relationship with Government Groups, Acting as both Information Receivers and Information Producers

A networked perspective underscores the bi-directional flows of information and communication between government parties and citizens. The interactive capacities of new ICT platforms such as blogs, wikis, and social networking sites not only provide audiences with access to information produced for them, but through actions such as commenting and liking, users also have the opportunity to author information and provide feedback that government agencies can use to inform their public policies. Knowing that audiences have the tendency to play both roles—consumers and producers—makes a traditional "push" strategy of government-citizen communication, whereby information is pushed downward from communication practitioners or topical specialists to lay citizens, seems naïve if not misguided (Bandura, 2001).

Personal influence is a more dynamic process that involves top-down and bottom-up vertical flows as well as intermediate, horizontal flows among citizens themselves (Erickson, 1988). In these contexts, citizens produce and consume information. And, as they consume information, they do so in active and passive ways. As such, knowing the degree to which campaign targets would actually utilize the interactive capacities of ICT to both produce and consume information and interact with government agencies is a crucial step toward effectively engaging audiences. In the context of the CCAP campaign, three types of data were collected and used to demonstrate audience dualities: the types of media outlets on which respondents relied to obtain information; the interactive capacities of the channels through which they would use to obtain information from organizational sources of information; and the extent to which respondents initiated interpersonal conversations to obtain information.

"Push" versus "pull" media outlets

From a comprehensive list of media outlets that represented print, broadcast, and web-based formats, respondents selected the media they would use to obtain information about household and community concerns, including those related to sustainability practices. Nearly 60% of the 290 respondents said they would use a *search engine* like Google to find information and 32% indicated that they would rely on a *web portal* like Yahoo. Both preferences imply respondents prefer media that allow them to actively search for the information they need, granting them control over the type and quality of information to which they are eventually exposed.

However, as noted earlier, despite the availability of new interactive information platforms, individuals do not necessarily replace their "old media" preferences with new ones. Thus, it was not surprising to also learn that respondents would still turn to more traditional media outlets like regional and local newspapers, as well as local network affiliates and public television. While there is no right or wrong way to obtain information, respecting audience members' typical approach to obtaining information is integral to facilitating effective communication. Learning that respondents considered both traditional "push" media and digital "pull" media to be viable sources of information warranted recommending a hybrid approach to communication outreach.

The interactive nature of communication channels

In addition to naming the organizations they would consult for information or advice about household and community related concerns, respondents were also asked to identify the communication channels they would use to access each source they named. Channels included *face-to-face, telephone, mail, website, social networking sites,* and *letter writing*. This was then followed by a forced choice question, whereby respondents selected the channel they most preferred using to communicate with organizations.

When communicating with organizations respondents revealed a preference for more traditional, intimate channels, like face-to-face and telephone. However, going to an organization's website was also commonly cited as a viable mode of obtaining information from an organization. The website is a far less intimate mode of communication and is one that grants less interaction between the producer and consumer of information. This implies that in some cases, individuals may not need or want to engage in two-way communication with an organization in order to obtain information.

Initiators versus initiatees in interpersonal conversation

During the process of learning about an issue, formulating an opinion, and making a decision, individuals are influenced by the people with whom they interact. Sometimes the focal person initiates these interactions, while at other times peer conversations draw in the focal person. Asking respondents to provide the names of people with whom they have had opportunities to discuss certain matters, tells researchers and strategists about the degree to which survey respondents actively seek out information (i.e., approaching others first for information) or are exposed to it by others.

In the CCAP studies, after naming the people with whom they *would* consult if they needed advice about climate change specific concerns, further inquiries were made regarding whether or not they had ever engaged in conversation about climate change related issues with any of their potential sources. Of those who had conversed with peers about environmental issues (n=63), 65% were initiators, 51% were initiates, and 16% of the aggregate of initiators and initiates demonstrated both tendencies.

In the end, for information campaigns to be effective in a networked society, they should accommodate audience members' proclivities to initiate the information consumption process through both traditional and contemporary channels. For example, to suit some citizens' preferences for traditional interactive channels like face-to-face and telephone-based modes of communication, campaign sponsors should make information available through front desk service points and patron service hotlines. These outlets should also be supplemented with information made available through new platforms like websites and social media to meet the demands of those who favor digital platforms.

That said, this should not be at the cost of also strategically creating moments of communication with the audience designed for passive information exposure through "push" platforms like print and broadcast media. In many cases, campaign audiences are unaware that they should want or need information in the first place, or they simply do not have the time, skills, or resources to obtain it on their own. As such, being exposed to information may increase an individual's awareness that a problem exists, alter their attitudes, and/or compel them to take active steps on their own to acquire further information.

Network assumption #2: Audiences are immersed in an information environment that is characterized by source and channel multiplexity

Several theories underscore the roles of intermediary information sources in the diffusion of ideas (Katz & Lazarsfeld, 1955; Rogers, 2003). As such, individuals are influenced by a variety of formal and informal sources. Intermediary sources of information, whether they are organizations, media outlets, or peers, are capable of facilitating the flow of communication between governments and citizens. However, if their role in the influence process is not anticipated and effectively managed these intermediate sources are also capable of challenging communication strategists' efforts to influence audiences in intended directions.

To get a sense for the breadth and depth of the information environments they sought to infiltrate, sponsors of the CCAP initiative strove to identify potential intermediate sources in advance. To begin, we found that on average respondents would consult 9.68 organizational sources, 4.07 media outlets, and 4.37 peers, revealing that residents of South Chicago possessed relatively diversified personal information networks. But this presents only a partial, generalized picture of the multiplexity of the information environment that the CCAP campaign must leverage. A more detailed picture emerges when we narrow our gaze to a particular type of source, for example organizations, and examine the nature of these sources and their relationships vis-à-vis one another.

To these ends, we mapped the organizational affiliation network among 50 organizational sources of information (see Figure 6.1). *Nodes,* demarcated by shapes, represent different types of organizations. The lines that connect the nodes are referred to as *ties* (or edges) and symbolize a relationship between nodes. In this case, a tie between two organizations represents their affiliation by virtue of

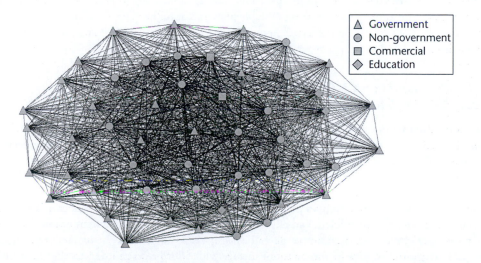

Figure 6.1   Organizational Affiliations by Citizen Patronage

being named as viable sources of information by the same individual. Finally, we weighted the ties to show which organizational pairs are more often co-named as viable sources of information than other pairs, one can see there are numerous ties between different types of organizations, many of them quite strong, indicating that, as a whole, individuals are inclined to diversify their selections of organizational sources of advice and information.

Another layer of multiplexity is found in the various channels (or modes) of communication that are used to interact with sources of information. Theories of channel choice, particularly *Media Richness Theory (MRT)* (Daft & Lengel, 1986), assume unique affordances are built into communication technologies that make their application for particular tasks more or less appropriate. From this perspective, the mode of communication an individual chooses should be a clear, logical choice given the complexity of the task or the depth of the information needed.

However, reality often tells a different story. In South Chicago, surveyed residents revealed a diverse repertoire of channel choices. In the context of Proposition #1 about audience dualities, we showed evidence for a range in channels that individuals preferred using to communicate with organizations about household and community related concerns. Thus, by holding the task and source type constant, the only explanation for the breadth of answers lies in differences between individuals and in their personal attitudes and experiences with each communicative platform.

Channel multiplexity is also evidenced in the modes of communication selected specifically for given sources. Regarding their communication with the 10 most cited organizational sources, respondents indicated they would rely on a relatively consistent, yet diversified repertoire of channels including face-to-face communication, telephone, and web-based modes of engagement.

However, when comparing channel choices across different types of organizations, slight variations emerge. Using the telephone to interact with organizations is a more popular mode of communication when reaching out to service providers like utility companies, whereas the website seems to be a strong choice for obtaining information from municipal agencies. These subtleties suggest there may be something about the nature of the organization itself as opposed to the task that informs channel selections.

In sum, individuals who adopt a repertoire of information sources and communication channels are able to access a more diversified pool of information on which to base their opinions and decisions. As such, they complicate others' efforts to influence them. For the sponsors of information in a communication campaign, managing how a message is interpreted is rarely, if ever, an easy task. However, the more diversified and multiplex an individual's information environment, the more difficult it becomes to maintain control over the message itself. For this reason, the more communication strategists can learn about these multiplexities and how they affect information flows in the environments they seek to influence, the greater their capacity to leverage these dynamics to their advantage as opposed to being thwarted by them.

Network Assumption #3: Source and Channel Selections Depend on the Situational Context

Our third assumption challenges the traditional suppositions made about human behavior when choosing sources of information and communication channels. While some studies have been conducted on the choice of information sources, most theoretical development and empirical studies focus on the process of choosing channels. MRT (Daft & Lengel, 1986) is by far the most well-known of these theories.

It posits that different informational needs require different communication channels in order for communication to be efficient and effective. The theory describes two types of tasks: *uncertainty tasks* motivated by a need for information and *ambiguity tasks* motivated out of a need for interpretation. Each warrants using communication media with affordances tailored to the nature of the communication task.

MRT delineates these affordances by the degrees of *richness* that a medium offers, which are based on four characteristics: immediacy of feedback; number of cues used; level of personalization; and possibility of language variety. Based on these criteria, face-to-face communication would be the richest medium given its possession of all four characteristics, and printed formal documents would be the least rich media type. According to the theory, rich media should be used for ambiguous tasks and lean media are better suited to resolve uncertainty.

While this idea is plausible, empirically validating the task–medium fit has proven more difficult. Many critics attribute MRT's validation problems to its underlying assumption that people are objectively rational in selecting communication media (Bozeman, 1993). Skepticism of full rationality arguments can be traced back to Simon's (1956) contention that people are unable to make fully rational decisions due to time constraints and cognitive limitations. Simon presented the strategy of *satisficing* as a softer form of rational behavior, whereby people do not seek to maximize their profit but try to attain satisfactory levels of decision making instead. This implies that people do behave rationally (in the sense of weighing alternatives), but do so within the limits of *bounded rationality*.

Satisficing, then, may be a more plausible explanation for why particular channels are chosen over others to meet one's information needs. Recent studies on channel and source choices (e.g. Pieterson, 2009; Van den Boer, Wijngaert, Pieterson, & Arendsen, 2012) lend support to the prevalence of satisficing tendencies, showing that *habits* and *situational elements* like proximity to a given source and the influence of peers drive channel choices more than *objective fit*. To learn what objective and situational features motivate source and channel selections amongst South Chicago residents, we asked study participants to indicate *why* they would rely on each source and channel they named. Possible explanations included *proximity, convenience, trust, expertise, familiarity* and *peer use*.

Overall, regarding source motivations, results show that peer consultations tend to be motivated out of *trust* (30.8%), *convenience* (22.5%), and *familiarity* (20.0%), all three of which suggest respondents are driven by the general ease of consulting peers with whom they interact frequently and are generally close. Conversely, if rationality drove source selections then one would expect to see *expertise* as the most important reason for consulting particular peers for advice. Perceptions of a source's *expertise* did motivate decisions in regards to the organizations people would turn to for assistance (34.7%). Taken together, these findings suggest that people are motivated differently depending on the nature of the information source.

The results of our study on sources and other studies on channels (e.g. Pieterson, 2009) do show the selection of the source and channel is not always a rational process, but is heavily dependent on the specific context in which the communication takes place. For strategic communication this implies the strategist should take this context into account, e.g. how familiar audience members are with certain information sources and which channels they use habitually, when planning communication campaigns.

Network Assumption #4: Information Flows are Embedded in a Relational Context that Enables and Constrains Information-Seeking Processes

In the paradigm shift from linear to networked models of communication, increased attention is brought to the relational context in which information and knowledge is generated and exchanged. Thus, the analytical focus of a network approach is on the communicative relationship between actors in a network rather than on individuals in isolation. Furthermore, the network structures that emerge out of these relationships have important consequences for the actors within them (Freeman, 2004), particularly in terms of their ability to access important resources like information. Therefore, for those who seek to promote attitudinal or behavioral changes within a community or social network, identifying the patterns of information exchange within a target population is a crucial step in being able to effectively gain support for those changes.

Ego-Network Composition

One approach to assessing the impact that relational embeddedness can have on information accessibility is to examine the composition of an individual's personal information network. Proponents of resource-based theories of social capital have argued that the degree to which an individual can obtain the resources they need to fulfill information needs and achieve upward social mobility is linked in part to the characteristics of the people to whom they have access (Lin, 1999; 2001; Marsden & Hurlbert, 1988). From this perspective, the socio-demographic traits of an individual's contacts are treated as proxies for the resources that they can reasonably be assumed to possess and, therefore, provide others access to by virtue of their association.

In the CCAP study we wanted to examine the extent to which the members of each respondent's network were demographically similar to the respondent. The relevance of the extent to which personal information networks are characterized by demographic similarity or diversity has to do with the types of resources one can reasonably expect to have access to when embedded in such networks. If we assume that individual characteristics like education, occupation, age, and gender speak to the types of resources one brings to a network, then being embedded in a network comprised of people who are similar to you has the potential to make your network redundant.

To these ends, we computed the mean similarity between each respondent and their respective peers. This was done on the basis of four demographic variables: *gender, education, age cohort,* and *race*. Mean similarity values range from 0 to 1, where a value of "0" represents a personal network that is characterized by completely dissimilar relationships whereas a value of "1" indicates a network comprised of completely similar relationships. A score of .5 is considered the threshold above which the personal relationships that comprise a respondent's core network become more similar than dissimilar.

Overall, we find a general tendency for respondents to consult peers that are similar to them in terms of age, gender, education, and race. While the personal networks of respondents exceeded the .5 threshold of similarity for all four attributes, this trend was particularly noticeable for race. On average a respondent's peer relationships were 76% racially homogenous.

Given that we were primarily concerned with the conditions that facilitate access to *unique* information (i.e., information that an individual does not personally possess), the overall homogeneity of respondents' personal networks could be interpreted as a constraint in that peers with similar traits as the respondent are less likely to provide novel insight. On the other hand, similarities foster trust. Thus, having relationships with peers who are similar to you is likely to facilitate more pronounced levels of trust in those people. And, in the context of advice seeking, an individual who trusts the person giving the advice may be more likely to take and follow the advice being sought.

Ego-Network Structure

Another approach to assessing the impact relationships have on information accessibility is to examine their structural properties. Some social capital theorists have suggested that an individual gains value (or capital) from being embedded in particular types of network structures (Wellman and Frank, 2001; Burt, 1992; Coleman, 1988). They have argued that the structural configuration of a network, specifically its density, conditions information flows in particular ways.

To demonstrate, Figure 6.2 shows four versions of the same ego (or personal) network on a scale of increasing network density. In each, the ego (i.e., the owner of the network) is depicted

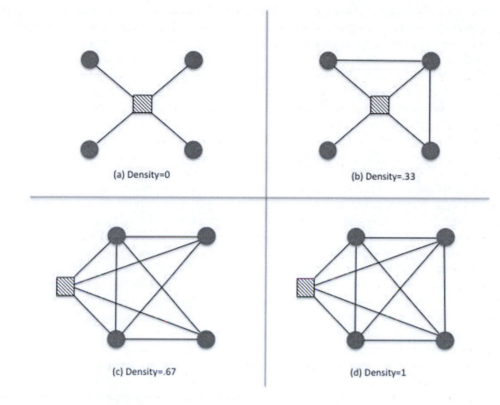

(a) Density=0

(b) Density=.33

(c) Density=.67

(d) Density=1

Figure 6.2   Ego-Networks With Varying Densities

as a square and her alters (i.e., peers) are shown as circles. Figure 6.2a represents a completely open network in which the ego is the only actor who connects all others. Whereas, Figure 6.2d shows a completely closed network in which the ego and her alters are directly connected.

Theorizing strategic advantage in organizational settings, Burt (1992) posits that an individual accrues the most benefit from her or his relational surroundings when she or he fills or invests in *structural holes,* as Figure 6.2a shows most prominently. As the absence of a tie between two unconnected actors, a structural hole represents an opportunity for a third party to fill that hole, thereby gaining access to the non-redundant resources that each unconnected party offers.

However, other social capital theorists like Coleman (1988) have contended that being embedded in dense *closed* networks, as is shown in Figure 6.2d, provides an individual with the most value. As an individual's relationships become more entwined and connected, the easier it is to gain access to the information that flows between them. Further, tightly connected networks foster trust between their members, making the advice that flows between people more likely to be adhered to.

The CCAP study found individuals in South Chicago tend to have relatively closed information networks with an average density of .836. Nearly 70% of the respondents were embedded in information networks that were completely closed, namely, where each peer the respondent named knew every other peer in the network. Conversely, about 17% of the respondents revealed personal networks that were proportionally more open than closed, which means they were filling structural holes and more likely to have access to non-redundant, unique forms of information.

Ultimately, what type of network structure facilitates better outcomes for an individual depends on the context of the information retrieval situation. If an individual wants access to unique, non-redundant sources of information it is probably best to be in a more open network. However, if that individual is not really interested in environmental issues *per se,* but is more interested in being informed about actions that are likely to have an effect on him or her, then being embedded in a dense network will have its own advantages. When a respondent's information sources are clustered, where everyone has a direct relationship with one another, information spreads rapidly and efficiently. Thus, having an accurate view of what personal information networks look like can inform decisions about how best to engage that audience in flows of communication and to see if trends or patterns exist across individual networks that can be leveraged or identified for intervention.

Inter-Organizational Network Structure

Another structural dimension of the information environment strategists should be made aware of is the interorganizational network that exists amongst sources of information. In a government-led initiative like CCAP, which seeks to influence people's attitudes and behaviors, the community-based interorganizational network often serves as the infrastructure for information dissemination, knowledge building, and social influence. Furthermore, the collaborative ties between organizations are like resource conduits, providing one organization's patrons with access to resources provided by another. These interorganizational connections are particularly useful for individuals living in lower-income communities, where access to local resources is generally hard to come by. Thus, it is important to have an accurate conception of the members of the interorganizational network and the collaborative relationships that bind them together.

To demonstrate, we mapped the information exchange network amongst a sample of 22 community-based organizations in South Chicago (Figure 6.3). Representatives from each organization were asked to name the organizations with which their organization exchanges information. Here, the directedness of ties is maintained, which means a tie represents one organization's perception that it has engaged in information exchange with another and not a mutually agreed upon relationship. Nodes are sized by their betweenness centrality, which is the extent to which an organization lies on the path between two unconnected organizations. As such, larger nodes represent network brokers

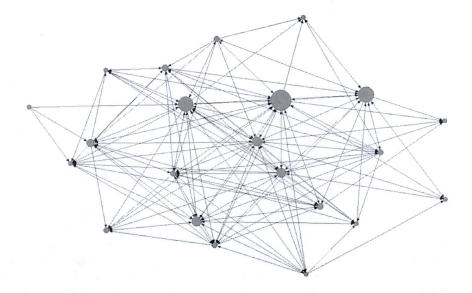

Figure 6.3 The Interorganizational Information Exchange Network

that have the ability to facilitate the flow of information between unconnected actors and who are likely to be exposed to non-redundant sources of information.

Further structural analysis shows that network density in the information exchange network was .364, which means that 36% of all possible ties were present. On average, actors had less than eight directed ties, about 38% of which were reciprocal (named by both). The greatest number of steps between any two nodes in the network (diameter) was 3, and the average number of steps between any two nodes was 1.648, indicating information would only have to travel about two steps to get to any given intended party. And finally, betweenness centralization is a measure of the variation in the number of times actors in the network lie on paths between other actors.

Social network maps and analyses, such as those highlighted here, are valuable diagnostic tools in making sense of the complex information environment. Network analysis can reveal if relevant organizations are missing or under-represented, the degree of integration across types of organizations, and gaps that might need to be filled. Network maps can also help network participants identify new partners, ideas, and resources they need for effective planning and management (Vance-Borland & Holley, 2011). Furthermore, one can also see how types of relationships at the micro level manifest into macro-level structural properties of an information environment, which have the potential to both enable and challenge strategic efforts to influence the flows and processes of communication that occur within them.

Discussion

In this chapter, we demonstrate the need for a revised approach toward conceptualizing and facilitating effective information and communication flows between governments and citizens. In light of the belief that information is the foundation of governing (Bimber, 2003; Mayer-Schönberger & Lazer, 2007), governments strive to improve relational communication with citizens. Over time, theories have been developed that carry with them particular assumptions about how communication flows work between institutions and the citizenry. These theories often reflect what is known about the capabilities of the present communication infrastructure and the way in which society is organized.

That said, given the emergence of new ICT in conjunction with a societal shift toward a networked logic, these theories of communication flows have likewise shifted from linear models to networked models. However, evidence shows government campaigns still reflect a linear approach to communication, pushing information via allocution mechanisms (Ebbers, Pieterson & Noordman, 2008) through mass media to citizens, leaving little opportunity for citizens to initiate dialogue with the governmental sponsors behind the campaigns.

We argue here that the assumptions inherent in traditional, linear models of communication are inadequate for understanding what is a far more complex communicative reality. By relying on outmoded assumptions governments contribute to their own communication ineffectiveness. Instead, we argue governments and government groups need to restructure their assumptions about communication processes to reflect a more networked perspective, (re)conceptualizing the communication relationship between institutional actors and citizens as multi-directional, multiplex, and structurally dependent.

Implications for Strategic Communication Practitioners

To demonstrate how these networked assumptions can and should be integrated into strategic communication planning, we use our experiences in the exploratory study of the information and communication networks in South Chicago to construct a template for practice. While results from this study are not generalizable beyond this community, we believe that our data collection procedures and findings highlight several practical insights for moving forward in designing and implementing effective strategic communication campaigns in community settings.

1. Before communication decisions are made, use network surveys and other related forms of exploratory data collection to learn more about the established information and advice seeking practices that exist amongst members of the targeted community. Investing in proactive research is a crucial preliminary step in strategic communication outreach between local governments and its citizens. Most strategic communication campaigns seek to influence a target population's knowledge, attitudes, or behaviors around a particular issue. However, to do so effectively, it behooves practitioners to have working knowledge of the communication network infrastructure that already exists within the boundaries of the target population. Facilitating or encouraging disposition changes is difficult enough. Even more difficult, though, is trying to communicate these goals in a way that is antithetical or countervailing to deeply entrenched systems of communication. Therefore, practically speaking, network surveys map the space that one will need to operate in and leverage.

2. Enlist the influence and prestige of organizations that people would consult as information intermediaries and strategic partners in planning and outreach. Communication practitioners are well aware of the salient role that organizations play in mediating social and communicative interactions between change agents and target populations. This is particularly true of community-based organizations (CBOs) that have established relationships with community residents and a working knowledge of the challenges and opportunities that the community faces. As such, organizations have the potential to participate as *collaborating change agents*, working with campaign sponsors in the design and implementation process, as *channels of communication*, disseminating information to clients and members, and as the *targets of change* itself.

But not all organizations are created equal; some are more likely to play these roles than others. A key determinant of an organization's role in a strategic campaign is how members of a target population perceive an organization as a potential source of information and assistance with regard to the issue of concern. For this reason, knowing where people *would* go, or *would not* go, if they needed help provides strategic communication practitioners with valuable insight regarding which outlets have the largest scope of influence and, therefore, which outlets will be most effective to work with during the campaign.

3. Use the information embedded in people's preferences for which organizations they would consult to better understand how they comprehend the issue of climate change. When people make choices regarding which organizations they would consult for assistance with a particular issue or concern, they are simultaneously providing insight about how they conceptualize the issue. For example, in the South Chicago study the Alderman's office was always cited as one of the "top 10" organizations that residents would consult for each of the four climate change themes, which suggests that residents view issues like energy efficiency, alternative transportation, and waste reduction as inherently "public" and "human-centered" ones that should be addressed in a civic capacity. Residents also mentioned conservation organizations more than any other type of organization as sources of advice for learning to adapt to a changing climate. This suggests that to them *adapting* means learning to interact with nature in a way that may be new to them. Thus, *climate change* is seemingly considered a problem facing both humans and the natural world.

As these examples show, mapping the dimensions of the relationships between residents and the community-based organizations that they turn to not only sheds light on the social structure of a community's information environment, but it also demarcates its semantic boundaries, revealing dimensions of a localized interpretation of the issue. For a practitioner, this insight is useful to the degree to which it can guide the design of a campaign that speaks to locally relevant perspectives.

4. Work with the existing interorganizational infrastructure to foster trust, build consensus, and develop a locally specific agenda for change within the community. In a government-led initiative that seeks to influence people's attitudes and behaviors, the community-based inter-organizational network often serves as the infrastructure for information dissemination, knowledge building, and social influence. Thus, to achieve success and effectively influence targeted community, it is incumbent for outsider entities, like many of the municipal, research, and private sector groups involved in campaign design and implementation, to leverage the system of insider collaborative relationships that bind a community together.

Structurally speaking, knowing which organizations collaborate, and how often, tells practitioners which organizations are perceived as authorities by other organizations. According to *Public Goods Theory,* these cohort authorities often become coordinating bodies that help build a unifying mission consensus amongst the other community-based organizations, and obtain resources to support community-based collective action. Further, it is important for change agents to realize that insider community-based organizations act as more than benign information repositories or quiescent assistants awaiting their instructions from above. Rather, insider organizations and the systems of collaboration that they have built over years of service to the community carry with them lessons learned from involvement in past campaigns as well as the responsibility to ensure that long-term behavior change occurs in the target community. For these reasons, the interorganizational environment within a community is a vital resource in any strategic communication campaign.

5. Leverage the capital that comes from interpersonal network composition and structure in order to facilitate information flows and social support. Like organizations, individual community members are embedded in their own interpersonal environments that provide them with certain types of value or network capital. As such, it is important for agents of change to gain a sense of what these personal networks look like, especially in terms of how they are structured, if their efforts to affect target populations are to succeed. When most or all of an individual's peers know one another, the individual is said to have a closed (or dense) personal network. These networks are thought to be well suited for rapid and efficient information diffusion as well as for providing social support required to adopt new attitudes and behaviors. Conversely, when an individual's peers do not know one another their network is thought to be open. Open networks are thought to be advantageous for accessing unique, non-redundant sources of information.

In that both closed and open networks provide value, the key for a practitioner is to match their communication outreach goals to what they can reasonably expect to achieve when working within the constraints of established interpersonal network environments. For example, in South Chicago, residents typically had dense personal information networks, seeking information from peers who were also highly connected. Further, many of the respondents who indicated belonging to dense networks also named family members as their primary contacts. With this information, the CCAP planners geared outreach efforts around enabling quick and easy diffusion of information, and capitalized on the familial nature of residents' personal networks by working through and with family-oriented programs and organizations such as health care clinics, churches, and schools.

6. Invest in modes of communication that members of the target audiences are most accustomed to and comfortable using, but recognize that these preferences are contingent on qualities of the information seeker and qualities of the information source. In a communication campaign like the CCAP initiative, an effective information diffusion strategy must take advantage of the communication channels utilized most by the target audience. However, it must also recognize that people are likely to utilize different communication channels when communicating with different types of sources. Survey respondents showed clear preferences for communicating with organizations and peers through traditional, more intimate channels like face-to-face and telephone. However, electronic channels like websites as well as social networking sites and text messaging were also revealed to be preferred channels for communicating with organizations and peers, respectively.

Attempts to raise awareness and influence change in communities must take advantage of these preferred channels of communication. For example, community-based organizations (CBOs) that are involved in the CCAP campaign should make information available "on location" as well as through websites. One way that organizations broker relationships between the City of Chicago and community residents is by serving as physical and digital repositories of information. Therefore, making information available and accessible within the actual physical space that the organization occupies would be a simple, yet strategic way to reach out to those who prefer in-person contact with community-based organizations. And, to meet the needs of those who prefer digital access, it would be most effective to encourage CBOs to post information about CCAP and provide links to the DOE and other relevant CCAP partners on their websites, which would also help build a digital information repository built around a web of connections fostered by the Internet.

Future Research

In moving forward, we suggest that to enhance and build on the networked propositions laid forth, future work should focus on further development and empirical testing across different campaigns and situational contexts. Only then can we integrate a collection of propositions into a more comprehensive networked theory of strategic communication that has utility for theorists as well as practitioners. As a field of scholarship, strategic communication is one part academic and one part pragmatic. Thus, bridges need to be created between practitioners and scholars to connect the pragmatic experiences and insights of the former with the theoretical and analytic expertise of the later. To these ends, campaigns can and should be reframed in design and implementation in terms of network theories that can facilitate understanding of the relational dynamics between targeted citizens and government change agents and the intermediary forces in between that contribute to campaign success.

References

Bandura, A. (2001). Social Cognitive Theory of Mass Communication. *Media Psychology, 3*(3), 265–299.

Baum, C., & Di Maio, A. (2000). *Gartner's four phases of E-Government model*. Location: Gartner Group, Research Note.

Bimber, B. (2003). *Information and American Democracy: Technology in the Evolution of Political Power*. Cambridge, England: Cambridge University Press.

Boase, J., Horrigan, J., Wellman, B., & Rainie, L. (2006). *The Strength of Internet Ties*. Washington, D.C.: Pew Internet & American Life Project.

Bozeman, D. P. (1993, August). Toward a limited rationality perspective of managerial media selection in organizations. *Academy of Management Proceedings, 1*, 278–282.

Burt, R. S. (1992). *Structural holes: The social structure of competition*. Cambridge, MA: Harvard University Press.

Castells, M. (1996). *Rise of the Network Society: The Information Age: Economy, Society, and Culture*. Oxford, England: Blackwell.

Castells, M. (2009). *Communication Power*. New York: Oxford University Press.

Coleman, J. S. (1988). Social capital in the creation of human capital. *American Journal of Sociology*, S95–S120.

Daft, R. L., & Lengel, R. H. (1986). Organizational Information Requirements, Media Richness and Structural Design. *Management Science, 32*(5), 554–571.

van Dijk, J. (2006). *The network society* (2nd ed.). London: Sage.

Dhanjal, C., Blanchemanche, S., Clémençon, S., Rona-Tas, A. & Rossi, F. (2012). Dissemination of Health Information within Social Networks. In B. Vedres & M. Scotti (eds.), *Networks in Social Policy Problems*. Cambridge: Cambridge University Press.

Downey, J., & Fenton, N. (2003). New Media, Counter Publicity and the Public Sphere. *New Media & Society, 5*(2), 185–202.

Ebbers, W., Pieterson, W., & Noordman, H. (2007). Rethinking Service and Channel Strategies after the Hype. In J. Makolm & Orthofer (Eds.), *ETaxation State & Perspectives*. Linz: Trauner Druck.

Ebbers, W. E., Pieterson, W. J., & Noordman, H. N. (2008). Electronic government: Rethinking channel management strategies. *Government Information Quarterly, 25*(2), 181–201.

Ellison, N. B., Steinfield, C., & Lampe, C. (2007). The Benefits of Facebook "Friends:" Social Capital and College Students' Use of Online Social Network Sites. *Journal of Computer -Mediated Communication, 12*(4) 1143–1168.

Erickson, B.H. (1988). The relational basis of attitudes. In B. Wellman & S.D. Berkowitz. (Eds.), *Social Structures: A Network Approach*. Cambridge: Cambridge University Press.

Estabrook, L., Witt, E., & Rainie, L. (2007). *Information searches that solve problems. How people use the internet, libraries, and government agencies when they need help*. Washington, DC: Pew Internet & American Life Project.

Fraser, N. (1990). Rethinking the Public Sphere: A Contribution to the Critique of Actually Existing Democracy. *Social Text,* 1990(25/26), 56–80.

Freeman, L.C. (2004). *The Development of Social Network Analysis: A Study in the Sociology of Science*. Vancouver, BC Canada: Empirical Press.

Heckathorn, D. D. (2002). Respondent-driven sampling II: deriving valid population estimates from chain-referral samples of hidden populations. *Social Problems, 49*, 11.

Jansen, J., Van de Wijngaert, L., & Pieterson, W. (2010) Channel choice and source choice of entrepreneurs in a public organizational context: The Dutch case. In Wimmer, M.A., Chappelet, J.-L., Janssen, M., Scholl, H.J. (eds.) *EGOV 2010*. LNCS, vol. 6228 (pp. 144–155). Heidelberg: Springer.

Katz, E. and Lazarsfeld, P.F. (1955). *Personal influence: the part played by people in the flow of mass communication*. New York: The Free Press.

Kinder, D. R. (1998). Communication and Opinion. *Annual Review of Political Science, 1*, 167–197.

Lasswell, H. D. (1948). The structure and function of communication in society. In L. Bryson (Ed.), *The communication of ideas* (pp. 37–51). New York: Harper.

Lazarsfeld, P. F., Berelson, B., and Gaudet, H. (1944). *The People's Choice*. New York: Duell, Sloan and Pearce.

Lin, N. (1999). Social Networks and Status Attainment. *Annual Review of Sociology, 25,* 467–487.

Lin, N. (2001). *Social capital: A theory of social structure and action*. New York: Cambridge University Press.

Marsden, P.V. & Hurlbert, J.S. (1988). Social resources and mobility outcomes: a replication and extension. *Social Forces, 66,* 1038–1059.

Mattelart, A. and Mattleart, M. (2004). *Theories of communication: a short introduction*. London, UK: Sage Publications.

Mayer-Schönberger, V., & Lazer, D. (Eds.). (2007). *Governance and information technology: From electronic government to information government*. Cambridge, MA: MIT Press.

McNeal, R., Hale, K., & Dotterweich, L. (2008). Citizen–Government Interaction and the Internet: Expectations and Accomplishments in Contact, Quality, and Trust. *Journal of Information Technology & Politics, 5*(2), 213–229.

Millard, J. (2006). eGovernment for an inclusive society: flexi-channelling and social intermediaries. Paper presented at the eGOV conference 2006, Krakow, Poland.

Monge, P.R. & Contractor, N. (2003). *Theories of communication networks*. New York: Oxford University Press.

Petty, R. E., Brinol, P., & Priester, J. R. (2009). Mass Media Attitude Change; Implications of the Elaboration Likelihood Model of Persuasion. In J. Bryant & M. B. Oliver (Eds.), *Media effects: Advances in theory and research* (3rd ed.). New York: Routledge.

Pieterson, W. (2009). *Channel choice: Citizens' channel behavior and public service channel strategy*. University of Twente, Enschede.

Pieterson, W., & Ebbers, W. (2008). The use of service channels by citizens in the Netherlands: Implications for multi-channel management. *International Review of Administrative Sciences, 74*(1), 95–110.

Putnam, R. D. (2000). *Bowling alone: The collapse and revival of American community*. New York: Simon and Schuster.

Ramirez, A., Walther, J. B., Burgoon, J. K., & Sunnafrank, M. (2002). Information-seeking strategies, uncertainty, and computer-mediated communication: Toward a conceptual model. *Human Communication Research, 28,* 213–228.

Reddick, C. G. (2005). Citizen interaction with E-government: From the streets to servers. *Government Information Quarterly, 22,* 38–57.

Resnick, P. (2002). Beyond bowling together: Social technical capital. In J. M. Carroll (Ed.), *HCI in the new millenium* (pp. 647–672). Boston, MA: Addison Wesley Professional.

Roberts, D. F. (2000). Media and Youth: Access, Exposure, and Privatization. *Journal of Adolescent Health* 27, 8–14.

Rogers, E.M. (2003). *Diffusion of innovations* (5th ed.). New York: The Free Press.

Rogers, E.M. and Kincaid, D.L. (1981). *Communication networks: toward a new paradigm for research*. New York: The Free Press.

Ronald, B. (1992). *Structural holes: The social structure of competition*. Cambridge, MA: Harvard University Press.

Savolainen, R., & Kari, J. (2004). Placing the Internet in information source horizons. A study of information seeking by Internet users in the context of self-development. *Library & Information Science Research, 26*, 415–433.

Shannon, C. and Weaver, W. (1949). *The Mathematical Theory of Communication*. Urbana and Champaign, IL: University of Illinois Press.

Simon, H. A. (1956). Rational choice and the structure of the environment. *Psychological Review, 63*, 129–138.

Symonds, M. (2000). The next revolution: a survey of government and the Internet. *The Economist, 355*, 1–34.

Uslaner, E. M. (2002). *The moral foundations of trust*. Cambridge: Cambridge University Press.

Vance-Borland, K. & Holley, J. (2011). Conservation stakeholder network mapping, analysis, and weaving. *Conservation Letters, 4*, 278–288. doi: 10.1111/j.1755–263X.2011.00176.x

Van den Boer, Y., Wijngaert, L., Van de, Pieterson, W., & Arendsen, R. (2012). On the interaction of source and channel choice in the government-to-business context. Electronic government, lecture notes in computer science. In H.J. Scholl, M. Janssen, M.A. Wimmer, C.E. Moe, L.S. Flak (Eds.): *EGOV 2012, LNCS 7443* (pp. 27–39). Heidelberg: Springer.

Weiss, J.A. & Tschirhart, M. (2007). Public Information Campaigns as Policy Instruments. *Journal of Policy Analysis and Management, 13*(1), 82–119.

Wellman, B., & Frank, K. (2001). Network capital in a multilevel world: Getting support from personal communities. *Social capital: Theory and research*, 233–273.

7

Contextual Distortion

Strategic Communication versus the Networked Nature of Nearly Everything

Priscilla Murphy

Strategic communication has been defined as "the purposeful use of communication by an organization to fulfill its mission" (Hallahan, Holtzhausen, Van Ruler, Verčič, & Sriramesh, 2007, p. 4). It is "not random or unintentional" (p. 27) although unintended consequences can ensue; it is not aimed at control but takes environment into consideration through dialogue or emergent strategy. From this standpoint, strategic communication is inclusive and flexible, but still fundamentally managed, purposive, and organization-centered—at least, within its home organization. This chapter focuses on the problem of what happens after such communication enters the public arena, where it shares space with random unwanted associations that distort the original intent of the message. Ultimately this chapter poses two questions that grow out of this contextual dependence:

1. How strategic can "strategic communication" be, given the distortions imposed by the environment outside?
2. What can organizations do to maintain some semblance to the original content and intent of their message after it leaves their hands?

Control has long been a troublesome issue in strategic communication. The lone organization that commands its own fate is rare, if it ever existed, and the positivist spark that illuminated earlier writing on public relations management by objectives (e.g., Nager & Allen, 1991) has faded considerably. Starting in the late 1990s, communication scholars began to try out multiple theories—some from communication, some not—to explore the lack of control that has become such a central problem in organizational strategy, particularly in the areas of issues management, reputation, and runaway news coverage. Early on, for example, Williams and Moffitt (1997) saw organizational image-making as a shifting, repeated process whereby "one image can emerge as strong at one moment in time, and another, contrasting image can emerge as dominant at a different moment in time because of the multiple and contradictory factors involved" in the audience's processing of organizational traits (p. 241). Botan and Soto (1998), and Berger (1999) proposed similar views of public relations as a shifting, recurrent process whereby an organization and its publics negotiate meaning through dynamic exchange between sender and receiver, organization and public.

Many scholars have tackled the problem of message management since then, but the issue remains open. For example, James (2011) recently circled back to the 1990s articles to redefine positioning in public relations as "the strategic attempt to stake out and occupy a site of intentional representation in the contested space where meanings are constructed, contested, and reconstructed" (p. 98). Molleda (2011) likewise noted the tendency of controversies involving multinational corporations to slide across national borders, to become entangled with local issues and prior coverage, and to be framed disparately by international news services that reflect their own national priorities even though organizations affected by the news have limited ability to shape it. Using the network theory of social capital, Ihlen (2005) noted that "competing interests" are "engaged in a continuous struggle to maintain or alter the distribution" of an organization's symbolic capital, which he defined in terms of its reputation (p. 493).

Currently, managing issues and messages looks more disorderly than ever. For example, Luoma-Aho and Vos (2010) recently described issues management in terms of "a multiplicity of 'issue arenas'" that are "comprised of organizational stakeholder networks and communication patterns" (p. 316). In this dynamic environment, the organization becomes, not a controlling force, but rather "one player among many, with the main focus on issues, not the organization" (p. 321); indeed, the content and outcomes of such issue arenas "are outside the organization's control" (p. 322). Publics and organizations have an equal stake in these issue arenas, which are composed of "simply a heterogeneous network of aligned interests" in which "actors are defined by their relations with others in the network" as well as by such influences as "surroundings, regulations, other people, and technology" (p. 318).

These studies have a number of themes in common. All of them depict communication outcomes as unruly, dynamic, and temporary, constantly needing to be renegotiated with multiple interest groups. All the studies emphasize that even when communication originates in a strategic plan, it is prone to unpredictable influence by other information that happens to occupy the same news space or public opinion environment. In this shifting arena, the negotiation of meaning is always local; it thereby eludes management by any one party and can take on novel and unintended meanings. For example, Curtin and Gaither (2006) noted that local meanings attached to smallpox, entirely unanticipated by the World Health Organization in its campaign to eradicate the disease, ranged from expensive nuisance (developed nations) to tool of neocolonialism (developing countries), to religious symbol (India, Nigeria). As a result, smallpox eradication became a "contested area of meaning that informed how the campaign unfolded" (p. 81).

These instances suggest that many of the problems related to control have to do with context, with launching a message into an opinion environment along with other messages that may create unanticipated or unwanted associations. The key element in this type of contextual distortion is connectedness—the relationship among interest groups, distribution technologies, events, messages, and other influences that mill around in the opinion environment. Given this emphasis on unpredictability, complex systems have been proposed as an appropriate model to issue arenas (e.g., Gilpin & Murphy, 2008). In this chapter, given the emphasis on interconnectedness, networks are suggested as an appropriate way to conceptualize message distortion and perhaps to suggest ways to mitigate these unwanted relationships.

Intersection of Theories of Social Networks and Complex Systems

Conceptually, the two bodies of theory—complex systems and social networks—intersect in many respects. Complex systems are composed of multiple actors, who interact locally and myopically to improve their immediate lot. However, these local interactions link together in a widening network of associations that quickly eludes control. The resulting pattern can have little resemblance to the original situation and can defy change by strategic communication (see Gilpin & Murphy, 2008).

As for networks, Borgatti and Foster (2003) defined a network as "a set of actors connected by a set of ties" (p. 992). The actors might be persons, teams, organizations, concepts, technologies—human or non-human, occupying any scale. Ties are inherently local and dyadic, although—like the local negotiations that characterize complex systems—each link between two actors ultimately adds up to elaborate social communication patterns. Network ties can be bidirectional (that is, shared) or unidirectional (going one way); the intensity of the relationship can be measured on a scale or the ties can simply be noted as present or absent. Actors are members of many different networks simultaneously—work, job, family—opening the possibility that information can spill over from one network to another. Conversely, actors can also reside in tight cliques where they have minimal awareness of what happens outside their own opinion environment.

In the past, social network analysis has often been discussed simply in terms of a methodological approach to data. In truth, however, social networks are much more than this: they propose a novel way of looking at the world, one that is very different from traditional substantialist perspectives. Network theory has not often been applied to strategic communication; in the communication discipline, most prior research has focused on organizational communication. Emphasizing the communication perspective, Monge and Contractor (2003) defined social networks as "patterns of contact that are created by the flow of messages among communicators through time and space" (p. 3). They cited personal networks, flows of messages between groups, strategic alliances, and globally networked organizations such as multinational corporations as examples of social networks.

In an effort to bring together complexity and network theories, Morçöl and Wachhaus (2009) defined a network as "a relatively stable and complex pattern of relationships among multiple interdependent and self-organizing elements (e.g., social, political, economic actors), which also constitutes a self-organizing system as a whole" (p. 45) They viewed the main differences between complexity and networks in terms of the perspective of scholars who study them: network scholars emphasize stability, whereas complexity scholars emphasize change.

The two bodies of theory are indeed similar. While emphasizing the dynamic nature of networks more than most traditional network theorists do, Morçöl and Wachhaus (2009) usefully summarized overlaps between social networks and complex systems. First, both have the ability to self-organize, although networks "self-organize in a manner that is constricted or guided by institutional rules" to a greater extent than complex systems do (p. 48). Second, when self-organizing, both networks and complex systems are "unpredictable (or predictable only in qualitative terms)" (p. 49)—that is, the relationship between cause and effect is not necessarily proportional but nonlinear. Third, both are dissipative: they tend not to settle in an equilibrium but rather lean toward an unstable state. Fourth, both networks and complex systems are best understood by observing the macro-level patterns that emerge as their agents interact, often through computerized simulations. Fifth, those who study networks or complex systems must accept a high level of uncertainty because of the radical nonlinearity fundamental to both networks and complex systems. Because a number of recent articles have applied complexity theory to communication (e.g., Gilpin, 2010, Murphy, 2000, 2010), this chapter will concentrate on network theories, drawing in complexity theory less frequently.

The evolution of both complexity theory and network theory reflects broader paradigm shifts within the social sciences in which they are grounded. Both express the decline of modernist, linear, reductionist ways of seeing the world; both show the shift, beginning in the mid-twentieth century, away from individualist and structuralist assumptions and toward a relational, contextual, systems-oriented perspective (Borgatti & Foster, 2003). Knox, Savage, and Harvey (2006) described network theory development in terms of three stages that parallel shifts in social science perspectives. First came an emphasis on individualism typified by the work of Granovetter (1973), whose work on weak ties will be discussed later in this chapter. Next, in the 1980s, came a reaction against individualism typified by the early work of White and others at Harvard (1970), described as "a thoroughgoing structuralism, where social networks became a means of mapping social structure" that "marks the apogee of the modernist project" (Knox et al., 2006, pp. 117, 119). More recently, social network theorists have recognized problems with excessive structuralism and have tried to develop the idea of a dynamic, culture-based approach to social networks. (See Freeman [2004] for an in-depth history of social network analysis; see Gilpin and Murphy [2008] for an overview of the parallel development of complexity theory.) This disciplinary evolution has left its mark on network theories in that they still maintain a tension between culture and structure, between agency to shape one's own network and determinism based on network position (e.g., Emirbayer, 1997). A similar tension, discussed throughout this chapter, manifests itself as a conflict in strategic communication between the management of messages and targeting of audiences on the one hand, and on the other hand the haphazard reception of messages by groups that share the same communication arena as equals.

In fact, we can learn much about strategic communication—its characteristics, its processes, and its limitations—by looking at it as one expression of the larger domain of social network theory. Since many of the possibilities and problems that we talk about in strategic communication have also caused debate among network theorists, propositions from that body of theory are for the most part germane to strategic communication. Some of these concepts that will be discussed in this chapter are:

- contagion, or the uncontrolled dissemination of information through an opinion environment;
- networks as pipes (dynamic but poorly controlled) or girders (structurally determined and static);
- network position: centrality, subgroups, and holes;
- types of ties between actors in the network; and
- network configuration: centralized or distributed networks.

A particularly useful way to conceptualize the passage of information through a network is in terms of the temporal and substantive distortion that occurs as a message is caught by various network nodes, its content attenuated by some and augmented by others and its passage hastened, slowed, or repressed altogether. The problems posed by a self-determining environment outside the control of an organizational communicator can be thus readily seen in distortions of an organization's public image or reputation.

Relatedly, Borgatti and Lopez-Kidwell (2011) noted that networks can be regarded in two different ways: first, as a set of "pipes" through which various resources—information, friendships, influence—pass; and second, as a set of "girders" that determine structure and establish the position of every element in relation to every other element. The first perspective—the "pipes" perspective—emphasizes problems raised by the dynamism of networks; in strategic communication, the way in which rumors elude control or pick up distortions as they pass from point to point, farther and farther away from the original source. The second perspective—the "girders" perspective—emphasizes the intransigence of an established point of view or set of relationships, making it difficult to move public opinion into an area more to an organization's liking. This tension between agency ("pipes") and determinism ("girders") underlies efforts by strategic communicators to steer a course between fast-spreading news or rumors and entrenched public opinions.

Centrality and Control

One of the chief determinants of a communicator's ability to control information flowing through a particular network is that person's centrality, or the pattern of connections between an actor and others in the network. Centrality captures how important an actor can be in monitoring and manipulating network flows—something that only a network-based perspective, with its ability to portray a holistic picture and to measure relationships, can discern. Different kinds of centrality give us ways to consider the possibilities for managing information and the possibilities for message distortion, either intentionally through the offices of a maladaptive gatekeeper or through message entropy as receivers get further away from the source. Thus, different types of centrality measure different ways in which an actor can manage or lose control of a network's resources. They aptly illustrate the old adage, "where you stand depends on where you sit."

The simplest type of centrality is *degree centrality,* which measures how many other actors are directly connected to a certain actor. An actor with high degree centrality is positioned at the center of an asterisk-like local network pattern. That actor has an advantage over less central actors in getting information, and can choose to pass on that information or repress it. A message recipient with high degree centrality looks very much like an opinion leader: an efficient conduit to pass along a message to the many others with whom the actor is connected. On the other hand, Yu and Lester (2008) pointed out that in an industry network, a highly central company so dominates the public consciousness that any scandal that touches it tends to spread easily to others that are connected to it, whether they are partners, suppliers, or competitors. In this light it is worse to be linked with a scandal-ridden company that dominates its industry than to be relegated to a link with an uninfluential company.

Somewhat more complicated is the concept of *closeness centrality,* which measures distances among the various actors in a network in terms of "degrees of separation" (Milgram, 1967), or how many actors one has to go through in order to reach the target. Actors who are globally central are at short distances from many others, so a central player tends to hear things first. Closeness centrality is epitomized by a quip attributed to Mark Twain to describe the provincialism of Cincinnati: "When the end of the world comes, I would like to be in Cincinnati because it's always twenty years behind the times" (http://www.twainquotes.com/Cincinnati.html). The same problem also interferes with an organization's ability to preserve the integrity of the messages after they leave the organization. Decreasing closeness centrality describes message entropy; control over message content and receivers' understanding diminishes substantially as information travels through a chain of receivers. In fact, network studies suggest that the originator's influence becomes inconsiderable after just two or three degrees of separation from the source (Kadushin, 2004). From the angle, strategic messages, the way an organization wants them, do not extend very far into public consciousness.

Another form of centrality, *betweenness centrality,* measures how often an actor lies along the shortest path between two others—that is, the extent to which an actor mediates between others as a gatekeeper, or a broker who can orchestrate relationships between otherwise separate groups in the network. In the role of boundary spanner, a public relations person traditionally has the highest betweenness centrality in any organization. From a network theory perspective, Burt (1992) examined the consequences of gaps in betweenness: structural holes that separated subgroups of actors in a network. He found that actors who could identify those holes, and position themselves as brokers to bridge the subgroups, held a great deal of power. However, this brokering power also signals problems with respect to communication. If an organization fails to keep its network together, it opens a structural hole that others will fill—perhaps with rumors or unfavorable frames. In fact, although he did not use network theory, this type of principle underlies Entman's (2003) model of "cascading activation" that explains how frames are strategically manipulated to encourage certain policy agendas at the expense of others. He observed that "Strategically maladroit administrations, such as the Carter and Clinton White Houses, often found news frames spinning out of their control. Poor strategy creates a power vacuum that opposing elites and journalists may enter with their own interpretations" (p. 422).

Finally, a specialized form of betweennness centrality—*eigenvector centrality*—measures whether an actor is connected with others who are also well connected. Borgatti and Lopez-Kidwell (2011) considered eigenvector centrality to be an indicator of enhanced popularity, of being well connected: an indicator of eliteness. A similar concept underlies Granovetter's (1983) propositions about the importance of bridges between groups: if one is not connected to important others, being connected is not an especially favorable position. In a communication context, eigenvector centrality helps to explain why peripheral organizations and activist movements—such the women's movement in the 1960s, or more recently, the LGBTQ movement—have had trouble getting onto the media agenda. One solution is to stage newsworthy events; however, the network-driven solution would be to forge an alliance with a more central actor. Hence in order to foster an environmentalist agenda the radical Friends of the Earth forged an alliance with the mainstream Sierra Club; to forward its animal-protection agenda, the SPCA created ties with celebrity quarterback and former dog-fighter Michael Vicks.

Network Configuration

In addition to individual actors' centrality, it is useful to consider the centralization patterns of an entire network: the degree to which a network focuses around one powerful actor or perhaps a handful of actors. Network centralization is clearly an indicator of control: For example, as Entman (2003) argued with respect to the control of media frames, if one actor, or a small number of sub-groups, mediates resource flows within a network, that actor or group has a high degree of control over the information that travels through the network.

Coming at the issues from different angles, both communication professionals and network theorists have long recognized the importance of homophily, or people's tendency to associate with others like themselves (McPherson, Smith-Lovin, & Cook, 2001). Depicting the configuration patterns of an entire network can show where communication between homophilous subgroups breaks down. Indeed, the costs of not having this holistic understanding of a communication network can be very high. For example, Garner's (2006) network analysis of internal communications at NASA leading up to the Columbia shuttle disaster clearly showed a breach between the reporting relationships depicted on NASA's organizational chart and the actual communication patterns of the team managing the shuttle flight. As in the earlier Challenger disaster, the NASA communication network showed a split between management and engineers so that information about the space shuttle's vulnerability was not passed along.

Homophilous groups within a network can seem like efficient targets for communication, but members' strong ties are also very difficult to break into. Associating with others like oneself tends to make qualities seem mainstream to group members when they might be viewed by the rest of the world as aberrant. For example, a series of studies by Christakis and Fowler (2007, 2008) showed that overweight people and smokers tend to associate with other people with the same characteristics in networks that can intensify the bad habits over time. By the same token, one might consider executive malfeasance in terms of a homophilous network. In this connection, Borgatti and Foster (2003), noted one important subset of network studies of "the so-called 'dark side" in which social ties imprison actors in maladaptive situations or facilitate undesirable behavior" (p. 994). One might argue that the cover-up of priestly abuse in the Catholic Church grew out of the imprisonment of Church authorities in homophilous ties they perceived as unbreakable. Similarly, financial abuses leading up to the Great Recession were fostered by a sense within the banking industry that extreme risk-taking was normal. In both cases, the densely homophilous groups were blind to the tidal wave of public opprobrium that overtook them.

Studying an overall network configuration may also expose numerous subgroups with little or no overlapping communications, and this is one sign of conflict between various audiences. Communication professionals may view these breaks in the network as one result of cultural dissonance, so that various interest groups may be debating the same phenomenon but with such different perspectives—cultural, ideological—that what they see does not coincide at all. For example, Garyantes and Murphy (2010) found that media coverage of the 2005 Iraq elections showed the origins of a cognitive split between U.S. perceptions of the war in Iraq and those of the Iraqi populace, the first sign of a growing ideological conflict that intensified in subsequent years. However, structural holes may also signal ways in which parties in conflict can be brought together. For instance, Pachucki and Breiger (2010) showed "how strikingly different narrative deployments of conflicting groups, each with their own understanding of self and others, create a hole in the discursive space that nonetheless manifests some common elements around its edges, creating possibilities for bridging in the stories told by individuals" (p. 216). Thus, studying the semantic networks of interest groups—a process akin to social network analysis but using words as actors—can show how strategic communication is advanced within an issue arena, and how it is received by various groups according to their own interests. (See Gilpin, 2010, and Murphy, 2010, for more examples of this type of study.)

In addition, the overall network configuration—especially centrality versus dispersion—profoundly influences what other actors are affected by a news event, even when they lack any ability to shape circumstances. For example, Yu and Lester (2008) showed that network position strongly determines whether or not an organization suffers harm when a similar company commits a malfeasance. Central organizations are associated with more stakeholders, are more easily able to influence others in the network, and receive more public scrutiny than less central ones so that news about them travels faster. Thus, being connected with a highly central organization can pose hazards for the other actors in a highly centralized network. They lose autonomy in establishing their own messages that might differentiate them from their malfeasant competition. As explained previously, if a crisis involves a central company, the blame is likelier to spread to innocent others simply because they are directly connected to the culpable organization. Molleda (2011), for example, pointed out that Mattel's involvement with lead-contaminated toys made in China became more intense and more difficult to limit because of prior news coverage about other Chinese products with life-threatening defects. Thus, highly centralized networks with strong ties carry both privileges and penalties.

Yu and Lester (2008) also examined the ramifications of less centralized networks. For example, a second kind of network configuration, termed a *scale-free network,* is less centralized, with a few disproportionately important (that is, highly connected) members who constitute hubs, although most other network members have very few connections at all. Examples of scale-free networks include Internet giants such as Google, through which websites essentially must be routed in order to communicate with Internet users at all. The near-monopoly on connections possessed by these hubs gives them disproportionate influence. They are free to impose their own standards and norms, much as important media outlets set the agenda and tone for coverage by less influential media.

However, these "aristocratic" networks are prone to failure from their own success: web sites with too many links become sluggish; public figures with too many connections lose their adaptiveness. Krackhart (1999) referred a similar phenomenon in terms of "ties that torture"—an excessive number of ties that attach an actor to issues or people in ways that create dissonance. This type of network arrangement causes strategic problems for organizations that wish to communicate different messages to different constituencies. One prototypical example is the dilemma faced by NASA supplier Morton Thiokol: The year after its defective O-rings contributed to the explosion of the Challenger space shuttle in 1986, the company's profits hit a new record; shareholders wanted to hear the good news about its earnings success but most other audiences wanted to see the company's penance continue. A similar problem afflicts public figures whose past ties can be used by competitors to manipulate public opinion: Barack Obama's prior associations with the radical Reverend Jeremiah Wright, or Republican presidential nominee Mitt Romney's inability to shake off prior liberal positions, illustrate the power of these "ties that torture."

What happens in a network where no one is central, where there is no leader? That pattern, termed a *distributed network,* is said to characterize terrorist cells set up to minimize key figures who might reveal information if captured, or rupture communications between other parts of the network if killed (Pedahzur & Perlinger, 2006). More important to most strategic communicators, emerging popular movements tend to follow a distributed pattern. The Egyptian revolution of Spring 2011 appeared to emerge in the form of a distributed network; similarly, protest movements such as the anti-World

Trade Organization (WTO) demonstrations have used the Internet to organize a distributed network of mass protests. Such networks evade control because there is no central leverage point but rather a diffused locus of control where resources are spread somewhat equally throughout the system. Messages therefore take more time to travel through a distributed network, and there is more potential for message distortion than there is when a central actor, or small group of influential actors, can be targeted. The WTO's inability to cope with the earliest Internet-organized diffused mass protests of 1999 in Seattle offers ample evidence of the difficulties in managing communications with distributed networks, as well as the strategic advantages conferred by anonymity on their key members.

Strong and Weak Ties

Network configurations are substantially influenced by the strength and character of relationship ties, which also tend to shape a network's mindset and its possibilities for change. One of the earliest and most persistent network theories involved the distinction between strong ties and weak ties (Granovetter, 1973, 1983). Strong ties arise when interactions are frequent, or emotionally intense, or both; when the parties involved are closely related, whether literally by blood or less literally by outlook; and generally when the actors closely resemble each other, as in opinions, profession, or relationships to others. In contrast, weak ties characterize less frequent, intense, or complicated interactions such as those with friends-of-friends or acquaintances, all of whom may have different mindsets and backgrounds.

Strong ties create a kind of close coupling that can facilitate the spread of information throughout a system, and—for better or for worse—also connect different organizations in the public mind. In particular, similar industries often appear to the public as strongly tied. Those ties present advantages when a focal organization has done a good deed. However, Yu and Lester (2008) pointed out that strong ties between organizations can imperil an entire industry's reputation after one of the member organizations has suffered a crisis. They applied network principles to explain why "stakeholders may evaluate the impact of a reputational crisis on a set of organizations based on their perceived relatedness to the damaged organization" (pp. 97–98). They focused primarily on two concepts taken from network theory. The first is the existence of direct ties (*proximity,* in network terms). For example, a company's reputation may suffer if its supplier has committed a malfeasance, as was the case when faulty auto tires affected the reputation not only of Japanese tire manufacturer Bridgestone but also the U.S. auto industry that bought the tires.

The second way in which strong network ties create problems for companies involves public perception that a culpable company is connected to others in the same way (*structural equivalence,* in network terms). For example, after the 2011 earthquake and tsunami, media coverage of the Japanese nuclear power industry frequently invoked the Chernobyl accident and ascribed dangers to nuclear power plants worldwide, even though the Japanese plants were unlike both the Russian plant and the more modern designs of nuclear plants elsewhere. Nuclear plant coverage illustrates the power of network relationships to exert a gravitational pull that brings entities together by reinforcing one characteristic while attenuating or ignoring other mitigating factors.

Furthermore, message control also fluctuates when variation in the strength of ties constrains or facilitates actors' ability to adapt to a changing environment. One of the most difficult problems in strategic communication is to dislodge entrenched ideas, regardless of whether or not those ideas have any connection to reality. The difficulty of breaking strong associations may be one important driver of recurring crises. For example, as discussed earlier, China has had to deal repeatedly with perceptions that its consumer products are not safe, as succeeding waves of media coverage recount and reinforce prior incidents. A further example of the imperviousness to change of historical patterns in complex systems is the continuing reputational woes of the powdered drink mix, Kool Aid. Since 1978, the mix has been linked to the mass suicide, through cyanide, of more than 900 members of a religious cult in Jonestown, Guyana. Even though the actual medium for the cyanide was a less well-known competitor named Flavor Aid, the Kool Aid/Jonestown link has remained so strong that decades later it has solidified into aphoristic advice for dealing with mistrusted groups: "Don't drink the Kool Aid" (Murphy & Gilpin, 2013).

In other ways, weak ties offer positive opportunities for strategic communication, particularly as they bridge separate groups. Through bridging, weak ties offer a low-risk way to test the waters, to explore commonalities with strangers without the deep commitment that strong ties express. Using the example of offering a cigarette to a stranger, Schultz & Breiger (2010) pointed out that weak ties "may be used strategically to reach outward" (p. 613). Many of those efforts take the form of what they call "weak culture," mutually shared taste in popular culture that often "binds together social actors so they can work together to accomplish instrumental aims" (p. 622).

Like frames, ties are important not only because they define members of a group but also because they define who is not in the group. This strategy has been used by U.S. cigarette manufacturers in a powerful strategic campaign to establish strong ties with working-class smokers. Some of the ties involved shared language; others involved pro-smoking membership groups created by tobacco companies. One of the strongest ways in which the tobacco companies created bonds with smokers was to exclude—to define as "other"—the public health actors in the network that tried to curtail smoking. Speaking for the common man, the average American, tobacco companies adopted the voice of the underdog, "'othering' the tobacco control community by making them 'appear in the public's mind as elitists (and even racists) who use 'social engineering' to impose their values on the vast middle and lower classes" (Katz, 2005, p. 35, quoted in Murphy, 2011, p. 11).

Strong and weak ties may also help to explain the differences in velocity with which a message spreads. Actors tend to develop strong ties with those most like themselves (Granovetter, 1983). If the target audience is excessively homophilous—a closed society—it will be hard for a new message to penetrate. If the target audience is sparsely connected, or lacks a strong center, the message may peter out before reaching many audience members. These problems led Granovetter (1983) to recommend a "division of labor" between strong and weak ties (p. 219). Weak ties lead to "a common cultural consciousness . . . in transmitting information and influences on stylistic matters, political judgments, and broad social trends" from group to group (Schultz & Breiger, 2010, p. 227). However, strong ties are effective in getting the new ideas actually adopted, because decision makers are influenced mainly by their strong relationships within their own group. The need to balance strong and weak ties was summarized by Granovetter (1983) in describing successful activist groups: "the initiators of successful groups were marginal individuals in the community . . . [who] were able to recruit people who had occupied leadership positions and were linked to a dense network of . . . activists" (p. 225). That suggests that "where innovations are controversial, a mobilization strategy based on the activation of weak ties is more likely to facilitate adoption of the goal" (p. 225).

Burt (1999) described a similar dynamic in terms of the "social capital of opinion leaders." He viewed opinion leaders as brokers who—perhaps contrary to normal expectations—"are not people at the top so much as at the edge, not leaders within groups so much as brokers between groups" (p. 47). Opinion leaders therefore use their weak ties to help new ideas gain a foothold in a group, whereupon their role ends as members of that group are motivated by their strong ties and competitive spirit to adopt the ideas. In terms of strategic communication, network balance of strong and weak ties is an important diagnostic that can identify interest groups and determine their receptivity to opinions outside of their immediate circle. For example, Adamic and Glance (2005) examined the citation patterns of 1000 liberal and conservative bloggers covering the 2004 presidential election. They discovered that the two groups linked mainly within their separate communities, "with liberal and conservative blogs focusing on different news articles, topics, and political figures" (p. 14). Conservative blogs linked to each other more frequently and more densely than did liberal blogs, but the analysis did not suggest that either group was receptive to opinions from the outside.

Finally, communication strategists should consider what types of ties exist among audience members, and should pair that assessment with the design of the message they wish to disseminate. Granovetter (1983) pointed out that in general, simple information is best passed along by weak ties, whereas more complicated or difficult information is best disseminated through strong ties. Yet, as anyone who has done media training knows, experts and upper managers often find it hard to match their messages appropriately to tie strength. For example, President Obama has clearly found it difficult to tailor messages according to tie strengths when framing communications about major policy issues such as the budget or health care, treating each as if he is dealing with a strong-tie network of policy experts and disregarding the distortions that may be passed along as the message travels among weak ties. Hence, in August 2009 a proposed provision in the health care reform sponsored by Obama that would have reimbursed doctors for discussing end-of-life issues with their patients became branded as "Death Panels" by Republican Sarah Palin. Fraught with cultural resonance, the term caught on in a process akin to the transmission of other popular culture fads that Schultz & Breiger (2010) described. The "Death Panel" sobriquet effectively shut down further discussion of the end-of-life funding provision.

Embeddedness and Multiplexity

Another influence that complicates efforts to manage message content, and control its distribution, is the network phenomenon of multiplexity. The term refers to an actor's membership in more than one network simultaneously. Embeddedness particularly describes an actor's shared membership in business and private networks; for instance, a golf match among friends may also be a gathering of people who share memberships on corporate boards.

Those who manage strategic communication are well aware of the positive potential of embeddedness. For example, media relations practitioners cultivate social relationships with key media sources; companies' efforts to be active in their communities also show the effectiveness of embeddedness. Although they did not invoke network theory, Williams and Moffitt's seminal work on reputation (1997) relies on the impact of embeddedness; they noted that after work, employees are neighbors, family members, and community volunteers; the company's strategic communications to them are attenuated and distorted as they pass through these multiplex networks.

Finally, multiplexity offers a new perspective on the phenomenon of cross-border conflict shifting noted by Molleda (2011) and his associates. A single crisis precipitated by the lead content of paint in children's toys brought together Chinese factories that manufactured the toys, the American company (Mattel) that distributed them, the Chinese and American governments that regulated toy safety differently, and media coverage that established a web of invidious connections to prior publicity about defective products made in China: toothpaste, milk powder, pet food, and others. Yu, Sengul, and Lester (2008) noted that companies have few options to avoid becoming entangled in other companies' crises to which stakeholders perceive them to be tied. One way would be to break the association altogether in a process termed "preferential detachment" (p. 463). That was Mattel's first impulse as it sought to place the blame for the defective toys solely on the Chinese manufacturer. However, Yu et al. acknowledged that public opinion often resists such efforts and in fact, Molleda showed that Mattel found it difficult to detach itself from the network of unwanted associations. It therefore chose to apologize to the people of China for its attempts to extricate itself from the negative associations; the U.S. government, meanwhile, worked to improve safety regulations. Yu and Lester (2008) described this fallback strategy as another attempt to weaken ties with the "stricken organization" by making "changes that fall within the range of legitimated features of their organizational form without being penalized or devalued for fully dissociating themselves from that original form" (p. 646). Thus, reinforcing ties with well-regarded actors can take the edge off associations with less well-regarded ones.

Contagion

Another side effect of multiplexity is contagion, the process by which ideas flow through a network—or from one network to another—regardless of their basis in fact, let alone their desirability to strategic communicators. Popularized by Gladwell (2000), the concept of contagion considers the speed with which ideas spread and tries to predict the threshold at which all the actors in a network can be expected to join in. Hence Burt (1999) founded his discussion of opinion leaders' machinations in part upon the operation of contagion between networks. He viewed "opinion brokers" as "network entrepreneurs" who connect otherwise disconnected groups and ascribed to them a "competitive advantage" because they move fast and adapt quickly. Nonetheless, Burt pointed out that contagion operates less through the brokers than through competition between actors in a network who hasten to adopt ideas because they see their neighbors reaping advantages.

The contagion process is related to the network concept of *preferential attachment,* according to which certain actors in a network who appear more attractive than others gradually acquire more and more connections as other actors seek to be associated with the attractive traits. Thus, the more well-connected an actor is, the more connections the actor acquires. Popular network writers (e.g., Buchanan, 2002) describe the trend as "the rich get richer"; the principle has been used to explain such phenomena as interlocking boards of directors (a director selected for one board appears more attractive to another) and the dominance of Google on the Internet.

Network studies show that contagion works toward homogenizing a network. As Borgatti and Foster (2003) described it, at the holistic network level, "actors are mutually influencing and informing each other in a process that creates increasing homogeneity within structural subgroups," whereas at the level of an individual actor, "adoption of a practice is determined by the proportion of nodes surrounding her that have adopted, while the timing of adoption is a function of the lengths of paths connecting her to other adoptees" (p. 1005). Borgatti and Lopez-Kidwell (2011) described this process as the "production of consensus through social influence" (p. 15). Once these messages or beliefs take root, strategic communication may find it very hard to manage a targeted change. For example, Hellsten (2003) traced the "rapid circulation and conventionalization of the metaphor of Frankenfood" during the decade from 1992 to 2002 through its adoption by various consumer groups on the Internet that saw genetic modification of food as "monstrous." Monsanto attempted to repair the damage through a strategic communication campaign that linked the Frankenstein story with a more positive view of genetic modification: scientific aspirations toward beneficial development and knowledge. Although its own version did not prevail, Monsanto was at least able to be active in the same issue arena defined by the consumerist propagators of the Frankenstein myth.

Even though contagion generally encourages homogeneity, it is important to keep in mind that networks are inherently unstable and therefore the patterns created by contagion are certain to change over time. In this respect, the concept of contagion in social networks comes particularly close to complexity theory's view that local interactions eventually lead to macro patterns in a society as a whole. The dynamism of the opinion environment can be modeled in terms of a fitness landscape, originally proposed by a complexity theorist (Kauffman, 1993) to model the process of evolution within complex biological systems. Species were viewed as populating a "landscape," or environment, alongside competing species. Each species' attempts to maximize its fitness—its survivability— "shift the fitness landscape shared by others, who likewise respond, creating an ongoing series of interactions and adaptations interspersed with temporary periods of stability" (Gilpin & Murphy, 2008, p. 171). Kauffman extended this network-based fitness landscape to model organizations' success within their own environments. The model illustrates one way in which communicators can exert some pressure to shape messages, by developing multiple contingent ways to communicate their points that depend on the network configuration at the time. Luoma-Aho and Vos (2010) made a similar point in their discussion of issue arenas: "Because various stakeholder interests are often competing, one strategy might no longer be the best alternative; instead different strategies should be applied depending on the need of each issues arena. . . . The result should be a dynamic mosaic of multiple strategies for multiple publics moved by multiple issues" (p. 323). Described thus, issue arenas offer alternative versions of Kauffman's network-based "fitness landscape": unstable opinion environments where everyone's strategy depends on everyone else's strategy.

Conclusion

Returning to the questions with which this chapter began, a network view of strategic communication tends to confirm the highly contingent characterization of "strategic" by Hallahan et al. (2007). In a complex, tightly linked opinion environment, strategic communication can be purposeful and mindful, but it cannot control. Organizations that operate in an older paradigm of "target" audiences and communication "objectives" need to be more aware of the limitations and even the dangers that such attempts pose in a networked context.

For strategic communication, the primary observation derived from social network analysis is that ties count. Communication professionals have long known that it is important to cultivate ties with important audiences. However, network theory leads us in a different direction from relationships as they have traditionally been defined, particularly in public relations. Network ties are more volatile and perilous than those envisioned by theorists who have viewed relationships as a process of building rapport with key audiences (e.g., Ledingham & Bruning, 2006). In addition, although directionality—whether communication is symmetric or nonsymmetric—tells us something about the nature of a relationship (e.g., Grunig, 2001), in network theory, equally important is the strength of the tie compared to all the other ties that exist in the network. It is that strength that determines whose message will prevail in the constantly negotiated fitness landscape.

A network perspective also shows us that "target" audiences are not clear-cut. They are intermixed with other groups and cannot be singled out for targeting any more than street fighters, intermixed with civilian populations, can be "targeted." As repeatedly pointed out above, network theory is attuned to a marketplace of ideas where multiple actors meet to construct public opinion. Thus, cultivating desired relationships entails accepting all the other relationships that are connected to that audience, whether we want to deal with them or not.

In this respect, network approaches are uniquely useful in giving a holistic view of the opinion arena in which communication takes place. As explained earlier, connections with certain key players are important, and can be cultivated purposefully; but the overall pattern of links among issues, communicators, and distribution technologies—all haphazardly stirred by unpredictable news developments—presents a challenge that lies well beyond anyone's control. In this environment, "management" means finding a way for strategic communicators to play a continuing role—not control, but a role—in shaping their messages, so they can at least participate in issue arenas that determine public opinion. Participating in an issue arena means accepting the dark side of networks that has been described throughout this chapter: ties that could constrain an organization's options later on, or force innocent actors to share the malfeasance of associates in the same space. It seems, then, that organizations have no choice but to attempt to communicate strategically, but the successful outcomes of these attempts will be as uncertain as the environment in which they take place.

References

Adamic, L., & Glance, N. (2005). The political blogosphere and the 2004 U.S. election: Divided they blog. *In LinkKDD 2005: Proceedings of the 3rd International Workshop on Link Discovery,* 36–43.

Berger, B. K. (1999). The Halcion affair: Public relations and the construction of ideological world view. *Journal of Public Relations Research, 11*(3), 185–203.

Borgatti, S. F., & Foster, P. C. (2003). The network paradigm in organizational research: A review and typology. *Journal of Management, 29*(6), 991–1013.

Borgatti, S. F., & Lopez-Kidwell, V. L. (2011). Network theory. In P. Carrington and J. Scott (Eds.), *The Sage Handbook of Social Network Analysis,* pp. 40–54. Thousand Oaks, CA: Sage Publications.

Botan, C. H., & Soto, F. (1998). A semiotic approach to the internal functioning of publics: implications for strategic communication and public relations. *Public Relations Review, 24*(1), 21-44.

Buchanan, M. (2002). *Small worlds and the groundbreaking science of networks.* New York: W. W. Norton & Company Inc.

Burt, R. S. (1992). *Structural holes: The social structure of competition.* Cambridge, MA: Harvard University Press.

Burt, R. S. (1999). The social capital of opinion leaders. *Annals of the American Academy of Political and Social Science, 566,* 37–54.

Christakis, N. A., & Fowler, J. H. (2007). The spread of obesity in a large social network over 32 years. *New England Journal of Medicine, 357,* 370–379.

Christakis, N. A., & Fowler, J. H. (2008). The collective dynamics of smoking in a large social network. *New England Journal of Medicine,* 358(21), 2249–2258.

Curtin, P. A., & Gaither, T. K. (2006). Contested notions of issue identity in international public relations: A case study. *Journal of Public Relations Research, 18*(1), 67–89.

Emirbayer, M. (1997). Manifesto for a relational sociology. *American Journal of Sociology, 103*(2), 281–317.

Entman, R. M. (2003). Cascading activation: Contesting the White House's frame after 9/11. *Political Communication, 20,* 415–432.

Freeman, L. C. (2004). *The development of social network analysis: A study in the sociology of science.* North Charleston, SC: BookSurge.

Garner, J. T. (2006). It's not what you know: A transactive memory analysis of knowledge networks at NASA. *Journal of Technical Writing and Communication, 36*(4) 329–351.

Garyantes, D., & Murphy, P. (2010). Success or chaos? Framing and ideology in news coverage of the Iraqi national elections. *International Communication Gazette, 72*(2), 151–170.

Gilpin, D. (2010). Organizational image construction in a fragmented online media environment. *Journal of Public Relations Research, 22*(3), 265–287.

Gilpin, D. R., & Murphy, P. (2008). *Crisis management in a complex world.* New York: Oxford University Press.

Gladwell, M. (2000). *The tipping point: How little things can make a big difference.* Boston, MA: Little, Brown & Co.

Granovetter, M. (1973). The strength of weak ties. *American Journal of Sociology, 78*(6): 1360–1380.

Granovetter, M. (1983). The strength of weak ties: A network theory revisited. *Sociological Theory, 1,* 201–233.

Grunig, J. E. (2001). Two-way symmetrical public relations: Past, present, and future. In Robert L. Heath (Ed.), *Handbook of public relations* (pp. 11–30). Thousand Oaks, CA: Sage Publications.

Hallahan, K., Holtzhausen, D., Van Ruler, B., Verčič, D., & Sriramesh, K. (2007). Defining strategic communication. *International Journal of Strategic Communication, 1*(1), 3–35.

Hellsten, I. (2003). Focus on metaphors: The case of "Frankenfood" on the web. *Journal of Computer-Mediated Communication, 8*(4).

Ihlen, Ø. (2005). The power of social capital: Adapting Bourdieu to the study of public relations. *Public Relations Review, 31,* 492–496.

James, M. (2011). A provisional conceptual framework for intentional positioning in public relations. *Journal of Public Relations Research, 23*(1), 93–118.

Kadushin, C. (2004). Some basic network concepts and propositions. In *Introduction to social network theory* (Chapter 2). Retrieved from http://construct.haifa.ac.il/~cerpe/papers/kadushin.html.

Katz, J. E. (2005). Individual rights advocacy in tobacco control policies: An assessment and recommendation. *Tobacco Control, 14*(suppl II) ii, 31–37.

Kauffman, S. (1993). *The origins of order: Self-organization and selection in evolution.* New York: Oxford University Press.

Knox, H., Savage, M., & Harvey, P. (2006). Social networks and the study of relations: Networks as method, metaphor and form. *Economy and Society, 35*(1), 113–140.

Krackhart, D. (1999). The ties that torture: Simmelian tie analysis in organizations. *Research in the Sociology of Organizations, 16,* 183–210.

Ledingham, J. A., & Bruning, S. D. (2006). *Relationship management: A relational approach to public relations.* Mahwah, NJ: Lawrence Erlbaum.

Luoma-Aho, V., & Vos, M. (2010). Towards a more dynamic stakeholder model: Acknowledging multiple issue arenas. *Corporate Communications, 15*(3), 315–331.

McPherson, J. M., Smith-Lovin, L., & Cook, J. (2001). Birds of a feather: Homophily in social networks. *Annual Review of Sociology, 2,* 415–444.

Milgram, S. (1967). The small world problem. *Psychology Today, 1,* 60–67.

Molleda, J.-C. (2011). Advancing the theory of cross-national conflict-shifting: A case discussion and quantitative content analysis of a transnational crisis' newswire coverage. *International Journal of Strategic Communication, 5*(1), 49–70.

Monge, P. R., & Contractor, N. (2003). *Theories of communication networks.* New York: Oxford University Press.

Morçöl, G., & Wachhaus, A. (2009). Network and complexity theories: A comparison and prospects for a synthesis. *Administrative Theory & Praxis, 31*(1), 44–58.

Murphy, P. (2000). Symmetry, contingency, complexity: Accommodating uncertainty in public relations theory. *Public Relations Review, 26*(4), 447–462.

Murphy, P. (2010). The intractability of reputation: Media coverage as a complex system in the case of Martha Stewart. *Journal of Public Relations Research, 22*(2), 209–237.

Murphy, P. (2011). Communicating with culturally unsympathetic audiences: Smokers as subaltern communities. Unpublished paper.

Murphy, P., & Gilpin, D. R. (2013). Complexity theory: Against reputation management. In Craig Carroll (Ed.), *The Handbook of Corporate Reputation,* pp. 166–182. Hoboken, NJ: Wiley-Blackwell.

Nager, N. R., & Allen, T. H. (1991). *Public relations: Management by objectives.* Lanham, MD: University Press of America.

Pachucki, M. A., & Breiger, R. L. (2010). Cultural holes: Beyond relationality in social networks and culture. *Annual Review of Sociology, 36,* 205–224.

Pedahzur, A., & Perlinger, A. (2006). The changing nature of suicide attacks: A social network perspective. *Social Forces, 84*(4), 1987–2008.

Schultz, J., & Breiger, R. L. (2010). The strength of weak culture. *Poetics, 38*(6), 610–624.

White, H. C. (1970). *Chains of opportunity: System models of mobility in organizations.* Cambridge, MA: Harvard University Press.

Williams, S. L., and Moffitt, M. A. (1997). Corporate image as an impression formation process: Prioritizing personal, organizational, and environmental audience factors. *Journal of Public Relations Research, 9*(4), 237–258.

Yu, T., & Lester, R. H. (2008). Moving beyond firm boundaries: A social network perspective on reputation spillover. *Corporate Reputation Review, 11*(1), 94–108.

Yu, T., Sengul, M., & Lester, R. H. (2008). Misery loves company: The spread of negative impacts resulting from an organizational crisis. *Academy of Management Review, 22*(2), 452–472.

8

Social Theories for Strategic Communication[1]

Øyvind Ihlen and Piet Verhoeven

Scholars have increasingly turned to social theory to study the practice and the consequences that strategic communication has in society. Important questions have been raised concerning issues such as trust and legitimacy, power and behavior. Using social theory, including sociological and culturally oriented approaches, practitioners and scholars focus on how organizations relate themselves to the public arena or society at large. This body of work often moves beyond the applied to discuss ethical and political consequences drawing on empirical data.

It must be said, however, that the approaches are widely disparate concerning most aspects. Some scholars have condemned the practice of forms of corporate strategic communication, in particular using critical theory (e.g., L'Etang & Pieczka, 1996, 2006) and postcolonial theory (e.g., Dutta-Bergman, 2005; McKie & Munshi, 2007; Munshi & Kurian, 2005). But the literature has also grown to include work that draws on other forms of social theory, like postmodernism (e.g., Holtzhausen, 2012; McKie & Munshi, 2007; Radford, 2012), feminism (e.g., Aldoory, 1998; Grunig & Hon, 2001; O'Neil, 2003; Toth, 2001), constructivism (e.g., Merten, 2004), communitarianism (e.g., Hallahan, 2004; Kruckeberg & Starck, 1988; Leeper, 2001; Starck & Kruckeberg, 2001), cultural theory (e.g., Banks, 1995; Leichty, 2003; Ristino, 2008, Hatch & Schultz, 2002), structuration theory (e.g., Durham, 2005), social constructionism (Tsetsura, 2010), systems theory (Holmström, 2010), complexity theory (Gilpin & Murphy, 2010), intersectionality theory (Vardeman-Winter & Tindall, 2010), agenda-setting and agenda building theory (Carroll & McCombs, 2003; Meijer & Kleinnijenhuis, 2006; Schultz, Kleinnijenhuis, Oegema, Utz & van Atteveldt, 2012) and framing (see Lim & Jones, 2010 for an overview in the field of public relations).

When talking about individual social theorists and strategic communication, it is particularly the work of Habermas that has received attention (e.g., Burkart, 2004; Jensen, 2001; Leeper, 1996; Maier, 2005; Meisenbach, 2005; Olasky, 1989; Pearson, 1989a, 1989b, 1990; Self, 2010), with Niklas Luhmann (e.g., Geist, 2001; Holmström, 1997, 2003; Merten, 2004; Ronnebeger & Rühl, 1992), Michel Foucault (e.g., Livesey, 2002; Motion, 1997; Motion & Weaver, 2005) and Pierre Bourdieu (e.g., Edwards, 2006, 2007; Ihlen, 2004, 2005) in tow. The use of social theory to analyze public relations in particular has been discussed in the edited volume *Public Relations and Social Theory: Key Figures and Concepts* (Ihlen, van Ruler, & Fredriksson, 2009), whereas cultural approaches have been explored more fully in other volumes (e.g., Edwards & Hodges, 2011).

This chapter somewhat boldly draws some general conclusions based on this multifaceted literature. We argue that to choose a social theoretical approach by implication means that:

1.   the domain of research includes the social level;
2.   a description of society is sought;
3.   key concepts like legitimacy and reflection come to the fore;
4.   key issues for research concerns power and language; and
5.   an empirical program based in social constructionism propels communication studies to the forefront (Ihlen & Verhoeven, 2009, 2012).

We will proceed to discuss these points accordingly.

Compass: Research Domain

Starting with the simple definition of strategic communication as "the purposeful use of communication by an organization to fulfill its mission" (Hallahan, Holtzhausen, van Ruler, Verčič, & Sriramesh, 2007, p. 3), we argue that social theoretical approaches will study this "use of communication" in relation to the social level. That is, we maintain that a focus on consequences and not only effectiveness is implied (Rakow & Nastasia, 2009). Research is not only focused on the organizational level, but supplements, also, the administrative perspectives with approaches that take a step back and evaluate the social and political influence. What place does the corporation or organization have in the social structure, in what the Germans call *Öffentlichkeit* ("in public") (Ihlen & van Ruler, 2007)? Öffentlichkeit is an outcome and a quality of the public communication system in a society (Ronnebeger & Rühl, 1992). All forms of strategic communication, as well as journalism, can help develop or destroy this public communication system in creating a symbolic reality. Research of strategic communication will therefore focus on organizational behavior, including meaning creation.

In an early study, Boorstin (1962/1992) wrote about how the communication industry created a "menace of unreality" through its staging of "pseudo events" that sought publicity (p. 247). The German theorist Jürgen Habermas, for his part, originally denounced strategic communication for undermining the critical public sphere: "For the criteria of rationality are completely lacking in a consensus created by sophisticated opinion-molding services under the aegis of a sham public interest" (Habermas, 1989, pp. 193–195). A similar criticism was voiced by Mayhew (1997) who argued that what we call *public opinion* is increasingly the result of marketing research that allows professional communicators to push the right buttons. Furthermore, a whole strand of books have been published that are critical of how the communication industry furthers corporate goals at the expense of the public interest (Dinan & Miller, 2007; Miller & Dinan, 2008).

Public relations textbooks in particular have had a tendency to present a progressive history of the profession where manipulative, self-interested practice has given way to ethical and enlightened communication forms (Duffy, 2000). When unethical practice is exposed in the media, a typical response from professional associations is that this is not representative of 'true' or 'good' strategic communication. Instead, it is pointed out that an association has defined ethical principles or a code of ethics. In the public relations literature it has been argued that the practice should be "goaded by the incentive to make society a better place in which to live and work" (Heath, 2010, p. xiv). Indeed, attempts have been made to give the practice a positive civic role: "*Public relations' role in society is to create (and re-create) the conditions that enact civil society* [original italics]" (Taylor, 2010, p. 7). In Europe, the majority (58%) of communication practitioners perceive that ethical issues are much more relevant today than they were in former times, due to the internationalization of organizations, media and society, the increasing number of compliance and transparency rules and the new ethical challenges that social media creates. About 67% of European professionals report encountering ethical challenges in their daily work and a vast majority of 93% of European professionals see a need for new ethical codes, to be provided by international and national associations of communication professionals (Zerfass, Verčič, Verhoeven, Moreno & Tench, 2012).

This heightened perception of ethics and the call for ethical reflection resonates well with what Heath (2010, p. xiii) phrased as strategic communication being less about making organizations more effective, than about making *society* effective. Here, research drawing on social theory has an obvious role to play, and also a role in asking the crucial question: effective for whom? In many respects, strategic communication still seems to be put to use for self-interested purposes, often tied to corporate interests where a key aim is "to achieve or resist change by persuasively advancing and potentially privileging particular meanings and actions" (Leitch & Motion, 2010, p. 103). This is of course only one side of the coin, because strategic communication is also a weapon used by those opposing corporate exploitation. Strategic communication in itself is not good or bad, but can be used for good or bad purposes. A research perspective building on social theory will recognize this.

Context: Description of Society

Social theory calls for analysis of how society works and questions the value and meaning of what we see around us. Social theory presents us with different diagnoses for social ills and social change. Society has seen several changes in its metanarratives, which have been described, for instance, as the change from a society where individuals acted in a manner that was based on tradition, to a society that is dominated by goal-oriented rationality (Wæraas, 2009, drawing upon Max Weber). Such a view, however, is contrasted by analyses that characterize society as postmodern and argue that emotional and value-oriented orders co-exist with rational ones. Pluralism, polycontextuality, and situated knowledge are defining characteristics of this situation (Lyotard, 1979). Even if truths were not always taken for granted in the pre-modern society, values and norms were concrete and fundamental and closed to reflection (Zijderveld, 2000). In modern society, an increasingly common view is the one forwarded by John Dewey in 1916 that society is not only maintained by communication, but is actually constituted by it (Kückelhaus, 1998). Strategic communication and public relations are therefore closely connected to modernity, especially in the economic context of commercial and administrative organizations.

If communication constitutes the modern society, strategic communication and public relations are important constituents of modernity. Versions of a social constructivist perspective seem to dominate the way social theorists describe the process by which modern and late modern society has come into being. Such a view necessarily also privileges a focus on language, communication and relations as when we interpret and de- and re-construct meaning. Constructing social reality is a shared process of meaning construction (Bentele & Rühl, 1993; van Nistelrooij, 2000).

During the last decade some theorists tried to bridge the theoretical and conceptual distinction between modernism and postmodernism by introducing so-called *second modernity* (Beck, Bonss & Lau, 2003) or *hypermodernity* (Lipovetsky, 2005). Second modernity, also called reflexive modernity, is a cosmopolitan theoretical perspective and a proposed research program that can overcome the relativism connected to postmodernism. Such a perspective suits strategic communication and public relations very well because the practical field of communication management is often accused of being relativistic and also contributing to postmodern relativism in society at large. In second modernity Beck, Bonss and Lau (2003) recognize that the modern society of the twentieth century has changed fundamentally, calling this a modernization of modernity. That is second or *reflexive modernity,* not signifying an "increase of mastery and consciousness, but a heightened awareness that mastery is impossible" (Latour, 2003, p. 36). Modern society becomes reflexive through "disenchanting and dissolving" (Beck et al., 2003, p. 3) its premises in the areas of, for example, the nation state, the welfare state, the legal system, the economy and governance. In second modernity boundaries between social spheres, between nature and society, scientific and unscientific statements are not institutionally guaranteed as in modernity, nor dissolved as in postmodernity. In second modernity boundaries become multiple and at the same time fundamental. This process raises the necessity of institutionalizing new fictive or negotiable boundaries self-consciously, and solving conflicts around responsibility and decision-making in society.

Contradictory scientific camps will grow in second modernity and the recognition of extra-scientific justifications will increase. Instead of forming a postmodern recognition of the arbitrary multiplicity and downplaying the need for justification of claims, second modernists try to find ways to take into account the unexpected side effects of policies and actions and search the closure of debates through ad hoc means of decision-making (Beck et al., 2003). It is not hard to picture an important role for strategic communication here in all sides of the debates. At the same time subjectivity becomes a central notion in second modernity. The necessity of the subjective drawing of boundaries in all aspects of social life (institutional, cultural and technical) and the recognition of those subjective boundaries as positive fictions, helps to solve social problems. This is different from the "bricolage mentality in postmodernism and the acceptance of a pluralized, defoundationalizing subjectivity" (Beck et al., 2003, p. 27). A perspective of second modernity can help to solve communication problems and conflicts between organizations, because it recognizes the private interests and the fundamentally subjective character of many strategic communication messages, as opposed to modern miscommunication, because of the assumed fixed boundaries between organizations. For instance, in first modernity the non-recognized subjectivity leads to miscommunication because an objective solution is expected, for example in societal debates about social and environmental issues.

Individualization is another important aspect of second modernity. Individualization is a result of the acceptance of the multiple bases on which an individual can be defined. Therewith the self-definition of individuals has become individualized (Beck et al., 2003). The development in the direction of more individualization is also found in theories about hypermodernity with the French philosopher Gilles Lipovetsky (2005) as its main representative. Hypermodernity is also a very suitable theoretical perspective for strategic communication because it not only recognizes the fundamental individualization and reflexivity of society, but also acknowledges the fundamental consumerist character of today's Western or even global society. As strategic communication is often functioning within an economic environment, the recognition of consumerism as a major force in society helps in theorizing about it.

Our "hyper modern society" as Lipovetsky (2005, p. 29) called this day and age, is characterized by hyperconsumption, hypermodernity and hypernarcissism as explained by Charles (2005). Consumption, modernity and narcissism are all three in overdrive today, in a 'hyper' state. Consumption is central to more and more aspects of social life and consuming is put more and more in a context of emotion and hedonism. Consumption has come to be about luxury, pleasure and sensation. Hypermodernity is a state of constant motion, fluidity and flexibility. The belief in science and technology and progress is still like it was in modernity, but it has become surrounded by criticism and skepticism as well. Hypernarcissism is not only a form of individualism. It is individualism linked to the expectation that every individual behaves in a responsible way on their own account. Postmodern hedonism is replaced by hypermodern responsibility (see Charles, 2005; Lipovetsky, 2005 for an introduction on hypermodernism). It is again not difficult to picture strategic communication in the theoretical perspective of hypermodernity: the centrality of consumption, the belief in modern welfare and progress and the responsibility of the individual for their own conduct, are close to the central professional values and beliefs in the field of strategic communication and public relations. Strategic communication is part of the hypermodern organization (Roberts & Armitage, 2006) and at the same time it plays an important role in its constitution and that of the hypermodern environment where the organizations are part of a society where conflict and difference are constant.

Social theorists differ as to how conflict and difference in society is perceived. The French scholar Bourdieu (1990) described society as structured, constituted, and reproduced through individual and collective struggle. Conflict and difference was seen as a fundamental core of human existence. His countryman, Foucault (1972), harbored similar thoughts in the sense that he wrote about how certain discourse coalitions produce modern knowledge and how power is expressed through these discourses. Other authors have drawn attention to how such power relations find their expression in how risk is distributed in society and how the macro structure of gender and patriarchy work (Fredriksson, 2009; Rakow & Nastasia, 2009). For instance, who has discursive control over what is accepted as a risk?

When social theorists present a societal diagnosis, by implication they will also often propose a remedy. The proposed solution might come in the form of acceptation or a call for *communicative action* (Habermas, 1984, 1987). Communicative action is a form of societal dialogue and consensus building and seen as opposing *strategic action* that only works for the realization of private interests and which could involve using other humans strategically. As pointed out above, some have also seen strategic communication as an important civic instrument (Heath, 2011; Taylor, 2010). Others have argued that we should draw lessons from how actors and actants construct our nonmodern condition from scratch (Verhoeven, 2009). Some calls have also been issued to focus on how strategic communication help perpetrate gendered, race and/or geographical dispersed social injustice. The communication practitioner is urged to become an activist on behalf of an organization's publics, and identify and learn to respect differences (Holtzhausen, 2012). Using a Marxist-feminist-deconstructivist perspective, Spivak (as cited in Dutta, 2009) pointed to how neo-liberal transnational capitalism breeds fundamental inequities. Studying strategic communication and its role in this project then becomes a remedy in itself. In short, using social theory can help strategic communication develop an ontology, something that public relations theory has been accused of lacking (Cheney & Christensen, 2001).

Concepts: Legitimacy and Reflection

A profound social change mentioned above is how social authorities have lost their previous privileged position and how decisions have to be legitimized on a continuous basis. Strategic communication will thus have to focus on such "constituents of thoughts" (*Stanford Encyclopedia of Philosophy*, 2011) as legitimacy and reflection. These are abstract ideas that structure knowledge and are structured by knowledge, and are helpful to understand strategic communication at its most fundamental level.

Social theory has offered up several definitions of legitimacy that are useful for strategic communication. Weber, for instance, defined it as "the justified right to exist" (as cited in Wæraas, 2009, p. 282). Organizations are bound by what the environment finds acceptable. Luhmann (1993, p. 28) argued it was the "generalized preparedness to accept decisions within certain boundaries of tolerance; decisions which are still undecided as regards contents." Habermas tied legitimacy to truth and using his work Burkart (2009) has suggested a model incorporating this aspect as a means to further understanding between organizations and their publics, which in turn might form the basis of legitimacy.

It could be argued that the most fundamental task of strategic communication is to see to it that the mission of the organization is considered legitimate (Holmström, Falkheimer, & Nielsen, 2010). With a fast changing society, organizations need to keep abreast and map their environments (Ihlen, 2008). Some would argue that strategic communication is a reflexive social expert system that assists in this endeavor (Falkheimer, 2009). Others, building on Luhmann, see strategic communication more as a functional system that has turned into a *reflective* practice on behalf of organizations (Holmström, 2009).

The increased demand for legitimacy is one driving factor, as is evident from the debate about corporate social responsibility (Ihlen, Bartlett, & May, 2011; May, Cheney, & Roper, 2007). Organizations have to maneuver among demands from several groups, stakeholders or publics in order to retain their "license to operate." Taking a cue from Holmström (2000, 2003), van Ruler and Verčič (2005) stated that in order to sustain this license to operate, those responsible for the management of organizations should take a reflective view of its communication management. The reflective model of communication management sees strategic communication as "engaged in constructing society by making sense of situations, creating appropriate meanings out of them and looking for acceptable frameworks and enactments" (van Ruler & Verčič, 2005, p. 266). This is a societal approach to strategic communication that takes society at large as the unit of analysis and looks at the organization from the outside, that is, from the perspective of the public sphere, the *Öffentlichkeit*. Communication management is defined then as being concerned with "maximizing, optimizing, or satisfying the process of meaning creation, using informational, persuasive, relational, and discursive interventions to solve managerial problems by coproducing societal (public) legitimation" (van Ruler & Verčič, 2005, p. 266).

Some single out legitimacy, either as an end in itself or as a means to realizing organizational goals. A social theory perspective makes it clear that legitimacy is conferred upon an organization by different publics, and hence it cannot be managed (Wehmeier, 2006). This leads to the conclusion that strategic communication has to do with the *negotiation* of knowledge, meaning, and behavior. In public relations, this thought is echoed by the so-called co-creational approach that sees publics and groups as co-creators of meaning (Botan & Taylor, 2004; Taylor, 2010).

Legitimacy and reflection are tightly intertwined and social theory also offers up other interesting concepts, such as trust (Bentele, 1994; Bentele & Wehmeier, 2007; Ihlen & Verhoeven, 2009). Such concepts also articulate ideas about what strategic communication is or could be about, which in turn largely spur on or are spurred on by certain concerns connected with the practice.

Concerns and Issues: Power and Language

Concerns or *issues* can be defined as *matters of discussion*. Put differently, issues are facts in the making. Concerns and issues can also lead to creative and fruitful discussions, in part as a result of involving the concepts discussed in the previous section.

Power is frequently discussed in the literature (e.g., B. K. Berger, 2005; Cottle, 2003; Courtright & Smudde, 2007; Edwards, 2006; Leitch & Motion, 2010; Plowman, 1998; Weaver, Motion, & Roper, 2006). Smudde and Courtright (2010) define power as having three dimensions: hierarchical, rhetorical, and social. Hierarchical power is based on a person's rank and position in an organization. Hierarchical power in an organization is still an issue because results from research on the power of communication professionals in organizations and how well they are connected to the dominant coalition (Grunig, 1992) are mixed. European research shows that not all practitioners are seated at the management table (Zerfass, Tench, Verhoeven, Verčič, & Moreno, 2010). Furthermore, European research also shows that female professionals perceive their influence to have less impact on the strategic decision making and planning of their organization than do male professionals (Verhoeven & Aarts, 2010). Issues such as salary inequity and a lack of women in higher management have far from disappeared (Wrigley, 2010).

Rhetorical power concerns the skills that are necessary to be effective with language and symbols. Rhetorical power relates to social theory also in the sense that it describes ability to influence the issues and values that are under public debate, in other words, issues that relate to the *public sphere* (Bentele & Nothhaft, 2010; Holtzhausen, 2010; Jensen, 2001). The public sphere is seen as a social construction of mankind. Ihlen (2002, 2004), for example, combines the rhetorical approach with the sociological approach and shows how strategic communication constitutes the struggle of actors in a public battlefield of meanings, thereby contributing to *the* public meaning and as such, to social reality. Meaning creation is at the heart of public relations and closely related to the concepts of organizational sense giving and sense making (Morsing & Schultz, 2006; Weick, Sutcliffe, & Obstfeld, 2005). With sense giving, organizations try to impose their interpretation of a phenomenon on others, often by means of one-way communication such as propaganda or public information. Combining sense giving and sense making in two-way communication processes makes room for multiple interpretations of and negotiation about the meaning that is produced in the communication process.

Social power binds the other two forms of power together: people acting together through communication to produce organizations, and to produce societies (Smudde & Courtright, 2010). To this could also be added mastery of the technological and social development of the media environment on a global level since the 1990s (see, e.g., Catalano, 2007). The rise of digital and social media and its use raises questions about their consequences for strategic communication. This is also recognizable in the top five most important issues for the profession in 2013, according to European communication professionals (Zerfass et al., 2010). Coping with digital evolution and the social web is seen as the most important issue.

The notion of social constructivism has already been alluded to. Berger and Luckmann (1966) argued that reality is a social construction and as such truth is inseparable from the way in which we use communication to interact with one another. This view is seen as opposing that of realists who think that objective knowledge is obtainable. To gain a better understanding of strategic communication in society, we have to look behind it and inquire into how strategic communication functions as the producer of certain dominating realities in society (B. K. Berger, 1999; Heide, 2009). Such processes have enormous implications for issues of power. They make strategic communication political as it establishes and/or reinforces particular truths (Motion & Leitch, 2009).

The articulation of all these particular truths from individuals, groups and organizations has become increasingly mediated, first since the rise of mass media in the twentieth century and secondly in the last few decades with the rise of computer mediated forms of (social) communication. Meaning construction nowadays increasingly takes place and materializes in the interplay between traditional mass media and the new social media systems, often on a global scale. Apart from the intentions of the communicating actors, all these messages and communications get a dynamic of their own that influences the meaning construction process and the meaning that is constructed about an issue. New research methods are called for to study this complex process of meaning construction and the dynamics of the communication in the field of strategic communication. New research methods should show a higher order structure in the discourses and allow for comparisons across time and across discourses. A higher order structure shows for example the structural characteristics of the language used and the structural characteristics of the communication or, in other words of the discourses. Also, next order analyses reveal the contextualization that is constructed in a domain by analyzing so-called implicit frames (Hellsten et al., 2010). Implicit frames show the latent dimension of communication content and the meaning that is created in those implicit frames. Such second order analyses that show meaning construction processes can be done with so-called semantic mapping methods that are used in information sciences and science and technology studies (see Leydesdorff, 2001; Leydesdorff & Hellsten, 2006). In the field of strategic communication such semantic mapping methods can show the different meanings constructed about an organization or issue by strategic communicators, journalists in the media and members of the active public on the Internet (Jonkman & Verhoeven, 2013; Verhoeven, Jonkman & Boumans, 2012) and the interplay between the different discourses (van der Meer & Verhoeven, in press).

Empirical Avenues: a Research Program

Drawing on social theory to analyze strategic communication opens up a wealth of possibilities for formulating empirical questions and hypotheses. Social theory is necessary to describe, understand,

and explain what happens to whom in the realm of strategic communication and with what consequences (Ihlen & Verhoeven, 2009). The most fundamental and shared premise would be that an empirical research program incorporates insights from what has been called the communicative, linguistic, or discursive turn. A fundamental constructivist starting point would entail micro studies of individual action to macro perspectives of system theory (Holmström, 2010; van Ruler & Verčič, 2005). A social theory perspective in this vein can help fill the gap between the descriptive and normative studies in the managerial paradigms and the individualistic psychological studies in the behavioral paradigm. Strategic communication can be seen as different forms of communication, ranging from symbolic, interpersonal and social communication to the non-personal communication function in system theory. It is possible to distinguish between mediated and non-mediated communication on the micro, meso, and macro levels.

Some of the questions raised by social theory would stem from the discussion in the previous sections and relate to the effects of strategic communication: what are the cognitive, attitudinal, and behavioral effects on different publics? Such studies can be conducted with the help of, for instance, theoretical perspectives of framing (Entman, 1993; Hallahan, 1999), agenda setting and priming (Scheufele, 2000), uses and gratifications (Ketelaar & van der Laan, 2009; Ruggiero, 2000), public opinion dynamics and formation (van Ginneken, 2003), cultural indicators (Gerbner, Gross, Morgan, & Signorelli, 1994), the spiral of cynicism (Cappella & Jamieson, 1997), the reception gap (Zaller, 1996), or new media theories about computer mediated communication (Neuman & Guggenheim, 2011), to name a few. A first step could be to conduct meta-studies about the effects of the numerous studies that have been conducted on this in the last 25 years.

Conclusion

In this chapter we have presented some key conclusions regarding social theory perspectives on strategic communication. First of all, we have argued that such a perspective addresses negative as well as positive effects of the practice of strategic communication. A social theory perspective studies all aspects, warts and all, and cannot only be judged as to whether or not it improves practice. A whole range of different descriptions of society is on offer in social theory. We have in particular discussed the notions of second modernity or hypermodernity, where communication is seen as an important constituting factor. One important contribution from such a perspective is the recognition of consumerism as a major force that strategic communication is related to. The function of strategic communication is occupied with creating legitimacy for organizations, something that might be achieved by reflecting on what demands society poses. Social theory calls attention to the negotiation around knowledge, meaning, and behavior in this sense. That is, issues of power and language follow. Social theory helps to see how strategic communication is influenced by and influences power structures in society through communication, i.e., symbol use. Finally, we have made some suggestions for how such processes can be studied empirically.

Strategic communication is used to help all kinds of organizations, and social theory calls attention to how this influences society. A good expression of this is how the corporation has become the dominant institution in modern society, and many studies have centered on the powerful role of the modern corporation and its (negative) impact on the public sphere and politics (e.g., Bakan, 2004; Boggs, 2000; Carey, 1995; Korten, 2001). Simple searches demonstrate how the revenue of many corporations surpasses the Gross Domestic Product of entire counties. For instance, the 2010 revenue of Walmart made this corporation the 25th largest economy in the world (Trivett, 2011). Using social theory to examine strategic communication can help to understand how such a position is legitimized. Such an undertaking goes beyond the administrative approaches found in many of the communication journals. Elsewhere (Ihlen & Verhoeven, 2009) we have posited a critical realist framework (Contu & Willmott, 2005; Reed, 2005) for this purpose. It is considered a perspective that can offer a solution for moving beyond the deadlock between positivists (or realists) and social constructionists in the social sciences. It is a realistic philosophical alternative for modern and post-modern analyses because it acknowledges the social construction of reality on the one hand and the existence of a reality independent of our interpretations on the other hand. Critical realism proposes to explain social phenomena at the real/deep level of the structures and mechanisms that underlie them (see, e.g., Bhaskar, 1978, 1979, 1986). In a critical realist framework all the elements proposed in this chapter can be combined in an effort to explain strategic communication as a social phenomenon. A research agenda for strategic communication in a critical realist framework does not impose a particular methodology or aim to produce one general theory of strategic communication. It opens up questions on different levels of analyses: from impressions, perceptions and sensations, events and states of affairs to the real/deep structures and mechanisms in the field. It can also account for the role of culture. This, however, is just one of the many possibilities on offer drawing from the indeed vast literature in the territory of social theory.

Note

1 This chapter is a development of Ihlen & Verhoeven (2009; 2012).

References

Aldoory, L. (1998). The language of leadership for female public relations professionals. *Journal of Public Relations Research, 10*(2), 73–101.

Bakan, J. (2004). The corporation: The pathological pursuit of profit and power. London: Constable.

Banks, S. (1995). *Multicultural public relations: A social-interpretive approach.* Thousand Oaks, CA: Sage.

Beck, U., Bonss, W., & Lau, C. (2003). The theory of reflexive modernization: Problematic, hypotheses and research programme. *Theory, Culture & Society, 20*(2), 1–33.

Bentele, G. (1994). Öffentliches Vertrauen: Normative und soziale Grundlage für Public Relations [Public trust: Normative and social fundamentals for Public Relations]. In W. Armbrecht & U. Zabel (Eds.), *Normative Aspekte der Public Relations. Grundlagen und Perspektiven* [Normative aspects of Public Relations. Fundamentals and perspectives] (pp. 131–158). Opladen, Germany: Westdeustscher Verlag.

Bentele, G, & Nothhaft, H. (2010). Strategic Communication and the Public Sphere from a European Perspective. *International Journal of Strategic Communication, 4*(2), 93–116.

Bentele, G., & Rühl, M. (Eds.). (1993). *Theorien öffentlicher Kommunikation [Theories of public communication].* München, Germany: Ölschläger.

Bentele, G., & Wehmeier, S. (2007). Applying sociology to public relations: A commentary. *Public Relations Review, 33*(3), 294–300.

Berger, B. K. (1999). The Halicon affair: Public relations and the construction of ideological world view. *Journal of Public Relations Research, 11*(3), 187–203.

Berger, B. K. (2005). Power over, power with, and power to relations: Critical reflections on public relations, the dominant coalition, and activism. *Journal of Public Relations Research, 17*(1), 5–28.

Berger, P., & Luckmann, T. (1966). *The social construction of reality: A treatise in the sociology of knowledge.* London: Penguin Books.

Bhaskar, R. (1978). *A realist theory of science.* London: Verso.

Bhaskar, R. (1979). *The possibility of naturalism: A philosophical critique of the contemporary human sciences.* New York: Routledge.

Bhaskar, R. (1986). *Scientific realism and human emancipation.* London, England: Verso.

Boggs, C. (2000). The end of politics: Corporate power and the decline of the public sphere. New York: Guilford.

Boorstin, D. J. (1992). *The image: A guide to pseudo-events in America.* New York, NY: Vintage Books. (Original work published 1962).

Botan, C H., & Taylor, M. (2004). Public relations: State of the field. *Journal of Communication, 54*(4), 645–661.

Bourdieu, P. (1990). *The logic of practice* (R. Nice, Trans.). Cambridge, UK: Polity.

Burkart, R. (2004). Consensus-oriented public relations (COPR): A concept for planning and evaluation of public relations. In B. van Ruler & D. Verčič (Eds.), *Public relations and communication management in Europe: A nation-by-nation introduction to public relations theory and practice* (pp. 459–465). Berlin: Walter de Gruyter.

Burkart, R. (2009). On Habermas: Understanding and public relations. In Ø. Ihlen, B. van Ruler & M. Fredriksson (Eds.), *Public relations and social theory: Key figures and concepts* (pp. 141–165). New York: Routledge.

Cappella, J. N., & Jamieson, K. H. (1997). *Spiral of cynicism: The press and the public good*. New York: Oxford University Press.

Carey, A. (1995). *Taking the risk out of democracy: Corporate propaganda versus freedom and liberty*. Urbana, IL: University of Illinois Press.

Carroll, G. E., & McCombs, M. (2003). Agenda-setting effects of business news on the public's images and opinions about major corporations. *Corporate Reputation Review, 6*(1), 36–46.

Catalano, C. S. (2007). Megaphones to the internet and the world: The role of blogs in corporate communications. *International Journal of Strategic Communication, 1*(4), 247–262.

Charles, S. (2005). Paradoxical individualism: An introduction to the thought of Gilles Lipovetsky. In Lipovetsky, G. *Hypermodern times* (pp. 1–28), Cambridge: Polity Press.

Cheney, G., & Christensen, L. T. (2001). Public relations as contested terrain: A critical response. In R. L. Heath (Ed.), *Handbook of public relations* (pp. 167–182). Thousand Oaks, CA: Sage.

Contu, A., & Willmott, H. (2005). You spin me round: The realist turn in organization and management studies. *Journal of Management Studies, 42*(8), 1645–1662.

Cottle, S. (Ed.). (2003). *News, public relations and power*. London: Sage Publications.

Courtright, J. L., & Smudde, P. M. (Eds.). (2007). *Power and public relations*. Cresskill, NJ: Hampton.

Dinan, W., & Miller, D. (Eds.). (2007). *Thinker, faker, spinner, spy: Corporate PR and the assault on democracy*. London: Pluto.

Duffy, M. E. (2000). There's no two-way symmetrical about it: A postmodern examination of public relations textbooks. *Critical Studies in Mass Communication, 17*(3), 294–315.

Durham, F. D. (2005). Public relations as structuration: A prescriptive critique of the Starlink global food contamination case. *Journal of Public Relations Research, 17*(1), 29–47.

Dutta, M. J. (2009). On Spivak: Theorizing resistance: Applying Gayatri Chakravorty Spivak in public relations. In Ø. Ihlen, B. van Ruler & M. Fredriksson (Eds.), *Public relations and social theory: Key figures and concepts* (pp. 278–300). New York: Routledge.

Dutta-Bergman, M. J. (2005). Civil society and public relations: Not so civil after all. *Journal of Public Relations Research, 17*(3), 267–289.

Edwards, L. (2006). Rethinking power in public relations. *Public Relations Review, 32*(3), 229–231.

Edwards, L. (2007). *Exploring power in public relations: A Bourdieusian perspective*. (PhD), Leeds Metropolitan University, Leeds, UK.

Edwards, L., & Hodges, C. E. M. (Eds.). (2011). *Public relations, society & culture: Theoretical and empirical explorations*. London: Routledge.

Entman, R. M. (1993). Framing: Toward clarification of a fractured paradigm. *Journal of Communication, 43*(4), 51–58.

Falkheimer, J. (2009). On Giddens: Interpreting public relations through Anthony Giddens' Structuration and Late Modernity Theory. In Ø. Ihlen, B. van Ruler & M. Fredriksson (Eds.), *Public relations and social theory: Key figures and concepts* (pp. 103–118). New York: Routledge.

Foucault, M. (1972). *The archaeology of knowledge and the discourse on language*. New York: Pantheon Books.

Fredriksson, M. (2009). On Beck: Risk and sub-politics in reflexive modernity. In Ø. Ihlen, B. van Ruler & M. Fredriksson (Eds.), *Public relations and social theory: Key figures and concepts* (pp. 21–42). New York: Routledge.

Geist, U. (2001). Om paradokser, usandsynligheder og tillid—en præsentation af Luhmanns teori om sociale systemer [About paradoxes, improbabilities and trust – a presentation of Luhmann's theory of social systems]. In M. Femø Nielsen (Ed.), *Profil og offentlighed: Public relations for viderekomne* [Profile and publicity: Public relations for the advanced] (pp. 301–334). Frederiksberg, Denmark.

Gerbner, G., Gross, L., Morgan, M. , & Signorelli, M. (1994). Growing up with television: The cultivation process. In J. Bryant & D. Zilmann (Eds.), *Media effects. Advances in theory and research* (pp. 17–41). Mahwah, NJ: Lawrence Erlbaum.

Gilpin, D. R., & Murphy, P J. (2010). Implications of complexity theory for public relations: Beyond crisis. In R. L. Heath (Ed.), *The SAGE handbook of public relations* (pp. 71–84). Thousand Oaks, CA: Sage.

Grunig, L. A. (1992). Power in the public relations department. In J. E. Grunig, D. M. Dozier, W. P. Ehling, L. A. Grunig, F. C. Repper & J. White (Eds.), *Excellence in public relations and communication management* (pp. 483-501). Hillsdale, NJ: Lawrence Erlbaum.

Grunig, L. A., & Hon, L. C. (2001). *Women in public relations: How gender influences practice*. New York: Guilford Press.

Habermas, J. (1984). *The theory of communicative action* (Vol. 1). Cambridge, UK: Polity Press.

Habermas, J. (1987). *The theory of communicative action* (Vol. 2). Cambridge, UK: Polity Press.

Habermas, J. (1989). *The structural transformation of the public sphere: An inquiry into a category of bourgeois society* (T. Burger, Trans.). Cambridge, MA: MIT Press.

Hallahan, K. (1999). Seven models of framing: Implications for public relations. *Journal of Public Relations Research, 11*(3), 205–242.

Hallahan, K. (2004). "Community" as a foundation for public relations theory and practice. *Communication Yearbook, 28*(1), 233–279.

Hallahan, K., Holtzhausen, D., van Ruler, B., Verčič, D., & Sriramesh, K. (2007). Defining strategic communication. *International Journal of Strategic Communication, 1*(1), 3–35.

Hatch, M. J., & Schultz, M. (2002). The dynamics of organizational identity. *Human Relations, 55,* 989–1018.

Heath, R. L. (Ed.). (2010). *The SAGE handbook of public relations.* Thousands Oaks, CA: Sage.

Heath, R. L. (2011). External organizational rhetoric: Bridging management and sociopolitical discourse. *Management Communication Quarterly, 25*(3), 415–435.

Heide, M. (2009). On Berger: A social constructionist perspective on public relations and crisis communication. In Ø. Ihlen, B. van Ruler & M. Fredriksson (Eds.), *Public relations and social theory: Key figures and concepts* (pp. 43–61). New York: Routledge.

Hellsten, L, Dawson, J., & Leydesdorff, L. (2010). Implicit media frames: Automated analysis of public debate on artificial sweeteners. *Public Understanding of Science, 19*(5), 590–608.

Holmström, S. (1997). The inter-subjective and the social systemic public relations paradigms. *Journal of Communication Management, 2*(1), 24–39.

Holmström, S. (2000, July 7). *The reflective paradigm turning into ceremony: Three phases of public relations—strategic, normative and cognitive in the institutionalisation of a new business paradigm, leading to three scenarios.* Paper presented at the 7th International Public Relations Research Symposium, Bled, Slovenia.

Holmström, S. (2003). *Grænser for ansvar* [Limits for responsibility]. Unpublished doctoral dissertation, Roskilde University, Roskilde, Denmark.

Holmström, S. (2009). On Luhmann: Contingency, risk, trust and reflection. In Ø. Ihlen, B. van Ruler & M. Fredriksson (Eds.), *Public relations and social theory: Key figures and concepts* (pp. 187–211). New York: Routledge.

Holmström, S. (2010). Reflective management: Seeing the organization as if from outside. In R. L. Heath (Ed.), *The SAGE handbook of public relations* (pp. 261–276). Thousand Oaks, CA: Sage.

Holmström, S., Falkheimer, J., & Nielsen, A. G. (2010). Legitimacy and Strategic communication in globalization: The cartoon crisis and other legitimacy conflicts. *International Journal of Strategic Communication, 4*(1), 1–18.

Holtzhausen, D. R. (2010). Communication in the Public Sphere: The political context of strategic communication. *International Journal of Strategic Communication, 4*(2), 75–77.

Holtzhausen, D. R. (2012). *Public relations as activism: Postmodern approaches to theory & practice.* New York: Routledge.

Ihlen, Ø. (2002). Rhetoric and resources: Notes for a new approach to public relations and issues management. *Journal of Public Affairs, 2*(4), 259–269.

Ihlen, Ø. (2004). *Rhetoric and resources in public relations strategies: A rhetorical and sociological analysis of two conflicts over energy and the environment* [Doctoral dissertation]. Oslo, Norway: Unipub forlag.

Ihlen, Ø. (2005). The power of social capital: Adapting Bourdieu to the study of public relations. *Public Relations Review, 31*(4), 492–496.

Ihlen, Ø. (2008). Mapping the environment of corporate social responsibility: Stakeholders, publics, and the public sphere. *Corporate Communications: An International Journal, 13*(2), 135–146.

Ihlen, Ø., Bartlett, J., & May, S. (Eds.). (2011). *Handbook of communication and corporate social responsibility.* Malden, MA: Wiley-Blackwell.

Ihlen, Ø., & van Ruler, B. (2007). How public relations works: Theoretical roots and public relations perspectives. *Public Relations Review, 33*(3), 243–248.

Ihlen, Ø., van Ruler, B., & Fredriksson, M. (Eds.). (2009). *Public relations and social theory: Key figures and concepts.* New York: Routledge.

Ihlen, Ø., & Verhoeven, P. (2009). Conclusions on the domain, context, concepts, issues and empirical avenues of public relations. In Ø. Ihlen, B. van Ruler & M. Fredriksson (Eds.), *Public relations and social theory: Key figures and concepts* (pp. 332–349). New York: Routledge.

Ihlen, Ø., & Verhoeven, P. (2012). A public relations identity for the 2010s. *Public Relations Inquiry, 1*(2), 159–176

Jensen, I. (2001). Public relations and emerging functions of the public sphere: An analytical framework. *Journal of Communication Management, 6*(2), 133–147.

Jonkman, J., & Verhoeven, P. (2013). From risk to safety: Implicit frames of third-party airport risk in Dutch quality news papers between 1992 and 2009. *Safety Science, 58,* 1–10.

Ketelaar, P. E., & van der Laan, M. P. (2009). A uses and gratifications approach to marketing communications: How to serve the interests of all stakeholder groups. In R. P. Konig, P. W. M. Nelissen & F. J. M. Huismans (Eds.), *Meaningful media: On the social construction of reality* (pp. 145–163). Nijmegen, the Netherlands: Tandem Felix.

Korten, D. C. (2001). *When corporations rule the world* (2 ed.). Bloomfield, CN: Kumarian Press.

Kruckeberg, D., & Starck, K. (1988). *Public relations and community.* Westport, CT: Praeger.

Kückelhaus, A. (1998). *Public Relations: die Konstruktion von Wirklichkeit: Kommunikationstheoretische Annäherungen an ein neuzeitliches Phänomen [Public Relations: The construction of reality: Communication scientific perspectives into a current phenomenon].* Opladen, Germany: Westdeustcher Verlag.

L'Etang, J., & Pieczka, M. (Eds.). (1996). *Critical perspectives in public relations.* London: International Thomson Business Press.

L'Etang, J., & Pieczka, M. (Eds.). (2006). *Public relations: Critical debates and contemporary practice.* Mahwah, NJ: Lawrence Erlbaum.

Latour, B. (2003). Is *Re*-modernization occurring—And if so, how to prove it? *Theory, Culture & Society, 20*(2), 35–48.

Leeper, R. V. (1996). Moral objectivity, Jürgen Habermas' discourse ethics and public relations. *Public Relations Review, 22*(2), 133-150.

Leeper, R. V. (2001). In search of a metatheory for public relations: An argument for communitarianism. In R. L. Heath (Ed.), *Handbook of public relations* (pp. 93–104). Thousand Oaks, CA: Sage.

Leichty, G. (2003). The cultural tribes of public relations. *Journal of Public Relations Research, 15*(4), 277–304.

Leitch, S., & Motion, J. (2010). Publics and public relations: Effective change. In R. L. Heath (Ed.), *The SAGE Handbook of Public Relations* (pp. 99–110). Thousand Oaks, CA: Sage.

Leydesdorff, L., (2001). *A sociological theory of communication: The self-organization of the knowledge-based society.* Leiden: DSWO Press, Leiden University.

Leydesdorff, L. & Hellsten, I. (2006). Measuring the meanings of words in contexts: Automated contexts of 'monarch butterflies,' 'Frankenfoods' and 'stem cells.' *Scientometrics, 67,* 231–258.

Lim, J., & Jones, L. (2010). A baseline summary of framing research in public relations from 1990 to 2009. *Public Relations Review, 36,* 292–297.

Lipovetsky, G. (2005). *Hypermodern times.* Cambridge: Polity Press.

Livesey, S. M. (2002). The discourse of the middle ground: Citizen Shell commits to sustainable development. *Management Communication Quarterly, 15*(3), 313–349.

Luhmann, N. (1993). *Legitimation durch Verfahren.* Frankfurt, Germany: Suhrkamp.

Lyotard, J. F. (1979). *La condition postmoderne [The postmodern condition].* Paris: Editions de Minuit.

Maier, C. T. (2005). Weathering the storm: Hauser's Vernacular Voices, public relations and the Roman Catholic Church's sexual abuse scandal. *Public Relations Review, 31*(2), 219–227.

May, S. K., Cheney, G., & Roper, J. (Eds.). (2007). *The debate over corporate social responsibility.* New York: Oxford University Press.

Mayhew, L. H. (1997). *The new public: Professional communication and the means of social influence.* Cambridge: Cambridge University Press.

McKie, D., & Munshi, D. (2007). *Reconfiguring public relations: Ecology, equity and enterprise.* New York: Routledge.

Meijer, M. M., & Kleinnijenhuis, J. (2006). Issue news and corporate reputation: Applying the theories of agenda setting and issue ownership in the field of business communication. *Journal of Communication 56,* 543–559.

Meisenbach, R. J. (2005). Habermas' discourse ethics and principle of universalization as a moral framework for organizational communication. *Management Communication Quaterly, 20*(1), 39–62.

Merten, K. (2004). A constructivistic approach to public relations. In B. v. Ruler & D. Verčič (Eds.), *Public relations and communication management in Europe: A nation-by-nation introduction to public relations theory and practice* (pp. 45–54). Berlin: Walter de Gruyter.

Miller, D, & Dinan, W. (2008). *A century of spin: How public relations became the cutting edge of corporate power.* London: Pluto Press.

Morsing, M., & Schultz, M. (2006). Corporate social responsibility communication: Stakeholder information, response and involvement strategies. *Business Ethics: A European Review, 15*(4), 323–338.

Motion, J. (1997). Technologising the self-an art of public relations. *Australian Journal of Communication, 24*(2), 1–16.

Motion, J., & Leitch, S. (2009). On Foucault: A toolbox for public relations. In Ø. Ihlen, B. van Ruler & M. Fredriksson (Eds.), *Public relations and social theory: Key figures and concepts* (pp. 83–102). New York: Routledge.

Motion, J., & Weaver, C. K. (2005). A discourse perspective for critical public relations research: Life sciences network and the battle for truth. *Journal of Public Relations Research, 17*(1), 49–67.

Munshi, D., & Kurian, P. (2005). Imperializing spin cycles: A postcolonial look at public relations, greenwashing, and the separation of publics. *Public Relations Review, 31*(4), 513–520.

Neuman, W. R., & Guggenheim, L. (2011). The evolution of media effects theory: A six-stage model of cumulative research. *Communication Theory, 21*(2), 169–196.

Nistelrooij, A. van. (2000). *Collectief organiseren: Een sociaal-constructionistisch onderzoek naar het werken met grote groepen [Collective organizing: A social-constructionistic research project into large scale group work].* Utrecht, the Netherlands: Lemma.

O'Neil, J. (2003). An analysis of the relationships among structure, influence, and gender: Helping to build a feminist theory of public relations. *Journal of Public Relations Research, 15*(2), 151–180.

Olasky, M. N. (1989). The aborted debate within public relations: An approach through Kuhn's paradigm. *Public Relations Research Annual, 1,* 87–95.

Pearson, R. (1989a). Beyond ethical relativism in public relations: Coorientation, rules, and the idea of communication symmetry. In J. E. Grunig & L. A. Grunig (Eds.), *Public Relations Research Annual* (Vol. 2, pp. 67–86). Hillsdale, NJ: Lawrence Erlbaum.

Pearson, R. (1989b). Business ethics as communication ethics: Public relations practice and the idea of dialogue. In C. H. Botan & V. Hazelton Jr. (Eds.), *Public relations theory* (pp. 111–131). Hillsdale, NJ: Lawrence Erlbaum.

Pearson, R. (1990). Ethical values or strategic values? The two faces of systems theory in public relations. In L. A. Grunig & J. E. Grunig (Eds.), *Public Relations Research Annual* (Vol. 2, pp. 219–234). Hillsdale, NJ: Lawrence Erlbaum.

Plowman, K. D. (1998). Power in conflict for public relations. *Journal of Public Relations Research, 10*(4), 237–261.

Radford, G. P. (2012). Public relations in a postmodern world. *Public Relations Inquiry, 1*(1), 49–67.

Rakow, L. F., & Nastasia, D. (2009). On feminist theory of public relations: An example from Dorothy E. Smith. In Ø. Ihlen, B. van Ruler & M. Fredriksson (Eds.), *Public relations and social theory: Key figures and concepts* (pp. 252–277). New York: Routledge.

Reed, M. (2005). Reflections on the 'Realist Turn' in Organization and Management Studies. *Journal of Management Studies, 42*(8), 1621–1644.

Ristino, R. J. (2008). The sociocultural model of public relations/communication management practice: A critical-cultural perspective. *International Journal of Strategic Communication, 2*(1), 54–73.

Roberts, J., & Armitage, J. (2006). From organization to hypermodern organization. On the accelerated appearance and disappearance of Enron. *Journal of Organizational Change Management, 19,* 558–577.

Ronneberger, F., & Rühl, M. (1992). *Theorie der public relations: Ein entwurf* [Theories of public relations: an introduction]. Opladen, Germany: Westdeutscher Verlag.

Ruggiero, T. E. (2000). Uses and gratifications theory in the 21st century. *Mass Communication and Society, 3*(1), 3–37.

Scheufele, D. A. (2000). Agenda-setting, priming, and framing revisited: Another look at cognitive effects of political communication. *Mass Communication and Society, 3*(2), 297–316.

Schultz, F., Kleinnijenhuis, J., Oegema, D., Utz, S., & van Atteveldt, W. (2012). Strategic framing in the BP crisis: A semantic network analysis of associative frames. *Public Relations Review, 38,* 97–107.

Self, C. C. (2010). Hegel, Habermas, and community: The public in the new media era. *International Journal of Strategic Communication, 4*(2), 78–92.

Smudde, P., & Courtright, J. (2010). Public relations and power. In R. L. Heath (Ed.), *The SAGE Handbook of Public Relations* (pp. 177–190). Thousand Oaks, CA: Sage.

Stanford Encyclopedia of Philosophy. (2011). Concepts. *Stanford Encyclopedia of Philosophy* Stanford, CA.

Starck, K., & Kruckeberg, D. (2001). Public relations and community: A reconstructed theory revisited. In R. L. Heath (Ed.), *Handbook of public relations.* Thousand Oaks, CA: Sage.

Taylor, M. (2010). Public relations in the enactment of civil society. In R. L. Heath (Ed.), *The SAGE handbook of public relations* (pp. 5–16). Thousand Oaks, CA: Sage.

Toth, E. L. (2001). How feminist theory advanced the practice of public relations. In R. L. Heath (Ed.), *Handbook of public relations* (pp. 237–246). Thousand Oaks, CA: Sage.

Trivett, V. (2011). 25 US Mega Corporations: Where they rank if they were countries. *Business Insider.* Retrieved December 3, 2012, from http://www.businessinsider.com/25-corporations-bigger-tan-countries-2011-6?op=1

Tsetsura, K. (2010). Social construction and public relations. In R. L. Heath (Ed.), *The SAGE Handbook of Public Relations* (pp. 163–175). Thousand Oaks, CA: Sage.

van Ginneken, J. (2003). *Collective behavior and public opinion: Rapid shifts in opinion and communication.* Mahwah, NJ: Lawrence Erlbaum.

Van der Meer, T. G. L. A., & Verhoeven, P. (in press). Public framing organizational crisis situations: Social media versus new media. *Public Relations Review.* Http://dx.doi.org/10.1016/j.pubrev.2012.12.001.

van Ruler, B., & Verčič, D. (2005). Reflective communication management: Future ways for public relations research. In P. J. Kalbefleisch (Ed.), *Communication Yearbook* (Vol. 29, pp. 239–274). Mahwah, NJ: Lawrence Erlbaum.

Vardeman-Winter, J., & Tindall, N. T. J. (2010). Toward an intersectionality theory of public relations. In R. L. Heath (Ed.), *The SAGE handbook of public relations* (pp. 223–236). Thousand Oaks, CA: Sage.

Verhoeven, P. (2009). On Latour: Actor-Network-Theory (ANT) and public relations. In Ø. Ihlen, B. van Ruler & M. Fredriksson (Eds.), *Public relations and social theory: Key figures and concepts* (pp. 166–186). New York: Routledge.

Verhoeven, P., & Aarts, N. (2010). How European public relations men and women perceive the impact of their professional activities. *PRism,* 7(4). Available at http:///www.prisonjournal.org.

Verhoeven, P., Jonkman, J., & Boumans, J. (2012). *Framebuilding van een nieuwe ziekte [Framebuilding of a new disease].* Paper presented at the Etmaal van de Communicatiewetenschap, Netherlands School of Communications Research (NESCoR). Leuven: February 9–10.

Weaver, K., Motion, J., & Roper, J. (2006). From propaganda to discourse (and back again): Truth, power, the public interest and public relations. In J. L'Etang & M. Pieczka (Eds.), *Public relations: Critical debates and contemporary practice* (pp. 7–21). Mahwah, NJ: Lawrence Erlbaum.

Wehmeier, S. (2006). Dancers in the dark: The myth of rationality in public relations. *Public Relations Review, 32*(3), 213–220.

Weick, K. E., Sutcliffe, K. M., & Obstfeld, D. (2005). Organizing and the process of sense making. *Organizational Science, 16,* 409–421.

Wrigley, B. J. (2010). Feminist scholarship and its contributions to public relations. In R. L. Heath (Ed.), *The SAGE handbook of public relations* (pp. 247–260). Thousand Oaks, CA: Sage.

Wæraas, A. (2009). On Weber: Legitimacy and legitimation in public relations. In Ø. Ihlen, B. van Ruler & M. Fredriksson (Eds.), *Public relations and social theory: Key figures and concepts* (pp. 301–322). New York: Routledge.

Zaller, J. (1996). The myth of massive media impact revived: new support for a discredited idea. In D. C. Mutz, P. M. Sniderman & R. M. Brody (Eds.), *Political persuasion and attitude change* (pp. 17–60). Ann Arbor, MI: Michigan University Press.

Zerfass, A., Tench, R., Verhoeven, P., Verčič, D., & Moreno, A. (2010). *European Communication Monitor 2009: Status quo and challenges for communication management in Europe: Results of an empirical survey in 46 countries.* Brussels, Belgium: EACD, EUPRERA.

Zijderveld, A. C. (2000). *The institutional imperative: The interface of institutions and networks.* Amsterdam: Amsterdam University Press.

Zerfass, A., Verčič, D., Verhoeven, P., Moreno, A., & Tench, R. (2012). European Communication Monitor 2012. Challenges and competencies for strategic communication. Results of an empirical survey in 42 countries. Brussels, Belgium: EACD/EUPRERA.

Part II

Institutional and Organizational Dimensions

9

Strategic Communication as Institutional Work

Magnus Fredriksson and Josef Pallas

Contemporary organizations operate in environments that require and expect strategic action in almost every sense. Recruitment, finance, product development, organizing, as well as communication, are expected to be strategic in the sense of being governed by rationality. Being strategic is not only commonly seen as crucial for an organization's ability to act autonomously in relation to its own objectives and expectations, but also as important for signaling security, sustainability, predictability and control to organizational constituents. The notion of strategy is thus strong in major theories about managerial practices as in *strategic communication*.

In short, strategic communication could be defined as "the purposeful use of communication by an organization to fulfil its mission" (Hallahan, Holtzhausen, van Ruler, Verčič, & Sriramesh, 2007, p. 3). It is a straightforward definition resting on the concepts of management, organization, and mission or goal, and in line with these the ideas of rationality, predictability, and free agency (Argenti, 1996; Cornelissen, 2008; J. E. Grunig & Hunt, 1984; Hallahan et al., 2007; Harlow, 1976; Long & Hazleton, 1987; Zerfass, 2009). Collectively these scholars described the activities of an organization as the result of the ideas, resources, and skills of the communicator, and those of her colleagues, along with organizational conditions. They also ascribed the communicator and the organization she works for decisive influence over the communication process. The goals, means and outcomes are predominantly seen as results of the organization's consideration, strategies and abilities and as such each organization is seen as exclusive (Argenti, 1996; Cutlip, Broom, & Center, 2006; Gregory & White, 2008; L. A. Grunig, Grunig, & Dozier, 2002; Heath, 2001).

However, taking a step backward and observing how organizations communicate, the exclusivity tends to disappear, as the activities in one organization are basically the same as those in another. Similar to the result from organizational research concerning the standardization and harmonization of business strategies or models (procedural conformity), organizational structures (structural conformity) as well as employment of individuals with certain competences or professional profile (Meyer & Rowan, 1977; Suchman, 1995), the practice of strategic communication is characterized by conformity. Some examples are the establishment of communication departments in organizations; the establishment of recommended educational paths; the demarcation of relevant competences; the production of communication policies, communication strategies and communication plans; the staging of press conferences; the distribution of press releases; media coaching, and the production of annual reports. All together most communication activities and communication products in organizational contexts are performed and produced without reflection over their actual benefits, relevance or purpose. It is activities and products that are expected to be performed or produced in an organization and as such they have become—more or less—self-evident.

These observations fit nicely with a sociological perspective on strategic communication where there is an ambition to analyze practice from macro, as well as meso and micro level (Edwards, 2012; Fredriksson, 2013; Ihlen, Ruler, & Fredriksson, 2009; Ihlen & Verhoeven, 2012). One line of thought in this stream of research is inspired by *neo-institutional theory* (Fredriksson, Pallas, & Wehmeier, 2013; Pallas & Fredriksson, 2011, 2013; Sandhu, 2009; Wehmeier, 2006), a tradition with its roots in political science, sociology and economics (DiMaggio & Powell, 1991). The institutionalization of practice is a central theme in neo-institutional theory pointing toward social structures as the major force of organizational governance. Rather than the individual, and the organizational, neo-institutional theory stresses the social in its explanations of why organizations function as they do and therefore resemble each other (Meyer & Rowan, 1977). Major arguments in these writings rest on recognizing regulative, normative, as well as cognitive structures as governing mechanisms for organizational performances (Scott, 2008).

Despite its strong exploratory power scholars in the field of strategic communication have used the neo-institutional perspective only sporadically and where such efforts are made (e.g. Bartlett, Tywoniak, & Hatcher, 2007; Sandhu, 2009; Wehmeier, 2006) the texts tend to turn over to a deterministic view of organizations. The analyses offered are inclined to see strategic communication as a result of regulative, normative and cognitive structures where communicators are more or less passively conforming to the requirements that the social context they are a part of generated and promoted. Thus the analyses usually end up in a rather deterministic interpretation of institutions and their influence on individuals and organizations.

This is a reaction to the dominant paradigm where the individual and the organizational are paramount. However, the insights from neo-institutional theory cannot be reduced to perceiving an organization's communication as mainly derived from prevailing institutional constraints. Institutions are not static or deterministic in the way they influence organizations and their behavior. On the contrary, institutions—in their coercive, normative and cognitive forms—are open for innovations and interpretations (Czarniawska & Joerges, 1996; DiMaggio, 1988; Lawrence & Suddaby, 2006; Lawrence, Suddaby, & Leca, 2009b; Oliver, 1991; Rövik, 2002). Thus, this chapter returns to and pays attention to the analysis of strategic communication as determined and conditioned by the institutional conditions. We argue that the dominant static view of institutions is unsatisfactory, and does not provide for a deeper understanding of the way organizations perform and handle their communication activities (Fredriksson et al., 2013). In view of this inadequacy, the chapter addresses the concept and mechanisms of *institutional work* through which organizations act to create, maintain and disrupt institutions (Brown, Ainsworth, & Grant, 2012; Lawrence & Suddaby, 2006; Lawrence, Suddaby, & Leca, 2011). In this context institutions are to be understood as taken-for-granted socially constructed templates that give meaning to actions and social exchange with democracy, market, and family as three concrete examples (Greenwood, Oliver, Sahlin, & Suddaby, 2008). The aim here is therefore to (a) confirm previous arguments about the constraining role of institutions; (b) argue that such conformity is neither holistic nor passive and that organizations have skills, knowledge and resources to take an active part in shaping and constructing their institutional environment; and c) re-address strategic communication both as bounded by and constitutive of institutional structures.

Strategic Communication and Institutions

Similar to other social activities, strategic communication is governed by rules, norms and cognitive structures. Communicators do as other communicators do not only because they are obliged or expected to according to legislation, professional norms, or predominant ideas, but also because the cost related to the infringement of these principles—to being different—is high in respect of monetary as well as social costs. This is not to say there is a lack of differences if we compare one organization with another but it is a way to point out that organizations tend to be different when it comes to details rather than concepts. Organizations choose different occasions for their media work (difference in detail) but all organizations carry out media work (similarity in concept) (Pallas & Fredriksson, 2011, 2013).

Neo-institutional theory holds that organizations—intentionally and unintentionally—relate to requirements and expectations from their environments. Therefore, organizational structures, processes, and responsibilities can be understood as responses to these requirements and expectations (DiMaggio & Powell, 1983; Meyer & Rowan, 1977). This argument is based on an assumption that organizations try to reduce risks and disturbances in their operations by complying to norms and ideas held by individuals and collectives who constitute and represent the most important resources in the organization's environment (Thompson, 1967). Common forms of uncertainty may include financial disturbances (i.e., a crisis in financial markets), technical transformations (i.e., development of new technologies, environmental degradation) and/or cultural or moral imperatives (i.e., decreasing expectations of corporate social responsibility). The goal of adaptation is to achieve legitimacy, credibility and authority. These are qualities necessary for the organizations' ability to survive in a society where a number of stakeholders groups scrutinize, audit and rank them (Power, 1997, 2007; Power, Scheytt, Soin, & Sahlin, 2009). By incorporating solutions, activities, units, models, and patterns of behavior that are perceived as rational, efficient, necessary and morally correct, organizations can minimize the risk of disturbances in their core activities (Meyer, 1994; Meyer & Rowan, 1977; Rövik, 2002; Scott, 2008). External demands on organizations are expressed in a number of ways pointing to three principles of influence: regulative, normative, and mimetic as expressed in rules, norms, and beliefs (Scott, 2008).

Legal Structures—Regulated Communication

The present has been described as increasingly regulated (Levi-Faur & Jordana, 2005). Laws, directives, regulations and codes constitute a major part of social reality that influences a wide range of organizational activities (Djelic & Sahlin-Andersson, 2006). Information dissemination regulations, accounting and reporting principles and regulations, and marketing and lobbying regulations are just a few examples of how such different regulative forms influence the communication activities of contemporary organizations (Sandhu, 2009). The rules and regulations are mandatory and they prescribe who has the right to demand information (journalists, the public, shareholders), the manner in which the information is to be distributed (press releases, reports, statements), what subjects it should include (new regulations, financial records, work and equality descriptions), and whom it should be addressed to (regulators, customers, shareholders, unions) (Callison, 2003; Fredriksson, 2008; Kent, Taylor, & White,, 2003; Pallas, 2007).

To ensure organizational compliance with these regulations there are various types of control and auditing mechanism such as fines and license issuance sanctioning behavior that deviates from or violates the existing regulatory framework (Jonsson, 2002; Jonsson, Greve, & Fujiwara-Greve, 2009; Power, 1997). The responsibility for designing and administrating the different control and auditing mechanisms is usually ascribed to governmental agencies and authorities. But there are also other rule-makers and auditors (i.e., accreditations and rating institutes or industry associations) who are involved in the development of regulatory frameworks. These can be more or less coercive and they often gain their power through their connection to standards, memberships and/or accreditations (Djelic & Sahlin-Andersson, 2006; see also Scott, 2004).

The existence of regulatory processes is based on the intention of the rule-makers to create rules of the game, rules that ensure predictability and stability in social contexts such as organizational fields, networks or markets (Hoffman, 1999). The degree of uncertainty is smaller if one can predict what an organization does in a particular situation. However, compliance with the regulatory conditions is not assured. If laws, directives, rules and codes are perceived as irrelevant or obsolete, the likelihood of organizations following these regulatory procedures decreases (Jonsson, 2002; Schneiberg & Soule, 2005). The same goes for organizations that are not dependent on rule-making actors in terms of different types of resources such as financial, technological or reputational assets (Leblebici, Salancik, Copay, & King, 1991; Maguire, Hardy, & Lawrence, 2004). The governing capacity of rules is then a direct result of the legitimacy of the rule-making actors (Suchman, 1995) and their ability to create dependency, and control and sanction mechanisms (Black, 2002; Power et al., 2009).

First and foremost political organizations locally (e.g., municipality or county), nationally (e.g., state) and internationally (e.g., EU) make up regulations. However, parallel to the globalization and the liberalization of the institutional landscape there is a trend towards new non-governmental actors getting involved in the creation, promotion and dissemination of novel or alternative rules in a variety of fields. Business and political networks, alliances, industry, and professional associations are just a few examples of soft rule makers influencing a number of different fields (Boli & Thomas, 1999; Djelic & Sahlin-Andersson, 2006; Higgott, Underhill, & Bieler, 2000; Mörth, 2004). The work of Global Alliance can be seen as an attempt to create regulative structures governing the work with strategic communication, first by the establishment of the Stockholm Accords and more recently the Melbourne Mandate. Both are documents covering the roles, responsibilities and principles Global Alliance and its members will see as mandates for communicators (Global Alliance for Public Relations and Communication Management, 2012).

Normative Structures—Adaptive Communication

Although the field of strategic communication is not regarded as a profession there is a tendency toward increasing professionalization. Recent research has shown that a majority of practitioners in the field have similar educational backgrounds—that is, a degree in media and communication studies, business administration or political science; belong to the same industry associations; and have remarkably similar work experiences and career paths (Gregory, 2008). The significance and importance of an occupational identity is striking and it also applies to semi-professionals. In strategic communication one can identify a set of ideas, ideals, models, methods and strategies that guide the way the work of practitioners is organized and performed. These ideals and beliefs, however contested and questioned, have been proven to resist most attempts to get modified or replaced; that is, they are considered to inform the most effective, moral, ethical, established and recognized communicative behavior for communication professionals.

Here the concept of *integrated communication* is a good example of the way normative processes operate. In short, integrated communication is an idea based on a conviction that all communication in an organization ought to be integrated and consistent with the values, understanding, and interpretations that management has made and presented (Schultz & Kitchen, 2004). The underlying rationale is to create a homogeneous image of the organization and its activities whereby consistency and unity are seen as prerequisite for organizational stability, rationality and predictability (van Riel, 1992). It is an understanding derived from a modernistic view where social actors are seen as coherent subjects with a single identity. To say two different things on two different occasions or to say one thing and do another is considered a marker of unreliability, or even schizophrenia, even though the causes might be fully reasonable. Therefore it is more or less impossible for someone working with strategic communication to disregard the idea of integrated communication. Communicators are assumed to take an active stand for the concept and its practice (Christensen, Morsing, & Cheney, 2008).

By way of shared ideas, models and expectations the normative elements of institutions stipulate desirable, ideal, or morally correct organizational behavior. These normative forms give rise to routines, conventions, techniques, and specific organizational forms and structures, as well as presentation and communication policies and strategies that organizations implement and adjust to. A highly relevant example of such normative pressure is the idea of marketization in areas such as healthcare, education, research, culture, and art (Brunsson & Sahlin-Andersson, 2000; Powell, Gammal, & Simard, 2005). These sectors, together with many other parts of our society, are expected to behave and conduct their communication and activities in accordance with market principles (Byrkjeflot & Angell, 2007; Wæraas, 2008; Wæraas, Byrkjeflot, & Angell, 2011).

Norms are not binding per se and therefore they differ from laws on a number of points. First, they are not coercive in the word's real sense. You can't be convicted in court for using a particular communication method, and there are no formal requirements for the way communication departments should be organized, or what should be included in an organization's communication policy. However, even if there are no formal sanctions attached to norms they are still very difficult to disregard (Ashforth & Gibbs, 1990; Jonsson, 2002; Jonsson et al., 2009; Suchman, 1995). Standards are generally accepted beliefs and facts that "introduce a prescriptive, evaluative, and obligatory dimension into social life" (Scott, 2001, p. 54). Second, as the work of professional carriers such as management consultants, universities and media creates, proliferates and disseminates norms, it is often presented as scientifically based and justified, which further enhances its status as inevitable and obligatory (Sahlin-Andersson & Engwall, 2002).

Norms and standards define, but are also defined, by relations and interactions between actors in terms of their responsibilities towards each other and the surrounding community. As such they constitute a more or less explicit frame of reference for achieving a desirable position in a given social context (Boström, Forssell, Jacobsson, & Tamm Hallström, 2004). In other words, standards and norms not only describe social obligations, they also create opportunities and privileges (Brunsson & Jacobsson, 2000). Declining or violating the prescriptive requirements may lead organizations to social isolation or punishment (Jonsson et al., 2009; Suchman, 1995). Damaged reputation, low ranking and missed accreditation are some examples of sanctions that often pose a greater threat than a fine or ban. The reverse is true when organizations display a sufficient convergence with the normative expectations such as those concerning organizational compliance with corporate social responsibility (CSR) standards or ethical marketing codes (Bartlett, Frostenson, & Pallas, 2013; Deephouse & Carter, 2005). Neo-institutional theorists refer to such adjustment to the normative pressures as based in *logic of appropriateness*; that is, logic that makes organizations strive for what is perceived as appropriate and desirable, rather than rational and most effective (Olsen & March, 2004; Sevón, 1996).

One example of the application of logic of appropriateness in the context of communication is ISO 10 668, which is a standard for valuation of brands, or professional ethical standards and guidelines industry associations create and proliferate. Communicators need to carry out their work in accordance with these standards in order to retain their membership in a professional body. Most of these associations have adopted the Code of Athens and the Code of Venice, leading towards new rules and norms stipulating the professional conduct of PR-practitioners vis-à-vis their organizations. Being able to show that organizations follow these norms and rules provides a basis for legitimacy and reputation not only for practitioners but also for their organizations and their entire professional field.

Another example of a practice with a strong normative force is industry awards and honors. These are clearly designed to highlight and recognize desirable and valued communication efforts and activities. In addition to the different awards there is also a large number of professional conferences, seminars and symposia that together create a strong normative environment that defines how individuals and organizations should organize and carry out their communication activities.

Cognitive Structures—Making Sense of Communication

Rules and norms are deliberate and explicit, as communicators are expected to know the laws and regulations they are supposed to follow. They are also expected to use the knowledge and skills they have gained in their education and experience, as well as take part in professional bodies, trainings and conferences. But instinctual and implicit assumptions about the work and its preconditions and accomplishments also govern the work they perform. These assumptions are more or less taken for granted, and they function as a frame of reference when the communicator sets her goal, chooses her aspirations and evaluates her results. The assumptions dictate what she will define as important, how she will create meaning and how she will act in different contexts. The French sociologist Pierre Bourdieu described these assumptions and patterns of actions using the concept *habitus* (Bourdieu, 1990).

One example of assumptions governing organizations' use of communication is how communication in itself is conceptualized. As Reddy (1979) pointed out we tend to think and talk about communication as transportation of meaning where information is more or less given physical properties and seen as moved from one place to another (see also Deetz, 1992; Krippendorff, 1993). Communication is then captured in the metaphor of a pipeline, depicting the communicator as a constructor of the right messages, transmitting them via the right medium to the right receiver to reach the desired effect(s) (Spicer, 1997). As with all metaphors it functions as a system of thought whereby one concept, that is, communication, is constructed in relation to other concepts such as knowledge, organization, society, and so forth. As a system of thought, a metaphor gives certain aspects precedence over others, and therefore it creates zones of meanings, legitimating certain goals and the acts used to reach them (Lakoff & Johnson, 1980). Certain communication methods and strategies thus become perceived as obvious and incorporated in the ideas of what kind of problems one could solve using communication, what means of communication one should use, and what results one could expect (Deetz, 1992).

To be able to understand the power of cognitive structures we need to understand the significance of sense-making and its frames. Sometimes sense-making is used in support of the subjective and individual; that is to say, our sense-making of the world is constructed around subjective and individual interpretations. This is a fallacy. Rather, the reasoning about cognitive structures has to be understood as an argument for the inter-subjective and collective. Our interpretations are made in interaction with others and in tune with rules and systems. Therefore there is little scope for individual interpretations (Berger & Luckmann, 1966). This is captured by the notions of "bounded rationality" and "embedded agency" suggesting that individual action (including interpretations and evaluations of the context in which the action is situated) is not autonomous. Individuals are always a part of collectively accepted norms, rules and values permeating a given social environment (March & Simon 1958; DiMaggio & Powell 1983). The significance of rules and systems is also amplified by the interaction between sense-making and practice, as those same rules and systems restrict and shape the preconditions for our acts. We do what we do simply because we don't see any alternatives. We have internalized our social systems (Bourdieu, 1984).

As sense-making is a collective process performed in relationship to other people as well as to social systems, individual interpretations could be aggregated to an organizational level. Organizations do also interpret and make sense of the world by the creation of collective interpretations of internal and external processes as well as the interaction between these two. Some of these interpretations are internalized in procedures, structures and distribution of responsibilities, creating standardization between organizations with similar preconditions. Driving this behavior is the actor's aversion toward insecurity and the sense of being the only one applying certain procedures, structures or competences.

Ideas are strong forces but they are not determinant. They do not prescribe a certain behavior but limit the alternatives to a very small number of conscious options. They do, however, create frames and internalize structures limiting the space of action for organizations. Therefore, particularly in times of insecurity, organizations tend to do as other successful organizations do with more or less consideration. By adopting what they see as functional solutions, such as creating particular structures

	Regulative	Normative	Cultural–cognitive
Communication	The principle of public access to official documents	Integrated communication	Pipe-line metaphor
Expression	Formal laws, rules, prescriptions	Norms, standards, models	Conceptions, ideas
Basis of legitimacy	Regulation	Moralization	Socialization
Sources	Governments, EU, UN	Profession, media	Schema, categories, symbols
Basis of compliance and legitimacy	Coercive—juridical/ financial sanctions	Normative—social sanctions and pressure	Mimetic—uncertainty, complexity, cultural support

Figure 9.1   Regulative, Normative and Cultural–Cognitive Conditions for Organizations

or recruiting professionals with certain competences, organizations search for stability, control and legitimacy. By implementing the concept of integrated communication, creating a communication department, and appointing communicators with a background in journalism, organizations strive for security on a conscious as well as subconscious level (Byrkjeflot & Angell, 2007; Engwall, 2009).

But it is not only the strengthening of self-esteem that is amplifying assimilation and standardization. It should also be seen as a maneuver to meet expectations from stakeholders and reduce their insecurity. Stakeholders expect certain structures, distribution of responsibilities, and procedures. A small business organization is expected to be run and organized in one manner and a large hospital in another. Therefore, to gain acceptance and legitimacy and appear as successful and moral, organizations adopt and assimilate what others do. Being the only organization doing things in a specific manner is often difficult as many resources have to be dedicated to convince stakeholders of its functionality (DiMaggio, 1983; Sevón, 1996). The internalization is rarely conscious or deliberate, or done after an evaluation of different alternatives. To a large extent it is a form of social learning, imitation or translation of successful concepts where organizations adapt, reshape, or add whole or parts of the concepts they find attractive (Czarniawska & Sevón, 1996, 2005).

Rules, norms and cognitive structures are strong forces with extensive significance for the practice of strategic communication, as summarized in Figure 9.1.

Strategic Communication and Alternation of Institutions

The preceding section has, by drawing upon lessons from classical neo-institutional analysis, illustrated how the concept of strategic communication can be contested. By adhering to regulative, normative and cognitive structures communicators are conforming to the requirements that the social context of which they are part generate and promote. The neo-institutional analysis thus serves to describe the underlying components of strategic communication more as a myth rather than factual practice, thus criticizing "the purposeful use of communication by an organization to fulfil its mission" (Hallahan et al., 2007, p. 3). But as we have argued initially, we should be careful in treating institutions as static or totalitarian in the way they influence organizations. Their behavior as social actors is not the behavior of *cultural dopes*. Neither should we understand the institutionally bounded notion of strategic communication as categorically disregarding or rejecting planned and intentional communication activities. Rather, we need to direct our attention to strategic communication as an organizational tool for alternation of the regulative, normative and cognitive pillars of institutions

(Pallas & Fredriksson, 2011, 2013). The following section develops this claim by connecting to the literature on institutional work and the neo-institutional understanding of communication as being placed at the heart of institutional processes (Lammers, 2011; Suddaby, 2011).

Institutional Work—The Creation, Maintenance and Disruption of Institutions

Departing from recent neo-institutional re-conceptualizations of strategic behavior, this section seeks to offer and develop the notion of strategic communication as an intentional and knowledge-able capacity of organizations to innovate and alter *institutional structures* (Barley & Tolbert, 1997; Giddens, 1984). By connecting to the research on *institutional entrepreneurship* in general (Battilana, Leca, & Boxenbaum, 2009; DiMaggio, 1988; Hoffman, 1999; Hwang & Powell, 2005; Oliver, 1991) and *institutional work* in particular (Lawrence & Suddaby, 2006; Lawrence et al., 2009b, 2011; Zietsma & McKnight, 2009) we address strategic communication as a means actors use to take active part in formation and transformation of institutional rules, norms and practices. Thus, we tie strategic communication to the reproductive and collaborative actions of organizations as they seek to main-tain, disturb or change the regulative, normative and cognitive constraints permeating their activities (Lammers, 2011; Suddaby, 2011).

Institutional entrepreneurship is a conceptualization whereby actors are given a central position in effecting, transforming and maintaining institutions (DiMaggio & Powell, 1991; Hoffman, 1999; Hwang & Powell, 2005). Here agency is seen as essential. However, in the effort to restore agency the concept tends to magnify the strategic realms and the liberties of actors' actions, leading to a con-ceited idea of actors as *heroes on steroids* (Lawrence & Suddaby, 2006; Lawrence, Suddaby, & Leca, 2009a; Lawrence et al., 2011). To balance and to offer a more complete view of the interplay between institutions, actors and agency, Lawrence and Suddaby (2006) coined the term institutional work, defined as "[t]he purposive action of individuals and organizations aimed at creating, maintaining, and disrupting institutions" (p. 215). Hereby the notion of institutional work emphasizes not only the formation and transformation of institutions in terms of new rules, norms, ideas and practices, but also the entire process of institutional ecology including persistence and de-institutionalization (Hwang & Colyvas, 2012). Lawrence and Suddaby (2006) argued that despite the acknowledgment of the intentional and knowledgeable capacity of actors to alter their institutional environments, these actors are not autonomous or independent of the very context that constrains their activities; neither are their intentions always accomplished (Lawrence et al., 2009a, 2011). This embeddedness of actors and the unintended consequences of their efforts underscore the importance of upholding the distinction between creating and creation, maintaining and maintenance, and disrupting and disruption of institutions (Lawrence et al., 2009a). Moreover, as institutions and the processes of de-institutionalization are complex and interrelated it is difficult to foresee and isolate the effects of individual intentions (Lounsbury & Crumley, 2007). This is amplified by the fact that other actors who defend the existing institutional orders or promote competing ones, often contest these efforts.

Keeping such limitations in mind the literature suggests that three sets of activities enhance insti-tutional innovation: collaborative arrangements; well-developed interactions; and extensive infor-mation flows. These are essential in institutionalization as well as in deinstitutionalization processes as they help actors to support or hinder new and old institutional forms to become legitimate and to spread (Battilana & D'Aunno, 2009; Lawrence, Hardy, & Phillips, 2002). The neo-institutional theorists suggest and describe a number of different forms and ways in which actors seek to cre-ate new or alter existing institutions (see Lawrence & Suddaby, 2006, for an overview). These can be ascribed three different aims. First, through changes in abstract categories of meaning (norms) and introduction of new coercive structures (rules), actors can actively and intentionally contrib-ute to *creation* of new institutions. Examples of such work include advocacy, mimicry, changes in normative associations, theorizing, and educating. Second, as institutions are not self-reproducing even though persistent mechanisms such as laws, regulations and norm systems protect them, they are open for interpretations and adaptation (Hirsch & Bermiss, 2009; Zilber, 2009). Thus *maintenance* of institutions is connected to active strategies such as embedding, routinizing, ritualizing, policing and mythologizing. The third form of institutional work includes activities where institutions are *disrupted* by being disconnected and disassociated from normative, regulative and moral foundations and values (Hirsch & Bermiss, 2009).

Strategic Communication and Institutional Work

With support from the conceptualization of institutional work, strategic communication can be understood as a means actors use to reach beyond particular organizational aims and missions (Fredriksson et al., 2013). From this perspective, strategic communication has to be viewed as a practice used to embed values and preferences into collaborative structures that help them to become widely spread and institutionalized, or to challenge and disrupt competing ones. This is an idea supported by the renewed view on social orders as constructed and imposed on actors through symbolical and communicative means and activities (Lammers, 2011; Suddaby, 2011). Strategic communication can then to be used as a carrier and translator of these institutional elements, as well as their maintainer and creator.

With this as a starting point and with additional support from earlier work on the different ways in which organizations enact media (Pallas, 2010; Pallas & Fredriksson, 2011) an understanding of strategic communication as having three general functions is possible:

1. *providing* signals of organizational adaptation to institutional values, norms and rules
2. *promoting* its own take on these institutional forms and
3. *co-opting* other organizations in their own work on institutions.

Providing

Organizations operating in strong normative and regulative regimes such as industries or organizational fields are expected, due to legal and legitimacy reasons (DiMaggio & Powell, 1983; Suchman, 1995), to explicitly and clearly declare they follow the "rules of the game" in those particular settings. Strategic communication can in such a context function as a protective activity since it might serve an organization by providing the relevant audience with evidence of being a recognized and legitimate actor. A major aim of such communicative efforts is to ensure stability and predictability. A systematic flow of formal and standardized information on which organizations can be evaluated in relation to, for instance, industry standards, prevailing market regulation, or professional expectations, can achieve this. By way of providing, organizations—mainly those that benefit from the prevailing conditions—contribute to the maintenance and protection of institutional structures (Lawrence & Suddaby, 2006; Pallas & Fredriksson, 2011).

Promoting

Organizations that find themselves threatened by existing rules, norms and values, for example, in the case of re-regulation of markets, or organizations that define these institutional forms as insufficient or malfunctioning, are more likely to use strategic communication as a promoting activity (Ihlen, 2009; Maguire et al., 2004). In this case promoting includes well-adjusted communicative efforts—regarding time, opportunity, form, channel, target group—which aim at introducing innovative ideas, norms and rules by way of making these interesting, or connected to or derived

	Providing	Promoting	Co-opting
Organizational strategy	Protecting	Establishing	Integrating
Institutional function	Maintaining	Creating	Transforming
Main approach	Conformity	Exclusivity	Interactivity
Appearance	Periodic	Selective	Continuous

Figure 9.2 Functions of Providing, Promotion and Co-Opting as Institutional Work

from legitimate models used in other contexts, as well as theoretically substantiated and rational (Fredriksson, 2009; Suddaby, 2011). These activities require a mixture of formal activities seeking to gain general acceptance of the alternatives offered, and highly informal interactions where the symbolic and rhetorical means serve in attracting resourceful and elite actors for support.

Co-Opting

Co-opting as a communication strategy focuses on establishing common platforms that reflect and integrate interests and needs of a variety of societal actors rather than communication efforts based on a pre-defined set of aims and goals (Pallas & Fredriksson, 2011). Here communication is mostly focused on creating strong collaborative contexts and issues and topics where relevance and importance are given priority to guide the work performed.

By addressing long-term effects and consequences and by appealing to values and common challenges, organizations seek to communicate with their audiences on the basis of collective good rather than self-interest. It is a general strategy, but used mainly by those who are dependent on long-term stability and predictability and those who are operating in areas that are generally questioned or criticized, such as the energy sector or tobacco industry (cf. Fredriksson, 2008; Pallas, 2007). Such communicative efforts are often conducted indirectly via involvement of third parties such as industry associations, expert groups, or PR consultants (Larsson, 2005).

The concepts of *providing, promoting* and *co-opting* bring to the fore the complex and multilevel institutional settings of organizations, which impose different and often conflicting requirements and expectations, as summarized in Figure 9.2.

Conclusion

Organizations are embedded in social webs. This is in itself rather an obvious assertion, but one that is still often overlooked when organizational practices are subjected to academic inquiry or empirical testing. In this chapter we have shown under what conditions strategic communication is performed and how legal, normative and cognitive structures govern these practices. With a number of illustrative examples this chapter has argued for a perspective whereby organizations' communication activities are characterized by structural and procedural conformity, where the use of communication is much more a search for security and predictability rather than distinction and uniqueness. In other words, it is a practice performed under the influence of social structures that define and constrain what to communicate, how, when and to whom.

However, the chapter also points to the limitations of such structural determinism, arguing individuals and organizations cannot be treated as cultural dopes. Rather, actors possess resources, intentions and skills, especially communicative ones, helping them to protect, challenge and re-shape the very context of which they are a part.

Thereby strategic communication is an essential means for organizations when they attempt to alter the institutional properties in which they are embedded. Such a perspective questions the traditional conceptualization of strategic communication on two accounts:

- Purpose: with focus on the determined and skilful enactment of institutional structures this reverses the traditional purpose of strategic communication arguing that communication activities often serve organizations in constituting these structures rather than acting upon them.
- Dynamics: strategic communication is nested in ongoing multi-level interactions and collaborations rather than being defined in relation to these interactions.

In general, this means strategic communication as concept and practice needs to relate to the structures of social life where organizations' communicative activities are both subordinated to and constitutive of commonly shared rules, norms and ideas.

References

Argenti, P. A. (1996). Corporate communication as a discipline. *Management Communication Quarterly, 10*(1), 73–97.

Ashforth, B. E., & Gibbs, B. W. (1990). The double-edge of organizational legitimation. *Organization Science: A Journal of the Institute of Management Sciences, 1*(2), 177–194.

Barley, S. R., & Tolbert, P. S. (1997). Institutionalization and structuration: studying the links between action and institution. *Organization Studies, 18*(1), 93–117.

Bartlett, J. L., Frostenson, M., & Pallas, J. (2013). Reputation rankings, certifications and accreditations. In C. E. Carroll (Ed.), *The handbook of communication and corporate reputation*. Chichester, England: Wiley & Blackwell.

Bartlett, J. L., Tywoniak, S., & Hatcher, C. (2007). Public relations professional practice and the institutionalisation of CSR. *Journal of Communication Management, 11*(4), 281–299.

Battilana, J., & D'Aunno, T. (2009). Institutional work and the paradox of embedded agency. In T. B. Lawrence, R. Suddaby & B. Leca (Eds.), *Institutional work. Actors and agency in institutional studies of organizations*. New York: Cambridge University Press.

Battilana, J., Leca, B., & Boxenbaum, E. (2009). How actors change institutions: towards a theory of institutional entrepreneurship. *The Academy of Management Annals, 3*(1), 65–107.

Berger, P., & Luckmann, T. (1966). *The social construction of reality: a treatise on the sociology of knowledge*. London, England: Penguin.

Black, J. (2002). Critical reflections on regulation. *Australian Journal of Legal Philosophy, 27*, 1–35.

Boli, J., & Thomas, G. M. (Eds.). (1999). *Constructing world culture: international nongovernmental organizations since 1875*. Stanford, CA: Stanford University Press.

Boström, M., Forssell, A., Jacobsson, K., & Tamm Hallström, K. (2004). *Den organiserade frivilligheten [The organized voluntariness]*. Malmö, Sweden: Liber.

Bourdieu, P. (1984). *Distinctions. A social critique of the judgment of taste*. Cambridge, MA: Harvard University Press.

Bourdieu, P. (1990). *The logic of practice*. Cambridge, MA: Polity Press.

Brown, A. D., Ainsworth, S., & Grant, D. (2012). The rhetoric of institutional change. *Organization Studies, 33*(3), 297–321.

Brunsson, N., & Jacobsson, B. (2000). *A world of standards*. Oxford, England: Oxford University Press.

Brunsson, N., & Sahlin-Andersson, K. (2000). Constructing organizations: the example of public sector reform. *Organization Studies, 21*(4), 721–746.

Byrkjeflot, H., & Angell, S. I. (2007). Dressing up hospitals as enterprises? The expansion and managerialization of communication in Norwegian hospitals. In P. Kjaer & T. Slaata (Eds.), *Mediating business: the expansion of business journalism in the nordic countries*. Copenhagen, Denmark: Copenhagen Business School Press.

Callison, C. (2003). Media relations and the Internet: How Fortune 500 company web sites assist journalists in news gathering. *Public Relations Review, 29*(1), 29–41.

Christensen, L. T., Morsing, M., & Cheney, G. (2008). *Corporate communications: convention, complexity, and critique*. London, England: Sage.

Cornelissen, J. (2008). *Corporate communications: guide to theory and practice*. London, England: SAGE Publications.

Cutlip, S. M., Broom, G. M., & Center, A. H. (2006). *Effective public relations* (9th ed.). Upper Saddle River, NJ Pearson Prentice Hall.

Czarniawska, B., & Joerges, B. (1996). Travels of ideas. In B. Czarniawska & G. Sevón (Eds.), *Translating organizational change* (pp. 13–48). Berlin, Germany: Walter de Gruyter.

Czarniawska, B., & Sevón, G. (Eds). (1996). *Translating organizational change*. Berlin, Germany: Walter de Gruyter.

Czarniawska, B., & Sevón, G. (Eds). (2005). *Global ideas: how ideas, objects and practices travel in the global economy.* Malmö, Sweden: Libris.

Deephouse, D. L., & Carter, S. M. (2005). An examination of differences between organizational legitimacy and organizational reputation. *Journal of Management Studies, 42*(2), 329–360.

Deetz, S. A. (1992). *Democracy in an age of corporate colonization. Developments in communication and the politics of everyday life.* Albany, NY: State University of New York Press.

DiMaggio, P. J. (1983). State expansion and organizational fields. In R. H. Hall & R. E. Quinn (Eds.), *Organizational Theory and Public Policy* (pp. 147–161). Beverly Hills, CA: Sage Publications.

DiMaggio, P. J. (1988). Interest and agency in institutional theory. In L. G. Zucker (Ed.), *Patterns and organizations: culture and environment* (pp. 4–21). Cambridge, MA: Ballinger Publishing Company.

DiMaggio, P. J., & Powell, W. W. (1983). The iron cage revisted: Institutional isomorphism and collective rationality in organizational fields. *American Sociological Review, 48*(April), 147–160.

DiMaggio, P. J., & Powell, W. W. (1991). *The new institutionalism in organizational analysis.* Chicago, IL: University of Chicago Press.

Djelic, M.-L., & Sahlin-Andersson, K. (2006). *Transnational governance: Institutional dynamics of regulation.* Cambridge, England: Cambridge University Press.

Edwards, L. (2012). Defining the 'object' of public relations research: A new starting point. *Public Relations Inquiry, 1*(1), 7–30.

Engwall, L. (2009). *Mercury meets Minerva: business studies and higher education: the Swedish case* (2nd, extended ed.). Stockholm, Sweden: Economic Research Institute, Stockholm School of Economics (EFI).

Fredriksson, M. (2008). *Företags ansvar marknadens retorik : en analys av företags strategiska kommunikationsarbete [Corporate responsibility marketplace rhetoric. An analysis of corporations strategic communication].* Gothenburg, Sweden: Göteborgs Universitet.

Fredriksson, M. (2009). On Beck: Risk and sub-politics in reflexive modernity. In Ø. Ihlen, B. van Ruler & M. Fredriksson (Eds), *Public relations and social theory key figures and concepts* (pp. 21–42). London, England: Routledge.

Fredriksson, M. (2013). European social theory and public relations. In R. L. Heath (Ed.), *Encyclopedia of public relations*. Thousand Oaks, CA: Sage.

Fredriksson, M., Pallas, J., & Wehmeier, S. (2013). Institutional perspectives on public relations. *Public Relations Inquiry, 2*(3).

Giddens, A. (1984). *The constitution of society: Outline of the theory of structuration.* Cambridge, MA: Polity Press.

Global Alliance for Public Relations and Communication Management (2012). *The Melbourne Mandate.* Retrieved January 3, 2013, from http://melbournemandate.globalalliancepr.org/

Greenwood, R., Oliver, C., Sahlin, K., & Suddaby, R. (2008). Introduction. In R. Greenwood, C. Oliver, K. Sahlin & R. Suddaby (Eds.), *The SAGE handbook of organisational institutionalism.* London, England: Sage.

Gregory, A. (2008). Competencies of senior communication practitioners in the UK: an initial study. *Public Relations Review, 34*(3), 215–223.

Gregory, A., & White, J. (2008). Introducing the Chartered Institute of Public Relations initiative: Moving on from talking about evaluation to incorporating it into better management of the practice. In B. van Ruler, A. T. Verčič & D. Verčič (Eds.), *Public relations metrics : research and evaluation* (pp. 307–317). New York: Routledge.

Grunig, J. E., & Hunt, T. (1984). *Managing public relations.* Fort Worth, TX: Harcourt Brace College.

Grunig, L. A., Grunig, J. E., & Dozier, D. M. (2002). *Excellent public relations and effective organizations: a study of communication management in three countries.* Mahwah, NJ: Lawrence Erlbaum.

Hallahan, K., Holtzhausen, D., van Ruler, B., Verčič, D., & Sriramesh, K. (2007). Defining strategic communication. *International Journal of Strategic Communication, 1*(1), 3–35.

Harlow, R. F. (1976). Building a public relations definition. *Public Relations Review, 2*(4), 34–42.

Heath, R. L. (2001). Shifting foundations: public relations as relationship building. In R. L. Heath (Ed.), *Handbook of public relations* (pp. 1–10). Thousand Oaks, CA: Sage.

Higgott, R. A., Underhill, G. R. D., & Bieler, A. (Eds). (2000). *Non-state actors and authority in the global system.* London, England: Routledge.

Hirsch, P. M., & Bermiss, Y. S. (2009). Institutional "dirty" work: preserving institutions through strategic decoupling. In T. B. Lawrence, R. Suddaby & B. Leca (Eds), *Institutional work. actors and agency in institutional studies of organizations.* Cambridge, England: Cambridge University Press.

Hoffman, A. J. (1999). Institutional evolution and change: environmentalism and the U.S. chemical industry. *Academy of Management Journal, 42*(4), 351.

Hwang, H., & Colyvas, J. (2012). Institutional work to maintain professional power: recreating the model of medical professionalism. *Organization Studies, 33,* 937–962.

Hwang, H., & Powell, W. W. (2005). Institutions and entrepreneurship. In S. Alvarez, R. Agrawal & O. Sorenson (Eds), *Handbook of entrepreneurial research: disciplinary perspectives.* New York: Springer.

Ihlen, Ø. (2009). Business and climate change: the climate response of the world's 30 largest corporations. *Environmental Communication—a Journal of Nature and Culture, 3*(2), 244–262.

Ihlen, Ø., Ruler, B. v., & Fredriksson, M. (2009). *Public relations and social theory key figures and concepts.* London, England: Routledge.

Ihlen, Ø., & Verhoeven, P. (2012). A public relations identity for the 2010s. *Public Relations Inquiry, 1*(2), 159–176.

Jonsson, S. (2002). *Making and breaking norms. Competitive imitation patterns in the swedish mutual fund industry.* Doctoral Thesis, Stockholm School of Economics, Stockholm, Sweden.

Jonsson, S., Greve, H. R., & Fujiwara-Greve, T. (2009). Lost without deserving: the spread of legitimacy loss in response to reported corporate deviance. *Administrative Science Quarterly, 59*(2), 195–228.

Kent, M. L., Taylor, Maureen, White, William J. (2003). The relationship between web site design and organizational responsivenes to stakeholders. *Public Relations Review, 29,* 63–77.

Krippendorff, K. (1993). Major metaphors of communication and some constructivist reflections on their use. *Cybernetics & Human Knowing, 2*(1), 3–25.

Lakoff, G., & Johnson, M. (1980). *Metaphors we live by.* Chicago, IL: University of Chicago Press.

Lammers, J. C. (2011). How institutions communicate: institutional messages, institutional logics, and organizational communication. *Management Communication Quarterly, 25*(1), 154–182.

Larsson, L. (2005). *Opinionsmakarna. En studie om PR-konsulter, journalistik och demokrati* [A study of PR-consultants, journalism and democracy]. Lund, Sweden: Studentlitteratur.

Lawrence, T. B., Hardy, C., & Phillips, N. (2002). Institutional effects on interorganizational collaboration: the emergence of proto-institutions. *Academy of Management Journal, 45*(1), 281–290.

Lawrence, T. B., & Suddaby, R. (2006). Institutions and institutional work. In S. Clegg, C. Hardy, T. B. Lawrence & W. Nord (Eds), *The Sage Handbook of Organization Studies (2nd ed.)* (pp. 215–254). London, England: Sage.

Lawrence, T. B., Suddaby, R., & Leca, B. (2009a). Introduction: theorizing and studying institutional work. In T. B. Lawrence, R. Suddaby & B. Leca (Eds), *Institutional work. actors and agency in institutional studies of organizations.* Cambridge, England: Cambridge University Press

Lawrence, T. B., Suddaby, R., & Leca, B. (Eds.). (2009b). *Institutional work. Actors and agency in institutional studies of organizations.* Cambridge, England: Cambridge University Press

Lawrence, T. B., Suddaby, R., & Leca, B. (2011). institutional work: refocusing institutional studies of organization. *Journal of Management Inquiry, 20*(1), 52–58.

Leblebici, H., Salancik, G. R., Copay, A., & King, T. (1991). Institutional change and the transformation of interorganizational fields: an organizational history of the U.S. radio broadcasting industry. *Administrative Science Quarterly, 36*(3), 333.

Levi-Faur, D., & Jordana, J. (2005). *The rise of regulatory capitalism.* Paper presented at the The Annals of APSA, London, England.

Long, L. W., & Hazleton, V. (1987). Public relations: A theoretical and practical response. *Public Relations Review, 13*(3), 3–13.

Lounsbury, M., & Crumley, E. T. (2007). New practice creation: an institutional perspective on innovation. *Organization Studies, 28*(07), 993–1012.

Maguire, S., Hardy, C., & Lawrence, T. B. (2004). Institutional entrepreneurship in emerging fields: HIV/Aids treatment advocacy in Canada. *Academy of Management Journal, 47*(5), 657–679.

March, J. G., & Simon, H. A. (1958). *Organizations.* New York: Wiley.

Meyer, J. W. (1994). Rationalized environments. In P. M. Scott, John (Ed.), *Institutional environments and organizations* (pp. 28–54). Thousand Oak: CA: Sage.

Meyer, J. W., & Rowan, B. (1977). Institutionalized organizations: formal structure as myth and ceremony, *American Journal of Sociology, 83*(2), 340–363.

Mörth, U. (2004). *Soft law in governance and regulation: an interdisciplinary analysis.* Cheltenham, England: Edward Elgar.

Oliver, C. (1991). Strategic responses to institutional processes. *The Academy of Management Review, 16*(1), 145–179.

Olsen, J. P., & March, J. G. (2004). *The logic of appropriateness.* ARENA Working Papers no 9. ARENA. Retrieved from http://ideas.repec.org/p/erp/arenax/p0026.html

Pallas, J. (2007). *Talking organizations: corporate media work and negotiation of institutions*. Doctoral thesis, Uppsala University, Uppsala, Sweden.

Pallas, J. (2010). Informatörerna och medierna [Communicators and media]. In J. Pallas & L. Strannegård (Eds), *Företag och medier* [Corporations and media]. Malmö, Sweden: Liber.

Pallas, J., & Fredriksson, M. (2011). Providing, promoting and co-opting: corporate media work in a mediatized society. *Journal of Communication Management, 15*(2), 165–178.

Pallas, J., & Fredriksson, M. (2013). corporate media work and micro-dynamics of mediatization. *European Journal of Communication, 28*, 420–435.

Powell, W. W., Gammal, D. L., & Simard, C. (2005). Close encounters: the circulation and reception of managerial practices in the San Francisco Bay area nonprofit community. In B. Czarniawska & G. Sevon (Eds), *Global ideas*. Malmö, Sweden: Liber & Copenhagen Business School Press.

Power, M. (1997). *Audit society: rituals of verification*. Oxford, England: Oxford University Press.

Power, M. (2007). *Organized uncertainty: designing a world of risk management*. Oxford, England: Oxford University Press.

Power, M., Scheytt, T., Soin, K., & Sahlin, K. (2009). Reputational risk as a logic of organizing in late modernity. *Organization Studies, 30*(2–3), 301–324.

Reddy, M. J. (1979). The conduit metaphor. In A. Ortony (Ed.), *Metaphor and thought*. Cambridge, England: Cambridge University Press.

Rövik, K.-A. (2002). The secrets of the winners: management ideas that flow. In K. Sahlin-Andersson & L. Engwall (Eds.), *The expansion of management knowledge: carriers, flows, and sources* (pp. 113–144). Stanford, CA: Stanford University Press.

Sahlin-Andersson, K., & Engwall, L. (Eds.). (2002). *The expansion of management knowledge: carriers, flows, and sources*. Stanford, CA: Stanford University Press.

Sandhu, S. (2009). Strategic communication: an institutional perspective. *International Journal of Strategic Communication, 3*(2), 72–92.

Schneiberg, M., & Soule, S. (2005). Institutionalization as a contested, multi-level process: politics, social movements and rate regulation in American fire insurance. In M. Zald, R. W. Scott & J. Davis (Eds.), *Social movements and organizations* (pp. 122–160). Cambridge, England: Cambridge University Press.

Schultz, D. E., & Kitchen, P. J. (2004). Managing the changes in corporate branding and communication: closing and re-opening the corporate umbrella. *Corporate Reputation Review, 6*(4), 347–366.

Scott, R. W. (2001). *Institutions and Organizations*. London, England: Sage.

Scott, R. W. (2004). Reflections on a half-century of organizational sociology. *Annual Review of Sociology, 30*, 1–21.

Scott, R. W. (2008). *Institutions and organizations. Ideas and interests*. Thousand Oaks, CA: Sage.

Sevón, G. (1996). Organizational imitation in identity transformation. In B. Czarniawska & G. Sevón (Eds.), *Translating organizational change* (pp. 49–68). Berlin, Germany: Walter de Gruyter.

Spicer, C. (1997). *Organizational public relations. a political perspective*. Mahwah, NJ: Lawrence Erlbaum.

Suchman, M. C. (1995). Managing legitimacy: strategic and institutional approaches. *Academy of Management Review, 20*(3), 571–610.

Suddaby, R. (2011). How communication institutionalizes: a response to Lammers. *Management Communication Quarterly, 25*(1), 183–190.

Thompson, J. D. (1967). *Organizations in action: social science bases of administrative theory*. New York: McGraw-Hill.

Wæraas, A. (2008). Can public sector organizations be coherent corporate brands? *Marketing Theory 8*(2), 205–221.

Wæraas, A., Byrkjeflot, H., & Angell, S. I. (Eds.). (2011). *Substans og framtreden; omdømmehåndtering i offentlig sektor [Substance and performances: reputation management in public service organizations]*. Oslo, Norway: Universitetsforlaget.

van Riel, C. B. M. (1992). *Principles of corporate communication*. Hemel Hempstead, England: Prentice Hall Europe.

Wehmeier, S. (2006). Dancers in the dark: The myth of rationality in public relations. *Public Relations Review, 32*(3), 213–220.

Zerfass, A. (2009). Institutionalizing strategic communication: theoretical analysis and empirical evidence. *International Journal of Strategic Communication, 3*(2), 69–71.

Zietsma, C., & McKnight, B. (2009). Building the iron cage: instutional creation work in the context of competing proto-institutions. In T. B. Lawrence, R. Suddaby & B. Leca (Eds.), *Institutional work. Actors and agency in institutional studies of organizations*. Cambridge, England: Cambridge University Press.

Zilber, T. B. (2009). Institutional maintenance as narrative acts. In T. B. Lawrence, R. Suddaby & B. Leca (Eds), *Institutional work. Actors and agency in institutional studies of organizations*. Cambridge, England: Cambridge University Press.

10

Cultural Influences on Strategic Communication

Kim A. Johnston and James L. Everett

Strategic communication is a central device organizations use to respond to environmental uncertainty. The inherent nature of the strategic response is premised on two key internal activities. The first requires management to monitor and interpret environmental conditions. The second requires the formulation of an appropriate response to that interpretation. Both are open to influences from features operating within the internal organizational environment.

Scholars studying strategy development have recognized the need to take a cultural perspective (Volberda & Elfring, 2001) to understand the internal organizational processes and influences on decision making (Craig-Lees, 2001; Weick, 2001). However, there has been little progress exploring these factors from a strategic management perspective (George, Chattopadhyay, Sitkin, & Barden, 2006) or from a public relations or communication management perspective (Sriramesh, 2007).

A cultural perspective on strategy formulation is built from the view that an organization's culture is a system of social knowledge that is shared among organizational members and transmitted by members across time (Durham, 1991; Everett, 1985, 1990; Schein, 1984). In these terms, strategy formulation requires a collaborative effort by organizational members to identify, interpret, and subsequently make decisions that create shared meaning about a complex situation in the effort to reduce environmental uncertainty (Lane, 2007; Selsky, Goes, & Baburoglu, 2007). Unpacking this collaborative effort to explore how frames of reference derived from culturally shared values and assumptions influence that process is a central conceptual challenge in strategy formulation (Bailey & Johnson, 2001).

Weick's (1969, 1979) sociocultural concept of organizing as an adaptive response to environmental equivocality frames the basic terms of this study. It is premised on the concept that organizations seek to reduce environmental equivocality by acting on an implicit or explicit consensus of environmental meanings (Kreps, 1990; Littlejohn, 1999; Weick, 1969). Weick (1969, 1979) contends managerial worldviews influence how managers interpret the environmental equivocality and subsequent organizational responses to manage their relationship with the environment. This perspective places the formulation of strategic communication in a cultural framework and focuses the need to understand how a group's shared and socially transmitted beliefs and values, that is, its culture, shape understanding and actions toward its environment (Dil, 1980; Milton, 1996). As a relational model, Weick's (1969, 1979) sociocultural approach provides a substrate to examine these processes as they interact to produce organizational strategic communication.

Strategic communication is an outcome of deliberate communication practices within an organization and it encapsulates the intentional, transactional activities of the organization's leaders, members, and communication practitioners to respond to environmental change. This conceptualization is based on descriptions of strategic communication as a goal-focused or purposeful communication effort combining knowledge-based decision-making and action. Hallahan, Holtzhausen, van Ruler, Verčič, and Sriramesh (2007) define strategic communication as "the purposeful use of communication by an organization to fulfil its mission" (p. 3). Strategic communication therefore equips an organization to confront the challenges of environmental uncertainty (Zerfass & Huck, 2007) through purposeful instrumental and strategic actions (Verhoeven, Zerfass, & Tench, 2011).

Clampitt, DeKoch, and Cashman (2000) view the development of strategy as a series of macro-level choices as a basis for action (p. 41). In these terms, strategic communication is an outcome of a transactional social activity within the organization (Marchiori & Bulgacov, 2012; Shockley-Zalabak, 2002), or a "social activity" (Jarzabkowski, Balogun, & Seidl, 2007, p. 8). Although some scholars (see for example, Botan, 2006; Steyn, 2003b) have argued that strategic communication is a managerial function, this chapter emerges from a transactional perspective; with the assumption that strategic communication encompasses processes of strategy identification and implementation. These should be expected to vary from a series of highly integrated to widely distributed processes as a function of such factors as organizational history, culture, and market condition.

With these assumptions in place, strategic communication results from both planned and emergent processes (Christensen & Cornelissen, 2011; Cornelissen, 2008). An interpretive approach to strategy formulation is based on a social contract view of strategy in which the organization is seen as "a collection of cooperative agreements entered into by individuals with free will" (Chaffee, 1985, p. 93). While other perspectives of strategic communication formulation are offered, the dominant paradigm in the literature is a rational, functional efficiency-oriented perspective (Sandhu, 2009). Similarly public relations and organizational communication literature often describe the formulation of strategic communication as a rational, linear and traditional process with a focus on the planning and tactical implementation of communication campaigns (Chia & Synnott, 2009; Seitel, 2007; Shockley-Zalabak, 2002; Steyn, 2003a; Stroh, 2007).

A cultural perspective of strategy formulation recognizes the fundamental significance of the efforts of organizational members to interpret environmental information and respond appropriately (Ansoff & Sullivan, 1993; Bourgeois, 1980; Hambrick, 1981; Mintzberg & Quinn, 2003). In this context, the effectiveness of the response relies on the ability of organizational members to interpret, understand, or translate equivocal environmental information (Beer, Voelpel, Leibold, & Tekie, 2005; Everett, 1993; O'Shannassy, 2003; Weick, 1988, 2001). This chapter explores the importance of collective influence, conceptualized as organizational culture, towards this effort.

Importance of Organizational Culture in Strategic Communication

In the anthropological literature, culture has traditionally been viewed as a mediating influence on human action that shapes action and meaning for members of a group and gives direction to organizing their lives (Dil, 1980; Durham, 1991; Milton, 1996; Norlin, Chess, Dale, & Smith, 2003). Following these terms, culture acts as a grounding and orienting force for interpretation that underpins human understanding, definitions, and actions towards the environment (Hatch, 1993; Milton, 1996). Culture therefore functions to give meaning and as a consequence it influences how events are viewed and interpreted (Bates, 2001). Geertz (1973) uses the analogy of a spiderweb to describe the concept of culture, arguing, "man is an animal suspended in webs of significance he himself has spun" (p. 5). Analysis of these cultural webs, according to Geertz, should be interpretive and focused on meaning.

Culture is defined as a system of shared meaning, values or beliefs, socially transmitted over time among a particular social group (Bates, 2001; Durham, 1991; Geertz, 1973; Keesing, 1981; Keyton, 2005). While many definitions of culture have been offered (Chick, 1997) and applications of central concepts differ (Sackmann, 1992), anthropologists generally agree that culture is cognitive phenomena (D'Andrade, 2001).

Key challenges remain in employing the culture concept in analysis of organizing, given the array of claims for what culture means in various literatures. Another challenge involves the existing conceptual diversity surrounding the concept of culture, making it difficult to operationalize (Sackmann, 1992). Adopting an ideational approach focuses the anthropological treatment of culture and offers "a more explicit and more analytic conceptualization of culture" (Durham, 1991, p. 3).

The view of culture as a system of social knowledge captures the role of culture in relating communities to their ecological settings (Keesing, 1974). Durham (1991) views culture as "systems of symbolically encoded conceptual phenomena that are socially and historically transmitted within and between populations" (p. 9). Culture operating as a learned system of shared knowledge assists members of a society to relate and cope with their environment (Bates, 2001). As a sociocultural system, it represents the "social realizations or enactments of ideational designs-for-living in particular environments" (Keesing, 1974, p. 82).

Cultural Schema

Schemes of interpretation operate as frameworks for people to make sense and understand events, actions and situations in unique ways, allowing meaning or a reality to be constructed (Chan, 2003). Weick (1979) argued that schema direct action, and have an effect of mediating or "bracketing portions of experience" (p. 154). Schema operate at an individual level as a framework for understanding the organizational way of life, or put more simply, "schemas influence individual interpretations, assumptions and expectations regarding organizational events" (Scroggins, 2006, p. 86). This view follows Pace (1988) who argued schema "consist of hypotheses or expectations about incoming information, which then provide plans for gathering, interpreting, and using this information" (p. 149). Lyles and Schwenk (1992) suggest schema held by organizational decision makers have an important influence on how environmental information is interpreted, framed and processed. This suggestion is in keeping with the perspective of this chapter, in which strategy emerges from a collective effort.

Cultural Selection

Cultural selection describes the capacity of an organization's cultural system to influence the nature of its own evolution (Durham, 1991). Cultural selection is defined as "the differential social transmission of cultural variants through human decision making" or simply as "preservation by preference" (Durham, 1991, p. 199). Cultural selection preserves cultural variation between different groups by reinforcing the differences over time. Cultural selection predicts that human decision making systems promote general patterns of fitness, that is, desirability, and sustains many of the differences in that group (Durham, 1992). It is during the social process that cultural material is influential in the selection process (Everett, 2002) supporting Weick's (1979) notion that selection pressures in organizations are the outcome of "schemes of interpretation and specific interpretations" (p. 131).

The theoretical importance of organizational culture in communication management has been articulated for nearly two decades with little advancement (Everett, 1993; Sriramesh, 2007). Grunig (1992a, 1992b) identified authoritarian and participative culture as the two key influencing concepts in organizational culture, and argued that these variables directly affected both the communication function of the organization and the success in achieving organizational outcomes. Cameron and McCollum's (1993) study of the relationship between organizational culture and the producers of communication highlighted the importance of alignment of beliefs (shared reality) about the organization by all levels of staff. More recent studies of organizational culture have continued to note culture's influence in ethical decision making (Bowen, 2004), and on practitioners in many different practice contexts (see for example, Diaz, Abratt, Clarke, & Bendixen, 2009; Rhee & Moon, 2009). More importantly, Kersten (2005) argued for the need to challenge assumed singular rationalities that exist in organizations' perceptions of reality.

These studies collectively document the significant interaction of organizational culture with the problems of strategic communication as they play out in organizational contexts, and the understanding of the nature of organizational communication more generally. The consistency of the findings of the studies confirms the significance of the culture of an organization as the lens through which the challenges of developing and implementing strategic communication should be observed and interpreted. Research exploring organizational culture in organizational and corporate communication practice has recognized that meaning and interpretation are central processes (Christensen & Cornelissen, 2011; Leichty & Warner, 2001). Cultural discourse conditions that influence these practices however, are not fully understood (Leichty & Warner, 2001).

Research

The central research problem reflects a core proposition that strategic communication emerges less as a direct, rational response by organizational members to objectively given environmental factors than as an outcome to cultural selection (Durham, 1992) acting on the processes of environmental enactment by organizational members. This perspective informs this chapter as it examines cultural influences on organizational processes of environmental interpretation and expectations by organizational members in a leading humanitarian organization in Australia in response to a key event. Two research questions guide this study:

1. What are the cultural influences on organizational processes of environmental interpretation and expectations?
2. What are the implications of these cultural influences for the identification and implementation of strategic communication?

According to Rabinow (1977), exploring culture is an interpretive act. As this study is attentive to issues of interpretation, ethnography is well suited to efforts to understand the process by which actors construct meaning out of collective experiences (Hammersley & Atkinson, 2007). This study employs an organizational ethnography to allow for deeper understanding and accommodate multiple perspectives of organizational processes (Fine, Morrill, & Surianarain, 2009). The value of ethnography as a method in such disciplines responsible for strategic communication (including public relations, marketing and organizational communication) centers on the ability to gain critical insights into the value of practice and discourse surrounding practice and its contribution to new theoretical directions (Daymon & Hodges, 2009; Everett & Johnston, 2012; Sriramesh, 1992).

An organizational ethnography is defined as an ethnographic study of an organization and their organizing processes (Ybema, Yanow, Wels, & Kamsteeg, 2009). It differs from traditional ethnography as people in a setting are organized around prescriptive goals and formalized rules governing status, relationships and behaviors within the context of the setting (Rosen, 1991).

The primary setting for this research is a major humanitarian organization and one of Australia's leading humanitarian and disaster response organizations. Employing nearly 2,000 staff nationally, the organization operated as a decentralized organizational structure through state based divisions. The focus on strategic communication centered the ethnography on organizational members involved in the enactment, selection and retention of environmental cues. As strategizing is often undertaken in group settings or communities of practice (Balogun, Huff, & Johnson, 2003), observation focused on scenes where the researcher anticipated decision- and sense-making would occur (Hammersley &

Atkinson, 1995) for strategic communication processes and outcomes. This included unit and senior management meetings, team leader and staff meetings, and workshops or project-specific meetings.

Qualitative research traditions offer three major approaches for data collection: "participant observation (experiencing), interviewing (enquiring) and studying materials prepared by others (examining)" (Wolcott, 1994, p.10). The prime sources of data for this work can focus on the words and actions of the members organized around direct experience, social action, talk and supplementary data (Lofland, Snow, Anderson, & Lofland, 2006). Data for this study included observation (approximately 787 hours) and 51 depth interviews. Interviews sought rich and complex data suited for exploratory and descriptive research (Cavana, Delahaye, & Sekaran, 2000), using semi-structured questions to stimulate the participant to talk about key topics (Hammersley & Atkinson, 1995).

The study derived from ethnoecological approaches to research that seek to understand how people perceive their environment and how they organize these perceptions (Frake, 1962). Through exploring the relationships between an organization and its environment, ethnoecology "seeks to provide an understanding of the systems of knowledge that local people have" (Gragson & Blount, 1999, p. ix). Ethnoecology therefore focuses on what local people know, classify, and how they use the knowledge of their environment (Sutton & Anderson, 2010). Iterative coupling of data collection, analysis and theory generation was applied to an inductive analysis of the data to generate an exploratory theory and explore the origins and nature of strategic communication as an organizational response to enacted environments (Marshall & Rossman, 1999; Patton, 1990; Strauss & Corbin, 1998). The progressive contextualization (Vayda, 1983) of the case setting looked for "systematic relationships among diverse phenomena, not for substantive identities among similar ones" (Geertz, 1973, p. 9). Data reduction followed the iterative stages of transforming data through description, analysis and interpretation (Wolcott, 1994, 2009).

In the first stage of description, fieldwork observation data were documented in journals and interviews transcribed. Observations were further reduced by memo writing in three contexts: in the field after directly witnessing an event, after a series of observations, and at the end of each observation day. Concept maps were also developed and refined as themes emerged and shifted. Memo and data sorting (reduction) were guided by the data's key emergent properties (Glaser, 1998). In all of these steps, the analytical goal was to allow the unique patterns of the case to emerge (Denzin, 2002). The first stage of enactment occurred at the individual level; therefore, categories, themes and patterns were identified to describe enacted events at the individual level and presented as cultural knowledge structures. The individual enacted environment represented what was going on that impacted on the organization. Variation at this level was captured in this analytical stage.

The role of culture at the collective group level was described as memes that represented patterns in the selection processes: that is, cultural data—schemas representing collective cultural material, or patterns of how collective beliefs of organizational members operated as cultural criteria. The analytical goal for this stage was to identify concepts that represent the cultural subsystems acting as selection biases collectively on enacted materials.

Description, topic, and analytical coding differentiate the purposes of each coding stage (Richards, 2005). At this first level of analysis, descriptive coding identified the cases and attributes of the data, including position, department, location, gender, age, qualifications, and length of time employed. Topic coding initially labelled expressions, sentences, and paragraphs into topics and categories that emerged from the data (Richards, 2005) and generated to build conceptual theory and clarify relationships.

The first research question seeks to identify the cultural influences on organizational processes of environmental interpretation by organizational members and their associated expectations. Knowledge structures and schemas representing participants' shared cultural knowledge in the case organization were identified to provide a conceptual foundation to explore the role of cultural influences in the development of strategic communication. The identification of classificatory schemas

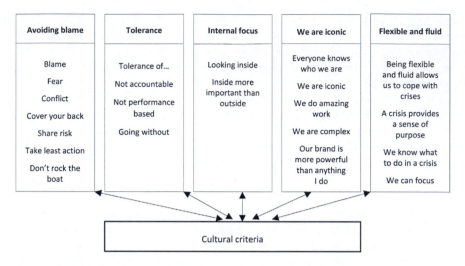

Figure 10.1 Cultural Schema Operating in the Focal Organization

Adapted from Johnston, 2011

derived from observations rather than preordained models is viewed as an important step in theory development (Pratt, 1994). Five schemas (Figure 10.1) emerged from the data, as core themes of coherent knowledge systems that were mapped to collectively act as criteria to guide selection in the selection process (Weick, 1979). Selection criteria were identified as units that are socially transmitted, had historical presence, and acted to inform or guide behavior (Durham, 1991). These criteria illustrate the five coherent systems the data yielded (see Figure 10.1): criterion around avoiding blame; criterion around tolerance; criterion around internal focus; criterion around being iconic, and finally, criterion around being flexible and fluid. According to Durham (1991), these units are learned and shared systems of knowledge and beliefs, and are socially transmitted over time.

Cultural schema depicted in Figure 10.1 operated to organize other cultural knowledge structures into a coherent selection system, and therefore are fundamental to identification of a cultural selection system operating in the selection process (Everett, 2003).

The second research question seeks to identify the implications of these cultural influences for the identification and implementation of strategic communication. Strategic communication is recognized as a multidisciplinary endeavor (Sandhu, 2009) and aligns with the management of communication on behalf of an organization (Heath, 2005). The formulation of strategic communication requires organizational members to interpret, understand or translate equivocal environmental information (Beer et al., 2005; Everett, 1993; O'Shannassy, 2003; Weick, 1979, 1995) and make decisions based on information available (Johnson, Scholes, & Whittington, 2008). The findings as they related to each cultural selection criterion are discussed in the following sections.

Cultural Selection Criterion: Five Schemas

1. Avoiding Blame

The cultural criterion of avoiding blame influenced the development of strategic communication in a number of ways. The avoiding blame criteria were instrumental in influencing the timing of communication responses. The stifled nature of contemplating communication actions and time spent on deliberating to get the response 'right' to avoid being blamed meant that workload was increased and responses were slowed. Time was spent on redefining the problem several times.

Organizational members followed precedents or scripts of action that had been historically established as acceptable. Members opted for replicating what had been done, or what they thought had been done previously, and therefore avoided taking risks. Cultural selection influenced the endorsement of a workplace that effectively avoided documentation of communication programs, activities or actions. This included a lack of planning in the form of written documents and evaluation of activities. The confluence of fluidity in these criteria rationalized the lack of documentation and planning with the need to be flexible and open to change because they argued they were a 'crisis' organization. For strategic communication this meant actions were reserved for reactive or directed items, leaving opportunities for exploring other options or communication actions unattended.

Cultural selection influenced the group to work in a way that avoided evaluation of performance and thus blame. Environmental scanning, such as media monitoring, was avoided as it challenged the status quo, and responsiveness was reduced as members struggled with high levels of bureaucracy in having communication tactics approved by senior management. Member efforts to avoid blame fractured sensitivity to the external environment. Decision making about external events and communication responses revealed members actively sought to avoid situations that challenged the status quo within the organization, For example, they ignored—did not see, or hear—external signals if what they saw challenged the current accepted view of the situation within the organization. Members were therefore unlikely to acknowledge the equivocality, or would actively avoid or ignore equivocality if it conflicted with internal dynamics. The criteria of avoiding blame meant that members sought direction and followed instructions without necessarily analyzing what they were told. Avoiding blame as criteria also influenced member avoidance of challenging power relations. For members this meant that even if the group felt the interpretation or action being taken was not correct, they avoided challenging or questioning this to maintain the status quo. This action was also acceptable to the group, being justified as the way the organization worked.

2. Tolerance

The cultural criteria of tolerance influenced the development of strategic communication in a number of ways. The strength of traditions and history in the organization, combined with the traditions of the federated structure and traditional roles of boards and community representatives, meant members were not inclined to embrace opportunities. The tendency to follow established precedent influenced members to keep to the routine, keep to the traditional ways of doing things, reduce or avoid risks and not try anything new. This also translated to other components of strategic communication including messaging and channel selection. In this case, messaging and channels were identified in ways that met expectations and satisfied 'old ways' of working. Old conceptualizations of communication problems propagated by ageing board members were accepted and unchallenged by more youthful members. Questioning or challenging board members' interpretation was viewed as disrespectful and not something that was done at [the organization].

The tolerance criterion was powerful in influencing performance and acceptance expectations of the group. The impact of this criterion on the development of strategic communication meant that members were not sensitive or responsive to the environment, but rather, were risk-averse, wanting to stay with or tolerate what was familiar. While it is not unexpected to find an organization to be risk-averse, collectively cultural selection affected communicative action. Selection criteria guided actions to avoid putting the individual or group at risk. As a way of working, this meant little was realized in terms of opportunities—only reactive responses to emergent issues and a general reluctance to embrace opportunity.

3. Internal focus

Cultural selection acted to influence a dominant internal focus for attention and response. First, organizational members did not view information from the external environment as important. This included identifying, analyzing and prioritizing information from the media or opinion leaders, and integrating stakeholder views for decisions. Members relied on power-holders in the organization to identify and interpret ecological change for meaning. The reliance on power-holders to define the environment delegated middle and lower members to a technician role. This reduced risk for team members through allowing power holders to define strategic communication problems and identify communication responses.

Second, members' high prioritization of internal relationships and low prioritization of external issues and external publics, created a lack of perspective of any influence or consequences caused by organizational actions on external publics. The dominance of power relationships in the organization meant that for members this was not a safe environment to take risks to challenge the internal focus. For members this meant that there were often conflicting directives from the different hierarchies.

Third, the internal focus created missed strategic communication opportunities for the organization. This, coupled with the avoiding blame criteria, meant the organization was not proactive, but remained reactive to issues.

4. We Are Iconic

The cultural criterion "we are iconic" was influential in the development of strategic communication in the organization through creating haughtiness or a sense of organizational superiority, particularly when exploring potential sponsorships or corporate partnerships. The linkages of being an iconic, large, globally important humanitarian organization meant potential relationships were assessed on criteria of whether the other party was worthy of partnering with the organization, rather than on other financially based criteria, such as return on investment or tangible strategic communication outcomes.

This schema was instrumental in directing a tendency to conceptualize communication problems historically, based on previous experiences. For example, because there was a cultural expectation that the organization was an iconic humanitarian organization that stakeholders held in high regard, members viewed local marketing, communication or public relations efforts as ineffectual. For them this meant their actions had little effect on influencing the reputation of the organization. In addition, old or traditional ways of working meant existing practices were left unchallenged or were accepted as the way of approaching stakeholder communication.

5. Flexible and Fluid

The cultural criterion of "flexible and fluid" encouraged a somewhat unstructured approach to communication in the organization, evidenced through minimal planning and documentation. This had four key influences on strategic communications.

The flexible criterion influenced fluidity in decision-making processes around strategic communication, resulting in little or no formal planning processes being developed around key programs or projects. The outcome of this meant there was little to no resource allocation for projects, and more critically, no evaluation of any communication outcomes.

While some members claimed they formally planned communication activities (strategically), no formal documentation (record) of strategic communication activities took place. The "flexible and fluid" criterion encouraged members to be variable in their approaches to communication tasks and functions. For some members this allowed them to work with little structure, resulting in a more reactive approach to prioritizing communication actions, but it provided little support for members to "push back" on projects, due to a lack of documentation of program priorities and goals.

Being flexible and fluid also hindered the progression of any developing campaigns as members felt they needed to attend to other priorities. For some members, this meant they were just "treading water until the next crisis"—meaning it was acceptable for programs to be left in a state of limbo. Finally, the criterion of flexible and fluid created additional pressure for members as there was a lack of performance benchmarks or structures around milestones. In response to these criteria, members would revert to old ways of doing things driven by a sense of security that comes from following historical precedents, and by reassurance from providing something to senior management that was familiar.

In summary, the preceding discussion presented an analysis of the role of cultural criteria, drawn from the five identified collective schema emerging from the data, acting in the selection process (Weick, 1969, 1979) to influence strategic communication in the organization. Each cultural selection criterion was found to influence strategic communication and was shown to be present both during free choice and imposition-based decision making (Durham, 1992) as members negotiated meanings and actions in their efforts to respond to environmental equivocality. This finding contributes to understanding how the internal organizational environment influences strategic decision making (Nutt & Wilson, 2010; Papadakis, Thanos, & Barwise, 2010) and more specifically for strategic communication (Johnston, 2011).

Culturally Derived Strategic Communication

Social ecology describes the relationships between parts of a system and reflects organizational needs in responding to a changing social environment (Emery & Trist, 1973). Ecology recognizes the interaction of the system, while social ecology highlights the interdependent relationship of the social environment and the organization. Set within an ecological context, strategic communication represents the organizational response to the social elements of an organization's operating environment, such as public opinion and the actions of stakeholder and special interest groups (Broom & Sha, 2012; Everett, 1993). Everett (2001) argues that the challenge of an organization to adapt to changes in its social environment is a problem central to organizational efforts to build and maintain relationships with its social environment. This adaptive challenge also highlights one of the most important considerations in assessing the effectiveness of strategic communication by an organization. Since all organizations seek the best adaptive outcomes to strategy, then an essential challenge for strategic communication is to identify and facilitate such outcomes in the social ecology of organizations.

The central task of strategic communication is to assist an organization in responding to the uncertainty that ultimately helps the organization achieve its needs for adaptation (Argenti, Howell, & Beck, 2005; Hallahan et al., 2007; Steyn, 2003b; Xavier, Johnston, & Patel, 2006). Clampitt et al. (2000) highlight the role of choice by management based on judgment. Culturally derived strategic communication reflects the influence of cultural selection on social cognition within organizations in their effort to formulate an adaptive response to the environment (Johnston, 2011), as illustrated in Figure 10.2. Culturally derived strategic communication, through the action of cultural criteria and cultural selection, is centrally placed in the ecological relationship of an organization and its efforts to adapt to its social environment. The centrality of cultural criteria at the collective group level is found to conservatively influence the core roles and functions undertaken by members to formulate strategic communication (Johnston, 2011).

Environmental scanning of factors in an organization's social environment including public opinion, media, and stakeholder groups, with subsequent interpretation and judgment about environmental equivocality, follows Alvesson's (2002) cultural view of strategy. This view highlights the reality of the external environment as a social construction by the group. He argues, "the consequences

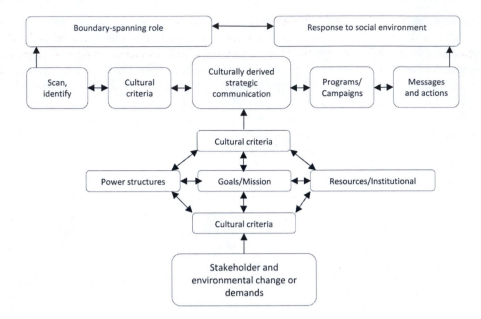

Figure 10.2 Ecological Relationships: Culturally Derived Strategic Communication Model

Adapted from Johnston, 2011

of the environment for the organization and the actions of organizational participants are revealed in the interpretations, frames of reference, perceptions and forms of understanding which character-ize the strategic actors as a collective" (p. 77). He cautions the need to understand how the group collectively attributed meaning and content to the environment. This understanding is provided through examining knowledge structures in organizations, and identifying cultural criteria operating in selection processes (Durham, 1991). Culturally derived strategic communication will therefore reflect the *internal* imperatives of the organization as much as it does the *external*. Therefore, the stronger the organizational culture (Geertz, 1973), the more likely that culture, rather than environ-mental variables, will be the dominant influence in the development of strategic communication. The outcome of this influence will eventually produce substantive differences between organiza-tional groups, even though they may face similar environmental challenges. These implications are discussed in the next section.

Understanding Influences on Strategic Communication

This chapter has explored the important and significant role an organization's culture plays in the formulation of strategic communication. We argue that the action of cultural selection criteria oper-ating on the collective knowledge system, that is, the culture of an organization, mediates strategic communication. When an organization's culture is seen as a constellation of collective knowledge structures, including beliefs and values, the guiding influence of cultural selection criteria on that knowledge system can create a significant influence on the communicative actions and messages used in the strategic communication process the organization developed. The identification of the influ-ence of these cultural selection criteria supports criticism of the received view in communication management disciplines that strategic communication is principally driven by responses to external drivers in the social environment of an organization. In contrast to this management-centric maxim, this study provides evidence that strategic communication may reflect outcomes to the action of cultural selection in the culture of an organization, as much as it reflects imperatives of the external social environment. More importantly, we argue that the culture of an organization should be recognized as a potentially significant influence on an organization's identification of strategic communication imperatives. Underpinning this central claim and a key theoretical perspective around which this chapter is organized is Weick's (1969, 1979) foundational perspective on organizational communication generally—organizations are first and foremost sociocultural systems.

Implications for the Management of Strategic Communication

Ecological perspectives to understand the efforts of organizations to meet adaptive requirements in their social environments through strategic communication have been most explicitly formulated in the public relations textbook tradition set by Cutlip, Center, and Broom (2000). Building on this perspective, the study and findings presented in this chapter contribute to understanding the significance of the cultural ecology of organizing by their identification and description of the role of culture and cultural selection in mediating the organization–environment relationship and the influence of organizational culture on responses to environmental change.

Astley and Fombrun (1983) emphasized the importance of "collective" forms of organizational adaptation to the environment. Exertion toward organizational adaptation is a key claim in public relations (Broom & Sha, 2012), organizational communication (Conrad & Poole, 2012) and strategic marketing (Drummond, Ensor, & Ashford, 2012) literatures. While Mintzberg and Lampel (1999) argued that strategy formulation is intuitive and judgmental, this approach is not reflected in the textbook traditions of core strategic communication (Steyn, 2007; Stroh, 2007).

Traditional conceptualizations of the organization–environment relationship reinforce the dominant role the environment has on choices made for organizational action (Astley & Fombrun, 1983). Following this tradition, student education in strategic communication focuses on the task of environmental scanning and analysis, with rational approaches remaining dominant (Steyn, 2007). However, a key imperative drawn from this study is that practitioners should also be trained in the analysis and description of an organization's culture to understand an essential context for the development of strategic communication. While senior management provide stewardship in strategy formulation and senior leaders provide the discipline and perspective for strategy (Porter, 1996), practitioners need to be better equipped for the task of understanding and describing how their work is influenced by an organization's culture. The significance of cultural selection to the development of strategic communication reinforces this view.

Everett's (1985, 1990) early work on the challenges of integrating the perspective of organizations as sociocultural systems identified the theoretical implications for organizational communication of organizational culture as an evolving system of social knowledge. This study extends Everett's perspective by identifying the role of cultural selection operating in the selection processes of organizing (Weick, 1969, 1979) as a key driver to understanding the social ecology of organizations. Weick's (1979) notion that the creation of causal maps from past organizational experiences creates templates to guide interpretations of equivocal information is extended in the culturally derived strategic communication model (Johnston, 2011), which model illustrates that the mechanism that creates these templates is the action of cultural selection in organizing (Weick, 1969, 1979).

The foundation of this chapter has set the context of understanding the role of cultural selection in organizing processes, and more specifically, in terms of organizations' development of strategic communication. At the organizational level, we should expect that over time the action of cultural selection would create increasing variation between similar types of organizations in a population, in terms of how they look at, understand, and react to environmental features. This process will eventually produce substantive differences between organizations even though they face similar environmental challenges. This macro level outcome is tightly coupled with the operation of selection criteria within organizations. In this context, there is an essential role for the action of cultural selection criteria within organizations when they engage with the problem of assessing significant imperatives of their social environment and determining what to do about those imperatives.

References

Alvesson, M. (2002). *Understanding organizational culture.* London: Sage.

Ansoff, H. I., & Sullivan, P. A. (1993). Optimizing profitability in turbulent environments: A formula for strategic success. *Long Range Planning, 26*(5), 11.

Argenti, P. A., Howell, R. A., & Beck, K. A. (2005). The strategic communication imperative. *MIT Sloan Management Review, 46*(3), 83.

Astley, W. G., & Fombrun, C. J. (1983). Collective strategy: Social ecology of organizational environments. *Academy of Management. The Academy of Management Review, 8*(4), 576.

Bailey, A., & Johnson, G. (2001). A framework for managerial understanding of strategy development. In H. W. Volberda & T. Elfring (Eds.), *Rethinking strategy* (pp. 212–230). London: Sage.

Balogun, J., Huff, A. S., & Johnson, P. (2003). Three Responses to the methodological challenges of studying strategizing. *Journal of Management Studies, 40*(1), 197–224.

Bates, D. (2001). *Human adaptive strategies: Ecology, culture and politics* (2nd ed.). Needham Heights, MA: Allyn and Bacon.

Beer, M., Voelpel, S. C., Leibold, M., & Tekie, E. B. (2005). Strategic management as organizational learning: Developing fit and alignment through a disciplined process. *Long Range Planning, 38*(5), 445–465.

Botan, C. H. (2006). Grand strategy, strategy, and tactics in public relations. In C. H. Botan & V. Hazelton (Eds.), *Public Relations Theory II.* Mahwah, NJ: Lawrence Erlbaum Associates.

Bourgeois, L. J. (1980). Strategy and environment: A conceptual integration. *The Academy of Management Review, 5*(1), 25–39.

Bowen, S. A. (2004). Organizational factors encouraging ethical decision making: An exploration into the case of an exemplar. *Journal of Business Ethics, 52*(4), 311–324.

Broom, G. M., & Sha, B. (2012). *Cutlip and Center's effective public relations* (11th ed.). New Jersey: Prentice Hall.

Cameron, G. T., & McCollum, T. (1993). Competing corporate cultures: A multi-method, cultural analysis of the role of internal communication. *Journal of Public Relations Research, 5*(4), 217–250.

Cavana, R. Y., Delahaye, B. L., & Sekaran, U. (2000). *Applied business research: qualitative and quantitative methods.* Brisbane: John Wiley and Sons Australia.

Chaffee, E. E. (1985). Three models of strategy. *Academy of Management Review, 10*(1), 89–98.

Chan, A. (2003). Instantiative versus entitative culture: The case for culture as a process. In R. Westwood & S. Clegg (Eds.), *Debating organization: Point-counterpoint in organization studies* (pp. 311–320). Malden, MA.: Blackwell.

Chia, J., & Synnott, G. (2009). *An introduction to public relations: From theory to practice.* Melbourne, Vic: Oxford University Press.

Chick, G. (1997). Cultural Complexity: The concept and its measurement. *Cross-Cultural Research, 31*, 275–307.

Christensen, L. T., & Cornelissen, J. (2011). Bridging Corporate and organizational communication: Review, development and a look to the future. *Management communication quarterly, 25*(3), 383–414.

Clampitt, P. G., DeKoch, R. J., & Cashman, T. (2000). A strategy for communicating about uncertainty. *The Academy of Management Executive, 14*(4), 41–59.

Conrad, C. R., & Poole, M. S. (2012). *Strategic organizational communication* Malden: Wiley & Blackwell.

Cornelissen, J. (2008). *Corporate communications – theory and practice* (2nd ed.). London: Sage Publications.

Craig-Lees, M. (2001). Sense making: Trojan Horse? Pandora's Box? *Psychology & Marketing, 18*(5), 513.

Cutlip, S., Center, A., & Broom, G. M. (2000). *Effective Public Relations* (8th ed.). Upper Saddle River, NJ: Prentice-Hall.

D'Andrade, R. (2001). A cognitivist's view of the units debate in cultural anthropology. *Cross-Cultural Research, 35*(2), 242.

Daymon, C., & Hodges, C. (2009). Researching the occupational culture of public relations in Mexico. *Public Relations Review, 35*, 429–433.

Denzin, N. K. (2002). The interpretive process. In M. B. Miles & A. M. Huberman (Eds.), *The qualitative researcher's companion.* Thousand Oaks: Sage.

Diaz, V., Abratt, R., Clarke, R., & Bendixen, M. (2009). PR practitioners in international assignments. *Corporate Communications, 14*(1), 78.

Dil, A. S. (Ed.). (1980). *Language and cultural description – essays by Charles O. Frake*. Stanford California: Stanford University Press.

Drummond, G., Ensor, J., & Ashford, R. (2012). *Strategic Marketing: Planning and Control* (2nd ed.). Oxford: Butterworth Heinemann.

Durham, W. H. (1991). *Coevolution—genes, culture and human diversity*. Stanford, CA: Stanford University Press.

Durham, W. H. (1992). Applications of evolutionary culture theory. *Annual Review of Anthropology, 21*(1), 331–355.

Emery, F. E., & Trist, E. L. (1973). *Towards a social ecology*. New York: Plenum Rosetta.

Everett, J. L. (1985). *Culture and ecology in the analysis of organizations*. (doctoral dissertation), University of Colorado, Boulder, CO.

Everett, J. L. (1990). Organizational culture and ethnoecology in public relations theory and practice. *Public Relations Research Annual, 2*(1–4), 235–251.

Everett, J. L. (1993). The ecological paradigm in public relations theory and practice. *Public Relations Review, 19*(2), 177–186.

Everett, J. L. (2001). Public relations and the ecology of organisational change. In R. L. Heath (Ed.), *Handbook of Public Relations* (pp. 311–320). CA: Sage Publications.

Everett, J. L. (2002). *Towards identification of cultural structures in Weick's model of organising*. Paper presented at the International Conference on Social Sciences June 12–15, 2002, Honolulu, Hawaii, USA.

Everett, J. L. (2003). *The culture pools of organizational populations*. Paper presented at the Second Hawaii International Conference on Social Sciences June 12–15, 2003, Honolulu, Hawaii, USA.

Everett, J. L., & Johnston, K. A. (2012). Toward an ethnographic imperative in public relations research. *Public Relations Review, 38*(4), 522–528.

Fine, G., Morrill, C., & Surianarain, S. (2009). Ethnography in organizational settings. In D. A. Buchanan & A. Bryman (Eds.), *The Sage handbook of organizational research methods* (pp. 603–619). Thousand Oaks: Sage.

Frake, C. O. (1962). Cultural Ecology and Ethnography. *American Anthropologist, 64*(1), 53–59.

Geertz, C. (1973). *The interpretation of cultures; Selected essays*. New York: Basic Books.

George, E., Chattopadhyay, P., Sitkin, S. B., & Barden, J. (2006). Cognitive underpinnings of institutional persistence and change: A framing perspective. *Academy of Management Review, 31*(2), 347–365.

Glaser, B. G. (1998). *Doing grounded theory; Issues and discussion*. Mill Valley, CA: Sociology Press.

Gragson, T., & Blount, B. (1999). *Ethnoecology: knowledge, resources, and rights*. Athens, Georgia: University of Georgia Press.

Grunig, J. E. (1992a). *Excellence in public relations and communication management*. New Jersey: Lawrence Erlbaum Associates.

Grunig, J. E. (1992b). Symmetrical systems of internal communication. In J. E. Grunig (Ed.), *Excellence in public relations and communication management* (pp. 531–575). Hillsdale, NJ: Lawrence Erlbaum.

Hallahan, K., Holtzhausen, D. R., van Ruler, B., Vercic, D., & Sriramesh, K. (2007). Defining strategic communication. *International Journal of Strategic Communication, 7*(1), 3–35.

Hambrick, D. C. (1981). Specialization of Environmental Scanning Activities Among Upper Level Executives. *The Journal of Management Studies, 18*(3), 299.

Hammersley, M., & Atkinson, P. (1995). *Ethnography: Principles in practice* (2nd ed.). London: Routledge.

Hammersley, M., & Atkinson, P. (2007). *Ethnography: Principles in practice* (3rd ed.). London: Routledge.

Hatch, M. J. (1993). The dynamics of organizational culture. *Academy of Management Review, 18*(4), 657–693.

Heath, R. L. (Ed.). (2005). *Encyclopedia of public relations*. Thousand Oaks, CA: Sage.

Jarzabkowski, P., Balogun, J., & Seidl, D. (2007). Strategizing: The challenges of a practice perspective. *Human Relations, 60*(1), 5–27.

Johnson, G., Scholes, K., & Whittington, R. (2008). *Exploring corporate strategy* (8th ed.). Harlow, UK: Prentice Hall.

Johnston, K. A. (2011). *The influence of cultural selection on strategic communication*. (PhD thesis), Queensland University of Technology, Brisbane.

Keesing, R. M. (1974). Theories of culture. *Annual Review of Anthropology, 3*, 73–97.

Keesing, R. M. (1981). *Cultural anthropology*. New York: CBS College Publishing.

Kersten, A. (2005). Crisis as usual: Organizational dysfunction and public relations. *Public Relations Review, 31*(4), 544–549.

Keyton, J. (2005). *Communication and organizational culture*. Thousand Oaks: Sage.

Kreps, G. L. (1990). Weick's model of organizing: Organization as a response to information equivocality. In G. L. Kreps (Ed.), *Organizational Communication: Theory and practice* (2nd ed., pp. 114–134). White Plains, NY: Longmann.

Lane, A. B. (2007). Empowering publics: The potential and challenge for public relations practitioners in creative approaches to two-way symmetric public relations. *Australian Journal of Communication Monographs, 34*(1), 71–86.

Leichty, G., & Warner, E. (2001). Cultural topoi: Implications for public relations. In R. L. Heath (Ed.), *Handbook of Public Relations* (pp. 61–74). CA: Sage Publications.

Littlejohn, S. W. (1999). *Theories of human communication*. Belmont, CA: Wadsworth.

Lofland, J., Snow, D., Anderson, L., & Lofland, L. (2006). *Analysing social settings*. Belmont, CA: Wadsworth Thomson.

Lyles, M., & Schwenk, C. (1992). Top management, strategy and organizational knowledge structures. *Journal of Management Studies, 29*(2), 155–174.

Marchiori, M., & Bulgacov, S. (2012). Strategy as Communicational Practice in Organizations. *International Journal of Strategic Communication, 6*(3), 199–211.

Marshall, C., & Rossman, G. B. (1999). *Designing qualitative research* (3rd ed.). Thousand Oaks, CA: Sage.

Milton, K. (1996). *Environmentalism and cultural theory: Exploring the role of anthropology in environmental discourse*. London: Routledge.

Mintzberg, H., & Lampel, J. (1999). Reflecting on the strategy process. *Sloan Management Review, 40*(3), 21–31.

Mintzberg, H., & Quinn, J. B. (2003). *The strategy process* (4th ed.). London: Prentice Hall.

Norlin, J. M., Chess, W. A., Dale, O., & Smith, R. (2003). *Human behavior and the social environment* (4th ed.). Boston MA: Allyn & Bacon, & Pearson Education.

Nutt, P. C., & Wilson, D. C. (2010). Discussion and implications: Toward creating a unified theory of decision making. In P. C. Nutt & D. C. Wilson (Eds.), *Handbook of decision making* (pp. 645–677). Chichester: John Wiley & Sons.

O'Shannassy, T. (2003). Modern strategic management: Balancing strategic thinking and strategic planning for internal and external stakeholders. *Singapore Management Review, 25*(1), 53–57.

Pace, T. M. (1988). Schema theory: A framework for research and practice in psychotherapy. *Journal of Cognitive Psychotherapy, 2*(3), 147–163.

Papadakis, V., Thanos, I., & Barwise, P. (2010). Research on strategic decisions: Taking stock and looking ahead. In P. C. Nutt & D. C. Wilson (Eds.), *Handbook of decision making* (pp. 31–69). Chichester: John Wiley & Sons.

Patton, M. Q. (1990). *Qualitative evaluation and research methods*. Newbury Park, CA: Sage Publications.

Porter, M. E. (1996). What is strategy? *Harvard business review, 74*(6), 61–79.

Pratt, C. B. (1994). Applying classical ethical theories to ethical decision making in pulblic relation: Perrier's Product Recall. *Management Communication Quarterly : McQ (1986–1998), 8*(1), 70.

Rabinow, P. (1977). *Reflections on fieldwork in Morocco*. Berkeley: University of California Press.

Rhee, Y., & Moon, B. (2009). Organizational culture and strategic communication practice: Testing the competing values model (cvm) and employee communication strategies (ecs) model in Korea. *International Journal of Strategic Communication, 3*(1), 52–67.

Richards, L. (2005). *Handling qualitative data: A practical guide*. London: Sage.

Rosen, M. (1991). Coming to terms with the field: Understanding and doing organizational ethnography *Journal of Management Studies, 28*(1), 1–24.

Sackmann, S. (1992). Culture and subcultures: An analysis of organizational knowledge. *Administrative Science Quarterly, 37*(1), 140–161.

Sandhu, S. (2009). Strategic communication: An institutional perspective. *International Journal of Strategic Communication, 3*, 72–92.

Schein, E. H. (1984). Coming to a new awareness of organizational culture. *Sloan Management Review, 25*(2), 3.

Scroggins, W. A. (2006). Managing meaning for strategic change: The role of perception and meaning congruence. *Journal of Health and Human Services Administration, 29*(1/2), 83–102.

Seitel, F. P. (2007). *The practice of public relations* (10th ed.). Upper Saddle River, NJ: Pearson Education.

Selsky, J. W., Goes, J., & Baburoglu, O. N. (2007). Contrasting perspectives of strategy making: Applications in 'Hyper' environments. *Organization Studies, 28*(1), 71–94.

Shockley-Zalabak, P. (2002). *Fundamentals of organizational communication* (5th ed.). Boston, MA: Allyn & Bacon.

Sriramesh, K. (1992). Societal culture and public relations: Ethnographic evidence from India. *Public Relations Review, 18*(2), 201–211.

Sriramesh, K. (2007). The relationship between culture and public relations. In E. Toth (Ed.), *The future of excellence in public relations and communication management* (pp. 507–526). Mahwah N.J: Lawrence Erlbaum.

Steyn, B. (2003a, July). *A conceptualisation and empirical verification of the 'strategist', (redefined) 'manager, and 'technical 'roles of public relations*. Paper presented at the 10th International PR Research Symposium, Lake Bled.

Steyn, B. (2003b). From strategy to corporate communication strategy: A conceptualisation. *Journal of Communication Management, 8*(2), 168.

Steyn, B. (2007). Contribution of public relations to organizational strategy formulation. In E. L. Toth (Ed.), *The future of excellence in public relations and communication management: Challenges for the next generation* (pp. 137–172). Mahwah, N.J: Erlbaum.

Strauss, A., & Corbin, M. J. (1998). *Basics of qualitative research: Techniques and procedures for developing grounded theory*. Thousand Oaks: Sage.

Stroh, U. (2007). An alternative postmodern approach to corporate communication strategy. In E. Toth (Ed.), *The future of excellence in public relations and communication management* (pp. 199–220). Mahwah, NJ: Lawrence Erlbaum Associates.

Sutton, M. Q., & Anderson, E. (2010). *Introduction to Cultural Ecology*. (2nd ed.). Lanham: AltaMira Press.

Vayda, A. P. (1983). Progressive contextualization: Methods for research in human ecology. *Human Ecology, 11*(3), 265–281.

Verhoeven, P., Zerfass, A., & Tench, R. (2011). Strategic Orientation of Communication Professionals in Europe. *International Journal of Strategic Communication, 5*(2), 95–117.

Volberda, H. W., & Elfring, T. (2001). *Rethinking strategy*. London: Sage.

Weick, K. E. (1969). *The social psychology of organizing*. Reading, MA: Addison-Wesley.

Weick, K. E. (1979). *The social psychology of organizing* (2nd ed.). NY: Newbery Award Records, Inc.

Weick, K. E. (1988). Enacted Sensemaking in Crisis Situations. *The Journal of Management Studies, 25*(4), 305.

Weick, K. E. (1995). *Sensemaking in organizations*. Thousand Oaks: Sage

Weick, K. E. (2001). *Making sense of the organization*. Oxford, UK: Blackwell Publishers.

Wolcott, H. F. (1994). *Transforming qualitative data*. Thousand Oaks, CA: Sage.

Wolcott, H. F. (2009). *Writing up qualitative research* (3 ed.). Thousand Oaks, CA: Sage.

Xavier, R. J., Johnston, K. A., & Patel, A. M. (2006). Exploring strategy : What public relations strategy means in practice. *Asia Pacific Public Relations Journal, 6*(2), 1–10.

Ybema, S., Yanow, D., Wels, H., & Kamsteeg, F. (Eds.). (2009). *Organizational Ethnography*. London: Sage.

Zerfass, A., & Huck, S. (2007). Innovation, communication and leadership: New developments in strategic communication. *International Journal of Strategic Communication, 1*(2), 107–122.

11

Strategic Communication

The Role of Polyphony in Management Team Meetings

Helle Kryger Aggerholm and Christa Thomsen

Strategy has been defined as "situated, socially accomplished activity" (Jarzabkowski, Balogun, & Seidl, 2007, pp. 7–8), who go on to state that "strategizing comprises those actions, interactions and negotiations of multiple actors and the situated practices that they draw upon in accomplishing that activity." Strategy work is thus connected with particular types of practices, such as strategy meetings (Jarzabkowski & Seidl, 2008) and strategy workshops (Prashantham, Bourque, Floyd, & Johnson, 2010; Seidl, MacIntosh & MacLean, 2006; Schwarz, 2009), which can be understood as focal points for the strategic activities of organizational members (Jarzabkowski & Seidl, 2008). One recommendation for analyzing strategic communication as a situated, socially accomplished activity is to focus on management teams and their communicative activities and practices in relation to strategy formulation (Jarzabkowski & Seidl, 2008).

Researchers have conceptualized the management team as the inner circle of executives, who collectively formulate, articulate, and execute the strategic and tactical moves of an organization (Raes, Heijltjes, Glunk, & Roe, 2011; Eisenhardt, Kahwajy, & Bourgeois, 1997). The basic assumption of this field of research is that management teams influence their organizations through formulating and implementing strategy (Hambrick & Mason, 1984; Love, Priem, & Lumpkin, 2002; Mintzberg, 1978). Communication can be seen as a lens to describe and explain organizations, the interest being in strategy formulation in terms of choice of a particular course of discursive or communicative action during management team meetings (Hendry, 2000; Habermas, 2006). Here the focus is on the process of organizing through interaction rather than on "communication" within an "organization" (Deetz, 2001, p. 5). Hence, in this view, the process of decision making is seen as a communication process itself, by which meaningful decisions are constructed (Deetz, 2001; Hallahan, Holtzhausen, van Ruler, Verčič, & Sriramesh, 2007).

Previous research has suggested the amount and type of information team members gather, interpret, and synthesize during decision making influences the quality of strategic decisions (Dooley & Fryxell, 1999; Galbraith, 1973; Tushman & Nadler, 1978). Hambrick and Mason (1984) argue the values, cognitions, and personalities of team members are important sources of difference in the information they bring in and that this diversity has consequences for the content and quality of strategic decisions. Empirical studies have since then supported this proposition. These results show how the diversity in team members' cognitive backgrounds, as well as interaction processes within team meetings in which task-related differences in information and opinions are openly discussed, is positively related to the quality of strategic decisions (Amason, 1996; Dooley & Fryxell, 1999; Olson, Parayitam, & Bao, 2007).

Despite this research, we know little about the role of discursive practices in the decision-making processes within management teams, and their subsequent influence on the formation of strategic communication in a broader organizational setting. In the last decade or so, we have seen an increase in academic interest in discursive-oriented studies within strategy research (e.g., Vaara, 2010; Vaara & Tienari, 2002; Vaara & Monin, 2010; Suddaby & Greenwood, 2005). Overall, this interest is understood as part of a more general linguistic turn in social sciences. Discursive analyses of strategy have, for example, increased our comprehension of the role of language in strategy implementation, and opened up new perspectives on strategy: perspectives which we believe are useful for studying strategic communication (c.f. Golsorkhi, Rouleau, Seidl, & Vaara, 2010; Jarzabkowski & Sillince, 2007, Pälli, Vaara, & Sorsa, 2009; Spee & Jarzabkowski, 2011). In line with this, discursive analyses within the field of management have increased our comprehension of specific linguistic phenomena, such as polyphony, which we also believe are useful for studying strategic communication (e.g., Kornberger, Clegg & Carter, 2006).

Many researchers have studied corporate executives' strategic use of frequent and continuous communication efforts to avoid contradictions, paradoxes, inconsistencies and tensions (Putnam & Fairhurst, 2001; Seo & Creed, 2002), Research findings indicated that executives instead create underlying bases and contexts for organizational consensus, unity and commitment (Jarzabkowski & Sillince, 2007; Quinn, 1981; Rapert, Velliquette & Garretson, 2002). At the same time, there seems to be a scholarly consensus that this managerial use of *strategic* communication—understood as the purposeful use of communication by an organization to fulfill its mission (Hallahan et al., 2007)—may inherently contain negatively associated elements of persuasion (Habermas, 2006) or at least some kind of malevolent intent (Foucault, 1984; Lyotard & Thébaud, 1985). This being said, it is far less accurately described by use of linguistic micro-analysis of how a multi-vocal setting, for example, a management team, on some occasions generates instances of polyphony (Kornberger et al., 2006). Consequently, the lack of knowledge within this area may have the potential to maintain an organizational unawareness with regard to elements of power and specific interests, which inevitably surface within communicated messages.

Based on the theoretically generated assumptions above, we intend in this chapter to contribute to a further development of how micro-level, discursive practices may assist in gaining a deeper understanding of strategic communication. On this basis, the focus of this chapter is three-fold. First, we shall study the role of communication in the process of strategy decision-making. Rather than studying communication practice as an organizational function, the focus in the chapter is to study how the presence of multiple viewpoints influences strategy making in upper management teams. Second, until now, strategic communication has been understood at a macro or meso level (c.f. Sandhu, 2009) not taking into consideration micro-level phenomena such as the proposal Kornberger et al. (2006) made on the interrelation of change and language. However, issues do not simply arise, but are defined by certain parties, confined within a certain linguistic frame of reference, and, most powerfully, identified discursively (Kornberger et al., 2006). Hence, the second focus of this chapter is the study of strategic communication at a micro-level in order to deepen our understanding of micro-level phenomena and bridge the micro and the macro. Third and finally, the chapter wants to challenge the inherently persuasive element of management's strategic communication. Organizations (or individuals) who want to alter the behavior of others have four tools at their disposal: physical force, patronage, purchase, or persuasion (Cutlip, Center, & Broom, 1995). The latter involves navigating between and translating heterogeneous discourses (Kornberger et al., 2006) and the use of strategic communication to promote the acceptance of ideas. Thus, persuasion has until now laid at the very center of strategic communication (Hallahan et al., 2007). However, this chapter will show by use of the notion of polyphony "how the existence of multivocality in some occasions potentially represents managerial persuasion" (Belova, King & Sliwa, 2008, p. 496), but how in practice multivocality prevents the acceptance and mutual agreement of the organizational reality.

Applying observation notes and tape recordings of four management team meetings, the chapter empirically investigates communication in management teams through the prism of polyphony. By use of linguistic theory (Nølke et al., 2004) focusing on incidents of polyphony, for example in the form of negations as a linguistic micro-element, the purpose of the chapter is to address the following research question:

How does polyphony occur in the discursive practices by management team members, and what are the implications for the subsequent strategic communication at an organizational level?

By answering this question, we aim to contribute to the ongoing discussion of the possible relevance of studying strategic communication and management teams from a linguistically-based, polyphonic perspective.

The chapter consists of four sections. First, we present the literature on strategic communication, organizational polyphony and ambiguity, arguing that complexity and ambiguity are central to strategic communication. Polyphony is a useful framework for the study of multivocality in the sense that it can be used to reveal different types of hidden interaction and uncover the many voices and discourses that constitute organizations (Hazen, 1993). Managers must navigate between and translate these voices and discourses (Kornberger et al., 2006) in order to fulfill the mission of the organization. Second, the empirical research design and analytic process, that is, polyphony, is explained. Third, we present the empirical findings in two sections:

1. showing how polyphony within a management team shapes the strategy and
2. illustrating how the occurrence of polyphony in the strategy authoring phase has implications for the subsequent communication of the strategy to the employees.

Finally, we discuss the results and their contribution to strategic communication.

Theoretical Background

In this section, we review the literature on strategic communication, organizational polyphony and ambiguity, the purpose being to identify relevant information and place existing research in the context of its contribution to the understanding of organizing and strategizing.

Perspectives on Strategic Communication

Traditionally, strategic communication is defined as "the purposeful use of communication by an organization to fulfill its mission" (Hallahan et al., 2007, p. 3). This definition implies that people will be engaged in deliberate communication practice on behalf of the organization, such as shaping meaning, building trust, creating reputation, and managing symbolic relationships with internal and external stakeholders in order to support organizational growth and secure the freedom to operate (Zerfass, 2004; Grunig, Grunig, & Dozier , 2002). According to traditional management theory, strategic efforts are characterized and evaluated in terms of their economic contribution to the core drivers of success (Deetz, 2001). Hallahan et al. (2007) argue that the term *strategic* in relation to communication in its traditional context privileges a management discourse and emphasizes upper management's goals for the organization as given and legitimate. Hence, strategic communication recognizes that purposeful influence is the fundamental goal of communications by organizations. In this instrumental view, communication is characterized as something managers do to accomplish something else (Conrad & Haynes, 2001, p. 53). However, this perspective also comprises a somewhat naïve recipient who supposes that a description stands for an object in a pure and unmitigated way that not only opens himself up to being deceived or misguided, but also forestalls any chance to trace the misinformation or to counter it (Arminen, 2006, p. 166). Thus, the term *strategic* in terms of communication becomes unavoidably connected to the organizational context and the recipient's interpretation.

In addition to the naïve recipient (Arminen, 2006), this intentionality within strategic communication also requires a purposeful actor, rational and deliberate decision making, and the implementation and evaluation of a strategic communication program (Hallahan et al., 2007, p. 12). However, more and more scholars in strategic management seem to question any such ability of actors to act rationally in a contingent environment (Balogun, 2006; Holtzhausen, 2002; Jenkins, Ambrosini, & Collier, 2007; Pettigrew, Thomas, & Whittington, 2002; Powell, 2002; Pozzebon, 2004; Sandhu, 2009). Thus, Hallahan et al. (2007) deconstruct the term *strategic* to determine whether it necessarily implies manipulative or deviant communication practices or whether it allows for alternative, more critical readings that could provide a home to many different types of scholars. Contrary to the passive and naïve agent described above (Arminen 2006), Giddens (1984) argues that agents have the potential to deliberately and effectively choose and carry out actions in defiance of established rules, and thus Giddens positions the agent as an active person who can navigate the impact of social structure on her or his life. From Giddens's perspective, the communication agent is able to reflexively resist domination and play an active role in shaping the organization through her or his (strategic) communication role in the organization (Hallahan et al., 2007).

Organizational Polyphony

Russian philosopher Mikhail Bakhtin introduced the polyphonic notion and defined the term as the "multiplicity of independent and unmerged voices and consciousnesses …each with equal right and its own world" (Bakhtin, 1984, p. 208). Polyphony in discourse (e.g., Bakhtin, 1981; Goffman, 1981; Klewitz & Couper-Kuhlen, 1999; Kotthoff, 1998) is manifested by the fact that speakers are forever switching into different voices of their own. Hence, the communication model moves away from the simplistic idea of strategic communication as message exchange between sender and receiver (Shannon & Weaver, 1949) to an understanding of communication as a complex, multivocal process.

According to Belova et al. (2008) polyphony can be used as a tool for analysing organizations as discursive spaces shaped by a multiplicity of dominant as well as peripheral voices "which together make up a contested and ever-changing arena of human action" (2008, p. 495). Thus, researchers advocate the application of a polyphonic lens in organization studies in order to understand strategic practice as a multi-centered, non-linear, and intersubjective discursive activity. For example a study on organizational learning by Oswick, Anthony, Keenoy, Mangham, and Grant (2000) suggests how the intertwining of various accounts of reality and complex interpretations constitutes organizational events as polyphonic rather than univocal sense-making. Hence, polyphony assists in viewing organizations as spaces with no universally agreed-upon central voice (Gergen & Whitney, 1996). Far from being an amalgamation of free-will and free-flowing points of view, organizations are constituted by complex webs of sense-making activities between groups and individuals whose understandings intersect, clash and interfere with each other (Hazen, 1993). In the polyphonic view of organizations, there is no overarching meaning of what is going on, but only partial, non-linear, elusive and constantly changing understandings that change depending on one's relation to others. Hence, Carter, Clegg, Hogan & Kornberger (2003) claim the omnipresence of polyphony in organizations even if it is often silenced by dominant voices, stating, "in most organizations, there is a persistent plurality of different linguistic constructions that shape organizational reality" (2003, p. 295).

Kornberger et al. (2006) suggest the various discourses that embody and reinforce differences between disparate groups and members of an organization constitute organizational polyphony.

The role of managers in managing polyphony is to translate these heterogeneous discourses by conveying the message with its context and underlying meanings without having to unify or erase differences that enrich organizational life. This insight is relevant for our study of strategic communication in organizations in the sense that it helps us to delimit crucial communication processes; that is, in our case, the process of strategy translation, which takes place at an organization-wide meeting in which managers convey apparently unclear messages. These unclear messages are a result of underlying meanings in management talk at previous management team meetings.

Ambiguity as a Communicative, Strategic Resource

As stated in the previous section, researchers recognize the unavoidable existence of polyphony or multiple viewpoints in organizations (Eisenberg, 1984). The ambiguity which subsequently arises from these varying viewpoints is often seen as a key dimension in all complex organizations. Weick (2001) argues ambiguity is central to and existent in "all aspects of organizational activity" (p. 44), ranging from formal to informal activities and including all organizational members. In line with this, it has been largely acknowledged in strategy research that ambiguity is a central feature of strategy work (Alvesson & Sveningsson, 2003; Davenport & Leitch, 2005; Jarzabkowski et al., 2010).

Lately there has been an increased awareness of the complexity of ambiguity in organizational communication in general and in strategy research specifically. The complexity entails both its potential for facilitating multiple understandings and its prospective challenge for organizational unity. As Jarzabkowski et al. (2010) put it, "On the one hand, ambiguity is a political resource that might help with generating action. However, ambiguity also enables partial and multiple meanings and interests to proliferate, which obscure action" (p. 221).

The notion of *strategic ambiguity* represents the assumption that ambiguity can be used as a resource within organizational communication. Eisenberg (1984) refers to the concept as "those instances where individuals use ambiguity purposefully to accomplish their goals" (p. 230), thus including an element of strategic intentionality inherent in the traditional notion of strategic communication (Hallahan et al, 2007; Zerfass, 2004; Grunig et al., 2002). Eisenberg (1984) states "there are many situations in which ambiguous communication can be more helpful than clear communication, particularly during periods of rapid change and uncertainty" (p. 230), thus emphasizing that management can use ambiguity intentionally to facilitate multiple understandings of specific activities relevant for the organization.

Davenport and Leitch (2005) follow the understanding of ambiguity as a discursive strategic resource by showing how strategic ambiguity can be a means to delegate authority in organizational discourse. They focus on the role of strategic ambiguity in change processes and show that strategic ambiguity can open up the opportunity for the co-creation of meaning between multiple stakeholder groups. Hence, their study gives insight into how ambiguity can be used strategically in order to enable creative responses from various stakeholders.

Jarzabkowski et al. (2010) also focus on ambiguity as a resource by showing how different strategic actors can use strategic ambiguity as a discursive resource in order to balance individual interests and collective organizational goals. Based on four rhetorical positions, they develop a conceptual framework to explain how strategic ambiguity can be used as a resource for collective action while at the same time facilitating individual interests.

As a response to the prevalent focus on ambiguity as a strategic resource, Giroux (2006) introduces the term *pragmatic ambiguity*. Pragmatic ambiguity seeks to acknowledge that more than one course of action can be the result of a specific initiative. Here, ambiguity is seen as something that can be exploited intentionally, but the notion also acknowledges that not all ambiguity is the outcome of intentional acts. Instead, ambiguity can emerge by itself, in that for example "published texts . . . acquire a life of their own, sometimes far removed from the intention of their authors" (p. 1232). Thus, pragmatic ambiguity acknowledges that several interpretations are inevitable, while at the same time highlighting that numerous interpretations do not necessarily have to challenge collectivity and unity. According to Giroux, "the equivocality of concepts allows for different courses of action while maintaining a semblance of unity" (p. 1232).

The exploration of the strategic potential of ambiguity in strategizing work as such is of minor interest to this chapter. Instead we wish to investigate in detail the role of discourse and communication during a process of strategy formulation for the way different strategizing actors make use of language, and how this language use prevents unity and hence the formulation of monovocal, strategic (intentional) messages to the rest of the organization. By doing so, we hope to contribute new insight into strategic management communication, and, at a more general level, into strategizing as a micro-level discursive practice. The above review shows that several studies in management and organization research have discussed the concepts of polyphony and have shown their importance in understanding organizing and strategizing. However, there is still a lot of unexploited potential in how to apply these concepts, especially in empirical analysis. Despite the fact that the above studies have concerned themselves with the study of language and discourse, the micro-level analysis of discourse has remained an under-researched area. This chapter intends to remedy this by addressing strategizing activities as a micro-level discursive practice.

A Microanalytical Framework for Studying Multivocality

Within the linguistic literature, features of discourse that bring about other texts and other voices, for example reported speech, presupposition, negation, and irony, have been researched for decades and used in discourse analysis. Fairclough (1992), for example, talks about manifest intertextuality and (implicit) intertextuality and interdiscursivity, exemplifying these and other features of discourse related to polyphony. Previous research on dialogue (e.g., Linell, 1998, 2009) also is to a great extent concerned with analysing intertextuality and multivocality.

Nølke et al. (2004) has presented a linguistically-based polyphonic perspective and analytical framework. We will claim that this perspective constitutes a useful framework for studying communication in management teams, in the sense that it helps to identify and describe different types of hidden interaction. It thus uncovers implicit and unclear messages resulting from multivocality in management teams. Whether multivocality in management teams is intentional is not really central to the theory of polyphony. Polyphony is rather seen as a phenomenon that is inherent in all words or forms and in all organizations. Talk by individual managers seems particularly multivoiced in the sense that they must take the voices and arguments of many different stakeholders into consideration, such as, for example, investors, board members, white-collar employees, and blue-collar employees. In the management discourse central to our study, we see that different voices are given the floor, if not explicitly (for example by citing specific stakeholders), then by some distinctive mark signaling polyphony such as negation particles, connectives, and adverbs. These voices may be refuted or accepted in various ways, and they are used in a complex set of controversy strategies and persuasion strategies, with clear elements of strategic ambiguity or "creative unclearness" (Fløttum, 2010, p. 992). According to the linguistically-based polyphonic perspective (Nølke et al., 2004):

> elements from different levels in the linguistic description contribute to the polyphonic structure of an utterance: pronouns, connectives, sentence adverbs, negations, presuppositions, information structures, reported speeches and many more. When the polyphonic structure is identified at an abstract micro-linguistic level, it gives us instructions as regards possible interpretations of

the utterance related to its discursive context, which allows us to talk about different polyphonic configurations.

Fløttum, 2010, p. 993

In our analysis, we intend to identify polyphonic configurations and relate these to the organizational context, which, according to Fløttum (2010, p. 993), is the level of analysis where it is possible to link the abstract linguistically-attested voice to a real person or group of persons.

The polyphonic configuration can be described as a "unit" which consists of four entities (Fløttum, 2010, p. 993):

1. The locuteur-constructor who is responsible for the utterance
2. The point of view (POV), which is a semantic entity, related to a source
3. The discursive beings, which are semantic entities that constitute the sources
4. The enunciative relations, which relate the POV to the discursive beings. There are two main relations: the responsibility relation, which is by far the most important, and the non-responsibility relation of which there are various types, for example argumentative, counter-argumentative, reformulative, refutative.

Figure 11.1 below illustrates the creation of a polyphonic configuration in organizational communication and positions the framework in relation to the traditional, functionalistic way of understanding communication. In our case, each member of the management team we are studying represents such a configuration.

As illustrated in Figure 11.2, the many points of view constitute a challenge to intentional, strategic communication in the sense that they all contribute to the corporate story composed by Common Starting Points (CSP). CSPs are considered as central strategic values that function as the basis for undertaking all kinds of communication by an organization envisages (van Riel, 1995, p. 19). Thus, based on this theoretical viewpoint, the CSPs might seem to be inevitably multivocal and open to many interpretations.

In the following paragraphs, we will show how management talk, which is univocal in form, may have an implicit polyphonic structure in that the individual manager integrates the voices of others. The identification of different voices and their intra- or extra-organizational sources reveals relations between the individual manager and the voices integrated in the manager's own

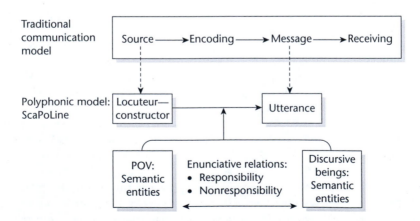

Figure 11.1 The Creation of Polyphonic Configurations

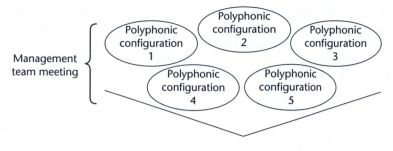

Figure 11.2   The Creation of Multivocal Common Starting Points

message. Identifying such relations is essential to the interpretation of the discourse as a whole and to defining relevant contextual layers (Fløttum & Stenvoll, 2009), for example, organizational layers.

We will limit our presentation to a few examples of markers of polyphony: the negation *not* in its polemical use and the connective *but* in its contrastive use. This selection is justified by the frequent use of these specific two markers in our data.

Research Design

The analysis is based on data extracted from a single-case study of a medium-sized enterprise (Yin, 2009). The enterprise was founded in 1993 and has specialized since 1997 in the private-label production of pet foods. In 2008, the enterprise was divided into two separate Strategic Business Units (SBUs): that is, the enterprise participating in this study (private label) and a separate enterprise (branded business) with limited synergies and collaborations. The company is organized in a functional structure headed by a chief executive officer (CEO) supported by an upper management group. The corporation is owned by a large capital fund, which has clearly voiced its intention to divest the SBUs if and when the price is right.

In the 12-month period in which the authors were in regular contact with the company at various stages of data collection (from first contact to actually collecting data and conducting research), the financial crisis became the major issue both in the public media and in the formal and informal discussions of the management group itself. The degree to which the crisis affected the enterprise and hence how the global recession affected its market situation became a recurrent topic within the upper management group in the period of data collection. Gradually, it became evident that the CEO and what we considered to be the core of the strategic management group (chief operating officer (COO), sales and marketing director, the financial director and HR director) had different opinions about the situation of the company, and the researchers often observed that multiple viewpoints and many voices dominated the meetings. The CEO typically defended the market position, whereas the COO in particular and the sales and marketing director were more skeptical and critical toward this stance. The primary interest of the CEO was how to prepare the company for sale, whereas the primary interest of other people, the COO in particular, in many ways appeared to be more long-term.

Data collection was centered on the development of a new market strategy over a six-month period (July–December, 2009). The empirical evidence for the project was collected by the use of a multi-sited fieldwork methodology, focusing on techniques for doing fieldwork on the move (Czarniawska, 2008; Nadai & Maeder, 2005). Data was collected in the form of participant observations and video recordings from six management team meetings. Moreover, we used participant observations and audio recordings of two organization-wide strategy information meetings to gain insight into the use of strategic communication following the management team meetings. Finally we conducted 12 semi-structured employee interviews to get an indication of the organizational members' reception of the management team's strategic communication.

For the purpose of this chapter, we have selected the most suitable examples to illustrate the role of polyphony in the discourse of the management team members.

Exemplary Analysis: Polyphonic Discourse in Management Teams

The six management team meetings around which our analysis centers could be characterized as basically consensus-oriented and very much dependent on the strategic context; that is, on strategic change and divestment. The meetings were held in July, August and September 2009 and lasted between two and three hours. The CEO, the COO, the sales and marketing director and the HR director participated in all six meetings, whereas the financial director was absent in two meetings. The head of production and the head of supply chain management participated in two of the meetings. The meetings were all held in the context of the financial crisis and at the same time in relation to the issue of divestment.

The topic of the management team meetings was the development and formulation of a strategic business plan where issues such as company history, price, distribution and so forth came up. In this setting, the CEO argued in favor of the success of the company and the management's control over the situation, whereas the COO and the sales and marketing director argued in favor of tackling the challenges in terms of the difficult market situation facing the company.

The organizational situation of divestment and the context of the financial crisis constitute an important background for the interpretation of the polyphonic constructions analyzed below. However, in the following, the emphasis will be on linguistic features. We have selected exemplary passages containing instances of use of the negation *not* and the contrasting and concessive connective *but* as markers of polyphony. The examples with *not* illustrate the polyphony in the CEO's discourse, whereas the examples with *but* illustrate the polyphony in the COO's and the sales and marketing director's discourse. Thus, the analysis reveals the different types of hidden interaction that management team members must navigate between and translate (Kornberger et al., 2006), in this case the hidden interaction in the CEO's discourse versus the hidden interaction in the COO's and sales and marketing director's discourse.

Authoring the Strategy in the Management Team

The CEO's positive perception of the company and control over the corporate situation is clearly present at the management team meetings. This perception is manifested in positive evaluative verbs and verb constructions such as *develop, continue to expand* and *aim at developing:*

1. CEO: *What we can do is to say that we believe that the market for our products will develop and continue to expand, and together with this description, we can say that next year, we aim at developing the market for our products for example in England, and here we need to make an effort.*

    Through the use of the pronoun *we,* the CEO transforms his statement into a polyphonic mix of what seems to be a mainstream top management voice mixed with the voices of the additional management team members, constructing thereby a discursive consensus. We argue that the above exchange can be characterized as "creative unclearness" (Fløttum, 2009, p. 992). For example, what is meant by expressions such as *developing* and *an effort?* And what does it mean that it is *we* who *say that next year, we aim at developing the market* and *we* who *need to make an effort?* Whose voices are actually included in this collective expression? Are all the voices of the management team members for example included?

The COO's and the sales and marketing director's perception of the company contrasts in many ways with the CEO's perception. The perception of the COO is manifested in rather negative evaluative verbs and verb constructions such as "the figures do not lie," "they are not positive" and "if prices go down further."

2. COO: *the figures do not lie . . . trends are important, and they are not positive . . . if prices go down further (interrupted by CEO: we don't know) . . . but if you look over the last three years, prices have gone down . . . discount will be rising . . . much . . . supermarket chains have been hard hit and are now making discount labels.*

The perception of the sales and marketing director (SMD) is manifested in the same type of negative evaluative verbs and verb constructions, for example "it only goes one way [downwards]:"

3. SMD: *it only goes one way on our home market [downwards] . . . we need a breakthrough elsewhere. In this country the market is saturated . . . the market development takes place on the other side of the pond [England].*

The COO's and the sales and marketing director's views on the company are imposed in a more categorical way. Through the use of the pronouns *you* and *we,* they transform their statements into a polyphonic mix of what seems to be an expert's or a market analyst's voice mixed with the voices of the management team, constructing a discursive consensus which points in the opposite direction, the polyphony and the opposite direction being marked by *not* (*the figures do not lie*) and an implicit initial *but.*

In the following, we will show how polyphony can help us to reveal the hidden interaction in the discourse, on one hand the discourse of the CEO and on the other hand the discourse of the COO and the sales and marketing director. In particular, we will show how the individual manager integrates the voices of others in his talk. The identification of different voices and their sources reveals relations (such as refusal or acceptance) between the individual manager and the voices integrated in his talk. Identifying such relations helps us to define relevant contextual layers, such as social, political and organizational, thus bridging the micro and the macro.

Similar to the previous analysis, we will limit our presentation to a few examples of markers of implicit polyphony, the negation *not* (in the discourse of the CEO) and the contrastive connective *but* in its concessive use (in the discourse of the COO and the sales and marketing director). The main issue discussed is the pricing strategy, for example in relation to a coming expansion on the British market. The CEO defends the position that price is not important, whereas the COO and the sales and marketing director defend the opposite position: that is, that price matters and that the market has come under pressure manifested by falling prices over the last years. We will first present the polyphony in the discourse of the CEO:

4. CEO: *Do we know whether it is important for our end users that a product costs eight or nine [currency] or isn't it so that a product is purchased when it is well positioned? You don't need to lower the price that much. We can document that the price is not an important factor.*

The polyphony in this example is marked by *not* and realized as a rebuttal of the implicit point of view: that "price matters." The argument is the following: Price is an important factor for some commodities (private label), but not so important for others. However, by the polyphonic negation, the CEO refutes the insistence on the price as an important factor.

At this point, the sales and marketing director raises an alternative voice to the voice represented by the CEO:

5.   SMD: . . . *but we are regarded as a wholesaler, we don't have the executive sales . . . we must crack the code in Germany, France and England . . . accessibility is our main concern . . . besides, I don't totally agree . . . price and distribution are the most important factors.*

Through the use of the polyphonic marker *but* in its contrastive and concessive capacity, the sales and marketing director takes responsibility for the point of view "but we are regarded as a wholesaler . . . we don't have the executive sales." The connective *but* gives us an instruction about the speaker making the concession that the point of view of the CEO is accepted, but not judged valid in the context and reasoning in question. The valid point of view here is the one presented by the sales and marketing director.

The voice of the sales and marketing director is more or less echoed by the COO:

6.   COO: *If we take a look at the last three years, then the price has been falling.*

Through the use of the pronoun *we,* the COO transforms his statement into a polyphonic mix of what seems to be the voices of the individual management team members, constructing a discursive consensus.

However, the CEO repeats his point of view, presenting it in a somewhat more pedagogical form:

7.   CEO: *It is more fun if we can expand our market . . . it is not relevant to compete on price. What is important is that the product is there . . . it is not like milk . . . there is not a natural need. It is us who create the demand, so theoretically the need is insatiable . . . what we miss is point-of-sales material to give to people.*

The polyphony in this example is marked by *not* (three times) and realized as a rebuttal of the implicit point of view: it is relevant to compete on price. By the polyphonic negation, the CEO once again refutes the insistence on the price as an important factor. In fact, what happened in this phase of the management team meeting was that the CEO closed the discussion about price and market situation, shifting the topic to communication strategy.

The COO and the sales and marketing director seemed to accept this topic shift. However, once again their view is different from the view the CEO presented, which the following statement by the sales and marketing director illustrates:

8.   SMD: *What is the purpose and the message . . . at the kick-off meeting [organization-wide information with all employees], for example . . . is it to convey the organization as picture perfect or is it to say 'this is what we're up against' . . . we've got a business where we have some challenges . . .*

Again, the polyphony is marked by an implicit point of view but followed by the two contrasting points of view, i.e. "the organization as picture perfect" and "this is what we're up against." It is this confrontational statement by the sales and marketing director that leads to the ambiguous or unclear statement by the CEO we saw in example 1:

9.   CEO: *What we can do is to say that we believe that the market for our products will develop and continue to expand, and together with this description, we can say that next year, we aim at developing the market for our products for example in England, and here we need to make an effort.*

Figure 11.3 sums up the above analysis of the various points of view on the pricing strategy. It illustrates the multivocality previous to the creation of the CSPs and the Corporate Sustainable Story formulated by van Riel (1995).

This lack of clarity explains the ambiguity when communicating the strategy to the employees.

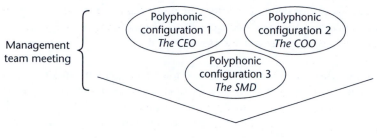

Common Starting Points

Figure 11.3   The Creation of Multivocal Common Starting Points in Management Teams

In the next section we will discuss this notion of ambiguity in light of the occurrences that followed the management team meetings. The purpose of this discussion is to illustrate our argument that polyphony manifests itself at the micro-level, first in the individual manager's discourse and next in the management team's discourse and finally in the communication at the organizational level, which consequently leads to uncertainty and confusion among employees, and ultimately lack of organizational persuasion.

Discussion

Following the six management team meetings, an annual meeting for the entire organization between upper management and the other organizational actors (middle management and employees) was arranged to convey or "translate" the strategic decisions made in relation to future sales and marketing efforts. The purpose of the meeting management formulated was to inform employees about the current situation, the development plans and the strategic goals, to establish and encourage a dialogue between management and employees, and to generate common commitment and corporate spirit across different functions. We consider this translation at the organization-wide meeting to be an exemplary instance of strategic communication in that the communicative focus is on conveying the strategic CSPs formally articulated and agreed upon in the written corporate strategy (the outcome of the line of management team meetings). At the organization-wide meeting the strategy team represented by the CEO, the COO, and the sales and marketing director presented the sales strategy and the market situation to the rest of the organization, including both front and back office employees and middle management, totaling 120 persons.

During his annual presentation on the state of the company, the CEO addressed the company's market situation by reassuring his audience that the organization is unaffected by the global financial crisis:

> What is special about [our company]—we can see it from the financial figures—it's not the financial crisis and things like that which affect us. It's something completely different. It's whether or not it snows during the winter. How many pets are there? Is the pet market developing satisfactorily or not? Because once you've got a dog or cat, then you'll feed them regardless of the financial crisis. In the same way as you feed your children or your grandparents. And if you feed your birds out in the garden, then you continue to do that. Because it doesn't amount to that much money. It's only a small item in the account, and in return you get excellent entertainment. But the unique thing about [our company] is that we are unaffected by the financial crisis . . . .

Subsequently, as can be seen from the following excerpt, the COO states the opposing point of view:

> YES, [the company] has definitely been hit by the global financial crisis—but not as severely as other exporting corporations in [home country]. Many of the products we produce are sold in the UK, and a lot has happened to the British pound.

Knowing what discursively happened during the various management team meetings leading up to the organization-wide meeting, it is not difficult to explain how the communicative inconsistency seems to arise. The two opposing rhetorical positions created by the CEO and the COO, respectively, very much seem to follow the polyphonic patterns of the team meetings, and the common starting point seems to have vanished.

Following the organization-wide meeting, the researchers conducted semi-structured interviews with 12 employees (a sample of 10% of the total organizational members) in order to create an understanding of the subsequent interpretations and sense-making processes occurring when the strategy text was recontextualized into an employee setting. Taking its point of departure in the CEO's rhetorical position of stability and non-crisis, the analysis of the interviews indicated disparate, rhetorical positions such as acceptance, ambiguity and rejection expressed in employee discourse as a way to expose the multivocality present in this third recontextualized setting.

One voice illustrated by the utterance of a non-salaried member of staff working on the production line attached little importance to the strategic and financial situation of the company and supported the discursive position of the CEO, namely, that the organization was unaffected by the global economic crisis. Acceptance of the CEO's translation of the strategic reality revealed a sense of security and trust in the management and the corporate strategic situation: "Oh well . . . the financial crisis is passing. It's a sound company." Another voice represented by a non-salaried member of staff working in the stockroom created a rhetorical position of ambiguity or confusion as he discursively reflected on the strategic initiatives the strategy team members presented:

> 'Well, I thought, 'so our company division will be sold, and the other division will also be demerged,' and my first thought was 'wonder if we will have permanent employment when someone else takes over.' That was my first thought. Afterwards, I talked to the warehouse manager, who has been with the company for 15 years, and he was calm and confident. So I thought, 'oh well, it's going to be all right.'

Hence, the employee expressed a position of uncertainty or ambiguity as to whether or not the external threats would result in a potential risk of being downsized. Finally, a third example of organizational voice constructed a negative discursive position in relation to the consequences of the global financial crisis, using a wavering discourse between a cognitive understanding of the financial situation of the capital fund owners and an emotional insecurity. This position is exemplified in the statement of an office worker in the purchasing department:

> In times like these, when you hear that venture capital funds are generally facing difficulties, and the capital base is no longer what it used to be, they can be forced into taking certain unexpected and unfavorable steps [such as a demerger]. This means that in reality we can suddenly be facing new owners, who might be a large player in the market. And who might want to gain considerable synergies by moving purchasing to for instance Germany, as their purchasing department is located there.

These rhetorical positions represent the multivocal interpretations or sense-making of the employees interviewed, illustrating once again the ambiguous understandings emerging on the basis of the situated context and priorities of each individual. Grounded in their own personal context, some employees might choose to ignore the threat of the financial crisis, preferring to express their interpretation of the strategy in terms of a positive rhetorical position instead. Others might be less averse to risk due to

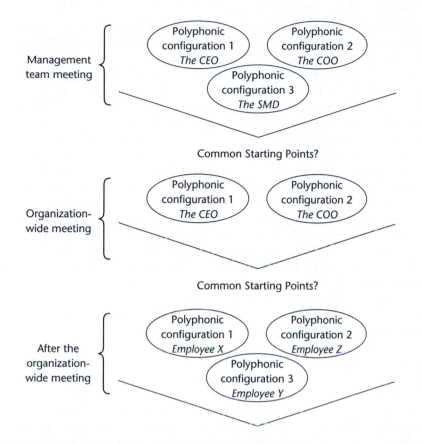

Figure 11.4 The Creation of Polyphonic Common Starting Points

personal characteristics such as a sense of empowerment, self-confidence, or family situation, so these individuals might be more willing to question the various rhetorical positions of management either by rejecting their translations or accepting the ambiguity created throughout the communication process. Consequently, the interpretation phase, in which the members of the organization perceived and interpreted the management's strategic discourse, was characterized by discursively articulated positions of acceptance, ambiguity, disorientation and contradictions—reactions that ultimately might affect the strategy implementation change processes (Lüscher & Lewis, 2008). As Kornberger et al. (2006, p. 13) noted, "issues do not simply arise, but are defined by certain parties, confined within a certain linguistic frame of reference, and, most powerfully, identified discursively." Thus, these examples illustrate how the communicative behavior of organizational actors through the various phases of strategizing are dependent on and influenced by the specific situated context. This results in a multivocal interpretation of strategy, questioning, thus, the intentionality of strategic communication. Using the concept of polyphony it becomes possible to circumscribe strategic management communication as discursive practice not dominated by a single, persuasive discourse, but driven by different discourses.

Figure 11.4 illustrates how polyphony in the various phases of strategizing results in polyphonic CSPs.

Conclusion

Through these few examples, we have tried to show how a micro-level polyphonic approach can contribute to the analysis of strategic management communication. We have also tried to indicate how macro-level organizational approaches might complement a micro-level approach, for example, in the implementation of the concept of CSPs, in order to reach a deeper understanding of the management discourse analyzed.

To conclude, one might ask what could possibly be the relevance of studying strategic communication from a micro-level polyphonic perspective?

From the organizational perspective of this case study, issues such as multiple voices, acceptance or refusal, points of view, and so forth, are interesting. They indicate points of convergence between micro-level and macro-level analyses. However, in order to give a macro-level interpretation of management discourse, micro-level polyphonic analysis needs assistance from broader managerial and organizational perspectives. These will help to determine to whom or what the linguistic sources correspond, for example, a stakeholder or a stakeholder group, or general opinion. This is a necessary step in order to understand "why a specific constellation of voices is put together, a specific content transmitted, or a specific relation between two given points of view presented" (Fløttum, 2010, p. 997). It is also necessary in order to understand the relationship between the utterances and the circumstances in which they appear, in our case change and divestment.

This analysis has integrated the broader perspective of strategic communication, in particular the concept of CSPs (van Riel, 1995). This has helped us to determine that the linguistic sources the CEO, the COO and the sales and marketing director used do not correspond to the same persons or group of persons, in our case different groups of customers. Whereas the COO and the sales and marketing director include for example the voice of discount chains in their discourse, these voices are not included in the discourse of the CEO. Taking into consideration the context of divestment, the personal (and maybe also financial) involvement of the CEO in the divestment and the difficulties of the COO and the sales and marketing director in getting access to, for example, discount chains, help us to understand what is happening in the discussion and, later on, when conveying the result of the discussion to the rest of the organization. Thus, the micro-level polyphonic analysis, conducted in this study combined with contextual information, reveals the multiple voices that are present in management team meetings and demonstrates how the multiple voices result in discrepancies in management team members' organization-wide articulation of the strategic, external context of the corporation. This leads to uncertainty and confusion among employees, and thereby ultimately a lack of organizational persuasion.

Doing so, the analysis queries the automatic association of management communication with inherent elements of strategy and persuasion and contributes both theoretical and empirical knowledge about the role of polyphony for strategic communication. In line with Kornberger et al. (2006, p. 19), the study suggests there is no meta-language or grand narrative that represent the different polyphonic realities accurately. Given that organizations are constituted through different discourses—including the discourse legitimated by top management—no single discourse can be identified that can cope with the complexities emerging from polyphony. Specifically, our analysis has shown how the element of overall intent and/or persuasion in the practice of strategic communication may vanish due to discursive discrepancies in management teams caused by the occurrence of polyphony. Further empirical research is needed within this area to grasp the true nature of polyphony in strategic communication and to advise managers on how to manage this challenge in relation to organizing and strategizing.

References

Alvesson, M., & Sveningsson, S. (2003). Good visions, Bad micro-management and ugly ambiguity: Contradictions of (non-) leadership in a knowledge-intensive organization. *Organization Studies, 24,* 961–988.

Amason, A. (1996). Distinguishing the effects of functional and dysfunctional conflict on strategic decision making: resolving a paradox for top management teams. *Academy of Management Journal, 39,* 123–148.

Arminen, I. (2006). *Institutional Interaction. Studies of Talk at Work.* Aldershot, England: Ashgate.

Bakhtin, M. M. (1981). Discourse in the novel. In C. Emerson & M. Holquist (Eds), *The dialogic imagination* (pp. 259–422). Austin, TX: University of Texas Press.

Bakhtin, M. M. (1984). *Problems of Dostoevsky's poetics* (trans. C. Emerson). Minneapolis, MN: University of Minnesota Press.

Balogun, J. (2006). Managing change: Steering a course between intended strategies and unanticipated outcomes. *Long Range Planning, 39*(1), 29–49.

Belova, O., King, I., & Sliwa, M. (2008). Introduction. Polyphony and organization studies: Mikhail Bakhtin and beyond. *Organization Studies, 29*(4), 493–500.

Carter, C., S. Clegg, J. Hogan, and M. Kornberger (2003). 'The polyphonic spree: The case of the Liverpool Dockers,' *Industrial Relations Journal 34*(4): 290–304.

Conrad, C., & Haynes, J. (2001). Development of key constructs. In F. M. Jablin & L. L. Putnam (Eds), *The new handbook of organizational communication: advances in theory, research, and methods* (pp. 47–77). Thousand Oaks, CA: Sage.

Cutlip, S. M., Center, A. H., & Broom, G. M. (1995). *Effective public relations.* Englewood Cliffs, NJ: Prentice-Hall.

Czarniawska, B. (2008). *Shadowing: and Other Techniques for Doing Fieldwork in Modern Societies.* Malmö: Liber and Copenhagen Business School Press.

Davenport, S., & Leitch, S. (2005). Circuits of power in practice: strategic ambiguity as delegation of authority. *Organization Studies, 26,* 1603–1623.

Deetz, S. (2001). Conceptual foundations. In F.M. Jablin & L.L. Putnam (Eds), *The new handbook of organizational communication. Advances in theory, research, and methods* (pp. 3–46). Thousand Oaks, CA: Sage.

Dooley, R.S., & Fryxell, G.E. (1999). Attaining decision quality and commitment from dissent: the moderating effects of loyalty and competence in strategic decision-making teams. *Academy of Management Journal, 42,* 389–402.

Eisenberg, E.M. (1984). Ambiguity as strategy in organizational communication. *Communication Monographs, 51,* 227–242.

Eisenhardt, K. M., Kahwajy, J. L., & Bourgeois, L. J., III. (1997). Conflict and strategic choice: how top management teams disagree. *California Management Review, 39*(2): 42–62.

Fairclough N., 1992, *Discourse and Social Change.* Polity Press, Cambridge.

Fløttum, K. (2010). EU discourse: polyphony and unclearness. *Journal of Pragmatics, 42,* 990–999.

Fløttum, K., & Stenvoll, D. (2009). Blair speeches in a polyphonic perspective. NOTs and BUTs in visions on Europe. *Journal of Language and Politics 8,* 269–286.

Foucault, M. (1984). What is Enlightenment? In P. Rabinow (Ed.), *The Foucault reader,* pp. 32–50. New York: Pantheon.

Galbraith, J. (1973). *Designing complex organizations.* Reading, MA: Addison-Wesley.

Gergen, K., & Whitney, D. (1996). Technologies of representation in the global corporation: power and polyphony. In D. Boje, R. Gephart, & T. Thatchenkery (Eds), *Postmodern management and organization theory,* pp. 331–357. Thousand Oaks, CA: Sage.

Giddens, A. (1984). *The constitution of society: Outline of the theory of structuration.* Cambridge, MA: Polity Press.

Giroux, H. (2006). 'It was such a handy term': Management fashions and pragmatic ambiguity. *Journal of Management Studies, 43*(6), 1227–1260

Golsorkhi, D., L. Rouleau, D. Seidl & E. Vaara (2010). *Cambridge handbook of strategy in practice,* Cambridge, England: Cambridge University Press.

Goffman, E. (1981). *Forms of talk.* Philadelphia: University of Pennsylvania Press.

Grunig, L. A., Grunig, J. E., & Dozier, D. M. (2002). *Excellent organizations and effective organizations: a study of communication management in three countries.* Mahwah, NJ: Lawrence Erlbaum.

Habermas, J. (2006). Political communication in media society—Does society still enjoy an epistemic dimension? The impact of normative theory on empirical research. *Communication Theory, 16*(4), 411–426.

Hallahan, K., Holtzhausen, D., van Ruler, B., Verc̆ic̆, D., & Sriramesh, K. (2007). Defining strategic communication. *International Journal of Strategic Communication, 1*(1), pp. 3–35.

Hambrick, D.C., & Mason, P.A. (1984). Upper echelons: The organization as a reflection of its top managers. *Academy of Management Review, 9,* 193–206.

Hazen, M. (1993). Towards polyphonic organization. *Journal of Organizational Change Management, 6*(5), 15–26

Hendry, J. (2000). Strategic decision making, discourse, and strategy as social practice. *Journal of Management Studies, 37*(7), pp. 955–977.

Holtzhausen, D. (2002). Towards a postmodern research agenda for public relations. *Public Relations Review, 28*(3), 251–264.

Jarzabkowski, P., Balogun, J., & Seidl, D. (2007). Strategizing: The challenges of a practice perspective. *Human Relations, 60*(1), 5–27.

Jarzabkowski, P., & Seidl, D. (2008). The role of strategy meetings in the social practice of strategy. *Organization Studies, 29* (11), 1391–1426.

Jarzabkowski, P., & Sillince, J. (2007). A rhetoric-in-context approach to building commitment to multiple strategic goals. *Organization Studies, 28*(11), 1639–1665.

Jarzabkowski, P., Sillince, J.A.A., & Shaw, D. (2010). Strategic ambiguity as a rhetorical resource for enabling multiple interests. *Human Relations, 63*(2), 219–248.

Jenkins, M., Ambrosini, V., & Collier, N. (2007). *Advanced strategic management* (2nd ed.). London, England: Palgrave.

Klewitz, G., & Couper-Kuhlen, E. (1999). Quote-unquote? The role of prosody in the contextualization of reported speech sequences. *Interaction and Linguistic Structures, 12,* 1–32.

Kornberger, M., Clegg, S.R., & Carter, C. (2006). Rethinking the polyphonic organization: Managing as discursive practice. *Scandinavian Journal of Management, 22,* 3–30.

Kotthoff, H. (1998). Irony, quotation, and other forms of staged intertextuality: Double or contrastive perspectivation in conversation. *Interaction and Linguistic Structures, 5,* 1–27.

Linell, P. (1998). *Approaching dialogue: talk, interaction and contexts in dialogical perspectives.* Amsterdam: John Benjamins.

Linell, P. (2009). *Rethinking language, mind and world dialogically.* Charlotte, NC: IAP Press.

Love, L. G., Priem, R. L., & Lumpkin, G. T. (2002). Explicitly articulated strategy and firm performance under alternative levels of centralization. *Journal of Management, 28,* 611–627.

Lüscher, L., & Lewis, M. W. (2008). Organizational change and managerial sensemaking: Working through paradox. *Academy of Management Journal, 51*(2), 221–240.

Lyotard, J.F., & Thébaud, J.L. (1985). *Just gaming,* Minneapolis, MN: University of Minnesota Press.

Mintzberg, H. (1973). *The nature of managerial work.* New York: Harper & Row.

Mintzberg, H. (1978). Patterns in strategy formation. *Management Science, 24*(9), 934–948.

Nadai, E., & Maeder, C. (2005). Fuzzy fields. Multi-sited ethnography in sociological research. *Forum: Qualitative Social Research, 6*(3). Retrieved August 1, 2014, from http://www.qualitative-research.net/fqs.

Nølke, H., Fløttum, K., & Norén, C. (2004). *ScaPoLine. La théorie scandinave de la polyphonie linguistique [ScaPoLine. The Scandinavian theory of linguistic polyphony].* Paris, France: Kimé.

Olson, B. J., Parayitam, S., & Bao, Y. (2007). Strategic decision making: the effects of cognitive diversity, conflict, and trust on decision outcomes. *Journal of Management, 33,* 196–222.

Oswick, C., Anthony, P., Keenoy, T., Mangham, I. and Grant, D. (2000), A dialogic analysis of organizational learning. *Journal of Management Studies, 37*(6), 887–901.

Pälli P., Vaara, E. and Sorsa, V. (2009). Strategy as text and discursive practice: A genre-based approach to strategizing in city administration. *Discourse & Communication, 3*(3), 303–318.

Pettigrew, A., Thomas, H., & Whittington, R. (2002). Strategic management: the strengths and limitations of a field. In A. Pettigrew, H. Thomas, & R. Whittington (Eds), *Handbook of strategy and management* (pp. 3–30). London, England: Sage.

Powell, T. C. (2002). The philosophy of strategy. *Strategic Management Journal, 23,* 873–880.

Pozzebon, M. (2004). The influence of a structurationist view on strategic management research. *Journal of Management Studies, 41*(2), 247–272.

Prashantham, S., Bourque, N., Floyd, S. W. & Johnson, G. (2010). The ritualization of strategy workshops. *Organization Studies, 31*(12), 1589–1618.

Putnam, L. L., & Fairhurst, G. T. (2001). Discourse analysis in organizations. Issues and concerns. In F. M. Jablin & L. L. Putnam (Eds), *The new handbook of organizational communication. Advances in theory, research, and methods* (pp. 78–136). Thousand Oaks, CA: Sage.

Quinn, J. B. (1981). Formulating strategy one step at a time. *Journal of Business Strategy, 1*(3), 42–63.

Raes, A.M.L., Heijltjes, M.G., Glunk, U., & Roe, R.A. (2011). The interface of the top management team and middle managers: a process model. *Academy of Management Review, 36*(1), 102–126.

Rapert, M. I., Velliquette, A., & Garretson, J. A. (2002). The strategic implementation process. Evoking strategic consensus through communication. *Journal of Business Research, 55,* 301–310.

Sandhu, S. (2009). Strategic communication: an institutional perspective. *International Journal of Strategic Communication, 3,* 72–92.

Schwarz, M. (2009). Strategy workshops facilitating and constraining strategy making. *Journal of Strategy and Management, 2*(3), pp. 277–287.

Seidl, D., MacIntosh, R.R., & MacLean, D. (2006). Strategy workshops and strategic change: toward a theory of endogenous strategic change. *Munich Business Research Paper,* No. 2006–2007.

Seo, M.G., & Creed, W. E. D. (2002). Institutional contradictions, praxis, and institutional change: a dialectical perspective. *The Academy of Management Review, 27*(2), 222–247.

Shannon, C., & Weaver, W. (1949). *The mathematical theory of communication.* Urbana, IL: University of Illinois Press.

Spee, A. P., & Jarzabkowski, P. (2011). Strategic planning as communicative process. *Organization Studies, 32*(9), 1217–1245.

Suddaby, R., & Greenwood, R. (2005). Rhetorical strategies of legitimacy. *Administrative Science Quarterly, 50,* 35–67.

Tushman, M. L., & Nadler, D. A. (1978). Information processing as an integrating concept in organizational design. *Academy of Management Review, 3,* 613–624.

Vaara, E. (2010). Taking the linguistic turn seriously: strategy as a multifaceted and interdiscursive phenomenon. *The Globalization of Strategy Research. Advances in Strategic management, 27,* 29–50.

Vaara, E., & Monin, P. (2010). A recursive perspective on discursive legitimation and organizational action in mergers and acquisitions. *Organization Science, 21*(1), 3–22.

Vaara, E., & Tienari, J. (2002). Justification, legitimization and naturalization of mergers and acquisitions: A critical discourse analysis of media texts. *Organization, 9*(2), 275–304.

van Riel, C. B. M. (1995). *Principles of corporate communication.* London, England: Prentice Hall.

Weick, K. E. (2001). *Making sense of the organization.* Malden, MA: Blackwell Business.

Yin, R. K. (2009). *Case study research: Design and methods* (4th ed.). Thousand Oaks, CA: Sage.

Zerfass, A. (2004). Unternehmensführung und Öffentlichkeitsarbeit. *Grundlegung einer Theorie der Unternehmenskommunikation und Public Relations* [Business management and the public sphere. *Foundations of a theory of corporate communications and public relations]* (2nd ed.). Wiesbaden, Germany: VS Verlag für Sozialwissenschaften.

12

Strategy as Communicational Practice in Organizations

Marlene Marchiori and Sergio Bulgacov

Communication is well established and recognized in the traditional literature of strategy as a functional mechanism of coordination (Srikanth & Puranam, 2011). This perspective has been involved in economic approaches adopted in studying company strategy. On the other hand, the relatively new phenomenon of the communication and strategy process and the growing complexity of organizational processes offer a context in which to examine a central question in the study of organizations: how communicational practices contribute to the construction of strategic practices. To see why strategy can be understood as a communicational practice and as a concept, this chapter will examine this phenomenon in the Itaipu Technological Park during the period 2008–2010.

The communication process is closely related to the notion that organization is a process of constant creation. Insight into this process can come from examining strategic practices as revealed within organizational environments. People create and modify everyday strategies based upon their interactions, meanings, and thoughts, while inserting new actors, resources, and environments into the process. The contemporary perspective on strategy is that it results from "the dynamics of sense making resulting from quotidian interactions" (Reis, Marchiori, and Casali, 2010, p. 173).

Interaction is a necessary condition for organizational existence (Cooren, 2006). Within the organizational context, strategies' meanings are constructed through the permanent relationships that exist in the organization: between the organization and people, and also by and between the people themselves, from the perspectives of communication and strategy. Organizations are built through interaction and relationships (Cheney, Christensen, Zorn & Ganesh, 2011). People, when learning about a new activity, making a decision, dealing with conflict, forming alliances, effecting change, or dealing with differences, are necessarily creating, stimulating, and developing processes. Furthermore, daily communication practices, the so-called "informal" ones, are the very substance of organizing (Mumby, 2011). "Organizing requires process thinking . . . replace static notions of organization(s) with a vision of continually evolving processes" (Hatch, 2011, p. 96).

Thus, this case study follows a course in which reality is inter-subjective and organizational behavior and strategy are socially constructed. Therefore, communication becomes a fundamental element for the creation, development and practice of strategies, when people interact. In order for the significance and practices revealed to be recognized as fundamental and strategic, it is first necessary that the participants recognize them. This recognition emerges with the consideration that communication is what brings a strategic process to life: "strategy has communication as one of its structural elements; in other words, communication is a constituent element of strategy" (Reis et al.,

2010, p. 169). Taylor and Roubichaud (2004, p. 398) argue "communication plays a key role in both the genesis and accomplishment of an activity, as well as in making sense of it."

It is from an organization's internal and external participants, based upon their capacity for agency, that strategy is constructed. Everyday practices and communication both enable and constrain social action in the sense that they are both created and modified by strategists through the sharing of meaning. In order to participate people need a series of continuous interactions (Stohl & Cheney, 2001) that allow for the construction of meaning. It is this continuity that gives life to the process and reignites in the nature of exchange the spaces for action. Individuals interact through communicative acts. Based upon this, it should be noted that actor agency during communicational processes, as well as during strategic practices, is an important element for analyzing strategic processes when both implementation and interpretation are considered.

In this manner, a strategic practice is conceptualized as a "socially accomplished activity" (Jarzabkowski, Balogun & Seidl, 2007, p. 5). The theoretical contribution of this chapter is to integrate and distinguish among communicational processes and strategy as practice by delving into the contributions of each of these, and empirically presenting the case of the Itaipu Technological Park in Brazil, which incorporated strategy as communicational practice in its communication department. The primary contribution of this study is to reveal and define the communicational practices that make up strategic practices at different organizational levels. In this matter, this study's question is how communicational practices contribute to the construction of strategic practices. Our goal is to enhance understanding of strategy as communicational practice as a concept that reveals that communication is constitutive of strategic practice, due to its procedural and interactive nature, in the reality of a Technological Park.

Specifically, the research objective is to reveal how communicational practices established and comprised the strategic practices of the Itaipu Technological Park during the period 2008–2010. It seeks to understand the communicational practices within a field of dialogue in which the coexisting strategists foment the creation and recreation of dynamic strategy. We shall start by discussing the concepts of strategy as practice and communication, and then delve into strategy as communicational practice before addressing the ways in which communication is part of strategy construction. The case study brings these ideas together by displaying the structure of organizational communication and changes in activities through interactional processes. Finally, a conclusion provides closure and encourages reflection on the possibilities for a future agenda of research in strategy as communicational practice.

Theoretical Foundation

Strategy as Practice and Communication

Whittington (2006) suggests that special attention must be given to participants in any given strategy's participants, as well as to the development of processes and practices. This in turn requires the examination of an organization within its own internal and external environments. Such context suggests to the field of study of strategy the idea that practices, through the involvement of people, become the main basis of organizational actions. This precludes the organization and actor-agents from being examined in isolation.

Organizational practices are understood as a process for constructing reality by means of social interaction in which micro-activities are essential (Whittington, 1996, 2004, 2006; Jarzabkowski, 2005; Haag, Helin & Melin, 2006; Spee & Jarzabkowski, 2008; Canhada, 2009). McAuley, Duberley, and Johnson (2007, p. 39) summarize this accurately: "What we perceive is a process in which we are active participants, not neutral receivers or passive observers. " For Jarzabkowski et al. (2007) there are three mandatory dimensions for understanding the approach of strategy as practice: praxis (the flow of socially performed activities), practices (cognitive, behavioral, discursive motivational and physical practices) and practitioners (actors who shape the construction of such practice by who they are, how they act and the resources they use). *Strategizing* takes place with the convergence of these three dimensions.

Organizations exist so that people may perform activities they would not perform alone (Hall, 2004). People, therefore, construct organizational reality and strategy through social interaction. This requires the consideration of communication as a constitutive process of that reality, which means moving beyond conceiving communication as a mere organizational process (Putnam & Nicotera, 2009). Communication is a fundamental process for the construction of strategy. It is a formative process that can challenge people's knowledge and it is the main process for individuals to build strategies through interaction. Communication therefore contributes to strategizing beyond finding ways to practice strategy. Strategy is then seen as something people do; that is, "a social practice and not only a property of the organization" (Bulgacov & Marchiori, 2010, p. 150). Strategy as a social practice implies the need to view it as a daily activity, and not as an eventual outcome (Reis et al., 2010, p. 273). Spee and Jarzabkowski (2008) suggest that by taking into account all of the participating actors, strategy can be seen as developing from routine practices. Activities may be understood through examining an organization's formal documents, such as written texts, planning practices, or messages, among others. Added to this emerging process of strategy development is the involvement of multiple actors from diverse organizational levels both inside and outside the organization (Johnson, Langley, Melin & Whittington, 2007).

As for the organizational change stemming from the involvement of people, emphasis is given to the quotidian: habitual activities, relationships, learning, knowledge exchange, discussions, dialogue, conflicts and interactions. In Johnson et al. (2007) the relevance of small interactions between people makes strategies potentially effective. According to Cheney et al. (2011), organizations' realities are actively constructed, dynamic, fluid and unstable. As people become more involved, they have a natural tendency to understand their own actions better, which enables the growth and exchange of knowledge in an organization. The strategic process takes place when people put into practice what they had in mind; in other words, the process is not complete if there is no practice. Practice is experienced through an organization's daily activities. These ideas embrace strategy as a practice made up of "interaction (communicational) between people" (Spee & Jarzabkowski, 2008).

Strategy as Communicational Practice

Based upon the works of Berger and Luckmann (1966/2003), Geertz (2008) and Giddens (2003), Canhada (2009) suggests that how stakeholders influence the development of strategy can be used as a paradigm to understand the perspective of strategy as a social practice from a predominately interpretative and social constructivist perspective. Social construction is concerned with how people produce meaning from their contexts (Westwood & Clegg, 2003). The process of constructing meaning can also be seen as a social activity (Gergen & Warhus, 2001). Interlocutors develop and stimulate knowledge, information and significance by interacting within an organization (Taylor & Van Every, 2000).

Thus, the organizational social reality and the strategy itself are two dependent aspects in constant association that are constructed through constant transition between the material world and the objectivity of the human conscience (Bulgacov & Marchiori, 2010). For these authors, the human interpretation individuals make occurs in a continuous movement as the subjective perception of reality takes place. During such movement, people lead themselves into social relationships in which they take part in the construction of meanings held in common. These common meanings, intermediated by language and communication, perpetuate and develop their knowledge and practices, and form what we conceive as human culture (Geertz, 2008). Therefore, Canhada (2009) understands that models of strategy can be seen as a symbolic system that conditions social practices mediated by language and human interpretation. The author also suggests that this is a crucial key for understanding why strategy, as a practice, validates the dominant discourses, models and strategic tools, as well as the interpretations the actors give of themselves and of their use in practice. The new interpretations that arise from the processes of interaction among interlocutors and that are rearranged in the organizational context as they create meanings, are part of this context.

Therefore, it can be assumed that a communicational practice, due to its procedural and interactive nature, constitutes strategic practice. It must be noted that this communication–strategy relationship is essentially dependent on the interlocution held by and between those involved with the process. Strategy as a practice is a translation of such a reality once it is understood to take place in micro activities. Strategies are essentially processes of interaction and construction of meaning whose expressiveness comes from communication and language. As a process, communication has its own momentum, and once it becomes a continuous process it cannot have a defined beginning, middle or end (Marchiori, 2010). Communication processes emerge and are made multi-dimensional and multi-directional due to differences of interests found in organizational contexts. Thus, it is fundamental that these differences be observed in contemporary society as this dynamic allows strategy to be seen as a practice, as "the opposite meaning of production of already crystallized meanings" (Pinto, 2008, p. 88), which highlights the differences of organizations and makes them essentially unique.

Therefore, the main argument is that communication is constituted by strategic processes and contexts. Organizational practices that take place in and by communication are a "generating source of knowledge" (Gherardi, 2009, p. 115), and are a type of active knowledge that constitutes knowledge in practice itself.

Research

This study follows an inductive and unique case study (Yin, 2003, p. 27) on strategy and communication practices. The Itaipu Technological Park was a particularly suitable organization for a case study because its key strategic decision makers could be interviewed, and organizational practices observed, during decision-making activities. The other aspect that makes the case interesting is the nature of the Technological Park itself. Created in 2003 by Itaipu Binacional, the biggest hydraulic power plant company from Brazil, the Parque Tecnológico Itaipu (PTI) has the mission of understanding and transforming the reality of the Iguassu Tri-National Region: Argentina, Brazil and Paraguay. It does so by articulating and fostering actions oriented towards the region's economic, scientific and technological development, all with a focus on solutions related to water, energy, and tourism through several integrated organizations such as university extensions and laboratories

Located in the former quarters of the workers who built the Itaipu Plant, PTI is an innovative setting for work in the fields of education, science, technology and entrepreneurship. Being part of the world's largest hydroelectric plant in terms of power generation, Itaipu also counts on the accumulation of know-how acquired over two decades of plant operations.

PTI is oriented toward the generation and distribution of knowledge at all levels in order to promote scientific and technological development and to generate employment opportunities and revenue. Actions are implemented by way of four programs: PTI Education, PTI Science & Technology, PTI Research & Development, and PTI Entrepreneurship. From this inception, the communications department perceived the need to expand the portfolio of activities and did not restrict themselves to events organization or public relations. Communication managers decided to construct a strategic plan for communication that could widen their field of action. The work was initially focused on complete and detailed knowledge about PTI, its strategic plan, and the structure of its projects. This process was the primary focus for this study, which investigated each step in the decision-making process and their respective implementation.

The research was conducted in three phases. The first consisted of document analysis of secondary data. The second involved field observation and in-depth interviews. There were 50 in-depth interviews of all of the organization's managers, including directors, managers and area assistants, as well as PTI program and project managers and communication team members. Having good relations with the managers and executives, the interviews were conducted in all of the organizations represented in the Park and the entirety of the communication department group and were conducted privately and regularly during a three-month period. Content analysis (Triviños, 1987) was used to treat the data. The third phase was used to triangulate all of the data in order to provide for objectivity, adequacy and validation.

In order to establish a reference for analysis, the research sought to observe any practices that emerged or were modified, as well as identify involved parties. The entrance and exit of new participants were seen to bring new elements of understanding of meanings to individuals and the group. These elements justified actions, as well as practices that were of interest to the involved group. Special attention was paid to individuals with greater power and to any events that instigated change. While observing the different sources of influence on practices, no clear rules for dynamics between individuals were either observed or established. Another methodological aspect uncovered during the first observations was that the communication process observed was multilevel due to the fact that the regulative aspects existed at international, national, regional, local, and organizational levels. The organization is also still in the process of defining its roles. However, greater emphasis was placed upon the regional and organizational levels.

Findings

The processes and the practices inherent in the communication department's proposal that the strategic managers made were based on strengthening and developing four structuring programs at PTI: science and technology, entrepreneurship, research and development, and education. The Itaipu Binational Tourist Complex was also a consideration. The proposal took into account a comprehensive discussion with the communication team about the steps to be taken towards empowering the team of eight participants at different hierarchical levels. As three veteran managers who dealt frequently with communication practices noted:

> We do not have a communication plan. We are trying to build it. We are building a bridge to foster new practices and mechanisms of communication. The newspaper for instance is great, the speech is clear and oriented to people in general.

> Communication practices is not the exclusive responsibility of the department of communication. The programs and projects have to be in the vein of everyone.

> We have to say it. The actual practices of communication are a way behind the strategic plan of PTI. The PTI Communication Plan has to understand the PTI dynamic and its velocity of change.

Workplace culture favored an attitude of team intimacy and motivation for conversation, awareness of points of views, the thinking process and exchange of ideas so as to have group members improve in terms of knowledge of their own field and of PTI as a whole. As the communication management team observed: "Communication has to be seen as a whole for the organization. This will be represented by the speeches, expressions and instruments of communication, practices in general, and mainly by the maturity of the communication team."

At the same time interviews revealed that the managers' understanding of communication was similar to what the team thought of it; that is, something more than just organizing events. They also understood that such an expectation demanded more than just background work; it required the development of different projects and programs. The following outcomes of communicational processes that developed organizational strategy were observed: a guide for dealing with stakeholders; empowerment of PTI's identity and image; PTI's institutionalization at regional, state and national levels; and further strategic communication measures.

Next, a proposal was made to establish PTI's communicational behavior. For this purpose, its mission, vision and objectives were carefully designed. PTI's communication mission, after several group meetings, was described thus:

> To articulate and support communication in public relationship networks, stimulating knowledge about and development of PTI. The vision: To be a sustainable entity acknowledged by the public through the communicational dynamic of PTI's actors. The following objectives materialized: to facilitate the communicational process among structuring programs, their projects and strategic partners, and expand the understanding of Park residents; to articulate and support PTI's internal, institutional, and public communication processes and practices; to develop relationships that may widen the understanding of PTI as a model Technological Park; to expand the relationships between ITAIPU and PTI over all work areas within the Park; and to strengthen the organizational identity, contributing to the solidification of PTI's image and reputation.

In addition to these perspectives, it was deemed necessary that the communication structure follow the same path of PTI's own structure, based upon defined projects. Therefore, the communications team, after considering which programs could lend support to the numerous PTI projects, decided that the following programs were the most imperative: "to inform and communicate with the public; to develop and manage internal and external relationships; and to approach and listen to stakeholders."

As shown in Figure 12.1 the proposed structure—developed, discussed, and defined by PTI managers and employees—gave the communication team flexibility in terms of creativity and attitude, thus providing more possibilities for action. The proposed structure was not fixed and limited within the traditional areas of communication, such as journalism, public relations, and propaganda, but changed depending upon the priorities of actions to be placed into practice by the group. This certainly promoted a continuous exchange between the areas and the further maturation of the team, the processes, and the practices that emerged or were practiced at PTI. This perspective is believed to be an innovative structure within organizational studies of communication.

The strategic guide focused on three pillars: internal communication, external communication, and stimulating relationship networks, as it would be fundamental for PTI to expand together with the stakeholders, as seen in Figure 12.2.

From that point on, the creation of strategies involved strategic thinking as practiced by the team. The strategies and scope as related to the stakeholders were then defined, as seen in Figure 12.3.

The whole proposal was central to rethinking communication as a strategic component for organizational development. For the final phase of the elaboration of the strategic planning of communication, the team worked on the creation of indicators of PTI's attitude toward the objectives being measured at three levels of achievements.

Discussion

The data concerning change show that the stakeholders and their practices have a significant influence over communicational processes as they further their own understanding of strategy-making in the institution. Based on the theoretical approach, the empirical data reveal that communication

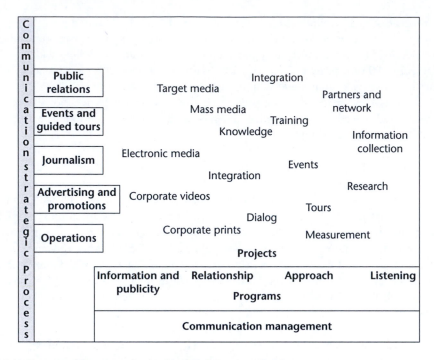

Figure 12.1 Proposed Structure for Institutional Communication

Authors' own work (reproduced with permission from Daniela Veronesi of Parque Tecnologico ITAIPU—PTI)

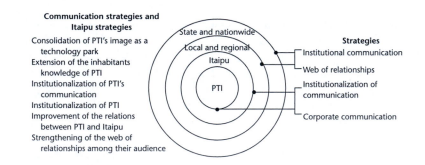

Figure 12.2 Spheres of Influence

Authors' own work (reproduced with permission from Daniela Veronesi of Parque Tecnologico ITAIPU—PTI)

management, as in the case of PTI, has been following contemporary trends from the field and stimulating processes for the interaction of strategic practices, as shown in the report and analysis presented here.

The constructivist perspective provokes the subjective construction of interpretations and understandings; something that happens naturally at PTI. Both instances of a social reality that its actors constructed were corroborated by a constant and dependent relationship between the organizational strategic reality and the subjectivity of interpretation and human values. Marchiori, Contani, and Buzzanell (2011, p. 18) suggest that "success in strategic interaction guided by dialogic principles means that humans can engage in processes of relevantly relating to others." We can see that these processes involve interaction and also construction of meaning.

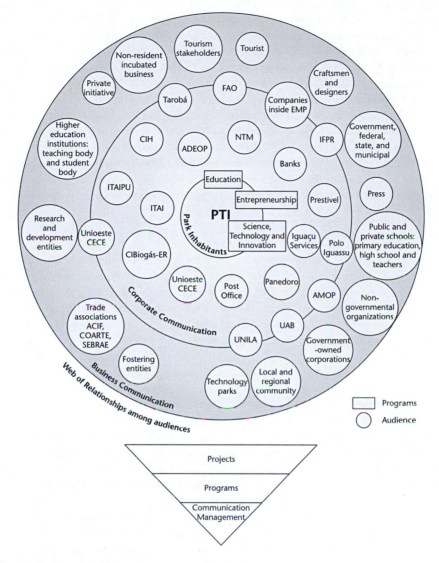

Figure 12.3   Stakeholders Mapping

Authors' own work (reproduced with permission from Daniela Veronesi of Parque Tecnologico ITAIPU—PTI)

The common meanings the team constructed were mediated by concepts collectively structured through the means of language and communication. Interviews provided evidence of shared senses, naturally attributed by the individuals to the interpreted reality. In PTI's organizational environment, one can see collectively operated values and meanings both in the routine activities and in the constitution of activities for the transmission of institutional purposes and practices.

It is important to highlight that the communication process at PTI is diversified, with different logics for action, but with a shared, significant and inter–subjective communication process constructed so that all participants have the same opportunity for action and interaction. As such, when also considering the theoretical approaches included in this chapter, it was observed that the construction of shared meaning through the communication process offers a common workspace for relatively individualized knowledge which in some ways hinders collective action. It isn't part of the participants' logic. The collective action of constructing strategic meaning can be identified as a result of dynamic communication. What emerges is that some aspects of understanding strategic and communicational processes are maintained, others are modified, and different references emerge in the context under analysis.

This study provides evidence of changes in people's behavior and as such it means that strategic practice, through interaction, brings about reflection and expands the knowledge and innovation capacity of those individuals who naturally foster communities of practice (Wenger, 1993). The greatest contribution lies in the communicational practices revealed in the *strategizing,* when the interlocutors produce and share sense making in a process marked by interaction and by the social-historical context (Maia and França, 2003). This interpretation could be used also in relation to the concept of communication as an organization process. Varey (2006, p. 194) conceives communication as acts of interaction and not as objects and artefacts. Interaction cannot be seen as an information process but as a process for the "construction and negotiation of meanings (a communication process)."

Conclusion

The purpose of this work is to describe and define the communicational practices that make up strategic practice at different levels. We have sought to reveal how communicational practices have influenced strategic practices at Itaipu Technological Park, specifically during the years 2008–2010. Our work was based in theory with the rationale of understanding communicational practices within the field of dialogue in which a coexistence of and with strategists allows the creation and recreation of a dynamic strategy. It understands that communication is a process of interaction and the negotiation of meanings.

The research was oriented towards the premise that the dynamic between communication and strategy is recursive. Inter-subjectivity could be observed through strategic practices consolidated by means of communication, building strategic senses developed and modified during the study. This study suggests that strategy as practice is revealed in communicational practices that construct meaning between different interlocutors, making these subjects practice processes they created and that certainly contribute to the existence of numerous and diverse environments, with meanings specific to those involved in their relationships. Looking at strategy as a communicational practice reveals that the contexts, history and interactive dynamics constitute the environments and meanings for these interlocutors, establishing the existence of diverse organizations in contemporary society. Therefore, the construction and negotiation of meaning is an interaction, understood by Varey (2006) as a communicational process and not as an information process.

The data concerning change show that the stakeholders and their practices have a significant influence over communicational processes as they further their own understanding of strategy-making in the institution. In the study, this was verified when, each time a participant entered or exited an event, the altered communicational conditions required a new understanding of what was happening, often resulting in modification of strategies, as was the case for defining external participants, as seen in Figure 12.2.

In this manner the team built common meanings intermediated by concepts that were collectively structured by language and communication. It is therefore confirmed that the socially constructed communication practices legitimated and institutionalized strategic practices based upon social interaction.

This study also revealed changes in people's behavior. A strategic practice that is part of the process of interaction brings about reflection and expands the knowledge and innovation capacity of those individuals who naturally foster "communities of practice" (Wenger, 1993). The greatest contribution lies in the communicational practices revealed in the *strategizing,* when the interlocutors produce and share senses in a process marked by interaction and social-historical context

(Maia & França, 2003). This emphasizes the importance of micro-actions and activities that happen day-by-day, minute-by-minute inside organizations, in which "human actors shape activity in ways that are consequential for strategic outcomes" (Jarzabkowski et al., 2007).

New research opportunities that take our findings into consideration might start by mapping organizational practices based upon pre-existing meanings, in order to verify how changes in communicational processes interfere with these meanings. Another aspect that might guide future research regards the differences between strategic practices and their communicational precursors. Future studies might develop multi-level, quantitative methods to analyze the positioning of communicational properties at different organizational levels, in order to verify and deepen understanding of those that relate to more stable strategies.

References

Berger, P. & Luckmann, T. (2003). *A Construção Social da Realidade*. [The social construction of reality]. (F. Fernandes, Trans.) Petrópolis: EditoraVozes. (Original work published in 1966).

Bulgacov, S. & Marchiori, M. (2010). Estratégia como prática: a construção de uma realidade social em processos de interação organizacional. [Strategy as practice: the construction of a social reality in processes of organization interaction]. In M. Marchiori . (Org) *Comunicação e Organização:* reflexões, processos e práticas (pp. 149–165). São Caetano, SP: Difusão Editora.

Canhada, D. I. D. (2009). Estratégia como prática social e resultados acadêmicos: o doutorado em administração no Brasil [Strategy as social practice and academic results: the doctoral course of administration in Brazil]. Master's thesis. Programa de Mestrado e Doutorado em Administração, Universidade Federal do Paraná, Curitiba, Brazil.

Cheney, G., Christensen, L.T. , Zorn, T.,Jr. , & Ganesh, S. (2011). *Organizational communication in an age of globalization: Issues, reflections, practices* (2nd ed.). Long Grove, IL: Waveland.

Cooren, F. (2006). Arguments for the in-depth study of organizational interactions: a rejoinder to McPhee, Myers, and Trethewey. *Management Communication Quarterly, 19,* 327–340.

Geertz, C. (2008). *A interpretação das culturas* [The interpretation of cultures]. Rio de Janeiro: LTC Editora.

Gergen, K. J. & Warhus, L. (2001). Therapy as social construction. In K. J. Gergen (Ed.), *Social constructions in context* (pp. 96–114). London, UK: Sage.

Gherardi, S. (2009). Introduction: the critical power of the 'practice lens.' *Management Learning, 40*(12), 115–128.

Giddens, A. (2003). *A constituição da sociedade. [The constitution of society].* São Paulo: Martins Fontes.

Hall, R. (2004). *Organização:* estruturas, processos e resultados [*Organization:* structures, processes and outcomes]. (8th. ed.), R. Galman, Trans.) São Paulo, SP: Prentice Hall.

Haag, K., Helin, J., & Melin, L. (2006, July). Practices of communication in the strategic context of succession. Paper presented at the 22nd European Group for Organizational Studies (EGOS) Colloquium, Bergen, Norway.

Hatch, Mary Jo. (2011). *Organizations: a very short introduction.* New York: Oxford University Press.

Jarzabkowski, P. (2005). *Strategy as practice: an activity-based approach.* Thousand Oaks, CA: Sage.

Jarzabkowski, P. , Balogun, J. ,& Seidl, D. (2007). *Strategizing:* the challenges of a practice perspective. *Human Relations, 60*(1), 5–27.

Johnson, G., Langley, A., Melin, L., & Whittington, R. (2007*). Strategy as practice: Research directions and resources.* Cambridge: Cambridge University Press.

McAuley, J., Duberley, J., & Johnson, P. (2007). *Organization theory: Challenges and perspectives.* Harlow, England: Pearson Education.

Maia, R. C., & França, V. (2003). A comunidade e a conformação de uma abordagem comunicacional dos fenômenos. [Community and the conformation of a communicational approach of events.]. In M. Lopes (Ed.), *Epistemologia da comunicação* (pp. 187–203). São Paulo, SP: Loyola.

Marchiori, M. (2010, September). Reflexões iniciais sobre a comunicação como processo nas organizações da contemporaneidade [Initial reflections on communication as a process in contemporary organizations]. Paper presented to the XXXIII Congresso brasileiro de Ciências da Comunicação (INTERCOM 2010), Caxias do Sul, Brasil.

Marchiori, M. R., Contani, M. L., & Buzzanell, P. M. (2011, April). *Dialogue as a possibility for knowledge in organizations.* Paper presented to the 13th Conference, Dialogue and Representation (IADA 2011), Quebec, Canada.

Mumby, D. K. (2011). *Reframing difference in organizational communication studies: Research, pedagogy, practice*. Thousand Oaks, CA: Sage Publications.

Pinto, J. (2008). Comunicação organizacional ou comunicação no contexto das organizações? [Organizational communication or communication in the context of organizations?]. In R. Ivone, L. Soares, & Ana T. Nogueira (Eds), *Interfaces e tendências da comunicação no contexto das organizações* (pp. 81–90). São Caetano, SP: Difusão Editora.

Putnam, L. L. & Nicotera, A. M. (Eds) (2009). *Building theories of organization: the constitutive role of communication*. New York: Routledge.

Reis, M. C., Marchiori, M., Casali, A. M. (2010). A relação comunicação estratégia no contexto das práticas organizacionais [The relation between communication and strategy in the context of organizational practices). In M. Marchiori (Org). *Comunicação e Organização:* reflexões, processos e práticas (pp. 165–187). São Caetano, SP: Difusão Editora.

Spee, A. P. & Jarzabkowski, P. (2008, July). Strategy formation as communicative process. Paper presented at the 24th EGOS Colloquium, Amsterdam, Holland.

Srikanth, K. & Puranam, P. (2011, August) Integrating distributed work: comparing task design, communication, and tacit coordination mechanisms. *Strategic Management Journal, 32*(8), 849–875.

Stohl, C. & Cheney, G. (2001). Participatory processes/paradoxical practices: communication and the dilemmas of organizational democracy. *Management Communication* Quarterly, *14,* 349–407.

Taylor, J. R., & Roubichaud, D. (2004). Finding the organization in the communication: discourse as action and sensemaking. *Organization,11,* 395–413.

Taylor, J. R., & Van Every, E. J. (2000). *The emergent organization: communication as its site and surface*. Mahwah, NJ: Lawrence Erlbaum.

Triviños, A. N. S. (1987). *Introdução à pesquisa em ciências sociais [Introduction to social research]*. São Paulo, SP: Atlas.

Varey, R. J. (2006). Accounts in interactions: implications of accounting practices for managing. In F. Cooren, J. R. Taylor, & E. J. V. Every (Eds.), *Communication as organizing: Empirical and theoretical explorations in the dynamic of text and conversation* (pp. 181–196). Mahwah, NJ: Lawrence Erlbaum.

Wenger, E. (1993) *Communities of practice: learning, meaning and identity*. Cambridge, MA: Cambridge University Press.

Westwood, R., & Clegg, S. (2003). *Debating organization: point-counterpoint in organization studies*. Oxford, UK: Blackwell Publishing.

Whittington, R. (1996). Strategy as practice. *Long Range Planning, 29*(5), 731–735.

Whittington, R. (2004). Estratégia após o modernismo: Recuperando a prática. *ERA - Revista de Administração de Empresas, 44*(4), 44-53.

Whittington, R. (2006). Completing the practice turn in strategy research. *Organization Studies, 25,* 613-634.

Yin, R. K. (2003). *Estudo de Caso:* planejamento e métodos *(Case study: planning and methods)*. (2nd ed.). Porto Alegre, RS: Bookman.

13

Good Governance and Strategic Communication

A Communication Capital Approach[1]

Patricia Riley, Gail Fann Thomas, Rebecca Weintraub, Allison Noyes, and Stephanie Dixon

---

What the eye does not see, the heart does not grieve about. Old English Proverb[2]

Good governance is a critical component in attaining human development, poverty reduction and peace-building in less developed countries (United Nations' Millennium Declaration, 2000). Good governance reform movements, where the goal is to build the capacity of both citizens and governments to work jointly for reforms that will improve the livelihoods of citizens, are becoming more prominent around the world. When used in the context of good governance, the concept of strategic communication encompasses the actors, organizations, infrastructure and systems that are necessary to ensure "a two-way flow of information and ideas between the government and the citizenry" (Mozammel & Odugbemi, 2005, p. 9).

As policymaking and security become more complex, typically, governance is defined in terms of the *actions and outcomes* considered necessary to promote and spread it.

> Good governance is effective, equitable and promotes rule of law. It also ensures that political, social and economic priorities are based on broad consensus in society and that the voices of the poorest and the most vulnerable are heard in decision-making over the allocation of development resources.
>
> *UNDP, n.d.*

This perspective often views governance as dependent on positive, sustainable, open relationships between government agencies and NGOs or CSOs (civil society organizations) as well as private sector organizations, and a knowledgeable public who can actively participate in their own governance.

As a process, strategic communication fosters support for governance reform by influencing opinion, attitude, and behavior change among leaders and policymakers (political will), mid-level bureaucrats (organizational will), and citizens (public will) (Odugbemi, 2010). Thus critical communication pathways are constituted between individuals, organizations and institutions, large and small, such as dialogue between government organizations and community groups or collaborations between information rights organizations and the media. Although the language is optimistic, this space is necessarily conflicted and problematic both practically and theoretically.

Strategic communication has been defined as "communication that is aligned with a company's overall strategy to improve its strategic positioning" (Argenti, Howell & Beck, 2005). Strategic communication has also been examined by researchers focusing on communicative practices in areas such as public relations (Waters & Lemanski, 2011), political campaigns (Holbert & Geidner, 2009), military campaigns and issues (Ward, 2011), and corporate marketing (Kitchen, Brignell, Li, & Jones, 2004). This practice-oriented approach to communication has been critiqued by scholars such as Deetz (2001) for being in the service of the managerial class at the expense of other organizational constituencies, and Habermas (1979) for its sometimes manipulative and non-transparent purposes. More recently, however, the concept of strategic communication has been conceived as neither inherently good nor bad, especially as the practice has become commonplace in agencies and organizations focused on the public good (e.g., Faccinetti, 2004). Research in this arena ranges from traditionally focused marketing-style campaign assessments to much larger projects that rigorously investigate the actors, actions and interpenetrating systems for their values, implementation practices and outcomes as well as other concerns (Hallahan, Holtzhausen, van Ruler, Verčič & Sriramesh, 2007).

Other constituencies that have begun to explore strategic communication include civil society groups and international development organizations (c.f. Botan & Taylor, 2005; Durán-Bravo & Fernández-Fuentes, 2010). Organizations involved in issues such as poverty reduction, health outcomes and good governance are currently creating new approaches to strategic communication as it is practiced and researched. This community retains the purposive connotation of strategic communication, but these scholar–practitioners are less focused on the communication of a particular organization and more concerned with engaging multiple organizations—large and small—to improve specified outcomes. This perspective creates a much larger framework for implementation than may be traditionally understood, and requires a new model for analysis.

Theoretical Framework

The strategic communication framework we use for good governance is a process that connects agency with institutions and mediated communication to produce both individual and collective action. Institutions in this sense are considered to be instantiated in communication practices (McPhee & Zaug, 2009; Putnam & Nicotera, 2009). This view, sometimes referred to as communication-as-constitutive, posits that communication generates the realities of organizations such as culture, power, networks, and the structure-agency relation (Ashcraft, Kuhn, & Cooren, 2009; Banks & Riley, 2006; Eisenberg & Riley, 2000). This conception of strategic communication is informed by Giddens's (1984) action theory perspective where human agency and social structure are not seen as two separate concepts or constructs, but as *duality of structure*. His analytical tool, structuration, explores the ways in which social systems are produced and reproduced through communication in social interaction. By positioning strategic communication within structuration theory, we are using a theoretical lens that is grounded in human interaction, focuses on the interpenetration of multiple systems, takes it as given that the complexity of systems of action often results in contradictions and unintended consequences, believes in the agency of actors, and features an ability to transcend time and space in human communication (Giddens, 1991; Poole, Seibold and McPhee, 1985; Riley, 1983).

The varying uses of structuration concepts have been innovative and demonstrate its expansive and elastic nature.[3] Subsequent to the development of structuration theory, Giddens (1991) elaborated on the social conditions of late modern society and focused on social constructs that are brought into relief in a rapidly changing, mass mediated, economically interdependent and networked world. Issues such as identity, security, skills, politics, and ecosystems all play a role in diverse but intersecting landscapes in Giddens's desire for a progressive life world (an agent-centered social philosophy somewhat analogous to Habermas's public sphere). Thus Giddens's work offers significant guidelines for a framework that sees strategic communication as a set of key constructs bound together in a purposive agenda; in this case with the progressive reform agenda of good governance.

Recently, though, the production, consumption, and relational nature of deliberative organizational- and systems-level communication processes have been altered by a number of dramatic societal changes. These include the increased speed of message and information development and transmission, as well as the proliferation of channels and platforms; a society that is growing more dense and diverse through urbanization and migration; organizational structures that have a great deal of variation in form and boundaries; and power shifts in governments, science, humanities and the arts. In this environment, the complexity of systems and the speed of change create both challenges and opportunities for reformists and others interested in strategic, planned change.

From a strategic, large-scale perspective, the praxis of human communication—the habitual nature of social relations and the means through which actors learn social behaviors and strategies (rules and resources in his parlance)—provide critical features for analysis (Giddens, 1986). The deeply ingrained behaviors and relationships found in various forms of social activity (e.g., families, communities, organizations, large governmental institutions) are especially important when researchers are attempting to identify their means of reproduction. These patterns may constitute engaging, innovative cultures that nurture great ideas or they might produce abusive, harassing organizations where behaviors that would not be tolerated elsewhere are taken for granted. In the case of government organizations and bureaucracies where mid-level civil servants outlast the leaders—and their initiatives—it is extremely important to investigate their rules and sources of power. Organizational change efforts and their strategic communication plans are thus often about altering or disrupting the underlying generative mechanisms that produce and reproduce the social structures that allow organizational members to be indifferent to change efforts.

A strategic communication perspective also allows us to examine the positioning of the existing relationships between agency and power focusing on the conditions under which actors perceive they "can do otherwise," and use their communication skills (agency) and knowledge from communication programs (rules and resources) to enhance their communication and social capital to advocate for, and effect, change. This may require, for example, an analysis of the embeddedness of disciplinary power (in a Foucauldian sense) in the personal or organizational lives of bureaucrats or leaders and a sophisticated examination of systemic resource allocations, because straightforward persuasive appeals may not be motivational even if they are credible and emotionally appealing.

A strategic repositioning of power can enhance opportunities for citizens to participate in the creation of information used in governance, and create a two-way flow of information. In this sense all members of NGOs or SCOs and interested citizens, can see themselves as important members of the interlocking systems of governance. They can then use this information, spread it through sustainable networks, and advocate for change. This is an example of individuals building up their resources, or what is known as *communication capital*[4].

A goal of communication processes should also be to increase the transparency of information produced by institutions, including knowledge about its ownership (Fairbanks, Plowman & Rawlins, 2007). This builds the communicative capacity of the system. Similarly, communication capacity can be built by growing collaborations and networks of people engaged in reform. Collective action, as a communicative phenomenon, always includes: "(1) identifying and connecting people who share a common private interest(s) in a public good, (2) communicating messages to these people, and (3) coordinating, integrating, or synchronizing individuals' contributions" (Flanigan, Stohl & Bimber, 2006, p. 32).

Strategic communication for governance helps combine knowledgeable, creative endeavors, such as issue framing and messaging, with the collaboration and coordination skills necessary for operational activities, such as coalition building and network development. In this conception, strategic communication is more than themes and messages or a campaign—it requires the examination of existing coalitions and policy negotiations; it calls for an understanding of institutional positioning

(McPhee and Zaug, 2009), and entails the analysis of structures such as competing networks, media argument frames, and organizational cultural changes (Riley, 2005).

Project Overview

Expert Interview Methodology

To better understand the strategic communication needs and challenges in the developing world, our partners in the CommGap program at the World Bank conducted in-depth interviews with regional communication professionals from governments, the private sector, and the World Bank who are all engaged in governance reform efforts in some capacity through their work. A total of 51 phone or face-to-face interviews were conducted with individuals from 17 countries in six regions, including: Africa (Ghana, Kenya, Nigeria, Rwanda, South Africa, Tanzania), the Middle East and North Africa (Morocco), Eastern Europe (Bosnia, Serbia, Romania), Latin America and the Caribbean (Guyana, Trinidad and Tobago), East Asia (Indonesia, Philippines, Thailand), and South Asia (India). The semi-structured interviews also provided input on the most critical governance reform skills and the target audience for a communication and governance reform workshop. The interviews were transcribed, and we analyzed the data both through a structurationist lens to identify the interlocking systems issues and through a thematic analysis looking for key issues (e.g., challenges and opportunities) (Boyatzis, 1998), which is the first step toward a larger content analysis study (see Roberts, 1997) to be conducted during the next phase of this research project.

Analysis

Analysis of the interview data showed the connections among communication-related governance challenges, the skills required to address these challenges, and the target audience for a communication and governance reform workshop that would teach participants the knowledge-base and skills required to address these challenges.

Communication-Related Governance Challenges

Participants were asked to identify key governance challenges that were consistent with their current experience in governance reform implementation. Responses were wide ranging, but four key themes emerged.

1. Challenges related to lack of political will. Respondents talked about the lack of political support for reform. Some spoke of vested interests and political agendas that got in the way of supporting needed reform. Others spoke of political promises that did not lead to significant reform. Still others referred to lack of transparency as a challenge. Among all of the challenges, political will was perceived as the most important challenge. Several made comments such as this: "Political will is the apex of the challenges."

2. Challenges related to lack of organizational will. Often related to political will is the lack of organizational/administrative will. One respondent said, "Political will and administrative will are key challenges. Communication plays an important role in providing links from policy to reform implementation." Of all of the comments, a large majority focused on challenges within the participants' organizations. A frequently mentioned issue was resistance from middle managers. Some claimed there were no incentives for middle managers to change; others suggested that middle managers had little knowledge or understanding of the reforms. Some mentioned a lack of leadership support, resource deficiencies, lack of continuity of government personnel, and sub-par coordination and collaboration. Overall, many respondents seemed to believe their organizations lacked the capacity to effectively implement governance reform.

3. Challenges related to a lack of public will. Several respondents mentioned a lagging engagement from their citizenry. This often showed up as citizen indifference or reform fatigue. Some respondents claimed that citizens lacked voice in the system or that there was no force to unite the people in support of governance reform. In some cases, interviewees spoke about public will as an ephemeral concept. For example, in some countries there is no push for reform and no consensus about what government should do. One interviewee said there is little understanding of public policy reforms and no request for accountability. Some felt that there really was no such thing as public opinion because some societies are so fragmented.

4. Lack of communication with the public. The fourth theme links organizational challenges to the lack of public will. Many respondents identified that their organizations needed to cast a broader communication net with a larger set of stakeholders. Some mentioned there was no concerted effort to communicate with the public. Others mentioned the lack of media management by reform managers.

Individual Skills Needed to Address Governance Challenges

The interviewees believed reform-related organizational skills were underdeveloped. Again, these data were wide ranging, but could be categorized under six themes, as follows.

1. Political, historical, and intercultural environment. Participants seemed to comprehend the importance of understanding the context of their reform initiatives. One participant stated they must know "how to maneuver and navigate the political landscape." Another noted, "Reform is linked to politics so an understanding of the evolution of the political culture is key." Several mentioned the importance of intercultural differences while others went beyond the typical intercultural concerns. For example, an interviewee claimed:

> Another example is Nigeria and their secret societies. They have parallel systems of government run by various societies and clans . . . these matter more to Nigerians than existing things. So what one needs to do is know a country quite well. If [you] want to change systems and individuals, there are other roadmaps that aren't known and need to be discovered.

2. Coalition building and stakeholder analysis. Many mentioned the importance of coalition building. For instance, one interviewee said it was critical to build coalitions that would address vested interests. Another said:

> Coalition building is key . . . trying to engage people in collective action is needed to support successful implementation. If there are no strong coalitions, communication may not get far. Building strategic interest groups are (*sic*) essential so people can take the message to the rest of the society.

There was widespread agreement that there would be a need for individuals from nonprofit organizations and think tanks that focus on reform and advocacy, academics, private sector communication consultants, and members of CSOs to engage in building communication capacity.

Others mentioned that members of trade associations or unions, communication professionals in donor organizations (e.g., DFID), people who worked in government agencies, those who interact with the media, senior political and civil service officials, and monitoring and evaluation specialists should be educated about the importance of communication. There were comments about adversaries; there were examples of counter-movements to stop reform because it means fewer jobs to be doled out under the current system, or lobbying by business to slow reforms and talk of people who feared their opponents. This, of course, gave rise to the desire for fearless individuals—people who would be passionate proponents for change. Related to coalition building is stakeholder analysis. Several mentioned the importance of analyzing and understanding the multiple stakeholders who are related to the reform. Stakeholder analysis is valuable for identifying key interests, sources of power, perceptions, and media preferences. This analysis would be an essential first step for trust building, knowing how to best frame issues, and learning how to manage conflict with various stakeholders.

3. Change management. Central to implementing reform is an understanding of change management. Several interviewees told stories of complications that were perhaps not totally unexpected but were still frustrating. One interviewee discussed the link between understanding the stakeholders and change management:

> In terms of information and changes between cultures, Afghanistan is an example. They get their information from the radio and TV but if you dig deeper, you see what really influences them to change are discussions inside the family unit when you want to reflect what they do and influence change.

4. Monitoring and evaluation. Interviewees were also concerned about research and evaluation skills. Many were interested in gathering data and analyzing metrics. One interviewee said, "The use of a metrics and evaluation framework is critical to track progress, identify constraints, and ensure productive results of work undertaken."

5. Problem solving and strategic-level thinking. Interviewees were interested in developing a more strategic approach for their reform work. Several mentioned the importance of strategic communication. Others spoke about the importance of developing problem-solving skills.

6. Role of professional communicators. Another interesting theme revolved around communication as a role, a profession. One respondent noted that communication professionals may be important, but

> depending on where you go, for example South Asia, in 8 out of 10 cases, the communications guy is 17 years old and they send him out to get sandwiches for meetings. At best he puts out a press release or two. This isn't the problem-solving coalition base you want to be dealing with.

Other respondents made a similar point, noting that communication professionals are undervalued, so the best audience for education interventions are high-caliber decision makers and senior managers from any functional position, not just communication, with the power to influence change. Others, however, noted communication professionals are *not* the people who need to learn that communication is central to governance reform. Some interviewees were concerned with the role of journalists. They noted that their regions were quite different from the West in that they lacked positions like *science writer* because the journalists tended to be generalists, not specialists like in the West.

The Communication and Governance Project

Out of the analysis of governance reform efforts and the communication and governance interview data, an executive course in communication and governance reform was developed along with a five-year program to build capacity and sustainability in governance reform. This section gives an overview of the long-range project on communication and government reform with our C@C research group at USC's Annenberg School in partnership with the Annenberg School at University of Pennsylvania and CommGap and WBI of the World Bank Group.

The program's goal is to ensure that governance reforms can be advanced and consolidated over the long term by those with the most at stake, namely, citizens of the countries themselves, whether through government or civil society. The program contains five interlocking and mutually support-ive components that promote coalition building for governance reform through a self-reinforcing cycle of capacity building, networking, and knowledge generation. These five components are as follows.

An executive course in communication and governance reform. This component will directly strengthen the capacity of communication and other professionals in supporting reform efforts in developing countries.

A network of students, scholars, and practitioners. This component will bring together networks of executive course graduates, scholars and practitioners. These networks will develop research agendas, foster talent, build ties with local, regional and international organizations, and improve their members' capacity to enhance and employ their expertise.

Peer-partnered research and analysis. This component seeks to develop North–South peer-partnered research by creating teams of early-career researchers working on issues of communication and governance reform in developing countries, and helping them make an impact on the broader conversation about governance and development.

Knowledge leadership, generation and sharing. This component extracts and shares knowledge from the other parts of the program. It acts as a global think tank on governance and communication issues, helping to lead the broader conversation on governance reform through policy-oriented research and convening discussion.

Operations-oriented advice. Drawing particularly upon the knowledge leadership and network elements of the program, this aspect connects organizations with hands-on, practical, operational advice on the communication-based aspects of governance reform.

Curriculum Development

The remainder of this chapter focuses on the development of the executive course, "World Bank–Annenberg Executive Course in Communication and Governance Reform." The initial phase of the program focuses on two regions in particular, Africa and the Middle East.

The concept for the course was originally rooted in the Bank's use of political economy approaches to better understand stakeholders and their reform contexts. The goal of the executive course is to move from simply analyzing policy to locating support that is critical to implementa-tion. The World Bank's broad experience shows one or more of the following issues produce serious challenges to successful governance: the need to strengthen political will and increase cli-ent ownership; overcoming bureaucratic resistance, especially from middle managers; managing a plurality of vested interests; confronting hostile public opinion; addressing collective action problems; and cultivating citizen demand for accountability. The interview data analyses generally supported this viewpoint.

We see these issues as problems that can be addressed through a strategic communication lens and by the structuring of communication capital and capacity. This is accomplished, for example, by building effective and efficient information systems and cultivating new networks of anti-corruption supporters and coalitions that can help address collective action problems and ultimately expand the existing spaces for reform.

The curriculum for the course was developed through a collaborative effort of the three project partners: the C@C research group at USC's Annenberg School in partnership with the Annenberg School at University of Pennsylvania and CommGap and WBI units of the World Bank Group. This took place over the nine-month period preceding the course pilot, which was held in July 2011 at the World Bank headquarters in Washington, DC. The World Bank put out a call for applications to individuals and organizations they thought might be interested. They received over 400 applications and through a rigorous process of review, 35 individuals were chosen to attend the pilot: 11 from North Africa and the Middle East, 11 from Africa, and three from other regions. Ten individuals representing development and donor organizations around the world (DFID, World Bank) also attended the pilot course.

Learning objectives called for the participants to be able to carry out the following tasks.

Interpret governance diagnostics and political economy analysis. Participants were expected to gain the knowledge and skills to become informed consumers of political economy analyses and governance diagnostics and be able to draw out adaptive, non-technical challenges amenable to communication-based solutions.

Craft and implement strategies for multi-stakeholder coalition building in support of reform. Participants were expected to be able to secure political will through broad leadership support for change; gain support of public sector middle managers; address vested interests by building coalitions of pro-change influentials; transform indifferent or even hostile public opinion into support for reform; and instigate citizen demand for good governance and accountability.

Provide implementation support. Participants were also expected to gain knowledge and skills in facilitating multi-stakeholder dialogue and negotiation toward a durable agreement; set up mechanisms for continuous gathering of political context updates for reform managers and country offices of international organizations; identify and draw on necessary high-quality expertise for implementation; and identify the necessary expertise mix for implementation.

Apply monitoring and evaluation frameworks. Last, participants were expected to be able to gain familiarity and skills in the actual use of evaluation frameworks, embedding monitoring and evaluation frameworks in the upstream planning processes; set up monitoring mechanisms to track outputs; and evaluate whether or not communication and governance interventions contributed to desired outcomes.

The 10-day course was organized around five key areas of learning:

1. communication and governance
2. sustaining coalitions and networks for governance
3. traditional media and social media and the fifth estate
4. metrics and evaluation frameworks
5. communication and self-mastery.

We review each area below in reference to the key learning areas and then reflect on the workshop as a whole and the process of curriculum development going forward.

Communication and Governance

The first module for the workshop focused on governance in the development context, specifically the central role of communication in the governance process. Participants learned about governance as a contested arena in development, including its evolution from a narrow view of public administration, exclusively focused on supply-side factors to today's much broader governance agenda that seeks to incorporate demand-side considerations along traditional concerns. Additionally participants learned that good governance can only be realized and sustained if public sector consumers (stakeholders and civil society) are involved in the decision-making process—whether via direct participation and/or accountability mechanisms.

Key concepts like public opinion and influence were reviewed through a communication lens. Political economy analysis helped participants develop a deeper knowledge of the "what, why, and how" of reform including the existing pathologies, the origin of the pathologies, and strategies for addressing the pathologies to successfully implement reform. Participants applied the principles with concrete examples of a bus system improvement project in Dhaka and journalistic methods in India.

Participants also learned to do stakeholder analysis and mapping, which helped them identify the winners and losers, the strong supporters and the powerful opponents of reform. Stakeholder analysis is one way of putting communication at the center of decision-making in organizations and society. It requires strategic communication planning and poses questions such as: Which stakeholders might best carry the message? How do we reach younger citizens? What members of coalitions are networked with the individuals who are likeminded but not involved in the reform?

Sustaining Coalitions and Networks for Governance

The second module emphasized the process of building coalitions to benefit reform efforts and sustain them through technologies and best practices that enhance knowledge sharing. A case study of coalition building in support of procurement reform policy in the Philippines offered participants a practical example of this process, and a related exercise gave them a chance to think about the initial phase of coalition building in their local contexts as an extension of stakeholder mapping and analysis. A presentation on *sustaining* coalitions introduced technologies and best practices that aid organizational knowledge sharing processes, which have the potential to turn coalitions built around a single reform into long-term information sharing networks. Participants had the opportunity to think about their own role in building lasting networks through an exercise on network leadership.

Traditional Media and Social Media (the Fifth Estate)

These sessions began with a focus on the media as one of the most important sources of data—on a macro, global scale and on a micro–local level. Lectures included a public diplomacy perspective on global media as well as a media use and messaging perspective that discussed the power of narratives and images and introduced concrete topics like message *stickiness,* framing and priming. Participants also focused on social media as a check on governments and corporations as well as the transformative impact of social media on traditional notions of *information* and *audience*. A mini case study was presented on a mobile social media research project called *Mobile Voices* as an example of citizen empowerment. The importance of building relationships with media outlets was a theme across all sessions. Recently, work by Jacobson and Jang (2002) has explored how the media can contribute to a global civil society through promoting peace as well as by providing coverage of democratic struggles. Taylor (2000) argued that media, especially independent media, are critical in helping activist organizations become involved in setting public agendas and stimulating public discourse.

Metrics and Evaluation Frameworks

This module highlighted one of the most important aspects of a strategic communication approach: metrics and evaluation. Participants learned how to develop measures for monitoring and evaluation and how to collect the data to enable these analyses. The module encompassed the traditional focus on monitoring and evaluation that is required in the 'donor world,' but with a twist. This set of elements develops the research on governance by setting up a web portal for the course and training participants to contribute data to a wiki. They were encouraged to be innovative at piloting and testing their own metrics and diagnostic tools and becoming what we call "field knowledge workers" who innovate, test and spread good practices. Participants discussed data that are needed for successful strategic communication, and discussed questions such as: How will this data be collected? What metrics should be used? How should progress be monitored? How shall the reform efforts be evaluated?

Communication and Self-Mastery

The final module centered on the process of building communication capital for participants as individuals. Leadership, vision and framing were explored through a scenario exercise that developed strategic thinking and foresight. A session on middle managers discussed how to deal with resistance to organizational change followed by a session on communication as risk mitigation and crisis communication. Finally, a lecture on negotiation and dialogue presented the idea of emotional intelligence and the communication tools and strategies that can be useful when dealing with "wicked" or intractable problems that are often made worse by the challenges of interpersonal and intercultural communication.

The course ended by analyzing a difficult case study about a fictitious country where most land is owned on a communal basis, with tenurial arrangements driven by traditional practices. However, due to changing economic and social conditions, customary land management is increasingly under pressure. Current law restricts the sale or lease of 80% of the country's arable land, thus stifling growth. Corruption is rampant, land laws are unclear at best and contradictory at worst, dispute resolution and enforcement mechanisms lack capacity and legal force, and administration is over-centralized and inefficient. There are frequent conflicts between municipal governments and traditional leaders over the authority to allocate land. Many powerful local bureaucrats, judges, and lawyers benefit immensely from the current land tenure confusion, charging inflated fees in order to navigate the convoluted land laws and land administrative systems. Many politicians continue to take advantage of the ambiguous land tenure system by strong-arming local officials and judges to provide them with enough land to use as a patronage resource. As a result, property rights are weak or unclear, and this rural insecurity has become a major obstacle to national development. Participants were also assigned roles and asked to apply the knowledge and skills that they had learned during the workshop.

Discussion

Increasing pressure is being felt around the world for good governance. Good governance is characterized by highly participative, two-way communication linking citizens and the government. Drawing on Giddens (1984), poor governance is a social system that is produced and reproduced in communication. Top-down, non-participative communication and corruption often characterize poor governance. Institutions are instantiated in engrained communication practices. To disrupt these patterns, reform managers must understand the deep structures of production, consumption, and relational organizational and systems-level processes.

For example, the governance challenge of collusion requires a solution involving transparency-building incentives. These incentives must be designed through ongoing dialogue with key stakeholders. This requires research efforts and stakeholder analysis to learn how the current system is produced and reproduced as well as a clear understanding of stakeholder values and assumptions. For example, what rules and norms reproduce the current behaviors what would count as evidence to a key stakeholder that the system was changing to become more transparent?

Interventions by reform managers require a strategic approach; one that links macro-level issues to micro-level actions. Reform managers must learn to be adept at building political will, organizational will, and public will—all issues that require increasing communicative capacity systemically and institutionally by first developing communication capital. Very few people were described as truly capable of the kind of self-mastery that can leverage the intersection of highly developed personal communication skills and successful engagement with governments, agencies and civil society organizations.

Interviewees made numerous comments about both the institutionalized roles of communication specialists and the need for communication skills in other roles. Individuals in both positions were seen as both helpful and inept, since being a communication specialist appears to confer no special skills in some regions. The resources that people have available to them to implement reform vary greatly.

Interviewees were consistent in their belief that middle managers are the keepers of resistant behaviors and while they could articulate the motivations and mental models that underpin these behaviors, they were less able to discuss how these practices were sustained over time. They also observed that most mass media systems remain powerful entities that can either enable or prevent change. Further analysis will be needed to better understand the deeper structuring processes of strategic communication in institutional reform efforts. Field-level data will need to be collected over several years, across state and regional contexts to uncover these patterns.

The interview showed that many citizens have little knowledge of the reform efforts in their countries or insight into the bureaucracies that sustain their governments. This lack of knowledge allows those in power to reproduce the surface-level structures that dominate their lives such as improper taxes or the unequal application of laws. Only a few country representatives mentioned the power of corporations, which is always a key institutional power broker in the West. So the question remains, why is this the case? Are those structures invisible or unmentionable? Also, remarkably few interviewees brought up the role of social media and new technology. This is likely due to the lack of communication technology and Internet access in many rural areas in Africa and the Middle East, yet there is a good deal of information on the growing role of mobile technology in many of these countries. These interviews were conducted during the same time frame as the "Arab Spring" 2011 movements. Initial media reports indicated that social media such as Facebook and Twitter played a significant role in the Tunisian and Egyptian uprisings and although it is likely that their role was more nuanced than initially reported, empirical research indicates a significant role was played by social media (Lotan et al., (2011)). We expect that the growth of smartphones and platforms will increase the interest in social media over time.

Reflections on the Experience and Moving Forward

We did brief exit interviews with a subset of the participants to get their perspective on the first iteration of the course. Although a systematic analysis of this data is still underway, one key theme that has emerged is the value of peer-to-peer knowledge-sharing in this kind of course. These individuals from different parts of the world each use a localized communication perspective to confront the challenges of governance reform in their own specific local contexts, but the challenges they are confronting have many common qualities and their work to confront these challenges has both local and global application.

The projects director for a Filipino think tank said:

> A lot of us are somewhat myopic in terms of our outlook, having practiced advocacy communication or governance reform only in our own respective territories. Being able to hear the experiences and stories of others . . . It helps you adopt a more global feeling in terms of approaches to advocacy communication and governance reform.

A PR spokesperson for the Romanian government also noted, "Although we come from different countries, different cultures with different histories, I identified common aspects and common challenges when it comes to reform. The transition process looks very similar and very difficult."

This 10-day program was not designed to replace graduate school, and the growing body of work on participatory research it adds to exemplifies the value of localized knowledge combined with media messaging. There is a great deal of concern about "research that works," so one of the analytic tools that was emphasized in the course is the cynefin model (Kurtz & Snowden, 2003). This systems model of management decision-making is a helpful diagnostic for those engaged in strategic communication and governance. It breaks situations or projects into five categories: simple, complicated, complex, chaotic and disordered. After individuals analyze their circumstances into one of these categories, the model helps determine the most appropriate response. In the first category there are best practices, in the second there are good practices that can be brought to bear, in the third there are emergent practices, in the fourth it is time to try a novel approach and in the fifth the disordered circumstances provide no guidelines. In the final instance strategic communication principles indicate that when all else fails, one should stop talking and just listen in order to build relationships (Taylor & Doerfel, 2003) and acquire communication capital that can effect change another day.

Notes

1 Partial funding for this project comes from CommGap, World Bank Group and partial funding is from the Annenberg Trust fund for the Annenberg Network on Global Communication. The authors would like to thank their partners in CommGap for their help and support.
2 Cited in Chambers, R. (1999). Rural development: Putting the last first. Longman London. Retrieved from http://www.eou.edu/socwomen/support/articles/chambers.pdf.
3 That is not to say that the theory is without its challenges (see Conrad, 1993). Nonetheless, Giddens is largely considered one of the two or three most significant social theorists alive today.
4 This is a new use of this term. Nando Malmelin (2007) uses the notion of communication capital as organizational asset but we began using the term at about the same time as an individual development concept and prefer the use of communication capacity at the organizational or institutional level.

References

Argenti, P., Howell, R.A., & Beck, K.A. (2005). The strategic communication imperative. *MIT Sloan Management Review, 46*, 83–89.
Ashcraft, K. L., Kuhn, T. R., & Cooren, F. (2009). Constitutional amendments: "Materializing" organizational communication. *The academy of management annals, 3*, 1–64.
Banks, S. P., & Riley, P. (2006). Structuration theory as an ontology for communication and research. In L. Putnam and K. Krone (Eds.), *Organizational communication, Vol. 1*. Thousand Oaks, CA: Sage Publications.
Botan, C., & Taylor, M. (2005). The role of trust in channels of strategic communication for building civil society. *Journal of Communication, 55*, 685–702.
Boyatzis, R.E. (1998). *Transforming qualitative information: Thematic analysis and code development*. Thousand Oaks, CA: Sage Publications.
Conrad, C. (1993). Rhetorical/communication theory as an ontology for structuration research. In S. Deetz, (Ed.) *Communication yearbook 16* (pp. 197–208).
Deetz, S. (2001). Conceptual foundations. In F. M. Jablin & L. L. Putnam (Eds.), *New handbook of organizational communication: Advances in theory, research and methods* (pp.3–46). Thousand Oaks, CA: Sage.

Durán-Bravo, P., & Fernández-Fuentes, M. (2010). Communication in third sector organisations. *Revista Latina de Comunicación Social, 65,* 595–603. Retrieved May 22, 2011, from Research Library. (Document ID: 2252652601).

Eisenberg, E.M. & Riley, P. (2000). Organizational culture. In F.M Jablin & L. Putnam, L. (Eds.). *The new handbook of organizational communication: Advances in theory, research, and methods* (pp. 291-322). Thousand Oaks, CA: Sage Publications.

Faccinetti, J. D. (2004). Making strategic communications work to prevent elder abuse. *Journal of Elder Abuse & Neglect, 14,* 11-20.

Fairbanks, J., Plowman, K. D., & Rawlins, B. L. (2007). Transparency in government communication. *Journal of Public Affairs, 7,* 23–37.

Flanigan, A., Stohl, C., & Bimber, B. (2006). Modeling the structure of collective action. *Communication Monographs, 73,* 29–54.

Giddens, A. (1984). *The constitution of society.* Cambridge: Polity Press.

Giddens, A. (1986). Action, subjectivity, and the constitution of meaning. *Social Research, 53,* 529-545.

Giddens, A. (1991). *Modernity and self-identity: Self and society in the late modern age.* Cambridge: Polity.

Habermas, J. (1979). *Communication and the evolution of society.* Boston, MA: Beacon Press.

Hallahan, K., Holtzhausen, D, van Ruler, B., Verčič, D. & Sriramesh, K. (2007). Defining strategic communication. *International Journal of Strategic Communication, 1,* 3–35.

Holbert, L. R., & Geidner, N. (2009). The 2008 election: Highlighting the need to explore additional communication subfields to advance political communication. *Communication Studies, 60,* 344–358.

Jacobson, T. L., & Jang, W. Y. (2002). Media, war, peace and global civil society. In W. B. Gudykunst & B. Mody (Eds.), *The handbook of intercultural and international communication* (pp. 343–358). Thousand Oaks, CA: Sage.

Kitchen, P. J., Brignell, J., Li, T., & Jones, G. S. (2004). The emergence of IMC: A theoretical perspective. *Journal of Advertising Research, 44,* 19–30.

Kurtz, C.F., & Snowden, D.J. (2003). The new dynamics of strategy: Sense-making in a complex and complicated world, *IBM Systems Journal, 42,* 462.

Lotan, G., Graeff, E., Ananny, M., Gaffney, D., Pearce, I., & boyd, d. (2011). The Arab Spring| The revolutions were tweeted: Information flows during the 2011 Tunisian and Egyptian Revolutions. *International Journal of Communication, 5,* 1/3, 75–1405. Retrieved from http://ijoc.org/index.php/ijoc/article/view/1246/643.

Malmelin, M. (2007). Communication capital: Modeling corporate communications as an organizational asset. *Corporate Communications, 12,* 298–310. Retrieved May 24, 2011, from ABI/INFORM Global. (Document ID: 1858590561).

McPhee, R. D., & Zaug, P. (2009). The communicative constitution of organization: A framework for explanation. In L. L. Putnam & A. M. Nicotera (Eds.), *Building theories of organization: The constitutive role of communication* (pp. 21–48). New York: Routledge.

Mozammel, M. & Odugbemi, S. (2005). *With the support of multitudes: Using strategic communication to fight poverty through PRSPs.* London: DFID.

Odugbemi, S. (2010, April 10). 'Why is the transparency revolution not taking off in Africa?' Retrieved from http://blogs.worldbank.org//publicsphere/why-transparency-revolution-not-taking-africa.

Poole, M. S., Seibold, D. R. & McPhee, R. D. (1985). Group decision-making as a structurational process. *Quarterly Journal of Speech, 71,* 74–102.

Putnam, L. L., & Nicotera, A. M. (Eds.). (2009). *Building theories of organization: The constitutive role of communication.* New York: Routledge.

Riley, P. (1983). A structurationist account of political culture. *Administrative Science Quarterly, 28,* 414-437.

Riley, P. (2005). Communication Centered Change (C3): engaging the public organization. In J. Simpson & P. Shockley-Zalabak (Eds.) *Engaging communication, transforming organizations: Scholarship of engagement in action.* Cresskill, NJ: Hampton Press.

Roberts, C.W. (Ed.) (1997). *Text analysis for the social sciences: Methods for drawing statistical inferences from texts and transcripts.* Mahwah, NJ: Lawrence Erlbaum Associates.

Taylor, M. (2000). Media relations in Bosnia: A role for public relations in building civil society. *Public Relations Review, 26,* 1–14.

Taylor, M. & Doerfelr, M. L. Building relationships that build nations. *Human Communication Research, 29,* 153–181.

UNDP (n.d.). Our work—Democratic governance. Retrieved from http://www.tj.undp.org/content/tajikistan/en/home/library/democratic_governance/

United Nations Millennium Declaration (2000). Retrieved from http://www.un.org/millennium/declaration/ares552e.htm

Ward, W.E. (2011). Strategic communication at work. *Leader to Leader, 59,* 33–38.

Waters, R.D., & Lemanski, J. L. (2011). Revisiting strategic communication's past to understand the present: Examining the direction and nature of communication on Fortune 500 and Philanthropy 400 web sites. *Corporate Communications: An International Journal, 16,* 150–169.

14

Adopting an Entrepreneurial Perspective in the Study of Strategic Communication

Emanuele Invernizzi and Stefania Romenti

Four Dimensions of Entrepreneurial Organization Theory

This chapter explores the ability of *Entrepreneurial Organization Theory* (Alvarez & Barney, 2004; Burns, 2005; Busenitz et al., 2003; Bygrave, 1989; Dew, Ramakrishna & Venkataraman, 2004; Foss & Klein, 2005; Ireland, Hitt & Sirmon, 2003) to provide a unique conceptual framework that can be used to integrate and evaluate each dimension of strategic communication.

Entrepreneurial organization theories (EOTs) support the development of processes for creating value in a firm because it has "the ability (. . .) to act entrepreneurially" (Stevenson & Jarillo, 1990, p. 23). "Thus, corporate entrepreneurship can form a basis for competitive advantage and technological growth in all types of firms that are oriented toward leadership and excellence in the new global economy" (Gupta, MacMillan & Surie, 2004, p. 243). Stevenson & Jarillo (1990) define corporate entrepreneurship as "a process by which individuals—either on their own or inside organizations—pursue opportunities without regard to the resources they currently control" (p. 23).

We have chosen to examine four dimensions of EOTs, which can be defined as *gate-keeping and networking; orientation to innovation; transformative leadership and visioning;* and *enactment*.

Gate-Keeping and Networking

Gate-keeping consists in gathering continuously updated outside information and knowledge regarding areas of interest for organizational development, such as the introduction of technological innovation or change in the market or within the organizational environment. This implies "(s)earching, filtering and evaluating potential opportunities from outside the organization, including related and emerging technologies, new markets and services, which can be exploited by applying or combining with existing competencies" (Tidd, Bessant, & Pavitt, 2001, p. 293). Gate-keeping can also be carried out within the organization by supporting and combining existing sources of knowledge and coordinating different work teams. "The examination of the internal environment involves the evaluation of novel combinations of existing technology, shelved concepts and ideas, and new applications for existing competencies" (McFadzean, O'Loughlin, & Shaw, 2005, p. 356). In particular, gate-keeping favors the development, maintenance and improvement of the so-called internal communication networks supporting work groups.

Creating a network of relationships based on trust and credibility in the gate-keepers facilitates building the social capital needed to spread information, feedback and knowledge. "Networks have been seen as important to entrepreneurial activity since Granovetter (1973) suggested that they, and not autonomous action, were the major driver of entrepreneurial activity" (Butler, Brown & Chamornmarn, 2003, p. 152). Entrepreneurship needs social interactions both within and outside the organization in order to generate support from others and to shape and develop new ideas (Sadler-Smith, Hampson, Chaston, & Badger, 2003). "Networks provided a way to link information to entrepreneurial perfor-mance, as a critical explanatory variable" (Butler et al., 2003, p. 153). Business networks provide useful business information, advice and access to informal alliances, while personal networks are key entre-preneurial ingredients and efficient channels for ideas (Kusuma Wardhani, McCarthy & Perera, 2009).

Cultivating networks gives a firm the resources needed to survive in the medium and long term (Stevenson & Jarillo, 1990). This means being able to develop and maintain relationships with cli-ents, suppliers, collaborators and competitors operating in different sectors (Hitt, Ireland, Camp, & Sexton, 2001). In this way the organization manages to find, within its own network, the resources of information, technology, and finance and the skills needed to successfully compete in the market (Hitt et al., 2001).

Social capital formed through the experience acquired within the organization's internal network is a theme of growing importance (Hitt et al., 2001; Tsai, 2000). Organizations are oriented toward building relationships of trust that allow them to work efficaciously with their partners. The rela-tionships based on mutual trust not only limit opportunistic behavior, but also represent a source of competitive advantage for the network (Davis, Schoorman, Mayer, & Tan, 2000). Advantages in terms of resources and legitimacy of work carried out, and membership in the network, may affect all its components (Hitt et al., 2001).

Orientation to Innovation

"A number of authors have emphasized entrepreneurship as the primary act underpinning inno-vation, which also resonates with Schumpeter's (1961) view of entrepreneurship, as the primary catalyst for innovation" (McFadzean et al., 2005, p. 351). Drucker (1985), for example, suggests that innovation is the primary activity of entrepreneurship. Also, Lumpkin and Dess (1996) argue that a key dimension of an entrepreneurial orientation is its emphasis on innovation. "Corporate entrepreneurship can be defined as the effort of promoting innovation in an uncertain environment" (McFadzean et al., 2005, p. 356).

Within the entrepreneurial organization innovation is promoted from an internal perspective, through the continuous evaluation of new potentialities and ideas and the alignment of different resources to exploit these potentialities (Li, Liu, Wang, Li, & Guo, 2009). This is the reason why McFadzean et al. (2005) use the terms *entrepreneurship* with *intrapreneurship* interchangeably.

Possessing innovative ability means knowing how to identify new market, technological and organizational opportunities, as well as knowing how to deal with possible problems or fill in gaps due to changes in the environment the organization operates in (Hayton & Kelley, 2006).

> Innovation can be defined as a process that provides added value and a degree of novelty to the organization and its suppliers and customers through the development of new procedures, solu-tions, products and services as well as new methods of commercialisation.
>
> *McFadzean et al., 2005, p. 353*

Entrepreneurial theories maintain that innovation is a discontinuous and non-linear process that involves an ample number of subjects, both inside and outside the firm. Corporate entrepreneurship is held to promote entrepreneurial behaviors within an organization (Echols & Neck, 1998).

Innovative ability cannot be concentrated in one or a few individuals. The reason for this is that innovating requires wide and specific knowledge of techniques and managerial practices in use for existing services and products (Knight, 1997; Prahalad & Ramaswamy, 2003). "The level of entrepreneurship within the firm is critically dependent on the attitude of individuals within the firm, below the ranks of top management" (Stevenson & Jarillo, 1990, p. 24). Successful implementation of strategies is a product of involving people throughout the organization (Morris, Kuratko, & Schindehutte, 2001; Morris & Kuratko, 2002). Gupta et al. (2004) argue:

> Fostering experimentation and autonomous initiatives in subordinates to promote autonomous strategic decision-making helps generate commitment and higher levels of involvement, raises morale and increases the capacity to address ambiguity by improving the ability to gain access to required information through multiple channels.
>
> *p. 244*

The entrepreneurial leader's challenging task is to mobilize the capacity of the organization and its stakeholders to do the above (Gupta et al., 2004, p. 245).

Transformative Leadership and Visioning

Entrepreneurial organization is based not only on the ability to create innovation but also on the ability to guarantee its development and use (Hayton & Kelley, 2006). Such ability is believed indispensable to the success of any organizational initiative (Schon, 1967), and, in entrepreneurship literature, has been identified in the qualities of championing, visioning or transformational leadership (Bass, 1985; Gupta et al., 2004; Hayton & Kelley, 2006; McFadzean et al., 2005). This means knowing how to unfold innovative potential in an organization, overcome critical obstacles, and resolve any opposition through constant search for commitment on the part of key stakeholders (Howell & Higgins, 1990). This requires a "vision to energise employees, help them to meet the challenges that face them" (McFadzean et al., 2005, p. 366).

Actively promoting innovative ideas and projects is a good way to create engagement, motivation, and sharing among the organization members (Hayton & Kelley, 2006; Howell & Higgins, 1990) and thereby obtain their support. An important characteristic of entrepreneurial organization is the effective communication of an entrepreneurial vision. Hitt et al. (2001) note the significance of developing, communicating and emphasizing specific shared values among organization members. Some authors "highlight the visionary role of top management in creating the context for transaction set altering changes (*sic*)" (Gupta et al., 2004, p. 244).

In this regard entrepreneurial organization draws inspiration from the theory of transformational leadership in the organizational environment (Bass, 1985; Hayton & Kelley, 2006; Howell & Higgins, 1990) and stresses the importance of formulating a vision of the project, thus encouraging organizational members involved to actively support the project and developing a relationship of trust and respect with every one of them. Sharing the objectives of the project to encourage participants to attain superior results, as well as fostering discussion regarding the project, and comparing different analytical points of view are equally important (Maidique, 1980). "We define entrepreneurial leadership as leadership that creates visionary scenarios that are used to assemble and mobilize a supporting cast of participants who become committed by the vision to the discovery and exploitation of strategic value creation" (Gupta et al., 2004, p.242). This definition emphasizes the challenge of mobilizing the resources and gaining the commitment required for value creation that the entrepreneurial leader faces, which involves creating a vision and a cast of supporters capable of enacting that vision. "The two challenges of forging a vision and building a cast of competent and committed supporters are interdependent since the former is useless without the latter" (Gupta et al., 2004, p. 242).

Enactment

The innovative ability of an *entrepreneurial organization* is closely tied to the ability to activate, build, and re-invent the organization's competitive environment. In other words, the organization carries out a process of *enactment,* a term used to indicate a process of activation and creation of the environment on the basis of individual interpretation, to which meaning is attributed (Daft, & Weick, 1984; Weick, 1995). In fact, the institutional setting may at times not understand the innovative solutions and behaviors the entrepreneurial organization carries out. As a result the organization may decide to either align itself with the environment or to carry out modifications and changes to its interpretation of the environment. "Strictly speaking, opportunities become real in the creative mind of the entrepreneur, as he or she uses observations and impressions from the external environment to activate unobserved or latent combinations of resources and customer demand" (Zander, 2007, p. 1144).

In such a case we speak of *enacted environment* (Daft & Weick, 1984; Smircich & Stubbart, 1985) or *selection environment* (Levinthal, 1994), within which an organization carries out behaviors, experiments with different solutions, or creates new markets on the basis of its own opinions and knowledge, ignoring past behavioral norms and consolidated traditional expectations. "There are no threats or opportunities out there in an environment, just material and symbolic records of action. But a strategist—determined to find meaning—makes relationships by bringing connections and patterns to the action" (Smircich & Stubbart, 1985, p. 726).

> An enactment model implies that an environment of which strategists can make sense has been put there by strategists' patterns of action—not by a process of perceiving the environment, but by a process of making the environment (. . . .). In summary, theories involving objective or perceived environments envision concrete, material organizations that are within, but separate from, real material environments. The relationships between the two are expressed in terms of cause and effect. On the other hand, enactment theory abandons the idea of concrete, material organizations/environments in favour of a largely socially-created symbolic world.
>
> *p. 727*

Gupta et al. (2004) describe two kinds of enactment: scenario and cast enactments. *Scenario enactment* consists of envisaging and creating a scenario of possible opportunities. *Cast enactment* is to convince the firm's network of stakeholders that it is possible to accomplish the objectives emerging from the scenario.

Finding Four Dimensions of Strategic Communication

Corporate communication and public relations literature has given diverse meanings to the concept of strategic contribution of communication, praising its multiple potentialities and delineating the implications in the process of creating corporate value (Hallahan, Holtzhausen, Van Ruler, Verčič, & Sriramesh, 2007). The present section will point out four components of strategic communication in the light of the four dimensions of Entrepreneurial Organization Theory (EOT). Their comparison will allow us to show the importance that each component of strategic communication exercises in creating competitive advantage and in contributing to the success of the firm. Above all, it will allow us to highlight the contribution that strategic communication makes to the different decision processes of the firm. Rereading the contributions of strategic communication in the light of the analyses carried out using EOT permits us to single out the following four dimensions: the *aligning* role of strategic communication, meaning both boundary spanning and environmental scanning, and the activity of bridging and engaging stakeholders; the *energizing* of internal stakeholders, stimulating their orientation to innovation; the *visioning* role of communication, meaning the activation of transformative leadership through the definition and diffusion of a vision, corporate strategies and guiding values; and the *constituting* role of strategic communication, meaning the enactment of competitive environment through the sense-making processes and the creation of organizational settings and company environments.

Aligning

The aligning component of strategic communication includes environmental scanning and boundary-spanning activities, as well as bridging and engaging ones.

Communication plays its role at the increasingly more and more porous and fragile boundary between the organization and its reference environment (White & Verčič, 2001). From this viewpoint, communication exercises a function of *boundary spanning*. The fact that it has a boundary function gives corporate communication a privileged position for observing and interpreting the context in which an organization operates, and this is considered a central theme in strategic management studies to guarantee long-term corporate survival.

The monitoring and interpretation of the ongoing dynamics in *environmental scanning* are thus an important component of the strategic contribution of communication to the decisional processes and can be conducted on two levels: the issue and public level and the company stakeholder level (Stoffels, 1994). Through such activities, communication stimulates management to formulate strategies and processes aligned with the ongoing dynamics in the company's social context and with the most relevant expectations of stakeholders, rather than just limiting itself to only considering its own interests (Steyn, 2007). This facilitates the progressive legitimization of the company in its environment, which is a necessary condition so as to maintain its long-term "operating license."

The decisions of the companies that use this type of approach end up being more sustainable, not only from the standpoint of financing, human resources, and technology, as traditionally occurs in the majority of corporations, but also from the communicative standpoint (Lurati & Eppler, 2006). Taking sustainable decisions from the communicative standpoint, therefore, means ensuring that the choices made are not only communicated, but also aligned with the expectations of the company stakeholders as well as with the public image and identity of the organization (Lurati & Eppler, 2006).

Together with boundary spanning and environmental scanning activities, the aligning component of strategic communication includes bridging with and engaging stakeholders.

Public relations scholars have traditionally identified the development of solid, lasting, and symmetric relations between the organization and its stakeholders as the strategic objective of communication (Grunig, 2001; Lan, 2006; Ledingham & Bruning, 2000). This role implies abandoning short-sighted management attitudes dedicated primarily to defending management's own areas of interest (*buffering*) in favor of dedicating their energies to encouraging greater open-mindedness on the part of the organization to its reference environment, welcoming *stimuli* coming from outside, and valuing the wealth of opinions, positions, and experiences which constitute the organizational context.

Assuming an approach of this type means building bridges between the organization and its most important stakeholders (*bridging*), as well as activating and facilitating the participation and involvement of company members, while taking care to maintain a balance between the weight of their voices and those of the management of the organization (Van den Bosch, & van Riel, 1998).

Beyond bridging, stakeholder engagement means activating co-decisional processes, building partnerships and stimulating supporting behavior from stakeholders. Activating co-decisional processes, for example through ad hoc stakeholder meetings and multi-stakeholder workshops, means incorporating stakeholders' points of view in managerial decision making. The result is shared choices that should be more aligned to meeting stakeholders' expectations. Building partnerships means working together with stakeholders to devise, plan and develop new business solutions. Stimulating support-ing behavior transforms stakeholders into real advocates for organizational projects.

Granarolo Case Study

Granarolo is a leading Italian dairy company and its reputation has been built on a solid network of stakeholder partnerships through which the company continuously improves organizational learning and develops new business solutions. In particular, the activation of co-decisional processes involv-ing stakeholders enabled the company to recover from a severe loss of confidence by investors in the second half of the 1990s.

The reputation development model Granarolo adopted focuses on the systematic engagement of stakeholders. The six reputation drivers—vision and leadership, financial performance, internal climate, social responsibility, quality of products, and innovation—become starting points for stake-holder engagement. For this reason, engagement has not been limited to listening to stakehold-ers' needs and expectations. They were involved first in the process of defining, disseminating and implementing new values and corporate identity. Second, employees were involved in work groups in order to implement shared solutions to make the working environment and the internal climate better, and to debate the future challenges that the company would face.

Other ways of engaging clients, local communities, NGOs and suppliers on issues of social, envi-ronmental and economic sustainability were adopted. Numerous partnerships with suppliers were set up in order to develop new products, packaging and production solutions. As a consequence, the company tripled its revenues between 1995 and 2008, and since then the market share has continued to grow.

The case study shows that the introduction of co-decisional processes involving stakeholders, the building of partnerships, and the stimulation of supportive behavior helped the company to over-come a severe crisis of trust among employees and shareholders. Putting stakeholder engagement at the center of reputation development enabled the company to satisfy the needs of multiple categories of stakeholders (Freeman, 1984), encouraged them to identify and agree with business projects, and guaranteed substantial and enduring consistency in communication, core values and organizational behavior.

Energizing

Strategic decisions should, therefore, be rooted in the interchange between the organization and its most important internal interlocutors, rather than being defined only autonomously by the domi-nant coalition (Stroh, 2007). This line of research is the concrete expression of what Knights (1997) defined as a postmodern approach to the strategic management of a corporation, where the efficacy of decision making increases proportionately to the number of participating members; that is, pro-portionate to the wealth of points of view and experiences.

Communication professionals acting as activists should concentrate more on facilitating rather than on managing communication, thus contributing to creating processes that have meaning and attribute priority to the strategic options of the organization (Holtzhausen, 2002). The postmodern approach emphasizes the fact that paradox, which originates in dialogue among its principle figures, continually characterizes corporate life. The meaning of organizational action, in fact, is created through constant interaction, participation, continuous change and self-regulation among the corpo-rate parts. Thus diversity contributes to feeding the decisional, managerial, and productive processes with ever-new knowledge.

Even the most recent contributions of *Innovation Communication* (Zerfass, 2005; Zerfass, & Huck, 2007) stress that strategic communication as a support of innovation has the creation of a collaborative culture and fertile climate as its goal. "Innovation Communication differs fundamentally from 'ordinary' communication which is based on the situation that organizations and employees generally act in concert and share a common corporate goal" (Zerfass, 2005, p. 16). Strategic communication supports management in reassuring employees regarding changes due to innovation, supplying adequate information, and, in particular, listening to what happens inside the organizational context (Zerfass, & Huck, 2007). Communication must be oriented to defining objectives with precision, facilitating their sharing, and creating surrounding forms of cooperation. "Internal Innovation Communication is essential for defining innovation goals, capitalizing existing knowledge, overcoming fear, enhancing motivation, and developing shared visions" (Zerfass, 2005, p. 18).

The latest contributions in the field of internal communication (Boswell, 2006; Welch & Jackson, 2007) stress the importance of empowering employees within the innovative process. "The internal corporate communication dimension is defined as communication between an organization's strategic managers and its internal stakeholders, designed to promote commitment to the organization, a sense of belonging to it, awareness of its changing environment and understanding of its evolving aims" (Welch & Jackson, 2007, p. 193). Communication has the aim of rendering employees responsible by virtue of their being of key importance in implementing innovative processes (Dougherty, 1996). Effective communication transmits an innovative spirit to all employees, stimulating them, supplying input, and giving every individual room for expression as well as defining his or her specific responsibility.

Ferrari Case Study

The re-birth of Ferrari, the well-known Formula One auto maker, following a period of extremely serious crisis during the 1980s, is tied to the strategies put into effect by the new CEO, Luca Montezemolo. Montezemolo is a former director of Corporate Communication of the FIAT Group, where he reached the position of CCO. He joined Ferrari, became its president in 1991, and started a program that he named *Formula Persona,* which consisted in continuously improving innovation and creativity, centering on each employee and on what she or he could contribute.

To this end, several buildings and work environments were designed to optimize the production process and emphasize employees' individual identity and sense of belonging. In addition, a system was designed to recognize the contributions of the employees and to implement a series of company-sponsored services, including outside services, to simplify and improve employees' lives. This package of benefits took into account various aspects of private life: health, physical fitness and financial support, specifically as regards buying a home and furthering education.

The idea on which the *Formula Persona* was based, was that these measures would communicate to the employees the value the company placed on them as well as the recognition of the contribution of every person to the company's success.

The results have been astonishing from the point of view of employee commitment and of the company's economic results. In the middle of the 1990s the economic bottom line turned up and in 1999 Ferrari started again to win the world championships non-stop up until 2008 (Invernizzi, Romenti, & Fumagalli, 2012).

Visioning

Some scholars (Argenti, 2008; Cornelissen, 2008; van Riel, 1995) define as strategic those communication activities that make known the contents of company strategy and important corporate decisions to key stakeholders, both internal and external. The communication activity focuses on what to communicate in order to obtain the desired effect (Stroh, 2007). In the case of internal stakeholders, communicating the decisions regarding strategic company choices serves to channel collective energy to a common goal, consistent with company mission and guiding values.

In the case of external stakeholders, strategic communication activities are essential to shaping a single, clear company position in the minds of stakeholders as well as to developing a solid long-term reputation (Cornelissen, 2008). These studies stress the importance of coordinating all communication activities to ensure the coherence of messages sent and the strategic intent of the organization (van Riel, 1995).

Appropriate coordination between the departments and professionals responsible for communication reinforces this coherence when consideration is given to the content, tone, and style of the messages (Argenti, 2008).

The visioning component corresponds to the dimension, which Zerfass (2008, p. 70) defined as the enabling role of communication, meaning that communication facilitates the implementation of company decisions. In this case the CCO contributes by following the actual decisional momentum and exercising influence on the ways in which decisions are communicated and carried out. Communication helps govern the activities, mainly tactical in nature, which are necessary for the implementation of the decisions themselves. In fact, communication enables the decisional processes by transmitting their contents to interested parties, involving and motivating human resources, supporting the exercise of leadership, helping plan and organize the managerial and operational activities, and making it possible to check the results obtained. Some authors define communication strategy (Argenti, 2008; Cornelissen, 2008; Steyn, 2007) as that which makes known, inside and outside the organization, the decisions regarding company strategy and business objectives, focusing the energies of the organization's internal and external members towards a shared goal (Fenton & Langley, 2011).

The visioning role includes the infrastructural role, traditionally attributed to communication, that is, the role of sustaining and supporting the company business (Kotler, 2001). It represents a crucial component as it substantially contributes to the efficacy and quality of the results in the decisional process. This component in the communication role does not, however, exercise influence on the content of the decision itself, but rather on the way in which the decision is carried out. The approach employs a functionalist matrix since it begins by asking which processes, structures, and communication systems are the most adequate and contribute the most to developing business decisions (Belasen, 2008).

Also, Hamrefors (2010) argues that a *communicative leader* has the specific role of *mediator,* that is, one who endeavors not only to transmit messages from outside to inside, but, above all, to create a common, comprehensible, shared meaning. In this particular case, the skill required is being able to negotiate and influence.

Pastificio Rana Case Study

Pastificio Rana is a successful maker of fresh pasta products, which in a few years has become a multinational corporation. The founder and current president, Giovanni Rana, has always made use of principles based primarily on communicative and relational objectives to govern his company and to lead it to success. Rana has always taken into serious consideration the communicative impact of every strategic choice in his most important strategic and operating decisions. He has always placed the relational and communicative aspects at the forefront of his decisions, even if they are of technical and commercial nature.

An example of a technical decision is the design and engineering of a machine to produce tortellini that would be very similar to home-made tortellini. And a decision was made to decline to enter the frozen foods market, not so much because the product would not have the same quality or be as pleasing to the palate as the fresh product, but rather because of the desire to maintain the perception of high quality coupled with high price. This has always been a characteristic of Rana products in the eyes of the consumer, maintained by the company even at the risk of a lower share of the market.

Other examples can be mentioned to show that the Giovanni Rana, and his son and current CEO, Gian Luca Rana, have always considered relationships as very important tools in managing their company.

First, the relationship between father and son is a tribute to the founder's ability to ensure gradual transition, without discontinuity, by activating a collaborative effort to transform the potential generational problem into generational synergy. This synergy is fundamental in facilitating the transition from a family-run to a managerial company: that is, to achieve what Giovanni Rana sees and defines as a boat run by two motors—a company able to grow and be successful in the face of international challenges.

The relationship with clients constitutes another important aspect, such as tortellini given away for free to potential customers as a way of promoting the product during the early phases of the company's history. Recently, Gian Luca Rana sent invitations to dinner to important customers (directors of large retail companies) at his villa on Lake Garda, where Gian Luca himself and his managers do the cooking and serve the guests.

The potent integration of values and culture, rooted in relationships, is a characteristic strongly cultivated, first by Giovanni Rana, and later by his son Gian Luca, who have built a successful company, starting from a small artisanal business to its present status as an important multinational corporation (Invernizzi, Romenti, 2013).

Constituting

The interpretation of the information gathered, and the attribution of sense and meaning to it, is part of the process that Weick (1995) defined as organizational sense-making. By including communication in the dominant coalition, the process of sense-making gains a more complete and articulated outlook of the company and of all the interested parties within it.

The role of sense making can be utilized within the corporation, looking outside it, and can consist of pinpointing in advance the communicative aspects of decisions taken, of the strategic options the organization has at its disposal, and of the specific strategic objectives. In particular, the relevant aspects include the attitudes and behaviors of the stakeholders, and the resulting impact that strategic decisions can have on the quality of the relationship network and on the value of the corporate reputation. Sense making from the outside to the inside of the organization is also essential to understanding the impact and the consequences of issues on the decisional, productive and managerial processes.

In this case, communication becomes something more than an infrastructural component of the business. Scholars who define the theories of *communication as constitutive of the organization* (Cooren, Taylor, & Van Every, 2006; Putnam & Nicotera, 2009, 2010; Reed, 2010; Sewell, 2010) consider communication as a constituting element and process of an organization, and base their theories on Weick's (1969) concept of organizational sense-making, according to which reality is created through a cognitive process of interpretation rooted in individual mental maps.

An organization is seen as a continuous entity constantly transforming the communicative actions of its members (Bisel, 2010; Cooren, Kuhn, Cornelissen, & Clark 2011; Kuhn, 2008). In this case, communication becomes something more than an infrastructural component of the business. It feeds the decisional process, influencing its contents even through reflective activities of analysis and interpretation of the internal and external context. Here the listening activity plays a different role from that of the enabling role of communication, where listening aims at aligning the communication of the decisions taken with the opinions and attitudes of the stakeholders.

The constitutive component plays a crucial role in the definition of the communicative aspects of decisions, completing the different ways in which communication contributes significantly to the corporate decision-making process.

Each of these components places special emphasis on given moments of the decisional, managerial and operational, processes.

For instance, through the aligning component, the strategic contribution of the activities that build symmetric relationships with key stakeholders is particularly important in the initial phase of the decisional process, the phase that defines the problems which catalyze the attention of the management. The problems which give rise to the decisional processes should, in fact, be rooted in an ongoing interchange between the organization and its reference environment. It is in this interchange that the communication professional can play the role of activist and facilitator.

In particular, the activity of analysis and interpretation of the organizational context can contribute to formulating the strategic options available to the manager as well as guiding him or her towards the most suitable choice. Through such activities managers can, in fact, understand which dynamics within the organizational context may have an impact on the decisional processes and, at the same time, what the communicative consequences could be of the various options available.

Visioning and energizing components of communication can make a strategic contribution to the corporation respectively by making known to key interlocutors the contents of company strategy and of the most relevant decisions taken, and by creating a work environment that facilitates innovation. The professionalism of the communicator is in these cases important in selecting the language best suited for the desired effect as well as in selecting the most appropriate techniques, messages and instruments.

Illycaffè Case Study

According to CEO Andrea Illy: "The real problem for Illycaffè is that the company has always aimed at a quality product whereas the average person thinks of coffee as a product to be consumed at a cafeteria bar while standing and, frequently, in a hurry. This way of having a cup of coffee makes it difficult to reward quality and makes the consumer reluctant to pay a higher price" (Andrea Illy, personal communication, December 2009).

For a number of years the goal of Illycaffè has been to bring clients to appreciate the quality of its product and, at the same time, to establish a strong link with the company. For this reason, Andrea Illy has been working hard on the *construction of relevance* of the product for customers and *building trust* towards the company.

The construction of relevance means making customers perceive a cup of coffee as an object of desire to be satisfied through various pleasant sensations, starting with those of the palate to those of a relational, cultural and environmental nature. In other words, it means raising expectations so as to be able to appreciate the quality of the product.

Building trust means working on the reputation of the company so that its customers are aware of the fact that it guarantees high levels in terms of the quality of the product, the selection and roasting of the raw material, and the respect with which it approaches the environment, people, cultures and aesthetics.

Communication assumes a strategic relevance for Illycaffè in upholding both relevance and trust and in creating synergy between the two. This vision of the strategic component of communication brings out a particularly interesting dimension that can be defined as an entrepreneurial component in the scenario enactment, whereby communication is used in support of corporate strategy to create a scenario of business opportunities, as previously mentioned.

The entrepreneurial dimension in the scenario enactment through communication is the component Illycaffè expects from communication in order to sustain the entrepreneurial nature of the company which, according to the CEO and to company history, is quite clearly evident, resting as the company does on four conceptual pillars. The first of these pillars is the high quality of the product and service attained; the second is the construction of relevance for the customers of a high quality product; the third is the building of trust that has been developed to benefit the customers and is rooted in the reputation the company has built over time; and the fourth—the truly unique nature of the company and its products—resonates with the aforementioned three factors, and strengthens Illycaffè's success.

An Entrepreneurial Communication Model

In this chapter we argue that entrepreneurial organization theories provide a conceptual framework which is useful in describing and evaluating the relevance of strategic communication. Adopting an entrepreneurial organization theory perspective allows us not only to describe the strategic role of communication as such, but also to describe the strategic role of communication in supporting the organizational decision-making processes. This means explaining the strategic communicative contents of the main organizational actions related to products, buildings and layouts, and the result of every significant managerial choice.

We have identified the most significant contribution made by the entrepreneurial organization theories (e.g., Busenitz et al., 2003) and we shall set out, now, the four dimensions best suited to interpreting and explaining the potentialities of strategic communication activity. Here we relate each of these four aspects of Entrepreneurial Organization Theory to one aspect of strategic communication, as shown in Figure 14.1.

By doing so, we elicit the entrepreneurial content of strategic communication. The result is what we call the entrepreneurial communication model, made up of *aligning, energizing, visioning* and *constituting* dimensions.

The four dimensions are not related to each other because each dimension must be evaluated by itself. Neither is there a specific point at which strategic communication begins to support and inform organizational decision making. Instead, as entrepreneurial organization theory and practice suggest, an entrepreneurial idea and activity can start from any phase or dimension of strategic communication and continue, following different paths.

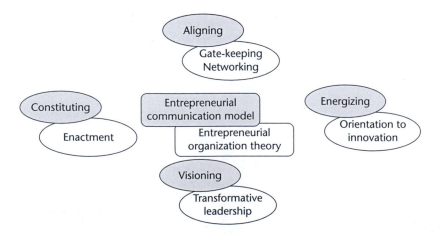

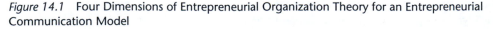

Figure 14.1   Four Dimensions of Entrepreneurial Organization Theory for an Entrepreneurial Communication Model

First, entrepreneurial studies say that strategic decisions are modelled by a continuous gate-keeping activity and the creation of social interactions, both within and outside the organization, in order to generate support and to shape and develop new ideas. Entrepreneurial communication, by means of its *aligning* component, can support organizations in scanning the environment, implementing boundary-spanning activities, and building supportive networks of stakeholders.

The Granarolo case study is presented as an example of aligning activity, mostly devoted to engaging stakeholders, such as in shaping new guiding values, developing new products and reducing costs.

Second, successful organizations should be innovation-driven, and entrepreneurial studies stress how important it is that a company striving to be innovative uses its resources, competences and capabilities in innovative ways, promoting entrepreneurial behaviors among internal stakeholders. Entrepreneurial communication supports the *energizing* of internal collaborative networks to drive innovation through the processes of new combinations of existing resources, creation of capabilities, and spread of knowledge.

The *Ferrari* case study shows how the "Formula Persona" project, based on the involvement of all internal stakeholders, drove the company back to economic success after a long period of losses.

Third, entrepreneurial organization studies highlight the transformative leadership role performed by management in modelling corporate strategies, creating a vision and defining guiding values around organizational projects. Entrepreneurial communication, by means of its *visioning* component, can help organizations create and share their mission and values, and deliver coherent messages.

The *Pastificio Rana* case study is an example of the extent to which company vision is based on product quality as an 'obsession,' and on the relationships with stakeholders as a must, guiding every action and communication activity including advertising.

Fourth, entrepreneurial scholars argue that organizations cannot develop a perfect knowledge of environments, but should enact their selective environments before taking strategic decisions (Weick, 1995). Enactment activity implies that the environment in which an entrepreneurial organization works will be socially created and therefore that opportunities become real in the mind of the entrepreneurial members.

The enactment of selective environments to shape strategic decisions presupposes the development of the *constituting* component of entrepreneurial communication, according to which the organization is seen as a product in constant transformation as a result of the communicative activities of its members.

The Illycaffè case study is an interesting example of how and to what extent communication helped the company to enact the external environment, transforming the product, a "cup of coffee," from a commodity into a high quality product.

Our conclusion is that each of the four dimensions of strategic communication shows a specific and relevant entrepreneurial content which allows us to formulate the entrepreneurial communication model. Our model is based on the discussion developed in this chapter on the conceptual relation between strategic communication and entrepreneurial organizational theories, and the empirical analysis of the four case studies. Further conceptual and empirical research is needed to consolidate the model.

References

Alvarez, S., & Barney, J. (2004). Organizing rent generation and appropriation: toward a theory of the entrepreneurial firm. *Journal of Business Venturing, 19,* 621–635.

Argenti, P. (2008). *Corporate communication.* New York: McGraw-Hill.

Bass, B. M. (1985). *Leadership and performance beyond expectations.* New York: Free Press.

Belasen, A. T. (2008). *The theory and practice of corporate communication.* Thousand Oaks, CA: Sage Publications.

Bisel, R. (2010). A communicative ontology of organization? A description, history, and critique of CCO theories for organization science. *Management Communication Quarterly, 24,* 124–131.

Boswell, W. (2006). Aligning employees with the organization's strategic objectives: out of line of sight, out of mind. *Human Resource Management, 17,* 1489–1511.

Burns, P. (2005). *Corporate entrepreneurship: building an entrepreneurial organization.* Basingstoke, England: Palgrave MacMillan.

Busenitz, L. W., West, G. P., Shepherd, D., Nelson, T., Chandler, G., & Zacharakis, A. (2003). Entrepreneurship research in emergence. *Journal of Management, 29,* 285–308.

Butler, L. E., & Brown, B., & Chamornmarn, W. (2003). Informational networks, entrepreneurial action and performance. *Asia Pacific Journal of Management, 20,* 151–174.

Bygrave, W. D. (1989). The entrepreneurship paradigm (I): a philosophical look at its research methodologies. *Entrepreneurship: Theory and Practice, 14,* 7–26.

Cooren, F., & Taylor, J. R., & Van Every, E. J. (2006). *Communication as organizing,* Mahwah, NJ: Lawrence Erlbaum.

Cooren, F., Kuhn, T., Cornelissen, & J. P., Clark, T. (2011). Communication, organizing and organization: an overview and introduction to the special issue. *Organization Studies, 32,* pp. 1149–1170.

Cornelissen, J. (2008). *Corporate communication.* London: Sage.

Daft, R.L., & Weick, K.E. (1984). Toward a model of organizations as interpretations systems. *Academy of Management Review, 9,* 284–295.

Davis, J. H., Schoorman, F. D., Mayer, R. C., & Tan, H. H. (2000). The trusted general manager and business unit performance: empirical evidence of a competitive advantage. *Strategic Management Journal, 21,* 563–576.

Dew, N., & Ramakrishna, V. S., & Venkataraman, S. (2004). Dispersed knowledge and an entrepreneurial theory of the firm. *Journal of Business Venturing, 19,* 659–679.

Dougherty, D. (1996). Organizing for innovation. In S. R. Clegg, C. Hardy, & W. R. Nord (Eds.), *Handbook of organization studies* (pp. 424–439). London, England: Sage.

Drucker, P.F. (1985). *Innovation and entrepreneurship: practice and principles.* New York: Harper and Row.

Echols, A.E., & Neck. C.P. (1998). The impact of behaviors and structure on corporate entrepreneurial success. *Journal of Managerial Psychology, 13,* 38–46.

Fenton C., Langley A. (2011). Strategy as practice and the narrative turn. *Organization Studies, 32*(9), 1171–1196.

Foss, N. J., Klein, P.G. (2005). Entrepreneurship and the economic theory of the firm: any gains from trade? In R. Agarwal, S.A. Alvarez, & O. Sorenson (Eds.), *Handbook of entrepreneurship research: disciplinary perspectives* (pp. 349–372). Dordrecht, Holland: Springer.

Freeman, R. E. (1984). *Strategic management: a stakeholder approach.* Boston, MA: Pitman.

Granovetter, M. S. (1973). The strength of weak ties. *American Journal of Sociology, 78,* 1360–1380.

Grunig, J. E. (2001). Two-way symmetrical public relations: past, present and future. In R. L. Heath (Ed.), *Handbook of public relations.* Thousand Oaks, CA: Sage.

Gupta, V., MacMillan, I. C., & Surie, G. (2004). Entrepreneurial leadership: developing and measuring a cross-cultural construct. *Journal of Business Venturing, 19,* 241–260.

Hallahan, K., & Holtzhausen, D., Van Ruler, B., Verčič, D., & Sriramesh, K. (2007). Defining strategic communication. *International Journal of Strategic Communication, 1,* 3–35

Hamrefors, S. (2010). Communicative leadership. *Journal of Communication Management, 14,* 141–152.

Hayton, J.C., & Kelley, D. (2006). A competency-based framework for promoting corporate entrepreneurship. *Human Resource Management***,** *45,* 407–427.

Hitt, M. A., Ireland, I. D., Camp, S. M., & Sexton, D. L. (2001). Guest editors' introduction to the special issue Strategic Entrepreneurship: Entrepreneurial Strategies for Wealth Creation. *Strategic Management Journal, 22,* 479–491.

Holtzhausen D. R. (2002). Towards a postmodern research agenda for public relations. *Public Relations Review, 28,* 251–264

Howell, J. M., & Higgins, C. A. (1990). The champions of technological innovation. *Administrative Science Quarterly, 35,* 317–341.

Invernizzi, E., Muzi Falconi, T., & Romenti, S. (Eds.), (2009). *Institutionalising PR and corporate communication.* Milano: Pearson.

Invernizzi, E., & Romenti, S. (2009). Institutionalisation and evaluation of corporate communication in Italian companies, *International Journal of Strategic Communication, 3,* 116–130.

Invernizzi, E., Romenti, S., Fumagalli, M. (2012). Identity, communication and change management in Ferrari. *Corporate Communications: an International Journal, 17,* 483–497.

Invernizzi E., Romenti S.(2013) Relationships and quality management. The Pastificio Rana case study. In J. M. T. Balmer, L. Illia, B. Gonzales (Eds.), *Contemporary perspectives on corporate marketing*. Abingdon, England: Routledge.

Ireland, R. D., Hitt, M. A., & Sirmon, D. G. (2003) A model of strategic entrepreneurship: the construct and its dimensions. *Journal of Management, 29,* 963–989.

Knight, G. A. (1997). Cross-cultural reliability and validity of a scale to measure firm entrepreneurial orientation. *Journal of Business Venturing, 12,* 213–225.

Knights, D. (1997). Organization theory in the age of deconstruction. *Organization Studies, 18,* 1–19.

Kotler, P. (2001). *Marketing management.* Englewood Cliffs, NJ: Prentice Hall.

Kuhn, T. A. (2008). Communicative theory of the firm: developing an alternative perspective on intra-organizational power and stakeholder relationships. *Organization Studies, 29,* 1227–1254.

Kusuma Wardhani, A., McCarthy, G., & Perera, N. (2009, December). Framework of entrepreneurial orientation and networking: a study of SME's performance in a developing country. Paper presented at the Australian and New Zealand Academy of Management Conference, Adelaide, Australia.

Lan, N. (2006). Relationships as organizational resources: examining public relations impact through its connection with organizational strategies. *Public Relations Review, 32,* 276–28.

Ledingham, J. A., & Bruning, S. D. (2000) (Eds.), *Public relations as relationship management.* Mahwah, NJ: Lawrence Erlbaum.

Levinthal, D. A. (1994). Surviving Schumpeterian Environments: an Evolutionary Perspective. In J. A. C. Baum, J. V. Singh (Eds.), *Evolutionary dynamics of organizations.* New York: Oxford University Press.

Li, Y., Liu, X., Wang, L., Li, M., & Guo, H. (2009). How entrepreneurial orientation moderates the effects of knowledge management on innovation. *Systems Research and Behavioral Science, 26,* 645—660

Lumpkin, G. T., & Dess, G. G. (1996). Clarifying the entrepreneurial orientation construct and linking it to performance. *Academy of Management Review, 21,* 135–172

Lurati, F., & Eppler, M. J. (2006). Communication and management: researching corporate communication and knowledge communication in organizational settings. *Studies in Communication Sciences, 6,* 75–98.

Maidique, M. A. (1980). Entrepreneurs, champions, and technological innovation. *Sloan Management Review, 21,* 59–76.

McFadzean, E., O'Loughlin, A., & Shaw, E. (2005). Corporate entrepreneurship and innovation part 1: the missing link. *European Journal of Innovation Management, 8,* 350–372.

Morris, M. H., & Kuratko, D. F . (2002). *Corporate entrepreneurship.* Fort Worth, TX: Harcourt College Publisher.

Morris, M. H., Kuratko, D. F., & Schindehutte, M. (2001). Towards integration: understanding entrepreneurship through frameworks. *Entrepreneurship and Innovation, 2,* 35–49.

Prahalad, C. K., Ramaswamy, V. (2003). The new frontier of experience innovation. *MIT Sloan Management Review, 44,* 11–18.

Putnam, L. L., Nicotera, A. M. (2009). *Building theories of organization: the constitutive role of communication.* New York: Routledge.

Putnam, L. L., & Nicotera, A. M. (2010). Communicative constitution of organization is a question: critical issues for addressing it. *Management Communication Quarterly, 24,* 158–165.

Reed, M. (2010). Is communication constitutive of organization? *Management Communication Quarterly, 24,* 151–157.

Sadler-Smith, E., Hampson, Y., Chaston, I., & Badger, B. (2003). Managerial behaviour, entrepreneurial style and small firm performance. *Journal of Small Business Management, 41,* 47–67.

Schon, D. A. (1967). *Technology and change.* New York: Delacorte.

Schumpeter, J. A. (1961). *The theory of economic development: an inquiry into profits, capital, credit, interest and the business cycle* (7th ed.). Cambridge, MA: Harvard University Press.

Sewell, G. (2010). Metaphor, myth, and theory building: communication studies meets the linguistic turn in sociology, anthropology, and philosophy. *Management Communication Quarterly, 24,* 139–150.

Smircich, L., & Stubbart, C. (1985). Strategic management in an enacted world. *Academy of Management Review, 10,* 724–736

Stevenson, H. H., & Jarillo J. C. (1990). A paradigm of entrepreneurship: entrepreneurial management. *Strategic Management Journal, 11,* 17–27.

Steyn, B. (2007). Contribution of public relations to organizational strategy formulation. In E. L. Toth (Ed.), *The future of excellence in public relations and communication management.* London, England: Routledge.

Stoffels, J. D. (1994). *Strategic issues management: A comprehensive guide to environmental scanning.* Tarrytown, NY: Elsevier.

Stroh, U. (2007). An alternative postmodern approach to corporate communication strategy. In E. L. Toth (Ed.), *The future of excellence in public relations and communication management.* London, England: Routledge

Tidd, J., & Bessant, J., & Pavitt, K. (2001). *Managing innovation: integrating technological market and organizational change* (2nd ed.). Chichester, England: John Wiley & Sons.

Tsai, W. (2000). Social capital, strategic relatedness and the formation of intraorganizational linkages. *Strategic Management Journal, 21,* 925–939.

van den Bosch, F. A. J., & van Riel, C. B. M. (1998). Buffering and bridging as environmental strategies of firms. *Business Strategy and the Environment, 7,* 24–31

van Riel, C. B. M. (1995). *Principles of corporate communication.* London: Prentice Hall

Weick, K. E. (1995). *Sensemaking in organizations,* Thousand Oaks, CA: Sage.

Welch, M., & Jackson, P.R. (2007).Rethinking internal communication: a stakeholder approach. *Corporate Communications: an International Journal, 12,* 177–198

White, J., & Verčič, D. (2001). An examination of possible obstacles to management acceptance of public relations contribution to decision making, planning and organisation functioning. *Journal of Communication Management, 6,* 194–200.

Zander, I. (2007). Do You See What I Mean? An Entrepreneurship Perspective on the Nature and Boundaries of the Firm. *Journal of Management Studies, 44,* 1141–1164.

Zerfass, A. (2005). Innovation readiness. A framework for enhancing corporations and regions by innovation communication. *Innovation Journalism, 2,* 1–27.

Zerfass, A. (2008). Corporate communication revisited: integrating business strategy and strategic communication. In Zerfass, A., van Ruler, B., Krishnamurthym, S. (Eds.), *Public Relations Research European and International Perspective and Innovations* (pp. 65–92), Wiesbaden: VS Verlag für Sozialwissenschaften.

Zerfass, A., & Huck, S. (2007). Innovation, Communication, and Leadership: New Developments in Strategic Communication. *International Journal of Strategic Communication, 1,* 107–122.

15

The Role of Communication Executives in Strategy and Strategizing

Finn Frandsen and Winni Johansen

In the 1950s and 1960s, the two words *strategy* and *strategic*—as in *corporate strategy* and *strategic management*—entered the world of business (Kiechel, 2010). Since then, managers in the private and public sectors have lived under the rule of a new strategy paradigm, which has become more and more dominant. Today, strategy has transformed into something that almost every organization has (or ought to have) and/or perform (or ought to perform); something that everybody talks about and/or identifies with in either a positive or a negative manner.

The two words *strategy* and *strategic* have also penetrated the area under investigation in the chapters of this handbook, that is, strategic communication defined as a specific organizational practice and a specific academic discipline. Today, communication professionals are expected to produce communication strategies for their organizations; at the same time, communication is more and more often perceived as a strategic management function reporting to or represented in the *dominant coalition* and contributing to or participating in its decision-making processes. Likewise, an increasing number of communication scholars have started examining what strategy, strategizing and strategists are and mean.

The new strategy paradigm penetrates at two different, but interrelated levels in relationship to the strategic communication of an organization: At the level of the *organizational practice* it emphasizes the need for a strategic understanding and approach to the external and internal communication activities as such, and to the relationship between these activities and the mission, vision, and strategy of the organization (an instrumental or functionalist perspective); and at the level of the *social status* of the communication executive it is understood to be part of the strategic work of the organization that provides the communication executive with a new and more powerful status (an institutional or symbolic perspective).

The aim of this chapter is to provide a state-of-the-art review of the research on the role of communication executives in strategy and strategizing, and we will address the following issues: the *role* communication executives perform in strategy and strategizing; their *competency* in strategic thinking; their self perception (*identity*) of their own strategic abilities; and how organizational members serving other managing functions, such as the CEO and other executives, perceive their strategic abilities (*legitimacy*).

Before we start addressing these issues, we need to clarify some of the key concepts. By *role* we do not only understand a specific behavioral program (the behavior that a communication executive is expected to enact, or that he or she actually enacts in a specific strategic and organizational context, as in the theory of organizational roles), but something more comprehensive transgressing the traditional boundaries of the concept (competencies, identity, and legitimacy). By *communication executive* (Wright, 1995) we do not only mean the highest ranking communication manager of an organization, but all types of communication managers who are involved in strategy and strategizing. Finally, by *strategy* we do not only mean the one-off result of rational decision-making, but also the less rational micro-level social activities whereby a strategy is produced and 'performed' (strategizing).

The chapter is divided into four sections. First, we give a brief account of how the study of strategy within the field of management research in general has developed since the 1960s following a series of important lines of development. This account is followed by an equally short section demonstrating how strategy has been thematized within the disciplines of public relations, corporate communication, and strategic communication. Then comes a longer section presenting the research conducted so far on the role, competencies, identity and legitimacy of communication executives in strategy and strategizing. We introduce the concept of *strategic work* as an overall term for this configuration of phenomena. The chapter concludes with a section on future research focusing on the insights about communication executives we have gained so far, and in particular the methods we have applied in order to do so. It answers the questions of what is it that we know something about, and which methods have we applied to get this knowledge. The chapter concludes with a discussion on whether a more *contextualized* approach will provide us with a new and better, that is, more realistic understanding of the strategic work of communication executives.

Understanding Strategy and Strategic Management: From Normative Idealism to Critical Realism

Frandsen and Johansen (2010) claim that "the concepts of strategy, management, and leadership are multidimensional concepts applied, with more or less diverging meanings, within a series of different theoretical and practical contexts" (p. 298). Instead of producing a long list of schools of thought within strategic management (e.g. Mintzberg, Ahlstrand & Lampel, 1998), they provide an overview by making a distinction between four important lines of development, which collectively present a shift from normative idealism to critical realism in management research. These lines of development will serve as the theoretical coordinating system for the rest of the chapter. The four lines of development are as follows.

From a Prescriptive to an Emergent Perspective on Strategic Management

According to the prescriptive perspective, strategy is the result of a linear, rational–analytical process in which a distinction is made between a series of clearly separated sequences such as *situational analysis, decision making (strategy formulation) implementation,* and *evaluation.* The prescriptive perspective is based on the idea that it is possible to define the objective of a strategy in advance and to develop its main elements, before it is implemented (Lynch, 2012, p. 35). On the contrary the emergent perspective holds that a strategy is seldom the result of such a process. Strategies do not always develop as planned or expected, but tend to emerge in organizations over time as a result of new opportunities, organizational learning or even accidental actions. Therefore, advocates of the emergent perspective claim that it is not possible to define the final goal of a strategy in advance, or to develop its main elements before it is implemented (Lynch, 2012, p. 40). This means that from an emergent perspective, it doesn't make sense to perceive decision-making and implementation as two clearly separated sequences in the strategy formation process.

McGee (2003) introduces a similar distinction between two worldviews: the programmatic view is "a mindset where the world is largely 'anticipated' and 'planned for'" (p. 150) and the emergent view is "a mindset where the world is viewed as uncertain and 'shaping' but also 'shapable'" (p. 150).

The prescriptive approach is much more widespread than the emergent perspective. It represents what we might call the *archetype* of strategic management. This is also the case in public relations, corporate communication and strategic communication, where one seldom meets the emergent perspective. Even in recent publications such as Moss and DeSanto (2011), who promote a managerial perspective on public relations, the authors claim that "much of the writing about communication/public relations shows little recognition of how thinking about management and managerial practice has evolved in recent years" (p. XV) and end up with a model based on the prescriptive perspective. Moss and DeSanto propose the C–MACIE framework consisting of four stages: *communication management analysis, communication management choice, communication management implementation*, and *communication management evaluation* (p. 41).

From an Intuitive to a Scientific Approach to Strategic Communication

Until the end of the 1960s and the beginning of the 1970s, strategic management was based on intuitive understanding, and not on scientific investigation, often with a reference to Fayol's (1916/1918) distinction between five managerial functions: to plan, to organize, to coordinate, to command, and to control. However, in 1973, Henry Mintzberg formulated his famous question: *What do managers really do when they manage?* It was the first in a series of empirical studies of what managers do or are expected to do (their behavior and activities, their functions and responsibilities), how they do what they do, whom they interact and communicate with, and what else they are doing (the informal aspects of managerial work). In his study, Mintzberg (1973) identified 10 basic management working roles, which he divided into three categories: interpersonal roles (the manager as figurehead, leader and liaison), informational roles (the manager as monitor, disseminator and spokesperson), and decisional roles (the manager as entrepreneur, disturbance handler, resource allocator and negotiator). Subsequently, other management scholars such as Hales (1986, 2001) and Stewart (1983, 1988)—including Mintzberg himself (see Mintzberg, 2009)—have discussed, not only the empirical results, but also the theoretical and methodological issues that are linked to the study of what managers really do when they manage.

Mintzberg (1973) represents a major breakthrough. However, as we will see in the second part of this chapter, the study of the role of communication executives that scholars in public relations, corporate communication and strategic communication have conducted has only to a very limited extent been inspired by this type of empirical management research.

From a Functionalist to a Critical Approach to Strategic Management

A third line of development is the shift from a functionalist to a critical approach to strategic management. Inspired among others by Critical Theory (the Frankfurt School), social constructivism, feminist theory, poststructuralism and "French Theory" (e.g., Foucault and Derrida), the critical approach questions the dominant management principles of organizing (such as efficiency, rationality, homogeneity, and masculinity), bringing new meanings to the concept of strategy.

Shrivastava (1986) reached the conclusion that strategic management was an *ideology* and that the discourse on strategy helped legitimize existing power structures and resource inequalities. Knights and Morgan (1991) draw a similar conclusion, defining corporate strategy as a "set of discourses and practices which transform managers and employees alike into subjects who secure their sense of purpose and reality by formulating, evaluating and conducting strategy" (p. 252).

Since the beginning of the 1990s, and the publication of Alvesson and Willmott (1992), critical management studies (CMS) has established itself as a subdiscipline adding a new and provocative dimension to the agenda of management studies. According to Alvesson and Deetz (2000), critical management research includes three tasks: an *insight* task demonstrating a commitment to "the hermeneutic, interpretive and ethnographic goals of local understandings closely connected to and appreciative of the lives of real people in real situations" (p. 17), a *critique* task counteracting the "dominance of taken-for-granted goals, ideas, ideologies and discourses which put their imprints on management and organization idea" (p. 17), and a *transformative redefinition* task demonstrating a commitment to the pragmatic aspects of a critical approach, "recognizing that insight and critique without support for social action leaves research detached and sterile" (p. 17).

A critical approach to strategic management in public relations, corporate communication, and strategic communication is still a rare sight. L'Etang (2008) is one of the few exceptions. She describes strategic management as a "Holy Grail for some PR academics and some PR practitioners," as an "ideological practice, focused on domination and power," and as a "form of civilian political warfare or *psyops*" (pp. 29–30). In the chapter on public relations and management in her book, new topics such as the creolization of management knowledge, power and gender issues, and management fashions and gurus are introduced. However, strategic management is only mentioned once, without any attempt to clarify the new discourse on strategy. Derina Holtzhausen is another critical scholar who takes a postmodern approach defining public relations as activism (Holtzhausen, 2012).

From a Macro-Level to a Micro-Level Approach to Strategic Management

The fourth important line of development is also the most recent: the move in the 2000s towards a micro-level approach to strategic management, introduced under the name of strategy as practice (Johnson, Langley, Melin & Whittington, 2007; Golsorkhi, Rouleau, Seidl & Vaara, 2010). This new community of scholars is first of all inspired by the 'practice turn' in the social sciences (Schatzki, Knorr Cetina & Savigny, 2001). Like Mintzberg (1973), they want to study what people actually *do* when working with strategy in organizations:

> Strategy as practice attempts a fundamental inversion of dominant conceptions of strategy. Whereas strategy has traditionally been seen as something an organization has—for example, a diversification strategy or an internationalization strategy—for strategy as practice researchers, strategy is something you do.
>
> *Jarzabkowski & Whittington, 2008, p. 101*

According to the *archetype* of strategic management, a strategy is something that an organization *has;* a strategy is the result of one-off decisions; a strategy is developed in specific places (e.g., the board room), at specific times (e.g., during strategy seminars), and by specific persons at the top of the organizational hierarchy (top management or the board of directors); and a strategy is always formulated before it is implemented. The strategy-as-practice researchers take a somewhat different approach. To them, strategy is first of all *strategizing,* something *people do,* an activity embedded in a specific organizational context. The result is a new focus on the complex micro-practices constituting the everyday activities of organizational life including strategy making. Viewed from this perspective, strategic management is not a disembodied and decontextualized activity, but an interactive and situated type of behavior in organizational settings.

To these four lines of development within the study of strategic management, one may perhaps add a fifth line of development, namely the shift from a *leader-oriented* perspective where strategy is understood as the result of the transmission of a manager's decisions to the employees, focusing on leader identity and/or leader behavior (as in most recently the theories of transactional versus transformational leadership), to a *follower-oriented* perspective, where strategy is understood as an outcome of the interaction between the manager and the employees (as in most recently the theories of shared, collective or distributed leadership, leader-member exchange, and the romance of leadership) (Shamir, Pillai, Bligh & Uhl-Bien, 2008). Thus far, Heide and Simonsson (2011) are among the very few scholars who have tried to develop a follower-oriented perspective within the field of strategic communication.

Strategy and Disciplines

In this section, we provide an overview of how strategy has been thematized within three important communication disciplines: public relations, corporate communication and strategic communication. These disciplines all pride themselves on their strategic approach to the communication activities between an organization and its publics or stakeholders. But what do they mean by *strategy* and *strategic?*

Public Relations

Public relations emerged as an academic discipline in the 1970s and the 1980s. In Excellence Theory, born out of the IABC funded Excellence Study, which was led by James E. Grunig from the mid-1980s until 2002, and which for a long period of time was defining for the discipline as such, the strategic approach to public relations is highlighted repeatedly as in the concept of *strategic public relations*. L. A. Grunig, J. E. Grunig and Dozier (2002) list five keywords describing Excellence Theory: "*managerial, strategic, symmetrical, diverse,* and *ethical*" (p. 306). Throughout the years, Grunig has defined his approach to public relations as a "*behavioral, strategic management paradigm* that focuses on the participation of public relations executives in strategic decision-making to help manage the behavior of organizations" (Grunig, 2006).

In the first of the three volumes presenting the results of the Excellence Study, J. E. Grunig and Repper (1992) promote a definition of strategy as the balancing of the internal structures and processes of the organization (the *mission* of the organization) with the external factors (the *environment* of the organization). A model of strategic management is presented that is clearly based on the prescriptive perspective, and strategy is viewed as a *symmetrical* concept: "[I]t is in the strategic interest of organizations to change their behavior when they provoke opposition from the environment as well as to try to change the behavior of environmental stakeholders" (p. 123). Finally, the relation between strategic management and public relations is conceptualized as participation in the overall strategic management process of an organization, and as the strategic management of public relations itself (pp. 119–123).

In Dozier, L. A. Grunig and J. E. Grunig (1995), the definition of public relations as the balancing of internal structures and processes of organizations with external factors is still present. However, in the third volume, L. A. Grunig, J. E. Grunig and Dozier (2002) define strategic management in a more metaphorical way as "the arena in which important organizational problems are identified and decisions are made about how to address those problems" (p. 143). The theoretical references also changed in a remarkable way and the authors cite Mintzberg and Weick together with Knight's and Morgan's postmodern view of strategic management. What characterizes public relations in relation to strategic management is still the fact that public relations "brings a different set of problems and possible solutions into the strategic management arena. In particular, it brings the problems of stakeholder publics into decision making—publics who make up the environment of the organization" (p. 143).

Corporate Communication

Corporate communication makes its appearance as an academic discipline in the 1990s defining itself as a *strategic management discipline* that examines how the external and internal communication activities of an organization can be integrated, and how relationships to key stakeholders can be built with the purpose of creating a favourable reputation (for definitions of corporate communication, see Frandsen & Johansen, 2014).

In one of the most popular textbooks on corporate communication, strategy is defined briefly as "[t]he ways or means in which the corporate objectives are to be achieved and put into effect" (Cornelissen, 2011, p. 7). In the very same book, however, two approaches to strategy formation are presented in more detail. In the one approach it is described as a deliberate, planned, analytical top-down process, and in the other as a spontaneous, emergent, visionary bottom-up process (Cornelissen, 2011, p. 83). In other words, we rediscover the first of the five lines of development presented in the previous section.

It must be emphasized that in contrast to the majority of textbooks on corporate communication, Cornelissen (2011) takes a rather progressive approach to strategy and strategizing. Most other textbooks either refrain from defining what they understand by *strategy* and *strategic,* or they support, explicitly, but mostly implicitly, the prescriptive perspective on strategy. Van Riel (1995) uses the term *corporate strategy,* but without defining it. Argenti (1994) prefers the term *organization strategy* which embraces three subsets: determining the objectives, deciding what resources are available, and diagnosing the organization's image credibility.

More recently Goodman and Hirsch (2010) talk about leadership defined either from a leader identity or from a leader behavior approach. The aim of these two authors is to establish normative guidelines putting corporate communication strategy into action in a global context—again, unfortunately, without specifying what they mean by strategy.

Strategic Communication

The last of the three disciplines, strategic communication, emerges as an academic discipline after the year 2000 defining its field of study as "the purposeful use of communication by an organization to fulfill its mission" (Hallahan, Holtzhausen, van Ruler, Verčič and Sriramesh, 2007, p. 3; see also Holtzhausen, 2008). The concept of organization has a very broad meaning in this context, including not only private and public organizations, but also advertising agencies and political parties (Hallahan, 2004). Strategic communication is the only discipline in which the word *strategic* forms part of the name itself. It is also a discipline that right from the beginning reflected on the meaning of *strategy* and *strategic* in a more sophisticated way.

Hallahan et al. (2007) make a distinction between a *modernist* and a *postmodernist* approach to strategy and strategic management. The modernist approach corresponds to what we labelled the prescriptive perspective in the previous section. The strategy formation process is viewed as rational and objective; that is, as a process detached from its political and cultural context. The critics of the modernist approach claim that this approach only takes into account the interests and goals of top management, thereby reducing strategic communication to asymmetrical, top-down communication from top management to employees. Strategy is therefor conceived as something negative. The postmodernist approach corresponds to what we called the emergent perspective in the previous section, but it also includes elements from what we have described as the shift to a critical or practice-oriented approach (comprising the issues of power and agency). Concerning the emergent perspective, it is emphasized that the strategy-making process always will be based on prior experience and actions, and that it also always will include actions and decisions made by employees at all levels of the organization. Thus, the postmodernist approach entails a critique of the traditional distinction, introduced by public relations scholars, between two roles: communication managers who take decisions or contribute to the decision-making process, and communication technicians who implement these decisions.

To summarize, then: the understanding of strategy and strategic management within the disciplines of public relations, corporate communication, and strategic communication has developed over a period of more than 30 years. Strategic orientation was already prominent as a topic of discussion in the 1980s, but it remained within the scope of the prescriptive perspective, without being very explicit about this. Since that time, and especially since the year 2000, the understanding of strategy and strategic management among communication scholars has clearly become more explicit and sophisticated. However, when compared to the research conducted within the field of management research, there still seems to be a gap that needs to be addressed. Among the scholars who have contributed to reducing this gap are Steyn (2007) and Raupp and Hoffjann (2010).

The Strategic Role of Communication Executives

Equipped with this understanding of how the study of strategy and strategic management has developed within the field of management research in general, and in the disciplines of public relations, corporate communication and strategic communication specifically, it is now possible to discuss the major concern of this chapter: the role of communication executives in strategy and strategizing. In order to conduct a state-of-the-art review, we have screened the most important journals in public relations, corporate communication, and strategic communication (such as *Public Relations Review, Journal of Public Relations Research, Corporate Communications: An International Journal, Journal of Communication Management*, and *International Journal of Strategic Communication*), as well as some of the most important research monographs and handbooks published between 1990 and 2013. The literature on the role of communication executives in strategy and strategizing is small but growing. The analysis yielded several variations on the theme, namely, how communication executives perceive themselves as strategists, how others perceive them, their strategic thinking, their view of social media and text genres such as the press release, and the role of communication executives in specific types of organizations (such as universities) and in specific countries (such as the United Kingdom). Behind all these variations lies the key question of the *institutionalization* of communication management in organizations (Grandien & Johansson, 2012; Frandsen & Johansen, 2013).

Space limitations preclude a review of all these research contributions. In this section, therefore, we will concentrate on the *role, competencies, identity* and *legitimacy* of communication executives as strategists, as explained earlier.

The Role of Communication Executives as Strategists

In the previous section, we claimed that so far public relations scholars have not approached the concept of strategy and strategic management in a very explicit or sophisticated way. However, this doesn't mean that the discipline of public relations has not contributed insights that are of interest to the study of the role of communication executives in strategy and strategizing. There are two areas in particular where public relations scholars have conducted relevant research regarding communication executives. The first area is the research on public relations practitioner *roles*. The second area is the research on the *access to and membership in the dominant coalition*.

Concerning the first line of research it seems possible to draw a rough distinction between a first generation of research on public relations practitioner roles, represented first of all by Broom and Dozier, which runs from the late 1970s until the beginning of the 2000s; and a second generation of research (represented, among others, by Moss, Steyn and Holtzhausen), which starts after the year 2000 (see the most recent literature review in Dozier & Broom, 2006). It is characteristic of the first generation that it is not very explicit regarding the practitioners' role as *strategists* and participants in the strategic work of organizations, whereas the second generation seems to be more aware of this role.

Broom and Smith (1979) established the first typology of practitioner roles based on the literature on organizational and consulting roles. Organizational role is defined as "abstractions, conceptual maps that summarize the most salient features of day-to-day behaviors of organizational members"

(Dozier and Broom, 2006, p. 137). Broom and Smith (1979) identified four conceptual roles: the expert prescriber (the practitioner as the authority on public relations), the communication facilitator (the practitioner as the mediator between the organization and its publics), the problem-solving process facilitator (the practitioner as the rational problem-solver collaborating with line management), and the communication technician (the practitioner as the producer of communication materials).

Subsequently, Dozier (1983, 1984) discovered that the first three types could be collapsed into a single role, thus creating the well-known role dichotomy that was dominant until the beginning of the 2000s: namely, the role of the *communication manager* versus the role of the *communication technician*. Regarding the content of the role of the communication manager, Dozier refers to decision-making and strategic planning, but seldom, and only in an indirect way, does he refer to strategy and strategizing as such, or to the practitioner's role as strategist.

In a series of articles, Moss and Green (2001), DeSanto and Moss (2004) and Moss, Newman and DeSanto (2005) highlighted some of the limitations of previous practitioner roles research, including Broom and Dozier's pioneering research in the 1980s and 1990s. First, the majority of the studies of practitioner roles had only provided a one-sided perspective of role enactment, "rather than examining the role-making process as a product of the interaction between 'role senders' and 'role receivers'" (Moss & Green, 2001, p. 122). This is a criticism that reflects the micro-level perspective of the *strategy as practice* research tradition presented above. Second, there had been a strong focus on the issue of gender discrimination. Third, there was also a strong focus on a US context. And finally, with an implicit reference to Mintzberg, "insufficient attention has been paid to examining critically how the nature of 'managerial work' in the public relations context has been defined" (p. 122); that is, "what public relations 'managers' do" (p. 127). According to Moss and his colleagues, the explanation is methodological: whereas public relations researchers have adopted a deductive approach to examine the validity of the conceptual role types identified by Broom and Dozier, management researchers have adopted an inductive approach using both quantitative and qualitative methods, such as participant observation, interviews and diaries.

Tindall and Holtzhausen (2011) were among the first scholars to conceptualize the communication executive's role of *strategist*. Inspired by Steyn (2002, 2007), they tested and measured public relations roles theory, conducting an online survey among 782 South African advertising, public relations, and government practitioners. It must be emphasized that the purpose of the study was not to test the existence of these roles *per se* but to contribute to theory building in strategic communication as defined by Hallahan et al. (2007).

Among the three research questions addressed by this study, RQ1 is the most relevant to this chapter: What are the roles performed by South African communication practitioners? A total of 32 items were used to measure nine different communication roles: the four roles conceptualized by Broom and Smith (1979) (cf. above), the four roles measured in a previous study (Holtzhausen, Petersen, & Tindall, 2003), and finally the new role of strategist. The four items used to measure the strategist role were

1. I am required to scan the environment for new stakeholder and societal trends that can be used in strategic planning.
2. I actively contribute to the strategic planning process of my organization/client on behalf of the communication function.
3. I am part of the strategic team that helps my organization/client adapt to the future.
4. I always consider the strategic implications of my work for my organization/client (pp. 83–84).

Interestingly, the results of Tindall and Holtzhausen's (2011) study showed that the role of strategist was the role most commonly used in South African communication practice. In addition, a factor analysis conducted to ensure there was no overlap between the roles also revealed that the strategist role actually included nine items, with two items from the expert prescriber role, and three items from the process facilitator role (p. 87).

Research on public relations roles now included the role of strategist (and not only communication manager), and has also been carried out in areas other than public relations, such as advertising and government communication. However, we still know very little about what respondents actually mean by *strategy* and *strategic* when they give answers to questions such as "I actively contribute to the strategic planning of my organization" and "I am part of the strategic team that helps my organization."

Membership in the Dominant Coalition

The second line of research that is of interest to the study of the communication executive's role in strategy and strategizing examines how public relations practitioners gain membership in the dominant coalition of an organization. By *membership* we mean a specific organizational status and a specific set of actions and reactions that manifest themselves in various forms, such as a move from temporary access to permanent membership, or from passive to active participation once inside the dominant coalition, or as attention and reliance from top management.

To define what dominant coalition means is far more challenging. Grunig (1992) defines the dominant coalition as "the powerholders of the organization" (p. 24). The prototype of a dominant coalition is still the CEO, the rest of the C-suite, or the board of directors who possess the formal authority and the control of decision-making processes, resources and outcomes. However, public relations researchers such as Berger (2005) have emphasized the shifting nature of dominant coalitions:

> [M]ost of the decision-making struggles occur beneath the BOD level among multiple-dominant coalitions. These are the intersecting power groups—loosely or tightly coupled—where public relations managers seek and are sometimes active in strategic roles. Some of these coalitions or power groups are relatively fixed and formal in nature, whereas others are more ad hoc and contingency based.
>
> *Berger, 2005, p. 10*

Bowen (2009) conducted a major study of how communication executives obtain membership in the dominant coalition and what kind of barriers there are to such a membership. Based on data from a large survey among members of IABC, four focus groups and interviews with 32 communication executives, she identified five different routes to short-term or long-term membership of the dominant coalition of an organization: serious organizational crises, ethical dilemmas, credibility gained over time, issues high on the media agenda and leadership.

In a series of studies that adopt a critical perspective including power as an important issue, Berger (2005, 2007) and Berger and Reber (2006) made an attempt to demystify the dominant coalition by opening it up for scrutiny. What happens inside the dominant coalition when the communication executive has finally gained membership? According to Excellence Theory, we can expect the communication executive to do the "right" thing, that is, contribute to the implementation of a two-way symmetrical model of public relations balancing organizational self-interest with the interest of key publics. However, the studies conducted by Berger and Reber revealed a somewhat different picture.

Based on interviews with 21 communication executives, Berger (2005) formulated six propositions (valid for large organizations), which shed light on our lack of realism when talking about the dominant coalition:

1. There is not just one dominant coalition: power relations occur in multiple dominant coalitions.
2. It is difficult to maintain permanent membership: venues for dominant coalitions shift back and forth, from formal to informal settings.

3. The CEO, often considered a leading member of the dominant coalition, is still very much "present," even when he or she is not there (during formal meetings): decisions still need to be 'blessed' by the CEO.
4. Decisions made by the dominant coalition are seldom final: the decision-making process often continues and it has multiple points of entry.
5. The dominant coalition may value the strategic advice of public relations, but it still demands a set of deliverables (texts) that highlight technical skills.
6. Public relations professionals are not immune to pressures of organizational compliance; that is, they do not always do the "right" thing.

Both Bowen (2009) and Berger (2005) emphasize the importance of gaining membership in the dominant coalition. Yet, they approach the topic from two different perspectives. Like most representatives of the Excellence Theory, Bowen views strategic management as a decision-making process to which communication executives may have access in specific situations and/or due to specific competencies, but does not discuss strategy as such. Berger, who presents himself as a critical scholar, is far more pragmatic in his approach, but sheds light neither on how communication executives understand and perform strategy, nor on what it means to them to be strategic.

Competencies

Much research has focused on the distinction between communication technicians and communication managers and on the idea that participation in strategic decision making and membership in the dominant coalition depends on the capability of the communication executive to enact the managerial role (Brønn, 2001). Brønn argues that because enacting the managerial role can be just the same as "performing high-level technical activities" (p. 313), what communication executives need is competencies in *strategic thinking*. Based on a review of literature and on models of strategic planning, issues management, and issues life cycle, Brønn identifies three major attributes associated with strategic thinking: using research-based information (generated from environmental scanning or information gathering); working from a plan (managerial planning: strategic and tactical plans); and being a member of the top management team with a boundary spanning role: that is, to communicate stakeholder views to senior managers and vice versa, and to participate in the decision-making process.

The Communication Executive as Perceived by Others

Whereas the vast majority of studies of the roles and competencies of communication executives are based on the practitioners' self-perception, only a few studies have examined how CEOs and managers of other departments such as marketing and HR departments perceive communication executives. Steyn (1999), Brønn (2001), and, especially, Brønn and Dahlen (2012) have tried to shed some light on this important aspect.

Steyn (1999) conducted a survey among 103 South African CEOs from public and private companies to determine the expectations of the CEO of public relations roles. The CEO expectations were assessed according to 25 statements that formed the index for measuring the roles of the PR technician, the PR manager and the PR strategist. According to the findings, the historical manager role could be split into the role of PR strategist and PR manager. In smaller organizations, one person might perform both roles, whereas these roles often are enacted by two different people at different organizational levels in larger organisations. The study also described the activities the CEO expected the PR strategist to perform: to provide the organization's strategy formulation processes with strategic information about strategic stakeholders, publics and activists and their concerns, and about the consequences of organizational policies and strategies for these groups.

In a study conducted among a large sample of private and public sector leaders in Norway to examine how they perceived the communication executive and the communication function, Brønn and Dahlen (2012) identified several gaps between the views of leaders and the views of communication practitioners in Norway. The leaders rated the communication executives' competencies regarding strategic thinking only as above average, and worse in the public sector than in the private sector. The competencies related to information collection, problem analysis, creativity, planning, organizational and external awareness, and change orientation. The leaders participating in the survey looked for competencies that mirrored activities performed by top management. If they found that the communication executive was able to make strategic contributions, they were more likely to value the communication executive and the communication department. This implies that having the right competencies, and also the support of top management, is critical if communication executives want to have more influence on strategic decision making, and to be invited to strategic meetings at the top level. It means that communication executives should have an "understanding of the appropriate external environment, the capabilities and objectives of the organisation, connections between loosely connected events, influencers, new opportunities and the seeing of strategies and solutions" (Hayes, as cited in Brønn & Dahlen, 2012). However, only 3% of the Norwegian communication practitioners indicated that their department was responsible for environmental scanning and issues management.

Legitimacy of Communication Executives

The legitimacy of the communication executive inside an organization, or in society at large, has been investigated by Johansson and Ottestig (2011). These two researchers were inspired by a survey the Swedish Public Relations Association conducted in 2009 among 200 CEOs about the future work of public relations practitioners. The survey showed that almost 80% of the communication executives were members of the senior management group, and that they were working chiefly with activities such as brand issues, relationship management, development of communication strategies, and coaching of managers in communication. The survey also showed that many communication executives are recruited without possessing any formal education in public relations or communication science.

Based on these findings, Johansson and Ottestig (2011) carried out in-depth interviews with communication executives from 10 organizations in order to find out if their internal and external roles enhanced the legitimacy of the communication function. The explorative study showed that the interviewees had a strategic or managerial role and that their work was clearly located at the managerial and strategic level. The external legitimacy of communication executives was perceived to be good. Externally they were considered official spokespersons on behalf of their organizations, they were treated as organizational leaders, and they had a good relationship with journalists. However, the study also showed that the internal legitimacy of communication executives was constantly negotiated inside the organization and that it differed a great deal from organization to organization. Even though internal legitimacy had increased in private as well as public organizations in Sweden (four out of five participants were members of the senior management group), a few interviewees indicated that they were not taken seriously, or that they sometimes had to legitimate their presence in the senior management group, for instance by taking initiatives and pursuing strategic organizational issues. Legitimacy varied over time, and it could be jeopardised due to the expectations of other managers. The lack of formal education in public relations or communication science among communication executives was also indicated as a contributing factor.

Shadowing Communication Executives

Inspired by Minzberg's *The nature of managerial work* (1973), Nothhaft (2010a, 2010b) conducted a shadowing study to examine what communication managers do when they manage, and why, in eight German companies. The study showed that it is possible to identify roles and functions of communication managers. However, the study also showed that there is much more to it than this. Nothaft (2010a, 2010b) introduces a distinction between *first-order* management and *second-order* management. First-order management is to influence the work of subordinates by managing it: for example by planning, organizing, and controlling. Second-order management is to influence the managing of others (peers) by institutionalizing certain concerns (of specific stakeholders or the general public) in an organization for the benefit of the organization.

The shadowing study showed that communication executives can enact at least three different roles when they perform second-order management, namely the missionary, the agent of common sense, and the buck's stop (Nothaft (2010a, 2010b). Although the role comes close to Mintzberg's figurehead, the *missionary* is not a special person. When he or she explains the company's brand values to new employees, he or she is just behaving as a "normal person inspired by a great idea" (Nothaft, 2010b, p. 135). The agent of common sense enacts Mintzberg's role of the disturbance handler. This type of communication manager is the diplomat trying to make parties stop quarrelling by talking some common sense into them, by using communication skills and public relations arguments. Finally, the buck's stop is the communication executive who has to shoulder the blame when something goes wrong. It is a more passive role, and more often than not it is imposed on the communication executive rather than actively taken by himself or herself. He or she is seen as somebody that covers the back of the others in communication matters. In second-order management, it is important that communication executives operate in a soft, influential and diplomatic way by influencing, advising and counselling rather than in a hard and 'managerial' way. In fact, Nothaft concludes that it is important for communication executives to be careful, when using power or claiming authority, to restrain their personal ego and not to steal the limelight from others.

Future Research: Opening Up the Black Box?

For decades, it has been a declared ambition for academics as well as practitioners in public relations, corporate communication and strategic communication to apply and to promote a strategic approach to their field of study or practice. However, there is still a stretch to accomplish before we have reached a more complete understanding of the concept of *strategy*. One of the most frequent ways of verbalizing about this topic is to use the expression *strategic decision-making,* but in most cases this expression is just another black box not allowing us to see what is meant by strategic and decision-making. (See Latour, 1987 concerning the status of concepts as black boxes.)

Future research on the role of communication executives in strategy and strategizing has the opportunity to develop along two parallel tracks: a theoretical track and a methodological track.

The theoretical track will first of all materialize as a cross-disciplinary combination of communication research and management research. Although a lot of progress has been made since the 1980s, the majority of scholars, especially in public relations and corporate communication, only seem to have eyes for the prescriptive perspective on strategic management. This applies in particular to the first generation of research on practitioner roles and membership in the dominant coalition. It is time to unfold the many dimensions of the concepts of strategy and strategic management, inspired by some of the other perspectives and approaches such as the emergent perspective or the strategy-as-practice approach.

The methodological track will most probably assume the form of a stronger combination of quantitative and qualitative research methods. On the one hand, surveys are still the most appropriate method when it comes to identifying recurrent patterns and generalizing across large populations of respondents, as in the study Tindall and Holtzhausen (2011) conducted. On the other hand, researchers such as Bowen (2009), Berger (2005), DeSanto and Moss (2004) and Nothhaft (2010a; 2010b) have demonstrated how both old and well-known qualitative research methods, such as interviews and focus groups, and new and perhaps less well-known research methods, such as shadowing and participant observation, can contribute with new insights concerning the roles and functions of communication executives in private and public organizations.

In response to these findings, we contend first that the increased application of qualitative methods will push us in the direction of a more contextualized approach to the study of strategic communication in general, and the roles and functions of communication executives and communication departments in particular. By *contextualized* we mean that strategic communication is not just a rational, instrumentalized function, but first and foremost a *contextually embedded organizational practice*. Second, and as an immediate consequence of the contextualized approach, a higher sense of critical realism should gradually appear in our ambitions and understanding of what strategy and strategic management are, and what they can do in organizations and to organizations.

References

Alvesson, M., & Willmott, H. (Eds.) (1992). *Critical management studies.* London, England: Sage.

Alvesson, M., & Deetz, S. (2000). *Doing critical management research.* London, England: Sage.

Argenti, P. (1994). *Corporate communication.* Boston, MA: Irwin McGraw-Hill.

Berger, B. K. (2005). Power over, power with, and power to relations: Critical reflections on public relations, the dominant coalition, and activism. *Journal of Public Relations Research, 17*(1), 5–28.

Berger, B. K. (2007). Public relations and organizational power. In E. L. Toth (Ed.), *The future of excellence in public relations and communication management: Challenges for the next generation* (pp. 221–234). Mahwah, NJ: Lawrence Erlbaum.

Berger, B. K., & Reber, B. H. (2006). *Gaining influence in public relations: The role of resistence in practice.* Mahwah, NJ: Lawrence Erlbaum.

Bowen, S. A. (2009). What communication professionals tell us regarding dominant coalition access and gaining membership. *Journal of Applied Communication Research, 37*(4), 418–443.

Broom, G. M., & Smith, G. D. (1979). Testing the practitioner's impact on clients. *Public Relations Review, 5*(3), 47–59.

Brønn, P. S. (2001). Communication managers as strategists? Can they make the grade? *Journal of Communication Management, 5*(4), 313–325.

Brønn, P. S., & Pedersen Dahlen, Ø. (2012). *Communication managers as strategists: Are they making the grade yet? A view of how other leaders view communication managers and communication in Norwegian private and public sector organizations.* Paper presented at annual the EUPRERA annual conference, Istanbul, Turkey.

Cornelissen, J. (2011). *Corporate Communication: A Guide to Theory and Practice* (3rd ed.). London, England: Sage.

DeSanto, B., & Moss, D. (2004). Rediscovering what PR managers do: Rethinking the measurement of managerial behavior in the public relations context. *Journal of Communication Management, 9*(2), 179–196.

Dozier, D. M. (1983). Toward a reconciliation of 'role conflict' in public relations research. Paper presented at the meeting of the Western Communication Education Conference, Fullerton, CA.

Dozier, D. M. (1984). Program evaluation and roles of practitioners. *Public Relations Review, 10*(2), 13–21.

Dozier, D. M., & Broom, G. M. (1995). Evolution of the managerial role in public relations practice. *Journal of Public Relations Research, 7*(1), 3–26.

Dozier, D. M., & Broom, G. M. (2006). The centrality of practitioner roles to public relations theory. In Botan, C., & Hazelton, V. (Eds). *Public Relations .Theory II* (pp. 137–170). London, England: Lawrence Erlbaum.

Fayol, H. (1918). *Administration industrielle et générale.* Paris, France: Dunod. (Originally published in the *Bulletin de la Société de l'Industrie Minérale, 1916*).

Frandsen, F., & Johansen, W. (2010). Strategy, management, leadership, and public relations. In Heath, R. L. (Ed.). *The SAGE handbook of public relations* (2nd ed., pp. 293–306). Thousand Oaks, CA: Sage.

Frandsen, F., & Johansen, W. (2013). Public relations and the new institutionalism: In search of a theoretical framework. *Public Relations Inquiry, 2*(2), 205–221.

Frandsen, F., & Johansen, W. (2014). Corporate communication. In V. Bhatia, & S. Bremner (Eds.). *The Routledge handbook of language and professional communication* (pp. 220–236). London, England: Routledge.

Golsorkhi, D., Rouleau, L., Seidl, D., & Vaara, E. (Eds.) (2010). *Cambridge handbook of strategy as practice*. Cambridge, England: Cambridge University Press.

Goodman, M. B., & Hirsch, P. (2010). *Corporate communication: strategic adaptation for global practice*. New York: Peter Lang.

Grandien, C., & Johansson, C. (2012). Institutionalization of communication management: A theoretical framework. *Corporate communication: an international journal, 17*(2), 209–227.

Grunig, J. E. (1992). Communication, public relations, and effective organizations: An overview of the book. In Grunig, J. E. (Ed.). *Excellence in public relations and communication management*, pp. 1–28. Hillsdale, NJ: Lawrence Erlbaum.

Grunig, J. E. (2006). *After 50 years: The value and values of public relations*. 45th Annual Distinguished Lecture, The Institute for Public Relations, The Yale Club, New York, November 9, 2006.

Grunig, L. A., Grunig, J. E., & D. M. Dozier (2002). *Excellent public relations and effective organizations: A study of communication management in three countries*. Mahwah, NJ: Lawrence Erlbaum.

Grunig, J. E., & Repper, F. C. (1992). Strategic management, publics, and isssues. In Grunig, J. E. (1992). *Excellence in public relations and communication management* (pp. 117–157). Hillsdale, NJ: Lawrence Erlbaum.

Heide, M., & Simonsson, C. (2011). Putting coworkers in the limelight: New challenges for communication professionals. *International Journal of Strategic Communication, 5*, 201–220.

Hales, C. P. (1986). What do managers do? A critical review of the evidence. *Journal of Management Studies, 23*(1), 88–115.

Hales, C. P. (2001). Does it matter what managers do? *Business Strategy Review, 12*(2), 50–58.

Hallahan, K. (2004). Communication management. In R. L. Heath (Ed.). *Encyclopedia of Public Relations* (Vol. 1, pp. 161–164). Thousand Oaks, CA: Sage.

Hallahan, K., Holtzhausen, D. R., Van Ruler, B., Verčič, D., & Sriramesk, K. (2007). Defining strategic communication. *International Journal of Strategic Communication, 1*(1), 3–35.

Holtzhausen, D., Petersen, B. K., & Tindall, N. T. J. (2003). Exploding the myth of the symmetrical/asymmetrical dichotomy: Public relations models in the new South Africa. *Journal of Public Relations Research, 15*(4), 305–341.

Holtzhausen, D. R. (2008). Strategic communication. In W. Donsbach (Ed.). *The International Encyclopedia of Communication* (pp. 4848–4855). New York: Wiley-Blackwell.

Holtzhausen, D. R. (2012). *Public relations as activism: postmodern approaches to theory and practice*. New York: Routledge.

Jarzabkowski, P., & Whittington, R. (2008). Hard to disagree, mostly. *Strategic Organization, 6*(1), 101–106.

Johansson, C., & Ottestig, A. T. (2011). Communication executives in a changing world: Legitimacy beyond organizational borders. *Journal of Communication Management, 15*(2), 144–164.

Johnson, G., Langley, A., Melin, L., & Whittington, R. (2007). *Strategy as practice: research directions and resources*. Cambridge, England: Cambridge University Press.

Kiechel, W. (2010). *The lords of strategy: The secret intellectual history of the new corporate world*. Boston, MA: Harvard Business Press.

Knights, D., & Morgan, G. (1991). Corporate strategy, organizations, and subjectivity: A critique. *Organization Studies, 12*(2), 251–273.

Latour, B. (1987). *Science in action: How to follow scientists and engineers through society*. Boston, MA: Harvard University Press.

L'Etang, J. (2008). *Public relations: Concepts, practice and critique*. London, England: Sage.

Lynch, R. (2012). *Strategic management* (6th ed.). Harlow, England: Pearson.

McGee, J. (2003). Strategy as orchestrating knowledge. In S. Cummings & D. Wilson(Eds.), *Images of strategy* (pp. 136–163). Malden, MA: Blackwell.

Mintzberg, H. (1973). *The nature of managerial work*. New York: Harper & Row.

Mintzberg, H. (2009). *Managing*. San Francisco, CA: Berrett-Koehler.

Mintzberg, H., Ahlstrand, B., & Lampel, J. (1998). *Strategy safari: The complete guide through the wilds of strategic management*. London, England: FT Prentice Hall.

Moss, D., & DeSanto, B. (2011). *Public relations: A managerial perspective*. London, England: Sage.

Moss, D., & Green, R. (2001). Re-examining the manager's role in public relations: What management and public relations research teaches us. *Journal of Communication Management, 6*(2), 118–132.

Moss, D., Newman, A., & DeSanto, B. (2005). What do communication managers do? Defining and redefining the core elements of management in a public relations/corporate communication context. *Journalism and Mass Communication Quarterly, 82*, 873–890.

Nothaft, H. (2010a). *Kommunikationsmanagement als eine professionelle Organisationspraxis. Theoretische Annäherung auf Grundlage einer teilnehmenden Beobachtung*. Leipzig, Germany: University of Leipzig.

Nothaft, H. (2010b). Communication management as a second order management function: Roles and functions of the communication executive: Results from a shadowing study. *Journal of Communication Management, 14*(2), 127–140.

Raupp, J., & Hoffjann, O. (2010). Understanding strategy in communication management. *Journal of Communication Management, 16*(2), 146–161.

Shamir, B., Pillai, R., Bligh, M. C., & Uhl-Bien, M. (Eds.) (2008). *Follower-centered perspectives on leadership: A tribute to the memory of James E. Maindl.* Greenwich, CT: Information Age.

Schatzki, T. R., Knorr Cetina, K., & von Savigny, E. (Eds.) (2001). *The practice turn in contemporary theory.* London, England: Routledge.

Shrivastava, P. (1986). Is strategic management ideological? *Journal of Management, 12*(3), 363–377.

Steyn, B. (1999). CEO Expectations in terms of PR roles. *Communicare, 19*(1), 20–43.

Steyn, B. (2002). A meta-theoretical framework for the role of the corporate communication strategist. *Communicare, 21*(2), 42–63.

Steyn, B. (2007). Contribution of public relations to organizational strategy formulation. In E. L. Toth (Ed.). *The future of excellence in public relations and communication management: Challenges for the next generation* (pp. 137–172). Mahwah, NJ: Lawrence Erlbaum.

Stewart, R. (1983). Managerial behavior: How research has changed the traditional picture. In Earl, M. J. (Ed.). *Perspectives on management* (pp. 82–98). Oxford, England: Oxford University Press.

Stewart, R. (1988). *Managers and their jobs: A study of the similarities and differences in ways managers spend their time.* London, England: Macmillan.

Tindall, N. T. J., & Holtzhausen, D. R. (2011). Toward a roles theory for strategic communication: The case of South Africa. *International Journal of Strategic Communication, 5*(2), 74–94.

van Riel, C. (1995). *Principles of corporate communication.* London, England: Prentice Hall.

Wright, D. K. (1995). The role of corporate public relations executives in the future of employee communications. *Public Relations Review, 21*(3), 181–198.

16

Organizational Goals and Communication Objectives in Strategic Communication

Kirk Hallahan

Strategic communication involves an organization communicating in a purposeful way to achieve its mission. Implied in the term *strategic* and the adjective *purposeful* is the notion that one or more outcomes are envisioned, planned and pursued (Hallahan, Holtzhausen, van Ruler, Verčič & Sriramesh, 2007).

Effective strategic communication begins with *analyzing situations* (problems or opportunities) that confront the entity through *research* (see chapter 24 in this volume). *Goals and objectives* that are specific provide the foundation for planning and *evaluating* the effort as well as for *strategy* and *message development* (see for example chapters 15 and 17 in this volume).

When strategic communication is viewed from a modernist perspective, strategically pursued outcomes smack of control and manipulation. Yet, in today's increasingly postmodern communication environment, entities of all types (organizations, products, services, personalities and causes) strive for desired outcomes—although the nature of those outcomes and methods for achieving them might be quite different from traditional modernist approaches.

This chapter examines the nature of goals and objectives as they apply to strategic communications across the various subdisciplines that comprise the field—including management communication, marketing communication, public relations, technical communication, political communication and public diplomacy, and health and pro-social information campaigns.

The Modernist Perspective: Management by Objectives

Despite any claims to the contrary, organized communication programs or campaigns by an entity are no different from other carefully planned organizational endeavors when viewed from the modern managerial perspective. Communicators must be accountable in order to earn the respect of organization leaders.

Perhaps representing the pinnacle of modern management theory, *management by objectives* (MBO) is a concept introduced by management guru Peter Drucker (1954; 1974, pp. 430–422) who argued that each manager's job must be focused on the success of the whole organization. He wrote:

> The performance that is expected of the manager must be derived from the performance goals of the business, his results must be measured by the contribution they make to the success of the enterprise. The manager must know and understand what the business goals demand of him in terms of performance, and his superior must know what contribution to demand and expect

of him—and must judge him accordingly. If these objectives are not met, managers are misdirected. Their efforts are wasted. Instead of team work, there is friction, frustration and conflict.

Drucker, 1954, p.121

MBO was later codified and popularized as management gospel by George Odiorne of the University of Michigan, who defined MBO as

a process whereby the superior and subordinate managers of an organization jointly identify its common goals, define each individual's major areas of responsibility in terms of the results expected of him, and use these measures as guides for operating the unit and assessing the contribution of its members.

Odiorne, 1965, pp. 55–56

He explained that MBO required no particular jargon because MBO is "essentially a system of incorporating into a more logical and effective pattern the things many people are already doing" but in a way that makes risks and responsibilities clear.

Communications professionals quickly embraced the value of objectives-based approaches. In 1961 Russell Colley called for advertising professionals to define advertising *goals* for measured advertising results (Colley, 1964). His DAGMAR model included specification of audiences and corresponding objectives (outcomes of the advertising message). Colley argued that advertising should be conceptualized fundamentally as a *communication* process, not merely in terms of sales. The latter approach had predominated advertising at the time. Colley extended the legendary AIDA model (Strong, 1925) by arguing that key steps included awareness, comprehension, conviction and action. Subsequently, others identified the importance of planning and specifying objectives in various strategic communication disciplines. This focus is most prevalent in advertising (Parente, 2006; Sheth & Sisodia, 2012), public relations (Austin & Pinkleton, 2006; Broom & Sha, 2013; Brody, 1988; J. E. Grunig & Hunt, 1984; Nager & Allen, 1984; Ross, 1977) and information campaigns (Lee & Kotler, 2011; Pfau & Parrott, 1993; Resnick & Siegel, 2013; Rice & Paisley, 1981; Rice & Atkin, 2013). Managerial communication and technical communication do not dwell as much on broad organizational goals or shorter-term objectives, although their purposes are unequivocal: enhanced productivity. In the case of managerial communication, the major focus is on leadership communication and is stated in terms of providing information and direction (Argenti, 2009; Munter, 2012). Technical communication similarly focuses on understanding and effective actions by providing information that can help organizational customers and staff perform tasks on a timely basis in a satisfying way (Carliner, 1998). Political communication similarly tends to focus on the achievement of short-term outcomes, such as winning elections or seeking adoption of a particular law or administrative rule sought by political interests. Yet, broader goals are often sought both by politicians (Baines, 2011, p. 120–122) and political activists (M. F. Smith & Ferguson, 2001, p. 294). These are grounded in the desire for long-term changes in public policy, social values and culture.

In the context of communications, Simmons (1990, pp. 115–116) argued that management by objectives

1. assures all concerned people are informed in writing
2. requires the statement of specific, observable or measurable outcomes
3. ensures campaign messages are clearly related to objectives
4. facilitates work delegation
5. provides accountability, and
6. confirms whether intended outcomes actually resulted from communications activities or from spurious forces in the environment.

The Postmodern Perspective: Role for Goals and Objectives

Today, many precepts of modern management and marketing are being challenged by alternative management theories and postmodern approaches (Boje & Dennehy, 1993; Firat & Venkatesh, 1995; Hatch & Cunliffe, 2006). Yet, as evidenced in a variety of fields, such as marketing (Brown, 2006, p. 223), modernist concepts continue to be deeply embedded.

Management theorists, for example, recognize that organizations are not monoliths with singular, rationale goals. They point out that organizational goal attainment can be often compromised by struggles over power and control *within* the organization's dominant coalition of leadership. Indeed, organizational interests trump personal self-interests only when organizations are threatened by external forces or become dependent on others (Pfeffer & Salancik, 1978). Individual managers seek to increase their authority or the prominence of their perspectives in organizational thinking. Thus strategic communicators strive to be recognized and trusted. They strive to become members of the dominant management coalition (or at least develop strategic alliances with the CEO or with factions if no single coalition exists) and seek to influence organizational, goals and strategies through their counseling role (Berger & Reber, 2006; L. A. Grunig, J. E. Grunig & Ehling, 1992, p. 78; J. E. Grunig & Hunt, 1984, p. 120).

Postmodernism's influence is readily evident in how organizations are structured and managed. Changes observed over the past three decades include the flattening of hierarchies, the delegation of responsibility, the rise of work teams, the shift from specific- to general-rules making, and the encouragement of innovation. In particular organizations have been implored to becoming responsive learning organizations (Senge, 1990) and to share information in all directions using technology ranging from intranets to knowledge management systems (Hislop, 2013).

Postmodernists similarly recognize the limitations of traditional linear approaches to strategy and planning. Chaffee (1985), for example, outlined three broad approaches to strategy: linear, adaptive and interpretive (see Moss & Warnaby, 1997). Separately, Mintzberg and Waters (1985) differentiated between purely prescriptive *deliberate strategies*, where outcomes are clearly specified and activities are painstakingly planned, versus a purely *emergent strategy*, where action evolves as the organization engages in strategic learning and responds to changing circumstances and external factors that cannot be controlled by an organization. The authors suggested most organizational strategies array along a continuum between these two extremes and combine elements of each. An emergent strategy can develop over time in the absence of specific mission or goals, or despite specifying a mission and goals, according to Mintzberg (1994). However, as a practical matter, managers often must impose their desires or intended outcomes (and intended action) on their organizations to provide a sense of direction. Furthermore, in certain circumstances (when required information is collected and environments are known), it might be appropriate to abandon emergent strategies and to pursue intentions with as much determination as possible (Mintzberg & Waters, 1985, p. 271).

Importantly, organizations today continue to be *results-oriented*, and *work units* remain accountable. It is only the *micromanagement* of every unit's activities by senior managers that has been eliminated. Indeed such scrutiny is impractical in light of the expertise required to manage various specialized functions found in organizations and the size and scope of large complex organizations.

Not surprisingly, professional communicators today act with increasing levels of autonomy in many organizations and are not merely responsible for execution of assigned tasks. Indeed, they have an obligation to be critical thinkers and leaders, not order takers (Nager & Truitt, 1987). Because of their considerable autonomy, even employees *within* organizations have become *agents* of the clients who hire them and have considerable independence and power to control their work and shape their environment. According to Derina Holtzhausen, the consequences of this type of agency are (a) expectation of self-assertion, (b) evaluation and judgment of performance based on concrete achievement, (c) initiatives to shape and change the environment to serve the agent's preconceived ideas, (d) independent actions, and (e) being influenced by developments from both outside and inside the organization (Holtzhausen, 2012, p. 213, see also Weick & Sutcliffe, 2007). Principal-agency Theory (PAT) suggests that experts (such as strategic communicators) have an advantage over principals (employers and clients) and often have divergent interests (Miller, 2005; Holtzhausen, 2012, pp. 216–217).

This postmodern perspective explains why goals and objectives continue to be important in contemporary strategic communication. First, goals and objectives are usually part of a communications plan that is presented to a client, and which essentially creates a *contract* that provides incentives for the agent to work in the client's interests. Second, plans containing goals and objectives are either *approved* or *determined* by clients (Crable & Vibbert, 1986, p. 209) or *negotiated* and/or *co-created* with them collaboratively. Third, goals provide an agreed-upon basis for which the results will be recognized. Fourth, goals and objectives can guide the activities of strategic communicators so that intended outcomes are actually achieved, which reinforces the communicator's professionalism or self-identity.[1]

Organizational Goals versus Communications Objectives

Confusion reigns among scholars and practitioners alike about the use of goals versus objectives, and the terms are often used interchangeably. Thus, Drucker might have written about management by goals. Importantly, *multiple outcomes* also might be sought in a strategic communication effort—outcomes that can be assessed at both the organizational and program levels. Although this distinction might appear arbitrary and contrary to how the terms have been (mis)used in everyday practice, this chapter argues that two inter-related sets of outcomes should be the focus of strategic communication (Hallahan, 2011). These are compared in Figure 16.1.

Organizational goals are end results pursued by an entity at the organizational, division or unit level, whether or not any communication activity is undertaken, whereas *communication objectives* are changes in behavior by people (or other entities) that are the direct outcome of strategic communication activities, and which aim (and are necessary) to achieve organization goals.

Importantly, both goals and objectives are creations of *planning processes*—goals as a result of organizational planning and communication objectives as a result of communication planning. Despite numerous advances, communications planning remains, at best, an imperfect art (and hardly can be considered an established science).

Authors have noted the dearth of empirical research about goal-setting at the organizational level (Smith, Locke & Barry, 1990; Young & K. G. Smith, 2013) and lamented the lack of proficiency among communicators in specifying outcomes. For example, Anderson, Hadley, Rockland and Weiner (2009, p. 4) noted that objectives are often "overlooked" components in public relations planning. Dozier (1985, p. 22) stated "practitioners don't know how to set measurable objectives." Pieczka (2000, p. 227) observed "poor skill in objectives setting and evaluation, or both" in her analysis of award-winning programs in the United Kingdom. In advertising, Sheth and Sisodia (2012, p. 12) opine that marketing departments typically operate with fuzzy goals and objectives that are not clearly articulated.

Consistent with the turn toward postmodern marketing approaches (Grant, 1999), Watkis (2010) observed that many marketers (and communicators) still consider their role to be a creative one that focuses on promotion, customer relationship management, and networking. Marketers, he says, perform their jobs with comparatively little regard to their responsibility for managing resources to achieve organizational goals.

According to Watkis, the most important activities for marketers are the establishment of objectives, a plan for their achievement, a budget to support the plan, and the management of assets and resources to achieve those objectives. Watkis contends that many marketers are found wanting in

Table 16.1 Goals and Objectives Compared

Organizational goals	Communication objectives
Higher-order outcomes that center on *organizational activities*	Lower-order outcomes that involve *people's behaviors*
Established as benchmarks to help attain an organization's mission or to fulfill its vision	Established to achieve a specified organizational goal in the context of a communication campaign, program or project
Measured in terms of regularly monitored organization activities, such as • units sold or donated • revenue • attendance at events • traffic to a facility • market share (of sales or as a service provider) • market position or rank in an industry or field • some specified accomplishment (such as winning an election) • reduction in the incidence of disease, or risky or antisocial behaviors	Measured in terms of people's response specifically to communications campaign • knowledge (mere awareness, recognition, recall, comprehension, understanding) • attitudes (affect, predispositions, beliefs) • intermediate actions (typically interactions or communications actions) • ultimate actions that benefit the organization *and* individual—buying, investing, donating or volunteering, working, voting, adopting a particular faith, etc. • post-action behaviors
Measured using data from extant or specially created organizational systems or from public sources.	Measured using data collected as part of the campaign, program or project using quantitative or qualitative research methods
Often identified by client or management as part of the annual or other planning activities; sometimes refined or restated by communicator for inclusion in a communication plan	Usually specified by *campaign planners* and recommended to a client based on stated goals. Some objectives might be for the communicator's own use

these critical skills—a problem that extends to many professional communicators. The consultant elaborates, "Unfortunately, many marketing objectives are subjective statements and therefore difficult to measure. Alternatively, objectives may be quantifiable but not usefully comparable to other measurements, a potential difficulty for marketers, especially when asked to give proof of their contribution to the business" (Watkis, 2010).

Goals: Outcomes Identified at Organizational Level

Goals are desired outcomes typically identified by the organization as a result of either formal or informal strategic planning processes (Abraham, 2011; Allison, 2011; Simerson 2011; see also Mintzberg, 1994). Corporate objectives (goals) are often established or ratified by a board of directors and then trickle down through the organization (Bart, 1997; Sheth & Sisodia, 2012, p. 11). Importantly, strategic communications can (and should) participate as advisers in helping organizational leaders to hone organizational goals (White & Mazur, 1995, p. 29).

According to Steyn (2007), goals more properly should be thought about as stemming from *strategic thinking*. Thus goals are only *refined* as part of any formal strategic planning exercise. Simply stated, strategic thinking and strategic planning involve identifying an organization's purpose and direction, the strategy that will be pursued based on current circumstances, and alternative courses of action. Strategic plans typically begin with a mission statement that succinctly describes the entity's purpose and what it does to achieve its reason for being (Bart, 1997; Haschak, 1998; Jones & Kahaner, 1995; McGinnis, 1981). A vision statement is an aspirational statement that outlines what the organization wants to be and how it might be ideally differentiated from similar entities (Lipton, 1996; Truitt, 2002).

In turn, goals are statements of outcomes an entity strives to achieve to fulfill its mission and vision and provide the basis for strategy (R. D. Smith, 2013). Goals can be long-term, intermediate-term or short-term ones, and ideally they should drive the nature and level of activities in which the entity engages over a specified planning cycle (which ends whenever planned activities conclude or will be evaluated). Entities can pursue multiple compatible goals (goal congruency), can cluster or nest related goals within one another (goal hierarchies), and can address goals in order (goal sequencing).

Management theorists such as Kaplan and Norton (2006) argue that organizations should adopt a *balanced scorecard* approach that takes into account four perspectives in setting goals and assessing organizational success. These include financial, customer, operational or internal, and innovation or learning perspectives (see also Fleisher & Mahaffy, 1997; Zerfass, 2008a, 2008b). Although goals have traditionally been internally driven, corporate goals increasingly reflect external conditions (Steyn, 2007) Elkington (1998) suggested three pillars for business success and accountability: profit, people and planet—an idea that has since been popularized as the "triple bottom line."

Psychologists since the 1960s have recognized the importance of *goals* and *plans* as constructs in communication and problem-solving (Eccles & Wigfield, 2002; Elliot & Dweck, 1998; Hawkins & Daly, 1988; Ryan, 1970). Kruglanski (1996, p. 600) writes that a goal describes "a desirable future state of affairs one intends to attain through action." As cognitive structures, goals involve knowledge both about what is goal-worthy and the processes required to achieve them, based on experience. Similarly, Miller, Galanter and Pribaum (1960/1986, p. 161) defined a *plan* as "any hierarchical process in the organization that can control the order in which a sequence of operations is to be performed." As cognitive structures, goals contain alternative paths or schemas (mental scripts) for goal attainment (Schrank & Abelson, 1977).

Goal-setting is clearly a component of management by objectives as well as planning more generally. Industrial psychologist Edwin M. Locke proposed *goal-setting theory* in the context of motivating employees, and led a program of research spanning four decades that stressed the importance of goals and incentives to enhance individual performance versus merely asking employees to do their best. That research was later extended to consider the impact of macro-level goal-setting on organizations. Locke and his colleague concluded that the goals provided the focus for activities, energized effort, fostered persistence, and provided specific communication strategies for success. Performance was found to be positively linked to the specificity and difficulty of the goal, and moderated by goal commitment, goal importance, self-efficacy, feedback, and task complexity. Satisfaction with performance and rewards, in turn, prompted willingness to commit to new challenges (Latham & Locke, 2002, p. 714). Goals, along with the self-efficacy (task-specific confidence) required to achieve them, are also influenced by factors such as personality, feedback, participation in decision making, job autonomy and monetary incentives (Locke & Latham, 2006).

Depending on the rigor with which planning is pursued, goals can be quite broad (such as a "Big Hairy Audacious Goal"—Collins & Porras, 1997) or quite specific. Effective goals have their most practical value when *specific* (identify clearly identifiable outcomes) and *measurable* (indicate verifiable results). Most importantly, goals are desired outcomes that can be *communicated* and shared widely in the organization as outcomes to be pursued (by strategic communication as well as by other units). Sometimes these are derived directly from written strategic, marketing, or other plans. However, goals also can be articulated by organizational leaders or by managers of the organization based on their *interpretation* of the organization's mission, vision or purpose without being extracted directly or summarized from any kind of official source. Indeed goals are *social constructions* co-created or enacted within organizations through the process of communication (Berger & Luckmann, 1966; Weick, 1995).

Ideally, strategic communicators, in their counseling role, are involved in helping formulate or clarify organizational goals (White & Mazur, 1995). Reflecting the autonomy enjoyed by strategic communicators acting as organizational agents, strategic communicators can help clients clarify or articulate extant explicit goals that serve as the basis for strategic communication. Brody (1988, p. 75) goes so far as to state about goals that public relations practitioners "should assume responsibility for creating them—at least to the extent necessary to developing an effective public relations program." Because communication goals do not need to be adopted verbatim, the power of communicators to focus and frame goals discursively reflects their ability to construct reality.

In addition to being shared throughout the organization, client organizations typically can measure the attainment of goals using extant monitoring, tracking or other feedback systems. Most entities routinely measure goals attainment where data are easily and directly available based on transactions or readily verifiable public information, such as the following.

- *Activity levels*: These include number of units sold, attendance at events, participation in programs, traffic to a facility, and so on. Although goals most frequently involve *increasing* activity levels, some communications programs focus on decreasing undesirable or anti-social activities (to lower incidence of disease, for example, or risky behaviors such as drinking and driving).
- *Revenue levels*: These are outcomes typically measured in financial terms, such as revenues, representing the monetary value of units sold, contributions received, or other finance-based accomplishments. Revenue is often used as a proxy measure for activity, but revenues from the same activity can vary based on accounting procedures. Thus activity levels (versus revenues) might be the purest measure.

Other common goals include the following.

- *Comparative accomplishments*: These goals involve comparing an organization's activity or revenues against others. Examples include percentage of *market share* (the proportion of activity compared to others in the arena) or *market ranking* enjoyed in an industry or field compared to others and achieved by moving up in a measured list of leading organizations. However, such goals can be problematic because they are predicated on the activities of all the organizations involved. A dramatic increase in activity by an organization could be emasculated by a similar increase by other players, while a decrease in market share or rankings might be purely a function of extraordinary accomplishments by others.
- *Specified accomplishments*: Sometimes goals involve achieving distinctions identified as priorities by the organization, such as winning an election, winning a prize or being selected for an award. Elections are an ideal example because all ostensible benefits go to the victor. Merely winning 45% of the vote (a plurality) is not itself sufficient if a majority is required. Winning a prize might be sought because it is viewed as an avenue to financial or other tangible rewards. But the direct value is mostly in the "bragging rights" associated with the distinction, which might or might not lead to higher activity or revenue levels.

Goals can vary based on circumstances. The key is to reach an agreement between the client and strategic communicator as to the outcomes to be sought and to be considered in the evaluation of a campaign, program or project.

Objectives: Outcomes Identified at Program Level

Whereas organizational goals are rooted in organization planning and culture and are either adopted directly or adapted by communications professionals, *communication objectives* are almost always formulated by communication professionals to facilitate communication planning. Communication objectives can be conceptualized as lower-order *outcomes* that contribute to achieving higher-order organizational outcomes. Notably, the process is not reciprocal; organizational goals do *not* lead to attaining communication objectives.

Pursuing behaviorally-based objectives is completely consistent with modernist views about deliberate strategy as well as postmodern adoption of emergent strategies. Indeed, nothing in postmodern management nor the postmodern marketing literature attempts to delegitimize or deconstruct goals or objectives per se. Postmodern approaches primarily challenge modernist institutional practices that involve centralization and the egregious exercise of power.

Depending on the circumstances, a strategic communicator becomes involved in influencing various aspects of human behavior. These include ultimate actions that can directly translate to the achievement of organizational goals as well as intermediate behavioral actions that lead individuals toward the desired response. These involve both changes in awareness and attitudes as well as intermediate behaviors. Figure 16.2 summarizes eight broad categories of organizational goals commonly found in various subdisciplines of strategic communication, as well as corresponding behaviors or communications objectives required to attain those goals (second column) and intermediate behaviors or steps that might be specified by a strategic communicator in attaining those organizational outcomes (goals).

Ultimate Behaviors

Communication objectives address the ultimate actions people can take that are consistent with an organizational goal. Although these are sometimes *implied* in stating organizational goals, the reality of the task that must actually be accomplished can be easily lost unless it is explicitly stated. For example, *generating sales* (whether for products, services, or tickets to cultural events) is probably the most universal behavior sought in marketing communications programs. But the underlying behavior that drives sales is *buying* (such as ordering by distributors and retailers and purchases by consumers). In a similar way, one of the most important functions of investor relations is to *attract capital* or funding, but the underlying behavior is *investing* (the term used in the case of commercial ventures, but also to seek major gifts to not-for-profit causes). Much managerial communication is directed to *enhancing performance and productivity*, but this can only be accomplished by shaping work habits of employees—getting them to apply for employment, be industrious, or work safely. Political communication seeks to *influence public policy*, but the underlying action is *voting* (balloting by the electorate as well as decision-making by lawmakers and government officials). Many information campaigns for worthy causes seek to *promote particular cultural values*, but such social or cultural change requires people to adopt *prosocial behaviors* (such as professing faith in a particular religion or sect or following sound environmental practices). In the same vein government agencies and non-government organizations (NGOs) often have the goal of *protecting public health and safety* through the eradication of disease or maladies—but such outcomes are only effected when people *avoid risky behavior* or *adopt healthy lifestyles*.

Intermediate Steps Toward Effecting Behavior

Figure 16.2 (third column) includes various intermediate steps that might be involved in effecting the ultimate communication objectives suggested in the second column. As most strategic communicators know, influencing people's behaviors is a complex process, which can involve what they know (cognition), how they feel (affect) and actual actions (conation). These intermediate steps are basic concepts in psychological processing (Christen & Hallahan, 2014) and are the bases for persuasion (McGuire, 1973). These are also found in hierarchy of effects models in advertising

Table 16.2 Eight Common Organizational Goals and Corresponding Communication Objectives

Organizational goals	Communication objective (ultimate behavior)	Intermediate steps to communication objective
Generate sales, revenue	Buying	**Knowledge**
Attract capital	Investing	• awareness (recognition, recall)
Enhance organizational performance	Working productively or safely	• comprehension or understanding
Influence public policy	Voting	• beliefs
Help others	Donating (financial resources)	• norms
	Volunteering (time and talent)	
Advance peace, reduce conflict	Co-operating	**Attitudes**
Promote cultural values	Supporting or participating in supportive cultural causes and activities	• arousal • affect • values
Protect public health and safety	Avoiding risky behaviors	• believability
	Engaging in healthy activities	• predispositions
		• trust
		• acceptance
		• preference
		Intermediate actions
		• intent
		• self-efficacy
		• message engagement
		• information seeking
		• information sharing
		• trial
		• self-observation
		Post-action behaviors
		• affirmation
		• reinforcement by others
		• information sharing or bolstering
		• repetition

and theories about the diffusion and adoption of innovations (Barry, 1987, 1990; Lavidge & Steiner, 1961; Rogers, 2003; Strong, 1925). These same notions are widely recognized in discussions about behavioral aspects of strategic communication (see Anderson, Hadley, Rockland & Weimer, 2009; Broom & Dozier, 1990; Coombs & Holladay, 2009, p. 70; Dozier, 1985; Dozier & Ehing, 1992, pp. 163–164; J. E. Grunig & Hunt, 1984, p. 125; Smith, 2013, p.74–77; Stacks, 2012, pp. 28–32; Tucker & Derelian, 1989, p. 45; Watson & Noble, 2005, p. 166), Wilcox & Cameron, 2012). These are effects that intervene between message production and action (Parente, 2006, p. 105).

- **Knowledge objectives** include but are not limited to *awareness* (measured in recognition and recall—the ability to retrieve information from memory on either an aided or unaided basis), *comprehension* or understanding (as exhibited in the ability to explain a concept), the adoption of *beliefs* (information in memory believed to be true), and the assumption of *norms* (contextual reference points to which information is compared).
- **Attitude-related objectives** include *arousal* (emotion excitation), *affect* (negative or positive emotion), *values* (emotionally based assessments that a topic is important or unimportant),

believability or verisimilitude (whether the message resonates with personal experience), *predispositions* (favorable or unfavorable assessments of a topic or idea), *trust* (whether the information is reliable, consistent or from a credible source), *acceptance* of claims or arguments (exhibited by lack of resistance to or counter-arguing) and *preference* (choice of a particular option versus alternatives).

- **Intermediate actions** involve conative or observable actions that people actually take. *Behavioral intent* involves an individual's conviction to undertake a particular action (not merely the expression of an opinion indicating favorability). *Self-efficacy* involves the person's belief (confidence) that they are capable of engaging in a particular behavior. Both are included under actions because they deal with the person's contemplation of specific actions, not merely generalized attitudes. *Information seeking* includes queries to obtain more information as well as efforts to verify information (which can take the form of personal visits, telephone calls, access to websites or online discussions, and conversing with family, friends or colleagues). *Message engagement* involves extended attention and processing of persuasive messages, such as re-reading or participating in an online activity such as a game or contest. *Information sharing* includes a variety of reinforcing behaviors in which people express opinions about their experience with a newly adopted idea. Today, information sharing is especially relevant in the online world and takes the form of ratings; online recommendations (such as liking or favoriting online content), forwarding e-mail, text or microblog messages; and sending or posting comments (essentially endorsements or complaints about their experience). *Trial* involves tentative adoption of the new idea, often for purposes of making a first-hand assessment. *Self-observation* is a form of learning reinforcement in which the person observes him- or herself taking an action as well as his or her response.
- **Post-Behavior actions** can lead to a pattern of habitual behavior based on satisfaction with the behavioral action taken. *Affirmation* involves personal validation of decision. *Reinforcement by others* entails receiving and taking into account social support that reinforces the behavior. *Information sharing/bolstering* encompasses communicating with others about an experience, which serves to reinforce personal assessments. *Repetition* involves taking the targeted behavior more than once.[2]

Setting communication objectives involves the same process of setting organizations and does not differ substantively in terms of the benefits that can be accrued. Although the ultimate behaviors called for can be extrapolated from organizational goals set by clients, the specification of the various intermediate steps that might be appropriate require substantial expertise on the part of the communicator that might or might be held by the client. Here again, strategic communicators exercise considerable control over specification of desired outcomes. Importantly, whereas client organizations often have the systems in place to measure the attainment of organizational goals, communications objectives require communications professionals to arrange the collection and analysis of relevant measures. The communicator exercises considerable power in terms of measuring and reporting results based on intermediate-level behavior objectives.[3]

Processes of Identifying Goals, Objectives, and Intermediate Behavioral Steps

Clarifying organizational goals and corresponding communications objectives is one of the most critical steps in the strategic communication planning process. It is typically based on formative research that examines the *organization* and the circumstances in which it operates, its focal *offering* (products, services or ideas that might be the basis for the program), the *opinions* of key constituents, and *opportunities* to communicate (past activities and potential media and channels). The resulting *situation analysis* attempts to synthesize the results into a coherent statement of problem or statement of opportunity and can incorporate a variety of popular analysis tools, such as SWOT analysis (Hill & Westbrook, 1997; Mind Tools, n.d.) and force-field analysis (Lewin, 1943; Tucker & Derelian, 1989).

Research includes interviewing client representatives as key informants (Anderson, Hadley, Rockland & Weimer, 2009). Clients are often able to articulate the outcomes they want to accomplish, especially when they have been directly involved in the development of an organizational strategic plan or an annual or quarterly operating plan. But many less-experienced clients are unable to articulate communications goals and objectives or are vague about specifying them. For example, a client might state the purpose of an effort is to "create awareness." But what they are really saying is that they know awareness leads to sales—*and sales are their actual goal*. Or consider the example of a political campaign. Every candidate wants to "get elected." The actual objective, however, might be stated as follows: "To obtain 50% plus one of all votes cast in the general election."

Well developed communication objectives provide a vital linkage with organizational goals (Steyn, 2007, pp. 155, 161) and are derived from organizational objectives or goals (Anderson, Hadley, Rockland & Weimer, 2009, p. 3). Moreover, communications objectives link organizational goals to the behaviors of important constituents (which might be variously labeled as audiences, publics, markets, constituents, stakeholders or communities).

Although a communicator might research and consider possible goals and objectives simultaneously, the process is best accomplished by setting organizational goals first. There is no point in conducting a communication program that does not address an organizational need. If not adopted directly from extant organizational plans, goals at least should be congruent with what the organizations seeks to accomplish.

One of the most important considerations in goal- and objective-setting is determining the *number* of outcomes that should be pursued. Where possible, organizations do better by focusing on the *fewest numbers of goals and objectives* at any one time, although multiple outcomes might be appropriate. For some plans, one goal, one objective and a few intermediate steps are sufficient. In a phased campaign, the initial period might focus merely on awareness, while a later phase emphasizes prompting actions among informed and positively predisposed audience members. This is consistent with the admonition by Intel CEO Andy Grove (cited in Sheth & Sisodia, 2012, p. 11) that organizations should pursue a small number of precisely articulated objectives (and then give managers considerable leeway in determining how to achieve them). Few authors address the specific criteria for comparing possible communication objectives that might contribute to achieving an organizational goal. One notable example in social marketing suggests objectives might be evaluated based on potential impact, audience willingness, measurability, opportunity and need (Lee & Kotler, 2011, p. 166–167).

Specifying communication objectives is especially important because audience members vary where they are situated on the pathway to ultimate actions based on their knowledge, attitudes and behavioral intent and self-efficacy. The specific challenge might be to crystallize, to intensify or reinforce, or to change responses (Pfau & Parrott, 1994). Research can be most useful to determine the *intermediate steps* required to effect behavior change. At least four situations are possible involving people's extant knowledge and attitudes.

- When an idea is new, the challenge is to create both supportive knowledge and positive attitudes so that desired behavior is possible.
- When knowledge is adequate, but attitudes are absent, the focus might be entirely on attitudinal steps.
- When the situation is reversed (knowledge is absent but attitudes are positive) the focus should be on raising knowledge and encouraging intermediate steps that facilitate education (such as information seeking).
- When both awareness and attitudes are positive, the need might be to simply overcome inertia and provide compelling incentives to prompt action.

Consider the case of a public information campaign where the general goal is to reduce HIV/AIDS. This goal could be refined and restated to focus on either a) reduction in the *incidence* of AIDS, i.e. the rate of infection or b) a reduction in *number of deaths* among victims, or preventing the unnecessary loss of life when treatment is available. These are quite different outcomes and several possible behavioral changes might be involved. For example, the objective might be to a) discourage casual sexual contacts, b) encourage the consistent use of condoms, c) promote regular screenings and the availability of treatment or d) encourage patients who test positive to actually obtain treatment.

In this example, general awareness of HIV/AIDS is already quite high in society, but specific knowledge about the dangers of casual sex with strangers, use of condoms, or the availability of treatment might not be readily accessible. Thus information is a key step. Similarly, attitudes might vary among target audience members whose fears might need to be reduced and self-efficacy increased to avoid risky situations, might need to be increased to use condoms consistently, or to seek testing or treatment.

When creating goals and objectives (and specifying the intermediate steps that can effect behavior), a useful procedure is to *brainstorm* all possible goals and objectives and then to mercilessly pare the list to the fewest possible outcomes. Resulting items should complement one another and eliminate contradictions or duplications. A long, unwieldy list of multiple outcomes can obfuscate the purpose, complicate assessment, and distract clients and staff members from priorities. (See following section about writing goals and objectives statements.)

For determining the required intermediate steps, the best strategy is to focus on the highest-order intermediate step whenever possible. Prompting actions usually is more desired than merely changing attitudes, and forming or crystallizing attitudes is usually more important than merely creating knowledge. Often these higher-level measures assume achievement of lower-level outcomes. However, depending on circumstances, merely enhancing knowledge or fostering positive attitudes might be sufficient, especially when no change in behavior is required and the desired behavior is understood or implied.

Writing Goals and Objectives

Goals and objectives are useful to the extent that they are precisely measurable.

In his DAGMAR model, Colley (1964) was among the first to stress the importance of clearly defined, written objectives. He stressed four key elements. According to Colley, a good objective should be concrete and measureable, target a specific audience, provide a benchmark and a measure for the degree of change sought, and specify a time period. Variations on these guidelines are suggested by authors in advertising today (see Duncan, 2002; Moriarty, Mitchell & Wells, 2012; O'Guinn, Allen & Semenik, 2009).

In the intervening years, various models and mnemonics have been proposed to suggest characteristics of effective objectives. The most prominent of these is the S.M.A.R.T. formula, which suggests a good objective should be specific, measurable, attainable, relevant and time-framed/timely (Doran, 1981; Meyer, 2003). Meanwhile, experts in personal planning suggest that objectives should follow a formula representing specific, measurable, achievable, and compatible ("Goal setting" n.d.) S.M.A.C. guidedlines. Duncan (2002, p. 199) applies a similar S.M.A.C. acronym to suggest that advertising objectives should be specific, measurable, achievable and challenging.[4]

Using a S.M.A.R.T. Approach to Write Precise Statements

One deceivingly simple—but critical—skill in strategic communication involves writing clear statements of organizational goals and communication objectives that withstand testing when included in a communication plan. The best goals and objectives statement are simple phrases that communicate a single concept, and begin with the infinite "To. . . ." As suggested in the S.M.A.R.T. formula, goals and activities include specific results that can be measured at a specific time in the future. The metrics used can be based on raw numbers or percentages, but those figures need to be attainable and realistic/relevant to qualify under the S.M.A.R.T. regimen.

The following are examples of well-written, notably brief outcome statements that might be appropriate in a strategic communication campaign.

Examples of S.M.A.R.T. Goal Statements

- to increase sales of XYZ product by 30% before Christmas, 2015
- to achieve sales of €375 million by year-end
- to raise 600 million euros in new capital through an initial public stock offering before December 31, 2015
- to become the largest reseller of kitchen cabinetry in Germany during 2010
- to gain a 20% market share among pet food sellers nationwide by June 30, 2015
- to eradicate reported incidents of food contamination in the western United States by October 31
- to become the most popular women's website in New York during 2015

Examples of S.M.A.R.T. Objectives Statements

- to create awareness of XYZ product among 35% of South American consumers by December 31.
- to increase consumer awareness by 10 percentage points (from 15% to 25%) by year end
- to increase the candidate's favorable (positive attitude) ratings in the polls from 45% to 55% by 10 days before the election
- to create a positive attitude about the new benefits plan among 35% of employees by the merger date (note: actual date is either unknown or implied)
- to generate 2,500 sales leads from Australian consumers by December 1.
- to increase traffic on the website by 50% prior to the movie's release date.
- to generate 6,000 sign-ups for the organization's new e-mail newsletter in May.

Several points are worth noting based on the above examples. First, metrics and time frames often can be *implied* in goals and objectives. For example, "eradicated" means 100% eliminated. Similarly, "by the merger date" implies an unknown, moving target but it is understood that the event will occur even though the date is uncertain. Yet the targeted outcomes are specific and measurable. Finally, goals and objectives are more valuable to clients when actual values (activity levels, revenues, market shares, etc.) are noted instead of mere percentage changes.[5] For additional considerations in writing objectives, see Ferguson (1999, pp. 38–39).

Goals and Objectives as the Basis for Evaluation

Specific and measurable organizational goals and communications objectives are widely acknowledged to play a critical role when assessing strategic communication initiatives (Broom & Dozier, 1990; Fill, 2009; Stacks, 2011; Watson & Noble, 2005). To be strategic, communication activities must be important to the organization and planned, and desired outcomes ought to be identifiable in advance. Without clearly stated purposes, communications activities might be valuable, but are not strategic.

Although many clients possess the systems and savvy to evaluate organizational-level outcomes (goals), they are frequently dependent on communications staff members or consultants for compiling and analyzing communication results. As suggested previously, the onus of responsibility is on the professional communicator to assure that required data and insights are available and delivered in keeping with the communicator's commitment to the client.

Evidence suggests that many communicators do not fully address organizational goals (Pieczka, 2000) and merely impute (rather than substantiate) the achievement of organizational goals in awards competitions (Bissland, 1990).

Measuring communications objectives independently of organizational goals is essential. Indeed, communication objectives ought to be conceptually linked to organizational goals, but they are not necessarily directly correlated. This notion has been recognized in the advertising field since Colley's argument that advertising (communication) results should be separate from sales activity. Thus, advertisers continue to resist efforts to link advertising results only to sales, but instead focus on a variety of measures such as awareness, attitude change, trial, repeated purchases and brand switching (McGuinn, Allen & Semenick, 2009, pp. 269–270; Parente, 2006, pp. 105–106). In a similar vein, the maintaining of a publicly traded company's stock price often drives executives to invest in investor relations activities, but IR officers overwhelmingly reject stock price as a valid measure of their efforts because so many other factors can influence financial markets (Laskin, 2011).

Indeed, various strategic communication programs can be cited that were highly effective in prompting people to take desired actions—yet organizational goals were not attained. Most frequently such failures result from external factors (such as market conditions or public controversy) or internal factors *not related to communication* (such as financial investment, lack of inventory, or staff performance). Fear of failure is one of the reasons some communicators are reluctant to be specific about goals and objectives. Yet, when multiple outcomes are sought, such as a measureable organizational goal in combination with one or more behavioral objectives, the ability to detect positive outcomes (and more meaningful insights) is enhanced.

Assessments of strategic communication can be based on impact, process or financial measures. *Impact measures* focus on the outcomes or results obtained, and thus goals and objectives are integral to outcome assessments. By comparison, *process measures* address factors such as the quality of materials produced (outputs), the number of exposure of messages, and audience response to a message (liking or engaging with the content). Yet process measures, at best, serve as proxies for measuring impact. Finally, *financial measures* can address the comparative costs of two or more strategies to determine which was more efficient (presuming the same impact or outcomes were attained) or can address *return on investment (ROI)* (the extent to which an activity contributed to an organization financially). Yet, like process measures, favorable efficiency or ROI are not reasons in themselves for organizations to undertake strategic communication activities. There must be a clear purpose (organizational goal or communication objective).

Effective evaluation of program impacts (outcomes) requires a philosophical commitment on the part of the communications professional, knowledge of evaluation methods, and allocation of resources to evaluation. Effective evaluation also requires creating an organizational culture that embraces evaluation as a strategic tool but also recognizes the importance of validity and reliability and limitations of evaluation research methods.

Discussion and Implications

Goals and Objectives as Distinct Outcomes

This chapter has presented a framework for distinguishing organizational goals and communications (behavioral) objectives that departs from other treatments of these two concepts.

The proposed approach conceptualizes goals as organization-level outcomes and is consistent with the approach of authors such as Brody (1988), who describes goals as *prerequisites* for public relations programs, and Ferguson (1999), who uses the objectives to refer to both types, but at least differentiates between *corporate objectives* and *functional objectives*. Others relegate goals to be a program-specific concept. For example, Broom & Sha (2013, p. 270) state goals are "broad summative statements that spell out the overall outcomes of a program." The authors don't specify at what level (organizational or program) these outcomes will be accomplished, only that they are "what will be accomplished if the objectives set for each of the publics are achieved."

Other authors use the terms interchangeably (Parente, 2006), while others convolute the distinction. Crable and Vibbert (1986, p. 209) state, for example, "Objectives are public relations goals . . . and provide for intermediate progress toward shared goals." Nager and Allen (1984, p. 56) use a metaphor to contrast goals as *general directions* whereas objectives are *specific destinations* (also cited in Watson & Noble, 2005, p. 162, and Austin & Pinkleton, 2006, pp. 36–40). Watson and Noble (2005, p. 160) dodge the issue by stating, "Here, we will be no more precise than accepting that goals and aims are frequently slightly broader and less closely defined than objectives and concentrate on understanding and applying the latter."

Others suggest that that a goal serves as a "generalized end" (Grunig & Hunt, 1984, p. 116; Dozier & Ehling, 1992, p. 163), as a "general, usually nonmeasurable end" (Hainsworth & Wilson, 1992, p. 12), as a "broader, more general outcome" (Bobbitt & Sullivan, 2005, p. 87), as a "general direction" (Rayfield, 1991, or as "any desired change or effect attempted in each target audience" (Moffitt, 1999). Similarly, this conceptualization is different from the approach suggested by Tucker and Derelian (1989), Kendall (1996), Austin & Pinkleton (2006) and Wilson and Ogden (2008)—all of whom suggest that a program goal is merely a statement that offers a *solution* to the problem or opportunity that is the basis for a campaign, program or project.

As used here, objectives are *not* generalized statements about any outcomes but refer specifically to outcomes measured at the conclusion of campaign dealing with *changes in people's behavior*. One noted campaigns theorist identified at least three ways that the term can be used: *global objectives* (broad outcomes to be achieved), *intermediate objectives* (tasks to be accomplished), and *terminal objectives* actually measured at the conclusion of an effort (Simmons, 1990; also cited by Austin & Pinkleton, 2006, p. 40). Others have similarly and superficially identified objectives as specific tasks to be accomplished or procedures to be followed (Hainsworth & Wilson, 1992; Kendall, 1996; Moffitt, 1996; Nager & Allen, 1984; Pavlik, 1987). The present conceptualization recognizes that intermediate steps or stages are involved, but these represent *behavioral states* of the target audience, not tasks to be undertaken by the communicator.

Regrettably, confusion between goals and objectives continues to reign in everyday practice. A handful of authors reverse the two concepts, using goals to denote specific metrics for measuring program objectives (e.g., Lee & Kotler, 2011, p. 165).

Pieczka (2000, p. 222) also lamented how winning entries in a British awards program routinely included two or three levels of organizational goals and objectives without distinguishing between them. Meanwhile, a popular book directed at public relations professionals identified four types of objectives (informational, motivational, statutory and financial) and then went on to use the term to cite *process objectives* versus *outcome objectives* (Bobbitt & Sullivan, 2005, p. 88; see also J. E. Grunig, 2008, pp. 104–106).

Paying More Attention to Goals and Objectives

Comparatively little formal research has been conducted in the various subdisciplines of strategic communication about practitioners' opinions about goals and objectives. Although the need for clear objectives is recognized in advertising (Corkindale, 1976; Huntington, 2008; U.S. Government Accountability Office, 2003; Welsh, 1965), academic research in advertising has abandoned any focus on studying the objectives of actual programs and their achievement (Preston, 1985; Smallianov

& Aiyeku, 2009). Other fields such as management communication, political communication and technical communication (Carliner, 1998) have paid virtually no attention to the topic.

In public relations, Hon (1997) observed that comparatively little research has been conducted pertaining to what public relations actually does for an organization. She argued that more needs to be done to understand how effectiveness can be defined. In a second study also involving depth interviews with practitioners and CEOs, she defined *effective public relations* as being achieved when "communications activities achieve communications goals (in a cost-efficient manner)" (p. 104) and argued that public relations outputs "increasingly must be tied to meaningful outcomes for organizations and clients" (p. 104). Although the practitioners she interviewed generally opined that setting goals and objectives was uncomplicated, her study revealed tremendous variability in respondents' explanations of their public relations goals and objectives. She concluded that setting goals and objectives and conducting evaluation are actually quite complicated tasks (Hon, 1998, p. 128).

One 2012 online poll of 54 public relations practitioners addressed reasons that programs failed and concluded that not enough strategic thought goes into program planning (Siegel, 2012a). To illustrate: More than half of respondents (57%) responded affirmatively when asked the question, "Was the failure tied in any way to not setting any PR goals (or setting unrealistic goals) at the start"?

Questioning the Value of Goals and Objectives

At least five problems can be identified in the processes of developing, negotiating and assessing organizational goals and especially communications objectives.

Misapplication

One fundamental problem is the flawed assumption that particular problems can be resolved merely through communication vis-à-vis substantive changes in organizational policies or practices. Goals and objectives also can fail to meet the SMART criteria by being unclear, inconsistent or unrealistic in terms of what can be achieved, or unreasonableness in terms of time frame. Although the strategic communicator enjoys great latitude in formulating goals and objectives as implemented, adequate research must be conducted and the quality of input from the client must be sufficient to assure that client and communicator expectations are in sync. This includes good communication between all levels of management—poor communication is a shortcoming that often leads to failure (Siegel, 2012b).

Obsession with Metrics

Although strategic communication and constructs such as planning, goals and objectives and measurements are vaunted in modern management theory, latter-day theorists do not uniformly embrace them. Mintzberg (2009, pp. 61–62) refers to management by objectives as "deeming," where subordinates are driven to perform when managers don't know what to do. He chides strategic planning as a formulaic process that focuses on analysis rather than synthesis, and one that fails to specify strategy (see also Mintzberg, 1994). Although an advocate of planning and the importance of outcomes, W. Edward Deming, a noted statistician and management expert who gained notoriety for his work in Japan, rejected the notion of management by objectives and called for the elimination of management by numerical goals. Instead, he called for leadership to be substituted for measurement (Walton, 1991).

Misused Metrics

Metrics or measurement levels for goals and objectives also can be misused. Some communicators or clients might purposely establish conservative goals and objectives levels that are too low and thus do not serve the needs of the organization. Or goals might be set low out of fear of missing more ambitious outcomes. Take the example of a goal involving a 4.0% increase in revenue. Attaining an increase of only 3.9% could be viewed either as failure or tantamount to success, depending on the culture of the organization or propensity of a particular manager to interpret such figures favorably or unfavorably to advance a particular agenda. This is consistent with the often-cited axiom "Figures can lie, while liars can figure." Falling short is to be expected if goals and objectives are purposefully ambitious, and allowing people to fall short is a necessity.

Postmodernists similarly challenge abuses involving goals and objectives. Although he does not address goals and objectives directly, French social theorist Jean-Francois Lyotard probably would describe them as devices that enable strategic planning to become a form of terrorism based on its slavish attention to measurement (Holtzhausen, 2012, p. 152; Lyotard, 1992, pp. 138–139) and productivity and efficiency (Holtzhausen, 2012, pp. 189–191; Lyotard, 1984, p. 51).

In critically examining how organizations exercise power, postmodern communications scholar Derina Holtzhausen provides a framework for considering how goals and objectives might be questioned from a critical perspective. Examples include their discursive nature, their reliance upon intelligence gathering and subsequent use for exploitation, their insertion of distance between organizations and others, their framing and focusing on particular ideas, and their creation of organizational metanarratives (Holtzhausen, 2012, especially pp. 108–111, 151–153, 217–219). She notes that such organizational metanarratives were rebutted by social philosopher Jürgen Habermas (1979, p. 210) as "deliberate pseudoconsensual communication" and by sociologist Zygmunt Bauman (1993, p. 205) as tools to assure prediction of and the "colonization" of the future.

Reification of Objectives

The importance of clearly differentiating goals from objectives is especially evident in the growing trend toward identifying desired outcomes in symbolic terms, including enhancement of an organization's *image* or *reputation* and *identity* or the fostering of *goodwill*. In the organizational behavior literature, Elsbach (2006) has carved out a niche for *organizational perception management*. According to the author, who never mentions the word "communication" as the underlying constitutive activity, organizational perceptions are managed through verbal accounts, categorization and labels, symbolic business behaviors, and physical markers. Similarly, Fill (2009, p. 326) notes that image, reputation and preferences of stakeholders toward the organization are commonly cited as promotional objectives.

Although these ideas can contribute to goal achievement, the concepts of image, reputation and identity are not themselves concrete outcomes that can be measured on a par with organizational activity or revenue levels. At best they might serve as intermediate constructs that can be used to measure core behavioral measures such as knowledge, attitudes and behavioral intent.

In a similar way, two other constructs popular today—*relationship* and *engagement*—are inappropriately cited as desired outcomes of communications programs. Although J. E. Grunig (1993) rejected any focus on symbols in favor of substance in public relations, his measures of relationships (trust, commitment, control mutuality and satisfaction) are based on *perceptions* of organizational public-relationships (Hon & J. E. Grunig, 1999). Indeed, marketers more properly focus on relationships as a pattern of interaction based on purchasing behavior between an organization and its customers or markets (Sheth & Parvatiyar, 2000). Engagement similarly is not a single construct, but an amalgam of behavioral components that encompass learning, attitudes, interactions, and depth of message processing involvement (Evans, 2010; Gambetti & Graffigna, 2010; Mollen & Wilson, 2010). Strategic communicators need to better clarify how some of these "fuzzy" concepts actually represent valuable and measurable outcomes that directly translate into client organization benefits.

Focusing Solely on Organizational Outcomes

A final critical question is whether goals and objectives are used only to advance the organization's own purposes (such as wealth creation) or also to better the quality of life or the interests of the publics, constituents, markets and communities it serves. Organizations no longer operate in an environment in which they can assume to be more knowledgeable or in more privileged positions to make decisions for others. Nor can they assume people share a common worldview of reality and would readily adopt organizational priorities if they could only be convinced to do so. Concocting clever, persuasive messages might capture attention but are not sufficient in an era when audiences are obstinate (Bauer, 1964), vary widely in their motivation and ability to process persuasive messages (Hallahan, 2000) and are co-creators of meaning.

Today strategic communicators must demonstrate a genuine concern for others and act ethically or demonstrate what Bauman (1993, pp. 10–15) called a genuine "moral impulse." To create organizational goals (or communications objectives) that only serve the interests of the organization are destined to failure in an era where audiences are skeptical and organizations are mandated to be socially responsible. Effective goals mutually benefit *both* the organization and its constituencies, and effective communications objectives should empower audiences to take mutually beneficial actions.

Notes

1 Various other benefits for clearly articulated goals and objectives might be cited (Hallahan, 1992, 2007). Broom & Sha (2013) suggest, for example, that objectives give focus and direction for developing a communication program, provide guidance and motivation to those implementing the program, and spell out criteria for monitoring progress and assessing impact. Anderson, Hadley, Rockland & Weimer (2009) suggest these provide a structure for prioritization, reduce potential for later disputes, focus resources and identify areas for prescriptive change. Dozier (1985 pp. 21–22) cites justification of communication as a management activity and accountability. Fill (2002, pp. 310) adds determining the time period in which the activity is to be completed and communicating the values and scope of the activity to participants.

2 Importantly, attitudes do not automatically lead to behavior; attitudes and behaviors can be inconsistent for a variety of reasons. Similarly, evidence suggests that the traditional order assumed in hierarchy of effects models (knowledge → attitudes → behavior) does not always apply, such as in conditions of low involvement or when people are forced to radically change their behaviors (Ray, Sawyer, Rothschild, Heller, Strong & Reed, 1973). High (or low) believability and trust do not always translate into positive (or negative) attitudinal or behavioral responses (Parente, 2006).

3 This chapter does not attempt to tackle the complex topic of strategy, or how to influence responses. However, strategy can include the organization proactively reaching out to people directly, responding to queries, utilizing mediated communications, or involving third-party influentials as intermediaries. The latter essentially requires a two-step persuasive process where the ultimate desired action is communication by the influential. The same intermediate steps toward action are required, including knowledge and positive attitudes, and especially behavioral intent and self-efficacy.

4 Other proposals include SAFE (see the end result; accept the end result; feel the end result; express the end result); RUMBA (reasonable, unambiguous, measurable, bounded by time, achievable); STEP UP (specific, time-bound, engaging, practical, under your control, progress management); STAR (specific, testable, achievable, relevant); GROW (goal, reality, options, will); and SMARTT (with targeted added to time-framed) and SMARTER or SMARTERS (specific, motivating, achievable, rewarding, tactical, evaluated, revisable, satisfaction). Various advisers have substituted words in these acronyms for their own purposes, while others have created other extended lists of characteristics, using numbering without acronyms, which include four to 11 desirable characteristics (Kotler, 2002; Parente, 2006; Simmons, 1990, pp. 119–121; Wilson & Ogden, 2008, pp. 78–80).

5 Stating goals and objectives in terms of percentages can be problematic. For example, increasing the number of customers by 50% sounds impressive, except when the reader finds that it means going from 6 customers to 9 customers. Percentages can be fraught with other problems: A change from 38% to 41% is not a 3% percentage change; it's an increase of *3 percentage points,* which actually represents a 7.8 % increase (41 is 107.8% of 38). Finally, a metric can be increased by a percentage if the starting point is zero. (An increase of 15% from

zero is mathematically equal to zero.) Thus, increasing awareness of a new product by 15% is impossible if no knowledge exists.

References

Abraham, S. C. (2011). *Strategic planning. A practical guide for competitive success*. Bingley, UK: Emerald Group.

Allison, M. (2011). *Strategic planning for nonprofit organizations. A practice guide and workbook*. Hoboken, NJ: John Wiley & Sons.

Anderson, F. W., Hadley, L., Rockland, D. & Weiner, M. (2010). *Guidelines for setting measurable public relations objectives: An update*. Gainesville, FL: The Institute for Public Relations. Retrieved July 7, 2014, from http://www.instituteforpr.org/topics/setting-measurable-objectives/

Argenti, P. (2009). *Corporate communication* (5th ed.). Boston: McGraw-Hill Irwin.

Austin, E. W. & Pinkleton, B. E. (2006). *Strategic public relations management: Planning and managing effective communication programs* (2nd ed.) Mahwah, NJ: Lawrence Erlbaum.

Baines, P. (2011). Political public relations and election campaigning. In J. Strömbäck & S. Kiousis (Eds.), *Political public relations. Principles and applications* (pp. 115–137). New York: Routledge.

Barry, T. E. (1987). The development of the hierarchy of effects: An historical perspective. *Current Issues & Research in Advertising, 10*(2), 251–295.

Barry, T. E. & Howard, D. J. (1990). A review and critique of hierarchy of effects in advertising. *International Journal of Advertising, 9*(2), 121–135.

Bart, C. K. (1997). Sex, lies and mission statements. *Business Horizons, 40*(6), 9–18.

Bauer, R. (1964). The obstinate audience: The influence process from the point of view of social communication. *American Psychologist, 19*(5), 319–328.

Bauman, Z. (1993). *Postmodern ethics*. Cambridge, MA: Blackwell.

Berger, P. L. & Luckmann, T. (1966). *The social construction of reality. A treatise on the sociology of knowledge*. Garden City, NY: Doubleday.

Berger, B. K. & Reber, B. H. (2006). *Gaining influence in public relations. The role of resistance in practice*. Mahwah, NJ: Lawrence Erlbaum.

Bissland, J. H. (1990). Accountability gap: Evaluation practices show improvement. *Public Relations Review, 16*(2), 25–35.

Bobbitt, R. & Sullivan, R. (2005). *Developing the public relations campaign. A team based approach*. Boston, MA: Pearson.

Boje, D. & Dennehy, R. (1993). *Managing in the postmodern world. America's resolution against exploitation*. Dubuque, IA: Kendall/Hunt.

Brody, E. W. (1988). *Public relations programming and production*. New York: Praeger.

Broom, G. M. & Dozier, D. (1990). *Using research in public relations. Applications to program management*. Englewood Cliffs, NJ: Prentice-Hall.

Broom, G. M. & Sha, B.-L. (2013). *Cutlip & Center's effective public relations* (11th ed.) Upper Saddle River, NJ: Prentice-Hall.

Brown, S. (2006). Recycling postmodern marketing. *The Marketing Review, 6*, 211–230.

Carliner, S. (1998). Business objectives: A key tool for demonstrating the value of technical communication products. *Technical Communication, 45*(3), 380–384.

Chaffee, E. E. (1985). Three models of strategy. *Academy of Management Review, 10*(1), 89–98.

Christen, C. T. & Hallahan, K. (2014). Psychological processing. In R.L. Heath (Ed.), *Encyclopedia of public relations* (2nd ed.) (vol. 2, pp.705-709). Thousand Oaks, CA: Sage.

Colley, R. H. (1964). *Defining advertising goals for measured advertising results*. New York: Association of American Advertisers.

Collins, J. C. & Porras, J. (1997). *Built to last: Successful habits of visionary companies*. New York: HarperBusiness.

Coombs, W. T. & Holladay, S. J. (2009). *PR strategy and application: Managing influence*. Hoboken, NJ: Wiley Higher Education.

Corkindale, D. (1976). Setting objectives for advertising. *European Journal of Marketing, 10*(3), 109–127.

Crable, R. E. & Vibbert, S. L. (1986). *Public relations as communication management*. Edina, MN: Burgess International/Bellwether Press.

Doran, G. T. (1981). There's a S.M.A.R.T. way to write management's goals and objectives. *Management Review, 70*(11), 35–36.

Dozier, D. M. (1985, Summer). Planning and evaluation in PR practice. *Public Relations Review, 11*(2), 17–25.

Dozier, D. M. & Ehling, W. P. (1992). Evaluation of public relations programs: What the literature tells us about their effects. In J. E. Grunig (Ed.), *Excellence in public relations and communication management* (pp. 159–184). Hillsdale, NJ: Lawrence Erlbaum.

Drucker, P. F. (1954). *The practice of management*. New York: Harper & Row.

Drucker, P. F. (1974). *Management. Tasks, responsibilities, practices*. New York: Harper & Row.

Duncan, T. (2002). *IMC. Using advertising and promotion to build brands*. Boston, MA: McGraw-Hill.

Eccles, J. S. & Wigfield, A. (2002). Motivational beliefs, values and goals. *Annual Review of Psychology, 53*, 109–132.

Elkington, J. (1998). Cannibals with forks: *the triple bottom line of 21st century*. Gabriola Island, BC ; Stony Creek, CT : New Society Publishers.

Elliott, E. S. & Dweck, C. S. (1998). Goals: An approach to motivation and achievement. *Journal of Personality and Social Psychology, 54*(1) 5–12.

Elsbach, K. D. (2006). *Organizational perception management*. Mahwah, NJ: Lawrence Erlbaum.

Evans, D. (2010). *Social media marketing: The next generation of business engagement*. Hoboken, NJ: John Wiley & Sons.

Ferguson, S. D. (1999). *Communication planning. An integrated approach*. Thousand Oaks, CA: Sage.

Fill, C. (2002*). Marketing communications. Contexts, strategies and applications* (3rd ed.) Harlow, England: Prentice-Hall.

Fill, C. (2009). *Marketing communications. Interactivity, community and content*. (5th ed.) Harlow, England: Prentice-Hall.

Firat, A. F. and Venkatesh, A. (1995), Liberatory postmodernism and the reenchantment of consumption. *Journal of Consumer Research, 22*, 239–267.

Fleisher, C. S. & Mahaffy, D. M. (1997). A balanced scorecard approach to public relations management assessment. *Public Relations Review, 23*, 117–142.

Gambetti, R. C. & Graffigna, G. (2010). The concept of engagement. A systematic analysis of the ongoing marketing debate. *International Journal of Market Research, 52*(6), 801–826.

Goal setting guidelines (n.d.) Retrieved July7, 2014, from http://www.affirmations-for-radical-success.com/goal-setting-guidelines.html

Grant, J. (1999). *The new marketing manifesto*. London, England: Orion.

Grunig, J. E. (1993). Image and substance: From symbolic to behavioral relationships. *Public Relations Review, 19*, 123–139.

Grunig, J. E. (2008). Conceptualizing quantitative research in public relations. In B. van Ruler, A. Tkalac Verčič & D. Verčič (Eds.), *Public relations metrics. Research and evaluation* (pp. 88–119). New York: Routledge.

Grunig, L.A., Grunig, J. E. & Ehling, W. P. (1992). What is an effective organization? In J. E. Grunig (Ed.), *Excellence in public relations and communication management* (pp. 65–90). Hillsdale, NJ: Lawrence Erlbaum.

Grunig, J. E. & Hunt, T. (1984). *Managing public relations*. New York: Holt, Rinehart and Winston.

Habermas, J. (1979). *Communication and the evolution of society*. Boston, MA: Beacon Press.

Hainsworth, B. E. & Wilson, L. J. (1992). Strategic program planning, *Public Relations Review, 18*(1), 9–15.

Hallahan, K. (1992). The paradigm struggle and the public relations practitioner. *Public Relations Review, 19*(4), 197–205.

Hallahan, K. (2000). Enhancing motivation, ability and opportunity to process public relations messages. *Public Relations Review, 26*(4), 463–480.

Hallahan, K. (2007). Integrated communication: Implications for and beyond public relations excellence. In Elizabeth L. Toth (Ed.), *The future of excellence in public relations and communication management: Challenges to the next generation* (pp. 299–337). Mahwah, NJ: Lawrence Erlbaum.

Hallahan, K. (2011). *Communication campaign/program organizer* (Ver. 5.0). Available http://lamar.colostate.edu/~pr/organizer.htm

Hallahan, K., Holtzhausen, D., van Ruler, B., Verčič, D. & Sriramesh, K. (2007). On defining strategic communication. *International Journal of Strategic Communication, 1*(1), 3–35.

Haschak, P. G. (1998). *Corporate statements: The official missions, goals, principles and philosophies of over 900 companies*. Jefferson, NC: McFarland.

Hatch, M. J. & Cunliffe, A. L. (2006). *Organizational theory: Modern, symbolic and postmodern perspectives*. New York: Oxford University Press.

Hawkins, R. P. & Daly, J. (1988). Cognition and communication. In R. Hawkins, J. Wiemann & S. Pingree (Eds.), *Advancing communication science: Merging mass and interpersonal* (pp. 191–223).Newbury Park, CA: Sage.

Hill, T. & Westbrook, R. (1997). SWOT analysis: It's time for a product recall. *Long Range Planning, 30*(1), 46–52.

Hislop, D. (2013). *Knowledge management in organizations. A critical introduction*. Oxford, England: Oxford University Press.

Holtzhausen, D. (2012). *Public relations as activism. Postmodern approaches to theory and practice*. New York: Routledge.

Hon, L. C. (1997). What have you done for me lately? Exploring effectiveness in public relations. *Journal of Public Relations Research, 9*(1), 1–30.

Hon, L. C. (1998). Demonstrating effectiveness in public relations: goals, objectives and evaluation. *Journal of Public Relations Research 10*(2), 103–116.

Hon, L. C. & Grunig, J. E. (1999, November). Guidelines for measuring relationships in public relations. Gainesville, FL: Institute for Public Relations. Retrieved July 7, 2014, from www.instituteforpr.org/measuring-relationships

Huntington, R. (2008, July 31) How can advertising succeed if it doesn't have a clear goal? *New Media Age*, p. 16. Retrieved July 7, 2014, from http://econsultancy.com/us/nma-archive/14414-how-can-advertising-succeed-if-it-doesn-t-have-a-clear-goal

Jones, P. & Kahaner, L. (1995). *Say it and live it: The 50 corporate mission statements that hit the mark.* New York: Currency Doubleday.

Kaplan, R. S. & Norton, D. P (2006). *Alignment: Using the balanced scorecard to create corporate synergies.* Boston, MA: Harvard Business School Press.

Kendall, R. (1996). *Public relations campaigs strategies. Planning for implementation.* New York: HarperCollins College Publishers.

Kotler, P. (2002). *Marketing management* (10th ed.). Upper Saddle River, NJ: Prentice-Hall.

Kotter, J.P. (1977, July-August). Power, dependence and effective management. *Harvard Business Review, 55*(4), 125–136.

Kruglanski, A.W. (1996). Goals as knowledge structures. In P. M. Gollwitzer & J. A. Bargh (Eds.), *The psychology of action* (pp. 599–618). New York: Guilford.

Laskin, A. (2011). How investor relations contributes to the corporate bottom line. *Journal of Public Relations Research, 23*(3), 302–324.

Latham, G. & Locke, E. A. (2002). Building a practically useful theory of goal setting and task motivation. *American Psychologist, 57*(2), 705–709.

Lavidge, R. J. & Steiner, G. A. (1961, October). A model for predictive measurements of advertising effectiveness. *Journal of Marketing. 25*, 59–62.

Lee, N. R. & Kotler, P. (2011). *Social marketing. Influencing behaviors for good* (4th ed.). Los Angeles, CA: Sage.

Lewin, K. (1943). Defining the "field at a given time." *Psychological Review. 50*, 292–310.

Lipton, M. (1996, Summer). Demystifying the development of an organizational vision. S*loan Management Review, 37*(4), 83–92.

Locke, E. & Latham, G. (2006). New directions in goal-setting theory. *Current Directions in Psychological Science, 15*(5), 265–268.

Lyotard, J.-F. (1984). *The postmodern condition: A report on knowledge.* G. Bennington & B. Massumi, trans. Minneapolis: University of Minnesota Press.

Lyotard, J.-F. (1992). Answering the question: What is postmodernism? In C. Jencks (Ed.), *The postmodern reader* (pp. 138–150). London, England: Academy Editions.

McElreath, M. P. (1999). *Managing systematic and ethical public relations campaigs* (2nd ed.). Madison, WI: Brown & Benchmark.

McGinnis, V. (1981). The mission statement: A key step in strategic planning. *Business, 31*(6), 41.

McGuire, W. J. (1973). Persuasion, resistance and attitude change. In I. de Sola Pool & W. Schramm (Eds.), *Handbook of communication* (pp. 216–252). Chicago, IL: Rand-McNally.

Meyer, P. J. (2003). *Attitude is everything: If you want to succeed above and beyond.* Meyer Resource Group, Incorporated.

Miller, G.J. (2005). The political evolution of principal-agency models. *Annual Review of Political Science, 8*, 203-225.

Miller, G. A, Galanter, E. & Pribaum, K. H. (1960/1986). *Plans and the structure of behavior.* New York: Adams Bannister. (Originally published 1960).

Mind Tools, Ltd. (n.d.) SWOT analysis. Discover new opportunities, manage and eliminate threats. *MindTools* [Website]. Retrieved July 7, 2014, from http://www.mindtools.com/pages/article/newTMC_05.htm

Mintzberg, H. (1994). *The rise and fall of strategic planning.* New York: Free Press.

Mintzberg, H. (2009). *Managing.* San Francisco, CA: Berrett-Koehler Publishers.

Mintzberg, H. & Waters, J.A. (1985). Of strategies, deliberate and emergent. *Strategic Management Journal, 6*, 257–272.

Moffitt, M.A. (1999). *Campaign strategies and message design. A practitioner's guide from start to finish.* Westport, CT: Praeger.

Mollen, A. & Wilson, H. (2010). Engagement, telepresence and interactivity in online consumer experience: Reconciling scholastic and managerial perspectives. *Journal of Business Research, 63*(9/10), 919–925.

Moriarty, S., Mitchell, N. & Wells, W.D. (2012). *Advertising. Principles and practice* (9th ed.) Upper Saddle River, NJ: Pearson Education.

Moss, D. & Warnaby, G. (1997). A strategic perspective for public relations. In P.J. Kitchen (Ed.), *Public relations: Principles and practice* (pp. 43–73). London, England: International Thomson Business Press.

Munter, M. (2012). *Guide to managerial communication: Effective business writing and speaking*. Boston, MA: Pearson.

Nager, N.R. & Allen, T.H. (1984). *Public relations management by objectives*. New York: Longman.

Nager, N.R. & Truitt, R.H. (1987). *Strategic public relations counseling. Models from the Counselor's Academy*. New York: Longman

O'Guinn, T.C., Allen, C.T. & Semenik, R.J. (2009). *Advertising and integrated brand promotion* (5th ed.). Cincinnati, OH: South-Western Cengage Learning.

Odiorne, G.S. (1965). *Managing by objectives*. New York: Pitman.

Parente, D. (2006). *Advertising campaign strategy. A guide to marketing communication plans* (4th ed.) Mason, OH: Thomson Higher Education/South-Western.

Pavlik, J.V. (1987). *Public relations: What research tells us*. Newbury Park, CA: Sage.

Pfau, M. & Parrott, R. (1993). *Persuasive communication campaigns*. Boston, MA: Allyn and Bacon.

Pfeffer, J. & Salancik, G.R. (1978). *The external control of organizations. A resource dependence perspective*. New York: Harper & Row.

Pieczka, M. (2000) Objectives and evaluation in public relations work: What do they tell us about expertise and professionalism? *Journal of Public Relations Research, 12*(3), 211–234.

Preston, I. L. (1985). The detachment of advertising research from the study of advertiser's goals. *Current Issues & Research in Advertising, 8*(1), 1–14.

Ray, M.L., Sawyer, A.G., Rothschild, M.L., Heller, R.M. Strong, E.C. & Reed, J. (1973). Marketing communication and hierarchy of effects. In P. Clarke (Ed.), *New models for communication research* (pp. 147–173). Beverly Hills, CA: Sage.

Rayfield, R. (1991). *Public relations writing. Strategies and skills*. Dubuque, IA: Wm. C. Brown.

Resnick, E.A. & Siegel, M. (2013). *Marketing public health. Strategies to promote social change* (3rd ed.). Burlington, MA: Jones & Bartlett.

Rice, R.E. & Atkin, C.K. (2013). *Public communication campaigns* (4th ed.). Los Angeles, CA: Sage.

Rice, R.E. & Paisley, W.J. (1981). *Public communication campaigns*. Beverly Hills, CA: Sage.

Rogers, E. M. (2003). *Diffusion of innovations* (5th ed.). New York: Free Press.

Ross, R.D. (1977). *The management of public relations*. New York: Wiley.

Ryan, T.A. (1970). *Intentional behavior*. New York: Ronald Press.

Schrank, R.C. & Abelson, R.P. (1977). *Scripts, plans goals and understanding. An inquiry into human knowledge structures*. Mahwah, NJ: Lawrence Erlbaum.

Senge, P.M. (1990). *The fifth discipline. The art and practice of the learning organization*. New York: Doubleday.

Sheth, J.N. & Parvatiyar, A. (Eds.) (2000), *Handbook of relationship marketing*. Thousand Oaks, CA: Sage.

Sheth, J.N. & Sisodia, R.S. (2012). *The 4A's of marketing. Creating value for customers, companies and society*. New York: Routledge.

Siegel, L. (2012a, October 9). Failure to meet PR goals and expectations: Why it happens; what can prevent it. *BridgeBuzz* [Web log post]. Retrieved July 7, 2014, from http://scottpublicrelations.com/failure-to-meet-pr-goals-and-expectations-why-it-happens-what-can-prevent-it/

Siegel, L. (2012b, October 14). Many comments: Factors contributing to PR failure. *BridgeBuzz* [Blog]. Retrieved July 7, 2014, from http://scottpublicrelations.com/many-comments-factors-contributing-to-pr-failure/

Simerson, B.K. (2011). *Strategic planning. A practical guide for strategy formulation and execution*. Santa Barbara, CA: Praeger.

Simmons, R.E. (1990). *Communication campaign management. A systems approach*. New York: Longman

Smallianov, P. & Aiyeku, J.F. (2009). Corporate marketing objectives and evaluation measures for integrated television advertising and sports event sponsorships. *Journal of Promotion Management, 15*, 79–89.

Smith, K. & Locke, E. A. & Barry, D. 1990). Goal setting, planning and organizational performance: An Experimental simulation. *Organizational Behavior and Human Decision Processes, 46*, 118–134.

Smith, M. F. & Ferguson, D. P. (2001). Activism. In R.L. Heath (Ed.), *Handbook of public relations* (pp. 291–300). Thousand Oaks, CA: Sage.

Smith, R. D. (2013). *Strategic planning for public relations* (4th ed.). New York: Routledge.

Stacks, D. W. (2012). *Primer of public relations research* (2nd ed.). New York: Guilford Press.

Steyn, B. (2007). Contribution of public relations to organizational strategy formulation. In E. L. Toth (Ed.), *The future of excellence in public relations and communication management. Challenges for the next generation* (pp. 137–172). Mahwah, NJ: Lawrence Erlbaum.

Strong, E.K. (1925). *The psychology of selling and advertising.* New York: McGraw-Hill.

Truitt, W.B. (2002). *Business planning. A comprehensive framework and process.* Westport, CT: Quorum Books.

Tucker, K. & Derelian, D. (1989). *Public relations writing. A planned approach for creating results.* Englewood Cliffs, NJ: Prentice-Hall.

U.S. Government Accountability Office (2003, September 19). Military recruiting: DOD needs to establish objectives and measures to better evaluate advertising's effectiveness: GAO-03–1005 [Report]. Washington, DC: GAO. Available www.gao.gov/products/GAO-03–1005

Walton, M. (1991). *Deming management at work.* New York: Perigee Books.

Watkis, N. (2010, November). Marketers won't succeed if they don't have objectives. *Marketing Magnified* (CMO Council e-Journal). Retrieved from http://www.marketingmagnified.com/2010/november/index.html

Watson, T. & Noble, P. (2005). *Evaluating public relations. A best practice guide to public relations, planning, research & evaluation.* London, England: Kogan Page.

Weick, K.E. (1995). *Sense-making in organizations.* Thousand Oaks, CA: Sage.

Weick, K.E. & Sutcliffe (2007). *Managing the unexpected. Resilient performance in an age of uncertainty.* San Francisco, CA: Jossey-Bass.

Welsh, S.J. (1965). Marketing and advertising: Setting objectives that get results. *Management Review, 54*(1), 4–12.

White, J. & Mazur, L. (1995). *Strategic communication management.* Wokingham, England: Addison-Wesley.

Wilcox, D. L. & Cameron, G.T. (2012). *Public relations strategies and tactics* (10th ed.). Boston: Allyn & Bacon.

Wilson, L.J. & Ogden, J.D (2008). *Strategic communications planning: For effective public relations & marketing* (5th ed.). Dubuque, IA: Kendall/Hunt Publishers.

Young, G. & Smith, K.G. (2013). Units, divisions and organizations: Macro-level goals setting. In E.A. Locke & G.P. Latham (Eds.), *New directions in goal setting and task performance* (pp. 311–328). New York: Routledge Academic.

Zerfass, A. (2008a). Corporate communication revisited: Integrating business strategy and strategic communication. In A. Zerfass, B. van Ruler & K. Sriramesh (Eds.). *Public relations research, European and international perspectives and innovations* (pp. 65–96). Wiesbaden, Germany: Verlag.

Zerfass, A. (2008b). The corporate communications scorecard. A framework for managing and evaluating communication strategies. In B. van Ruler, A. Tkalac Verčič & D. Verčič (Eds.), *Public relations metrics. Research and evaluation* (pp. 193–153). New York: Routledge.

Part III

Implementing Strategic Communication

17

A Theoretical Framework for Strategic Communication Messaging

Kelly Page Werder

The program of research reviewed in this chapter seeks to identify, describe, and explain the message variable in the strategic communication process. While discipline-specific public relations scholarship provides the strategic messaging framework advanced in this program, the multidisciplinary nature of strategic communication facilitates the integration of theories and concepts from many fields to enable a fuller understanding of organizational communication processes and outcomes. This chapter reviews the theoretical growth of this program of research from a discipline-specific public relations approach to a multidisciplinary approach positioned in the strategic communication domain.

The focus of this area of inquiry is on the message variable in the communication process, rather than source and receiver variables, which have historically been the unit of analysis in public relations scholarship. According to Hallahan (2000), creating effective messages to reach strategically important publics is a critical function of public relations; however, public relations theorists have failed to develop message strategies for communicating with publics (p. 464). Similarly, Springston and Keyton (2001) stated that, although scholars have described the need for delivering strategic messages concurrently to multiple publics, a theoretically grounded methodology for assessing and analyzing messages sent to publics has not been offered (p. 117).

Although strategic messaging has received limited attention in public relations scholarship, the theoretical framework provided by the *public relations process model* (Hazleton & Long, 1988) describes public relations as goal-driven message strategies used by organizations to interact with target publics in their environment. As part of the model, Hazleton (1992, 1993) identified six functions of messages at the psychological level that reflect message effects common to public relations: informative, persuasive, facilitative, coercive, co-operative problem-solving, and bargaining. The findings of numerous studies indicate that the message strategy taxonomy is a valid conceptualization of the communication behavior of organizations (Förster & Werder, 2011; Gallo, 2009; Guilfoil, 2010; Page, 2000a, 2000b; Page & Hazleton, 1999; Werder, 2005, 2006a, 2006b; Werder & Holtzhausen, 2009; Werder & Mitrook, 2011; Werder & Schuch, 2008; Werder & Schweickart, 2013).

Although the public relations process model provides a useful theoretical framework, it does not define the receiver variables important to achieving organizational goals by means of strategic messaging. Nor does it specify the effects of strategic messaging in various contexts and situations. Thus, a broader perspective is needed: one that integrates these concepts to provide a more robust understanding of strategic messaging. This chapter presents theories from different academic domains and attempts to synthesize these theories into a comprehensive and parsimonious framework that facilitates identification, description, and explanation of the message variable in the strategic communication process.

Identifying Strategic Communication Messages

According to Hazleton and Long's public relations process model,[1] public relations is a communication function of management through which organizations establish relationships necessary to adapt to, alter, or maintain their environment for the purpose of achieving organizational goals (Hazleton, 1993; Hazleton & Dougall, 2007; Hazleton & Long, 1988; Long & Hazleton, 1987). As such, public relations can be conceptualized as an open system consisting of a multi-dimensional environment and three subsystems. At the macroscopic level, the environment is the system, and public relations input, transformation, and output processes are made up of the organization, communication, and target audience subsystems (Hazleton & Long, 1988, p. 82).

The communication subsystem provides a boundary-spanning function among the environment, organization, and target audience subsystems. The function of this boundary-spanning role is the encoding and delivery of messages (Hazleton & Long, 1988, p. 85). Public relations behavior in organizations is enacted through communication strategies designed to achieve organizational goals (Hazleton, 1993). Communication strategies are manifest in the form of messages that serve as inputs to target audiences located in the environment. This manifestation is a functional result of the communication process—a process based on the analysis of symbols.

Hazleton (1993) stated that symbols are observable tangible parts of the communication process. In order for communication to be effective, symbols or symbol systems must be shared or at least understood by both source and receiver in the communication process. As socially constructed objects that take physical form and have predictable effects, symbols may be viewed as organizational resources. Organizations expend other types of resources to develop and use symbolic resources in order to accomplish organizational goals (Hazleton, 1993, p. 89).

Therefore, it is possible to analyze messages as symbolic communication that contains unique physical, psychological, and social properties. "Physically, messages are tangible stimuli that can be perceived. Psychologically, meanings attributed to messages by receivers can be specified. Socially, significant others influence individual message evaluation processes" (Hazleton & Long, 1988, p. 85).

Hazleton (1993) used these concepts to develop a matrix for the analysis of public relations messages as symbolic communication. This matrix is illustrated in Figure 17.1. The top of the matrix reflects increasing levels of abstraction of the audience in terms of message effects and message processing. At the first level, messages are seen as physical objects to be apprehended and processed by individuals. At the second level, messages are seen as objects to be understood by individuals, so their psychological impact is considered. At the third level, the impact of social processes on symbol effects is considered (p. 91).

The left side of the matrix consists of three general concepts—content, structure, and function—that reflect assumptions about the characteristics of messages. Although these concepts are present at every point in the communication process, they are aspects of symbolic messages that can be viewed independently. As a result, they can be recognized and understood without knowing the motive or the characteristics of the message source.

Content refers to the manifest characteristics of messages. Structure refers to the distribution and frequency of communication elements within a particular level of analysis. Function references the audience and reflects assumptions about message effects. According to Hazleton (1993), "The classification of messages according to their functional characteristics must take into account characteristics of the audience for the message. Specifically, strategic choices reflect assumptions about motivational, cognitive, and behavioral characteristics of audiences" (p. 91).

	Physical	Psychological	Sociological

Content	• graphic-visual
	• oral-aural
	• tactile
	• olfactory
	• taste
		A. *Reference*
		    • denotative
		    • connotative
		B. *Style*
		    • logical
		    • interesting
		    • emotional
		    • assertive
		    • face-preserving
		    • concise
		    • ambiguous
		    • factual
			• rhetorical visions
			• fantasy themes
			• symbolic cues
			• fantasy types
			• sagas

Structure	• intensity
	• contrast
	• special order
	• chronological order
		A. *Organic*
		    • spatial
		    • chronological
		    • types
		B. *Psychological*
		    • cause/effect
		    • problem/solving
		    • climax/anti-climax
			A. *Distribution*
			    • network size
			    • network shape
			    • symmetry
			    • relationship
			B. *Frequency*
			    • activity
			    • topic/symbol

Function	A. *Attributions to symbols*
	    • repeat
	    • contradict
	    • substitute
	    • complement
	    • accent
	    • verify
	B. *Attributions to communicators*
	    • relationship
	    • status
	    • affect
		Facilitate
		
		Inform
		
		Coerce/empower
		
		Bargain
		
		Solve problems
		
		Persuade
			A. *Task performance*
			    • problem identification
			    • solution identification
			    • behavior regulation
			    • information exchange
			B. *Group maintenance*
			    • socialization
			    • consciousness raising
			    • conflict resolution
			    • leadership

Figure 17.1   Matrix for the Analysis of Public Relations Symbols

Source: Hazleton, 1993

Hazleton (1993) identified six functions of messages at the psychological level that reflect public relations strategies used by organizations when communicating with publics. These functions represent the goals of public relations in terms of the impact messages have on audiences and the meanings audiences attribute to messages. The six functions are: facilitate, inform, persuade, coerce, bargain, and solve problems.

The first four functions—facilitate, inform, persuade, and coerce—derive from social change literature and include concepts for planned change identified by Zaltman and Duncan (1977). Although there is no definitive way of categorizing these strategies, they are considered to lie on a continuum of degree of pressure exerted (p. 60). In addition, Zaltman and Duncan stated that multiple strategies might be employed to accomplish a desired outcome. The last two functions identified in the matrix—bargaining and problem-solving—incorporate J. E. Grunig's ideas about direction and purpose of communication (J. E. Grunig & Hunt, 1984). These strategies reflect characteristics of the two-way asymmetrical and two-way symmetrical models of public relations described in J. E. Grunig's excellence theory (1992).

Hazleton (1992) used these six psychological functions of messages to develop a taxonomy of public relations strategies that organizations use when communicating with publics. Hazleton labeled the strategies informative, facilitative, persuasive, power (formerly referred to as coercive), bargaining, and co-operative problem-solving.

Informative Strategies

An informative strategy is based on the presentation of unbiased facts and assumes a rational and motivated audience. Informative messages do not draw conclusions, but instead presume the public will infer appropriate conclusions from accurate data. Informative messages may suggest a variety of alternative solutions to problems. In addition, they are characterized by the use of neutral language and organic, or natural, patterns of organization to create greater ease of comprehension.

Research indicates that time-on-task and frequency of exposure to messages are positively related to learning; therefore, informative strategies are most effective when behavioral change within a target public does not have to occur quickly. Zaltman and Duncan (1977) stated that informative strategies are effective in enhancing problem recognition, so they may be used to build a foundation for future learning. However, it may not be desirable to mention a specific solution, especially a controversial one, until a clear need has been established. Informative strategies can be effective in creating awareness of a problem and establishing perceptions that a known problem can be resolved (i.e., reducing constraint recognition), but when an organization does not possess the resources to sustain a needed long-term involvement, an informative strategy alone will not be effective (p. 132).

In addition, informative strategies are useful at the awareness stage of the change process. They are effective in inoculating individuals against appeals to resist change or to revert back to a previous pattern of behavior. When resistance to change is high, informative strategies require more time to be effective. Furthermore, informative strategies are indicated when a public does not possess the knowledge or skills necessary to implement a change, and they are most effective with highly motivated publics.

Facilitative Strategies

A facilitative strategy is accomplished by making resources available to a public that allow it to act in ways that it is already predisposed to act. Resources may be tangible artifacts, such as tools or money, or they may be directions for accomplishing specific tasks.

According to Zaltman and Duncan (1977), facilitative strategies are useful when the public recognizes a problem, agrees remedial action is needed, is open to external assistance, and is willing to engage in self-help. Facilitative strategies are most effective when used with a program that creates awareness among the public of the availability of assistance. In addition, an organization using a facilitative strategy must determine if the continuation of the strategy will require continued resource expenditures after the initial implementation of the change. Facilitative strategies may be used to compensate for low motivation and are indicated when target publics lack the resources needed to implement or maintain a change. Furthermore, if the resistance to change is great, a facilitative strategy is less likely to succeed.

Persuasive Strategies

A persuasive strategy is characterized by appeals to a public's values or emotions. This strategy may include a selective presentation of information. It may use language that is not neutral and reflects the importance of the issue and/or the involvement of the source in the situation. Persuasive messages are directive in that they contain a call for action, either tacitly or explicitly. According to Zaltman and Duncan (1977), persuasive strategies are indicated when a problem is not recognized or considered important by a public, when involvement is low, or when a particular solution is not perceived to be effective. Persuasive strategies are useful when it is necessary to induce a public to reallocate resources from one program or activity to an alternative advocated by the organization. These strategies are often used when an organization does not have direct control over a public through the manipulation of resources valued by the public, and persuasive strategies are useful when time constraints are great and the ability to use power is low (p. 151).

In addition, persuasive strategies may be useful when a public's motivation to change is low, but they are not feasible when a target public lacks resources to sustain change. These strategies are particularly useful at the legitimation and evaluation stages of the change process and when the magnitude of change is considered to be great or perceived to be risky. Persuasion may be necessary when trial is not possible, changes are difficult to understand, or there is no visible relative advantage. Furthermore, greater resistance to change in target publics indicates a greater need for persuasive strategies; however, resistance to change increases when members of a public are aware of an intention to persuade.

Power Strategies

Both promise and reward and threat and punishment strategies are defined by their use of power to gain compliance; therefore, they are considered to be coercive techniques. A promise and reward strategy includes a directive and contingent outcome that may be explicitly or tacitly linked to performance of the directive request. This strategy uses positive coercion in that it implies the source of the message controls an outcome desired by the receiver of the message. In contrast, a threat and punishment strategy employs negative coercion. This strategy implies the source of the message controls an outcome feared or disliked by the receiver of the message.

Power strategies are useful when a public's perceived need for change is low; however, a power strategy will not be effective if a target group does not have the resources required to accept change and the organization cannot provide them (Zaltman & Duncan, 1977). A power strategy may be effective in getting a public to reallocate resources to initiate and sustain change. Power strategies also are useful when there is anticipated resistance to change, a solution to a problem has to be implemented in a short period of time, and change must occur quickly. In addition, an organization must be able to control outcomes for target publics for power strategies to be effective: therefore, these strategies often require more resources than other strategies. Power strategies are more effective when behavioral change is the goal and psychological change is not important. If psychological change is important, power strategies must be combined with other strategies. Finally, promise and reward strategies are easier to use than threat and punishment strategies because they are more socially acceptable.

Bargaining Strategies

Bargaining strategies are characterized by an organized exchange of messages between communicators. Strategic withholding of information, and deception designed to mislead others concerning an acceptable range of alternatives and to discover the other party's acceptable range of alternatives, are used. Bargaining communication is characterized by the use of contrasting symbols that differentiate groups, such as "we", and "they." This strategy reflects characteristics similar to J. E. Grunig's (1992) two-way asymmetrical model in that organizations and publics are likely to have incompatible goals and information withholding is a common tactic.

Bargaining strategies are indicated when interdependence is high. This means that all parties to the bargaining situation are dependent on the co-operation of the other parties to achieve their goals. This is a constraint in that bargaining is a competitive situation. Bargaining is likely to be a more viable strategy when the goals of differing parties are less compatible; however, bargaining is not likely to be effective unless all parties have a range of acceptable alternatives from which a solution can be achieved.

Co-Operative Problem-Solving Strategies

A co-operative problem-solving strategy reflects a willingness to jointly define problems and solutions to problems. Messages derived from this strategy are characterized by an open exchange of information that establishes a common definition of the problem and common goals, and leads to the sharing of positions and responsibilities about the issue. These strategies use inclusive symbols, such as 'we.' In addition, this strategy reflects characteristics of J. E. Grunig's (1992) two-way symmetrical model in that there is a sense of interdependence among the organization and its publics. Co-operation is effective when the organization and the public recognize their interdependence and feel a need for each other's participation in the identification of problems and the development of alternative solutions. The more compatible the goals of differing parties are, the more likely that a co-operative problem-solving strategy will be effective. All parties must be able to agree on a common problem definition and common solution to the problem; therefore, openness and fairness characterize these strategies.

Describing Message Strategy Use and Effectiveness

The public relations process model and its accompanying taxonomy of public relations strategies offer a much-needed framework for understanding the messaging behavior of organizations. An underlying assumption of the model is that it is situational, asserting that an organization's perception of the audience it is communicating with at a given time guides the organization's strategy selection (Hazleton, 1993). Attributes of publics can be identified by organizations during the research and analysis phase of the public relations decision process and used to select public relations strategies most appropriate and effective in achieving organizational goals. In this way, organizational goals are aligned with attributes of publics to facilitate strategy use, and public relations strategies become the functional link between organizational goals and publics. Moreover, by viewing public relations strategies as symbolic messages guided by attributes of publics, it is possible to predict the effectiveness of strategies in achieving organizational goals.

Numerous studies have validated Hazleton's message strategy taxonomy by measuring the frequency of strategy use in organizations, the influence of attributes of publics on strategy use and effectiveness, and the effect of message strategies on receiver variables. Research has also investigated the relationship between organizational management variables and message strategy use and effectiveness in achieving organizational goals. The findings of these studies are reviewed below.

Frequency of Strategy Use in Organizations

Six studies have been conducted that measure the frequency of strategy use in organizations. The results of these studies, which employed survey methods and content analysis, are shown in Tables 17.1 and 17.2.

In the first empirical study using the message strategy taxonomy, Page and Hazleton (1999) surveyed members of the Public Relations Society of America (PRSA) via direct mail to measure strategy use in the implementation of public relations campaigns. Using a repeated measures design,

Table 17.1 Comparison of Frequency of Message Strategy Use Across Studies Using Survey Methods

Werder & Holtzhausen (2009)	Werder (2005)	Page (2000a)	Page & Hazleton (1999)
Persuasive	Persuasive	Informative	Persuasive
Informative	Informative	Persuasive	Informative
Facilitative	Facilitative	Co-operative	Co-operative
Co-operative	Co-operative	Facilitative	Facilitative
Power		Promise/reward	Promise/reward
		Threat/punishment	Bargaining
		Bargaining	Threat/punishment

Table 17.2 Comparison of Frequency of Message Strategy Use Across Studies Using Content Analysis

Werder (2006a, 2006b)	Page (2000b)
Persuasive	Informative
Informative	Persuasive
Co-operative	Facilitative
Facilitative	Co-operative
Promise/reward	Threat/punishment
Threat/punishment	Promise/reward
Bargaining	Bargaining

the survey instrument provided the definition of each of the seven strategies and asked practitioners to rate their use of the strategy using a five-point scale anchored by the statements, *This organization has frequently used this strategy*, and *This organization has never used this strategy*. Page and Hazleton found significant differences in frequency of strategy use across strategies and reported that strategy type accounted for approximately 40% of the variance in frequency of strategy use measures. Specifically, the study found that organizations use persuasive strategies most frequently. Informative strategies were found to be the second most frequently used, followed by co-operative problem-solving and facilitative strategies. Promise and reward, bargaining, and threat and punishment strategies were found to be the least frequently used by practitioners.

Two subsequent studies produced similar results. In one study, Page (2000a) surveyed public relations practitioners who were members of the PRSA Counselor's Academy, using an online questionnaire. Results indicated that the informative strategy was used most often in the implementation of public relations campaigns. Specifically, the informative strategy was used 48.8% of the time. Practitioners reported using the persuasive strategy 18.8% of the time, followed by the co-operative problem-solving strategy (14.6 %), and the facilitative strategy (12.2%). The promise and reward strategy was used 4.9% of the time and the threat and punishment strategy was used only 1.2% of the time. No use of the bargaining strategy was reported in this study.

In another study, Page (2000b) conducted a content analysis of public relations strategy use in 100 randomly selected news releases distributed by organizations via the PRNewswire Web site (www.prnewswire.com). Results indicated that the informative strategy was used most frequently in news releases. The persuasive strategy was the second most frequently used strategy, followed by the facilitative strategy, the co-operative problem-solving strategy, the threat and punishment strategy, the promise and reward strategy, and the bargaining strategy.

This content analysis was replicated five years later (Werder, 2006a) with slightly different results. Specifically, persuasive strategies were most often used by organizations in the later sample of news releases, followed by informative, co-operative problem-solving, facilitative, promise and reward, threat and punishment, and bargaining strategies.

In 2005, Werder replicated the Page and Hazleton (1999) survey of PRSA members with a larger sample size (N=403); however, only the four most frequently used strategies, as indicated by previous findings, were tested. Statistically significant differences in frequency of strategy use were found across strategies. Specifically, 16.6% of the variance in frequency of use measures was accounted for by strategy type. The results were nearly identical to Page and Hazleton's findings, with practitioners reporting they used persuasive strategies most often, followed by informative, facilitative, and co-operative problem-solving strategies.

Finally, in a large-scale study of organizational communication management practices, Werder and Holtzhausen (2009) surveyed 885 PRSA members and found statistically significant differences in frequency of use across five strategies tested. The eta-squared score indicated that strategy type accounted for 69% of the variance in frequency of strategy use measures. Their study produced the same frequency of strategy use reported by Werder (2005); however, they also tested power strategies, which were found to be the least frequently used among practitioners in their sample.

The results of these six studies validate Hazleton's public relations message strategy taxonomy and suggest a good fit between the conceptual definitions and operationalizations of the strategies. Furthermore, the finding that frequency of strategy use varies across strategies indicates that the strategies have unique usage characteristics—organizations use some strategies more than others and some not at all. This supports Hazleton's assertion that public relations message strategy use is situational.

The Influence of Attributes of Publics on Strategy Use and Effectiveness

To explain why organizations use different message strategies in different situations, Page and Hazleton (1999) argued that strategy use by communication practitioners is influenced more by receiver variables than by organizational management variables, which have been the focus of much public relations scholarship to date. They attempted to describe the relationship between attributes of publics, strategy use, and strategy effectiveness by testing attributes of publics derived from J. E. Grunig's situational theory of publics (J. E. Grunig & Hunt, 1984), including problem recognition, constraint recognition, level of involvement, information processing, and information seeking. In addition, Page and Hazleton (1999) conceptualized and tested goal compatibility as a key attribute of publics that influences an organization's strategic message choices. Their study found that strategy type accounted for 72.6% of the variance in attributes of publics across strategies. Specifically, practitioners' perceptions of problem recognition, information seeking, and goal compatibility in publics were found to be the most important variables in practitioners' message strategy selection (p. 17).

Page and Hazleton (1999) also predicted that attributes of publics are related to perceived effectiveness of message strategies in achieving organizational goals. Multiple regression analysis yielded significant results for attributes of publics and effectiveness for six of the seven strategies tested in their study. Specifically, the variables of goal compatibility, problem recognition, level of involvement, and information seeking were significant predictors of strategy effectiveness. However, Page and Hazleton argued that goal compatibility functions as a primary predictor of strategy effectiveness, since it was found to be the main contributor to unique variance in effectiveness for five of the strategies tested. According to the authors, the attribute of goal compatibility becomes even more important when organizations have a limited ability to process information. "Under conditions that limit an organization's capacity to evaluate multiple attributes of publics, goal compatibility may function as a primary factor in both strategy use and effectiveness" (1999, p. 23).

These results were supported by Page (2000a), who conducted follow-up research to develop a better understanding of goal compatibility and how it relates to strategy effectiveness. Results indicated a significant positive correlation between goal compatibility and strategy effectiveness ($r = .412$, $p < .001$).

In Werder's 2005 study, multiple-item measures of problem recognition, constraint recognition, involvement, and goal compatibility were used to examine the influence of attributes of publics on strategy use. According to the results of repeated measures ANOVA, strategy type accounted for 58% of the variance in attributes of publics across strategies. Univariate analysis indicated that measures of problem recognition and constraint recognition produced the largest effect sizes, and measures of goal compatibility and involvement produced the smallest effect sizes.

Werder's 2005 study also found that perceived attributes of publics account for a large percentage of the variance in the effectiveness of informative, facilitative, persuasive, and co-operative problem-solving strategies. Specifically, measures of goal compatibility, problem recognition, and involvement accounted for approximately 33% of the unique variance in informative strategy effectiveness. Measures of goal compatibility, problem recognition, involvement, and information processing accounted for approximately 40% of the unique variance in facilitative strategy effectiveness. Measures of goal compatibility, problem recognition, information processing, involvement, and constraint recognition accounted for approximately 42% of the unique variance in persuasive strategy effectiveness. Measures of goal compatibility, involvement, problem recognition, and information processing accounted for approximately 52% of the unique variance in effectiveness for the co-operative problem-solving strategy.

Using these results, Werder (2005) proposed the foundation for a positive theory of public relations message strategy use and effectiveness in organizations that links the message and receiver variables inherent in the public relations process. She posited the following hypotheses and related propositions for future empirical testing:

H1:   Perceived attributes of publics influence public relations strategy use in organizations.

P1.1:   When informative strategies are used, practitioners perceive the public as having low problem recognition and low goal compatibility.

P1.2:   When facilitative strategies are used, practitioners perceive the public as having moderate problem recognition, high goal compatibility, high involvement, and information-processing behavior.

P1.3:   When persuasive strategies are used, practitioners perceive the public as having low problem recognition, low goal compatibility, low involvement, and information-seeking behavior.

P1.4:   When co-operative problem-solving strategies are used, practitioners perceive the public as having high problem recognition, high goal compatibility, and information-seeking behavior.

H2:   Perceived attributes of publics are predictors of public relations strategy effectiveness.

P2.1:   Informative strategy effectiveness is predicted by perceived goal compatibility and problem recognition.

P2.2:   Facilitative strategy effectiveness is predicted by perceived goal compatibility and information-processing behavior.

P2.3:   Persuasive strategy effectiveness is predicted by perceived goal compatibility.

P2.4:   Co-operative problem-solving strategy effectiveness is predicted by perceived goal compatibility and problem recognition.

The Effect of Message Strategies on Receiver Variables

Numerous experimental studies have attempted to determine which public relations message strategies are most effective in achieving organizational goals in various situations. These studies have primarily focused on message strategy effects on receiver cognitions related to issues. In an effort to broaden the application of public relations message strategies, Page (2003) tested their effect on receiver variables using the theory of reasoned action (Fishbein & Ajzen, 1975), a commonly used framework in advertising and marketing research. The theory of reasoned action provides a model for measuring people's beliefs, attitudes, and intentions toward a behavior in order to predict their actual behavior (Fishbein & Ajzen, 1975; Ajzen & Fishbein, 1980). The theory specifies that

1. behavior is determined by intention to engage in behavior,
2. intention is determined by attitude toward the behavior and subjective norm
3. attitude is determined by behavioral beliefs and evaluations of the salient outcomes
4. subjective norm is determined by normative beliefs and motivation to comply with the salient referents (Fishbein & Ajzen, 1975).

The theory assumes that attitude and behavior are related because humans are rational beings who systematically process the information available to them in a reasonable way to arrive at a behavioral decision (Ajzen & Fishbein, 1980). In most cases, people act consistently with their stated attitude (Fishbein & Ajzen, 1975; Ajzen & Fishbein, 1980).

Using an experimental design, Page (2003) applied the theory of reasoned action (Fishbein & Ajzen, 1975) to examine the influence of public relations strategies on individuals' beliefs, attitudes, and behavioral intentions toward an organization responding to activism. Results indicated that co-operative problem-solving strategies produced the most positive attitudes and behavioral intentions toward the organization. In contrast, threat and punishment strategies produced the least effective outcomes for the organization.

In a similar study using the variables of the situational theory of publics (J. E. Grunig & Hunt, 1984), Werder (2006b) found that message strategy type had a significant effect on individuals' problem recognition and level of involvement toward an organization responding to activism. Specifically, the facilitative strategy produced the highest level of problem recognition among publics, followed by the co-operative problem-solving strategy. Informative strategies were the least effective in producing problem recognition among publics. The persuasive strategy produced the highest level of involvement among publics, followed by the facilitative strategy. Informative and threat and punishment strategies produced the lowest involvement among publics.

Werder and Schuch (2008) replicated Werder's (2006b) study, but examined message strategies from the perspective of the activist organization rather than the corporation responding to activism. Their study combined variables from both the situational theory of publics and the theory of reasoned action and found that message strategies influence problem recognition, goal compatibility, attitude toward strategy, and attitude toward behavior. In addition, their results suggested that persuasive and power strategies are most effective in making publics active toward an activist organization's cause.

Gallo (2009) employed an emergency management context to examine the effect of message strategy type on receiver responses to hurricane evacuation messages. Results indicated that problem recognition and level of involvement among message receivers were significantly affected by strategy type. The threat and punishment strategy produced the highest problem recognition among message receivers, followed by the persuasive and promise and reward strategies. The threat and punishment strategy also produced the highest level of involvement among message receivers, followed by facilitative and co-operative problem-solving strategies. In addition, the threat and punishment strategy produced the highest level of information-seeking behavior, and the persuasive strategy produced the lowest level of information-seeking behavior among message receivers.

Using a similar experimental design, Guilfoil (2010) explored the effect of message strategies on beliefs, attitudes, and behavioral intentions of non-boaters and active boaters regarding boater safety.

Table 17.3 Interaction of Issue Involvement and Message Strategy on Communication Behavior

Level of involvement	Strategy type	M	Std. error
Low issue involvement	Co-operative problem solving	3.731	.286
	Facilitative	3.500	.292
	Threat and punishment	3.250	.286
	Persuasive	3.210	.292
	Promise and reward	2.846	.286
	Informative	2.594	.298
High issue involvement	Co-operative problem solving	4.705	.276
	Persuasive	4.040	.292
	Threat and punishment	4.000	.271
	Promise and reward	3.540	.292
	Informative	3.458	.298
	Facilitative	3.330	.311

Results indicated that power strategies—threat and punishment and promise and reward—were most effective when communicating to a passive public.

In an attempt to better understand the relationship between involvement and message strategy effects, Werder and Mitrook (2011) tested the main and interaction effects of message strategies and issue involvement on relational outcomes and communication behavior. They used a 2 × 6 factorial design (N = 333) to examine the effects of six message strategies on trust, satisfaction, commitment, control mutuality, and communication behavior in high and low issue involvement conditions. Their study sought to determine the most effective message strategies and involvement conditions for producing positive relational outcomes and motivating publics to act. While the message strategies did not have a significant effect on the relational variables, the results indicated that nearly 13% of the variance in communication behavior of publics was due to the interaction between message strategy type and issue involvement. Furthermore, co-operative problem-solving strategies were the most effective in motivating publics to act in both low and high issue involvement conditions. The means for message strategy effectiveness in motivating communication behavior among publics for both low and high involvement issues are shown in Table 17.3.

In a similar study, Förster and Werder (2011) employed an interdisciplinary and multi-cultural perspective to examine message strategy effects on variables common to marketing research—brand associations and purchase intentions—and the role of product involvement and cultural values in moderating these effects. Their study found that product involvement acts as a moderator for message strategy effects—it influences the strength of the message effect, which is stronger for high involvement than for low involvement conditions.

Förster and Werder (2011) found that, for highly involved audiences, the most effective message strategy for increasing purchase intention among consumers is persuasive, and for low involved audiences, power strategies are most effective. These results are contrary to the assumptions of Zaltman and Duncan (1977) and the message strategy taxonomy originally identified by Hazleton, as well as previous research. The literature suggests that informative and co-operative problem-solving strategies are most effective for high involvement conditions, and facilitative and persuasive strategies are most effective for low involvement situations. Förster and Werder (2011) argued that their results might be due to the fact that their study was carried out in a marketing product-driven context, rather than a public relations issue-driven context. They concluded that message strategy effects are complex and highly situational.

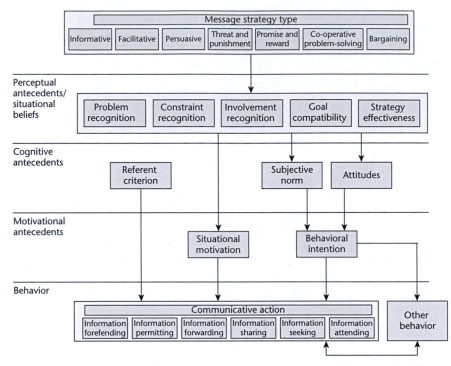

Figure 17.2 An Integrated Model for Explaining the Communication Behavior of Publics

Source: Werder and Schweickart (2013).

In an attempt to synthesize the results of these previous studies, Werder and Schweickart (2013) proposed and tested an integrated model for explaining the communication behavior of publics, shown in Figure 17.2. They applied an interdisciplinary perspective that integrated the independent and dependent variables of the situational theory of problem-solving (Kim & J. E. Grunig, 2011; J.-N. Kim, Ni, S.-H. Kim, & J. R. Kim, 2012) and the theory of reasoned action (Fishbein & Ajzen, 1975) to provide a more comprehensive, robust way of understanding and explaining why publics engage in communication behavior—and other behaviors—related to organizational activities and goals.

The integrated model places each variable of the situational theory of problem solving (an extension of the situational theory of publics) and the theory of reasoned action on the appropriate antecedent level that reflects its function. Specifically, the model posits that message strategies communicated from organizations influence individuals' situational beliefs. According to the situational theory of problem-solving, situational beliefs influence situational motivation in problem-solving, which in turn operates with referent criterion to predict communicative action. Similarly, the theory of reasoned action posits that situational beliefs influence attitudes and subjective norm, which in turn predict intention to engage in behavior. An important aspect of the integrated model is its addition of behavioral intention to the variables that predict communicative action. The model draws from the issues management framework offered by the situational theory of problem-solving to suggest that attitudes toward the organization and the issue are also important in predicting behavioral intention and influencing communicative action in publics. It draws from the theory of reasoned action to suggest that behavioral intention, specifically purchase intention, is a factor that should be considered when attempting to understand communicative action, and other behaviors of publics that impact organizational activities and goals.

The results of Werder and Schweickart's (2013) test of the model provide support for the relationships proposed. They found that message strategies influence attitudes toward the issue, organization, and behavior through their influence on perceived strategy effectiveness. In addition, perceived strategy effectiveness was a significant contributor to situational motivation in problem solving and behavioral intention was a significant predictor of communicative action.

Organizational Management of Strategic Messaging

Several studies have explored the relationship between organizational management variables and message strategy use and effectiveness in organizations. Specifically, the influence of management-level variables such as organizational structure, communication practitioner decision-making behavior, practitioner leadership style, and practitioner roles have been examined to determine how they may influence message strategy use in organizations.

Werder (2009) examined the influence of organizational structure and practitioner decision-making behavior on message strategy use and effectiveness. The results of her study suggest that network structures are predictors of informative and co-operative problem-solving strategy use and co-operative problem-solving strategy effectiveness. Matrix structures were found to predict use and effectiveness of facilitative and co-operative problem-solving strategies. Virtual structures predicted informative strategy use, and multidivisional structures predicted persuasive strategy use.

In addition, practitioner decision-making behavior was found to influence use of all of the strategies except the persuasive strategy and effectiveness of all of the strategies tested. Specifically, information acquisition decision making was found to be a predictor of informative and co-operative problem-solving strategy use, as well as informative, facilitative, persuasive, and co-operative problem-solving strategy effectiveness. Technology-oriented decision-making behavior was a predictor of facilitative and power strategy use, and power strategy effectiveness. In addition, risk assessment decision-making behavior was a predictor of power strategy use and facilitative strategy effectiveness, and group decision-making behavior was a predictor of co-operative problem-solving strategy use.

A study by Werder and Holtzhausen (2008) showed limited, albeit statistically significant, effects of communication practitioner roles on the use and perceived effectiveness of message strategies by practitioners. While communication strategists, communication facilitators, and technicians repeated more use of informative strategies, this did not translate into perceptions of strategy effectiveness. The communication strategist and media relations roles were related to the perceived effectiveness of informative strategies. The process facilitator role was related to the perceived effectiveness of facilitative messages, and the expert prescriber role contributed to the perceived effectiveness of persuasive message strategies. The communication facilitator role led to the use and perceived effectiveness of co-operative message strategies. While the expert prescriber, communication facilitator, and strategist roles led to use of power message strategies, none of these roles contributed to the effectiveness of power message strategies.

Finally, the results of research by Werder and Holtzhausen (2009) suggest that transformational leadership style is related to the use of facilitative and power strategies, and the perceived effectiveness of persuasive and co-operative problem-solving strategies. In addition, inclusive leadership style is related to the use of facilitative, co-operative problem-solving, and power strategies, and the perceived effectiveness of informative and facilitative strategies.

Explaining Message Strategy Use and Effectiveness

The findings of the research reviewed here demonstrate that the message strategy taxonomy proposed by Hazleton provides a useful framework for understanding the message variable in the strategic communication process. The triangulated perspective provided by the various research methods used to study the message strategies suggests their efficacy in both practice and scholarship.

The Theory of Strategic Communication Messaging

This program of research provides the foundation for a positive theory of strategic communication messaging in organizations. Based on the findings of these studies, the following hypotheses are proposed as the basis for this theory. These hypotheses originate from the studies conducted by Page and Hazleton (1999) and Werder (2005); however, they have been modified to reflect the findings of the research reviewed here. Hypotheses 1 through 4 relate to message strategy use, and Hypotheses 5 through 10 relate to message strategy effectiveness in achieving organizational goals.

H1: Informative strategies are used when the public is perceived as having moderate problem recognition, moderate constraint recognition, moderate involvement, moderate goal compatibility, and information-seeking behavior.

H2: Facilitative strategies are used when the public is perceived as having low problem recognition, low constraint recognition, low involvement, high goal compatibility, and information-processing behavior.

H3: Persuasive strategies are used when the public is perceived as having low problem recognition, moderate constraint recognition, moderate involvement, low goal compatibility, and information-processing behavior.

H4: Co-operative problem-solving strategies are used when the public is perceived as having high problem recognition, high constraint recognition, high involvement, high goal compatibility, and information-seeking behavior.

H5: Informative strategies are effective when publics exhibit moderate problem recognition, moderate involvement, and moderate goal compatibility.

H6: Facilitative strategies are effective when publics exhibit low problem recognition, low involvement, high goal compatibility, and are not actively seeking information.

H7: Persuasive strategies are effective when publics exhibit low problem recognition, moderate involvement, low constraint recognition, low goal compatibility, and are not actively seeking information.

H8: Co-operative problem-solving strategies are effective when publics exhibit high problem recognition, high involvement, high goal compatibility, and are actively seeking information.

H9: Promise and reward strategies are effective when publics exhibit high goal compatibility.

H10: Threat and punishment strategies are effective when publics exhibit high goal compatibility and high involvement.

These hypotheses can be more concisely presented in the form of two tables. Table 17.4 shows the perceived attributes of publics when message strategies are used in organizations. Table 17.5 shows the perceived attributes of publics when message strategies are effective in achieving organizational goals.

The results of the program of research described in this chapter provide the foundation for a positive theory of strategic communication messaging in organizations. Future research should aim to deepen understanding of the message strategies and how they are applied across situations and organizational contexts to achieve organizational goals. This research makes an important contribution to the strategic communication body of knowledge, as it supports the notion that an effective communication manager must engage with multiple interactants (i.e., consumers, publics, audiences) and should, therefore, understand how different interactants require different strategic messaging approaches. This is the unique domain of strategic communication.

Table 17.4 Relationship of Attributes of Publics and Strategy Use

Strategy type	Problem recognition	Constraint recognition	Level of involvement	Goal compatibility	Info. seeking
Informative	Moderate	Moderate	Moderate	Moderate	High
Facilitative	Low	Low	Low	High	Low
Persuasive	Low	Moderate	Moderate	Low	Low
Co-operative	High	High	High	High	High

Table 17.5 Relationship of Attributes of Publics and Strategy Effectiveness

Strategy type	Problem recognition	Constraint recognition	Level of involvement	Goal compatibility	Info. seeking
Informative	Moderate		Moderate	Moderate	
Facilitative	Low		Low	High	Low
Persuasive	Low	Low	Moderate	Low	Low
Co-operative	High		High	High	High
Promise and reward			High	High	
Threat and punishment			High	High	

Note

1 For a complete review of the public relations process model, see Hazleton and Dougall (2007) and Werder (2005).

References

Ajzen, I., & Fishbein, M. (1980). *Understanding attitudes and predicting social behavior.* Englewood Cliffs, NJ: Prentice Hall.

Fishbein, M., & Ajzen, I. (1975). *Belief, attention, intention, and behavior: An introduction to theory and research.* Reading, MA: Addison-Wesley.

Förster, K., & Werder, K. P. (2011, May). *The persuasive power of messages: An interdisciplinary analysis of product involvement and values as moderators of public relations message strategy effects.* Paper presented at the 2011 Conference of the International Communication Association, Boston, MA.

Gallo, A. M. (2009). *Risk communication: An analysis of message source and function in hurricane mitigation/preparedness communication.* Unpublished master's thesis. University of South Florida, Tampa, FL.

Grunig, J. E. (1992). *Excellence in public relations and communication management.* Hillsdale, NJ: Lawrence Erlbaum Associates.

Grunig, J. E., & Hunt, T. (1984). *Managing public relations.* New York: Holt, Rinehart & Winston.

Guilfoil, E. N. (2010). *Nautical knowledge: An experimental analysis of the influence of public relations strategies in safe boating communication.* Unpublished master's thesis. Tampa, FL: University of South Florida.

Hallahan, K. (2000). Enhancing motivation, ability, and opportunity to process public relations messages. *Public Relations Review, 26,* 463–480.

Hazleton, V. (1992). Toward a system theory of public relations. In H. Avenarius & W. Ambrecht (Eds.), *Ist public relations eine wissenschaft?* [Is public relations a science?] (pp. 33–46). Berlin: Westdeutscher Verlag.

Hazleton, V. (1993). Symbolic resources: Processes in the development and use of symbolic resources. In W. Armbrecht, H. Avenarius, & U. Zabel (Eds.), *Image und PR: Kann image Gegenstand einer Public Relations-Wissenschaft sein?* [Image and PR: Can image be a subject of public relations science?] (pp. 87–100). Wiesbaden, Germany: Westdeutscher Verlag.

Hazleton, V., & Dougall, E. (2007). New directions for the public relations process model. *Proceedings of the 8th Annual International Public Relations Research Conference.* Gainesville, FL: Institute for Public Relations.

Hazleton, V., Jr., & Long, L. W. (1988). Concepts for public relations education, research, and practice: A communication point of view. *Central States Speech Journal, 39*, 77–87.

Kim, J-N, & Grunig, J. E. (2011). Problem-solving and communicative action: A situational theory of problem-solving. *Journal of Communication, 61*, 120–149.

Kim, J-N, Ni, L., Kim, S-H. & Kim, J. R. (2012). What makes people hot? Applying the situational theory of problem-solving to hot-issue publics. *Journal of Public Relations Research, 24*(2), 144–164.

Long, L. W., & Hazleton, V., Jr. (1987). Public relations: A theoretical and practical response. *Public Relations Review, 13*(2), 3–13.

Page, K. G. (2000a, August). *Determining message objectives: An analysis of public relations strategy use in press releases.* Paper presented to the Public Relations Division of the Association for Education in Journalism and Mass Communication. Phoenix, AZ.

Page, K. G. (2000b, June). *Prioritizing relations: Exploring goal compatibility between organizations and publics.* Paper presented to the Public Relations Division of the International Communication Association. Acapulco, Mexico.

Page, K. G. (2003, May). *Responding to activism: An experimental analysis of public relations strategy influence on beliefs, attitudes, and behavioral intentions.* Paper presented to the Public Relations Division of the International Communication Association. San Diego, CA.

Page, K. G. & Hazleton, V. (1999, May). *An empirical analysis of factors influencing public relations strategy use and effectiveness.* Paper presented to the Public Relations Division of the International Communication Association. San Francisco, CA.

Springston, J. K., & Keyton, J. (2001). Public relations field dynamics. In R. Heath (Ed.), *Handbook of public relations* (pp. 115–126). Thousand Oaks, CA: Sage.

Werder, K. P. (2005). An empirical analysis of the influence of perceived attributes of publics on public relations strategy use and effectiveness. *Journal of Public Relations Research, 17*(3), 217–266.

Werder, K. P. (2006a). Exploring the link between strategy and tactic: An analysis of strategic message content in news releases. *Conference Proceedings of the Ninth Annual International Public Relations Research Conference.* Gainesville, FL: Institute for Public Relations.

Werder, K. P. (2006b). Responding to activism: An experimental analysis of public relations strategy influence on attributes of publics. *Journal of Public Relations Research, 18*(4), 335–356.

Werder, K. P. (2009, March). *An analysis of the influence of organizational structure and practitioner decision-making behavior on public relations strategy use and effectiveness.* Paper presented at the 12th Annual International Public Relations Research Conference. Miami, FL.

Werder, K. P., & Holtzhausen, D. (2008, August). *The emergence of the communication strategist: An examination of practitioner roles, department leadership style, and message strategy use in organizations.* Paper presented to the Public Relations Division of the Association for Education in Journalism and Mass Communication. Chicago, IL.

Werder, K. P., & Holtzhausen, D. (2009). An analysis of the influence of public relations leadership style on public relations strategy use and effectiveness. *Journal of Public Relations Research, 21*(4), 1–24.

Werder, K. P., & Mitrook, M. A. (2011, August). *Motivating Publics to Act: An Analysis of the Influence of Message Strategy and Involvement on Relational Outcomes and Communication Behavior.* Paper presented to the Public Relations Division of the Association for Education in Journalism and Mass Communication. St. Louis, MO.

Werder, K. P., & Schuch, A. (2008, May). *Communicating for social change: An experimental analysis of activist message strategy effect on receiver variables.* Paper presented to the Public Relations Division of the International Communication Association. Montreal, Canada.

Werder, K. P., & Schweickart, T. (2013, March). *An experimental analysis of message strategy influence on receiver variables: Advancing an integrated model for explaining the communication behavior of publics.* Paper presented at the 16th Annual International Public Relations Research Conference. Miami, FL.

Zaltman, G., & Duncan, R. (1977). *Strategies for planned change.* New York: Wiley.

18

Framing as a Strategic Persuasive Message Tactic

Kenneth E. Kim

It is essential to design effective message tactics for a successful strategic communication campaign. A large body of persuasion literature has documented that one or a combination of communication variables (i.e., message source, message itself, message channel, and message recipient) can lead to cognitive and behavioral changes (see Perloff, 2003; Salovey, Schneider & Apanovitch, 2002; Kahneman & Tversky, 1984). Of these communication elements, the concept of framing as psychological processing of persuasive messages has received a great deal of attention in the areas of strategic communications, including health campaigns (Salovey & Williams-Piehota, 2004; Williams, Clarke, & Borland, 2001; Block & Keller, 1995), marketing campaigns (Shiv, Britton, & Payne, 2004; Grewal, Gotlieb, & Marmorstein, 1994), and political campaigns (Druckman, 2001; Kanner, 2004).

Despite the confusion about its conceptual and operational definitions in a wide range of disciplines (see Scheufele & Tewksbury, 2007; Maule & Villejoubert, 2007; Hallahan, 1999), message framing generally refers to the ways in which a choice problem is strategically phrased in a message, and framing effect is related to how mental representations of the choice problem, partly developed by message framing, influence cognitive or behavioral responses, including judgment and choice (Kahneman, 2003; Tversky & Kahneman, 1981), attitudes (Putrevu, 2010; S. M. Smith & Petty, 1996), and behavioral intentions (Y.-J. Kim, 2006; Jones, Sinclair & Courneya, 2003; Meyerowitz & Chaiken, 1987).

According to prospect theory, a classical approach to framing effect, people are more likely to accept loss-framed (i.e., negative outcome-focused) arguments than corresponding gain-framed (i.e., positive outcome-focused) arguments under risky or uncertain decision contexts (Kahneman & Tversky, 2000). However, scholars have criticized framing literature for failing to reach a consensus that supports the robustness of loss advantage (see Fagley & Miller, 1987; Frisch, 1993; Salovey, Schneider, & Apanovitch, 2002; Levin, Schneider, & Gaeth, 1998). In the past few decades, a substantial body of research has demonstrated that gain framing is more effective than loss framing, or that there is no difference between the two (Marteau, 1989; Levin, 1987; Salovey et al., 2002).

To resolve this confusion, framing scholars have identified potential moderating factors of the framing effect. For instance, the impact of gain–loss message framing may differ based on the order of the framed argument in a persuasive message; that is, whether the framed argument is presented at the beginning or end of the message (Buda, 2003). Decision contexts also moderate the message framing effect. For example, the impact of gain–loss framing differs depending on the level of the temporal proximity of an event, like whether outcome events occur in the near or distant future (McElroy & Mascari, 2007). Also, the message framing impact may be dependent on whether a decision is made in a real or hypothetical context (Levin, Chapman, & Johnson, 1988; Kühberger, Schulte-Mecklenbeck, & Perner, 2002). Scholars further revealed that the gain–loss framing effect differs based on the type of product category in advertising campaigns, such as established (familiar) products versus new (unfamiliar) products (K. Kim & Park, 2010; Chang, 2007; G. E. Smith, 1996), and the type of required health behaviors in health campaigns, such as detection versus prevention behaviors (see Rothman, Bartels, Wlaschin, & Salovey, 2006; Salovey et al., 2002). Framing effects also vary depending on individual-level variables , such as issue involvement (Maheswaran & Meyers-Levy, 1990), the need for cognition (S. M. Smith & Levin, 1996; Zhang & Buda, 1999), the level of perceived risk or uncertainty (Scott & Curbow, 2006; Broemer, 2002), the type of self-regulatory focus (Dijkstra, Rothman, & Pietersma, 2012; Kees, Burton, & Tangari, 2010), and education level (Smith, 1996).

Recent work directs attention to the difference in the framing manipulations as a possible explanation for the reversed or null effect (Putrevu, 2010; Krishnamurthy, Carter & Blair, 2001; Levin, Gaeth, Schreiber, & Lauriola, 2002). For instance, some research focuses on the characteristics of a choice problem or choice object in a positive or negative sense (e.g., "more than 80% of the users of this vaccine did not experience side effects" versus "less than 20% of the users of this vaccine experienced side effects"), while other framing research deals with different outcomes or goals of a choice problem in a positive (gain) or negative (loss) way (e.g., "taking this vaccine will prevent you from contracting the disease and other infections" versus "without taking this vaccine, you would suffer from the disease and other infections") as framing manipulations. Each approach implies an equivalent expected value of the choice options, but the difference only exists in the selection of message-framing tactic (whether to focus on attribute or outcome (goal) of a choice problem) and framing valence (positive versus negative). The recent framing literature has reported empirical evidence that gain–loss framing effects are influenced by the attribute–goal framing tactic (Ferguson & Gallagher, 2007; Levin et al., 2002). This conclusion deserves attention because this approach not only provides theoretical implications for developing robust framing hypotheses across different framing types (i.e., attribute framing versus goal framing; individual framing versus societal-level framing), but it also provides important practical implications for developing effective messages in strategic communication campaigns.

Gain–loss framing and the framing hypothesis

A frame is defined as "decision makers' conception of acts, outcomes, and contingencies associated with a particular choice" (Tversky & Kahneman, 1981, p. 453). Prospect theory provides a framework for the gain–loss framing hypothesis under uncertain or risky decision contexts. Prospect theory was first proposed to challenge expected utility theory, the normative perspective that dominated the early risky decision paradigm in which reason-based judgments were believed to control individual decision process (see Tversky & Kahneman, 1986; Dawes, 1998). Under the expected utility paradigm, it was postulated that people's choices are constant regardless of the way the choice problem is presented because human beliefs and values are hardly affected by situational changes and their choices are always determined by the invariable belief systems (Newell, Lagnado, & Shanks, 2007). Prospect theory rejects the expected utility perspective, suggesting instead that people often make choices that conflict with their underlying beliefs because the relative value of behavioral outcomes (that is, either gain or loss) represented by a situation is more important to the decision process than preexisting values or beliefs. (Tversky & Kahneman, 1986). Hence, prospect theory suggests framing as a key determinant that guides individual judgments and choices (Kahneman & Tversky, 1984; Hogarth, 1987).

The gain–loss framing domain has been the typical framing manipulation under prospect theory. A gain-framed message emphasizes the positive prospects that result from performing the choice option (e.g., chances of contracting cervical cancer decrease by 80% if you get the human papillomavirus vaccine), while a loss-framed message highlights the negative outcomes as a result of not accepting or performing the required behavior (e.g., the chance of contracting cervical cancer increases by 20% unless you get the human papillomavirus vaccine). These two messages have the exactly same goal, but the only difference is in the domain or valence of outcomes that may guide different choice behaviors. The gain–loss framing hypothesis under prospect theory suggests that loss framing is more effective than gain framing when a choice option involves uncertainty or risk elements (Kahneman & Tversky, 2000).

Although early prospect theory limits the framing effects to actual choice and judgment, Kahneman, one of the pioneers of the theory, documented in his recent article that "framing effects are not restricted to decision making" (Kahneman, 2003, p. 703), suggesting that the psychological principle postulated in the theory can be applied to more diverse social science disciplines. A large body of evidence has demonstrated that gain- and loss-framed messages have diverse effects on human perceptions, cognitive responses, and behavioral outcomes (Yi & Baumgartner, 2009; A. M. O'Connor, Pennie, & Dales, 1996; Apanovitch, McCarthy, & Salovey, 2003; Shah, Kwak, Schmierbach, & Zubric, 2004). For example, Venkatraman, Aloysius, & Davis (2006) found that the decision-framing effects on behavioral intention are mediated by both perceived riskiness and perceived ambiguity. Further, a number of studies in applied health have reported that gain–loss framing have distinct effects on the level of perceived health-related risk, medical decisions (see Ferguson, Leaviss, Townsend, Fleming, & Lowe, 2005), healthcare product purchase intentions (Chang, 2007), attitudes (Sibley, Liu, & Kirkwood, 2006), and health behaviors (see Rothman et al, 2006; Salovey et al., 2002).

Confounding framing effects

Despite a large body of evidence that supports the gain–loss framing hypothesis, confounded or null results also have been consistently reported in the framing literature. For instance, D. B. O'Connor, Ferguson, & R. C. O'Connor (2005) tested the gain–loss framing hypothesis in the context of hormonal male contraceptive use, perceived as a risky option for men compared to other methods of contraception. The researchers found no significant difference in intentions to choose the contraceptive pill between gain and loss framing.

A number of scholars suggest several possible accounts for the confounding results. First, the conflicting results may be attributable to different operational definitions of message framing across studies. The original framing manipulation involves using the numeric information with probabilities (see Kahneman & Tversky, 1979). However, a large number of framing studies, particularly in health decisions, defined the gain versus loss distinction in terms of qualitative scenarios (e.g., if you decide to get HIV tested, you may feel the peace of mind that comes with knowing about your health) (see Apanovitch et al., 2003). Williams et al. (2001) distinguish the gain–loss framing manipulation into behavior framing and statistical framing, suggesting that the confounding findings of framing effects may be due to the inconsistent use of framing manipulations. Behavior framing emphasizes either gain or loss outcomes as a function of complying or not complying with the promoted behavior without the statistical (probability) information, whereas statistical framing focuses on the statistical information of different outcomes as a function of either selecting or not selecting the choice option. For instance, out of 100 people who opted for the medical surgery, 25% were diseased but 75% survived. The majority of early framing studies (e.g., Tversky and Kahneman's (1981) disease framing study) conducted using prospect theory employed the outcome probability information in the frames, whereas the majority of framing research on health behaviors has examined the effects of behavior framing (see Rothman et al., 2006; Williams et al., 2001). Based on this distinction, Williams et al. compared the two formats of framing in the context of public health campaigns that promoted breast-cancer-related perceptions and behaviors. The researchers found no evidence of the statistical framing effects on breast self-examination (BSE) intention, perceived susceptibility to breast cancer, self-efficacy in performing BSE, perceived early detection risk, and anxiety about the cancer. However, partial support for perceived susceptibility to breast cancer and BSE-related behavioral change was reported in the behavior framing conditions such that participants presented with loss-framed information showed greater perceived susceptibility to breast cancer and performance of BSE than participants receiving gain-framed information.

Further, research on health campaigns suggests that the gain–loss framing effects vary based on the different types of health behavior (Rothman & Salovey, 1997; Salovey et al., 2002). Salovey et al. (2002) suggest that a gain-framed health message has a greater advantage than its loss-framed counterpart when promoting behaviors for disease prevention, such as the promotion of sunscreen use and physical exercise. In contrast, a loss-framed health message is more persuasive than its gain-framed counterpart when promoting disease detection behaviors such as HIV screening and breast self-examination. The rationale for this theorizing is based on the idea that disease detection behaviors are deemed as a risk-taking option because people generally experience uneasiness or fear at the prospect of having a serious disease when engaging in the early disease screening process (Meyerowitz & Chaiken, 1987). Prospect theory suggests that individuals tend to accept a risk-taking option to avoid potential losses (i.e., diseases) and seek safety in the future. Loss framing is likely to facilitate a safety-seeking mindset and thus has more impact when promoting risk-taking health behaviors (Lee & Aaker, 2004).

Chang (2007) provided empirical evidence supporting the prevention-detection perspective in healthcare product advertising. He classifies healthcare product types in terms of prevention versus detection functions and suggests that persuasive effects of message framing vary according to such product distinctions. The study found that gain framing was more persuasive for preventive health-care products such as mouthwash and dental chewing gum, whereas loss framing was more effective for detection healthcare products such as disclosing gum. However, these results were observed only for the healthcare products already familiar to consumers, and the interactive effect of gain–loss framing and product type was not statistically significant for products unfamiliar to consumers (i.e., new, innovative products).

Recent work in direct-to-consumer (DTC) pharmaceutical advertising suggests that the level of product knowledge moderates the gain–loss framing effects on product attitudes and intentions (K. Kim & Park, 2010). The study found that a loss-framed ad had more persuasive impact than a gain-framed ad for an emergency contraception medicine, which falls in the low product knowledge category, while gain- and loss-framed DTC ads were equivalent in their effectiveness for the category of allergy medicine, which falls in the high product knowledge category. The study findings suggest that product familiarity and subjective product knowledge matter in predicting the impact of message framing in pharmaceutical advertising.

Individual level variables such as involvement have received considerable attention as a moderating factor in the gain–loss framing literature. For instance, Maheswaran and Meyers-Levy (1990) reported that compared with a gain-framed message, a loss-framed message generated more favorable attitudes and intentions regarding the diagnostic blood test under the high involvement condition, whereas the relative benefits of gain framing were observed under the low involvement condition.

Recent theorizing in framing (Dijkstra, et al., 2012; Y.-J. Kim, 2006) suggests that the relative effectiveness of gain- and loss-framed persuasive messages varies as a function of individuals' self-regulatory orientation. According to self-regulatory focus theory (see Higgins, 2002), people are motivated to organize their thinking and behaviors in the light of their dominant regulatory focus; that is, whether *promotion focus* or *prevention focus* is predominant. The theory suggests that, when promotion focus is activated at the moment of processing of external information, individuals are preoccupied with an accomplishment- or ideal-seeking mindset and hence come to give better attention to the presence or absence of positive outcomes: that is, gains (Yi & Baumgartner, 2009). In contrast, when prevention focus momentarily is salient, a responsibility- or safety-seeking mindset takes over, and people come to give heed to the presence or absence of negative outcomes: that is, losses (Higgins, 1998). This self-regulatory framework suggests the advantage of loss framing is most likely to be found when the audience mindset is preoccupied with a responsibility- or safety-seeking mindset, whereas accomplishment-minded people tend to favor gain-framed messages (K. Kim & Park, 2010; Idson, Liberman, & Higgins, 2004; Lee & Aaker, 2004).

Zhang and Buda (1999) investigated the moderating role of the need for cognition in the message framing, incorporating prospect theory and the elaboration likelihood model. They found a positively framed message more effective than a negatively framed message for all dependent variables, including the attractiveness of the product, perception of product performance, and willingness to purchase the product.

Attribute–goal framing and the framing hypothesis

Recent theorizing in framing effects has focused on two distinct types of frames: *attribute* and *goal* (Putrevu, 2010). *Attribute framing* focuses on the attributes of a choice being promoted in either negative or positive terms (Levin, et al., 1998), while goal or outcome framing emphasizes the outcomes of a choice in either negative or positive terms (Nan, 2007). Attribute and goal frames have been shown to have different persuasive effects depending on the valence of frames (Levin, et al., 2002). Oft-cited studies on attribute-framing effects include Levin and Gaeth's (1988) study on evaluation of ground beef where the message frames of 75% lean meat versus 25% fat meat were applied, and Marteau's (1989) medical decision study where the message was framed as either an 80% survival rate or a 20% death rate. Attribute-framed persuasive messages encourage people to consider the generic nature of a choice problem by stressing either its positive characteristics or its negative aspects in diverse settings such as health decisions (Wilson, Kaplan, & Schneiderman, 1987) and medical decisions like contraceptive use (Linville, Fischer, & Fischhoff, 1993). Work in attribute framing suggests that a positively framed message is more effective than a negatively framed message (Putrevu, 2010; Krishnamurthy, et al., 2001; Levin & Gaeth, 1988; Marteau, 1989).

Studies on *goal framing* effects abound, especially in health psychology (see Maheswaran & Meyerslevy, 1990; Meyerowitz & Chiken, 1987). Goal framing is similar to behavior framing (Williams et al., 2001) and to gain–loss framing in prospect theory in that goal-framed messages highlight either positive or negative behavior outcomes. As abundantly documented in the framing literature, research on goal framing effects suggests that a message framing negative outcomes (loss-framed persuasive messages) is more effective than a message framing positive outcomes (gain-framed persuasive messages).

Recent empirical studies have confirmed reliable interactive effects of attribute–goal framing tactics and valence framing such that a positively framed persuasive message tends to be more effective than a negatively framed message in the context of attribute framing, whereas negative framing has more persuasive impact than positive framing in the context of goal framing (see Keren, 2007; Ferguson & Gallagher, 2007; Levin et al., 2002). For instance, Ferguson and Gallagher, (2007) investigated the interaction of attribute–goal framing and valence framing in promoting flu vaccination. Their study findings showed the pattern of the interaction such that a negative goal-framed message was more effective than a positive goal-framed message and a positive attribute-framed message had more impact than a negative attribute-framed message when participants perceived the flu vaccination as risky.

Keren (2007) found experimental subjects evaluated a negative attribute-framed message (25% fat meat) as more trustworthy than a positive attribute -framed message (75% lean meat), but positive attribute framing was more effective than negative attribute framing in promoting a meat product.

Despite the general assumption that high credibility perception leads to greater persuasiveness, Keren's study showed an asymmetric relationship between actual choice and message content credibility as a result of message framing.

Individual–societal framing and the framing hypothesis

Individual–societal framing relates to whether a persuasive message emphasizes *societal-level situations* or whether it focuses on *individual level situations*. Specifically, a societal frame highlights how important an issue discussed in a message is for a community or society, as in the availability of medical abortion for women in the community. An individual frame focuses on how important the issue is for the individual, as in whether medical abortion is available for you or your friends (see Shah et al, 2004; Nan, 2007). Work in individual- and societal-level framing suggests that each elicits different cognitive responses in message reception. For instance, Shah et al. (2004) found that people in the societal gain framing condition engaged in more in-depth processing of a message than those in the societal loss and individual gain framing conditions, contemplating the message arguments in terms of causes and consequences of the problem and its solutions. Similar patterns were observed for people in the individual loss framing condition. *Social cognition theory* suggests that cognitive responses are an important factor that determines the attitude change in message processing (Fiske & Taylor, 2008). Persuasion scholars have revealed that the persuasiveness of a message is based on the level of elaboration in certain conditions. Specifically, when other cues such as message source or prior knowledge are unavailable, people who are highly motivated and able to think about the arguments of the message are likely to engage in careful thinking and thus form or change attitudes (Petty, Priester, & Brinor, 2002). Although Shah et al. (2004) did not consider judgment and choice as outcome measures—which classic prospect theory posits as relating to the gain–loss framing function— or other persuasion variables (i.e., attitude and intention), their study findings suggest that societal gain and individual loss frames generates more detailed thoughts about the arguments in a persuasive message and thus may facilitate people's judgments or choices.

Nan (2007) further suggests that societal-level framing encourages people to think about the consequences of a problem for socially distant entities, such as other people in your country, rather than for socially proximal entities, such as your close friends or yourself. He found that the persuasive effect of societal-level framing increased significantly when a judgment was made for psychologically distant others. However, there was no significant impact of individual framing when decisions were made either for socially distant or for proximal individuals.

Explanatory studies

Message framing is a complex area of study and the many variables that affect framing outcomes can be confusing. The following two studies help explain the application and interpretation of message framing in different contexts.

Study 1: Attribute–goal framing

This study investigated the interactive effects of attribute–goal framing and valence framing (positive versus negative term) in the context of direct-to-consumer (DTC) human papilloma virus (HPV) vaccine advertising. Overall, the framing literature suggests that a positive attribute frame is more persuasive than a negative attribute frame, whereas a negative goal frame is more effective than a positive goal frame. The attribute-framed DTC ads focus on absence or presence of a desirable attribute, in this case drug efficacy, of the prescription drug (see Krishnamurthy et al., 2001, for a similar study). The goal-framed DTC ads emphasized a desirable or undesirable health outcome of the drug option.

Design and procedure

Typically, the effects of message frames are tested using experimental design. This study employed a 2 (attribute or goal framing) × 2 (positive or negative framing) between-subjects design. Previous studies suggest that the effectiveness of message framing is likely to be influenced by pre-experimental factors such as knowledge, previous attitudes, product experience, involvement, and demographics (G. E. Smith & Wortzel, 1997; G. E. Smith, 1996). Therefore, despite the fact that study participants were randomly assigned in the sampling procedure, the study performed a series of analysis of covariance (ANCOVA) as a primary statistical method to analyze these interaction effects. This allowed the researcher to control for the effects of product knowledge, personal importance, and perceived risk of side-effects of HPV vaccines.

Participants

This study recruited one of the primary target segments of HPV vaccines. Research sample groups consisted of female college students between the ages of 18 and 25 years, who had never had the HPV vaccine. Subjects who had already had the vaccine were excluded from the study to control the effect of previous experience with the drug. A total of 105 female college students participated, and they were randomly assigned to one of four conditions. The average age of the sample was 21 years and in terms of identification with the ethnic origin classifications presented to study participants, approximately 70% of participants were European American, 18% were African American, 6% were Hispanic American, and 6% were Asian American.

Message frames

Four versions of a DTC print drug advertisement for a fictitious HPV vaccine prescription drug brand were created to manipulate the four message frames. All versions of the advertisement shared the same characteristics in terms of any visual and textural elements except the manipulations. Table 18.1

Table 18.1 Attribute–Goal Framing Manipulations

	Attribute frame	Goal frame
Positive frame	Research shows that the HPV vaccine drugs are effective in protecting against four types of human papilloma virus in 80% of cases. In more than 80% of cases for both women and men HPV vaccine use prevents warts in the genital area.	By taking the HPV vaccine drugs you take advantage of the best method of defense against 4 types of human papilloma virus, ensuring your health. If you take the HPV vaccine drugs in time, you can reduce the risk of developing warts in the genital areas by 80%, and women can lower by 50% their chance of getting two types of cervical cancer.
Negative frame	Research shows that the HPV vaccine drugs are not effective in protecting against four types of human papilloma virus only in 20% of cases. Less than 20% of HPV vaccine users, women and men, experience warts in the genital area.	If you don't take the HPV vaccine drugs you fail to take advantage of the best method of defense against 4 types of human papilloma virus, which would help safeguard your health. If you don't take the HPV vaccine drugs in time, you may fail to take advantage of an 80% increased chance of preventing the development of warts in the genital area, lowering by 50% your chance of getting two types of cervical cancer.

shows four different message-framing manipulations for the current study. The combinations of framing tactic and framing valence manipulations were adapted from previous studies (e.g., Krishnamurthy et al., 2001; Ferguson et al., 2005).

In this study, the framing tactic was classified into two dimensions: attribute versus goal. Attribute framing focuses on attributes of a product. For this study, a positive attribute frame stresses the efficacy of the vaccines in preventing HPV, while a negative attribute frame emphasizes the relatively low level of its inefficacy.

Goal framing emphasizes outcomes of the use of a drug product. In the DTC context, the drug product outcomes are associated with health benefits or disease prevention as results of the drug use. Therefore, positive goal versus negative goal framed ad messages can be manipulated by focusing on either the presence of positive health benefits of a drug or the absence of negative health outcomes of the drug use versus absence (presence) of positive health benefits (negative health outcomes) as a result of failing to use the drug (see Salovey et al, 2002). For this study, positive goal framing was manipulated by focusing on the positive health benefits of the drug use and relative absence of negative health outcomes, while negative goal framing was constructed through emphasizing negative health outcomes as the result of not taking the HPV vaccine drugs.

Dependent measures

Two dependent measures were introduced: attitudes toward HPV vaccine drugs and behavioral intentions.

Attitudes toward HPV vaccine drugs. Attitudes toward the HPV vaccine were measured on nine 7-point semantic scales developed by Oliver & Berger (1979): *foolish/wise, safe/risky, harmful/beneficial, pleasant/unpleasant, waste of time/wise use of time, good for me/bad for me, useful/useless, worthless/valuable,* and *ineffective/effective* (α = .93).

Behavior intentions. According to Huh, DeLorme, and Reid (2005), DTC ads tend to promote three different types of behavior, which comprise communication with doctors, seeking more information about treatment options, and talking with others. Based on the items to measure these behaviors, different types of DTC-related behavior intentions were developed for this study. First, intention to seek more information about HPV vaccine drugs was measured with a two–item, seven-point scale modified from Huh et al. (2005). On a seven-point scale (1 = *very unlikely*, 7 = *very likely*), participants rated the likelihood that they would: (a) participate in a free educational program about HPV vaccines and HPV-related diseases if the University Health Services offered the program; and (b) go to other media sources to get more information about HPV vaccine drugs (α = .76). Second, intention to consult doctors was measured using a single item, seven-point scale adapted from Huh et al. On a seven-point scale (1 = *very unlikely*, 7 = *very likely*), participants rated the likelihood that they would consult doctors about HPV vaccine drugs if University Health Services offered a free opportunity. Last, intention to take HPV vaccine drugs was measured with a single item, seven a-point scale (1 = *very unlikely*, 7 = *very likely*). Participants rated the likelihood that they would take HPV vaccine drugs.

Control variables

Although the study's experimental group is based on random assignment, pre-experimental factors, such as demographic variables, subjective knowledge level, pre-existing beliefs and other psychological variables, may influence the dependent variables (see Shah et al, 2004). To remove such confounding effects, the study included three control variables as covariates: product knowledge, personal involvement, and perceived side effects. These measures have been considered to influence on attitude or belief and intention associated with health-related outcomes (Salovey et al., 2002).

Personal involvement. Five 7-point semantic differential scale items adapted from Mittal (1995) were used to measure a person's involvement in a particular issue. These included: "HPV vaccine drugs are *important/unimportant; mean a lot to me/mean nothing to me; matter to me/do not matter; significant/insignificant; of no concern/of concern to me*" ($\alpha = .90$).

Subjective knowledge about HPV vaccine drugs. Two 5-point Likert scale items (1 = *Little or no knowledge*, 5 = *A great deal of knowledge*) adapted from Bloch, Ridgway, & Sherrell (1989) were used to measure a person's self-reported familiarity with a particular issue. These included: "How do you rate your knowledge of HPV vaccine drugs relative to other people?"; and "How do you rate your knowledge of HPV vaccine drugs relative to most of your friends" ($\alpha = .91$).

Perceived side-effect. Two 7-point Likert scale items (1 = *Strongly disagree*, 7 = *Strongly agree*) were used to measure a person's self-reported feeling about the side-effects of HPV vaccines. These included: "When I think about the side effects of HPV vaccines, I feel nauseous"; and "the side effects of HPV vaccines could put my life in danger" ($\alpha = .72$).

Results

Effects of message frames on attitudes toward HPV vaccine drugs

The obtained data indicates a significant interaction effect of attribute–goal framing by valence framing on attitudes at $p < .05$. In addition, analyses of simple effects revealed that a positive attribute frame generated more favorable attitudes toward the HPV drug than a negative attribute frame. In contrast, there was no significant difference in attitudes toward the HPV drug between a positive goal frame and a negative goal frame ($p > .05$).

Effects of message frames on DTC drugs-related behavioral intentions

The overall ANCOVA tests, with intention to seek more information, intention to consult doctors, and intention to take the HPV vaccine drugs as the dependent variables, revealed that there were no significant interactions between attribute–goal framing and gain–loss framing.

ANCOVA contrast analyses

ANCOVA contrast analyses were conducted to investigate the relative advantages of the framing combinations. Contrast testing revealed that goal–gain framing produced more favorable attitudes than the attribute–loss framing, and the effect of goal–loss framing on attitudes was significantly greater than the attribute-loss framing. The effects of the rest of the framing combinations on attitudes did not approach statistical significance.

The participants in goal–gain framing conditions induced stronger intentions to seek more information about the HPV vaccine drugs than those in the attribute–gain framing condition and, similarly, goal–gain framing produced stronger intentions to seek more information than the attribute–loss framing. However, the effects of the rest of the framing combinations were not significant on intentions to seek more information. For intentions to consult doctors about the HPV vaccine drugs, the effects marginally approached statistical significance between goal–gain framing and the attribute–loss framing. The effects of the rest of the framing combinations were not statistically significant in terms of intention to consult doctors. For intention to take the HPV vaccine drugs, the effects of the framing combinations were not statistically significant.

Study 2: Individual-societal framing

The purpose of study 2 was to investigate the interactive effects of *individual-societal framing* and *valence framing* (a gain versus loss term) in the context of a health advocacy campaign. Overall, the literature on framing effects that observed potential for the interactive effect between individual-societal framing and gain–loss framing in the context of controversial decisions suggests that an individual loss frame is more persuasive than a societal loss frame, whereas a societal gain frame is more persuasive than an individual gain frame. The primary goal of health advocacy campaigns is to persuade people to take action to ensure a healthy life. Because advocacy campaigns often deal with controversial and divisive issues, such as the use of hormonal medicines, medical abortion pills, performance enhancement drugs, or hormone replacement therapy, one of the major challenges for campaign practitioners is to provide strong, persuasive messages supporting their point of view.

Design

The study employed a 2 (individual- or societal-level framing) × 2 (positive or negative framing) between-subjects design. Similar to Study 1, this study also controlled for pre-experimental factors such as knowledge, previous attitudes, product experience, involvement, and demographics (G. E. Smith & Wortzel, 1997; G. E. Smith, 1996). The researchers performed a series of analysis of covariance (ANCOVA) as a primary statistical method to analyze these interaction effects while controlling HPV vaccine drugs product knowledge, the level of personal importance, and perceived risk of side-effects.

A total of 147 college students in a southeastern state university participated in the experimental study, and they were randomly assigned to one of four conditions; females comprised 64%, and the average age of the sample was 21 years. In terms of identification with the ethnic origin classifications presented to study participants, approximately 67% of participants were European American, 12% were African American, 11% were Hispanic American, 7% were Asian American, and 3% were others.

Message framing

Framing of the benefits of medical abortion for young women was manipulated between subjects by exposing them to different versions of information about medical abortion (see Table 18.2). As in the case of previous research, the factual contents and message goal were the same, but each framing condition focused on different behavioral outcomes (see Shah et al, 2002; Nan, 2007).[1]

Dependent Measures

The dependent factors were measured on judgment on medical abortion, attitudes toward medical abortion, and intentions for choosing or recommending medical abortion pills. The item for the judgment measure was modified from Tewksbury, Jones, Peske, Raymond, & Vig, (2000). The item was measured on a 7-point Likert scale: "Women should be allowed to choose the medical abortion option." Attitudes toward medical abortion and intentions to choose or recommend the medical abortion option also were assessed. Attitudes toward the medical abortion option were measured with a nine-item, seven-point semantic differential scale developed by Oliver and Berger (1979): foolish/wise, safe/risky, harmful/beneficial, pleasant/unpleasant, waste of time/wise use of time, good for me/bad for me, useful/useless, and worthless/valuable ($\alpha = .93$). Intention to seek more information was measured with a three-item, seven-point scale adapted from Huh et al. (2005). On a

Table 18.2   Individual–Societal Message-Framing Manipulations

	Individual frame	Societal frame
Positive frame	Remember, support for availability of medical abortion can improve your access to safe abortion services and thus help reduce maternal health risks that may be caused by surgical abortion. Medical abortion is an important component of reproductive health care to which you are entitled.	Remember, support for availability of medical abortion can improve women's access to safe abortion services and thus help reduce maternal health risks that may be caused by surgical abortion for thousands of women in your community. Medical abortion is an important component of reproductive health care, to which all women are entitled.
Negative frame	Remember, if you do not support the availability of medical abortion, chances to improve your access to safe abortion services will be lost, which might increase maternal health risks that may be caused by a surgical abortion. Medical abortion is an important component of reproductive health care to which you are entitled.	Remember, if you do not support the availability of medical abortion, chances to improve women's access to safe abortion services will be reduced, which could increase maternal health risks that may be caused by surgical abortions for thousands of women in your community. Medical abortion is an important component of reproductive health care to which all women are entitled.

seven-point scale (1 = *very unlikely*, 7 = *very likely*), participants rated the likelihood that they would: (a) retain useful information about new or other medical abortion in the future; (b) go to other media sources to get information about medical abortion in the future; and (c) learn more about medical abortion in the future (α = .91). Intention to consult health providers was measured using a two-item, seven-point scale (1 = *very unlikely*, 7 = *very likely*) adapted from Huh et al. Participants rated the likelihood that they would: (a) talk with a doctor about medical abortion and their medical conditions if they were given a free consultation with the doctor, and (b) ask their doctor intelligent questions about medical abortion and their medical conditions if they were given a free consultation with the doctor (α = .95). Intention to choose the option was measured with a two-item, seven-point scale modified from Huh et al. On a seven-point scale (1 = *very unlikely*, 7 = *very likely*), participants rated the likelihood that they would: (a) choose the medical abortion option, and (b) recommend others to choose the medical abortion option (α = .92).

Control Variables

As mentioned, to remove confounding effects, the study included four control variables as covariates: general attitude toward abortion, religious/moral conviction, personal importance (issue involvement) and prior knowledge about the medical abortion pills. According to Spence, Elgen, and Harwell (2003), religious conviction is a principal factor for college women not to consider the use of an emergency contraceptive. Given that the abortion issue encompasses opposing ethical perspectives, such as pro-life versus pro-choice, the pre-existing attitude toward abortion was also included as a covariate. The other two measures, personal importance and individual knowledge, have also been considered to influence on attitude and intention associated with health-related outcomes (see Salovey et al., 2002).

Attitudes toward abortion. Four 7–point semantic differential scale items adapted from Burton and Lichtenstein (1988) were used to measure a person's attitude toward abortion. These included: "My attitude toward abortion (pro-choice) is favorable/unfavorable; bad/good; harmful/beneficial; attractive/unattractive" (α = .94).

Religious/moral conviction. Three 7-point Likert scale items adapted from McMahon and Byrne (2008) were used to measure a person's moral/religious obligation regarding a particular issue. These included: "My decision not to use medical abortions is in line with my moral conviction;" "I feel morally obliged not to use medical abortion;" and "My religious conscience calls me to not use medical abortion" ($\alpha = .93$).

Personal importance (issue involvement). Five 7-point semantic differential scale items adopted from Mittal (1995) were used to measure a person's involvement in a particular issue. These included: "Medical abortion: is important/unimportant; means a lot to me/means nothing to me; matters to me/does not matter; significant/insignificant; of no concern/of concern to me" ($\alpha = .93$).

Subjective knowledge about the issue. Two 5-point Likert scale items adopted from Flynn and Goldsmith (1999) were used to measure a person's self-reported familiarity with a particular issue. These included: "How do you rate your knowledge of medical abortion relative to other people?"; and "How do you rate your knowledge of medical abortion relative to most of your friends" ($\alpha = .83$).

Results

Effects of frames on judgment

The overall ANCOVA contrasts model, with framing combination as the independent variable and judgment as the dependent variable, was statistically significant. The contrasts revealed significant difference between individual–gain framing and individual–loss framing; and societal-loss framing and individual-loss framing. Also, the difference between societal-gain framing and individual-loss framing approached significance. The difference between the societal-gain framing and individual-gain framing was not significant. The difference between the societal-loss framing and societal-gain framing also was not significant, similar to the difference between societal-loss framing and individual-gain framing.

Effects on attitudes

The overall ANCOVA model, with framing combination as the independent variable and attitudes as the dependent variable, did not approach significance. The only statistically significant difference was observed when individual-gain framing was contrasted with societal-gain framing.

Effects on intention to seek more information

The overall ANCOVA test, with intention to seek information as the dependent variable, was not significant. Contrast testing revealed that no frame combination yielded significant difference on participants' intention to seek more information.

Effects on intention to choose the medical abortion option

Again, the overall ANCOVA test, with intention to choose the option as the dependent variable, was not significant. Contrast testing revealed that no framing combination yielded significant difference on this variable.

Effects on intention to consult health providers

The overall ANCOVA test, with intention to consult with doctors as the dependent variable, was not significant and no frame combination yielded significant difference on this variable.

General Discussion

Implications of the Framing Studies for Message Frames

While judgments and behavior changes in strategic communications emerge through multiple layers of influence, the research initiative in this chapter focused on the relative persuasiveness of distinct message frames in the context of controversial women's medical decisions: HPV vaccination and medical abortion.

Study 1 attempted to test the attribute–goal framing hypothesis in the context of DTC HPV vaccine advertising. The study predicted that attribute–goal framing effects on persuasion would differ based on valence framing. An attribute-framed drug ad emphasizes the attributes or efficacy of a drug, while a goal-framed drug ad focuses on the health benefits or risks of the drug. The data showed that the *positive framing* effects on attitudes toward the drug product and DTC drugs-related behavioral intentions were more pervasive than *negative framing* in attribute-framed advertisements, which is consistent with the results of previous work (see Krishnamurthy et al, 2001; Levin et al, 1998). On the other hand, negative-frame advantages were not observed in this study. Although the results were not statistically significant, the data suggested that *positive goal framing (gain framing)* was more effective than *negative goal framing (loss framing)*, which is quite inconsistent with the findings of classic gain–loss framing research. Interestingly, positive goal framing had the strongest effects on both attitudes and intentions.

Salovey et al. (2002) provide an insight into the gain-framing advantages in the context of pharmaceutical advertising. Based on empirical findings, they suggest that gain-framed health or medical messages have more persuasive effects than the corresponding loss-framed messages when promoting disease prevention behaviors such as flu vaccination, sunscreen use, and regular physical exercise. HPV vaccination is also an important medical decision for young women to prevent cervical cancer and thus we may conclude that the advantages of gain framing are more prevalent regardless of attribute-focused and goal (outcome)-focused messages.

This study did not support the framing effects on DTC drugs-related behavioral intentions although previous framing studies supported the effect of framing on behavior intentions (Kim & Park, 2010; Salovey & Williams-Piehota, 2004). It might be that other important confounding factors should be considered in the context of medical decisions. For instance, ambivalence regarding the health behavioral option might be a factor that influences dependent variables. According to Broemer (2002), consumers' ambivalent feelings toward exercise moderated the gain–loss framing effect on intention. Future research on this topic should ensure a well-constructed design that proves the relative advantages of goal–loss framing and attribute–gain framing as documented in the framing literature by considering additional critical confounding factors and considering improved experimental procedures.

The data from Study 2 provided partial support for the prediction that the advantage of *loss framing* is observed when health advocacy campaigns focus on individual-level health outcomes, whereas *gain framing* is more likely to benefit from being combined with public (societal)-level health outcomes. Specifically, participants in the individual loss-framing condition demonstrated significantly more favorable judgment to the medical abortion option than those in the other conditions, namely, individual-gain, societal-loss and societal-gain framing. The overall pattern of effects is consistent with the prospect theory's proposition that judgment under risk is more likely to be influenced by loss than gain outcomes. Moreover, the results support the theorizing that the effectiveness of a loss frame may increase when combined with an individual-level frame because this mix is likely to generate more detailed mental descriptions of the arguments in a message (Shah et. al, 2004). Thus, this has important implications for the design of strategic health messages targeting a very narrowly defined audience segment of the population.

However, Study 2 failed to show the predicted pattern for behavioral intentions. To control participants' pre-existing beliefs and perceptions regarding abortion, Study 2 included four control variables, including attitudes toward abortion, religious conviction, issue knowledge, and personal importance. Given that the relationships did not hold for intentions, other individual characteristics might have influenced health-related behavioral intentions: for example, perceived susceptibility or the perceived risk of the side-effects of the medical abortion pill (see Lalor & Hailey, 1990).

The data also suggest that societal-gain framing may yield more positive attitudes toward medical abortion than individual-gain framing. Although the relative advantage of societal-gain framing over societal-loss framing was not observed, the pattern of effects is closely linked to the recent theorizing that a gain-framed persuasive message may have stronger impact when an issue framed at the societal level encourages people to consider its consequences on psychologically distant entities (i.e., public) rather than psychologically proximal entities (i.e., oneself or a close friend) (see Nan, 2007). This has valuable implications for building effective public health strategies in that many public health advocacy campaigns are aimed at generating public-level solutions, such as "policy change rather than individual behavior as a solution to health problems" (Brown & Walsh-Childers, 2002, p. 478). Thus, strategic public health campaigns could benefit from the societal-level gain framing strategy.

Implications for Strategic Communicators Across Strategic Communication Disciplines

The findings of the experimental studies in this chapter have a range of implications for the practice of strategic communications. First, the results suggest the relative effectiveness of a specific message frame to other frames based on the nature of a choice problem. First, Study 1 showed positive frames were more effective for a HPV vaccine in both attribute and goal framing conditions. Considering the nature of the drug is preventing a potential disease, this provides valuable insight into how to build effective messages for preventive medications. For instance, when promoting a healthcare product such as vitamins, the results of Study 1 suggests both positive attributed- and positive goal-frames could be more effective than the corresponding negative frames, because one of the key functions of vitamins is preventing disease.

The findings from Study 2 provide a range of insights into the practice of strategic communication campaigns, especially when dealing with controversial public issues. For instance, as the Study 2 findings suggest, a gain frame could be more effective than a loss frame in public health and political campaigns targeting broader audiences because the focus of public campaigns is likely to be on societal level responsibilities, solutions, or consequences. Further, the Study 2 findings suggest that societal-level frames may have greater persuasive impact than individual-level frames in countries where collectivistic values predominate, such as Asian countries, because societal-level frames are likely to facilitate people to consider societal-level consequences and values (i.e., the public interest). On the other hand, individual loss-framed persuasive messages could be more effective when reaching people in highly individualistic cultures, such as Western countries, because losses outweigh the corresponding gains when the consumer mindset is preoccupied with individual responsibility (see Shah, 2004).

Research findings on individual and societal frames also provide political campaign professionals with valuable insights into how to design effective message for election campaigns. For instance, a political ad can be designed to emphasize either societal or individual level consequences of voters' decisions on the targeted candidate. The impact of these societal frames may differ based on variations in issues or voters. That is, voters may be more sensitive to a societal gain frame than a societal loss or individual loss frame when the issue of the ad focuses on public issues such as wars on terrorism. On the contrary, an individual loss-framed political ad could be more effective than a societal loss- or societal gain-framed ad when focusing on issues such as gay marriage, which is considered a matter of individual choice.

Further, findings on the gain–loss framing effects provide insight into strategic message design in negative political advertising, which has received limited attention in the message-framing literature. An important goal of negative political advertising experts is effectively conveying negative information about a targeted candidate and, as a result discouraging voters not to support for the target. Based on the gain–loss framing perspective, a negative ad message framing either positive or negative consequences of voters' choice can be strategically designed. For instance, K. Kim (2012) reported that a negative political ad containing loss-framed arguments about the targeted candidate had stronger impact on college student voters' attitudes toward the candidate than a negative ad containing gain-framed arguments when the targeted candidate was from their supporting party. The findings suggest that a Democratic Party candidate in a conservative state, such as Wyoming or Oklahoma, could effectively attack a Republican candidate by incorporating loss-framed arguments in his or her campaigns. Future investigators should take this research initiative further by applying it to a wider range of issues, consumer segments, and media contexts, so that the message-framing literature contributes to specifying a set of solid guidelines on which strategic communication professionals can act.

A potential limitation in most message-framing research is that the experimental stimuli were text-based to allow for effective manipulations of the content elements. It would be meaningful to replicate the findings in this chapter using more realistic versions of strategic communication campaigns. Indeed, channel differences may play a role in the way media advocacy messages are perceived. Future studies may want to consider framing strategies in broadcast settings or online advertising. Another potential limitation is that most framing studies were conducted in laboratory settings. Real strategic campaign settings may produce different framing effects from those observed in hypothetical settings (Kühberger et al., 2002). Hopefully, the findings in this chapter will spur further investigation on the effects of message frames, especially individual–societal and attribute–goal frames, and provide a guideline for developing effective messages by illuminating how strategic communication experts can utilize and adapt message frames across strategic communication disciplines.

Note

1 The manipulation messages were based on the contents of the following website www.abortion.gen.nz/docs and modified for the study manipulations.

References

Apanovitch, A. M., McCarthy, D., & Salovey, P. (2003). Using message framing to motivate HIV testing among low-income, ethnic minority women. *Health Psychology, 22*(1), 60–67.

Broemer, P. (2002). Relative effectiveness of differently framed health messages: the influence of ambivalence. *European Journal of Social Psychology, 32*, 685–703.

Buda, R. (2003). The interactive effect of message framing, presentation order, and source credibility on recruitment practices. *International Journal of Management, 20*(2), 156–163.

Bloch, P. H., Ridgway, N. M., & Sherrell, D. L. (1989). Extending the concept of shopping: An investigation of browsing activity. *Journal of the Academy of Marketing Science, 17*(1), 13–21.

Block, L. G., & Keller, P. A. (1995). When to accentuate the negative: The effects of perceived efficacy and message framing on intentions to perform a health-related behavior. *Journal of Marketing Research, 32*, 192–203.

Brown, J. D., & Walsh-Childers, K. (2002). Effect of media on personal and public health. In J. Bryant & D. Zillmann (Eds.), *Media Effects: Advances in Theory and Research* (pp. 453–488). Mahwah, NJ: Lawrence Erlbaum Associates.

Burton, S., & Lichtenstein, D. (1988). The effect of ad claims and ad context on attitude toward the advertisement. *Journal of Advertising, 17*, 3–11.

Chang, C. (2007). Health-care product advertising: The influences of message framing and perceived product characteristics. *Psychology & Marketing, 24*(2), 143–169.

Dawes, R. M. (1998). Behavioral decision making, judgment, and inference. In D. T. Gilbert, S. T. Fiske & G. Lindzey (Eds.), *The handbook of social psychology* (pp. 589–597). Boston, MA: McGraw-Hill.

Dijkstra, A., Rothman, A., & Pietersma, S. (2012). The persuasive effects of framing messages on fruit and vegetable consumption according to regulatory focus theory. *Psychology & Health, 26*(8), 1036–1048.

Druckman, J. N. (2001). The implications of framing effects for citizen competence. *Political Behavior, 23*, 225–256.

Fagley, N. S., & Miller, P. M. (1987). The effects of decision framing on choice of risky vs. certain options. *Organizational Behavior and Human Decision Processes, 39*, 264–277.

Ferguson, E., & Gallagher, L. (2007). Message framing with respect to decisions about vaccination: the roles of frame valence, frame method and perceived risk. *British Journal of Psychology, 98*(4), 667–680.

Ferguson, E., Leaviss, J., Townsend, E., Fleming, P., & Lowe, K. C. (2005). Perceived safety of donor blood and blood substitutes for transfusion: the role of informational frame, patient groups and stress appraisals. *Transfusion Medicine, 15*(5), 401–412.

Fiske, S. T., & Taylor, S. E. (2008). *Social cognition: From brains to culture.* New York: McGraw-Hill.

Flynn, L. R., & Goldsmith, R. E.B (1999). A short, reliable measure of subjective knowledge. *Journal of business Research, 46*(1), 57–66.

Frisch, D. (1993). Reasons for framing effects. *Organizational Behavior and Human Decision Processes, 54*, 399–429.

Grewal, D., Gotlieb, J., & Marmorstein, H. (1994). The moderating effects of message framing and source credibility on the price-perceived risk relationship. *Journal of Consumer Research, 21*(1), 145–153.

Hallahan, K. (1999). Seven models of framing: Implications for public relations. *Journal of Public Relations Research, 11*(3), 205–242.

Higgins, T. E. (1998). Promotion and prevention: Regulatory focus as a motivational principle. In M. P. Zanna (Ed.), *Advances in experimental social psychology* (Vol. 30, pp. 1–46). New York: Academic Press.

Higgins, T. E. (2002). How self-regulation creates distinct values: The case of promotion and prevention decision making. *Journal of Consumer Psychology, 12*(3), 177–191.

Hogarth, R. M. (1987). *Judgment and choice: The psychology of decision.* New York: Wiley.

Huh, J., DeLorme, D. E., & Reid, L. N. (2005). Factors affecting trust in on-line prescription drug information and impact of trust on behavior following exposure to DTC advertising. *Journal of Health Communication, 10*, 711–731.

Idson, L. C., Liberman, N., & Higgins, E. T. (2004). Imagining how you'd feel: The role of motivational experiences from regulatory fit. *Personality and Social Psychology Bulletin, 30*(7), 926–937.

Jones, L., Sinclair, R., & Courneya, K. (2003). The effects of source credibility and message framing on exercise intentions, behaviors, and attitude: An integration of the elaboration likelihood model and prospect theory. *Journal of Applied Social Psychology, 33*(1), 179–196.

Kahneman, D. (2003). A perspective on judgment and choice: Mapping bounded rationality. *American Psychologist, 58*(9), 697–720.

Kahneman, D., & Tversky, A. (1979). Prospect theory: An analysis of decisions under risk. *Econometrica, 47*(2), 263–292.

Kahneman, D., & Tversky, A. (1984). Choices, values, and frames. *American Psychologist, 39*(4), 341–350.

Kahneman, D., & Tversky, A. (2000). Prospect theory: An analysis of decision under risk. In D. Kahneman & A. Tversky (Eds.), *Choices, values, and frames.* New York: Cambridge University Press.

Kanner, M. (2004). Framing and the role of the second actor: An application of prospect theory to bargaining. *Political Psychology, 25*(2), 213–239.

Kees, J., Burton, S., & Tangari, A. H. (2010). The impact of regulatory focus, temporal orientation, and fit on consumer responses to health-related advertising. *Journal of Advertising, 39*(1), 19–34.

Keren, G. (2007). Framing, intentions, and trust–choice incompatibility. *Organizational Behavior and Human Decision Processes, 103*(2), 238–255.

Kim, K. (2012). Paper presented in Political Communication Interest Group at the annual convention of the Association for Education in Journalism and Mass Communication, Chicago, IL, August 9 – 12, 2012.

Kim, K., & Park, J. (2010). Message framing and the effectiveness of DTC advertising: The Moderating role of subjective product knowledge. *Journal of Medical Marketing, 10*(2), 165–176.

Kim, Y.-J. (2006). The role of regulatory focus in message framing in antismoking advertisements for adolescents. *Journal of Advertising, 35*(1), 143–151.

Krishnamurthy, P., Carter, P., & Blair, E. (2001). Attribute Framing and goal framing Effects in health decisions. *Organizational Behavior and Human Decision Processes, 85*(2), 382–399.

Kühberger, A., Schulte-Mecklenbeck, M., & Perner, J. (2002). Framing decisions: Hypothetical and real. *Organizational Behavior and Human Decision Processes, 89*, 1162–1175.

Lalor, K. M., & Hailey, B. J. (1990). The effects of message framing and feelings of susceptibility to breast cancer on reported frequency of breast self-examination. *International Quarterly of Community Health Education, 10*, 183–192.

Lee, A. Y., & Aaker, J. L. (2004). Bringing the frame into focus: The influence of regulatory fit on processing fluency and persuasion. *Journal of Personality and Social Psychology, 84*, 205–218.

Levin. I. P. (1987). Associative effects of information framing. *Bulleting of the Psychonomic Society, 25*(2), 85–86.

Levin, I. P., Chapman, D. P., & Johnson, R. D. (1988). Confidence in judgments based on incomplete information: An investigation using both hypothetical and real gambles. *Journal of Behavioral Decision Making, 1*(1), 29–41.

Levin, I. P., & Gaeth, G. J. (1988). How consumers are affected by the framing of attribute information before and after consuming the product. *Journal of Consumer Research, 15*(3), 374–378.

Levin, I. P., Gaeth, G. J., Schreiber, J., & Lauriola, M. (2002). A new look at framing effects: Distribution of effect sizes, individual differences, and independence of types of effects. *Organizational Behavior and Human Decision Processes, 88*(1), 411–429.

Levin, I. P., Schneider, S. L., & Gaeth, G. J. (1998). All frames are not created equal: A typology and critical analysis of framing effects. *Organizational Behavior and Human Decision Processes, 76*(2), 149–188.

Linville, P. W., Fischer, G. W., & Fischhoff, B. (1993). AIDS risk perceptions and decision biases. In J. B. Pryor & G. D. Reeder (Eds.), *The social psychology of HIV infection* (pp. 5–38). Hillsdale, NJ: Lawrence Erlbaum.

Maheswaran, D., & Meyers-Levy, J. (1990). The influence of message framing and issue involvement. *Journal of Marketing Research, 27*(3), 361–367.

Marteau, T. M. (1989). Framing of information: Its influence upon decisions of doctors and patients. *British Journal of Social Psychology, 28*, 89–94.

Maule, J., & Villejoubert, G. (2007). What lies beneath: Reframing framing effects. *Thinking & Reasoning, 13*(1), 25–44.

McElroy, T., & Mascari, D. (2007). When is going to happen? How temporal distance influences processing for risky-choice framing tasks. *Social Cognition, 25*(4), 495–517.

McMahon, R., & Byrne, M. (2008). Predicting donation among an Irish sample of donors and nondonors: extending the theory of planned behavior. *Transfusion, 48*(2), 321–331.

Meyerowitz, B. E., & Chaiken, S. (1987). The effects of message framing on breast self-examination attitudes, intentions, and behavior. *Journal of Personality and Social Psychology, 52*(3), 500–510.

Mittal, B. (1995). A comparative analysis of four scales of involvement. *Psychology & Marketing, 12*, 663–682.

Nan, X. (2007). Social distance, framing, and judgment: A construal level perspective. *Human Communication Research, 33*(4), 489–514.

Newell, B. R., Lagnado, D. A., & Shanks, D. R. (2007). *Straight choices: The psychology of decision making*. Hove, UK: Psychology Press.

O'Connor, A. M., Pennie, R. A., & Dales, R. E. (1996). Framing effects on expectations, decisions, and side effects experienced: the case of influenza immunization. *Journal of clinical epidemiology, 49*(11), 1271–1276.

O'Connor, D. B., Ferguson, E., & O'Connor, R. C. (2005). Intentions to use hormonal male contraception: the role of message framing, attitudes, and stress appraisals. *British Journal of Psychology, 96*, 351–369.

Oliver, R. L., & Berger, P. K. (1979). A path analysis of preventive health care decision models. *Journal of Consumer Research, 6*, 113–122.

Perloff, R. M. (2003). *The dynamics of persuasion: Communication and attitudes in the twenty first century*. Mahwah, NJ: Lawrence Erlbaum.

Petty, R. E., Priester, R, J., & Brinor R. (2002). Mass media attitude change: Implications of elaboration likelihood model of persuasion, in J. Bryan and D. Zillmann (Eds.), *Media Effects: Advances in Theory and Research* (pp. 453–488). Hillsdale, NJ: Lawrence Erlbaum.

Putrevu, S. (2010). An examination of consumer responses toward attribute- and goal-framed messages. *Journal of Advertising, 39*(3), 5–24.

Rothman, A. J., Bartels, R. D., Wlaschin, J., & Salovey, P. (2006). The strategic use of gain- and loss-framed messages to promote healthy behavior: How theory can inform practice. *Journal of Communication, 56*(1), 202–220.

Rothman, A. J., & Salovey, P. (1997). Shaping perceptions to motivate healthy behavior: The role of message framing. *Psychological Bulletin, 121*(1), 3–19.

Salovey, P., Schneider, T. R., & Apanovitch, A. M. (2002). Message framing in the prevention and early detection of illness. In J. P. Dillard, & M. Pfau (Eds.), *The persuasion handbook: Developments in theory and practice*. London, England: Sage.

Salovey, P., & Williams-Piehota, P. (2004). Field experiments in social psychology: Message framing and the promotion of health protective behaviors. *American Behavioral Scientist, 47*(5), 488–505.

Scheufele, D. A., & Tewksbury, D. (2007). Framing, agenda-setting, and priming: The evolution of three media effects models. *Journal of Communication, 57*(1), 9–20.

Scott, L. B., & Curbow, B. (2006). The effect of message frames and CVD risk factors on behavioral outcomes. *American Journal of Health Behavior, 30*(6), 582–597.

Shah, D., Kwak, N., Schmierbach, M., & Zubric, J. (2004). The interplay of news frames on cognitive complexity. *Human Communication Research, 30*(1), 102–120.

Shiv, B., Britton, J. A. E., & Payne, J. W. (2004). Does elaboration increase or decrease the effectiveness of negatively versus positively framed messages? *Journal of Consumer Research, 31*(1), 199–208.

Sibley, C. G., Liu, J. H., & Kirkwood, S. (2006). Toward a social representations theory of attitude change: The effect of message framing on general and specific attitude toward equality and entitlement. *New Zealand Journal of Psychology, 35*(1), 3–13.

Smith, G. E. (1996). Framing in advertising and the moderating impact of consumer education. *Journal of Advertising Research, 36*(5), 49–64.

Smith, G. E., & Wortzel L. H. (1997). Prior knowledge and the effect of suggested frames of reference in advertising. *Psychology and Marketing, 14*(2), 121–143.

Smith, S. M., & Levin, I. P. (1996). Need for cognition and choice framing effects. *Journal of Behavioral Decision Making, 9*(4), 283–290.

Smith, S. M., & Petty, R. E. (1996). Message framing and persuasion: A message processing analysis. *Personality and Social Psychology Bulletin, 22*(3), 257–268.

Spence, M. R., Elgen, K. K., & Harwell, T. S. (2003). Awareness, prior use, and intent to use emergency contraception among Montana women at the time of pregnancy testing. *Maternal and Child Health Journal, 7*(3), 197–203.

Tewksbury, D., Jones, J., Peske, W. M., Raymond, A., & Vig, W. (2000).The Interaction of News and Advocate Frames: Manipulating Audience Perceptions of a Local Public Policy Issue. *Journalism & Mass Communication Quarterly, 77*(4), 804–829.

Tversky, A., & Kahneman, D. (1981). The framing of decisions and the psychology of choice. *Science, 211*(4481), 453–458.

Tversky, A., & Kahneman, D. (1986). Rational choice and the framing of decisions. *Journal of Business, 59*(4), 251-278.

Venkatraman, S., Aloysius, J. A., & Davis, F. D. (2006). Multiple prospect framing and decision behavior: The mediational roles of perceived riskiness and perceived ambiguity. *Organizational Behavior and Human Decision Processes, 101*(1), 59–73.

Williams, T., Clarke, V., & Borland, R. (2001). Effects of message framing on breast-cancer-related beliefs and behaviors: The role of mediating factors. *Journal of Applied Social Psychology, 31*(5), 925–950.

Wilson, D. K., Kaplan, R. M., & Schneiderman, L. (1987). Framing of decisions and selections of alternatives in health care. *Social Behavior, 2*, 51–59.

Yi, S., & Baumgartner, H. (2009). Regulatory focus and message framing: A test of three account. *Motiv Emot, 33*, 435–443.

Zhang, Y., & Buda, R. (1999). Moderating effects of need for cognition on responses to positively versus negatively framed advertising message. *Journal of Advertising 28*(2), 1–15.

19

Image Repair Theory in the Context of Strategic Communication

William L. Benoit

This chapter explicates image repair theory. First, I explain why image is important and discuss the nature of image. Then I argue that it is vital to understand the nature of threats to image. Next, I present the assumptions of image repair theory and explain the possible image repair strategies. Then I discuss the importance of the audience and look at crisis preparation and response.

Image Matters

People and organizations—including companies, governments, and non-profit organizations—frequently face accusations or suspicions of wrong-doing. A glance at newspaper headlines, televised news stories, or Internet news confirms the ubiquitous nature of threats to image. For example, we have heard and read about alleged scandals including JP Morgan, which lost two billion dollars, BP's Gulf of Mexico oil spill, or Rupert Murdoch's newspaper's illegal hacking of telephone messages and bribes to police. So, threats to image are common in modern society.

Threats to an image are inevitable for at least four reasons. First, our world has limited resources—there is only so much time, money, or resources. We often have to compete for limited resources, which means allocation of these resources can make those who desired a different distribution of resources unhappy. Second, events that are out of our control sometimes keep us from meeting our obligations. We can be delayed by traffic and arrive late to meetings, documents may become lost, or a colleague may not inform us that the time or location of an important meeting changed. Third, we as humans are simply not perfect and sometimes we commit misdeeds, make honest errors, or allow our behavior to be guided too much by our self-interests. Alcohol, drugs, or lack of sleep can affect our judgment and impair performance of our duties. Finally, the fact that we are individuals with different priorities can create conflict arising from our competing goals. For example, do we want the most effective prescription drugs (patients) or the least expensive drugs (insurance companies)? Should a company spend more money and effort on research and development or on marketing? How do we balance protecting society from criminals with preserving rights of those accused of crimes? Together, these four factors combine to ensure that actual or perceived wrong-doing is a recurrent feature of human activity. These elements can apply to organizations as well as to individuals.

When such inevitable misbehavior (actual or perceived) occurs, others are very likely to criticize us and our behavior. They may object to things we said or did, complain about things left unsaid or undone, or criticize the way we performed an action or phrased an utterance. Persuasive attacks are messages that attempt to create unfavorable attitudes about a target (person or organization) and these messages have been investigated in several studies (see, e.g., Benoit & Delbert, 2010; Benoit & Dorries, 1996; Benoit & Harthcock, 1999; Benoit, Klyukovski, McHale, & Airne, 2001; Benoit & Stein, 2009). An organization does not have to be the target of an explicit attack to need image repair, because it can respond to anticipated image problems, but attempts to rehabilitate reputation are often prompted by criticism.

These attacks on our reputation are serious matters, for our image or reputation is extremely vital to us. A damaged reputation can hurt our persuasiveness because credibility generally and trustworthiness in particular are important to persuasion (see, e.g., W. L. Benoit, & P. J. Benoit, 2008[1]; Benoit & Strathman, 2004) and credibility can be impaired by fallout from actual or perceived wrong-doing. We may be liable to punishment such as fines or even jail time for misdeeds. Although organizations, including companies, may not feel embarrassed, officers, workers, and shareholders do have feelings and those feelings can be hurt when their organization is the target of accusations. Furthermore, other companies or organizations could take their business elsewhere when an image is damaged. People and companies jealously guard their reputations and work hard to repair tarnished images. Hence, attacks on an image can be very serious concerns, and most people recognize the importance of these threats to reputation.

When image is threatened, we usually feel compelled to offer explanations, defenses, justifications, rationalizations, apologies, or excuses for our behavior. This chapter focuses on messages that respond to perceived damage to reputation—image repair strategies—because threats to image are pervasive, reputation is important, and communication has the potential to mend our face or reputation.

Defensive utterances or image repair messages are persuasive attempts to reshape the audience's attitudes: creating or changing beliefs about the accused's responsibility for an act and/or creating or changing values about the offensiveness of those acts. Human behavior includes both physical acts and communication. Communication includes a variety of contexts, including health communication, political communication, and crisis communication. Image repair discourse can be distinguished from crisis communication, a broader category. Crisis communication includes image repair discourse, but it also includes messages about other kinds of crises, such as natural disasters and terrorism. Image repair discourse consists of messages intended to improve images tarnished by criticism and suspicion (it is also possible for an organization to try to preempt anticipated criticism).

The Nature of Image

Image is all about perceptions—it is the impression others have about us. Saying this does not necessarily mean that image is false or does not reflect reality. Our perceptions of people and organizations are shaped by our direct experience with the organization and by what others say about the organization and how they behave toward it (vicarious experience). Furthermore, organizations and people are very complex and we rarely, if ever, know everything about them. Incomplete knowledge means that our impressions are limited. For example, before the BP Gulf of Mexico oil spill, many people knew BP from its gas stations. Those who live and work in the Gulf area learned about the spill from their first-hand experiences, but most of us watched it on television or read about it in newspapers or on the Internet (residents also learned about this vicariously through word of mouth, watching TV, reading newspapers, and other communication means). These messages (news stories and reports) shaped our knowledge about the oil spill and BP and influenced our attitudes toward the company. Many had an unfavorable impression of the company based on news reports. These unfavorable impressions were a threat to BP's image and in fact BP responded in many ways, including a series of television and newspaper advertisements designed to counteract the public's negative impressions. The fact that our knowledge of a person or organization is usually incomplete also means that different people will often have somewhat different impressions because each has some information that the others lack.

So, image is an impression we have of a person or organization. Our image is a perception that develops out of what the organization says and does as well as by what others say about the organization and how others behave toward it: for example, fines assessed against a company by the government. Many of our images are based in large part on messages about the target (vicarious experiences). Image repair theory is about using communication to improve images threatened by bad behavior and/or reports of bad behavior.

The Nature of Threats to Image

An unfavorable image has two key components: responsibility and offensiveness. For example, BP's oil wells in the Gulf of Mexico leaked. This spill was, at least in part, BP's fault. Other companies (e.g., those who supplied equipment) may have been partly to blame. but BP was definitely responsible. Other companies, such as Mobil Oil or (to stress the point of organizations totally unrelated to the act in question) Microsoft or Bank of America did not face threats to their images because the oil spill was in no way their fault. Responsibility for an act is essential for a threat to image to occur.

Second, the act for which an organization is responsible must appear offensive before image is at risk. If BP had not had an oil spill, but had done a completely different kind of act (distributed food to the poor, hired workers, helped with Hurricane Katrina—or, again, to stress the point, did something innocuous such as repainted its offices) that was not offensive, its image would not be at risk. But the oil spill depressed tourism, hurt wildlife, and damaged businesses, so it was offensive. BP's image was damaged because it was (at least partly) to blame for an offensive act. This analysis gives an insight into how image repair works. If the organization can persuade the audience that it was not to blame (difficult in BP's case but sometimes possible) or that the action it performed was not offensive (again, difficult in BP's case), its damaged image might be helped.

Understanding the accusations or suspicions that threaten an image is vital to image repair. First, you must know what the threats are to be able to attempt to counteract them. An organization may decide an accusation is too trivial to address, but it is a mistake to ignore an important accusation. You must know the accusations to decide which require defense. Second, you need to understand both blame and offensiveness for each accusation in order to decide how to respond.

Assumptions of Image Repair Theory

Image repair theory rests on two key assumptions. First, communication is a goal-directed activity. Second, maintaining a positive reputation is one of the central goals of communication. Each of these assumptions will be discussed separately here.

Communication is a Goal-Directed Activity

The first assumption made by this theory is that communication is a goal-directed activity. With few exceptions, most rhetorical theorists consider rhetoric to be the art of persuasion, a declaration typically carrying with it the assumption that rhetorical discourse is purposeful (see, e.g., Arnold & Frandsen, 1984; Bitzer, 1968; Richards, 1936; Rowland, 1982; or Scott, 1980). The assumption that communication is goal-directed can also be found in the literature on communication theory (see e.g., Halliday, 1973). H. H. Clark and E. V. Clark, for example, declare that "speaking is fundamentally an instrumental act" (1977, p. 223). Craig (1986) even declares that "a practical discipline of communication in which the concept of goal would not be central is difficult to imagine; and the pragmatic language of goal, decision, and consequence is in fact the common coin of the discipline of speech communication that has emerged in the United States in this century" (p. 257). The key point here is that the view of communication as goal-directed pervades writing in communication, transcending particular contexts of interpersonal communication or rhetorical theory. Hence, it is appropriate to construe communication and rhetoric as goal-driven activities.

Any assumption as broad as this one is likely to require qualifications, and this one is no exception. First, an organization can have multiple goals that are not completely compatible. In such cases, messages that further one goal may well interfere with other goals. Still, people and organizations try to achieve the goals that seem most important to them at the time they act, or to achieve the best mix of the goals that appears possible (considering the perceived costs of the behavior enacted in pursuit of the goals, and the importance of those goals).

Second, at times a person's goals, motives, or purposes are vague, ill-formed, or unclear. An organization can be made of many people who are not equally aware of all goals or do not accept all goals equally. Nevertheless, to the extent a person's or organization's goals are clear, he, she, or it will attempt to accomplish those goals. Furthermore, even when a communicator has a clear conception of a goal, that does not necessarily mean that he or she knows or is willing and able to use the most effective means for achieving that goal. However, to the extent a particular goal is salient to a communicator, he or she will pursue that goal by enacting the behavior that the communicator believes is likely to achieve that goal and has tolerable costs.

Third, I do not claim that people devote the same amount of attention to each and every communicative encounter, micro-managing all utterances and all characteristics of an utterance, constantly identifying goals and unceasingly planning behavior to accomplish them. In situations that are particularly important to us, however, we do plan aspects of our utterances as carefully as we can. In other cases we spend as much effort in developing goal-directed messages as seems reasonable and necessary.

Finally, even when an individual's goals are relatively clear, it may be difficult for others to identify that person's goals. Of course, multiple goals (including "hidden agendas") complicate matters. Another problem in identifying a person's goal(s) arises because people sometimes attempt to deceive others about their goals. Despite these reservations, communication generally is best understood as an intentional activity. Communicators attempt to develop messages that they believe will best achieve the goals that are most salient to them when they communicate.

Maintaining a Favorable Image is a Key Goal of Communication

The second key assumption of image repair theory is that maintaining a favorable impression is an important goal in interaction. One useful typology of communication purposes is advanced by R.A. Clark and Delia (1979), who indicate that there are three

> issues or objectives explicitly or implicitly present for overt or tacit negotiation in every communicative transaction: (1) overtly instrumental objectives, in which a response is required from one's listener(s) related to a specific obstacle or problem defining the task of the communicative situation, (2) interpersonal objectives, involving the establishment or maintenance of a relationship with the other(s), and (3) identity objectives, in which there is management of the communicative situation to the end of presenting a desired self image for the speaker and maintaining a particular sense of self for the other(s).
>
> *p. 200*

Furthermore, Fisher (1970) distinguishes between four goals in communication about identity. He argues that there are "Four motives, or kinds of rhetorical situations: . . . affirmation, concerned with giving birth to an image; reaffirmation, concerned with revitalizing an image, purification, concerned with correcting an image, and subversion, concerned with undermining an image" (p. 132). Persuasive attacks, which can prompt image repair, are what Fisher calls subversion, or messages intended to damage an image, mentioned above. This chapter focuses on Fisher's motive of purification, namely, messages attempting to repair a damaged image.

Thus, our vulnerability to criticism leads to (internal) guilt and (external) threats to our face, both of which motivate a reaction from the actor. What happens when we believe that negatively perceived events threaten our reputation? Goffman explains, "When a face has been threatened, face-work must be done" (1967, p. 27). Notice also that R.A. Clark and Delia (1979) identify the identity objective as a key goal in communication and Fisher (1970) suggests one of the basic motives of rhetoric is purification of an image.

Why is face or image so important that persuasive attacks motivate defensive responses? Because one's face, image, or reputation is so significant, Brown and Levinson (1978) observe that "people can be expected to defend their faces if threatened" (p. 66). Empirical evidence confirms the claim that perceived embarrassment is positively correlated with the amount of facework (Modigliani, 1971). Therefore, when our reputation is threatened, we feel compelled to offer explanations, defenses, justifications, rationalizations, apologies, or excuses for our behavior. Because blame and criticism or complaints occur throughout human society and because face is important for virtually everyone, this phenomenon, a felt need to cleanse one's reputation through discourse, occurs in all our lives, public and private.

Image Repair Strategies

Image repair theory develops out of the nature of persuasive attacks. One component of persuasive attack is blame: the accused is responsible for an act. This means image repair efforts can attempt to reject blame (denying responsibility, shifting blame to others, or reducing responsibility). The second element of persuasive attack is the action of the accused is offensive. Image repair messages can try to reduce perceived offensiveness of the action. Beyond responding to blame and offensiveness, it is possible to admit wrong-doing (not challenging blame or offensiveness) and ask for forgiveness or to promise to fix the problem. Table 19.1 lists the general image repair strategies and specific strategies, giving definitions and examples of each.

This typology (see also Benoit, 2015) has been applied to image repair messages in a variety of contexts, including corporate (e.g., Benoit, 1995b; Benoit & Brinson, 1994; Benoit & Czerwinski, 1997; Benoit & Hirson, 2001; Blaney, Benoit, & Brazeal, 2002; Brinson & Benoit, 1996, 1999), political (e.g., Benoit, 2006a, 2006b; Benoit, Gullifor, & Panici, 1991; Benoit & Nill, 1998a; Blaney & Benoit, 2001; Kennedy & Benoit, 1997; Len-Rios & Benoit, 2004), celebrities and athletics (e.g., Benoit, 1997a; Benoit & Hanczor, 1994; Benoit & Nill, 1998b; Blaney, Lippert, & Smith, 2013; Wen, Yu, & Benoit, 2009), international contexts (e.g., Benoit & Brinson, 1999; Drumheller & Benoit, 2004; J. Zhang & Benoit, 2004; W. Zhang & Benoit, 2009; Wen, Yu, & Benoit, 2012), health care, and religion (e.g., Blaney & Benoit, 1997; Miller, 2002).

The Importance of Audience

It is important to remember that in image repair we are dealing with perceptions. The actor responds to perceived threats to her or his character. In the case of organizations these attacks are important to the organization when the attacks are believed to reduce the organization's reputation in the eyes of a group or audience who is salient to the source. As Tedeschi and Reiss put it, "Central to the realization that one faces a predicament is the belief that *others* [emphasis added] attribute to oneself causality and responsibility for the event in question" (1981, p. 271). Of course, an organization's perceptions of the audience's image of the source may or may not reflect the *audience's actual perceptions* of the

Table 19.1 Corporate Image Repair Strategies

Strategy	Key characteristic	Example
Denial		
Simple denial	Did not perform act	Tylenol: did not poison capsule
Shift the blame	Another performed act	Tylenol: a "madman" poisoned capsules
Evasion of responsibility		
Provocation	Responded to act of another	Firm moved because of new taxes
Defeasibility	Lack of information or ability	Executive not told meeting changed
Accident	Mishap	Tree fell on tracks causing train wreck
Good intentions	Meant well	Sears wants to provide good auto repair service
Reducing offensiveness of event		
Bolstering	Stress good traits	Exxon's "swift and competent" clean-up of oil spill
Minimization	Act not serious	Exxon: few animals killed in oil spill
Differentiation	Act less offensive than similar acts	Sears: unneeded repairs were preventative maintenance, not fraud
Transcendence	More important values	Helping humans justifies testing animals
Attack Accuser	Reduce credibility of accuser	Coke: Pepsi owns restaurants, competes directly with you for customers
Compensation	Reimburse victim	Disabled movie-goers given free passes after denied admission to movie
Corrective action	Plan to solve/prevent recurrence of problem	AT&T promised to spend billions to improve service
Mortification	Apologize	AT&T apologized for service interruption

Source: Benoit, W. L. (1995a, 1997b)

organization's image. However, the organization's perceptions of the audience's reaction to attacks are all the source has available to prompt and guide image restoration efforts. Hence, when trying to understand the source's perception of and response to an attack, critics must consider the source's point of view—the source's perceptions of the audience's beliefs. If the critic elects to assess the success or effectiveness of the defensive discourse in restoring the organization's reputation with the audience, the critic must also consider the audience's actual perception of the source before and after the image restoration attempt if possible.

This analysis leads to the idea that, in a sense, there are at least two "audiences" for a given image restoration attempt. The organization addresses an external audience consisting of those for whom the accused is most concerned with restoring his or her face. There are three possibilities for this external audience. First, it may consist solely of the person who objected to the apologist's behavior. For example, if Jill criticizes her husband Steve, Steve may wish to restore Jill's impression of him (and be concerned only with Jill's perceptions of him). Here, the source is trying to restore reputation with the accuser. Second, John may criticize Arthur in front of several coworkers, and Arthur may wish to repair John's perceptions as well as the perceptions of the other coworkers aware of John's charges. In this case, the source is trying to restore reputation with the accuser and others aware of the accusation. A final form of external audience occurs when a third party levels the charges before a relevant group. For example, if an activist protests against a company, that company's spokesperson may wish to reassure customers and/or stockholders but be completely (or largely) unconcerned about whether the protester is convinced by the image restoration effort. In this third case, the source is more concerned with restoring reputation with those aware of the accusations than with the accuser. Thus, it is important to realize that an apologist's accuser may or may not be part of the audience for whom the image restoration attempt is designed. Similarly, because the accuser may or may not be the alleged victim of the offensive act, sources may be concerned primarily with restoring their reputations with victims, or with other audiences, or both.

As suggested earlier, incomplete knowledge and different priorities or values mean that different people frequently have different impressions of a person or organization. This is exceptionally clear during a presidential election, such as the one of 2012, when Republicans and Democrats had very different impressions of President Obama and Governor Romney. Even in these extreme situations some of our perceptions overlap: Democrats and Republicans alike agreed that Mitt Romney had been governor, had run the Utah Olympics, and was married to Ann Romney. They also agree that Barack Obama had won the presidency in 2008, had participated in the auto bailouts of 2009, and was married to Michelle Obama. Audiences are complex because individuals in an audience have (some) different information and (some) different priorities. This complexity can make image repair very challenging.

Preparing Crisis Response Plans

Crisis response plans are contingency plans: Their purpose is to anticipate potential threats to image and prepare responses without stress and time pressure. In a crisis, these plans should be adapted to the specific situation and implemented thoughtfully, not followed blindly. Furthermore, crisis response plans should be reviewed periodically and revised or updated as appropriate.

First, the organization should reflect on which crises can be anticipated. We cannot know when a crisis will emerge and we cannot anticipate every possible crisis. However, some crises can be anticipated and crisis response plans developed. For example, restaurants and restaurant chains face the possibility of food poisoning. Airlines often experience delays and, unfortunately, sometimes planes crash. Utilities can have their service to customers interrupted. Organizations should anticipate potential crises and prioritize them by likelihood and importance. Crisis response plans should be developed for the crises which are highest on the list. The organization should also consider other goals, e.g., profitability, that could conflict with image repair efforts.

Second, the crisis plan should address several questions:

- What actions should be taken (e.g., shut down production)?
- Who in the organization needs to be informed, and what should they be told?
- Who outside the organization needs to be informed, and what should they be told?
- Who will be the organization's spokesperson? Is this the same person who will design (and approves) Image Repair messages?
- How will the message be disseminated? If there are multiple messages, when and to whom will they be distributed?
- What are the precise accusations and who are the most important audiences?
- Are there conditions when the image repair message(s) should be changed?
- When should image repair efforts cease?
- Can a potential crisis be averted before it happens?

The organization should review its response in the light of the outcome, and revise it as necessary. The more contingency plans that are developed, and the more frequently they are revised and updated, the more effective the crisis response. The actual image repair messages should be created with four factors in mind: which accusations/suspicions need the most attention, what does the most important audience believe is true, what evidence and other resources does the organization have, and what media will best connect the message with the audience. The image repair message should not lie or deceive: the truth often comes out, whereupon the organization is threatened not only by the original offensive act but also by having lied about it.

Conclusion

Image, the perceptions of a person or organization held by others, is vital in human affairs. Threats to image are inevitable. People and organizations need to understand how to deal with threats to image. Image repair theory is an approach to this situation. Research has applied this theory in many case studies to help understand this complex phenomenon.

Note

1 The rest of the citations for Benoit in this chapter are for W. L. Benoit.

References

Arnold, C. C., & Frandsen, K. D. (1984). Conceptions of rhetoric and communication. In C. C. Arnold & J. W. Bowers (Eds.), *Handbook of rhetorical and communication theory* (pp. 3–50). Boston, MA: Allyn & Bacon.

Benoit, W. L. (1995a). *Accounts, excuses, apologies: A theory of image restoration discourse.* Albany, NY: State University of New York Press.

Benoit, W. L. (1995b). Sears' repair of its auto service image: Image restoration discourse in the corporate sector. *Communication Studies, 46,* 89–105.

Benoit, W. L. (1997a). Hugh Grant's image restoration discourse: An actor apologizes. *Communication Quarterly, 45,* 251–267.

Benoit, W. L. (1997b). Image restoration discourse and crisis communication. *Public Relations Review, 23,* 177–186.

Benoit, W. L. (2004). Image restoration discourse and crisis communication. In D. P. Millar & R. L. Heath (Eds.), *Responding to crisis: A rhetorical approach to crisis communication* (pp. 263–280). Mahwah, NJ: Lawrence Erlbaum.

Benoit, W. L. (2006a). Image repair in President Bush's April 2004 news conference. *Public Relations Review, 32,* 137–143.

Benoit, W. L. (2006b). President Bush's image repair effort on *Meet the Press:* The complexities of defeasibility. *Journal of Applied Communication Research, 34,* 285–306.

Benoit, W. L. (2015). *Accounts, excuses, apologies: Image repair theory and research* (2nd ed.). Albany: State University of New York Press

Benoit, W. L., & Benoit, P. J. (2008). *Persuasive messages: Balancing influence in communication.* Oxford, England: Blackwell.

Benoit, W. L., & Brinson, S. (1994). AT&T: Apologies are not enough. *Communication Quarterly, 42,* 75–88.

Benoit, W. L., & Brinson, S. L. (1999). Queen Elizabeth's image repair discourse: Insensitive royal or compassionate Queen? *Public Relations Review, 25,* 145–156.

Benoit, W. L., & Czerwinski, A. (1997). A critical analysis of USAir's image repair discourse. *Business Communication Quarterly, 60,* 38–57.

Benoit, W. L., & Delbert, J. (2010). Get a Mac: Mac vs. PC TV spots. *Relevant Rhetoric, 1.* Accessed 4/14/12: http://relevantrhetoric.com/wp-content/uploads/Get-A-Mac1.pdf.

Benoit, W. L., & Dorries, B. (1996). *Dateline NBC*'s persuasive attack of Wal-Mart. *Communication Quarterly, 44,* 463–477.

Benoit, W. L., Gullifor, P., & Panici, D. (1991). President Reagan's defensive discourse on the Iran-Contra affair. *Communication Studies, 42,* 272–294.

Benoit, W. L., & Hanczor, R. (1994). The Tonya Harding controversy: An analysis of image repair strategies. *Communication Quarterly, 42,* 416–433.

Benoit, W. L., & Harthcock, A. (1999). Attacking the tobacco industry: A rhetorical analysis of advertisements by The Campaign for Tobacco-Free Kids. *Southern Communication Journal, 65,* 66–81.

Benoit, W. L., & Hirson, D. (2001). *Doonesbury* versus the Tobacco Institute: The Smoke Starters' Coupon. *Communication Quarterly, 49,* 279–294.

Benoit, W. L., Klyukovski, A. A., McHale, J. P., & Airne, D. (2001). A fantasy theme analysis of political cartoons on the Clinton-Lewinsky-Starr affair. *Critical Studies in Media Communication, 18*, 377–394.

Benoit, W. L., & Nill, D. M. (1998a). A critical analysis of Judge Clarence Thomas's statement before the Senate Judiciary Committee. *Communication Studies, 49*, 179–195.

Benoit, W. L., & Nill, D. M. (1998b). Oliver Stone's defense of JFK. *Communication Quarterly, 46*, 127–143.

Benoit, W. L., & Stein, K. A. (2009). *Kategoria* of cartoons on the Catholic Church sexual abuse scandal. In J. R. Blaney & J. P. Zompetti (Eds.), *The rhetoric of Pope John Paul II* (pp. 23–35). Lanham, MD: Lexington, Rowman & Littlefield.

Benoit, W. L., & Strathman, A. (2004). Source credibility and the Elaboration Likelihood Model. In R. Gass & J. Seiter (Eds.), *Readings in persuasion, social influence, and compliance gaining* (pp. 95–111). Boston, MA: Pearson.

Bitzer, L. F. (1968). The rhetorical situation. *Philosophy & Rhetoric, 1*, 1–14.

Blaney, J. R., & Benoit, W. L. (1997). The persuasive defense of Jesus in the Gospel according to John. *Journal of Communication and Religion, 20*, 25–30.

Blaney, J. R., Benoit, W. L., & Brazeal, L. M. (2002). Blowout! Firestone's image restoration campaign. *Public Relations Research, 28*, 379–392.

Blaney, J. R., Lippert, L. R. & Smith, J.S. (Eds). (2013). *Repairing the athlete's image: Studies in sports image restoration*. Lanham, MD: Lexington Books: Rowman & Littlefield.

Brinson, S., & Benoit, W. L. (1996). Dow Corning's image repair strategies in the breast implant crisis. *Communication Quarterly, 44*, 29–41.

Brinson, S. L., & Benoit, W. L. (1999). The tarnished star: Restoring Texaco's damaged public image. *Management Communication Quarterly, 12*, 483–510.

Brown, P., & Levinson, S. (1978). Universals in language usage: Politeness phenomena. In E. Goody (Ed.), *Questions and politeness: Strategies in social interaction* (pp. 56–310). Cambridge, England: Cambridge University Press.

Clark, H. H., & Clark, E. V. (1977). *Psychology and language.* New York: Harcourt, Brace, Jovanovich.

Clark, R. A., & Delia, J. G. (1979). *Topoi* and rhetorical competence. *Quarterly Journal of Speech, 65*, 187–206.

Craig, R. T. (1986). Goals in discourse. In D. G. Ellis & W. A. Donohue (Eds.), *Contemporary issues in language and discourse processes* (pp. 257–273). Hillsdale, NJ: Lawrence Erlbaum.

Drumheller, K., & Benoit, W. L. (2004). USS Greeneville collides with Japan's Ehime Maru: Cultural issues in image repair discourse. *Public Relations Review, 30*, 177–185.

Fisher, W. R. (1970). A motive view of communication. *Quarterly Journal of Speech, 56*, 131–139.

Goffman, E. (1967). *On face work. Interaction ritual: Essays in face-to-face behavior* (pp. 5–45). Chicago, IL: Aldine.

Halliday, M. A. K. (1973). *Explorations in the functions of language.* London: Edward Arnold.

Kennedy, K. A., & Benoit, W. L. (1997). The Newt Gingrich book deal controversy: A case study in self-defense rhetoric. *Southern Communication Journal, 63*, 197–216.

Len-Rios, M., & Benoit, W. L. (2004). Gary Condit's image repair strategies: Squandering a golden opportunity. *Public Relations Research, 50*, 95–106.

Miller, B. A. (2002). *Divine apology: The discourse of religious image restoration.* Westport, CT: Praeger.

Modigliani, A. (1971). Embarrassment, facework, and eye contact: Testing a theory of embarrassment. *Journal of Personality and Social Psychology, 17*, 15–24.

Richards, I. A. (1936). *Philosophy of rhetoric.* New York: Oxford University Press.

Rowland, R. C. (1982). The influence of purpose on fields of argument. *Journal of the American Forensic Association, 18*, 228–245.

Scott, R. L. (1980). Intentionality in the rhetorical process. In E. E. White (Ed.), *Rhetoric in transition: Studies in the nature and uses of rhetoric* (pp. 39–60). University Park, PA: Pennsylvania State University Press.

Tedeschi, J. T., & Reiss, M. (1981). Verbal strategies in impression management. In C. Antaki (Ed.), *The psychology of ordinary explanations of social behavior* (pp. 271–326). London, England: Academic Press.

Wen, J., Yu, J., & Benoit, W. L. (2009). Our hero can't be wrong: A case study of collectivist image repair in Taiwan. *Chinese Journal of Communication, 2*, 174–192.

Wen, W-C., Yu, T., & Benoit, W. L. (2012). The failure of "scientific" evidence in Taiwan: a case study of international image repair for American beef. *Asian Journal of Communication, 22*, 121–139.

Zhang, J., & Benoit, W. L. (2004). Message strategies of Saudi Arabia's image restoration campaign after 9/11. *Public Relations Review, 30*, 161–167.

Zhang, W., & Benoit, W. L. (2009). Former Minister Zhang's discourse on SARS: Government's image restoration or destruction. *Public Relations Review, 35*, 240–246.

20

Images with Messages

A Semiotic Approach to Identifying and Decoding Strategic Visual Communication

Janis Teruggi Page

Strategic communication is the "purposeful use of communication by an organization to fulfill its mission" (Hallahan, Holtzhausen, van Ruler, Verčič, & Sriramesh , 2007, p. 4). It provides particular information, influences desired attitudes, and encourages specific behaviors. This chapter focuses on how one can identify strategic approaches in an organization's *visual* communication and decode it from a critical perspective. Visual theory offers ways to recognize and understand how strategic intent may influence construction of a visual image's form and content, embedding it with a dominant ideology and guiding receivers toward a preferred reading. This essay will review theories that help explain the various ways a visual image might be designed and experienced. It will then apply one theory, semiotics, to analyze a specific artifact located in public common areas of Abu Dhabi city, the capital of the United Arab Emirates (UAE). Here government-influenced signage reinforcing Emirati identity is integrated into people's everyday patterns of living. Particular contexts of the UAE as a 40-year-old fast-developing nation bounded by Islam, authoritarian rule, tribal cultural norms, and a majority expatriate population are considered. Applying semiotics to visual communication as a sense-making tool offers a way to look at how an image structures thought, and how it moves the viewer to find some unity and meaning.

Privilege of the visual

This chapter considers the visual as an important mode of strategic communication because we live in an image-dominated culture—image in the sense of pictorial representation of the 'real,' and dominated in the sense of both plentiful and powerful. The force of the visual is greater now than ever before due to the intensity of visual stimulation in our lives. More than fifteen years ago, visual culture theorist Mitchell announced that the "pictorial turn" had supplanted the "linguistic turn" in the study of culture (1994, p. 15). The subsequent explosion of digital technologies that invite easy manipulation and fast, global dissemination through the Internet has greatly elevated the role of the visual. Thus the ease of image-making and sending now makes the viewer more reliant than ever before on an ability to critically engage and interpret visual messages. If not, we are forced to rely on the credibility of the producers, their standards and institutional merits, and to accept that their interpretive frames are honest.

While visual communication has experienced a cultural resurgence, the power of the visual is an old story. Beginning with the sixteenth century invention of the camera obscura and continuing through the nineteenth century stereoscope and first Kodak, Crary (1992) cites the developing technology's gradual imposition of a normative vision on the observer. By the mid–nineteenth century, reality was understood to *be* images. Society preferred the image to the thing, copy to original, representation to reality, and appearance to being, Crary writes, and society was aware of this. The chief activity of society became producing and consuming images. As technology developed in the twentieth century, semiotician Roland Barthes and historian Daniel Boorstin echoed concerns about the "dangers of a society saturated with pseudo-images," (Barnhurst, Vari, & Rodriguez, 2004). Wariness of the 'real,' its intent, and its creator became rooted in the cultural landscape.

"Every image embodies a way of seeing," proclaimed Berger (J. Berger, 1972, p. 10) in his seminal book inspired by the television series *Ways of Seeing*: " ... the photographer select(s) that sight from an infinity of other possible sights," choosing subject and frame among other determinants. The photographic image is rhetorical and compelling, engaging the spectator. Visuals are more emotive and as heuristics are more easily and quickly 'read.' As Langer (1942) explained, presentational or pictorial symbols are often better equipped than discursive symbols for expressing sentiment because the mind is able to read them in a flash and preserve them in a disposition or an attitude. Sontag (1977) locates this flash in the power of the camera: "Images that have virtually unlimited authority today are mainly photographic images" (p. 153). As a trace or reflection of the *real*, the photographic image immediately lures the beholder. Barthes (1977) also noted the powerful role of the visual image as a transparent window into unsullied fact, playing a key role in shaping cultural perceptions (Stein, 2001). Decades later, despite technological advances in photo manipulation that obfuscate the *real*, Brugioni (1999) deemed photos to be instruments of powerful believability. Barbatsis (2005) noted that while the photographic quality of images so transparently appears to merely record and represent the *real*, viewers are challenged to explain how it makes sense of raw experience and how it structures thought to so powerfully constitute reality.

If the photograph is always potentially a means of control as a rhetorical construction of reality, the development of mass mediated film, television, Internet communication, and digital technologies have heralded myriad ways to influence the viewer. As the twenty-first century began, Gitlin (2002) expressed concern about the immensity of our media experience, or rather media torrent, which imposes its super-saturation on society. Noting the present age as one of cybernetic technology and electronic reproduction, Mitchell (1994) cautions that "a culture totally dominated by images has now become a real technical possibility on a global scale" (p. 16). The need for critique of visual culture seems inescapable.

Understanding the visual

Among the many ways to understand visual messages, established theories of Gestalt, cognition, and semiology help to explain how creators might encode, and receivers might decode an image. Before demonstrating one specific method—semiotic analysis—a brief overview of a few theories helps to provide a foundation for understanding the breadth of visual analysis.

Gestalt theories involve *groupings of elements* in a composition. The Gestalt concept comes from Wertheimer's conclusion that the whole is different from the sum of its parts (Zakia, 2007, p. 28–29). In other words, meaning results from a combination of sensations and not of individual sensations. The principle of *similarity* causes the viewer to concentrate on the simplest, most stable grouping of similar forms, i.e. they appear as a single unit amid disparate shapes. The principle of *proximity* induces the eye to more closely associate objects that are near to each other more so than it does objects that are set apart. The *continuation* principle recognizes that the eye prefers smooth line continuity over sudden or unusual changes in direction. The law of *common fate* causes a viewer to mentally group items that appear to point in the same direction. Applying these various Gestalts through purposeful design prompts the viewer to become a participant in meaning construction, a strategy common in advertising to shift ownership of a message to the receiver (Williamson, 1978/1987). The Gestalt principle of *closure* involves content with missing parts—parts that rest within the viewer who is then called to draw upon memory, latent knowledge, or impressions or desires collected from cultural experiences to complete the idea or image. A simple example might be a face with missing features, violating everyday reality and summoning the viewer to 'see' the mouth and draw conclusions about the meaning of its absence (Figure 20.1).

Figure 20.1 Seeking Closure

Moving on from Gestalt, cognitive theories require the viewer to assign a more complex meaning to what is seen. With the cognitive approach, viewers actively arrive at conclusions. For example, contradictions and abnormalities will stimulate attention and encourage comprehension because they violate familiar expectations. Also, stimuli that are *salient* to certain viewers will carry more meaning, as in the cricket game that excites Indian fans of the sport and leaves American baseball fans confused. Lester (2011, p. 62–66) provides good explanations of how cognitive visual theories work. *Memory* is a very important mental activity involved in accurate visual perception. People have long used pictures as memory aids to help them recall certain events. *Projection* comes into play when a person's mental state of mind is 'projected' onto an inanimate object. This is the principle behind the Rorschach inkblot test in psychology (Lester, 2011). *Expectation* is the cognitive theory that explains how preconceived expectations (for example, how one's old neighborhood should look) often lead to false or missed visual perceptions. *Selectivity* explains how people unconsciously process a complicated visual experience. With large numbers of images, or multi-element images, the mind focuses only on significant details within a scene. For example, if you are trying to locate a friend sitting in the packed bleachers, all the other unknown faces in the crowd will have little significance. *Habituation* allows the mind to protect itself from over-stimulation and unnecessary pictures; as with selectivity, the mind tends to ignore visual stimuli that are a part of a person's every day habitual activities. Lester suggests that one way not to become ambivalent about the habitual barrage of imagery is to constantly search out new ways to think about familiar objects. *Dissonance* theory helps us to understand the difficulty when trying to read with a television or stereo loudly playing in the same room. The mind really can concentrate on only one activity or the other. Visual messages become more focused in contexts without competing formats. *Cultural* and *historical* manifestations will be more meaningful to those who identify with a specific culture or past. Envision a photo of the *Souk* (marketplace) at Central Market, Abu Dhabi, taken in

1962 when the city's population was estimated at less than 4,000. While an Emirati grandmother might study the image intently, looking back in time to remember the moment and perhaps to identify some of the indistinct faces, feeling sad her world has changed so much (Bristol-Rhys, 2010, p. 2–3), her granddaughter might just say, "Cool, a vintage photo!"

Following Gestalt and cognitive theory, the third theoretical perspective is semiology; it considers all texts (visual images, music, words) as signs with meanings below the surface that the receiver must work to grasp (Leiss, Kline, and Jhally, 1990, p. 201–2). Through this process, the receiver is led toward realizing a predetermined message. Often it is a heuristic process. The texts appear to be the ordinary representing of day-to-day cultural experiences. The field of British cultural studies identified culture as ideological—the "taken-for-granted realities of everyday life" (Burgin, 1982, p. 46) that reinforce a dominant worldview. Ideology is generally defined as a body of beliefs and representations that sustain and legitimate current power relationships; it promotes the values and interests of dominant groups within society (Eagleton, 1991, p. 5–6).

A semiotic analysis begins with the understanding that there are no neutral signs; they function to persuade as well as to refer, yet their ideology is often masked in naturalized framings of the common-sense 'way things are' of the dominant societal coalition. Thus, if signs do not merely reflect reality but are involved in constructing and reinforcing it, then those who control the sign systems control the construction of reality (Chandler, n.d.). Semiotic analysis questions how a text is organized to construct meaning. The analyst searches for what is hidden beneath the obvious and can lead to insights on whose view of reality is being privileged and what may be challenged.

While semiology stems from various theorists, including Saussure, Pierce, Eco, Barthes, Hall, and Hartley, the following analysis is guided by Barthes (1983/1967, 1972). A sign consists of a signifier (image) and what's signified (meaning), which carry both denotation (literal meaning) and connotation (subjective meaning). Barthes's early work offered guidelines for semiotic analysis from a perspective of inherent meaning—cultural, mythological, or ideological. In *Mythologies* (1972), he demonstrated the relationship between image and ideology, analyzing the front cover of an issue of the magazine *Paris Match*—an explanation now considered a classic example of semiotic analysis. It pictured a young Black soldier in a French uniform, appearing to salute the French flag. Through a socio-historical reading Barthes identified the image as a sign for French imperialism.

Public signage in Abu Dhabi

The above semiotic analysis approach will now be applied to a visual campaign in Abu Dhabi city, a site of complex historical and socio-cultural conditions. An undeveloped coastal encampment with illiterate and impoverished occupants only 50 years ago, today it is the capital of the UAE, located in the wealthiest oil-rich state of the seven emirates. While its grandmothers remember the hard and spare conditions of their upbringing, due to the dispersal of oil wealth among UAE citizens their daughters and granddaughters know only lives lived in lavish family compounds with maids, cooks, personal drivers, and unlimited consumption of luxury material goods. Exponentially accelerated modernization has attracted millions of expatriate workers to the UAE, many in low-skilled service and construction jobs, resulting in a population in 2012 that is only 11% Emirati.

The rapid growth and changes are viewed by some indigenous people as a threat to Emirati social and religious identity in this very conservative country. Although personal wealth has fast-tracked them into the modernity of the material world, family and tribal traditions with strict Islamic interpretations often have a firm hold on their worldviews and behaviors. Alongside these deeply ingrained codes of personal behaviors, the government retains absolute control over all public order and policy in this generous welfare state.

Abu Dhabi now is leading a mission toward Emiratization, an effort both to recapture the nation from the professional expatriate workforce and to reaffirm Emirati national identity. Educational reforms, hiring quotas, and public image campaigns proliferate. Under the direction of the ruling Al Nayhan tribe, whose leader Sheikh Zayed bin Sultan Al Nahyan led the country for 38 years until his death in 2004, the Abu Dhabi government reinforces national identity through outdoor signage communicating UAE political heritage and its hierarchal paternalistic society that privileges the male.

The following examples of value-laden public signage are prominently displayed in central Abu Dhabi city. Figure 20.2, depicting the founding sheikhs at the old fort Al Hosn, appears on a barrier around the old fort currently undergoing renovation as a cultural center. In the same location are poetry and praise for the patrilineal succession of Abu Dhabi's rulers (Figure 20.3). Along the city's main road, a government building features portraits of current UAE rulers (Figure 20.4). In a

Figure 20.2 Al Hosn

Figure 20.3 Zayed Poetry

promotional campaign for the government-owned cable TV/Internet utility, Etisalat, an idealized Emirati son, appears in various poses (Figure 20.5, Figure 20.6). A bank displays a typical representation of the Emirati family: parents with son (Figure 20.7); and a rare representation of just the Emirati female—and son—is located in a city park (Figure 20.8).

Outdoor advertising surrounds the Souk situated in one of Abu Dhabi city's most historic commercial locations, once known as the Central Market and now branded as the World Trade Center Abu Dhabi. To illustrate how visual communication functions strategically in an applied situation, this article analyzes one of these public signs (Figure 20.9). Aldar Properties, an Arab real estate company founded and supported by the Abu Dhabi government, is developing this significant site that for many decades before oil was the one major trading area. This analysis considers the ideological meanings behind public images in the contexts of contemporary Abu Dhabi. It is a fast-emerging economy controlled by an autocratic ruling family. It has an indigenous population that is economically privileged yet dominated by tribal inequalities and suppression of women's rights. Abu Dhabi also lacks any tangible democratic developments: an elected parliament, voting rights, an open press, freedom of speech, or freedom to publically assemble.

Barthes suggests beginning by making explicit the meanings of apparently neutral objects and then moving on to consider the social and historical conditions they obscure. A defining feature of signs is that they 'stand for' or represent other things, so this analysis ultimately asks what concepts

Figure 20.4 UAE Rulers

Figure 20.5   Etisalat Ad One

Figure 20.6 Etisalat Ad Two

Figure 20.7   Bank Poster

the composition stands for. It is particularly useful to critically analyze photographic images in that they are typically judged to be the most 'realistic' of images. This realism helps to naturalize the underlying symbolic message. The following section considers the composition of the image through content and form, the possible relationships between the elements, and their associations with cultural/historical knowledge. It responds to the basic questions in semiotic analysis.

Visual Analysis

The Significance of Choosing This Image

This public sign (Figure 20.9) is placed in an important site of cultural heritage for Emiratis, the old Souk at the Central Market, which the government is refashioning into a global center for trade

Figure 20.8 Public Park Image

Figure 20.9 Souk Outdoor Ad

and tourism. Its display during site renovations allowed the signage to stand in place of the Souk for many months. It remains, now that the Souk is open. On the surface it is just an ad for the Souk, yet considering its content, considering it is government-sponsored communication, and considering the cultural gender norms in the UAE, its imagery suggests layers of possible meaning beyond mere retail promotion. Past research reveals advertising texts as decidedly visual expressions of culture and society, often having a superficial transparency that cloak persuasive suggestion (Messaris, 1996; A. A. Berger, 2008; Lester, 2011). Most ads feature a product, however there is no product here; rather, a female Emirati mystique appears to be the offer.

The Denoted Elements in the Sign (Literally What We See)

The elements include an attractive Emirati woman likely in her twenties wearing the traditional *sheilah* (black head cover), two Emirati men wearing the traditional *kandoura* (white body cover) and the *ghutra* headcloth, and one or two golden chandeliers. The color scheme is black, browns, whites, and gold. The background has vague architectural elements. There are no words.

What is Dominant?

The woman's eyes dominate the image, gazing toward the left of the image, in which the two men are standing, after which we notice her mouth that is full-lipped and slightly open. The Arabian woman's eyes are iconic for expressiveness because in very traditional dress, the *niqab* (face veil) reveals only the eyes (Figure 20.10).

Figure 20.10 Woman with Niqab

What is of Secondary Importance?

Of secondary importance are the two men—as the viewer follows her gaze to them. They both have their backs turned to her and appear to be outside, with sun shadows reflecting on their kandouras. She appears to be inside with a beaded curtain drawn back from her face.

What is the Significance of the Clothing?

Although a deeply stratified society, the UAE is visually homogenous due to a universal adoption of national dress. Along with the floor-length black *abayah* covering, Emirati women wear the sheilah to cover their hair and neckline. Both clothing items are often adorned with decorative embroidery, fabric, or jeweled trim to make a statement on personal style or wealth. Men wear a long neatly tailored white kandoura along with a ghutra and *ogal* (black rope) that secures it to the head. The ogal is purposefully iconic of the rope used to tie down a camel. This national dress was adopted by Emiratis to distinguish themselves from the many foreign Arabs living in the UAE 'after oil.' The dress is not traditional. Pre-oil, keeping this costume would have been impossible without running water, washing machines, irons, and so forth. Typical dress for men then came in browns and black. While the abayah did exist back then, women were hardly ever in public view so it was not worn frequently (Bristol-Rhys, 2010, pp. 111—112). Now, the abayah makes young women feel powerful—it represents wealth and commands respect and privileged service.

What are the Connoted Messages (Drawing from Common Cultural Knowledge to Decode or Unpack Values)?

The sheilah, kandouras, and ogals connote Emirati nationality, wealth, pride, and general Islamic values. Chandeliers connote luxury and elegance. The woman's sophisticated face suggests modernity. In fact, the magnification of the woman's face, commanding all other elements in the ad, also suggests privilege, importance, power, pride, and exposure, whereas the remote positioning of the men, with their faces turned away, connotes the unknown and unknowing, the detached and inaccessible. As simply an ad, it appears to indicate that women identify with the Souk; men, far less so.

Through form perspectives, distance is established between the men and the woman, yet her gaze is directed toward the left of the image, in which the two men are standing. She appears motionless, trapped in a moment of desire, hesitation, or anticipation? Moving about freely in public is often rigidly curtailed for many Emirati women from conservative families. In permissible situations (shopping or dining), she typically must be accompanied by a personal assistant or male relative. At the university, female students are segregated from males and must swipe ID cards in and out through security gates, leaving campus only when their drivers are waiting to chauffeur them home. She is very rarely in public alone. Here, she is.

While her motives remain unknown, she is the picture of a perfect Arabian princess, evoking the admiration of viewers. If this advertising is well targeted, it is deliberative and effective, and the Emirati female will see herself in the model. The aesthetic for young Emirati women is an ideal of luxury, beauty, stylishness, and modesty. It can be assumed then that young Emirati women may be attracted to and admire this female ideal. While she is not seen by the Emirati men appearing in the image, she is fully and intimately disclosed to all pedestrians and seems to have deliberately revealed herself (sweep of bead curtain) to be objectified by the viewer's gaze. As an ad exposed to all publics passing by, the many Westerners might understand the Souk as a place to see exotic Emiratis in their national costume. It also promises Western eyes a close *look* at the very private Emirati. Her representation functions as both a *reveal* and a lure into the Souk.

The black and brown-toned colors communicate 'Arabness,' yet due to their darkness and shadows, also a sense of mystery. While the colors are calming—in stark contrast to the restlessness of Abu Dhabi with its congested traffic and booming construction—the darkness combined with the imagery also suggests a tease of wariness. In this tension of unknowing, something is hidden, unrevealed, yet pulls the viewer toward some resolution. As an ad, it promises that the fulfillment and solution of the mystery is at the Souk, where the woman in the ad may satisfy her gaze on desirable and totally permissible material goods.

What Story does this Scene Suggest?

Without accompanying words, there is a dramatic tension in the image. Something significant must be coming. Curiosity is invoked, along with a desire for that Gestalt concept of *closure,* for the scene to be completed. The flawless beauty of the model has a powerful halo effect, helping to suggest a noble Emirati woman with a strong character. Her prominent eyes, the image's focal point, evoke clairvoyance. Yet this perfect being chooses to hide herself and her beauty from unknown men. The beaded curtain alludes to the Arabic word *hijab,* meaning curtain or cover: in wider definitions it refers to any type of modest dressing that covers the entire body except the face and hands while in public. The hijab also has a deeper meaning of privacy, morality and modesty in Islam. For young Emirati women, it is an affirmation of cultural expectations: to aspire toward a combination of modesty and morality with elegance, beauty, and 'stylish' tradition. In these, she is 'free' to *be.*

Does the Composition Evoke Any Other Images?

The staging of the photo evokes ads targeting women throughout various media products. The vast majority of the images of women found in Arab media (TV, movies, ads) are negative (Allam, 2008), mainly using their bodies "as sexual commodities or a vehicle for sexual arousal" (p. 3). Similar advertising in the Middle East sells fashion, makeup, or styling services through appeals to idealized self-image: beauty, boldness, desire, availability, and so forth. The images in other outdoor ads surrounding the Souk echo these appeals (Figures 20.11, 20.12, and 20.13). The text which accompanies the image in Figure 20.11 translates to "Center of Your World." The other two appear on the website for the World Trade Center Abu Dhabi alongside the words "enchanted" and "distinct". This series of Souk promotional photos also might evoke a scene from a television drama or music video, as advertising often relies on these popular culture frames of reference. These associations help invite the viewer to engage in the visual image to understand its message and take away its proposition.

Conclusion

Past scholarship recognizes that images of Arab women, sometimes controversial, sometimes liberating, frequently market the Middle East to the world—as well as influence native identity (Al Jenaibi, 2011; Gökariksel and McLarney, 2010; Allam, 2008). In present-day Abu Dhabi, where tradition is often contested by modernity, Islamic values mix with Western representations as Muslim identities are constructed through commodities and consumer capitalism, according to Gökariksel and McLarney (2010). The marketing of Arab images to reflect the territory as a welcoming and exotic tourist destination is common—and Arab women are central to this branding (Al Jenaibi, 2011). Like much Western advertising that fetishizes the female body (Reichert, 2003) and constructs women as consumers (Lancaster, 1995), ad images of woman in fast-evolving Abu Dhabi sometimes function on these levels, as shown here, but critical analysis uncovers more.

The Souk ad image (Figure 20.9), while on the surface a somewhat common, provocative appeal to multiple viewers, also carries a bipolar message to the Emirati woman. It challenges her to uncover her beauty, reveal her power, and unleash her desire to interact more freely with men and engage more boldly in society. However, taking into consideration the sum of its denotations

Figure 20.11   Center of Your World

Figure 20.12   Enchanted

and connotations, the overall proposition of the image reinforces the dominant culture of female suppression. The Emirati woman is honored for her femininity, beauty, respect for tradition, and staying 'in place.' It is stylish to be traditional. Modernity must be tempered by tradition. Figure 20.9 emphasizes the agency women have to make the culturally prescribed 'right' choice of covering,

Figure 20.13 Distinct

and to find self-actualization in their appearance and in material consumption. The Emirati woman personifies the Souk experience as one of luxury, mystery, intimacy, 'trendy' tradition, and freedom.

The ideological meaning establishes the Emirati woman as an object of beauty, mystique, and desire, with freedoms that fall within narrow societal norms. She may satisfy her needs at the new Souk. The representations in this sign legitimate the current power relationships in Emirati society that dictate women will dishonor their families if they uncover in public or socially interact with men outside their family. Yet the sign also tells of the paradox of modern times, when the government is promoting real opportunities for women to educate and infiltrate the workforce, while their families continue to frown on and even forbid change due to tribal traditions. With this deeper understanding of the cross-currents within the UAE today, we can judge this sign as possibly an attempt by the state to promote more liberal conditions for women, yet as it struggles with the ingrained tribal constraints, the 'safe' and acceptable (and economically valuable) message is for women to continue to locate themselves and their freedoms in the marketplace. Gökariksel and McLarney write, "a Muslim woman is constantly negotiated, defined and redefined through or in reaction to the images, narratives, and knowledges about Muslim womanhood constructed in the marketplace" (2010, p. 2).

Strategic visual communication lets culturally recognized frames work for it. If these frames work to influence, what ideology are they promoting in the process? This reading suggests the cultural meaning of outdoor ad signage in Abu Dhabi and how it constructs its audiences within specific contexts.

Although advertising's primary function is to sell, Williamson's (1978/1987) seminal study *Decoding Advertisements* asserts that ads also create structures of meaning in which they are selling us ourselves (p. 13). In an autocracy where legal and societal norms are interlinked with the fundamentals of Islam, the state-controlled communication that pervades the public sphere is designed to reinforce its ideology.

Semiotic analysis reveals that this particular public image communicates a strategic imposition of prescribed values into the collective national identity. While this chapter only presents the analysis of a single ad, the examples of other public signs support a highly visible and widely coordinated strategy of message enforcement. They function to legitimate and sustain the cultural identity of the marginalized female within a society of uneven power relationships. The analysis demonstrates the power of strategic communication in applied situations and underscores the need for visual literacy to critically decode pictorial messages and respond with acceptance, negotiation, or rejection.

References

Al Jenaibi, B. N. A. (2011). The changing representation of the Arab woman in Middle East advertising and media. *Global Media Journal, Arabian Edition, 1*(2), pp. 67–88.

Allam, R. (2008). Countering the negative image of Arab women in the Arab media: Toward a "Pan Arab Eye" media watch project. *The Middle East Institute Policy Brief, 15*, 1–8.

Barbatsis, G. (2005). Narrative theory. In K. Smith, S. Moriarty, G. Barbatsis, & K. Kinney (Eds.), *Handbook of visual communication: Theory, methods and media.* (pp. 329–349). Mahwah, NJ: Erlbaum.

Barnhurst, K. G., Vari, M., & Rodriguez, I. (2004). Mapping visual studies in communication. *Journal of Communication, 54,* 4, 616–644.

Barthes, R. (1972). *Mythologies.* Trans. by A. Lavers. New York: Hill and Wang.

Barthes, R. (1977). *Image, music, text.* (S. Heath, Trans.). New York, NY: Hill and Wang.

Barthes, R. (1983). *Rhetoric of the image.* Trans. by S. Heath. New York: Hill and Wang. (Original edition published 1967).

Berger, A. A. (2008). *Seeing is believing.* New York: McGraw-Hill.

Berger, J. (1972). *Ways of seeing.* London, England: BBC/Penguin.

Bristol-Rhys, J. (2010). *Emirati women: Generations of change.* London, England: Hurst & Company.

Brugioni, D. A. (1999). *Photo fakery: The history and techniques of photographic deception and manipulation.* Dulles, VA: Brassey.

Burgin, V. (1982). Photographic practice and art theory. In V. Burgin (Ed.), *Thinking photography* (pp. 39–83). London, England: Macmillan.

Chandler, D. (n.d.). Semiotics for beginners. Retrieved from http://www.aber.ac.uk/media/Documents/S4B/semiotic.html

Crary, J. (1992). *Techniques of the observer: On vision and modernity in the nineteenth century.* Cambridge, MA: MIT Press.

Eagleton, T. (1991). Ideology: An introduction. New York: Verso.

Gitlin, T. (2002). *Media unlimited: How the torrent of images and sounds overwhelms our lives.* New York: Metropolitan Books.

Gökariksel, B. & McLarney, E. (2010). Introduction: Muslim women, consumer capitalism, and the Islamic culture industry. *Journal of Middle East Women's Studies, 6,* 3, pp. 1–18.

Hallahan, K., Holtzhausen, D., van Ruler, B., Verčič, D., & Sriramesh, K. (2007). *Defining strategic communication. International Journal of Strategic Communication, 1*(1), 3–35.

Lancaster, B. (1995). *The department store: A social history.* London, England: Leicester University Press.

Langer, S.K. (1942). *Philosophy in a new key.* Cambridge, MA: Harvard University Press.

Leiss, W., S. Kline & S. Jhally. (1990). *Social communication in advertising: Persons, products and images of well-being* (2nd ed.). London, England: Routledge.

Lester, P. M. (2011). *Visual communication: Images with messages, 5th ed.* Boston, MA: Wadsworth.

Messaris, P. (1996). *Visual persuasion: The role of images in advertising.* Thousand Oaks, CA: Sage.

Mitchell, W.J.T. (1994). *Picture theory.* Chicago, IL: University of Chicago Press.

Reichert, T. (2003). *The erotic history of advertising.* Amherst, NY: Prometheus Books.

Sontag, S. (1977). *On photography.* New York: Picador.

Stein, S. (2001). Legitimating TV journalism in *60 Minutes:* The ramifications of subordinating the visual to the primacy of the word. *Critical Studies in Media Communication, 18,* 3, 249–269.

Williamson, J. (1987). *Decoding advertisements.* London, England: Marion Boyers. (Original work published 1978).

World Trade Center Abu Dhabi. http://www.wtcad.com/, accessed 1–21–2013.

Zakia, R. (2007). *Perception and imaging: Photography—a way of seeing* (3rd ed.). Burlington, MA: Focal Press.

21

Relationship Cultivation Strategies in Strategic Communication

Eyun-Jung Ki

Strategic communication is an organization's planned and purposeful communication aimed at achieving its goals. Public relations has been identified as a fundamental element of strategic communication (Hallahan, Holtzhausen, Van Ruler, Verčič, & Siramesh, 2007; Holtzhausen, 2008). Hallahan et al. (2007) specified that the field of public relations can play a part in the development of strategic communication by emphasizing developing theory to determine how an organization can "establish and maintain beneficial relationships with key constituencies" (p. 6). In the public relations scholarship, relationship management has been a primary paradigm since Ferguson's call in 1984 (Ferguson, 1984). This chapter will review the extent to which relationship cultivation strategies are relevant to the field of strategic communication and how this program of research can be applied beyond the publics in the public relations process.

Literature examining relationship management has highlighted the following three elements of organization–public relationships: antecedents of relationships, cultivation strategies, and relationship quality (Broom, Casey, & Ritchey, 1997; Hon & J. E. Grunig, 1999). An antecedent of a relationship represents the impetus for an organization and its public to establish a relationship. Cultivation strategies consist of the communication activities between an organization and its publics that can improve or prevent deterioration of the relationships. Relationship quality is the outcome of the relational interaction by both parties involved in the relationship.

Since evaluating relationship quality has been regarded as equivalent to measuring the effectiveness and value of public relations, scholars have devoted themselves to establishing reliable and valid measures of relationship quality outcomes (e.g., Bruning & Ledingham, 1999; Ferguson, 1984; L. A. Grunig, J. E. Grunig, & Ehling, 1992; Hon & J. E. Grunig, 1999; Huang, 1997, 2001; Jo, 2006; Ki & Hon, 2007; Y. Kim, 2001). Recently, the academic focus in relationship management has shifted from measuring relationship quality outcome to identifying and evaluating relationship cultivation strategies (Hung, 2004; Ki & Hon, 2009a, 2009b; Shen, 2011). This chapter attempts to integrate relationship cultivation strategies with the strategic communication process in order to attract both more scholarly and practical attention to these strategies, which can proactively improve the relationship quality outcomes.

Relationship Theory in Public Relations

Relationship cultivation strategies effectively fit into strategic communication due to several shared commonalities. First, strategic communication practice is deliberate and intentional as it attempts to achieve a certain outcome (Holtzhausen & Zerfass, 2013). Organizations utilize relationship cultivation strategies to gain better relational outcomes with their stakeholders. Second, one or more practitioners tend to partake in strategic communication or communication activities on behalf of a communicative entity (Holtzhausen & Zerfass, 2013). Multiple practitioners often apply relationship cultivation strategies on behalf of their organizations, which are called *communicative entities* in strategic communication. Finally, strategic communication occurs in the public sphere (Holtzhausen & Zerfass, 2013). As such, relationship cultivation strategies should also occur in the public sphere.

Relationship Cultivation Strategies

Although strategic communication theory prefers the broader term of stakeholders, the concept of *publics* stays relevant to this discussion because relationship cultivation theory has been developed in the context of public relations theory. Organizational research has demonstrated that any organization's behavior can affect the status of its relationship with its strategic publics. Organizations cannot simply maintain relationships with their publics, but should devote time and resources to improve their relationships and/or restore any damaged relationships. In order to properly cultivate relationships with their strategic publics or stakeholders, organizations can incorporate a variety of relationship cultivation strategies into their daily communication activities. In this respect, this chapter defines *relationship cultivation strategies* as organizational behavioral efforts to improve a relational condition with strategic publics or stakeholders.

Relationship cultivation strategies originated from theories of interpersonal relations, specifically romantic relationships (Canary & Stafford, 1994; Stafford, Dainton, & Hass, 2000). Public relations scholars (e.g., J. E. Grunig & Huang, 2000; Hon & J. E. Grunig, 1999) transformed the concept of relationship cultivation strategies in interpersonal communication and applied the strategies to organization–public relationships (OPRs). Relationship cultivation strategies are daily communication activities employed by an organization to improve the quality of its relationships with various publics or stakeholders and are often considered proactive approaches to fostering high quality relationships.

The most effective strategies, which have been identified to produce positive relationship outcomes, are *access, positivity, openness, sharing tasks, networking,* and *assurances* (J. E. Grunig & Huang, 2000; Hon & J. E. Grunig, 1999; Hung-Baesecke & Chen, 2013; Ki & Hon, 2006, 2009a). J. E. Grunig and Huang (2000) categorized these strategies as being symmetrical. Below is a brief description of each strategy.

Access

This strategy involves providing channels of communications for both sides of the relationship. Specifically, publics or representatives of publics offer communication avenues for public relations professionals, who provide similar levels of access to members of publics in order to share their opinions regarding an organization (J. E. Grunig & Huang, 2000; Hon & J. E. Grunig, 1999). Making individuals available to the other party, an organization and its publics can engage one another. Since relationship cultivation theory is considered organizational behavior, access strategy can be conceptualized as the attribute of organizational behavioral efforts that provide communication channels to help its strategic publics or stakeholders to reach an organization (Ki & Hon, 2009a).

With the development and popularity of advanced communication technologies, coupled with the use of traditional communication channels, an organization should consider providing more interactive communication channels as an access strategy.

Positivity

In interpersonal communication, positivity is often described as individuals' effort to maintain enjoyable interactions. Canary and Stafford (1994) provided examples of this strategy, such as joyful and affectionate behavior, polite communication, and avoiding criticism of the other. In the area of interpersonal relationships, this strategy is often regarded as a prerequisite to control mutuality and relational satisfaction, which are primary relationship quality outcomes indicators (Canary & Stafford, 1992, 1993; Dainton, 1991; Stafford & Canary, 1991).

In organization–public relationships, the concept of '*positivity*' is defined as "anything the organization or publics do to make the relationship more enjoyable for the parties involved" (Hon & J. E. Grunig, 1999, p. 14). They contend that positivity strategy can be effective for conflict resolution. A few examples of this strategy include offering encouraging feedback, joyful behaviors, polite communication, and avoiding criticism of the parties involved in the relationship.

Based on relationship cultivation strategy as an organizational behavior, positivity can be defined as "the degree to which strategic publics can benefit from the organization's efforts to make the relationship more enjoyable" (Ki & Hon, 2009a, p. 246).

Openness and disclosure

Scholars of interpersonal relationships have explained openness as the willingness to explicitly express and discuss feelings and opinions about a relationship (Canary & Stafford, 1994). In a romantic relationship, openness was found to have the least predictive power of relationship quality (Stafford & Canary, 1991).

This openness strategy was introduced into public relations scholarship as the expression of concerns and opinions among the parties involved in organization–public relationships (Hon & J. E. Grunig, 1999). While openness does not automatically contribute to a positive relationship, the party with more power should justify that any safeguarding of information is in the interest of the less powerful party (Bok, 1989). Scholars agree that openness is a predictor of relationship quality, including satisfaction (Ledingham & Bruning, 1998) and trust (Dimmick, Bell, Burgiss, & Ragsdale, 2000). Moreover, L. A. Grunig et al. (1992) demonstrated openness as being a fundamental component of a quality relationship. The study by Ki and Hon (2009a), however, demonstrated an insignificance of openness strategy and argued openness is a fundamental dimension of all relationship cultivation strategies. Based on the approach that considers relationship cultivation strategy as an attribute of organizational behavior, *openness* can be defined as "an organization's behavioral efforts to provide information about the nature of the organization and what it is doing that affects its strategic publics" (Ki & Hon, 2009a).

Sharing tasks

Scholars examining interpersonal relationships conceptualized sharing tasks as the distribution of routine tasks and equitable sharing of responsibilities (Canary & Stafford, 1994; Stafford & Canary, 1991). Sharing household chores is an example of this strategy in interpersonal relationships. Like other strategies, sharing tasks has been confirmed as a significant predictor of relationship quality, including control mutuality (Canary & Stafford, 1994) and satisfaction (Huston, McHale, & Crouter, 1986; Wilmot & Sillars, 1989).

In public relations scholarship, *sharing tasks* has been defined as a strategy through which an organization and its stakeholders all perform their relevant responsibilities to solve problems and address concerns, so that both parties are able to reach their interdependent goals (Hon & J. E. Grunig, 1999). Some examples of this strategy include working together to reduce pollution, supporting philanthropic efforts, providing employment opportunities, or remaining competitive (J. E. Grunig & Huang, 2000). These tasks might be of interest to either an organization or stakeholders or both parties. Because the idea of sharing tasks is similar to corporate social responsibility for an organization, this strategy can be evaluated through an organization's corporate social responsibility reports, which demonstrate the degree to which an organization has made an effort to work with its stakeholders to address issues or common concerns (Ki & Hon, 2009b).

As this chapter considers cultivation strategy as an organizational behavioral effort, sharing tasks can be conceptualized as "an organization's behavioral efforts to share in working on projects or solving problems of common interest between an organization and its strategic publics" (Ki & Hon, 2009a).

Networking

In interpersonal relationships, this strategy involves individuals' willingness to network common friends and affiliations to maintain relationships (Canary & Stafford, 1994). Networking has been determined to affect relationship quality outcomes such as control mutuality (Canary & Stafford, 1992, 1993; Stafford & Canary, 1991) and liking (Canary & Stafford, 1992, 1994).

Hon and J. E. Grunig (1999) expanded the concept of *networking strategy* to organization–public relationships and defined networking as an organization's willingness to form relationships with groups associated with its strategic publics, such as environmentalists, unions, or community groups. Networking in particular was found to be a catalyst in relationship-building in Asian countries such as China because it is a culture that emphasizes the importance of personal relationships (Hung, 2002).

Assurances

This strategy involves efforts between individuals to reinforce and reassure one another of the importance of their relationship and of each other (Canary & Stafford, 1994). This strategy was found to be the most important for promoting a commitment to relationship quality outcomes, and it is also a significant predictor of trust (Canary & Stafford, 1992, 1993; Stafford & Canary, 1991).

In organization–public relationships, *assurance* is defined as an effort to communicate how an organization values the relationship with its stakeholders (Hon & J. E. Grunig, 1999). L. A. Grunig, J. E. Grunig, and Dozier (2002) describe the importance of assurance thus: "each party in the relationship attempts to assure the other that it and its concerns are legitimate and to demonstrate that it is committed to maintaining the relationship" (p. 551). An organization can employ this strategy by communicating and demonstrating the extent to which it values its publics. Hung (2000) indicates that providing assurances can be effective as it influences satisfaction and commitment among the parties involved in the relationship. This strategy can be conceptualized as "an organization's effort to assure its strategic publics that they and their concerns are attended to" (Ki & Hon, 2009a).

Measures of Relationship Cultivation Strategies

As the focus of relationship management has shifted from the measurement of relationship quality outcomes to identifying relationship cultivation strategies, several scholars have attempted to establish a way to measure relationship cultivation strategies. Ki and Hon (2009b) conducted one of the first studies to develop a measure of relationship cultivation strategies based on the multiple scale development steps suggested by Spector (1992). They gathered the six cultivation strategies—*access, positivity, openness, sharing of tasks, networking,* and *assurances*—from the literature and conceptualized them based on organizational behavioral perspectives:

- *Access:* "the degree of effort that an organization puts into providing communication channels or media outlets that assist its strategic publics in reaching it."
- *Positivity:* "the degree to which members of publics benefit from the organization's efforts to make the relationship more enjoyable for key publics."
- *Openness:* "an organization's efforts to provide information about the nature of the organization and what it is doing."
- *Sharing of tasks:* "an organization's efforts to share in working on projects or solving problems of mutual interest between the organization and its publics"
- *Networking:* "the degree of an organization's effort to build networks or coalitions with the same groups that their publics do, such as environmentalists, unions, or community groups."
- *Assurances:* "any efforts by an organization to assure its strategic publics that they and their concerns are attended to."

Ki and Hon (2009b) drafted multiple initial items to measure each of the six strategies based on feedback from in-depth interviews with top public relations practitioners. Multiple steps were taken to improve the scale, and the final measure was evaluated by surveying a large number of organization members. They concluded that the scale was both reliable and valid.[1]

Recently, following examination of relationship cultivation strategies based on the two typologies—symmetrical and asymmetrical—Shen (2011) extended Ki and Hon (2009b)'s measure of relationship cultivation strategies in an organization–employee context. She discovered that a six-factor measurement model could act as a meaningful representation of organizations' relationship cultivation efforts for their employees. The six effective strategies include *openness*, *assurances of legitimacy*, *networking*, *distributive negotiation*, *avoiding*, and *compromising*. These two studies contribute to theoretical and operational development in the area of relationship management research, specifically relationship cultivation strategies.

Application of Relationship Cultivation Strategies

Only a handful of studies have examined relationship cultivation strategies across diverse relationship types, and these studies have added new cultivation strategies. Ki and Hon (2009a) applied the six relationship cultivation strategies to the relationships between a membership organization and its members. They found the four relationship cultivation strategies—access, positivity, sharing of tasks, and assurances—to be significant predictors of relationship quality outcomes. However, the other two strategies, openness and networking, did not significantly influence any of the relationship outcomes in the context of membership organization. Waters (2009) applied the six relationship cultivation strategies to relationships between nonprofit organizations and donors and stressed that cultivation strategies play an essential role in fundraising success. Bortree (2010) investigated relationship cultivation strategies in the context of non-profit organizations and adolescent volunteers. She added *guidance* as a new cultivation strategy, specifically as it applied to adolescent volunteers, and concluded that guidance, assurances, and shared tasks are key predictors of relationship quality outcomes in the context of relationships between adolescent volunteers and a non-profit organization.

Discussion and Research Agendas

This chapter introduces and summarizes the effect of relationship cultivation strategies on relationship outcomes. As relationship cultivation strategies have started to gain attention, this area of research offers many opportunities. First, the strategies should be applied to more diverse contexts to determine if they effectively influence relationship outcomes. Specifically, relationship cultivation strategies were primarily examined in the context of non-profit organizations (Bortree, 2010; Waters, 2009) and membership organizations (Ki & Hon, 2009a). Therefore, scholars may consider developing a measure of relationship cultivation strategies to fit other types of organizations such as healthcare organizations, governmental organizations, corporations, and other types of contexts, such as marketing, advertising, health communication and political campaigns, to mention but a few. Specifically, as the majority of business is profit-driven, the consumer is the most important stakeholder in that regard. The importance of positive relationships has continuously been confirmed in organization–consumer relationships (Bach & S. Kim, 2012; Hong & Yang, 2009). For example, Hong and Yang (2009) tested the link between relationship quality and word-of-mouth intention and affirmed that customer satisfaction levels serve as a good predictor of positive word-of-mouth intentions. Although these studies are meaningful for learning the importance of quality relationship formation between an organization and its customer stakeholder group, it is difficult to understand specific tactics or strategies that foster quality relationships. Therefore, scholarly attention is necessary in order to identify relationship cultivation strategies within organizational contexts, which have not yet been effectively examined. More importantly, scholars should test if the measure is an effective evaluation of relationship outcome across the various environments in order to ultimately assess a more general measure of cultivation strategies.

Second, the aforementioned studies primarily applied relationship cultivation strategies in an offline setting. Rapidly growing social media is an essential organizational communication channel today and it can be employed to increase strategic communication efficiencies. Relationship cultivation strategies should be explored in the context of new communication platforms to understand and evaluate their effectiveness. Scholars have primarily applied a theoretical framework designed by Kent and Taylor (1998) as a guide for relationship building in online settings. They introduced five relationship cultivation strategies: dialogic loop, usefulness of information, generation of return visits, intuitiveness/ease of the interface, and the rule of conservation of visitors. In follow-up research (Kent & Taylor, 2002), they highlighted the dialogic approach as an ethical relationship management method and expanded the strategies by adding features such as mutuality, propinquity, empathy, risk, and commitment. Recently, Men and Tsai (2012) explored relationship cultivation strategies on social media platforms from a cross-cultural perspective by applying Kent and Taylor's theoretical framework. They examined the ways organizations use social network sites to communicate with stakeholders in two culturally different countries—China and the United States. Men and Tsai (2012) discovered that organizations in both countries frequently use the dialogic strategies of disclosure, information dissemination, and interactivity. Although it is natural to apply a theoretical framework specifically designed for online environments in order to identify effective relationship cultivation strategies in online settings, it is necessary to test various strategies to determine which of those are most appropriate and effective. Hopefully, this chapter will guide and inspire further scholarly efforts to refine the existing strategies and identify more effective and strategic ways of communicating with stakeholders in online contexts.

Third, given the importance of global public relations, it is necessary to consider culture as an important variable in cultivating relationships with these foreign publics or stakeholder groups. While effective public relations practices may share universal principles, they are not immune from the impacts of politics, media, economic development and cultural values (Verčič, J. E. Grunig, & L. A. Grunig, 1996). Typology of *high-* and *low-context* cultures by E. T. Hall (1989) has been applied as a useful approach in order to explain the differences between Western and Eastern countries (H. Kim, Coyle, & Gould, 2009). In E. T. Hall's (1989) typology, context is the situational information that one needs in order to understand the meaning of an event or subject, and cultures can be categorized into either high and low based on the extent to which context is necessary for such understanding. In high-context situations, "most of the information is already in the person, while very little is in the coded, explicit, transmitted part of the message," while low-context situations involve "just the opposite, i.e., the mass of the information is vested in the explicit code" (E. T. Hall & M. R. Hall, 1990, p. 8). Thus, high and low contexts act as an important variable for considering the development of effective relationship cultivation strategies for foreign publics. For example, because Western culture is known to be high-context according to Hall (1989), public relations messages geared toward this audience should be developed in clear and explicit ways. Relationship cultivation strategies have been applied to an Asian context, and *personal networking* was often found to be a key strategy (Hung, 2002, 2004). Future research should explore ways to cultivate relationships with publics in other unexplored countries while considering cultural and situational variables.

Fourth, different *types of publics* should be considered to develop more effective relationship cultivation strategies. Ni and Kim (2009) organized types of publics based on a framework of communicative action in problem solving (CAPS) and characteristics of problem solving among publics. They predicted and confirmed that the three different problem-solving characteristics—*openness to approaches* in problem solving, *the extent of activeness* in problem solving, and *the time or history* of problem solving—explain the features of communication behaviors of publics, such as transmitting or selecting information. Moreover, Ni and Kim (2009) noted the publics' perceptions about the given problems or situations might explain the communication process. Scholars may need to consider this new classification of segmented publics established by Ni and Kim (2009) whose aim was to find more effective way of communication with these publics and to develop more specific relationship cultivation strategies.

Fifth, relationship cultivation strategies might influence or be affected by types of relationships. Hung (2005) identifies seven relationship types: covenantal relationships,[2] symbiotic relationships[3], communal relationships,[4] exchange relationships, contractual relationships[5], manipulative relationships[6] and exploitive relationships.[7] The extent to which each relationship cultivation strategy might be applied would depend on the type of relationship an organization has with its stakeholders. For example, an organization that practices the manipulative relationship type would probably be less likely to prioritize the openness strategy.

Last, the three elements—relationship antecedents, cultivation strategies, and relationship outcomes—are suggested as essential components in the organization–public relationship literature (Broom, Casey, & Ritchey, 2000). This chapter only addresses the element of relationship cultivation strategies. Therefore, scholars might consider applying all three of the components in diverse settings in order to empirically document evidence of the linkages among these three elements.

Strategic communication is planned and purposive communication in which a communication agent participates with the aim of achieving an organization's goal (Holtzhausen & Zerfass, 2013). Such goals may include, but are not limited to, winning market share, winning a political campaign, building a positive reputation, and influencing social change. In many situations, organizational goals can be more effectively reached by fostering favorable relationships between the organizations and their strategic publics or stakeholders. To develop a favorable and healthy relationship with stakeholders, an organization should apply effective relationship cultivation strategies. Hopefully this chapter will attract greater scholarly and practical attention to the development and testing of these strategies.

Notes

1 To see a complete measure of relationship cultivation strategies, please refer to Ki & Hon (2009b).
2 A covenantal relationship is one in which both parties make a commitment to a common good through their open exchanges and the norm of reciprocity (Hung, 2005, p. 398).
3 The symbiotic relationship is an interdependent relationship, in which both parties need to work together to coexist (Hung, 2005, p. 416).
4 A communal relationship incorporates the concern that one party has regarding the other's welfare, whereas an exchange relationship depends upon economic exchanges (Clark & Mills, 1979 cited in Hung, 2005).
5 Hung (2005) explains that contractual relationships begin when the parties make an agreement about what each should do in the relationship. This type of relationship is not necessarily an equal one.
6 A manipulative relationship occurs when a party asserts power to obtain what she or he wants through an asymmetrical communication approach (Hung, 2005).
7 Exploitive relationships occur when one party in a relationship takes advantage of the other, or when one party does not fulfill his or her obligations or responsibilities in the relationship (Clark & Mills, 1993, cited in Hung, 2005).

References

Bach, S. B., & Kim, S. (2012). Online consumer complaint behaviors: The dynamics of service failures, consumers' word of mouth, and organization-consumer relationships. *International Journal of Strategic Communication, 6,* 59–76.

Bok, S. (1989). *Secrets-on the ethics of concealment and revelation.* New York: Vintage Books.

Bortree, D. S. (2010). Exploring adolescent-organization relationships: A study of effective relationship strategies with adolescent volunteers. *Journal of Public Relations Research, 22*(1), 1–25.

Broom, G. M., Casey, S., & Ritchey, J. (1997). Toward a concept and theory of organization-public relationships. *Journal of Public Relations Research, 9*(2), 83–98.

Broom, G. M., Casey, S., & Ritchey, J. (2000). Toward a concept and theory of organization-public relationships: An update. In J. A. Ledingham & S. D. Bruning (Eds.), *Public relations as relationship management: A relational approach to public relations* (pp. 3–22). Mahwah, NJ: LEA.

Bruning, S. D., & Ledingham, J. A. (1999). Relationships between organizations and publics: Development of a multi-dimensional organization-public relationship scale. *Public Relations Review, 25*, 157–170.

Canary, D. J., & Stafford, L. (1992). Relational maintenance strategies and equity in marriage. *Communication Monographs, 59*, 239–267.

Canary, D. J., & Stafford, L. (1993). Preservation of relational characteristics: Maintenance strategies, equity, and locus of control. In P. J. Kalbfleisch (Ed.), *Interpersonal communication: Evolving interpersonal relationships* (pp. 237–259). Hillsdale, NJ: Erlbaum.

Canary, D. J., & Stafford, L. (1994). Maintaining relationships through strategic and routine interaction. In D. J. Canary & L. Stafford (Eds.), *Communication and relational maintenance* (pp. 3–22). San Diego, California: Academic Press.

Clark, M. S., & Mills, J. (1979). Interpersonal attraction in exchange and communal relationships. *Journal of Personality and Social Psychology, 37*, 12–24.

Clark, M. S., & Mills, J. (1993). The difference between communal and exchange relationships: What it is and is not. *Personality and Social Psychology Bulletin, 19*, 684–691.

Dainton, M. (1991, May). *Relational maintenance revisited: The addition of physical affection measures to a maintenance typology.* Paper presented at the meeting of International Communication Association, Chicago, IL.

Dimmick, S. L., Bell, T. E., Burgiss, S. G., & Ragsdale, C. (2000). Relationship management: A new professional model. In J. A. Ledingham & S. D. Bruning (Eds.), *Public relations as relationship management: A relational approach to the study and practice of public relations* (pp. 117–136). Mahwah, NJ: Erlbaum.

Ferguson, M. A. (1984). *Building theory in public relations: Interorganizational relationships.* Paper presented at the meeting of Association for Education in Journalism and Mass Communication, Gainesville, FL.

Grunig, J. E., & Huang, Y.-H. (2000). From organizational effectiveness to relationship indicators: Antecedents of relationships, public relations strategies, and relationship outcomes. In J. A. Ledingham & S. D. Bruning (Eds.), *Public relations as relationship management: A relational approach to the study and practice of public relations* (pp. 23–53). Mahwah, NJ: Erlbaum.

Grunig, L. A., Grunig, J. E., & Dozier, D. M. (2002). *Excellent public relations and effective organizations: A study of communication management in three countries.* Mahwah, NJ: Lawrence Erlbaum.

Grunig, L. A., Grunig, J. E., & Ehling, W. P. (1992). What is an effective organization? In J. E. Grunig, D. M. Dozier, W. P. Ehling, L. A. Grunig, F. C. Repper & J. White (Eds.), *Excellence in public relations and communication management* (pp. 65–90). Hillsdale, NJ: Lawrence Erlbaum.

Hall, E. T. (1989). *Beyond culture.* New York: Anchor Books/Doubleday.

Hall, E. T. & Hall, M. R. (1990). *Hidden differences.* New York: Anchor Books/Doubleday.

Hallahan, K., Holtzhausen, D., van Ruler, B., Verčič, D., & Siramesh, K. (2007). Defining strategic communication. *International Journal of Strategic Communication, 1*(1), 3–35.

Holtzhausen, D. R. (2008). Strategic communication. In W. Donsbach (Ed.), *The international encyclopedia of communication.* Malden, MA: Wiley-Blackwell.

Holtzhausen, D. R., & Zerfass, A. (Eds.). (2013). *Strategic Communication—Pillars and Perspectives of an Alternative Paradigm.* Wiesbaden, Germany: Springer VS.

Hon, L. C., & Grunig, J. E. (1999). *Guidelines for measuring relationships in public relations.* Gainesville, FL: Institution for Public Relations.

Hong, S. Y., & Yang, S.U. (2009). Effects of reputation, relational satisfaction, and customer–company identification on positive word-of-mouth intentions. *Journal of Public Relations Research, 21*(4), 381–403.

Huang, Y. H. (1997). *Public relations strategies, relational outcomes, and conflict management strategies.* Unpublished doctoral dissertation, University of Maryland, College Park, MD.

Huang, Y. H. (2001). OPRA: A cross-cultural, multiple-item scale for measuring organization-public relationships. *Journal of Public Relations Research, 13*, 61–90.

Hung, C. J. F. (2000). *Organization-public relationships, relationship maintenance strategies, and relationship outcomes.* March. Paper presented at the Educator's Academy, Public Relations Society of America, Miami, FL.

Hung, C. J. F. (2002). Relationship types, relationship cultivation strategies, and relationship outcomes: How multinational and Taiwanese companies practice public relations and relationship management in China. Unpublished doctoral dissertation, University of Maryland, College Park.

Hung, C. J. F. (2004). Cultural influence on relationship cultivation strategies: Multinational companies in China. *Journal of Communication Management, 8*(3), 264–281.

Hung, C. J. F. (2005). Exploring types of organization-public relationships and their implications for relationship management in public relations. *Journal of Public Relations Research, 17*, 393–425.

Hung-Baesecke, C.-j. F., & Chen, Y.-R. R. (in press). Factoring Culture into relationship management theory: Cultivation strategies and traditional Chinese value orientations. In E.-J. Ki, J.-N. Kim & J. Ledingham (2nd Eds.), *Public relations as relationship management: A relational approach to the study and practice of public relations.* New York: Routledge.

Huston, T. L., McHale, S., & Crouter, A. (1986). When the honeymoon's over: Changes in the marriage relationship over the first year. In R. Gilmour & S. Duck (Eds.), *The emerging field of personal relationships* (pp. 109–132). Hillsdale, NJ: Erlbaum.

Jo, S. (2006). Measurement of organization-public relationships: Validation of measurement using a manufacturer-retailer relationship. *Journal of Public Relations Research, 18*(3), 225–248.

Kent, M. L., & Taylor, M. (1998). Building dialogic relationships through the world wide web. *Public Relations Review, 24,* 321–334.

Kent, M. L., & Taylor, M. (2002). Toward a dialogic theory of public relations. *Public Relations Review, 28,* 21–37.

Ki, E. J., & Hon, L. C. (2006). Relationship maintenance strategies on Fortune 500 company web sites. *Journal of Communication Management, 10*(1), 27–43.

Ki, E. J., & Hon, L. C. (2007). Validation of relationship quality outcome measurement. *Journalism & Mass Communication Quarterly, 84*(3), 419–438.

Ki, E. J., & Hon, L. C. (2009a). The causal linkages between/among relationship cultivation strategies and relationship quality outcomes. *International Journal of Strategic Communication, 3*(4), 242–263.

Ki, E. J., & Hon, L. C. (2009b). A measure of relationship cultivation strategies. *Journal of Public Relations Research, 21,* 1–24.

Kim, H., Coyle, J. R. & Gould, S. J. (2009). Collectivist and individualist influences on website design in South Korea and the U.S.: A cross-cultural content analysis. *Journal of Computer-Mediated Communication,* 14(3), 581–601.

Kim, Y. (2001). Searching for the organization-public relationship: A valid and reliable instrument. *Journalism and Mass Communication Quarterly, 78,* 799–815.

Ledingham, J. A., & Bruning, S. D. (1998). Relationship management in public relations: Dimensions of an organization-public relationship. *Public Relations Review, 24,* 55–65.

Men, L. R., & Tsai, W. H. S. (2012). How companies cultivate relationships with publics on social network sites: Evidence from China and the United States. *Public Relations Review, 38*(5), 723–730.

Ni, L., & Kim, J. N. (2009). Classifying publics: Communication behaviors and problem-solving characteristics in controversial issues. *International Journal of Strategic Communication, 3*(4), 1–25.

Shen, H. (2011). Organization-employee relationship maintenance strategies: A new measuring instrument. *Journalism & Mass Communication Quarterly, 88*(2), 398–415.

Spector, P. E. (1992). *Summated rating scales construction: An introduction.* Newbury Park, CA: Sage.r

Stafford, L., & Canary, D. J. (1991). Maintenance strategies and romantic relationship type, gender, and relational characteristics. *Journal of Social and Personal Relationships, 8,* 217–242.

Stafford, L., Dainton, M., & Hass, S. (2000). Measuring routine and strategic relational maintenance: Scale development, sex versus gender roles, and the prediction of relational characteristics. *Communication Monographs, 67,* 306–323.

Verčič, D., Grunig, J. E. & Grunig, L. A. (1996). Global and specific principles of public relations: Evidence from Slovenia. In H. Culbertson, & N. Chen (Eds.), *International public relations: A comparative analysis* (pp. 31–65). Mahwah, NJ: Erlbaum.

Waters, R. D. (2009). The importance of Understanding Donor Preference and Relationship Cultivation Strategies. *Journal of Nonprofit & Public Sector Marketing, 21,* 327–346.

Wilmot, W. W., & Sillars, A. L. (1989). Developmental issues in personal relationships. In J. F. Nussbaum (Ed.), *Life-span communication: Normative process* (pp. 119–135). Hillsdale, NJ: Lawrence Erlbaum.

22

Strategic Communication in Participatory Culture

From One- and Two-Way Communication to Participatory Communication Through Social Media

Jesper Falkheimer and Mats Heide

In contemporary literature in strategic communication, public relations, and corporate communication, co-creation of meaning is often claimed to be a core objective (e.g., Coombs & Heath, 2006). The aim of this chapter is to review the literature on social media and strategic communication and develop arguments for why we believe the new communication structure is challenging old concepts and perspectives. The chapter discusses social media as technologies woven into a social and cultural communication structure, defined through participatory communication. It also addresses some of the challenges, opportunities, threats and changed practices that an organization's approach to participatory communication, through use of social media, can cause. The chapter is, as mentioned, a literature review and it also contains a conceptual analysis, using different examples. The theoretical approach is to a certain extent founded in the cocreational tradition, but it follows a social constructionist perspective where communication is viewed as constitutive of reality. This approach may be interpreted as a current example of a paradigm struggle, forecast by Botan and Taylor (2004, p. 659):

> We expect the period starting in the early 2000s and extending into the next decade to be characterized by a paradigm struggle away from symmetrical research. The future state of the field of public relations lies with whichever cocreationist model emerges as the most useful, the most theoretically valuable, and perhaps, the one that situates public relations theory as a foundational member of the field of communication.

From a contextual and societal level our perspective is linked to the postmodern critique of public relations theory (Holtzhausen, 2012), where strategic communication is viewed as a more relevant concept than public relations for understanding the transboundary communication processes taking place in contemporary liquid organizations and society.

Pointing to great change and its consequences are quite risky. On the one hand, such attempts may lead to simplification of history. On the other hand, there are reasons for research to point to contemporary trends and change when they have the support of theory and empirical research. Discussion of new and social media is a good example of how difficult the distinction is. From a historical perspective, all media were new at some point and it is possible to see media development as a long and continuous development process. While one can argue that technology itself is quite unexciting, what is interesting is how the forms of communication, that is, how we create common meaning, are reformed or renewed. In the popular context consultants and analysts tell us about how the new media have transformed our entire social, cultural, political and economic communications structure over the past few years. This is undoubtedly a grave simplification. We believe it may be true that the new media, and forms of communication they provide, may be interpreted as a paradigm shift, but note that this is something that happens over a long period of time.

Paradigm shift is a difficult and grandiose concept. When it was launched in the philosophy of science (Kuhn, 1962) it led to much debate. Put simply, as Kuhn stated, the paradigm denotes the dominant approach to what is considered as normal during a certain era—or the pattern of science within which scientists subsume themselves. Discrepancies or anomalies emerge gradually and if they get enough support there is a scientific revolution. Kuhn's perspective is grand, approaches centuries rather than decades, and focuses primarily on natural science. But it is possible to translate the paradigm theory also to the history of communications. In strategic communication research, which has a relatively short history, it may be difficult to analyze the trend in the field, but there is reason to believe that in recent decades a possible paradigm shift and new pattern in scientific thought is emerging. This new pattern is forming in conjunction with practice, since strategic communication as a research field is based on studies of a practice.

In this chapter we aim to describe how technological innovation interacts with social and communication forms, without resorting to technological determinism. Initially we discuss the historical context, and then we embody what new forms of communication are emerging. Next, we discuss participatory orientation as the most important feature of the new forms of communication and link this with examples from corporate branding, the media industry, and strategic communication. We also summarize past and current research on new media and strategic communication.

The Third Industrial Revolution

From a historical perspective, the emergence of new media is seen as a development of the third industrial revolution, which can be linked to the breakthrough development of the micro-electronics or micro-processor, which took place in the 1970s. This is in accordance with the analysis of the economic historian Schön (2006), who highlighted three industrial revolutions in the development of modern society. The first revolution was connected to the steam turbine, and the second revolution to the electric motor and combustion engine. The three revolutions have led to innovations in technology and organization, and have had implications for all areas of society.

Within social theory the division above is usually described as the development phases of modernity, beginning with the specific characteristics of the Enlightenment in the 1700s, which encompassed the first industrial revolution. The Enlightenment characteristics of rationality, individualism, mechanization, progress, and science are taking new forms in postmodern or late modern thinking. There are social scientists who believe that we now live in late modernity, characterized by risk, networks, globalization, media saturation and increased uncertainty (Bauman, 2000). There are also those who argue that our contemporary modernity can be seen as a break with the previous form of society and that we have entered a postmodern society where truth and reason are no longer relevant, but instead highlight increasing relativism and the crisis of modern values and authorities. In this postmodern world there is no longer any link between the existing world and the symbols that represent it; instead we find ourselves in a hyper-reality where the characters communicate with each other and create an imaginary reality (Baudrillard, 1988).

Strategic communication as a research field or practice cannot be isolated from this historical and social theoretical context, but should be viewed both as a contributing force and a consequence of the development. In a historical sense strategic communication grew as a practice parallel to the second industrial revolution, as a tool to manage the new relationships that emerged between organizations and society. Conflicts between different organizations and groups created a need for professionals who could handle them, not least in relation to the increasingly independent media. The same trend was creating a need for theories on organizations' internal communication, as relations between management and employees were becoming more complex and sometimes conflicting. This trend gained momentum mainly in the United States while many European countries, including Sweden, put more emphasis on the need for agencies to inform or enlighten their surroundings. Despite differences between the U.S. and Europe, the basic purpose was quite similar. It was about building consensus among organizations, their employees, and various external stakeholders, primarily in order to legitimate those organizations. A pioneer of public relations, Edward Bernays (1955), termed this mission as the *engineering of consent*. Bernays, who had an elitist view of the general public, meant that the general public was irrational, and for this reason propaganda was needed to manage public opinion. Paradoxically, Bernays also believed that the primary purpose of propaganda was to defend democracy. Although Bernays's approach to the public or those whom he did not count as society's elite was extreme, there are similarities with the approach that dominated strategic communications during this period. Strategic communicators considered the masses as passive recipients of messages, not as participants in the communication process.

From Centralization to Decentralization

During the 1900s a solid communication structure was established with professional owners of media technology, centralized communication organizations, and professional communicators, such as public relations or communication officers, journalists, graphic designers, and advertising professionals. Research and education were established in different times in different nations, but in most cases communication theories gathered from previous research on mass communication were used. *Transmitter, receiver, feedback* and *target* were concepts that dominated, all in accordance with the forms of communication made possible by the second industrial revolution.

From the 1960s, oppositional expressions toward the dominant social order became common in society and journalism also became more professionalized. It became increasingly clear that the communication professional had one main purpose: to create, strengthen or defend the legitimacy of organizations both internally in relations between management and employees and externally to various stakeholders. The power of media technology and distribution were, however, still in the hands of the professionals. When the personal computer became popular in the 1980s the tools for creating information became more accessible to ordinary people. Now everyone could design his or her own magazine or brochure. Internet penetration in the 1990s and its development during the 2000s challenged the communication infrastructure and power distribution. Decentralized networks disseminated through new technologies to a wider audience challenged the established ownership of media technologies and former professional communicators were joined by everyone who wanted to communicate to a wider group of people: "[A]nyone in the developed world can publish anything anytime, and the instant it is published, it is globally available and readily findable" (Shirky, 2009, p. 71). The 1990s were marked by the question whether state or market actors would have responsibility for different tasks in society. The new technologies have created new opportunities for collective organization beyond the established players and organizations, Shirky argued.

In the same vein, Jenkins (2006) pointed to three key characteristics of the new communications structure, which all have high relevance for strategic communication. First, he noted that we live in a convergent media culture, where old and new media interact and new forms of communication open up. The forms and genres that were established during the modern era are still here, but are influenced and are slowly being changed by new media. Limit overrun occurs in all areas: private confluences with public ones, entertainment with information; media move into each other (see, for example, how newspapers have brought out iPad versions). Second, Jenkins pointed to the emergence of participatory culture. This culture follows the collapse of the one-way communication culture. Through the new media direct feedback is made possible and collective processes are set in motion beyond the domains of professional actors. In future, strategic communication between organizations and stakeholders will be less relevant to how common meaning is created and will be comparable with the communication that takes place between stakeholders, that is, between participant to participant. Third, the developments strengthen the creation of collective intelligence: problems are resolved through communication with various partners who contribute different parts to a whole. One question in a digital network gets answers from different people, and gradually an answer or a discussion is created.

Convergence, participatory culture and collective intelligence are all highly relevant for contemporary and future strategic communications. Basically, this challenges traditional power relations between management and employees and between organizations and its stakeholders.

Participatory Strategic Communications

The reverse communication structure that is emerging, in which the roles of transmitter and receiver becomes less clear, challenges the boundaries between strategic communication and marketing, particularly branding. In their research on corporate branding, Hatch and Schultz (2009, 2010) tried to apply a participatory approach. The catchword in their studies is co-creation, a concept collected from research in product innovation. The leading innovation researchers Prahalad and Krishnan (2008) described the value of co-creation, based on both participatory orientation and an individual focus:

> The way in which the principle N = 1 goes beyond mass customization is that it is about understanding the behavior, needs, and skills of individual customers and co-creating with them a value proposition that is unique to them. Customers play an active role in co-creating value, and firms leverage a broader resource base to deliver value.
>
> *p. 27*

A first, fairly trivial, but clear example of participatory orientation is the Build-A-Bear toy stores (www.buildabear.dk) where children themselves may determine how their teddy bear should look. They co-create the product and thereby increase its value to themselves.

Another example is the art exhibition "The Fifth Floor: Ideas Taking Place" at Tate Modern in Liverpool during 2008. Traditionally exhibitions are planned inside and out; experts come together and decide what the audience should take part in. This time the museum chose to send out artists and art educators to schools, clubs, workplaces and other places in the city. Nearly 1,000 people were asked the question: If you had the chance to put on an exhibition at Tate Liverpool, what would you do? The next step was to invite 12 international artists or artist groups to process all the ideas. The exhibition program was a success and drew a large crowd of visitors, many of whom had not previously been in an art museum (Kultur Skåne, 2009).

A third example can be gathered from the newspaper industry, which is doing everything it can to create new forms of participation from readers and establish itself as a necessary actor in the new structure. So far this has mainly entailed opportunities to write comments after news articles, and readers' blogs, photos, and reports from the scene of action. A Swedish study (Hedman, 2009) showed that the players behind the online magazine publishers were convinced that the importance of user-created content would increase each year. The reasons for investing in user-created content were twofold, they concluded: first, the belief that it increased the loyalty of users, and second, the belief that the material attracted new readers. The same study also noted that there were problems with opening the content creation of online magazines to all readers because they might lack an understanding of media ethics and legal constraints. Reader comments tended to be rather extreme and polarized.

Within marketing, there are historical examples of how users are getting involved. When it comes to product innovation, consumers have increasingly been given an important role to play. Traditional market research survives but is supplemented with qualitative participation in the actual innovation processes. Hatch and Schultz (2009, 2010) studied the LEGO Group in Denmark. This privately owned company, founded in 1932, had major problems in the market at the beginning of the 2000s. Since then the company has undergone a renaissance, based on clear participatory orientation. LEGO Group bases its business on a corporate brand platform and cherishes transparency. What has happened is that the company has gone from

> [p]olitely responding to customers' letters of gratitude and complaints, to finding themselves in need of a more public response to enthusiastic consumers who, within hours of its launch on the website, hacked into the software that runs mindstorms, the company's highly successful robotics product.
>
> *Hatch & Schultz, 2010, p. 596*

The self-interest groups around Lego have been invited to participate in various events and their ideas for new products are taken seriously in the production process. The company also introduced the LEGO Ambassador Program, which each year invites Lego enthusiasts from all over the world to participate in the innovation process.

Social Media and Strategic Communication

Social media is widely used by people to expand human knowledge and to find information. As mentioned earlier, Jenkins (2006, p. 4) emphasized that collective intelligence is created and made possible with the help of social media: "[N]one of us can know everything; each of us knows something; and we can put the pieces together if we pool our resources and combine our skills." A typical example is when people interact through social media to ask questions and get answers from others. In other words, social media provides a new way of communicating that is intimately associated with their interactive elements. The major breakthrough of social media has led to talk of a new media revolution (e.g. Cooke & Buckley, 2008). Cooke and Buckley have identified factors that explain the social importance of the media. First, there is the emergence of *user-generated content* that blurs the traditional boundaries between professional and user-produced content. Second, the use of social media is based on how users themselves *retrieve the information* they are interested in, instead of information being pushed out to different audiences through traditional media. Third, users have the freedom to *produce their own story*. For example, viewers can choose the images or videos they want to see on Flickr and YouTube. Social media offers micro parts that consumers can use and put together to form their own narrative, rather than being limited to the only composition and narrative that a publisher dictates. Fourth, the *social interactions* that are developed around the content are a key to understanding the importance of user-generated content. Many interactions arise through users' abilities to rate, comment and review, and these opportunities can also be seen as important keys to social media success. Cooke and Buckley described social media as a media revolution that has had and will have significant impact on how people act, think and understand our age:

> In short, we are witnessing the emergence of a population that is ever more willing to record, and share, their experiences: mash them up and submit them to their friends and other community members for evaluation, and allow their 'reputations' to be built via these assessments.
>
> *2008, p. 274*

In a similar fashion, Hart (2011) proposed five roughly defined attributes of social media: authenticity, transparency, emphasis on a decentralization of authority, rapid and consistent release of information, and engagement of users in a collaborative effort. This means that if organizations were to take full advantage of social media, they would have to engage in genuine two-way communication with different stakeholders and not use social media as an additional venue for one-way information delivery. Stakeholders would instantly recognize standardized responses, and leave the platform. Hart argued that social media users expect organizations they follow or communicate with to be transparent. Social media also give possibilities for decentralizing communication responsibility, meaning increasing communication between groups and individuals on a horizontal level inside and outside an organization, instead of traditional top-down communication. While social media offers possibilities to maintain relationships with different stakeholders, it also makes it easier to quickly respond with information in different situations, for example during a crisis. Finally, organizations that put a lot of energy into maintaining a durable communication with stakeholders and engage them in collaborations have clear advantages in building and upholding long-term relationships.

Marken (2005) asserted that social media has a great potential for strategic communication, since they promote both one- and two-way communication and can be used for both interpersonal and mass communication. Hence, the border between interpersonal and mass communication seems to be erased with social media (Cho & Huh, 2010). The enhanced opportunities for interactivity make it more realistic for communication professionals to reach the ideal of symmetric communication (J. E. Grunig, L. A. Grunig, & Dozier, 2006) and joint decision-making (Coombs & Heath, 2006). Research indicates that interactive blogs can produce personal relations between organizations and users, which often facilitate positive attitudes towards the organization (Yang & Kang, 2009). Also, Aula (2011) maintained that communication online can foster a stronger relationship between organizations and their stakeholders, and even increase an organization's social capital.

Social media is unique in the sense that communication professionals have never before had access to a medium where it is fairly easy to create and maintain dialogue with a large number of people in different audiences (Briones, Kuch, Liu, & Jin, 2011). However, it is an open question whether dialogic opportunities in social media are actually used to any great extent. There are not many examples of research on how social media is used within strategic communication (some exceptions are Briones et al., 2011; Diga & Kelleher, 2009; Kent, 2008; Steyn, Salehi-Sangari, Pitt, Parent, & Berthon, 2010). A comparative study of Australian and European organizations' use of social media for strategic communication reveals that the practice is still rather experimental and ad hoc (Macnamara & Zerfass, 2012). Besides the great potential for dialogue with a large number of people, social media has another major advantage. It is reasonably easy to identify, observe and map different stakeholders, their activities and opinions. Hence, issues management is significantly improved through the use of social media.

Thus, social media offers other possibilities than the conventional media and can be regarded as more open and democratic media. These media create and promote the emergence of numerous social networks whose objectives may be to promote knowledge about a particular topic or interest, strengthen a public's special interest, or create and consolidate people's social identity. At the same time, research shows that many organizations still do not use the dialogic or interactive side of websites (Taylor, Kent, & White, 2001) or social media (Bortree & Seltzer, 2009). All too often social media is only used to place user-friendly information at different groups' disposal (Rybalko & Seltzer, 2010). Bortree and Seltzer (2009) underlined that organizations must stick to Kent and Taylor's (1998) principles—by always responding to stakeholders' questions, for example, and by keeping their information updated, and publishing useful information. And of course, as Kent and Taylor emphasized, if a relationship built on online communication were to survive in the long run, the goal of the relationship would have to be that communication actually took place. Hence, one can question whether organizations really are interested in communicative actions the way Habermas

(1984) saw it (co-operative action performed by individuals, based upon mutual deliberation and argumentation) or if they are only interested in strategic communication (attempting as efficiently as possible to distribute information in order to affect receivers). This critical view may be interpreted as extreme: valid, perhaps, in the second stage of the industrial revolution, but not taking into account current developments in society and organizations.

Are Organizations Losing Control?

Historically, organizations have had fairly good control over the information that was available, through strategically placed press releases and skilled practitioners' work (Kaplan & Haenlein, 2010). Since the mid-1990s there has been an extraordinary diffusion, adaption and development of Internet technology, and consequently prerequisites for communication have changed dramatically (González-Herrero & S. Smith, 2010). Strategic communication that earlier was characterized by a single source diffusing information to many has now been displaced by communication where many communicate with many. Accordingly, there has been a change from a push culture, with traditional analogue mass media where publics had little influence on the content, to a pull culture, where publics are expected to search for and collect the information they are interested in (González-Herrero & S. Smith, 2008; Telleen, 1997).

Social media brought about a power shift from organizations to stakeholders, which have a greater potential to influence than they used to have. The low admission barriers to get access to new media contribute to the great diffusion of social media. Information traditional mass media previously censured is accessible today for most people, and is not limited by time and space (Mei, Bansal, & Pang, 2010). This also means that social media challenges the traditional journalistic channels, while stakeholders quite easily can produce an alternative agenda (Domingo & Heinonen, 2008). Traditional mass media's gatekeeping function is not applicable on the Internet. Internet technology and social media allow laypeople to act as journalists and produce news. Long before the introduction of social media, Chaffee and Metzger (2001, p. 375) wrote "the key problem for agenda-setting theory will change from what issues the media tell people to think about to what issues people tell the media they want to think about." Consequently the power position of the public has changed with social media.

Solis and Breakenridge (2009) suggested that social media challenges the traditional understanding of public relations (which is the concept they use) in that the users themselves can create strategic messages and make them publicly available. The use of social media has also made journalists and communication professionals confused, when 'ordinary' people can fairly easily make a strategic message publicly available. B. G. Smith (2010) similarly talked about a social model for strategic communications, with communication professionals' traditional responsibilities transferred to the users of social media. This applies to both internal and external stakeholders. Organizational members, who are dedicated and committed, talk about and discuss their work and organization in different blogs. They are hence important ambassadors who have new opportunities to spread the message of the organization. The organizational image co-workers spread is naturally more differentiated than the official image communication professionals mediate, but on the other hand it is probably many times more in line with employees' organizational identity. When it comes to marketing there is a tendency for users to act on behalf of an organization. Hast (2010) stresses that on YouTube there is a wide variety of movies—everything from amateur videos to professional commercials that companies are trying to spread through viral marketing. The idea is that individuals should flag films that somehow raise others' interest within their network. Hast and Ossiansson (2008) maintain that the emergence of user-generated content has increasingly blurred the boundary between materials amateurs and professionals create. Consumers have become transmitters instead of passive recipients. In their view, the reason that social media has become so popular is the medium's potential to let individuals rate, comment and interact with others. In other words, there is no longer a clear and given border between communication professionals and laymen. Through social networks, consumers can act as marketers promoting various products they like. For instance, Dhar and Chang (2008) show that artists' albums that were mentioned 40 times on different blogs increased their sale by three times compared to the average.

B. G. Smith (2010) studied how various external stakeholders used Twitter during the earthquake that hit Haiti's capital Port-Au-Prince in January 2010, and how those publics thereby become active strategic communicators. Twitter, Smith argued, is more than just a message platform; it is a platform for social connections between people and for marketing. In Smith's social model an audience using social media initiates strategic communication-related activities based on user interactivity. Smith's study confirmed previous studies that people's online interactivity is based on interest in a topic. This stands in contrast to the common notion that people only use social media for self-fulfillment and to construct and shape their own identity (Rettberg, 2009). People often seem to be more interested in focusing on an issue and on belonging to a community, than in expressing personal opinions (B. G. Smith, 2010). Searching, retrieving and distributing information through social media is included in this interactivity. The messages distributed through Twitter comprise many retweets, a retweet being a message that is sent with a reference to the person who originally wrote it. The forwarded message usually begins with *RT* or *Retweet*. Smith saw this as proof that people do not only use social media as a tool for self-realization. Furthermore, Smith stated that the presence of the hashtag was further proof that people were using social media to disseminate messages. A hashtag is a way to find information about a topic on Twitter, using a common tagging. For example, if you want to know what has been written about the iPhone, you write *#iPhone*.

We argue that professional communicators do not lose control over information to social media. J. E. Grunig and L. A. Grunig (2010) pointed out that communications professionals have never been able to define who is part of a public and almost never have been able to influence them to do what the organization wishes. With social media, the dreams that many practitioners have about controlling publics become even more illusory.

Deleted Borders and Transparency

It has been claimed that the border between internal and external communication is difficult, or even impossible, to draw (Christensen, Morsing, & Cheney, 2008; Falkheimer & Heide, 2007). Internal communication does not stop within organizational boundaries without reaching out to other stakeholders, and external communications that are primarily meant to affect actors outside the organization also greatly affect the employees. For example, it is a fairly high probability that employees who read a newspaper article about their organization will be affected in some way. If the article describes the organization's success, it will probably strengthen the employees' perception of the organization's excellence and the organizational identity is, in most cases, strengthened. And, vice versa, if the article is more negative or critical to the organization and its activities, the employee's attitude toward the organization would not be improved: rather the contrary.

With social media the unclear border between internal and external communication is accentuated ever further, since the external public's opinions are much more accessible to organization members, who also have great potential to disseminate information about the internal situation in the organization. Published information can have a major impact, and negative writings can definitely damage an organization's reputation. One example comes from the police in southern Sweden, where a police officer mocked people through a private blog. Among other things, the policeman wrote about how he shook a deceased person's hand, as he and his colleagues had learned to shake hands at a first meeting, in an ethics course, and that the police officers present then laughed at the situation (Mattsson, 2010). The Swedish Police decided to give the blogging police officer a warning.

Such talk and actions have always existed, but with social media the dissemination and transparency of communication is much more apparent. This example shows how the boundary between internal and external, and private and professional communication is removed. Another example comes from Danish DSB First, a large train operator in Denmark and southern Sweden, where two employees were suspended from their jobs after they had posted pictures of trains, railway and a signal-man on Facebook (Nylund, 2010). The employees had taken the pictures during work and published them on Facebook in their spare time; the employer found this action very inappropriate. Other organizations have gone even further and given notice of termination to employees who have published negative or damaging information about an organization.

There seems to be a fear that organization members spend too much time communicating through social media. A special report on social networking in *The Economist* (2010) noted that staff's use of social media cost 14 billion USD annually in lost productivity. The same article reported that the U.S. firm Nucleus Research estimated that their productivity would increase by 1.5% if their staff did not use Facebook during work time. A survey by the consulting firm Blue Coat showed that Facebook, among other sites, took up most of an organizations' network capacity (Lindström, 2010). However, it should be noted that this exercise in math was based on the assumption that employees do not do anything else during their workday than work. After all there are many other activities staff might engage in, such as a smoking break, drinking water, and talking to colleagues in the hallway. In addition, many people have their own mobile phone or smart phones where they can surf the Internet. In other words, the criteria for the study were warped. The fact that staff members are engaged in private communication by e-mail, phone calls and Facebook will in most cases, if not abused, not affect their work or productivity.

The Double-Edged Sword

"From a public relations standpoint, blogs can be a blessing and a curse" (Smudde, 2005, p. 35). Organizations can effectively use social media to establish good and long-term relationships with various stakeholders, and as a tool for environmental scanning and issues management. Different stakeholders can also use this media in a negative way against the organization, cause major damage and be a primary source of an organizational crisis. Social media can also be dangerous for organizations, due to the high speed with which material can be published and spread over the Internet and thereby become accessible to large numbers of people. Mei, Bansal and Pang (2010) underlined that social media is a double-edged sword. One example is the U.S. carrier JetBlue Airways, whose passengers on Valentine's Day 2007 on Flight 751 stood on the runway at the John F. Kennedy International Airport for eight hours (CNN Travel, 2007). It was a very cold winter and when the plane was on its way to the runway, the captain had orders to stop because of a sudden weather change. While they were waiting for a change in weather, the wheels froze to the ground and were fixed. Because the airplane was already loaded, there was no available gate. During the wait passengers had no information about what was happening and no food or drinks were served. Two days later the first passengers started to publish pictures and video footage from inside the plane on YouTube, and discussed JetBlue on various blogs. For this company the crisis escalated when the passengers began to upload videos on the Internet (Mei et al., 2010).

In market research, scholars emphasize the danger of not putting enough resources into communicating with different stakeholders, not least when it comes to consumers. In the same way that consumers are able to act for an organization and in their networks discuss and market different products, services and organizations, they are also able to spread negative messages about an organization. This applies to commercial businesses, as well as public authorities and universities. In the worst cases such messages can have an incredibly fast and wide dissemination. Research has shown that consumer websites dedicated to complaints, so-called sucks.com sites, always get listed at the top when an online search for an organization is conducted (Ward & Ostrom, 2006). Ward and Ostrom's analysis shows that consumers are spreading negative information to demonstrate their power and possibilities to influence and take revenge on an organization, and to urge others to do the same thing. Consumers create websites for support of other consumers, while encouraging others to oppose a certain organization. Hence, a community of discontent can be produced through which both individual and social identities are created and confirmed when participants interact. This is another example of how social media has led to a power shift from organizations to stakeholders. With social media, consumers and other groups have an effective tool to make their voices heard and exert the ability to influence others' thinking and behavior (Hast & Ossiansson, 2008).

On the Internet there are plenty of examples where activities in various social media have had negative consequences for organizations. One example is the door lock Evo, which the Swedish company Assa Abloy manufactured. During 2008 videos were published on YouTube, where different people, such as a six-year-old boy with various tools, such as a popsicle stick, quickly lock-picked Assa Abloy locks. These videos attracted the attention of many journalists, who wrote numerous articles, and even Swedish television reported on the case. In sum, this resulted in a substantial weakening of the brand, reputation and goodwill of Assa Abloy, especially given that people felt their security threatened.

A phenomenon that has had a renaissance—it has a long history in the PR industry—is "astroturfing," which means a campaign that is planned by an organization and masked to create the impression of being spontaneous and carried out at grass roots level (AstroTurf is a brand of synthetic turf—designed to look like the genuine, living lawn). An example of contemporary astroturfing (through a viral video) is a controversial social media campaign by the Danish tourism organization Visit Denmark, launched in September 2009. In the YouTube video a Danish mother, named Karen, asked the audience to help her find the foreign father of her newborn baby. The heartbreaking story, which later turned out to be a fake, created huge interest and was spread all over the world. Astroturfing as a communication method is obviously very risky for an organization. If the campaign gets revealed, it will damage the organization's reputation considerably. For example, Mazda's reputation has deteriorated significantly since their astroturfing campaign for the car model M3 was revealed in 2004 (Cox, Martinez, & Quinlan, 2008). It is therefore vital that organizations allocate adequate resources to respond to various stakeholders, enter into dialogue, and exploit the potential of dialogue that social media provide.

Communication Professionals and Participatory Strategic Communication

J. E. Grunig and L. A. Grunig (2010) suggested the capabilities and benefits of social media rarely are fully exploited. Often social media are used primarily as a platform to spread organizational messages. There seems to be a widespread assumption that social media *per se* will reach expected outcomes automatically and that published information also will be read and interpreted in a certain way. This is wishful thinking among many communication professionals and is likely derived from a desire to gain access to an effective medium in which the results are obvious and predictable. Media history verifies that new technologies and media always initially bring forth a technological determinism.

Recently, a number of more critical articles on blogs have been published (e.g., Kent, 2008), which stressed that many authors are too one-sidedly positive toward blogs and that more research is needed before it is possible to comment on their different effects. A master's thesis (Sternvad & Wendel, 2009), showed that organizations primarily used blogs to monitor the surrounding society, while many organizations wanted more dialogue with different audiences. The dialogue that took place tended to be asymmetrical and organizations were listening to audiences in order to adjust their strategies and then more efficiently affect beneficiaries.

Is a paradigm shift taking place? With reference to the historical description in this chapter and the overview of social media's role for strategic communication, there is little doubt that a shift is taking place. This shift affects many sectors of society, but strategic communication is in a key position to experience it. The earlier models on which strategic communication is based come mainly from mass communication research. The concepts from this field, such as transmitter, target groups and beneficiaries, are of doubtful relevance for strategic communications in the third industrial revolution. There are optimistic case studies, such as Briones et al. (2011) who claimed that the communication professional must update strategies and practices if they want to build relationships through social media. Their research on the American Red Cross's usage of social media showed that an organization can give faster service to different stakeholders, get more media coverage and obtain more feedback, both positive and negative, which they can use to improve their work. Further, they concluded that social media is an ideal communication platform, when an organization and its stakeholders share similar values, beliefs and interests. Still, it is important to avoid technological determinism. If corporations and governments are serious about listening more and being more democratic, a focus on media technologies and communication distribution are not enough. Deetz and Brown (2004) concluded that what was really needed was new forms of management, leadership and organizational culture.

While there is reason not to exaggerate what is happening right now, progress should be viewed over the long term. It is important to realize that a paradigm shift in communications could take place over a longer timeline—in decades rather than in particular years. Even if there is available technology, it takes time to change the dominant approach to strategic communications. What is clear is that social media's emergence has highlighted the fact that communication rarely can be controlled in the way that organizations wish.

References

Aula, P. (2011). Meshworked reputation: Publicists' views on the reputational impacts of online communication. *Public Relations Review, 37*(1), 28–36.

Avery, E. J., Lariscy, R. W., & Sweetser, K. D. (2010). Social media and shared—or divergent—uses? A coorientation analysis of public relations practitioners and journalists. *International Journal of Strategic Communication, 4*, 189–205.

Baudrillard, J. (1988). Simulacra and simulations. In M. Poster (Ed.), *Selected writings* (pp. 166–184). Stanford, CA: Stanford University Press.

Bauman, Z. (2000). *Liquid modernity*. Cambridge, England: Polity Press.

Bernays, E. L. (1955). *The engineering of consent*. Oklahoma: University of Oklahoma Press.

Bortree, D. S., & Seltzer, T. (2009). Dialogic strategies and outcomes: An analysis of environmental advocacy groups' Facebook profiles. *Public Relations Review, 35*(3), 317–319.

Botan, C. H., & Taylor, M. (2004). Public relations: State of the field. *Journal of Communication, 54*(4), 645–661.

Briones, R. L., Kuch, B., Liu, B. F., & Jin, Y. (2011). Keeping up with the digital age: How the American Red Cross uses social media to build relationships. *Public Relations Review, 37*(1), 37–43.

Chaffee, S. H., & Metzger, M. J. (2001). The end of mass communication? *Mass Communication & Society, 4*(4), 365–379.

Cho, S., & Huh, J. (2010). Content analysis of corporate blogs as a relationship management tool. *Corporate Communications: An International Journal, 15*(1), 30–48.

Christensen, L. T., Morsing, M., & Cheney, G. (2008). *Corporate communications: Convetion, complexity, and critique*. London, England: Sage.

CNN Travel. (2007). Passengers trapped on runway for 8 hours. Retrieved November 18, 2010, from http://articles.cnn.com/2007–02–15/travel/passengers.stranded_1_jetblue-flights-passengers-flight-attendants?_s=PM:TRAVEL

Cooke, M., & Buckley, N. (2008). Web 2.0, social networks and the future of market research. *International Journal of Market Research, 50*(2), 267–292.

Coombs, W. T., & Heath, R. L. (2006). *Today's public relations*. Thousand Oaks, CA: Sage.

Cox, J. L., Martinez, E. R., & Quinlan, K. B. (2008). Blogs and the corporation: Managing the risk, reaping the benefits. *Journal of Business Strategy, 29*(3), 4–12.

Deetz, S. A., & Brown, D. (2004). Conceptualizing involvement, participation and workplace decision precesses: A communication theory perspective. In D. Tourish & O. Hargie (Eds.), *Key issues in organizational communication* (pp. 172–187). London, England: Routledge.

Dhar, V., & Chang, E. A. (2008). *Does chatter matter? The impact of user-generated content on music sales. CeDER Working Paper: CeDER-07–06.* New York: New York University, Leonard N. Stern School of Business.

Diga, M., & Kelleher, T. (2009). Social media use, perceptions of decision-making power, and public relations roles. *Public Relations Review, 35*(4), 440–442.

Domingo, D., & Heinonen, A. (2008). Weblogs and journalism: A typology to explore the blurring boundaries. *Nordicom Review, 29*, 3–15.

Falkheimer, J., & Heide, M. (2007). *Strategisk kommunikation: En bok om organisationers relationer* [Strategic communication: A book on organizations' relations]. Lund, Sweden: Studentlitteratur.

González-Herrero, A., & Smith, S. (2008). Crisis communications management on the web: How Internet-based technologies are changing the way public relations professionals handle business crises. *Journal of Contingencies & Crisis Management, 16*(3), 143–153.

González-Herrero, A., & Smith, S. (2010). Crisis communication management 2.0: Organizational principles to manage crisis in an online world. *Organization Development Journal, 28*(1), 97–105.

Grunig, J. E., & Grunig, L. A. (2010). *Public Relations Excellence 2010.* Paper presented at the PRSA International Conference, Washington, DC. Retrieved from http://www.instituteforpr.org/files/uploads/Third_Grunig_Lecture_Transcript.pdf

Grunig, J. E., Grunig, L. A., & Dozier, D. M. (2006). The excellence theory. In C. H. Botan & V. Hazleton (Eds.), *Public relations theory II* (pp. 21–62). Mahwah, NJ: Lawrence Erlbaum.

Habermas, J. (1984). *The theory of communicative action.* London, England: Polity Press.

Hart, L. (2011). Social media. In J. Doorley & H. F. Garcia (Eds.), *Reputation management: The key to successful public relations and corporate communication* (pp. 113–133). Boca Raton, FL: CRC Press.

Hast, L. (2010). Klagande kunder på nätet värda att tas på allvar [It's worth taking complaining customers on the net seriously]. Retrieved February 28, 2011, from http://www.brandnews.se/se/article_print.php?id=444103

Hast, L., & Ossiansson, E. (2008). Konsumtionsmakt 2.0 [Consumer power 2.0], *CFK-rapport 2008:01.* Göteborg, Sweden: Göteborgs universitet, Handelshögskolan.

Hatch, M. J., & Schultz, M. (2009). Of bricks and brands: From corporate to enterprise branding. *Organizational Dynamics, 38*(2), 117–130.

Hatch, M. J., & Schultz, M. (2010). Toward a theory of brand co-creation with implications for brand governance. *Journal of Brand Management, 17*, 590–604.

Hedman, U. (2009). Läsarmedverkan: Lönande logiskt lockbete [Reader co-operation: Profitable logical bait]. Working Report 56. Göteborg, Sweden: Göteborg University, JMG.

Holtzhausen, D. R. (2012). *Public relations as activism: Postmodern approaches to theory and practice.* New York: Routledge.

Jenkins, H. (2006). *Convergence culture: Where old and new media collide.* New York: New York University Press.

Kaplan, A. M., & Haenlein, M. (2010). Users of the world, unite! The challenges and opportunities of social media. *Business Horizons, 53*, 59–68.

Kent, M. L. (2008). Critical analysis of blogging in public relations. *Public Relations Review, 34*, 32–40.

Kent, M. L., & Taylor, M. (1998). Building dialogic relationships through the World Wide Web. *Public Relations Review, 24*(3), 321–334.

Kuhn, T. S. (1962). *The structure of scientific revolutions.* Chicago, IL: University of Chicago Press.

Kultur Skåne [Regional development of arts and culture] (2009). Paper presented at *Vår Konst Publik* [Our Art Public] conference, Malmö, Sweden.

Lindström, K. (2010). Facebook i topp [Facebook on top]. *Computer Sweden.* Retrieved from http://www.idg.se/2.1085/1.356156/facebook-i-topp

Macnamara, J., & Zerfaß, A. (2012). Social media communication in organizations: The challenges of balancing openness, strategy, and management. *International Journal of Strategic Communication, 6*(4), 287–308.

Marken, G. A. (2005). To blog or not to blog: That is the question? *Public Relations Quarterly, 50*, 31–33.

Mattsson, A. (2010). Polis hånar offer i sin blogg [Police officer scoffs victims in his blog]. *Kvällsposten.* Retrieved July 7, 2014, from http://www.expressen.se/kvp/polis-hanar-offer-i-sin-blogg/

Mei, J. S. A., Bansal, N., & Pang, A. (2010). New media: a new medium in escalating crises? *Corporate Communications: An International Journal, 15*(2), 143–155.

Nylund, S. (2010, January 15). Facebookbilder fick anställda avstängda [Facebook pictures got employees shut off], *Sydsvenskan.* Retrieved from http://sydsvenskan.se/ekonomi/article620576/Facebookbilder-fick-anstallda-avstangda.html

Prahalad, C. K., & Krishnan, M. S. (2008). *The new age of innovation: Driving cocreated value through global networks.* New York: McGraw-Hill.

Rettberg, J. W. (2009). "Freshly generated for you, and Barack Obama": How social media represent your life. *European Journal of Communication, 24*(4), 451–466.

Rybalko, S., & Seltzer, T. (2010). Dialogic communication in 140 characters or less: How Fortune 500 companies engage stakeholders using Twitter. *Public Relations Review, 36*(4), 336–341.

Schön, L. (2006). *Tankar om cykler: Perspektiv på ekonomin, historien och framtiden* [Thoughts on cycles: Perspectives of the economy,the history and the future]. Stockholm, Sweden: SNS förlag.

Shirky, C. (2009). *Here comes everybody: How change happens when people come together.* London, England: Penguin.

Smith, B. G. (2010). Socially distributing public relations: Twitter, Haiti, and interactivity in social media. *Public Relations Review, 36*(4), 329–335.

Smudde, P. M. (2005). Blogging, ethics and public relations: A proactive and dialogic approach. *Public Relations Quarterly, 50*(3), 34–38.

Solis, B., & Breakenridge, D. (2009). *Putting the public back in public relations: How social media is reinventing the aging business of pr.* Upper Saddle River, NJ: Pearson Education.

Sternvad, F., & Wendel, J. (2009). *Bloggar—Organisationernas Heliga Graal? En kritisk diskussion kring organisationers möjlighet att uppnå dialogbaserad kommunikation genom bloggar* [Blogs—The holy grail of organizations? A critical discussion on organizations' possibility to achieve dialog-based communication through blogs]. Unpublished master's thesis. Lund, Sweden: Lund University. Retrieved from http://www.lu.se/o.o.i.s?id=19463&postid=1465317w

Steyn, P., Salehi-Sangari, E., Pitt, L., Parent, M., & Berthon, P. (2010). The social media release as a public relations tool: Intentions to use among B2B bloggers. *Public Relations Review, 36*(1), 87–89.

Taylor, M., Kent, M. L., & White, W. J. (2001). How activist organizations are using the Internet to build relationships. *Public Relations Review, 27*(3), 263–284.

Telleen, S. (1997). The intranet paradigm. Retrieved September 8, 2002, from http://www.iorg.com/papers/paradigm.html

Ward, J. C., & Ostrom, A. L. (2006). Complaining to the masses: The role of protest framing in customer-created complaint web sites. *Journal of Consumer Research, 33*(2), 220–230.

Yammering away at the office: A distraction or a bonus? (2010, January 28). Special report. *The Economist.*

Yang, S.-U., & Kang, M. (2009). Measuring blog engagement: Testing a four-dimensional scale. *Public Relations Review, 35*(3), 323–324.

Part IV
Domains of Practice

23

Institutionalization in Public Relations

Another Step in Examining its Place in Strategic Communication

Robert I. Wakefield, Kenneth D. Plowman, and Alex Curry

No matter how much they champion innovation, greater competitive advantage, or enhanced services, virtually all organizations must also harbor enduring values and practices. Typically, these fundamentals are developed through persistent trial and error coupled with ongoing theoretical assessment from the best and, in some cases, failed practices within a given industry or field. Many domains (accounting, business management, economics, law, the political sciences, etc.), have accumulated a body of knowledge that guides entire entities or specific functions within those entities in their efforts to achieve maximum effectiveness.

In organizational literature, a state or environment where widely accepted fundamentals of an industry endure even in the midst of change is best characterized as *institutionalization*. Institutionalization is defined as the process of infusing 'rule-like' values and procedures into an organization and sustaining them over time, regardless of circumstances or of the individual personalities and philosophies of the entity's main leaders (Zucker, 1977). In institutionalizing their processes and patterns, organizations are able to establish ongoing legitimacy for themselves in the various contexts in which they function (Suchman, 1995). Some critics argue that institutionalization makes organizations too rigid and resistant to necessary change (Oliver, 1992), but others counter that institutionalization need not preclude adaptability. Rather, the enduring fundamentals of institutionalization offer the very stability that organizations need to persist despite the inevitable changes and adaptations they must deal with in their daily activities and encounters (Selznick, 1957; Scott, 1987).

With institutionalization being a debated yet vital aspect of organizational theory, a natural corollary to that debate addresses the field of strategic communication or public relations—its role, if any, in fostering organizational institutionalization, and whether or not strategic communication should itself be institutionalized. This question is relevant to theory building because public relations is often seen as the main organizational function that anticipates and guides strategic change. Yi (2005) argued that strategic public relations can help organizations recognize relationships in the environment and continually facilitate changes in those relationships (Yi, 2005). It may be asked how public relations can do this if it becomes institutionalized and then, as some suggest, more resistant to change (Oliver, 1992).

The concept of institutionalization should also be important to strategic communication because it can help legitimize the function in organizations and society. Understanding this, scholars and veteran practitioners are always attempting to establish a body of knowledge about the fundamental principles needed to effectively practice public relations and to make it valuable to the organizations it serves. Yet, James E. Grunig (2006) said, "a major task remains . . . in institutionalizing strategic public relations as actual practice in most organizations" (p. 171). His assumption was that public relations efforts too often depend not on enduring standards or principles of effectiveness but on the philosophies of senior organizational executives or public relations managers who are in charge at any given time. Frequently, when one regime leaves an entity and is replaced by another, within a short time the public relations program looks entirely different to how it looked before the transition. Sometimes these changes create needed improvements but more often than not they simply reflect the whims of a given group of managers.

In his challenge to institutionalize public relations, J. E. Grunig (2006) argued that most public relations practices today center around tactical support processes instead of strategic implementation of values that genuinely assist the ongoing legitimacy of the organization. He cited research by Yi (2005), which indicated that whatever institutionalization of public relations may exist, it centers on buffering organizations against outside pressures rather than on the more essential bridging or linkage activities that, in the long run, help organizations adapt better to change and, as a result, make them more successful in their missions.

This chapter represents a qualitative multiple-case study of institutionalization in several organizations that have experienced a turnover of public relations executives or top management. A study was conducted that determined whether the public relations programs remained intact or changed significantly as a result of the transition—and, if changes occurred, why? The study observed whether changes that took place were positive or harmful, or made little difference. This chapter also assesses whether these cases suggest that strategic public relations should be more enduring in organizations regardless of who may be supervising the program.

Theoretical Basis for Institutionalization

Institutionalization offers the perpetuation of basic values, norms, and processes that are widely accepted or prescribed within a given domain or societal context. Meyer and Rowan (1977) proposed that institutionalization is the construct "by which social processes, obligations, or actualities come to take on a rule-like status in social thought and action" (p. 341), partly because these, processed, are passed down from generation to generation (Sandhu, 2009). Scott (1987) explained further that through institutionalization, "individuals come to accept a shared definition of social reality—a conception whose validity is seen as independent of the actor's own views or actions but . . . as defining the 'way things are' and/or the 'way things are to be done'" (p. 496). Yi (2005) said: "Institutionalists argue that within an organizational field, there would be a dominant form or practices that are taken for granted" (p. 8).

Strategic Communication

Institutionalization is a form of and could be considered subordinate to strategic communication. Argenti, Howell and Beck in 2005 defined strategic communication "as communication aligned with the company's overall strategy, to enhance its strategic positioning."

The term *strategic* in a military sense is usually referring to the highest levels of command and to large, far-reaching military campaigns (Harvard Business Essentials, 2003). Ideally, it would occur at the highest or leadership levels of an organization and be carried out at the lowest or tactical levels. It educates and informs publics; but the most effective strategic communication changes behavior. Strategic communication sets measureable communication goals and considers the long-term effects on key publics or strategic stakeholders while constantly scanning the organizational environment for issues that might affect the organization (J. E. Grunig & White, 1992).

In the seminal article on strategic communication in the inaugural issue of the *International Journal of Strategic Communication,* Hallahan, Holtzhausen, van Ruler, Verčič, and Sriramesh (2007) covered the origins of strategic communication from a number of fields. Strategic communication as defined by these authors fits more under changing behavior and psychological operations in the military. They addressed the term *strategic* as well, citing its origins as coming from warfare, the art of war. The authors also focus on the term *communication* and the process of communication that is the key ingredient for this study. The authors define communication "as the constitutive activity of management" (p. 27). Under the article's section on management they write of the focus on rational decision-making using the SWOT Analysis (strengths, weaknesses, opportunities, and threats) as part of the process of goal setting, strategy formulation and implementation, and evaluation (Porter, 1985). They later cite Mintzberg (1990) about environmental scanning of stakeholders, issues management and the integration of the communications functions. In 1994 Mintzberg defined strategy as a plan for a future course of an action and broadened that definition to include strategy as a pattern, consistency in behavior over time. This consistency is usually a combination of deliberate and emergent strategies. Deliberate strategies are realized or fulfilled whereas emergent strategies are realized but not expressly intended. These emergent strategies include the influence of stakeholders incorporating the concept of relationships from Botan, 2006; Hallahan et al., 2007; Hon & Grunig, 1999; Ledingham & Bruning, 2000).

Leadership

Admiral James G. Stavridis of the U.S. Navy spoke about strategic communication in the following terms:

> Effective communication requires leaders of an organization to take an early and persistent role in deciding how ideas and decisions are shaped and delivered. Certainly in the national security context, a leader can improve the effects of operational and policies planning by ensuring communications implications of that planning are considered as early as possible in the process. If planning is done in that fashion, then it is likely that the communications associated with it will indeed be strategic in its effects.
>
> *Stavridis 2007, p. 4*

This quote adds further to the planning and leadership aspects of strategic communication as well as negotiating how these ideas are shaped and delivered. Argenti, Howell and Beck (2005) and Plowman (1995, 1998), as well as many others in the field of public relations, have argued for public relations having a seat at the management decision table so that the ideas discussed above have a better chance to make it in final strategic communication plans.

Leadership plays a vital role in institutionalization. "The key tasks of leaders," Fleck (2007) explained, "include the definition of institutional mission and role; the institutional embodiment of purpose; the defense of institutional integrity; and the ordering of internal conflict. It is up to leadership not only to create but to preserve values" (p. 68).

Of course, all creations eventually decay or get demolished. In human-built systems, some changes come through simple evolution: individual entities, communities, or societies arise anew, gradually institutionalize, and then reassess, adapt, change, or even disappear (Fleck, 2007). Other changes are purposefully imposed by societal mandate or individual whim. Oliver (1992) referred to these change processes as *deinstitutionalization*. Deinstitutionalization is seen as a theoretical opposition to institutionalization—the needs and desires for change instead of the push for stability.

Oliver (1992) noted several conditions that would render organizations and industries susceptible to deinstitutionalization. Just a few of these conditions are organizational crises, pressures from important internal or external constituents, loss of competitive advantage, and alterations in the social, political, or economic environment in which the entity operates. Whatever the impetus for organizational change, it can come suddenly and dramatically, imposed by people or forces seeking to overthrow entrenched traditions and norms, or through prolonged neglect and atrophy.

If change amidst stability seems contradictory, scholars have explained how it is possible. Selznick (1957) perceived that organizations can be adaptive if they are institutionalized around values rather than technical processes. "To institutionalize," he explained, "is to *infuse with value* beyond the technical requirements of the task at hand" (p. 17). Scott (1987) added that with bureaucratized technical processes, adaptation is difficult; but if stability stems from enduring values and culture instead of the imposition of processes, adaptation is possible.

The chapter to this point has looked at institutionalization as a principle of leadership and a necessary requirement for stability and legitimacy. This is coupled with an ability to adapt to needed changes through shared value systems. Institutionalization can be sustained in organizations, industries, and entire societies. Stability is not inherently a static phenomenon, however; various factors within and outside the entity or industry can lead to desired and even necessary changes. Therefore, a critical decision point for leaders in the institutionalization process is to wisely strike the proper balance between stability and change (Selznick, 1996).

From here, this chapter will explore how these observations affect strategic communication. As mentioned above, institutionalization is important for establishing legitimacy for a given industry. As Scott (1987) said, a given industry is rewarded with greater legitimacy when it is institutionalized because people outside that industry can then clearly understand its core principles and functions as well as its inherent value to the greater society in which it operates.

Perhaps surprisingly for a field that has existed for a long time, "very little attention has been paid to institutionalization as a relevant . . . perspective for public relations" (Jensen, 2009, p. 113). Scholars and practitioners have only recently advocated the need to institutionalize the field. For example, J. E. Grunig (2007) said, "the practice of public relations is in dire need of conceptualization . . . about what public relations is, what its value is to organizations and society, and what its core values should be (p. 1). Given this concern, he advocated for "institutionalizing strategic public relations" (J. E. Grunig, 2006, p. 171). Arnold (1995), Hutton (2001), and Macnamara (2006) are among the many more who have argued for institutionalization of the industry. Nielsen (2006) observed: "The standing and reputation of our own profession could benefit from a coming together around a shared set of values that speak about what we believe our responsibilities are and what we hold as important about what we do" (p. 1).

To a limited extent, encouragements toward more institutionalization are starting to be answered. In 2008, the annual conference of the European Public Relations Education and Research Association (EUPRERA) emphasized the subject, but only a handful of the papers actually addressed it. A special issue of the *International Journal of Strategic Communication* in 2009 also focused on the subject. The introduction to that issue cited as one of the first discussions on the topic an earlier version of this study presented by Wakefield (2008) at the International Public Relations Research Conference in Miami (Zerfass, 2009).

Several scholars have reflected the concept proposed by Scott (1987), that institutionalization would make public relations more legitimate if centered on overall strategic communication values instead of technical processes. Macnamara (2006), however, contended that if any institutionalization had occurred it was in the wrong direction, emphasizing the tactical over the strategic. He said, "public relations [has] continued down its practical path . . . based on outdated assumptions about the effects of communication" (p. 6). This path, he added, begins in university curriculum, where students learn "how to write news releases, brochures, advertisements and scripts, work with producers and designers to arrange events—but with little or no understanding of what effects if any their work might produce within the groups that they target" (p. 9). Others, like J. E. Grunig (2006) and Falconi (2006) have agreed that the persistent focus on tactics and techniques instead of strategic principles robs the field of respect. This focus hardly seems to be rectified by the more recent obsession towards creating blogs, tweets, and viral videos.

When the institutionalization of strategic values of environmental scanning, issues anticipation, relationship building and reputation management is encouraged, as opposed to technical functions like publicity or marketing support (J. E. Grunig, 2007; Macnamara, 2006), public relations can then accomplish what it was intended to do. It can help entities maintain enduring stability and legitimacy within their respective environments. But to enact these strategic processes, the industry itself must have its own enduring legitimacy.

So, if the institutionalization of strategic public relations placed highly within the entity helps to build legitimacy for the field, then it seems it would be valuable to determine to what extent public relations may be institutionalized around these fundamental values and principles. This chapter has investigated the relationship of leadership, adaptation, change and legitimacy in the institutionalization of public relations in organizations. The idea was to determine to what extent institutionalization is occurring; and, if so, whether it is at the strategic or tactical level. If the study were to indicate that institutionalization of strategic public relations is occurring in organizations, then it could be possible that the field itself may be institutionalizing and thus gaining legitimacy. If, however, institutionalization is occurring at the tactical level, then Scott's (1987) characterizations could hold true—that this would make the field unable to help entities respond to changes in their environment. A cross-case analysis of common themes seemed the next step in this research. Specific questions to be investigated included:

1. To what extent is public relations an institutionalized function in entities that practice strategic communication?
2. What factors (leadership) foster institutionalization *or* deinstitutionalization of public relations in a given entity?
3. If practitioners can best serve as change agents in an entity, how does institutionalization occur without losing the ability to foster change?
4. If strategic communication is institutionalizing in entities, does it stand to reason that the field is gaining legitimacy? Why would that be the case, or why not?

Method for the Study

According to Yin (2009), a case study design should be considered when the focus of the study is to answer "how" and "why" questions and when behavior of those involved in the study (in this case organizational leaders) cannot be manipulated. A multiple case study (or collective: Stake, 1995) enables the researcher to explore differences within and between cases. The goal is to replicate and compare findings across cases. Such a design has advantages and disadvantages, and generally control for bias through a triangulation of sources of data and comparisons by researchers is requisite. Overall, the evidence created from a multiple-case study is considered robust and reliable (Baxter & Jack, 2008). However, this particular study was exploratory in nature—the intent was to examine a few organizations to determine whether there might be any factors that contribute to the potential for institutionalization in organizational public relations.

Data Sources and Analysis

One key strength of case study research is the use of triangulation through multiple data sources, a strategy which also enhances data credibility (Fisher, Ury, & Patton, 1991; Yin, 2009). For this study, five of Yin's (2009) six sources of evidence were used: interviews, physical artifacts, documentation, direct observation, and participant-observation. This data was converged in the individual cases and then the strongest common themes across the cases were coded for in the multiple cases. This convergence adds strength to the findings but there are weaknesses involved. One is that the findings are not generalizable to a population (Baxter & Jack, 2008; Yin 2009), but they are generalizable to theory with the strength being that they can be replicated across cases. Another weakness is the enormous amounts of data that require management and analysis. This was the situation in this study because it involved six cases.

Yin (2009) described a number of techniques for analysis. The ones chosen for this study were pattern matching, linking the guiding research questions, and cross-case synthesis. For this study, six entities were analyzed. Selection of these entities was purposeful—partly because we as researchers had access to them—but we also intended to examine organizations that were quite different in terms of size, structure, and industry or service. The study included six organizations: two transnational corporations, a small university, a political office, and two military units. The first four of these entities were headquartered in the United States (with those various locations stretching from the east coast to the west coast), but each of them also had significant operations or reach outside the United States. The two military units were based in the Middle East. The first corporation was a major *Fortune 500* firm with hundreds of public relations practitioners around the world (Entity A); and the second was a mid-sized corporation (annual turnover of about $1 billion per year) that operated in consumer products industries (Entity B). The university was a private, not-for-profit educational institution (Entity C), and the political office was that of a governor of one of the states in the USA, with a communications staff of more than a dozen people (Entity D). The two military entities included multinational force units in Iraq during Operation Iraqi Freedom encompassing almost 160,000 personnel and over 200 public affairs-related officers (Entities E and F).

Data for the study were gathered through extensive emails and personal telephone or face-to-face interviews, ranging from 40 minutes to one hour, with current and former heads of public relations or related functions in each of these entities. In some cases, interviews were conducted with other public relations personnel who supervised specific aspects of public relations. The authors of this chapter also examined related or relevant internal emails, organizational and industry newsletters, communication plans, PowerPoint presentations, organizational charts, and other documents. Direct or participant observation was also incorporated into four of the organizations.

Results

As mentioned earlier in this chapter, this study was considered to be an introductory exploration into the possibility of institutionalization in public relations—both as a function within organizations and as an industry. Nevertheless, it was possible to show some patterns related to the theory of institutionalization. The results are organized by entity with the characteristics and factors mentioned previously: leadership in the organization or the public relations function; organizational adaptation to change; and legitimacy of the public relations function within each organization described. Table 23.1 below shows the transition from method to results that specifically addresses change, organizational response and evidence of institutionalization—to what degree it is strategic or tactical.

Entity A. The main analysis of Entity A, the *Fortune 500* firm, came from a 50-minute interview with a senior public relations executive who has worked in this particular entity for several years. We also spoke with another public relations staff member in the organization and examined newsletters and other documents that are widely used within the industry. More than 400 employees serve in various areas of public relations in this corporation, and the firm has an overall communications budget that can approach $200 million.

Table 23.1 Methods and Results Summary for Seven Organizations

Organization type	Organization size	Study methods employed	Potential change agent	Organization response	Evidence of institutionalization?
A: Transnational corporation— Midwest U.S.	Fortune 500 firm—400 PR employees	Interviews, review of industry newsletters and other documents	Top PR officer retired; replacement from other firm; stockholder expectations, environmental groups, etc.	Kept basic procedures in place when staff change occurred, following industry standards	Yes, for the most part
B: Transnational corporation— Mountain West U.S.	$1B firm, operations in some 40 nations	Interviews, review of emails and other entity documents	Change in corporate leadership; value of PR minimized	PR staff radically cut over time; many strategic PR functions dissolved or reduced	No
C: University— West Coast	3,000 students, 45% from outside United States	Interviews, review of communication plans and other documents	President replaced after 13 years in office	New president disbanded all PR except for media relations	No
D: Governor's office—West United States	Two dozen PR employees, highly mechanistic government bureaucracy	Interviews, review of emails and other documents, direct and participant observation	Many changes in senior ranks and PR staff; expectations of voters, legislature, other stakeholders	Ongoing program but also changes at whim of executives or senior PR staff	Some
E & F: Multinational Forces—Iraq	160,000 Soldiers, Sailors, Marines and Air Force Personnel from 27 countries; 200 public affairs personnel	Review of communication plans and other documents; and participant observation	Changes in all ranks due to year-long rotations of personnel including public affairs	Basic public affairs doctrine followed with many exception based on evolving conflict situation in Iraq	Yes, in part

About two years ago, the senior public relations executive left the firm, thus necessitating a change in leadership. Yet, with the change, according to the interviewee, basic missions, strategies, and activities remained intact. The reporting system also did not change, as the senior public relations executive continued to report directly to the chief executive officer. The change in the organization, therefore, had no major impact. "I believe institutionalization is built into our company because we are in an industry that mandates effective outreach to our stakeholders," the interviewee reported. "In our company, we have a long history of communication; it has always been given high priority, and it cannot be underestimated. It would be hard for someone to change it, because too much stake is put into it. A lot of people have a strong commitment to the traditions of our organization." The interviewee described scenarios reflecting Zucker's (1977) explanations that in highly institutionalized entities, it is difficult for outsiders to make changes. "We've had employees come in from different companies and try to change things. They resist our procedures, fight it, but sooner or later they conform," the respondent said.

Despite the earlier claim that the industry demands highly responsive public relations and that the executive's own company adapts to those demands, the interviewee did acknowledge that other firms in the industry have not been so institutionalized in their procedures. One firm, for example, has had considerable volatility over the past two or three decades, including different ownership. Under yet another new chief executive, the company restructured its highest levels and replaced a vice president of communications with a lower-level executive who would report to a human resources vice president.

But Entity A continues to operate its public relations in a manner consistent with Scott's (1987) contention that organizations can adapt to their environment even when institutionalized, as long as the institutionalization has occurred at the strategic and cultural levels rather than at the tactical levels. For example, the organization was among the first major companies to create and build a unit focused specifically on communicating and building relationships through social networking. "We spend a lot of money on social networking and on working with activists and non-governmental organizations," said the respondent. "We identify major cities or areas, we even communicate with people who are highly critical of us, and we bring them to our headquarters and show them what is going on there in the company. We don't give up on people very quickly; we feel there is nobody's mind we cannot change if given the opportunity, or at least we can convert people to a mutually neutral situation."

The respondent for Entity A expressed strong belief in the processes of institutionalization. The executive stated that public relations must show its value to the entity at the highest levels, assisting with corporate reputation through sound relationship building and through accurate and honest communication of the entity's products and services. In addition, the respondent realized the important role of public relations in creating change, in "transforming the organization to new heights. Organizations should be dynamic and open to their stakeholders," the respondent explained. "Communications can be the tail that leads the dog. In our company, we have resolved a lot of issues, and we are in a position to be very competitive."

In summary of Entity A, then, it appeared that the company has institutionalized its public relations programs regardless of who supervises the function. Perhaps size and company history influenced this institutionalization, as well as the philosophies and vision of those who had led both the organization and the public relations units. The industry's need for responsiveness and adaptation to stakeholders was also described as a factor, but this was not supported by the mention of other companies in the industry that did not have records of institutionalization. Even with Entity A's established traditions, it was apparent as well that the company and its public relations unit actively support and are engaged in changes and improvements to become even more responsive to stakeholders as society changes. It seems that the company's public relations units have gained a great element of legitimacy among senior officers and other functions in the firm.

Such institutionalization did not occur with either Entity B or Entity C. In fact, quite the opposite took place. Both of these entities experienced leadership changes, but the first changed at the senior level of public relations and the second underwent a change in the entity's senior executive. Nevertheless, in each case, changes in leadership drastically affected the public relations programs in the entity.

Entity B. The person interviewed for this mid-size transnational corporation started out as director of communications and then became vice president of corporate communication for about eight years. When hired, he replaced another vice president who had been brought into the firm specifically to help resolve a nationwide public relations crisis. The first executive had convinced senior leadership that a long-term, strategic public relations approach was necessary not only to survive the crisis but to ensure that such a situation would not occur again. The interview respondent had carried on most of the programs initiated by the first vice president, despite fairly regular pressures by some in senior management to reduce public relations efforts "now that the crisis is passed and we don't need all of this anymore." When he was hired, the company's public relations department had 15 employees; when he left, it had 100. "I took over the PR department in this corporation when it had been vacant for a year. And I felt there were things that needed to be done that hadn't been done, and so it became a process then of making people aware and selling the idea of what we needed to do. And so the changes were pretty significant over the first year or so."

For close to 13 years, the staff included a dozen employees dedicated to media and community relations, international communication, issues management, and other public relations functions. Another 30 to 40 employees, depending on the year, assisted these efforts with graphic design, photography, and visual production. These activities all continued as the organization expanded its product lines and geographic reach around the world, became a public company, and slowly improved its reputation in its home state, nationally, and internationally. Both vice presidents and other senior managers guided these efforts with the veteran leadership that reflected their decades of experience in the field. Whenever one employee would leave, another would be hired who was known and trusted by these vice presidents, and the culture of the public relations unit was maintained as one of experience, strategic thinking, and teamwork.

The interviewee stated that the company's communications strategy was impacted "in part by values and in part by events. For example, if the company decided that it wanted to expand into overseas markets, then that drove what we did—although the way we did it was very much impacted by values." However, the steps taken to carry out public relations strategies were in large measure dependent on who was in charge and on selling the ideas to the senior executives. "We made a concerted effort to put together a strategic plan to explain to the company why the company needed to do those things in order to achieve its desired results. . . . There was always a selling process going on."

This need to "sell" the public relations department's value, or to establish legitimacy of the function within senior management ranks, was something the interviewee touched on time and again during the interview: "It was a never-ending education process. We had an ongoing effort to educate the people at the top of the business and to cut us in when they were contemplating major changes." During the interviewee's time with the company, this 'selling' process was effective in that it gave him and his department the latitude to make many of the company's communications decisions. Those decisions were put into action by a written mission statement "that was a reflection of the business plan of the company. And so, it was basically an identification of what the PR department was going to do to help realize the results that they were seeking. But it took a lot of reminding because there was an inclination on the part of some senior executives not to see the PR organization as a player. And so it was a never-ending education process." When senior executives bought into his ideas, they generally endured during his tenure. With his departure, however, came a swift demise of the changes that he had put into place, and much returned to the way it had been prior to his time with the company. Arguably, even, the state of public relations returned to how it was before this interviewee's predecessor came in to save the company from a major public relations crisis—many of the needed strategic functions again became virtually non-existent. When asked if the communications efforts remained in place no matter who was in charge, the interviewee responded that it "depended on who was there. In my case, I took over the PR department, was elevated to a vice-president level, and the public relations department remained pretty strong players until about a year after I retired. At that time they just dismantled and changed things because they didn't have anybody who was strongly pushing it anymore. And so, it went back to the way it originally was."

In 2004, this company suffered a prolonged sales slump and decided to reduce its workforce. Several top managers, including the respondent to this study, were offered early retirement incentives.

The respondent and several other long-term public relations employees accepted the retirement package or were simply laid off. As a result, the staff which had once numbered more than 50 was reduced to less than 20. Of those who remained, none had experience in or inclination toward long-term relationship-building strategies. The leadership over the broad area of "public relations" was reduced to the media relations specialist, a former graphic design manager, and a person who had been the chief executive's special projects manager.

So, why did the institutionalization process fall apart in this case? Most likely, the respondent surmised, it was because many in the senior managerial positions outside of public relations never fully supported the department's creation in the first place. They assumed that once the original crisis had passed, the entity would no longer need costly strategic communication efforts. As the years went by and no other major crisis occurred, this confirmed the idea in their minds that public relations was no longer needed. Senior managers seemed to believe that the company was naturally satisfying stakeholder expectations and that no continual adaptation to stakeholders was worth expenditures for a strategic public relations program.

As the respondent explained, "At the beginning the concept and practice of building bridges with our stakeholders was not encouraged by upper management, supposedly because of their lack of understanding of the responsibilities and value of corporate communication experts. But the CEO realized the value of the function in helping a much-needed effort to improve the company's reputation, so the function survived for many years. Ultimately, when the CEO kind of stepped away from daily management of the company, his influence over managerial decisions waned and other influential managers were finally able to get their way. And getting their way included getting rid of most of the public relations function."

Entity C. One of the people interviewed for this small, private university had worked there for more than 15 years, serving mostly as a director of alumni relations. The respondent had seen the evolution of public relations from virtually nothing to a full-scale program that included a new identity movement; hosting of dignitaries and other special guests; media, community, government, and alumni relations; special events management; international outreach; creation, supervision, and production of print communication collateral materials, including a biennial magazine; and visual production of a variety of communication messages. These tasks were led by a vice president over development, a director of communications who joined the university in 2001 as the first-ever to serve in such a position, and a director of alumni relations, with support from photographers, graphic designers and visual production supervisors. This made up a total staff of up to 20 individuals. The staff had strong support from the entity's president and most of the vice presidents. As another public relations staff member said, "We had great freedom to be innovative and to accomplish the tasks we felt were needed to improve our relationships and to build awareness and understanding among constituents."

In 2007, after serving for more than 13 years, the president of the institution retired. The board of trustees replaced him with a president brought in from another state, and arguably from a considerably different cultural and philosophical background (he had been an accounting professor at a university in the eastern United States). The new leader, according to the respondent to this study, possessed managerial values that differed vastly from those the long-standing organizational culture was accustomed to, and the leader also carried a mandate from the entity's board to significantly streamline costs and personnel. This new approach apparently sent shock waves throughout the organization, and changes were made rapidly over the next year or two.

Among the changes was a wholesale reordering of the vice presidents of the institution. The vice president of development retired right after the new president arrived, and the director of communications left the university shortly before the presidency changed. The remaining communication functions were restructured under an executive who had served as the previous president's administrative assistant. The respondent said that this person had no real communication background but was asked to supervise a new director of communication who had more than 30 years of experience in the field—mostly in broadcast production. Therefore, visual production remained in this unit, as well as graphic design—however, the strategic oversight of the communications area largely went away when the new president arrived. Graphic design was drastically reduced (the full-color biennial magazine reaching out to important alumni, for example, ceased production), and visual production was changed from an outreach tool to mostly a means for supporting distance learning programs. The alumni relations director was assigned to another position entirely, and the alumni relations role was given to a junior executive in the student services department.

In this case, the changes in public relations were implemented by the new president despite strong support for the function by the previous administration and throughout the organization and community. Many of these stakeholders lost considerable influence in the organization in the months after the new president arrived. The function which had evolved into a full-scale strategic unit became separated into new reporting roles and relationships and marginalized in the university, according to the interviewee. Many employees in the previous public relations unit either immediately or eventually left the university.

The first respondent reported that some of the broader organizational alterations were necessary—the previous administration had become entrenched in traditional thinking and the financial situation did need to be tightened. However, the respondent did state that the administration's relationships, both inside the university and with the small local community, became worse because of the changes. "Obviously," the respondent added, "I have to be careful about what I say, because I want to support the new president and be positive." Judging from many of the decisions made by and under the new president, it is apparent that the president saw no value for public relations; therefore, there is a need all over again to establish legitimacy for the function in this university.

Entity D. This governor's office serves a large and diverse population. An interview was conducted with a former chief deputy communications director and chief speechwriter who worked in the office for three years in the mid-2000s. Not only was he involved in and privy to the discussions surrounding major communications decisions, he also witnessed numerous transitions in communications, press, and other senior staff leadership. The interviewee indicated that the overarching communications goal in the office was to communicate the governor's energy and agenda to the citizens of the state. This goal informed the communications decisions that were made, and although the tactics and strategies used to realize the goal changed at times, this change had less to do with the personalities inside the office than with circumstances outside the office. In other words, changes in communication strategy "would have happened even without a new communications chief and new chief of staff," according to the interviewee.

According to the respondent, the personalities in charge did play an important role in how communications challenges were met on a day-to-day basis and on how goals were conveyed to others in the office. Decision making came from the governor and the senior communications executives: "the governor had ideas, of course, and goals—but the strategy for the most part was hatched by the very strong chief of staff and the communications director. The staff contributed ideas and were encouraged to weigh in, but for the most part it was a top-down approach. There was a tendency on the part of the chief of staff and communications director to keep information close to the vest so staff was sometimes left to . . . guess what the strategy was from day to day."

Another issue that contributed to changes in communication tactics was that at certain times the governor's office had a particular issue of focus (including getting re-elected) that required strategizing about the communications message. For example, senior staff "held regular and frequent meetings . . . when the re-election was paramount, and we were all clear on the objectives. When the urgency diminished in the natural course of political cycles, the strategy was not as clear and the meetings not as frequent."

In defense of the changes to strategy and tactics, the respondent was clear that the nature of political work made adaptable communications efforts paramount to the success of the office and agenda. "The pace is so fast in an office like the governor's and outside forces are examining and reacting to everything you do so quickly and so reflexively that you are constantly changing gears and reacting to what happens outside the office. You try, of course, to stick to your basic message but chaos rules much of the time and it's easy to get knocked off track."

When asked if communications strategy and programs endured despite who was leading the communications team, he said: "I think for the most part it endured. Obviously, there is a shift in emphasis and different levels of success when it comes to execution. But the overall strategy . . . stayed pretty constant." Therefore, it seems that in this case the public relations function operated under some sense of legitimacy.

It should be noted that one of the authors of this paper was a participant observer and worked in this same governor's office for more than five years as a member of the communications team, and his own experiences confirm those of the respondent. This author concludes that the enduring and overarching goals of the administration guided mostly tactical communications efforts that shifted with political trends that render adaptability as highly necessary. Most of the changes were generally well received by public relations staff members as long as they were consistent with the office's long-term goals.

Entities E and F. The U.S. military is unique in that public relations is practiced as information operations, psychological operations, public affairs, civil affairs, and strategic communications. The difference among these terms is still evolving (Army Public Affairs Handbook, 2007). This state of flux affects how public affairs are practiced in the military. There is public affairs doctrine that calls for education of publics as in the public information model (J. E. Grunig & Hunt, 1984). There is also information operations and strategic communications doctrine that allows for influence and behavioral change (Joint Chiefs of Staff, 2006; U.S. Department of Defense, 2010). That doctrine, however, is largely limited to international publics. So, the institutionalization structure is in place but is highly adaptable to the changing military operations at hand in Iraq and other military operations abroad. Public affairs operators have also had to act quickly to counter social media and Internet abilities by opposition forces, and therefore strategic communications plans are highly flexible according to the "situation on the ground" and how local military commanders want to address the various public affairs situations that arise.

Initially for Iraq, 100-page strategic communication plans were written but were not used because public affairs operations were reacting so quickly to changing circumstances. By policy (APAH, 2007), a Public Affairs Operations Center, or PAOC, was established in Iraq to handle public affairs for the entire theater of operations. That PAOC later evolved into an expanded media credentialing and news conference operation. News conferences were held twice a week in the Green Zone in Baghdad. Initially, just U.S and other multinational force commanders in Iraq (MNF-I) conducted those news conferences attended by international and Pan-Arab media. By 2008, this responsibility for the news conferences was split with Iraqi commanders.

The other organization that evolved under MNF-I was a division of communications under the Strategic Effects Command. That division developed four internal sections involved in public relations activities. Those included

- a communication section that acted as a liaison with public affairs officers in the government of Iraq for strategic planning, training, expansion of capacity message alignment, and performance support;
- a measurement and analysis section that developed quantitative and qualitative analysis of public affairs efforts and achievement of objectives; and

- a special forces section that planned and coordinated operations and intelligence activities as well as "declassified imagery requirements," and that also oversaw the process of obtaining permissions for detainee photo releases.

The fourth and perhaps most important section was a media operations section that, among other duties, supervised Western, Pan-Arab and Iraqi media monitoring, responded to media inquiries, produced media releases, and developed and promulgated such documents as Public Affairs Guidance, Questions and Answers, talking points and fact sheets (Unclassified documents, Communication Division, 2008).

As can be seen, then, from a partial description of how these organizations operated in public affairs, it was highly institutionalized, but adapted for the situation at the time in those areas of operation. This was also the case in Operation Iraq Freedom, the name of the operation up until 2010 in Iraq. The communications division was organized in a manner unique to the operation but functional for the demands of the situation and the commander. Policy mandated the use of a public affairs operations center, but by 2005–2006 that had evolved into the communications division that continues today.

This description could be interpreted to mean that the institutionalization of public affairs was adapted from normal policy in a large bureaucracy that was strategic in focus but nevertheless answered the needs of the current tactical situation. Although the changing bureaucracy was large and cumbersome, as might be expected, it matched the various levels of command in Iraq at the time and therefore was not as rigid as might be expected. Organizational change moves slowly in such a bureaucracy but it was adapted relatively quickly given the very real threat from enemy forces.

Another factor that affected institutionalization was the relative rapid rate of change of personnel in the operation. Most personnel at all levels of command were on tours in the country for an average of one year, and at staggered intervals. So although there was usually an overlap of personnel to ensure institutionalization, the situation on the ground was constantly evolving. New commanders always had new ideas about how to proceed, and then there were the ideas and skills of those personnel changing at the operational and tactical levels. These skill sets or instances of expertise deteriorated somewhat as rotations of personnel increased as fewer fully trained personnel were able to be deployed. There were limits on the number of tours personnel could do and the continuing operational tempo began to deplete the pool of trained personnel available.

Conclusions and Perspectives

At this point, then, what do we know about institutionalization in public relations, based on these cases and related discussions in the literature? Institutionalization certainly suggests that there should be some common inception of basic principles and procedures wherever a given function is practiced and regardless of who may be in charge of the given organizational units. For example, it can be argued that the legal and accounting professions have institutionalized to the point that when attorneys or accountants enter any organization where their function is practiced, they likely would recognize a certain stability surrounding the basic principles, standards, and even regulations comprising the function, no matter whose name was attached to the function's directorship or to senior management of the organization. The first research question in this chapter asked to what extent is public relations institutionalized within organizations? Does it share the same status as some of these other professions? A look at the cases examined in this chapter suggests that public relations does not share this same status and is not close to the same level of institutionalization as the professions with which its practitioners interact in given organizations.

The observation of Entity A indicates that institutionalization can occur around a strategic mission and an ongoing commitment to open, honest relationship building. It also shows that institutionalization need not preclude the ability to adjust to changing needs and mandates of stakeholders. In fact, if the recent creation of the social media unit within Entity A serves as an indicator, institutionalized strategic public relations programs can actually adapt rapidly and be strong innovators in the communication arena without losing the fundamental values of relationship building and open communication inherent to the practice.

By contrast, Entities B and C, as well as the industry competitor mentioned by the Entity A respondent, indicate that attempts to institutionalize public relations still seem to be subject to the whims, value systems and overall understanding of public relations by organizational leaders in too many organizations. Even many years of solid public relations programs can be overturned in a short period of time, and often by leaders who hold power in the organization but who understand little about the practice or fundamental purposes of public relations. With these capricious reductions of staff or elimination of vital programs, organizations are again rendered vulnerable to future public relations problems and perhaps even major crises. Regrettably, as has too often been the case over the years, senior executives do not realize or even seem to care about the liabilities created in their own entities when public relations programs are deinstitutionalized.

Entity D seems to mirror the direction of both Entity A and Entities B and C. It was similar to Entity A in that imperatives of the stakeholder environment dictated to at least some extent the need for ongoing fundamental values and practices of public relations, regardless of the people directing each program. In both cases, long-term goals were in place to help the public relations program survive changes in personnel; yet, the political situation, like the adaptation of social media in Entity A, also influenced the ability to quickly determine changes in tactics. However, the respondent in the case of Entity D also recognized the inherent short-term nature within political public relations, noting that goals and strategies were much more focused before an election period than during other times. Related to this is the inevitability of electoral turnover, whereupon an entire office staff can then be changed in a matter of months.

Entities E and F represented extremely large organizations of the U.S. armed forces and other militaries around the world. In these entities, public relations is evolving at different rates. The inherent military culture tends to be so cumbersome that institutionalization is protected by sheer bureaucratic size, and inability to change rapidly. In an environment where stability and complete loyalty can be the difference between life and death, this rigidity can be a strength as well as a burden. Public relations in these entities retains continuity across cases as in Entity A, and because of the absolute requirement to adapt to oppositional activities in the Middle East, new policies are being written especially for counter-insurgency operations (U.S. Army/Marine Corps, 2007) that aggressively use strategic communication to discredit enemy propaganda and provide a more compelling alternative to the insurgencies.

So, results of this multiple-case analysis and other current investigations show support for institutionalization in certain cases. The second and third research questions in this chapter asked what factors would lead to institutionalization? For a start, it may be possible to correlate the institutionalization of the larger organization with the institutionalization of the public relations function. Larger organizations tend to be more bureaucratic, with more ingrained structure, policies, and traditions than the smaller organizations have had time to set up. In this study, the larger corporation has existed for a century, and most of the firms in its industry have certainly become highly stratified (as evidenced in this case by the 400 employees in the public relations function alone). Partly as a result of this, even when changes occurred in the public relations leadership there were few changes in the function. By contrast, the second corporation is much more entrepreneurial, and it had existed for less than 20 years when the public relations officer changed. Some of the company's original leaders had never supported public relations, and so it was easy for them to use the change in the senior public relations officer as an excuse to disband the strategic aspects of the function in favor of continued publicity alone.

The environment in which the organization operates also seems to be a factor. For the military, it was extremely important for everyone to be on the same page, as it were, to maximize self-preservation of all soldiers. For the large firm, the tight competition and traditions of the industry helped foster continuity. The environment was also mentioned in the governor's office, with an electorate that carried expectations regardless of who was in office at a given time. In all of these cases, it seemed that strategic outcomes were seen as more important than any specific tactics. However, individual whims and philosophies of the organizational leaders still carried too much weight in most of the organizations studied.

The fourth and fifth questions proved much more difficult to answer. The public relations field may be growing in legitimacy because of the increasingly dynamic environment that affects organizations. And yet it seems that the field still has far to go before being permeated by institutionalization of values and standards. In smaller organizations, particularly those that are less affected by their environments and more affected by changes in leadership and personnel, institutionalization may be even less promising. The study also revealed little information regarding any correlation between institutionalization and the ability of public relations officers to serve as change agents within the organizations (and perhaps there may even be a reverse correlation—this study was not able to determine that either way).

Coombs and Holladay (2008) suggested that public relations literature often emphasizes the need for institutionalizing public relations as part of organizational management, helping to make key decisions for the organization. They believe that such efforts could be successful if they were linked to, for example, corporate social responsibility. Similarly, in a study on Chinese public relations, Chen (2009) noted that the debate on institutionalization typically hones in on two key issues: "first, the necessity to 'legitimize' the practice of public relations; and second, the importance of empowering PR practitioners to play strategic roles." She then added:

> Once incorporated into existing norms and values as well as recognized internally, the institutionalizing process will bring about certain advantages. These may include: first, an empowered position within organizations that enables PR people to play an important role in strategic decision-making process; second, skepticism on the "legitimacy" of PR practice can be minimized; third, PR people could avoid getting into a "tug of war" fighting for resources needed to get their jobs done; and fourth, public relations could be practiced in a more coherent and consistent way. With such coherence, public relations will become a generally accepted practice—a crucial step toward recognition as a profession, contributing to the effectiveness of organizational achievements (p. 188).

Sadly, and perhaps somewhat ironically, if any institutionalization of the function is occurring today—if perceptions of the field are coalescing—it may be towards tactical elements of the field, instead of around strategic processes. Steyn (2008), for example, argued that the technical aspects of public relations have become more or less institutionalized; the managerial aspects are only partly institutionalized and the strategic functions are not institutionalized at all. Chen (2009) added, "Though put in charge of making communication-related decisions, most PR people remain outside of 'dominant coalitions,' still having little chance to participate in strategic planning" (p. 188).

James E. Grunig (2011) put forward the same argument: "In the minds of most people, public relations has become institutionalized as a messaging activity whose purpose is to make organizations look good . . . rather than as a management activity that improves relationships among stakeholders" (p. 12). He then added, "Practitioners who follow [this] paradigm emphasize messages, publicity, media relations, and media effects," as opposed to "the participation of public relations executives in strategic decision-making so that they can help manage the behavior of organizations" (p. 13). Of course, much more research needs to be conducted to fully understand the possibilities and effects of the institutionalization of public relations. This particular study serves as an early view into how public relations is actually positioned in organizations in relation to leadership, adaptability, and institutionalization. It seems to be legitimate and institutionalized in some organizations and not institutionalized at all in other organizations. And yet, as an exploration, this study only really serves to more closely examine the theory of institutionalization in public relations as well as the possibility of how it can be replicated for other similar cases. More case studies certainly are needed, with more specific questions and operationalization. Additional research methods should also be devised in order to provide more understanding of the process. Future research also could better delve into specifics about how organizations should be both institutionalized and adaptable at the same time. This study touched on the notion that these concepts are both important, but did not go into detail about how they interact. So, certainly there is much more room for qualitative and quantitative studies into these concepts.

Future research also could better delve into specifics about how organizations should be both institutionalized and adaptable at the same time. This study touched on the notion that these concepts are both important, but did not go into detail about how they interact. So, there is certainly much more room for qualitative and quantitative studies into these concepts. This approach of institutionalization and adaptation could even key on J. E. Grunig's institutionalization of *strategic management* in public relations (2011), although he fears that a strategic management function might ossify (p. 28) the practice of public relations as much as an *interpretive approach* has in the past. By strategic management he refers to his model that incorporates the communication process with management decisions, stakeholders and publics, and relationship outcomes. It assumes the participation of public relations in strategic decision making to help manage the behavior of organizations. The interpretive approach assumes that public relations "strives to influence how publics interpret the behavior of organizations after they occur and that its purpose is to secure the power of decision-makers who chose those behaviors" (p. 13). The bottom line for this study is to be able to adapt institutionalization as it is being created; as Larissa A. Grunig (2007) stated, public relations must continue to evolve and continually reinstitutionalize itself as change occurs in organizations, communication technologies and societal expectations.

References

Argenti, P. A., Howell, R. A., & Beck, K. A. (2005). The strategic communication imperative. *MIT Sloan Management Review, 46*(3), 83–89.

Army Public Affairs Handbook. (2007). ST 45-07-01. Army Public Affairs Center, Ft. Meade, Maryland.

Arnold, J. (1995). IMC: Much ado about little. *The Public Relations Strategist, 1*(4), 29–33.

Baxter P., & Jack, S. (2008). Qualitative case study methodology: Study design and implementation for novice researchers. *The Qualitative Report, 13*(4), 544–559.

Botan, C. H. (2006). Grand strategy, strategy and tactics in public relations. In C. H. Botan & V. Hazleton (Eds.), *Public relations theory II* (pp. 223–248). Mahwah, NJ: Lawrence Erlbaum.

Chen, N. (2009). Institutionalizing public relations: A case study of Chinese government crisis communication on the 2008 Sichuan earthquake. *Public Relations Review, 35*(3), 187–198.

Communications Division (2008). Unclassified documents. Strategic Communications Division. Operation Iraqi Freedom. Baghdad, Iraq.

Coombs, W. T., & Holladay, S. J. (2008). *Corporate social responsibility: missed opportunity for institutionalizing public relations?* Paper presented to the Annual Congress of the European Public Relations Education and Research Association (EUPRERA), Milan, Italy.

Falconi, T. M. (2006). How big is public relations (And why does it matter)?: The economic impact of our profession. Gainesville, FL: Institute for Public Relations. Retrieved from http://www.instituteforpr.org/files/uploads/Falconi_Nov06.pdf.

Fisher, R., Ury, W., & Patton, B. (1991). *Getting to yes: Negotiating agreement without giving in* (2nd ed.). New York: Penguin Books.

Fleck, D. (2007). Institutionalization and organizational long-term success. *Brazilian Administration Review, 4*(002), 64–80.

Grunig, J. E. (2006). Furnishing the edifice: Ongoing research on public relations as a strategic management function. *Journal of Public Relations Research, 18*(2), 151–176.

Grunig, J. E. (2007). After 50 years: The value and values of public relations. Annual distinguished lecture, The Institute for Public Relations. Retrieved from http://www.instituteforpr.org/edu_info/values_after_50_years/.

Grunig, J. E. (2011). Public relations and strategic management: Institutionalizing organization-public relationships in contemporary society. *Central European Journal of Communication, 1,* 11–31.

Grunig, J. E., & Hunt, T. (1984). *Managing public relations.* New York: Holt, Rinehart & Winston.

Grunig, J. E. & White, J. (1992). The effect of worldviews on public relations theory and practice. In J. E. Grunig (Ed.), *Excellence in public relations and communication management* (pp. 31–64). Hillsdale, NJ: Lawrence Erlbaum.

Grunig, L. A. (2007). *Public relations in the chaos and change of transformational societies: The potential of evolutionary theory*. Paper presented at the Annual Conference of the International Communication Association (ICA), San Francisco, CA.

Harvard Business Essentials (2003). *Negotiation*. Boston, MA: Harvard Business Publishing.

Hallahan, K., Holtzhausen, D. R., Van Ruler, B., Verčič, D., & Sriramesh, K. (2007). Defining strategic communication. *International Journal of Strategic Communication*. *1*(1), 3–35.

Hon, L. C., & Grunig, J. E. (1999). *Guidelines for measuring relationships in public relations*. Gainesville, FL: The Institute for Public Relations, Commission on PR Measurement and Evaluation.

Hutton, J. G. (2001). Defining the relationship between public relations and marketing. In R. L. Heath (Ed.), *Handbook of Public Relations* (pp. 205–214). Thousand Oaks, CA: Sage.

Jensen, I. (2009). Institutionalization—the social reality of corporate communication. In E. Invernizzi, T. M. Falconi, & S. Romenti (Eds.), *Institutionalising PR and corporate communication: Proceedings of the EUPRERA 2008 Milan Congress* (Vol. 1, pp. 100–119). Milan, Italy: Pearson.

Joint Chiefs of Staff. U.S. Department of Defense (2006). *Joint publication 3–13 information operations*. Washington, DC: U.S. Government I-10.

Ledingham, J. A., & Bruning, S. D. (2000). Public relations as relationship management. Mahwah, NJ: Lawrence Erlbaum.

Macnamara, J. (2006). *The fork in the road of media communication practice and theory*. Paper presented at the 4th Annual Summit on Measurement, Portsmouth, NH.

Meyer, J., & Rowan, B. (1977). Institutionalized organizations: Formal structure as myth and ceremony. *American Journal of Sociology, 83*(2), 340–363.

Mintzberg, H. (1990). The design school: Reconsidering the basic premises of strategic management. *Strategic Management Journal, 11,* 171–195.

Mintzberg, H. (1994). *The rise and fall of strategic planning*. New York: The Free Press.

Nielsen, B. (2006). *The singular character of public relations in a global economy*. Annual distinguished lecture of the Institute for Public Relations, London, UK, October 11.

Oliver, C. (1992). The antecedents of deinstitutionalization. *Organization Studies, 13*(4), 563–588.

Plowman, K. D. (1995). *Congruence between public relations and conflict resolution: Negotiating power in the organization* (Unpublished doctoral dissertation). College Park, MD: University of Maryland,

Plowman, K. D. (1998). Power in conflict for public relations. *Journal of Public Relations Research, 10*(4), 237–262.

Porter, M. (1985). *Competitive advantage: Creating and sustaining superior performance*. New York: Free Press.

Sandhu, S. (2009). Strategic Communication: An Institutional Perspective. *International Journal of Strategic Communication, 3*(2), 72–92.

Scott, R.W. (1987). The adolescence of institutional theory. *Administrative Science Quarterly, 32*(4), 493–511.

Selznick, P. (1957). *Leadership in Administration*. New York: Harper & Row.

Selznick, P. (1996). Institutionalism 'old' and 'new.' *Administrative Science Quarterly, 32*(4), 493–511.

Stake, R. E. (1995). *The art of case study research*. Thousand Oaks, CA: Sage.

Stavridis, J. G. (2007). Strategic communication and national security. *Joint Forces Quarterly, 46*(3), 4–7.

Steyn, B. (2008). *Institutionalizing the strategic role of public relations*. Slide deck presented to the Annual Congress of the European Public Relations Education and Research Association (EUPRERA), Milan, Italy.

Suchman, M. C. (1995). Managing legitimacy: Strategic and institutional approaches. *Academy of Management Review, 20*(3) 571–610.

U.S. Army/Marine Corps (2007). *Counterinsurgency field manual 3–24 and 3–33.5*. Chicago, IL: University of Chicago Press.

U.S. Department of Defense (2010). *Quadrennial defense review report*. Washington, DC: United States Government.

Wakefield, R. I. (2008). *Institutionalizing Public Relations: Progress or Pipe Dream?* Paper presented at the 11th International Public Relations Research Conference, Coral Gables, FL.

Yi, H. (2005). *The role of communication management in the institutionalization of corporate citizenship: Relational convergence of corporate social responsibility and stakeholder management*. Unpublished master's thesis. College Park, MD: University of Maryland.

Yin, R. K. (2009). Case study research: Design and methods (4th ed.) Thousand Oaks, CA: Sage.

Zerfass, A. (2009). Editor's introduction—Institutionalizing strategic communication: Theoretical analysis and empirical evidence. *International Journal of Strategic Communication, 3*(2), 69–71.

Zucker, L. G. (1977). The role of institutionalization in cultural persistence. *American Sociological Review, 42*(5), 726–743.

24

Strategy in Advertising

Tino G. K. Meitz and Guido Zurstiege

Strategy in Advertising

Strategic communication is at the center of communication studies, whether we link strategic communication to intentionally motivated purposes or define the strategic aspect as an inherent part of every communication. In either case, we face an attribution, we make an assessment relating to our observations, and we assign a specific value to communication. Then again, defining strategic communication in the realms of organizational communication is by nature a deliberative operation: the purposeful use of communication to fulfill an organization's mission (Hallahan, Holtzhausen, van Ruler, Verčič & Sriramesh, 2007). However, regardless of the impact of strategic communication in terms of ethical considerations, the nature of the term *strategic* reveals one aspect in particular: Strategic communication provides legitimacy for actors to achieve specific goals. More specifically, beyond the attribution of strategic purposes in communication, and beyond the suspicion towards communication *as* strategic intent, there is a transparent field of application—in corporate communications, public relations and, especially, advertising—whose *raison d'être* is accounted for by the expectation that goals will be achieved: A mission has to be accomplished for communication to be effective. Strategic communication is thus always related to actor groups who are in charge of *doing strategy*.

Doing strategy brings one face to face with issues that define, not only strategy per se, but also what it means to take conscious action by doing strategy to fulfill an organization's mission. Considering the overriding topic of this chapter, it is hardly necessary to define advertising as a specific form of strategic communication, which does not make any secret about its strategic intentions with regard to effectiveness and economic purposes. Nevertheless, advertising and advertising strategy cannot be detached from corporate organization's overall strategic considerations: thus we have to address hierarchies of strategies.

Ordinarily, classifications of advertising from a business point of view place advertising under the aegis of marketing planning, and doing strategy in terms of marketing planning routinely ends up with textbook definitions that tend to describe organizations' strategic objectives on a formal level, rather than the *practice* of doing: "[B]ases for strategic planning are the global analysis of the potential of a corporation's success and the development of ideas in order to safeguard the corporation's future in the long run" (Berndt, 1996, p. 7—our translation). A definition of strategy itself fails to appear. Nevertheless, management theory, at least, has undertaken efforts to define strategy in a paradigmatic attempt. For example Furrer, Thomas and Goussevkaia (2008) carried out a content analysis, investigating strategic management journal articles over a 26-year period (1980–2005). Within the data corpus of 2,125 articles published in the *Academy of Management Journal (AMJ)*, *Academy of Management Review (AMR)*, *Administrative Science Quarterly (ASQ)* and *Strategic Management Journal (SMJ)*, Furrer et al. identified 26 main keywords associated with strategy definitions and strategy modeling. The most common keyword, appearing in 777 articles, was *performance,* which included sub-categories like *risk, wealth creation, profitability,* and so on. Other frequent keywords were in the following order: *environment* (543 articles), *capabilities* (518 articles) and *organization* (492 articles). Although the authors were able to show an interesting evolution of management theory that traces a paradigmatic shift in economics' understanding of the term strategy—towards a more organizational theory-oriented approach—most of the evolutionary stages of strategy perception tend to atomize strategy from a corporate-based view. "Therefore, future research questions should be related to the integration of corporate and competitive strategies and its implication for firms' performance and competitive posture" (Furrer et al., 2008, p. 16). These competitive strategies are defined as socially complex competitive resources such as trust, change and choice, capability and, in particular, *creativity.*

The question is: How do we implement these varying statements of strategic intent? How, and under which conditions, is strategy *done?* As David Seidl (2007) remarked, "[u]nder the label 'strategy as practice' there have recently been increasing calls for closer attention to the ways in which strategizing in organizations is influenced by 'macro-social' structures" (p. 197). Seidl's critical review of paradigmatic accounts in strategy research that disregard the multitude of strategy discourses is a suitable point of departure. Beginning with Seidl's assumption that strategy can be defined neither as a cohesive procedure of action nor as a unified field of research and scientific discourse, we turn towards another hurdle that enters the limelight: the aforementioned hierarchy of strategies. Understanding strategy *as practice* on the one side—as proposed by Seidl's re-description of the entire field of strategy as an ecology of strategy discourses—may cast a light on the manifoldness of practices in doing strategy, but on the other side these practices refer to differing rationalities. As Zerfass (2008) stated with regard to corporate communications' efforts to integrate communication activities:

> This suggests itself as a sensible idea inasmuch as these component areas of corporate communication do [. . .] contribute in distinct ways to the realization and effective execution of strategy. A separation of this sort is also current amongst service-providers and agencies [. . .]. Hand in hand, however, with this necessary specialization goes, again and again, the danger that the view may be lost of the common reference of communication to the strategy as a whole.
>
> *pp. 87–88)*

Focusing on advertising agencies, as a relevant service-provider in corporate communications, the concept of strategy as a whole is challenged more than ever. Corporations' marketing divisions and advertising agencies operate on varying grounds that differ in organizational cultures, and yet both take responsibility for corporations' brand management. In order to incorporate versatile aspects of strategy as a practice, we have to start with a thorough engagement in communicator research focusing on the advertising system and the conditions under which advertising is planned, produced, and finally distributed. As a result we talk about *doing* strategy because we want to stress that in advertising, strategy has become a somewhat taken-for-granted omni-relevant concept, organizing the manifold activities within the whole advertising process.

Doing Strategy in Advertising

Rival Conceptions of Advertising

Since the beginning of the twentieth century we face two principal conceptions of what professional advertising should be: (1) the 'technical' and the (2) 'creative' conception of advertising

(Zurstiege, 2001). The technical conception of advertising draws on reason and sound judgment on the basis of standard measures helping to appraise efforts within the process of the planning, production, and distribution of advertising objectively. Siegert and Brecheis (2010, p. 116) have argued, in view of Zurstiege's (1998, 2005) systems theoretical approach to a theory of advertising, that research deciphers the distinct codes applied by the economic system, on the one hand, and the media system, on the other hand. Similarly, the sociologist Cronin (2004) has suggested that drawing on research fulfills a specific function in the relationship between the advertising practitioner and the advertiser and, moreover, between the brand manager and his superiors: "Indeed, research data can be used as a kind of alibi by those brand managers to justify to their superiors' decisions they have made about the campaign. In this way, brand managers can deploy research as a way of negotiating their (relatively powerless) position in the management structures of client firms, rather than as any benchmark of actual consumer preferences" (p. 350). What is the optimum advertising budget (Jones, 1999)? Which compensation system will motivate the advertising practitioner to provide best service most efficiently (Spake, D'Souza, Crutchfield & Morgan, 1999)? What are the most significant testing methods that help to appraise advertising effects? Does the use of advertising agency consultants lead to a more successful relationship between the advertiser and the advertising practitioner (Beard, 2002)? These are but a few of the generic problems investigated from this perspective. To answer these questions one must exercise sound judgment, and deliver good reasons for which one might be held accountable.

The creative conception of advertising, on the contrary, draws on *artistic license* and thus establishes a strong tie between art and advertising. Despite the fact that most practice-oriented research assumes that the appreciation of applied creativity was sparked of by the *creative revolution* of the 1960s, the creative conception of advertising is much older. Marchand (1986) indicated that— since the beginning of the twentieth century—art has become an instrument of advertising in order to accomplish a cultural uplift. Modern art offered an "aura of both rarefied aesthetic quality and an up-to-date tempo" (p. 140). Even though many authors have complained that research in advertising creativity has received insufficient empirical attention (Stewart, 1992; Zinkhan, 1993; Reid, Whitehill, King & DeLorme, 1998; West & Ford, 2001; Koslow, Sasser & Riordan, 2003; 2006), at least as many authors again have dealt with creativity in advertising by approaching this subject matter from a broad range of perspectives. The individual characteristics of the creative personality have been scrutinized as well as the creative decision process or the (creative) *philosophy* of advertising agencies (West, 1993; West & Ford, 2001). Organizational influences on the creativity of agency personnel (Ensor, Cottam & Band, 2001; Pratt, 2006) have been under discussion, as well as changes in creative advertising, monitored over time (Reid, Whitehill, King & DeLorme, 1998).

Among the different contributors to this field of research there is a strong mutual agreement that stressing applied creativity means that in advertising, for example, as distinct from art, creativity is not employed for its own sake, but rather, to achieve some other (commercial) end. Yet, as research has indicated clearly, in order to enhance creativity it is essential that the creative personnel of the advertising agency perceive encouragement by their co-workers, supervisors, and high-level superiors to take risks. Practically speaking this means a high degree of operational autonomy on the job, liberating the creative personnel from the advertiser's restraints (Amabile, Conti, Coon, Lazenby & Herron, 1996; Ensor, Cottam & Band, 2001). Therefore, whoever establishes a strong tie between art and advertising places emphasis on good sense rather than sound judgment, mutual trust rather than rational inter-subjectivity, inspiration rather than reason, and autonomy rather than control. The creative conception of advertising presupposes a more co-operative business-building relationship between the advertiser and the advertising practitioner.

Fostering research in regard to these rival conceptions of advertising admittedly faces some constraints. Fröhlich (2008) has stated: "representative research concerning occupational structures within the German advertising industry [. . .] is not available." (p. 18: our translation). Without limitation the same holds true for representative communicator research concerning the German advertising industry. Due to this fact, within the German-language research context little is known about the question of how and under which conditions advertising is planned, produced, and distributed. Yet, this interplay between actor groups within the advertising industry, and their respective struggles for power, authority and professional identity, are of considerable importance for the functionality of the media system.

Biting the Bullet or Pulling Together? Power, Authority and Professional Identity in the Advertising Industry

The relationship between the main actor groups can be observed most clearly by asking two different, yet related questions: What are the cornerstones of professionalism in advertising, and what are the key features of best practice in co-operative work between the actors involved? Contributions concerning the first question have put strong emphasis on the latent—or, as the case may be, manifest—conflicts between the members of the different actor groups involved in the planning, production, and distribution of advertising. Taking account of these conflict-laden relationships within the practice of advertising, one of the first thorough investigations was made by the sociologist Tunstall (1964). If the scientific community had appreciated Tunstall's comprehensive analysis properly then he could have been called the founder of this research tradition. This, however, has not been the case until today. If referred to within the field of advertising research at all, Tunstall's pioneering study is usually mentioned in connection with the notion that the effects of advertising and subsequently, the efficiency of advertising are hard to appraise because advertising is but one factor among many others determining the advertiser's business success (1964, p. 16). This is a recurrent theme both in advertising practice and in advertising research.

Tunstall's (1964) interest in advertising research, however, far exceeded the question of how to appraise advertising effects. Instead, he concentrated on another subject: the problem of how the different actors within the advertising business operate in the midst of such uncertainty. On the basis of research subsequent to Tunstall's early contribution it may be stated that at all stages of the advertising process, uncertainty and, moreover, the management of the conflicts accompanying this uncertainty, are a characteristic, if not a vital feature, of the advertising business.

In view of Tunstall's enlightening research we turn to the implications of different actors and differing rationalities within the advertising business.

Implementing Strategy in Advertising Agencies' Services

The implementation of strategy in advertising agencies allows for three relevant lines of argument within this field of research, as follows.

- Power. Advertising agencies and their clients struggle for power in their mutual relations. The problems arising from this constellation have often been scrutinized, for example from the perspective of agency theory: Who gains power in the relationship, and what are the means, respectively, to gain or to check, power?
- Complexity. The production of advertising is a complex process executed by experts who belong to different intellectual "milieus," as pointed out from an organization theory standpoint by Chris Hackley and Arthur J. Kover (2007), among others.
- Integration. This complex process needs, on a personal level, people who can span the boundaries between these different milieus. The complex process also needs, on a rather conceptual level, an organizing idea.

In the last few decades discussion has covered two main organizing ideas: *creativity* and *efficiency*. Currently, we can observe the gradual coming forth and consolidation of a third organizing idea, and this idea is epitomized by the somewhat vague term *strategy*.

Filling a Gap—the Origins of Planning

Reflecting on advertising agencies' strategic impact on communications compulsorily leads to a brief retrospection of *account planning*. 'Fireside tales' of account planning in advertising often render a historic plot, enclosing two outstanding figures in British advertising in the 1960s, namely Pollit and King, and without any doubt, their 'midwifery' plays a vital role in establishing planning within agency cultures. However, *establishing* and *assertiveness* in a business context represent a whole other world. First, there was no sweeping success for account planning within Britain's 1960 advertising agencies; second, as Fletcher (2008) rightly remarks, account planning is a "lousy name" (p. 102), as there has always been planning in advertising, and third, the ambition of 'early stage planners' is anything but consistent.

King, who could claim authorship of the term "account planning" in 1968 (Treasure, 2007), started the institutional deployment of strategic thought at *J. Walter Thompson* (JWT) in order to integrate the consumers' perspective into the creative strategy, as he claimed that JWT's "objective must be a certain state of mind in the potential buyer, not a certain type of advertisement" (p. 14). On this note, in 1964 King introduced the *T-Plan* (Target Plan) in order to orientate the most creative personnel towards brand planning requirements required of potential buyers. Interestingly enough, the deployment of account planning at JWT is not the 'genesis' of strategic thought within the agency's history. According to John Treasure, who became director of research and marketing at JWT in 1960, it mirrored the preceding years' organizational dysfunctions. At that time 27 executives were working for the department. In November 1962, the number of executives had increased to 42, and although Treasure has no doubt that research and marketing executives 'planned' JWT's advertising strategies for clients, they did this duty alongside other tasks. "I can certainly remember that they all were very busy but it is difficult even for me now to understand (given the size of JWT at that time) why we needed so many people" (p. 13).

Pollit, co-founding an agency—*Boase Massimi Pollit* (BMP)—in 1968, focused mainly on strategic aspects of planning within the *intra-agency* context in terms of mediating marketing requirements within a creativity-focused environment. Pollit's approach had already taken shape in 1965 when he became responsible for the research department at Pritchard Wood Partners, his former employer.

> At just this time there was a considerable increase in the quality and quantity of data that was relevant to more professionally planned advertising such as company statistics, available consumer and retailer panel data and so on. This posed a paradox as more data relevant to sharper advertising planning were becoming in, more and more people qualified to handle it were leaving the agencies.
>
> *Pollit, 1979/2000b, p. 5*

Comparing King and Pollit's initial situation reveals significant differences in their approach to personnel expenditure in a changing market. Whereas King, as Treasure depicts, discovered a situation where personnel capacities were inefficiently allocated, Pollit hints at a reverse situation: a sudden lack of qualified personnel to fill a gap originally triggered by clients' own efforts to integrate market research and marketing departments into their corporation's hierarchy. Thus, the erosion of advertising agencies' own research departments presents two sides of the same coin. In agencies with an abundance of staff, the added value of research departments was jeopardized. Reduction in staff, however, led to the implementation of an increasing amount of externally produced research data, whose counterpart could no longer be produced within the advertising agencies.

Albeit that the paths followed by BMP and JWT might be seen to differ when they are appraised in detail, they seem pertinent examples in an illustration of the history of planning in advertising agencies. In this respect, it seems misleading to render account planning as a commonly agreed inception of strategic thinking, planning and development of advertisements and campaigns. Rather it stands to reason that the 'renaming' of planned advertising creation should be considered in the light of changing markets, which thereafter changed business models and logics, and not least, advertising agencies' resource-based reactions to these modifications of their business segment. As Fletcher (2008) stated, the consequences of marketing departments' relocation to the client's side included a rigid regime of success metrics, which suited advertising creation only to a limited extent but filled the needs for the reporting standards of agency clients.

> More importantly, as the new breed of client marketing specialists extended their territorial powers, they began to draw up inflexible rules, disciplines, and evaluation systems for their advertising. These were usually based on simplistic research tools, the best known being 'Day After Recall' (DAR), used by Procter & Gamble, the world's largest advertiser. [. . .] If its recall is worse than average, the new commercial will be taken off air and either tweaked or ditched. DAR is the basis of 'tracking studies,' today's standard means of monitoring campaigns [. . .]. But it cannot be carried out until after a commercial has been made and transmitted.
>
> *p. 103*

Consequently, the logic of measurement did not suit quality requirements for the process of creating advertisements anymore; rather it had been installed to justify marketing budget spending and budget allocation, which went hand in hand with the shifting of research in the aftermath of changes in advertisement production.

The Coevolution of Strategic Planning

Under these conditions, the installment of account planners in the 1960s appears as an unavoidable necessity that above all filled a gap that advertising agencies' partially created by the downsizing of internal research departments, a process that Lewin and Volberda (1999) outlined as organizations and environments' *coevolution*. Coevolution, as the authors state, characterizes the "joint outcome of managerial intentionality, environment, and institutional effects" (p. 526). The point of departure for Lewin and Volberda's concept of coevolution is founded in the very basic assumption that change is mainly a phenomenon derived from interacting populations of organizations: an observation which similarly finds use in systems theory in the description of system–environment relations (Luhmann, 1999). "Change can be driven by direct interactions and feedback from the rest of the system. In other words, change can be recursive and need not be an outcome of either managerial adaptation or environmental selection but rather the joint outcome of managerial intentionality and environmental effects" (Lewin & Volberda, 1999, p. 526).

Doing strategy in advertising, at least from a research perspective, is therefore a challenging process. *Doing* strategy is also rewritable as a dynamic process that gears towards conditions that secure advertising agencies' significance in a competitive market environment in which the roles filled by providers of strategic advice, such as brand agencies, strategy consultancies, public relations professionals, and court clients' marketing departments are constantly synchronizing. Along these lines, one of the main factors for pressing ahead in strategic planning within advertising agencies is *standing ground*. Day and Wensley (2002, p. 101) explain this thus: "*[T]he positioning of each firm within a market space (relative to rivals) over time,*[emphasis added] is a second level of evolutionary process. Individual firms make constraint positioning choices, and these choices develop over time to become what we may label individual market strategies".

These considerations imply that strategy—above the operative workflow of strategic planning in advertising creation—is a core benefit-promise and the one organizing idea concerning the service being provided by the advertising practitioner, as well as the advertising agencies' external stakeholders. In what follows, we expound on how advertising practitioners define the term strategy (*defining strategy*), why and to which ends strategy is possibly gaining its central role within the advertising business (*positioning complexity*), and how drawing on strategy may serve to manage the relation between the advertising agency and the advertising client (*implementing strategy*). Finally, we address how drawing on strategy serves to manage the relation between the different professionals within an advertising agency, and how advertising agencies demonstrate their strategic commitment in terms of the justification of advertising efficiency.

The Operationalization of Strategic Planning in Advertising Agencies

Defining Strategy

To review how strategic planning fits into the workflow of advertising agencies, we interviewed agency CEOs, board members, and senior executive personnel in advertising agencies (Meitz & Zurstiege, 2012). In this context, it seems timely to arrive at a working definition of strategy, and of strategic planning or the synonymic notion of account advertising practitioners, insofar as these terms apply to advertising practitioners. "Perhaps ironically, several times in the last few years at the AAAA [American Association of Advertising Agencies] Account Planning Conference participants and presenters have struggled to explain exactly how to define account planning and how one does it" (Koranda, 2007, p. 627). Such 'voiceless-ness' holds true for the term strategy itself: How do advertising practitioners define the term? In brief, the answer is: They don't! Although both within advertising agencies and externally, strategy is highlighted as a means by which clients' expectations of advertising efficiency can be met, strategy definitions are not available. Executives' attempts to develop definitions ad hoc betoken self-justification—for example, explaining the diversification of the professional field as a shortcoming. Against the background of these statements it is obvious that the term strategy is at least as cloudy as the term creativity, which is still functioning as the most important organizing idea within the advertising practice. Despite this fact, however, we maintain that the term strategy functions as an 'organizing idea,' as it were, within the advertising business.

Why and to what end, however, does strategy possibly gain this central role within the advertising business? Most decision makers draw a clear distinction between the classic and the new digital era of advertising, and most interviewed executives leave no doubt about the fact that the proliferation of channels and media has changed the advertising business profoundly under these new conditions of what one might call *multi-channel options*. Advertising executives display their uncertainty concerning the question of how to reach target groups effectively. In this situation strategic planning promises to represent the intractable target group, which has left the TV couch and hit the road in order to undertake countless digital adventures. Talking about strategy means talking about all possible channels, and this means talking with all possible channel-managers. For instance, when asked what strategic planning meant to him, an executive officer pointed out: "we try to implement a vision of the *campfire:* people, come together, come together, come together!" (Meitz & Zurstiege, 2012, p. 47).

Regardless of the actual outcomes of these 'campfire talks,' however, one can say as a first line of argument that the terms strategy and planning implement as it were a *medium of consent,* the "operative fiction" (Schmidt, 1996) which means that despite the proliferation of options the advertising process can be organized around one central idea. The second line of argument, concerning the central role of strategy, also affects the matter of integration, but in this case it does not focus on the processes within the advertising agency but in the relation between the advertising agency and its client. "In the moment that is my approach to strategy, I think, we work much more backstage and try to make connections for our clients they don't see" (Meitz & Zurstiege, 2012, p. 47).

Reading the statements of decision makers in advertising agencies closely, it becomes apparent that advertising agencies' promise to deliver strategy can be understood as a strategy itself, to fill in a blank position within the hierarchies of the agencies' corporate clients and thus to gain power in the relationship: a blank position that is situated above the marketing department and that in the past has been filled by consulting.

Implementing Strategy

The essential task for an agency in order to regain influence within a client's decision-making processes is the integration of *experts* in a client's decision-making process. Insofar as the basic application of strategy in client–agency relationships implies alignment with executive decision makers, strategy is an alignment in order to regain visibility. There is no general attempt to implement strategy in order to draw customers' attention to the offered planning services. The processes of strategy implementation are mainly driven by factors that are likely to be described in Mintzberg's (1979; and Mintzberg & McHugh, 1985) organizational concept of *adhocracy*, which they describe as "an extraordinary flexible organizational form specialized for ad hoc tasks." At this point our argument could be summarized thus: There is no planned management of strategy issues in client–agency relationships. Nevertheless, this 'lack of concept' is mainly caused by predominating daily business concerns and the limited amount of power held by agency professionals' counterparts.

Considering these constraints, agencies have developed alternative paths to ensure executive decision makers' awareness of the issue of strategy. Three such paths can be identified, illustrating the advertising agency's exclusive competence with regard to strategy implementation:

1. Networking into a client's hierarchy: To support the agency's interests in networking with the client, for example, agencies seem to favor workshops as a means of establishing a visible framework for the customer's executive decision makers in order to draw attention to the agency's range of services as well as to maintain a get-together atmosphere. But networking can also be regarded as a long-term face-to-face engagement, whereby an agency member tries to support his or her direct counterpart on the client's side in order to lift him or her up within the organizational hierarchy and finally benefit from his or her professional advancement. These processes refer to the second factor with influence to regain or expand agencies' influence in customer's decision-making processes: sustainability.

2. Sustainability in relationships: An agency seeks to persuade executive decision-makers of the agency's strategic potential by performing a steady progression of strategic tasks. "As a matter of course [account planning] also is a customer-loyalty-tool ... for the agency, in terms of a long-term planning with the customer" (Meitz & Zurstiege, 2012, p. 48). While clear focus on the strategic impact of the agencies' work is missing, the evidence of the necessity and success of strategy is finally often seen in the creative output.

3. Post-rationalization: constructing a 'vision of strategy' whose impact is verifiable by the agency's creative output. This means that when an agency is dealing with the complexity of client–agency relations, the conception level and inter-relation of "creativity and efficiency" have a special quality. As senior advertising executives unanimously report, efficiency originates from strategic planning but is in itself concealed to the client's view. Therefore, in order to provide a 'vision of strategy,' agencies tend to define a campaign's success or at least customer satisfaction with the creative output of a project: the *coming alive* of a strategy's effectiveness. Strategy comes alive by post-rationalizing the creative workflow: "[A]s a matter of course, an agency will always

be evaluated by creative awards. And I dare to claim that planning has a considerable proportion on what keeps creative excellence relevant [. . .]" (Meitz & Zurstiege, 2012, p. 50).

Bridging the Gap—the Role of Boundary-Spanners

The interplay of strategic planning as the trigger for efficiency that is borne out by creative excellence, on the one hand, and the creative potential of an agency, on the other hand, is not only an external alliance, referring to customers. By definition, boundary-spanners bridge distinct spheres of interest. They notoriously "wear two hats," as it were, and are therefore as important for the advertising process as they are susceptible to role ambiguity. Focusing on the advertising system there are mainly three fields of action in which boundary-spanners serve their function: (a) the relationship between the advertiser and the advertising practitioner, (b) the relationship between the creative personnel and the management personnel, and (c) the relationship between the advertising practitioner and the media marketer.

In the first field of action the account executive serves as a boundary-spanner, mediating between the personnel of the advertising agency on the one hand and the advertiser's marketing manager on the other hand. Account executives accomplish their mediating function on the basis of their proficiency in the advertiser's business as well as on the basis of their professional authority within the advertising agency. The account executive's most important relationship is towards his boundary-spanning counterpart in the advertiser's company: the marketing manager. Due to this fact—from the advertising agency's perspective—it is highly important to establish a good personal relationship between the account executive and the marketing manager in order to acquire and maintain long-term, mutually rewarding relationships with their clients. Advertising agencies therefore typically consign to a given account those account executives that are similar in educational background and taste to the advertiser's marketing manager (Ewing, Pinto, & Soutar, 2001; Crutchfield, Spake, D'Souza, & Morgan, 2003). Thus, it can be said that account executives and marketing managers fulfill their respective functions because an emphasis has been placed on role-correspondence.

In the second field of action the account planner and other "connectors," informally called "runners," serve as boundary-spanners with a view to reconciling differences between the highly specialized experts of account management, the creative department and experts for special services (Kover & Goldberg, 1995; Steel, 1998; Hackley, 2000; 2003a; 2003b; Morrison & Haley, 2003). Account planners help to bridge the gap between the two different milieus within an advertising agency: the liberal arts milieu and the scientific milieu of management (Hackley & Kover, 2007, p. 65).

Summarizing briefly, boundary-spanners by definition bridge distinct spheres of interest composed by members who conform to different standards and norms. The research topic underlying this function of boundary-spanners, of course, is that of a conflict between the members of the different actor groups involved in the planning, production, and distribution of advertising. The internal role of professionals in strategic planning units thus goes far beyond that of classical "ad tweaking" (Pollit, 2000a); it is a profession of facilitating between account management as mainly driven by economic ratio and the 'artists' of the creative units. On that note, boundary-spanning refers to the implementation of strategic planning as an internal 'translation-service' within agencies that negotiates the terms of collaboration between different intellectual milieus.

Unequal Conditions and Strategic Rituals

The attempts and efforts within the advertising agencies in order to regain clients' awareness—as we have shown—are driven by the integration of techniques and knowledge as well as social alignment processes. However, it remains whether these efforts echo in clients' organizational patterns. Likewise, it is doubtful if clients are able to incorporate agencies' strategic offers within their organizational structures, if they are able to mirror agencies' adhocracy from a structural perspective, and if they deem the revaluation of advertising practitioners in decision-making processes a necessity.

Yet, focusing on intra-organizational aspects of strategic planning in advertising, strategy in itself has a utility value, a ritual function that bridges the interests of differing intellectual milieus. "We get a hint of what may be the deeper function of the art, cult and ritual of various occupations. They may provide a set of emotional and even organizational checks and balances against both the subjective and objective risks of the trade" (Hughes, 1958/1981, p. 97).

Verifying Strategic Performance

Regardless of strategy's ritualistic value for balancing these milieus, it still serves as a legitimate benchmark in order to justify advertising budget allocation and spending. Advertising must not happen without a cause, and for this reason efficient accounting for expenditure naturally escorts the notion of strategy in advertising. As we have pointed out already, the legitimization of the creative outcome of advertising campaigns is consistently accompanied by post-rationalizing decisions *as* strategic, which is expressed in terms of *research measures* in order to verify campaigns' effectiveness.

As advertising awards mark a central indicator for advertising campaigns' success, researching for evaluation measures in the context of award-submissions for professional awards or prize-winning campaigns appears quite logical (Raupp, 2008). With reference to the primary implication of research data, we refer once back to Pollit:

> The main problems that arose in the use of all these measurements, despite their essentially common-sense origins, have been that they have produced results, which have been very difficult to reconcile with any reasonable judgment expectations about particular advertisements and campaigns. They did not provide common-sense answers.
>
> *Pollit, 2000a, p. 30*

Certainly, Pollit's remarks pertain to the early 1960s when market research divisions were still an integral part of advertising agencies. The outsourcing of market research divisions in the course of the professionalization of market research, however, did not remove the barrier to understanding research-data and creative workflows; nor did the advertising industry's attempt to establish its own internal research cultures, which are prominently labeled as *strategic* or *account planning* in advertising agencies, lead to independency from market research measures. The professionalization of market research and the establishment of internal research cultures, however, did nurture the distinction between varying intellectual milieus, and functional fixedness with regard to concurring rationalities.

However, this distinction is at risk when strategic planning follows the task of post-rationalization, a task that unambiguously aims at meeting the requirements of accountability. To consider the question of whether internal research cultures play a pivotal role in this regard, it seems apposite to take a closer look at one of the prestigious *efficiency-led* awards within the advertising business: the *Effie Awards*. Effie Worldwide licenses its award scheme to national associations. If the implementation of research is a key factor for agencies' success with regard to receiving awards, the case studies of short-listed agencies provide revealing information. Based on case-studies for the German Effie Awards in the period 1995–2011 ($N = 666$), discrete research achievements of strategic planning departments within advertising agencies are nearly insignificant. Concerning strategic planning's own contributions, post-rationalization relies—at least when edited and graphically displayed for these case studies—on the 'usual suspects,' namely the major players in market research (Table 24.1).

Table 24.1 Top Five External Market Research Corporation's Designation Within German Effie Awards Shortlisted Case Studies (1995–2011)

(n)	2009	2011
AC Nielsen Reseach	161	189
Gesellschaft für Konsumforschung (GfK)	140	165
Icon Added Value	52	63
tns Research International	49	61
Milward Brown	29	34
Total of designated top 5 research corporations	431	512
N	728	889

Results of a continuing content analysis of submitted and short-listed Effie-awards case studies

Table 24.1 displays the designation of external research corporations whose research results are graphically displayed within Effie-awards case studies in order to justify advertising success (multiple answers)

Such results indicate that the success of agencies' efforts to establish research-based strategic planning is somewhat doubtful, all the more so as the commissioner of these research datasets in most cases can be identified as the agency's client. On this note, agencies simply align their clients' benchmarks of success to the requisite standards, although measures like revenue, turnover, or even brand likeability are very rarely suitable markers to employ in verifying the accomplishment of strategic planning.

As a last point, the re-introduction and institutionalization of market research displays similarities to the historical development of public opinion research. As Raupp (2007) stated, more recent history of the public opinion research market has shown vivid indications of an increasing internationalization and concentration of the market. Raupp traced the recent history of *Emnid*, an established German enterprise that delivers public opinion research for Germany's mass media. "From 1990–1997 Emnid predominantly belonged to the French Sofres-Group. Since the merger of the French Sofres-Group with the British market-research enterprise Taylor Nelson AGB, London, Emnid belongs to the TNS-Group" (p. 132 our translation).

The historical similarities between public opinion research and advertising-related market research are barely surprising and are evident if we pursue Raupp's line of enquiry: In 2008 the TNS-Group was acquired by Kantar, owner of Added Value (comprising Added Value, Icon Brand Navigation and Diagnostic Research), and rebranded as TNS Global Research. Kantar in turn is a consultancy division of WPP, an enterprise-network that displays itself as "world's largest communications services group" (WPP, 2011), pooling such illustrious advertising-agency names like Bates, Grey, J. Walter Thompson (JWT), Ogilvy & Mather, Scholz & Friends, Young & Rubicam, and so on. Based on that balance of power in market research and advertising, the progressive concentration in the business sectors is worth mentioning, not least as asking *who is watching the watchdogs* in the process of advertising efficiency evaluation becomes a matter of delicacy.

What we finally face by these processes of internationalization and market consolidation is apparent as the convergence of research cultures. It is not that we persist in saying that certain methods of market research and consumer behavior research are disappearing but that a specific perception in regard of research and its relevance in general is pre-shaped by the daily experience of advertising agencies when market research data are delivered on behalf of clients. This specific perception is mainly driven by agencies' expectations and anticipations towards clients' ideas of advertising efficiency. Except for Pollit's objection in regard to these data-sets' "numeracy" (2000a, p. 31), the convergence of research cultures influences advertising agencies if the *effect* of advertising communication is taken into account. Once again, *doing* strategy in advertising shows up as a process that maintains the gap between creativity and efficiency—the proof of the concept, the verification of the creative production's effect is ordinarily accomplished by post-rationalization.

References

Amabile, T. M., Conti, R., Coon, H., Lazenby, J., & Herron, M. (1996). Assessing the work environment for creativity. *The Academy of Management Journal, 39*(5), 1154–1184.

Beard, F. K. (2002). Exploring the use of advertising agency review consultants. *Journal of Advertising Research, 42*(1), 39–50.

Berndt, R. (1996). *Marketing 1. Käuferverhalten, Marktforschung und Marketing-Prognosen.* [Marketing 1. Consumer behavior, market research and marketing prognoses] Berlin, Germany: Springer.

Cronin, A. M. (2004). Currencies of commercial exchange. Advertising agencies and the promotional imperative. *Journal of Consumer Culture, 4*(3), 339–360.

Crutchfield, T. N., Spake, D. F., D'Souza, G. & Morgan, R. M. (2003). "Birds of a feather flock together": Strategic implications for advertising agencies. *Journal of Advertising Research, 43*(4), 361–369.

Day, G. S., & Wensley, R. (2002). Market strategies and theories of the firm. In B. Weitz & R. Wensley (Eds.), *Handbook of Marketing.* London, England: Sage.

Ensor, J., Cottam, A., & Band, C. (2001). Fostering knowledge management through the creative work environment: A portable model from the advertising industry. *Journal of Information Science, 27*(3), 147–155.

Ewing, M. T., Pinto, T. M., & Soutar, G. N. (2001). Agency–client chemistry: Demographic and psychographic influences. *International Journal of Advertising, 20*(2), 169–187.

Fletcher, W. (2008). *Powers of Persuasion. The Inside Story of British Advertising: 1951–2000.* Oxford, England: Oxford University Press.

Fröhlich, R. (2008). Werbung in Deutschland—Auf dem Weg zu einem Frauenberuf? [Advertising in Germany—On the way to a female profession?] In C. Holtz-Bacha (Ed.), *Stereotype? Frauen und Männer in der Werbung* [Stereotypes? Women and men in the advertising business] (pp. 14–39). Wiesbaden, Germany: Verlag für Sozialwissenschaften.

Furrer, O., Thomas, H., & Goussevskaia, A. (2008). The structure and evolution of the strategic management field: A content analysis of 26 years of strategic management research. *International Journal of Management Reviews, 10*(1), 1–23.

Hackley, C. (2000). Silent running: Tacit, discursive and psychological aspects of management in a top UK advertising agency. *British Journal of Management, 11*(3), 239–254.

Hackley, C. (2003a). Account planning: Current agency perspectives on an advertising enigma. *Journal of Advertising Research, 43*(2), 235–245.

Hackley, C. (2003b). How divergent beliefs cause account team conflict. *International Journal of Advertising, 22*(3), 313–332.

Hackley, C., & Kover, A. J. (2007). The trouble with creatives: Negotiating creative identity in advertising agencies. *International Journal of Advertising, 26*(1), 63–78.

Hallahan, K., Holtzhausen, D, van Ruler, B., Verčič, D., & Sriramesh, K. (2007). Defining strategic communication. *International Journal of Strategic Communication, 1*(1): 3–35.

Hughes, E. C. (1981). *Men and their work* Westport, CT: Greenwood Press. (Original work published 1958).

Jones, J. P. (1999). Budgeting for advertising and the advertising-intensiveness curve. In J. P. Jones (Ed.), *The advertising business: operations, creativity, media planning, integrated communications* (pp. 77–88). London, England: Sage.

Koranda, D. (2007). Advertising account planning: A practical guide [book review]. *Journalism & Mass Communication Quarterly, 84*(3), 627–628.

Koslow, S., Sasser, S., & Riordan, E. A. (2003). What is creative to whom and why? Perceptions in advertising agencies. *Journal of Advertising Research, 43*(1), 96–110.

Koslow, S., Sasser, S., & Riordan, E. A. (2006). Do marketers get the advertising they deserve? Agency views of how clients influence creativity. *Journal of Advertising, 35*(3), 81–101.

Kover, A. J., & Goldberg, S. M. (1995). The games copywriters play: Conflict, quasi-control, a new proposal. *Journal of Advertising Research, 35*(4), 52–68.

Lewin, A. Y., & Volberda, H. W. (1999). Prolegomena on coevolution: A framework for research on strategy and new organizational forms. *Organization Science, 10*(5), 519–534.

Luhmann, Niklas. (1999). *Die Wirtschaft der Gesellschaft* [The economy of society] (3rd ed.). Frankfurt am Main, Germany: Suhrkamp.

Marchand, R. (1986). *Advertising the American dream. Making way for modernity, 1920–1940.* Berkeley, CA: University of California Press.

Meitz, T. G. K., & Zurstiege, G. (2012). Die Werbeforschung der Werbepraxis [Advertising research of advertising practitioners]. In H. Haas & K. Lobinger (Eds.), *Qualitäten der Werbung—Qualitäten der Werbeforschung* [Quality of advertising—quality of advertising research] (pp. 45–57). Köln, Germany: Herbert von Halem.

Mintzberg, H. (1979). *The structuring of organisations*. New York: Prentice Hall Inc.

Mintzberg, H., & McHugh, A. (1985). Strategy formation in an adhocracy. *Administrative Science Quarterly, 30*(2), 160–198.

Morrison, M. A., & Haley, E. (2003). Account planners' views on how their work is and should be evaluated. *Journal of Advertising, 32*(2), 7–16.

Pollit, S. (2000a). Has anything gone wrong with advertising research? In P. Feldwick (Ed.), *Pollit on planning* (pp. 27–38). Henley-on-Thames, England: Admap.

Pollit, Stanley. (2000b). How I started account planning in agencies. In P. Feldwick (Ed.), *Pollit on planning* (pp. 1–9). Henley-on-Thames, England: Admap. (Original article published in 1979).

Pratt, A. C. (2006). Advertising and creativity, a governance approach: A case study of creative agencies in London. *Environment and Planning, 38*(10), 1883–1899.

Raupp, J. (2007). *Politische Meinungsforschung. Die Verwendung von Umfragen in der politischen Kommunikation* [Political public opinion research. The use of surveys in political communication]. Konstanz, Germany: UVK.

Raupp, J. (2008). Evaluating strategic communication: Theoretical and methodological requirements. In A. Zerfass, B. Ruler & K. Sriramesh (Eds.), *Public Relations Research* (pp. 179–192): VS Verlag für Sozialwissenschaften.

Reid, L. N., Whitehill King, K., & DeLorme, D. E. (1998). Top-level agency creatives look at advertising creativity then and now. *Journal of Advertising, 27*(2), 1–16.

Schmidt, S. J. (1996). *Kognitive Autonomie und soziale Orientierung. Konstruktivistische Bemerkungen zum Zusammenhang von Kognition, Kommunikation, Medien und Kultur* [Cognitive autonomy and social orientation. Constructivistic remarks on the interrelation of cognition, communication, media and culture] (2nd ed.). Frankfurt am Main, Germany: Suhrkamp.

Seidl, D. (2007). General strategy concepts and the ecology of strategy discourses: A systemic-discursive perspective. *Organization Studies, 28*(2), 197–218.

Siegert, G., & Brecheis, D. (2010). *Werbung in der Medien- und Informationsgesellschaft. Eine kommunikationswissenschaftliche Einführung* [Advertising in media- and information societies. A communication research introduction] (2nd ed.). Wiesbaden, Germany: Springer VS.

Spake, D. F., D'Souza, G., Crutchfield, T. N. & Morgan, R. M. (1999). Advertising agency compensation: An agency theory explanation. *Journal of Advertising, 28*(3), 53–72.

Steel, J. (1998). *Truth, lies, and advertising. The art of account planning*. New York: Wiley & Sons.

Stewart, D. W. (1992): Speculations on the future of advertising research. *Journal of Advertising, 21*(3), 1–18.

Treasure, John. (2007). The origins of account planning. In J. Lannon & M. Baskin (Eds.), *A masterclass in brand planning. The timeless works of Stephen King* (pp. 13–18). Chichester, England: Wiley & Sons.

Tunstall, J. (1964). *The advertising man in London advertising agencies*. London, England: Chapman & Hall.

Weick, K. E. (1979). *The social psychology of organizing*. New York: McGraw-Hill.

West, D. (1993). Cross-national creative personalities, processes, and agency philosophies. *Journal of Advertising Research, 33*(5), 53–62.

West, D., & Ford, J. (2001). Advertising agency philosophies and employee risk taking. *Journal of Advertising, 30*(1), 77–91.

WPP (2011). Who we are. Retrieved 04.11.2011, from http://www.wpp.com/wpp/about/whoweare/

Zerfass, A. (2008). Corporate communication revisited: integrating business strategy and strategic communication. In A. Zerfaß, B. van Ruler & K. Sriramesh (Eds.), *Public relations research: European and international perspectives and innovations* (pp. 65–96). Wiesbaden, Germany: Springer VS..

Zinkhan, G. M. (1993). Creativity in advertising: Creativity in the *Journal of Advertising. Journal of Advertising, 22*(2), 1–3.

Zurstiege, G. (1998). *Mannsbilder—Männlichkeit in der Werbung. Eine Untersuchung zur Darstellung von Männern in der Anzeigenwerbung der 50er, 70er und 90er Jahre.* [Male representations in advertising. A study on the representation of males in print advertising of the 1950s, 1970s and 1990s]. Opladen, Germany: Westdeutscher Verlag.

Zurstiege, G. (2001). Good girls go to heaven, bad girls go everywhere—advertising under suspicion. *Poetics, 29*, 273–282.

Zurstiege, G. (2005). *Zwischen Kritik und Faszination. Was wir beobachten, wenn wir die Werbung beobachten, wie sie die Gesellschaft beobachtet* [Between critique and fascination. What we observe when we observe advertising, observing society]. Köln, Germany: Herbert von Halem.

25

The Strategic Context of Political Communication

Spiro Kiousis and Jesper Strömbäck

Although political communication has been a thriving field of study in communication scholarship since its inception, the major focus of this area of research has been to explore the interrelationships among policymakers, news media, and public opinion with a heavy emphasis on one-way information flow and the role of news in impacting public perceptions, attitudes, and voting behavior (Knott Martinelli, 2011). For example, the classic studies of Lazarsfeld and colleagues examined the influence of news media on public opinion and voting behavior during the 1940 and 1944 U.S. presidential elections and explicated the two-step and multi-step flow models of communication (e.g., Katz & Lazarsfeld, 1955; Katz, 1957). More recent research on agenda setting, priming, the spiral of silence, and framing has continued this trend of examining news media–public opinion relationships (e.g., Iyengar & Kinder, 1987; McCombs, 2004; Scheufele, 1999).

Similarly, the pattern in most strategic communication scholarship has been to investigate the impact of corporate communication, advertising, public relations, and marketing messages within a business setting. The focus of this research, albeit important, has left the influence of strategic communication in a political context under-examined from both a theoretical and an empirical standpoint, although there are exceptions (e.g., Manheim, 1991; 2011). Thus, the central emphasis of this chapter is to probe the role of strategic communication in politics. The aim is not to be totally comprehensive but to provide a broad overview of major perspectives and contexts in this area of strategic communication scholarship. To accomplish this, the chapter will compare the meta-perspectives on strategic political communication offered by political marketing and political public relations, explore the strategies prevalent in strategic political communication, offer a conceptual model and specific theoretical perspectives that are useful for understanding its impact, and conclude by presenting directions for future research.

Conceptual Orientations

A natural starting point for considering strategic communication in a political context is to identify its core qualities by looking at different definitions. According to Hallahan, Holtzhausen, Ruler, Verčič and Sriramesh (2007), strategic communication is defined as "the purposeful use of communication by an organization to fulfill its mission" (p. 3). From a corporate communication perspective, Argenti, Howell and Beck (2005) define it as "communication aligned with the company's overall strategy, to enhance its strategic positioning" (p. 83). Finally, the term has been used in military circles and defined as "the orchestration and/or synchronization of actions, images, and words to achieve a desired effect" (U.S. Department of Defense, 2008, p. 4). Thus, one major characteristic that separates strategic communication from other types of communication is that it is intentional and objectives-driven. In politics, the two major aims that strategic communication supports are campaigning and governing, although these aims are often separated, as shown during elections when staff for an incumbent's campaign are typically separate from his or her governance personnel. At the same time, the rise of permanent campaigning has served to blur the boundaries between campaigning and governing (Blumenthal, 1980). In either case, strategic political communication can be used to achieve objectives in elections and policymaking. It can also be used for aims such as increasing internal cohesion or shaping media coverage.

Another major theme in definitions of the term is the emphasis on being "strategic." Prior research suggests four major contexts where a strategic orientation is important in politics: the electoral arena, internal arena, parliamentary arena, and media arena (Sjöblom, 1968a; Nord, 1997; Strömbäck, 2007). According to Botan (2006), the term "strategic" subsumes the two overlapping concepts of grand strategy and strategy. Grand strategy refers to "the policy-level decisions an organization makes about goals, alignments, ethics, and relationship with publics and other forces in its environment," strategy to "the campaign-level decision making involving maneuvering and arranging resources and arguments to carry out organizational grand strategies," and tactics to "the specific activities and outputs through which strategies are implemented—the doing or technical aspect of public relations" (Botan, 2006, p. 225–226). For strategic communication to be effective, their practitioners must be involved when making decisions on both grand strategy and strategy, and not confined to the role of technicians carrying out the tactics (Botan, 2006; Grunig & Repper, 1992; Hallahan et al., 2007; Pfau & Wan, 2006). For example, in political communication, an example of grand strategy is the approach used to win elections or govern effectively. An example of strategy might be to complete a fund-raising drive in support of a particular politician, and a tactic may comprise the specific social media messages used to complete such an effort.

To address what meta-perspectives provide the best understanding of strategic communication in politics, the authors suggest that political marketing and political public relations are perhaps the most promising (Strömbäck, Mitrook & Kiousis, 2010). Broadly speaking, political marketing has been defined as:

> . . . the application of marketing principles and procedures in political campaigns by various individuals and organizations. The procedures involved include the analysis, development, execution, and management of strategic campaigns by candidates, political parties, governments, lobbyists and interest groups that seek to drive public opinion, advance their own ideologies, win elections, and pass legislation and referenda in response to the needs and wants of selected people and groups in society.
>
> *Newman, 1999, p. xiii*

In comparison, Strömbäck and Kiousis (2011a) define political public relations as

> the management process by which an organization or individual actor for political purposes, through purposeful communication and action, seeks to influence and to establish, build, and maintain beneficial relationships and reputations with its key publics to help support its mission and achieve its goals.
>
> *p. 14*

The benefit of this comprehensive definition of political public relations is that it does not simplify it as news management or media relations, thereby relegating it to merely a technical function (e.g., Froehlich & Rüdiger, 2006).

The concepts of strategic political communication, political public relations, and political marketing are closely related. In particular, all three underscore the need for purposeful communication and management being focused in the sense that they should advance organizational missions and objectives. They are also all concerned with the interrelationships among multiple groups in the political arena. Nonetheless, there do seem to be some critical distinctions, especially between political marketing and political public relations. We suggest that political marketing and political public relations offer competing meta-perspectives for conceptualizing the role of strategic communication in a political context. Political marketing draws from consumer behavior literature and tends to treat political communication in much the same way as businesses selling products to customers (e.g., Cwalina, Falkowski & Newman, 2010; Scammell, 1999; Kotler, 1974). Thus, candidates are products, voters are consumers, and so forth. The flow of information is often viewed as a top-down, one-way transmission of messages and information. Some of the major strengths of political marketing, though, are its focus on reputation cultivation and controlled candidate communications in the political process, as well as its emphasis on continuously gathering market intelligence (Lees-Marshment, 2012).

One important aspect where political public relations differs from political marketing is that the latter deals with a wider range of stakeholders, such as members, interest groups and politicians from other parties, whereas the former tends to zero in more on voters than other groups (Strömbäck & Kiousis, 2011a). Nonetheless, Hughes and Dann (2009) offer an instructive list of at least 17 stakeholder groups that can be identified as paramount in strategic political communication, political marketing, and political public relations: alternative political providers; electoral commissions, parliaments, government offices; industry lobby groups; issue competitors; media organizations; party donors; party members and supporters; political candidates; political opponents; private lobbyists; social pressure lobby groups; citizens and society at large; splinter interest groups; voters at election time; and voters between elections. Although this may not be the definitive list—as it depends on the organization and thus is contextual—it illustrates that there are a large number of organizations and groups that are relevant in the context of strategic political communication.

Other important ways in which political public relations differs from political marketing are that it underscores both short-term and long-term engagement with stakeholders, views the flow of information as multi-way among political organizations and their stakeholders, encompasses both organizational communication and action (Kaid & Holtz-Bacha, 2008; Strömbäck & Kiousis, 2011b), and focuses less on the specific context of election campaigns, which political marketing tends to focus on. For these reasons, it can be argued that political public relations supplies a more comprehensive and inclusive view of strategic communication in politics than political marketing. The broader view of political engagement offered in political public relations incorporates not only a reputation management framework (short-term) but also a relationship cultivation framework (long-term) that both have significant theoretical, empirical, and practical implications for strategic political communication (to be explained further in the next section). Although a political public relations framework for understanding strategic political communication is to be preferred, it is not without its limitations, as political marketing may be more appropriate for studying specific tools such as political ads or particular campaigns.

Political Public Relations Strategies

Returning to the explication of Botan (2006) concerning grand strategy, strategy, and tactics, another benefit of adopting a political public relations framework is that a greater range of elements can be identified as being a part of the strategic communication process in politics. Smith (2009) explicates a variety of general public relations strategies that are defined as proactive versus reactive and are easily adapted to a political public relations and strategic communication setting. The proactive ones include organizational performance, audience participation, special events, alliances and coalitions, sponsorships, activism, newsworthy information, and transparent communication. The reactive ones are prebuttal, attack, embarrassment, threat, denial, excuse, justification, concession, ingratiation, disassociation, relabeling, concern, condolence, regret, apology, investigation, corrective action, restitution, repentance, and silence. It is noteworthy that these involve both communication and action, consistent with this chapter's advocacy of a political public relations framework for studying strategic political communication.

Another perspective on strategies is offered by Hendrix (2007) but has a more specific emphasis on government relations and politics. Among the most effective are fact finding, coalition building, direct lobbying, grassroots activities, political action committees, political education activities, communications on political issues, and political support activities. A specific set of strategies developed for government media relations was offered by Baker (1997), who suggested most political communicators use approaches that are active, proactive, combination, or just "winging it." The last is, of course, the least desirable, but it is important to note that the practice of strategic political communication may not coincide with normative ideals about how it should occur. Finally, Froehlich and Rüdiger (2006) asserted that framing can be viewed as a mobilization strategy in political public relations inasmuch as it brings certain topics and how they are portrayed into public and policymaking discourse.

Theoretical Perspectives

With respect to the concept of adopting a political public relations framework the better to understand strategic political communication, a common theme in the literature and definitions is a ubiquitous concern with both *reputation* and *relationship* development and maintenance. Applying the ideas of Hutton, Goodman, Alexander and Genest (2001) to a political context, political public relations and strategic communication can be seen as critical to all stages of stakeholder engagement, whether the latter involves an adolescent developing an allegiance to a political party or a lifelong volunteer for a civic organization aiming to recruit new voters. Important in this context is also the multiplicity of publics that are germane to political organizations, broadly conceived. Therefore views of political public relations and strategic communication that reduce these spheres to media relations, news management or voter relations, or that only focus on either short-term *or* long-term interactions between organizations and key publics, should be rejected. The concepts of reputation and relationship management are *both* central to capturing this short-term and long-term orientation regarding the engagement of political organizations and the multiplicity of their key stakeholders.

From this viewpoint, political public relations, in particular, is not limited to simple information dissemination and exchange for peripherally involved publics, but it is also not centered solely in the engagement of highly involved stakeholder groups such as major donors or activist groups. Consequently, conceptualizing political public relations and strategic political communication along a continuum of stakeholder engagement with reputation and relationship quality at each end can be

Low engagement
(Reputation quality)

High engagement
(Relationship quality)

Figure 25.1 Stakeholder Engagement in Political Public Relations and Strategic Political Communication

Based on a figure from Kiousis, S., & Strömbäck, J. (2011)

useful for understanding its study and practice (Kiousis & Strömbäck, 2011). Figure 25.1 illustrates this conceptualization.

Relationship Cultivation

A relationship cultivation approach has the most direct application to the right-hand side of the aforementioned engagement continuum (Figure 25.1). From this perspective, strategic political communication should be employed to develop and maintain quality relationships between political organizations and their key stakeholders. This can be conceptualized in terms of relationship maintenance strategies, indicators of relationship quality, and relationship outcomes (cf. Broom, Casey & Ritchey, 1997). In other words, this explication identifies relationship antecedents, processes, and consequences. In a study of the 2008 U.S. presidential election, Seltzer and Zhang (2008) explored the impact of the relationship maintenance strategies of mediated communication, social activities, interpersonal communication, and online communication on relationship quality with political parties along the dimensions of trust, satisfaction, commitment, control mutuality, and supportive behaviors. Their findings indicated that mediated communication was a significant predictor of relationship quality. In addition, strategies that were perceived as two-way and symmetrical were positively associated with relationship quality. Providing a final link to outcomes, they observed that voters with favorable relationships towards their own political party were more likely to vote for that party's candidate. Collectively, this evidence offers empirical support for the continuum proposed earlier.

From a general public relations standpoint, Hon and Grunig (1999) identified the following as indicators of relationship quality: control mutuality, trust, satisfaction, and commitment. Ledingham (2011) identified the dimensions of trust, openness, satisfaction, access, mutual control, and responsiveness as arguably the most critical in determining relationship quality in a political public relations setting. It is worth recognizing that this approach goes beyond defining political public relations as communication to include actions and behaviors. Relevant outcomes in strategic political communication include favorable attitudes towards political candidates, parties, or legislation and supportive behaviors such as vote choice, vote intention, volunteering, donating, attending events, joining an organization, protesting, or engaging in activism (see Strömbäck & Kiousis, 2011b).

Connected to the aforementioned engagement continuum, a natural application of the relational perspective is a better understanding of highly engaged constituencies such as major donors, volunteers, lobbyists, and highly partisan voters. Ledingham (2011) argues that the use of interpersonal communication and symbolic or actual behaviors is key to success in the political arena when a relational approach is being used. One caveat, though, with this type of perspective in a political context is that it is probably not feasible to adopt a fully relational interaction with all constituencies. At the same time, when strategic communication is applied to governing, all citizens can be considered stakeholders. For more low involvement publics, a reputation cultivation and management perspective may however be more appropriate and is explicated in further detail below.

Reputation Management

A second perspective that is useful for our understanding of strategic political communication is reputation management. According to Wartick (1992), corporate reputation is defined as "the aggregation of a single stakeholder's perception of how well organizational responses are meeting the demands and expectations of many corporate stakeholders" (p. 34). Elsewhere, Gotsi and Wilson (2001), in a comprehensive review of several definitions, asserted that it is

> a stakeholder's overall evaluation of a company over time. This evaluation is based on the stakeholder's direct experiences with the company, any other form of communication and

symbolism that provides information about the firm's actions and/or a comparison with the actions of other leading rivals.

p. 25

Looking at it from a multidimensional vantage point, Carroll (2010) notes that corporate reputation includes a "firm's public prominence, its public esteem, and the series of qualities or attributes for which a firm is known" (p. 3). Similarly, Fombrun and Gardberg (2000) suggest the dimensions of vision and leadership, products and services, emotional appeal, work environment, social responsibility, and financial performance for defining reputation.

The application of reputation management to strategic political communication requires, of course, that it be moved out of the traditional business context. That is, the reputation concept is applied to political parties, leaders, nations, and so forth. A growing body of research has confirmed this application (Donsbach & Brade, 2011; Scammell, 1999). For example, Yang, Shin, Lee and Wrigley (2008) found a positive association between a perceived positive reputation of South Korea and preference for personal communication, national television, cable television, national newspapers, and libraries to obtain information about the country among a sample of U.S. citizens in 2006. Favorable reputations were connected with more supportive behavioral intentions towards the country. Country reputation in that study was defined as emotional appeal, physical appeal, financial appeal, leadership appeal, cultural appeal, global appeal, and political appeal. Wang (2006) suggested that positive country reputation is linked with favorable economic outcomes but did not test this empirically.

Also linked to agenda building and framing (described below), a related body of work on political candidate images has also illustrated the importance of reputation in strategic political communication. Such research has examined how the portrayals of political leaders in candidate communications, news media messages, and public opinion can closely correspond to one another. Among the most common attributes of the candidate images studied were credibility (does the candidate seem believable?), morality (do the candidate's actions reflect well on his or her ethics or integrity?), intelligence (is this reflected in his or her knowledge or skills?), leadership (is he or she charismatic or inspiring?), ideology and issue positions (what are his or her policies?), and biographical information (details of his or her hometown or family) (Kiousis, Mitrook, Wu & Seltzer., 2006; Weaver, Graber, McCombs & Eyal, 1981). McCombs, Lopez-Escobar and Llamas (2000) found close links between the aspects of candidate images emphasized in political ads, news content, and voter perceptions during the 1996 Spanish general elections.

Although the application of corporate reputation to government communication and politics is not pervasive, scholars have noted that strategic communication is a key influence driving reputation in this setting (Canel & Sanders, 2012). Based on the explication earlier, reputation is distinguished in the literature from identity (what an organization is) and image (what stakeholders perceive). Given our emphasis on adopting a political public relations perspective, organizational action is obviously a major force impacting reputation as well. Based on the continuum, the application of a reputation management perspective in strategic political communication is most relevant for low engagement stakeholders. This is evident in the crisis communication literature that stresses the importance of effective crisis management to protect an organization's reputation (Coombs, 2007). Such stakeholders might include last-minute voters, tourists, and temporary residents in a country.

Agenda Building

The third major theoretical approach from political public relations that is relevant to strategic communication is agenda building. Whereas the traditional focal point of agenda setting research has explored the transfer of issue salience from the media to public opinion, the expanded view of agenda building has considered the reciprocal influence among various political stakeholders in the process of salience formation, exchange, and transfer (Berger, Hertog & Park, 2002; Kiousis, Laskin & Kim, 2011; Kiousis et al. , 2006; Kiousis, Bantimaroudis & Ban, 1999; McCombs, 2004). Major political constituencies involved in this process include candidates, parties, government agencies, news media, voters, donors, volunteers, activists, and others.

Originally conceptualized in terms of issue salience, this also encompasses the salience of a variety of political objects and their attributes. Issues are but one category of object that includes stakeholders, political candidates, nations, and so forth. Attribute salience links the agenda building construct to framing by indicating that groups outside the media and public opinion play a major role in impacting how topics are discussed and portrayed in political discourse. Political public relations efforts, for instance, emphasize certain attributes while ignoring others and may thus lead to different interpretations, opinions, and behaviors connected to issues and policies.

Empirical support for agenda building has been gleaned in a number of investigations (e.g., Cobb, Ross & Ross, 1976; Kim, Xiang & Kiousis, 2011; Kiousis & Strömbäck, 2010; Kiousis & Wu, 2008; Ragas, Kim & Kiousis, 2011). The primary strategy for activating news attention in agenda building is the use of information subsidies. According to Gandy (1982), information subsidies can be defined as "efforts to reduce the prices faced by others for certain information in order to increase its consumption" (p. 8). Lieber and Golan (2011) succinctly define these types of subsidies as "the currency of the trade within the marketplace of information" (p. 60). The three most common forms of information subsidies are materials, spokespersons, and events (Hallahan, 2011).

Perhaps the most widely used and most studied type of information subsidy is the standard news release. News releases have been shown to play a meaningful role in shaping news coverage. Research, for example by Sweetser and Brown (2008), indicates that up to 80% of news content is generated from information subsidies, particularly in the form of news releases. A robust body of research has offered strong empirical support to suggest that the salience of objects in news releases contributes to the media agenda (McCombs, 2004; Turk, 1986; Wanta & Ghanem, 2007). Hopmann, Vliegenthart, Elmelund-Praestekaer, Albaek and De Vreese (2010), offered empirical evidence to confirm that the salience of issues in political party-controlled news releases shaped the salience of issues in media coverage during the 2007 national elections in Denmark, but the effectiveness of these news releases varied based on the party's relevance to the country's political system.

The stakeholder engagement continuum explicated above can be valuable in agenda building from a strategic communication standpoint. Questions that might arise during such a process might include: does a common set of priorities between a political organization and multiple stakeholder groups lead to stronger relationships and reputations? Such questions can be probed for both object and attribute salience, having key implications for strategic political communication messages, programs, and campaigns.

Issues Management

Related to agenda building, issues management in politics refers to the process by which politicians, campaigns, parties, and other political groups identify, prioritize, develop, and convey positions on key issues (Heath & Waymer, 2011). A fundamental early step in effective political issues management involves formative research where groups investigate the perceptions, attitudes, and behaviors of major constituencies concerning policy preferences and problems. Strategic political communication is a major part of how political groups aim to influence political discourse and policymaking during election and law-making periods.

A vital factor impacting the issues management process involves meaningfully classifying different types of issues. Research has offered several systems for categorizing issues. Specifically, the difference between obtrusive issues (those with which citizens have direct experience) and unobtrusive issues (those with which citizens have little direct experience) has proved critical with regard to media influence on public perceptions of issue importance (Zucker, 1978). Research suggests that mass-media impact is greatest for unobtrusive issues. A similar distinction has been drawn between abstract and concrete issues, with empirical work detecting stronger media influence on perceptions for the latter issue type (Yagade & Dozier 1990). Beyond issue type, the tone and frames associated with issues are also relevant for issue-management purposes because they shape *how* issue portrayals are generated and the subsequent effects of these issue portrayals on various constituencies.

As in agenda building, the use of information subsidies by political groups or organizations to exert influence on news media, voters, and other groups represents a widespread approach for effective issues management via strategic communication. Among the most commonly used information subsidies are news releases, interviews, news conferences, social media messages, and "op-ed pieces." Op-ed pieces are editorials written from a party other than a news outlet to advocate for a position on an issue relevant to the news organization and its community. From the realm of political marketing, political advertisements are also paramount in political issues management.

A major application of issues management in the aforementioned stakeholder engagement continuum is that it can be used to identify and develop strategies for emerging issues: those that are rising in policymaking and public circles, those that are receiving heavy attention, and those that have fallen off a major agenda. Various expositions of the lifecycle of an issue in the political science and communication literature could be enhanced with the incorporation of the stakeholder engagement continuum (Downs, 1972).

Framing

Although framing scholarship has an extensive literature in the general mass communication and political communication arenas, its application to strategic political public relation and communication merits additional scholarly attention. Hallahan (1999) explained the role of framing in public relations:

> In developing programs, public relations professionals fundamentally operate as *frame strategists*, who strive to determine how situations, attributes, choices, actions, issues and responsibility should be posed to achieve favorable objectives. Framing decisions are perhaps the most important strategic choices made in a public relations effort.
>
> *p. 224, emphasis in original*

In political public relations, Hallahan (2011) later identified seven areas where framing is crucial, including situations, risks, supporting arguments, issues, responsibility, and stories. What distinguishes these perspectives on framing is that they do not solely consider the impact of framing on the relationship between news and public opinion. Just as multiple stakeholders and groups contribute to agenda building, the same can be said of those constituencies' contribution to framing in the areas outlined by Hallahan (2011).

In looking at the use of framing by political leaders, Hänggli and Kriesi (2012) pinpointed three major framing choices made by politicians to gain a strategic advantage during campaigns: the "substantive emphasis choice", the "oppositional emphasis choice" and the "content emphasis choice." In the first, candidates must highlight which frames of their own they hope to emphasize through the campaigning period. For the second, they decide which frames from their opponent (or opponents) they will seek to emphasize. Presumably, it will be those in which they hold a perceived advantage. Finally, the third choice involves how much they will highlight the campaign competition itself. Among their findings are that candidates tend to highlight just one or two frames in their own communication activities and that they pay more attention to their opponents' frames that are emphasized in media coverage as opposed to political ads.

Framing not only impacts strategic political communication in terms of campaigning but in terms of governing as well. Sellers (2010) explained the process by which members of the U.S. Congress use strategic communication to impact the salience and framing of issues in media coverage with the purpose of ultimately affecting policy outcomes. This process contains four stages. In the first, members of Congress create the message by identifying the issue, arguments, and frames that they want to emphasize in it. The second stage involves promoting the message through a collective effort with their political party. The third step involves engaging journalists to draw attention to it through various publicity efforts. In the final stage, journalists highlight the messages in news coverage, which subsequently impacts public opinion and feeds back to impacting policymakers.

A recent conceptual development in agenda setting and agenda building that is important to framing in strategic political communication is that the *connections* among elements on different agendas can impact the salience formation and transfer process (Guo & McCombs, 2011a; 2011b; Schultz, Kleinnijenhuis, Oegema, Utz & van Atteveldt, 2011; Schultz et al., 2012), as summarized by Vu, Guo and McCombs (2012):

> Our new approach, which we have named the Network Agenda Setting Model, suggests that the news media can actually bundle different objects and attributes and make these bundles of elements salient in the public's mind simultaneously. Drawing from Lang's (2000) theoretical framework, the NAS model hypothesizes that the more likely the news media mention two elements in tandem, the greater chance that the audience will perceive these two elements as interconnected.
>
> *pp. 6, 9*

Hence, the co-occurrence of certain attributes and/or objects with one another leads to a greater likelihood that they will be perceived as salient *together*. This could range from a few elements on an agenda to the entire pattern of connections among elements. In political public relations and strategic communication, this can have major ramifications for how politicians and issues are portrayed and perceived in public affairs discourse. In turn, this can greatly influence outcomes in terms of campaigning and governing. For example, had the George W. Bush administration been unsuccessful in pairing Saddam Hussein and weapons of mass destruction in political discourse during its first term, it is possible that a different policy outcome might have been been generated in dealing with Iraq as a threat to the United States after the 9/11 attacks.

Thus, framing processes are critical to the two fundamental aims of strategic political communication. The engagement continuum's application to framing may be to serve as a heuristic device for understanding the process of frame resonance. Although the literature has identified both macro-level generic frames and micro-level topic-specific frames, the factors that make certain frames prominent even though others are marginalized remains unclear. Examining what types of frames are more consistently linked with reputation outcomes and relationship outcomes may offer insight into such questions.

Crisis Communication

Within the context of this chapter, the conclusive area central to the understanding of strategic communication in politics comprises crisis communication and management. Although typically viewed through the lens of business or non-profit organizations, the role of crisis communication in politics is critical (Coombs, 2011). Whether initiated by natural causes (e.g., a major earthquake) or engendered by humans (e.g., a military attack), the government's crisis communication efforts are crucial to successful crisis management. Such efforts should be proactively developed and purposeful, and therefore are included as a part of strategic political communication. Although this falls under the governance aspect of strategic political communication, the success in which governments at the local, state, regional, or national levels handle crises can alter election outcomes.

At a basic level, most scholars conceptualize crises in three phases: pre-crisis, crisis, and post-crisis (Coombs, 2012). Yet Coombs (2011) suggested that although there are similarities between political crisis communications and corporate crisis communication, major differences include crisis managers, crisis types, crisis constraints, and what defines indicators of success. In the first area, political crisis managers can be grouped in the following four categories: elected politicians, elected agencies, appointed bureaucrats, and appointed bureaucratic agencies where corporate crisis managers are normally appointed executives from within a company's management structure. In the second area, Coombs notes that most corporations seek to avoid playing the "hero" role in a crisis whereas this possibility greatly increases in political crisis. In the third arena, politicians are much more likely to use an apology strategy because they are not as constrained by financial considerations as are businesses and corporations. In the fourth arena, government bureaucrats or agencies handling crisis management may take longer to respond to crisis situations because they do not face the same job security concerns as those who have been elected or who are in corporate communication circles.

Returning to the engagement continuum, we can see several applications to crisis communication. In particular, crisis communication strategies aimed at protecting reputation would be more appropriate for dealing with low-involvement stakeholders whereas those aimed at protecting relationships are most suitable for highly involved or engaged constituencies. For the former, an informative communication strategy may be most appropriate, whereas rectifying behavior and action may be necessary for the latter.

Conclusion

In summary, the role of strategic communication in politics is important and has been studied from an empirical and theoretical standpoint, although there is still a lack of empirical research firmly anchored in theories of political public relations and political marketing. The purpose of this chapter has been to trace this role in some detail. Set against the backdrop of two major meta-perspectives of political public relations and political marketing, the framework offered by political public relations has been suggested as the most comprehensive for understanding the influence of strategic political communication. An integrative conceptual model of stakeholder engagement has been offered to understand strategic political communication in terms of both reputation management and relationship cultivation. This chapter has demonstrated the application of the engagement continuum to areas such as agenda building, issue management, framing, and crisis communication. Given its potential in these settings, the authors believe there are applications for several other arenas of strategic political communication not covered in this chapter, such as fund raising and public diplomacy. The authors suggest future research could possibly explore these applications, which might expand theoretical, empirical, and practical knowledge associated with strategic political communication.

References

Argenti, P. A., Howell, R. A., & Beck, K. A. (2005). The strategic communication imperative. *MIT Sloan Management Review, 46*(3), 83–89.

Baker, B. (1997). Public relations in government. In Caywood, C. L. (Ed.), *The handbook of strategic public relations & integrated communications* (pp. 453–480). New York: McGraw-Hill.

Berger, B. K., Hertog, J. K., & Park, D. (2002). Political role and influence of business organizations: A communication perspective. *Communication Yearbook, 26*, 160–200.

Blumenthal, S. (1980). *The permanent campaign. Inside the world of elite political operatives.* Boston, MA: Beacon Press.

Botan, C. H. (2006). Grand strategy, strategy, and tactics in public relations. In C. H. Botan & V. Hazleton (Eds.), *Public relations theory II* (pp. 223–248). Mahwah, NJ: Erlbaum.

Broom, G. M., Casey, S., & Ritchey, J. (1997). Toward a concept and theory of organization-public relationships. *Journal of Public Relations Research, 9*(2), 83–98.

Canel, M. J., & Sanders, K. (2012). Government communication: An emerging field in political communication research. In H. A. Semetko & M. Scammell (Eds.), *The SAGE handbook of political communication* (pp. 85–96). London, England: Sage.

Carroll, C. E. (2010). International perspectives on agenda-setting theory applied to business news. In C. E. Carroll (Ed.), *Corporate reputation and the news media: Agenda-setting within business news coverage in developed, emerging, and frontier markets* (pp. 3–14). New York: Routledge.

Cobb, R., Ross, J-K., & Ross, M. H. (1976). Agenda building as a comparative political process. *The American Political Science Review, 70*(1), 126–138.

Coombs, W. T. (2007). *Ongoing crisis communication: Planning, managing, and responding* (2nd ed.). Los Angeles, CA: Sage.

Coombs, W. T. (2011). Political public relations and crisis communication: A public relations perspective. In J. Strömbäck & S. Kiousis (Eds.), *Political public relations: Principles and applications* (pp. 214–234). New York: Routledge.

Coombs, W. T. (2012). *Ongoing crisis communication: Planning, managing, and responding* (3rd ed.). Thousand Oaks, CA: Sage.

Cwalina, W., Falkowski, A., & Newman, B. I. (2010). Towards the development of a cross-cultural model of voter behavior: Comparative analysis of Poland and the US. *European Journal of Marketing, 44*(3), 351–368.

Donsbach, W., & Brade, A. (2011). Nothing is as practical as a good theory: What communication research can offer to the practice of political communication. *International Journal of Press/Politics, 16*(4), 508–522.

Downs, A. (1972). Up and down with ecology: The issue attention cycle. *Public Interest, 28*, 38–50.

Fombrun, C. J., & Gardberg, N. (2000). Who's tops in corporate reputation? *Corporate Reputation Review, 3*, 13–17.

Froehlich, R., & Rüdiger, B. (2006). Framing political public relations: Measuring success of political communication strategies in Germany. *Public Relations Review, 32*(1), 18–25.

Gandy, O. H. Jr. (1982). *Beyond agenda-setting: Information subsidies and public policy.* Norwood, NJ: Ablex.

Gotsi, M., & Wilson, A. M. (2001). Corporate reputation: Seeking a definition. *Corporate Communications, 6*, 24–30.

Grunig, J. E., & Repper, F. C. (1992). Strategic management, publics, and issues. In J. E. Grunig (Ed.), *Excellence in public relations and communication management* (pp. 117–158). Hillsdale, NJ: Erlbaum.

Guo, L., & McCombs, M. (2011a, August). *Toward the third level of agenda setting theory: A Network agenda setting model.* Paper presented at the annual conference of the Association for Education in Journalism & Mass Communication, St. Louis, MO.

Guo, L., & McCombs, M. (2011b, May). *Network agenda setting: A third level of media effects.* Paper presented at the annual conference of the International Communication Association, Boston, MA.

Hallahan, K. (1999). Seven models of framing: Implications for public relations. *Journal of Public Relations Research, 11*, 205–242.

Hallahan, K. (2011). Political public relations and strategic framing. In J. Strömbäck & S. Kiousis (Eds.), *Political public relations: Principles and applications* (pp. 177–213). New York: Routledge.

Hallahan, K., Holtzhausen, D., van Ruler, B., Verčič, D., & Sriramesh, K. (2007). On defining strategic communication. *International Journal of Strategic Communication, 1*(1), 3–35.

Hänggli, R., & Kriesi, H. (2012). Frame construction and frame promotion (strategic framing choices). *American Behavioral Scientist, 56*(3), 260–278.

Heath, R. L., & Waymer, D. (2011). Corporate issues management and political public relations. In J. Strömbäck & S. Kiousis (Eds.), *Political public relations: Principles and applications* (pp. 138–156). New York: Routledge.

Hendrix, J. A., & Hayes, D. C. (2007). *Public relations cases* (7th ed.). Belmont, CA: Thomson Wadsworth.

Hon, L. C., & Grunig, J. E. (1999). *Guidelines for measuring relationships in public relations.* Gainesville, FL: The Institute for Public Relations.

Hopmann, D. N., Vliegenthart, R., Elmelund-Praestekaer, C., Albaek, E. & De Vreese, C. H. (2010). Party media agenda-setting: How parties influence election news coverage. *Party Politics, 15*, 101–123.

Hughes, A., & Dann, S. (2009). Political marketing and stakeholder engagement. *Marketing Theory, 9*(2), 243–256.

Hutton, J. G., Goodman, M. B., Alexander, J. B., & Genest, C. M. (2001). Reputation management: The new face of corporate public relations? *Public Relations Review, 27*(3), 247.

Iyengar, S., & Kinder, D. R. (1987). *News that matters: Television and American opinion*. Chicago, IL: University of Chicago Press.

Kaid, L. L., & Holtz-Bacha, C. (Eds.). (2008). *Encyclopedia of political communication*. Thousand Oaks, CA: Sage.

Katz, E. (1957). The two-step flow of communication: An up-to-date report on a hypothesis. *Public Opinion Quarterly, 21*(1), 61–78.

Katz, E., & Lazarsfeld, P. F. (1955). *Personal influence: The part played by people in the flow of mass communications*. Glencoe, IL: The Free Press.

Kim, J. Y., Xiang, Z., & Kiousis, S. (2011). Agenda building effects by 2008 presidential candidates on global media coverage and public opinion. *Public Relations Review, 37*(1), 109–111.

Kiousis, S., Bantimaroudis, P., & Ban, H. (1999). Candidate image attributes: Experiments on the substantive dimension of second level agenda setting. *Communication Research, 26*(4), 414–428.

Kiousis, S., Laskin, A., & Kim, J. Y. (2011). Congressional agenda building: Examining the influence of congressional communications from the speaker of the house. *Public Relations Journal, 5*(1), 1–14.

Kiousis, S., Mitrook, M., Wu, X., & Seltzer, T. (2006). First- and second-level agenda-building and agenda-setting effects: Exploring the linkages among candidate news releases, media coverage, and public opinion during the 2002 Florida gubernatorial election. *Journal of Public Relations Research, 18*(3), 265–285.

Kiousis, S., & Strömbäck, J. (2010). The white house and public relations: Examining the linkages between presidential communications and public opinion. *Public Relations Review, 36*(1), 7–14.

Kiousis, S., & Strömbäck, J. (2011). Political public relations research in the future. In J. Strömbäck & S. Kiousis (Eds.), *Political public relations: Principles and applications* (pp. 314–323). New York: Routledge.

Kiousis, S., & Wu, X. (2008). International agenda-building and agenda-setting: Exploring the influence of public relations counsel on US news media and public perceptions of foreign nations. *International Communication Gazette, 70*(1), 58–75.

Knott Martinelli, D. (2011). Political public relations: Remembering its roots and classics. In J. Strömbäck & S. Kiousis (Eds.), *Political public relations: Principles and applications* (pp. 33–53). New York: Routledge.

Kotler, P. (1974). Marketing during periods of shortage. *Journal of Marketing, 38*(3), 20–29.

Lang, A. (2000). The limited capacity model of mediated message processing. *Journal of Communication, 50*(1), 46–71.

Ledingham, J. A. (2011). Political public relations and relationship management. In J. Strömbäck & S. Kiousis (Eds.), *Political public relations: Principles and applications* (pp. 235–253). New York: Routledge.

Lees-Marshment, J. (Ed.). (2012). *The Routledge handbook of political marketing*. London, England: Routledge.

Lieber, P. S., & Golan, G. J. (2011). Political public relations, news management, and agenda indexing. In J. Strömbäck & S. Kiousis (Eds.), *Political public relations: Principles and applications* (pp. 54–74). New York: Routledge.

Manheim, J. B. (1991). Political communication and elections. *Congress & the Presidency, 18*(2), 181.

Manheim, J. B. (2011). *Strategy in information and influence campaigns: How policy advocates, social movements, insurgent groups, corporations, governments, and others get what they want*. New York: Routledge.

McCombs, M. (2004). *Setting the agenda: The mass media and public opinion*. Malden, MA: Polity.

McCombs, M., Lopez-Escobar, E., & Llamas, J. P. (2000). Setting the agenda of attributes in the 1996 Spanish general election. *Journal of Communication, 50*(2), 77–92.

Newman, B. I. (1999). *The mass marketing of politics: Democracy in an age of manufactured images*. Thousand Oaks, CA: Sage.

Nord, L. (1997). *Spelet om opinionen*. Lund, Sweden: Studentlitteratur.

Pfau, M., & Wan, H-H. (2006). Persuasion: An intrinsic function of public relations. In C. H. Botan & V. Hazleton (Eds.), *Public relations theory II* (pp. 101–136). Mahwah, NJ: Erlbaum.

Ragas, M. M. W., Kim, J., & Kiousis, S. (2011). Agenda-building in the corporate sphere: Analyzing influence in the 2008 Yahoo!–Icahn proxy contest. *Public Relations Review, 37*(3), 257–265.

Scammell, M. (1999). Political marketing: Lessons for political science. *Political Studies, 47*(4), 718.

Scheufele, D. A. (1999). Framing as a theory of media effects. *Journal of Communication, 49*(1), 103.

Schultz, F., Kleinnijenhuis, J., Oegema, D., Utz, S., & van Atteveldt, W. (2012). Strategic framing in the BP crisis: A semantic network analysis of associative frames. *Public Relations Review, 38*(1), 97–107.

Sellers, P. (2010). *Cycles of spin: Strategic communication in the U.S. Congress*. New York: Cambridge University Press.

Seltzer, T., & Zhang, W. (2009, March). *Impact of antecedents and relationship maintenance strategies on perceived relationship with political parties during the 2008 presidential general election*. Paper presented at the meeting of the International Public Relations Research Conference, Miami, FL.

Sjöblom, G. (1968). *Party Strategies in a Multiparty System*. Lund: Studentlitteratur.

Smith, R. D. (2009). *Strategic planning for public relations* (3rd ed.). New York: Routledge.

Strömbäck, J. (2007). Antecedents of political market orientation in Britain and Sweden: Analysis and future research propositions. *Journal of Public Affairs, 7*(1), 79–89.

Strömbäck, J., & Kiousis, S. (2011a). Political public relations: Defining and mapping an emergent field. In J. Strömbäck & S. Kiousis (Eds.), *Political public relations: Principles and applications* (pp. 1–32). New York: Routledge.

Strömbäck, J., & Kiousis, S. (Eds.). (2011b). *Political public relations: Principles and applications.* New York: Routledge.

Strömbäck, J., Mitrook, M. A., & Kiousis, S. (2010). Bridging two schools of thought: Applications of public relations theory to political marketing. *Journal of Political Marketing, 9*(1), 73–92.

Sweetser, K. D., & Brown, C. W. (2008). Information subsidies and agenda-building during the Israel-Lebanon crisis. *Public Relations Review, 34*(4), 359–366.

Turk, J. V. (1986). Information subsidies and media content. *Journalism Monographs, 100,* 1–29.

U.S. Department of Defense (2008). *Principles of strategic communication.* Retrieved from http://www.au.af.mil/info-ops/documents/principles_of_sc.pdf

Vu, H. T., Guo, L., & McCombs, M. (2012, August). *Exploring "the world outside and the pictures in our heads": A network agenda setting study.* Paper presented at the annual meeting of the Association for Education in Journalism and Mass Communication, Chicago, IL.

Wang, J. (2006). Managing national reputation and international relations in the global era: Public diplomacy revisited. *Public Relations Review, 32*(2), 91–96.

Wanta, W., & Ghanem, S. (2007). Effects of agenda setting. In R. W. Preiss, B. M. Gayle, N. Burrell, M. Allen, & J. Bryant (Eds.), *Mass media effects research: Advances through meta-analysis* (pp. 37–51). Mahwah, NJ: Erlbaum.

Wartick, S. L. (1992). The relationship between intense media exposure and change in corporate reputation. *Business and Society, 31*(1), 33–49.

Weaver, D. H., Graber, D. A., McCombs, M. E., & Eyal, C. H. (1981). *Media agenda-setting in a presidential election: Issues, images, and interest.* New York: Praeger.

Yagade, A., & Dozier, D. M. (1990). The media agenda-setting effect of concrete versus abstract issues. *Journalism Quarterly, 67*(1), 3–10.

Yang, S., Shin, H., Lee, J., & Wrigley, B. (2008). Country reputation in multidimensions: Predictors, effects, and communication channels. *Journal of Public Relations Research, 20*(4), 421–440.

Zucker, H. G. (1978). The variable nature of news media influence. *Communication Yearbook, 2,* 225–245. New Brunswick, NJ: Transaction.

26

Communicating Strategically in Government

Kirsten Kozolanka

Despite the proliferation of mainstream political voices and issues in the media, the modern state has hungered for even more predictive ways to dominate how it communicates with its citizens. An extensive and growing communications apparatus both in political offices and in the permanent government that supports them feeds a political obsession to ensure lengthy if not permanent occupancy of the highest office in the state.

The chances are that the above description applies to a good many Western countries, if not many other states around the world. It is late democracies in the West, however, that make allegiance to democratic governance while engaging in struggles with—for the most part—privately owned media for the right to make meaning in ways that benefit and extend their political mandates. These late democracies engage in such struggles while expressing concern publicly over the democratic deficit that has characterized their society and that some (Putnam, 2000; Aucoin & Turnbull, 2003; Nadeau & Giasson, 2003) believe manifests itself in generally less engagement by citizens in political life and the troubling fall in voter turnout at election time. However, generally left out in any discussion on citizen engagement are the benefits to politicians of voter disenchantment: the capability to target the most receptive audiences for their research-led political messages, while courting strategies that discourage other citizens from the perceived need to vote at all (Bennett & Manheim, 2001). Moreover, technological developments have transformed the political playing field by extending election and other campaigns permanently and making political messages available endlessly. It could be claimed that there has never been another recorded era in which strategic political communication in its many guises reigns so supreme. One might say that it is a good time to be a politician or a business that supplies strategic communications advice to politicians.

This chapter examines the nature and evolution of strategic communication in politics as it has developed in Canada and discusses how recent political parties in government in Canada have used the communications and information apparatus of the state to construct positive perceptions and images of their policies and actions, and conflate the government (or state apparatus) with the political party in power with the goal of gaining public support. The chapter takes a critical communication approach to strategic communication through analysis that is holistic, contextual, historical, and that foregrounds relations of power and dominance. A critical approach can further understanding of how contemporary communication practices in politics both extend and challenge the concept of "strategic" as applied to the terrain of political communication. Insights explored using this approach and the case of Canada may shed light on developments in strategic communication in politics in other countries or serve as a warning to tread carefully when using strategic communication for political and hegemonic purposes.

Specifically, the chapter draws on the work of Jay G. Blumler (1990), who first identified a disturbing direction in political communication in the UK of what he called "the modern publicity process." This process was a struggle for influence and control over political events and issues that was akin to "the irresistible force of a magnet," capable of "altering messages, issues, terms of political combat" and, finally, "perspectives and choices of citizens themselves" (pp. 101, 113). Peter Golding (1992) situated this modern publicity process and its bureaucratic apparatus within what he called a "public relations state" that built up its own publicity activities in order to manage the media and fund information campaigns to promote its programs. It has become routine for political communication scholars to discuss the "public relations democracy" (Lilleker, 2006), "PR state" (Ward, 2007), "propaganda society" (Sussman, 2010), and, more obliquely, "symbolic government" (O'Shaughnessy, 2004). The latter concept will be discussed later in this chapter.

If we are concerned about the role of the citizen in the modern publicity state, as politicians themselves claim to be, the concept of the commodification of audiences also needs to be examined. As Vincent Mosco (2009) explained, communication is a commodity that is very different from other commodities because it "contains symbols and images whose meaning helps to shape consciousness" (p. 134). Furthermore, the audience—in political communication, citizens—is a commodity in which the dominated (citizens) agree to be dominated in "reciprocal relationships" with those who dominate, here, the state or its representatives (p. 137; Fuchs, 2010, p. 32). There is no tangible product to purchase, just persuasive communications messages from the state that can contradict the factual reality, but make the audience complicit in their successful execution. Currently, in state publicity, it is the depth and breadth of that reciprocity that is in question.

Moreover, the audience commodity can be considered as endless in its capacity to extend its reach beyond the primary commodity. Commodities, in fact, produce their own commodities in a process Mosco called "immanent commodification" (p. 141), and commodification itself "demands the use of measurement procedures to produce commodities and monitoring techniques to keep track of production, distribution, exchange and consumption" (p. 141). Marketing studies are included in Mosco's examples of monitoring techniques; for this chapter's purpose, public opinion research analysis would be another such example that can "grow out of the development of generalized monitoring and surveillance procedures" (p. 142).

The field of strategic political communication has undergone conceptual change in response to a more commodified society. Kirk Hallahan (2004, p. 6) identified six different specialties in strategic communication, including marketing and political communication. Along with others, I contend in this chapter that the boundaries between two of these distinct categories have already blurred. As this chapter will demonstrate, within a Canadian context (Paré & Berger, 2008), marketing communication and political communication are seen to have already joined to produce the hybrid of political marketing (Lees-Marshment, 2001) now used by Canada and the United Kingdom, both by the state (by the elected political party) and within the state (by communications officers within the public service). It is clear from this recent scholarship that a connection exists between the two specialties. In addition, it is important to keep in mind that, for this chapter's analysis, the largely uncritical acceptance of a marketing–politics merger actually works to give it credence and veracity as the way forward in political communication literature, thus permanently linking the two fields as a natural and normal alliance in political communication. Instead, the appropriateness of a state as an organization that "presents and promotes itself through the intentional activities of its leaders, employees, and communication practitioners" needs to be interrogated (Hallahan, Holtzhausen, van Ruler, Verçiç & Sriramesh 2007, p. 7). Even if a case can be made for such use of communication, it need not be accepted as a natural and inevitable marriage. In fact, communication thus "relegated to an instrument merely used to reach managerial or marketing-based goals" (p. 25) can be considered an unvoiced and presumably non-consensual process or occurrence that challenges, even defies, identification and analysis.

In addition, as noted in Hallahan et al., a critical perspective that situates communication practice rather than organizational function as part of a strategic process reveals the broader power and control that lie behind how such practices "transform both organizations and societies" (p. 14). These practices are not normally transparent or apparent without deliberative examination of hierarchical power. This is due to a presumption that neutral administrative power as traditionally imagined and applied remains in the inner workings of the state, when clearly such neutrality has been breached by recent communication-focused governments, as this chapter will lay out.

A key question to be probed is: how does the commodification of targeted audiences through strategic political communication co-habit with state accountability to all citizens, when such purposeful communication is by definition exclusionary?

Development of Government Communication

Strategic communication cannot be divorced from the conditions under which it developed. W. Lance Bennett and Jarol B. Manheim (2001, p. 279) examined the post-WW2 pluralism of late democracies, with its underlying ideal that "the views of citizens are effectively and equitably represented through competing organized interests." Critiquing the view that a free flow of quality information in a society is sufficient to ensure equal governance, even if elite policy capture is at play, they suggested instead that "information is typically publicized to mobilize and demobilize segments of the public to serve narrow strategic objectives, often masking the identity or intent of the communicator in the process" (p. 280) at the expense of both information transparency and inclusiveness. Bennett & Manheim concluded that an emerging neo-pluralist order based on the decline of stable group affiliation, the introduction of technology as an enabler to identify multiple targeted publics, and the rise of strategies of groups that lobby government not for influencing policy in itself but for reaching target audiences through them, has worked against the transfer of knowledge to citizens, and has both mobilized and demobilized publics for their own strategic ends. Later analyses echoed Bennett and Manheim contending that these shifts were made possible because of the fewer constraints on and the increasing free flow of information enabled by technology and its deregulation (Skinner & Gasher, 2005; Kozolanka, Mazepa & Skinner, 2012). Moreover, suggested Bennett and Manheim, an examination of strategic political communication campaigns illustrates how such campaigns work in a largely rule-free and instrumental environment in which whatever works strategically becomes paramount (p. 285); this can be related to the consequences of the uncritical embrace of political marketing.

Specifically examining the Westminster model of governance in the Canadian political environment, the beginnings of communication can be traced within the state and the public service that supported it back to the post-WW2 years, in which a war propaganda bureau became a permanent part of the state bureaucracy (Rose, 2000). This early communication, which is not unique to Canada, was perfunctory and generally not criticized in a time when the state was expanding and when most of the news disseminated was considered good for a growing society. Thus, such communication was merely considered the benign output of the normal management of government.

The concept of being strategic in state communication does not emerge until the post-war consensus began to exhibit cracks in the 1970s and 1980s due to economic crises that Keynesianism did not seem able to resolve. These crises in late democracies, with their large state apparatus to support the social welfare policies of Keynesianism, provided opportunities for economic libertarianism in the form of neo-liberalism and socially regressive neo-conservatism to develop over time and coalesce as The New Right (Gutstein, 2009). A key element in the social shift from the post-war consensus, with its collective system-led responses to social and economic issues, towards the New Right was the emergence of an ethos of individualism that manifested itself through one's economic ability to choose for oneself from a marketplace of both goods and ideas. In addition, the New Right strategically used the specter of economic crisis in communicating its perception of the need for restraining what it considered to be a bloated and inefficient state apparatus (Kozolanka, 2007). As New Right thinking coalesced and found success in elections at different levels of government, the concept of "citizen" itself vis-à-vis its relation to the state narrowed into "consumers" and into the even smaller group of "users." This represented a paradigm shift from the universality of the social welfare state to individualism and had an impact on how citizens themselves used their votes, shifting their allegiances to whichever party of the moment spoke to their personal needs and wants. Thus the eventual retrenchment of the state in late democracies such as the UK, the US, New Zealand, and Canada represented not only different economic goals, but also specifically New Right economic goals.

Mosco (2009) points specifically to the shift to the New Right as an example of how the state has been transformed through commodification processes that have turned its "public service communication with social commitments to universal access and content that reflects the broad range of society into commercial communication that provides access to those who can afford it and content that delivers audiences to advertisers" (pp. 130–131). Just as a renewed neo-liberalism/neo-conservatism itself was expressed politically in the New Right, a private-sector management ethos became the administrative model of choice for emerging New Right governments. As New Public Management (NPM) within a de-funded, de-layered, back-to-basics bureaucracy, governance itself was transformed to focus on services and measurement. Overall, it was an acceptance of a more market-based organizing structure and orientation for the state (Havemann, 1998; Savigny, 2008). Within the politics of retrenchment, however, the role of communication was renewed and strengthened (Davis, 2002). The emphasis was placed on strategic communication—a concept borrowed from the private sector—to manage the cutbacks and expectation of citizens, made possible by adding to communication budgets and taking on the functions normally found outside of the public sector, such as risk management and crisis management (Kozolanka, 2006). In fact, the idea of "crisis" was a profound two-pronged animus: it was both the underlying rationale for crisis management and also the communication message itself that ensured that a crisis was seen as the horrific end result of not taking action to protect the economy. In management in the public service in Canada and other countries, strategic communication was "not random or unintentional," but a "constitutive activity of management" (Hallahan et al., 2007, p. 27).

In practice, the inculcation of strategic communication into the state bureaucracy was based on the instrumental methods of political marketing to achieve its hegemonic goals. This included not only the use of practices from public relations, but also extensive public opinion research. The latter was already in use in government in order to fine tune information on government programs for the generally accepted purpose of finding out the opinions of the populace, but now it was used for identifying target audiences of citizens so that the government in power could adjust and tailor the right messages to the right sectors for maximum approval ratings and, eventually, votes. Thus, citizens were commodified as audiences for strategic political communication messages and campaigns to sell public policy.

This chapter now examines the emergence of strategic communication as a key element in political communication in Canada. It draws on examples from two political parties that used different and emerging political communication tactics—strategic communication and political marketing—during their time in office and assesses their varied success, attributing it to developments in socio-economic and political conditions as well as advances in political communication. It finds that political marketing can be considered the communication arm of the New Right ideology of management and governance. The chapter concludes that political marketing is an effective instrumental tool that can be useful for electoral success, but that is not suitable for use by governments, as it fosters a commercial relationship with consumer–voters, rather than accountability to citizens.

Government Communication in Canada

Canada has a parliamentary system based on the Westminster model in the UK. Although it is a multi-party system with various political parties represented in Parliament, in practice, only two major parties, the Liberals and the Conservatives, have formed governments in the last 100 years. Over time, the Liberals have been seen as the party of government, as they have been in power far more than the Conservatives and are hegemonic in their approach to governing, and hence in their (to them) non-problematic use of promotional communications. Since 2006 however, a renewed Conservative Party has challenged them and, in addition, a major shift in the fortunes of two of the parties in the 2011 general election has changed the political environment in a major way, with the left-leaning New Democratic Party replacing the centrist Liberals as the official opposition. This shift dominated the other major change in that election: after two minority governments, the Conservatives won a majority mandate from the Canadian populace.

Just as with other late democracies, Canada has faced slipping voter turnout in federal elections. This is thought to be related to many factors (Norris, 2000), including distrust by citizens of governments that do not follow through on election promises, and governments that do not disclose information needed for citizenship, because such information might put the government in a bad light (Rubin & Kozolanka, 2013). This perception affects not only voter turnout, but also trust of and accountability in government, a key issue in recent Canadian political history. Due to its strong political and structural ties to the UK, as illustrated by its similar parliamentary system, political communication in the UK tends to foreshadow similar developments in Canada. The policies and communication strategies used by the neo-liberal Conservative government of Margaret Thatcher (1979–1990) and, later, Tony Blair's Labour government (1997–2007)—many successful, some not—are often echoed in the Canadian political environment. British examples include the failure of the government's poll tax campaign in Thatcher's Britain (Deacon and Golding, 1994) and subsequent prime minster Blair's successful media management while in office (Scammell, 2001). In addition, close proximity to the USA, with its presidential style of politics, also influences political behavior in Canada.

Other social and political conditions that have an impact on how governments and political parties in Canada and elsewhere communicate have changed over time as well. The 24-hour news cycle keeps the media hungry for content and also provides broader opportunities for politicians to publicize themselves and their policies. In addition, the Internet has given immediate access to information and opinions on everything, although not necessarily reliable information. These and other conditions have changed politics from a discrete election period, after which a government governs, into what political commentators call the permanent campaign (Bowman, 2000).

The politics of the New Right has also influenced policy making. In the post-war politics of consensus, labor and civil society groups were consulted and had influence on public policy. However, as politics shifted towards the New Right, civic groups were replaced by business, lobbyists for interest groups, and communications consultants (Dobbin, 1998; Gutstein, 2009). A further shift in the policy process was a legislative strategy that crunched public consultation into a shorter time-frame, often in tandem with curtailed scrutiny by the parliamentary opposition in all-party committees. For example, in 2012, the new majority Conservative government used a 457-page omnibus bill strategically as a budget bill to overwhelm opposition and push through many controversial changes to legislation at once. In prior times, omnibus bills were considered housekeeping that tidied up small points in existing legislation. Used in broader contexts, these tactics challenge parliamentary and broader opposition on many fronts at once, effectively curtailing the right of citizens to communicate fully with their elected representatives.

Canada's public service grew as the state grew throughout the last half of the twentieth century. In the 1990s, however, the country experienced severe cutbacks in response to global monetary crises, which sparked the move to more streamlined and smaller government. As a result of this shift in the state, communication in government took on new importance as a strategic activity, and the "natural" and uncritical use of communication began to change. In a continued time of fiscal restraint, the size of communications staff and operations grew across government. Communication took on many new responsibilities, including, as mentioned earlier, risk management, which was intended to minimize uncertainty and neutralize opposition in a downsized bureaucracy. Basically, it was understood that strategic communication was needed to sell the unpopular cuts to citizens. To achieve the government's goals, communication became embedded within the policy cycle in government operations, becoming progressively institutionalized, centralized and politicized (Kozolanka, 2012).

One important aspect of communication in government changed over time, and has also accelerated in recent years: this was the role of the Prime Minister's Office (PMO), composed of political appointees and including both research and communication branches, and the role of the Privy Council Office (PCO), the administrative body of the permanent bureaucracy composed of bureaucrats that works closely with the PMO to implement policy. Not only have both offices increased in size, but their respective communication components, including budgets, have also increased significantly. From time to time, governments have made token cuts to these offices, but they remain the nucleus of policy direction—and communication—for the bureaucracy. Although its mandate is to work closely with the PMO, the PCO has been criticized in recent years for participating actively in partisan goals of the party in power, rather than just administering the government's policies that are intended to boost the party's in power's approval ratings from the public, including direction of the communication of those policies, with additional funds for that purpose (Kozolanka, 2012).

The Liberals and Strategic Communication

At the time of state retrenchment in the 1990s, the Liberal Party was in power. Throughout the 1980s and 1990s in Canada, a political situation existed in which the country's largest province, Quebec, was building public opinion to secede from the Canadian state. Throughout these years, Canadian politics was rife with debates on national unity. The Liberals had a huge personal stake in Quebec remaining in Canada: quite simply, Quebec was a vote-rich province for them. The response of the Liberals to the threat to their party and their continued dominance in federal electoral politics was to fan the flames of national unity and pour money into Quebec, with the help of strategic communications strategies and tactics.

This was the broad period in which communications in government increased dramatically and was formalized as "strategic communications" in its operations. As noted above, even during the time of state retrenchment in the mid-1990s, with thousands of public employees either laid off or their positions terminated, communication directorates in government rebounded quickly (Kozolanka, 2006). In 1998, the Liberals also took the unprecedented step of centralizing all communication within a new government department called "Communication Canada." This would be akin to having a Secretary of Communication in the US or a Secretary of State for Communication in the UK (Canada already had an office for communication that was headed by a coordinator within the Privy Council Office). This meant that advertising, public opinion research, public information campaigns and other tools were contracted, approved and managed. Budgets for all these activities continued to rise sharply. In the same year, the Liberals established a Committee of Cabinet on Communications to oversee all government communications. The committee's remit ranged from major advertising campaigns and large public opinion research budgets on issues of concern to the Liberals, to a fairs and exhibits program that promoted government across the country, and mass mailings (targeted at "householders") to citizens across the country on issues deemed through research as issues on which Canadians wanted to see action. As a further sign of the strategic turn in communication, the 1988 government policy on communications was revised in 2002 to include many more communications tools, including marketing, fairs and exhibits, risk management, crisis communications and sponsorships (Canada, 1988).

So untouchable was the hegemony of the majority Liberal government that its efforts to try to persuade Quebec to stay in Canada went beyond acceptable communication practices and tipped into illegality that benefitted the Liberal party itself. What became known as the "sponsorship scandal" ended the government's obsession with national unity. Its lack of accountability for public money was also seen to be a cause of the eventual fall of the Liberal government in 2006. The purpose of the sponsorship program was to inform Canadians, heighten federal awareness, and build a strong and united Canada. What it more or less amounted to was the federal government paying advertising companies to have the country's word-mark or the logo (a stylized Canadian flag and the word "Canada") used at sporting events and other public activities across the country, and market Canada to Canadians in the same way that products get marketed.

Over several years, media reports began to note the huge costs of the program, then the Auditor General of Canada, an independent official with a mandate to examine public expenditure, investigated the program and produced two reports detailing its failures and overblown costs. This was followed by a public inquiry, which revealed that the scandal was caused partly by a lack of checks and balances in a streamlined bureaucracy, and partly by the control of communication that was centered within the Prime Minister's Office itself. In addition, as it turned out, a disproportionate amount of this federal visibility was focused in Quebec. In all, the cost to Canadians was $145 million in inflated commissions and production costs to Liberal-friendly businesses in Quebec; and $100 million in kickbacks from advertising companies to the Quebec Liberal Party (Canada, 2005).

In the wake of the sponsorship scandal, most of the strategic communications apparatus that was built up in the bureaucracy was dismantled. The sponsorship scandal also provided an opportunity for the opposition Conservatives to use accountability and trust in government as a major plank in their election platform. In 2004, the Liberals lost their majority and then, in 2006, after a gap of 15 years, they were replaced by a Conservative minority government.

Important to note is that the scandal also hurt the reputation of those engaging in legitimate practices of information and communication in government. Overall, it was becoming more difficult to differentiate between public information necessary for citizenship and strategic communication that promoted the particular party in power.

The Conservatives and Political Marketing

As the transition of power from the Liberals to the Conservatives was taking place in Canada, developments in political communication theory and practice based on the UK experience were pointing to new ways that political parties were utilizing communications to promote themselves and their policies with the aim of gaining political office.

Jennifer Lees-Marshment (2001) conceptualized a "marriage" between political communication and political marketing that groups political parties into three types based on the communications strategies they employ. Lees-Marshment's subsequent research demonstrated the success of those political parties that had embraced new forms of strategic communication that drew on political marketing (Lees-Marshment & Lilleker, 2005; Lees-Marshment, 2011). She suggested that parties can be product-oriented, sales-oriented, or market-oriented.

Parties that have a *product* orientation are traditional parties that simply stand for what they believe in. They have an ideology and ethos that is clearly visible in their policies and election strategies. They maintain their beliefs and believe that the best product will win. The implication in political marketing is that these parties are old-fashioned and risk losing electoral power by standing on principle. In the *sales* orientation, parties realize that to gain support for their policies or win elections they must actively promote or sell their beliefs and create demand for their product; even a good product will not win without promotion. The third orientation for political parties is the *market* orientation, in which parties change their beliefs and behavior to match what the voters want, which they discover from marketing research. The party then delivers the policies or beliefs that people want, and creates a product that citizens respond to favorably—and vote for, which represents the "fulfillment" dream of advertisers. The implication is clear for political parties: if you want to gain power, you will take on a market orientation.

The idea of political marketing is deceptively simple. It speaks to the desire if not the need of politicians to achieve their ultimate goal of electoral success. The deterministic promise of political marketing is a powerful narcotic in the world of politics, yet it carries a high cost. First, it decouples ideology from politics. For electoral success, ideology is not needed; in fact, it can impede progress towards victory, as flexibility on the part of the party is an important element. For success, the party must go where the results of marketing take it. Second, political marketing privileges a consumer response to a product over a citizen response to a policy, thus commodifying the audience. Voters are encouraged to pick and choose as individuals which political product is best for them personally and not as citizens with the welfare of the community or the country at stake. Thus a link is created between political marketing and an ethos of individualism and consumerism. In effect, it can be seen as the public communication arm of New Public Management or, as it has now become fully implemented in government bureaucracies, New Public Governance (Osborne, 2010).

Some background is needed on organized conservatism in Canada. The shift away from the post-war consensus and towards the New Right manifested itself differently than in it did in the UK, New Zealand and Australia. Here it appeared first in provincial governments in British Columbia, Alberta and Ontario. In the industrial heartland of Ontario, the Conservatives came to power in 1995. Typically Ontario had elected Progressive Conservative governments for much of the post-war period. However, the Conservative government of Premier Mike Harris introduced the "common sense revolution"—the name of its party platform—with a stated goal of transforming the state-citizen relationship that was very unlike the former benign and middle-of-the-road "progressive" conservatism seen previously in the province. Using the tried and true "blitzkrieg" tactics formulated earlier in New Zealand (Easton, 1994)—also called a "communication offensive" in the UK context (Golding, 1992)—the new Conservative government packed in as much restructuring policy and legislation as quickly as possible, including a precedent-setting omnibus bill in its first six months in office. This ushered in two and a half years of relentless state restructuring and counter-response from civic society that at one point saw 250,000 people in Toronto demonstrate against the government (Macleod, 1999). Despite this, the Harris government stayed the course, even being re-elected for a second term. My own research demonstrates the importance of strategic communication to the Harris government, underpinned by extensive and finely targeted public opinion research that identified favorable sub-audiences and messaging for government communication with the public (Kozolanka, 2007).

However, the downside to the blitzkrieg approach to regime shifts was the extended and exhausting public struggle between the government and its opponents, from opposition politicians to social justice groups. By the time the federal Conservative party was re-building to replace the Liberals, the political strategy had changed. Like the Harris government in Ontario, the aim was to shift Canadians from their liberalism to a right-wing hegemony; however, the short-term blitzkrieg strategy was replaced by an under-the-radar incrementalism (Flanagan, 2007)—moving slowly towards their policy goals—supported by comprehensive strategic communication. This was for several reasons: the precarity of a minority government, which can be defeated at any time; the party's realization that the Canadian public was generally liberal in political orientation and needed to be moved slowly to take New Right positions; and, importantly, the desire to avoid challenges from civil society that would take them off-track in achieving their ultimate goal of a conservative hegemony.

After the 2006 election, the federal Conservative march forward started with a decidedly controversial—and even counter-intuitive—media strategy. Instead of courting journalists in Ottawa, who mostly represented national or larger media, and winning them over to the Conservative way, the new government deliberately bypassed the parliamentary press gallery, preferring regional media outside parliament's reach. When the Conservatives wanted or needed national media attention, they would select the reporters they felt would provide positive coverage. If they held a media conference, they would use a pre-arranged (and much shortened) list of journalists, in the U.S. presidential style. It was a high-stakes gamble, but the government knew that media owners would sooner play by the Conservatives' rules and get the story than protest and be bypassed for interviews with cabinet ministers. The new government also instituted a cumbersome process for the media to use when attempting to interview cabinet ministers and subject specialists within the bureaucracy. The process was so lengthy that the need for comment or explanation was long past by the time approval from the Prime Minister's Office was received (Blanchfield & Bronskill, 2010).

An interesting aspect of the Conservatives' broader communication strategy is the diffused use they make of new media, blogging in particular, to disseminate their messages. Although blogging was once a communication tool rarely thought of as controllable or even well-informed, the government also stimulates and encourages carefully targeted citizen participation across the country through a large group of Blogging Tories, who network online to disseminate the party's position under the radar from traditional politics in Ottawa. The Blogging Tories played a role in amplifying the Conservatives' position in a political crisis that occurred when the two opposition parties in parliament attempted to form a coalition government soon after the 2008 election (Kozolanka, 2012).

The Conservatives have continued to conduct in-depth consumer-based research to target citizens. They have also delayed or denied public access to information requested by the media, the political opposition, or members of the public. Also, they have conflated the party with government in public communication, as "Canada's New Government" when they were first elected and later as "The Harper Government." This is in violation of rules that state that the appropriate and non-partisan title is "Government of Canada."

As this strategy unfolded and included the 2008 general election, in which the party was returned as a minority government, the Conservatives continued to centralize power within the Prime Minister's Office, especially power over communication, and in the government bureaucracy. Moreover, the role and nature of the PMO itself changed considerably under the new government. Not only did it increase in size, it added to its communication strength, although its policy component remained quite small in comparison, at one-fifth that of communication in 2007 (Kozolanka, 2012). As the PMO took on more communication strength, communication directorates in the bureaucracy were losing the strategic focus that had been built up under the Liberals, and the PMO returned to its previous role of merely implementing communication strategies. These included work undertaken by the Privy Council Office, which had inherited the administration of advertising and public opinion research after the sponsorship scandal (Kozolanka, 2012). Given the Conservative government's extreme focus on self-promotion, in effect the PMO could be considered the executive office for its corporate communication (Hallahan et al., 2007, p. 18).

Nowhere were their self-promotion efforts more evident than in the Economic Action Plan, the government's response to the worldwide recession of 2008. Forced by the opposition parties to take measures to stimulate the economy, public communication about the plan also reinforced the Conservatives' ongoing tactic of re-styling all public communication to make the connection to the party as government. This was clearly promotional, as well as partisan, rather than informational. In addition, costly saturation advertising to promote the plan, funded by taxpayers, continued well beyond the period in which the plan's funds were dispersed and continued from January 2009 until the next federal election was called in April 2011 and then resumed after the election, which gave the Conservatives their majority, well after the plan's funds were depleted. (In Canada, governing parties cannot use public money for advertising and public opinion research during election periods, which have become ever shorter, and rarely exceed five weeks.)

The Conservatives also took over the logo of the Economic Action Plan, now firmly connected to the Conservative party, using it as the theme and backdrop for all government announcements. This made it very clear that the plan promoted the party, rather than the government program, and thus the advertising and the signs became part of the permanent election campaign. Importantly, the Conservatives directed the communication for the Economic Action Plan out of the Prime Minister's Office, with its large numbers of communication experts, and with the Privy Council Office managing only the implementation of the plan (Canada. Privy Council Office, 2010).

Although the Conservatives at last gained a majority in the 2011 general election, they did so even as their popular vote rose only marginally, as the party successfully targeted and concentrated advertising, public opinion research, and their campaign events in a handful of ridings. Since the election, there have been allegations that the Conservatives may have gone beyond legal boundaries to convince citizens to vote for them, and that in a number of key constituencies they used voter suppression tactics that made a difference to the outcome of the election. It is alleged that the Conservatives used automated "robocalls" to misdirect non-supporters to the wrong voting stations on election day. At the time that this chapter was being written, these allegations were being investigated by Elections Canada (Milewski, 2012).

For better or worse, the Conservatives had become a market-based party, targeting voters based on precise public opinion research and selling voters' own positions on issues back to them. In using the bureaucratic apparatus of government and the Privy Council Office as adjunct offices for support of its communication and information plans, the PMO had in effect been using PCO as its own version of Communication Canada, the short-lived, self-standing department formed by the previous Liberal government, and had firmly established New Public Governance in the bureaucracy (Hallahan et al., 2007, p. 7; Osborne, 2010.

Conclusion

In their time in power, the hegemonic Liberals were adept at building a huge communication apparatus in government, concentrating power within the Prime Minister's Office and politicizing communication efforts in the bureaucracy. The ensuing sponsorship scandal has been seen as the biggest scandal ever in Canadian politics, and the Liberals were voted out of office. The Conservatives also built communication capacity in government, enlarged the Prime Minister's Office and controlled PCO and communication within it. Numerous small scandals were endured over five years of this minority government. In particular, the government breached their promise of greater transparency many times in ways that shocked political veterans, other parties and the media. They were rewarded, not with defeat, but with a majority government.

To the extent that scholars have been able to document strategies that are proprietary to the Conservative party, it is clear that the difference between the outcomes for the two parties lies in the Conservatives' use of political marketing. Through information gained from political marketing, the Conservatives targeted the right groups of voters with the messages that would appeal to them and framed the issues in ways these voters could support. They did not allow themselves to be diverted from their core messages, even when faced with sustained negative media coverage and political opposition. In this way, moving incrementally over the period of five years as a minority government, they convinced just enough targeted voters that they were not scary right-wingers, and that they deserved their vote. Their next goal—a Conservative hegemony—will take a generation to reach.

The Conservatives came to power on a platform that emphasized accountability to citizens after the excesses of the Liberals. However, although they established different mechanisms and passed a law on accountability, they broke the rules themselves. For example, they established a Parliamentary Budget Office, headed by their own appointee, but refused to give the PBO the information it needed to assess government accountability. Instead, the government challenges such attempts to uncover their practices, often through the courts, but also by stonewalling the opposition in daily parliamentary Question Period and avoiding media questioning, thus impeding transparency by withholding or manipulating information needed for citizenship.

Political marketing offers an attractive array of strategic communication tools and opportunities with promising results for late democracies beyond Canada. It is also an extremely useful and successful stratagem for political parties that strategize to campaign and govern for certain segments of society only, and whose communication strategies rely on the increasing non-attention, lack of trust and eventual lack of political participation by citizens that the parties themselves have fostered in campaigns both prior to and while in office. Seen as manipulation by the public, these communication practices foster political inattention and discourage citizens other than partisans and targeted voters from engaging in political life. The public cannot readily discern the difference between a public communication campaign such as the Economic Action Plan, which should be non-partisan, and actual communication products emanating from a political party, because the former has become politicized. It will remain difficult to decipher what, if anything, can be taken as neutral in politics and what is interested and purposeful.

Political marketing solidifies marketing behavior as a more technologized and advanced version of strategic communication. Its use in politics, in an era of downsized governments with fewer checks and balances, and the market ethos of NPM, coupled with the urge of political parties to centralize and dominate through the use of marketing methods in their strategic communication, could soon be the norm in the permanent campaigns of the future.

However, it is difficult to reconcile political marketing with the needs of citizens and with the extensive form of democracy envisaged in the post-WW2 era. Strategic communication is always interested and purposeful when used by powerful entities such as the state to, in effect, purchase that audience at a critical juncture that benefits the perpetrator. As Hallahan et al. (2007) point out, such communication excludes, narrows and focuses in ways that are incompatible with democratic communication to citizens (p. 4). The examples here show that even government information campaigns to inform citizens involve some subtle or overt layer of persuasion that aids the government in power, and, increasingly, they involve many different practices of publicity in massive, expensive, multi-media campaigns disseminated widely but selectively.

Given the political environment analyzed in this chapter, it is difficult to believe that strategic communication and political marketing serve the public interest. Such communication suggests impoverishment of the public's ability truly to make political choices. Social actors also have more opportunities to intervene in politics; however, we need to acknowledge as well that there are power imbalances that impede citizen challenges to government actions. Civil society groups themselves can and do use strategic communication to counter and resist government strategies and messages; however, this is not necessarily from a position of power, which has a direct impact on the ability of these social actors to be heard in a crowded media landscape. Moreover, such audience denigration may represent a return to the one-way transmission model of communications conceptualized and critiqued by James Carey (1989), instead of the more democratic and interactive ritual model that "helps us explain how we build shared reality and culture in social groups, including in organizations, even as we account for constant change" (Bell, Golombisky, & Holtzhausen, 2002, p. 5, cited in Hallahan et al., 2007). The media, which are relied on to interpret political behavior on behalf of the public, face their own structural constraints in fulfilling their democratic function, a reality (and an opportunity) not lost on politicians and governments.

On their own, the issues facing the public and the media draw needed attention to the ethical dimension of strategic communication in politics, both in Canada and elsewhere. Given the intransigence of the Conservative government in not governing transparently or in the interests of the public—the whole public, not just targeted segments of it—as one example, how can suitable strategic communication, and its political marketing offshoot, be used in public environments, especially when the state–public relationship is already asymmetrical?

The superficial banality of political marketing implies that it is a neutral tool, when in fact it is imbued with the differentiated power of those who purchase it and those who consume it. Lost in the middle is any notion that information is different from other commodities, with its dual material and symbolic aspects (Mosco, 2009), and thus needs to be handled carefully and ethically in public applications. This, of course, is at odds with the instrumental understanding of political marketing in that it gets results and that such results are neutral. For political communication, in the short term, that self-interested result is electoral success. In the long term, however, it is hegemony: an ideological regime shift.

In conclusion, a critical communication approach reveals the unequal power relations between state and citizen relations that impoverish political culture. It also reveals the nature of the growing use of strategic communication in recent Canadian political history, as well as the reach of the New Right's coalescence of its market hegemony (Lilleker & Scullion, 2008, p. 3). Furthermore, and more broadly, this approach allows us to see how the instrumental use of political marketing commodifies citizens as consumers. Political marketing can claim considerable electoral success in the short term, but risks further alienation of citizens over time and should be considered cautiously by governments that value a vibrant public sphere.

References

Aucoin, P., & Turnbull, L. (2003). The democratic deficit: Paul Martin and parliamentary reform, *Canadian Public Administration, 46(4)*, 427–449.

Bennett, W. L., & Manheim, J. B. (2001). The big spin: Strategic communication and the transformation of pluralist democracy. In W. L. Bennett & R. M. Entman (Eds.), *Mediated politics: Communication in the future of democracy* (pp. 279–98). Cambridge, England: Cambridge University Press.

Blanchfield, M., & Bronskill, J. (2010, June 7). Documents reveal extreme steps Conservatives use to control all federal events, announcements. *The Toronto Star*, p. A1.

Blumler, J.G. (1990). Elections, the media and the modern publicity process. In M. Ferguson (Ed.), *Public Communication: The new imperatives* (pp. 101–113). London, England: Sage.

Bowman, K. (2000). Polling to campaign and to govern. In N.J. Ornstein, & T.E. Mann (Eds.), *The permanent campaign and its future* (pp. 54–74). Washington DC, WA: American Enterprise Institute and The Brookings Institution.

Canada. (1988). *Government communications policy of the government of Canada*. Ottawa, ON: Treasury Board of Canada Secretariat.

Canada. (2005). *Commission of inquiry into the sponsorship program and advertising activities. Who is responsible? Phase 1 report*. Ottawa, Canada: Government of Canada (Gomery Inquiry).

Canada. Privy Council Office (2004). *Table A-1—Resources by strategic outcomes and business lines*, DPR 2003–4 (Departmental plans and priorities). Retrieved from http://www.collectionscanada.gc.ca/webarchives/20060120012007555553/http://www.tbs-sct.gc.ca

Canada. Privy Council Office (2010). *Report on plans and priorities 2010–11*. Retrieved from www.tbs-sct.gc.ca/rpp/2010–2011/inst/pco/pco-eng.pdf

Carey, J. W. (1989). *Communication as culture: Essays on media and society*. Winchester, MA: Unwin Hyman.

Davis, A. (2002). The expansion of public relations and its impact on news production. In *Public relations democracy: Public relations, politics and the mass media in Britain* (pp. 19–41). Manchester, England, and New York: Manchester University Press.

Deacon, D., & Golding, P. (1994). *Taxation and representation: The media, political communication and the poll tax*. London, England: John Libbey.

Dobbin, M. (1998). *The myth of the good corporate citizen: Democracy under the rule of big business*. Toronto, Canada: Stoddart.

Easton, B. (1994). How did the health reforms blitzkrieg fail? *Political Science, 46(2)*, 215–233.

Flanagan, T. (2007, September 22). Thou shalt not lean too far to the right. *The Globe and Mail*, p. A1.

Fuchs, C. (2010). Grounding critical communication studies: An inquiry into the communication theory of Karl Marx. *Journal of Communication Inquiry, 34*(1), 15–41.

Golding, P. (1992). Communicating capitalism: Resisting and restructuring state ideology. *Media, Culture and Society, 14*(4), 503–522.

Gutstein, D. (2009). *Not a conspiracy theory: How business propaganda hijacks democracy.* Toronto, Canada: Key Porter.

Hallahan, K. (2004). Integrated communication: Implications for public relations beyond excellence. In E.L. Toth (Ed.), *The future of excellence in public relations and communication management: Challenges for the next generation* (pp. 299–336). Mahwah, NJ: Lawrence Erlbaum.

Hallahan K., Holtzhausen, D., van Ruler, B., Verçiç, D., & Sriramesh, K. (2007). Defining strategic communication. *International Journal of Strategic Communication, 1*(1), 3–35.

Havemann, P. (1998). Social citizenship, re-commodification and the contract state. In E. A. Christodoulidis (Ed.), *Communitarianism and citizenship* (pp. 134–57). Aldershot, England: Ashgate.

Kozolanka, K. (2006). The sponsorship scandal as communication: The rise of politicized and strategic communication in the federal government. *Canadian Journal of Communication, 31*(2), 343–366.

Kozolanka, K. (2007). *The power of persuasion: The politics of the new right in Ontario.* Montreal, CA: Black Rose Press.

Kozolanka, K. (2012). 'Buyer beware': Pushing the boundaries of market communications in government. In A. Marland, T. Giasson & J. Lees-Marshment (Eds.), *Political marketing in Canada* (pp. 107–22). Vancouver, CA: UBC Press.

Kozolanka, K., Mazepa, P., & Skinner, D. (2012). Introduction: Considering alternative media in Canada: Structure, participation, activism. In K. Kozolanka, P. Mazepa, & D. Skinner (Eds.), *Alternative media in Canada* (pp. 1–22). Vancouver, CA: UBC Press.

Lees-Marshment, J. (2001). The marriage of politics and marketing. *Political Studies, 49*(4), 692–713.

Lees-Marshment, J. (2011). *The Political Marketing Game.* Hampshire, UK: Palgrave Macmillan.

Lees-Marshment, J., & Lilleker, D. G. (Eds.) (2005). *Political marketing: A comparative perspective.* Manchester: Manchester University Press.

Lilleker, D. G. (2006). *Key concepts in political communication.* London, England: Sage.

Lilleker, D. G., & Scullion, R. (2008). Introduction. In D. G. Lilleker & R. Scullion (Eds.), *Voters or consumers: Imagining the contemporary electorate* (pp. 1–11). Newcastle, England: Cambridge Scholars Publishing.

Macleod, C. (1999). Introduction. In V. Pietropaolo, *Celebration of resistance: Ontario's days of action,* pp. 1–3. Toronto: Between the Lines.

Milewski, T. (2012). Tories trying to block new evidence in robocalls case. CBC News. Retrieved from http://www.cbc.ca/news/politics/story/2012/08/03/pol-hamilton-council-canadians-robocalls.html

Mosco, V. (2009). *The political economy of communication* (2nd ed.). Thousand Oaks, CA: Sage.

Nadeau, R., & Giasson, T. (2003). *Canada's democratic malaise: Are the media to blame?* Montreal, CA: Institute for Research on Public Policy.

Norris, P. (2000). *A virtuous circle: Political communication in postindustrial societies.* Cambridge, England: Cambridge University Press.

O'Shaughnessy, N.J. (2004). *Politics and propaganda: Weapons of mass seduction.* Ann Arbor, MI: University of Michigan Press.

Osborne, S. P. (2010). *The new public governance?: Emerging perspectives on the theory and practice of governance.* London, England: Routledge.

Paré, D., & Berger, F. (2008). Political marketing Canadian style? The Conservative party and the 2006 general election. *Canadian Journal of Communication, 33,* 39–63.

Putnam, R. (2000). *Bowling alone: The collapse and revival of American community.* New York: Simon and Schuster.

Rose, J. (2000). *Making "pictures in our heads": Government advertising in Canada.* Westport, CT: Praeger.

Rubin, K., & Kozolanka, K. (2013). Managing information: Too much publicity, not enough information. In K. Kozolanka (Ed.), *Publicity and the Canadian state.* Toronto, Canada: University of Toronto Press.

Savigny, H. (2008). The construction of the political consumer (or politics: What not to consume. In D. G. Lilleker & R. Scullion (Eds.). *Voters or consumers: Imagining the contemporary electorate* (pp. 35–50). Newcastle, England: Cambridge Scholars Publishing.

Scammell, M. (2001). The media and media management. In A. Seldon (Ed.). *The Blair effect* (pp. 509–533). London, England: Little, Brown.

Skinner, D., & Gasher, M. (2005). So much by so few: Media policy and ownership in Canada. In D. Skinner, J. R. Compton & M. Gasher (Eds.), *Converging media, diverging politics: A political economy of news media in the United States and Canada* (pp. 51–76). Oxford, England: Lexington Books.

Sussman, G. (2010). *Branding democracy: U.S. regime change in post-soviet Eastern Europe.* New York: Peter Lang.

Ward, I. (2007). Mapping the Australian PR state. In S. Young (Ed.). *Government communication in Australia* (pp. 3–18). Cambridge, England: Cambridge University Press.

27

Strategic Health Communication

Theory- and Evidence-Based Campaign Development

Constanze Rossmann

Health Communication

Health communication is a central field of health prevention and health care. The field embraces any type of communication about health and illness that either occurs incidentally, for example in the transmission of health information via soap operas on television, or is initiated with the intention to inform or educate, promote health or prevent diseases. Health communication has been defined in various ways. Due to its broad scope it seems reasonable to define the area rather broadly. In the words of Jackson and Duffy (1998, p. ix-x), the "study of health communication focuses on the interaction of people involved in the health care process and the elucidation and dissemination of health-related information."

Health communication can be found on four different levels:

- intrapersonal communication—psychological and communicative processes within individuals;
- interpersonal communication—the exchange of information between individuals (e.g., provider–patient interaction);
- organizational communication in the context of health institutions (e.g., public relations of hospitals); and
- mass media communication (Signitzer, 2001).

Within the latter field, different areas can be identified according to the traditional research areas in communication science: journalism studies (e.g., medicine journalism), media content (e.g., depiction of health issues in the media), media use (e.g., selective exposure to health content), and media effects (e.g., impact of media on health-related perceptions, attitudes, and behavior; and suitability of message types to persuade and motivate individuals to engage in healthy behavior) (Viswanath, 2008; Walsh-Childers & Brown, 2009). One of the central questions in the history of mass media health communication is the development of communication campaigns for health promotion and prevention, the focus of the present chapter.

Health Communication Campaigns

As with health communication in general, health communication campaigns are defined in several ways. One of the most cited definitions stems from E. M. Rogers and Storey (1987, p. 821).

According to them, four elements are crucial for communication campaigns: "(1) a campaign intends to generate specific outcomes or effects (2) in a relatively large number of individuals, (3) usually within a specified period of time, and (4) through an organized set of communication activities." Rice and Atkin (2009) expanded their definition and describe public communication campaigns as:

> (1) purposive attempts (2) to inform, persuade, or motivate behavior change (3) in a relatively well-defined and large audience, (4) generally for noncommercial benefits to the individuals and/or society at large, (5) typically within a given time period, (6) by means of organized communication activities involving mass media, and (7) often complemented by interpersonal support (p. 436).

Even if the term "health campaigns" is often used in everyday language many scholars (e.g., E. M. Rogers & Storey, 1987; Rice & Atkin, 2009) refer to the broader term "communication campaigns," indicating that it applies to health issues as well as other social issues. Communication campaigns are only one strategy among several to solve social problems such as health problems. Accordingly, social problems can only be solved effectively by combining technical developments (e.g., pharmaceuticals), legal regulations (e.g., smoking ban), and economic regulations (e.g., tobacco tax) with communication campaigns. Although they are related, communication campaigns are not equal to advertising, marketing, public relations, mass media communication, or interpersonal communication; however, they make use of these elements (Bonfadelli & Friemel, 2010).

Even in the early eighteenth century, sporadic trials to improve public health with communicative measures were being implemented: to impede the smallpox epidemic (Atkin & Marshall, 1996), for instance. It was not until the mid twentieth century, however, that campaign developers and scholars began to collaborate in order to improve campaign design and implementation. The acknowledgement of individual lifestyles as important determinants of health beyond biological and genetic factors played a major role in strengthening the impact of health promotion; this connection was established in the "Ottawa Charter for Health Promotion" by the World Health Organization (World Health Organization, 1986; Fertman, Allensworth, & Auld, 2010).

Classification of Health Communication Campaigns

Health communication campaigns as an important measure of health promotion appear in numerous different forms and can be differentiated along several dimensions. First, they vary according to the *health domain*. Frequently addressed domains are tobacco consumption, coronary diseases, alcohol and drug abuse, and cancer prevention (Wakefield, Loken & Hornik, 2010). Furthermore, campaigns vary according to the *stakeholder* involved: governmental organizations (e.g., Center for Disease Control and Prevention, USA, or European Center for Disease Control and Prevention), non-profit institutions (e.g., foundations, associations), health insurances, or pharmaceutical companies. Campaigns also vary according to the *receiver* they address. They address a certain target group either directly or indirectly via individuals or groups who influence their peers via interpersonal communication (opinion leaders, peer groups, role models). If communication campaigns use a policy strategy, they address politicians at first who in turn are to change the relevant social and legal conditions (Rice & Atkin, 2009, p. 440).

A further fundamental distinction refers to the question of whether a campaign is aimed at health promotion (healthy behavior such as physical activity is to be enforced or stabilized) or prevention (unhealthy behavior, e.g. drug abuse, is prohibited) (Silk, Atkin & Salmon, 2011). Furthermore, campaigns can be distinguished according to the *outcome* they address. On the individual level communication campaigns address affective, cognitive, behavioral, or physiological outcomes. Affective outcomes are emotional reactions to health information (trust, fear, uncertainty), cognitive outcomes refer to knowledge, perceptions, or attitudes, behavioral outcomes become evident in altered health or information behaviors. Also physiological effects play a role in the health domain: for instance, weight reduction or a reduced blood cholesterol level (Kreps, O'Hair, & Clowers, 1994). As E. M. Rogers (1994) pointed out a characteristic of health communication as compared to other communication domains is its general focus on positive outcomes. Indeed, health communication campaigns are usually intended to have a positive effect, such as improving people's health behavior. However, sometimes they are also intended to cause negative emotional reactions first in order to reach positive behavioral outcomes in the end (e.g., fear appeals causing fear in order to provoke behavior change: see below).

Further distinctions of health communication campaigns refer to the use of different *message types* (informing, explaining, persuasive) that are distributed via different *channels* or combinations of channels (television, radio, print media, interactive media, mobile media, interpersonal communication) (Wakefield et al., 2010; for further classifications see Rice & Atkin, 2009, p. 436).

Effectiveness of Health Campaigns

According to E. M. Rogers and Storey (1987), research on campaigns can be divided into three eras. The 1940s and 1950s mark the peak of the *era of minimal effects*. In this early stage of campaign research most of the campaigns failed to reach their target outcomes. The 1960s and 1970s fall into the *era in which campaigns could succeed,* if they "were carried out in a more strategic way" (p. 829) using formative evaluation, setting reasonable campaign goals, audience segmentation, and considering the role of interpersonal communication. Thus scholars began to detect, formulate, and standardize the principles of campaign development and design. With this approach more successful campaigns were implemented with promising results, one of which was the outstanding "Stanford Heart Disease Prevention Three Community Program" (Maccoby & Altman, 1988). The 1980s and 1990s designate the *era of moderate effects.* The effectiveness of campaigns further increased, while scholars examined both the conditions that increased campaign effectiveness and their limitations. Supplementing these three eras Noar (2006) identified a new era of campaign research beginning in the new millennium and still continuing at present: the *conditional effects era* (p. 22). During this era the developed and learned principles of campaign development have been implemented more effectively and creatively, whereby the effectiveness of campaigns has been further increasing.

However, the effectiveness of campaigns varies according to the addressed outcome. Specifically, the impact of communication campaigns on knowledge or risk perception seems to be stronger as compared to their impact on attitudes, which in turn are influenced more easily as compared to health behavior (Silk et al., 2011). Several meta-analyses (Derzon & Lipsey, 2002; Snyder & Hamilton, 2002) and reviews (Silk et al., 2011; Wakefield et al., 2010) identified factors that are able to increase campaign effectiveness even in the context of behavior change.

First, a high reach has a positive influence on the effectiveness of campaigns. Furthermore, enforcement messages, new information, and distribution via audiovisual and multiple channels are effective factors. At the same time, the chance to introduce new behaviors is higher as compared to changing existing behaviors. Singular or episodic behavior (e.g., skin cancer screening) can be influenced more easily than recurring habitualized behavior (e.g., nutrition, physical activity). Policy measures and public relation activities as complementary strategies to conventional mass media campaigns are also able to increase campaign effectiveness. Not least, interpersonal communication and communication via new technologies (interactive web applications, mobile media) are important ways to improve campaign effects. In contrast, campaign effectiveness is reduced by opposing messages in media coverage, entertainment or advertising (e.g., advertisements for unhealthy food); by social norms (e.g., tobacco consumption within certain peer groups); by addiction; and by the increasing fragmentation of media audiences that makes it harder to reach target groups via specific channels. Further factors that can lead to reduced campaign effects are distorted risk perceptions (e.g., optimistic bias or third-person perceptions; see Chapin, 2000; Weinstein, 1980) as well as reactance (e.g., Hong & Faedda, 1996) and boomerang effects (for an overview, see Wakefield et al., 2010).

Strategic Campaign Development

Because the effectiveness of communication campaigns depends on numerous factors, determinants, and conditions, one of the most important requirements to enable effective campaigns is a strategic campaign development.

As mentioned earlier, E. M. Rogers and Storey (1987) indicated four strategies to design successful communication campaigns, which had previously been identified in the 1960 and 1970s era of potential campaign effects: formative evaluation, reasonable campaign goals, audience segmentations, and interpersonal channels. Later on further important strategies were identified. Even if there is no clear consensus as to the labels and order of the strategic steps, there is a broad consensus among health communication scholars as to which strategic steps are essential in order to improve campaign effects (e.g., Bonfadelli & Friemel, 2010; Noar, 2006; Silk et al., 2011).

Strategic Steps

1. The starting point is the problem identification and situational analysis examining the present situation, its causes, determinants, and opportunities for change (also *formative evaluation*). In this context the central determinants of a target behavior are to be identified against theory- and evidence-based knowledge. If the available evidence (e.g., from previous research or literature reviews) is insufficient, this step also comprises the implementation of qualitative or quantitative studies (e.g., focus groups, surveys).
2. Another important step in campaign development involves the specification of the target group or several target groups (*audience segmentation*). The target group can be specified against the background of several relevant criteria, which typically include demographic attributes (e.g., age, gender, education), media consumption behavior, and lifestyle patterns. These criteria may also include the degree to which individuals of a certain target group are affected by the health problem or risk behavior in question, behavioral determinants, and the preparedness to change behavior (described as "stage of change" in Prochaska, Redding, & Evers, 2008). As a general rule a combination of these criteria should be applied in order to identify and describe the target group that is to be addressed; in no case is it advisable to address a campaign to the general population without any further specification.
3. Also the *goals of the campaign* have to be clearly specified. In this context the direct receiver of the campaign messages and the specific outcomes are defined. In some cases the specified target group is directly addressed; in other cases the campaign is addressed to relevant social groups (e.g., parents, teachers), which in turn disseminate the messages to the target group (e.g., their children). As with the classification of outcomes mentioned above, campaigns can be aimed at cognitive, affective, behavioral, or physical outcomes. In some cases the appropriate outcome is public awareness: for example, if the problem is rather unknown. In other cases it is appropriate to aim the campaign at behavior change.
4. Against the background of the previous steps an adequate *campaign strategy* is to be chosen. Which message is suitable to reach the target group? Which message appeals are to be used (e.g., fear appeals, gain-framed messages, humor, or erotic appeals)? Should the tone of the message be informing, explaining, or persuasive?

5. The next step refers to the *implementation of the campaign*. Campaign developers have to decide which media channels, specific genres, and programs to use, and which ways of interpersonal communication to choose for the dissemination of the campaign messages. These decisions again depend on the previous steps and decisions (e.g., the target group will affect the implementation).

6. The last step refers to the *evaluation of the campaign effectiveness*. Within this step are a few things that have to be kept in mind. First, the evaluation results largely depend on the intended outcomes and campaign goals. Second, it is important to distinguish between effects (any changes in outcome variables that can be traced back to the campaign), effectiveness (effects consistent with the previously defined campaign goals), and efficiency (economic balance between costs and outcomes) (Bonfadelli & Friemel, 2010). Third, evaluation embraces *summative evaluation*, after a campaign has been run; *formative evaluation*, previous to the campaign development (problem analysis); evaluation during campaign development (test of messages and message types); and evaluation during the implementation of a campaign.

In short, the crucial strategies for successful campaign planning, development, implementation, and evaluation are (Noar, 2006, p. 25) as follows: formative evaluation (problem identification), theory-based campaign development, segmentation of the target group, development and design of messages suitable for the target group, dissemination via channels the target group uses, summative evaluation with adequate methods (for an overview see also Bonfadelli & Friemel, 2010; Finnegan & Viswanath, 2008; Silk et al., 2011).

Theoretical Foundation

As outlined above, use of theory is an essential strategy in order to increase the effectiveness and efficiency of a campaign (Finnegan & Viswanath, 2008; Noar, 2006). Apart from epidemiological and medical findings on the effectiveness of lifestyle and health behavior changes (e.g., increasing physical activity in order to prevent diabetes type 2), results from communication science on the uses and effects of mass media channels, findings from cognitive psychology and communication research on information processing and persuasion strategies, and knowledge from health psychology explaining the determinants of health behavior are important to consider (Rossmann, 2010a; see also Figure 27.1).

Behavioral Theories

Social psychology and health psychology provide several theories explaining (health) behavior and behavioral determinants, for example social-cognitive theory (Bandura, 2001), transtheoretical model (Prochaska et al., 2008), health belief model (Champion & Skinner, 2008), and theory of planned behavior (TPB) (Ajzen, 2005; Fishbein & Ajzen, 2010). Basically, each theory is useful to determine the relevant factors of a specific behavior. Specifically, the well-established TPB together with the Integrated Behavioral Model (IBM) (Montano & Kasprzyk, 2008), which adapted the TPB to the health domain and integrated further relevant constructs, provides a good theoretical starting point. These two models not only identify the main factors but also the underlying beliefs determining behavioral intentions and behavior. Hence, referring to TPB and IBM enables health scholars to measure the determinants of health behaviors—for example, physical activity—very precisely. Figure 27.2 shows an integrated version of the model as adapted to physical activity in the context of diabetes prevention.

According to the TPB, behavior (e.g., physical activity) depends on the intention to perform the behavior (e.g., "Do I want to engage in physical activity?") in the first place (Ajzen, 2005; Fishbein &

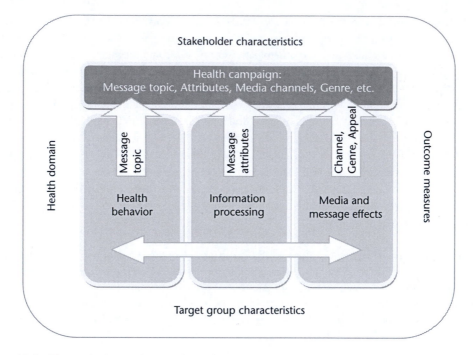

Figure 27.1   Theoretical Foundation of Health Campaigns

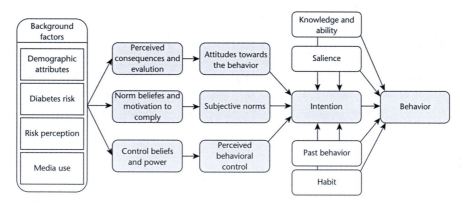

Figure 27.2   Theory of Planned Behavior and Integrated Behavioral Model Applied to Physical Activity

Based on Ajzen (2005) and Montano & Kasprzyk (2008)

Ajzen, 2010). The intention to perform a behavior is driven by three specific components: attitude towards the behavior (e.g., "Is it good to engage in physical activity?"), subjective norm (e.g., "Do important others think it is good to engage in physical activity?," "Are important others engaged in physical activity?"), and perceived behavioral control (e.g., "Am I able to engage in physical activity?"). These three components are determined by specific beliefs. Attitude towards the behavior depends on so-called behavioral beliefs, which consist of perceived consequences of a behavior (e.g., "Physical activity makes me feel better") and the evaluation of these consequences (e.g., "It is good to feel better"). Subjective norms describe the perceived social pressure to perform a specific behavior. They are also a function of specific beliefs (normative beliefs): a person's belief that important others approve or disapprove of performing the behavior (e.g., "My husband thinks it is good to engage in physical activity"), that they are engaged or not engaged in the behavior (e.g., "My husband is engaged in physical activity"), and the motivation to comply with this person or group (e.g., ""What my husband thinks is important"). Perceived behavioral control, the third major determinant of intentions, is a function of the so-called control beliefs, which are based on perceived factors facilitating or impeding the performance of a behavior (e.g., "I don't have time to engage in physical activity") and the perceived power of the factor to facilitate or inhibit the performance of the behavior (e.g., "Having no time hinders me very strongly from engaging in physical activity").

In the past decades numerous studies and several meta-analyses have been carried out which confirm the assumptions of the TPB for different issues both in the health domain and in other contexts (Albarracín, Johnson, Fishbein & Muellerleile, 2001; Armitage & Conner, 2001; Sheeran & Taylor, 1999; Sheppard, Hartwick & Warshaw, 1988. For an overview see Fishbein & Ajzen, 2010; Rossmann, 2010b). To provide an example, research consistently confirms the TPB in the context of physical activity behavior. Based on a meta-analysis of 31 studies Hausenblas, Carron, and Mack (1997) concluded that physical activity could well be explained by the TPB components. Hagger, Chatzisarantis, and Biddle (2002) confirmed this observation with a meta-analysis of 72 studies. However, including past behavior and self-efficacy as additional behavioral determinants (beyond attitudes, subjective norms, and perceived behavioral control) improved the model. It was able to explain 60% of the variance for intentions to engage in physical activity and 47% of the variance for actual behavior. Downs and Hausenblas (2005) conducted a further meta-analysis of 111 studies and confirmed the power of the TPB in explaining physical activity.

Application of Behavioral Theories to Identify the Key Message

Hence, the TPB provides a fruitful theoretical tool for the development of health campaigns to promote physical activity. Specifically, the TPB should be applied to formative research in order to identify the most important determinants of health behavior, such as physical activity, together with the underlying behavioral, normative, and control beliefs. Even if most studies indicate that behavioral intentions are influenced by attitudes, subjective norms, and perceived behavioral control, one can assume the individual effect sizes for the three components to be unequal. Research has shown subjective norms to have a smaller impact on intentions as compared to the other two components (Singh, Leong, Tan, & Cheong Wong, 1995). In addition, scholars have observed different effect sizes for the three components depending on varying target groups (see Trinh, Rhodes & Ryan, 2008, for differences between women and men; and Plotnikoff, Karunamuni & Brunet, 2009, for differences between patients with type 1 and type 2 diabetes). Depending on the effect sizes of attitudes, subjective norms, and perceived behavioral control within a specific target group, it will be adequate to address the campaign message to one of the components. Assuming perceived behavioral control has a strong impact on intentions to engage in physical activity, whereas attitudes and subjective norms are only marginally related to these intentions, it will be reasonable to address a campaign to the perceived behavioral control component. Knowing that perceived behavioral control is the crucial determinant one has to identify which control beliefs are most strongly related in the next step. Thus, it is possible to identify factors and thus message content that should be most effective in changing health behavior.

Exemplary Studies

Maddock, Silbanuz, and Reger-Nash (2008) applied this strategy to the identification of effective messages for a mass media campaign to promote physical activity in the USA. The authors conducted a TPB study among the target group, in order to find out which of the TPB components had the strongest impact on intentions to go for a walk for at least 30 minutes a day. Their results showed that perceived behavioral control was the strongest determinant of regular physical activity. Perceived behavioral control in turn depended most strongly on lack of time: that is, the more people felt they didn't have enough time to go for a walk every day, the less they felt able to perform the behavior. Against this background, the authors developed the so-called "Step it up" campaign with the message that it was easy to go for a walk for at least 30 minutes a day if one separated the time-span into three 10-minute walks (see Hawaii Department of Health, 2009).

Also, Rossmann (2013) applied this strategy to the identification of the determinants of physical activity among German adults between 30 and 60 years of age. At first, they conducted qualitative interviews with ten German adults aged between 30 and 60 years in order to identify diabetes-specific beliefs with regards to physical activity behavior within this subpopulation. The most frequent answers were selected and integrated into the quantitative survey. With regards to perceived consequences of regular physical activity (behavioral beliefs) the participants mentioned "I feel better", "I am in a better mood" or "I lose weight" fairly often; important others (normative beliefs) were partners, children, parents/siblings, colleagues, and friends. Factors facilitating or impeding the performance of physical activity (control beliefs) were "being active with someone else", "having people who motivate me", "being close to exercise facilities", "being physically active is expensive", "being physically active is time consuming" or "suffering from physical discomfort." As a second step, computer-aided telephone interviews were conducted with a random sample of German adults between 30 and 60 years of age (n = 1006 respondents). The TPB components (behavioral intentions, attitudes towards physical activity, subjective norms, perceived behavioral control, as well as behavioral, normative, and control beliefs) were collected following the guidelines to the measurement of TPB constructs as provided by Ajzen (2006; also see Rossmann, 2010b). Further data were collected on self-efficacy, habit, knowledge about causes and consequences of diabetes, health prevention behavior, and past physical activity behavior. For the background factors demographics, media use, diabetes risk, as well as reactance, third-person perception, and optimistic bias were assessed.

The results revealed a consistent pattern. Altogether, the TPB components explained people's intentions fairly well, whereas the impact of perceived behavioral control was considerably stronger as compared to attitudes and subjective norms. In the next step, the control beliefs underlying perceived behavioral control were analyzed. The results showed some of the beliefs to be more important than others. Specifically, the belief that it is easier to engage in physical activity if one has other people joining one, turned out to be the most important one. In sum, the results indicated that German adults aged between 30 and 60 years would be more willing to be physically active, if they believed they were able to do so. Perceived behavioral control was strong, if people had others accompanying them. Therefore, campaigns addressing perceived behavioral control in combination with companionship and community should be more effective than campaigns addressing knowledge, attitudes, or subjective norms.

This strategy allows for the identification of *message content* able to reach the specific target group and change their respective behaviors. Even if the effectiveness of the identified messages still has to be evaluated for the studies described above, a series of evaluations in other health domains has demonstrated interventions addressed to one of the TPB components to be effective in changing different health behaviors (Albarracín et al., 2003; Albarracín et al., 2005; J. B. Jemmott, L. S. Jemmot & Fong, 1992; Kalichman, 2007; Kamb et al., 1998; Rhodes, Stein, Fishbein, Goldstein & Rotheram-Borus, 2007).

Design and Dissemination of the Campaign Message

Knowing just the message content that is suitable to reach and convince a specific target group might not be enough to actually reach the campaign goals. In the next steps, theories and empirical evidence from cognitive psychology and communication theory as well as knowledge of media use patterns within the target group in question have to be considered in order to decide how to present the message, whether to confront the target group with fear appeals or humorous appeals, and whether to spread the campaign via information or entertainment programs on television, newspapers, or posters.

Message Design

In general, health messages can be framed in many different ways. One of the most common, but also most challenged ways is the use of fear appeals. Fear appeals are defined as "persuasive messages designed to scare people by describing the terrible things that will happen to them if they do not do what the message recommends" (Witte, 1992, p. 329). Fear appeals comprise three different elements: fear, perceived threat (severity and susceptibility), and perceived efficacy (self-efficacy and response efficacy) (R. Rogers, 1975; Witte & Allen, 2000). As research shows, fear appeals do not always yield positive results; indeed they can provoke (usually unintended) negative effects, such as ignorance or reactance (Witte & Allen, 2000). Therefore, health messages should always combine fear appeals stressing the health risks or negative consequences of unhealthy behavior with information on how to reduce these risks. Since Janis and Feshbach's (1953) pioneer study researchers have produced a vast amount of literature on this topic (Ordoñana, González-Javier, Espín-López, & Gómez-Amor, 2009, p. 195). Also a series of meta-analyses have been conducted. Confirming previous meta-analyses (Boster & Mongeau, 1984; Mongeau, 1998; Sutton, 1982) Witte and Allen (2000, p. 595) found a positive relationship between the strength of a fear appeal and message effectiveness: The greater the perception of threat and efficacy, the stronger its influence on attitudes, intentions, and behavioral change. Thus, findings of earlier studies that indicated a curvilinear relationship (e.g., Kohn, Goodstadt, Cook, Sheppard, & Chan, 1982) or a negative relationship (e.g., Janis & Feshbach, 1953) have not been confirmed. More recently, de Hoog, Stroebe, and de Wit (2007) conducted a meta-analysis and differentiated the influences of vulnerability and severity of a risk. They found slightly different effects for vulnerability and severity, although the general tendency of the results was consistent with those of previous meta-analyses (e.g. Witte & Allen, 2000).

Fear appeals can appear as drastic phrases presented within a written text (e.g., the worst possible consequences of a certain disease) or as threatening images (e.g., an image of a damaged lung on a cigarette packet). Images seem to be especially effective in communicating health risks. In general, research has shown that threatening or nauseating images increase the attention paid to and the time spent with a health message (e.g., Leshner, Vultee, Bolls, & Moore, 2010; Zillmann, Knobloch, & Yu, 2001). In their meta-analysis, de Hoog et al. (2007) compared two ways of operationalizing severity: images (pictures or films) and written information. They found only slight differences between the effects of fear-arousing images and written information, but both had a significant positive effect on attitudes, intentions, and behavior.

Even if promising in many cases, under some circumstances fear appeals might not be the adequate way to present and illustrate campaign messages. Considering, for instance, the exemplary studies on physical activity described above, a fear appeal does not seem to be suitable, because the crucial determinant of physical activity was not fear or risk perception but the perceived ability to engage in physical activity. In this case, other message appeals might be more effective, for example gain-framed messages (O'Keefe & Jensen, 2008), messages with humor (Conway & Dubé, 2002), with sex appeal (e.g., Reichert, Heckler & Jackson, 2001; C. Struckman-Johnson, D. Struckman-Johnson, Gililand & Ausman, 1994), or with exemplars or narrative information (e.g., Betsch, Ulshöfer, Renkewith & Betsch, 2011; Jansen, Croonen & de Stadler, 2005; Kim, Bigman, Leader, Lerman & Cappella, 2012).

As discussed in the context of fear appeals, messages can be transported via written texts (e.g., slogans) or images. Sometimes a picture might say even more than words. This was the conclusion of a study the author carried out in the context of physical activity promotion among German adults. In order to evaluate the effectiveness of the identified message (see above) an online experiment was conducted with a convenient sample of adults aged between 30 and 60 years (n = 513). The subjects saw fictive campaign posters with a slogan and an image, depicting people engaged in physical activity (e.g., cycling, hiking). The posters were varied in a three by two design. Factor 1 was the slogan, which was varied according to the three TPB-components (slogan 1 addressed the attitude component: for example, "exercising is healthy"; slogan 2 addressed the norm component: for example, "the others do it, too"; slogan 3 addressed the perceived behavioral control component, e.g. "it is easier together"). Factor 2 was the type of the image, which showed either one person engaged in physical activity or a group of people. According to the results of the TPB study outlined above, the slogan with the behavioral control component and the picture with a group of people was expected to be more effective than the other versions. However, the results showed that the slogan itself did not have an effect on people's perceptions, attitudes, and behavioral intentions, whereas the image did have an effect. Specifically, the image depicting a group of people had a stronger impact as compared to the image depicting only one person. Consequently, in this case, the illustration of the campaign message in the picture was more effective as opposed to the merely textual message.

Considering the numerous possibilities to frame a campaign message (fear appeals, gain frame, humor, sex-appeal, etc.) and the different ways to depict them (words, pictures) it becomes clear that the best way is not easy to find. Therefore, it is advisable to test different possibilities in a subsample of the target group before finally implementing a campaign.

Media Channels

No matter how well a campaign message is prepared it will only have an effect on individuals' cognitions and behaviors if it reaches them. Due to their high reach the traditional mass media channels (television, radio, newspapers, magazines) provide a good way to reach many people all at once. However, it is important to be aware of the specific media use patterns of the target group that is to be addressed. To illustrate that, we return to the already mentioned campaign to increase physical activity among German adults. As part of the telephone survey (n = 1006) media use was assessed. The results showed that television and radio were the main media sources within this target group similarly to typical media patterns in Germany. Among the relevant television genres, German adults were specifically interested in information, health, and, most importantly, entertainment programs. This pattern holds true for many other target groups as well. Accordingly, various scholars suggest that the entertainment–education approach is an effective strategy to promote health: "[E]ntertainment-education is the process of purposely designing and implementing a media message to both entertain and educate, in order to increase audience members' knowledge about an educational issue, create favorable attitudes, shift social norms, and change overt behavior" (Singhal, Cody, Rogers & Sabido, 2004, p. 5). In the course of this process, health messages are implemented, for instance, into the plot of a soap opera, which enables viewers to learn health messages incidentally.

Print media, too, are a suitable channel for campaign messages aimed at increasing physical activity among German adults aged between 30 and 60 years. Because the target group reads at least one newspaper, six days per week, and two magazines per month, this channel is a good way to disseminate information, in spite of the decreasing importance of print media in the general population, especially among age groups born before 1984.

Besides the traditional mass media channels the Internet has become an increasingly important channel. As the survey results showed, the Internet is a major source of information for German adults between 30 and 60 years, but it is even more important for target groups under 30 years of age.

The relevance of the Internet for conveying health messages was acknowledged in the early days of the web (Suggs, 2006). Indeed, online health information has great potential because the Internet is comfortable to use, cheap, and rather independent of time and place. Hence, it reaches target groups traditional channels often fail to reach. Furthermore, online health information is interactive and can be tailored to the particular needs of single target groups, if not individual users (Kreuter, Farrell, Olevitch, & Brennan, 1999; Strecher, Shiffman & West, 2005). Hence, health promotion via the Internet combines mass media's broad reach with the strong effects of interpersonal communication, thus improving intervention effectiveness (Neuhauser & Kreps, 2003).

In recent years scholars have emphasized Web 2.0 applications as a promising way to disseminate health messages. Besides their hybrid character, combining the reach of traditional mass media with the interactivity and dynamism of interpersonal communication, social media provide the opportunity to become an active part of information creation and dissemination, in that users are able to create their own blogs, videos, or posts with regard to health risk issues. In the course of doing so, users' involvement increases, which in the end amplifies potential effects on risk perception, attitudes, and behavior. Furthermore, social media provides an easy opportunity to express support for an issue and forward information to friends without any great effort: for example, just by one mouse click on the "Like Button" or "Forward to a Friend" link . In this way, not only do health risk messages reach a greater audience but, more importantly, they are also disseminated by people whom the originators of the messages know and trust and who are thus, it can be argued, more influential than strangers in shaping beliefs, attitudes, and behavior (Betsch et al., 2012; Abroms & Lefebvre, 2009; Thackeray, Neiger & Hansons, 2008).

Finally, mobile media and mobile health applications (e.g., text messages, apps), providing the opportunity to reach individuals anywhere, anytime, and regularly, with tailored health messages, have also been discussed as promising tools to disseminate messages for health promotion (Noar & Harrington, 2012).

Challenges and Perspectives

No matter how well a communication campaign is developed and implemented it will always be difficult to change perceptions, attitudes, and behaviors in the population, not only in the health domain but also in other areas of strategic communication (e.g., political communication, environmental communication, advertising). People are surrounded by numerous influences and messages in their everyday life. Behaviors are not easy to change due to deeply ingrained habits (e.g., eating habits), due to addiction, and due to the belief that certain behaviors (e.g., unhealthy behavior such as buying fast food) are easier than other behaviors (e.g., healthy behavior such as cooking healthy meals). Moreover, the channels campaigns use for disseminating their messages (e.g., television) transport numerous messages at the same time, thus contradicting campaign messages and diminishing their effects (e.g., unhealthy messages such as smoking protagonists on soap operas, advertising for sweets and fast food).

Another problem that comes along with communication campaigns is that they are often accompanied by a series of unintended effects. Cho and Salmon (2007) identified 11 types of unintended campaign effects in the health domain that can also be adapted to other fields of strategic communication: (a) campaigns can cause misperceptions of health risks (*obfuscation*), (b) they can cause *dissonance* reactions, which in the worst case lead to (c) *boomerang* effects. Also (d) exaggerated sorrows (*epidemic of apprehension*) or (e) *desensitization* against health risks are possible consequences of health communication campaigns. Although the previous effects directly affect individuals, further unintended effects rather pertain to the societal level, specifically (f) unintended *social norming*, (g) distorted causal attributions (*culpability*), (h) *opportunity costs*, (i) *social reproduction* of existing attitudes or behaviors, (j) enforcement or image-promotion of engaged stakeholders (*enabling*), and finally (k) influences on social groups who in turn moderate campaign effects on the actually addressed target group (*system activation*).

Against this background, ethical questions may arise (Rice & Atkin, 2009, p. 439) that go beyond the manipulation debate in other fields of strategic communication such as advertising, public relations, and political communication. Campaign developers have to rely on medical and epidemiological findings as to what is the right way to prevent a certain disease. But also epidemiological findings can change (e.g., knowledge on nutrition, such as fat, cholesterol, sugar, sweetener, etc.), thus, messages that seem to be true today, might turn out to be false in future. Consequently, we have to ask ourselves whether it is right to disseminate certain messages if they might be wrong or might harm people. Furthermore, the population has to face not one, but numerous health issues (e.g., obesity, diabetes, coronary diseases, cancer, vaccination). Who decides which health issue is important enough that a communication campaign in this domain is more urgent than one in another domain? When deciding which audience to address, again ethical questions arise, because it is not easy to decide who is most in need while acknowledging that other target groups might be ignored at the same time. Furthermore, campaigns might not have the same positive influence on all target groups. For instance, a campaign against obesity might help overweight people to change their behavior, but it might also reinforce unhealthy eating habits of people with eating disorders. Are fear appeals ethically justifiable, if they intentionally provoke negative emotions, such as fear? And finally, can we justify strategies that disseminate health messages and persuade people without letting them know that they are persuaded, such as entertainment–education approaches do?

One can argue that dealing with health messages means dealing with pro-social messages, that are spread in order to help people. However, as outlined before, the actual benefits or harm are not always evident. Of course, this ethical dilemma cannot be solved within this chapter. Nevertheless, one step in the right direction is to reveal persuasion intentions. In the context of entertainment–education, research indicates that the disclosure of persuasion intentions does not have a negative effect on the effectiveness of the program (Lampert, 2007). In the end, the solution cannot be to stop communicating health issues. However, scholars and practitioners should be aware of these questions in order to communicate about health effectively and ethically in future.

References

Abroms, L. C., & Lefebvre, R. C. (2009). Obama's wired campaign: Lessons for public health communication. *Journal of Health Communication, 14,* 415–423.

Ajzen, I. (2005). *Attitudes, personality and behavior.* Milton Keynes, England: Open University Press & McGraw Hill.

Ajzen, I. (2006). Constructing a TPB questionnaire: Conceptual and methodological considerations. Retrieved 21 August, 2008, from http://people.umass.edu/aizen/pdf/tpb.measurement.pdf

Albarracín, D., Gillette, J. C., Earl, A. N., Glasman, L. R., Durantini, M. R., & Ho, M.-H. (2005). A test of major assumptions about behavior change: A comprehensive look at the effects of passive and active HIV-prevention interventions since the beginning of the epidemic. *Psychological Bulletin, 131,* 856–897.

Albarracín, D., Johnson, B. T., Fishbein, M., & Muellerleile, P. A. (2001). Theories of reasoned action and planned behavior as models of condom use: A meta-analysis. *Psychological Bulletin, 127,* 142–161.

Albarracín, D., McNatt, P. S., Klein, C. T. F., Ho, R. M., Mitchell, A. L., & Kumkale, G. T. (2003). Persuasive communications to change actions: An analysis of behavioral and cognitive impact in HIV prevention. *Health Psychology, 22,* 166–177.

Armitage, C. J., & Conner, M. (2001). Efficacy of the theory of planned behavior: A meta-analytic review. *British Journal of Social Psychology, 4,* 471–499.

Atkin, C. K., & Marshall, A. (1996). Health communication. In M. B. Salwen & D. W. Stacks (Eds.), *An integrated approach to communication theory and research* (pp. 479–495), Mahwah, NJ: Erlbaum.

Bandura, A. (2001). Social cognitive theory of mass communication. *Media Psychology, 3,* 265–299.

Betsch, C., Brewer, N. T., Brocard, P., Davies, P., Gaissmaier, W., Haase, N., … Stryk, M. (2012). Opportunities and challenges of Web 2.0 for vaccination decisions. *Vaccine, 30,* 3727–3733.

Betsch, C., Ulshöfer, C., Renkewitz, F., & Betsch, T. (2011). The influence of narrative v. statistical information on perceiving vaccination risks. *Medical Decision Making, 31,* 742–753.

Bonfadelli, H., & Friemel, T. N. (2010). *Kommunikationskampagnen im Gesundheitsbereich. Grundlagen und Anwendungen* [Communication campaign in the health domain. Basics and applications]. Konstanz, Germany: UVK.

Boster, F. J., & Mongeau, P. (1984). Fear-arousing persuasive messages. In R. N. Bostrom, & B. H. Westley (Eds.), *Communication Yearbook 8* (pp. 330–375). Newbury Park, CA: Sage.

Champion, V. L., & Skinner, C. S. (2008). The health belief model. In K. Glanz, B. K. Rimer, & K. Viswanath (Eds.), *Health behavior and health education: Theory, research, and practice* (pp. 45–65), San Francisco, CA: Wiley & Sons.

Chapin, J. (2000). Third-person perception and optimistic bias among urban minority at-risk youth. *Communication Research, 27,* 51–81.

Cho, H., & Salmon, C. T. (2007). Unintended effects of health communication campaigns. *Journal of Communication, 57,* 293–317.

Conway, M., & Dubé, L. (2002). Humor in persuasion on threatening topics: Effectiveness is a function of audience sex role orientation. *Personality and Social Psychology Bulletin, 28,* 863–873.

de Hoog, N., Stroebe, W., & de Wit, J. B. F. (2007). The impact of vulnerability to and severity of a health risk on processing and acceptance of fear-arousing communications: A meta-analysis. *Review of General Psychology, 11,* 258–285.

Derzon, J. J., & Lipsey, M. W. (2002). A meta-analysis of the effectiveness of mass-communication for changing substance-use knowledge, attitudes, and behavior. In W. D. Crano, & M. Burgoon (Eds.), *Mass media and drug prevention: classic and contemporary theories and research* (pp. 231–258). Mahwah, NJ: Lawrence Erlbaum.

Downs, D. S., & Hausenblas, H. A. (2005). The theories of reasoned action and planned behavior applied to exercise: A meta-analytic update. *Journal of Physical Activity Health, 2,* 76–97.

Fertman, C. I., Allensworth, D. D., & Auld, M. E. (2010). In C. I. Fertman, & D. D. Allensworth (Eds.), *Health promotion programs: From theory to practice* (pp. 3–27), San Francisco, CA: Jossey-Bass.

Finnegan, J. R., & Viswanath, K. (2008). Communication theory and health behavior change. The media studies framework. In K. Glanz, R. K. Rimer, & K. Viswanath K (Eds.), *Health behavior and health education: Theory, research, and practice* (pp. 363–387). San Francisco, CA: Wiley & Sons.

Fishbein, M., & Ajzen, I. (2010). *Predicting and changing behavior. The reasoned action approach.* New York: Taylor & Francis.

Hagger, M. S., Chatzisarantis, N. L. D., & Biddle, S. J. H. (2002). A meta-analytic review of the theories of reasoned action and planned behavior in physical activity: Predictive validity and the contribution of additional variables. *Journal of Sport and Exercise Psychology, 24,* 3–32.

Hausenblas, H. A., Carron, A. V., & Mack, D. E. (1997). Application of the theories of reasoned action and planned behaviour to exercise behaviour: A meta analysis. *Journal of Sport & Exercise Psychology, 19,* 36–41.

Hawaii Department of Health (2009). Step It Up Hawaii Media Campaign. Retrieved 21 July, 2009, from http://www.healthyhawaii.com/about/about_start_living_healthy/step_it_up_hawaii_media_campaign.htm

Hong, S. M., & Faedda, S. (1996). Refinement of the Hong Psychological Reactance Scale. *Educational and Psychological Measurement, 56,* 173–182.

Jackson, L.D., & Duffy, B.K. (Eds.) (1998). *Health Communication Research. A Guide to Developments and Directions.* Westport, CT: Greenwood Press.

Janis, S., & Feshbach, S. (1953). Effects of fear-arousing communications. *The Journal of Abnormal and Social Psychology, 48,* 78–92.

Jansen, C., Croonen, M., & de Stadler, L. (2005). 'Take John, for instance.' Effects of exemplars in public information documents on HIV/AIDS in South Africa. *Information Design Journal and Document Design, 13,* 194–210.

Jemmott, J. B., Jemmott, L. S., & Fong, G. T. (1992). Reductions in HIV risk—associated sexual behaviors among black male adolescents: Effects of an AIDS prevention intervention. *American Journal of Public Health, 82,* 372–377.

Kalichman, S. C. (2007). The theory of reasoned action and advances in HIV/AIDS. In I. Ajzen, D. Albarracín, & R. Hornik (Eds.), *Prediction and change of health behavior. Applying the reasoned action approach* (pp. 265–272), Mahwah, NJ: Erlbaum.

Kamb, M. L., Fishbein, M., Douglas, J. M. Jr, Rhodes, F., Rogers, J., Bolan, G., ... Peterman, T. A. (1998). Efficacy of risk-reduction counseling to prevent human immunodeficiency virus and sexually transmitted diseases. *Journal of the American Medical Association, 28,* 1161–1167.

Kim, H. S., Bigman, C. A., Leader, A. E., Lerman, C., & Cappella, J. N. (2012). Narrative health communication and behavior change: The influence of exemplars in the news on intention to quit smoking. *Journal of Communication, 62,* 473–492.

Kohn, P. M., Goodstadt, M. S., Cook, G. M., Sheppard, M., & Chan, G. (1982). Ineffectiveness of threat appeals about drinking and driving. *Accident Analysis and Prevention, 14,* 457–464.

Kreps, G. L., O'Hair, D., & Clowers, M. (1994). The influences of human communication on health outcomes. *American Behavioral Scientist, 38:* 248–256.

Kreuter, M. W., Farrell, D., Olevitch, L., & Brennan, L. (Eds.) (1999). *Tailoring health messages: Customizing communication with computer technology.* Mahwah, NJ: Lawrence Erlbaum.

Lampert, C. (2007). *Gesundheitsförderung im Unterhaltungsformat. Wie Jugendliche gesundheitsbezogene Botschaften in fiktionalen Fernsehprogrammen wahrnehmen und bewerten* [Health promotion in entertainment programs. How adolescents perceive and evaluate health-related messages in fictional television programs]. Baden-Baden, Germany: Nomos.

Leshner, G., Vultee, F., Bolls, P., & Moore, J. (2010). When a fear appeal isn't just a fear appeal: The effects of graphic anti-tobacco messages. *Journal of Broadcasting & Electronic Media, 54,* 485–507.

Maccoby, N., & Altman, D. G. (1988). Disease prevention in communities: The Stanford Heart Disease Prevention Program. In R. H. Price, E. L. Cowen, R. P. Lorion, & J. Ramos-McKay (Eds.), *Fourteen ounces of prevention: A casebook for practitioners* (pp. 165–174). Washington, DC: American Psychological Association.

Maddock, J. E., Silbanuz, A., & Reger-Nash, B. (2008). Formative research to develop a mass media campaign to increase physical activity and nutrition in a multiethnic state. *Journal of Health Communication, 13,* 208–215.

Mongeau, P. (1998). Another look at fear arousing messages. In M. Allen, & R. Press (Eds.), *Persuasion: Advances through meta-analysis* (pp. 53–68). Cresskill, NJ: Hampton Press.

Montano, D. E., & Kasprzyk, D. (2008). Theory of reasoned action, theory of planned behavior, and the integrated behavioral model. In K. Glanz, B. K. Rimer, & K. Viswanath (Eds.), *Health behavior and health education: Theory, research, and practice* (pp. 67–96), San Francisco, CA: Wiley & Sons.

Neuhauser, L., & Kreps, G. L. (2003). The advent of e-health: How interactive media are transforming health communication. *Medien & Kommunikationswissenschaft, 51,* 541–556.

Noar, S. M. (2006). A 10-year retrospective of research in health mass media campaigns: Where do we go from here? *Journal of Health Communication, 11,* 21–42.

Noar, S. M., & Harrington, N. G. (2012). *eHealth applications. Promising strategies for behavior change.* New York: Routledge.

O'Keefe, D. J., & Jensen, J. D. (2008). Do loss-framed persuasive messages engender greater message processing than do gain-framed messages? A meta-analytic review. *Communication Studies, 59,* 51–67.

Ordoñana, J. R., González-Javier, F., Espín-López, L., & Gómez-Amor, J. (2009). Self-report and psychophysiological responses to fear appeals. *Human Communication Research, 35,* 195–220.

Plotnikoff, R.C., Karunamuni, N., & Brunet, S. (2009). A comparison of physical activity-related social-cognitive factors between those with type 1 diabetes, type 2 diabetes and diabetes free adults. *Psychology, Health & Medicine, 14,* 536–544.

Prochaska, J. O., Redding, C. A., & Evers, K. E. (2008). The transtheoretical model and stages of change. In K. Glanz, B. K. Rimer, & K. Viswanath (Eds.), *Health behavior and health education: Theory, research, and practice* (pp. 97–121), San Francisco, CA: Wiley & Sons.

Reichert, T., Heckler S.E., & Jackson, S. (2001). The effects of sexual social marketing appeals on cognitive processing and persuasion. *Journal of Advertising, 30,* 13–27.

Rhodes, F., Stein, J. A., Fishbein, M., Goldstein, R. B., & Rotheram-Borus, M. J. (2007). Using theory to understand how interventions work: Project RESPECT, condom use, and the integrative model. *AIDS and Behavior, 11,* 393–407.

Rice, R. E., & Atkin, C. K. (2009). Public communication campaigns: Theoretical principles and practical applications. In J. Bryant, & M. B. Oliver (Eds.), *Media effects. Advances in theory and research* (pp. 436–468). New York: Lawrence Erlbaum.

Rogers, E. M. (1994). The field of health communication today. *American Behavioral Scientist, 38,* 208–214.

Rogers, E. M., & Storey, J. D. (1987). Communication campaigns. In C. R. Berger, & S. H. Chaffee (Eds.), *Handbook of communication science* (pp. 817–846), Newbury Park, Beverly Hills, London & New Delhi: Sage.

Rogers, R. (1975). A protection motivation theory of fear appeals and attitude change. *The Journal of Psychology, 91,* 93–114.

Rossmann, C. (2010a). Zur theorie- und evidenzbasierten Fundierung massenmedialer Gesundheitskampagnen [Theory- and evidence-based foundation of mass-mediated health campaigns]. *Public Health Forum, 18,* 16–17.

Rossmann, C. (2010b). *Theory of reasoned action—Theory of planned behavior.* Baden-Baden, Germany: Nomos.

Rossmann, C. (2013). Strategic campaign development. Identifying effective messages for the promotion of physical activity in Germany. *International Journal of Communication and Health, 1,* 1–11.

Sheeran, P., & Taylor, S. (1999). Predicting intentions to use condoms: A meta-analysis and comparison of the theories of reasoned action and planned behavior. *Journal of Applied Social Psychology, 29,* 1624–1675.

Sheppard, B. M., Hartwick, J., & Warshaw, P. R. (1988). The theory of reasoned action: A meta-analysis of past research with recommendations for modifications and future research. *Journal of Consumer Research, 15,* 325–343.

Signitzer, B. (2001). Ansätze und Forschungsfelder der Health Communication [Approaches and research fields in health communication]. In K. Hurrelmann, & A. Leppin (Eds.), *Moderne Gesundheitskommunikation* (pp. 22–35). Bern, Göttingen, Toronto, Seattle: Huber.

Silk, K. J., Atkin, C. K., & Salmon, C. T. (2011). Developing effective media campaigns for health promotion. In T. L. Thompson, R. Parrott, & J. F. Nussbaum (Eds.), *The Routledge handbook of health communication* (2nd ed., pp. 203–251). New York, London: Routledge.

Singh, K., Leong, S. M., Tan, C. T., & Wong, K. (1995). A theory of reasoned action perspective of voting behavior: Model and empirical test. *Psychology & Marketing, 12,* 37–51.

Singhal, A., Cody, M. J., Rogers, E. M., & Sabido, M. (Eds.) (2004). *Entertainment-Education and social change. History, research, and practice.* New York: Routledge.

Snyder, L. B., & Hamilton, M. A. (2002). A meta-analysis of U.S. health campaign effects on behavior: Emphasize enforcement, exposure, and new information, and beware the secular trend. In R. C. Hornik (Ed.), *Public health communication. Evidence for behavior change* (pp. 357–383). Mahwah, NJ: Lawrence Erlbaum.

Strecher, V., Shiffman, S., & West, R. (2005). Randomized controlled trial of a web-based computer-tailored smoking cessation program as a supplement to nicotine patch therapy. *Addiction, 100,* 682–688.

Struckman-Johnson, C., Struckman-Johnson, D., Gililand, R.C., & Ausman, A. (1994). Effect of persuasive appeals in AIDS PDSAs and condom commercials on intentions to use condoms. *Journal of Applied Social Psychology, 24,* 2223–2244.

Suggs, L.S. (2006). A 10-year retrospective of research in new technologies for health communication. *Journal of Health Communication, 11,* 61–74.

Sutton, S. R. (1982). Fear-arousing communications: A critical examination of theory and research. In J. R. Eiser (Ed.), *Social psychology and behavioral medicine* (pp. 303–337). London: Wiley.

Thackeray, R., Neiger, B. L., Hansons, C. L., & McKenzie, J. F. (2008). Enhancing promotional strategies within social marketing programs: Use of Web 2.0 social media. *Health Promotion Practice, 9,* 338–343.

Trinh, L., Rhodes, R. E., & Ryan, S. M. (2008). Gender differences in belief-based targets for physical activity intervention among adolescents. *Social Behavior & Personality, 36,* 77–86.

Viswanath, K. (2008). Health Communication. In W. Donsbach (Ed.), *The International Encyclopedia of Communication* (pp. 2073–2087). New York: Wiley.

Wakefield, M. A., Loken, B., & Hornik, R. C. (2010). Use of mass media campaigns to change health behavior. *The Lancet, 376,* 1261–1271.

Walsh-Childers, K., & Brown, J. D. (2009). Effects of media on personal and public health. In J. Bryant, & M. B. Oliver (Eds.), *Media effects. Advances in theory and research* (pp. 469–489). New York, London: Routledge.

Weinstein, N. D. (1980) Unrealistic optimism about future life events. *Journal of Personality & Social Psychology, 39,* 806–820.

Witte, K. (1992). Putting the fear back into fear appeals: The extended parallel process model. *Communication Monographs, 59,* 329–349.

Witte, K., & Allen, M. (2000). A meta-analysis of fear appeals: Implications for effective public health campaigns. *Health Education & Behavior, 27,* 591–615.

World Health Organization (1986). *Ottawa Charter for Health Promotion.* Retrieved 13 September, 2011, from www.who.int/hpr/NPH/docs/ottawa_charter_hp.pdf.

Zillmann, D., Knobloch, S., & Yu, H. (2001). Effects of photographs on the selective reading of news reports. *Media Psychology, 3,* 301–324.

28

Strategic Activism for Democratization and Social Change

Cheryll Ruth Soriano

Introduction

In the online space, minorities from the developing world, previously underrepresented in mainstream media, can rewrite their history and collection of struggles that have been erased in the national narratives of the dominant culture. This possibility for self-production of political expression is relevant for minority groups who have long suffered as objects of others' image-making and issue-framing practices as it provides them with the platform for strategic mobilization to achieve political goals. However, there is skepticism about the actual value of online spaces in effecting agency in an Internet-mediated environment. Critical perspectives on strategic communication raise this debate on the organization's ability to resist power, domination and control (Bourdieu, 1977). Techno-utopian promises that online media will empower the voiceless have also been challenged as issues of cultural objectification, commercialism, and state controls shed doubt on whether online media can truly be localized and emancipatory for minorities (Landzelius, 2006; Belausteguigoitia, 2006; Ginsburg, Abu-Lughod, and Larkin, 2002; McCallum & Franco, 2009; Brooten, 2010). Moreover, unlike businesses, government, or well-resourced transnational organizations, minorities are faced with conditions that complicate their position as activists and as users of technology. Yet, as minorities are often understood as diaspora communities in the West, and given the understudied nature of minorities from developing societies as online activists, the question of whether online media can be strategically used by minority groups to advance their political goals remains devoid of the empirics of social and political mediation.

This chapter explores strategic communication in the context of online political mobilization by minorities from developing Asia. To what extent is the use of online spaces by minority groups "strategic"? What does it mean for minority groups to communicate strategically within a techno-logical discourse? For what purposes do minority groups use online spaces and how do they use them to achieve their purposes? Concerns about minorities' engagement with online media are critical of over-optimistic views about the benefits of the Internet communication technologies. However, this perspective seems to propagate previous depictions of minorities as helpless, passive actors that are easily harmed by the structures surrounding them. It is important to probe not only the instances where minorities are compromised by the use of technology, but to surface instances where they are able to carve out discursive spaces for expression and control. This includes exploring the conditions that allow them to assimilate media to advance their own political and cultural goals.

This chapter first defines strategic communication and activism in practice and then moves on to present the dialectical tensions as well as the enabling and constraining structures surrounding minorities' online political mobilization. Using findings from case studies of an indigenous social movement organization and a Muslim minority revolutionary group from the Philippines, I discuss the dominant strategies underlying minority online political mobilization. The chapter seeks to surface new understandings of political formations and strategic communication in the context of minorities, as enabled, constrained, and shaped by the features of online media.

Strategic Communication and Activism in Practice

Strategic communication is defined broadly as "communicating purposefully to advance its mission" (Hallahan, Holtzhausen, van Ruler, Verčič & Sriramesh, 2007, p. 2). This definition highlights the purposeful and "intentional" nature of strategic communication, and in the context of organizations, it focuses on how the organization presents and promotes itself through the intentional activities of its leaders, members, and communicators. However, the theory and practice of strategic communication still tend to focus more on profit corporations and governments. In the public relations field, attention to non-profit organizations and the use of online new media is increasing, although most of these explore the effects and outcomes of online interactivity, for example, in building more productive dialogic relationships with stakeholders (Bortree & Seltzer, 2009; Taylor, Kent, & White, 2001; Waters, Burnett, Lamm, and Lucas, 2009) or as an equalizing effect on the PR performance of non-profits that have varying fund capacities (Kang & Norton, 2004; Sriramesh, Rivera & Soriano, 2013). While some studies have explored the role of public relations in activism (e.g., Dutta & Pal, 2007; Taylor, Kent & White, 2001; Kim & Sriramesh, 2009), there remains a broad space for exploration in the field of activism and strategic communication, particularly when these emanate from marginalized communities, and in instances where there is a focus on meaning-making and intention of use. Similarly, much literature on minority media focuses on use and effects, with assumptions that the use of technology will automatically empower minority groups despite uncertainty on whether media enables or challenges the workings of power or the potential of activism. There is also limited understanding of purposes of use and what they seek to achieve with online mediation. Without the activist's voice, the study of strategic communication would seem to continue to remain as a "parcel of the maintenance of metanarratives and domination of society" (Holtzhausen, 2000, p. 100).

Moreover, strategic communication used to be associated with a description of tactics and practice, with little room to contextualize the social, economic, or political circumstances in which organizations operate: circumstances that make such "tactics" possible and meaningful (Hallahan, et al., 2007, p. 11; Mintzberg, 1988). The use of institutional theory in strategic communication expands the scope of analysis beyond the single organization and stresses the importance of the social and political embeddedness of organizations, including the specific institutional setting and the logic of the media system (or the framing of decisions influenced by the media) it operates in (Sandhu, 2009, p. 18). According to Holtzhausen (2000, p. 109), the context in which strategic communication takes place should be emphasized, and excellence should be measured "against the ability of the practitioner to deal with a particular event, in a particular place, within a just and moral framework." This is where the exploration of the conditions and contexts that shape communication strategies would be important in determining what it means to communicate strategically—particularly when communicators are in less privileged positions or are engaged in sensitive relations with the state (i.e., minorities). This is important because previous studies on Internet use for activism and social change have shown that the mediation of dissent by one group may be strategic for one, but not strategic for another, and this implies that differential contexts and particular situations of power can influence strategic communication.

Further, "strategic communication comprises of activities that are 'strategic,' not random or unintentional—even though unintended consequences of communication can adversely impact the ability of an organization to achieve its strategic goals" (Hallahan et al., 2007, p. 22). Sandhu (2009) described strategic communication as "intentional" communication that requires a purposeful actor, and rational and deliberate decision-making. For example, an organizational strategy is described in terms of intention and motivation based on certain goals, such as competing in the marketplace and with organizational survival and efficiency as motivating factors, or planning communication with important publics to gain trust (Tench, Verhoeven, & Zerfass, 2009). However, what constitutes "purpose" and how an organization arrives at intention and strategy, should be further explored. Others argued, for example, that the purposes of minority media may not emanate from the grass-roots community being represented, but may be influenced by funders or by the hype to use technology (Latufeku, 2006; Landzelius, 2006; Ginsburg et al., 2002).

Moreover, the term strategic formerly evoked a one-sided "management" approach that was based on asymmetrical or top-down communication to protect the interest of the organization. However, how does the organization's understanding of its audience and anticipation of the audience's response and expectations affect strategic communication? To what extent does communicating strategically necessitate an assessment of how the message would be received and what the recipient would do with the message? Or does strategic communication lie solely in expression or execution of a tactic? An organization's purpose can be complex and have a dynamic evolving character, and the crafting of purpose and intention can result from a confluence of factors in the organization's environment. King (2009) developed the concept of "emergent communication strategies" that take into consideration "audience-response" and "situated context." Developing the concept from Mintzberg's (1988) work on emergent business strategies, King argues that "communication strategies will emerge based on audience response and practitioners design a series of pre-messages . . . establishing a design/test cycle to better achieve communicative goals and inform future message" (2009, p. 35). This implies that strategic communication may in reality entail a more dynamic, iterative approach that probes the response of target audiences and adjusts according to the realities of the political or socio-economic environment.

Philippine Minorities and the Socio-Political Context of Online Political Mobilization

A minority group is "a group of people who, because of physical or cultural characteristics, are singled out from others in the society in which they live for differential and unequal treatment, and who therefore regard themselves as objects of collective discrimination" (Wirth, 1945, p. 347). A minority group is not a statistical concept that accounts for less in number count or representation. Instead, its existence in society "implies a corresponding dominant group enjoying higher social status and greater privileges" (Wirth, 1945, p. 348). Minoritization can emanate from race, ethnicity, language, religion (Wirth, 1945; Capotorti, 1991; He & Kymlicka, 2005), gender and sexuality (Hacker, 1951), physical characteristics (Wirth, 1945), as well as other grounds, and the members of minority groups are usually held in lower esteem and may even be objects of contempt, hatred, ridicule, and violence. However, when the sentiments of a disadvantaged group are articulated, when they clamor for emancipation and equality, a minority group can become a political force to be reckoned with.

Across Asia, minority groups have been overlooked by government policies and have also been affected by ongoing processes of economic and social change and development initiatives (Clarke, 2001, p. 419; He & Kymlicka, 2005; Brown & Ganguly, 1997). By virtue of their remote locations or their discriminated identities, they are marginalized from markets and government services and have limited access to mainstream media to articulate their causes. Commonly, they are underrepresented politically at local, regional and national levels and often stereotyped as backward and inferior others.

With respect to the treatment of minorities, the Philippines may be judged as a relatively bright spot in Southeast Asia. For ethnic (indigenous) and religious minorities (*Moro* Muslims), the nation has passed legislation addressing the concerns of minority peoples, and the indigenous and Muslim minorities have won significant economic, political and cultural concessions from government (Eder & McKenna, 2004). However, it is important to locate such state response and political openings alongside the long history of unmet grievances and atrocities experienced by minorities that underlie their continued expressions of dissent.

For example, the 1987 constitutional provision of autonomous regions in Muslim Mindanao and the Cordillera region sought to respect the "common and distinctive historical and cultural heritage, economic and social structures, and other relevant characteristics" (Rood, 1989) of these minorities, and a significant departure from centrism and national integration that marked earlier constitutions. After years of lobbying, the Indigenous Peoples' Rights Act was also passed in 1997 to protect the rights of indigenous peoples to their ancestral domain, and to preserve their culture and institutions. However, indigenous communities have continued to suffer from the illegal encroachment of business such as mining or logging activities in their ancestral lands. Members of an indigenous activist community have also condemned the "sudden disappearances" of some of their members in what they suspect to have been government military-led operations (*Cordillera Peoples Alliance* members, personal communication, May 2010), and retain in their memories the deaths of some of their past indigenous leaders in their historical fight against large-scale dam and mining projects.

The Muslim struggle in the Philippines, on the other hand, is considered as one of the longest struggles of ethno-religious minorities globally (Jubair, 1999, 2007). Alongside the failure of the autonomous government in Muslim Mindanao to give meaningful autonomy to Muslims, an armed group of Muslim rebels formed the Moro Islamic Liberation Front (MILF), and have pursued earlier demands for secession. The term *Moro* refers to Muslims indigenous to Christian-dominated Philippines. Historically it had a derogatory connotation, originating from the word 'moors', although the Moro revolutionary organizations have used the term to define an identity for their struggle. As with the deaths of past indigenous leaders from other ethnic groups, the violent mass killings of Moro intellectuals in 1968, dubbed the "Jabidah Massacre," has catalyzed modern Moro insurgencies (Jubair, 2007, 1999). The armed conflict and sporadic clashes between the Moro rebels and the military has caused thousands of deaths and millions of displacements. However, there has been some respite during this conflict, as the government has continued to engage the Moro rebels in peace negotiations overseen by the International Monitoring Team and other international actors. In a long-awaited peace agreement signed with the Philippine government in March 2014, the MILF has shifted its demand for secession to a new autonomous government, which would be part of (and not separate from) the Philippine state. Following this peace agreement, the parties are in the process of constructing the implementing mechanisms for the governance, power, and wealth sharing in the contested lands.

Minority online political mobilization also needs to be situated within the reality of simultaneous freedom and restraint underlying conditions for political expression. The Philippines has been widely recognized for having the freest media in Southeast Asia, and the 1986 "People Power Revolution" and post- martial law regime have seemingly created a climate of tolerance toward expressions of dissent. Yet, there is a "militarization of the media" in the country, which involves direct censorship, violence, killings, and other human rights violations against journalists, and the use of libel and defamation laws to silence dissent (Brooten, 2011, p. 244). Thus, the commercial and militarized media in the country are far from exemplary in terms of meeting the communication rights of the most marginalized groups.

Although Internet penetration in the Philippines remains at approximately 29% of the population (International Telecommunications Union, 2012) and is still concentrated in urban areas, minority groups have begun to gain substantial online presence in websites, blogs, and other social media. The call center industry has expanded beyond the capital Metro Manila and into Philippine provinces, and this has created a demand for, and fast-tracked the establishment of, Internet and telecommunications services in some geographically remote areas (R. De Chavez, W. Bolinget & A. Anongos, personal communication, April and May, 2011). This is accompanied by a national community telecenter program, which has made Internet kiosks available in different parts of the country, and a rise in local enterprises such as Internet cafes, which have brought access to the Internet in smaller towns. International and local development organizations have also embarked on projects to assist minority communities in using new media technologies. In terms of surveillance or filtering, the OpenNet Initiative reported that "there is no evidence of national filtering" of the Internet in the Philippines (OpenNet Initiative, 2009). However, these same technologies can be used by the military to monitor the so-called enemies of the state, and use the same information for counter-intelligence operations (Magno, 2009).

These findings show that despite some gains and forms of response from the state and openings for political expression, the overt and covert forms of control and repression as well as the sensitive relations between the state and minorities serve as significant grounds for problematizing the condition of minorities in Philippine society, and provide a significant context for understanding the character of their online political mobilization.

Dialectical Tensions of Online Self-Mediation

A variety of online media platforms are now available for ordinary people to express themselves in public, strategically mobilize, and participate in the forms of meaning-making that constitute them (Bakardjieva, 2003; Ginsburg et al., 2002). The many-to-many reach of communication technologies allows marginalized groups to penetrate the scene of politics by broadening the scope of the "political" beyond the nation state and disrupting structures of normalcy and democracy (Dutta, 2011). The absence of mass-media style editorial control also opens up possibilities for new forms of political engagement, giving minorities the opportunity to create new informational resources about their history of grievances, aspirations, and struggles.

However, concern about whether the global character of online media can be used to articulate minority agendas and allow the meaningful production of culture is tied to views that global technologies can challenge, distort, or undermine locality's production. The pervasiveness of the neoliberal and capitalist logic in technology (Hassan, 2008; Dean, 2002; Armitage, 1999; Ginsburg et al., 2002), coupled by state controls on Internet-mediated activism (Zhou, 2006; Kelly & Etling, 2008; York, 2011) have raised some very crucial questions on the value of the Internet for social change movements from the margins. For example, Hughes and Dallwitz (2007) warned that allowing important cultural material to be publicly accessible on the Internet could pose challenges in restricting access to local cultural knowledge. Others raised concern over activist organizations' goals being driven by "media-centered political activism" where organizations treat online mediation as the end in itself (Sobieraj, 2012). Moreover, it is important to explore, while presenting the possibilities generated by online articulations, how participatory elements of performance are shaped and influenced within the agendas of dominant institutions (Dutta, 2011, p. 219).

This relationship between new media technologies and participatory practices is captured in the "democratization of technology" and "technologization of democracy" dialectic (Chouliaraki, 2010). Democratization of technology (Hartley, 2010) focuses on the empowering potential of new media technologies for counter-hegemonic, emancipatory practices. Technologization of democracy, on the other hand, addresses self-mediation from the perspective of the regulative potential of new media technologies in controlling the discourses and in reproducing existing unequal power relations (Chouliaraki, 2010, p. 227). It is important to explore minorities' intention, meaning-making, and negotiations behind such online mediations within the lens of this dialectical tension.

Case Studies

A component of a larger study, the case studies for this chapter, Cordillera Peoples Alliance *(CPA)* and *Moro Islamic Liberation Front* (MILF) were selected purposively (Yin, 2009, p. 91) based on the legitimacy of the organization (e.g., not fly-by-night), scope of network based on expert interviews and secondary research, online activity, and agreement to participate in the research. Face to face, online, and telephone interviews with organizations' leaders, information officers, and members, as well as experts and civil society members significantly involved with the group's activities, were conducted in April and May 2010 and February and May 2011. To triangulate findings from interviews, the form, content, and style of political mobilization in the online spaces were also reviewed and analyzed at three time periods, January to May 2010 (in preparation for and during field interviews), October to December 2010, and May to July 2011. Thematic categories were generated from recurring topics that appeared in both interviews and online spaces (Ryan & Bernard, 2003). The case study inquiry relies on multiple sources of evidence, with data converging in a triangulating fashion and benefits from the prior development of theoretical propositions to guide data collection and analysis (Yin, 2009, pp. 15, 101–114). Following Yin's (2009) methods for case study analysis, these themes were juxtaposed with theoretical propositions concerning minority media culled from earlier literature that were used as bases for possible interpretations (i.e., "propositions" and "rival propositions"). The quoted messages are excerpts of interviews in their original form, except for those that had to be translated from local language.

The CPA, founded in 1984, is a federation of people's organizations, most of them grassroots-based among the indigenous communities in the Cordillera region of the Philippines. CPA mobilizes "for the defense of ancestral domain and for self-determination" and promotion of social justice and indigenous people's rights (www.cpaphils.org). CPA was selected for this study because of its activist roots and its strong linkages with other Cordillera civil society and grassroots organizations, having the historical association of leading the indigenous movement. The CPA launched its website in 2004 with assistance from the Swedish Society for Nature Conservation. Aside from its website, CPA also maintains an e-group for internal communication (CPA members, personal communication, May 2010, Feb 2011).

The MILF, on the other hand, is considered the biggest organization leading the Muslim minority struggle for self–determination in the Philippines. The group has been engaged in a violent armed conflict with the Philippine military but at the same time it is a major party in the peace negotiations with government. The Moro struggle is rooted in the failure to recognize the Moro people's entitlement to land (Mindanao) and livelihood resources that they lost through the transmigration of Christians in Mindanao and the establishment of multinational companies in the region. This resettlement policy led to the Moros' minoritization in Mindanao, where Muslims were reduced from about 75% of Mindanao's population in the 1900s to 25% in the late 1960s (Rodil, 2004). Aside from dispossession of land and statistical minoritization in Mindanao, the situation of resentment against the Philippine state is caused by the relative poverty of the Muslim dominated provinces vis-à-vis other provinces in the country (Philippine Human Development Network, 2009). To communicate its struggle to a broader audience, MILF launched its main website (www.uwaran.com) in 1998. Now, it maintains four websites. One of these sites is an Arabic website, http://www.Luwaran.net/arabic/, aimed at attracting the sympathy and support of the larger Islamic community. In addition MILF has two active Facebook accounts, and Twitter and MySpace pages which as of July 2011 have no content.

Findings: Strategic Online Activism from the Margins

It will be recalled that some past studies have perceived minority groups to have a lack of control over technology, and therefore potentially to be further marginalized by its use. Based on findings from the case studies, this section discusses the different strategies that foreground strategic online activism from the margins.

Balancing Relevant Modes of Activist Communication Media

Although CPA has computers and a shared wireless connection in its main office in Baguio City, many of its grassroots organizational partners either have no direct access to the Internet, or have to travel significant distances to get it. Given this reality, CPA has clarified the purposes of its online spaces, and how they maintain other relevant forms of communication to reach grassroots members. As many of the organization's members do not have access to the Internet or need to travel kilometers to access Internet cafés, they retain their offline modes of organizational management and communicating information. They also balance sophistication of site versus ease of access by members with slow connections.

> The Internet is just one medium, equal in importance to other media such as print and radio. But because not all our members in the Cordillera can access the Internet; not all the public in the far-flung mountainous communities whom we want to reach through our advocacies and public information campaigns have Internet . . . so we still release our quarterly publications of magazines and newsletters to our local partners. We know that when they see the magazine or newsletter, they immediately read it. When we send the position papers via email, we are not sure if our members will read it . . . in terms of security, for example, in our provinces, if it is really important we still send a hard copy by bus.
>
> *CPA leader, personal communication, May, 2010; some phrases translated from Filipino*

Like CPA, MILF is also a grassroots organization with most members without access to the Internet. Thus, MILF also targets the mainstream media and international community as the main audience of its online interventions, seeking to draw their attention to MILF's own version of Moro history and struggle. Using the websites for internationalization is aimed at making their claims more audible and legitimate, bolstering the struggle, and exerting greater pressure to receive more serious attention from important Philippine and international bodies, while also building financial resources. To reach its grassroots members, offline communication and mobilization strategies, which have been the pervasive strategy for the group, are the norm.

Strategizing amidst the Realities of the Socio-Political Environment

My interviews with both CPA and MILF revealed that they plan their online mediations to negotiate technological, state, and capitalist controls. For example, contrary to concerns in the literature that minorities may be unknowingly threatened by the dangers of online mediation (Landzelius, 2006; Ginsburg et al., 2002), CPA and MILF leaders and members appear to have a clear understanding of the varied threats posed by possible government surveillance of their sites, and therefore control the public discussion of sensitive opinion pieces and tactics.

> We always assume that our emails are monitored . . . so that is the danger. So in our website, we don't put everything there. Especially the internal matters not for public consumption, we don't put them there. We discuss about what we post or upload. Matters that are delicate, we don't

normally put there. As a political movement, we always assume that our website and emails are monitored. Our landlines and phones are bugged. Because in our experience for the past 26 years many of our members have been abducted . . . the extra judicial killing . . .

CPA member, personal communication, May, 2010; some phrases translated from Filipino

Awareness of the dangers of security threats in the online spaces also pushed the groups to strategize resources to minimize such threats, such as disabling interactive forums or chat facilities in their websites. CPA's members manage the website internally to maintain control over content. Minorities are also not automatically "objectified" by commercial forces as they engage with the online medium. CPA, which has a leftist orientation related to its historical struggle against large-scale mining and capitalist projects in the Cordillera, shared that conscious efforts to veer away from capitalist pulls such as website advertisements are conducted at the expense of not having interactive chat facilities. They also exercised caution over the publication of indigenous knowledge online and had set rules that ritual-based indigenous knowledge must not be published online (for an extensive discussion, see Soriano, 2012).

The MILF, on the other hand, has experienced more explicit instances of "intrusion" in its website, such as the replacement of their banner with photographs of pigs as an insult to their Muslim faith. This compelled them to invest in more secured website hosting services in the United States. The MILF also strategically uses symbolic forms and creative online strategies to communicate particular messages about their struggle given their sensitive relations with the state. For example, the *Luwaran* website banner carries photographs of its past and present leaders to inspire feelings of support from the broader Islamic community of supporters and to chronicle the long history of its struggle. But MILF also shared that it does not publish the photographs of all its leaders in the website:

> For example, we have there the photograph of Salamat Hashim, our deceased former leader. It is about symbolism, the continuity of what the Chairman has started. And also mysticism. In the sense that we do not expose all of our leaders. If you will look at the photographs on top of the banner, those who(m) we already make accessible to the media are there, but there are others who are not exposed. Because although we are engaged in the Peace Process, which is an open engagement, at the same time we also engage in underground operation. Meaning not all of our leaders can be exposed . . . so we cannot put all of our eggs in one basket, otherwise, all of them may break . . . the MILF has that kind of sophistication, which is still a part of the struggle. We need for more and more members and other people to understand the dynamics, the nuances, of the struggle. It's part of the learning process and also a struggle for us.
>
> *MILF Web Team, Personal communication, some sentences translated*
> *from Filipino & local dialect, May 2010*

A MILF leader explained that this is an important strategy because although they are involved in the peace negotiations, which are open engagements, they also conduct underground operations in the armed struggle with the government. In this sense, identifying all their leaders may be risky for their military operations in times of armed conflict. This also implies that despite the expectations that they can seal a workable peace agreement with the government, they continually suspect a possibility of war.

Quotes from MILF's deceased leader, Hashim Salamat, are also used in the website to enliven the sentiment of Muslim supporters based in the Philippines and globally. According to the historians interviewed for this case study, Salamat is a well-respected leader of the Moro community and a key actor in the internationalization of the Bangsamoro struggle (R. Pendaliday & R. Rodil, personal communication, May 2011 & Oct 2011). Thus, the use of his writings is a strategic move by the MILF web team to elicit both local and international support.

Defining a Unique Identity to Legitimize Political Claims

The CPA recounted the lengthy process of website planning and how members debated on how best to represent the organization's indigenous identity in the online space. The process of presenting their struggle online aided the organization into determining "what makes them indigenous" and "how to present themselves and their struggles to the general public." This might be construed as "objectification of culture," yet CPA explained that articulating their difference as indigenous people is an important way to justify the historical and political basis of their political claims. For example, demanding the protection of their ancestral lands from certain "development projects" can only be explained using the rituals and cultural meanings attached to such lands. As stated within previous research by the author of this chapter (Soriano, 2012), Philippine indigenous organizations' online experiences reflect a process different from simply buying into the hype of having an online space, involving as it does a careful rethinking of their indigenous identity in the process of articulating their claims in the online medium. Inasmuch as the website "represents" and "constructs" them as a people, it has aided them to recollect from history and from present struggles what elements would constitute this indigenous identity.

Like CPA, crucial in the internationalization of the *Bangsamoro* struggle through participants' online spaces is defining a Moro identity distinct from the rest of the Filipinos. MILF members explained that their own communicative space, the website, allows them to overcome the limitations of their lack of control over mainstream media forms. *Luwaran*, for them, has become an important platform for communicating their alternative version of history of their struggle, and constructing a unique Moro identity:

> *Luwaran* was formed so that it can help achieve the aims of the Bangsamoro struggle. To do this . . . the international community needs to know that there are people in the South of the Philippines that have a different nationality. It is also important for the people of Mindanao to know that they are Bangsamoro. So you have people of Mindanao, that is us; and the people in Mindanao, the Christian settler. We refused to be assimilated. We refused to be integrated because we have our own identity. Now, I believe we are successful . . . that is the international community's acceptance that we are native inhabitants of Mindanao, that we have a distinct identity of being a Bangsamoro people.
>
> *MILF leader, personal communication, May, 2010*

This implies assertion of the difference, first in terms of nationality; and at an individual and collective level, in terms of identity. To make the distinction, the Moros emphasize the difference between "people in Mindanao" and the "people of Mindanao." The MILF explained that it is an important goal for the organization to get others, as well as their own Bangsamoro people, to recognize this distinction as it provides the basis to their ultimate claim for the right to govern themselves, which is also the fundamental consideration in the ongoing peace negotiations with the Philippine government. Like CPA, this assertion of difference is not to "essentialize one's culture," but to establish the foundation for the political claims that they make in terms of protection of their right to self-determination. In Philippine discourses, the Moros are considered as Filipinos despite the prejudice that they receive as minorities. In fact, a recognition of "difference" in identity may exist, but commonly for the purpose of casting Muslims in a negative light (e.g. Muslims as violent, or Muslims as robbers) (Jubair, 1999, 2007). With the use of online media, both CPA and MILF are in a better position to defend what they consider their legitimate rights and patrimony.

Countering Prejudice and Building Credibility

Both CPA and MILF admitted the reality of the need to constantly attract external support as national minorities. However, they argue that their clamor for "external support" is not mainly aimed at generating funds but more on gaining strength through solidarity with like-minded activists and supporters in other parts of the world. Nonetheless, having a website also allows them to establish their credibility as legitimate organizations and build networks while at the same time challenging existing misconceptions. For example, according to a CPA member:

> We saw this as a good opportunity for fast networking, for wider projection of our issues and struggles that we cannot do using local newspaper or radio. This allows us to reach international supporters, partners, and other indigenous organizations. That is what drove us to develop and continue this. In networking, we meet people in conferences but there, you can't talk thoroughly about your struggles. Sometimes, you just exchange cards, or say, 'please visit our website.' In the websites, we can share strategies. We also post all our position papers there. It is the same for funders because not all the funders can come over. And if you have a website which is updated, it adds to your credibility as an organization. Because we also want to debunk, as I joked earlier, that misconception, that indigenous peoples are backward as national minorities. That we cannot defend ourselves. That we are left behind. But CPA as a grassroots alliance has disproven that. So even if our website is not that sophisticated, in terms of substance and content, people who visit our website applaud the content because they learn about our struggle more. And of course because they see the website that is updated with rich content, they see that this organization is alive and existing. So their doubts will be allayed that it is not like other fake NGOs.
>
> *CPA leader, personal communication, May 2010*

Like CPA, the MILF noted that based on its website statistics, they are aware that the international audience, particularly those from the United States and supporters from the Middle East, are visiting their websites. The MILF also emphasized the effort they make in showing through their online spaces that they veer away from terrorism, as the organization seeks the support and assistance of the United States, which played a role in historical roots of the conflict (Soriano & Sreekumar, 2012; Jubair, 2007) in its political negotiations with the Philippine government. As mentioned in an earlier quote, the organization considers as a benchmark of success the assumption that "the distinction [of Bangsamoro from Filipino identity] is recognized by the international community," regardless of whether the international community is prepared to challenge Philippine national sovereignty. This is with the expectation that internationalization will highlight and legitimize their claims, attract the notice of important Philippine and international bodies, and boost financial resources. The group also ensures that documentation of their meetings with representatives of international organizations is posted in their website to support this "anti-terrorism" position. Considering that Muslims are often treated as a homogeneous entity in Philippine discourses, this effort is also undertaken, they argue, to differentiate themselves from the extremist organization, the Abu Sayyaf Group.

Assessing the Outcomes of Technological Mediation of Activism

Scholars have contended that those critical of strategic communication view all strategic communication as manipulative, although others view it as purposive of achieving specific goals. According to Holtzhausen (2010, p. 75), strategic communication entails an assessment of which strategy is viewed as most effective. During interviews, both organizations shared their assessment of what they considered to be achievements, in terms of internationalizing their struggle, that have encouraged them to continue investing in their website.

As an organization with limited funds, CPA specifically emphasized the importance for them to rationalize the investment they make in terms of funds and human resources by considering what they have achieved with online mediation. Such assessment of the real outcomes of their online investment is consonant with King's (2009) conceptualization of emergent communication strategies based on an assessment of audience-response and the overall consequences of communication interventions:

> ... for example, our campaign against destructive mining has reached the international community and therefore generated much support. The same for our human rights campaign against extra-judicial killings, we used our website to target the international community's support: NGOs, civil society organizations, parliamentarians, and multilateral bodies like UN agencies or European Union. They received it quickly and their response was fast. In the past, we would fax, or send by post. It can be very costly and time-consuming. The Internet also allowed us to disseminate our appeals to those we don't expect to reach. So for that issue on extra-judicial killings, regarding our hit list ['death list' of CPA members], the forced disappearance of *James Balao* [CPA member], they all sent a barrage to *Malacanang* [seat of Philippine Presidency] about the issue. We were able to call Malacanang's attention and the issue got popularized in mainstream media.
>
> *CPA leader, personal communication, May 2010*

As members of a national minority, the group emphasized the limited support afforded by government and other local institutions to indigenous causes, making it necessary for them to seek support from and be in solidarity with indigenous communities from outside the nation-state to help them gain the attention of government and mainstream media. According to Dutta (2011), such interventions are crucial because they can facilitate the disruption of the discourses of normalcy, and vital where inability to challenge such discourses perpetuates the maintenance of the status quo. In this instance, Moro and indigenous performances online "disrupt the status quo symbolically" (Dutta, 2011) by situating the dominant rhetoric of democracy and peace beside the lived experience of conflict, encroachment of ancestral lands, prejudice, hunger and marginalization of Moro and indigenous communities. As some of the issues they advance concern multinational companies or government that have significant control of local mainstream media, they consider their online space as their platform for communicating their causes and claims that can reach a broader international audience. However, over time, CPA has also realized that internal organization and coordination could benefit from the online spaces. This has allowed them to save time in terms of having an archive of their statements, history, and position papers that are available for their members and supporters and that they are able to preserve, given the reality of office movement and calamities. The process of online networking also provides them the opportunity to learn about similar issues and strategies from other minority actors in other parts of the globe, attract understanding and support from the external community, and obtain strength through solidarity and belonging with minorities of similar experiences. At the same time, they facilitate the production of their own resources as well as archives of statements and histories that they intend to pass on to inspire future struggles.

Summary

The Internet is providing opportunities for minority groups such as CPA and MILF to construct public spaces online, an opportunity for expression by groups of people who have experienced colonization and marginalization from various media forms. A privileged knowledge of these organizations' meaning-making surfaces the rationale of their strategies for using online spaces to advance their particular political goals in light of the realities of their condition as minorities. Although their online spaces can be viewed publicly, these strategies are often invisible to the uninformed. The organizations' online spaces, as a component of their broader political communication strategy, serve as their platform for narrating their own version of their history, present discourses alternative to those offered by government, and reach out to a broader, global audience for support. Yet, as online spaces are considered public spaces and are possibly under surveillance, the crafting of purpose, cautious negotiation of the risks and possibilities of technology, assessment of what aspects of information to make public, and embedding of symbolic messages under the blanket of ambiguity, are key to the groups' strategic communication.

Discussion and Conclusion: Online Strategic Communication from the Margins

Many previous studies on the "democratization of technologies" have focused on overt forms of online activism, or Internet-mediated political engagements of prominent activists. Similarly, many studies on strategic communication focus on observable strategies and well-planned and organized action. However, there are subtle nuances in the conditions underlying minority groups' online political mobilization—particularly those situated in developing country contexts—that help expand the way strategic communication can be understood. These conditions include not only the dialectical tensions involved in Internet-mediated engagements, but also the tension between the political openings and subtle controls of the state and capital. In the midst of these dialectical tensions, it is important to think analytically about how minority groups' experiences of online media engagement constitute strategic communication. This exploration of the meaning-making of the purposes and strategies of two particular minority groups' online spaces has surfaced the following foci for thoughts on strategic activism for democratization and social change: (a) balancing relevant modes of activist communications media, (b) defining a unique identity to legitimize political claims, (c) countering prejudice and building credibility, (d) strategizing amidst the realities of the socio-political environment, and (e) assessing the outcomes of technological mediation.

First, the Internet is viewed as most useful for publicity, image-building, and networking with Internet-connected local and international organizations. In interactions with local networks that are highly grassroots-based the minority groups in this study still rely on more relevant media such as face-to-face, print, radio, and telephone communication. This implies that, for minority groups, to communicate strategically is to be adept at engaging tools relevant for reaching particular audiences and using online media to complement traditional, effective modes of communication.

Second, the organizations' use of online spaces is strongly driven by a need to assert their unique identities, which allows them to emphasize the historical and political basis of their political claims as minorities.

Third, strategic communication entails the re-construction of the organizations' maligned identities and the articulation of alternative versions of history that work alongside their efforts to build their credibility as legitimate political actors. In the process, they use the online spaces to construct their identities while challenging prejudiced representations and misconceptions about them as minorities. As the groups developed the content for their online space, they realized that having websites also functions to challenge dominant stereotypes of minorities as "backward," or as "terrorists."

Fourth, minorities employ symbolic and creative strategies to communicate political messages while circumventing the limits of socio-political conditions of their minoritization. Some of their political acts may be concealed; still minorities communicate important messages to their target audience. Covert political action does not invalidate such articulations, which communicate important meanings concerning minorities' engagement with technology, their view of the controls and forces surrounding technology, and their use of technology to achieve political goals in light of structures and conditions of use. Such strategies create new dimensions in understanding strategic communication and technological possibilities for actors from the margins.

Finally, the experiences of these minority groups in using online media for activism imply that strategic communication can be rethought from being a purposive form of communication predetermined by organizations in accordance with set goals, towards one that arises out of practice. Here we find strategic communication to be of a more emergent (King, 2009) and dynamic nature, as it develops with a continued engagement and reflection by the actors of the implications of technology use for the group and the struggle. The organizations have pre-set purposes for particular communication strategies, yet such purposes developed over time. The decision of the indigenous and Moro organizations to continue with the use of the online space also developed after these groups learnt how to negotiate technological engagement. The two case studies also show the ways in which both the organizations achieved organizational growth through their online experiences. The online spaces primarily target the broader projection of the organizations' issues to their international audiences, in order to internationalize their struggle and solicit support. Over time, the spaces have generated archives, 'screen memories', to borrow from Ginsburg et al., (2002), which document not only the groups' histories, but also the development of their political struggle and position statements, and records of their activities over time. Although they remain cautious about its possible dangers, the groups have learnt to manage their use of technology in ways that can help to construct their identity, build solidarity, and strengthen their impact. This shows that online discourse can also shape practice, and that being able to communicate strategically not only works to influence others, but also may change the organization itself. If strategic communication is focused only on well-planned, purposive strategies of business, government, or well-resourced civil society organizations, a range of possibilities for strategic activism and communicative action in light of unique socio-political and technological circumstances can be neglected. An exploration of the experiences in marginalized contexts can inspire a rethinking of what constitutes strategic communication.

Fraser (1990) argued that minorities are important in balancing the views within any rational critical discourse, and that encountering new opinions would encourage people to rethink their views, reconsider their biases and predilections, and foster reflection and understanding. However, the circuits, reach, and interpretations of online messages are unpredictable, and the posts can also be used by antagonists to reinforce prejudices, further segregate minorities, and nullify the seriousness of their demands (Bailey & Harindranath, 2006). Furthermore, uncontrolled exchanges can expose the organizations' competing ideologies, covert operations, or internal conflicts. Thus, marginal groups will continue to navigate the multiple challenges and possibilities of online media, create their own screen memories, negotiate their political voice, construct their struggles, and define themselves in the online platform. In the context of minority online political mobilization, communicating strategically entails a continuing balancing act between the challenges and opportunities posed by online mediation.

References

Armitage, J. (1999). Resisting the neoliberal discourse of technology. The politics of cyberculture in the age of the virtual class. Retrieved from http://www.ctheory.net/articles.aspx?id=111

Bailey, O. G., & Harindranath, R. (2006). Ethnic minorities, cultural difference and the cultural politics of communication. *International Journal of Media and Cultural Politics, 2*, 299–316.

Bakardjieva, M. (2003). What knowledge? Whose fingertips? Negotiating and serving diverse identities through information technology. *Canadian Ethnic Studies, 35*(3), 133–149.

Belausteguigoitia, M. (2006). On line, off line and in line: The Zapatista Rebellion and the uses of technology by Indian women. In K. Landzelius (Ed.), *Native on the net: Indigenous and diasporic peoples in the virtual age* (pp. 97–111). New York: Routledge.

Bortree, D.S., & Seltzer, S. (2009). Dialogic strategies and outcomes: An analysis of environmental advocacy groups' Facebook profiles. *Public Relations Review, 35*, 317–319.

Bourdieu, P. (1977). *Outline of a theory of practice*. Cambridge, England: Cambridge University Press.

Brooten, L. (2010). Indigenous peoples' media. In J. Downing (Ed.), *Encyclopedia of social movement media*. New York: Sage. Retrieved from www.www.sage-ereference.com/

Brooten, L. (2011). Media, militarization, and human rights: Comparing media reform in the Philippines and Burma. *Communication, Culture & Critique, 4*, 229–249.

Brown, M. & Ganguly, S. (Eds) (1997). *Government policies and ethnic relations in the Asia-Pacific*. Cambridge, MA: MIT Press.

Capotorti, F. (1991). *Study on the Rights of Persons Belonging to Ethnic, Religious and Linguistic Minorities*. Geneva: United Nations Center.

Chouliaraki, L. (2010). Self mediation: New media and citizenship. *Critical Discourse Studies, 7*(4), 227–232.

Clarke, G. (2001). From ethnocide to ethno-development? Ethnic minorities and indigenous people in Southeast Asia. *Third World Quarterly, 22*(3), 413–436.

Dean, J. (2002). *Publicity's secret: How technoculture capitalizes on democracy*. Ithaca, NY: Cornell University Press.

Dutta, M. (2011). *Communicating social change: Structure, culture and agency*. New York: Routledge.

Dutta, M., & Pal, M. (2007). The Internet as a site of resistance. The case of the Narmada Bachao Andolan. In S. Duhe (Ed.), *New media and public relations* (pp. 203–216). New York: Peter Lang.

Eder, J., & Mckenna, T. (2004). Minorities in the Philippines: Ancestral lands and autonomy in theory and practice. In C. Duncan (Ed.), *Civilizing the margins. Southeast Asian government policies for the development of minorities* (pp. 86–115). Ithaca, NY: Cornell University Press.

Fraser, N. (1990). Rethinking the public sphere: A contribution to the critique of actually existing democracy. *Social Text, 25/26*, 56–80.

Ginsburg, F.L., Abu-Lughod, L., & Larkin, B. (2002). *Media worlds: Anthropology on new terrain*. Berkeley, CA: University of California Press.

Hacker, H. M. (1951). Women as a minority group. *Social Forces, 30*(1), 60–69.

Hallahan, K., Holtzhausen, D., van Ruler, B., Verčič, D., & Sriramesh, K. (2007). Defining strategic communication. *International Journal of Strategic Communication, 1*(1), 3–35.

Hartley, J. (2010). Silly citizenship. *Critical Discourse Analysis, 7*(4), 233–248.

Hassan, R. (2008). *The information society*. Digital media and society series. Cambridge, England; Malden, MA: Polity Press.

He, B., & Kymlicka, W. (2005). *Multiculturalism in Asia*. Oxford, England: Oxford University Press.

Holtzhausen, D. (2000). Postmodern values in public relations. *Journal of Public Relations Research, 12* (1), 93–114.

Holtzhausen, D. (2010).Communication in the public sphere: The political context of strategic communication. *International Journal of Strategic Communication, 4*(2), 75–77.

Hughes, M., & Dallwitz, J. (2007). Ara Irititja: Towards a culturally appropriate IT best practice in remote Indigenous Australia. In L. E. Dyson, M. Hendriks, & S. Grant (Eds.), *Information technology and indigenous people* (pp.146–158). Hershey, PA: Information Science Publishing.

International Telecommunications Union (2012). Percentage of individuals accessing the internet 2001–2011. Retrieved from http://www.itu.int/ITU-D/ict/statistics/

Jubair, S. (1999). *A nation under endless tyranny*. Kuala Lumpur, Malaysia: IQ Marin.

Jubair, S. (2007). *The long road to peace. Inside the GRP-MILF peace process*. Cotabato, Philippines: Institute of Bangsamoro Studies.

Kang, S., & Norton, H. E. (2004). Nonprofit organizations' use of the World Wide Web: Are they sufficiently fulfilling organizational goals? *Public Relations Review, 30*(3), 279–284.

Kelly, J., & Etling, B. (2008). *Mapping Iran's online public: Politics and culture in the Persian blogosphere*. Internet and democracy case study series. Retrieved from http://cyber.law.harvard.edu/sites/cyber.law.harvard.edu/files/Kelly&Etling_Mapping_Irans_Online_Public_2008.pdf

Kim, J. N., & Sriramesh, K. (2009). Activism and public relations. In K. Sriramesh & D. Verčič (Eds.) *The global public relations handbook: Theory, research, and practice, 2nd. ed.* (pp. 79–98). New York: Routledge.

King, C. (2009). Emergent communication strategies. *International Journal of Strategic Communication, 4*(1), 19–38.

Landzelius, K. (2006). Introduction: Native on the net. In K. Landzelius (Ed.), *Native on the net: Indigenous and diasporic peoples in the virtual age* (pp. 1–42; 292–301). New York: Routledge.

Latufeku, A. (2006). Remote indigenous communities in Australia: Questions of access, information, and self-determination. In K. Landzelius (Ed.), *Native on the Net: Indigenous and Diasporic Peoples in the Virtual Age* (pp. 43–60). New York: Routledge.

Magno, F. (2009). *Internet Surveillance in the Philippines*. Paper presented at the Living the Information Society conference 2. QC, September, Ateneo de Manila University, Philippines.

McCallum, K., & Franco, P. (2009). Community business: The Internet in remote Australian indigenous communities. *New Media and Society, 11*(7), 1230–1251.

Mintzberg, H. (1988). Five Ps for strategy. In J. B. Quinn, H. Mintzberg & R. James, (Eds.), *Readings in the strategy process* (pp. 10–18). New Jersey: Prentice Hall.

OpenNet Initiative (2009). Internet filtering in Asia 2009. Retrieved from http://opennet.net/research/regions/asia

Philippine Human Development Network (2009). *Institutions, politics and human development: Philippine human development report 2008–2009*. Retrieved from http://hdn.org.ph/

Rodil, R. (2004). *The minoritization of the indigenous communities of Mindanao and the Sulu archipelago*. Davao City, AFRIM. Philippine Ed.

Rood, S. (1989). *Issues on creating an autonomous region for the Cordillera, Northern Philippines*. Baguio City, Philippines: Cordillera Studies Center.

Ryan, G., & Bernard, R. (2003). Techniques to identify themes. *Field Methods, 15*(1), 85–109.

Sandhu, S. (2009). Strategic communication: An institutional perspective. *International Journal of Strategic Communication, 3*(2), 72–92.

Sobieraj, S. (2012). *Soundbitten: The perils of media-centered political activism*. New York: New York University Press.

Soriano, C.R. (2012). The Arts of Indigenous Online Dissent: Negotiating technology, indigeneity, and activism in the Cordillera. *Telematics and Informatics, 29*, 33–44.

Soriano, C.R., & Sreekumar, T.T. (2012). Multiple Transcripts as Political Strategy: Social media and conflicting identities of the Moro liberation movement in the Philippines. *Media, Culture and Society, 34*, 1028–1039.

Sriramesh, K, Rivera, M., & Soriano, C.R. (2013). Websites for stakeholder relations by corporations and non-profits: A time-lag study in Singapore. *Journal of Communication Management, 17(2)*, 122–139.

Taylor, M., Kent, M., & White, W. (2001). How activist organizations are using the Internet to build relationships. *Public Relations Review, 27*, 263–284.

Tench, R., Verhoeven, P., & Zerfass, A. (2009). Institutionalising strategic communication in Europe—An ideal home or mad house? Evidence from a survey in 37 countries. *International Journal of Strategic Communication, 3*(2), 147–164.

Waters, R. D., Burnett, E., Lamm, A., & Lucas, J. (2009). Engaging stakeholders through social networking: How nonprofit organisations are using Facebook. *Public Relations Review, 35*(2), 102–106.

Wirth, L. (1945). The problem of minority groups. In R. Linton (Ed.), *The science of man in the world crisis* (pp. 347–372). New York: Columbia University Press.

Yin, R. K. (2009). *Case study research: Design and field methods* (4th ed.). Los Angeles, CA: Sage.

York, J. (2011, June 7). *When social networks become tools for oppression*. Bloomberg. Retrieved from http://www.bloomberg.com/news/2011–06–07/when-social-networks-become-tools-of-oppression-jillian-c-york.html

Zhou, Y. (2006). Understanding Chinese Internet politics. In M. Mohr (Ed.), *China and democracy: A contradiction in terms*. Asia program special report, no 131. Washington, DC: Woodrow Wilson International Center for Scholars. Retrieved from http://www.wilsoncenter.org/sites/default/files/FinalASIA_131.pdf

29

Strategic Dimensions of Public Diplomacy

Martin Löffelholz, Claudia Auer, and Alice Srugies

Public Diplomacy as Strategic Communication

The question "How strategic is public diplomacy?" is seldom posed in public diplomacy literature. Instead, academic studies take the strategic alignment of public diplomacy activities to be a natural condition for the success of a nation's public diplomacy. Only a few researchers dare to identify concrete strategic dimensions of public diplomacy. This leads to four characteristic interpretations of the correlation between public diplomacy and strategic communication. Some authors see public diplomacy and strategic communication as analogous concepts; others see them as distinct concepts; still others see either strategic communication or public diplomacy as the overarching concept (e.g., Gregory, 2005; Wimbush, n.d.; Deutsch, 2010; Hayden, 2010; Leonard, Stead, and Smewing, 2002; Nye, 2004; Tatham, 2008; Department of Defense, 2004; Taylor, 2009; van Dyke & Verčič, 2009; Pamment, 2009). The conflicting opinions demonstrate that a theoretical grounding of public diplomacy, strategy, and strategic communication needs to be accomplished. The goal of this chapter is therefore to provide a new theoretical perspective on the relations between strategic communication and public diplomacy. In order to create such a theoretical basis, we will first review the state of research on public diplomacy. That section will conclude with a definition of the concept that reflects the broad areas of agreement. Then, we will consider the research on strategy and strategic communication. Based on that, we will identify the strategic dimension of public diplomacy. In the next step, this dimension will be used to review case studies of public diplomacy in different countries and regions (selected according to their respective relationships to the research) to evaluate to what extent public diplomacy is conducted strategically in practice.

Definition of *Public Diplomacy*

Edmund A. Gullion, the then Dean of the School of Law and Diplomacy at Tufts University, coined the term "public diplomacy" in 1965 in an attempt to free it from any propagandist tendencies (Cull, 2009b, p. 19). Since then, the concept has been continually adapted to developments in the international arena. Definitions in modern, post-Gullion times have shifted in communication mode and target structure on an axis from persuasion to mutual understanding, as well as in terms of the actors. Writing during the Cold War, Gullion defined public diplomacy as "the means by which governments, private groups and individuals influence the attitudes and opinions of other peoples and governments in such a way as to exercise influence on their foreign policy decisions" (Edward R. Murrow Center of Public Diplomacy, n.d.). After the Cold War ended, with its dichotomous perceptions of international politics, definitions of public diplomacy focused on generating understanding for the communicator. At that time, Tuch (1990), for instance, described public diplomacy as "a government's process of communicating with foreign publics in an attempt to bring about understanding for its nation's ideas and ideals, its institutions and cultures, as well as its national goals and current policies" (Tuch, 1990, pp. 3–4). After the 9/11 attacks in the USA, academic orientations shifted toward mutual understanding, reflecting terms like "engagement" or "relationship-building." Leonard et al. (2002, p. 8), for example, state that "public diplomacy is about building relationships: understanding the needs of other countries, cultures and peoples; communicating our points of view; correcting misperceptions; [and] looking for areas where we can find common cause." Until today however, a comprehensive, consensus definition has been lacking. However, broad areas of agreement can be identified, to the effect that public diplomacy

- describes the direct or mass-mediated communication activities by individuals, governmental and non-governmental organizations to a foreign government and/or foreign publics and/or the domestic public;
- aims at directly or indirectly reducing negative clichés and prejudices, generating sympathy and understanding for a nation's ideals, goals, (foreign) policies, its institutions, culture and model of society;
- aims furthermore at building positive images and relationships, facilitating closer political ties or alliances, and encouraging tourism and foreign direct investments.

The theoretical and empirical knowledge on public diplomacy is internationally gained, but geographically disproportionally distributed. The majority of the institutions and authors dealing with public diplomacy is situated in the USA (USC Center on Public Diplomacy, 2009) and studies the USA as the main object of analysis (e.g., Adelman, 1981; Blinken, 2002; Critchlow, 2003; Cull, 2009a; Duffey, 2009; Hoffman, 2002; Laqueur, 1994; C. Lord, 1998; K. M. Lord, 2009; Mueller, 2009; Reinhard, 2009; Ross, 2002; Snow, 2004; Sun, 2008; Vlahos, 2009; von Eschen 2005), but the concept has either not been applied at all, or has only been applied for a few years, in most nation-states in Eastern Europe. Similarly most Asian, African and South American countries are at an early stage in exploring the relevance of addressing foreign citizenship through public diplomacy (e.g., Chitty, 2009; Ehteshami, 2009; Heine, 2009; Ndhlovu, 2009; Ogawa, 2009; Starr, 2009; Szondi, 2009). In Western Europe researchers started no earlier than the beginning of the 1990s to analyze the concept (e.g., Gramberger, 1994; Leonard et al., 2002; Melissen, 2005, 2006; Signitzer, 1993, 1995; van Ham, 2001, 2002). Therefore, research is still quite biased—most analyses are conducted from U.S. perspectives neglecting Asian, African, European or Latin American interests.

Although researchers have already related public diplomacy to propaganda (e.g., Plaisance, 2005; Snow, 2004; Snow & Taylor, 2006; Taylor, 2002; Zaharna, 2004), diplomacy (e.g., Bolewski, 2008; Gregory, 2008; Melissen, 2005;), public relations (e.g., Kruckeberg & Vujnovic, 2005; Lee, 2007; Petersone, 2008; Signitzer, 1993, 1995, 2008; Yun, 2006, 2008), marketing (e.g., Benoit & Zhang, 2003; Kendrick & Fullerton, 2004; Kotler & Gertner, 2002; Sun, 2008) and nation branding (e.g., Anholt, 2006; Copeland, 2006; Olins, 2002; Szondi, 2008), its relationship to strategic communication has been widely neglected so far.

Nonetheless, few publications on public diplomacy go without using the attribute "strategic" or the concept "strategic communication" (c.f. Dutta-Bergman, 2006; Manheim 1994a, 1994b; Wang

& Chang, 2004; Zaharna, 2005): Especially those studies containing recommendations for a more effective public diplomacy put out a call to advance strategic goals, a strategic framework or a strategic planning of public diplomacy -related activities (Epstein & Mages, 2005). As Gregory (2005) correctly stated: "Strategy is a theme in most public diplomacy studies issued since 9/11" (p. 3). However, the widespread use of the term "strategic" does not imply a consensus over its meaning (Gregory, 2005, p. 4). Only a few authors deal with the difficulty of defining public diplomacy and strategic communication in order to keep them apart. Instead, the meaning of the concepts seems to be taken for granted resulting in contradicting attributions, as follows.

- Some authors use public diplomacy and strategic communication as analogous concepts "to describe a blend of activities by which governments, groups, and individuals *comprehend* attitudes, cultures, and mediated environments; *engage* in dialogue between people and institutions, *advise* political leaders on the public opinion implications of policy choices, and *influence* attitudes and behavior through strategies and means intended to persuade" (Gregory, 2005, p. 39). They understand strategic communication in a broader sense.
- Some authors present public diplomacy and strategic communication as distinct concepts, however without clearly defining and differentiating them (e.g., Deutsch, 2010; Hayden, 2010; Wimbush, n.d.).
- Others subordinate strategic communication to public diplomacy (e.g., Leonard et al., 2002; Nye, 2004). Leonard et al. (2002) for example classified it as one of three dimensions of public diplomacy, beside news management and relationship building. Strategic communication is defined by them in a more narrow sense as "[p]roactively creating a news agenda through activities and events which are designed to reinforce core messages and influence perceptions" (Leonard et al., 2002, p. 11).
- Still others consider strategic communication as the overarching concept (e.g., Department of Defense, 2004; Pamment, 2009; Tatham, 2008; Taylor, 2009; van Dyke & Verčič, 2009;). These are mostly political–military approaches. They are based on the concept of strategic communication that was fostered by the Department of Defense, which came up with the concept to better co-ordinate public diplomacy, public affairs and military psychological operations (C. Lord, 2006, p. 32).

It can be assumed that there are several reasons for these contradicting statements regarding strategic communication and public diplomacy. First, both public diplomacy and strategic communication signify a practice *and* an academic concept with respectively varying meanings. Second, the contradiction might be rooted in the fact that there is no agreement yet on the meaning of the disparate concepts. Public diplomacy definitions in the modern post- Edmund Gullion sense differ with regard to the communication mode, target structure, and actor (see above). Strategic communication, analogously, lacks consensus over its analytical boundaries. Synonymously used for it are for example public relations, strategic communication management, and information work (Kristensen, 2010, p. 137). Kristensen (2010) traces it back to the fact that strategic communication draws on several traditions. Instead of being restricted to specific professional, organizational or communicative contexts or dimensions of work, the adjective "strategic" rather underlines that the conducted communication uses "strategically intended, planned, and purposeful mechanisms" (Kristensen, 2010, p. 137).

In sum, research on public diplomacy and on its relationship to strategic communication is deficient and highly fragmented in its attributions. Most publications relate public diplomacy and strategic communication without clear definitions. Thus, research still needs to theoretically analyze the relationship between public diplomacy and strategic communication—which is the endeavor of this article.

Defining Strategic Communication

The terms "strategy" and "communication" can be combined in different ways with different meanings: "Strategy communication" describes the communication of the organizational leadership's strategic vision to internal and external stakeholders (Moss & Warnaby, 1998, p. 135). "Communication strategy" refers to the development of a strategy of the organizational communication function. Finally, "strategic communication" indicates that communication is organized and carried out strategically (Moss & Warnaby, 1998). Such a diverse interlocking suggests first, that "communication" plays a significant role in the strategic process and second, that "strategy" is of relevance in organizational communication functions. Interestingly however, strategic communication literature—with only a few exceptions (e.g., Hallahan, Holtzhausen, van Ruler, Verčič & Sriramesh, 1997)—pays little attention to the underlying term "strategy." Likewise, reference to communication as an element of the strategy process is just as rare in strategy literature. As a consequence thereof, communication is allocated two different roles: Whereas strategy literature mostly assigns a rather tactical, promotional function to communication (Moss & Warnaby, 1998, p. 131), public relations literature demands a more strategic role for communication in organizations (c.f. Cutlip, Center & Broom, 1994; J. E. Grunig & Repper, 1992;). Central to this chapter are therefore the questions: What does "strategic" mean and what does it mean to communicate strategically?

Research on strategy provides the first indications, although in itself it is diverse and has yielded a number of varying definitions and typologies (for a good overview see Hax & Majluf, 1996; Raupp & Hoffjann, 2012). According to Hax and Majluf (1996, p. 2) "one of the oldest and most classical views of the concept of strategy" is an understanding of strategy "as a means of establishing the organizational purpose in terms of its long-term objectives, action programs, and resource allocation priorities." Chaffee (1985, p. 90) describes this type of strategy as linear because it focuses the linear sequence of strategy planning on how to deal with competitors when striving to achieve one's organizational goals. With the adaptive strategy that concerns the adjustment of the organization to align it with internal and external conditions (management of opportunities and risks), and the interpretive strategy that is related to the conveyance of meaning to conceptualize and guide individual attitudes to motivate stakeholders in ways that favor the organization (management of cooperation), he labels two other types of strategy (Chaffee, 1985, pp. 91–94; Hax & Majluf, 1996, pp. 4–14). With its focus on desired relationships, the aforementioned interpretive strategy, in particular, gains relevance for the analysis of public diplomacy strategies. It has to be acknowledged however that the three models of strategy are not independent of each other, but may be interrelated in practice. These definitions of strategy list essential dimensions: the goals, programs, analysis of external and internal conditions, stakeholders, and allocated resources.

With regard to public diplomacy, another approach is especially helpful. Steyn (2003) hints at the fact that different organizational levels have different strategies. Accordingly, this author (2003, pp. 172–174) differentiates strategies by organizational level, goals, and stakeholders and makes a distinction between the

- enterprise strategy that determines the role of the organization in society (or in a public diplomacy network) and focuses on the achievement of non-financial goals (e.g., reputation, social responsibilities),
- corporate strategy that determines the organization's profile (the portfolio of business) (also in relation to public diplomacy),
- business-unit strategy that determines the organization's approach in a specific segment, often related to a specific product or group of related products (or to a specific public diplomacy activity),

- functional strategy that determines the co-operation of the functional areas of an organization (e.g., marketing, finance) to support the enterprise, corporate and business level strategy, and
- operational strategy that relates to implementation strategies.

This classification indicates that different strategies might exist in one organization and it also hints at the relevance of the external environment (society), the organizational mission, and the organizational internal dimension of strategy (functional strategy).

Academically, strategic communication can be regarded as an interdisciplinary field with no underlying distinct epistemology or core body of knowledge (Kristensen, 2010, p. 138). Marketing, management, corporate communication, political communication, public relations, and disciplines like political science or cultural studies have all contributed to shaping and contextualizing the term strategic communication (Hallahan et al., 2007; Langer, 2005) and highlight different aspects of the concept. Whereas strategic communication promotes understanding of an organization's mission and vision as well as its values from a management point of view (Hallahan et al., 2007, p. 5), scholars focusing on political communication, for example, emphasize strategic communication as an attempt to influence the political agenda and the public opinion through mediated communication (Tils, 2005, p. 125). From this perspective, political actors apply strategic communication in order to establish relevant topics in the public sphere and the media (Brettschneider, 1998, p. 635). Schwan (2011) relates strategic communication to a country's external communication and defines it as a management function in the foreign policy of a country. Thus, so far, a consensus on a definition of strategic communication is missing: "In professional communication involving organizations, there is no single overarching or unifying conceptual framework to inform the work of the many disciplines relating to the field of strategic communication" (Hallahan et al., 2007, p. 5).

In accordance with the classical, linear view of strategy, Hallahan et al. (2007) perceive strategic communication as the "purposeful use of communication by an organization to fulfill its mission" (Hallahan et al., 2007, p. 3). They thereby target the word organization in its broadest sense, "referring to corporations, for-profit and nonprofit organizations, activist groups, nongovernmental organizations, organizations promoting various forms of social change, political parties or movements, and governmental organizations" (Hallahan et al., 2007, p. 4). The concept of strategic communication thus embodies how entities intentionally attempt to communicate or create meaning as well as comprehend factors that impede sharing meaning between an organization and its constituents (Hallahan et al., 2007, pp. 22–24). Kristensen (2010) accentuates that the concept is not merely equal to a set of supporting communication tactics, but to "strategically intended, planned and purposeful mechanisms aimed at changing the attitudes or actions of specific target groups with a potential value and mandate in relation to the communicating organization as such in relation to its surroundings" (Kristensen, 2010, p. 137). Strategic communication can therefore be distinguished from spontaneous and routine actions because the latter do not take alternatives into account (Raupp & Hoffjann, 2012). Raupp and Hoffjann (2012, p. 157) therefore define strategic communication management as "communication management which deliberatively creates such decision-making situations in which several alternatives of action are evaluated."

According to Kristensen (2010), strategic communication can be studied from two points of view. The communication-internal perspective, that this article has focused on so far, is related to the interdisciplinary and practice-based nature of the concept. To adopt a communication-external perspective, on the contrary, is to scrutinize the integration and the priority given to strategic communication within an organization (Kristensen, 2010, p. 135). Findings of institutional theory prove to be particularly helpful in understanding and substantiating this communication-external view on strategic communication: Institutional theory stresses the influence of institutional frameworks on organizations (Sandhu, 2009, p. 73). "Institutions are comprised of regulative, normative and cultural-cognitive elements that, together with associated activities and resources, provide stability and meaning to social life" (Scott, 2008, p. 48). They enable and constrain organizations and, hence, strategic communication. Organizations do not operate independently, but they "are embedded in a social web of rules, norms and cognitive assumptions, which form expectations for the organizations that enable, shape or constrain strategic communication" (Sandhu, 2009, p. 75). These expectations are transmitted by agencies like the state, the media or professional institutions, and they influence the process and the outcome of strategic communication to a great deal. Therefore, one can assume that "[o]rganizations in similar fields are experiencing the same kind of societal expectations. Therefore organizations tend to adopt similar strategies to cope with external demands" (Sandhu, 2009, p. 76). The success of strategic communication is also determined by its institutionalization within an organization. Its institutionalization is based on three main criteria: The access to the top decision-making platform of an organization (*power*), its autonomy as an organizational function in comparison with other functions (*independence*) and its level of *specialization* (Sandhu, 2009, p. 85).

Strategic Dimensions of Public Diplomacy: Theoretical Analysis

As laid out in the previous section, strategic communication is often regarded as an overarching concept combining public diplomacy, public affairs, international broadcasting and information operations as done by the political–military sector (C. Lord, 2006, p. 32). However, van Dyke & Verčič point out that this practical convergence might "mov[e] beyond a theoretical explanation" (van Dyke & Verčič, 2009, p. 822). They give voice to the concern that, "without a theoretical framework to guide these programs, the boundaries between communication functions could erode" (van Dyke & Verčič, 2009, p. 822) and threaten the integrity of the single concepts. This article contributes to developing such a framework by theoretically exploring the strategic dimensions of public diplomacy.

The different definitions of strategy and strategic communication have helped to identify areas of agreement as to what strategic dimensions of public diplomacy might be. With short explanations, these areas of agreement are listed in bullet points below (Raupp & Hoffjann, 2012; Steyn, 2003; Samansky, 2003; Moss & Warnaby, 1998; Hallahan et al., 2007; Hax & Majluf, 1996; J. E. Grunig & Repper, 1992; Chaffee, 1985):

- orientation in the course of the current mission;
- the strategy process, which comprises
  - situational and environmental analysis (the analysis of organizational stakeholders, publics, and issues), a dimension that corresponds to "listening", one of the five core components that Cull (2008, p. 32) identifies to characterize public diplomacy, involving
    - analysis of the internal environment (e.g., analysis of profile, mission, values, policies; and of internal stakeholder perspectives) and
    - analysis of the external environment (e.g., analysis of societal norms, values, expectations; and of stakeholders and issues) (e.g., by issues management, segmentation of publics, or in terms of J. E. Grunig and Hunt's (1984) two-way asymmetrical or symmetrical communication);
  - selection of key issues and their stakeholders;
  - identification and selection of goals and objectives;
  - evaluation and deliberate selection of alternatives of action;
  - implementation;
  - evaluation of strategy: the measurement of progress and achievement; and
  - adaption of strategy;

- content of strategy, which encompasses

  o clearly stated goals and objectives;

  o issues;

  o specific communication programs, with

    ▪ tactics, and
    ▪ key messages;

  o means, implying

    ▪ instruments or types of media (Löffelholz, Auer, Krichbaum & Srugies, 2011, pp. 8–10) and
    ▪ resources: staffing needs, non-staff costs; and

  o timeframe;

- strategic communications plan; and
- alignment of strategies.

These dimensions serve as an analytical instrument to evaluate whether public diplomacy is in practice conducted strategically. Based on this list, we can conclude that there are strategic and non-strategic forms of public diplomacy, meaning that some communication could be public diplomacy, but not strategic communication, or, at least, not well executed strategic communication. Reactive efforts are not automatically an indication for non-strategic public diplomacy, but they can be part of the strategy that might set proactive and reactive efforts in line with the strategy. Strategic public diplomacy demands conscious decision-making against the background of recognized alternatives (Raupp & Hoffjann, 2012, p. 157).

The list of strategic dimensions is rather descriptive and does not make any normative statements about the structural embedding of the strategic communicator in his or her organization, or about his or her preferred styles of strategy formulation. However, we can assume from public relations literature that—while thus attaching a strategic role to communication—the strategic communicator should have access to top-level management to participate in strategy formulation (L. A. Grunig, J. E. Grunig, & Dozier, 2002). Above all, scholars have learned from strategy literature that strategy may be related to different organizational levels, whose respective strategies have different aims, which has to be acknowledged in any analysis. Strategy literature has also stated that the strategies of the different functional units should be co-ordinated. Transferred to the context of the public diplomacy of a nation, this might also mean that the different actors should align their strategies. These criteria are in keeping with the criteria proffered in works on excellence in public relations (L. A. Grunig et al., 2002) and public diplomacy (e.g., Yun, 2006).

Strategic Dimensions of Public Diplomacy in Selected Countries

Based on the theoretical deduction of strategic dimensions of public diplomacy, this section will examine the reality of strategic public diplomacy in the international practice. This analysis is by no means exhaustive: it focuses on selected countries.

The selection of countries reflects the state of research on public diplomacy: The USA is not only the dominant object of analysis (see for example Höse, 2008; Schatz & Levine, 2010)—it is also home to the majority of public diplomacy scholars and research institutions. At the start of the 1990s, European researchers started engaging in public diplomacy, and they shed light on the public diplomacy practice in Great Britain (see for example Leonard, Small, & Rose, 2005) and Germany (Löffelholz et al. 2011; Zöllner, 2006, 2009). Löffelholz et al. (2011) have conducted a comprehensive, empirical study on the understanding and practice of public diplomacy in 31 organizations.

Furthermore, a number of scholars have also addressed the public diplomacy of small and medium-sized states within Europe. This section will discuss strategic dimensions of public diplomacy in the North European countries. In recent years, public diplomacy in Asia has received particular scholarly attention (see for example Lee & Melissen, 2011; Rawnsley, 2009; Wang, 2008). A few scholars have also assessed public diplomacy in East European countries (see for example Ociepka & Riniejska, 2005) or in Australia (see for example Byrne, 2009, 2011). Public diplomacy scholars have also started to examine South America and Africa. Due to a lack of space, studies on public diplomacy in South America and Africa are not discussed in detail in this chapter. Follow-up studies need to consider the degree of strategy in South American and African public diplomacy initiatives.

Public diplomacy research has predominantly drawn on nation states as a frame of reference. However, it has not been limited to countries, but has also been applied on a supranational (see for example studies on the public diplomacy of the European Union by Cross, 2010, 2012; Rasmussen, 2010) and a sub-national level (see for example Huijgh, 2009). This recent development will be illustrated by a short discussion on the European Union as well as discussions of Quebec and Catalonia.

United States of America

The United States of America have a long tradition in research and practice of public diplomacy. One might trace "this type of cross-national communication to the advent of the country" (Wang, 2007, p. 22). In his analysis of historical U.S. public diplomacy, Wang (2007. p. 21) concludes that "U.S. public diplomacy has been principally an ad hoc instrument of American foreign policy to meet wartime exigencies and has been underscored by the promotion of American values or democracy and freedom." Although interest in public diplomacy strongly decreased at the end of the Cold War resulting in budget restrictions, cuts in public diplomacy programs, and the closing of the United States Information Agency (Sun, 2008; Snow, 1997), among other effects, 9/11 re-set public diplomacy on the agenda of political actors. As Hughes (2007), former under-secretary for public diplomacy and public affairs, stated: "PD is back and is now a high priority at the highest levels of government."

Academic and practitioners' analyses agree that since then the US has been in a difficult situation: Foreign publics do like the American people, but not what their government does (Snow, 2009, p. 4). Accordingly, today's mission of American public diplomacy as stated by the under-secretary of public diplomacy and public affairs, is "to support the achievement of U.S. foreign policy goals and objectives, advance national interests, and enhance national security by informing and influencing foreign publics and by expanding and strengthening the relationship between the people and government of the United States and citizens of the rest of the world" (U.S. Department of State, n.d.). The focus is on education and exchange programs, teaching English, promoting U.S. higher education, and humanitarian and development initiatives.

The strategic plan for public diplomacy issued in 2010 by the under-secretary of public diplomacy and public affairs explicitly demanded a strategic character for public diplomacy: among other points, it stressed the alignment with foreign policy objectives and a strategic focus to how public diplomacy programs, resources and structures should support those objectives. Furthermore, it defined five issues of twenty-first century public diplomacy along with concrete tactics, which included tactics for shaping a narrative, tactics to combat violent extremism, and tactics to better inform foreign policy about attitudes of foreign publics (Under Secretary of Public Diplomacy and Public Affairs, 2010). Snow (2009, p. 7), however, came to the conclusion that the communication strategies were "crisis-driven and self-preservation oriented."

Wang (2007, p. 28), too, concluded "there has been constant tension concerning the ultimate role of public diplomacy as a strategic, policy function versus merely as a 'mouthpiece' within the foreign affairs apparatus" that still reverberates in today's practice (Wang, 2007, p. 21). This might also be rooted in the fact that between 1999 and 2010 the position of the under-secretary of public diplomacy and public affairs was vacant 30% of the time: the position was unoccupied for 1375 1,375 days, according to a 2011 report of the U.S. Advisory Commission on Public Diplomacy (which was itself not reauthorized by Congress for 2012) (U.S. Advisory Commission on Public Diplomacy, 2011, p. 2). Furthermore, the commission critically reviewed the evaluation efforts of U.S. public diplomacy in its 2010 report. They deduce, among other conclusions, that public diplomacy and public affairs departments do not co-operate and that there is an inadequate relationship between program planning and evaluation (U.S. Advisory Commission on Public Diplomacy, 2010). Dale, Cohen and Smith (2012, p. 2) also criticize that U.S. public diplomacy neglects the internal stakeholders: "[T]oo often, operational decisions are constrained by bureaucratic misinterpretations of the U.S. Information and Educational Exchange Act (known as the Smith–Mundt Act), a post-World War II measure aimed at preventing the party that holds the White House from using the State Department to 'propagandize' Americans," whereas Americans do have access to other nations' public diplomacy activities. More access to U.S. positions would "help Americans better understand and evaluate their government's foreign policies, allow better oversight, and make public diplomacy spending more accountable" (Dale et al., 2012, p. 2).

In sum, U.S. public diplomacy actors put a lot of effort into strategically conducting public diplomacy. The multitude of actors however makes a strategic alignment of the different strategies difficult. Also the evaluation of programs and adjustment is not matured. Although the U.S. has a long tradition in the practice of public diplomacy, its activities are not strategic in every case. Dale et al. (2012, p. 1) conclude: "[W]hat is needed in Washington is more focused commitment to public diplomacy, prioritization of programs, better organization of instruments, better trained and experienced personnel, and stricter oversight of resources."

Europe

Public diplomacy in the United Kingdom is dominated by three key actors: The Foreign and Commonwealth Office, the British Council and the BBC World Service. All three organizations are part of the Public Diplomacy Strategy and Performance Measurement Board that is "responsible for agreeing the strategy, advising on resource allocation, and for performance measurement and monitoring" (Lord Carter of Coles, 2005, pp. 14–15).

The resources allocated to public diplomacy are divided into the Public Diplomacy Campaign Fund, that covers major initiatives in the most important target countries, and the Public Diplomacy Challenge Fund. The Public Diplomacy Challenge Fund addresses "innovative" public diplomacy activities of overseas posts of the Foreign and Commonwealth Office (2005) in support of local public diplomacy goals and strategies . With regard to the evaluation of public diplomacy strategies and activities, the British Council serves as a model for international public diplomacy actors. The British Council combines quantitative and qualitative evaluation methods: "The British Council operates a performance scorecard. Through it we assess our performance in a range of dimensions including customer and stakeholder satisfaction, our reputation, the perceptions of our staff and the impact of our projects" (British Council, 2008, pp. 6–7). This scorecard is based on quantitative data analysis. Additionally, the British Council uses "storyboards" as a qualitative evaluation tool in order to document the experiences of individual participants of British Council programs (Pamment, 2011, pp. 189–190). All in all, British public diplomacy is coined by a strong emphasis on developing a coherent, consistent strategy that goes beyond the individual goals of single public diplomacy actors and builds on a close network of public diplomacy actors.

Based on guided expert interviews and a document analysis, Löffelholz et al. (2011) conducted a comprehensive, empirically grounded analysis of the functions, strategies, structures and instruments of public diplomacy in Germany. The analysis revealed that public diplomacy actors in

Germany pursue individual strategies to reach their organizational aim. The organizations set their goal priorities regarding the subsystems they are acting in. Sandhu (2009) explained this observation by stating that "[o]rganizations in similar fields are experiencing the same kind of societal expectations. Therefore they tend to adopt similar strategies to cope with external demands. This in turn leads to isomorphism of practices and structures in the field" (Sandhu, 2009, p. 76). Leonard et al. (2002) defined three dimensions or subsystems that public diplomacy actors operate in: the political and military dimension, the social and cultural dimension, and the economic dimension. Löffelholz et al. (2011, p. 14) extended this typology by introducing a fourth public diplomacy dimension: education and research.

The organizations analyzed operate worldwide, but they usually focus on specific target regions that are constituted by the organizations' mission statements, policy priorities, regional expertise and structural conditions. They apply both mid- and short-term activities that serve as the basis for long-term strategies and activities. Depending on situational factors, the organizations implement both asymmetric and symmetric public diplomacy tools. However, the interviewees accentuated a general preference for dialogue-oriented instruments that could be described as a central characteristic of German public diplomacy. The interviewees admitted shortcomings regarding the extent, institutionalization and professionalization of evaluations. So far, the majority of the organizations have only measured single public diplomacy activities such as events and workshops and have neglected the evaluation of entire public diplomacy strategies. A lack of human and financial resources causes obstacles to conducting public diplomacy strategically. Unlike public relations, public diplomacy has not been institutionalized as an organizational function (yet): the analysis of organizational charts confirms that, in most cases, departments below the executive level that are already concerned with communication activities take the responsibility (Löffelholz et al., 2011). This observation on public diplomacy is also reflected in research on strategic communication by Bakka and Fivelsdal (2003) that noted that strategic communication had long been a staff function on classic organizational terms designed to support the other organization's (line) functions (Bakka & Fivelsdal, 2003, p. 46). "In the strategic management literature communication is regarded as an enabling function facilitating the successful implementation of strategic decisions" (Steyn, 2007, p. 143). Thus, both public diplomacy and strategic communication refer directly to the top management as analysts and advisors, but mostly they do not possess any final decision-making power. The majority of public diplomacy organizations rely financially on the Federal Foreign Office as well as the other German federal ministries, as they command and distribute the lion's share of public diplomacy resources. The organizations give voice to the concern that the resources allocated to public diplomacy are too limited, constraining a proactive approach to public diplomacy as well as a more flexible application of the concept (Leonard et al. 2002, p. 97). In addition to the budget restrictions, the annual allocation of financial resources causes obstacles to conducting public diplomacy strategically. Public diplomacy practitioners can be characterized by a very heterogeneous educational and professional background. It is striking, however, that only a very small number of practitioners have specialized in communications in their education. Competencies that are crucial to conducting public diplomacy as well as communication competencies in general are primarily acquired "on the job." Thus, (further) training in public diplomacy as a means of professionalization and strategic conduct of the concept is not yet fully recognized by the organizations.

The analysis of German public diplomacy on a macro level indicates that the organizations do not opt for a general German public diplomacy strategy. This is based on two notions: first, especially the non-governmental organizations want to keep their independence and do not want to be perceived as an instrument of the government. Based on the experiences with national socialist monopoly structures, any semblance of an instrumentalization of organizations by the state as well as state-run centralization ought to be avoided. Second, the organizations would rather present a pluralistic image of Germany. In effect, the public diplomacy actors follow a strategy that comprises partial and even contradictory strategies in order to depict Germany as a diverse, multifaceted state. The analysis shows that public diplomacy on a macro level is primarily characterized by co-operations within the single public diplomacy subsystems. However, an overall German public diplomacy strategy cannot be detected.

The public diplomacy of Scandinavian countries focuses on few core areas that guide the definition of target groups and target countries as well as the development of public diplomacy strategies, activities and messages. Norway, for example, tries to distinguish itself from other countries as a mediator and carrier of peace and focuses on a small number of target regions (Leonard & Small, 2003). Swedish and Danish public diplomacy actors emphasize the economic dimension of public diplomacy. Their understanding and practice of public diplomacy is strongly influenced by the concept of nation branding (Pamment, 2011; Meiner-Jensen, 2012). Therefore, Meiner-Jensen (2012) points to the fact that public diplomacy is only a small part of a much bigger nation branding budget in Denmark. The Swedish focus on nation branding is also exemplified by "Brand Sweden," a brand platform depicting Sweden as a progressive country that is based on four core values: openness, authenticity, care and innovation (Swedish Institute, 2008, p. 7). Brand Sweden focuses on enhancing the coherence of public diplomacy activities and messages. However, the notion of Brand Sweden and, for that matter, of a centralized public diplomacy strategy and a uniform image of Sweden abroad, has also met with skepticism and rejection. Pamment (2011, p. 216) argued that this strategy undermines the plurality of public diplomacy actors and their individual goals and activities. The relevance attributed to public diplomacy in Scandinavian countries is reflected by the institutionalization of the concept within organizations: In the Finnish Ministry of Foreign Affairs, "[t]he Unit for Public Diplomacy is responsible for the planning, development, coordination and country-specific support of strategic public diplomacy in foreign affairs" (Ministry for Foreign Affairs of Finland, n.d.). The Norwegian foreign ministry has established a Department for Culture, Public Diplomacy and Protocol. In addition, the Norwegian Foreign Minister Jonas Gahr Støre created the Norwegian Public Diplomacy Forum in 2007 (Ministry of Foreign Affairs of Norway, 2007). The forum was designed to "encourage debate and dialogue between the authorities, business sector, academia and other actors on how and in which areas we can develop cohesive public diplomacy strategies" (Norway Communicates, n.d.). In sum, public diplomacy in Scandinavian countries can be characterized by a focus on a few core areas and core values as well as the development of a consistent, overarching public diplomacy strategy.

Asia

Asian public diplomacy is a special case of public diplomacy considering "its political systems and bilateral relationships that cannot be found within the Western world, its distinct cultural setting, and its own ideational preferences and normative frameworks" (Melissen, 2011a, p. 248). The countries can build their public diplomacy efforts on many different assets, and also the "region's increasing economic power provides fertile ground for its states to look forward and build up their soft power" (Lee & Melissen, 2011, p. 4). Besides public diplomacy, the concept of *soft power* has gained special popularity in Asian countries (Melissen, 2011a; Wang, 2011; Wang, 2008) and is seen as having "strategic value" (Melissen, 2011a, p. 250). Melissen (2011b, p. 23) described the Asian approach to public diplomacy as having "a more strategic perspective on public diplomacy than has been observable in the West." It attaches more importance to the long haul than to correct short-term damage to national reputations, and focuses on regional dimensions with the capacity to assist in regional community-building and co-operation (Melissen, 2011a, p. 250; 2011b, p. 24).

Mutual understanding and lasting relationships within and across its borders is also one of the major goals of the Association of South East Asian Nations (ASEAN). Besides, it aims at promoting its increasing role in regional and international stages (Bui, 2011, p. 47). It does so by means of dialogue communication and collaboration. Bui (2011, p. 47) however criticizes that ASEAN lacks a forum for daily communication to disseminate information. It deploys several public diplomacy activities, which are mostly run by elites and not by non-state actors, while its member states follow their own ways of achieving their goals (Bui, 2011, p. 3). Besides the regionally focused public diplomacy strategies going beyond individual national images (Melissen, 2011b, p. 24), Melissen (2011a, p. 250) concludes with regard to East Asia that "soft power issues [. . .] are closely linked to nations' domestically contested self-perceptions of government-initiated constructs of national identity." In the individual countries, the identity issues can facilitate (Indonesia) or constrain (Japan) the countries' endeavor to develop public diplomacy strategies (Melissen, 2011a, p. 250).

In China, public diplomacy aims to serve domestic politics and national cohesion (d'Hooghe, 2011, p. 165; Wang, 2008, p. 260) which leads to a mixture of public diplomacy and public affairs. "The public diplomacy department of China's Ministry of Foreign Affairs, for example, mainly organizes activities to inform domestic, not international, audiences about China's foreign policy and diplomacy" (d'Hooghe, 2011, p. 165). There is no single organ of public diplomacy; instead it is shared by several political institutions, e.g., the Division for Public Diplomacy in the Information Department of the Ministry of Foreign Affairs, among others (Wang, 2008, p. 260). An alignment of the different organizations and their strategies is missing. Therefore, it "is difficult to make long-term strategic arrangements to practice public diplomacy" (Wang, 2008, p. 264). The fundamental goal of Chinese diplomacy is to build "an objective and friendly publicity environment" (cf. Wang, 2008, p. 264). With a specific focus on Europe, China wants to build itself an image of a trustworthy and responsible member of the international political community (d'Hooghe, 2011, p. 167). Wang (2008, p. 264) views this as the foundation for Chinese diplomats to understand public diplomacy strategically. In its image management, China pays a lot of attention to the role of Chinese media, while censoring them and thus undermining the growth of Chinese soft power (d'Hooghe, 2011, pp. 165, 184). The State Council Information Office also puts a lot of effort in situational analysis by monitoring and evaluating media coverage on China (d'Hooghe, 2011, p. 165). China's greatest threat to soft power is its own negative image abroad (for more details on European perceptions see d'Hooghe, 2011, p. 174; Wang, 2008, p. 257) and the fact that China misconceives its international image (for more details see Wang, 2008, p. 261). D'Hooghe (2011, p. 169) identifies the enormous gap between European and Chinese ideas and values as a major problem in the relation between the two actors, "a factor that Chinese policymakers often fail to grasp." China's policies with regard to the absence of human rights, democratic institutions, and processes, collide with public diplomacy efforts to a great extent. Therefore, "it is difficult to persuade the democratic international community to look beyond economics and to perceive China as a credible diplomatic and political power" (Rawnsley, 2007). China needs to better manage the external risks of its negative image abroad and adapt the strategy accordingly, for example the foreign perception of China.

South Korea and Indonesia are seen as good examples of how "countries in transition can be effective in developing a public diplomacy that supports strategic policy objectives overseas, while underlining the appositeness of public diplomacy in one's own civil society for purposes of national cohesion" (Melissen, 2011b, p. 24). Indonesia especially stands out "by making the twin theme of Islam and democracy the centerpiece of its public diplomacy strategy" (Melissen, 2011a, p. 254). However, the return of Islam into politics has raised much anxiety in the international community (Sukma, 2011, p. 112). Also Taiwan has to pay attention to matching messages sent out with what is done at home: it must re-build on its democratic development so as not to weaken its soft power (Chu, 2011, p. 135).

In sum, Asian countries show similarities and differences in their approaches to public diplomacy. Most of them struggle with a negative image abroad that either results from their huge economic growth or their discrepancy between politics and communication messages. All the Asian countries mentioned here are in need of better situational analysis of the international environment and respective adaption of their strategies.

Australia

There is little empirically grounded knowledge on public diplomacy in Australia. Byrne (2009) was the first to provide a detailed analysis of the role of public diplomacy in Australian foreign policy in her doctoral thesis. This author characterized Australian public diplomacy as "fragmented, ad hoc and disconnected from Australia's strategic foreign policy interests" (Byrne, 2009, p. 309). According to Byrne (2009), public diplomacy can only be effective if it is co-ordinated with foreign policy outcomes and based on close co-operation among actors. Byrne identified many individual public diplomacy messages and activities that had received but little co-ordination from the Australian Department of Foreign Affairs and Trade (Byrne, 2009, pp. 309–313).

The European Union

The public diplomacy of the European Union (EU) represents both one supranational organization and the 27 member states that constitute this supranational power. Cross (2012, p. 1) pointed to the fact that the EU is a major normative power in areas like humanitarian aid or environmental sustainability; its actions, however, are not reflected by the external visibility of the EU. Scholars have traced this lack of visibility back to the complex structure of the organizations, its constant transformation and the public diplomacy of the EU (Szondi, 2010, p. 340).

Szondi stated that a common public diplomacy understanding was missing which impeded the identification and selection of public diplomacy goals and strategies. Moreover, Szondi called for a "more strategic and holistic approach" (Szondi, 2010, p. 341) to public diplomacy. According to Cross (2011, p. 22), this approach needs to include the development and implementation of an overarching core message that is communicated not only by the EU itself, but also by the EU member states.

Lynch (2005) remarked that the EU was passing up the chance of integrating public diplomacy into EU foreign policy thinking and the policy-making process (Lynch, 2005, p. 12). He alleged that the public diplomacy of the EU could not tap its full potential due to insufficient staffing and a very limited budget (Lynch, 2005, p. 12). A number of these deficiencies were addressed by the Lisbon Treaty in 2007: Prior to the Lisbon Treaty, the Council Presidency and security policy were taken over by a different member state every six months making a continuous public diplomacy strategy next to impossible (Szondi, 2010, p. 340). Duke and Courtier (2011) pointed to the "establishment of a 'new' leadership architecture in the EU": [T]he appointment of Herman van Rompuy as President of the European Council and Catherine Ashton as a High Representative of the Union for Foreign Affairs and Security Policy and Vice-President of the Commission (HR/VP), as well as the return of José Manuel Barroso as President of the Commission" (Duke & Courtier, 2011, p. 2) serve as a basis for a more coherent and strategic public diplomacy practice. Moreover, the European External Action Service (EEAS), launched in December 2010, incorporates a "strategic planning" division, a "strategic communication" division, and a "public diplomacy" division. The EEAS was designed to unify the external representation of the EU and it has the potential to improve the horizontal coherence of EU public diplomacy by communicating the different foreign policy issues of the EU via one administrative structure (Duke, 2012; Duke & Courtier, 2011).

Federal entities: Quebec and Catalonia

Increasingly, federal entities recognize the potential of public diplomacy and develop their own, individual public diplomacy strategies. This section focuses on Quebec in Canada as well as Catalonia in Spain, as both federated entities consider public diplomacy an important part of their foreign affairs strategy. According to Huijgh (2009), Quebec goes beyond the public diplomacy of most federal entities that is often coined by a number of single, unconnected public diplomacy initiatives that lack co-ordination. The Ministry of International Relations developed a strategic plan for the years 2011 to 2014 that defined five objectives. Each objective was divided into several priorities that were accompanied by key initiatives (Gouvernement du Québec, 2006; Le ministère des Relations internationales, n.d.) carried out by the ministry in cooperation with other organizations like *Les Offices jeunesse internationaux du Québec*.

The government of Catalonia recognizes public diplomacy as "a flexible, innovative instrument for promoting international projection activities that supplement the conventional channels of international law" (Government of Catalonia, 2010, p. 71). Its "Foreign Affairs Strategy 2010—2015" defines the goals and the building blocks of a Catalonian public diplomacy strategy (Government of Catalonia, 2010, pp. 108–109). In a first step, the government seeks to identify the most important values that have the capacity to successfully project Catalonia to target audiences. The already established image of Barcelona serves as a starting point. In this way, other federal entities have also built on prior experiences using city diplomacy (La Porte, 2012). City diplomacy comprises communication strategies and activities of local governments and other local actors to communicate their citizens' interests in an international arena. The Catalonian government does not view itself as sole public diplomacy actor, but seeks to co-ordinate its public diplomacy initiatives closely with the different governmental agents and civil society (Government of Catalonia, 2010, pp. 72–73).

Comparison: Strategic Dimensions of Public Diplomacy in Selected Countries

This brief overview over public diplomacy in selected regions and countries has shown that the cultural setting, the ideational preferences, and the size and population of a country have a direct impact on the practice of public diplomacy. Bigger states like the USA, Germany, or the UK apply broader public diplomacy strategies that cover a wide range of issues, as they command a comparatively large amount of resources allocated to public diplomacy. Small and medium-sized countries like Norway or Sweden operate on a smaller budget. Hence, they concentrate on specific public diplomacy goals, strategies, messages, instruments and target groups and aim at carving their own public diplomacy niche (Bátora, 2005). According to Melissen (2011b, p. 23), public diplomacy can be regarded as strategic if it is conducted in the long run. He emphasizes the strategic dimension of public diplomacy in Asian countries: Public diplomacy in Asia attaches more importance to influencing long-haul perceptions rather than short-term national reputations. Moreover, Asian public diplomacy often focuses on the regional dimensions with the capacity to assist in regional community-building and co-operation (Melissen, 2011a, p. 250; 2011b, p. 24).

Conclusion and outlook

Is an overarching public diplomacy strategy, focusing on a number of core messages and values as well as on a centralized public diplomacy structure (e.g., UK, Sweden), automatically more strategic than a more pluralistic, decentralized approach (e.g., Germany)? Not necessarily. In the case of Germany, the coexistence of several individual public diplomacy strategies and a multitude of voices and actors contributes to a unique strategy that seeks to present a pluralistic image of Germany abroad, and dissociate German public diplomacy from the centralized propaganda efforts in the Third Reich.

The analysis in this chapter has identified a number of factors impeding a more strategic conduct of public diplomacy. Asian countries are in need of better situational analysis of the international environment and the key publics that public diplomacy strategies are targeted at. This situational and environmental analysis serves as a basis for defining public diplomacy goals, strategies and instruments. Moreover, the analysis discloses shortcomings regarding public diplomacy evaluation. The majority of public diplomacy actors tend to evaluate single public diplomacy activities rather than entire public diplomacy strategies and their impact. Because of this, public diplomacy actors miss the opportunity to determine the effectiveness and impact of their own strategies that could serve as a starting point for developing new public diplomacy strategies. Shortcomings regarding the extent, the institutionalization and the professionalization of strategies can also be traced back to the notion that resources allocated to public diplomacy are insufficient—a view that is voiced by scholars and practitioners alike. The institutionalization of public diplomacy differs between the countries analyzed: Whereas public diplomacy has not yet been institutionalized as an organizational function in Germany, smaller countries like Norway and Finland have already set up a public diplomacy division in their foreign ministries.

The case of the EU has shown the considerable challenge of defining public diplomacy goals and strategies, as well as co-ordinating public diplomacy on a supranational level. This is particularly striking when national and supranational actors pursue individual, conflicting public diplomacy goals, or member states use the EU as a scapegoat (Cross, 2012).

Federal entities are emerging actors that have started to develop their own public diplomacy strategies. The example of Catalonia illustrates that federal entities can build on previous experiences with city diplomacy as well as public diplomacy tools such as cultural exchanges. Just as supranational and national public diplomacy affect each other, the public diplomacy of federal entities can either add to already existing public diplomacy strategies on a national level or undermine the public diplomacy of nation states by communicating unique, distinct features and achievements of particular regions, especially when federal entities strive for a higher degree of autonomy.

The state of research has disclosed four contradictory correlations between public diplomacy and strategic communication. This chapter has contributed to the clarification of this relationship. The analysis of definitions and theoretical conceptions of strategic communication has helped to identify a number of criteria for determining the degree to which public diplomacy is strategic. These criteria have been applied to the public diplomacy practice in selected countries. This chapter advances the hypothesis that public diplomacy can be regarded as strategic communication, but is not strategic per se. There is no single most effective public diplomacy strategy. The strategies pursued by public diplomacy actors range along a continuum from centralized approaches to public diplomacy to decentralized, pluralistic strategies. The analysis of the public diplomacy practice in selected countries points to a number of factors that impede the strategic conduct of public diplomacy: insufficient budgeting and staffing, and shortcomings regarding the extent and professionalization of public diplomacy evaluations, as well as an inadequate institutionalization of public diplomacy within organizations.

This chapter's contribution can be regarded as a starting point for further discussion of the relationship between public diplomacy and strategic communication. The reference criteria that were defined within this chapter may serve as a basis of further empirical studies that discuss the question: To what extent can public diplomacy be regarded as strategic communication from an internationally comparative view?

References

Adelman, K. L. (1981). Speaking of America: Public diplomacy in our time. *Foreign Affairs, 59*(4), 913–936.

Anholt, S. (2006). Public diplomacy and place branding: Where's the link? *Place Branding, 2*(4), 271–275.

Bakka, J.F. & Fivelsdal, E. (2003). *Organisationsteori. Struktur, kultur, processer* [Organization theory. Structure, culture, processes]. Copenhagen, Denmark: Handelshøjskolen Forlag.

Bátora, J. (2005). *Public diplomacy in small and medium-sized states: Norway and Canada.* The Hague, Netherlands: Netherlands Institute of International Relations "Clingendael."

Benoit, W., & Zhang, J. (2003). *The message strategies of Saudi Arabia's image restoration campaign after 9/11.* Paper presented at the annual meeting of the International Communication Association. Retrieved from http://www.allacademic.com/meta/ p_mla_apa_research_citation/1/1/2/2/1/p112215_index.html

Blinken, A. J. (2002). Winning the war of ideas. *The Washington Quarterly, 25*(2), 101–114.

Bolewski, W. (2008). Diplomatic Processes and Cultural Variations: The relevance of culture in diplomacy. *The Whitehead Journal of Diplomacy and International Relations,* Winter/Spring, 145–160.

Brettschneider, F. (1998). Agenda building. In O. Jarren, U. Sarcinelli, & U. Saxer (Eds.), *Politische Kommunikation in der demokratischen Gesellschaft* [Political communication in the democratic society] (p. 635). Opladen/ Wiesbaden, Germany: Westdeutscher Verlag.

British Council (2008). Annual report 2007–2008. Retrieved from http://www.britishcouncil.org/annual-report/global_scorecard.htm

Bui, A. D. (2011). Public diplomacy in ASEAN and the cases of Vietnam and Singapore. Dissertation, University of Leeds. Retrieved from http://ics.leeds.ac.uk/files/2011/12/Anh-Bui.pdf.

Byrne, C. (2009). *Public diplomacy in an Australian Context: a policy-based framework to enhance understanding and practice.* Doctoral thesis. Sydney: Bond University.

Byrne, C. (2011). *Public diplomacy in an Australian Context: a policy-based framework to enhance understanding and practice.* The Hague, Netherlands: Netherlands Institute of International Relations "Clingendael."

Chaffee, E. E. (1985). Three models of strategy. *Academy of Management Review* 10 (1), 89–98.

Chitty, N. (2009). Australian public diplomacy. In N. Snow & P.M. Taylor (Eds.), *Routledge handbook of public diplomacy* (pp. 314–322). New York: Routledge.

Chu, Y. (2011). Taiwan's soft power and the future of cross-strait relations: Can the tail wag the dog? In S. J. Lee, & Melissen, Jan (Eds.), *Public diplomacy and soft power in East Asia* (pp. 117–137). New York: Palgrave.

Copeland, D. (2006). *Public diplomacy and branding.* Retrieved from http://uscpublicdiplomacy.org/index.php/newswire/cpdblog_detail/060403_public_diplomacy_and_branding/

Critchlow, J. (2003). The power of public diplomacy. How to make friends and influence the world. *The New Leader,* September/October, 12–14.

Cross, M. K. D. (2010). *EU foreign policy and the challenge of public diplomacy.* Retrieved from http://stockholm. sgir.eu/uploads/Mai%27a%20Cross%20EU%20PubD%20paper.pdf

Cross, M. K. D. (2012). *Perspectives from IR theory.* Paper presented at the author's workshop "European public diplomacy: Soft power at work." Los Angeles, CA: University of Southern California.

Cull, N. J. (2008). Public diplomacy: Taxonomies and histories. *Annals of the American Academy of Political and Social Science, 616,* 31–54.

Cull, N. J. (2009a). Designing out the mess: A historically literate approach to re-booting U.S. public diplomacy. *Public Diplomacy Magazine, 1*(1), 13–18.

Cull, N. J. (2009b). Public diplomacy before Gullion. The evolution of a phrase. In N. Snow & P. M. Taylor (Eds.), *Routledge handbook of public diplomacy* (pp. 19–23). New York: Routledge.

Cutlip, S. M.; Center, A. H., & Broom, G. M. (1994). *Effective public relations* (7th ed.) Englewood Cliffs, NJ: Prentice Hall.

d'Hooghe, I. (2011). The limits of China's soft power in Europe: Beijing's public diplomacy puzzle. In S. J. Lee & J. Melissen (Eds.), *Public diplomacy and soft power in East Asia* (pp. 163–190). New York: Palgrave.

Dale, H. C.; Cohen, A., & Smith, J.A. (2012). Challenging America: How Russia, China, and other countries use public diplomacy to compete with the U.S. *Backgrounder,* No. 2698, pp. 1–6. Retrieved from http://thf_media.s3.amazonaws.com/2012/pdf/b2698.pdf

Department of Defense (2004). *Report of the Defense Science Board Task Force on strategic communication.* Retrieved from http://www.acq.osd.mil/dsb/reports/ADA428770.pdf

Deutsch, R. D. (2010). Ambassadors to the world. A new paradigm for public diplomacy and strategic communication. *Joint Forces Quarterly, 56*(1), 3–5.

Duffey, J. (2009). How globalization became U.S. public diplomacy at the end of the Cold War. In N. Snow & P. M. Taylor (Eds.), *Routledge handbook of public diplomacy* (pp. 325–333). New York: Routledge.

Duke, S. (2012). *The European External Action Service and public diplomacy.* Paper presented at the author's workshop "European public diplomacy: Soft power at work." Los Angeles, CA: University of Southern California.

Duke, S., & Courtier, A. (2011). *The EU's external public diplomacy and the EEAS—cosmetic exercise and intended change?* European diplomacy policy paper 7. Retrieved from http://dseu.lboro.ac.uk/Documents/Policy_Papers/DSEU_Policy_Paper07.pdf

Dutta-Bergman, M. J. (2006). U.S. public diplomacy in the Middle East: A critical cultural approach. *Journal of Communication Inquiry, 30* (102), 102–124.

Edward R. Murrow Center of Public Diplomacy (n.d.). *Definitions of public diplomacy.* Retrieved from http://fletcher.tufts.edu/Murrow/Diplomacy/Definitions

Ehteshami, A. (2009): Iran as a middle power. *Public Diplomacy Magazine: Middle Powers. Who they are. What they want, 2,* 54–56.

Epstein, S. B., & Mages, L. (2005). *Public diplomacy: A review of past recommendations.* (CRS report for Congress, RL33062). Retrieved from https://www.policyarchive. org/bitstream/handle/10207/2547/RL33062_20050902.pdf?sequence=1

Foreign and Commonwealth Office (2005). *A modern, creative, diverse and relevant UK reaches out to the world* – Report on the Public Diplomacy Challenge Fund 2004-2005. London: Foreign and Commonwealth Office.

Gouvernement du Québec (2006). *Québec's International Policy. Working in concert*. Québec: Gouvernement du Québec.

Government of Catalonia (2010). *Government of Catalonia foreign affairs strategy 2011–2015*. Retrieved from: http://www20.gencat.cat/docs/Departament_de_la_Vicepresidencia/0-WEB_AEC_CHCC/Afers_Exteriors_Cooperacio/Documents/PAEC/Pla_Accio_Exterior_EN.pdf

Gramberger, M. R. (1994). *Wider den häßlichen Deutschen: die verständnisorientierte Öffentlichkeitsarbeit der Bundesrepublik Deutschland in den USA* [Against the ugly German: understanding-oriented public relations of the Federal Republic of Germany in the United States]. Münster, Germany: Lit.

Gregory, B. (2005). *Public Diplomacy and Strategic Communication: Cultures, Firewalls, and Imported Norms*. Paper presented at the American Political Science Association conference on international communication and conflict. Retrieved from http://www8.georgetown.edu/cct/apsa/papers/gregory.pdf

Gregory, B. (2008). Public diplomacy: Sunrise of an academic field. *Annals of the American Academy of Political and Social Science, 616*, 274–290.

Grunig, J. E., & Hunt, T. (1984). *Managing public relations*. Fort Worth, TX: Harcourt Brace.

Grunig, J. E., & Repper, F. C. (1992). Strategic management, publics and issues. In J. E. Grunig (Ed.), *Excellence in public relations and communication management* (pp. 117–157). Hillsdale, NJ: Lawrence Erlbaum.

Grunig, L. A., Grunig, J. E., & Dozier, D. M. (2002). *Excellent public relations and effective organizations: A study of communication management in three countries*. Mahwah, NJ: Lawrence Erlbaum.

Hallahan, K., Holtzhausen, D., van Ruler, B., Verčič, D., & Sriramesh, K. (2007). Defining strategic communication. *International Journal of Strategic Communication, 1*(1), 3–35.

Hax, A. C., & Majluf, N. S. (1996). *The strategy concept and process. A pragmatic approach*. London, England: Prentice-Hall.

Hayden, C. (2010). The role of audience in public diplomacy argumentation. In D. Gouran (Ed.), *The Functions of Argument and Social Context* (pp. 164–171). Washington, D.C.: National Communication Association.

Heine, J. (2009). Middle powers and conceptual leadership. *Public Diplomacy Magazine: Middle Powers. Who they are. What they want 2*, 41–45.

Hoffman, D. (2002). Beyond Public Diplomacy. *Foreign Affairs, 81*(2), 83–95.

Höse, A. (2008). Selling America: Die Public Diplomacy der USA vor dem Irakkrieg 2003 [The public diplomacy of the United States for the Iraq War, 2003]. In T: Jäger & H. Viehrig, Henrike (Eds.), *Die amerikanische Regierung gegen die Weltöffentlichkeit? Theoretische und empirische Analysen der Public Diplomacy zum Irakkrieg* [The American government against world public affairs? Theoretical and empirical analyses of public diplomacy toward the Iraq War] (pp. 79-107). Wiesbaden: VS Verlag für Sozialwissenschaften.

Hughes, K. (2007). *Strategic communication and public diplomacy: interagency coordination*. Remarks at the Department of Defense conference on strategic communication. http://2001–2009.state.gov/r/us/2007/88630.htm

Huijgh, E. (2009). *The public diplomacy of federated entities. Excavating the Quebec model*. Clingendael diplomacy paper 23. The Hague, Netherlands: Netherlands Institute of International Relations 'Clingendael.'

Kendrick, A., & Fullerton, J. A. (2004). Advertising as Public Diplomacy: Attitude change among international audiences. *Journal of Advertising Research*, September, 297–311.

Kotler, P., & Gertner, D. (2002). Country as brand, product and beyond: A place marketing and brand management perspective. *Brand Management, 9*(4–5), 249–261.

Kristensen, N. N. (2010). Nice to have—or Need to Have? The professional challenges of the communication sector. *Nordicom Review, 31*(2), 135–150.

Kruckeberg, D., & Vujnovic, M. (2005). Public relations, not propaganda, for US public diplomacy in a post-9/11 world: Challenges and opportunities. *Journal of Communication Management, 9*(4), 296–304.

La Porte, T. (2012). *City Diplomacy*. Paper presented at the workshop "European public diplomacy: Soft power at work." Los Angeles, CA: University of Southern California.

Langer, R. (January, 2005). Hvad er kommunikationsvidenskab? Status og fremtid for et udisciplineret diskursfælleskab [What is communication science? Status and future for an undisciplined discourse community]. *Dansk Tidsskrift for Kommunikation*, pp. 1–28. Retrieved May 10, 2011, from www.kommunikationsforum.dk/file.asp?id=536

Laqueur, W. (1994). Save public diplomacy: Broadcasting America's message matters. *Foreign Affairs, 73*(5), 19–24.

Lee, H. M. (2007). *Public diplomacy as international public relations: Speculation on national determinants of world governments' web public diplomacy interactivity*. Paper presented at the annual meeting of the International Communication Association, TBA, San Francisco, CA. Retrieved from http://www.allacademic.com/meta/p_mla_apa_research_citation/1/7/0/5/5/p170558_index.html

Lee, S. J., & Melissen, J. (2011). Introduction. In: S. J. Lee & J. Melissen, Jan (Eds.), *Public diplomacy and soft power in East Asia* (pp. 1–9). New York: Palgrave.

Le ministère des Relations internationales Québec (n.d.). *2011–2014 Plan stratégique*. Québec: Le ministère des Relations internationales Québec.

Leonard, M., & Small, A. (2003). *Norwegian public diplomacy*. London, England: The Foreign Policy Centre.

Leonard, M., Small, A., & Rose, M. (2005). *British public diplomacy in the 'Age of Schisms.'* London, England: The Foreign Policy Centre.

Leonard, M., & Stead, C. & Smewing, C. (2002). *Public diplomacy*. London, England: The Foreign Policy Centre.

Löffelholz, M., Auer, C., Krichbaum, S., & Srugies, A. (2011). *Public diplomacy as external organizational communication. Structures and strategies of state and non-state actors shaping Germany's image abroad.* Paper presented at the annual meeting of the International Communication Association, Boston, MA.

Lord, C. (1998). The past and future of public diplomacy. *Orbis,* Winter, 49–72.

Lord, C. (2006). *Losing hearts and minds? Public diplomacy and strategic influence in the Age of Terror.* Westport, CT: Praeger Security International.

Lord, K. M. (2009). The USA World Trust: Bringing the power of networks to U.S. public diplomacy. *Public Diplomacy Magazine, 1*(1), 19–31.

Lord Carter of Coles (2005). *Public diplomacy review*. London, England: British Council.

Lynch, D. (2005). *Communicating Europe to the world: What public diplomacy for the EU?* EPC working paper 21. Brussels, Belgium: European Policy Centre.

Manheim, J. (1994a). *Strategic public diplomacy and American foreign policy: The evolution of influence.* Oxford, England: Oxford University Press.

Manheim, J. (1994b). Strategic public diplomacy: Managing Kuwait's image during the Gulf conflict. In W. L. Bennet & D. L. Paletz (Eds.), *Taken by storm: The media, public opinion, and U.S. foreign policy in the Gulf War* (pp. 131–148). Chicago, IL: University of Chicago Press.

Meiner-Jensen, N. (2012). *Danish public diplomacy—a dialogic approach to international relations between states and publics.* Roskilde, Denmark: Roskilde Universitet.

Melissen, J. (2005). *The new public diplomacy. Soft power in international relations.* New York: Palgrave Macmillan.

Melissen, J. (2006). *The new diplomacy: Soft power in international relations.* Houndsmill, UK: Palgrave Macmillan.

Melissen, J. (2011a). Concluding reflections on soft power and public diplomacy in East Asia. S. J. Lee & J. Melissen, Jan (Eds.), *Public diplomacy and soft power in East Asia* (pp. 247–262). New York: Palgrave.

Melissen, J. (2011b). Beyond the new public diplomacy. *Clingendael Paper,* No.3. The Hague, Netherlands: Institute of International Relations 'Clingendael.'

Ministry for Foreign Affairs of Finland (n.d.). Unit for Public Diplomacy. Retrieved from: http://formin. finland.fi/public/default.aspx?nodeid=15988&contentlan=2&culture=en-US.

Ministry of Foreign Affairs of Norway (2007). *Norwegian Public Diplomacy Forum launched today.* Retrieved from: http://www.regjeringen.no/en/dep/ud/press/news/2007/Norwegian-Public-Diplomacy-Forum-launche. html?id=467754.

Moss, D., & Warnaby, G. (1998). Communications strategy? Strategy communication? Integrating different perspectives. *Journal of Marketing Communications, 4* (3), 131–140.

Mueller, S. (2009). The Nexus of U.S. public diplomacy and citizen diplomacy. In N. Snow & P. M. Taylor (Eds.), *Routledge handbook of public diplomacy* (pp. 101–107). New York: Routledge.

Ndhlovu, J. T. (2009). World Cup 2010: Africa's time has come. *Public Diplomacy Magazine: Middle Powers. Who they are. What they want. 2,* 46–48.

Norway Communicates (n.d.). Norwegian public diplomacy. Retrieved from: http://www.norwaycommunicates. com/diplomacy.html].

Nye, J. S. (2004). *Soft power. The means to success in world politics.* New York: Public Affairs.

Ociepka, B., & Riniejska, M. (2005). *Public diplomacy and EU enlargement: the case of Poland.* The Hague, Netherlands: Netherlands Institute for International Relations 'Clingendael.'

Ogawa, T. (2009). Origin and development of Japan's public diplomacy. In N. Snow & P. M. Taylor (Eds.), *Routledge handbook of public diplomacy* (pp. 270–281). New York: Routledge.

Olins, W. (2002). Branding the nation—the historical context. *Brand Management, 9*(4–5), 241–248.

Pamment, J. (2012). American strategic communication in Iraq: The "Rapid Reaction Media Team". *Online Journal of Communication and Media Technologies, 2*(2), 1-18.

Pamment, J. (2011). *The limits of the new public diplomacy. Strategic communication and evaluation at the U.S. State Department, Foreign & Commonwealth Office, British Council, Swedish Foreign Ministry and Swedish Institute.* Doctoral thesis. Stockholm, Sweden: Stockholm University.

Petersone, B. (2008). *Increasing a nation's diplomatic capabilities through relationship management: Public relations contributions to middle power diplomacies.* Paper presented at the annual meeting of the International Communication Association, Montreal, Quebec, Canada.

Plaisance, P. L. (2005). The propaganda war on terrorism: An analysis of the United States' "Shared Values" public–diplomacy campaign After September 11, 2001. *Journal of Mass Media Ethics, 20*(4), 250–268.

Rasmussen, S. B. (2010). The messages and practices of the European Union's public diplomacy. *The Hague Journal of Diplomacy, 5*(3), 263–287.

Raupp, J., & Hoffjann, O. (2012). Understanding strategy in communication management. *Journal of Communication Management 16*(2), 146–161.

Rawnsley, G. (2007). A survey of China's public diplomacy. *CPD Blog*. Retrieved from http://uscpublicdiplomacy. org/index.php/newswire/cpdblog_detail/070502_a_survey_of_chinas_public_diplomacy/.

Rawnsley, G. D. (2009). China talks back. Public diplomacy and soft power for the Chinese century. In: N. Snow & P. M. Taylor (Eds.), *Routledge handbook of public diplomacy* (pp. 282–291). New York, NY: Routledge.

Reinhard, K. (2009). American business and its role in public diplomacy. In N. Snow & P. M. Taylor (Eds.), *Routledge handbook of public diplomacy* (pp. 195–200). New York: Routledge.

Ross, C. (2002). Public diplomacy comes of age. *The Washington Quarterly, 25*(2), 75–83.

Samansky, A. W. (2003). Successful strategic communications plans are realistic, achievable, and flexible. *Public Relations Quarterly, 48*(2), 24–26.

Sandhu, S. (2009). Strategic communication: An institutional perspective. *International Journal of Strategic Communication, 3*(2), 72–92.

Schatz, E. & Levine, R. (2010). Framing, Public Diplomacy, and Anti-Americanism in Central Asia. *International Studies Quarterly, 54*(3), 855–869.

Schwan, A. (2011). *Werbung statt Waffen. Wie strategische Außenkommunikation die Außenpolitik verändert* [Advertising instead of weapons. How strategic external communication changed foreign policy]. Wiesbaden, Germany: VS Verlag für Sozialwissenschaften.

Scott, R. W. (2008). *Institutions and organizations. Ideas and interests.* Thousand Oaks, CA: Sage.

Signitzer, B. H. (1993). Anmerkungen zur Begriffs- und Funktionswelt von Public Diplomacy [Notes on the conceptual and functional world of public diplomacy]. In W. Armbrecht, H. Avenarius & U. Zabel (Eds.), *Image und PR – Kann Image Gegenstand einer Public Relations-Wissenschaft sein?* [Image and PR. Image as a subject of public relations science?] (pp. 199–211). Opladen: Westdeutscher Verlag.

Signitzer, B. H. (1995). Public relations und public diplomacy. In W. A. Mahle & A. Walter (Eds.), *Deutschland in der internationalen Kommunikation* (pp. 73–81). Konstanz, Germany: UVK.

Signitzer, B. H. (2008). Public Relations and Public Diplomacy: Some conceptual explorations. In A. Zerfass, B. van Ruler & K. Sriramesh (Eds.), *Public relations research* (pp. 205–220). Wiesbaden, Germany: VS Verlag für Sozialwissenschaften.

Snow, N. (1997). United States Information Agency. *Foreign Policy in Focus, 2*, 1–4.

Snow, N. (2004). From bombs and bullets to hearts and minds: U.S. public diplomacy in an age of propaganda. In Y. R. Kamalipour & N. Snow (Eds.), *War, media and propaganda: A global perspective* (pp. 17–24). Oxford, England: Rowman & Littlefield Publishers.

Snow, N. (2009). Rethinking public diplomacy. In N. Snow & P. M. Taylor (Eds.), *Routledge handbook of public diplomacy* (pp. 3–11). New York: Routledge.

Snow, N. & Taylor, P. M. (2006). The Revival of the Propaganda State. US propaganda at home and abroad since 9/11. *The International Communication Gazette, 68*(5–6), 389–407.

Starr, P. K. (2009). Mexican public diplomacy. *Public Diplomacy Magazine: Middle Powers. Who they are. What they want. 2*, 49–53.

Steyn, B. (2003). From strategy to corporate communication strategy: A conceptualisation. *Journal of Communication Management, 8* (2), 168–183.

Steyn, B. (2007). Contributions of public relations to organizational strategy formulation. In: E. L. Toth (Ed.), *The future of excellence in public relations and communication management* (pp. 137–172). Mahwah: Lawrence Erlbaum.

Sukma, R. (2011). Soft power and public diplomacy: The case of Indonesia. In: S. J. Lee & J. Melissen (Eds.), *Public diplomacy and soft power in East Asia* (pp. 91–115). New York: Palgrave.

Sun, H. H. (2008). International political marketing: a case study of United States soft power and public diplomacy. *Journal of Public Affairs, 8*, 165–183.

Swedish Institute (2008). *Brand Sweden. The road to an updated image of Sweden abroad.* Retrieved from: http:// www.si.se/upload/sverigebilden%202.0/FINAL_ENG_080117.pdf

Szondi, G. (2008). *Public diplomacy and nation branding: Conceptual similarities and differences.* Netherlands Institute of International Relations 'Clingendael.' The Hague. (Discussion papers in diplomacy). Retrieved from http://www.clingendael.nl/ publications/2008/20081022_pap_in_dip_nation_branding.pdf.

Szondi, G. (2009). Central and Eastern European public diplomacy: A transitional perspective on national reputation management. In: N. Snow & P. M. Taylor (Eds.), *Routledge handbook of public diplomacy* (pp. 292–313). New York: Routledge.

Szondi, G. (2010). Communicating with the world: An interdisciplinary approach to European Union public diplomacy. In: C. Valentini (Ed.), *Public communication in the European Union: History, perspectives and challenges* (pp. 335–361). Cambridge, England: Cambridge Scholars Publishing.

Tatham, S. (2008). *Strategic communication: A primer.* Shrivenham, England: Defence Academy of the United Kingdom. Retrieved from http://smallwarsjournal.com/documents/stratcommprimer.pdf

Taylor, P. M. (2002). Strategic communications or democratic propaganda? *Journalism Studies, 3*(3), 437–452.

Taylor, P. M. (2009). Public diplomacy and strategic communications. In N. Snow & P. M. Taylor (Eds.), *Routledge handbook of public diplomacy* (pp. 12–16). New York: Routledge.

Tils, R. (2005). *Politische Strategieanalyse: konzeptionelle Grundlagen und Anwendung in der Umwelt- und Nachhaltigkeitspolitik* [Political strategy analysis: conceptual foundation and applications in environmental and sustainability policies]. Wiesbaden, Germany: VS Verlag für Sozialwissenschaften.

Tuch, H. N. (1990). *Communicating with the world: U.S. public diplomacy overseas.* New York: Institute for the Study of Diplomacy.

Under Secretary of Public Diplomacy and Public Affairs (2010). *Public diplomacy: Strengthening U.S. engagement with the world.* Retrieved from http://www.carlisle.army.mil/DIME/documents/Public%20Diplomacy%20US%20World%20Engagement.pdf.

U.S. Advisory Commission on Public Diplomacy (2010). Assessing U.S. public diplomacy. A notional model. Retrieved from http://www.state.gov/documents/organization/149966.pdf

U.S. Advisory Commission on Public Diplomacy (2011). *Staff report of the U.S. Advisory Commission on Public Diplomacy.* Retrieved from http://www.state.gov/documents/organization/179370.pdf

U.S. Department of State (n.d.). *Under Secretary for Public Diplomacy and Public Affairs.* http://www.state.gov/r/.

USC Center on Public Diplomacy (2009). *Resources—PD organizations.* Retrieved from http://uscpublicdiplomacy.com/index.php/resources/pd_organizations.

van Dyke, M. A., & Verčič, D. (2009). Public relations, public diplomacy, and strategic communication: An international model of conceptual convergence. In K. Sriramesh & D. Verčič (Eds.), *The global public relations handbook. Theory, research, and practice* (pp. 822–842). New York: Routledge.

van Ham, P. (2001). The rise of the brand state. The postmodern politics of image and reputation. *Foreign Affairs,* September/October, 2–6.

van Ham, P. (2002). Branding territory: Inside the wonderful worlds of PR and IR theory. *Millennium—Journal of International Studies, 31*(2), 249–269.

Vlahos, M. (2009), Public diplomacy as loss of world authority. In N. Snow & P. M. Taylor (Eds.), *Routledge handbook of public diplomacy* (pp. 24–38). New York: Routledge.

von Eschen, P. M. (2005). Enduring public diplomacy. *American Quarterly, 57*(2), 335–343.

Wang, J. (2007). Telling the American story to the world: The purpose of U.S. public diplomacy in historical perspective. *Public Relations Review, 33,* 21–30.

Wang, J. (2011). *Public diplomacy with Chinese characteristics.* Post on the CPD Blog. Retrieved from http://uscpublicdiplomacy.org/index.php/newswire/cpdblog_detail/public_diplomacy_with_chinese_characteristics/.

Wang, J., & Chang, T. K. (2004). Strategic public diplomacy and local press: How a high-profile "head of state" visit was covered in America's heartland. *Public Relations Review, 30*(1), 11–24.

Wang, Y. (2008). Public diplomacy and the rise of Chinese soft power. *ANNALS, 616,* 257–272.

Wimbush, E. S. (n.d.). *Fixing public diplomacy and strategic communications.* Hudson Institute. Retrieved from http://www.hudson.org/files/publications/Wimbush%20-%20final%20low%20res%20(2).pdf

Yun, S. H. (2006). Toward public relations theory-based study of public diplomacy: Testing the applicability of the excellence study. *Journal of Public Relations Research, 18*(4), 287–312.

Yun, S. H. (2008). Cultural consequences on excellence in public diplomacy. *Journal of Public Relations Research, 20,* 207–230.

Zaharna, R. S. (2004). From propaganda to public diplomacy in the Information Age. In Y- R. Kamalipour & N. Snow (Eds.), *War, media and propaganda: A global perspective* (pp. 219–225). Oxford, England: Rowman & Littlefield Publishers.

Zaharna, R. S. (2005). The network paradigm of strategic public diplomacy. *Foreign Policy in Focus, 10*(1), 1–4.</list>Zöllner, O. (2006). A Quest for Dialogue in International Broadcasting: Germany's Public Diplomacy targeting Arab Audiences. Global Media and Communication, 2(2), 160-182.

Zöllner, O. (2009). German Public Diplomacy: The Dialogue of Cultures. In: N. Snow and P. M. Taylor (eds.): *Routledge Handbook of Public Diplomacy* (pp. 262-269). New York, London: Routledge.

30

Strategic Communication Practice of International Nongovernmental Organizations

Andreas Schwarz and Alexander Fritsch

In the last few decades, nongovernmental organizations (NGOs) have become influential actors in creating awareness of international social, political, environmental and economic causes in global society. Management scholars have recognized them lately as "high profile actors within public policy landscapes at local, national and global levels" (D. Lewis, 2003, p. 326) and "strategically mature organizations" (Lambell, Ramia, Nyland & Michelotti, 2008, p. 75). Many NGOs, such as Oxfam, Plan International or Reporters Sans Frontières, operate in culturally diverse and institutionally complex contexts. At the same time "as they have looked to expand their role in global governance, NGOs have faced mounting pressure to establish their legitimacy in the eyes of a range of stakeholders, including the media, governments, inter-governmental organizations and other civil society actors" (Lambell et al., 2008, p. 80). Hence, the use of public relations (PR) and other types of strategic communication should be crucial for NGOs to establish and maintain legitimacy as well as to achieve their goals. However, these organizations have not received much attention in research on international PR (Tkalac & Pavicic, 2009). NGOs were typically studied in their role as activists; the organization's perception of being 'acted' on was the center of inquiry, rather than the activists' strategic communication itself (Dozier & Lauzen, 2000).

This is surprising insofar as NGOs are assumed to have tremendous impact on global society (L. Lewis, 2005) and largely use communication to achieve their goals. In many cases, these goals are related to some public purpose or even to the "public good." International NGOs (INGOs) operate by encouraging voluntary participation at a global and a local level, which presumably makes them the most important agents in global civil society. Therefore, we need to understand how INGOs use and organize PR as a subset of strategic communication in international environments to achieve their goals. This is also relevant because most INGOs have a Western (or Northern) background and influence not only policies and business, but also cultural values and nation images around the world. As the literature does not offer sufficient insights into these issues the findings of a survey of communication professionals in INGOs conducted in 2010 will be reported and analyzed in this chapter.

The research question of this study was: How do INGOs manage PR across borders? This question has three major aspects. First, the study assessed to what extent these organizations implement strategic PR planning and control (Broom, Cutlip & Center, 2009, p. 324). Second, the data sheds light on how NGOs coordinate PR between headquarters and subsidiaries in terms of centralization or decentralization. Third, the importance of several contextual national and cultural factors for planning and conducting communication internationally was analyzed to explain strategic choices between global integration and local responsiveness. An understanding of the way INGOs balance the global and the local facilitates assessment of the extent to that INGOs adapt communication programs to participate in their local environments, or rather try to impose ethnocentric views, and goals developed at central units.

Literature Review

Defining NGOs and International PR

From a normative perspective, NGOs are thought to contribute to the global development of civil society and democracy (Taylor, 2005). They belong to the so-called third sector, which means they are a type of organization that is different from government agencies and business organizations. According to Salamon and Anheier (1999), such organizations have five key common characteristics: (a) they are organized and possess some institutional reality; (b) they are private and institutionally separate from the government; (c) they do not return profits to directors or owners; (d) they are independent and have broad control over their own activities; and (e) they involve a certain degree of voluntary participation at the level of activity or governance.

NGOs form a subset of the larger category of nonprofit organizations as the latter include a wider range of organizations such as museums, schools or universities. Tkalac and Pavicic (2009) argue that the main difference between NGOs and other nonprofit organizations is the significant dedication of NGOs to advocacy. However, NGOs that mainly provide services such as humanitarian relief or social welfare organizations do exist. "The principal point, however, is that service delivery organizations differ from advocacy organizations in the sense that the latter seek primarily to change the status quo" (Young, 1992, p. 4). In many cases, NGOs combine both service provision and advocacy (Lambell et al., 2008). Therefore, we conceptualize NGOs as organizations that fulfill the five characteristics outlined by Salamon and Anheier (1999), which include a focus on service provision and/ or advocacy. Many organizations in the broader nonprofit category, in contrast, are owned, financed or controlled by governments and therefore were not included in this study.

In the last two decades, NGOs have had to face several challenges related to globalization, such as major complex emergencies, new forms of global poverty, weakened national governments, outmoded global institutions, the internationalization of business and new pressures to respond globally (Lindenberg & Bryant, 2001). Many issues on NGO agendas are global in character: for example, world peace, global warming, social justice, or economic prosperity. These issues need to be addressed with operations and communications in more than one country. Young (1992) states: "[I]f voluntary efforts are to have major impacts, they will require cooperation across national boundaries, suggesting the development of international associations" (p. 2). Although some NGOs are based in a single country, trying to resolve issues of global importance, others are truly international in scope and participation (e.g., Oxfam and Amnesty International). International PR is expected to play a major role in these NGOs. They are subsequently termed international nongovernmental organizations (INGOs) and they represent the main object of this study.

International PR is defined in the literature as "the practice of public relations in an international or cross-cultural context" (Culbertson, 1996, p. 2) and refers to the strategic communication efforts of companies, governments and nonprofit organizations to establish mutually beneficial relationships across nations or cultural borders (Banks, 1995; Wilcox, Ault, Agee & Cameron, 2000). This may involve planned and organized communication with host publics in countries where an international organization operates as well as transnational publics that simultaneously act in several locations (Molleda, 2009).

Research on International PR of NGOs

INGOs have been growing in number and importance since the 1990s. They managed to gain high consultation status within major intergovernmental organizations like the UN or the World Trade Organization. In addition, they are among the most important communicators in creating awareness and influencing public opinion with regard to international social, environmental and political issues (Lambell et al., 2008). Between 1960 and 1980, the number of INGOs doubled (Boli & Thomas, 1997), and between 1990 and 2000, they grew by almost 20% (United Nations Development Programme, 2002). Although it has been recognized that effective PR is central to the success of NGOs and that these organizations use communication as a main tool to achieve their goals, "public relations literature on this subject is rather thin" (Tkalac & Pavicic, 2009, p. 807). L. Lewis (2005) stated the same conclusion in research on "important managerial and communicative issues" (p. 240) in the broader nonprofit sector.

Most of the research on international PR has been limited to descriptions of the PR practice in a certain country, whereas studies on PR of multinational corporations or nonprofit organizations were rare (Molleda & Laskin, 2005). NGOs have primarily been studied as activist publics from the perspective of for-profit organizations, thus NGOs have not been focused on as organizations in their own right. Only in the last ten years have PR scholars been urged to study NGOs' unique ways of using strategic communication (Dozier & Lauzen, 2000; Taylor, Kent, & White, 2001).

Most of the studies on NGOs were not explicitly designed to analyze the international dimensions of their strategic communication. The majority of these studies focused on crisis-related case studies of larger NGOs (Murphy & Dee, 1992; Sisco, Collins & Zoch, 2010) and the NGOs' use of the Internet to communicate with their stakeholders (e.g., Naudé, Froneman & Atwood, 2004; Seo, Kim & Yang, 2009; Taylor et al., 2001). Studies on NGO's use of the Internet basically come to the same conclusion as Taylor et al. (2001). "The data suggest that activist organization Web sites are not fully employing the dialogic capacity of the Internet as expected" (p. 277).

Regarding their international public perceptions, NGOs seem to be the most trusted institutions, exceeding business organizations, government authorities, and the media (Edelman, 2011). They were considered to be sophisticated communicators that evolved from small brands of activists into the new "super brands" in the global marketplace (Wootliff & Deri, 2001). However, several scandals and critics have seriously challenged the reputation of NGOs. Tkalac and Pavicic (2009) discussed some of the reasons why NGOs, especially INGOs, have to face such problems. In some cases the status of INGOs was abused to achieve latent political or religious goals, or goals that differed from the official mission of an NGO. One of the most prevalent threats to the legitimacy of NGOs is the misuse of financial resources. Embezzlement, misappropriation of funds and fraud are among the most frequently reported cases (Gibelman & Gelman, 2000). With increasing size and complexity, INGOs can become unproductive and bureaucratic. In addition, certain partnerships with multinational corporations (MNCs), the involvement of INGOs in commercial market activities (e.g., the Oxfam–Cafédirect case) or governmental agencies' influence on NGOs through partial funding (Tkalac & Pavicic, 2009) can jeopardize their reputation. Another major threat may result from the culturally heterogeneous environments in which INGOs operate. "Large international NGOs from developed countries sometimes develop standards based on 'western' traditions and expect these standards to be universally applicable. The so-called effect of 'westernizing' can be observed as a serious image problem" (Tkalac & Pavicic, 2009, p. 813).

Public perception problems and growing global competition among INGOs has caused them to increasingly depend on professional and strategic approaches to manage their international PR. This applies to both the internal efficiency of their management processes and the external effectiveness of their communication programs. External effectiveness means that PR goals are achieved with specific relevant stakeholders. INGOs have to address a wide variety of stakeholders from multiple national and cultural backgrounds, which represents a major challenge. Tkalac and Pavicic (2009) stated:

> Given these differences across cultures on various environmental variables, it seems logical that the publics in different countries may have different ways of deciding whom to trust, different levels of involvement toward the same cause, and so on. Considering the lack of relevant research in the area of international public relations of NGOs, this question remains unanswered
>
> p. 817

Although INGOs' need to adapt their communication activities to local stakeholders is widely acknowledged in the literature, little is known about their internal structures, or the strategic communication planning necessary to put this adaptation into practice. PR scholars mainly shed light on MNCs and on how they coordinate, control and conduct cross-national communication activities (Lim, 2010; Molleda & Laskin, 2010; Verčič, 2003; Wakefield, 2000). This stream of research will be reviewed in the next few sections. Although one should be cautious about adopting models and findings produced for international PR of MNCs for INGOs, Blood (2005) argues that they are equivalent on several criteria, such as internal organization or degree of internationalization. Therefore, the findings and concepts of international PR research on MNCs will be used, at least, as a heuristic and starting point for the study of INGOs in the next section of this chapter.

Global Integration and Local Responsiveness in Strategic Communication

Balancing the needs for global integration and adaptation to specific cultural contexts has been one of the most delicate questions in terms of strategic decisions on the communication management of MNCs (Molleda & Laskin, 2010). Therefore, a large body of scholarship has been produced in PR, marketing and the broader field of management studies (Lim, 2010).

Proponents of global integration of communication programs usually refer to the need of MNCs to achieve higher cost-efficiency and to maintain consistency in creating brands and in disseminating messages globally. As a consequence, such organizations would have to establish strong coordination systems and control between headquarters and local subsidiaries (Bartlett & Ghoshal, 2002; Lim, 2010).

On the other hand, several scholars concluded from their observations that multinational organizations have to understand national and cultural variability across and within countries in which they operate, as international publics respond distinctively to messages and actions. Taylor (2000), for instance, showed that Coca Cola failed with its "one market, one strategy" approach when the company tried to resolve an international crisis in Western Europe. The failure was mainly attributed to the inflexible centralized structures and the lack of understanding of the different cultural contexts that shaped publics' responses to the crisis in various European countries. Such culture-sensitive aspects, in contrast to ethnocentric approaches, were also advocated by Banks (1995) and Botan (1992). Taylor and Kent (1999) concluded from in-depth interviews with seven PR managers in Malaysia that "for 'international public relations' to be truly effective, it must account for the 'international' dynamic in various contexts." Sriramesh and Verčič (2001) proposed a list of contextual variables that presumably influence PR practice in different countries and help practitioners to localize their strategies and tactics. The list consists of three factors that comprise further variables: the infrastructure of a country (including the political system, the level of economic development, the legal environment and the role of activism in a country); the media environment (including media control, media outreach and media access); and societal culture (referring to different dimensions of cultural values as well as corporate culture).

To date, there is some consensus among scholars that the strategic decisions for global integration and local responsiveness in international PR are not either/or choices (Huck, 2005; Lim, 2010; Wakefield, 2001). Rather, MNCs increasingly have to balance the global and the local by means of specific mechanisms of coordination and control between headquarters and subsidiaries. This notion was tentatively supported by Wakefield (2000) who conducted interviews with approximately 80 experts of international PR from more than 30 countries. Based on excellence theory and two qualitative studies, he proposed a normative model of 'world-class PR' for MNCs and outlined basic elements of presumably effective PR programs. According to this model, effective organizations have a global instead of a "central-mandate" philosophy. They coordinate communication both at headquarters and internationally. The PR officers they hire are full-time trained experts who represent the diversity of the MNC's transnational publics. They employ dual-matrix reporting relationships between headquarters and subsidiaries and offer frequent opportunities for informal and formal interaction. PR officers work as a global team with horizontal reporting relationships and a central person who acts as team leader rather than mandate giver.

Lim (2010) suggested: "coordinating between integration and responsiveness can be achieved by giving tactical autonomy to local subsidiaries within the boundary in which the MNC's mission, goals, and specific program's themes are kept" (p. 310). Tentative evidence that supports this relationship between the centralization or decentralization of the PR function on the one hand and the standardization or localization of PR programs on the other hand was produced by Huck (2005). This author conducted in-depth interviews with the PR managers of 20 MNCs based in Germany. The findings showed that the more MNCs centralized their communication function and the more headquarters controlled their subsidiaries, the less they localized their PR messages and activities. The more they decentralized their communication function by giving local subsidiaries more autonomy and the more they developed PR programs collaboratively between subsidiaries and headquarters, the more they adapted communication activities to local and cultural contexts. In fact, most companies used decentralized structures and localized their PR efforts to some degree. Molleda (2000) also supported these findings and found that 60% of the MNCs he studied had medium levels of centralization, meaning that headquarters were responsible for 50% of the coordination and control, and local units were responsible for the other 50%. To achieve global coordination, MNCs use integrative communication devices such as annual reports, corporate websites, intranets, teleconferences, newsletters or codes of conduct and ethics (Molleda, 2000). According to Huck (2005), organizations that make use of decentralized PR structures and develop their programs collaboratively between headquarters and subsidiaries reported higher needs of coordination.

Although some knowledge has been produced for MNCs, almost no studies that analyzed how and to what degree INGOs organize, coordinate and localize their international communication activities have been found. For this lack of research, the broader management literature was reviewed to identify different types of INGOs in terms of headquarters–subsidiary relationships and coordination.

Coordination and Control in INGOs

INGOs usually operate in complex and turbulent environments. Together with increasing competition for donations and higher pressure for accountability they need efficient management processes and organizational structures, including the PR functions that are able to accommodate these developments (Tkalac & Pavicic, 2009). They all have in common that for their international scope in membership and operations they "must structure [themselves] in a manner that is effective in developing and maintaining support and coordinated action by participating members in different countries" (Young, 1992, p. 10). In addition, Young (1992) suspected that "those which succeed do so, in part, because they have found organizational structures that accommodate the unique challenges to organizing at an international level" (p. 2). Common problems in this context were reported to be difficulties in communication between headquarters and local units, and lack of leadership capacity and professional human resources management, as well as problems with financial and institutional planning (Stark Biddle, 1984).

Young (1989) identified five different types of NGOs placed on a continuum between highly centralized, hierarchical and decentralized, segmented organizations. The unitary model refers to the most centralized type of NGO with strong headquarters that take all decisions for local branch offices in different countries, which have to implement these decisions. In the federation-type of INGOs decision-making mainly resides in central headquarters that set standards and acquire resources, but local units have their own leaders and implementation capacity. Confederations consist of strong affiliates that partially delegate coordination, resource allocation and standard setting to headquarters. However, central decisions are taken by consensus between larger subsidiaries and the central office. INGOs consisting of rather autonomous local organizations that established weak coordinating mechanisms represent the so-called umbrella model. The most decentralized type of INGO does not have any central office with decision-making or coordination authority. In this model separate national organizations sharing a common name are completely autonomous and co-operate on an ad hoc basis.

On the basis of several case studies of bigger INGOs such as Oxfam, Médecins Sans Frontières, or Plan International, Lindenberg and Bryant (2001) observed that some INGOs had abandoned organizational structures that were placed at both ends of the centralization–decentralization continuum. Care USA, for instance, moved from the unitary to the confederation model in the 1980s, and Save the Children changed its structure from separate independent organizations in the 1970s to the confederation model in the late 1990s. Therefore, these authors believed that three dominant forms of Northern relief and development NGOs would emerge: (a) competitive, independent national organizations with a weak umbrella coordinating structure, like Médecins Sans Frontières; (b) federations like Plan International; and (c) confederations like Care International. Young (1992) concluded from a number of case studies on international advocacy NGOs that over time they "will become more decentralized once they have established a formal federal structure." Although Young assumed that the federation model would be most appropriate for accommodating challenges of national diversity and international coordination, Hudson and Bielefeld (1997) stated that INGOs operating in multiple national settings are most likely to be structured as umbrella organizations. They supported the notion that unitary, hierarchical structures are less common in NGOs, and probably less convenient for them.

How and whether these structures are related to organizing and coordinating international PR at INGOs has not been studied systematically so far and, thus, represents the point of departure for this study.

Research Questions and Hypotheses

The main research question of this study was:

> RQ1: How do INGOs manage strategic communication across borders in terms of centralization or decentralization of the PR function?

As research on MNCs suggested that major strategic decisions (mission, goals, etc.) should be made co-operatively between headquarters and subsidiaries although local units should be autonomous on the level of tactics (Lim, 2010), we aimed at a differentiated analysis of the different steps in strategic PR planning. In addition, Molleda (2000) found that MNCs employ varying degrees of centralization for different disciplines of international PR such as media relations, shareholder relations or government relations. Similarly, within this chapter different PR disciplines at INGOs (e.g., crisis communication, advocacy, media relations) were examined.

Management research on INGOs found that over time and with growing international scope, INGOs leave behind rigid centralized and hierarchical structures (unitary model) although others strive for a minimum of coordination by abandoning the model of completely independent national organizations that only share a common name. Therefore a first hypothesis was developed:

H1:   The older and the more international in scope an INGO is, the more likely its PR function will be structured as federation, confederation or umbrella-type as opposed to completely centralized or decentralized structures.

The second research question refers to the use of integrative communication devices (Molleda, 2000) as an indicator of coordination efforts and interaction between headquarters and local units:

RQ2:   Which and how many integrative communication devices do INGOs use to coordinate their international PR programs?

The need for the use of internal communication to coordinate PR between central and local units should rise with increasing levels of involvement of these units in their international communication strategies:

H2:   INGOs where decision-making on PR resides in completely autonomous local subsidiaries or highly centralized headquarters implement significantly fewer communication devices or forms of co-operation compared to INGOs that involve both central and local units in strategic communication.

Third, scholars assumed that INGOs have to face substantial pressure to adhere to local standards and the cultural environment in order to avoid being perceived as Western intruders (at least in the case of Northern INGOs) (Tkalac & Pavicic, 2009). Hence, international PR programs of INGOs to be effective have to be adapted to varying national and cultural contexts. The resulting research question was:

RQ3:   To what extent do PR professionals in INGOs account for contextual factors in their strategic and tactical decisions?

As earlier studies on MNCs suggested a relationship between degrees of centralization of the PR function and the degree of local adaptation of PR programs, a third hypothesis was developed:

H3:   The more INGOs centralize their PR function the less they will account for contextual factors in their strategic and tactical communication decisions.

Method

Sample and Procedure

To identify different types of INGOs and their ways of managing international communications, an online survey was conducted with professionals who lead international PR departments or programs. The study's target population was NGOs with substantial international scope in their operations and communications. The Yearbook of International Organizations is a large database that has been proven useful in drawing samples of INGOs (Boli & Thomas, 1997). It provides data on more than 63,000 INGOs and intergovernmental organizations (IGOs) all over the world in all fields. The database is particularly useful for studying transnational actors in PR because it strictly includes only those organizations that are truly "international" based on the following criteria: (a) the aims of an INGO should involve the international level; (b) the membership of an INGO should be of international character; (c) the structure of the INGO should be formal or should have a permanent office and possess some continuity; (d) the INGO should be independent; and (e) the INGO should not provide profits to its members. These criteria were regarded as being viable in comparison to the NGO definition discussed previously.

The yearbook's online database contains more than 12,000 active INGOs. However, this population was reduced by certain criteria to include only those INGOs with a very strong international orientation. The yearbook divides INGOs into federations of international organizations, universal membership organizations, intercontinental membership organizations, and regionally defined membership organizations. Regionally defined membership organizations containing members from only one continent were not included in the survey, as it was assumed that international PR played a less important role. According to Boli and Thomas (1997), the yearbook is incomplete for the years immediately preceding its publication. They found that it takes 10 years before 80% to 90% of the organizations are included. It was therefore decided that only organizations established before 2000 would be included. As a result, the final population relevant to this study included 5,092 INGOs. The online database provides contact details for all organizations, so we aimed to conduct a census of this population. However, only 4,477 INGOs' email addresses could be retrieved from the database.

After pre-screening with some PR managers of INGOs, the questionnaire was abridged, and the wording was simplified. On March 23, 2010, personalized email invitations were sent to 4,477 organizations. After the first wave of invitations, several hundred emails were returned undelivered because of inaccurate email addresses or other issues. Alternative email addresses for the respective organizations were investigated, and further invitations were sent. A total of 250 email invitations could not be delivered, meaning that a total of 4,227 organizations received invitations. After an additional reminder email, a total of 485 INGOs completed the questionnaire. Thus, a response rate of 11.5% was achieved. Although such response rates are commonly reported in online survey research (Couper & Bosnjak, 2010), the high dropout ratio is a study limitation in terms of representativeness. Nevertheless, we expected that more than 400 cases would cover a broad range of approaches to international PR within INGOs.

During the process of data collection, the deficiencies of the Yearbook of International Organizations became apparent. Several organizations sent individual responses, claiming that their organization was not an independent entity or was dormant or dissolved. Others had no formal structure, no headquarters or they were not international in scope. Therefore, the yearbook data should be treated with caution. Moreover, a methodological limitation stems from the survey technique. For each INGO only one individual PR professional was expected to be the only information source for his or her international organization including its numerous international subsidiaries. For some INGOs that are very complex in terms of internal structure and international scope, the actual knowledge of these individuals about structures and PR strategies might be limited.

The Questionnaire

The online questionnaire contained questions in four main areas of interest: general questions about the organization, the structure of the international PR function, forms and tools of international coordination, and the importance of environmental variables for planning and conducting international PR. The first area included questions about the structure of communications at organizational headquarters and the extent of international operations, measured by the number of countries and the specific continents the INGOs cover with their operations.

Questions regarding the forms of coordination inquired about how headquarters and local units share responsibilities for each of the following elements in the process of planning and conducting PR (Broom, Cutlip & Center, 2009): (a) carrying out research; (b) setting objectives; (c) definition of target groups; (d) the development of strategies; (e) the development of messages; (f) deciding measures (e.g., press releases); (g) deciding channels; and (h) the evaluation of PR activities. For each element, respondents were asked to indicate the particular leadership at the respective INGO (headquarters, local units, both independently, both collaboratively, or no one). At the same time this operationalization captures to what extent international PR is planned strategically in INGOs. The same response options were applied to measure where decision-making resides with regard to the following disciplines of PR: advocacy, crisis communication, donor relations, fundraising, marketing, international media relations, local media relations, and the production of materials.

To assess the use of integrative communication devices to coordinate PR between headquarters and subsidiaries (Molleda, 2000) respondents had to state which of the following devices were used in their organization: formal guidelines, global code of practice, global media strategy, regular newsletters, online community, online knowledge base, regular meetings, regular phone conferences, showcasing of examples, skill-share meetings, training sessions, and email lists.

In addition, participants were asked to rate the importance of 21 contextual variables and their influence on strategic decisions in international PR activities (1—not important; 5—very important). These items were derived from Sriramesh and Verčič (2001) who proposed a list of variables that pertain to one of three factors: societal culture, national infrastructure, and the media environment. Based on Fritsch's (2010) exploratory study, which consisted of in-depth interviews with PR managers of four major INGOs, additional variables were added to that list. These included (a) the history of a country, (b) the relative importance of an issue in a country, (c) national language, and (d) the diversity of languages in a certain country.

Data Analysis

To identify different types of INGOs in terms of their coordination of international PR between headquarters and local units (centralized or decentralized), two-step cluster analysis was used. One advantage is that it can include both categorical and continuous variables simultaneously. The algorithm also easily handles bigger samples and "is thought to behave reasonably well when the assumptions are not met" (Norušis, 2011, p. 394). These assumptions include the use of continuous variables with normal distribution, categorical variables with a multinomial distribution and the independency of all variables. Follow-up analyses of variance (ANOVA), comparing mean values between clusters as well as post hoc tests (Tukey-HSD) were used to test the hypotheses.

Regarding the 21 contextual variables that presumably influence strategic choices in international PR, an exploratory factor analysis (principle component analysis) was used to reduce them to a lower number of underlying dimensions. Oblimin was applied as a method of factor rotation due to the resulting factors being assumed as correlated. The Kaiser–Meyer–Olkin (KMO) measure was used to assess sampling adequacy, with values above 0.8, indicating a reliable factor solution. Bartlett's test of sphericity assesses whether the data shows sufficient inter-correlations and should be significant ($p < 0.05$). Factor scores were calculated with the regression method and used for subsequent analysis.

Results

General Findings

After data cleansing, a total of 440 INGOs were included in the analysis. So-called Northern INGOs, stemming from developed countries, clearly dominated the sample. 64% of these had established their headquarters in Europe, 17% in the US or Canada, and 2% in Australia. Among the Southern NGOs, 4% were from Asia, 3% from Africa, and 2% from Latin America; 5% had no permanent headquarters or only rotating headquarters. Most of the INGOs were professional associations or worked in the trade or business fields (27%), followed by organizations in research and education fields (21%), environmental protection (7%), religion (6%), human rights or peace (6%), culture, sports, or recreation (6%), and health care (5%). Further INGOs in the fields of politics, social welfare, humanitarian relief and development made up groups of approximately 3% each, and 13% of the analyzed organizations simultaneously worked in several fields or fell into another category not specified in the questionnaire.

Regarding their position, most of the respondents identified themselves as CEO or president (26%), head of PR (12%) or senior PR officer (6%). However, a great variety of positions and titles existed among the respondents. Many of them used the open-ended question to specify their position, such as president, vice president, chairman, general secretary, or secretary. Accordingly, for most of the INGOs the CEO or president was responsible for PR (31%). 16% had a separate department. In 12% of the cases, a single PR officer was in charge, and 10% of the INGOs had each department carrying out PR on its own. In 7% of the INGOs, PR was part of the marketing department. A fairly large group of 20% carried out PR through individual part-time employees.

The vast majority of the respondents (94%) said that communication activities of INGOs are very important (69%) or important (25%) for attaining their strategic goals. Only two respondents felt strategic communication is not important for their organization. Hence, strategic communication is highly valued by PR professionals and/or CEOs in these INGOs.

Centralization or Decentralization of International PR (RQ1)

To assess whether systematic differences existed between the INGOs with respect to the degree of centralization or decentralization of international PR all the variables that referred to the elements of the PR management process (research, strategy, target groups, etc.) were entered into a two-step cluster analysis using the Schwarz Bayesian Criterion (BIC). The algorithm calculated a solution with four clusters (Table 30.1). The silhouette coefficient of cohesion and separation, ranging from -1 to +1, indicated a "fair" cluster solution (0.3), meaning that the average distance of a case to members of its own cluster is smaller than the average distance to cases in the other clusters (Norušis, 2011).

The first cluster was the largest and contained 132 INGOs (33.6%). This group was clearly dominated by highly centralized PR functions. For almost all steps in the communication management process, decision-making resided at the INGOs' headquarters. Decisions on measures, the development of strategies and messages, objective setting and the definition of target groups were the central office's main tasks. Only in conducting research was the cluster composition more heterogeneous.

Table 30.1 Cluster Solution for Centralization or Decentralization of Different Elements of PR Management

Element of strategic PR management	Cluster 1	Cluster 2	Cluster 3	Cluster 4
	50% headquarters	59% both collaboratively	54% both independently	40% no-one
Research	15% both independently 14% both collaboratively	12% no one 11% local units	21% both collaboratively 11% headquarters	25% local units 13% both independently
	77% headquarters	74% both collaboratively	67% both independently	30% both collaboratively
Setting objectives	14% both collaboratively 6% both independently	22% headquarters 2% both independently	23% both collaboratively 9% headquarters	24% no-one 22% local units

	72% headquarters	*80% both collaboratively*	*75% both independently*	*35% no-one*

	72% headquarters	*80% both collaboratively*	*75% both independently*	*35% no-one*
Defining target groups	14% both collaboratively 7% both independently	7% both independently 7% headquarters	19% both collaboratively 4% headquarters	30% local units 24% both collaboratively
	80% headquarters	*87% both collaboratively*	*62% both independently*	*24% no-one*
Developing strategies	17% both collaboratively 2% both independently	8% headquarters 4% both independently	23% both collaboratively 14% headquarters	22% both collaboratively 22% local units
	80% headquarters	*76% both collaboratively*	*66% both independently*	*29% local units*
Developing messages	9% both collaboratively 9% both independently	14% headquarters 5% both independently	19% both collaboratively 14% headquarters	22% both collaboratively 21% no-one
	87% headquarters	*89% both collaboratively*	*89% both independently*	*38% local units*
Deciding measures	8% both collaboratively 3% both independently	7% headquarters 4% local units	6% both collaboratively 4% headquarters	32% no-one 13% both collaboratively
	72% headquarters	*86% both collaboratively*	*92% both independently*	*49% local units*
Deciding channels	14% both independently 9% no-one	5% local units 5% no-one	4% no-one 2% both collaboratively	38% no-one 10% both independently
	67% headquarters	*69% both collaboratively*	*74% both independently*	*48% no-one*
Evaluation	11% both collaboratively 11% no-one	17% headquarters 8% no-one	13% no-one 6% both collaboratively	29% local units 19% both independently
Totals (N = 393)[a]	132	85	113	63
Totals in %	33.6%	21.6%	28.8%	16%

[a]The reduced number of cases is due to missing values

Note. All percentages except totals are within-cluster proportions. In each cell, the two categories with highest within-cluster proportions are displayed

In the second cluster, which contained 85 organizations (21.6%), most of the PR planning was performed collaboratively by headquarters and local units, especially the definition of target groups, the development of strategies and messages, and the decisions on measures and channels. Again, conducting research was distributed more heterogeneously.

The third cluster was the second largest with 113 INGOs (28.8%), predominantly containing organizations in which both headquarters and local units coordinated their PR independently. In these cases, the tactical considerations, such as the decisions on measures and channels, primarily fell in this category (approx. 90%), followed by the definition of target groups (75%) and evaluation (74%). Both headquarters and local units also developed strategies, objectives, and messages independently (values above 60%). However, for a considerable percentage of cases, these more strategic functions were coordinated either collaboratively by both units or solely by the central office.

The fourth cluster, containing 16% of the INGOs, was the most diverse in terms of coordinating international PR. It primarily included INGOs whose local units were exclusively in charge of a certain PR function, and those in which the function was not implemented at all. Specifically, research (40%) and evaluation (48%) was not employed at any unit of many INGOs. In most cases local units made tactical decisions about channels (49%) and measures (38%). Decisions about strategies, objectives, and messages were almost evenly distributed among the different forms of coordination.

The descriptive analysis of centralization or decentralization of the PR management process across the four clusters showed that strategy, objective setting and message formulation were the most centralized functions. Decisions on communication channels and research were the most decentralized functions.

A second cluster analysis was conducted for the different disciplines of international PR, including advocacy, crisis communication, donor relations, fundraising, marketing, international media relations, local media relations, and the production of materials (e.g., leaflets). A total of 371 INGOs for which the respondents gave answers in each category was clustered into four groups (silhouette coefficient = 0.3</eq; Table 30.2). The fields of donor relations, fundraising and marketing were especially decisive in separating the clusters. A similar pattern was found for PR disciplines compared to the previous cluster solution.

Again, the first cluster contained mostly INGOs that coordinate the different fields of PR centrally from their headquarters, especially donor relations, fundraising and international media relations.

Table 30.2 Cluster Solution for Centralization or Decentralization of Different Specialized Functions of PR/ Communications

	Cluster 1	Cluster 2	Cluster 3	Cluster 4
PR function	*68% headquarters*	*39% both collaboratively*	*60% both independently*	*67% no-one*
Advocacy	13% both collaboratively 10% no-one	29% headquarters 16% local units	22% both collaboratively 11% headquarters	16% both independently 16% headquarters
	68% headquarters	*44% both collaboratively*	*51% both independently*	*81% no-one*
Crisis communication	14% no-one 10% both collaboratively	31% headquarters 13% local units	18% both collaboratively 16% headquarters	9% both collaboratively 5% local units
	82% headquarters	*53% both collaboratively*	*81% both independently*	*84% no-one*
Donor relations	13% no-one 3% both collaboratively	31% local units 11% headquarters	10% no-one 6% both collaboratively	5% both independently 5% headquarters

	81% headquarters	*60% both collaboratively*	*87% both independently*	*65% no-one*
Fundraising	8% no-one 7% both independently	28% local units 9% headquarters	7% both collaboratively 2% local units	21% headquarters 9% both independently
	71% headquarters	*55% both collaboratively*	*83% both independently*	*70% no-one*
Marketing	11% both independently 9% both collaboratively	18% local units 13% both independently	9% both collaboratively 6% no-one	16% both independently 9% both collaboratively
	74% headquarters	*42% both collaboratively*	*50% both independently*	*47% no-one*
International media relations	13% both collaboratively 11% both independently	36% headquarters 11% no-one	31% headquarters 16% both collaboratively	28% both independently 19% headquarters
	32% headquarters	*55% local units*	*59% both independently*	*42% no-one*
Local media relations	27% local units 22% both collaboratively	34% both collaboratively 8% both independently	39% local units 1% both collaboratively	30% both independently 23% local units
	66% headquarters	*60% both collaboratively*	*79% both independently*	*33% no-one*
Production of materials	19% both collaboratively 10% both independently	23% both independently 10% headquarters	18% both collaboratively 2% local units	25% headquarters 23% both independently
Totals (N = 371)[a]	139	93	82	57
Totals in %	37.5%	25.1%	22.1%	15.4%

[a]The reduced number of cases is due to missing values
Note. All percentages except totals are within-cluster proportions. In each cell, the two categories with highest within-cluster proportions are displayed

Only local media relations were in some cases assigned to local units (27%) or coordinated between both units (22% collaboratively). This was the largest cluster with 38% of all cases.

The collaborative approach was dominant in the second cluster with 25% of all INGOs. However, the distribution of the different forms of coordination between central and local offices was rather heterogeneous. Advocacy, crisis communication and international media relations were either coordinated collaboratively or exclusively assigned to the central office. Donor relations, fundraising and marketing were either both planned and conducted collaboratively by central and local units or autonomously by the local units. Local units were responsible for local media relations in most cases of INGOs in this cluster (55%), followed by INGOs with a collaborative approach (34%).

The third cluster contained 82 organizations (22%) where central and local units planned and conducted the specific PR functions rather independently. This applied primarily to fundraising, marketing, donor relations and the production of materials. For crisis communication, a considerable proportion of INGOs assigned this function exclusively to their headquarters (16%) or at least involved the central office on a collaborative basis (18%). In the case of international media relations, 31% of the INGOs in the cluster controlled this function from the central office. However, for all the variables organizations with rather independent central and local units represented the majority of cases.

In the fourth cluster most INGOs did not implement the specific communication functions at all. In particular, crisis communication (81% of the cluster), donor relations (84%) and marketing (70%) were not coordinated by any unit. The analysis of the degree of centralization or decentralization across all clusters revealed that international media relations, crisis communication and advocacy were the most centralized PR disciplines in these INGOs compared to the other disciplines. Local media relations and marketing were the most decentralized PR functions.

Besides this descriptive analysis of centralization or decentralization of international PR, we looked for differences between the four clusters in terms of their age and their international scope to test H1. The latter was measured by the number of continents that the INGOs covered with their operations according to the respondents. Hence, older INGOs and organizations with higher degrees of geographical range are most likely to be found in the clusters with collaborative or rather autonomous units as opposed to the centralized INGOs and the residual cluster. ANOVA was used to test this assumption by comparing the mean age and the mean number of continents. The assignment of INGOs to one of the four clusters was the independent variable.

For the age of INGOs no significant relationship was found ($F(3, 371) = 2.4$; $p = 0.06$). The operational scope of the INGOs across continents was significantly related to the centralized or decentralized coordination of PR ($F(3, 389) = 9.1$; $p < 0.01$). INGOs with local units and central offices that are both involved in the process of communication management and work rather independently had the highest international scope with an average of 4.3 continents that they cover with their operations. Slightly lower values were found for the collaborative cluster ($M = 3.6$). INGOs with very centralized PR functions were lowest in international scope ($M = 2.9$), followed by the INGOs in the fourth cluster ($M = 3.3$). Similar results were calculated for the second cluster solution. Again, the clusters failed to produce a significant effect on the age of the INGOs ($F(3, 353) = 1.7$; $p = 0.17$), but the number of continents differed significantly between the four types of organizations ($F(3, 367) = 6.5$; $p < 0.01$). The cluster of independent INGOs with both central and local units involved in PR planning showed the highest average of continents ($M = 4.3$) followed by the INGOs with collaborative units ($M = 3.9$). The organizations in the residual cluster ($M = 3.1$) and in the cluster with centralized INGOs ($M = 3.2$) were lowest in international scope. Thus, H1 was confirmed regarding the international scope of INGOs, although they did not significantly differ with respect to their age.

The Use of Integrative Communication Devices (RQ2)

With the second research question we were interested in the communication devices and forms of co-operation that central and local units at INGOs use to coordinate their international communication activities. Out of a list of 12 such devices respondents were asked to indicate which were used in their organizations. On average they used four communication devices ($M = 4.0$; $s = 2.5$). Regular meetings, online communities and regular newsletters were most frequently used in almost half of the INGOs (Table 30.3). Online knowledge databases (34%), formal guidelines (28%), email lists (26%) and regular phone conferences (24%) were less common. Even less used were global codes of practice (20%) or skill-share meetings (17%).

In addition to the overall use of coordination methods, we compared the four different clusters of INGOs in terms of the total number of integrative communication devices they use. The highest average

Table 30.3 Use of Integrative Communication Devices and Forms Of Collaboration

Communication device	Total (N = 440)	Total in %
Regular meetings	210	47.7
Online community	204	46.4
Regular newsletters	199	45.2
Online knowledge base	149	33.9
Formal guidelines	121	27.5
Email lists	113	25.7
Regular phone conferences	106	24.1
Training sessions	98	22.3
Global code of practice	88	20.0
Skill-share meetings	76	17.3
Showcasing of examples	70	15.9
Global media strategy	57	13.0

coordination efforts were found for the clusters with INGOs that involve both central and local units in the coordination of their international communication efforts, either collaboratively (M = 4.6) or rather independently (M = 4.6). The lowest use of integrative communication devices made the organizations in Cluster 4 (M = 3.3) where either no-one or the local units alone are responsible for international PR. INGOs in the cluster of centralized PR functions used on average 3.7 devices. These differences were significant (F(3, 389) = 6.6; p < 0.01). Post-hoc tests showed significant differences between highly centralized and highly decentralized INGOs on the one hand (Clusters 1 and 4) and INGOs with collaborating central and local units (Clusters 2 and 3) on the other hand. H2 was confirmed.

The difference in the use of integrative communication devices between these clusters was most notable in the cases of regular meetings (Chi^2(3) = 12.5; p < 0.01) as well as online communities (Chi^2(3) = 12.3; p < 0.01). These communication devices were used much more often in INGOs that involve both central and local units in the PR management process (Clusters 2 and 3) compared to highly centralized INGOs and INGOs with autonomous local units and/or missing PR functions (Clusters 1 and 4).

Local Responsiveness and the Centralization or Decentralization of International PR (RQ3)

Besides levels and forms of centralization and coordination we analyzed to what extent practitioners at INGOs consider contextual factors in designing and implementing their communication strategies. To test H3, the list of 21 context variables was first reduced to a lower number of dimensions with principal component analysis. A reliable solution with three factors was obtained with a total explained variance of 67% (KMO = 0.94; Bartlett's test: Chi^2(210) = 6886; p < 0.01). With some restrictions, this factor solution is comparable to the three factors of contextual variables proposed by Sriramesh and Verčič (2001). The first component predominantly contained characteristics of the national media systems and public communication (Table 30.4). However, legal restrictions on activism and public attitudes towards activism loaded on this factor. The second factor that emerged was most similar to the factor of societal culture suggested by Sriramesh and Verčič (2001). However, respondents provided similar answers with respect to the importance of language, recent issues and events, history and corporate culture in the local units. The levels of economic and technological development, the political system and legal restrictions on communication formed the third component. With the exception of the activism variables, the third component corresponds roughly to the factor of national infrastructure described by Sriramesh and Verčič (2001).

All factor scores were calculated with the regression method and were used as dependent variables to test H3. The four cluster solutions regarding the centralization or decentralization of the PR management process were used as the independent variable. The three factors of contextual variables (media, infrastructure, and culture) were used as dependent variables. The results showed significant effects on all three contextual factors with the strongest effect on the social/cultural context $(F(3, 389) = 7.2; p < 0.01, Eta^2 = .005)$. The different models of centralization or decentralization also influenced the INGOs' consideration of the media/communication context $(F(3, 389) = 3.0; p < .05; Eta^2 = 0.02)$ as well as the national infrastructure $(F(3, 389) = 3.1; p < 0.05; Eta^2 = 0.02)$.

The lowest scores for all three contextual factors were found in Cluster 4 where the PR function was exclusively assigned to local units or was not implemented at all. The media factor and the culture factor were both rated as most important by respondents in the two clusters of collaborative and rather independent units. Lower scores were calculated for the cluster of centralized INGOs. For the consideration of national infrastructure, however, the INGOs with a strongly centralized PR function had the highest scores, followed by the cluster with collaborative units. Hence, for the media and the culture variables lower degrees of centralization were related to higher degrees of local responsiveness of communication programs. The INGOs in Cluster 4 with autonomous local units and/or a complete lack of certain PR functions were the exception as they operate on a highly decentralized basis, but nevertheless do not consider contextual factors to be important for their international PR activities. For the national infrastructure, an opposite relationship was found. These

Table 30.4 Principal Component Analysis of Contextual Variables that Influence PR

Contextual variable	Components		
	Structures and dynamics of public communication/media	Social and cultural context	National infrastructure
Legal restrictions on journalism	.98		
Legal restrictions on PR	.96		
Degree of media censorship	.93		
Attitude of journalists towards PR	.70		
Structure of media ownership	.69		
Legal restrictions on activism	.67	.31	
Level of literacy among population	.63		
Public attitudes towards activism	.59	.40	
Reach of different media	.57	.20	
National language		.77	
Importance of an issue in the country		.74	
Diversity of languages		.72	
History of the country		.70	.23
Level of activism in that country	.30	.64	
Cultural values	.26	.64	
Recent events in that country		.58	.24
Corporate culture in local units	.26	.52	
Level of economic development			.86
Level of technological development			.79
Political system		.27	.65
Legal restrictions on communication	.47		.51

Note. Rotation method: oblimin direct; total variance explained = 67%; KMO = .94; Bartlett's test: Chi²(210) = 6886; p < .01; factor loadings below .2 were suppressed contextual variables were most considered at centralized INGOs, although the more decentralized INGOs attributed less importance to such factors.

However, these relationships are only descriptive and do not represent sufficient evidence that confirms H3 because additional post hoc tests failed to produce significant differences between the clusters. In fact, only INGOs in Cluster 4 with very low scores of local responsiveness differed significantly from the INGOs in the remaining three clusters with higher levels of local responsiveness in their PR programs.

Discussion and Implications for NGO Communications

This study's primary goal was to gain better insight into how organizations in the global civil society sector manage communication across borders. The results suggest that, with some restrictions, INGOs should indeed be regarded as strategically mature. It was found that they highly value their strategic communications functions for attaining organizational goals. However, as INGOs often operate in resource-scarce environments, they do not always have the ability to establish an entire department for PR to integrate all communication functions. Consequently, this function is often assigned to the INGO's most senior manager (CEO or president) in both central and local units. Although they regard strategic communication a primary asset for their success, this might limit INGOs' ability to achieve their international communication goals as the PR function is not sufficiently separated from other functions and CEOs in many cases might lack the necessary background and time resources for setting up professional international PR programs. Thus, INGOs should look for ways to compensate for the lack of resources dedicated to international PR. A possible solution, which is already practiced by many INGOs such as the World Wide Fund for Nature (WWF), is the formation of alliances with MNCs. Actually, business organizations increasingly try to improve their reputation and perceptions of corporate social responsibility by partnering with NGOs. However, this may also result in conflict, reputational risks and financial dependency, especially for the INGOs. Given these risks, which in the case of the WWF already resulted in major reputational crises in 2011, INGOs might be better advised to form networks with other civil society organizations co-operating and sharing the PR function. This way they would be more likely to benefit from synergy effects and improve their international coordination and advocacy.

To measure local responsiveness in the communication programs of INGOs we applied the three-factor structure of variables influencing PR across borders proposed by Sriramesh and Verčič (2001). This taxonomy turned out to be empirically viable. However, the factor analysis also revealed slight differences. Respondents regarded public attitudes towards activism and legal restrictions on activism to be characteristic of the media environment rather than the national infrastructure. This might be due to the practitioners' understanding of the term "public attitudes," which they probably construed as the tone of the media coverage on activism in a certain country. In addition, legal restrictions on activism constrain INGOs' access to media organizations and the national media agenda. This might explain the strong correlation of this item with the media–public communication factor. In contrast, the level of activism in a certain country was correlated with the factor of culture as it refers to the historically grown disposition of people to engage in activism and to commit themselves to social causes. Our findings also revealed additional aspects of the cultural environment of a country (national history, recent events, importance of an issue, language and diversity of languages), which were perceived by practitioners to influence their decisions on international strategic communication. Future studies should add these variables and apply confirmatory factor analysis to validate the three-factor structure.

Another goal of the present study was to identify the prevailing types of structures and coordination mechanisms used by NGOs that manage strategic communication across nations and cultures. The results suggest that management scholars' assumptions regarding NGO structures (Lindenberg

& Bryant, 2001) are also viable in terms of the PR function. With the help of cluster analysis, four types of INGOs were identified: (a) organizations with strongly centralized PR functions that use local units to implement their decisions; (b) organizations with central and local units that develop and conduct their international PR collaboratively; (c) organizations that allow their local units to operate quite autonomously, but still undertake substantial efforts to coordinate their activities; and (d) INGOs that seem to be strategically immature as they do not cover many steps of strategic communication planning and lack some of the basic PR functions.

The first cluster is most similar to what Young (1992), as well as Lindenberg and Bryant (2001), described as the "federated model", because headquarters possess most of the decision-making power. To a certain extent this group may even include some INGOs of the "unitary corporate" type. In the second type of INGO that was found, local subsidiaries have much more influence on communication programs, especially on the tactical level. However, they still involve the central unit in almost all steps of managing PR. That is why we tend to classify such organizations as examples of a more decentralized type of federation. The third cluster contained INGOs with very autonomous local units, although they still made substantial efforts of international coordination. This type best fits what has been described as the "confederated model." The smallest group of organizations was assigned to the fourth cluster. The central and local units in these organizations are only loosely coupled and seem to lack efforts of cross-national coordination. In addition, they do not have a real strategic approach in their communication programs, which is probably due to their lack of financial resources or staff.

An overview of these four types of INGOs in terms of their approach to international PR is presented in Table 30.5. Future studies will have to show whether this classification is viable. In addition, this might serve as a benchmark to compare individual INGOs to existing models or to track changes in the predominant management models over time.

The data that was produced by this survey does not say anything about the actual effectiveness of the management models and structures that were identified. This will be the task of future research that should relate internal structures and different strategic communication approaches to indicators of external effectiveness of international PR. Usually, standardized approaches (global integration) were related to higher levels of internal efficiency, and higher degrees of local responsiveness of PR programs were assumed to increase external effectiveness (Lim, 2010). Based on these assumptions, the confederated model might be most suited to achieving strategic goals across borders, as these INGOs seem to be most aware of cultural, social and communication-related context variables in their strategic choices. Indeed, increasing complexity in terms of international scope seems to favor or even require such a model. INGOs of this type were found to cover the highest number of continents in this study. On the other hand, it was shown that these organizations need to attribute more resources to their internal coordination, which means their communication management is more costly and time consuming. However, given the reputational risks that stem from being perceived as ethnocentric, Western-based or bureaucratic and ineffective organizations, these resources are a worthwhile investment.

Conclusions

Surveying communication managers at 440 INGOs, with 70% of the organizations operating on more than one continent and 30% on six continents, produced insights into structures and strategic orientations in the international communication management practice of civil society actors in the twenty-first century. Although their importance has been recognized in the management literature (L. Lewis, 2005), international PR of INGOs were barely examined. In addition, most of the international PR literature has been limited to descriptions of PR in various countries and has taken into account neither civil society organizations nor the extent to which organizations take contextual factors into consideration in their communication strategies. Therefore, this study will help to advance the study of truly international PR as practiced by transnational organizations.

Table 30.5 Classification of INGOs According to Their International Orientation and Coordination Mechanisms in PR

Type of INGO[a]	Role of central units[a]	Role of local units[a]	Co-ordination efforts[b]	Strategic consideration of contextual factors[c]	International scope in membership/operations[d]
Federations with dominating headquarters	Strong headquarters take most of the strategic decisions	Implement decisions made in central units	Moderate, less interactive	Consideration of national infrastructure; tendency to neglect cultural and communication-related context	Low
Collaborative federations	Decision-making based on consensus between central and local units; delegation to headquarters for some strategic issues (e.g., crisis communication, international media relations)		High, more interactive	Consideration of cultural and communication-related context; lesser importance of national infrastructure	Moderate
Confederations	Umbrella-type co-ordination role with occasional decision-making power in overarching questions (e.g., crisis communication)	Rather independent, on the tactical level; occasional collaboration with central unit or delegation to central unit on the strategic level	High, more interactive	Great consideration of cultural and communication-related context; lesser importance of national infrastructure	High
Strategically immature INGOs	Scant involvement in strategic issues; certain PR functions do not exist	Tactical autonomy; lack of strategic orientation; certain PR functions do not exist	Very low, less interactive	Tendency to neglect contextual factors	Low

[a]This classification is based on a validated two-step cluster analysis
[b]The differences in the use of co-ordination devices between these types of INGOs were significant (p < .05)
[c]The differences in the consideration of contextual factors between these types of INGOs are only descriptive and did not reach statistical significance (p > .05)
[d]measured by the number of continents the INGOs cover; these differences were significant (p < .05)

Our findings seem to confirm the suspicions of some management and communication scholars: INGOs should be viewed as relevant actors with strong strategic orientation in the global arena of business and politics. This applies to the ways they organize and implement strategic communications across national and cultural borders. In our study, approximately two thirds of the respondents stated that their organizations cover all elements of strategic planning, implementation and evaluation with respect to their international PR programs. Almost all communication professionals claimed that they highly value communications for attaining strategic organizational goals. Thus, research on international PR should increasingly investigate INGOs as organizations "in and of their own right" (Lambell et al., 2008, p. 75) alongside governments, intergovernmental organizations and MNCs. However, almost half of the INGOs in this study either had highly centralized PR functions (Cluster 1) or had failed to establish well-coordinated communication programs (Cluster 4). It is questionable whether these organizations are able to cope with their culturally heterogeneous stakeholders (including voluntary members) or if these organizations can manage to balance the global and the local in their communication strategies. Based on our insights from the literature, these INGOs should move towards more collaborative models of coordination of international PR that involve both central and local units with differing degrees of autonomy (Clusters 2 and 3). These two types of INGOs (confederations and collaborative federations) correspond most closely to common recommendations in the literature on international PR management of MNCs (Lim, 2010; Wakefield, 2000). They coordinate communication at both headquarters and internationally, they offer more opportunities for interaction between staff of central and local units, and they tend to give tactical autonomy to local subsidiaries even though their global strategy is coordinated internationally.

Perspectives for Strategic NGO Communications

The presumably increasing professionalism of INGOs, in terms of managing their reputation and influencing public perceptions of a broad range of globally relevant issues, will have a greater impact on global politics, international business and cultural dynamics in the future. This finding highlights the need for more systematic research on this type of organization and more detailed investigations of the ways that INGOs practice strategic communication beyond "fashionable case studies" (Tkalac & Pavicic, 2009, p. 812) of well-known INGOs. International NGOs organize and coordinate their communication functions in manifold ways which roughly correspond to the models of managing international strategic communication at MNCs (Huck, 2005). Future research will have to produce further insights into the relationship between these models and the external effectiveness of the NGOs' communication programs. This will also allow for a better understanding of the actual impact of NGO communication on the global political agenda, nation images and important international issues such as global warming and social justice.

NGOs often have to struggle with a lack of resources and staff, for which they have to compensate by means of voluntary participation, donations and cheaper ways to attain their communication goals. In many NGOs, CEOs and presidents are the key persons that manage strategic communication. Future research will have to answer the question of who these persons are and what background they have, especially with regard to communication. Another important aspect will be the measurement of communication processes and results. To date, NGOs still lack sophisticated models for measuring their reputation. In addition, NGOs need reliable and affordable tools to link strategic communication activities to the achievement of program goals (e.g., lower poverty rates or increasing school attendance of children in certain regions). Communication scholars have only just begun to focus their research on these issues.

Another trend in NGO communications seems to be the establishment of strategic alliances between major NGOs and MNCs. The question of whether NGOs really benefit from this approach, also in terms of their communication goals, urgently needs further research. In many cases this might lead to the consequence that NGOs have to face reputational crises and allegations of fraud. In the crisis communication literature, however, NGOs have played a marginal role. As in PR research in general, they have mostly been studied in their role as inconvenient stakeholders of MNCs. Neither the crisis preparedness of NGOs nor their use of crisis response strategies have been systematically analyzed, although various NGO scandals and crises (Gibelman & Gelman, 2000) might indicate that the so-called "new super brands" (Wootliff & Deri, 2001) are eroding with regard to reputation and trust.

Further research in this respect would also allow for a better understanding of the role of strategic communication in the globalization process and its contribution to "social good" in an international environment (Sriramesh & Verčič, 2007). The systematic study of the peculiarities of NGO communications, such as their often sophisticated use of online communication and social media, would also help to assess the impact NGOs have on possible changes in the PR profession in terms of strategies, ethics and role perception. Future research on strategic communication of NGOs should extend beyond the PR discipline and look at related and/or overlapping types of strategic communication such as public diplomacy where NGOs have been regarded as top priority on the research agenda (Gilboa, 2008).

References

Banks, S. P. (1995). *Multicultural public relations. A social-interpretive approach*. Thousand Oaks, CA: Sage Publications.

Bartlett, C. A., & Ghoshal, S. (2002). *Managing across borders: The transnational solution* (2. ed.). Boston, MA: Harvard Business School Press.

Blood, R. (2005). Should NGOs be viewed as "political corporations"? *Journal of Communication Management, 9*(2), 120–133.

Boli, J., & Thomas, G. M. (1997). World culture in the world polity: A century of international non-governmental organization. *American Sociological Review, 62*(2), 171–190.

Botan, C. (1992). International public relations: Critique and reformulation. *Public relations Review, 18*(2), 11.

Broom, G. M., Cutlip, S. M., & Center, A. H. (2009). *Effective public relations* (10th ed.). Upper Saddle River, NJ: Prentice Hall, Pearson.

Couper, M. P., & Bosnjak, M. (2010). Internet surveys. In J. D. Wright & P. V. Marsden (Eds.), *Handbook of survey research* (2nd ed., pp. 527–550). Bingley, England: Emerald.

Culbertson, H. M. (1996). Introduction. In H. M. Culbertson & N. Chen (Eds.), *International public relations: a comparative analysis* (pp. 1–13). Mahwah, NJ: Lawrence Erlbaum.

Dozier, D. M., & Lauzen, M. M. (2000). Liberating the intellectual domain from the practice: Public relations, activism, and the role of the scholar. *Journal of Public Relations Research, 12,* 3–22.

Edelman (2011). 2011 Edelman Trust Barometer: Findings. *Edelman trust barometer: Annual global opinion leaders study.* Retrieved from http://www.edelman.com/trust/2011/uploads/Edelman%20Trust%20Barometer%20Global%20Deck.pdf

Fritsch, A. (2010). *Implementing specific principles of global public relations: The case of international non-governmental organizations.* Unpublished diploma thesis, Department of Media Studies, Ilmenau University of Technology, Ilmenau, Germany.

Gibelman, M., & Gelman, S. R. (2000). *Very public scandals: an analysis of how and why nongovernmental organizations get in trouble—a working paper.* Paper presented at the International Society for Third-Sector Research (ISTR) Fourth International Conference, Dublin, Ireland. Retrieved from http://www.istr.org/conferences/dublin/workingpapers/gibelman.pdf

Gilboa, E. (2008). Searching for a theory of public diplomacy. The annals of the *Amercian Academy of Political and Social Science, 616,* 55–77.

Huck, S. (2005). *Internationale Unternehmenskommunikation: Ergebnisse einer qualitativen Befragung von Kommunikationsverantwortlichen in 20 multinationalen Großunternehmen* [International corporate communication: Results of qualitative interviews with communication professionals in 20 big multinational corporations] (Working paper). Department of Communication Studies and Journalism,University of Hohenheim, Stuttgart, Germany.

Hudson, B. A., & Bielefeld, W. (1997). Structures of multinational nonprofit organizations. *Nonprofit Management and Leadership, 8*(1), 31–49.

Lambell, R., Ramia, G., Nyland, C., & Michelotti, M. (2008). NGOs and international business research: Progress, prospects and problems. *International Journal of Management Reviews, 10*(1), 75–92.

Lewis, D. (2003). Theorizing the organization and management of non-governmental development organizations: Towards a composite approach. *Public Management Review, 5*(3), 325–344.

Lewis, L. (2005). The civil society sector: A review of critical issues and research agenda for organizational communication scholars. *Management Communication Quarterly, 19*(2), 238–267.

Lim, J. S. (2010). Global integration or local responsiveness? Multinational corporations' public relations strategies and cases. In G. J. Golan, T. J. Johnson & W. Wanta (Eds.), *International media communication in a global age* (pp. 299–318). New York: Routledge.

Lindenberg, M., & Bryant, C. (2001). *Going global: Transforming relief and development NGOs.* Bloomfield, CT: Kumarian Press.

Molleda, J.-C. (2000). *Integrative public relations in international business: the impact of administrative models and subsidiary roles.* Unpublished doctoral dissertation. University of South Carolina, Columbia, SC.

Molleda, J.-C. (2009). Global public relations. *Essential knowledge project.* Retrieved from http://www. instituteforpr.org/topics/global-public-relations/

Molleda, J.-C., & Laskin, A. V. (2005). Global, international, comparative and regional public relations knowledge from 1990 to 2005: A quantitative content analysis of academic and trade publications. Retrieved May 12, 2011, from http://www.instituteforpr.org/topics/pr-knowledge-2005/

Molleda, J.-C., & Laskin, A. (2010). Coordination and control of global public relations to manage cross-national conflict shifts. In G. J. Golan, T. J. Johnson & W. Wanta (Eds.), *International media communication in a global age* (pp. 319–344). New York: Routledge.

Murphy, P., & Dee, J. (1992). Du Pont and Greenpeace: The dynamics of conflict between corporations and activist groups. *Journal of Public Relations Research, 4*(1), 3–20.

Naudé, A. M. E., Froneman, J. D., & Atwood, R. A. (2004). The use of the internet by ten South African non-governmental organizations: a public relations perspective. *Public Relations Review, 30*(1), 87–94.

Norušis, M. J. (2011). *IBM SPSS statistics 19 statistical procedures companion.* Upper Saddle River, CA: Pearson.

Salamon, L. M., & Anheier, H. K. (1999). *The emerging sector revisited: A summary* (2nd ed.). Baltimore, MD: Institute for Policy Studies, Center for Civil Society Studies, Johns Hopkins University.

Seo, H., Kim, J. Y., & Yang, S.-U. (2009). Global activism and new media: a study of transnational NGOs' online public relations. *Public Relations Review, 35,* 123–126.

Sisco, H. F., Collins, E. L., & Zoch, L. M. (2010). Through the looking glass: A decade of Red Cross crisis response and situational crisis communication theory. *Public Relations Review, 36*(1), 21–27.

Sriramesh, K., & Verčič, D. (2001). International public relations: A framework for future research. *Journal of Communication Management, 6*(2), 103–117.

Sriramesh, K., & Verčič, D. (2007). Introduction to this special section: The impact of globalization on public relations. *Public Relations Review, 33*(2), 355–359.

Stark Biddle, C. (1984). *The management needs of private voluntary organisations.* Washington, DC: USAID.

Taylor, M. (2000). Cultural variance as a challenge to global public relations. A case study of the Coca-Cola scare in Europe. *Public Relations Review, 26*(3), 17.

Taylor, M. (2005). Nongovernmental organizations (NGOS). In R. L. Heath (Ed.), *Encyclopedia of public relations* (Vol. 2, pp. 576–578). Thousand Oaks, CA: Sage.

Taylor, M., & Kent, M. L. (1999). Challenging assumptions of international public relations. When government is the most important public. *Public Relations Review, 25*(2), 14.

Taylor, M., Kent, M. L., & White, W. J. (2001). How activist organizations are using the Internet to build relationships. *Public Relations Review, 27,* 263–284.

Tkalac, A., & Pavicic, J. (2009). Nongovernmental organizations and international public relations. In K. Sriramesh & D. Verčič (Eds.), *The global public relations handbook: Theory, research, and practice* (2nd ed., pp. 807–821). New York, NY: Routledge.

United Nations Development Programme. (2002). Human development report 2002: Deepening democracy in a fragmented world. *Human Development Report.* New York, NY: Oxford University Press.

Verčič, D. (2003). Public relations of movers and shakers: Transnational corporations. In K. Sriramesh & D. Vercic (Eds.), *The global public relations handbook. Theory, research and practice* (pp. 478–489). Mahwah, NJ: Lawrence Erlbaum.

Wakefield, R. I. (2000). World-class public relations: A model for effective public relations in the multinational. *Journal of Communication Management, 5*(1), 59–71.

Wakefield, R. I. (2001). Effective public relations in the multinational organization. In R. L. Heath (Ed.), *Handbook of public relations* (pp. 639–647). Thousand Oaks, CA: Sage.

Wilcox, D. L., Ault, P. H., Agee, W. K., & Cameron, G. T. (2000). *Public relations: Strategies and tactics* (6th ed.). New York: Addison-Wesley Longman.

Wootliff, J., & Deri, C. (2001). NGOs: The new super brands. *Corporate Reputation Review, 4*(2), 157–164.

Young, D. R. (1989). Local autonomy in a franchise age: structural change in national voluntary associations. *Nonprofit and Voluntary Sector Quarterly, 18*(2), 101–117.

Young, D. R. (1992). Organising principles for international advocacy associations. *Voluntas: International Journal of Voluntary and Nonprofit Organizations, 3*(1), 1–28.

31

Terrorism as Strategic Communication

Liane Rothenberger

[A]n act of terrorism is in reality an act of communication. For the terrorist the message matters, not the victim. [. . .] In our view terrorism can best be understood as a violent communication strategy. There is a sender, the terrorist, a message generator, the victim, and a receiver, the enemy and/or the public. [. . .] Without communication, as we have said at the beginning of this chapter, there can be no terrorism.

Schmid & de Graaf, 1982, p. 14–15

Terrorists do not communicate nonsensically; they calculate and follow an intrinsic logic (Crenshaw, 1998). This chapter discusses how far the concept of strategic communication can be applied to terrorist groups. Therefore, it is necessary to review the state of research related to terrorism and strategic communication, before presenting the results of various case studies.

Defining terrorism

The word "terror" comes from Latin "terror, terroris" and signifies "scare" or "fright". The Latin verb "terrere" means "I scare (sb.)" (Stowasser, 1994, p. 510). Early perpetrators of terrorist deeds were the Zealots and the Sicarii in Antiquity as well as the Assassins in the Middle Ages. Their goal was "a common and long lasting state of fear and uncertainty of the ruling elites" (Heine, 2004, p. 61). The term "terrorism" appeared for the first time in everyday speech during the Jacobin regime: the reign of Maximilian de Robespierre at the end of the French Revolution (1793–1794) was called "régime de la Terreur" because of the mass executions by guillotine. "In its origins, the term [terrorism] usually meant violence carried out by a government or a ruling order, rather than, as later, the actions of antigovernment rebels" (P. Jenkins, 2003, p. 27). This was the case in the 19th century when anarchists Pierre Proudhon and Mikhail Bakunin made a point for the legitimacy to overthrow the Russian Tsarist regime by the help of terrorist deeds. In times of democracy, they argued, terrorist deeds were not acceptable, because of other possibilities of participation.

Keeping this evolution in mind, it can already be stated that terrorism is a heterogeneous and socially constructed phenomenon, which is considered differently depending on the (cultural, linguistic etc.) context. In the following section, relevant definitions of terrorism and common characteristics will be elaborated on. The biggest pool of definitions can be found in political science, for example in the works of B. Hoffman (2007) and B. M. Jenkins (1981), but also social scientists, such as Waldmann (2000, 2005), historians, such as Laqueur (1978, 1982), and communication scientists, such as Picard (1993), have dealt with the topic.

What is terrorism? Historian Walter Laqueur described it as the use of covert violence by a group for political purposes (Laqueur, 1982, p. 100). Normally, terrorism is directed against governments, more seldom against other groups, classes or parties. Schmid and Jongman state: "[T]errorism is a method of combat in which random or symbolic victims serve as an instrumental *target of violence*" (italics in the original) (Schmid & Jongman, 1988, p. 1). When Schmid and Jongman counted the words in 109 definitions of terrorism, they found that the words "violence," "force," "political," "fear" and "threat" were used most often (Schmid & Jongman, 1988, p. 5).

Also in the 1980s, Signorelli and Gerbner investigated definitions of terrorism and stated a general consensus: "[A] terroristic act is typically defined as one involving violence by, among, or against states or other authorities in order to spread fear and to make a statement, usually political" (Signorelli & Gerbner, 1988, p. xi). This definition includes "terror from above," that means, violence conducted by a government. Other definitions exclude this explicitly, defining terrorists as subnational actors committing violent deeds against civilians (Richardson, 2007, p. 64). Martin, like Signorelli and Gerbner, also analyzed various definitions of terrorism, settling on the following list of common characteristics: "[T]he use of illegal force, Subnational actors, Unconventional methods, Political motives, Attacks against 'soft' civilian and passive military targets, Acts aimed at purposefully affecting an audience" (Martin, 2006, p. 47).

The amount of literature on the topic of terrorism increased significantly in the 1970s and 1980s following more and more terrorist acts that were triggered by the development of more far-reaching and faster media coverage (Alali & Eke, 1991, p. 1). Having in mind the "mass-mediated terrorism," Nacos defined terrorism as "political violence against noncombatants/innocents that is committed *with the intention to publicize the deed, to gain publicity and thereby public and government attention*" (italics in the original) (Nacos, 2007, p. 26).

Resonance in public is one of the main goals of terrorists for committing their acts. Furthermore they want to destabilize the political, economic and/or social system they deem illegal or oppressive. Thus,

> Terrorism can be briefly defined as coercive intimidation or more fully as the systematic use or murder, injury, and destruction or threat of same to create a climate of terror, to publicize a cause, and to coerce a wider target into submitting to its aims.
>
> *Wilkinson, 1990, p. 27*

Wilkinson added unpredictability and arbitrariness of the attack as essential characteristics of terrorism (Wilkinson, 1990, p. 28).

Similarly, Picard stated: "[A]n important objective of many terrorist attacks is the creation of the *propaganda of the deed,* that is, the act itself carrying messages" (italics in the original) (Picard, 1993, p. 13). The message then is that not all people support the state's status quo, that the authorities do not have everything under control, and that the terrorists' demands have to be taken seriously.

Miller sustained the notion of propaganda. In his opinion, terrorism is "an instrument of political violence [. . .]. The propaganda of the deed as a means of creating political change through fear" (Miller, 1982, p. v). Furthermore he stated that "terrorism was then and is now a mixture of propaganda and theatre" (Miller, 1982, p. v). Terrorists want to provoke the government by breaking civil norms and standards without any respect for humanitarian conventions. That is what distinguishes terrorism from war. "It is, after all, one of the outstanding features of terrorism that there is no battle, that one armed organization commits atrocities against unarmed, unprepared civilians who offer no resistance, against neutrals and mere bystanders" (Schmid & Jongman, 1988, p. 13). Bockstette viewed one of the main characteristics of terrorism as exploiting the media to achieve a goal. "Terrorism is defined as political violence in an asymmetrical conflict that is designed to induce terror and psychic fear (sometimes indiscriminate) through the violent victimization and destruction of noncombatant targets (sometimes iconic symbols). Such acts are meant to send a message from an illicit clandestine organization. The purpose of terrorism is to exploit the media in order to achieve maximum attainable publicity as an amplifying force multiplier in order to influence the targeted audience(s) in order to reach short- and midterm political goals and/or desired long-term end states" (Bockstette, 2008, p. 8). Bockstette substantiated: "[T]errorism uses a strategy that primarily relies on the symbolic strength of the act. The use of terror serves not primarily the purpose of fighting, injuring or destroying the opponent. Rather, its primary purpose lies in the conveying of messages to the target audience(s)" (Bockstette, 2008, p. 8).

Terrorists systematically and purposefully challenge governments; it is a struggle for power, relying on physical and psychological effects (B. Hoffman, 2007, p. 23). "Terrorism is the exercise of violence or the threat of violence against an unarmed and/or unsuspecting population to coerce it to meet the demands of the aggressor" (Biernatzki, 2002, p. 5). But how do terrorists force the population or at least the government to react or bring about changes? How can they reach a big audience if their bomb detonates locally? The media play a crucial role in the process of distribution of a message. How media forms part of terrorists' communication strategy, will be examined after a focus on definitions of strategic communication.

Defining Strategic Communication

As there are various classifications for strategic communication, the focus within this chapter will fall on definitions that can be applied to terrorist groups as organizations. The approach taken by Hallahan and his colleagues seems the most fitting one. These authors defined strategic communication as "purposeful use of communication by an organization to fulfill its mission" (Hallahan, Holtzhausen, van Ruler, Verčič & Sriramesh, 2007, p. 3). In the present case, the organization is a terrorist group. Theoretically speaking, it can be seen as a proper and self-contained communicative entity. "Strategic communication focuses on how the organization presents and promotes itself through the intentional activities of its leaders, employees, and communication practitioners" (Hallahan et al., 2007, p. 7). These activities can include "a variety of persuasive, cooperative, and coercive instruments" (Gregory, 2005, p. 7). Regarding terrorist groups, coercive and forceful instruments prevail, but instruments of persuasion and co-operation are getting more and more important. "A strategy is a plan for action that sets priorities and uses resources to achieve goals. Strategic logic in any endeavor involves determination of specific goals (ends) and choices among instruments (means) needed to achieve them" (Gregory, 2005, p. 7). Gregory distinguished between discourse logic and instrumental logic to achieve goals. Discourse logic refers to "reasoned discourse on ideas and values with the goal of reaching shared understandings" (Gregory, 2005, p. 39), and instrumental logic includes "advocacy activities that seek to influence opinions, decisions, and actions" (Gregory, 2005, p. 39). For ordinary political or civil groups, norms and values limit the choice of action in the public sphere. The actions of terrorist groups, however, deliberately and intentionally differ from norms and societal values, provoking the government by breaking communication rules and even military fighting conventions. Terrorists often employ their strategies *against* the existing political system but they also can fight *for* a specific interest. "At its core, terrorism is a tactic that individuals and groups choose to employ in the service of political goals" (Wright-Neville 2010, p. xi). It is contestable that the term "tactic" suffices to describe the sophisticated protocol of terrorist actions. Following Bockstette's approach, it should rather be referred to as "strategic communication management." "Strategic communication management is defined as the systematic planning and realization of information flow, communication, media development and image care in a long-term horizon. It conveys deliberate message(s) through the most suitable media to the designated audience(s) at the appropriate time to contribute and achieve the desired long-term effect" (Bockstette, 2008, p. 9). From a more general point of view, one should not limit strategic communication to a long-term horizon, but also include short- and midterm goals.

An overall strategy consists of different single tactics, which will be described in the following paragraph. Some of them accord with Bockstette's (2008, p. 9) scheme of a strategic communication management planning process. The overall goal of the strategy is to state objectives and communicate causes. This can be seen in the light of persuasion (e.g., via violence or physical force and persuasion techniques such as letters claiming responsibility). "Strategic communication is about informational, persuasive, discursive, as well as relational communication when used in a context of an organization's mission" (Hallahan et al., 2007, p. 17). The ultimate goal for which the strategies are applied, is legitimization and finally power. Harmon, summarizing Sendero Luminoso leader Guzmán, speaks of the dimension of "construction" which goes along with the dimension of "destruction" (Harmon, 2008, p. 39).

Most of the time terrorist groups concentrate on one main message and its repetition. The main message sometimes can already be derived from the group's label, name or branding (e.g. "freedom," "homeland," a certain date). Furthermore, the different audiences play a crucial role. It is not only choosing targets, victims, a certain (ethnic or intercultural) public, and recruits that makes different communication strategies necessary. The group also has to think about competitors, analyze their strategy and apply a different one (see for example the IRA (Irish Republican Army) splinter groups in Northern Ireland) (Korstian, 2008). In every case, strategic communication has to be adapted to available human and material resources, such as technical equipment and financial and moral support of the diaspora network. The terrorist groups are in need of efficient structures and talented people to implement their strategic communication concepts. Strategic communication also refers to advertising, product marketing, looking for suitable media for message-transfer, including organizations' own publications and interpersonal communication. Key questions could therefore be: Which goal? Which channel? Which audience? Which message? And of course, evaluation and feedback also form part of the communication plan.

Regarding the choice of channel, there has been a significant change. "During the 1990s, terrorists communicated with their audience(s) by more traditional means, such as journalist interviews, fax, face-to-face propaganda and even press conferences" (Bockstette, 2008, p. 12). The discovery of TV as a very important channel or stage for transmitting messages had already taken place at the beginning of the 1970s. For example, when in 1972 the Palestinian terrorist group Black September took members of the Israeli Olympic team hostage, millions of viewers watching the Olympic Games turned to watching the hostage taking, thus providing a huge audience for the terrorists. In these times, terrorism was transformed to an international phenomenon. And today, the importance of the Internet in regard to strategic communication should not be underestimated (Rothenberger, 2012).

Stakeholders in the Terrorism Process

If terrorists want to communicate strategically, they have to know about their respective target groups, in terms of the recipients of their (political) messages. In times of mass media, one of the main channels for message distribution is the (online and offline) media. The media do not just mirror the conflict, but actively frame the discussion and assess facts and opinions. The locally limited audience, which witnessed the terrorist act, will be replaced by a dispersed mass audience when the mass media communicate the deed to a broad public. Thus, the media present a stage for the terrorist act, inviting a big audience to watch; the media act as a multiplier and reach the whole (political, societal, etc.) system, which might be scared by the news.

Besides the media and civilians, politicians represent another pivotal target for terrorists. In this rectangle of (inter)national communication between terrorists, politicians or government, and media

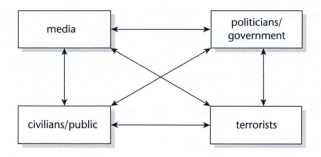

Figure 31.1   Rectangle of Communication

and civilians or publics, depicted in Figure 31.1, every stakeholder can communicate uni-, bi- or multilaterally, not forgetting internal communication within the respective group as well as communication to competing groups such as political opponents, rival publishers and competitors from other terrorist groups. Very often, the communication processes take place synchronously; hence, it is the terrorists' task to attend on multiple relations. The rectangle indicates that the terrorists' target group is not the people killed in the terror attack, but the wider circle of all the people who share certain attributes—albeit that those people merely belong to the nation that the terrorist group is challenging. "[T]he political terrorist's victim is symbolic. A victim is chosen who is representative of a target group that is strategically involved in the terrorist's political goals" (Schaffert, 1992, p. 44). But the target group is not limited to the wider public, the government, and the national majority contradicting the terrorists' goals; the terrorist group also wants to reach the social class or minority they claim to fight for, as well as competing political or social movements.

The stakeholders have different goals and therefore have to apply different communication strategies. The politicians want to get re-elected, the media strive for a high print run or audience ratings, the civilians aspire to security and wealth, and the terrorists want to change the political status quo and recruit like-minded people. A good example for unsuccessful political strategic communication is the diverging government–media framing in the aftermath of the Madrid bombing in March 2004 (Canel, 2011).

History provides many examples for terrorists' target-oriented communication, such as sending letters of responsibility to the media or politicians, talking to journalists or providing them with written statements during a kidnapping, and providing internal information via password-protected Internet sites. If the terrorists communicate successfully, they will induce fear and insecurity in society and even change public opinion. This can be done in a two-step flow of action and communication: The terrorist act creates a climate of fear (step one): the government restricts civil rights for security reasons, and the people reject these restrictions and suddenly turn against the government. The destabilization of the social order can even culminate in a societal collapse (Townshend, 2005, p. 25), clearing the way for revolution (step two). Thus, the terrorists have reached their goal via a counter-reaction of the ones in power. The media provide the terrorists with feedback on their success in changing public opinion, because public discussions will be reflected and commented on in the media.

Terrorism as Label

One of the main factors determining the audience's reception of terrorist events is how the group is labeled in the media. As stated above, it is one of the terrorists' goals not to be called "terrorists" in public, because of the very negative impact of the term, so they call their group something with more positive connotations, like "freedom fighter" or "rebels." To a large extent, communication is language. In this respect, terrorists have to be very sensitive if they want to communicate successfully. One of their strategies is to label the group with a term that transmits a connotation of legitimacy.

According to Rapoport (1977, p. 46) the Russian anarchists in the nineteenth century proudly called themselves "terrorists," and later on Trotsky spoke of the benefits of the "Red terror." But regarding modern terrorism, these aspects are different:

> [T]he first group to describe *itself* as a terrorist organization was the one widely known as 'The Stern Gang' [. . .]. Today, the term has so many abusive connotations that no terrorist will ever call himself one publicly, and he will make every effort to pin that term on his enemy.
>
> *Rapoport, 1977, p. 46*

Labeling the enemy a terrorist forms part of the strategic communication by means of which a party legalizes its own actions. "It has become an axiom that terrorism describes acts of violence committed by others and that similar violence committed by one's own nation, or by those with whom one sympathizes, is legitimate violence" (Picard, 1993, p. 3).

Calling someone a terrorist is ascribing to them attributes like inhumanity, delinquency, and lack of political assertiveness:

> [T]o label is to call something or someone by a name. *Terrorism* itself is, after all, a label. [. . .] In discourse, labeling provides quick, shorthand identification for whatever is labeled. Using the word *terrorism* to identify a violent attack on civilians in a marketplace gives this violence a quick and easily understood name.
>
> *Tuman, 2003, p. 32*

All political negotiations with terrorist groups are *a priori* forbidden. From the government's point of view, it is an asymmetrical conflict against an illegal perpetrator. Jenkins decried using the term "terrorist" just because it sounds dramatic and raises public awareness:

> [I]t is generally pejorative. Some governments are prone to label all violent acts as terrorism, committed by their political opponents, while antigovernment extremists frequently claim to be the victims of government terror. What is called terrorism thus seems to depend on one's point of view. Use of the term implies a moral judgment; and if one party can successfully attach the label 'terrorist' to its opponent, then it has indirectly persuaded others to adopt its moral viewpoint. Terrorism is what the bad guys do.
>
> *Jenkins, 1981, p. 3*

Terms that signify (illegal) opposition against a status quo or government include rebel, insurgent, guerrilla fighter, revolutionary, and of course terrorist. Weimann and Winn (1994) studied the meaning of terms used for terror groups and constructed a framework of reference for negotiating this communicational field (Weimann & Winn, 1994, p. 193). Negative labels included such terms as murderers, gunmen, saboteurs, terrorists, criminals or kidnappers. Neutral labels were for example guerrilla, army, underground, separatists, organization or movement. And the "positive" category comprised terms such as freedom fighter, liberation movement, nationalists or patriots.

For an analysis of strategic communication, it is important to understand which terms are used by terrorist groups to label themselves. These terms are primarily in the "positive" category, for example names including the terms liberation, national, people, popular, unity, salvation, democracy and resistance (Weimann & Winn, 1994, p. 193). First and foremost separatist groups like LTTE (Liberation Tigers of Tamil Eelam) in Sri Lanka or ETA (Euskadi Ta Askatasuna [Basque Homeland

and Freedom]) in Spain used the term "liberation" to indicate their struggle against an "oppressor." Newspapers, on the other hand, mostly used negative labels, especially in cases of hijacking (Weimann & Winn, 1994, p. 203).

Labels are not limited to oral or written attributions but can also be visual or iconic representations. The terrorist group uses visual symbols and colors that are catchy and memorable and carry a meaning for the causes for their existence: for example, the red star behind the submachine gun of the RAF (Red Army Faction), or the fist and kalashnikov of Hezbollah. The colors also form part of strategic communication, red being the color of social–revolutionary groups, green the color of Islam, black mostly standing for anarchism (Elter, 2008, p. 35). The weapons signify the group's determinedness and propensity to violence.

Terrorism as Strategic Communication

Not the terrorist act itself, but the continued communication about it, the interpretations and explanations, are the important issues for terrorist groups. Only via this continued communication will the seemingly "senseless" act be given a meaning. "Acts of terrorism are thus symbolic acts designed to carry messages from the perpetrators of the violence to various audiences. [. . .] terrorism is a form of communication [. . .]. In the majority of incidents, the most important element in communication about terrorist acts is not the acts themselves but the meaning assigned to the acts by media, authorities, and the populace" (Picard, 1993, p. 4). Keeping this in mind, it seems obvious that the psychological impact of terrorism by far outnumbers the physical impact of direct violence, because it is the communication about the act (and not only the act as such) that triggers the climate of terror in society; "this impact is more media-created than intrinsic to the act" (Bassiouni, 1982, p. 128). Bassiouni further explains: "[T]errorism is a term used to describe a strategy of violence designed to inspire terror within a particular segment of a given society. [. . .] The very word terrorism has come to acquire an ominous meaning triggering an almost automatic reaction of fear" (Bassiouni, 1982, p. 128). To put it plainly: Terrorism primarily is a communication strategy (Waldmann, 2000, p. 13). That is why terrorists often choose specific spaces of communication and order such as department stores or banks for their deeds. At these locations, an attack is extraordinarily surprising, causes massive disorder and thus raises great fear. Another option is to choose symbolic targets like military facilities or government buildings which represent a certain power and form of government. Destroying the buildings symbolizes destroying part of the opponent's power.

The media play a key role in the terrorists' communication strategy because they are the key to public awareness providing a stage and an audience. This media-oriented terrorism gathers strength even as the news and information technologies become faster and more easily accessible—just think of the possibilities the Internet offers. Schmid and de Graaf (1982, p. 53–54) present an extensive list of terrorists' active and passive uses of news media. Some examples are given in Table 31.1. Of course—as the case studies will also demonstrate—most of the time, the groups do not apply all of these uses.

Harmon (2008, pp. 39–44) uses a more concise list when naming the five most common terrorist strategies which "all meld violence and propaganda in some form to gain public effect" (Harmon, 2008, p. 39):

- Create or further a sense of societal dislocation, fear, and even anarchy.
- Discredit, diminish, or destroy a particular government and replace it with another
- Create economic damage (directly harm property owners or government, oppose existing trade patterns).
- Render damage to the state's military forces or infrastructure.
- Commit terrorist acts for international effect.

Table 31.1 Insurgent Terrorist Uses of News Media

Active uses (examples)	Passive uses (examples)
• Polarizing public opinion • Making converts, attracting new members to terrorist movement • Demanding publication of manifesto under threat of harm to victim • Linking message to victim • Misleading enemy by spreading false information • Advertising terrorist movement and cause represented • Arousing public concern for victim to pressure government to concessions	• Learning new coercive techniques from media reports on terrorism • Obtaining information about identity and status of hostages • Obtaining information on counter measures by security forces • Identifying future targets for terroristic violence • Obtaining information about public reaction to terroristic act • Benefitting from media exaggeration of own strength to create fear in the enemy

Adapted from Schmid & de Graaf, 1982, p. 53–54

What kind of deed is it that triggers international media coverage and high public resonance? According to news value theory, it is, of course, one with high "news values." B. Hoffman said that suicide terrorism is first and foremost an instrumental strategy with the goal of publicity at the highest possible price (B. Hoffman, 2007, p. 258). The more horrible the atrocity, the more expansive the media coverage, reaching even a "perverted form of entertainment" (my translation) (B. Hoffman, 2007, p. 272). The terrorists can use the mechanisms of the media system for their own means. The event shall preferably attract attention for a long time. This will be the case only if there is no "noise" disturbing the flow of communication, for example many violent deeds or other important events at the same time. This is why democracies, in which there is a low level of violence, are preferred areas for terrorists to commit their attacks. Psychologically speaking the unexpected event carries the possibility of a high level of fright or paralysis; it charges participants with emotion and triggers spontaneous reactions. Some societies might react to terror attacks with stock market crashes or a collapse in tourist travel to certain regions, as demonstrated by the aftermath of the attacks in the USA, the Philippines and Indonesia. It is part of the terrorists' strategic communication that the high economic damage should wear down Western democracies and lead to overreactions. The agitator relies on the reaction of the challenged regime for his success. Hardly any governments can withstand the provocation, and rather they will react emotionally, verbally and/or physically to the terrorists' nondirect communication via violence.

But getting public attention is not the ultimate goal of the terrorists: "[M]ost terrorists are not aiming at publicity for its own sake. The publicity obtained is *instrumental* and serves the final aim of the terrorist movement" (Gerrits, 1992, p. 32). However, sometimes the midterm goal advances to the main purpose of the terrorists' strategies. For example, fighting against opponents or freeing prisoners seems to matter more to autonomous and religious terrorist groups than does the (political and organizational) embodiment of, for example, an autonomous Basque Country, or the ultimate caliphate. Gerrits pointed out various psychological strategies and tactics used by terrorist groups to engage public awareness.

The classification depicted in Table 31.2 shows the two main goals of terrorist attacks: demonstration of own strength and exhibition of vulnerability of the authorities (Gerrits, 1992, p. 36). On the one side, the attack has a strengthening, on the other side a demoralizing effect.

Gerrits, who analyzed various memoirs of terrorists, did not consider attacks and media coverage to be the main components of strategic communication:

Table 31.2 Terrorists' psychological strategies and tactics of publicity

Chosen method of action: insurgent terrorism	
Psychological strategies (examples)	*Tactics of publicity (examples)*
• Demonstrating the vulnerability of authorities • Demoralizing the government and its adherents and troops • Winning or increasing public sympathy • Radicalizing the people or polarizing the political situation • Presenting violent deeds as necessary or heroic	• Committing violent deeds because of their news value • Choosing optimal time and place for action • Issuing statements • Bringing powerful symbols into play

Source: Adapted from Gerrits, 1992, p. 33

Terrorists do not depend exclusively on radio, television, and newspapers to accomplish their psychological aims. They spend a great deal of time and energy on other ways of promoting their movements and ideals. Gatherings, as well as self-made brochures, pamphlets, and periodicals, remain important in the dissemination of information on movements and their ideas. The mass media are an important and attractive instrument, but not the only vehicle for terrorist propaganda.

Gerrits, 1992, p. 59

Strategic communication is not limited to the mass media, as can be seen in the case studies.

Crelinsten held that it is a necessary attribute of terrorism that an attack should deliver a message: "The victimization must be designed to generate messages to others about the possibility of future victimization, or it is not terrorism" (Crelinsten, 1992, p. 214). Furthermore, he stated: "[I]n this communication model of terrorism, the terrorist act constitutes a sign or a message within a wider political discourse. It is a claim for attention, for recognition as a player in political life and, ultimately, for legitimacy as a valid representative of a particular political cause" (Crelinsten, 1987a, p. 419). Crelinsten challenged researchers with a concept of comprehensive investigation. "To study, for example, the actions of insurgent terrorists in isolation from the reactions of intended and unintended audiences is to ignore a key element of the terrorist phenomenon—its communicative nature" (Crelinsten, 1987b, p. 7). His perspective is based on symbolic interactionism and conflict theory.

In the interactionist paradigm, the meaning of a particular action derives from the social reaction which it evokes. This in turn defines that action in a particular way, labeling it and thereby confining its meaning to a particular interpretation. The conflict approach recognises that groups compete for resources and power and that institutions of social control serve as instruments in such conflicts.

Crelinsten, 1987b, p. 8

Terrorism, as became clear hitherto, is not only ideology but also strategy. Terrorist groups may differ highly in their ideologies, but their communication strategies seem to be very much alike. A very typical form of their communication includes statements of responsibility.

Excursus: Claims of Responsibility

In the field of ordinary crime, the perpetrators normally want to stay unrecognized. In contrast to this, terrorist groups very often publish communiqués or upload video messages to claim their responsibility for a deed. Criminals do not intend to send messages; they are mostly interested in material value. Terrorists however, want to enhance their symbolic communication and "explain" the act.

In the 1970s and 1980s, European terror groups following Marxist–Leninist ideology, such as RAF (Rote Armee Fraktion [Red Army Faction]) in Germany sent their statements to news agencies or TV channels explaining and trying to legitimize their deeds. Today, terrorist groups no longer depend on traditional media as their transmitter; they can issue their statements via the Internet. This message reaches not the specific target audiences of certain media, but a far-flung, dispersed public.

Some terrorist groups changed their strategy from issuing statements not after the attack happened, but in advance (A. C. Hoffmann, 2008, pp. 241–242). TAK (Teyrêbazên Azadîya Kurdistan [Kurdistan Freedom Falcons]), close to the Kurdistan workers' party PKK (Partiya Karkerên Kurdistan), over a long period of time used to attack Turkish civilians, quite ignored by the international media. After about 25 attacks, in Spring 2006, they changed their tactic and announced that they were going to target tourists in holiday areas. Of course, the international media promptly reported this, and also broadcast the problems of the Kurds in Turkey in general, before any attack had happened.

There have also been cases of free-riders. In Summer 2009, a few days after an accident in a Russian hydro-electric power plant resulting in 70 people dead, a group of Russian Muslims stated their responsibility for the "attack" in a letter to the Chechen website Kavkaz Center (Ludwig, 2009). The accident had obviously happened without any attack but the group wanted to disseminate fright and fear of further attacks. In this way, strategic communication sometimes results in plain propaganda.

Terrorism as Propaganda of the Deed

"Propaganda is a form of communication that attempts to persuade or manipulate opinions or actions of an individual or group toward political, religious, military, economic, or social ends" (Picard, 1993, p. 45). This description shows that strategic communication, in its extreme form, results in propaganda. In other words: propaganda essentially is powerful strategic communication and that is the reason why a closer look at the concept of terrorism as "propaganda of the deed" is required.

By means of their communication (acts, statements etc.) terrorists want to persuade the public of their righteousness.

> Propaganda and terrorism are identical insofar as they both seek to influence a mass audience in a way that is intended to benefit the sponsor. But while terror has a singular purpose—inducing fear and uncertainty—propaganda can and does serve every imaginable purpose from religion to politics to commerce.
>
> *Tugwell, 1987, p. 409*

Who first coined the term of "propaganda of the deed," cannot positively be identified. It might have been Italian revolutionary Carlo Pisacane (1818–1857), French anarchist Paul Brousse (1844–1912) or nineteenth century German anarchist Johann(es) Most (Elter, 2008, p. 63). In his publication "liberty" Most certainly stated that the right deed at the right time and place would be of more than the literary or oratory propaganda of thousands of agitators (Laqueur, 1978, p. 88).

In any case, coverage of terrorist acts is in no way positive propaganda (Herman & O'Sullivan, 1989). Mostly, journalists report about victims, and dramatize and write "against" the inhumane perpetrators. Most people do not feel attracted by, or positively influenced to support the terrorists' causes, but rather feel repelled and horrified. The terrorists cannot control the framing of coverage. The problem is that journalists again and again cover only the media event, the attack. But counterterrorist measures should allow for coverage of the groups' causes in times of calm, too, so as not to force the group to resort to violence as the main type of communication (Waldmann, 2005, p. 15). Many terrorist groups have founded political arms in order to have the possibility of conducting legal propaganda. But the groups justify their attacks, saying their causes would not have been heard otherwise. Thus, the terror groups compensate for their military and civic participation shortcomings by extensive (violent) propaganda campaigns.

Terrorism is an organized campaign of violence as communication. The terrorists operate in secret until the day of the attack, when they make their causes public in a most massive and powerful way. Terrorists can also use techniques of persuasion in their statements of responsibility or in interviews—for example, repetition of arguments, putting their ideas in a positive context or contrasting them with something negative, association with (positive) emotions (Picard, 1993, p. 41). In return, disadvantageous facts and circumstances will be omitted or trivialized. A characteristic of the terrorists' propaganda is that they present their causes and (violent) measures as absolutely justified; "because of their belief in their own righteousness, the terrorists can portray their opponents not as simply misguided but as totally evil, as corrupt oppressors" (Wilkinson, 1990, p. 29).

Case Studies: Applying Characteristics of Strategic Communication to Terrorist Groups

Terrorists have plans, and a strategy consists of accurately planned courses of action and communication. Terrorist acts do not take place spontaneously, but are rationally and systematically planned. Terrorists want to defeat their enemy not militarily, but mentally. Wilkinson puts the four main goals of terrorists as follows (Wilkinson, 1997, pp. 56–57):

1. inducing fear and horror by propaganda of the deed,
2. attracting the public's attention in regard to the groups'—in their eyes—justified causes,
3. weakening and provoking the government or challenged system to employ undemocratic counter measures, and
4. recruiting new sympathizers and raising funds.

In two graduate-level seminars at Ilmenau University of Technology, several case studies were conducted in 2009, 2010 and 2011 to find out more about the strategic communication of several terrorist groups. The research focused on groups with separatist and social–revolutionary motivation. In terms of determining which factors led to the groups being identified as terrorist groups, researchers followed the criteria of Elter (2008, pp. 24–25), who not only demarcated the phenomenon of "terrorism," but also defined the actors, the terrorist organizations. The approach was qualitative and exploratory. Documents were collected and analyzed, and social media, product sales, political pamphlets, and databases such as the Global Terrorism Database (GTD) (for example Lafree & Dugan, 2007) were looked at, as well as secondary literature.

In the following section some of the results of the case studies are presented, and some points are highlighted in Table 31.3.

In the groups studied here, contact with their respective diaspora seems to be a crucial element in their communication plans. The diaspora have to be informed about the group's activities and be committed to its causes; they have to get some feedback about what happened to their money, otherwise there would be no more fundraising abroad. The LTTE and IRA have a very strong diaspora. The LTTE was not only dependent on the diaspora's money but also on actions such as demonstrations of Tamils in Hamburg, Berlin, or Frankfurt in recent years, in which they tried to attract attention to the difficult situation of the Tamils in Sri Lanka.

Table 31.3 Comparing Strategic Communication of Various Terrorist Groups

	RAF	IRA	GAM	LTTE	FARC
Motives	Socialist, anarchist	Separatist and religious	Separatist	Separatist	Social-revolutionary
Short-term goals	Free members	Gain public attention and support	Public support, autonomy	Language, laws	Better conditions for people
Long-term goals	Change of government	Unify Ireland	Islamic state	Tamil Eelam	Fight US imperialism, Marxist–Leninist state
Duration	1970s–1998	1919–	1976–2005	1976–2009	1964–
Diaspora	Left-wing, Stasi, Al-Fatah, bank robberies	NORAID, legal and illegal businesses	Leader in exile (Sweden), resources from international companies, military from Libya	Europe, North America, Australia finance & morality	No diaspora, resources: coca-plantations
Targets	Embassies, Springer press, representatives of economy	Religious targets (churches), infrastructure, police, army, (civilians)	Javanese government, international businesses	Sinhalese / Muslim civilians, politicians, army	Army, Ingrid Betancourt, politicians, US-American citizens
Nature of main attacks	Kidnappings, shootings	Bombings (cars), shootings	Bombings, burning of schools	Suicide bombings (women), civil war	Bombings, shootings, kidnappings
Labeling	Urban guerrilla, socialists	Revolutionary army, freedom fighters	Liberation fighters	Liberation tigers	Revolutionary army, social fighters
Evaluation	Press clippings, professional way of evaluating	Director of publicity?	Attacking journalists after negative coverage	Influencing journalists, Nitharsan Unit	Inviting journalists
Achievements	Imprisoned, self-liquidation, official dissolution	Public attention, lifted broadcasting ban	Peace agreement, sympathy of East Timor, political party	Defeated	Control over certain areas & drugs
New media	TV, phone, polaroi photos	Propaganda videos, internet, USB-sticks	Not very common	Online-nation, fundraising, social networks, blogs	Websites, social networks, blogs, YouTube
Public perception/ coverage	Not much public support (because of violence)	Public is threatened, negative perception	International media: atrocities of Indonesian government; Indonesian media restricted in reporting	Sri Lankan people: negative global; negative, but also negative on Sri Lankan government	Negative: association with drugs
Guidelines	Concept paper on urban guerrilla, Marx's manifesto	Green Book	East Timor blueprint as example, no SC guideline found	Prabhakaran, Nitharsan Unit directives	How to do propaganda videos

The targets are nearly always symbolic. Embassies, business or government buildings, banks, military facilities, but also representatives of other ethnic or ideological groups have been attacked. That states the message: You—if you are on "the enemy's" side—could be next.

The media, utilized to communicate to various stakeholders or to address letters of responsibility, have shifted from traditional to new media, above all the Internet. The analyzed terrorist groups (except the Gerakan Aceh Merdeka [Free Aceh Movement]/ (GAM)), frequently make use of Youtube, blogs and forums (Rothenberger, 2012). LTTE even tried to create an "online nation" of all Tamil citizens to advance their cause of separation from Sri Lanka (Tekwani, 2004). The terrorists know exactly which channels to use to address which public. The "Fuerzas Armadas Revolucionarias de Colombia" [Revolutionary Armed Forces of Colombia] (FARC), for example, use radio stations to communicate their causes and propaganda within the rural regions of Colombia, because radio is still the most important medium for the peasants.

The coverage of the terrorist groups and in consequence also the public perception is mainly negative. But in international media the reactions of the respective governments are discussed, too, and, at least in articles about counterstrategies of the Sri Lankan and Indonesian government, journalists have thoroughly criticized the military courses of action.

What about relationships between media content and terrorist reaction? Interestingly, almost all terrorist groups deem coverage very important and evaluate articles and newscasts. GAM terrorists attacked journalists after negative coverage. FARC, on the other hand, offered them their own (of course manipulated) picture of the situation. RAF was very professional and even created press clippings.

Also of interest is whether there exist professional communication guidelines. In most cases, terrorists had followed a manifesto created by their group's founder or another historic person, which not only contained political norms, goals, and advice, but also rules for communication. The IRA *Green Book*, for example, states that members are not allowed to talk to anybody about IRA activities, not even to members of their own families. LTTE had their press offices in London and an own unit, called the *Nitharsan Unit*, to take pictures and capture video recordings for propaganda purposes.

Bockstette (2008), after analyzing the strategic management techniques of jihadist terrorists, concluded that

> the jihadist terrorist know (*sic*) how to apply strategic communication management techniques. The mass media and especially the Internet have become the key enablers and the main strategic communication assets for terrorists and have ensured them a favorable communication asymmetry. With these assets, terrorists are able to compensate for a significant part of their asymmetry in military might. [. . .] They craft their strategies based on careful audience analysis and adapt their messages and delivery methods accordingly, adhering to the fundamental rules underlying any communication or public relations campaign.
>
> *Bockstette, 2008, p. 5*

Thus, they are able to recruit new members and terrorize their so-called enemy. In order to reach their own followers, the jihadist terrorists also apply "face-to-face methods utilizing prayers, speeches and sermons in mosques and Koran schools" (Bockstette, 2008, p. 18). The more channels the organization has at its disposal, the more multi-faceted strategies it can add to its portfolio. Bockstette names the three primary communication goals of terrorists in which all these activities have a share: "[T]he propagation and enlargement of their movement, the legitimization of their movement and the coercion and intimidation of their enemies" (Bockstette, 2008, p. 5).

Conclusion and Perspectives

The results of the case studies show that the ultimate goal of the group (i.e. legitimization and power) is subordinated to preliminary goals, which include stating objectives and communicating causes. Therefore terrorists use violence and persuasion techniques such as letters claiming responsibility. Strategic communication has to be adapted to the available resources. For instance, if a group has a strong diaspora community, it is easier to apply a greater variety of communication techniques. Of course, technologies like the Internet, which allow illegal groups to circumvent gatekeepers' selection processes, play a major role, but interpersonal communication remains important.

Coming to a conclusion, it can be stated that the concept of strategic communication can be applied to terrorist groups. They can—and should be—treated like professional organizations seeking maximum publicity. Also, communication and terrorism studies could advance their methodological pool and examine the terrorism communication process in greater depth. Path analyses of the distribution and framing of messages, critical discourse analysis of published documents of all parties involved (i.e., politicians, terrorists, nongovernmental organizations or citizens' groups) as well as media content lend themselves to exploring the field in detail. Moreover, visuals as key elements of persuasion and emotional effects should form part of future research.

Besides their attacks and atrocities, terrorists give much significance to winning people over to their ideas. This is why research and anti-terrorism measures should focus more on this perhaps not so spectacular field of counteraction. "Developing an effective counter strategic communication plan, which exploits weaknesses and contradictions [. . .], is vital in winning the asymmetrical conflict" (Bockstette, 2008, p. 20). Therefore, not only to eliminate the root causes of terrorism, but also to explore the terrorists' communication strategies, will remain an endeavor for future research. Only if researchers, educators, governments, and other actors know about the hitherto very successful communication strategies of terrorists, will they be able to know how to respond to and counter their rhetoric and actions.

References

Alali, A. O., & Eke, K. K. (1991). *Media coverage of terrorism. Methods of diffusion*. Newbury Park, CA: Sage.

Bassiouni, C. M. (1982). Media coverage of terrorism: The Law and the public. In *Journal of Communication, 32*(2), 128–143.

Biernatzki, W. E. (2002). Terrorism and mass media. In Centre for the Study of Communication and Culture (Ed.), *Comunication Research Trends, 21*(1), 1–42.

Bockstette, C. (2008). *Jihadist terrorist use of strategic communication management techniques*. Garmisch-Partenkirchen, Germany: George C. Marshall Center.

Canel, M. J. (2011). Communicating strategically in the face of terrorism: The Spanish government's response to the 2004 Madrid bombing attacks. In *Public Relations Review, 38*(2), 214–222.

Crelinsten, R. D. (1987a). Power and meaning: Terrorism as a struggle over access to the communication structure. In P. Wilkinson, & A. M. Stewart (Eds.), *Contemporary Research on Terrorism* (pp. 419–450). Aberdeen, Scotland: Aberdeen University Press.

Crelinsten, R. D. (1987b). Terrorism as political communication: The relationship between the controller and the controlled. In P. Wilkinson, & A. M. Stewart (Eds.), *Contemporary Research on Terrorism* (pp. 3–23). Aberdeen, Scotland: Aberdeen University Press.

Crelinsten, R. D. (1992). Victims' perspectives. In D. L. Paletz, & A. P. Schmid (Eds.), *Terrorism and the media* (pp. 208–238). Newbury Park, CA: Sage.

Crenshaw, M. (1998). The logic of terrorism: Terrorist behavior as a product of strategic choice. In W. Reich (Ed.), *Origins of terrorism. Psychologies, ideologies, theologies, states of mind* (pp. 7–24). Washington, DC: Woodrow Wilson Center Press.

Elter, A. (2008). *Propaganda der Tat. Die RAF und die Medien*. Frankfurt am Main, Germany: Suhrkamp Verlag.

Gerrits, R. P. J. M (1992). Terrorists' perspectives: Memoirs. In D. L. Paletz, & A. P. Schmid (Eds.), *Terrorism and the media* (pp. 29–61). Newbury Park, CA: Sage.

Gregory, B. (2005). *Public diplomacy and strategic communication: Cultures, firewalls, and imported norms.* Paper presentation at the American Political Science Association Conference on International Communication and Conflict. Washington, DC.

Hallahan, K., Holtzhausen, D., van Ruler, B., Verčič, D., & Sriramesh, K. (2007).Defining Strategic Communication. In *International Journal of Strategic Communication, 1*(1), 3–35.

Harmon, C. C. (2008). *Terrorism today* (2nd ed.). London, England & New York: Routledge.

Heine, P. (2004). *Terror in Allahs Namen. Extremistische Kräfte im Islam* [Terror in Allah's name. Extremist Islamic factions]. Lizenzausgabe für die Bundeszentrale für politische Bildung. Bonn, Germany: Bundeszentrale für politische Bildung.

Herman, E. S. & O'Sullivan, G. (1989). *The "terrorism" industry. The experts and institutions that shape our view of terror.* New York, NY: Pantheon Books.

Hoffmann, A. C. (2008). Multiplikatoren des Schreckens. Medien spielen Terroristen (unfreiwillig) in die Hände [Multipliers of terror. Media (involuntarily) play into the hands of the terrorists]. In M. Löffelholz, C. F. Trippe, & A. C. Hoffmann (Eds.), *Kriegs- und Krisenberichterstattung. Ein Handbuch* [War and crisis coverage. A handbook] (pp. 240–245). Konstanz, Germany: UVK.

Hoffman, B. (2007). *Terrorismus—der unerklärte Krieg. Neue Gefahren politischer Gewalt* [Terrorism – the unexplained war. New threats of political violence] Bonn, Germany: Bundeszentrale für politische Bildung.

Jenkins, B. M. (1981). The Study of terrorism: Definitional problems. In Y. Alexander & J. M. Gleason (Eds.), *Behavioral and quantitative perspectives on terrorism* (pp. 3–10). New York: Pergamon Press.

Jenkins, P. (2003). *Images of terror. What we can and can't know about terrorism.* New York: de Gruyter.

Korstian, S. (2008): Der Nordirlandkonflikt [The Northern Ireland Conflict]. In: T. Bonacker, R. Greshoff, U. Schimank (eds.): *Sozialtheorien im Vergleich* [Comparison of Social Theories], pp. 15–31. Wiesbaden, Germany: Springer VS.

Lafree, G. & Dugan, L. (2007): Introducing the Global Terrorism Database. *Terrorism and Political Violence, 19*(2), 181–204.

Laqueur, W. (1978). *Zeugnisse politischer Gewalt. Dokumente zur Geschichte des Terrorismus* [Evidence of political violence. Documents of terrorism history] Kronberg im Taunus, Germany: Athenäum.

Laqueur, W. (1982). *Terrorismus* [Terrorism]. Frankfurt am Main, Germany: Suhrkamp.

Ludwig, M. (2009). Rebellen prahlen mit Anschlag auf Kraftwerk [Rebels boast about attack on power plant]. In *Frankfurter Allgemeine Zeitung.* Retrieved from www.faz.net.

Martin, G. (2006). *Understanding terrorism. Challenges, perspectives, and issues.* Thousand Oaks, CA: Sage.

Miller, A. H. (1982). *Terrorism, the media and the Law.* Dobbs Ferry: Transnational.

Nacos, B. L. (2007). *Mass-mediated terrorism. The central role of the media in terrorism and counterterrorism.* New York: Rowman & Littlefield.

Picard, R. G. (1993). *Media portrayals of terrorism. Functions and meaning of news coverage.* Ames, IA: Iowa State University Press.

Rapoport, D. (1977). The politics of atrocity. In Y. Alexander, & S. M. Finger (Eds.), *Terrorism. Interdisciplinary perspectives* (pp. 46–61). New York: John Jay Press.

Richardson, L. (2007). Britain and the IRA. In R. J. Art, & L. Richardson (Eds.), *Democracy and counterterrorism: Lessons from the past* (pp. 63–104). Washington, DC: United States Institute of Peace Press.

Rothenberger, L. (2012). Terrorist groups: Using Internet and social media for disseminating ideas. New tools for promoting political change. In *Romanian Journal of Communication and Public Relations, 14*(3), 7–23.

Schaffert, R. W. (1992). *Media coverage and political terrorists. A quantitative analysis.* New York: Praeger.

Schmid, A. P., & de Graaf, J. (1982). *Violence as communication. Insurgent terrorism and the Western news media.* London, England: Sage.

Schmid, A. P., & Jongman, A. J. (1988). *Political terrorism. A new guide to actors, authors, concepts, data bases, theories, and literature.* New Brunswick, NJ: Transaction.

Signorelli, N., & Gerbner, G. (1988). *Violence and Terror in the Mass Media. An Annotated Bibliography.* New York: Greenwood Press.

Stowasser, J. M. (1994). Stowasser. Lateinisch–deutsches Schulwörterbuch [Latin–German Learners' Dictionary]. Munich, Germany: Oldenbourg Schulbuchverlag.

Tekwani, S. (2004).*Constructing a nation online: Tamil nationalism and the Internet.* Paper presented at the annual meeting of the International Communication Association, New Orleans, LA.

Townshend, C. (2005). *Terrorismus. Eine kurze Einführung* [Terrorism. A short introduction]. Stuttgart, Germany: Reclam.

Tugwell, M. (1987). Terrorism and propaganda: Problem and response. In P. Wilkinson, & A. M. Stewart (Eds.), *Contemporary research on terrorism* (pp. 409–418). Aberdeen, Scotland: Aberdeen University Press.

Tuman, J. S. (2003). *Communicating terror. The rhetorical dimensions of terrorism*. Thousand Oaks, CA: Sage.

Waldmann, P. (2000). Terrorismus als weltweites Phänomen: Eine Einführung [Terrorism as a worldwide phenomenon: An introduction]. In K. Hirschmann, & P. Gerhard (Eds.), *Terrorismus als weltweites Phänomen* (pp. 11–26). Berlin, Germany: Berlin Verlag Arno Spitz.

Waldmann, P. (2005). Terrorismus und öffentliche Wahrnehmung [Terrorism and public perception]. In J. Klußmann (Ed.), *Terrorismus und Medien. Eine komplexe Beziehung. Dokumentation der Tagung 25/2004 vom 6. bis 8. September 2004* [Terrorism and media. A complex relationship. Documentation of the conference 25/2004 from September 6 to September 8, 2004] (pp. 9–20). Bonn, Germany: Evangelische Akademie im Rheinland.

Weimann, G., & Winn, C. (1994). *The theater of terror. Mass media and international terrorism*. New York: Longman.

Wilkinson, P. (1990). Terrorism and propaganda. In Y. Alexander & R. Latter (Eds.), *Terrorism & the media. Dilemmas for government, journalists and the public* (pp. 26–33). Washington, DC: Brassey's.

Wilkinson, P. (1997). The Media and terrorism: A reassessment. In *Terrorism and Political Violence, 9*(2), 51–64.

Wright-Neville, D. (2010). *Dictionary of terrorism*. Cambridge, MA: Polity Press.

the official

the manager

32

Strategic Intent and Crisis Communication

The Emergence of a Field

W. Timothy Coombs and Sherry J. Holladay

UNIVERSITY OF CENTRAL FLORIDA

Crisis communication is a relatively new applied communication field of study, with its origins traced to the 1980s. In the early days the field reflected a strong tactical focus in efforts to redress the problems created by crises. A crisis can be defined as "the perception of an unpredictable event that threatens important expectancies of stakeholders and can seriously impact an organization's performance and generate negative outcomes" (Coombs, 2012, p. 2). As its theories developed and matured, crisis communication research evolved from a tactical to a strategic focus. Crisis communication research emphasizes solving the problems organizations such as corporations and non-governmental organizations (NGOs) face in a crisis. This chapter reflects the organizational-centric focus by examining the ways managers intentionally utilize crisis communication to prevent or to reduce the problems generated by a crisis. Crisis communication refers to a variety of communicative interventions that are utilized as part of the crisis management process and employed during all three phases of crisis management:

1. pre-crisis (prevention and preparation),
2. crisis response, and
3. post-crisis (learning and recovering) (Coombs, 2009).

Crisis communication is a form of strategic communication. Strategic communication is about the intentional "application of communication and how an organization functions as a social actor to advance its mission" (Hallahan, Holtzhausen, van Ruler, Verčič & Sriramesh, 2007, p. 7). Crisis communication involves the strategic application of communication to limit the harm a crisis inflicts on an organization and its stakeholders—it is designed to advance the organization's mission. Moreover, crisis and strategic communication share an emphasis on influence. Many applications of crisis communication do try to influence people's reactions to a crisis and their perceptions of organizations in crisis (Coombs, 2010).

The crisis communication array provides a means of organizing the various types of crisis communication. The various crisis communication applications can be divided into: (a) managing meaning and (b) managing information. Managing information includes all efforts used to collect and to analyze information. Managing meaning includes making efforts to shape how people perceive the crisis and the organization in crisis. These two categories can be crossed with the three crisis phases to create the 2 × 3 crisis communication array. The six cells in the crisis communication array are:

1. pre-crisis managing information,
2. pre-crisis managing meaning,
3. crisis response managing information,
4. crisis response managing meaning,
5. post-crisis managing information, and
6. post-crisis managing meaning (Coombs, 2009).

[handwritten margin note: presentation]

The bulk of the crisis communication research examines the fourth cell, crisis response managing meaning. This chapter reflects crisis communication literature by emphasizing managing meaning during a crisis response, the dominant research area in crisis communication.

This exploration of crisis communication as strategic communication unfolds in three parts. The first part details the common outcomes associated with crisis communication. The outcomes provide a strategic focus by establishing what an organization hopes to achieve through its crisis communication. The second part discusses the primary crisis response strategies crisis managers utilize. There is a need to outline these crisis response strategies and to understand what effects they are intended to have upon their target audiences. This section builds upon the outcomes by explaining how various crisis response strategies can be used to pursue different outcomes. The third part examines how crisis communication fits with related strategic communication fields. This entails exploring the relationships of crisis communication with issues management, reputation management, and risk communication.

Crisis Communication Outcomes

Strategic communication is intentional and thus it tries to generate specific reactions from the target audiences. Crisis managers employ crisis communication as a way to lessen the negative effects of a crisis upon the organization and stakeholders. Crisis communication serves to protect the organization and stakeholders from the myriad potential harms a crisis can inflict upon it. Crisis managers do seek specific outcomes from their crisis communication efforts. The outcomes of crisis communication can be divided into three areas (Coombs, 2012): (a) attitudes and affect, (b) potential supportive behaviors, and (c) media coverage. Obviously these three areas may overlap and influence one another. The attitudes and affect shape potential supportive behaviors, whereas media coverage can influence the other two. Still the distinctions are useful for organizing the discussion of the crisis communication impacts.

Attitudes and Affect

[handwritten margin note: value of reputations]

Attitudes and affects include reputational assets (attitude) and the various emotions commonly associated with a crisis (affect). The term "reputation" can be defined as how people perceive and evaluate an organization. Reputations have an evaluative dimension to them. People assess an organization by determining if the organization is "good" or "bad" (see Fombrun & van Riel, 2004). Reputations are valuable, intangible assets that organizations seek to cultivate and to protect. Reputations have value because they can accrue any or all of the following benefits: attracting and motivating employees, attracting customers, creating positive media coverage, and generating investment interest (Alsop, 2004; Davies, Chun, da Silva, & Roper, 2003; Dowling, 2002; Fombrun & van Riel, 2004). Crises may pose threats to an organization's reputation (Barton, 2001).

It is logical that a large percentage of crisis communication research should be dedicated to organizational reputation protection or restoration. The major research lines of corporate apologia (Hearit, 1994; 2006), image repair (Benoit, 1995), and *situational crisis communication theory* (*SCCT*) (Coombs, 1995; 2007) all feature reputation as a primary crisis communication outcome. The desired outcome

[handwritten margin note: presentation]

Example of a time when your reputation was damaged in a crisis situation.

Strategic Intent and Crisis Communication

for crisis communication is to limit or to prevent reputational damage. The idea is that the use of crisis communication reduces or even eliminates the potential reputational damage generated by a crisis.

Crises can generate a wide range of emotions among stakeholders. The most common emotions associated with crises are anger, anxiety, and sympathy. Anger and anxiety represent negative affective responses. As anger from a crisis increases, people are more likely to engage in negative word-of-mouth and to experience a greater reduction in purchase intention (Coombs & Holladay, 2007). The *Integrated Crisis Mapping* (*ICM*) model presents the most detailed analyses of affect in crisis communication. The ICM uses two axes to describe responses:

1. the X-axis is the public coping strategy and
2. the Y-axis is the level of organizational engagement.

Publics cope by either acting (conative coping) or by changing their interpretations of the situation (cognitive coping). Organizational engagement is the level of resources an organization commits to the crisis and this level ranges from high to low. The two axes create four quadrants representing different types of crises and identify the emotions associated with the crisis, how publics are likely to cope, and the amount of organizational engagement. The assumption is that crisis communication should be consistent with the emotions and coping strategies of the publics. Research using the ICM model reports that anxiety is the most common emotional reaction by publics during crises, followed by anger. Conative coping was the most common public response and organizations tend to have moderate engagement (Jin & Pang, 2010).

Crises can disrupt organizational operations and these disruptions create anxiety for employees, suppliers, and customers. Employees are concerned about their pay, benefits, and job security. Suppliers wonder if they will be paid and if the standing orders will be modified. Customers worry whether or not they will have access to products and how long that access might be denied. The outcome for crisis communication is to reduce the amount of anger and anxiety people feel as a result of a crisis.

Sympathy is a positive affect; people feel sorry for someone or something. When an organization is the victim of a crisis, such as in a product-tampering crisis, people can feel sympathy for an organization. Sympathy leads people to support an organization. This type of support can include purchase intention or positive word-of-mouth. The outcome for crisis communication is to increase or to facilitate sympathy when the organization is a victim of the crisis.

Behaviors

There are two types of behaviors that characterize crisis response: public safety and potential supportive behaviors. Many crises, such as chemical accident and product harm crises, involve a threat to public safety. In such crises, public safety is the number one priority for crisis managers. Communication is used to protect public safety. People are told that a threat exists, the nature of that threat is explained, and people are told how to avoid or protect themselves from the crisis. A product harm crisis illustrates the public safety communication. People are told what specific product could be harmful, why the product presents a danger to them, and what they should do to protect themselves from that harm. For example, people are given details and instructions on how to determine if the product they have is part of the recall and if they should return the product or seek some corrective action necessary to make the product safe to use. The outcome for crisis communication is to prevent further harm from the product and to have that product returned or corrected.

Potential supportive behaviors refer to actions people can take which serve to benefit the organization in some way. The most researched potential supportive behavior is purchase intention. Marketing-oriented crisis communication demonstrates a strong interest in how crises impact customers (see Jorgensen, 1996). This research has found that crises do decrease purchase intentions.

The outcome for crisis communication is to reduce or to eliminate the negative effects of the crisis on purchase intentions.

Word-of-mouth is another potential supportive behavior that is favored by marketing-oriented crisis communication research. Word-of-mouth can have a profound effect on customers and in how any stakeholder might view an organization. In essence word-of-mouth is related to both purchase intention and reputation. Aside from physical harm, the greatest danger from a crisis is that it stimulates negative word-of-mouth. Negative word-of-mouth can harm reputations and suppress purchase intention (Coombs & Holladay, 2007). The outcome for crisis communication is to reduce or eliminate negative word-of-mouth.

Organizations generally do not like new government regulations because regulations typically increase costs for organizations (Baker, Conrad, Cudahy & Willyard, 2009). Crises create the potential for new regulations. A crisis can become a focusing event, as illustrated by Fishman (1999), who adapted Birkman's (1997) notion of this concept. A focusing event draws attention to some issue. In a crisis, attention is drawn to the factors that gave rise to the crisis.

Stakeholders worry that, if not addressed properly, the conditions that created the crisis will linger and the potential for additional crises remain. The focusing event can create pressure on policy makers to create policies designed to redress the conditions that created the crisis. The crisis managers need to reassure stakeholders, especially government officials, that the conditions that created the crisis are no longer a threat and that necessary corrective actions have been taken. If an organization is perceived to be in control and has adequately addressed the crisis, then there would be no need for the government to impose external corrections. The outcome for crisis communication is to prevent new regulations from emerging after a crisis.

A final behavior is media coverage. We are using the term *media* broadly to include both traditional media and digital media. Media outlets are drawn to crises because they have the dramatic elements that appeal to media consumers. Crisis managers are concerned about the quality, quantity, and duration of the media coverage. The starting point should be the quality of crisis media coverage. The quality of media coverage is whether the "story" portrays the organization in a negative light. In most cases, crisis media coverage is negative for an organization because it is associated with a negative event (Barton, 2001). The quantity of the media coverage is represented by the number of stories generated by the crisis. Obviously, if most crisis stories were negative, crisis managers would prefer to attract as little media coverage as possible. Reputation management dictates that organizations should minimize negative media coverage while maximizing positive media coverage (Carroll & McCombs, 2003; Meijer, 2004). In general, if people are talking about the crisis, that is negative for an organization. However, some crisis response strategies can seek to place positive information about the organizations into the stories. The duration is the length of time the media covers the story. Media coverage of a crisis keeps the story alive for stakeholders and will perpetuate the discussion of negative information. Ideally, the duration of the crisis media coverage will be short. The outcome for crisis communication is to limit the amount and duration of negative media crisis coverage. In a few cases, the outcome for crisis communication is to add positive information about the organization to the media coverage.

Crisis Response Strategies: Dynamics and Types

As noted earlier, crisis communication is a complex process when viewed as strategic and therefore crisis managers may choose from a variety of crisis response strategies. The choices should be guided by the desired outcomes. Informing this choice are the dynamics that underlie crisis communication. This section begins by detailing the basic dynamics involved in crisis response communication and then examines the specific crisis response strategies and their relationships to various outcomes.

Dynamics

Attribution theory has contributed significantly to our understanding of crisis communication. Attribution theory posits that people seek to find causes for events they experience. When something like a crisis happens, people naturally try to explain *why* it happened. People tend to attribute the cause of an event to internal or external factors (Weiner, 1986; 2006). For instance, did the person spill the red wine because he was drunk (internal) or because someone bumped his arm (external)? People naturally generate attributions of crisis responsibility when they are engaged with a crisis. Crisis responsibility is the amount of responsibility for the crisis people attribute to the organization.

Marketing researchers were the first to identify the importance of attributions of crisis responsibility to crisis communication (e.g., Mowen, 1980). Situational crisis communication theory (SCCT) has refined and extended the role of crisis responsibility in crisis communication (Coombs & Holladay, 2002). Experimental research consistently finds that increased crisis responsibility produces greater reputational damage and more anger, and creates a strong reduction in purchase intention (Coombs, 2007; Schwarz, 2008).

When crisis responsibility is the key variable, three dynamics can be identified for understanding how crisis response strategies are related to the desired outcomes. First, crisis response strategies can be used to separate the organization from the crisis. If an organization is perceived to have no responsibility for the crisis, it suffers no harm, and crisis damages are avoided. Second, crisis response strategies can seek to reduce attributions of crisis responsibility. If stakeholders perceive the organization has little responsibility for the crisis, the crisis damages are minimized. Third, crisis response strategies seek to provide positive actions to counter the negatives created by the crisis. The crisis response strategies attempt to buffer the crisis damages (Coombs, 1995).

Types of Crisis Response Strategies

Crisis managers have a number of crisis response strategies at their disposal during a crisis. Typically each crisis communication effort combines a number of crisis response strategies. Sturges (1994) recommended dividing crisis response strategies into three categories:

1. instructing information,
2. adjusting information, and
3. reputation management.

Our discussion of the types of crisis response strategies begins with these three message categories. As we discuss the crisis response strategies, we will return to the outcomes because specific strategies are linked to particular outcomes.

Instructing information involves messages designed to physically protect stakeholders from the harm produced by the crisis. Stakeholders must know what actions they can take to protect themselves from the physical harm a crisis can generate. There is a strong connection between instructing information and the public safety outcome derived from this focus on physical safety. Examples of instructing information include alerts about product recalls, public health warnings, and orders or alarms to evacuate an area or to *shelter in place* (Coombs, 2012).

Adjusting information, the second category of strategies, includes messages intended to help people cope psychologically with a crisis. Crises can be traumatic for victims (those affected by the crisis). Crisis managers can take actions to ease the burden on victims. Expressions of sympathy, corrective actions designed to prevent a reoccurrence of the crisis, and information about what happened in the crisis are examples of adjusting information. People expect organizations to express sympathy and show concern for the crisis victims (Patel & Reinsch, 2003). Research shows expressions of concern

501

reduce anxiety and anger (Cohen, 2002). Corrective action refers to the steps taken to prevent a repeat of the crisis. The corrective action reassures stakeholders by demonstrating the organization's commitment to their safety (Sellnow, Ulmer & Snider, 1998). Simply providing details that reduce uncertainty about what happened in a crisis produces reassurance as well. Providing information about the crisis event reassures people by reducing their uncertainty (Ammerman, 1995).

Reputation management crisis response strategies, the third category of strategies, are the words and actions designed to protect or to repair the reputational damage posed by a crisis. Sturges (1994) argues that instructing and adjusting information must be prioritized in a crisis, and reputation management addressed only after the other two have been provided. The concern with reputation management has produced the greatest volume of research in the crisis communication literature (Coombs, 2009). The three dynamics of crisis response communication provide an excellent framework for organizing and explaining the various reputation management crisis response strategies. The reputation management response strategies are classified into three strategies: denial, diminish, and repair. Table 32.1 provides a list of the commonly used reputation management crisis response strategies.

The reputation management strategies can be tied directly to the earlier discussion of the three dynamics that explain how crisis communication achieves the desired outcomes. Denial reputation management strategies work by disconnecting the organization from the crisis. If the organization bears no responsibility for the crisis, the crisis should not harm the organization's reputation. Why should stakeholders punish an organization if they do not believe it is responsible for the negative events? Diminish reputation management strategies seek to minimize attributions of crisis responsibility. There is a relationship between crisis severity and attributions of crisis responsibility (Coombs & Holladay, 2004). By recognizing that the crisis created only minimal damage, stakeholders should perceive minimal attributions of crisis responsibility. By arguing that the organization had limited

Table 32.1 Crisis Response Strategies

Response strategies		Definition
Category	*Type*	
Instructing information		Help people protect themselves physically
	Warning information	Alert people to a danger
	Basic information	Tell what happened during the crisis
Adjusting information		Help people to cope psychologically
	Sympathy	Express concern for victims
	Corrective action	Take steps to prevent a repeat of the crisis
Reputation management		
	Attacking the accuser	Confront those claiming a crisis exists
	Denial	Claim organization is not involved in crisis
	Scapegoating	Blame someone else for the crisis
	Excusing	Minimize organizational responsibility for the crisis by denying intention to do harm or lack of control
	Justification	Claim that the damage from the crisis was minor
	Compensation	Offer money or gifts to victims
	Apology	Accept responsibility and ask for forgiveness
	Reminding	Remind people of past good actions by the organization
	Ingratiation	Praise those who helped with the crisis
	Victimage	Explain that the organization is a victim of the crisis too

control over the crisis events, crisis managers claim that the organization had little responsibility for the crisis. A crisis has less negative effects when attributions of crisis responsibility are low. Lastly, repair or reputation management strategies accept responsibility for the crisis and offer positive actions as a means to offset the negatives created by the crisis (Coombs, 2012).

At this point it is useful to connect the crisis response strategies to specific crisis communication outcomes. Earlier we noted some connections between crisis response strategies and outcomes; this section elaborates on how the two are related. Table 32.2 summarizes the relationships between the crisis response strategies and crisis communication outcomes.

Instructing information is designed for the public safety outcome. Moreover, the information provided about protective actions also should help to reduce anxiety. Adjusting information directly targets anxiety by providing reassurance. Corrective action can prevent government regulation because the corrective actions indicate there is no need for action beyond the steps taken by the organization. The expressions of sympathy should serve to reduce anger by demonstrating concern for the victims.

The denial and diminish reputation management strategies should protect an organization's reputation, reduce anger, maintain purchase intention, and reduce the likelihood of negative word-of-mouth. If there is no crisis, the reputation is unharmed, purchase intentions should remain intact,

Table 32.2 Crisis Response Strategies and Crisis Outcomes

Response strategies		Outcome
Category	*Type*	
Instructing information		
	Warning information	Public safety
	Basic information	Anxiety
Adjusting information		
	Sympathy	Anger and anxiety
	Corrective action	Anger, anxiety, and regulation
Reputation management		
	Attacking the accuser	Reputation, purchase intention, anger, and word-of-mouth
	Denial	Reputation, purchase intention, anger, and word-of-mouth
	Scapegoating	Reputation, purchase intention, anger, and word-of-mouth
	Excusing	Reputation, purchase intention, anger and word-of-mouth
	Justification	Reputation, purchase intention, anger, and word-of-mouth
	Compensation	Reputation, purchase intention, anger, and word-of-mouth
	Apology	Reputation, purchase intention, anger, word-of-mouth, and media coverage (quality, quantity, and duration)
	Reminding	Reputation, purchase intention, anger, word-of-mouth, and media coverage quality
	Ingratiation	Reputation, purchase intention, anger, and word-of-mouth
	Victimage	Reputation, purchase intention, anger, word-of-mouth, and media coverage quality

and there is no need for anger or negative word-of-mouth. Establishing minimal responsibility for a minor crisis limits the reputational damage and danger as well as the adverse effect on purchase intention and the desire to engage in negative word-of-mouth. In addition, the denial strategies should reduce the quantity and duration of media coverage. If there is no crisis there, then there is no need for crisis coverage in the media.

The repair reputation management strategies seek to reduce the reputational damage, the negative effect on purchase intention, anger, and negative word-of-mouth. Crisis managers realize the crisis will inflict damage in all four of those categories, but providing positive words and/or actions seeks to reduce that damage. Apology, reminding and victimage strategies can influence the quality of media coverage by indirectly encouraging media to include positive information about the organization (the apology, past good works, or how the organization has suffered from the crisis). Victimage seeks to increase sympathy by reminding people the organization is a victim in the crisis. In addition, apology can help reduce the amount and duration of media coverage. An apology ends the crisis narrative. The organization accepts responsibility and asks for forgiveness (Hearit, 2006). The villain accepts the punishment, thus ending the crisis narrative and reducing media and stakeholder interest in the crisis.

Other Crisis Communication Variables

Research has identified two other variables that have an impact on crisis communication that are independent of the crisis response strategies: timing and channels. Timing refers to whether the organization or some other entity, typically the media, are the first to report about the crisis. This research is known as "stealing thunder." Experimental studies provide evidence that an organization suffers less reputational damage from a crisis when it is the first actor to report the crisis. In other words, if the first report of a crisis comes from another source, the organization suffers more damage from the same crisis than if the organization had been the first to announce the crisis (Arpan & Pompper, 2003; Claeys & Cauberghe, 2010).

Initial studies also suggest that stealing thunder has an effect on crisis response strategies. Essentially, no benefits, such as reputation protection, are derived from crisis response strategies if the organization is the first to report the crisis (Claeys, 2012). It appears that the favorable outcomes are achieved with either timing or crisis response strategies. However, combining the two does not increase the benefits associated with stealing thunder.

An emerging area of research has begun to examine the channel effects of crisis communication. This research tries to determine if the channels that are used to deliver the crisis information and crisis response strategies have an effect on attributions of crisis responsibility and the desired crisis communication outcomes. Research thus far has produced only speculative results. The comparison of print and video presentations of crisis information and responses revealed little difference between the two types of presentation (Coombs & Holladay, 2011).

More recently researchers have compared how people react to messages delivered via social media channels and other communication channels. The examination of social media channels is embryotic and the conclusions are tentative at best. The difficulty with social media channels is that source and timing can complicate the results. In addition to examining a channel, examining the source of the information in a social media channel reveals that sources range from friends of the recipient, to the organization in crisis, to an unknown person. The research by Freberg (2012) and Schultz, Utz and Goritz (2011) provides excellent examples of work seeking to identify source factors and source effects among various social media. For example, Freberg's (2012) research on food recall messages found that organizational sources (the government) created more compliance than user-generated content (social media). The source might be the reason for an effect. Also, people may assume that if the organization is the source of a social media message, it is the first to report about the crisis. In this case timing might be the reason for any effects found in the study. Hence, we have some tentative evidence that the use of social media channels might change how people perceive and react to crisis response strategies (Liu, Austin & Jin, 2011).

Crisis Communication and Related Areas of Strategic Communication

The preceding discussion has linked crisis communication to reputation management and issues management. Risk management can be added as a third area of strategic communication that has close ties to crisis communication. Each of these four areas of strategic communication has an effect upon the others. Hence, crisis communication should not be considered in isolation from the other three areas of strategic communication.

Reputation management involves efforts designed to influence how people perceive and evaluate the organization. Crises can have a negative effect on reputations when stakeholders lessen their perceptions of an organization because of a crisis. Research still needs to determine the length of time a crisis suppresses the organization's reputation. Prior reputation has an effect on how people perceive crisis responsibility. In some cases, a strong, positive pre-crisis reputation reduces the reputational damage from a crisis (Dean 2004; Ulmer, 2001). Moreover, a negative pre-crisis reputation intensifies the reputational damage from a crisis by increasing attributions of crisis responsibility (Coombs & Holladay, 2006). It is nearly impossible to separate crisis management from reputation management.

Issues management involves the identification of issues (problems whose resolution can impact an organization) and attempts to resolve the issues (Heath, 1990). Issues management can be part of crisis prevention. Efforts to manage an issue simultaneously are efforts to prevent a crisis threat from manifesting into a crisis. A crisis can result from a failed issues management effort (González Herrero & Pratt, 1996). As noted earlier, a crisis can become an issue. Crises can focus attention on an issue and increase pressure by policy makers to take action in order to prevent a repeat of the crisis (Fishman, 1999). For certain crisis communication efforts, there is a close connection with issues management.

The risk assessment aspect of risk management seeks to reduce the vulnerabilities an organization faces to reduce crisis threats. Risk assessment and efforts to reduce the identified risks are essential to crisis prevention. Once a crisis threat manifests itself in a crisis, there may be a need for crisis managers to engage in risk communication. Risk communication seeks to understand how stakeholders perceive the risk and to explain the nature of the risks as well as the organization's efforts to protect people from those risks (Palenchar, 2005).

This section has emphasized the relationship between crisis communication and reputation management, issues management, and risk management and communication. Yet all four functions are strongly interrelated. Risks and issues can impact reputations, and reputations can limit or facilitate efforts to manage issues or risks. Moreover, a risk can create an issue or an issue can generate risks. All four of these strategic communication areas can be used proactively to address organizational concerns. The point is that the strategic nature of crisis communication is influenced by its relationship to the strategic communication areas of reputation management, issues management, and risk management.

Conclusion

Crisis communication began to emerge as a distinct entity in the late 1980s. The early writings were presented by practitioners who developed simple lists of what crisis managers should and should not do during a crisis. The field began with a simple tactical focus on *what* to do. We would argue this is a common "origins story" for an applied field of communication. As research and theory has advanced in crisis communication, the field has moved toward explaining "why" certain communicative interventions should be initiated. This research-based movement represents significant improvement over simplistic "practitioner wisdom." This chapter has documented the strategic focus of crisis communication with a focus on managing meaning during a crisis response. This focus was selected because the vast majority of crisis communication research examines the managing meaning during the crisis response.

The chapter began by detailing the desired outcomes for crisis communication. Strategic communication must be intentional and the outcomes for crisis communication are its intentions. The focus then shifted to how the various crisis response strategies could be used in pursuit of the various crisis communication outcomes. The analysis of crisis response strategies included an explanation of the dynamics by which crisis communication achieved its intended effects. This chapter concludes with a review of the connections between crisis communication, reputation management, issues management, and risk management to illustrate the relationships between these four types of strategic communication.

Crisis communication is developing as a unique field of strategic communication. Its research has identified a variety of crisis response strategies and offered an understanding of how each can produce certain outcomes. In crisis communication, crisis managers have a body of knowledge that guides them in their efforts to achieve a wide range of intended outcomes through the utilization of crisis communication. Crisis communication has evolved from its tactical start and should be considered a significant strand of strategic communication.

References

Alsop, R. J. (2004). *The 18 immutable laws of corporate reputation: Creating, protecting, and repairing your most valuable asset*. New York: Free Press.

Ammerman, D. (1995). What's a nice company like yours doing in a story like this? In L. Barton (Ed.), *New avenues in risk and crisis management* (Vol. 3, pp. 3–8). Las Vegas, NV: University of Nevada Las Vegas, Small Business Development Center.

Arpan, L.M., & Pompper, D. (2003). Stormy weather: Testing "stealing thunder" as a crisis communication strategy to improve communication flow between organizations and journalists. *Public Relations Review, 29*(3), 291–308.

Baker, J. S., Conrad, C., Cudahy, C., & Willyard, J. (2009). The devil in disguise: Vioxx, drug safety, and the FDA. In R. L. Heath, E. L. Toth & D. Waymer (Eds.), *Rhetorical and critical approaches to public relations II* (pp. 170–194). New York: Routledge.

Barton, L. (2001). *Crisis in organizations II* (2nd ed.). Cincinnati, OH: College Divisions South-Western.

Benoit, W. L. (1995). *Accounts, excuses, and apologies: A theory of image restoration*. Albany, NY: State University of New York Press.

Carroll, C. E., & McCombs, M. E. (2003). Agenda-setting effects of business news on the public's images and opinions about major corporations. *Corporate Reputation Review, 6*, 36–46.

Claeys, A. S. (2012). *The impact of the content and timing of organizational crisis communication on reputation repair*. Unpublished doctoral dissertation. Ghent, Belgium: University of Ghent.

Claeys, A .S., & Cauberghe, V. (2010). Crisis response and crisis timing strategies: Two sides of the same coin. *Public Relations Review, 38*(1), 83–88.

Cohen, J. R. (2002). Legislating apology: The pros and cons. *University of Cincinnati Law Review, 70*, 819–895.

Coombs, W. T. (1995). Choosing the right words: The development of guidelines for the selection of the "appropriate" crisis response strategies. *Management Communication Quarterly, 8*, 447–476.

Coombs, W. T. (2007). Protecting organization reputations during a crisis: The development and application of situational crisis communication theory. *Corporate Reputation Review, 10*(3), 163–177.

Coombs, W. T. (2009). Conceptualizing crisis communication. In D. O'Hair & R. L. Heath (Eds.), *Handbook of risk and crisis communication* (pp. 99–118). Mahwah, NJ: Lawrence Erlbaum.

Coombs, W. T. (2010). Crisis communication: A developing field. In R. L. Heath (Ed.), *Handbook of public relations*, (2nd ed., pp. 477–488). Thousand Oaks, CA: Sage Publications.

Coombs, W. T. (2012). *Ongoing crisis communication: Planning, managing, and responding* (3rd ed.). Thousand Oaks, CA: Sage Publications.

Coombs, W. T., & Holladay, S. J. (2002). Helping crisis managers protect reputational assets: Initial tests of the situational crisis communication theory. *Management Communication Quarterly, 16*, 165–186.

Coombs, W. T., & Holladay, S. J. (2004). Reasoned action in crisis communication: An attribution theory-based approach to crisis management. In D. P. Millar & R. L. Heath (Eds.), *Responding to crisis: A rhetorical approach to crisis communication* (pp. 95–115). Mahwah, NJ: Lawrence Erlbaum.

Coombs, W. T. & Holladay, S. J. (2006). Halo or reputational capital: Reputation and crisis management. *Journal of Communication Management, 10,* 123–137.

Coombs, W. T., & Holladay, S. J. (2007). The negative communication dynamic: Exploring the impact of stakeholder affect on behavioral intentions. *Journal of Communication Management, 11,* 300–312

Coombs, W. T. & Holladay, S.J. (2011). An exploration of the effects of victim visuals on perceptions and reactions to crisis events, *Public Relations Review, 37*(2), 115–120.

Davies, G., Chun, R., da Silva, R. V., & Roper, S. (2003). *Corporate reputation and competitiveness.* New York: Routledge.

Dean, D. H. (2004). Consumer reaction to negative publicity: Effects of corporate reputation, response, and responsibility for a crisis event. *Journal of Business Communication, 41,* 192–211.

Dowling, G. (2002). *Creating corporate reputations: Identity, image, and performance.* New York: Oxford University Press.

Fishman, D. A. (1999). ValuJet flight 592: Crisis communication theory blended and extended. *Communication Quarterly, 47*(4), 345–375.

Fombrun, C. J., & van Riel, C. B. M. (2004). *Fame and fortune: How successful companies build winning reputations.* New York: Prentice Hall.

Freberg, K. (2012). Intention to comply with crisis communicated via social media. *Public Relations Review, 38,* 416–421.

González Herrero, A., & Pratt, C. B. (1996). An integrated symmetrical model of crisis communications management. *Journal of Public Relations Research, 8*(2), 79–106.

Hallahan, K., Holtzhausen, D., van Ruler, B., Verčič, D., & Sriramesh, K. (2007). Defining strategic communication. *International Journal of Strategic Communication, 1*(1), 3–35.

Hearit, K. M. (1994). Apologies and public relations crises at Chrysler, Toshiba, and Volvo. *Public Relations Review, 20*(2), 113–125.

Hearit, K. M. (2006). *Crisis management by apology: Corporate response to allegations of wrongdoing.* Mahwah, NJ: Lawrence Erlbaum.

Heath, R. L. (1990). Corporate issues management: Theoretical underpinnings and research foundations. In J. E. Grunig & L. A. Grunig (Eds.), *Public relations research annual* (Vol. 2, pp. 29–66). Hillsdale, NJ: Lawrence Erlbaum.

Jin, Y., & Pang, A. (2010). Future directions of crisis communication research: Emotions in crisis—the next frontier. In W. T. Coombs & S.J. Holladay (Eds.), *Handbook of crisis communication* (pp. 677–682). Malden, MA: Blackwell Publishing.

Jorgensen, B. K. (1996). Components of consumer reaction to company-related mishaps: a structural equation model approach. *Advances in Consumer Research, 23:* 346–51.

Liu, B.F., Austin, L., & Jin, Y. (2011). How publics respond to crisis communication strategies: The interplay of information form and source. *Public Relations Review, 37*(4), 345–352.

Meijer, M.M . (2004). *Does success breed success? Effects of news and advertising on corporate reputation.* Amsterdam, Netherlands: Aksant Academic Publishers.

Mowen, John C. (1980). Further information on consumer perceptions of product recalls. *Advances in Consumer Research, 8,* 519–523.

Palenchar, M. J. (2005). Risk communication. In R. L. Heath (Ed.), *Encyclopedia of public relations* (Vol. 2, pp. 752–755). Thousand Oaks, CA: Sage.

Patel, A., & Reinsch, L. (2003). Companies can apologize: Corporate apologies and legal liability. *Business Communication Quarterly, 66,* 17–26.

Schultz, F., Utz, S., & Goritz, A. (2011). Is the medium the message? Perceptions of and reactions to crisis communication via Twitter, blogs and traditional media. *Public Relations Review, 37*(1), 20–27.

Schwarz, A. (2008). Covariation-based causal attributions during organizational crises: Suggestions for extending situational crisis communication theory. *International Journal of Strategic Communication, 2,* 31–53.

Sellnow, T. L., Ulmer, R. R., & Snider, M. (1998). The compatibility of corrective action in organizational crisis communication. *Communication Quarterly, 46,* 60–74.

Sturges, D. L. (1994). Communicating through crisis: A strategy for organizational survival. *Management Communication Quarterly, 7,* 297–316.

Ulmer, R. R. (2001). Effective crisis management through established stakeholder relationships. *Management Communication Quarterly, 14,* 590–615.

Weiner, B. (1986). *An attributional theory of motivation and emotion.* New York: Springer Verlag.

Weiner, B. (2006). *Social motivation, justice, and the moral emotions: An attributional Approach.* Mahwah, NJ: Lawrence Erlbaum.

33

Crisis Communication and Improvisation in a Digital Age

Mats Eriksson

In the network landscape, information and communication technologies (ICTs) and social media have tended to become increasingly important tools in the strategic communicator's toolbox (see, e.g., Eyrich, Padman, & Sweetser, 2009; Verhoeven, Tench, Zerfass, Moreno, & Verčič, 2012; Waters, Tindall, & Timothy, 2010). Due to the possibilities presented by communication technology, new work methods for and approaches to crisis communication have emerged (see, e.g., Eriksson, 2009; 2012; González-Herrero, & Smith, 2008, 2010; Hallahan, 2009; Hughes, & Palen, 2012). Via social media, many organizations today communicate with their surroundings in a more undirected and situation-oriented way through which the perception of a crisis is developed in interaction with the user. These working methods tend to be in line with the "new" late modern and/or postmodern crisis management perspectives, which argue that modern crisis managers have to improve their ability to improvise (see, e.g., Czarniawska, 2009; Gilpin, & Murphy, 2006, 2008, 2010; Weick, & Sutcliffe, 2007). Watchwords like *control* and *steering* in crisis communication have tended to become *passé,* or are at least changing in the networked world (see, e.g., Liu, Palen, Sutton, Hughes, & Vieweg, 2009; Palen, Vieweg, Liu, & Hughes, 2009; Wigley & Fontenot, 2010). The question is how crisis communicators' attitudes toward previously developed crisis management plans and strategies change in such a context. What happens to the strategy logic—with its roots in the military sphere—that has so long characterized the field of crisis management when the communicator is forced to improvise to an ever-increasing degree?

The research on strategic communication and social media in a crisis communication context is only in its infancy. Although the research is not extensive, several researchers in crisis management, public relations, marketing, and informatics proclaim that the greatest thing about social media and the Internet from the organization's point of view is the possibility to work with issues and knowledge management for signal detections and analysis of opinions and public behavior in potential crisis situations (see, e.g., Eysenbach, 2009; González-Herrero & Smith, 2008; Palenchar & Freberg, 2012; Wang & Belardo, 2009). Some researchers in marketing, such as Cova and White (2010), on the contrary, argue that social media mainly opens up dangerous possibilities for consumers to develop potential opposition. They conclude that online grouping generates "alter brands and counter brands that present opportunities and threats for existing brand managers" (p. 256). However, research is still lacking discussions of how this user-generated and situation-oriented communication landscape affects possibilities for those practitioners who need to apply traditional strategies, plans, and tactics in their strategic crisis communication.

The aim of this chapter is, therefore, to analyze and examine the role of classic crisis management strategy, planning, and tactics in a digital landscape of crisis communication, where far too rigid plans and guidelines seem to risk tying the hands of the crisis communicator. The chapter presents a qualitative case study of Scandinavian Airlines' work with social media in their crisis communication during the eruptions of the Icelandic volcano, Eyjafjallajökull, and the following closure of most of Europe's airspace from 15 to 20 April 2010. This chapter's main research questions are: (a) how did the involved crisis communicators combine today's possibilities for improvisation (via social media) with drilled strategies, tactics, action patterns and routines? And (b) how can we understand the concepts of classical strategy, planning and tactics in this new crisis communication context?

Strategy, Crisis Communication and Improvisation

Traditional concepts of strategy, planning and tactics have to be partly rephrased in the light of recent knowledge about crisis management and crisis communication. A short reflection on these concepts highlights the need for improvisation in modern crisis communication.

Defining Strategy, Planning and Tactics

The history of the concept of *strategy* is long and multifaceted, with a wide range of applications in politics, military and business (see, e.g., Gilbert, Hartman, Mauriel, & Freeman, 1988; Liddell Hart, 1967; Mintzberg, 1987; Schelling, 1960). Broadly stated, strategy is, in its original meaning, the planning, coordination, and general direction of military operations to meet overall military objectives. Strategy originally signified purely military planning and it comes from the Greek *strategos,* which means "the art of the general." From this point of view, strategy is an action or plan—with clear military roots and logic—to handle a specific situation and to achieve certain specific goals. To equate strategy with concrete management plans and planning is also the most common way to consider the strategy concept in the field of strategic communication. As Smith (2005) states: "strategy is the heart of planning for public relations, marketing communication and related areas" (p. 67). According to this view, strategy is a management function, which includes the mapping of the organization's course toward its overall destination, and the development of the organization and its strategic communications goals and objectives. In this approach, the general role of strategy is to guide the organization's members in their work. Another dimension of the classical view of strategy is the use of tactics. From the military point of view, *tactics* is the application of strategy at a field level (Liddell Hart, 1967). Recontextualizing the military definition, tactics are the more visible elements of public relations, marketing communication or crisis communication. Tactics include the use of a variety of "weapons", such as different media channels and messages, to reach the public.

The concepts of strategy, planning and tactics are, however, not clearly differentiated in the wide range of organizational management and communication management research. Sometimes the terms are equated with one another, and sometimes they are regarded as different steps in a single work process. The most common view is, however, that strategy is a result of good management planning: that is, that strategy is a consequence of planning. Mintzberg (1987, 2000) and Mintzberg and McHugh (1985) argued, however, for an alternative view of strategy and strategic planning. Mintzberg contended that the traditional view of senior managers planning detailed strategies (senior managers formulating courses of action that everyone else would implement) should be replaced with an approach where, instead, the organization's members *craft strategy.* This approach differs considerably from the classical strategy perspective in that craft "evokes traditional skill, dedication, perfection through the mastery of detail" (1987, p. 66). The craftsmen are involved and have a feeling of intimacy with the material at hand, and they develop their skills through long and extensive experience. Therefore, Mintzberg argued, from his alternative perspective on strategy, that: "(1) strategies are both plans for the future and patterns from the past; (2) strategies need not be deliberate—they can also emerge; (3) effective strategies develop in all kinds of strange ways; (4) to manage strategy is to craft thought and action, control and learning, stability and change" (Mintzberg, 1987, p. 67–73).

The Classical Approach to Strategic Crisis Management and Crisis Communication

Based on the military slant on the functions in management and bureaucracy of strategy, planning, and tactics, the classical approach to strategic crisis management and crisis communication has been developed. According to Gilpin and Murphy (2006; 2008; 2010), the classical approach to crisis management, in brief, is based on three categories of proposition that are taken for granted; these are: (a) specific *philosophical* assumptions, (b) assumptions about the *organization*, and (c) assumptions about *crisis management*. In short, the philosophical assumptions are characterized by the belief that it is possible to control events and the perception of events with the right kind of communication and actions. A typical assumption about the organization is that it is like a mechanical system, with clear boundaries between itself and its external environment. From this point of view, an organization and its crisis communicators are considered as the center of crisis communication with a view of communication as transmission and the organization as the transmitter. Another important element of this traditional approach is that the first aim of crisis management is to limit the loss of organizational resources as quickly as possible through restoration of organizational reputation and legitimacy. To adapt well to its environment, an organization should learn as much as possible of that same environment through research and issue management. The traditional approach is also based on assumptions colored by bureaucratic management logic, with a focus on top-down control and decision chains in an organization (Gilpin & Murphy, 2006; 2008; 2010). In practice, traditional crisis managers centralize information and decision-making in a smaller crisis management team or a single press officer (see, e.g., Kauffman, 1999). Also of great importance in the classical approach is following prepared crisis plans when time-sensitive and stressful situations are to be handled. The idea is that stressed crisis managers should act reflexively when a real crisis occurs. The main aim of crisis exercises and training is, therefore, to test whether or not the plans are well rehearsed (Falkheimer & Heide, 2010).

The New Approach to Strategic Crisis Management and Crisis Communication

There are, however, several researchers in crisis management who suggest that the classical approach to strategy, with its rigid focus on planning and control, can be destructive. Classical crisis plans are criticized as being fanciful, rather than reality-based (Clarke, 1999), and McConnell and Drennan (2006) argue that it is "mission impossible" to take control of today's crises through rigorous planning. The need for a new approach to crisis management and crisis communications is relatively broadly stated and the need for fewer written plans and routine exercises is emphasized. Instead, mental preparation and learning processes are proposed for those working with crisis management in practice (Falkheimer & Heide, 2010; Robert & Lajtha, 2002). In the field of public relations, Gilpin and Murphy (2006) argue, for example, that too much planning and detailed guidance in a crisis "narrows the vision [. . .]rather than expands it" (p. 376). Inspired by Weick's theory of organization enactment (1988, 1993), and theories of chaos and complexity (Richardson & Cilliers, 2001; Murphy, 1996), Gilpin and Murphy highlight the need for a change from the current dominant approach to crisis management because it "attempts to eliminate or control ambiguity, paradox and uncertainty rather than accept these as unavoidable and uncontrollable characteristics inherent in our world" (2006, p. 379). Instead, they argue for a new crisis management/crisis communication paradigm working with improvisation and chaos as underlying forces. The new approach to crisis management and crisis communication necessitates not only greater daring in abandoning controlling plans, but also an understanding of the need for a style of crisis organization and communication that develops in symbiosis with the particular crisis at hand (see also Czarniawska, 2009; Falkheimer & Heide, 2010; Holder, 2004; McConnell, & Drennan, 2006).

Modern, strategic crisis managers and communicators, inspired by the "new" approach, are urged to look at the work models within improvisational theater for the ideal logic (see, e.g. Finch & Welker, 2004). With neither a script nor a preordained, rehearsed series of actions to provide reassuring support and guidance, the theater ensemble using improv successfully navigates a challenging, spontaneous theatrical journey: "[I]mprovisation expands participants' abilities to perceive and reduces the need for intense and specific scripted preparation" (2004, p. 192). The idea is that the organization's and the crisis communicator's ability to improvise and to take action in a crisis can be trained much like the abilities of a theater ensemble—all in the name of finding the best work methods for a particular situation rather than following the rules, directions and plans that characterized the classic crisis communication logic. Modern crisis managers think, therefore, that it is impossible to center crisis communication in a single person or a crisis management team; instead, the crisis communication revolves around networks of several co-operating crisis communicators. He or she prefers interpersonal communication and micro communication, conducted directly with smaller audiences, to mass communication with a broader public (Falkheimer & Heide, 2009). Another characteristic of the modern crisis manager is the notion that total control and totally uniform messages in crisis communication constitute a utopia. Finally, the modern "new" approach is characterized by a view that the organization's crisis training is not done to test proposed strategies and plans; instead, the aim is to get crisis managers used to uncertainty and chaos (Gilpin & Murphy, 2006; 2008; 2010).

The Case of Scandinavian Airlines (SAS)

This section presents a case study of SAS's experiences of social media use in their crisis communication during the eruption of the Icelandic volcano, Eyjafjallajökull, in Spring 2010. After the crisis, SAS won the *SimpliFlying Awards of Excellence* award for the best use of social media in crisis communication. The award honored SAS's work to provide their customers with information via Facebook during the period of five days in April when flight traffic in large parts of Europe was canceled. The case of SAS was chosen as a valuable focus for study because of the way in which the organization and its practitioners experienced the new phenomenon of social media in strategic crisis communication. The empirical material was collected from six qualitative interviews with the head of corporate emergency response planning, the head of online communication, public relations officers, marketing managers, and staff working with customer relations and other strategic communication functions at the company. All the respondents had, in different ways, worked with social media as a tool in the company's crisis communication during the period of the ash cloud crisis.

The analytical work used an abductive research logic (see Dubois & Gadde, 2002) where prevailing concepts such as Mintzberg's (1987) view of strategy as crafting and Gilpin and Murphy's (2006; 2008; 2010) "new" approach to crisis management initiate questions and comparisons pertaining to the current phenomenon of crisis communication using social media. The study focuses, therefore, on the specific circumstances of crisis communication with social media, based on "classical" and "new" assumptions and directions about crisis management and crisis communication strategy. In particular, it identifies a number of tensions between the visions of classical and new approaches for crisis management and crisis communication, and the realities of crisis work using social media. The research logic was not to prejudice these a priori hypotheses; instead these non-formulated hypotheses guided the study's analytical work from the outset (see e.g., Layder, 1993). The aim was to organize new concepts about the realities for strategic crisis management and crisis communication in the context of social media. After the interviews, in a first analytical step, the material was grouped into three descriptive and analytical themes: (a) organizing, (b) messages and tactics, and (c) emergence of (new) structures. The thematic categorization was based on themes from the theoretical framework, the interview questions, and the crisis communication practitioners' experiences expressed during the interviews.

SAS's Experiences of Social Media Use in Crisis Communication

Organization

When the ash cloud crisis occurred, social media was not a prior channel for crisis management and crisis communication at SAS. Before the crisis, the director of online strategy and communications had begun to plan how the company could possibly handle the social media flows of information in future, extraordinary situations. She had, among other things, started to arrange a solution where the company's already existing phone-based customer service could also answer questions asked by customers and others on Facebook. This service had, however, not started, when the ash cloud traffic disruption occurred. Instead, at this time, she started to organize the crisis communication after she had had her attention drawn to the expanding discussions of the issue on Facebook. Several practitioners interviewed in this study argued that it was customers' needs that set the pace and the agenda in this initial phase of the crisis:

> [I]f we hadn't had a page, we might have chosen not to start one. But we saw now that there was a need. So we started completely based on the customer. We realized that we simply couldn't shut the channel down just because we weren't ready yet [. . .] We absolutely couldn't shut down and say that we didn't have time to answer. There was such a huge need.
>
> *Project manager, customer relations*

During the first hours, the director of online strategy and communications ran the company's Facebook conversation on her own. But she soon realized she needed help to handle the increasing number of issues. She asked two colleagues from other communication-related departments in the company for help. The two colleagues were experienced Facebook users:

> [She] chose us mainly because she knew that we hung out on Facebook. We were quite familiar with the language—it's important that you use the right language and approach. And we were fast. And we were hungry and curious. And above all fearless.
>
> *Project manager, customer relations*

> That she called me was probably because I had helped before at certain times with portals and so on and was there as a resource. It was a coincidence. I don't think we had a plan. I think it just happened. After that, we improvised while it happened.
>
> *Head of internal online communication*

In this initial phase of the crisis, there were no emergency and/or crisis management plans, and so forth, to dictate who should work with the company's online crisis communication on Facebook. Instead, the choice of co-workers was related to previous experience of the medium. An important criterion in the selection of people was also that they would have the confidence to act and communicate without detailed guidance. Step by step, in the second phase of the crisis, more skills were added to the team. The new team members were people with expertise in fields such as legal issues, repayments, travel guarantees. At most, five people worked together at the same time. In the evenings, nights and early mornings, the members in the Facebook team worked from home. The team interacted with each other and organized their work via Skype and through an internal company blog. Using these communication tools, they also sought answers to customers' questions by contacting internal colleagues. The daytime work was at an office in the company's communication department. The team members were assigned different roles by the head of online communication: "We had different roles in the room [. . . .] I was in charge of all communication and decided what was what. That we used all channels. I coordinated the message and had a coordinating role" (head of online strategy and communication).

Overall crisis communication through social media was, however, only indirectly controlled by the organization's predetermined crisis management plans and routines, even though the head of online communication tried to organize the work and give it some structure: "We never mentioned the emergency file or that we could take something from it and apply it directly to this" (head of internal online communication). Instead, the routines and patterns that characterized the work grew more in interaction with incoming questions and the nature of the discussions in the social media: "The work wasn't structured—it was created there and then and it worked. It was 'try and seek.' Calling it a new paradigm is to exaggerate—but for us it was a change" (head of corporate emergency response planning).

These more improvised working methods were perceived as a success, although some of the team members also faced a problem in the sense that pre-established plans, guidelines and manuals were overlooked: "I am the kind of person who likes checklists so that everyone knows what to do. That's not what it was like. [. . .] Next time I hope we use the file more" (head of internal online communication).

Messages and Tactics

Initially, customers and other incoming queries almost exclusively set the message agenda on Facebook. Even if the head of online communication tried to coordinate the communication, in the initial phase of the crisis the co-workers were forced to act quickly and under uncertainty when they answered Facebook users' questions. The unspoken goal that emerged during the work was to provide the most prompt information service possible. But gradually, from the company's strategic point of view, more coordinated messages were delivered through social media:

> In the beginning it was very much about responding to questions. But as our colleagues around the world got organized, arranged buses, fixed alternative routes and so on, they phoned us. The station manager in Madrid could call and let us know that they had five coaches. "Can you go on Facebook and tell them that they leave from the station and on to . . . " Towards the end, or in the middle, once we had organized alternative routes, we started using targeted messages.
>
> *Head of internal online communication*

In the second phase of the crisis, message tactics emerged that advocated that a single crisis communicator at the company should deliver short uncomplicated, concise and positive Facebook messages. The team who normally worked with customer relations introduced the tactics. Using such tactics it was, according to the interviewees, quite often possible to reach the underlying goal, which was to take command of the forthcoming discussions:

> We were very good at closing discussions. We had help from Customer Relations. "Try closing the discussion! So that topics don't get too long because people refuse to give up!"
>
> *Head of internal online communication*

At its worst, of course the customer is in control. You can't consider your responses. At the same time, I think we had an enormous amount of influence because we had the very explicit idea of not getting hooked by customers and trying to turn something negative into positive. And not focusing on the small stuff. We gave customers alternatives and focused on making it positive. So I think that on the whole we were in control. We've got lots of concrete examples where we had negative flows which we totally turned.

Project manager, customer relations

Another emerging tactic was that the messages should have an informal and personal touch, as it was considered as appropriate in social media: "We must get rid of the formalities—we can't sit and write 'Dear customer' on Facebook—it doesn't fit!" (Project manager, customer relations). And, to avoid distributing old information and to transfer some of the liability for the Facebook content, the team used web links to other web pages in their messages. Using hypertext links to Scandinavian Airlines' everyday web pages, they tried to provide updated information about cancelled flights:

When we provided information, we didn't always have concrete answers—but we tried to refer people to pages on the web site. If they, for example, asked about buses, we had a page we could link to and that page was constantly being updated. If they had questions about rebooking, we linked to that. We always gave the impression that we were helping and that we cared. We tried not to write specifically that there would be a bus at a certain. Because, before you knew it, everything changed.

Project manager, customer relations

The co-workers in the Facebook team played, so to speak, the role of guides in the Internet flow of information concerning the ash cloud crisis; guides who, to some degree, tried to influence the image of the crisis through their choice of messages.

The Emergence of (New) Structures

The use of social media in crisis communication, however, shapes new patterns and structures in crisis management. One such structure identified in the case study was that the crisis communicators thought they should be more informal and spontaneous in their communication because the information communicated through Facebook was not published on the company's formal website. Therefore, on the company's Facebook group page, both reputation-oriented and company-verified information was presented side by side:

It was quite good. They were the ones posting on the page. We weren't responsible for it. And everyone knew that as well. This is from Kalle and SAS is not to be held accountable . . . So we never had to check info. If you want to take Kalle's advice, that's entirely up to you. It's not something we published. And that was good. It didn't take the time we usually need to check up on things.

Head of internal online communication

Thus, Facebook came to be a forum for the SAS Group's own employees who, for various reasons, needed to communicate and keep themselves informed about how the crisis was evolving. The reason was that the reputation-oriented information on Facebook, to some degree, stayed ahead of the information on the company's website: "Actually, eventually there was more up-to-date information on Facebook than on the website. We're a large group and it was more complex to update all our sites" (project manager, customer relations). Through the medium's ability to establish instant communities and blur the boundaries between the internal and external, a strong positive feeling of cohesion developed around the common problems, according to the crisis communicators involved:

> A pilot, who had been stranded in Chicago, could write "I'll just tie my tie, get to the airport and fly you home." And someone would respond "God, that's great/good." Everyone became friends; there was a great feeling of community. With our employees around the world. Everyone thought it was a blast to be able to help.
>
> *Head of internal online communication*

These developments were seen mostly as positive. But the crisis communicators involved were also, paradoxically, concerned about internal issues being mixed with public issues.

Discussion

The case study shows some structural concepts and trends that pave the way to a new understanding of crisis communication in the landscape of social media. The key insights might be summarized in three theses.

1. Crisis Management Using Social Media Highlights Important Tensions Between Old and New Approaches for Crisis Management and Crisis Communication

According to the case presented in this chapter, crisis communication practitioners working in the digital landscape are forced to accept ambiguity and uncertainty to a higher degree than before. With access to social media, they are also willing to improvise to a higher degree then they might have done earlier. Such improvisation takes place both when they are organizing the work, and when they are choosing the messages in their crisis communication. However, despite this higher level of improvisation, paradoxically, some assumptions connected to the classical approach to crisis management influence the practitioners' view of best practice in crisis communication (see González-Herrero & Smith, 2010). The practice of crisis communication including social media tends, therefore, to emerge in an interaction between the standards and ideals belonging to the classical perspective on crisis communication (such as the need for clear boundaries between internal and external, clearly defined roles and centralization of decision making and message design to pre-established crisis management teams) and assumptions related to the digital age, such as instant communities, cross-bordering timeless networks and relentless connectivity.

2. Crisis Management Using Social Media Develops the Need for a New Metaphor for the Understanding and Practice of Future Crisis Communication

A crisis manager and/or crisis communicator from the classical normative crisis management point of view can metaphorically be seen as a *commander-in-chief*. Such a crisis communicator is likened to an authoritative military figure fighting for control over the flow of information. In the digital age, this normative metaphor for best practice of crisis communication seems to be under transformation. On the one hand, today's crisis communicators still use social media to seek to control and direct the image of the organization and of a particular crisis. But on the other hand, this "new" crisis communicator communicates, paradoxically, in a more decentralized, undirected and user-generated manner when he or she adapts to the digital network society's expectations and possibilities for a more user-driven communication. Such a digital age practitioner of crisis management and crisis communication could metaphorically be described as an *improvising real-time director*. In Grunig's (see, e.g., L. A. Grunig, J. E. Grunig, & Dozier, 2002) terms, such a metaphor can be considered as a "mixed motive" approach where asymmetrical logics and practices are combined with more symmetrical ones. Hopefully, such a metaphor for understanding crisis work in the digital age can be useful from several perspectives. First, for researchers who want to understand the phenomenon of strategic crisis communication in a new way. Second, for crisis communication practitioners in need of appropriate new working approaches and logics.

3. Crisis Management Using Social Media Highlights the Need for a Redefinition of the Concept of Strategy in Strategic Communication and Crisis Communication

Phillips and Young (2009) argued that both researchers and practitioners in the field of public relations and strategic communication are in need of "new ways in which communications strategies can be re-evaluated, redefined and developed in order to succeed" (p. 136) in the age of social media. One way, according to this study, is to complement or redefine the classical viewpoint of strategy with one that accepts higher levels of uncertainty than have erstwhile been accepted in the field. Such an understanding of strategy was, as already mentioned, favored by Mintzberg in the 1980s when he claimed that effective strategies evolved "in the strangest places and develop[ed] through the most unexpected means" (1987, p. 70), rather than in the course of careful planning at the top management level. Mintzberg also argued that these are effective "grass-roots" strategies or *crafting* strategies wherever people have the capacity to learn. Also typical for such crafting of strategy is, according to Mintzberg, the combination of "deliberation and control with flexibility and organizational learning" (1987, p. 70). With such a broad view of strategy in the crisis management context, opportunities for a complementary framework for understanding successful management in crisis communication within social media are created. It is a framework that highlights crisis managers' and crisis communicators' own experience, commitments, and abilities to improvise and learn, as much as it highlights the application of bureaucratic plans prepared at the top management level.

Conclusions and Perspectives

There is, as declared, a tension between the need for planning and structuring versus the need for improvisation and adaption in crisis management, according to several crisis management researchers. This chapter stresses the fact that the conditions for crisis communications in the digital age further reveal such tensions. Within the practitioner who is engaged in crisis communication through social media there occurs a mental struggle between the "classical" logic and the "new" logic for understanding and practicing crisis management and crisis communication. On the one hand, the digital crisis communicator improvises and interacts with his or her surroundings to a greater extent than ever before. On the other hand, crisis communicators are still influenced by ideals that advocate centralized decision-making, control of information flows, and detailed crisis management plans. The final conclusion is, however, that, more than ever before, crisis communication practitioners working in the digital landscape improvise and rid themselves of the requirement to implement dictated crisis management rules and plans. The question is, however, how both researchers and practitioners should understand the concept of strategy in this context. Could it be that strategy has now played out its role as a tool in this situation-oriented context of crisis management and new media? Or is the meaning of the concept changing? According to this study, an alternative explanation and understanding of the strategy concept is needed in the context of effective digital crisis management. There is also a need for new understanding of how successful strategies emerge in this context. If we assume that Scandinavian Airlines' award-winning crisis communication through social media was effective and successful, we can from this case study draw some interesting conclusions about how such effective strategies apparently develop. Effective crisis communication seems not to be about senior crisis and/or emergency managers sitting in the office dictating successful courses. Instead, it is more about experienced and involved crisis communicators who improvise in close relation with the material at hand. Effective strategies seem to develop by the practitioners being in close contact with the situation. The practice of effective strategic crisis communication in the digital age can, therefore, be compared to the *craftsman logic*. According to Mintzberg (1987) the craftsman has an "intimate knowledge of her work, her capabilities, and her markers" (p. 66). The craftsman also "senses rather than analyzes" because her "knowledge is tacit" (p. 66). Craft strategy is, therefore, more about devotion, involvement with material and learning. Such a crafting perspective on strategy seems also, finally, to be in alignment with Gilpin and Murphy's (2010) complexity approach on crisis management and crisis communication where ambiguity "encourages adaptive learning and sensemaking" (p. 684) is demanded. Effective strategy in today's new digital environment for crisis management and crisis communication is, therefore, according this study, more about *crafting strategy*, in Mintzberg's terms, than implementing strategy.

In conclusion, some reflections about the limits of the case study's research design. First, it is just a single case study and there is, therefore, no basis for scientific generalization. The purpose was, instead, to generalize theoretical and conceptual propositions (see the *Discussion* section of this chapter). Second, the company did not initially consider the ash cloud incident as a crisis; it was seen more as a major traffic disruption. If it had been a serious accident, such as an airplane crash, probably a different scenario of crisis or emergency management would have occurred, working more in line with the "classical" logic of crisis management, according to the interviewees. Third, this case study took place at a moment when social media was not yet implemented in the company's emergency plans and guidelines. These circumstances explain, in some part, the high level of improvisation and the effective grassroots strategies identified in the crisis work. Therefore, for a more nuanced knowledge, future studies are required of (a) the use of social media as a strategic tool in other kinds of crises—for example, crises without an insidious chain of events and/or crises where the organization has to repair images; and (b) the use of social media at the stage when it is already implemented in pre-established crisis management plans and guidelines.

The insights from this chapter add tentative knowledge about strategy work and crisis planning in the digital age to the body of knowledge in strategic communication. According to this chapter, an alternative explanation of the strategy concept is needed in digital crisis management. In such situations, effective strategy work seems to be more about crafting strategy than implementing strategy. This chapter, like most of the existing research on digital crisis communication, concerns macro-level questions about policy and planning rather than questions about argumentation and conversation between stakeholders. Therefore, further research is needed on the latter item, and especially studies concerning the "crafting" of the content in organizations. How are, for example, strategic crisis communication messages developed in interaction with comments and questions from audiences on the Web? Research methods from linguistics and speech communication (e.g., conversation analysis) may be used to deal with matters such as these, which are, from the viewpoint of strategic communication, highly important.

References

Clarke, L. (1999). *Mission improbable. Using fantasy documents to tame disaster*. Chicago, IL: University of Chicago.

Cova, B., & White, T. (2010). Counter-brand and alter-brand communities: the impact of Web 2.0 on tribal marketing approaches. *Journal of Marketing Management, 26,* 256–270.

Czarniawska, B. (Ed.) (2009). *Organizing in the face of risk and threat*. Northampton, MA: Edward Elgar.

Dubois, A., & Gadde, L-E. (2002). Systematic combining: An abductive approach to case research. *Journal of Business Research 55,* 553–560.

Eriksson, M. (2009). *Nätens kriskommunikation* [Crisis communication and the net]. Lund, Sweden: Studentlitteratur.

Eriksson, M. (2012). On-line strategic crisis communication: In search of a descriptive model approach. *International Journal of Strategic Communication, 6,* 309–327.

Eyrich, N., Padman, M. L., & Sweetser, K. D. (2008). PR practitioners' use of social media tools and communication technology. *Public Relations Review, 34,* 412–414.

Eysenbach, G. (2009). Infodemiology and infoveillance: Framework for an emerging set of public health informatics methods to analyze search, communication and public behaviour on the Internet. *Journal of Medical Internet Research, 11*(1):e11.

Falkheimer, J., & Heide, M. (2009). Crisis communication in a new world: Reaching multicultural publics through old and new media. *Nordicom Review 30,* 55–65.

Falkheimer, J., & Heide, M. (2010). Crisis communicators in change: From plans to improvisations. In W. T. Coombs & S. J. Holladay (Eds.), *The Handbook of Crisis Communication* (pp. 511–525). Malden, MA: Wiley-Blackwell.

Finch, M., & Welker, L. (2004). Informed organizational improvisation: A metaphor and method for understanding, anticipating, and performatively constructing the organization's precrisis environment. In D. P. Millar & R. L. Heath (Eds.), *Responding to crisis: a rhetorical approach to crisis communication* (pp. 189–200). Mahwah, NJ: Lawrence Erlbaum.

Gilbert, D. R,, Hartman, E., Mauriel, J., & Freeman, R. E. (1988). *A logic for strategy.* Cambridge, MA: Ballinger Publishing Company.

Gilpin, D., & Murphy, P. J. (2006). Reframing crisis management through complexity. In C. H. Botan & V. Hazleton (Eds.), *Public Relations Theory II* (pp. 375–392). Mahwah, NJ: Lawrence Erlbaum.

Gilpin, D. R., & Murphy, P. J. (2008). *Crisis management in a complex world.* New York: Oxford University Press.

Gilpin, D. R., & Murphy, P. J. (2010). Complexity and crises: A new paradigm. In W. T. Coombs & S. J. Holladay (Eds.), *The Handbook of Crisis Communication* (pp. 683–690). Malden, MA: Wiley-Blackwell.

González-Herrero, A., & Smith, S. (2008). Crisis communications management on the Web: How Internet-based technologies are changing the way public relations professionals handle business crises. *Journal of Contingencies and Crisis Management, 16,* 143–153.

González-Herrero, A., & Smith, S. (2010). Crisis communication management 2.0: Organizational principles to manage crisis in an online world. *Organizational Development Journal, 28,* 97–105.

Grunig, L. A., Grunig, J. E., & Dozier, D. M. (2002). *Excellent public relations and effective organizations: a study of communication management in three countries.* Mahwah, NJ: Lawrence Erlbaum.

Hallahan, K. (2009). Crises and risk in cyberspace. In R. L. Heath & D. O'Hair (Eds.), *Handbook of risk and crisis communication* (pp. 412–445). New York: Routledge.

Holder, T. (2004). Constructing response during uncertainty: Organizing for crisis. In D. P. Millar & R. L. Heath (Eds.), *Responding to crisis: a rhetorical approach to crisis communication* (pp. 51–62). Mahwah, NJ: Lawrence Erlbaum.

Hughes, A. L., & Palen, L. (2012). The evolving role of the public information officer: An examination of social media in emergency management. *Journal of Homeland Security and Emergency Management, 9(1),* Article 22, 1–20

Kauffman, J. (1999). Adding fuel to the fire: NASA's crisis communication regarding Apollo 1. *Public Relations Review, 25,* 421–432.

Layder, D. (1993). *New strategies in social research: an introduction and guide.* Cambridge: Polity Press.

Liddell Hart, B. H. (1967). *Strategy. The indirect approach.* London, England: Faber and Faber.

Liu, S., Palen L., Sutton, J., Hughes, A., & Vieweg, S. (2009). Citizen photojournalism during crisis events. In S. Allan & E. Thorsen (Eds.), *Citizen journalism: Global perspectives* (pp. 43–65). New York: Peter Lang.

McConnell, A., & Drennan, L. (2006). Mission impossible? Planning and preparing for crisis. *Journal of Contingencies and Crisis Management, 14,* 59–70.

Mintzberg, H. (1987). Crafting strategy. *Harvard Business Review,* July–August, 66–74.

Mintzberg, H. (2000). *The rise and fall of strategic planning.* London, England: Prentice Hall.

Mintzberg, H., & McHugh, A. (1985). Strategy formation in an adhocracy. *Administrative Science Quarterly, 30,* 160–197.

Murphy, P. (1996). Chaos theory as a model for managing issues and crises. *Public Relations Review, 22*(2), 95–113.

Palen, L., Vieweg, S., Liu, S., & Hughes, A. (2009). Crisis in a networked world: Features of computer-mediated communication in the April 16, 2007 Virginia Tech Event. *Social Science Computing Review, 27,* 467–480.

Palenchar, M. J., & Freberg, K. (2012). Emergency management planning: Risk, crisis, issues and social media. In B. A. Olaniran, D. E. Williams & W. T. Coombs (Eds.), *Pre-crisis planning, communication, and management: preparing for the inevitable* (pp. 147–169). New York: Peter Lang.

Phillips, D. & Young, P. (2009). *Online public relations: a practical guide to developing an online strategy in the world of social media* (2nd ed.) London: Kogan Page

Richardson, K.A., & Cilliers, P. (2001). What is complexity science? A view from different directions. *Emergence, 3*(1), 5–22.

Robert, B., & Lajtha, C. (2002). A new approach to crisis management. *Journal of Contingencies and Crisis Management, 10,* 181–191.

Schelling, T.C. (1960). *The strategy of conflict.* Cambridge, MA: Harvard University Press.

Smith, R. D. (2005). *Strategic planning for public relations* (2nd ed.). Mahwah, NJ: Lawrence Erlbaum.

Verhoeven, P., Tench, R., Zerfass, A., Moreno, A., & Verčič, D. (2012). How European PR practitioners handle digital and social media. *Public Relations Review, 38,* 162–164.

Wang, W. T., & Belardo, S. (2009). The role of knowledge management in achieving effective crisis management: A case study. *Journal of Information Science, 35,* 635–659.

Waters, R., Tindall, N., & Timothy, M. (2010). Media catching and the journalist–public relations practitioner relationship: How social media are changing the practice of media relations. *Journal of Public Relations Research, 22,* 241–264.

Weick, K. E. (1988). Enacted sense-making in crisis situations. *Journal of Management Studies, 25,* 305–317.

Weick, K. E. (1993). *Organizational redesign as improvisation. Organizational change and redesign: ideas and insights for improving performance.* New York: Oxford University Press.

Weick, K. E., & Sutcliffe, K. M. (2007). *Managing the unexpected: Resilient performance in an age of uncertainty.* San Francisco, CA: Jossey-Bass.

Wigley, S., & Fontenot, M. (2010). Crisis managers losing control of the message: A pilot study of the Virginia Tech shooting. *Public Relations Review, 36,* 187–189.

34

Strategizing Risk Communication

Juliana Raupp

More than ever before, in the current day, organizations act in a social environment characterized by a high public awareness of uncertainty, threats and dangers. Political organizations, public authorities and corporations have to make and communicate strategic decisions fraught with risk: deliberately or not, they are involved in risk communication. However, what level of risk is perceived as tolerable is inherently subjective and constantly renegotiated in public. Strategic risk communication is confronted with various and contradicting perceptions of risk by actors and groups inside and outside an organization. The purpose of this chapter is to bring theories of risk communication research to the field of strategic communication. Strategy is an under-researched topic in risk communication research (Chess & Johnson, 2010) and, likewise, scholarship on communication management is barely concerned with matters of risk communication.

A baseline in sociological risk research is the recognition of risk as socially constructed. Another common albeit disputed assumption in risk research is the distinction between public risk assessments and expert ones. Furthermore, the influential social amplification of risk (SARF) concept takes into account the distortions by socially "amplified" risk perceptions in public discourse. Thus risk communication is confronted with various and often conflicting risk perceptions. Strategy within the framework of risk communication must respond to divergent risk perceptions and therefore it will be conceptualized as an emergent sense-making and framing activity under the conditions of perceived uncertainties and dangers. By developing this conceptual framework for examining strategy in risk communication, this chapter aims to enhance the research on risk communication. Next to this, it offers a new perspective on strategic communication by applying risk communication theories to the field of organizational communication.

Risk and Risk Communication

Defining Risk

Risk relates to occurrences in the future associated with damage and loss, sometimes also with opportunities (Ale, 2009). While societies have always been exposed to risk and dangers, modern societies seem especially prone to risks (Beck, 1992). According to Beck (1992) present societies create modern risks such as ecological risks, technological and radiological hazards, and risks related to globalization. The threats and dangers related with these risks are not easily detectible and are difficult to quantify. Furthermore, dealing with these risks is always confrontational, as the risks and benefits are not equally distributed in societies.

The dominant paradigm in defining risk, however, stems from the exact sciences. Specialists who are professionally engaged in the study of risk work mainly in the health sector, in the domains of technology and engineering, and in insurance companies. The relevant categories within which risk experts think are statistic probabilities, projections and limit values. A baseline definition poses risks as "probabilistic occurrences that can have positive or negative outcomes of various magnitudes" (Proutheau & Heath, 2010, p. 40). Risk assessment consists of the identification of potential adverse events, of modeling and quantifying probabilities, and of consequences (Ale, 2009). Within that context, risk is defined as the likelihood of a specific event occurring multiplied by the magnitude of consequences associated with that event. Based on that definition, risk assessment aims on minimizing over- or underestimations of vulnerability to risk and hazards (for an overview, see Renn, 1998a).

Risk Communication

Peter Sandman (1987), a communication professional, challenged this notion from a risk communication perspective. He pointed to the gap between risk as framed by the rationality of hard sciences and the public way of perceiving risks. According to Sandman, there is a (low) correlation between a risk's *hazard* (how much harm it is likely to do) and its *outrage* (how upsetting it is likely to be to many people). His formula *risk = hazard + outrage* added the public perception of risks to the definition of risk.

Underlying this definition is the assumption of a gap between public perception and experts' perception of risk. It was this assumed gap that prompted social scientists to re-define risk. Risks were no longer considered solely as probabilities that could be measured and quantified. Also, the distinction between the "objective" risk assessment by experts and the "subjective" risk perception by the non-professional public was questioned (Fischhoff, Watson & Hope, 1984). Social and cultural sciences consider the perception of risk as principally contingent. Whether a condition is regarded as hazardous is based not on "hard" facts and first-hand experience but on second-hand information and the documentations of experts (Beck, 1992). One important contribution of social and cultural sciences was to demonstrate the importance of social values in risk perception and risk acceptance (R. E. Kasperson et al., 1988; Rayner, 1992; Sjöberg, 2000). Such assumptions are part of what Ben-Ari and Or-Chen (2009) called the contextualist perspective in risk research. Also, socio-cultural approaches stress the fact that risks are inseparably linked to conflicts over the distribution of power in society (Beck, 1992; Tansey & Rayner, 2010).

Thus, with risk definitions in the social sciences, context is seen as decisive in determining which occurrences constitute a risk and which do not. However, depending on their underlying theoretical framework, scholars disagree on how to judge positivist risk assessments. Some authors, especially those who argue from a behaviorist point of view, have accepted that there is some "truth" in probabilistic risk assessment. Yet they have claimed that there is another, additional "truth" grounded in the way human beings process information (J. X. Kasperson, R. E. Kasperson, Pidgeon & Slovic, 2003). Information processing is naturally biased and managerial decision making under the conditions of risk is especially likely to be guided not only by some degree of overestimation but also by risk avoidance (Kahneman & Tversky, 1979). From this perspective, calculating risk is one of the many ways of dealing with the problems of decision making in the face of uncertainty. Others argue from a more radical constructionist view and claim that positivist risk assessments are themselves constructions. Slovic (1999) summarized the constructionist view in the simple statement: "[T]here is no such thing as 'real risk' or 'objective risk'" (p. 690). Beck (1992) argued, moreover, that experts who deal professionally with risks are not at all independent or objective. Instead, they are inherently value-driven, so their risk perception is as subjective as is the public risk perception.

Apart from the ontological dimension that all that we perceive can be regarded as socially constructed since there is no straightforward correspondence between our experiences and the world outside our heads, there is also a political dimension inherent in the social-constructionist perspective. Scholars have stressed the fact that experts are part of a societal conflict on framing a problem as risk: Risk assessment has become a "battlefield" (Slovic, 1999; see also Douglas & Wildavsky, 1982; Fischhoff et al., 1984; Stern, 1991). Altering the fundamental question of risk–benefit analysis— "How safe is safe enough?" (Fischhoff, Slovic & Lichtenstein, 1978)—Rayner and Cantor (1987) proposed to ask, "How fair is safe enough?" (p. 3). Competing and conflicting interests negotiate risks and their consequences; the question as to which definition of risk becomes the generally accepted one becomes a question of power. As Stern aptly stated: "Risk communication is not information transfer, but a type of political discourse." (Stern, 1991, p. 100).

Drawing on those insights, risk communication research widened its perspective. Originally, risk communication ought to ventilate and translate expert knowledge and educate the public as to how to behave in the face of risks. The basic idea in risk communication research in the 1980s and 1990s was that understanding public risk perception would promote the design of effective risk communication models (Gurabardhi, Gutteling & Kuttschreuter, 2004). The focus of empirical risk communication research was on measuring the effectiveness of risk messages. In fact, until the present day, communication effects research has formed a large part of risk communication research. Moreover, with the paradigmatic turn in media effects research from its previous concentration on a more or less passive audience, risk communication research became more refined in terms of specifying attitudes, information-seeking behavior and knowledge of special target groups as important variables for explaining the success or failure of risk communication campaigns (McGuire, 2001). This approach towards risk communication is commonly defined as instrumental or technical (Hayenhjelm, 2006; Renn, 1998b).

With the proliferation of constructionist, contextual, and situational perspectives, scholars and professionals acknowledged that risk communication must accomplish more than merely conveying experts' knowledge to the public. Risk communication now includes participatory practices like public hearings, stakeholder decision groups and referenda (Heath, Palenchar & O'Hair, 2010; McComas, Arvai & Besley, 2010; Renn, 1998a, 1998b). This new approach towards risk communication is categorized as democratic or dialogic (Hayenhjelm, 2006; Renn, 2003). Interaction is now part of the US National Research Council's definition of risk communication as "an interactive process of exchange of information and opinion among individuals, groups and institutions. It involves multiple messages about the nature of risk and other messages, not strictly about risk, that express concerns, opinions, or reactions to risk messages or to legal and institutional arrangements for risk management" (cited in Ulmer, Seeger & Sellnow, 2010, p. 184). Participation and deliberation have become buzzwords in parts of risk communication research. But although there is a general agreement that the public has to be involved in order to be reached by risk communication efforts, there is considerable disagreement on the degree to which the public should also be involved in risk decision making. The expectancy is that people condone a decision if they have been involved in the decision-making process (Heath, Palenchar & O'Hair, 2010). However, the success of participatory risk communication is difficult to evaluate empirically (Renn, 2003; McComas, Arvai & Besley, 2010). Also, participatory risk communication may result in a relativization of power relationships. After all, as Coombs and Holladay (2010) state dryly in their textbook on public relations: "effective risk communication requires corporations to share their power with constituents" (p. 230). The option for more participation in the risk decision-making process depends on the political and social values of its proponents (R. E. Kasperson, 1986). When one sees experts' and public perceptions of risk as principally equal, or when one even claims that the public has a better intuition for what is potentially harmful, then the participation of the public in the risk decision-making process is vital. On the other hand, when one acknowledges that there is a gap between the experts' and the public risk assessment, but regards the experts' view as better informed, then the focus is on involving the public in the risk communication process in order to gain understanding and acceptance. Hayenhjelm (2006) provides a helpful suggestion for seeing this problem in a differentiated way. She distinguishes between different roles in the risk communication context. Participants in the communicative role possess the power to define the agenda and take the initiative for the communication. The informational and epistemological role is characterized by influence in terms of expertise and knowledge about hazardous activities and its consequences. The risk role is associated with influence over precautionary and mitigating decisions. Based on that distinction, Hayenhjelm (2006) identifies three dimensions of asymmetry: communicative, informational and risk role asymmetry. In principle, all participants in a risk communication process can take on all three different roles, but usually the roles and the distribution of influence are clustered around specific parties. For example, the party who initiates the communicative process—for example, the regulating governmental agency—is most likely also the one with the most knowledge and influence over a situation. In light of that fine-grained picture of the risk communication setting, Hayenhjelm (2006) concludes that when the aim is to provide impartial information about a scope of potential dangers, "then asymmetry as such need not be a problem" (p. 13). In the decision-making process, however, asymmetries must be handled with care.

The Social Amplification of Risk Framework

A deficiency in much risk communication research is that the complexity of communication is not adequately reflected. Risk communication involves various groups of players—not only risk managers, experts and the public. One notable exception is the concept of social amplification of risk (J. X. Kasperson et al., 2003; R. E. Kasperson, 1992; R. E. Kasperson, et al., 1988). This concept regards risk communication as a process that is amplified by several social processes, which together lead to a spread of impact: the much-cited "ripple effect" of risk events. One core argument of the concept is that risks that experts estimate to be relatively low will be amplified by societal and social political developments whereas other, potentially more harmful hazards will receive less public attention, leading to risk attenuation. The social amplification of risk framework acknowledges that not only professional risk communication agencies but also other agents play an important role in the risk communication process: individuals, groups, news media, politicians, public agencies and interest groups can and do function as amplification stations. Risk signals in the mass media often lead to dramatic shifts in the risk discourse, its symbols and pictures.

The mechanistic metaphor of amplification may provoke the association of linear information processing. But as the authors stress there is no simple causal relationship between, for example, amplification by mass media and the public perception of risks; a greater amount of media coverage does not necessarily lead to the amplification of risk (J. X. Kasperson et al., 2003). Nevertheless, critics argue that the role of the news media is simplified (Murdock, 2010; Murdock, Petts & Horlick-Jones, 2003; Petts, Horlick-Jones & Murdock, 2001). When it comes to risk and crisis communication, possible effects of news media are highly dependent on how the people make use of them and of other means of communication (Neuwirth, 2010). Also with regard to the content of media coverage, there is no clear media effect. While, for example, intense media coverage could result in amplification, messages of self-efficacy may attenuate this effect (McComas, 2006; Wahlberg & Sjoberg, 2000). Furthermore, amplification is dependent on other factors, such as trust. Trust in communication refers to the expectancy that the information provided is true. Therefore, trust and credibility are seen as important variables in risk communication research (Renn & Levine, 1991; Siegrist & Cvetkovich, 2000; Siegrist, Cvetkovich & Roth, 2000).

The analytical value of the social amplification of risk framework lies in the integration of "patterns of interacting amplification mechanisms, the nature of risks and risk events, and social contextual effects" (J. X. Kasperson et al., 2003, p. 40). Yet, the framework should be augmented in order to better depict the non-linear interaction processes between the actors and the feedback processes that constantly shape risk perception. Also, whereas the original model focuses on the impact of risk in economic terms, an enhanced model that takes into account various types of organizations—such as public authorities or non-profit organizations—must take into account intangible impacts like the loss of credibility.

The Peculiarities of Risk Communication

When it comes to applying the concept of strategy to risk communication, one may ask: What distinguishes risk communication from other forms of strategic communication? Both risk communication and public relations are, after all, forms of strategic communication that, according to Palenchar and Heath (2007), may add value to society. But risk communication has two peculiarities: first, more than other forms of communication, risk communication deals with uncertainty (Ulmer, Sellnow & Seeger, 2010). As techniques of risk assessment become more sophisticated, so too grow the challenges for risk communicators to inform others about variability and uncertainty (Thompson, 2002). Secondly, risk communication is an exceptionally conflict-ridden field of communication (Plough & Sheldon, 1987; Slovic, 1999; Stern, 1991). Its practitioners must deal with conflicting perceptions of risks, crises and disasters. The public is highly sensitive to risks nowadays, and many groups and individuals want to be included in making policy choices (R. E. Kasperson, 1986; Palenchar, 2010b). These communicative challenges stress the importance of a proper understanding of strategy in risk communication. However, up to now only a few authors have explicitly addressed the role of strategy in risk communication. Smillie and Blissett (2010) propose a model for risk communication strategy that takes into account the varying risk appraisals of the stakeholders. Leiss (2003) explicitly addresses the controversial nature of risk issues in his account on the relevance of public policy in risk communication. From a managerial point of view he stresses the importance of managerial competence as decisive for trusting public risk managers. But the major part of risk communication research has attended, as Chess and Johnson (2010) notice, "to public perception to a greater extent than organizational behavior—even though organizations vitally shape the communication process and messages" (Chess & Johnson, 2010, p. 323). That explains why the formation of risk communication strategies—as organizational behavior—is barely explored in detail. In the next part of this chapter, research on strategy in communications will be outlined. This forms the basis for the last part in which the role of strategy in risk communication will be discussed.

Strategy, Strategic Communication and the Strategic Role of Communication

Strategy research, particularly in management, originated several prescriptive concepts for strategic decision making. As the concept of strategy originally stems from the military, strategy relates to situations in which opponent parties compete with each other (King, 2010). The aim of applying a strategy is to have an advantage over the opponent. In prescriptive strategy literature, strategy is regarded as the result of a planning process that consists of a sequence of decisions: on the evaluation of the current situation, on formulating goals, on specifying suitable ways of implementation and, eventually, on evaluating the effectiveness of the decisions.

Also, in strategic communications literature, the prescriptive perspective on strategy prevails. In many textbooks on public relations and strategic communication, strategic communication is depicted as a chronological sequence of several steps. Recently, however, scholars in communication management have reconsidered the presumptions of the prescriptive approach and developed new perspectives on strategy in communications, such as the strategy-as-practice-approach, emergent, interpretive or constructionist views (Christensen, Morsing & Cheney, 2008; Frandsen, 2010; Hallahan, Holtzhausen, van Ruler, Vercic & Sriramesh, 2007; Holtzhausen, 2010; King, 2010;

Marchiori & Bulgacov, 2012; Raupp & Hoffjann, 2012; Ströh, 2007). In contrast to the prescriptive view those approaches can be subsumed as *descriptive perspective*, as the common focus is on the question of how and why strategies are developed (Frandsen, 2010; King, 2010; Raupp & Hoffjann, 2012). An important issue in descriptive strategy research is the notion of "bounded rationality" (March & Simon, 1993; March & Olsen, 1975). The assumed rationality of strategic decision making is limited by a lack of time, by insufficient information, and by other factors of the decision-making environment. Going against the prevailing rational and technical approaches in his day, Lindblom (1959)—in an effort to get a better description of the daily decision-making processes in administrations—coined the phrase "the science of muddling through." Mintzberg (1978) specified strategy formulation by drawing a distinction between intended and realized strategies, unrealized strategies, and strategies that were unintended but that have been realized. The latter he specified as emergent strategies.

Recently, communication scholars who stress the interactive nature of communication and the resulting unpredictability have taken on the idea of emergent strategies. King (2010) illustrated by an in-depth analysis how an organizational strategy emerges. Murphy (2007) drew on complexity theory, and stated that while the interactions of agents are dynamic, patterns of communication emerge that have an impact on the communicating system. The strategy-as-practice framework (Jarzabkowski, 2004; Jarzabkowski, Balogun, & Seidl, 2007; Jarzabkowski & Fenton, 2006; Johnson, Melin, & Whittington, 2003; Whittington, 2003; 2006) examines on a micro-level the process of how strategy is enacted in daily practices. As in complexity theory, the strategy-as-practice-framework also links strategy to organizing and thus attributes a structuring function to strategy (Jarzabkowski & Fenton, 2006).

Scholars of public relations and communication management have addressed the question of how communication strategies contribute to an organization's strategy (Christensen et al., 2008; Cornelissen, 2008; Zerfass, 2008). Public relations scholars have long demanded the involvement of public relations in corporate strategic decision making. In doing so, these scholars have also engaged with the concept of power. The question of power is addressed with particular regard to internal conflicts concerning the degree of influence public relations mangers should have in shaping an organization's overall strategy (Berger, 2005; L. A. Grunig, 1990; L. A. Grunig, J. E. Grunig & Dozier, 2002). A participative organizational culture and flat hierarchies should enhance the scope of action for public relations and corporate communication. Scholars argue that public relations and communication management should participate in overall strategic decision making because organizations have to act in complex environments. Segments of an organization have to develop their own rationalities of action in order to respond to the requirements of their particular environment. Steyn (2004; 2007) argues that as functional strategies, communication strategies should direct overall organizational strategy. The importance of communication management at the level of the overall organization lies in its capacity to legitimize organizational decisions by interpreting and evaluating the organization's environment so as to provide information on stakeholder expectations (Raupp & Hoffjann, 2012; Steyn, 2007). This "outside-in approach" (Steyn, 2007) defines the special importance of public relations to an organization. Organizations make use of various functions to this end, such as environmental scanning or issues management (Daft & Weick, 1984; Heath, 1997, 2002). Scanning procedures can serve to collect information (Choo, 2002). Through interpretation and transmission of environmental information inwards, communication strategies contribute to changing an organization's self-perception and self-descriptions.

Communication strategies have long been regarded as supportive strategies for an organization's overall strategy. Recently, however, as Christensen, Morsing, and Cheney (2008) proposed, communication has been attributed a far more strategic role for the organization. These authors distinguished between first- and second-order-strategies: the former aims to analyze an organization's environment and to react to contingencies from within; the latter aspire to actively influence and shape the organization's environment. "Organizations apply second-order strategies when they seek to define and shape the *conditions* for their strategies" (Christensen et al., 2008, p. 27). Communication contributes to an organization's strategic ability by actively enacting the organizational environment. The strategic function of communication management is thus considered to contribute to the creation of favorable preconditions for organizational strategy making.

Strategizing Risk Communication

The aim of this section of the chapter is to bring together insights from research on strategy with risk communication research. In doing so, the concept of strategy in risk communication will be discussed along two dimensions: a process-oriented dimension, and a structural one. The process-oriented dimension refers to risk communication activities enacted by individuals, and to the question of how risk communication strategies are formulated and enacted. The structural dimension, on the other hand, covers the organizational factors that constrain and shape the process of strategic risk communication. It highlights the strategic environment for risk communication.

The Process of Developing Risk Communication Strategies

Risk communication is expected to serve different purposes. As pointed out earlier within this chapter, institutional risk communication has the task to inform, to educate the public and to initiate risk dialogues. Developing strategies for those ends means to apply various instruments and to react constantly in the ever-changing organizational environment. In order to meet growing public expectations of transparency and participation, risk communicators are expected first of all to provide as much information as possible on a certain risk. Providing information seems to be a basic and rather uncomplicated communication strategy, compared to two-way communication strategies (J. E. Grunig & Hunt, 1984). But in risk communication, even informing is a challenging task. That is because what is defined as a risk is ambiguous and open to various and conflicting interpretations (Fischhoff, et al., 1984). Also, risk information is usually provisional and must be updated constantly (Slovic, 1987). The preliminarity and ambiguity inherent in risk messages allows competing actors to frame the risk according to their own interests and rationale. This holds true not only for the public communication of risks, but also to communicating risks within an organization. Risk communicators do not only inform the public and relevant stakeholders about potential threats and hazards, they also inform decision makers within the organization. And not only is it the public arena of risk communication that is highly politicized. When one applies the idea of politics and politicking to organizations (Bacharach & Lawler, 1980; Pfeffer, 1992), the internal risk perception and the assessment of risks become a disputed issue as well. Internal stakeholders, like political decision makers or members of the top management, hold their own definitions of risk based on their specific cognitive frames. Kaplan (2008) portrays managerial framing in strategy making as highly contested and intertwined with the political pursuit of interests. It is likely that varying definitions of risk will lead to internal risk framing contests as well. Wittingly or unwittingly, those who implement risk communication are involved in internal processes of sense-making and framing risk issues.

The strategic value of risk communication is that as risk communicators are situated in boundary-spanning positions of an organization, they are not only confronted with internal risk assessments but also with public perceptions on risk issues. By scanning and monitoring the organizational environment, risk communicators may bring additional definitions of risk to the other organizational members. Informing on risks means first of all to make sense of the various and potentially conflicting perceptions of risk within the organization and in public.

The educational function of risk communication comprises the task of raising awareness for risk issues. This is an especially difficult task because risks are by definition related to future events. In contrast to crisis situations, which can be seen as manifested risks (Heath, 2006) when public attention is high, educational risk communication is concerned with non-obtrusive issues for which it is difficult to get public attention (Covello, 2010; Neuwirth, 2010). As there is no direct demand for information that has no current relevance for most people, one could draw the conclusion that there is also no demand for risk communication management. After all, why should there be risk communication management at a time when there is no public problem? Organizations also could perform internal risk assessment and only communicate when there are substantial threats (but when is a threat "substantial"?). The strategic task of risk communication in those (commonly occurring) phases of low risk awareness is first of all to conceive communication in itself as strategic. Its function is to serve as an early-warning system by scanning the organizational environment and detecting potential threats. Also, as risks can easily turn into crises (Palenchar, 2010a; Reynolds & Seeger, 2005; Veil, Reynolds, Sellnow & Seeger, 2008), scanning the environment serves as part of a pre-crisis communication strategy.

As risk communication management has a legitimizing function, initiating and maintaining a dialogue with potentially affected groups is another strategic goal of risk communication (Hayenhjelm, 2006; Palenchar & Heath, 2007; Renn, 1992, 1998a). Developing a participatory communication strategy is the most demanding task in risk communication. Processes of organizational decision-making become transparent and have to be explained. As mentioned above, engaging the public to participate in risk decision-making may also result in a loss of decision-making power of an organization. In the long run, taking part in collaborative decision making may improve the strategic ability of an organization. But in the short term, collaborative decision making is often seen as impracticable. The reservations about deliberative and participatory risk assessment are strengthened by the mixed results of evaluations. As Renn (2003) illustrated, the possibilities of deliberative and participatory risk assessment processes and risk decision making are limited. Discursive procedures seem to dissolve fundamentalist views but it is unlikely that conflicting parties will give up their previously held positions. Public authorities, corporations and activist groups will maintain polarized views on risk definition.

What follows on from that in terms of considering the role of strategy in risk communication? The underlying concept of strategy in risk communication management, be it informative, educational or dialogic, has to be that of an adaptive and emergent strategy. Developing strategies in risk communication involves an ongoing process of sense-making of ambiguous information and the detection and interpretation of weak risk signals. Furthermore, it comprises processes of framing and re-framing risk issues in highly confrontational settings. As risk communication can turn into crisis communication quite easily, communication strategies must be malleable at short notice.

Organizational Factors Influencing Risk Communication

The process of developing risk communication strategies is shaped and constrained by external factors, that is, the structural dimension of risk communication. The social amplification of risk framework takes into account the importance of external factors like the organizational environment and the societal risk culture for the process and outcome of risk communication.

Institutional theorists in particular stress the impact of external factors on organizational practices (Scott, 2008; Zucker, 1987). The organizational environment is composed of norms, values, and beliefs, which make up the organizational field in which an organization operates. DiMaggio and Powell (1983) speak of an organizational field as a set of organizations that develop similar features. In order to understand how risk management strategies are developed by risk communicators within organizations, one has to consider the specific organizational fields of the organizations that are involved in the risk communication process. For example, a governmental agency that is responsible for risk assessment has to adapt to certain normative, legal and political requirements. The agency will establish rules and activate resources that are equipped to meet the legal and political expectancies. A social movement organization concerned with nuclear risk issues, on the other hand, faces different institutional requirements and will employ another risk communication strategy; most likely a more partisan and mobilizing one.

Next to the organizational field, the prevailing risk culture of a society is another institutional factor that shapes risk communication management. A risk culture is characterized by the way societies deal with (un)certainty. Hofstede (1991) categorized cultures along several dimensions. One of them is what he called "uncertainty avoidance": the way a society deals with ambiguity and uncertainty. The more rules there are regarding safety and security, the higher is a culture's uncertainty avoidance level—and vice versa. Risk culture manifests itself in rules and laws; it is reflected in the way the news media depict risks and dangers and in the way specific risks are attributed to individual or corporate actors, or to abstract entities or higher forces. The relevance of different manifestations of risk culture is especially important in light of the transboundary character of risks and crises (Boin, 2009).

Notwithstanding the impact of the organizational field and the societal risk culture, pro-active risk communication strategies are possible. Risk communication is a rather dynamic and interactive process, and although their respective organizational environments shape their organizational foundations, organizations also play an active role in shaping and creating those environments (Daft & Weick, 1984; Meyer & Rowan, 1977). Risk communication management interprets signals as risk issues and defines the organizational position towards matters of risk and uncertainty. Strategic risk communication includes first- and second-order strategies in the sense of Christensen et al. (2008). By detecting and defining risks, risk communication contributes to the strategic capability of an organization.

Much risk communication research treats organizations as "black boxes". In view of the above it becomes clear that organizations are not unified entities or solely "amplification stations". Strategizing risk communication rather includes sense-making and framing divergent interpretations of risks within an organization and in public. By engaging in strategic risk communication management, organizations contribute to risk amplification not only by magnifying risks in an assumingly negative way. They also collectively manage meaning by defining and framing risks and thus contribute to the origin of public risk discourse.

Discussion and Perspectives

The purpose of this chapter was to elaborate the concept of strategy with respect to risk communication. It was argued that risk is a highly contested social construction that depends on contextual factors. Risk communication is a conflict-laden negotiation process. Several agents, each of them following specific rationales, take part in risk communication. Literature in risk communication, especially as an applied field, offers plenty of advice on how to communicate risks. One might think that success lies in finding the right strategy, but the peculiarities of risk communication demand a critical and reflective approach to strategy. Linear, prescriptive concepts of strategy are insufficient to grasp the complexity of risk communication. Instead, constructionist and practice-oriented approaches to strategic decision making are considered especially useful for exploring the role of strategy in risk communication. In the light of those concepts, risk communication has been elaborated as a sense-making and framing activity under the conditions of contingency and perceived uncertainty.

What are the implications of that conceptualization of risk communication? First, a clear separation between risk management and risk communication appears to be nearly impossible. Risk management is based on risk perceptions and definitions and in turn influences risk perception. Risk communication is of strategic importance for risk management, and it is a constitutive part of the risk management process. In the context of risk societies (Beck, 1992) that are characterized by an ongoing dispute on the degree of uncertainty and safety a society is willing to accept, situating risk communication as subsidiary to risk management is insufficient. Second, there can be no generic organizational risk communication strategy (Stern, 1991). Risk confronts organizations with multiple situational requirements, conflicting goals, and irresolvable conflicts. This results in ambiguity, which may affect strategic decision making in a negative or positive way. Eisenberg (1984) pointed to the fact that ambiguity is not necessarily an appalling characteristic but forms a part of the strategy itself. He regarded strategic ambiguity as essential to organizing, as it facilitates organizational change. Arguing along the same line, Christensen and Langer (2009) suggested that organizations use inconsistencies and differences proactively to highlight their potential for change and improvement. Developing strategies in risk communication should be seen as an occasion for organizational learning.

The implications for strategy making have been referred to in a general way in this chapter. Empirical researchers on risk communication could step forward to distinguish between the strategic use of different modes of communication in dealing with different types of risk and different phases of the risk communication process.

References

Ale, B. J. M. (2009). *Risk: an Introduction. The concepts of risk, danger.* New York: Routledge.

Bacharach, S. B., & Lawler, E. J. (1980). *Power and politics in organizations.* San Francisco, CA: Jossey-Bass.

Beck, U. (1992). *Risk society. Towards a new modernity.* London, England: Sage.

Ben-Ari, A., & Or-Chen, K. (2009). Integrating competing conceptions of risk: A call for future direction of research. *Journal of Risk Research, 12*(6), 865–877.

Berger, B. K. (2005). Power over, power with, and power to relations: Critical reflections on public relations, the dominant coalition, and activism. *Journal of Public Relations Research, 17*(1), 5–28.

Boin, A. (2009). The new world of crises and crisis management: Implications for policymaking and research: Introduction to the special issue. *Review of Policy Research, 26*(4), 367–377.

Chess, C., & Johnson, B. (2010). Risk communication by organizations: The back story. In R. L. Heath & D. H. O'Hair (Eds.), *Handbook of risk and crisis communication* (pp. 323–342). New York: Routledge.

Choo, C. W. (2002). *Information management for the intelligent organization: The art of scanning the environment.* Medford, NJ: Information Today.

Christensen, L. T., & Langer, R. (2009). Public relations and the strategic use of transparency. Consistency, hypocrisy, and corporate change. In R. Heath, E. Toth & D. Waymer (Eds.), *Rhetorical and critical approaches to public relations II* (pp. 127–153). New York: Routledge.

Christensen, L. T., Morsing, M., & Cheney, G. (2008). *Corporate communications: Convention, complexity, and critique.* Los Angeles, CA: Sage.

Coombs, T. W., & Holladay, S. J. (2010). *PR strategy and application. Managing influence.* Malden, MA: Wiley-Blackwell.

Cornelissen, J. (2008). *Corporate communication. A guide to theory and practice* (2nd ed.). London, England: Sage.

Covello, V. T. (2010). Strategies for overcoming challenges to effective risk communication. In R. L. Heath & D. H. O'Hair (Eds.), *Handbook of risk and crisis communication* (pp. 143–167). New York; London, England: Routledge.

Daft, R. L., & Weick, K. E. (1984). Toward a model of organizations as interpretation systems. *The Academy of Management Review, 9*(2), 284–295.

DiMaggio, P. J., & Powell, W. W. (1983). The iron cage revisited: Institutional isomorphism and collective rationality in organizational fields. *American Sociological Review, 48*(2), 147–160.

Douglas, M., & Wildavsky, A. (1982). *Risk and culture. An essay on the selection of technical and environmental dangers.* Berkeley, CA: University of California Press.

Eisenberg, E. M. (1984). Ambiguity as strategy in organizational communication. *Communication Monographs, 51*(3), 227–242.

Fischhoff, B., Slovic, P., & Lichtenstein, S. (1978). How safe is safe enough? A psychometric study of attitudes towards technological risks and benefits. *Policy Sciences, 9*, 127–152.

Fischhoff, B., Watson, R. S., & Hope, C. (1984). Defining risk. *Policy Sciences, 17*, 123–139.

Frandsen, F. (2010). Strategy, management, leadership, and public relations. In R. L. Heath (Ed.), *The SAGE handbook of public relations* (pp. 293–306). Thousand Oaks, CA: Sage.

Grunig, J. E., & Hunt, T. (1984). *Managing public relations.* New York: Holt, Rinehart and Winston.

Grunig, L. A. (1990). Power in the public relations department. *Public Relations Research Annual 2*(1–4), 115–155.

Grunig, L. A., Grunig, J. E., & Dozier, D. M. (2002). *Excellent public relations and effective organizations: A study of communication management in three countries*. Mahwah, NJ: Lawrence Erlbaum.

Gurabardhi, Z., Gutteling, J. M., & Kuttschreuter, M. (2004). The development of risk communication: An empirical analysis of the literature in the field. *Science Communication, 25*(4), 323–349.

Hallahan, K., Holtzhausen, D. R., van Ruler, B., Verčič, D., & Sriramesh, K. (2007). Defining strategic communication. *International Journal of Strategic Communication, 1*(1), 3–35.

Hayenhjelm, M. (2006). Asymmetries in risk communication. *Risk Management, 8*(1), 1–15.

Heath, R. L. (1997). *Strategic issues management. Organizations and public policy challenges*. Thousand Oaks, CA: Sage.

Heath, R. L. (2002). Issues management: Its past, present and future. *Journal of Public Affairs, 2*(4), 209–214.

Heath, R. L. (2006). Best practices in crisis communication: Evolution of practice through research. *Journal of Applied Communication Research, 34*(3), 245–248.

Heath, R. L., Palenchar, M. J., & O'Hair, D. H. (2010). Community building through risk communication infrastructures. In R. L. Heath & D. H. O'Hair (Eds.), *Handbook of risk and crisis communication* (pp. 471–487). New York; London, England: Routledge.

Hofstede, G. (1991). *Cultures and organizations: Software of the mind*. London, England: McGraw-Hill.

Holtzhausen, D. R. (2010). Communication in the public sphere: The political context of strategic communication. *International Journal of Strategic Communication, 4*(2), 75–77.

Jarzabkowski, P. (2004). Strategy as practice: Recursiveness, adaptation, and practices-in-use. *Organization Studies, 25*(4), 529–560.

Jarzabkowski, P., Balogun, J., & Seidl, D. (2007). Strategizing: The challenges of a practice perspective. *Human Relations, 60*(1), 5–27.

Jarzabkowski, P., & Fenton, E. (2006). Strategizing and organizing in pluralistic contexts. *Long Range Planning, 39*(6), 631–648.

Johnson, G., Melin, L., & Whittington, R. (2003). Micro strategy and strategizing: Towards an activity-based view. *Journal of Management Studies, 40*, 3–22.

Kahneman, D., & Tversky, A. (1979). Prospect theory: An analysis of decision under risk. *Econometrica, 47*(2), 263–291.

Kaplan, S. (2008). Framing contests: Strategy making under uncertainty. *Organization Science, 19*(5), 729–752.

Kasperson, R. E. (1986). Six propositions on public participation and their relevance for risk communication. *Risk Analysis, 6*(3), 275–281.

Kasperson, R. E., Renn, O., Slovic, P., Brown, H. S., Emel, J., Goble, R., Kasperson, J.X., & Ratick, S. (1988). The social amplification of risk: A conceptual framework. *Risk Analysis. An International Journal, 8*(2), 177–187.

Kasperson, R. E. (1992). The social amplification of risk: Progress in developing an integrative framework. In S. Krimsky & D. Golding (Eds.), *Social theories of risk* (pp. 153–178). London, England: Praeger.

Kasperson, J. X., Kasperson, R. E., Pidgeon, N., & Slovic, P. (2003). The social amplification of risk: Assessing fifteen years of theory and research. In N. Pidgeon, R. E. Kasperson & P. Slovic (Eds.), *The social amplification of risk* (pp. 13–46). Cambridge, England: Cambridge University Press.

King, C. L. (2010). Emergent communication strategies. *International Journal of Strategic Communication, 4*(1), 19–38.

Leiss, W. (2003). Searching for the public policy relevance of the risk amplification framework. In N. Pidgeon, R. E. Kasperson & P. Slovic (Eds.), *The social amplification of risk* (pp. 355–373). Cambridge, England: Cambidge University Press.

Lindblom, C. E. (1959). The science of "muddling through". *Public Administration Review, 19*(2), 79–88.

March, J. G., & Olsen, J. P. (1975). The uncertainty of the past: Organizational learning under ambiguity. *European Journal of Political Research, 3*(2), 147–171.

March, J., & Simon, H. (1993). *Organizations*. Cambridge, MA: Blackwell.

Marchiori, M., & Bulgacov, S. (2012). Strategy as communicational practice in organizations. *International Journal of Strategic Communication, 6*(3), 199–211.

McComas, K. A. (2006). Defining moments in risk communication research: 1996–2005. *Journal of Health Communication, 11*, 75–91.

McComas, K. A., Arvai, J., & Besley, J. C. (2010). Linking public participation and decision making through risk communication. In R. L. Heath & D. H. O'Hair (Eds.), *Handbook of risk and crisis communication* (pp. 364–385). New York: London: England: Routledge.

McGuire, W. J. (2001). Input and output variables currently promising for constructing persuasive communications. In R. E. Rice & C. K. Atkin (Eds.), *Public communication campaigns* (3rd ed., pp. 22–48). Thousand Oaks, CA: Sage Publications.

Meyer, J. W., & Rowan, B. (1977). Institutionalized organizations: Formal structure as myth and ceremony. *The American Journal of Sociology, 83*(2), 340–363.

Mintzberg, H. (1978). Patterns in strategy formation. *Management Science, 24*(9), 934–948.

Murdock, G. (2010). Shifting anxieties, altered media: Risk communication in networked times. *Catalan Journal of Communication & Cultural Studies, 2*(2), 159–176.

Murdock, G., Petts, J., & Horlick-Jones, T. (2003). After amplification: Rethinking the role of media in risk communication. In N. Pidgeon, R. E. Kasperson & P. Slovic (Eds.), *The social amplification of risk* (pp. 156–178). Cambridge, England: Cambridge University Press.

Murphy, P. (2007). Coping with an uncertain world: The relationship between excellence and complexity theories. In E. L. Toth (Ed.), *The future of excellence in public relations and communication management* (pp. 119–134). New York, NY: Routledge.

Neuwirth, K. (2010). Risk, crisis, and mediated communication. In R. L. Heath & H. D. O'Hair (Eds.), *Handbook of risk and crisis communication* (pp. 398–411). New York: Routledge.

Palenchar, M. J., & Heath, R. L. (2007). Strategic risk communication: Adding value to society. *Public Relations Review, 33*, 120–129.

Palenchar, M. J. (2010a). Historical trends in risk and crisis communication. In R. L. Heath & H. D. O'Hair (Eds.), *Handbook of risk and crisis communication* (pp. 31–52). New York: Routledge.

Palenchar, M. J. (2010b). Risk communication. In R. L. Heath (Ed.), *The SAGE handbook of public relations* (pp. 447–460). Thousand Oaks, CA: Sage Publications.

Petts, J., Horlick-Jones, T., & Murdock, G. (2001). *Social amplification of risk: The media and the public.* Birmingham, AL: HSE Books.

Pfeffer, J. (1992). *Managing with power. Politics and influences in organizations.* Boston, MA: Harvard Business School Press.

Pidgeon, N., Kasperson, R. E., & Slovic, P. (Eds.). (2003). *The social amplification of risk.* Cambridge, UK: Cambridge University Press.

Plough, A., & Sheldon, K. (1987). The Emergence of Risk Communication Studies: Social and Political Context. *Science, Technology, & Human Values, 12*(3/4), 4–10.

Proutheau, S., & Heath, R. L. (2010). Precautionary principle and biotechnology: Regulators are from Mars and activists are from Venus. In R. L. Heath & D. H. O'Hair (Eds.), *Handbook of risk and crisis communication* (pp. 576–590). New York: Routledge.

Raupp, J., & Hoffjann, O. (2012). Understanding strategy in communication management. *Journal of communication management, 16*(2), 146–161.

Rayner, S. (1992). Cultural theory and risk analysis. In S. Krimsky & D. Golding (Eds.), *Social theories of risk* (pp. 83–116). London, UK: Praeger.

Rayner, S., & Cantor, R. (1987). How fair is safe enough? The cultural approach to societal technology choice. *Risk Analysis, 7*(1), 3–9.

Renn, O., & Levine, D. (1991). Trust and credibility in risk communication. In R. E. Kasperson & P. J. Stallen (Eds.), *Communicating risks to the public* (pp. 175–218). London, UK: Kluwer Academic Publishers.

Renn, O. (1992). Risk communication: Towards a rational discourse with the public. *Journal of Hazardous Materials, 29*(3), 465–519.

Renn, O. (1998a). Three decades of risk research: accomplishments and new challenges. *Journal of Risk Research, 1*, 49–71.

Renn, O. (1998b). The role of risk communication and public dialogue for improving risk management. *Risk Decision and Policy, 3*(1), 5–30.

Renn, O. (2003). Social amplification of risk in participation: Two case studies. In N. Pidgeon, R. E. Kasperson & P. Slovic (Eds.), *The social amplification of risk* (pp. 374–401). Cambridge, England: Cambridge University Press.

Reynolds, B., & Seeger, M. W. (2005). Crisis and emergency risk communication as an integrative model. *Journal of Health Communication, 10*, 43–55.

Sandman, P. (1987). Risk communication: Facing public outrage. *EPA Journal (ed.: U.S. Environmental Protection Agency)* (November 1987), 21–22.

Scott, R. W. (2008). *Institutions and organizations. Ideas and interests* (3rd ed.). Los Angeles, CA: Sage.

Siegrist, M., & Cvetkovich, G. (2000). Perception of hazards: The role of social trust and knowledge. *Risk Analysis, 20*, 713–720.

Siegrist, M., Cvetkovich, G., & Roth, C. (2000). Salient value similarity, social trust, and risk/benefit perception. *Risk Analysis, 20*(3), 353–362.

Sjöberg, L. (2000). Factors in risk perception. *Risk Analysis, 20*(1), 1–12.

Slovic, P. (1987). Perception of risk. *Science, 236*(4799), 280–285.

Slovic, P. (1999). Trust, emotion, sex, politics, and science: Surveying the risk-assessment battlefield. *Risk Analysis, 19*(4), 689–701.

Smillie, L., & Blissett, A. (2010). A model for developing risk communication strategy. *Journal of Risk Research, 13*(1), 115–134.

Stern, P. C. (1991). Learning through conflict: A realistic strategy for risk communication. *Policy Sciences, 24*(1), 99–119.

Steyn, B. (2004). From strategy to corporate communication strategy: A conceptualisation. *Journal of Communication Management, 8*(2), 168–183.

Steyn, B. (2007). Contribution of public relations to organizational strategy formulation. In E. L. Toth (Ed.), *The future of excellence in public relations and communication management* (pp. 137–172). Mahwah, NJ: Lawrence Erlbaum.

Ströh, U. (2007). An alternative postmodern approach to corporate communication strategy. In E. L. Toth (Ed.), *The Future of Excellence in Public Relations and Communication Management* (pp. 199–220). New York: Routledge.

Tansey, J., & Rayner, S. (2010). Cultural theory and risk. In R. L. Heath & H. D. O'Hair (Eds.), *Handbook of risk and crisis communication* (pp. 53–79). New York: Routledge.

Thompson, K. M. (2002). Variability and uncertainty meet risk management and risk communication. *Risk Analysis, 22*(3), 647–654.

Ulmer, R. R., Sellnow, T. L., & Seeger, M. W. (2010). *Effective crisis communication: Moving from crisis to opportunity* (2nd ed.). Thousand Oaks, CA: Sage.

Veil, S., Reynolds, B., Sellnow, T. L., & Seeger, M. W. (2008). CERC as a theoretical framework for research and practice. *Health Promotion Practice, 9*(4), 26–34.

Wahlberg, A. A. F., & Sjoberg, L. (2000). Risk perception and the media. *Journal of Risk Research, 3*(1), 31–50.

Whittington, R. (2003). The work of strategizing and organizing: For a practice perspective. *Strategic Organization, 1*(1), 117–125.

Whittington, R. (2006). Completing the practice turn in strategy research. *Organization Studies, 27*(5), 613–634.

Zerfass, A. (2008). Corporate communication revisited: Integrating business strategy and strategic communication. In A. Zerfass, B. van Ruler & K. Sriramesh (Eds.), *Public Relations research. European and international perspectives and innovations* (pp. 65–96). Wiesbaden, DE: VS Verlag für Sozialwissenschaften.

Zucker, L. G. (1987). Institutional theories of organization. *American Review of Sociology, 13*, 443–464.

35

Strategic Communication During Change

Rita Järventie-Thesleff, Johanna Moisander, and Mikko Villi

Change seems to be the normal condition of organizational life. Continuously changing operating environments, competitive landscapes, and legislative infrastructures, together with unpredictable shifts in customer behavior and technological development, all pose significant strategic challenges to contemporary business organizations. And to cope with these changes, organizations engage in a myriad of strategic change projects, constantly inventing and implementing new strategies, policies, and practices for carrying out their mundane operative activities.

This chapter elaborates on the challenges that managing top–down initiated change projects and emergent change processes at the same time brings about for *strategic communication*. The focus is especially on what top and middle managers need to know about the processes and practices of communication through which top–down initiated change projects and emergent change processes are managed and coordinated. Here the notion of strategic communication refers to the purposeful use of communication by an organization to fulfill its mission. Strategic communication is concerned with the processes and practices through which the organization presents and promotes itself, in the intentional activities of its leaders, employees, and communication practitioners (Hallahan, Holtzhausen, van Ruler, & Verčič, 2007). Although strategic communication is premised upon the active participation and commitment of the entire personnel, it is argued that the management plays a particularly important role in introducing discursive templates as well as in communicating and coordinating change (Tsoukas & Chia, 2002).

This chapter covers both *emergent* and *top–down initiated strategic change*. A *strategic change process* refers to organizations as emergent properties of change (Thomas, Sargent, & Hardy, 2010; Tsoukas & Chia, 2002; Carlsen, 2006). By contrast, a *strategic change project* is a change initiative that involves either a redefinition of organizational mission or a substantial shift in overall priorities and goals to reflect new emphasis or direction (Gioia, Thomas, Clark, & Chittipeddi, 1994, p. 364). In this context, *multi-change* refers to a bundle of either simultaneous or partly overlapping change projects, each of which contains project specific goals and meticulously expressed directions.

To examine the communication challenges that multi-change situations involve, this chapter draws on the concept of *sense making*. Organizational sense making is fundamentally a social process, meaning that organization members interpret their environments in and through interactions with others, constructing accounts that allow them to comprehend the world and act collectively (Maitlis, 2005, p. 22). A part of organizational sense making is understanding the different organizational

Table 35.1 Key concepts in strategic communication during change

Concept	Definition	References 1
Strategic communication	Purposeful use of communication by an organization to fulfill its mission. How the organization presents and promotes itself through the intentional activities of its leaders, employees and communication practitioners	Hallahan, Holtzhausen, van Ruler and Verde 2007: 3, 7
Corporate brand	Is based on a promise given by the organization to its key stakeholders. The success and reliability of the corporate brand depends on how well the entire organization gives content to and delivers on the given promise.	Järventie-Thesleff, 2011
Strategic change project	A change initiative that involves 'either a redefinition of organizational mission or a substantial shift in overall priorities and goals to reflect new emphasis or direction'	Gioia, Thomas, Clark & Chittipeddi 1994: 364
Strategic change process	Refers to organizations as emergent properties of change	Thomas, Sargent and Hardy 2010; Tsoukas and Chia 2002; Carlsen 2006
Multi-change	Refers to a bundle of either simultaneous or partly overlapping change projects, each of which contains project specific goals and meticulously expressed directions.	
Organizational sense making	Fundamentally a social process, meaning that organization members interpret their environments in and through interactions with others, constructing accounts that allow them to comprehend the world and act collectively	Maitlis 2005:22
Practices	'Routinized types of behaviour which consist of several elements, interconnected to one other: forms of bodily activities, forms of mental activities, things and their use, a background knowledge in the form of understanding, know-how, states of emotion, and motivational knowledge'	Reckwitz 2002: 249

practices. Here the term "practice" refers to coherent and consistent patterns of purposive activity, which is performed in the organization through several interconnected mental and bodily behaviors (Reckwitz, 2002, pp. 249–250). Practices are grounded in and guided by particular collective structures of knowing, reasoning, and understanding.

As one viable solution, the chapter proposes *corporate branding* as a tool for managing and coordinating strategic communication in a multi-change environment. Corporate branding is based on the vision and mission of the company, and it crystallizes the message for all stakeholders of the company. The corporate brand is based on a promise given by the organization to the stakeholders. The success and reliability of the corporate brand depend on how well the entire organization gives content to and delivers on the given promise (Järventie-Thesleff, 2011). During a change situation, moreover, it is important to support a *change affirmative culture*. This refers to a culture characterized by communicative practices that support continuous change. A vignette at the end of the chapter provides an illustration of an actual multi-change situation and highlights the importance of building a strong corporate brand and promoting a change affirmative culture.

Organizational Change

In the literature on strategic and organizational change, the importance of communication in explaining organizational change processes has long been discussed and generally acknowledged (Lewis, 1999). Communication and organizational change implementation are generally viewed as inextricably linked (Lewis, 1999), as change is inevitably a process that is created, sustained, and managed in and by communication (Ford & Ford, 1995, p. 560).

Organizational change can be conceptualized in several distinctive ways (Pettigrew, Woodman, & Cameron, 2001). Mintzberg and Westley (1992), for example, distinguish deductive and inductive change. Deductive change proceeds from thought to action, whereas inductive change evolves from concrete to conceptual in an emergent fashion. Deductive change is in line with deliberate strategy making and inductive change is connected to emergent strategy. In addition, Weick and Quinn (1999) draw a line between change that is episodic, discontinuous, and intermittent, and change that is continuous, evolving, and incremental. Continuous change is similar to inductive change, since small continuous adjustments that are created simultaneously across organizational units can accumulate and create substantial change.

Tsoukas and Chia (2002, p. 579) are also proponents of a less intentional way of conceptualizing change, arguing that "change in organizations occurs without necessarily intentional managerial action as a result of individuals trying to accommodate new experiences and realize new possibilities." This view is based upon the belief that change is inherent in human action and that human action also changes continuously in the organizational context. However, in their argument, Tsoukas and Chia (2002) still reserve a role for managerial intentionality. Managers are privileged to introduce new discursive templates, to lead the members of the organization to notice new issues and see new connections.

The notion of a continuous change has been discussed particularly in the literature on "organizational becoming" (Tsoukas & Chia, 2002; Carlsen, 2006; Thomas et al., 2010). This approach to organization studies subscribes to a theoretical reorientation from a substance ontology to a flux ontology (Tsoukas & Chia, 2002), which emphasizes movement, flux, emergence and process over end-states, entities, stability and discrete periods (Pettigrew, 1992; Carlsen, 2006). Thus, attention is directed towards "becoming" rather than "being," and reality is understood in terms of ceaseless process, flux and transformation rather than as a stable world of unchanging entities (Nayak & Chia, 2011, p. 281). Based on the perspective of "becoming," we look at organizations as emergent properties of change and as unfolding enactments of continuously changing practices (Thomas et al., 2010; Tsoukas & Chia, 2002; Carlsen, 2006).

Rather than seeing organizational change as a realization of a top-down initiated plan, the perspective of "becoming" treats change as an ongoing normal condition of organizational life (Ford & Ford, 1995; Weick & Quinn, 1999; Tsoukas & Chia, 2002). Change is grounded in continuous updates of work processes (Brown & Duguid, 1991) and social practices (Tsoukas, 1996). The interest is directed to the dynamic, unfolding and emergent nature of change, and organizations are assumed to consist of situation-specific webs of social relations (Tsoukas & Chia, 2002).

Next, we will discuss the strategic communication challenges during change by following the division introduced above, between top-down initiated change projects and change as a normal condition of organizational life.

Communication Challenges During Change

In the practice of organizations, the basic task and objectives of strategic communication vary depending on the nature of organizational change that needs to be managed. If change is carried out as a senior-management-initiated intervention, top-down, strategic communication is understandably geared at supporting the successful implementation of the change intervention. If, however, organizational change is something that needs to be managed as an ongoing process as the normal condition of organizational life (Brown & Duguid, 2001; Tsoukas, 1996), the focus of strategic communication shifts to facilitating the social and communicative processes through which all members of the organization effectively and constructively make sense of the change.

Communication of Top-Down Change Projects

In the case of top-down–initiated change projects, the aim of strategic communication is to create and disseminate messages that are clear and unambiguous as well as to ensure the reliability of communication processes and exchange processes so as to encourage participation and to avoid uncertainty. Communication is thus used as an instrument for management control, and directed at making change as bearable or tolerable as possible, by trying to play down fear, for example (Hübner, 2007). In these contexts, the basic task of strategic communication is to support three basic practices of change management (Johnson, Scholes, & Whittington, 2008; Balogun, 2001): education, showing direction, and collaboration.

Education: Informing versus Facilitating Learning

Education refers to the textual and interpersonal communication through which the top management communicates and explains the reasons for change and presents the means of strategic change (Johnson et al., 2008). It is about explaining, giving sense to the objectives and logic of the strategic change, and building trust in top management, mainly through top-down and lateral processes of communication.

The objective of this type of communication is to have the employees understand and deliver the change as planned, effectively and cost-efficiently. The challenge is to design the communication strategies and practices of communication that support active employee sense making and self-directed learning. It is important that employees themselves make sense of the strategic change and the associated changes in strategic vision and goals in a way that helps them to deliver the change in active, flexible and context-specific ways (Järventie-Thesleff, 2011).

The challenge here is to avoid an outcome where the educational communication of strategic change boils down to mere information transfer: Strategic change communication is geared at transferring information from the top management to the employees without engaging them in the learning process as active participants in processes of strategic change (Järventie-Thesleff, Moisander, & Laine, 2011). Another challenge is to overcome the shared understandings and taken-for-granted ideas that are embedded in existing organizational practices through which the employees attempt to make sense of the change initiative.

Showing Direction: Authoritative versus Charismatic

Showing direction is about informing, persuading and convincing stakeholders through processes of one-way communication (Johnson et al., 2008). It is based on the use of authority to set direction and means of change, utilizing top-down processes of communication-communicating information and orders through cascading processes of communication.

The objective of this type of communication is to establish a clear strategy for the organization and a plan for implementing the strategy. This may sometimes be accompanied by the use of organizational control and power to impose particular work practices, standards and explicit rules on the employees.

The challenge here is to be able to communicate the managerial, strategic vision in a convincing manner and to persuade the stakeholders about the strategic intent and the critical success factors and priorities involved. There is a need to design communication strategies that show direction in a supportive, charismatic manner, instead of merely imposing the strategy on the employees in an authoritative manner through hierarchical power relations.

Collaboration: Enrolling versus Engaging

Collaboration refers to interpersonal communication, both bottom-up and lateral processes of communication, through which the change recipients—employees—are engaged in strategy work (Johnson et al., 2008; Balogun, 2001). The goal is to get the employees involved in the development of the change agenda, setting up priorities, and drawing up action plans. The fundamental objective is to build a sense of ownership and commitment to the change agenda among the employees, thereby increasing readiness and capability for change.

The challenge here is to design communication strategies and practices of collaboration that not only elicit consent and enroll the employees in strategic change, but also acknowledge the strategic agency of the employees. It is important to appropriate the knowledge and expertise of the employees in strategy work, not only as change agents and change recipients, but also as knowledgeable practitioners who may provide valuable inputs in the development of the change agenda and the practices and policies through which change is implemented in the organization.

Communication During Emergent Change

From a communicational perspective on managing organizational change (Hübner, 2007) organizations can be viewed as essentially constituted by communication (Cooren, Kuhn, Cornelissen, & Clark, 2011). Communication, in this view, is not to simply one of the many factors involved in organizing. It is rather the means by which organizations are established, composed, designed, and sustained (Cooren et al., 2011, p. 1150). From this perspective, change may be understood as a continuous process that gradually unfolds, emerging through different kinds of discursive and organizational activities, of which the management has only partial control (Thomas et al., 2010, Tsoukas & Chia, 2002).

In dealing with this kind of emergent change, all members of the organization—and the top management in particular—need to understand that communication is not merely a simple tool for management control and discursive leadership. It is not only something that helps the middle management to transmit information and implement the change initiative effectively and in a way that helps them steer clear from negative or unintended organizational consequences. Rather, communication may have an important *performative* role (Cooren et al., 2011) in the organization: it actively contributes to and shapes the processes and practices through which change emerges in the day-to-day of organizational life.

In the context of emergent change, therefore, communication cannot be reduced to effectively providing and obtaining information, creating understanding, and building ownership (Ford & Ford, 1995, p. 542) through carefully planned internal communication strategies, implemented by the communications department. It is rather necessary to create practices and policies through which change can be embedded in the deep structures of the organization (Hübner, 2007), and to make sure that all members of the staff, on all organizational levels, are capable and motivated to make sense of the change process in the course of their daily activities, both individually and collectively.

In the practice of organizational life, "making change from below" in this way requires specific types of practical knowledge and skills (Dutton, Ashford, & O'Neill, 2001, p. 732). Since the meaning of organizational change is negotiated among actors in their communicative interactions (Thomas et al., 2010), it is important, in particular, that all members of the organization learn how to talk effectively and constructively with each other—across functional and status boundaries (Ashkenas & Jick, 1992, p. 271).

Overall, this means that both the top management and the corporate communications function have only a part to play in social and communicative activities through which the top-down initiated change projects are managed in organizations. Although the management has an elementary role in introducing discursive templates, as well as in communicating and coordinating the change, it is crucially important to engage all organizational units, departments and teams on multiple levels of organizational hierarchy in the change communication process as well as to create conditions and practices that foster and support active participation in the processes of individual and collective sense making through which the change emerges in the organization.

Moreover, as Cheney, Christensen, Zorn and Ganesh (2004, p. 328) remind us, it is important to keep in mind that the solutions for specific change communication problems always need to be examined within the specific contexts of their occurrence.

Making Sense of Change

In this chapter strategic communication is viewed as a two-way process, the aim of which is to create a sense of collective understanding and engagement. In other words, during change it is important to promote and support *organizational sense making*.

Organizational change projects engage various members of the organization in complementary and reciprocal sense making and sense-giving activities (Gioia & Chittipeddi, 1991; Thomas , Clark, & Gioia, 1993; Gioia, Schultz, & Corley, 2000a, 2000b; Balogun & Johnson, 2005). According to Weick (1995), sense making refers simply to how we make sense of the world we live in. In order to make sense of the world, people select certain information to which to pay attention and then decide how to interpret that information. Ultimately, sense making is a process of social construction (Berger & Luckman, 1966) in which individuals attempt to interpret and explain sets of cues from their environments (Maitlis, 2005). Weick, Sutcliffe and Obstfeld (2005) describe sense making as an effort to create orderly and coherent understandings that enable change.

Rouleau (2005, p. 1415) defines the reciprocal sense making activities as follows:

> Sense-making has to do with the way managers understand, interpret, and create sense for themselves based on the information surrounding strategic change. Sense-giving is concerned with their attempts to influence the outcome, to communicate their thoughts about the change to others, and to gain their support.

The above definitions of sense making and sense giving apply to the initial phase of all change projects, for example, to the phase when the objective is formulated and a rough implementation plan is drafted. This chapter, however, focuses on both collective and organizational sense making and sense giving activities encompassing several change projects. Boyce (1995, p. 109) defines collective sense making as the process whereby groups, both in the corporate center and the operative level, interactively create social reality. Similarly, Maitlis (2005, p. 22) regards organizational sense making as a fundamentally social process, meaning that members of the organization interpret their environments in and through interactions with others, constructing accounts that allow them to comprehend the world and act collectively. Accordingly, strategic communication is viewed as a two-way process, the aim of which is to create a sense of collective understanding and engagement instead of solely transmitting information. In the contemporary competitive environment, organizations are characterized by multiple, overlapping smaller and bigger change projects that might well be perceived to have conflicting objectives. "Customer focus" with an emphasis on understanding the needs and wants of the customers and aggressive cost-saving projects can be perceived as giving conflicting guidance to everyday operational activities. Dynamic contexts characterized by features of multi-change can intensify experiences of complexity and ambiguity.

As a consequence, various members of the organization might run the risk of "change burnout," which is conceptualized as the termination of a capacity or willingness to continue to participate in change projects (Lewis, 2006, p.27). In a case of change burnout, the change projects cease to make sense.

Managing and Coordinating Strategic Communication

In order to remain competitive, organizations are compelled to initiate a myriad of strategic change projects, and they constantly incorporate new ways of carrying out their mundane operative activities. As stated above, a continuous flow of change projects can pose a challenge to employees' endurance, engagement and feeling of significance (Lewis, 2006). Next, corporate branding and the framework of continuous change cycle (Lawrence, Dyck, Maitlis, & Mauws, 2006) are discussed as two practical approaches to strategic communication that can support the management in engaging the personnel in continuous change.

Corporate Branding

It can be argued that the concept of corporate brand has the potential to provide guidance to the processes and practices of strategic communication through which the top-down initiated change projects and the continuous, emergent change processes are managed and coordinated. In the current, fast-changing global competitive environment, corporate branding has become an important source of sustainable competitive advantage and a central element of corporate strategy that can be used as an umbrella construct giving direction and linking the variety of change and innovation efforts together (Balmer & Gray, 2003; Hatch & Schultz, 2003, 2008; Knox & Bickerton, 2003; Järventie-Thesleff et al., 2011). With the help of corporate branding, companies can communicate their competitive position and their long-term strategy to both internal and external stakeholders of the organization.

In marketing literature, the corporate brand is usually conceptualized as the visual, verbal and behavioral expression of an organization's identity and its unique business model (Balmer, 2001; Knox & Bickerton, 2003). It is typically referred to as a proposition, a "brand promise," that represents the organization and reflects its heritage, values, culture, people and strategy (Aaker, 2004). It thus serves as a crystallization of the company's competitive advantage in the market (Balmer & Gray, 2003), and may be viewed as a strategic asset or strategy tool with which the organization seeks to create difference and preference within its target markets. Hatch and Schultz (2003), for example, theorize corporate branding in terms of a set of brand alignment tasks through which the value of the brand asset base is continuously produced and sustained.

In the realm of marketing, corporate branding is one of the activities that can function as a useful platform for communicating the competitive positioning or the total offering of a company both externally and internally (Balmer, 2001; Balmer & Grey, 2003; Aaker, 2004). Corporate branding has a broad scope, and it addresses all stakeholder groups of the company. Furthermore, it requires perseverance and commitment and, as a consequence, the responsibility of corporate branding cannot be limited to marketing and communication departments; instead, importantly, all employees need to participate in building the corporate brand. Recent research on employee branding has highlighted the importance of brand affirmative ambiance within the organization (Macrae, 1999; Ind, 2001; Urde, 1994, 1999, 2003; Morrison, 2001; Kunde, 2000, 2002). In order to be able to support the building of the corporate brand, employees need to understand what the brand and the required changes are about. Understanding means that everyone in the organization knows who the company is, where the company is going, and what needs to be done to get there (Morrison, 2001; Fairhurst, 1993). Furthermore, it should be possible for the employees to participate in, and commit themselves to, developing and delivering the brand promise. The participation and commitment of the employees is believed to be more successful if they feel proud of the brand.

In this study, we build on the following definition of the corporate brand (Järventie-Thesleff, 2011):

> The corporate brand is based on a promise given by the organization to its key stakeholders. The success and reliability of the corporate brand depends on how well the entire organization gives content to and delivers on the given promise.

Recent research has provided a multitude of frameworks and models on corporate branding. However, the understanding of the day-to-day brand building activities or the dynamics that either support or slow down the corporate brand building process has largely been left unanswered (Kärreman & Rylander, 2008). The "doing" of the corporate brand consists of continuous improvisation enacted by organizational actors who try to make sense of the corporate brand and act coherently (Orlikowski, 1996). According to this view, corporate branding consists of an ongoing change rather than intentionally managed and controlled episodic events (Tsoukas & Chia, 2002). We claim that corporate branding can be conceived as an umbrella strategy that, on the one hand, can be implemented by initiating a number of specific, top-down initiated change projects, and on the other, can function as a strategic communication tool providing guidance and coordination to the emergent, bottom-up initiated change processes.

Practices of Strategic Communication in a Change-Affirmative Culture

The other practical approach to strategic communication that is suggested here builds on the cycle of continuous change (Lawrence et al., 2006). The objective in building the strategic communication on the framework of continuous change cycle is to make sure that all members of the staff, on all organizational levels, are capable and motivated to make sense of the change process in the course of their daily activities, both individually and collectively. By drawing on the continuous change cycle, people in managerial positions can create practices and policies through which change can be embedded in the deep structures of the organization (Hübner, 2007).

This framework depicts the underlying structure of continuous change in terms of four phases, illustrated in Figure 35.1.

The first phase, "using influence to sell ideas," focuses on the idea—an insight, intuition or belief—that motivates someone to question the way things are done. This idea needs to be articulated and communicated in order to influence change. During this phase strategic communication should concentrate on selling the idea to key organizational members. Different, persuasive communication strategies should be used to approach different stakeholder groups. The second phase, "using authority to change practices," focuses on change support that is communicated and which emphasizes what it takes to translate the idea into action. Strategic communication is needed especially to support the change, to decrease possible anxiety, and to deal with possible resistance. The third phase, "embedding change in technology," focuses on the systems or designs necessary to embed the change into corporate routines. Often this requires some technological change. During this phase strategic communication is very much information oriented. The fourth phase, "managing culture to fuel the cycle of change," emphasizes the importance of an innovative culture. During this phase the strategic communication should support employees in gaining expertise and motivation so that they would be able to both enact change and to extend and elaborate on it (Lawrence et al., 2006).

Since the meaning of organizational change is negotiated among actors in their communicative interactions (Thomas et al., 2010), it is important to create a culture that encourages all members of the organization to talk constructively with each other—across functional and status boundaries (Ashkenas & Jick, 1992, p. 271).

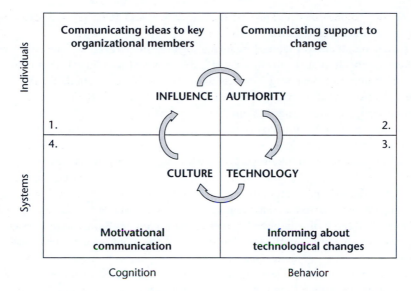

Figure 35.1   Communication in a change affirmative culture (adapted from Lawrence et al., 2006)

Vignette

Struggle Between Sense Making and Sense Dimming

The case company ("Basico") is a large, industrial, transnational company (TNC). Its roots and history go back more than 100 years. Led by visionary and audacious industrialists, the company grew based on large investments, heavy expansion and utilization of the latest technology. The company formed into its present state at the end of the 1990s as a result of a merger of equals. Soon after the merger, the company grew by acquiring smaller companies from its major markets; it acquired production units all over the world and capitalized on an extensive sales network. The formation of Basico created a truly global operator in its line of business. Simultaneously, however, the formation of Basico brought together different strategies, different ways of operating, and different company cultures. Consequently, the post-merger phase was characterized by several change projects aimed at creating uniform processes, integrated ways of working, and a common company culture. Basico started also to build its corporate brand and it linked the brand promise into a dynamic, continuously improving and customer-focused way of operating.

Generally speaking, a continuous flow of change initiatives posits high demands both on strategic communication and organizational sense making. Organizations should keep the flow of change communication continuous, yet they should avoid such an information overload that makes it difficult for the employees to recognize what is important, and what is not.

In the case company Basico, the corporate brand building endeavor was a top-down initiated change project, the aim of which was to motivate the personnel to continuously improve their mundane operative activities. Simultaneously the corporate brand was supposed to act as an overarching change program that would link together smaller, individual change projects. In Basico, the practice of multi-change communication was characterized by the dominance of formal communication at the expense of informal face-to-face communication between colleagues. Furthermore, the flow of communication varied. Right after the launch of a new change project, there was a high intensity of formal communication through intranet, personnel magazines and distributed PowerPoint presentations. The latest change projects were also usually included in unit-specific routine meetings.

However, closures, evaluations or connections between various change projects were seldom covered in the communication channels.

The corporate brand did not succeed in linking together the individual change projects, nor did it inspire the personnel to translate the meaning of the corporate brand into their mundane activities. On the contrary, some of the change projects were considered to be conflicting with each other and the personnel struggled in making sense of the overall change of the company. Furthermore, the conflicting change projects tended to dim sense among the personnel. By *sense-dimming* we refer to confusion, ambiguity and contradictory interpretations of the multiple change projects and their corresponding objectives.

Basico had an ambitious attitude to corporate branding, which however was not supported by communicative practices or policies that would have supported a culture of continuous change. By following the processes and practices of strategic communication in order to create a change-affirmative culture, the corporate brand as a uniting purpose would probably have functioned better. Basico should have invested more time in informal face-to-face communication during its corporate brand –building process. At the outset of the branding endeavor, the emphasis should have been in a convincing introduction of the corporate purpose in the form of the corporate brand. Trying to increase employees' courage to bring up ideas about corporate brand-related operative change initiatives would probably have supported the change-affirmative culture. Furthermore, Basico should have supported employees in gaining expertise and motivation in giving content to the corporate brand.

As stated before, it is crucially important to engage all organizational units, departments and teams on multiple levels of organizational hierarchy in the change communication process as well as to create conditions and practices that foster and support active participation in the processes of individual and collective sense making through which the change emerges in the organization.

Conclusions

This chapter has discussed strategic communication during change, focusing particularly on the challenges that people in managerial positions face when dealing with several simultaneous top-down initiated change projects and emergent change. According to Balogun and Johnson (2004), middle management has two interlinked roles in tackling these challenges: to act as change recipients and as implementers of change. Overlapping, top-down initiated change projects and emergent change processes pose a strategic communication challenge for them. If change is conceptualized as a top-down project, strategic communication needs, first and foremost, to support the implementation of change. By contrast, in the context of emergent change, internal communication strategies implemented by the communications department are not the right approach. Rather, the focus of strategic communication lies on all members of the organization on all levels of organizational hierarchy, and on their ability and motivation to make sense of the change process. Therefore, the aim of strategic communication is to create a sense of collective understanding and engagement by supporting active participation in the processes of sense making. Communication in a change situation should, thus, not consist only of transmitting information.

For supporting middle managers in their demanding roles as change agents, the chapter has emphasized the importance of building strong corporate brands and change-affirmative organizational cultures, so as to better guide and coordinate the activities of strategic communication through which the top-down initiated change projects and emergent change processes are managed and the personnel is engaged in continuous change. Corporate branding is offered primarily as a tool for creating an overarching goal that links together the different change projects. Corporate branding functions as an umbrella strategy that can be implemented by initiating specific, top-down change projects. It also provides guidance to the emergent, bottom-up change processes.

Furthermore, the chapter has suggested that people in managerial positions work towards a change affirmative culture that supports continuous change. It seems important to create communication practices and policies through which change can be embedded in the deep structures of the organization. With the help of such a change-affirmative culture, all members of the organization would be enabled and encouraged to make sense of the change process in the course of their daily activities, both individually and collectively.

References

Aaker, D. A. (2004). *Brand portfolio strategy*. New York: The Free Press.

Ashkenas, R. N., & Jick, T. D. (1992). From dialogue to action in GE work-out. In W. Pasmore and R. Woodman (Eds.), *Research in organizational change and development* (Vol. 6, pp. 267–287). Greenwich, CT: JAI Press.

Balmer, J. M. T. (2001). Corporate identity, corporate branding and corporate marketing—Seeing through the fog. *European Journal of Marketing, 35*(3/4), 248–291.

Balmer, J. M. T., & Gray, E. R. (2003). Corporate brands: what are they? What of Them? *European Journal of Marketing, 37*(7/8), 972–997.

Balogun, J. (2001). Strategic change. *Management Quarterly, 10*, 2–11.

Balogun, J., & Johnson, G. (2004). Organizational Restructuring and Middle Manager Sensemaking. *Academy of Management, 47*(4), 523–549.

Balogun, J., & Johnson, G. (2005). From intended strategies to unintended outcomes: The impact of change recipient sensemaking. *Organization Studies, 26*(11), 1573–1601.

Berger, P., & Luckmann, T. (1966). *The social construction of reality: A treatise on the sociology of knowledge.* Harmondsworth, England: Penguin.

Boyce, M. E. (1995). Collective centering and collective sense making in the stories and storytelling of one organization. *Organization Studies, 16*(1), 107–137.

Brown, J. S., & Duguid, P. (2001). Knowledge and organization: A social-practice perspective. *Organization Science, 12*(2), 198–213.

Carlsen, A. (2006). Organizational becoming as dialogic imagination of practice: The case of the indomitable Gauls. *Organization Science, 17*(1), 132–149.

Cheney, G., Christensen, L. T., Zorn, T. E. & Ganesh, S. (2004). *Organizational communication in an age of globalization.* Long Grove, IL: Waveland Press.

Cooren, F., Kuhn, T., Cornelissen, J. P., & Clark, T. (2011). Communication, organizing and organization: An overview and introduction to the special issue. *Organization Studies, 32*(9), 1149–1170.

Dutton, J. E., Ashford, S. J., O'Neill, R. M., & Lawrence, K. (2001). Moves that matter: Issue selling and organizational change. *Academy of Management Journal, 44*(4), 716–736.

Fairhurst, G. T. (1993). Echos of the vision: When the rest of the organization talks Total Quality. *Management Communication Quarterly, 6*, 331–371.

Ford, J. D., & Ford, L. W. (1995). The role of conversations in producing intentional change in organizations. *Academy of Management Review, 20*(3), 541–570.

Gioia, D. A., & Chittipeddi, K. (1991). Sensemaking and sensegiving in strategic change initiation. *Strategic Management Journal, 12*(6), 433–448.

Gioia, D. A., Thomas, J. B, Clark, S. M., & Chittipeddi, K. (1994). Symbolism and strategic change in academia: The dynamics of sense making and influence. *Organization Science, 5*(3), 363–383.

Gioia, D. A., Schultz, M., & Corley, K. G. (2000a). Organizational identity, image and adaptive instability. *Academy of Management Review, 25*(1), 63–81.

Gioia, D.A., Schultz, M., & Corley, K. G. (2000b). Identity dialogues: Where do we go from here? *Academy of Management Review, 25*(1), 145–147.

Hallahan, K., Holtzhausen, D., van Ruler, B., & Verčič, D. (2007). Defining strategic communication. *International Journal of Strategic Communication, 1*(1), 3–35.

Hatch, M. J., & Schultz, M. (2003). Bringing the corporation into corporate branding. *European Journal of Marketing, 37*(7/8), 1041–1064.

Hatch, M. J. & Schultz, M. (2008). *Taking brand initiative: How companies can align strategy, culture, and identity through corporate branding.* San Francisco, CA: Jossey Bass.

Hübner, H. (2007). *The communicating company—towards an alternative theory of corporate communication.* Heidelberg, NY: Springer/Physica.

Ind, N. (2001). *Living the brand: How to transform every member of your organization into a brand champion.* London, England: Kogan Page.

Järventie-Thesleff, R. (2011). *Building the corporate brand in a stream of sense-making and sense-giving activities, a practice perspective,* Published doctoral dissertation, Aalto University School of Business, Aalto, Finland..

Järventie-Thesleff, R., Moisander, J., & Laine, P. (2011). Organizational dynamics and complexities of corporate brand building—a practice perspective. *Scandinavian Journal of Management, 27,* 196–204.

Johnson, S., Scholes, K. & Whittington, R. (2008). *Exploring corporate strategy* (8th ed.). Harlow, England: Pearson Education.

Knox, S., & Bickerton, D. (2003). The six conventions of corporate branding. *European Journal of Marketing, 37*(7/8), 998–1016.

Kunde, J. (2000). *Corporate religion: Building a strong company through personality and corporate soul.* Harlow, England: Pearson Education.

Kunde, J. (2002). *Unique now or never: The brand is the company driver in the new value economy.* Harlow, England: Pearson Education.

Kärreman, D., & Rylander, A. (2008). Managing meaning through the case of a consulting firm, *Organization Studies, 29*(1), 103–124.

Lawrence, T. B., Dyck, B., Maitlis, S., & Mauws, M. K. (2006). The underlying structure of continuous change. *MIT Sloan Management Review, 47*(4), 59–66.

Lewis, L. K. (1999). Disseminating information and soliciting input during planned organizational change: Implementers' targets, sources and channels for communicating. *Management Communication Quarterly, 13*(1), 43–75.

Lewis, L. K. (2006). Employee perspectives on implementation communication as predictors of perceptions of success and resistance. *Western Journal of Communication, 70*(1), 23–46.

Macrae, C. (1999). Brand reality editorial. *Journal of Marketing Management, 15,* 1–24.

Maitlis, S. (2005). The social process of organizational sensemaking. *Academy of Management Journal, 48*(1), 21–49.

Mintzberg, H., & Westley, F. (1992). Cycles of organizational change. *Strategic Management Journal, 13*(S2), 39–59.

Morrison, D. P. (2001). B2B branding: Avoiding the pitfalls. *Marketing Management, 10*(3), 30–34.

Nayak, A., & Chia, R. (2011). Thinking becoming and emergence: Process philosophy and organization studies. In H. Tsoukas and R. Chia (Eds.), *Philosophy and organization theory* (*Research in the Sociology of Organizations,* Vol. 32) pp. 281–309.

Orlikowski, W. (1996). Improvising organizational transformation over time: A situated change perspective. *Information Systems Research, 7*(1), 63–92.

Pettigrew, A. M. (1992). The character and significance of strategy process research. *Strategic Management Journal, 13(S2),* 5–16.

Pettigrew, A. M, Woodman, R. W. & Cameron, K. S. (2001). Studying organizational change and development: Challenges for future research. *Academy of Management Journal, 44*(4), 697–713.

Reckwitz, A. (2002). Toward a theory of social practices. A development in cultural theorizing. *European Journal of Social Theory, 5*(2), 243–263.

Rouleau, L. (2005). Micro-practices of strategic sensemaking and sensegiving: How middle managers interpret and sell change every day. *Journal of Management Studies, 42*(7), 1413–1441.

Thomas, J. B., Clark, S. M. & Gioia, D. A. (1993): Strategic Sensemaking and Organizational Performance: Linkages Among Scanning, Interpretation, Action and Outcomes. *Academy of Management Journal 36*(2), 239–270.

Thomas, R., Sargent, L. D. & Hardy, C. (2011). Managing organizational change: Negotiating meaning and power-resistance relations. *Organization Science, 22*(1), 1–20.

Tsoukas, H. (1996), The firm as a distributed knowledge system: A constructionist approach. *Strategic Management Journal, 17,* 11–25.

Tsoukas, H., & Chia, R. (2002). On organizational becoming: Rethinking organizational change. *Organization Science, 13*(5), 567–582.

Urde, M. (1994). Brand orientation: A strategy for survival. *The Journal of Consumer Marketing, 11*(3): 18–32.

Urde, M. (1999). Brand orientation: A mindset for building brands into strategic resources. *Journal of Marketing Management, 15,* 117–133.

Urde, M. (2003). Core value-based corporate brand building. *European Journal of Marketing, 37*(7/8), 1017–1040.

Weick, K. E. (1995). *Sensemaking in organizations.* Thousand Oaks, CA: Sage.

Weick, K. E., & Quinn, R. E. (1999). Organizational change and development. *Annual Review of Psychology, 50,* 361–386.

Weick, K. E., Sutcliffe, K. M., & Obstfeld, D. (2005). Organizing and the process of sensemaking. *Organization Science, 16*(4), 409–421.

36

Social Media and Strategic Communication

An Examination of Theory and Practice in Communication Research

Bobbi Kay Lewis and Cynthia Nichols

Social media has made a major impact around the world. From assisting in connecting people on a day-to-day basis to being a catalyst in democratic revolutions, social media has changed the perspective and relationship that individuals have with the media and with each other. Social media, including social networking, blogs, video platforms, and micro-blogs, is used to create instant one-way and two-way communication between individuals, communities, and corporations. This type of communication between groups is powerful, and has made online services such as Facebook, Twitter, Youtube, Pinterest, Google+, and LinkedIn a part of users' daily lives. In the spring of 2013, Facebook had more than 1.1 billion users (Facebook, 2013), Twitter was the fastest growing social media site with nearly 21% of the world's internet population using it every month (Smith, 2013), and YouTube visitors watched 6 billion hours of video every month (Bullas, 2013). Macnamara and Zerfass (2012) examined how social media is being used by organizations in Europe and Australia and the challenges of openness, strategy and management. Consistent with studies of social media in the United States, the types of social media most used by organizations in these countries were social networks (e.g., Facebook), microblogging (e.g., Twitter), and video sharing (e.g., YouTube).

As more users access social media mobile through smartphone technology, the presence of social media will only grow stronger. People are using social media, not only for information and interpersonal communication, but also as an extension of experiencing and participating in society. Activities such as watching television, cheering on your team at a sporting event, and attending a concert, all now include participation in social media. According to Nielsen's 2012 "State of the media" report, due to the ubiquity of smartphones, tablets and ultrabooks as well as the proliferation of social media networks like Facebook and Twitter, 88% of the 70 million tablet owners and 86% of the 100 million smartphone owners in the USA use their mobile devices while watching TV at least once a month (Nielsen, 2012). Even more significant, roughly half of both groups use their "second screen" to express their opinions about what they're watching on a daily basis (Turner, 2013). Because of the growing tide of interest and activity in social media, both scholars and practitioners have begun to explore the uses and impacts of this area. In this chapter, we will discuss the scholarly research of social media from a theoretical perspective, and the role of social media in the field of strategic communication. We will then examine social media and strategic communication through Communities of Practice.

Social Media Research

In the burgeoning field of social media research, there has been numerous studies looking at the impact and influence of social media on our society (Khang, Ki, and Ye, 2012). Scholars have begun to explore how social media has the ability to influence various aspects of media, politics, societal norms, and even dating. One drawback to this flurry of recent research, however, is that scholars are often relying on common-sense and pure data analysis to explain social media as opposed to using grounded scientific theory. Upon reflection on this thought, one might ask if the scientific community is figuratively grasping at the social media straw without the theoretical groundwork needed to expand the current knowledge base (Anderson, 2008). This may be due to the relative newness of social media, and the possibility that some theories just don't apply and new concepts should be developed.

It could be argued that some research may not be approaching social media from a theoretical perspective, but rather is trying to connect the social media dots, to provide much needed context for theory development. Although this method of research is one of the first steps in hypothesis and theory building, social media research has been examined since 1997, when the blog first emerged (McCauliff, 2011). For nearly 15 years, scholars have been attempting to explain the influence and impact of social media. But, if we are to truly understand the influence of social media, scholars must take the time to systematically collect data, analyze patterns, and construct a basis for theory in social media. This process of theory construction can undoubtedly lead to a greater understanding of this developing digital world. If the current theories do not work or provide meaningful context to how social media works, then existing theories must be reconstructed or new theories posited.

Fortunately, most scholars are using theory as a basis of their research. One study that examined social media research in 17 of the top advertising, communication, marketing, and public relations journals found that 436 articles were published on the topic between 1997 and 2010 (Khang et al., 2012). The proportion of these articles varied from 5.5% to 43.6% of all the articles published during this period and also indicated a variety of topics—methodologies, effects, forms, theories, advancements, and social media itself were examined. However, only 40% of the articles used explicit theoretical frameworks. Although this may offer a certain level of theoretical rigor to these articles, Khang et al. noted "the majority of articles examined either utilized or replicated existing theoretical frameworks, rather than suggesting alternative frameworks that could entail better solutions for understanding and applying social media phenomena" (p. 292). The process of using existing theoretical frameworks to explain scientific anomaly is not a new concept. According to Kuhn's work on the structure of scientific revolutions (1970), these anomalies are often explained by using existing frameworks until a new paradigm can be established. As such, social media currently fits into this phase, and it is essential for scholars to establish, utilize, and explore theoretical frameworks that can better explain the phenomena of social media (Khang et al., 2012).

Theories Used in Social Media Research

In the 436 articles examined by Khang et al. (2012), several theoretical patterns began to emerge. The most frequently applied theories were *social information processing theory, uses and gratifications theory, relationship management theory, agenda setting or framing theory,* and *diffusion of innovation theory.* The following section will explore the main theoretical frameworks in which to explain social media. These frameworks should contribute to our existing knowledge on social media and how users interact with it.

Social Information Processing Theory

Introduced at the dawn of social media, social information processing theory (*SIP*) explains how interpersonal relationships develop online without the standard nonverbal cues that exist in face-to-face conversation (Walther, 1992). According to Walther, computer-mediated relationships develop at a slower pace than traditional relationships; however, once established these relationships hold to the same standards and values. Walther established that by interpreting textual or verbal cues in computer-mediated messages—as opposed to the normal nonverbal cues from face-to-face conversation—people form impressions of others with linguistic impressions. These impressions then build over an extended period of time depending on the interaction and feedback between the sender, receiver, and channel being used. The more positive the impression is, the faster the relationship forms. This process is known as the *hyperpersonal model* (Walther, 1992).

SIP has been used by a variety of scholars to explain relational intimacy online (e.g., Ellison, Heino, & Gibbs, 2006), to understand marketing on social media (e.g., Lin & Peña, 2011), as well as to understand user interaction within different age groups (e.g., Valkenburg & Peter, 2007). However, critics of the theory have argued that a lack of defined visual cues can be detrimental to establishing a solid and real relationship, something that must be overcome at some point. Tokunaga (2009) argued that relationships cannot be maintained online for an extended period of time, nor can this theory apply to a collectivist society.

When this theory is used to establish and understand strategic communication in social media, it can explain the interaction and attachment that individuals form toward a certain product or person. As a brand establishes itself online, it implements relationship-building efforts designed to create socio-emotional connections with the end user to a product or concept (Lin & Peña, 2011). By utilizing the framework of SIP, textual and nonverbal cues are created and interpreted by people who are already interested in a product or service. Much like parasocial interaction, these messages are often positively interpreted and a stronger more realistic relationship is established in the mind of the consumer, thus helping to explain the popularity and interaction of users in blogs, and on Facebook, Twitter, and other social media sites.

Uses and Gratifications Theory

A popular way to explain and interpret media usage in communication research is through uses & gratifications theory (*UGT*), which attempts to understand how and why people use specific media (Blumler & Katz, 1974). Within this theoretical framework, the importance of the individual, how they use media, and what they get out of it is very prevalent. UGT posits that every individual has different reasons for engaging with media—typically to satisfy their needs for information, entertainment and mood management (Shao, 2009). Additionally, the attributes of the media (such as its timeliness, level of involvement, and interactivity) and the context of use (space and time), play a significant role in how users engage with it.

UGT posits that individuals actively seek out information that will enhance their knowledge or provide companionship, or will allow for relaxation, diversion, or escape from reality. By interacting with others on social media sites, users can often satisfy their own needs by creating content used for enhancing socializing and status seeking, entertainment, information, self-expression and self-actualization (Park, Kee & Valenzuela, 2009; Raacke & Bonds-Raacke, 2008).

Critics of the research have argued that UGT is not theoretically sound as it does not examine psychological antecedents to behavior, the data is difficult to collect, and that users often don't select their own media (Straubhaar, LaRose, & Davenport, 2011). However, social media research has relied greatly on UGT because it helps explain the popularity of the medium. Additionally, it refutes some critics in that social media allows users to have control of the message, affording greater gratification to users (Shao, 2009). However, the ability to create the message and allow for greater gratification has led to privacy issues. At times, when an individual or group in the public eye gives an opinion that is controversial or disliked by the general public, unintended consequences and backlash can occur (Debatin, Lovejoy, Horn, & Hughes, 2009), leading, thus, to the argument that private and public individuals' uses and need for gratification on social media are different.

Relationship Management Theory

Since maintaining and developing relationships is one of the key tenets in strategic communication is it not surprising that relationship management theory is a major theory in social media research. Under the framework of relationship management, the role of strategic communication is to serve as a conduit for communication between the organization and the public (Ledingham, 2003). According to the theory, strategic communication should serve as a central role between parties; have a management function that utilizes the four-stop management process of research, action planning, implementation, and evaluation; identify public attitudes, knowledge, behavior and relationships; and be constructed around the standards and policies that the organization follows when communicating with its publics. Different types of strategies, such as openness, networking, dual concern, and avoiding, can be used when maintaining relationships between publics. According to Bruning and Ledingham (2000), these strategic communication strategies are designed to initiate, nurture, and sustain mutually beneficial relationships between groups.

Due to the changing nature of communication, however, the same basic standards must additionally be maintained and adapted for strategic communications. As practitioners learn to fully integrate social media into their strategies and standards of the organizations they represent, they are also becoming more aware of the need for their expertise (Diga & Kelleher, 2009). Before 2006, it was almost unheard of for an organization to create a social media presence, and thus the standards on relationship management were not fully embraced. However, when social networking sites began to allow business pages, both for-profit and non-profit organizations utilized the resource to strengthen their existing brand. Although some organizations made the assumption that a mere profile on social media would create awareness for them, this was not the case (Waters, Burnett, Lamm, & Lucas, 2009). As users became savvy to social media, tepid one-way communication became unsatisfactory to the consumer and two-way strategic communication was needed to manage the relationship between organizations and stakeholders (Sweetser, 2010). In order to develop relationships with stakeholders on social networks, careful planning and research through the tenets of the relationship management theory must be utilized.

Agenda Setting or Framing Theory

Introduced in 1968 by McCombs and Shaw, agenda setting theory explains how media coverage influences the public agenda. The more than 400 studies that have explored how the media frames a story since the initial Chapel Hill study have relied on two underlying assumptions. First, that media does not reflect reality, but rather filters and frames it (McCombs & Shaw, 1993). Second, when the media focuses on an issue, the public will also focus on that issue and deem it an important part of the public agenda. Since media have access to information and stories that the general public does not, they often act as *gatekeepers,* filtering the information that goes to the general public. Additionally, accessibility, or the frequency in which an issue is covered by the media and accessible to the public, also influences the public conversation—the more it is presented, the more it is important to the public agenda (McCombs & Shaw, 1993). This in turn, affects the agenda of public policy. Critics of classic agenda setting research point out the broad assumptions of the theory—that the public reacts *en masse,* that they are passive in how they consume media, and that they can be categorized into very large groups (which creates inflated results)—indicating a lack of theoretical rigor (Rogers, Hart & Dearing, 1997).

Agenda setting can be used to understand social media and its role in strategic communication. Organizations integrate their own social media (owned media: Facebook, blogs, Twitter, etc.) with their public relations (earned media) and advertising (paid media) in order to generate buzz, which involves consumers and media outlets communicating about the organizations. Any brand, political figure, or public entity can utilize the power of these media to create the public agenda and create public policy. According to Ragas and Roberts (2009) agenda setting can be used in virtual brand communities to control the message path and dampen unexpected negative relationships between the media and public agenda. This type of agenda setting has been implemented for brands online, through social media, and even for political campaigns (Sweetser & Lariscy, 2008). Additionally, some scholars have argued that with a changing media landscape agenda setting has taken on a certain level of role-reversal and the media can now ask the public what the agenda should be (Waters, Tindall, & Morton, 2010). Social media has shifted the theoretical perception of agenda setting and allowed organizations such as Help-A-Reporter-Out (HARO) to give importance and value to a story that the public deems important.

Diffusion of Innovation

As technology develops, so does the level of adoption in society (Rogers, 2003). This process of adoption of new technology in tandem with the spread of new ideas is known as diffusion of innovation (or diffusion of innovations) theory, by means of which an innovation can be seen to be influenced by its diffusion through the social system, and through time, which diffusion has consequences for the adopter, and for the innovation itself. The innovation of social media has spread quickly; it is relatively self-sustaining and has been widely adopted by society. According to Rogers (2003), people fall into one of five adoption categories: innovators adopting a product or technology first, followed by early adopters, early majority, late majority, and, finally, laggards. Additionally, every person goes through a five-step adoption process: Awareness, interest, evaluation, trial, and adoption are integral to this theory. At any point in this process, a person can choose to reject the innovation, idea, or technology.

Critics of diffusion of innovation theory have argued that the adoption of new technology does not necessarily happen in such a systematic pattern, as all populations are not equal, nor do they view technology the same way (Rogers, 2003). Critics have also pointed out the adoption process relies on one-way communication, something that does not exist in social media. However, because social media is such a prevalent new technology, it is no surprise that this theory is used so frequently. As scholars have pursued diffusion of innovation in relation to social media certain tenets hold firm—adoption of the innovation is dependent upon the innovativeness of the person (Chang, Lee, and Kim, 2006); the ease, complexity, and relative advantage of the innovation (Peslak, Ceccucci, and Sendall, 2010); and the adaption of the product by peers (Gulati & C. Williams, 2011).

Theories to Explore and Consider for Social Media Research

Although these five theories were the most frequently cited theories in the most well-respected communication journals, scholars attempting to explain social media have used other frameworks. Theories such as knowledge gap (see Effing, van Hillegersberg, & Huibers, 2011), cultivation (Stefanone, Lackaff, & Rosen, 2010), social identity (Barker, 2009), polymedia (Madianou & Miller, 2013), social feedback loop (Evans, 2008), socialgraphics theory (Owyang, 2010), McLuhan's media theory (e.g., Pan & Crotts, 2012), and communities of practice (Yukawa, 2010; Lewis & Nichols, 2012a, 2012b) have all been used to explain social media phenomena.

Social Media and Strategic Communication

As indicated in the literature, the rapid success of social media has had implications on society in various areas including communication, government, business, education, and religion. As stated in the Nielsen

2012 "State of the media" report, social media and social networking are no longer in their infancy, they are coming of age (Nielsen, 2012). Social media is considered to be transformative for democratic societies, invigorating the public sphere conceptualized by Habermas (1989) as a place where citizens come together and confer freely about matters of general interest (Macnamara & Zerfass, 2012, p. 287). Social media is also very important to the field of strategic communication. Strategic communication is a multidisciplinary endeavor with roots in diverse threads of social sciences (Hallahan, Holtzhausen, van Ruler, & Verčič, 2007). Strategic communication is dependent on institutions and implies intentional communication of an organization (Sandhu, 2009, p. 75). It is important to understand the distinction of strategic communication from integrated communication, which involves the emphasis on the strategic application of communication and how an organization functions as a social actor (Hallahan et al., 2007). "Strategic communication focuses on how the organization itself presents and promotes itself through the intentional activities of its leaders, employees, and communication practitioners" (Hallahan et al., 2007, p. 7). It is also important to note that the definition of strategic communication assumes that its function is part of the management structure that makes key organizational decisions (Coombs and Holladay, 2009). Understanding strategic communication as a management function rather than a technical function is a critical distinction in understanding how to effectively employ social media as a strategic communications tool.

Social media offers communication channels for organizational members to share information and talk to various stakeholders (Meredith, 2012). In the era of globalized media, social media provides an ideal forum to enable organizations to reach transnational audiences and offer them dialogic communication (Avery, Lariscy & Sweetser, 2010). Social media is being employed by virtually all fields to communicate with their various stakeholders. For example, the medical community and the business practices therein are also tapping into the resource of social media to engage the online community in order to better fulfill their missions (Samuel, 2012). Social media is being used to extend the authenticity provided by museums by enabling a museum to maintain a cultural dialogue with its audiences in real time (Russo, Watkins, Kelly, & Chan, 2008). In a multi-method study of the current uses of social media for communication by enterprises, political organizations and non-profit organizations, Linke and Zerfass (2012) offer insights into future trends in social media. The Delphi study indicates that organizations are evolving from experimentation to social media governance, and that guidelines will be more widely adopted and implemented.

The ownership or responsibility of social media within an organization remains a topic of debate. Some argue that only communication professionals should handle corporate or organizational social media, whereas others maintain that social media communication should be holistic, with all members of the organization participating. And there are arguments along the entire spectrum in between the two opposing points of view. Most of the social media literature emerged out of the areas of public relations and strategic communication (Falls 2008; Odden, 2006; Rose, 2008; Lewis, 2010; Luoma-aho & Vos, 2010; Toledano & Wolland, 2011; Wright & Hinson, 2009, 2010). Social media also falls within the areas of information technology, marketing, advertising, and customer service (Avery, Lariscy & Sweetster, 2010). Scott Elser, co-founder of a New York ad agency, argued in a recent article of *Inc.* magazine that social media is a natural fit within the discipline of public relations for several reasons, but because of the maturation and evolution of social media into a place for people to stay connected to products, promotions and developments, social media is starting to require the expertise of advertising professionals (Elser, 2013). The discipline of marketing has been aggressively addressing the need for content relating to social media and many MBA programs are offering courses in social media (Meredith, 2012). Moreover, the use of social media can be applied to all six relevant disciplines of strategic communications as defined by Hallahan et al. (2007): management, marketing, public relations, technical communication, political communication and social marketing. However, social media for organizations goes beyond communications departments, as social media applications are used in nearly every part of an organization.

Through a survey of 140 corporate social strategists, the Altimeter Group identifies five common frameworks for organizing social business (Owyang, 2013). The first model is titled "organic," or "decentralized." Approximately 10% of corporations use this model, which involves social media efforts bubbling up from the edges of the company, and no one department manages or coordinates the efforts. A little more than 29% of companies utilize the second model of social media structure, called "centralized." In this model, one department, such as corporate communications, manages all of the social media activities. The majority of corporations, 36%, use the "hub and spoke" model, which involves a cross-functional team sitting in a centralized position helping various business units. Corporations using this model recognize that social media has an impact on every customer touch point, both internally and externally. The centralized cross-functional team (hub) makes most of the strategic decisions, with input from the various business units (spokes). About 24% of corporations use the fourth model, known as the "dandelion," or multiple hub and spoke. This model, as the nickname suggests, is similar to the hub and spoke model with application to multinational companies where several companies act nearly autonomously from one another while being under one brand umbrella. The Altimeter Group maintains that this model will continue to grow year after year as it involves coordination at the center of the organization while multiple business units have the freedom to make decisions and manage within guidelines, (Owyang, 2013). Finally, only 2.4% of corporations are using the "holistic" model, which includes everyone in the company using social media "safely and consistently across all organizations" (Owyang, 2013). Companies such as Dell and Zappos are taking a holistic approach to their social media management structure. Very few corporations will ever work up to the holistic framework, as it stems from an internal culture that cannot be forced, as reported by Owyang (2013).

As the data from the Altimeter Group suggests, with more than 70% of corporations using a social media structure that utilizes a centralized unit (Owyang, 2013), social media has emerged as a prominent communication tool in strategic communication. It is no longer a matter of whether a company should utilize social media to communicate with audiences, but rather how and with what platforms (Walaski, 2013). Fortune Magazine annually compiles a list of America's largest corporations, aptly named the "Fortune 500" (F500) given their size and wealth. The University of Massachusetts Dartmouth Center for Marketing Research have been conducting an annual study of the social media adoption of these hugely influential companies, in order to gain insights into the future of commerce. Barnes, Lescault and Andonian (2012) report 73% of Fortune 500 companies were active on Twitter in 2012, and more than 80% of executives believed social media engagement led to increased sales.

The ultimate goal of social media is positive communication about the organization from individuals outside the organization. In other words, people are more likely to trust their friends, family and acquaintances than they are an organization, business or brand. When used effectively, social media is best used by "fans" of an organization to champion the goods, products, services and efforts of the organization to their social media friends and followers. However, the biggest asset of social media is also a matter of great concern. Using social media effectively requires not only relinquishing control of the message, but also a clear strategy on how to get fans talking about an organization without directly engaging them. The two concepts upon first glance appear to be mutually exclusive. How can you create a strategy while giving up control? In many instances, organizations only do one or the other. Many organizations have merely relinquished control, such as turning it over to interns with little direction or supervision, based on the notion that being "digital natives" makes millennials effective social media managers. However, Lewis and Nichols (2012a, 2012b) report that education has a more positive impact on college students' perception of using social media strategically than has personal social media use alone. Even if you have an intern who understands how to use social media strategically, he or she still needs to be trained in the communication strategy for the company (Huhman, 2013). Relinquishing control of the message is about getting fans to talk about the product, brand or organization organically and in their own words. It is not about relinquishing control to one employee or department.

Other organizations have developed clear strategies for engaging audiences, but fail to relinquish control. For example, in February 2007 Sara Rosso, an American blogger living in Italy, created World Nutella Day, celebrating Italy's chocolate–hazelnut spread with a website and social media presence on Facebook and Twitter. After almost seven years, in May 2013, Nutella's corporate parent, Ferrero SpA, set out to put an end to the fan-led product promotion sending out a cease and desist letter to Rosso. Because of Rosso's championing of Nutella through social media, more than 50,000 people were celebrating Nutella through Facebook, Twitter, Pinterest and blogs. In a final post on the World Nutella Day site, Rosso wrote:

> The cease-and-desist letter was a bit of a surprise and a disappointment, as over the years I've had contact and positive experiences with several employees of Ferrero, SpA., and with their public relations and brand strategy consultants, and I've always tried to collaborate and work together in the spirit and goodwill of a fan-run celebration of a spread I (to this day) still eat.

After considerable backlash on social media against Ferrero's actions, the corporation dropped the cease and desist. This is an excellent example of a corporation not understanding the benefits of fan-based social media for a brand (Crick, 2013). The importance of control completely overshadowed the situation that most brands would love to be in: an annual event that promotes the brand/product, organized by a fan, recognized internationally with no cost to the company (Crick, 2013).

Organizations must have strong relationships with their stakeholders and great trust in their attitude and communication about the organization. Zappos, an online shoe and clothing shop, is often discussed as a best practice case study in the marketing and organizational leadership circles (Perschel, 2010). Part of Zappos's communication strategy is to be customer-centric and strive to make customers happy. As a result, Zappos's customers want to share their positive experiences with their friends. This focus on customer service requires a high level of trust in the Zappos employees. Customers are encouraged to call Zappos and ask questions via social media, such as Facebook, Twitter and YouTube (Fernandez, 2010). A key aspect to the Zappos customer service model is that nothing is scripted. Employees are given autonomy in their decision-making and discussions with customers. Employees are encouraged to spend as much time with customers, either on the phone or through social media, as needed to make their shopping experience pleasurable and memorable. Zappos is an example of a company developing a clear communication strategy that recognizes the importance and value of relinquishing control of the message.

Among the most prominent ways that organizations are employing social media to fulfill their mission include: management and internal communications, promotion of corporate social responsibility, crisis communications, public relations, and building brand communities and brand loyalty.

Management and Internal Communications

When looking at strategic communications from a postmodern perspective, internal communications also need to be included in the discussion of social media as a function of strategic communication. As Smith (2013) points out, "Postmodern perspectives illuminate the role of negotiation, persuasion, and change on internal activities that ultimately influence the external communication product" (p. 67). Social media can be utilized for internal communications, which can in turn translate into more effective external communication. In a 2009 study of 1,700 business executives worldwide, 64% of companies reported using social media for effective internal communications (Culnan, Patrick, McHugh, & Zubillaga, 2010). Huang, Baptista and Galliers (2013) conducted a study of the impact of social media on internal communications. Their findings reveal that social media has played a role in reconceptualizing the rhetorical practices in organizations. They defined rhetoric in an organizational context and reported that it is used with specific intent, often to generate consensus in situations of uncertainty and emerging possibilities. The authors maintained that social media adds multivocality, increases organizations' reach and richness in communication, and enables simultaneous consumption and co-production of rhetorical content. When facilitated by social media, multivocality is beneficial in "stimulating employees' engagement and facilitating cross-functional innovation by providing a means by which different ideas, viewpoints and concerns are freely expressed, effectively exchanged, consulted, and consolidated" (Huang et al., 2013, p. 112). Their findings suggest that organizational use of social media allows for more voices and messages and less distinction between rhetor and audience. This is supported in Perschel's analysis of Zappos (2010).

Huang et al. (2013) maintain that when organizations embrace the emancipating characteristics of social media they improve communication flows and allow for the co-creation of strategic initiatives. Kesavan, Bernacchi & Mascarenhas (2013) recommend that organizations train employees on how to effectively use social media and encourage them to use it to promote the corporate brand. Many organizations prohibit or discourage employees from using social media because of an unfounded fear of abuse (Kesavan et al., 2013). Remidez and Jones (2012) maintain that project managers can enhance communication effectiveness by incorporating social media.

Utilizing social media from a management and internal communications perspective is better served with guidelines that keep the strategic communication consistent with an organization's image and culture. Linke and Zerfass (2012) argue that organizations should include employees and organization members in the process of developing the social media guidelines in order for the guidelines to be relevant and accepted by members of the organization.

It is also important for organizations to prepare employees to facilitate customer service via social media platforms, otherwise known as social care. The younger the customer, the more likely they are to contact a company by social care than they are by phone. Almost half of all global social media users engage in social care, taking part in such activities as asking questions by writing on a company's Facebook page or complaining to a company's Twitter username (Nielsen, 2012). If organizations do not have the people and guidelines in place to field these inquiries and comments, they are missing out on an opportunity not only to engage their audiences and change perceptions, but also to reach other audiences with whom they have yet to connect. In the Delphi study of communications professionals in Germany, notable increases were reported in the areas of availability of budget and support from top management with regard to social media (Linke & Zerfass, 2012). This suggests that consumers can expect increasingly more effective and strategic use of social media by corporations and brands.

Corporate Social Responsibility

Social marketing or communicating corporate social responsibility (CSR) activities via social media has been advocated and established in the literature. For example, Kesavan et al. reported that Kraft Foods Group is utilizing Facebook to communicate their efforts to help feeding less fortunate families in the United States. Kraft donates 6 meals to hungry families whenever a consumer joins Kraft's Facebook page. TOMS, an American footwear company in Santa Monica, California, is founded on the concept of donating a pair of shoes to a child in need for every pair of TOMS shoes sold. The company uses Twitter to communicate its "one for one" shoe donation program to needy kids in 60 developing countries (Kesavan et al., 2013). According to Ros-Diego and Castelló-Martínez (2012), social media assists organizations in improving interaction with customers and placing consumers in the center of the relationship with brands. This interaction and relationship-building climate allows organizations to highlight their responsible actions in their communication. Social media programs for

CSR communications need to be integrated with other efforts such as community events or executive outreach (Kesavan et al., 2013). Communicating an organization's social mission can lead not only to improved sales and profit, but also to growing a loyal fan base that "evangelizes" for the brand.

Crisis Communications

Organizations are also utilizing social media as part of their crisis communications. Social media is gaining acceptance as a strategic means of communicating warnings, risks and emergencies. Utilizing social media in a crisis requires considerable strategic planning. According to Walaski (2013), organizational integration of social media into risk and crisis communications hinges on developing trust and credibility with an audience well in advance of a crisis event. In March 2012, the American Red Cross launched its Digital Operations Center, which constantly monitors the social media space, so that when an emergency arises the Red Cross can evaluate the needs on the ground. A study in 2012 by American Red Cross reported that social media sites are the fourth most popular sites for obtaining information during an emergency (American Red Cross, 2013). Following the severe tornados in Joplin, Missouri in 2011, Rebecca and Genevieve Williams and David Burton co-authored a field guide to setting up a disaster recovery site via Facebook. The guide reports that utilizing social media for disaster recovery takes knowledge, expertise and dedication. "Collectively, the five person core team for Joplin Tornado Info was experienced in professional social media management, marketing, PR, crisis intervention, IT, journalism, copywriting, construction, logistics, nursing, and meteorology" (R. Williams, G. Williams & Burton, 2012).

Public Relations

Public relations practitioners have been at the forefront of adopting social media technologies and using them to achieve organizational goals (Eyrich, Padman, & Sweetser, 2008; Porter, Sweetster, & Chung, 2009; Wright & Hinson, 2009, Lewis & Nichols, 2012a, 2012b). Social media not only allow public relations practitioners to reach out and engage their publics in two-way symmetrical communication; they also provide an avenue to strengthen media relations. In a study of journalism and public relations coorientation, Avery, Lariscy, and Sweetser (2010) suggest that as journalists and public relations practitioners increase their use of social media, they may be sharing sources, information and insights which could lead to more agreement among the two groups, confirming accuracy of information. The authors maintain that this byproduct of social media signals not only that public relations practitioners can reach a key strategic public (journalists) through social media to the desired effect, but also that the use of the co-orientation model presents an intuitive approach to understanding the effect of strategic communication.

Building Brand Communities and Brand Loyalty

Utilizing social media in branding activities is also well established in the literature, despite debate over whether it is a welcomed practice by consumers (Laroche, Habibi, & Richard, 2013). Social media provide an opportunity for organizations to build brand communities. A brand community is a "specialized, non-geographically bound community, based on a structured set of social relations among admirers of a brand" (Muniz & O'Guinn, 2001, p. 412). Brand communities involve a common understanding of shared identity and can be found both in face-to-face interactions and via online technology (Muniz & O'Guinn, 2001). Brand communities based in social media provide an opportunity for gathering customers together, engaging them in conversation, encouraging conversation among themselves, and enabling them to obtain information about the brand from various sources (Laroche, Habibi, Richard, & Sankaranarayanan, 2012). Social media based brand communities enhance customer relationships, provide benefits to their members by facilitating information sharing and increasing customers' bonds to each other (Laroche, Habibi, & Richard, 2013). Kurikko and Tuominen (2012) maintain that online brand communities empower members by creating value and a sense of belonging. Brand communities provide a "place" for organizations and stakeholders to develop integrated ties that constitute loyalty (Lobschat, Zinnbauer, Pallas & Joachimsthaler, 2013; Laroche et al., 2012). Although the personal computer is still at the top, connecting to social media through mobile devices is one of the major and growing trends in social media; app usage accounts for more than a third of social networking time (Nielsen, 2012). Mobile is particularly strong in Asia-Pacific. Given the growth of mobile and increased adoption of apps for social media access, brand communities can establish that sense of place and belonging for their stakeholders while they are on the go.

Building community can also be accomplished with the fusion of television and mobile. As discussed in the introduction and often referred to as the "second-screen effect," social media users are interacting with others via social media on their mobile devices while watching TV. These multimedia users particularly enjoy watching and commenting about live events, including but not limited to the following: sporting events, awards shows, and contest and reality programs. Twitter is leading the social TV conversation. Simultaneous smartphone and tablet usage while watching TV is also a growing trend, not only in the United States, but globally. In a survey of more than 28,000 global consumers with internet access, more 60% of consumers in the Middle East and Africa and more than 50% in Latin America reported that they are interacting with social media while watching TV (Nielsen, 2012).

Social Media, Strategic Communication and Communities of Practice

Social media have changed the way organizations communicate both internally and externally. Since the inception of social media, organizations have been in an "on-the-job training" environment, learning to navigate the changing landscape of technology and strategic communication. Traxler (2007) reported that "mobile, personal and wireless devices are now radically transforming societal notions of discourse and knowledge, and are responsible for new forms of art, employment, language, commerce, deprivation and crime, as well as learning" (p. 2). According to Castronovo and Huang (2012), organizations are leveraging social media to actively engage with audiences, but the strategic execution of using social media has yet to be robustly identified. Although professional development has always been a part of organizations, communication, and business, changes in technology and the explosion of social media over the last decade have brought learning to the forefront. In addition, strategic communication has always been about information sharing and value creation within a specific context, which is essentially social learning at its core. Thus, social learning theory or situated learning is a natural lens for an examination of social media with respect to strategic communication. Etienne Wenger (2000) has maintained that the success of organizations depends on their ability to design themselves as social learning systems.

In a study of situated learning, mobile technology and learning language, Comas-Quinn, Mardomingo and Valentine (2009) reported that mobile technologies provide an opportunity for a situated and informal learning experience that encourages interaction and a sense of community among learners. The situated learning experience gives the learners the freedom to engage with the activity in their own way. The teacher or school is no longer mediating the context for the learners, but is inviting them to experience it for themselves in the hope that this will result in a more personalized and meaningful learning experience. It requires a transfer of control of the activity to the learners, which also requires a diminished degree of control for instructors (Comas-Quinn, Mardomingo & Valentine, 2009). Although this study is about mobile education, it is a mirror image of what is happening with social media and strategic communication. Practitioners and organizations must be willing to give their audiences the freedom to engage with social media activity in their own way. Organizations have to welcome the shifting balance of power in order for their stakeholders to gain a personal and meaningful experience with them via social media.

Lave and Wenger (1991) designate learning as a function of the activity, context and culture in which it occurs: learning is "situated." According to Wenger (1998), a social learning theory must integrate four components necessary to characterize social participation, namely: (a) Meaning: learning as experience, (b) practice: learning as doing, (c) community: learning as belonging, and (d) identity: learning as becoming (p. 5). Situated learning is framed by the concept that knowledge is best learned and retained in an authentic context (Moore, 2009). Likewise, effective strategic communication through social media involves experience, practice, community, and identity.

Born out of situated learning theory, Lave and Wenger coined the term *community of practice* while studying apprenticeship as a learning model, as reported by Wenger (1999). The term refers to the community that acts as a living curriculum for the apprentice. Through further investigation of the concept, Lave and Wenger realized the existence of the practice of a community went far beyond the formal apprenticeship system (Wenger, 1999).

Communities of Practice

Communities of Practice (CoP) are informal, pervasive, and an integral part of our daily lives. Knowledge and skills are obtained by participation in activities that expert members of the community would perform. Learners become involved in a CoP, which embodies certain beliefs and behaviors to be acquired through legitimate peripheral participation (Wenger, 1998). According to Annabi and McGann (2013), CoP have long been considered powerful knowledge management mechanisms, but are often viewed independently from organizational goals and structures. In their article, "Social media as the missing link," they argue that when supported by social media, CoP have great potential to contribute to organizational goals, such as business strategy. Among the findings of their study, they report that a change in culture is required at all levels of the organization. Employees from the top down must change their perception of CoP and social media in order to strike a balance between alignment with organization structure and strategy (Annabi & McGann, 2013).

Communities of Practice have been described as tools used to improve an organization's capacity to develop and share knowledge. These communities provide the opportunity to develop strong relationships and trust, which are essential for effective communications (Wenger, 1996). In today's connected world, organizational CoP can be both internal (management and employees) and external (organization and various stakeholders). Social media also can help facilitate an organization's capacity to develop and share knowledge. Like CoP, social media and online social networks bring organizations together through social ties that lead to strong relationships, trust and exchange of knowledge. A 2012 report from McKinsey showed that a majority of the estimated $1.3 trillion in untapped value from social technologies lies in "improved communications and collaboration within and across enterprises" (Barnes, Lescault & Andonian, 2012).

Traditional media, by contrast, is most often one-way communication where the message is simply broadcast from the producer to the receiver. When using only traditional media, organizations produced and distributed their messages to specific audiences through various media. With social media, the balance of control for both production and distribution of content is now being shared by the organization and its stakeholders. This shared control concept was and still is somewhat frightening to most executives and organizational leaders from a marketing and business perspective in the early stages of social media. They want to maintain control of the message and the distribution. But practitioners with a strategic communication perspective better understand and appreciate the value of social media and its ability to include the audience in production and distribution of an organization's message. In the article "Defining strategic communication," Hallahan et al. (2007) explain that communication is a "two-way process that is interactive and participatory at all levels" (p. 23). Social media is also interactive and participatory, fitting seamlessly within strategic communication. Social media is a tool for organizations to become social learning systems both internally and externally, informing and becoming informed about the organization via communication with various stakeholders. The organizations and its stakeholders are both empowered by the social learning systems created out of CoP and social media. Organizations and stakeholders are each creating value for themselves and for one another.

Conclusions

Social media plays a large role in the field of strategic communication today. Social media provides a meeting place for individuals, from all walks of life, who find each other to share information, emotion, beliefs and belonging. Organizations are also utilizing the social media space to become involved in that sharing of information, emotion, beliefs and belonging in order to connect with people on a sustaining level. Numerous theoretical perspectives are being used to examine the social media phenomenon, including the following theories examined in this chapter: *social information processing theory, uses and gratifications theory, relationship management theory, agenda setting or framing theory,* and *diffusion of innovation theory.*

The social media literature has implications for numerous fields of study as it is affecting so many areas of modern society, including but not limited to technology, political science, medicine, and, of course, communication. Within the field of strategic communication, many disciplines have made an attempt to take ownership of social media from an organizational perspective, such as public relations, marketing, advertising, and management. According to the literature, social media is a tool that can be employed effectively in each of these disciplines. However, we would argue that in order for that to be true, the social media plan needs to be positioned in the strategic communication of an organization, meaning it is a part of the management structure that makes all of the key organizational decisions. If social media is used as a mere tactic, independently from the various disciplines such as marketing or public relations and informed by no integrated strategy therefrom, its effectiveness is considerably diminished. By looking at social media and strategic communication through the lens of CoP, we can see the importance of learning through meaning, practice, community, and identity. In order to provide the right climate for CoP and effective knowledge management through social media, organizations need to give stakeholders the opportunity to experience Wenger's (2000) three modes of belonging: engagement, imagination, and alignment. To capture these different forms of participation, the strategic communication efforts have to be adopted by, if not born from, the organizational leadership and integrated from the top down.

References

American Red Cross (2013). *American Red Cross Annual Report.* Washington, DC. Retrieved from http://www. redcross.org/images/MEDIA_CustomProductCatalog/m18071523_Red-Cross-2012.AnnualReport.pdf

Anderson, C. (2008). The end of theory: The data deluge makes the scientific Method obsolete. *Wired Magazine, 16*(7), 16–07.

Annabi, H., & McGann, S. T. (2013). Social media as the missing link: Connecting communities of practice to business strategy. *Journal of Organizational Computing and Electronic Commerce, 23,* 56–83.

Avery, E., Lariscy, R., & Sweetser, K. D. (2010). Social media shared—or divergent—uses? A coorientation analysis of public relations practitioners and journalists. *International Journal of Strategic Communication, 4*(3), 189–205.

Barker, V. (2009). Older adolescents' motivations for social network site use: The influence of gender, group identity, and collective self-esteem. *CyberPsychology & Behavior, 12*(2), 209–213.

Barnes, N. G., Lescault, A. M., & Andonian, J. (2012). *Social Media Surge by the 2012 Fortune 500: Increase in Use of Blogs, Twitter and More.* Retrieved from http://www.umassd.edu/cmr/socialmedia/2012fortune500/statistics-2013–231748416.html

Blumler, J. G., & Katz, E. (1974). *The uses of mass communication.* Newbury Park, CA: Sage.

Bruning, S. D., & Ledingham, J. A. (2000). Perceptions of relationships and evaluations of satisfaction: An exploration of interaction. *Public Relations Review, 26*(1), 85–95.

Bullas, J. (2013, May 5). 21 Awesome social media facts, figures and statistics for 2013. *Yahoo Small Business.* Retrieved from http://smallbusiness.yahoo.com/advisor/21-awesome-social-media-facts-figures

Castronovo, C., & Huang, L. (2012). Social media in an alternative marketing communication model. *Journal of Marketing Development and Competitiveness, 6*(1), 117–131.

Chang, B. H., Lee, S. E., & Kim, B. S. (2006). Exploring factors affecting the adoption and continuance of online games among college students in South Korea: Integrating uses and gratification and diffusion of innovation approaches. *New Media & Society, 8*(2), 295–319.

Comas-Quinn, A., Mardomingo, R., & Valentine C. (2009). Mobile blogs in language learning: Making the most of informal and situated learning opportunities. *European Association for Computer Assisted Language Learning, 21*(1), 96–112.

Coombs, W. T., & Holladay, S. J. (2009). Corporate social responsibility: Missed opportunity for institutionalizing communication practice? *International Journal of Strategic Communication, 3*(2), 93–101.

Crick, P. (2013, June 18). Social media case study: Nutella. *Cre8ive: Creative Advertising LTD Blog.* Retrieved from http://cre8ive.co.nz/2013/06/social-media-case-study-nutella/

Culnan, M., Patrick, J. McHugh, P. & Zubillaga, J. (2010). How large U.S. companies can use Twitter and other social media to gain business value. *MIS Quarterly Executive, 9*(4), 243–259.

Debatin, B., Lovejoy, J. P., Horn, A. K., & Hughes, B. N. (2009). Facebook and online privacy: Attitudes, behaviors, and unintended consequences. *Journal of Computer-Mediated Communication, 15*(1), 83–108.

Diga, M., & Kelleher, T. (2009). Social media use, perceptions of decision-making power, and public relations roles. *Public Relations Review, 35*(4), 440–442.

Effing, R., van Hillegersberg, J., & Huibers, T. (2011). Social media and political participation: Are Facebook, Twitter and YouTube democratizing our political systems? *Electronic Participation* (pp. 25–35). Berlin, Heidelberg, Germany: Springer.

Ellison, N., Heino, R., & Gibbs, J. (2006). Managing impressions online: Self-presentation processes in the online dating environment. *Journal of Computer-Mediated Communication, 11*(2), 415–41.

Elser, S. (2013). Is social media advertising or PR? *Inc.* (May 1, 2013). Retrieved May 15, 2013 from http://www.inc.com/scott-elser/is-social-media-advertising-or-pr.html

Evans, D. (2008). *Social media marketing: An hour a day.* Indianapolis, IN: Sybex.

Eyrich, N., Padman, M. L., & Sweetser, K. D. (2008). PR practitioners' use of social media tools and communication technology. *Public Relations Review, 34*(4), 412–414.

Facebook (2013). *Quarterly Earnings Slides: Q1 2013.* Retrieved from: http://files.shareholder.com/downloads/AMDA-NJ5DZ/2462702744x0x659143/b4c0beda-da0a-4f8e-9735-9852ef08adb1/FB_Q113_InvestorDeck_FINAL.pdf

Falls, J. (2008). Philosophy, public relations, social media. *Social Media Explorer.* Retrieved March 15, 2013, from www.socialmediaexplorer.com/2008/07/18.

Fernandez, C. (2010) *Zappos Customer Loyalty Team: Pay, Benefits, and Growth Opportunities.* Retrieved from http://www.youtube.com/watch?v=OB3Qog5Jhq4

Gulati, G., & Williams, C. (2011). *Diffusion of Innovations and Online Campaigns: Social Media Adoption in the 2010 US Congressional Elections.* Retrieved from: http://papers.ssrn.com/sol3/papers.cfm?abstract_id=1925585

Habermas, J. (1989). *The structural transformation of the public sphere.* Cambridge, England: Polity (original work published in 1962).

Hallahan, K., Holtzhausen, D., van Ruler, B., Verčič, D., & Sriramesh, K. (2007). Defining strategic communication. *International Journal of Strategic Communication, 1*(1), 13–39.

Huang, J., Baptista, J., & Galliers, R. D. (2013). Reconceptualizing rhetorical practices in organizations: The impact of social media on internal communications. *Information & Management, 50*(2–3), 112–124.

Huhman, H. (2013, July 28). Why social media internships should never be unpaid. *Mashable.* Retrieved from http://mashable.com/2013/07/28/social-media-internships/

Kesavan, R., Bernacci, M., & Mascarenhas, O. (2013). Word of Mouse: CSR communication and social media. *International Management Review, 9*(1), 58–66.

Khang, H., Ki, E. J., & Ye, L. (2012). Social media research in advertising, communication, marketing, and public relations, 1997–2010. *Journalism & Mass Communication Quarterly, 89*(2), 279–298.

Kuhn, T. S. (1970). *The structure of scientific revolutions.* Chicago and London: University of Chicago Press.

Kurikko, H., & Tuominen, P. (2012). Collective value creation and empowerment in an online brand community: A netnographic study on LEGO builders. *Technology Innovation Management Review,* June, 12–17. Retrieved from: http://timreview.ca/sites/default/files/article_PDF/KurikkoTuominen_TIMReview_June2012.pdf

Laroche, M., Habibi, M. R., & Richard, M. O. (2013). To be or not to be in social media: How brand loyalty is affected by social media? *International Journal of Information Management, 33*(1), 76–82.

Laroche, M., Habibi, M. R., Richard, M. O., & Sankaranarayanan, R. (2012). The effects of social media based brand communities on brand community markers, value creation practices, brand trust and brand loyalty. *Computers in Human Behavior, 28*(5), 1755–1767.

Lave, J. & Wenger, E. (1991). *Situated Learning: Legitimate peripheral participation*. New York: Cambridge University Press.

Ledingham, J. A. (2003). Explicating relationship management as a general theory of public relations. *Journal of Public Relations Research, 15*(2), 181–198.

Lewis, B. K. (2010). Social media and strategic communication: Attitudes and perceptions among college students. *Public Relations Journal, 4*(3).

Lewis, B. K., & Nichols, C. (2012a) Attitudes and perceptions about social media among college students and professionals involved and not involved in strategic communications. In H. S. Noor Al-Dean & J. A. Hendricks (Eds.), *Social media: Usage and impact* (pp. 129–144). Lanham, MD: Lexington.

Lewis, B. K., & Nichols, C. (2012b). Social media and strategic communication: A two-year study of attitudes and perceptions about social media among college students. *Public Relations Journal, 6*(4).

Lin, J. S., & Peña, J. (2011). Are you following me? A content analysis of TV networks' brand communication on Twitter. *Journal of Interactive Advertising, 12*(1), 17–29.

Linke, A., & Zerfass, A. (2012). Future trends in social media use for strategic communication: Results of a Delphi study. *Public Communication Review, 2*(2), 17–29.

Lobschat, L., Zinnbauer, M.A., Pallas, F. & Joachimsthaler, E. (2103). Why Social Currency Becomes a Key Driver of a Firm's Brand Equity – Insights from the Automotive Industry. *Long Range Planning, 46*(1-2), 125-148

Luoma-aho, V., & Vos, M. (2010). Towards a more dynamic stakeholder model: Acknowledging multiple issue arenas. *Corporate Communications: An International Journal, 15*(3), 315–331.

Macnamara, J., & Zerfass, A. (2012). Social media communication in organizations: The challenges of balancing openness, strategy, and management. *International Journal of Strategic Communication, 6*(4), 287–308.

Madianou, M., & Miller, D. (2013). Polymedia: Towards a new theory of digital media in interpersonal communication. *International Journal of Cultural Studies, 16*(2), 169–187.

McCauliff, K. L. (2011). Blogging in Baghdad: The practice of collective citizenship on the blog Baghdad Burning. *Communication Studies, 62*(1), 58–73.

McCombs, M. E., & D. L. Shaw (1993). The evolution of agenda-setting research: Twenty-five years in the marketplace of ideas. *Journal of Communication, 43*(2), 58–67.

Meredith, M. (2012). Strategic communication and social media: An MBA course from a business communication perspective. *Business Communication Quarterly, 75*(1), 89–95.

Moore, J. (2009, August). *Working social media before it works you: Best practices in advertising and public relations*. Paper presented at the Association for Education in Mass Communication Annual Convention, Boston, MA.

Muniz, A., & O'Guinn, C. T. (2001). Brand community. *Journal of Consumer Research, 27*(4), 412–432.

Nielsen. (2012). *State of the media: The cross-platform report Q2*. New York, NY. Retrieved from http://www.nielsen.com/us/en/reports/2012/state-of-the-media—cross-platform-report-q2–2012.html

Odden, L. (2006). *Resources for new media and social media PR*. Online Marketing Blog. Retrieved from www.toprankblog.com/2006/08/resources

Owyang, J. (2013.) *Altimeter Research: Social business spreads across the enterprise.*. Retrieved from http://www.web-strategist.com/blog/2013/05/08/altimeter-research-social-business-spreads-across-the-enterprise/

Pan, B., & Crotts, J. C. (2012). Theoretical models of social media, marketing implications, and future research directions. In M. Sigala, E. Christou, E. & U. Gretzel (Eds.), *Social media in travel, tourism and hospitality—Theory, practice and cases*, pp. 73–86, Burlington, VT: Ashgate.

Park, N., Kee, K. F., & Valenzuela, S. (2009). Being immersed in social networking environment: Facebook groups, uses and gratifications, and social outcomes. *CyberPsychology & Behavior, 12*(6), 729–733.

Perschel, A. (2010). Work-life flow: How individuals, Zappos, and other innovative companies achieve high engagement. *Global Business and Organizational Excellence, 29*(5), 17–30.

Peslak, A., Ceccucci, W., & Sendall, P. (2010). An empirical study of social networking behavior using diffusion of innovation theory. Proceedings from 2010 CONISAR: *Conference on Information Systems Applied Research* (pp. 1–14). Nashville, TN: EDSIG. Retrieved from http://proc.conisar.org/2010/pdf/1526.pdf

Porter, L., Sweetser, K. & Chung, D. The blogosphere and public relations: Investigating practitioners' roles and blog use. *Journal of Communication Management, 13*(3), 250–267.

Raacke, J., & Bonds-Raacke, J. (2008). MySpace and Facebook: Applying the uses and gratifications theory to exploring friend-networking sites. *CyberPsychology & Behavior, 11*(2), 169–174.

Ragas, M. W., & Roberts, M. S. (2009). Agenda setting and agenda melding in an age of horizontal and vertical media: A new theoretical lens for virtual brand communities. *Journalism & Mass Communication Quarterly, 86*(1), 45–64.

Remidez, H., & Jones, N. (2012). Developing a model for social media in a project management communications. *International Journal of Business and Social Science, 3* (3), 33–36.

Rogers, E. M. (2003). *Diffusion of innovations* (5th ed.). New York: Free Press.

Rogers, E. M., Hart, W. B., & Dearing, J. W. (1997). A paradigmatic history of agenda-setting research. In S. Iyengar & R. Reeves (Eds.) *Do the media govern? Politicians, voters, and reporters in America* (pp. 225–236). Thousand Oak, CA: Sage.

Ros-Diego, V. R., & Castelló-Martínez, A. (2012). CSR communication through online social media. *Revista Latina de Comunicación Social, 67*, 47–67.

Rose, M. (2008). *Digital/new media drives PR growth.* Retrieved March 15, 2013, from www.prblognews.com/2008/03/18/digital.

Russo, A., Watkins, J., Kelly, L., & Chan S. (2008). Participatory communication with social media. *Curator, 51*(1), 21–31.

Samuel, S. (2012). Embracing the social media revolution. *In Practice, 34*, 48–51.

Sandhu, S. (2009). Strategic communication: An institutional perspective. *International Journal of Strategic Communication, 3*(2), 72–92.

Shao, G. (2009). Understanding the appeal of user-generated media: A uses and gratification perspective. *Internet Research, 19*(1), 7–25.

Smith, T. (Jan 28, 2013) Twitter now the fastest growing social platform in the world. *Global Web Index.* Retrieved from http://www.globalwebindex.net/twitter-now-the-fastest-growing-social-platform-in-the-world/

Stefanone, M. A., Lackaff, D., & Rosen, D. (2010). The relationship between traditional mass media and "social media": reality television as a model for social network site behavior. *Journal of Broadcasting & Electronic Media, 54*(3), 508–525.

Straubhaar, J., LaRose, R., & Davenport, L. (2011). *Media now: Understanding media, culture, and technology.* Boston, MA: Wadsworth.

Sweetser, K. D. (2010). A losing strategy: The impact of nondisclosure in social media on relationships. *Journal of Public Relations Research, 22*(3), 288–312.

Sweetser, K. D., & Lariscy, R. W. (2008). Candidates make good friends: An analysis of candidates' uses of Facebook. *International Journal of Strategic Communication, 2*(3), 175–198.

Tokunaga, R. S. (2009). High-speed internet access to the other: The influence of cultural orientations on self-disclosures in offline and online relationships. *Journal of Intercultural Communication Research, 38*(3), 133–147.

Toledano, M. & Wolland, L.F. (2011). Ethics 2.0: Social media implications for professional communicators. *Ethical Space: The International Journal of Communication Ethics, 8*(3/4), 43–52.

Traxler, J. (2007) Defining, discussing and evaluating mobile learning: The moving finger writes and having writ. . . . *International Review of Research in Open and Distance Learning, 8*(2), 1–12.

Turner, S. (2013). The evolution of the second screen. *Wired* (May 23, 2013). Retrieved from http://www.wired.com/insights/2013/05/the-evolution-of-the-second-screen/

Valkenburg, P. M., & Peter, J. (2007). Preadolescents' and adolescents' online communication and their closeness to friends. *Developmental psychology, 43*(2), 267–277.

Walaski, P. (2013). Social media: Powerful tools for SH&E professionals. Published in *Professional safety: Program development,* by ASSE. pp. 40–49. Retrieved from: http://www.asse.org/professionalsafety/docs/F1Wala_0413.pdf

Walther, J. B. (1992). Interpersonal effects in computer-mediated interaction A relational perspective. *Communication Research, 19*(1), 52–90.

Waters, R. D., Burnett, E., Lamm, A., & Lucas, J. (2009). Engaging stakeholders through social networking: How nonprofit organizations are using Facebook. *Public Relations Review, 35*(2), 102–106.

Waters, R. D., Tindall, N. T., & Morton, T. S. (2010). Media catching and the journalist–public relations practitioner relationship: How social media are changing the practice of media relations. *Journal of Public Relations Research, 22*(3), 241–264.

Wenger, E. (1996). Communities of practice: The social fabric of a learning organization. *HealthCare Forum Journal, 39*(4), 20–26.

Wenger, E. (1998). *Communities of practice: Learning, meaning, and identity.* Cambridge, England: Cambridge University Press.

Wenger, E. (1999). Communities of practice: The key to a knowledge strategy. *Knowledge Directions, 1(2),* 48–63.

Wenger, E. (2000). Communities of practice and social learning systems. *Organization, 7*(2), 225–246.

Williams, R., Williams, G., & Burton, D. (2012). *The use of social media for disaster recovery.* Retrieved from http://extension.missouri.edu/greene/documents/PlansReports/using%20social%20media%20in%20disasters.pdf

Wright, D., & Hinson, M. (2009). Examining how public relations practitioners actually are using social media. *Public Relations Journal, 3*(3).

Wright, D., & Hinson, M. (2010). An analysis of new communications media use in public relations: a five-year trend study. *Public Relations Journal, 4*(2).

Yukawa, J. (2010). Communities of practice for blended learning. Toward an integrated model for LIS education. *Journal of Education for Library and Information Science, 51*(2), 54–75.

37

Global Strategic Communication

From the Lens of Coordination, Control, Standardization, and Localization

Juan-Carlos Molleda and Sarabdeep Kochhar

In today's global marketplace, corporations are members of a worldwide community, rather than merely members of their city, town, or state (Maignan & Ferrell, 2004). We are in an era where advances in communication technologies and increased access to information affect and empower every individual. The advent of innovative information technologies has multiplied the influence large corporations have on their communities. The "goldfish bowl" transparency created by globalization, the Internet, and the media (Steger, 2003) has emphasized the importance of trust and relationship between an organization and its stakeholders. The relationship any corporation shares with its stakeholders and consumers is crucial because the identity and values a corporation creates in society determine how much power it gains in the given social system (Ordeix-Rigo & Duarte, 2009).

Globalization and Strategic Communication

Globalization has even shifted stakeholders and corporations' focus of attention towards developing countries rather than developed countries (Amann, Khan, Salzmann, Steger & Ionescu-Somers, 2007). Established multinational corporations (MNCs) from developed economies are striving to expand their business operations in developing and, in particular, emerging countries. Consumers and stakeholders from different echelons of society now have access to claims and offerings of organizations and their diverse products, services, ideas, and causes. They are being empowered by innovative and interactive communication technologies. Their choices in the marketplace or "marketspace" are expanding and, at times, becoming specialized and even tailored to meet their needs. Thus, the dynamic process of reaching out to stakeholders through coordinated strategic communication strategies is essential for MNCs to gain credibility in their host markets.

Stohl (2004) examined the theories of globalization and found communication to be central to this contemporary phenomenon, better to help plan and implement strategic communication campaigns. But what exactly strategic communication is and what it includes is highly debated (Paul, 2011). The role of strategic communication has been widely studied in MNCs, national policy making (Paul, 2012), supranational organizations, and military operations (Orgad, 2011). The term "strategic communication" is often prone to interpretation depending on the political, social, economic, or cultural factors of a society. This discussion will be relevant when attempting to provide a working definition of global strategic communication later in this chapter.

Purpose of the Chapter

The advent of globalization has made it imperative to comprehend strategic communication from a global perspective. Global strategic communication can be best understood as the strategies employed by organizations in any environment to engage in effective bidirectional communication with their stakeholders in an effort to build enduring symbiotic relationships with them. These environments are no longer isolated from each other, meaning that the influence an organization has on its stakeholders at home (where it is headquartered) impacts its influence on publics elsewhere, and vice versa. The impact may occur though marketing communication campaigns, crisis situations, or political or socioeconomic upheavals. Equally important is the transnational environment in which groups and institutions' activities can have a simultaneous impact in several world locations and, perhaps, globally. As a consequence, organizations planning, executing and evaluating global strategic communication programs should understand this multi-geographic and virtual dynamic. This chapter will focus on the mechanics of strategic communication from a global perspective. The first part of the chapter will explain further what strategic communication is and present a definition to help clarify the concept. The second part of the chapter will look at how MNCs are planning, implementing, and managing their global strategic communication efforts. Strategies such as coordination, control, standardization, and localization are frequently refined by MNCs to carry out their strategic communication functions and practices around the globe.

The chapter will delve into the coordination and control mechanisms required to manage the global strategic communication function while aiming to strike a balance between standardization and localization. The third part of the chapter will look specifically at the growing field of international tourism promotion and will also analyze a case study as an illustration of the theoretical framework. The case study is on a global tourism campaign developed by the Costa Rican Institute of Tourism called "Costa Rica: No artificial ingredients." The last part of this chapter will provide suggestions for research and practice in global strategic communications.

Defining Global Strategic Communication

The term strategic communication has been applied to any planned communication efforts by organizations (Botan, 1997). The planned efforts can result in achieving organizational goals and enhance corporate reputation through corporate diplomacy initiatives, corporate social responsibility campaigns, crisis communication, institutional or commercial advertising, and marketing campaigns, among others. Strategic communication incorporates planning and implementation involving all the organizational aspects and abilities (Hallahan, Holtzhausen, van Ruler, Verčič, & Sriramesh, 2007). Botan and Soto (1998) emphasized the components, such as comprehensive research, planning, and evaluation of strategic communication, that differentiate strategic communication from public relations.

PRSA led an international effort to modernize the definition of public relations and defined public relations as a strategic communication process that builds symbiotic relationships between organizations and their publics (Public Relations Defined, 2012). Public relations process comprises a set of objectives and goals, identifying the specific public, planning the strategies for each public with organizational goals in mind, implementing the strategies and tactics, and finally measuring the effectiveness of those strategies and tactics for the achievement of established measurable goals and objectives. This also is typically the process of strategic communication (Pfau & Wan, 2006) with the additional practice of other persuasive and goal-oriented communication and marketing techniques and efforts. The focus of strategic communication is on the end result of persuasion and hence the communication starts and ends with stakeholders and consumers in mind (Botan & Hazelton, 2006).

Thus, the essence of strategic communication is purposive and its deliberate efforts to advance the mission of organizations from an integrated, multidisciplinary perspective (Hallahan et al., 2007). The term is used as a unifying framework for coordinating communication functions (e.g., advertising, marketing, and public relations) and their plans, strategies, and tactics to achieve organizational goals. These functions support all types of sectors and industries both domestically and across geographical borders. In this chapter, *global strategic communication* is defined as a pursuit that multinational and multilateral organizations undertake to efficiently manage and effectively engage with stakeholders and consumers worldwide. The management process is performed through careful coordination and control of centralized or decentralized operations and activities, whereas stakeholders' and consumers' engagement is achieved by the continuous attempt to balance standardization and localization. Global strategic communication can, therefore, be seen as a strategically planned and structurally applied approach to communication, which integrates analysis and evaluation at each stage of design and implementation.

Strategic communication has specifically changed in the emergent media landscape. Communication through the emergent interactive media is based on how stakeholders and consumers are engaged so that corporations can be active producers and participants in a true dialogue. According to Lewis (2010), social media continues to have great influence on both the theory and practice of advertising, public relations, and marketing professions and practices. McCorkindale (2009) reported that around 69% of the *Fortune* 2000 companies use social networking sites. As cited by Wright and Hinson (2010), Burson-Marsteller reported the extensive use of social media platforms (i.e., Twitter, Facebook, YouTube, and corporate blogs) by 79% of the *Fortune* Global 100 companies. The growth every year is indicative of the fact that social media is being increasingly used by organizations to actively interact with their target audiences. Both scholars and practitioners of public relations, particularly, share the opinion that technology plays a crucial role in fostering meaningful dialogue and relationships with important publics (Heath, 1998; Kent & Taylor, 1998), which has created opportunities in managing strategic communication globally. Strategic communication in interactive media will aim at not controlling but facilitating or mediating the discussions. Friedman (2005) stated how media has the potential to bridge cross-cultural gaps and brings people closer together around the world. The globalization of markets constitutes management challenges for MNCs that necessitate an international orientation of their strategic communication decisions and actions.

Coordination and Control

Lenovo, the second world-largest personal computer manufacturer (Shah, 2012), has principal operations in China, Singapore, and the United States; seven research centers in China and one each in Japan and the United States; sales headquarters in China, France, Singapore, and the United States; and four manufacturing centers in China and one each in India, Mexico, and the United States ("Our locations," 2012). This complex structure is typical of corporations operating globally, which requires coordination and control of functional areas, including marketing—advertising and public affairs or public relations, among other related communication functions.

Coordination has been defined as "the linking or integrating of activities into a unified system" and control systems as "the measurement of performance so companies can respond appropriately to changing conditions" (Daniels, Radebaugh & Sullivan 2013, p. 646). Examples of coordination mechanisms are all the components of the global supply chain, as well as supplier relations, logistics, and the administration between the headquarters and subsidiaries of all marketing and communication programs and activities. Examples of control systems include structure and performance assessments. MNCs use coordination and control mechanisms "to synchronize, integrate, and evaluate value activities" (Daniels et al., 2013, p. 574). In particular, the coordination and control of global marketing—advertising and public relations or public affairs have been conceptualized and documented though cultural and transnational crisis perspectives (e.g., de Mooij, 2010; Molleda & Laskin, 2010).

The techniques and efforts to integrate and evaluate global operations follow three principles: efficiency, learning, and flexibility or responsiveness (Bartlett & Ghoshal, 2002). These principles, in a global strategic communication context, take different connotations that are described next. Global efficiency means the coordination and control, with various degrees of centralization or decentralization, of the management of programs, campaigns, plans, and daily activities or tactics. Worldwide learning refers to documenting, sharing, analyzing, and perhaps awarding and/or compensating the best domestic and multi-national practices. Finally, multinational flexibility or national responsiveness describes the need to adapt or conform to country-specific legal or social regulations, as well as stakeholders' and consumers' expectations and needs. Two out of the three principles, efficiency and flexibility or responsiveness, imply a continuum between two extremes: standardization and localization, which will be addressed next.

Standardization and Localization

The main assumption of coordination by standardization is operational consistency, which entails the application of "rules and precise procedures" that help a multinational (an MNC) "leverage its core competency as well as minimize inefficiencies" (Daniels et al., p. 574). In global strategic communication, standardization means the consistency of programs and strategies across dispersed world markets of the MNC. Coordination by standardization entails "universal rules and procedures that apply to units worldwide" (Daniels et al., p. 574). That also includes policies, rules, and procedures for global strategic communication and its various areas of specialization. On the other hand, localization is about understanding and accepting the unique local challenges.

The decision on standardization or localization definitely goes beyond just product, pricing, or distribution to include the choice of communication strategy adopted by the MNCs (Schmid & Kotulla, 2011). Pudelko & Harzing (2008) suggested considering both the internal and external factors to choose between standardization and localization. Molleda, Kochhar and Wilson (2012) reviewed the literature on standardization and localization from a multi-disciplinary perspective to conceptualize and empirically test the extent of localization practiced by MNCs. They conducted a content analysis of the online newsrooms of U.S. based MNC subsidiaries in China, India, and the United Kingdom. The study found a high extent of localization in the form of localized newsrooms on organizational websites and found news releases to be the most common localized information subsidy on the corporate portals. The extent of localization was also found to be dependent on the industry type and the level of impact the corporation has on its stakeholders (Molleda, Kochhar & Wilson, 2012).

A similar study done by Halliburton and Ziegfeld (2009) analyzed how major European multinationals communicate using their organizational websites and create a corporate identity. The study found evidence that the organizations adopt a "glocal" approach that varies according to the industry type. The discussion on standardization versus localization is significant for the tourism industry because of the uniqueness of the industry. Gotham (2005) analyzed how tourism, a truly global industry, integrates with local actions to develop different forms of the industry. Tourism is seen as a process that symbolizes the differences and commonalities between standardization and localization (Gotham, 2005). The following sections of this chapter will connect the theories of coordination and control with the theories of standardization and localization by applying these theories to tourism industry practices.

Tourism in Costa Rica

Tourism is one of the world's largest industries, or economic sectors, contributing trillions of U.S. dollars annually to the global economy, creating jobs and wealth, generating exports, boosting taxes, and stimulating capital investment (Travel & Tourism, 2011). In 2011, the World Travel and Tourism Council expected it to contribute almost USD 6 trillion to the global economy, or 99% of global gross domestic product. Eco-tourism has especially become popular because of the increased awareness of global environment degradation. Hence, tourists are more likely to spend their leisure time visiting natural areas (Wight, 2002).

Tourism has been a key area of economic growth for Costa Rica and its contribution to the global economy (Rivers-Moore, 2007). Since 1987, the socioeconomic dynamics of Costa Rica have been increasingly affected by the impact of foreign tourism (Céspedes, Gómez & Becerra, 2010). Tourism has grown to become Costa Rica's most important source of income and, in 2011, more than two million tourists visited the country, the vast majority from the United States (Costa Rica Tourism, 2011).

According to the United Nations Statistics Division (2010), Costa Rica's 4.5 million residents enjoy a relatively high standard of living compared to other Latin American countries. The average per capita income in Costa Rica is USD 5,800 a year, and the adult literacy rate is 96%, which further helps promote and develop tourism in the country.

Costa Rica's extensive national park system represents 25% of the country and provides a perfect example of ecotourism (Cook, 2007). Apart from the adventure tourism activities like hiking, bird-watching, observation of flora and fauna, and visiting volcanoes (Céspedes, Gómez, & Becerra, 2010), medical tourism is also a growing aspect of tourism in this Central American nation (Bristow, Yang, & Lu, 2011).

Allan Flores, serving his second term as Costa Rica's tourism minister, cited the strength of Costa Rican tourism as marketing a potent national identity (cited in Tellez, 2011). The *NoNArtificial Ingredients* campaign has delivered great results since 2002 and has helped Costa Rica build a "country brand," with emphasis on eco-friendly aspects of the country and examples of its culture, people, and history. As the campaign has been termed one of the most successful campaigns in tourism, the chapter will next examine the case study to understand the use of coordination and control, and standardization and localization strategies adopted in the campaign.

Case Study—"Costa Rica: No Artificial Ingredients"— A Global Campaign Of The Country's Tourism Board[1]

The government's participation in tourism development began in 1930, with the creation and promotion of the first privately owned luxury hotel, Gran Hotel Costa Rica ("History and institutional," n.d.). Foreign tourists entered the country via the Port of Limón (Atlantic coast), and then commuted to San José (capital city) by train. In 1931, the first regulation of tourism activity was decreed, by means of Law 91, on June 16, when the National Tourism Board was created. It operated until 1955, when the *Instituto Costarricense de Turismo* was created by Law 1917. The Costa Rican Tourism Board (*ICT* Spanish acronym hereafter) is a governmental organization that promotes and regulates the tourism industry in this Central American country. The ICT is responsible for promoting tourism attractions and destinations nationally and internationally; establishing tourism norms, regulations, and incentives; and certifying Costa Rica's hotels, travel agencies, rental cars, and other tourism service providers under its Certification of Sustainable Tourism program (E. Obando, personal communication, October 2, 2012). The ICT coordinates and controls all global promotional efforts of Costa Rica with internal human and material resources and the outsourcing of specialized advertising and public relations agencies with a global reach.

In 1997, the ICT launched the global campaign No Artificial Ingredients to promote the natural environment. Costa Rica is 31,600 sq. miles in area, which represents 55% of the Earth's biodiversity ("Costa Rica's natural heritage," 2010). A quarter of the country's landmass is protected by law as national parks and/or wildlife refuges (J. Perlaza & E. Obando, personal communication, January 12, 2010). In 2009, a research firm evaluated the branding effort of Costa Rica and concluded that the brand was very strong and well positioned. Burson-Marsteller's Latin American hub in Miami has been the global public relations agency in North America since 2007 (J. Perlaza & E. Obando, personal communication, January 12, 2010).

According to ICT's statistics, Costa Rica's main market is North America (more than 50%). U.S. tourists come from Florida, Texas, New York, Indiana, and California. Canadian tourists mainly come from Toronto, Vancouver, and cities in Quebec. Europe is an important market for Costa Rica, too (close to 20%). The majority of the European visitors come from UK, France, Germany, Holland, Italy, Spain, and Switzerland. European tourism in Costa Rica happens year-round but peaks in the winter (summer for Costa Rica). Since the end of 2012, the ICT has worked with a promotion agency in Spain named the Central America Tourism Agency (CATA). The economic crisis that started in 2008–2009 forced the ICT to increase its visibility and promotion in the European market, especially in markets such as UK, France, Germany, Spain, and other markets such as Belgium, Russia, Sweden, and Switzerland (E. Obando, personal communication, October 2, 2012). In 2008, two million tourists visited the country, generating two billion USD. In 2009, the number of tourists declined by 99% ("Instituto Costarricense de Turismo," 2010). The visits of foreign tourists had increased more than 10% by the end of 2011 ("International tourist arrivals," 2011). Overall, tourism represents 7.4% of Costa Rica's GDP and 19% of total exports.

The ICT's main strategy has been to educate and attract all demographics (e.g., families, students, eco-tourists, adventure seekers, etc.) that may find the characteristics of Costa Rica interesting. Allan Flores explained the offerings of the destination for a variety of tourists:

> Tourists can also go diving among a wealth of marine species, sport fishing, bird watching, surfing, hiking through forests, canopying, white-water rafting, and kayaking. There are also dozens of beaches that offer year-round open air [sic] activities thanks to the beautiful tropical forests and pleasant temperatures throughout the country.
>
> *Flores, 2012, para. 3*

The ICT sponsors and carries out formal and informal research to understand the media use of the identified tourists, and that helps ICT develop, execute, and measure effective campaigns. ICT has successfully developed and included social media and interactive online campaigns in its communication efforts to attract potential foreign tourists.

How is the Global Strategic Communication Function Structured?

The ICT's vision is "to be the leading and rector institution for the country's tourism activity" ("Vision," n.d.). Its mission is stated in a *National Development Plan*, quoted on the ICT website: "Promote a wholesome tourism development, with the purpose of improving Costa Ricans' quality of life, by maintaining a balance between the economic and social boundaries, environmental protection, culture, and facilities" ("Mission," n.d). ICT's main functions are:

> strengthening of the processes of formulation and implementation of planning for tourism development, attraction and assessment of investors, development of quality and competitiveness systems, development of marketing in an integral way, tourist attention, generation of information for decision-making, reinforcement of processes for improving administration (comptrollership services, income, administrative analysis, among others)".
>
> *"Functions," n.d., par. 2.*

In particular, the Director of Marketing is in charge of global strategic communication efforts through the departments of Research and Evaluation and Promotion (Instituto Costarricense de Turismo,

2008). The ICT Director of Marketing coordinates its campaigns with the network of embassies and consulates of Costa Rica worldwide, as well as with advertising and public relations firms and travel agency operators. The ICT's institutional policies state: "All of the international and national promotion will be done according to specific plans that have been designed keeping in mind the private sector's and related communities' proposals, responding to a vision and the country's tourism goals at large" (Institutional policies, n.d., para. 9).

What are the Outsourcing Marketing, Advertising, and Public Relations Agencies Employed?

The agency in charge of the advertising efforts in North America and other markets is 22Squared. This agency is located in Atlanta, Georgia. Burson-Marsteller handles the public relations for North America, the rest of the markets are handled through CATA or in-house (E. Obando, personal communication, October 2, 2012). The ICT is also interested in developing domestic tourism among Costa Ricans, especially during the low season of international tourism. The ICT targets domestic tourists and encourages travel through local public relations and advertising campaigns. The goal is to use the extensive tourist infrastructure to spread awareness among citizens about the importance of the tourist industry and the preservation of the natural environment Costa Rica has to offer to the world. The domestic agency for the ICT is Comunicación Corporativa Ketchum, which is an affiliated agency of the Omnicom Group with roots in Costa Rica. ICT works closely with its various outsourcing agencies, both local and global, to develop specialized campaigns and drive efforts to attract domestic and international tourists.

How was the Campaign Planned, Executed, and Evaluated in terms of Coordination and Control?

The planning of the "no artificial ingredient" campaign was carried out by the ICT Director of Marketing and McCann Erickson Worldwide, a marketing communication agency of the Interpublic Group of Companies. The approval of the global strategic communication plan and its objectives, strategies, and tactics was granted by the ICT Board of Directors (E. Obando, personal communication, October 2, 2012). The execution is also the responsibility of both the agency and the ICT marketing team. The main evaluation efforts have focused on the assessment of the country brand. These global branding efforts were still underway while this chapter was being written. A highly standardized approach was adopted for the campaign, in which the ICT (client) exercised the control and McCann Erickson (marketing communication agency) coordinated the effort. A moderate level of centralization was followed for the content of communication materials, in which language and currency accounted for a degree of localization, with the rest of the content standardized.

No Artificial Ingredients has been one of the hallmark campaigns of ICT, and the tourism branding efforts, including advertising, sales promotion, marketing, and public relations, are still being used to promote Costa Rica globally. The branding efforts of the destination have been effective according to the studies ICT has commissioned (E. Obando, personal communication, October 2, 2012). The Foreign Agents Registration Act (FARA) reports the money spent on media relations campaigns carried out by Burson-Marsteller for the Costa Rican Tourism Board since 2009. A total of $2,966,082 has been spent on monitoring and analyzing news coverage, writing news releases, distributing to the key media, organizing events with travel industry partners for consumers and agents, fulfilling media inquiries, and organizing media familiarization trips to Costa Rica (Foreign Agents Registration Act, 2011).

Media relations techniques were part of the strategic plan. The most successful efforts resulted from familiarization tours, in which media professionals had a direct encounter with the land of "no artificial ingredients." The following section focuses on one aspect of the ICT global strategic communication efforts to cultivate effective global media relations.

Familiarization Tours: Teaming Up With Foreign Media Professionals

Invited by the ICT, the first author of this chapter participated in a familiarization tour throughout Costa Rica in Summer 2010. This opportunity was used to conduct participant observations. This section of the chapter summarizes the first author's observations of the global media relations activity that was conducted by ICT. Guided by the no artificiality theme, the author's itinerary included an eco-lodge, a grand tourism hotel with national and global sustainability certifications, hot springs, zip lining, marine life and wildlife watching, volcano sights, national parks, pristine beaches, and an indigenous territory. The familiarization tour also entailed talks on sustainable development and indigenous cultural preservation given by managers of the lodge and hotel where the author stayed.

The process of familiarization tours are controlled by ICT and coordinated by the public relations agency. Foreign journalists and media professionals request guided tours or are invited strategically by the ICT, targeting various media outlets of specific markets with their potential to reach prospective tourists. Once the list of invitees is finalized, sent out, and confirmed, the marketing team assesses the needs and expectations of the professional guests through emails and telephone conversations. The logistics are planned in detail, and the marketing team sends out regulatory paper work (including visa documents or formal invitations), itineraries, logistics, timelines, welcome guides, and information regarding the assigned trained guides and/or drivers. The ICT is always very careful in explaining and setting expectations for the media guests regarding rules and conditions of travel expenses and sponsorships. Upon arrival, media guests are assigned to their respective guides or drivers who are responsible for ensuring a successful stay for the guests. Each media guest's requests for language translators and assistance in overcoming other cultural barriers and time orientations are specially arranged.

English is an international language that facilitates the work with media representatives from various markets of the world, and it is the preferred language for the ICT familiarization tours, unless otherwise specified by the media guests. The guides and drivers have experienced a variety of behaviors and attitudes from visiting media professionals, and find it easier to interact with and relate to some guests more than others. Rapport and empathy between guides and guests inform interpersonal relations on the tours, and, ultimately, may affect guests' impressions of their visit. The ICT marketing and promotion team is aware of how preparation, coordination, and personal treatment of visiting media professionals may influence the perceptions they have or develop regarding not only the professionalism and qualities of ICT personnel, but also, more importantly, Costa Rican tourism itself.

The first author's guide and driver explained some sensitive issues that should be treated carefully during familiarization tours, such as the exchange of gifts and valuable perks, the safety and comfort of guests, and hotel and tour operators' expertise on environmental and sustainability issues, among other subjects. Close coordination and constant communication between the ICT administrative headquarters and the guides and drivers guarantee a smooth running of the media professionals' familiarization tours. Any change or delay in the agenda is immediately reported and adjustments are subsequently made. Almost all aspects of familiarization tours for international media are guided by written policies, especially those which refer to guides or drivers' allowed behaviors and interactions with guests. Administrators and guides or drivers issue standard final reports with evaluations and recommendations. These reports are intended to support stated objectives and register best practices.

At the end of the familiarization tour, the slogan "no artificial ingredients" acquired a different meaning for the first author. It became a tangible subject with multiple reinforcements. The campaign's claims and promises were fulfilled greatly in the context of the tour. Media familiarization tours are one of the examples of how ICT strengthens its global strategic campaign. These tours support the solid foundations of tourism in Cost Rica by emphasizing the country's long-term programs to preserve and enhance their natural, human, and cultural environments. This is a universal theme that should resonate with today's international tourists, and will resonate for generations of tourists to come.

Conclusions and Perspectives

The complexity of global strategic communication increases because of the existence of a multiplicity of home, host, and transnational stakeholders and consumer groups. They are exposed constantly to claims, promises, and calls for action from a variety of organizations with domestic and foreign roots. Organizations operating in multiple markets face the challenge of being consistent with their core messages and yet relevant to local needs and expectations. Coordination, control, and standardization are essential to the success of multinational campaigns. Regarding the standardization—localization continuum, the approach taken by an MNC is not as important as the core foundation and distinctiveness of its offerings and rewards. Here the authors have presented an international case in which standardization was the strategic preference over localization in certain management functions. Costa Rica, as described in this chapter, is a unique case in that it offers a tourist destination with appealing characteristics for domestic and international tourists who are in search of natural and safe environments.

The case study was a unique way of applying the fundamentals of strategic communication in a tourism setting. However, in terms of research, studying other economic sectors will help determine the use of specific coordination and control mechanisms and the extent of standardization or localization of global strategic communication strategies and tactics. Further research is important to understand how organizations, operating in a diverse but interconnected world, can accomplish their goals and objectives through the adaptation of coordination control and standardization and localization efforts.

Research in strategic communication should analyze political, social and economic factors that can influence any organization. Comparative research of these determinants can guide organizations to deal with environmental complexity and reinforce a clear brand identity. Thus, organizations ought to invest in global strategic communication that accounts for challenges in strategically planning and effectively executing communication campaigns.

Note

1 The authors of this chapter would like to acknowledge ICT representatives Silvia Rodríguez, Evelyn Obando, and Johanna Perlaza for their contributions to and information provided for the development of this case study.

References

Amann, W., Khan, S., Salzmann, O., Steger, U., & Ionescu-Somers, A. (2007). Managing external pressures through corporate diplomacy. *Journal of General Management, 33*(1), 33–49.

Bartlett, C., & Ghoshal, S. (2002). *Managing across borders: The transnational solution* (2nd ed.). Boston. MA: Harvard Business School Press.

Botan, C. (1997). Ethics in strategic communication campaigns: The case for a new approach to public relations. *Journal of Business Communication, 34,* 187–201.

Botan, C. H., & Hazelton, V., Jr. (2006). Public relations theory in a new age. In C. H. Botan & V. Hazelton, Jr. (Eds.). *Public relations theory* (pp. 1–18). Mahwah, NJ: Lawrence Erlbaum.

Botan, C., & Soto, F. (1998). A semiotic approach to the internal functioning of publics: Implications for strategic communication and public relations. *Public Relations Review, 24*(1), 21–44.

Bristow, R. S., Yang, W. T., & Lu, M. T. (2011). Sustainable medical tourism in Costa Rica. *Tourism Review, 66*(1), 107–117.

Céspedes, D., V., Gómez, E. G., & Becerra, A. T. (2010). Demand indicators for adventure tourism packages in Costa Rica: An exploratory analysis. *Tourism and Hospitality Research, 10*(3), 234–245.

Cook, W. (2007). Costa Rica: From ecotourism leader to world class healthcare provider. *Medical Tourism at a Glance, 1,* 20–29.

Costa Rica Tourism (2011). Tourism statistical yearly report 2011. Retrieved October 16, 2012, from http://www.visitcostarica.com/ict/pdf/anuario/Statistical_Yearly_Report_2011.pdf

Costa Rica's natural heritage. (2010).Retrieved September 14, 2012, from http://www.smithsonianjourneys.org/blog/tag/biodiversity/page/2/

Daniels, J. D., Radebaugh, L. H., & Sullivan, D. P. (2013). *International business environments and operations* (14th ed.). Upper Saddle River, NJ: Prentice Hall.

de Mooij, M. (2010). *Global marketing and advertising: Understanding cultural paradoxes* (3rd ed.). Thousand Oaks, CA: Sage.

Flores, A. (2012). *With open arms!* Retrieved August 2, 2014, from http://www.venturecostarica.com/adventure-ecotourism

Foreign Agents Registration Act. (2011). *FARA reports to Congress.* Washington, DC: Retrieved from http://www.fara.gov/annualrpts.html

Friedman, T. L. (2005). *The world is flat: A brief history of the twenty-first century.* New York: Farrar, Straus, and Giroux.

Functions. (n.d.). Retrieved September 14, 2012, from http://www.visitcostarica.com/ict/paginas/Tourism Board.asp

Gotham, K. V. (2005). Tourism from above and below: Globalization, localization and New Orleans's Mardi Gras. *International Journal of Urban and Regional Research, 29*(2), 309–326.

Hallahan, K., Holtzhausen, D., Van Ruler, B., Verčič, D., & Sriramesh, K. (2007). Defining strategic communication. *International Journal of Strategic Communication, 1*(1), 3–35.

Halliburton, C., & Ziegfeld, A. (2009). How do major European companies communicate their corporate identity across countries? An empirical investigation of corporate internet communications. *Journal of Marketing Management, 25*(9), 909–925.

Heath, R. L. (1998). New communication technologies: An issues management point of view. *Public Relations Review, 26,* 31–51.

History and institutional legal framework. (n.d.). Retrieved September 14, 2012, from http://www.visitcostarica.com/ict/paginas/TourismBoard.asp

Institutional policies. (n.d.). Costa Rica Tourism Board website. Retrieved September 14, 2012, from http://www.visitcostarica.com/ict/paginas/TourismBoard.asp

Instituto Costarricense de Turismo. (2008). Organizational chart.Retrieved September 14, 2012, from http://www.visitcostarica.com/ict/paginas/images/Organigrama_noviembre_2008.jpg

Instituto Costarricense de Turismo. (2010). Plan nacional de turismo sostenible de Costa Rica 2010–2016: Resumen ejecutivo. San José, Costa Rica.

International tourist arrivals by month and nationality. (2011).Retrieved September 14, 2012, from http://www.visitcostarica.com/ict/pdf/anuario/Statistical_Yearly_Report_2011.pdf

Kent, M., & Taylor, M. (1998). Building dialogic relationships through the World Wide Web. *Public Relations Review, 24*(3), 321–334.

Lewis, B. K. (2010). Social media and strategic communication: Attitudes and perceptions among college students. *Public Relations Journal, 4*(3). Retrieved September 14, 2012, from http://www.prsa.org

Maignan, I., & Ferrell, O. C. (2004). Corporate social responsibility and marketing: An integrative framework. *The Journal of the Academy of Marketing Science, 32*(1), 3–19.

McCorkindale, T. C. (2009). Can you see the writing on my wall? A content analysis of the *Fortune* 50's Facebook social networking sites. Paper presented to the 12th Annual International Public Relations Research Conference, Coral Gables, Florida March 13.

Mission. (n.d.). Retrieved September 14, 2012, from http://www.visitcostarica.com/ict/paginas/TourismBoard.asp

Molleda, J. C., & Laskin, A. (2010). Coordination and control of global public relations to manage cross-national conflict shifts: A multidisciplinary perspective for research and practice. In G. J. Golan, T. J. Johnson, & W. Wanta (Eds.), *International media communication in a global age* (pp. 319–344). New York: Routledge.

Molleda, J. C., Kochhar, S., & Wilson, C. (2012). Theorizing the global-local paradox: Comparative research on information subsidies' localization by U.S.-based multinational corporations. Paper presented at the Association for Education in Journalism and Mass Communication's 100th Annual Convention, Division of Public Relations, Chicago, USA.

Ordeix-Rigo, E., & Duarte, J. (2009). From public diplomacy to corporate diplomacy: Increasing corporation's legitimacy and influence. *American Behavioral Scientist, 53*(4), 549–564.

Orgad, M. S. (2011). NATO's strategic communication as international public relations: The PR practitioner and the challenge of culture in the case of Kosovo. *Public Relations Review, 37,* 376–383.

Our locations. (2012). Lenovo website. Retrieved September 28, 2012, from http://www.lenovo.com/lenovo/us/en/locations.html

Paul, C. (2011). *Strategic communication: Origins, concepts, and current debates.* Westport, CT: Praeger Security International.

Paul, C. (2012). Challenges facing U.S. government and department of defense efforts in strategic communication. *Public Relations Review, 38,* 188–194.

Pfau, M., & Wan, H. H. (2006). Persuasion: An intrinsic function of public relations. In C. H. Botan & V. Hazleton (Eds.). *Public relations theory II* (pp. 101–136). Mahwah, NJ: Lawrence Erlbaum.

Public relations defined. (2012, January 1). Retrieved from http://www.prsa.org/aboutprsa/public relationsdefined/#.U–bkBoBdWel

Pudelko, M., & Harzing, A. W. (2008). The golden triangle for MNCs: Standardization towards headquarters practices, standardization towards global best practices and localization. *Organizational Dynamics, 37*(4), 394–404.

Rivers-Moore, M. (2007). No artificial ingredients: Gender, race and nation in Costa Rica's international tourism campaign, *Journal of Latin American Cultural Studies: Travesia, 16*(3), 341–357.

Schmid, S., & Kotulla, T. (2011). 50 years of research on international standardization and adaptation: From a systematic literature analysis to a theoretical framework. *International Business Review, 20,* 491–507.

Shah, A. (2012). Lenovo gains over Dell as world's second-largest PC maker. *PCWorld* online. Retrieved September 28, 2012, from http://www.pcworld.com/article/253622/lenovo_gains_over_dell_as_worlds_secondlargest_pc_maker.html

Steger U. (2003) *Corporate diplomacy: The strategy for a volatile, fragmented business environment,* London, England: John Wiley.

Stohl, C. (2004). Globalization theory. In S. May & D. K. Mumby (Eds.), *Engaging organizational communication theory and research* (pp. 223–261). Thousand Oaks, CA: Sage. .

Tellez, R. (2011, May 27). Costa Rica's new tourism minister talks about marketing the future. *McClatchy—Tribune Business News,* pp. n/a. Retrieved September 14, 2012, from http://search.proquest.com/docview/868782286?accountid=10920

Travel & Tourism. (2011).Retrieved September 14, 2012, from http://www.wttc.org/site_media/uploads/downloads/traveltourism2011.pdf

United Nations Statistics Division. (2010). Statistics. Retrieved September 20, 2012, from http://unstats.un.org/unsd/default.htm

Vision. (n.d.). Retrieved September 14, 2012, from http://www.visitcostarica.com/ict/paginas/TourismBoard.asp

Wight, P. (2002). Supporting the principles of sustainable development in tourism and ecotourism: Government's potential role. *Current Issues in Tourism, 5,* 222–243.

Wright, D. K., & Hinson, M. D. (2010). How new communications media are being used in public relations: A Longitudinal Analysis. *Public Relations Journal, 4*(3). Retrieved September 14, 2012, from http://www.prsa.org.

Index